The Unredeemed Conscience

In Psychotherapy and
Spiritual Development

by

Jerome W. Vreeland, Ph.D.

Copyright © 2011, 2012 by Jerome W. Vreeland

Cover Design by Jerome W. Vreeland

FOR

God Beyond All Understanding

The Holy Spirit and Jesus Christ

TABLE OF CONTENTS

	FORWARD	vii
	INTRODUCTION	1
CHAPTER I:	THE UNREDEEMED CONSCIENCE	3
	Endnotes for Chapter I	41
CHAPTER II:	THEORETICAL PREMISES AND CONSTRUCTS	57
	Endnotes for Chapter II	97
CHAPTER III:	A MANUAL FOR USING THE *LIGHT* IN THERAPY	109
	Endnotes for Chapter III	152
CHAPTER IV:	THE CHRIST WITHIN US	159
	Endnotes for Chapter IV	211
CHAPTER V:	EXPLORING MIND: EMOTIONAL SELVES IN THE CONTEXT OF OPPOSITES	223
	Endnotes for Chapter V	347
CHAPTER VI:	CHRIST AND THE ISSUE OF TEMPORAL AUTHORITY	367
	Endnotes for Chapter VI	422
CHAPTER VII:	MORAL AUTHORITY AND THE REDEMPTION OF CONSCIENCE	429
	Endnotes for Chapter VII	673

Table of Contents (Continued)

CHAPTER VIII:	RELATIONAL AUTHORITY	681
	Endnotes for Chapter VIII	790
APPENDIX I:	WORKING WITH SEXUAL ENERGY	801
APPENDIX II:	WHO IS YOUR HIGHER POWER?	809
	Endnotes for Appendix II	813

FORWARD

This work describes a large number of psycho-imaginative interventions using a spiritual methodology. All of them were developed in a clinical psychology setting using active imagination to explore and treat a wide range of clinical issues. The methodology involves a luminous sphere of *Light*, which the client uses to express willingness, and the evocation of a Christ image or comparable higher power able to channel the Holy Spirit. The interventions have proven effective for the redemption of conscience, the removal of its shaming enthrallments, and the correction of gender distortions in the images of self and others.

I confess the book is inordinately long. Some chapters are easily the equivalent in size of many books published today. But each chapter follows the other in what I hope is an organic whole. I could have shortened them greatly by offering abbreviated verbatims. But those capture the 'nitty-gritty' of actual practice; and hopefully provide the reader a realistic sense of what takes place when a client goes inside. You can skip through them on the initial reading, but I expect the practitioner will want to read them more closely if s/he ventures to offer the methodology to clients.

I am deeply indebted to my clients who have received positive benefits from these methodologies and allowed me to publish their results. They are the true authors of this book.

I am also indebted to my 'first editor,' Dr. Peg Hess, whose suggestions and enthusiasm were instrumental in helping me to finalize the work.

Last but not least, I most value Emily's continuing love and support through all the years consumed by this work.

J.W. Vreeland
Hunting Island, SC
May, 2011

INTRODUCTION

Imagine entering your Mind and finding a small sphere of *Light* that answers only to your willingness. Now imagine using this *Light* to find your image of Jesus Christ or comparable higher power. Imagine further, that this image can channel the Holy Spirit, which has the power to forgive and transform every image and event in your Mind provided you are willing. This type of psychotherapy is called *Light* therapy. It provides a nearly inexhaustible resource for the exploration of Mind, Soul, and Ego dynamics; and the power to heal most forms of mental illness addressed in psychotherapy as well as psychosomatic dis-eases. This methodology also demonstrates the inordinate power of parental images and their effects on the Ego; and the restitutive power of Jesus Christ when he is allowed to interact with those images. In this work, shame is treated as the root cause of most Ego dysfunction; and Christ channeling the Holy Spirit is seen as an unerring source of forgiveness able to completely dispel accumulated shame. It is the only kind of psychotherapy capable of doing so. Shame is a 'white elephant' in the therapy rooms of most mental health providers. It is rarely addressed in a secular context because only a spiritual power has the wherewithal to decisively end an individual's enthrallment to this most painful of all emotions, which most people and cultures still treat as unforgivable.

The initial focus of this book is conscience, which is treated as unredeemed so long as it remains in the thrall of shaming judgments and blocks the 'still quiet voice' within our hearts. Unredeemed conscience manifests in children as an archetypal energy that constellates Moral authority in parents, who then impede the expression of conscience as a Voice for God by their over reliance on shaming judgments. In this work, *consciousness* is also treated as unredeemed because it is largely governed by the Ego's excessive use of the pride-shame axis. This gravely and tragically constrains the Ego's options. Both conditions are treated as arbitrary limitations that can be decisively changed by a higher power channeling the Holy Spirit.

Use of the *Light* and Christological interventions can provide psycho-imaginative access to all major archetypal constellations and provide for their healing as needed. The archetypal energy responsible for an unredeemed conscience is called the Empowering archetype, which imbues parental images with god-like powers. Another archetypal energy – the Gendering archetype – also uses parental images to constellate our earliest and most enduring self-images. These can be shown to govern our most intimate, conflicted, and enduring relationships. The Gendering archetype dictates the masculine/feminine interaction sustaining every image within the Mind; and parents serve as the prototypes of its earliest and most enduring constellations. The constellations of both archetypes can be decisively altered by use of the *Light* and an image of Christ channeling the Holy Spirit.

The first half of this book is primarily theoretical and methodological. Theory has been of value to the extent it can inspire effective interventions, but it is the methodology

(Christ and the *Light*), and the client's use of it, that have dictated the results. The second part of the book describes systematic interventions and outcomes and extensive verbatims illustrating the process.

I hope this book will be of value to experienced psychotherapists who are spiritually inclined and spiritual directors of all denominations.

CHAPTER I

THE UNREDEEMED CONSCIENCE

The processive character of knowing reminds us that we are always on the way to a fuller account of all that makes up the moral reality of action.
-Richard Gula[1]

OVERVIEW

I have yet to find any contemporary writings on conscience that refer to it as other than 'conscience.' But the etymology of the word changes significantly when translated from Hebrew to Greek to Latin. In English all of these differences are reduced to one word making it a concept very much in need of clarification. This is especially true in view of the conundrum introduced by Freud this past century, which asserts that conscience is the punishing voice of parental dictates. At the very least, a distinction needs to be made between the traditional description of conscience as a 'Voice for God' and parental manifestations that are merely god-like in authority. To that end, I will define and build on three definitions of conscience: Heart conscience, Ego conscience, and the Christ conscience process.

In the Hebrew Old Testament, the heart – not the head – was considered the center of a person and the conduit of God's voice, i.e. the Holy Spirit. Likewise, in this work, Heart conscience will always refer to the Holy Spirit speaking directly to the Mind through the Heart.[2] But Heart conscience is nearly impossible to discern while parents speak with god-like authority because their voices can significantly block the heartfelt flow of that 'still quiet voice' by their use of shaming judgments. Later, when the Ego learns to emulate parents, it too will block the Holy Spirit by exercising the power to self-shame. Since both impediments are nearly universal occurrences, what is commonly referred to as 'conscience' seems better described as Ego conscience, which I also call the unredeemed conscience or Voice-of-conscience. Stated another way, Ego conscience is a complex created by archetypal authority that constellates Moral authority in parents. In turn, this obliges the Ego to create ego-aspects [3] that strive to cope with that authority by exercising the power to self-shame. That definition is based on Carl Jung's conception of archetype and complex, which I draw upon in my own conceptualizations of conscience.

It will be argued here that the process of *redeeming* conscience, so it can speak as a Voice for God, will always require the intervention of a higher power that can reliably channel the Holy Spirit within the human Mind while that 'Voice for God' is otherwise blocked by Ego and archetype. I will advocate for Jesus Christ as the most reliable channel of the Holy Spirit in Western culture. For that reason, I generally refer to the redemption of conscience as a *Christ conscience process* since it is Christ that redeems it by acting as an unimpeded channel of the Holy Spirit wherever the Ego becomes willing. The Christ conscience process is not a state of being. It is best thought of as ongoing series of interventions by which the Heart's conscience is gradually restored. I do accept that other higher powers can also channel the Holy Spirit, and in the clinical chapters of this book I examine that potential as well.

The thought of Jesus Christ 'channeling' the Holy Spirit may put off some readers who associate the concept with 'psychics' channeling spirits of the dead or individuals channeling spirits who purport to be enlightened. But I use it for that very reason: the Holy Spirit is the uncaused cause of the world of Spirit, the *unblemished* source of all that is Spirit over the face of the waters.[4] In this work, the *image* of Christ – and his ability to be an unimpeded conduit of the Holy Spirit, is crucial to most of the interventions described herein. To my way of thinking, Christ does more than 'evoke' the Holy Spirit. His *image* literally embodies the Holy Spirit, and he willingly extends its power to all who ask in his name.[5] His *image* is a channel – an unerring conduit, of the living Spirit, which he offers freely to any who ask.

The Spirit of God has 'hovered over the waters' from time immemorial; so while the Holy Spirit flows unhesitatingly through Christ, it is not restricted to his image. It can flow through myriad sources, just as it touched and inspired all the prophets and writers of the Old and New Testament. Today, it can flow through human beings who evoke it in the name of Jesus Christ. Finally, I accept that the higher powers of other religions and other cultures can also channel the Holy Spirit; that the Spirit of God, which hovers over the waters, can incarnate in any vessel that seeks to bring us closer to God ineffable. My personal preference, and that of most of my clients, is that Christ be that higher power; but it is only that: a personal preference. No image has a monopoly on the Holy Spirit. And that is notably true in clinical settings, which have provided most of the data supporting my theses.

Wherever possible, I will use Ego conscience, Heart conscience, and the Christ conscience process to describe the sense of conscience under discussion; but where I use the word alone it will almost always refer to Ego conscience as this is the unspoken frame of reference of most other writers on the subject. In this work, that egoistic sense of conscience will always refer to manifestations of archetype and Ego that constrict or block the conscious experience of the Holy Spirit in the Mind. In contrast, Heart conscience will always refer to the unimpeded flow of the Holy Spirit through the Heart directly into the Mind. It represents an ideal state modeled for us by Jesus Christ.

The Christ conscience process will always refer to *the power of the Holy Spirit channeled through the imaginal presence of Jesus Christ as he strives to restore Heart conscience*. The redemption of conscience is best thought of as a work in progress rather than a one step transformation. It is the ideal realized by Christ and offered to each of us through his discernment and the forgiving power of the Holy Spirit. So long as any aspect of the Ego insists on being self-reliant, it has the power to block the flow of Christ's discernment and the Holy Spirit from the portion of consciousness it organizes. But wherever an ego-aspect becomes willing, Christ can remove that sense of separation.

It has taken me many years to understand what is meant by commonly held conceptions of conscience and its perpetuation by parents, culture, and Ego. What I have finally deduced is that *Ego conscience is the unintended creation of an Empowering archetype, whose primary function is the constellation of Temporal authority in parental images.* But intended or not, this archetype imparts godlike authority to the actions of parents. More to the point, Temporal authority will evolve into Moral authority when the child is old enough to grasp absolute opposites governing the Mind. The growing awareness of absolute opposites must precede the emergence of conscience. That emergence occurs around age seven when the child is said to reach the 'age of reason.' At this age the child is said to acquire a conscience. Once the child becomes an adult, an internalized image of Jesus Christ, imbued with the power of the Holy Spirit, can terminate the Temporal and Moral authority constellated in the parental images. (I have observed this repeatedly in my clinical practice.) The internalized Christ has the power to nullify the constellational effects of the Empowering archetype without having to assume that authority. The Holy Spirit empowers Christ to further redeem Ego conscience by baptizing, convicting, converting, and consecrating the Ego's aspects until there is an unimpeded flow of the Spirit through the Heart to all aspects of the Ego willing to receive its grace. In Christ's own words it is the Holy Spirit who is the source of this power and forgiveness.[6]

Christ's inherent power, coupled with his power to channel the Holy Spirit, can manifest in five different ways: 1) it empowers him to staunch the flow of the Empowering archetype in any parental image, which effectively terminates the image's authority both temporally and as a Voice-of-conscience; 2) it empowers him to release any ego-aspect held in shameful bondage by baptizing it; 3) it empowers him to offer the power of his discernment to any ego-aspect who willingly asks for it; 4) it empowers him to purify the Heart for the indwelling of the Holy Spirit; and 5) it empowers him to convict any image with the power of the Holy Spirit and thereby transform it. The transformation of Ego conscience is a long and arduous process even with Christ's empowerment by the Holy Spirit; but it is doable if the therapist and client are willing.

Traditionally, Christian theology insisted on the primacy of Ego conscience on the assumption that it spoke as the Voice for God. In the 20th century that assertion was challenged by Freudian psychoanalysis, which amply demonstrated that parental images are imbued with a god-like authority that generally contradicts the Voice for God by being unforgivably punishing. Psychoanalysis does not use the concept of archetype to explain how parents become this Voice-of-conscience, but Freud leaves no doubt in the reader's mind that the father's voice is that voice and that it is both superordinate and mercilessly punishing in his clinical experience.[7] The conflicting assertions of theology and Freudian psychology have brought the two disciplines to an impasse this past century, to a point where one hears little of conscience from either side. In this work, I seek to resolve their conflict by conceptualizing conscience within a theory of levels wherein conscience can only function as a Voice for God when *it manifests through a freely chosen higher power such as Jesus Christ channeling the Holy Spirit*. Where the Holy Spirit is blocked by constellations of the Empowering archetype, and there is no higher power to redress this blockage, the individual is seen to remain in the thrall of a Voice-of-conscience expressed thru parental images and the individual's own Ego creations. Stated another way, for the vast majority of people conscience merely expresses the dictates of parents and ego-aspects created to cope with their archetypally generated Temporal and Moral authority. The goal of treatment, as regards Ego conscience, is the termination of this authority by a higher power who can then act as a freely chosen conduit of the Voice for God.

It will be argued here that the power undergirding the Voice-of-conscience (i.e. Ego conscience) exists a priori; that it is a genetically determined archetypal function. It is most like a Jungian archetype with parents forming the initial complex defining it. As formed by parents, the character of Ego conscience seems best described as *unredeemed*, and remains so while it only speaks with a parental voice, or the voice of other mortals claiming a parent's Moral authority.[8] By contrast, a *redeemed* conscience would be a freely chosen incarnation of God that provides discernment and forgiveness. From a Christian perspective, *that incarnation is Jesus Christ channeling the Holy Spirit.*[9]

Historically, Ego conscience has shown itself exceedingly resistant to change once constelled by parents – in no small measure because its god-like authority *has been mistaken* for the Voice for God. Yet this need not be so. In my work, I have found it is possible to dramatically alter a person's felt experience of Ego conscience provided the client is willing to interiorize an image of Jesus Christ that can channel the Holy Spirit.[10]

The Mind's Voice-of-conscience has been a source of study and revelation for several thousand years. The foundation and fall of civilizations may well flow from the moral convictions shaped by a culture's collective Voices-of-conscience.[11] Ancient Greeks personified it as "furies" older than the Greek pantheon.[12] In Catholic moral theology since Thomas Aquinas, it has been treated as the final moral arbitrator of thought and behavior. Since its formulation by Thomas Aquinas, Roman Catholic tradition:

> "...affirm[s] the inherent freedom of the human person to make choices for good or bad. The instrument of this choice in the area of morality is conscience which one is bound to follow even when mistaken. Experience, scripture, and Church teaching agree that judgments of conscience can be in error...Still, conscience holds primacy and must be followed; if one acts against one's conscience, one is certainly in the wrong." [13]

Given this sense of primacy, which I believe is a discernible felt experience in many people, the particular formation of an individual's Voice-of-conscience will have significant consequences for the individual as well as those in their relational field.

My own interest in conscience grew out of a desire to understand the archetypal, god-like, authority that my adult clients attribute to parental images, even when the client's past and present experience of those parents is clearly abusive. For the longest time, it did not even occur to me to consider Ego conscience as a critical variable since it is rarely, if ever, addressed in the current psychological literature.[14] But, finally, I recalled Freud's assertion that what we call conscience was essentially the introjection of parental values.[15] He assigned it considerable, if pejorative, power in shaping the individual's personality and resistance to treatment. His assertions effectively and justifiably weakened its traditional role as *vox Dei,* i.e. Voice for God.[16] As a consequence, today we speak of situational ethics as distinct from the moral absolutes imposed by a Voice-of-conscience. We rightly minimize its power as a Voice for God.

We seek other ways to explain the effects of Ego conscience, and its 'cure' by other means (e.g. drugs, prescribed and illicit).

The Analytical Psychology developed by Carl Jung offers an alternate view of conscience. Jung believed conscience could be better understood as an archetypally determined psychic function that had the potential of judging parents and culture, as well as merely reflecting them.[17] When Ego conscience is treated as an archetype, then the Voice-of-conscience can be seen as using parents to express itself, rather than vise versa (as Freud asserted). While archetypal imprinting can persist indefinitely, it can also be dramatically altered by radical experiences with other archetypally defined images such as the incarnation of Jesus Christ in the Mind. The parentification of conscience can be nullified because the Empowering archetype exists apart from the parental images it constellates. Parents are not the Empowering archetype; rather the Empowering archetype imparts Temporal and Moral authority to their voices and actions, and under the right conditions that authority can be stripped from the images.

Before proceeding to my clinical observations for redeeming Ego conscience, I think it important for the reader to have a greater appreciation of the psychological and theological perspectives, historical and current, that have sought to define conscience. I make no effort to be exhaustive, as thousands of chapters have been written on this subject; but, hopefully, I can provide a frame of reference for evaluating my own observations and conclusions. As regards the psychological perspective, I will restrict my findings to Freud and Jung. By identifying it as a subset of his super-ego construct, Freud legitimized the study of conscience as a psychological phenomenon. His own observations have decisively shaped the perspective of several generations of psychologists, philosophers, and theologians. Jung's conception of the Voice-of-conscience – particularly as to its origin – is in marked contrast to Freud. He allowed it could be treated as an archetype of the collective unconscious, but also felt it was 'psychoid' in nature, i.e. open to spiritual influence. Both men have strongly influenced my own thinking. My theological understanding of conscience is grounded primarily in the Greek Orthodox and Roman Catholic traditions, though I also draw on theological sources outside those traditions. Throughout the entire Christian era, the Greek and Roman traditions have consistently sought to define and inform conscience. While other sects and denominations may legitimately disagree with their perspectives, it seemed best to reference them as primary sources given their prominence over so many centuries.

Assertions concerning the inherent nature of conscience are bound to disagree. The minimalist view – which only gained prominence in the 20th century, draws heavily on psychoanalytic conceptualizations that treat conscience as dependent upon parents and culture for its creation and maintenance; in effect, it strips the concept of any Godly connection and reassigns that power to parents and culture. By contrast, Jung argued that, "We...give priority to the assertion which conscience itself makes – that it is a voice of God. This view is not a contrivance of the intellect, it is a primary assertion of the phenomenon itself: a numinous imperative which from ancient times has been accorded a far higher authority than the human intellect."[18] Traditional moral theology also treats conscience as the repository of God's will for us when not otherwise blunted by culture or willfulness. These distinctions are subtle but significant: conscience cannot claim primacy while it is treated solely as the creation of parents since it must be able to judge parental and cultural values not simply conform to them. The reader must grapple with these divergent views as s/he reads this chapter. The question I seek to answer is whether Heart conscience retains its innate potential to express the Voice for God, even when initially blocked by constellations of the Empowering archetype and the ego-aspects created to cope with those constellations. Or stated another way, can Ego conscience – though originally in the thrall of parents and culture, be transformed, through relationship with Christ, into a reliable conduit of the Voice for God?

THE PSYCHOLOGICAL PERSPECTIVE

Freud's Superego

Freud's definition of conscience challenged its historical position as a Voice for God. Simultaneously, its inclusion in his tripartite system of dynamics (i.e. id, ego, super-ego) made it an integral part of his study of personality.[19] Other theorists, notably Jung, disagree with Freud as to whether it was parents or parents-constellated-by-archetype that shaped conscience. But few would question the observation that parents are crucial to the initial expression of Ego conscience as most people experience it; and Freud must be credited with obliging us to take this more critical view of it.

It was Freud's contention that, "Although it is amenable to every later influence, it [Super-ego/conscience] preserves throughout life the character given it by its derivation from the father-complex, namely, the capacity to stand apart from the ego and to rule it.... the mature ego remains subject to its domination. As the child was once compelled to obey its parents, so the ego submits to the categorical imperative pronounced by its super-ego".[20] C.S. Hall was an expositor of Freud. His primer on Freudian psychology was widely read in the mid 20th century. Hall reiterates Freud's thesis: "It [super-ego] represents the ideal rather than the real, and it strives for perfection rather than for reality or pleasure. The super-ego is the person's moral code. It develops out of the ego as a consequence of the child's assimilation of his parents' standards regarding what is good and virtuous [ego-ideal] and what is bad and sinful [conscience]. By assimilating the moral authority of his parent, the child replaces their authority with his own inner authority. The internalization of parental authority enables the child to control his behavior in line with their wishes, and by doing so to secure their approval and avoid their displeasure [brackets added]."[21]

Freud conceptualized the super-ego as comprised of two parts: the ego ideal and the conscience. In his conceptualization, the ego ideal reinforced the good with pride while conscience punished the bad with guilt and shame. Thus, the role of conscience is always negative in Freud's paradigm. Whereas the ego ideal rewards with a sense of pride, conscience is seen as the internal source of punishment for bad thoughts and actions. To paraphrase C. S. Hall, the super-ego has the same control over the child's ego as the parents had over the child. It holds the ego responsible for moral and immoral acts. Moreover, the ego could be punished for merely thinking of doing something. A thought was the same as a deed in the eyes of the super-ego. Punishment could be experienced as guilt or shame, or other negative feelings, or even injury, illness or loss.[22]

Freud's view of conscience was pessimistic as well as negative. He felt that its unrealistic, unforgiving morality was atavistic and unhealthy, particularly, in light of the ego's ability to "realistically" defer gratification of id impulses. "The super-ego forces the ego to see things as they should be and not as they are. The id forces the ego to see the world as the id wishes it would be. In either case, the secondary process, reality testing, and the reality principle are perverted by irrational forces." [23] In the mid 20th century, Ayn Rand championed Freud's appreciation of the ego, *in extremis*, in such novels as *Fountainhead* [24] and *Atlas Shrugged*;[25] and her philosophy, in turn, was used by Brandon [26] to develop his psychology of self-esteem. Ayn Rand touched a cord in the agnostic, upwardly mobile, post-war generation by her espousal of rational self-interest as the basis for action, and productive achievement as the noblest endeavor. That notwithstanding, and even as Freud denigrated and secularized conscience, and sought at every turn to undermine its authority, a close reading of his papers will show that he also imbued it with an "almost daemonic power" to decisively cripple the very ego he championed.[27] In the end, Freud was forced to conclude that conscience was truly overbearing, exceedingly resistant to therapeutic intervention, and often the primary cause of neurotic characterological development such as found in depressive, hysterical, and obsessive compulsive disorders.[28]

"There is no doubt that there is something in these people that sets itself against their recovery and dreads its approach as though it were a danger...In the end we come to see that we are dealing with what may be called a "moral" factor, a sense of guilt, which is finding atonement in the illness and is refusing to give up the penalty of suffering. We are justified in regarding this rather disheartening explanation as conclusive. But as far as the patient is concerned this sense of guilt is dumb; it does not tell him he is guilty; he does not feel guilty he simply feels ill. This sense of guilt expresses itself only as a resistance to recovery which is extremely difficult to overcome...This description we have given applies to the most extreme instances of this state of affairs, but in a lesser measure this factor has to be reckoned with in very many cases, perhaps in all severe cases of neurosis." [29]

One reason for Freud's inability to alter conscience appears to be his unwillingness to address shame. In his early writings he acknowledged the role of shame in the repression of 'incompatible ideas,' [30] but failed to focus on shame as the primary reason for repression. Melvin Lansky, a senior training analyst, writing in the Journal of the American Psychoanalytic Association, reviews all of Freud's major writings plus those of major contributors to psychoanalytic thought over the past eleven decades, and concludes that *the discipline has utterly failed to address the central role shame plays in the function of conscience.*[31] His concluding speculation as to why is very telling. To quote him:

Perhaps this turning away from shame is due to the fact that the shame of others makes us feel about ourselves what we do not like to feel: vulnerable, weak, powerless, dependent, contingent, disconnected, and valueless. By contrast, the guilt of others, for all of its severity and pain, gives both the person experiencing that guilt and us as onlookers a sense of power. Despite the pain from the judgments of the guilty person's conscience, we as psychoanalysts feel about ourselves something of the sense of completeness, autonomy, and power that we would like to feel. One might speculate that the emerging shame of the other stirs up our own difficulty bearing shame, our helplessness, and our anxiety that we may prove defective and fail in our professional roles *because we, in facing the patient's incipient experience of shame, will be found to have nothing effective to offer.* Perhaps the prospect of experiencing the shame of another—especially someone who has turned to us for help—so stirs up in us feelings of helplessness, ineffectiveness, powerlessness, and worthlessness as analysts, thereby signaling the danger of our experiencing shame in our professional roles, that we turn away, unable to bear it. In the analyst's counter transference the idea of the actual or incipient shame of the other, then, becomes our incompatible idea—which must be pushed away from our clinical or theoretical awareness because the emotional dangers to us seem too overwhelming and, in our status as professionals, unbearable [italics added].[32]

In a later section I highlight a number of parallels between Freud's definition of Ego conscience and theology. Here, I consider it worthy of note that neither discipline has definitively addressed the role of shame as it manifests in Ego conscience. In fact, theologians tend to argue that we need to accept the verdicts of a shaming Ego conscience, not attempt to alter it. That argument assumes it is the Voice for God that shames us. Freud asserts – and in this I heartily agree with him, that it is the parent's shaming that condemns us, not God. But without question, in the absence of Christ's redeeming power, Ego conscience will convict with shame. Only Christ – or a comparable higher power capable of channeling the Holy Spirit, appears able to mitigate that emotion with love and forgiveness. So any therapist *unwilling* to call upon a higher power will be an insufficient resource as regards the redemption of conscience.

The Archetypal Conscience Described by Jung

I need to begin this section by emphasizing that Jung did not refer to conscience as a constellation of the Empowering archetype, nor did he refer to the normative manifestation of conscience in most people as Ego conscience. For Jung, conscience is only hypothetically archetypal. If he had named it, he would probably have called it the Conscience archetype, but in his sole paper on the subject he refers to it only as conscience. Likewise, neither Freud nor Jung referred to conscience as both archetypal and Ego derived. Ego conscience is my term for a synthesis incorporating Jung's archetypal hypothesis and my clinical observations of the Ego's dominant role in amplifying the Voice-of-conscience by the creation of Dominant selves with the power to self-shame. I will argue later that both constructs are necessary for an operational definition of Ego conscience as it manifests in most people. Jung acknowledges that for most people 'conscience' is like Ego conscience as I describe it, but he also argues for a definition that would allow for a spiritual dimension, what I have identified as the Christ conscience process.

Jung wrote one essay on conscience late in his life.[33] Thus, on the one hand he wrote very little on the subject (18 pages in 20 volumes), but on the other hand what he said was based on a fully developed theory of psychology and the wisdom of years of reflection and experience. In this essay he is tentative about reducing conscience to an archetype: "...I would suggest reducing the notion of the *vox Dei* to the hypothesis of the archetype, for this at least is understandable and accessible to investigation. The archetype is a pattern of behavior that has always existed, that is morally indifferent as a biological phenomenon, but possesses a powerful dynamism by means of which it can profoundly influence human behavior."[34] However, he then goes on to say: "... by the concept of the archetype nothing final is meant, and that it would be wrong to suppose that the essence of conscience could be reduced to nothing but the archetype. The *psychoid nature* of the archetype contains very much more than can be included in a psychological explanation [italics added]."[35,36] Thus, he concludes:

> For this reason I have not been able to confine myself exclusively to the psychological [archetypal] nature of conscience, but have had to consider its theological aspect. From this point of view it cannot be presupposed that the act of conscience is something that, of its own nature, can be treated exhaustively by means of rational psychology. *We have, rather, to give priority to the assertion which conscience itself makes – that it is a voice of God.* This view is not a contrivance of the intellect, it is a primary assertion of the phenomenon itself: a numinous imperative which from ancient times has been accorded a far higher authority than the human intellect [brackets and italics added].[37]

Jung's definition of conscience treats it as both archetypal and psychoidal (i.e. bounded by the world of Spirit and susceptible to spiritual influence).[38] Thus, while conscience is hypothetically archetypal, 'conscience' could also be far more. But Jung's formally stated theoretical position did not really allow for the psychoidal, so that concept is really left undefined except for one example in his paper (described below).

The concept of archetype has gained credence over the past fifty years, but there are still many misconceptions as to what it means. Stevens'[39] discussion of archetypes, coupled with his review of all the research in support of the concept, is one of the best I have come across, and I lean heavily on it in this summary. He begins by offering a contrast with Freud.

> Whereas Freud had assumed that most of our mental equipment was acquired individually in the course of growing up, Jung asserted that all the essential psychic characteristics that distinguish us as human beings are determined by genetics and are with us from birth. These typically human attributes Jung called archetypes. He regarded archetypes as basic to all the usual phenomena of human life. While he shared Freud's view that personal experience was of critical significance for the development of each individual, he denied that this development was a process of accretion or absorption occurring in an unstructured personality. On the contrary, for Jung, the essential role of personal experience was to *develop what is already there* – to actualize the archetypal potential already present in the psychophysical organism.[40]

Conscience, as an archetype, can be likened to other processes that appear universally in human beings - mothering, the heart-felt, shadow qualities, free will, contra-sexual qualities, intuition, etc. None of these words have precise meanings but all have feeling tones and values that make it hard to imagine a total life experience without them. The Heart, for example, cannot be defined by any particular definition or image of heart (certainly no one would restrict its meaning to physical anatomy); rather, it bespeaks a psychic reality few would deny, and only then if they are willing to define themselves as 'heartless.' Archetypal energy patterns exist a priori – they organize experience by *constellating* images, i.e. authorizing them with a particular power, and directing the individual via the images they constellate. Once constellated, the image acquires the quality of a categorical imperative. The source of archetypal energies resides in and defines the collective unconscious (which I will elsewhere define as the *conscious domain of Soul*). They are quickened to activity by an individual's life experiences. When there is a discernible 'absence' of conscience, the individual is labeled psychopathic and considered dangerously untrustworthy.[41]

The relevance of archetypes is well illustrated by the Mothering archetype whose constellation appears to be absolutely essential to a child's survival. Imagine within your Mind a number of magnets each different in what each attracts and how each affects the individual once something is attracted to it. Actuating a magnet completes a circuit connecting Soul with Mind. This analogy is particularly apt because, while the magnet is always active, it is only actuated (made conscious) when some content in the Mind is drawn to it. By way of illustration, let us call one of these magnets the *Mothering* archetype. This archetype constellates and organizes images, actions, feeling tones, and motifs that will define *mothering* for the child. In effect, this particular magnet has the power to constellate anything related to *mothering*, and authorize whatever it attracts with the power to govern *a child's responses to mothering*. The magnetic force has no shape of its own; rather it expresses itself by constellating experiential images that resonate with its particular energies, thereby shaping the child's consequent behavior. It distinguishes the images it constellates from all others, and assigns unique values and emotions to what it identifies.

Archetypes play a superordinate role in human behavior. For example, the role of the mothering archetype is so vital to an infant's well being that if there is no experience constellated by this archetypal energy the infant is likely to languish and die. Think of an archetype as a kind of psychic organ whose activity is absolutely critical to our very being, not unlike the heart, lungs or stomach. If these physical organs are absent or irreparably dysfunctional we die. Likewise, if the mothering archetype is not constellated in an infant's psyche, i.e. becomes a conscious experience in the infant, the lack will irreparably damage or kill it - an observation conclusively and tragically documented by Spitz more than sixty years ago.[42]

As a rule, individuals do not choose whether an archetype constellates images.[43] Fate (i.e. 'nurture') determines its initial activation and how it affects the individual once it is activated. Archetypal constellations are never considered pathological, but they can be cloaked in a personally conditioned conflict.[44] If images, symbols, and feeling tones expressing the archetype are threatening to a conscious sense of self, then the Ego can repress or defy them - always a regrettable action. The most common experience of this is the Western male's fear of feminine qualities constellated by his anima, which he summarily projects rather than owns; or a woman's comparable fear of masculine qualities. Once activated, an archetype will make itself felt one way or another. If it is denied conscious awareness, it will simply make itself felt in a negative way as in nightmares, psychosomatic illnesses, obsessions, compulsions, addictions, enthrallment, projections, etc. We can never repress archetypal images with impunity once they are constelled in the Mind. Even if conflictual, the archetype will pose a conflict "that it has been incumbent on man to suffer and solve from time immemorial."[45]

An archetypal constellation need not conform to *expected* parameters, since it is the archetype that gives shape and meaning to experience not visa versa. For example, we would generally expect female, maternal images to quicken and define the *mothering* archetype in a child, but if a father were obliged to enact that role from birth then *his image and actions* could well be identified by the infant's responses as 'good enough' to actuate and define the archetype.[46] It is the archetype that defines the experience as good enough. If the father's activity fits the parameters needed to constelle a sense of adequate mothering, the infant will live, and likely even thrive.

Hopefully, the forgoing provides an adequate description of conscience as the manifestation of an archetype. But it does not help us to understand how conscience can go against prevailing moral beliefs. We have examples of this in some of our most revered historical figures, e.g. St. Paul, Joan of Arc, Martin Luther, and Gandhi. Martin Luther's challenge to the Catholic Church is good example.[47] Luther seems quite justified from the perspective of history, but he did not have a Protestant reformation backing him the day he hammered his edicts to the church doors - only his conscience impelling him to act against the superiors he had vowed to obey. Sometimes the impelling primacy of conscience is even more dramatic as in the case of Satan's testing of Job. In Job's heart, his conscience remained clear, even though his afflictions, family, and neighbors judged him guilty.[48] His conscience upheld him despite the condemnation of all around him. If conscience as a psychic function is not superordinate to the morality it appears to support it could not stand against the prevailing morality in transcendent events. Jung highlights this characteristic of the conscience to stand against established mores by distinguishing what he calls the moral (Ego) and ethical (Heart) character of conscience:

Conscience, in ordinary usage, means the consciousness of a factor, which in the case of a 'good conscience' affirms that a decision or an act accords with morality and, if it does not, condemns it as 'immoral' [Ego conscience]. This view, deriving as it does from the *mores,* from what is customary, can properly be called 'moral.' Distinct from this is the ethical form of conscience, which appears when two decisions or ways of acting, both affirmed to be moral and therefore regarded as 'duties,' collide with one another. In these cases, not foreseen by the moral code because they are mostly very individual, a judgment is required which cannot properly be called 'moral' or in accord with custom.[49] Here the decision has no custom at its disposal on which it could rely. The deciding factor appears to be something else: it proceeds not from the traditional moral code but from the unconscious foundation of the personality. The decision is drawn from dark and deep waters. It is true that these conflicts of duty are solved very often and very conveniently by a decision in accordance with custom, that is, by suppressing one of the opposites. But this is not always so. If one is sufficiently conscientious the conflict is endured to the end, and a creative solution emerges which is produced by the constelled archetype and possesses that compelling authority not unjustly characterized as the voice of God. The nature of the solution is in accord with the deepest foundation of the personality as well as with its wholeness; it embraces conscious and unconscious and therefore transcends the ego [brackets added].[50]

Jung's view of the 'creative solution' comes closest to my definition of conscience as a Voice for God or Heart conscience. It is, as he notes, relatively rare. More often, when faced with two equally moral but opposing choices, we simply suppress one and act on the other. That is characteristic of an Ego conscience.

Where I differ with Jung is his attribution of the moral and ethical solutions to the same archetype. I would argue that Jung's 'ethical' solutions must derive from a force other than the Empowering archetype (or whatever name he would give it). Jung's 'moral' conscience is a complex of parental and cultural mores that cannot be repressed with impunity. Only under special circumstance, which Jung can point at but not define operationally, can conscience function as something more than an archetypal constellation. I am calling that 'something more' a Christ conscience or – in the case of Job, a Heart conscience. For most people, Jung's archetypal conscience is an Ego conscience; and only on rare occasions does it seem to manifest as something more than the Voice-of-conscience. Finally, I would note that Jung's understanding of conscience reflects the perspective of conscience since its translation into Latin, i.e. *conscientia*. That translation represented a significant shift theologically and is discussed at length in the next section. Basically, the 'conscientia' understanding of conscience asserts that it can *guide behavior* as well as punish wrongful behavior. Although *conscientia* is consonant with Freud's superego, which functions as both conscience and ego ideal, *conscientia* is quite different from the original Greek understanding of conscience, which is restricted to shaming condemnation.

Taken together, Freud and Jung have accurately discerned the dynamics of conscience as it has evolved theologically. Freud accurately described the dynamics of an Ego conscience. His understanding of conscience as the voice of the parental dictates helps us to understand why conscience has so often failed as a Voice for God these past two thousand years. Jung's treatment of conscience as archetypal allows for the constellation of Moral authority in parents, which places the source of their authority in an archetype rather than the parent. He also asserts the possibility that conscience can function as more than an archetype; that it has a psychoid nature that could allow it to speak as a Voice for God, i.e. the Holy Spirit. While Jung's writings do not point to a method whereby conscience might be transformed into a Voice for God, he did allow that a higher power could effect powerful changes in an individual. For example, he unknowingly inspired the Twelve Steps of Alcoholics Anonymous when he told a patient that only a spiritual conversion was likely to get him sober.[51] But he never said that a higher power per se was necessary for the alteration of conscience from moral to ethical; he only concluded that it was possible for it to speak as a Voice for God based on its historical manifestations across cultures and millennium.

The Theological Perspective

In the following review, most of the discussion implicitly addresses Ego conscience as constellated by the Empowering archetype. I have yet to find a definitive treatment of conscience as an expression of the Holy Spirit channeled by Jesus Christ, i.e. the Christ conscience process. Theology allows for the existence of a Heart conscience but only as an ideal. Theological discussions most often focus on the failure of Ego conscience to realize this ideal and the reasons for that failure.

Christian theology is always derived, in whole or part, from Scripture; and particularly, as regards the concept of conscience, that is where we need to begin. Old Testament writers defined the Judaic sense of conscience as an attribute of the Heart. "God is spoken of frequently as probing the heart (Jeremiah 11:20; 17:10; Proverbs 21:2; Psalm 26:2)."[52] "Job insists: '...my heart does not reproach me for any of my days' (Job 27:6). Fidelity to heart (conscience) is a central theme in the whole book of Job, as it is in the call of the prophets to fidelity to the Covenant and to the Law (Ezekiel 11:14-21; Jeremiah 31:31-34)."[53] In sum, the Old Testament identified the heart as the center of a person, and it was through the heart that God spoke to the individual.[54]

The Greek word for conscience is quite different from Old Testament words describing conscience as a function of the heart though the effect could be the same. The Greek word – *syneidesis*,[55] appears in the epistles of St. Paul, *and only there*. In the Hebrew Old Testament, the heart encompasses a great deal more than the Greek sense of conscience: the Heart is quite literally the center of Self, whereas *syneidesis* refers only to the Greek experience of conscience. Except for one reference in the Wisdom literature (Wisdom 17:11),[56] *syneidesis* is not found in Greek translations of the Old Testament or New Testament Gospels, which effectively retain the equivalency of the Voice of God speaking through the Heart. In those books, reference is always to the Heart. It is only in St. Paul's epistles that conscience is described as *syneidesis* and distinct from the heartfelt sense of conscience. But it is St. Paul's definition that partially defines conscience as theology has come to understand it in the 21st century.

Syneidesis

Syneidesis first appears in scripture in the writings attributed to St. Paul. "The word occurs twenty-five times in the Pauline writings, including Hebrews, three times in 1 Peter, and twice in the Acts of the Apostles, both times uttered by Paul."[57] C.A.Pierce argues that "... *conscience* was introduced into Christianity under pressure from Corinth, as bound up with a controversial issue."[58] Specifically, St. Paul was obliged to address the concept of Ego conscience in order to resolve a controversy over the eating of meat sacrificed to idols. The concept of syneidesis was strongly rooted in Greek culture. Their mythology and philosophers often assigned it the final moral authority as a governor of behavior.[59] Consequently, a number of influential members of the Greek Christian community at Corinth would argue that if an action did not bother their conscience, it was not wrong. St. Paul argued that while conscience should be obeyed where it judges an act to be wrong, its silence could not be relied upon as assent for an action. Thus St. Paul says: "I have nothing on my conscience, yet am I not hereby justified (I Cor. 4:4)." As Pierce [60] shows, exhaustively, almost all uses of conscience, as used in the Greek translations, fall in the category of moral absolute negatives and are, thereby, insufficient as a justification for action:

> The defect of [Ego] conscience as an ethical norm is common to every man: even if in all other respects it is 'functioning perfectly' it still remains negative only. Conscience comes into operation when the moral limits of a man's own nature are transgressed: but the simplest way to avoid walking over an edge is to stand still. The demands of God are positive, according to St. Paul – standing still is rebuked as sternly by Jesus in the parable of the talents as a gross sin....The onset of the pain of conscience must always, certainly, be taken as proof that the sufferer has done something wrong. The absence of such pain does not mean he has done right or good. It may mean that he has done nothing at all; or it may mean that he has in some way deadened his capacity to feel this pain to a greater or lesser extent – that in fact, his conscience is defective [bracket added].[61]

It was believed that conscience could be weakened, defiled, even subjugated to evil – though never without eventually destroying the individual's humanity. This 'scarring' of conscience is addressed in the Letters of Titus and Timothy, and also Romans. To quote Pierce:

> A single (supposedly) wrong act, according to his master [St. Paul], *wounds* or *defiles* the conscience – smites it and leaves a scar (Tit.1:15). If this sin be not repented and repudiated, and if other sins be committed, the *conscience* becomes in time all scar and no conscience. It is when it is thus completely *defiled* that it ceases to be effective in its proper office: it is callous or cauterized. If the Romans (Rom. 13:5) image be employed, each assault on the created limits of man's nature weakens them; if they be not repaired after each assault at the last they become so elastic, or are beaten down so low, that they can be overstepped with impunity [brackets and italics added].[62]

Despite its fallibility and negativity, conscience was still seen in Greek culture, and by St. Paul, as a final arbitrator of morality when aroused. The reason for this is that the other moral faculty – the thinking Mind, could also be corrupted or persuaded to act wrongly and then conscience was all that remained to correct the wrongful action by making the individual shamefully aware. In effect, the reasoning Mind and Ego conscience were seen as the two bulwarks of morality without which human nature would collapse upon its self, lose form and become void. "*Mind* can be so often beclouded otherwise than by sin – by inadequate knowledge of the facts, by honest error, by defective logic. It is, in fallen man, the earlier to be breached. *Conscience* is the last line of defense, itself a negative thing, a *pis aller*, but better than nothing."[63] This idea of final arbiter is also linked to the concept of choice or free will. "Choice is *prior*, and *Conscience*, if it arise at all, subsequent, to action."[64] Thus conscience, while itself fallible, has the power to refute or challenge bad choices or willfulness, though not the power to override them.

The moral limitation of conscience is its inability to prejudge an action. The effect of an aroused conscience, i.e. shame if caught, guilt if kept hidden, *always follows action*, never precedes it. However, both Greek philosophers and Christian theologians did contend that an act committed in the *Heart* could also arouse conscience, e.g. an individual could feel the *wrongness of coveting* his neighbor's wife. But for St. Paul, *syneidesis* could not inform the individual as to whether an action was good before the fact. Thus, it could not be used as a preeminent guide for morality; at best, it could only inform us when we actually left the path.

Fallible or not, the Greek philosophers and all writers of the Bible agreed that conscience should not be knowingly defied. When aroused it could be merciless and incapacitating on to death. Robert Graves interprets St. Paul's initial response, after his vision of Christ on the road to Damascus, as a Greek experience of conscience that threatened to kill him. According to Graves, Paul shows all the signs of suffering the merciless pangs of conscience for persecuting Christ's followers. In Greek mythology, the Erinnyes or Furies "were personified pangs of conscience, such as are still capable, in pagan Melanesia, of killing a man who has rashly or inadvertently broken a taboo. He will either go mad and leap from a coconut palm, or wrap his head in a cloak, like Orestes, and refuse to eat or drink until he dies of starvation; even if nobody else is informed of his guilt. Paul would have suffered a similar fate at Damascus but for the timely arrival of Ananias (Acts 9:9 ff)." [65] After arriving blind at Damascus, Paul refused food and water for three days. Ananias, at the bidding of God in a vision, lays hands on Paul, "that you may regain your sight and be filled with the Holy Spirit. And immediately something like scales fell from his eyes, and his sight was restored. Then he got up and was baptized, and *after taking some food*, regained his strength (Acts 9: 17-19, italics added)."

In the Damascus story, and others, Christ has the power to quicken conscience so acutely that individuals *stop* their shameful actions. This seems clearly the case for St. Paul. According to Pierce, the early Christians also saw this as occurring during Christ's ministry. [66] In the story of the adulterous woman in which the scribes and Pharisees want Christ to authorize her stoning, Christ is shown quickening their consciences such that their own shame forces them to withdraw at which point he forgives her sins. In this case, their shame is in wrongfully using Mosaic Law to entrap Christ. In effect, Christ has the power to stir conscience, but even more important, he has the power to redeem it, to forgive the unforgivable. According to Old Testament law the sin of the adulterous woman was unforgivable and therefore she had to be stoned not forgiven. Following his resurrection, Christ continues to forgive through the Holy Spirit as in the case of St. Paul.

The significance of Christ's incarnation is his power to immediately forgive the otherwise unforgivable. The trials of Orestes mentioned above were well known in the Greek-speaking world. There are numerous variations on this story but essentially all find Orestes condemned for killing his mother for her part in killing his father. He is ordered to kill her by no less than Apollo or suffer leprosy. But, historically, matricide was the most unforgivable sin; and for it the Furies hound Orestes without mercy. The Furies were "...older than Zeus or any of the other Olympians. Their task is to hear complaints brought by mortals against the insolence of the young to the aged, of children to parents, of host to guests, and of householders or city councils to – and to punish such crimes by hounding the culprits relentlessly, without rest or pause, from city to city and from country to country....In their hands they carry brass-studded scourges, and their victims die in torment."[67] Not Apollo, nor even Athene, can completely reverse Orestes' torment. Only after years of trial, and finally wresting away the image of Artemis, is he finally said to be free of their fury.

Contrast this legend with the power of the Holy Spirit through Jesus Christ to forgive Paul's sin after three days, or Christ's immediate release of the adulterous woman from her sin.

The Greeks were not alone in having little or no relief from an aroused conscience. Under Biblical Law – the original covenant made between God and his people Israel, Levitical sacrifices could not cleanse the *inner guilt* that resulted from sin.[68] "There was no provision in the Old Testament for atoning sacrifice for deliberate and defiant sins, only for 'unwitting' offenses committed by the ignorant and wayward." [69] "But whoever acts high handedly, whether a native or an alien, affronts the Lord, and shall be cut off from among the people. Because of having despised the word of the Lord and broken his commandment, such a person shall be utterly cut off and bear the guilt (Numbers 15:30-31)." But finally, after untold generations, this was prophesied to change under a new covenant announced by Jeremiah (as quoted in Hebrews): "...after those days, says the Lord: I will put my laws in their minds, and write them on their hearts, and I will be their God....For I will be merciful toward their inequities, and I will remember their sins no more (Hebrews 8: 10-12)." For Christians, the death and resurrection of Jesus Christ inaugurated this new covenant. For the first time a power was manifest in the world that could forgive, i.e. release an individual from the merciless pangs of conscience. The Letter to the Hebrews addresses conscience in this new way and is significantly different from anything written before it. For the first time we hear that Christ is the perfect sacrifice for our sins: "...the blood of Christ, who through the eternal Spirit offered himself without blemish to God, purify our conscience from dead works to worship the living God! (Hebrews 9:14)." Christ's willing submission to the will of God (Thy will not mine be done) is the perfect sacrifice for our sins, and has the power to release us from the torment and ostracism otherwise suffered at the hands of an unremitting conscience.

Imagine a worldview in which hardly anything had the power to release an individual from an aroused Ego conscience. In all our written history, only Jesus Christ by the power of the Holy Spirit willingly cleanses our conscience, purifies it and sets it to rest. There is not one of us who has not experienced the shame and guilt of conscience; and while the Ego has developed a number of strategies for dealing with these affects - such as prideful distain or defensive anger, all appear to worsen the individual's condition over the long run.[70] That was Freud's conclusion and final observation concerning the super-ego. We suffer conscience today no less than throughout recorded history. But for the past two thousand years we have also had a redress if we are able to receive the forgiving power of the Holy Spirit embodied in the person of Jesus Christ.

From Syneidesis to Conscientia

Conscientia is the Latin translation of *syneidesis*. Pierce makes the following observation regarding this translation from Greek to Latin:

> In Greek, as was seen, MA [moral absolute] was always MBA [moral bad absolute]; but this is far from the case in Latin, in which *conscientia* could be used absolutely to mean either a *good conscience* (in the modern sense) or a *bad conscience* quite indifferently. Further the word is far from being appropriated to a moral context to anything approaching the extent to which it [syneidesis] was in Greek in general, and in the N.T. in particular. In

conscience which is a realistic judgment of reason. The childhood conscience lays the necessary groundwork for the mature conscience, but if too punitive and perfectionistic or too permissive and chaotic it breeds neuroses that undermine mature judgment. We must recognize that today many Catholics suffer neurotic guilt, or rebel against all moral restrictions, because their childhood training was unsound.[83]

Unfortunately, while Freud's "modern psychology" has definitely highlighted the fallible humanity of conscience, it offers little in the way of correction: certainly it has not offered a means by which one obtains a more "realistic judgment of reason." Freud railed against conscience for undermining his beloved reality principle! So the problem remains: how do you reconcile the desire for conscience to express the Voice for God with the punishing guidance of fallible human parents? How do you supplant parental authority with something more akin to Christ's understanding of the world?

Conscience and the Wrath-of-God

Before moving to an integration of psychological and theological perspectives, I need to examine one other facet of conscience mentioned by St. Paul. In Romans, Paul says that we are subject to the Law not only because of conscience but also because of wrath (Rom.13:5). 'Wrath,' also known as the Wrath-of-God, is referred to often in the Old and New Testaments (261 times). The modern mind has difficulty accepting the idea of a Wrathful God coming into play when individuals or nations appear to exceed the limits ordained by God, but it is really not so difficult to understand. Consider, for example, the defeat of Germany and Japan in World War II. Both aggressively exceeded their territorial boundaries and grievously trespassed on other nations. This weakened their moral integrity both individually and collectively. America suffered likewise by denying the integrity of an ethnic people in the Vietnam War. Countries, like individuals, are weakened when they transgress against others. The same observation is made for territorial animals. They are strongest in defending their territory and progressively weaker as they seek to range into another's territory.[84] Very likely, our planet will express this Wrath-of-God as we continue to exceed its limits. And there is no dearth of examples for persons. Individuals all too frequently provoke the *Wrath-of-God* in their daily lives. Obesity is one of the most commonly observed examples in today's culture. *The Body has lawful limits.* When these are exceeded or abused, the effects place us at risk. Overeating leads to numerous health problems (sic) Wrath. This is true of most addictions, e.g. habitual smoking can lead to cancer, excess drinking to sclerosis of the liver, excessive spending to bankruptcy, etc. Whenever we *persistently exceed* the Body's lawful limits - whatever the reason, there are consequences, if not immediately, then most definitely over the long term.

The Wrath-of-God is a natural consequence of the created limits of flesh. When those limits are exceeded, whether by the Soul, Mind, or Body, the flesh is destroyed. Conscience is expected to warn us when those limits are exceeded. This is what St. Paul means when he says: "Therefore one must be subject, not only because of wrath but also because of conscience (Romans 13:5)." Pierce arrives at a similar conclusion: "We have discovered conscience in the N.T. to be the internal counterpart and complement of *the wrath*. It is the painful consciousness that man has of his own sins, past or, if present, begun in the past. It [Wrath] is *of God* in that it is the reaction of man's nature, as created, and so delimited, by God, against moral transgressions of its bounds [brackets added]."[85] In effect, conscience serves "...to turn man back from every attempt to break from the bounds imposed upon him by his Creator – 'Hitherto shalt thou come - but no further' (Job 38:11)."[86]

Where conscience functions properly, as in the above definition, it functions as a messenger warning us of Wrath. But a basic premise of this book is that conscience needs to be treated as unredeemed, and only potentially redeemable. If our thesis is correct, then its unredeemed state must actually produce Wrath *if it actively blocks the Voice for God*. If conscience truly speaks as a Voice for God, *then God must have a way of telling us when conscience fails to speak as a Voice for God*. The Wrath-of-God serves that function. Wrath will warn us when conscience fails to speak as a Voice for God. An unredeemed conscience will provoke Wrath when the Voice for God is blocked. Freud was the first clinician to observe this wrathful consequence when he noted that the mental anguish caused by an unredeemed Ego conscience was largely responsible for the most severe neuroses. Depression, for example, is by any definition wrathful. It can anguish the Mind until even suicide is preferable. If we accept Freud's conclusion that a guilty conscience causes depression and a host of other maladies, then we are obliged to conclude that Wrath warns us when conscience is dysfunctional – *when it persists in speaking as a voice of parents and Ego rather than a Voice for God as expressed by Christ*.

Confession, penance, and absolution can offer the Ego temporary reprise from a shaming conscience. But, ultimately, these are little better than bulimic purging if the shame is unremitting. Likewise, the Ego can temporarily silence the Voice-of-Conscience with any number of 'medications' such as excessive use of food, alcohol, and illicit drugs, as well as prescribed medications such as anti-depressants. These 'medications' can mask the mental anguish of frequent shaming and the fear of being shamed, but their excessive use will also produce Wrath (sic) the iatrogenic effects of excessive use. Just about any psychotropic medication has adverse side effects. Mental health providers actually foster Wrath when they prescribe medications to treat symptoms and fail to address their causes. Too often, medications are simply used to mask mental anguish rather than addressing it, as if a 'chemical imbalance' caused the illness rather than mirroring it. (For years, people in AA have joked about how frequently their doctors treated alcoholism as a 'valium deficiency.') But however depression is defined, it is clearly a manifestation of Wrath. Left untreated, depression is the number one cause of suicidal behavior, of failure to care for self, and of myriad other self-destructive coping behaviors such as alcoholism and eating disorders. If treated merely as a chemical imbalance, then Wrath will produce iatrogenic effects.[87] In short, unmitigated attack on the self – whether by an unredeemed Ego conscience shaming the individual or by the side effects of masking that pain with any kind of 'medication,' will exceed the brain's created limits. That is what depression is telling us. However the individual responds to a shaming conscience – short of redeeming it, the unintended side effects of merely coping will exceed our physical and psychological limits.

The 'mental Wrath' defined as personality disorders tells us that an unredeemed Ego conscience is exceeding God's law of created limits. Unredeemed conscience is, as Jung named it, a personally conditioned conflict "that it has been incumbent on man to suffer and solve from time immemorial." [88] Whatever the particular form of medication (e.g. absolution, alcohol or valium), we will suffer Wrath for its long-term use. In sum, an unredeemed conscience can generate Wrath as well as being its harbinger. The further Ego conscience is from redemption, the more Wrath it generates.

Conscience can only speak as a Voice for God, and warrant the name of Vox Dei, when it embodies a 'vessel' that unerringly channels the Holy Spirit. That voice can proactively guide us and warn us when we exceed our limits as God created them. Wrath occurs when that guidance is blocked, distorted, or goes unheeded. Stated another way, to the extent that a particular manifestation of conscience distorts or blocks the Voice for God, it will bring Wrath upon the Mind and flesh. By its very nature, an *unredeemed* conscience is bound to precipitate such Wrath. So long as the Voice for God is distorted by parental, institutional, and personal shaming, it cannot be otherwise. In the following sections, I will identify two primary reasons for the generation of Wrath while conscience remains unredeemed. First, an unredeemed conscience precipitates the creation of Ideal-selves whose standards frequently exceed the Ego's level of ability, thereby setting off repetitive rounds of shaming. That fact notwithstanding, these Ideal-selves are exceedingly resistant to change because they function as idols or graven images. Second - and here I introduce a totally new consequence, the unredeemed conscience holds Rejected selves in bondage by shaming them to such an extent they believe themselves unworthy of redemption. The Ego's attempts to cope with these Rejected selves and the toxic shame that surrounds them invariably leads to Wrath of one form or another. But the Rejected selves per se are not the primary cause of accumulated, undischarged, toxic shame in the Body. Rather the primary progenitors are Dominant selves and Egos-in-conflict. Both can generate shame on a daily basis that remains undischarged in the Body's emotional field. It is that accumulation which is hypothesized to be primary cause of all major chronic and recurrent dis-eases of Wrath.

WHEN IDEAL SELVES ARE CONSIDERED

To best appreciate the following discussion, a distinction must to be made at the outset between dissociation and repression. Dissociation is most often identified with Multiple Personality Disorder, now called Dissociative Identity Disorder. But several clinical models – including my own, amply demonstrate the pervasive presence of multiple selves in everyone, which is easily observable once the client is taught to access the Mind via active imagination. Dissociation is the Ego's earliest defense mechanism. Basically, the child's Ego fragments when severely stressed and this precipitates the creation of opposite selves in a reflexive effort to evade further stress. The emotion most likely to fragment the Ego is intense or repetitive shame. The earliest manifestations of Ego conscience – prior to age seven, are created by dissociation. During the earliest period of development, Ego conscience is comprised of a dissociative complex that minimally includes a parentified Voice-of-conscience embodying Temporal authority, one or more Rejected-selves, and several Coping aspects. With the maturation of moral development during the juvenile period (ages 7-12), most individuals will develop a new ego-aspect aptly called the Dominant self. A distinguishing characteristic of that self is its use of self-shame to usurp the role of the archetypal Voice-of-conscience. The Dominant self uses shame to *repress* shameful events. Essentially, the Dominant self learns the power of self-shame, which effectively hides shameful experiences within the Heart. So far as I can determine the import of this Dominant self has gone largely unrecognized by clinicians, though it is clearly dominant in the psyche of most individuals. Basically, this Dominant self *internalizes* all of the dynamics present in the dissociative complex within itself to evade further dissociation. The Dominant self enacts the Repressive dynamic.

A Dominant self uses the power of self-shame to preempt the Voice-of-conscience. It strives to emulate the activity of the Voice-of-conscience so it can effectively become its own conscience. To cope with the tension created by its 'solution,' the Dominant self must then learn to use one or more socially acceptable behaviors in excess in order to temporarily assuage the angst it creates by shaming itself. This excessive use of socially acceptable behaviors invariably results in Wrath. The discussion that follows will focus on the precursors of the Dominant selves, i.e. the dissociative complex, as well as the Dominant self. The Dominant self incorporates each function of these precursors. When the Dominant self is addressed in therapy each of the precursor elements will have to be addressed in the process of healing. The 'redemption' of a Dominant self is crucial to the redemption of Ego conscience, but these selves are rarely redeemable before the client and therapist have worked with the precursors defined by the dissociative complex. (In stating the forgoing, I am getting well ahead of the reader; but I have to start 'planting the seeds' someplace. The Dominant selves are described in great detail in Chapters VII and VIII, as well as the interventions for working with them. But they will 'show' themselves throughout the work so I need to begin sensitizing the reader to their existence.)

The Ideal Selves

Very little has been said till now about Ideal-selves, what Freud defined as the ego ideal. Recall that the ego ideal is the *prideful* aspect of the super-ego, which Freud paired with conscience. As used here, 'Ideal-self' and 'ego ideal' are interchangeable. In clinical practice, I prefer the term 'Ideal-self' since clients seem to identify it more easily. Ego-aspects identified as Ideal-selves strive to emulate the ideal attributes garnered from the parents' positive feedback and/or the *absence* of negative feedback expressed by the Voice-of-conscience. An Ideal-self is very much the product of the Greek understanding of conscience: the *absence* of shaming becomes tantamount to approval by a Voice-of-conscience. Ideal-selves strive to become a source of pride, but the mere absence of shaming will often suffice, since their initial 'ideal' is most often the diametric opposite of a Rejected-self held in bondage to shame.[89]

Clinically, the Voice-of-conscience and Ideal-selves function co-dependently, just as Freud defined them. In active imagination, however, their manifestations are distinctly different.

First, whereas the Voice-of-conscience will be constellated as a parental image or voice, *Ideal-selves are always identified as self-images decisively shaped by the Voice-of-conscience*. To complicate matters, Ideal-selves can manifest in three distinctly different ways. In the early dissociative phase of development they will manifest as the diametric opposite of a Rejected-self. I call these opposites Coping aspects and examine them at length in later chapters. During a brief transitional period, the Ideal-self will manifest as a Familial personality. This is essentially an archetypal constellation of parental gender values. This will be quickly incorporated into a Dominant self when the Ego discovers the power to self-shame. The Familial personality is generally not evident until the Dominant self has been redeemed.

The Dominant self completes the transition to the repressive phase of development. Henceforth, it will assume the role of Ego conscience. Its power to self-shame allows it to hide shameful events within the Heart and preempt the Voice-of-conscience. Clients and theologians are rarely aware of the connections between the Voice-of-conscience and Dominant self. Without reflection, the verdicts of conscience seem to emanate from a Dominant self that effectively drowns out the Voice-of-conscience. But when clients become willing to enter Mind through the psycho-imaginative process, *conscientia* is identifiable as *an idealized self that self-prides for adherence to standards garnered from a parent's behavior and self-shames failures in order to preempt the Voice-of-conscience.*

Most theological discussions of conscience implicitly recognize the existence of Dominant selves as the major impediment to the proper functioning of conscience. Those discussions generally highlight the Dominant self's experience of pride as a primary motivator of its behavior. Most theologians, and scripture, assert that pride is the "mother of evils." [90] At first glance, this theological disparagement of pride seems odd since pride is actively sought after in most cultures. It feels good. When forthcoming, ego-aspects seem to bask in it, though often covertly so as not to seem arrogant. When the individual experiences a deficit of pride, we speak of low self-esteem, which our culture treats as an anathema. This conflicting view of pride is a conundrum for many people. Even though the ways of the world and Ego conscience definitely encourage pride, the very act of seeking this approbation is said to be sinful and – I would argue, wrathful.

Theologically, what makes pride sinful is self-love (philautia). Theologians assert that it is self-love that makes us susceptible to evil; and to the extent that *a Dominant self makes us susceptible to self-love we are in danger of sinning*.[91] To quote Harakas, a Greek Orthodox theologian, "If we are to avoid evil, then there is need above all to recognize that self-love needs to be controlled and watched over with great care. It is powerfully deceptive and there is need for constant vigilance to overcome its ever present influence." [92] The source of this "ever-present influence" appears to be the Dominant self, which essentially functions as its own conscience in a concerted effort to preempt the Voice-of-conscience.

When the Dominant self is closely examined, several characteristics generally emerge. First, it will personify as a self imbued with qualities the individual values above others. For one person, it might be a quality of 'fierce independence,' or 'self-reliance' or 'tough invulnerability,' or 'perfectionism,' or 'high achievement' or 'being rational,' or 'being in control,' and for yet another 'Christ-like detachment,' or 'sensitivity and caring.' A Dominant self can even have the character of a 'turning the other cheek' martyr. In practice, *these qualities can be as varied as the parents who shaped them*, but whatever the particular qualities, the aspiration will be a driving force in the life of the client. Second, the ego-aspects imbued with these qualities appear to function under a rigid, unbending mandate. Even as adults, when we might feel constrained by such qualities, they still enforce themselves with unrelenting authority. Third, and most important, *these Dominant selves always manifest as their own highest Moral authority*; and as such will fail to recognize any other authority other than the parental image that created them. Whether we call this self-love or hubris the effect is the same. A Dominant self will treat itself as 'perfect' and the preemptive silencing of its Voice-of-conscience is seen as confirming this self-assessment. Other parts of the self may need to be saved but not these selves. Whatever the particular qualities of a Dominant self, it will see itself as establishing a standard that is above repute as defined *by the silence* of its Voice-of-conscience. This establishes it as a power onto itself. *It becomes god-like in its derived authority and henceforth has no need for a higher authority other than the parent who created it. An unredeemed Dominant self becomes quite literally an idol, a graven image.* The power to become your own highest Moral authority is hubristic by any measure. But the Ego can disavow this hubris by acceding to the Voice-of-conscience that created the standard, if only by its silence. Nonetheless, to the extent that a Dominant self acknowledges no authority beyond its own standard and the silence of a Voice-of-conscience, it becomes a graven image of God, and a violation of the first commandment.[93]

In Greek mythology, hubris refers to the act of assuming god-like powers, always to our detriment. The most enduring myth concerning hubris is that of Daedalus and his son, Icarus. Daedalus made wings with beeswax and bird feathers that allowed him and his son to escape the island of Crete. But despite his father's insistence on moderation, Icarus became caught up in his god-like power of flight, flew too close to the sun and melted his wings, whereupon he fell into the sea and drowned. Whenever we directly assume god-like powers we risk Icarus' fate. But a Dominant self seemingly protects itself from hubris (which is clinically described as ego inflation). Given that the Voice-of-conscience is not cognitively or willfully amenable to persuasion, the Dominant self *can disclaim responsibility for Ego conscience and the ideal it generates.* And having created it, we would not expect a Voice-of-conscience to challenge its own creation. Once in place, it is easy to understand how a Dominant self could promote hubristic self-love and be resistant to most attempts aimed at changing it.

Hubris notwithstanding, a Dominant self created by the Voice-of-conscience has definite liabilities. First and foremost, the Voice-of-conscience is never forgiving. Consequently, the Dominant self tends to be perfectionistic since mistakes are treated as unforgivable. It seeks to be perfect whatever its particular values. This compulsive adherence is particularly strong for clients whose parents used excessive shame, guilt, or ostracism to shape the standards internalized by a Dominant self. And when parents are downright abusive – emotionally, physically and/or sexually, the internalized pain can be intensified sevenfold. The conflicted standards generated by those parents are likely to be impossible, leaving the individual to cope with more or less constant states of anxiety, fear, low self-esteem, or worse. But however a Dominant self manifests, the most tragic consequence is an active blocking of movement toward God's power to redeem its condition because it is unable to acknowledge any authority greater than itself or the parent that shaped it. Lacking discernment, and imbued with the Moral authority of self-shaming, a Dominant self becomes the felt understanding of what 'God' expects of us, however harsh the standard. By early adolescence, most Dominant selves will acquire a number of defenses to assuage their unmitigating perfectionism. Most of those defenses will fall in the category of 'self-medicating,' which will invariably generate Wrath if the underlying dynamic is not addressed.

The creation of a Dominant self by the Ego is unavoidable; and it has become the modus operandi by which children are inculcated into adult society throughout the civilized world. Ego conscience cannot be prevented, only transformed. Moreover, the process of transformation cannot be rational or willful. Those have little effect on the Voice-of-conscience or Dominant self. Transformation requires psycho-imaginative processes and the grace of God. Once the Empowering archetype has constellated images within the Mind, only a higher power can change the dynamics it constellates, and even then, not by a direct assault on either the Voice-of-conscience or Dominant self. Their embodiment of Moral authority assures that other ego-aspects will experience them as superordinate and complete, if unremittingly harsh and punishing. But there is a way to challenge this sovereignty if clients are willing to look into the darker recesses of their Mind and Heart.

THE REJECTED-SELF

A Rejected-self is created by a parent's use of shame and/or angry physical force directed at an infant or young child. Children are defenseless in the face of such attacks and always experience them as unbearably painful constrictions of their free will. Such attacks will force the archetypal Ego to dissociate the 'offending sense of self' and create a reactive self. This reactive self generally becomes the prototype for an Ideal-self. While I often speak of the Rejected-self in the singular, in fact the Voice-of-conscience can generate numerous Rejected selves. What they all share in common is a dissociative trauma that abandons them to a state of shameful bondage. The Rejected-self can be logically deduced if one accepts the premise that all extremes require an opposite for definition, as light requires dark and good requires bad. An Ideal-self, i.e. Coping and Dominant selves, seemingly without flaw, *are invariably a reactive creation necessitated by the prior dissociation of a Rejected-self*. The Ego would have no need to create a reactive self if no ego-aspect was stripped of its free will by shameful assault and dissociation.

The Rejected-self is akin to Freud's Id or Jung's Shadow, and equally condemned by the combined forces of any Ideal-self and Voice-of-conscience. The Rejected-self is perpetually shamed by the Voice-of-conscience and perceived as an object of unremitting disgust, guilt, and fear by its ideal counterpart. Essentially, Rejected-self is that part of our selves that has *most strongly experienced the parent's shaming behavior expressed emotionally and/or physically*. It could, for example, be the image of a child being angry, if anger was severely shamed by the parents; or the image of a sexually active child, if the parents were sexually repressive, or the image of a silenced child if parents shamed interruptions, or a self perceived as weak, if the parents put a high value on being strong and unemotional. But it can also account for suppressed development of the feeling function, if the child is ridiculed for expressions of feeling; or even the suppression of basic trust if parents frequently violated boundaries. In many cases, the Rejected-self can also embody our contra-sexual aspect, i.e. the feminine in a man or masculine in a woman. But whatever the specific nature of a Rejected-self, it will be clothed in shame. Essentially, it epitomizes the shamefully unforgivable. In practice, there is rarely just one and, in almost all cases, these selves will be recreated over several developmental epochs, repeatedly providing the negative anchor defining what is unforgiveable.

Whitfield [94] popularized a comparable image in his concept of the 'wounded child' but did not connect it with conscience, and failed to appreciate its shameful origins. Likewise, in Eric Bern's Theory of Transactional Analysis, parent-child scripts ascribed the inner critic quality of conscience to parents, but his cognitive approach failed to dethrone the parent. [95] Jung's concept of the shadow comes closest to my definition of the Rejected-self. [96] The two are comparable though by no means identical. In Jung's theory, the shadow seems far broader in scope. [97] They are comparable in that it is possible in both cases to transform their negative energy into something very positive. As I demonstrate further on, the redemption of conscience requires that the Rejected-self become 'the corner stone rejected by the builders.'

The Rejected-self is always disowned by other ego-aspects in its role as *the opposite of whatever Ideal-self emerges to supplant it.* Even so, some individuals are quite sensitive to a Rejected-self and if discerned early in the process can use it to further clarify the Ideal-self and parentified Voice-of-conscience. For example, a Rejected-self identified as homosexual will point to an Ideal-self that actively disowns that identity and a parent who is equally shaming of homosexuals. Paradoxically, individuals often identify it as 'closer' to the core of who they are than the values demanded by an Ideal-self. It is the part of themselves they seek to hide from others, and in the hiding, paradoxically push it deep within the Heart toward the center of Self.

What makes the Rejected-self so significant – quite apart from its seemingly noxious and painful existence, is its 'odd-man-out' role in the triad comprising itself, the Voice-of-conscience, and Ideal-self. Of these three, the Rejected-self is the only one that will *readily acknowledge the need for Christ's healing*. It will always accept Christ as a higher power if given the opportunity. In turn, it is that part of the Ego most sought after by Christ. Unlike the Voice-of-conscience and Ideal-self, which are self-perceived as god-like and therefore self-perceived as un-needful of redemption, this Rejected-self knows it is unworthy. It accepts the verdict of the god-like powers that shame it. It personifies the cornerstone spoken of by Christ. [98] Once the triadic relationship between the Voice-of-conscience, Ideal-self and Rejected-self is identified and understood, most individuals will readily accede that the Rejected-self best fits the description of the lost sheep or prodigal son. In sum, this part of ourselves most condemned by the Voice-of-conscience and Ideal-self (i.e. the good son), is the part of us most receptive to Christ's redemptive presence and protection. Moreover, once the Rejected-self and Christ *can be brought into relationship*, the transformation of conscience has begun. The Rejected-self, by itself, has no power to sway the self-absorption of a Voice-of-conscience or Ideal-self, and regrettably the same is true of the Christ figure alone; but when Christ can join with the Rejected-self, he can effect a change the other two cannot evade. Where the

Aware-ego [99] can bring Christ and the Rejected-self together in active imagination, Christ can take the first step toward the redemption of conscience by *baptizing* the Rejected-self and liberating it from all shame. That observation is one of the most significant discoveries I have made in my initial explorations of conscience. And once Christ has liberated the Rejected-self, he can then begin offering the individual a loving source of guidance and forgiveness.

The Dissociative Triad

What forms the dissociative triad of an Ego conscience comprised of a Voice-of-conscience, Ideal-selves and Rejected selves? Clearly, the authorization of parents by the Empowering archetype is requisite; it is that power which authorizes a parent's shaming behavior. Following the creation of a Rejected-self, the parents' shaming judgments will precipitate the development of *avoidance* strategies, i.e. fearful selves that merely seek to avoid a repetition of the shaming experiences. Later, when Ego has a developmental grasp of absolute opposites, and access to gender attributes shaped by the parents (i.e. the Persona core), the Ego can trigger the creation a prideful self who will seek to usurp the parental Voice-of-conscience by exercising its own power to self-shame. But providentially, this polarization of opposites also insures our ongoing receptiveness to God's redemptive work in the world. An Ideal-self, by itself, is all but indifferent to the redeeming message of Jesus Christ. An Ideal-self is perfect in its own eyes and this perception is silently reinforced by the Voice-of-conscience that shaped it. Without a Rejected-self there would be no self-perceived need for a higher power that could remove the shame holding a Rejected-self in its thrall, or the exponentially greater shame that Ideal-selves will generate.

Once the Rejected-self is identified and felt, the Aware-ego (though powerless to change it of its own accord) can call on Christ. This 'stone' is most receptive to Christ. When the Aware-ego can finally orchestrate Christ's contact with the Rejected-self, the new relationship forged by Christ's baptismal redemption of the Rejected-self can begin to counter the condemnation, self-absorption, and idolatry. It cannot be overstressed that the Rejected-self is totally incapable of challenging the parental Voice-of-conscience by itself. From the point of view of the Ideal-self and Voice-of-conscience, the Rejected self's mere existence is unforgivable, absolutely condemnable and unremittingly punishable, and that is how it experiences itself in the triadic relationship. Only within the arms of Christ – often quite literally, can the Rejected-self know a different experience and regain the free will to return to full consciousness and participate in the emergence of a Voice for God. If the therapist and the client's Aware-ego can facilitate it, Christ has the power to redeem the Rejected-self, nullify the incessant condemnation of a Voice-of-conscience, and reconcile the opposites by opening them to the power of his discernment.

Ideal -self, Rejected-self, and Free Will

Often, I use the phrase 'in bondage to shame' to describe the unredeemed state of the Rejected-self. By this I mean an ego-aspect in the constant thrall of shame. This effectively reduces its access to free will to the point of nullity. Shame paralyzes, freezes, and isolates; and a shamed self can be indefinitely held in that bondage, though not without causing pain to the rest of the psyche. In contrast, the Ideal-self has unencumbered access to free will; it is above reproach. It is completely willful in the sense that it perceives no reason to be the subject to anything other than its own judgment. Ideal-selves such as the Dominant self can be made to feel ashamed, but this can be ameliorated by feeling guilty remorse, making amends, and trying harder. But a Rejected-self is held in perpetual bondage until liberated by Christ. However, once liberated, a Rejected-self can be shown – clinically, to regain complete access to free will. Free will gives it the power to choose; specifically, to choose for the first time who will function as its higher power.

THE REDEMPTION OF CONSCIENCE

Chapters VII and VIII focus on clinical interventions designed to identify and liberate Rejected selves, terminate the power of the Voice-of-conscience, and address the hubristic inflation of the Dominant self that so threatens the Body's wellbeing. The rest of this chapter focuses on the role of Christ in redeeming Ego conscience in concert with the Holy Spirit. The Holy Spirit is absolutely indispensable for the redemption of conscience. It is possible to alter conscience without specifically evoking an image of Jesus Christ, but without question the forgiving, convicting, power of the Holy Spirit is indispensable. Whatever image is offered as a channel of redemption within the Mind, it must be able to channel the 'Voice for God.' *Christ is Christ because he willingly extends the Holy Spirit to any and all who ask it of him*. The Holy Spirit is rarely given such an active role in mainline churches. Their focus is primarily on God the Father and Jesus Christ. But Christ is only Christ because he is conceived by and a perfect conduit for the Holy Spirit. Without the *forgiving* power of the Holy Spirit, Christ would only be a wise teacher or prophet. Only the Holy Spirit *flowing* through Christ's image has the power to forgive our sins. Christ was conceived by the Virgin Mary of the Holy Spirit and baptized by the Spirit of God at the River Jordon at the beginning of his Ministry. Thereafter he became a perfect conduit for the will of God. And before his ascension, he called down the Spirit upon his disciples at Pentecost – empowering them, as the first of many, to exercise all the gifts of the Spirit in his name, and his image retains that power to this day.

Remember too, the Empowering archetype is the source of Temporal and Moral authority in parental images. The Empowering archetype cannot be forced to constellate a particular image, but once an image is constellated, *only a power greater than the archetype can alter the constellated flow of archetypal energy*. The collective unconscious - what I am calling the domain of Soul, is the archetypal origin of Moral authority. Ego-aspects are creatures of the Mind, created to organize the Body's activity with free will intentionality. Ego-aspects cannot alter archetypal constellations except by their *willingness* to call on a higher power such as Christ. (Railing against this thesis is sound and fury signifying nothing.) Only a higher spiritual power is capable of intervening on behalf of mortal images held in the thrall of archetypal energies. If such intercessions could be accomplished by merely mortal images (sic) ego-aspects, there would be no need of Christ or any of the thousands of gods and goddesses in our mythological pantheons. [100] That said, the role of the Aware-ego is also crucial by virtue of its willingness for a higher power to intervene. *Once the process of conscience formation is understood, acts of willingness by the client's Aware-ego are absolutely necessary to initiate interventions by Christ. The Aware-ego's willingness is always a prerequisite to Christ entering the psycho-imaginative space and forming a relationship with the Rejected-self, who cannot act on its own behalf while held in the thrall of shame.*

The transformation of Ego conscience that allows Christ to become a Voice for God requires a large number of interventions. I only focus on the first three in this chapter. The first intervention requires that the client's Aware-ego arrange for Christ to engage the Rejected-self. That interaction allows Christ to bring about a decisive transformation of the Rejected-self by *Interior baptism*, i.e. filling the Rejected-self with the Holy Spirit. In the second set of interventions, the Aware-ego and the now baptized Rejected-self ask Christ to terminate the parents' Moral authority. Finally, the Rejected-self voluntarily opens itself to Christ's power of discernment, which is expected to guide it thereafter. These initial interventions set the stage for the voluntary conversion of ego-aspects that function as Ideal-selves, most particularly, the Dominant self. Their acceptance of Christ as a higher power is crucial to conscience becoming a Christ centered process. Those further steps are all discussed in Chapters VII and VIII. The transformation of the Rejected-self and Christ's termination of the parents' Moral authority is comparatively easy; the conversion of Dominant ego-aspects can require numerous sessions over a period of months. At each step in the process, the individual's *willingness* to seek out and engage these images remains a crucial factor. Free will cannot force a parental image or Ideal-self to change; only the willingness to call on a higher power can bring this about. The therapist's role is to assist the client in discovering the relevant images and bringing them into relationship with Christ. The discovery process can be arduous and inevitably humbling particularly as regards Ideal-selves. Dominant selves are well-entrenched and self-imbued with Moral authority, i.e. the power to reward with pride and self-shame unmercifully. The idea of opening to a higher power is always unpalatable at the outset.

A Number of Obstacles

When initially offered the opportunity, most people are ambivalent – if not outright fearful, at the prospect of actualizing a Christ conscience process. The first difficulty seems to rest with the pervasive experience of Ego conscience as unforgiving. The initial reaction of individuals is to equate Christ with the Ego conscience's power of condemnation. Scripture, especially in the story of the adulterous woman, elegantly demonstrates that quite the opposite is true. We need only imagine the Pharisees and scribes in that story as the 'the conscience of the father' to fully appreciate the contrast between an unredeemed conscience and the forgiving power offered by Christ:

> Early in the morning he came again to the temple. All the people came to him and he sat down and began to teach them. The scribes and the Pharisees brought a woman who had been caught in adultery; and making her stand before all of them, they said to him, "Teacher, this woman was caught in the very act of committing adultery. Now in the law Moses commanded us to stone such women. Now what do you say?" They said this to test him, so that they might have some charge to bring against him. Jesus bent down and wrote with his finger on the ground. When they kept on questioning him,

he straightened up and said to them, "Let anyone among you who is without sin be the first to throw a stone at her." And once again he bent down and wrote on the ground. When they heard it, they went away, one by one, beginning with the elders; and Jesus was left alone with the woman standing before him. Jesus straightened up and said to her, "Woman, where are they? Has no one condemned you?" She said, "No one, sir." And Jesus said, "Neither do I condemn you. Go your way, and from now on do not sin again." (John 8:1-11)

Clearly, Christ can discern our misuse of authority, and expose our shameful motivations to ourselves (as in the case of the Pharisees), but he will not condemn us for what we have already done. He is quick to forgive completely whatever we are willing for him to see. Contrast this with the old Covenant, which insists on stoning – or the unrelenting torment of the Furies, when faced with our shame. If there is anything that distinguishes a Christ conscience process from Ego conscience, *it is this quality of complete forgiveness, rather than punishment, for our trespasses.*

A second reason for client ambivalence is the issue of pride. The Ideal-selves are the primary recipients of *prideful self-love*. A Christ conscience process never reinforces our actions with pride. Feelings of peace or serenity, a sense of conviction or loving approbation, compassion, and forgiveness are all possible responses of a Christ conscience process, but never pride. In effect, every Ideal-self must forgo prideful self-love as a source of motivation and be reconciled with its rejected core. In effect, they must forgo all prideful attachments, most especially, the power to self-shame. That will call for a great deal of patience on the part of therapist as well as tenacity and discernment. Basically, the therapist must also learn to use the client's image of Christ at every turn.

Another difficulty in transforming conscience is definitely cultural. While mainstream churches and theology seemingly advocate for conscience as a new creation in Christ, to the best of my knowledge, *none offer a ritual in which Jesus Christ is specifically asked to transform conscience by making it a new creation enlivened by the Holy Spirit*. If the thesis of this book is correct, parents will always constellate Ego conscience in the first six years of a child's life and - almost without exception, it will be unforgiving. [101] Yet there is no ritual that takes this enduring distortion into account and seeks to reform it. Why is that? It could be that denominations, which are entrenchedly patriarchal – as a number of feminine theologians have argued [102, 103] – lack the motivation to transform Ego conscience. Basically, it underpins the religious and secular authority of patriarchy. Freud was quite clear that the conscience of his understanding spoke with a father's voice. My own clinical experience supports his conclusion. Even where the Voice-of-conscience is matriarchal, all too often her authority is derived from a father, grandfather or male religious leader. In the preponderance of cases, an unredeemed conscience assigns Moral authority to a *patris image*, and by generalization, to other patriarchal figures (e.g. kings, Popes, Bishops, male priests, lawyers, professors, senators, judges, etc.). It is hard to imagine patriarchal churches advocating for a transformation of conscience that undermined the patriarchal, hierarchal, underpinning of their organization.

It may be that no organized ritual can adequately facilitate the transformation of Ego conscience. I can identify the conditions needed to redeem it, but I cannot describe a group ritual that might achieve it. It may be that such rituals did exist in the early church, as I discuss further on, but they all disappeared once Christianity became the State religion of the very patriarchal Roman Empire. For the foreseeable future, I think the process will continue to require a one-on-one relationship such as that offered by therapists, ministers, and spiritual directors. They, at least, should be familiar with the machinations of an Ideal-self long recognized by mystics, such as Saint John of the Cross, [104] and the Greek monastics recorded in the Philokalia. [105]

Another difficulty in the transformation of conscience is the crucial role played by the Holy Spirit. *The therapist must actively support the image of Christ as a channel of the Holy Spirit*. I have intimated this throughout the chapter. In the next section I address it in detail. Essentially, the client's image of Christ must be empowered to channel the Holy Spirit. The Gospels are clear that the Holy Spirit is the source of forgiveness. But many clergy in mainstream Christianity are decidedly uncomfortable with evoking the Holy Spirit in a way that is emotionally transformative.

A Final Hurdle: Entering the Heart

While only touched on briefly in this chapter, work with the Repressive dynamic – as manifest in a Dominant self, is crucial to the transformation of conscience. The Dominant self repressively hides its shame rather than dissociating it. Essentially, it strives to become its own conscience by exercising the power of self-shaming. This repressive act creates a core of accumulated shame hidden within the Heart. To redeem that shameful core Christ must enter the Heart of the Dominant self to purify and consecrate it for the conscious indwelling of the Holy Spirit. In doing so he penetrates the Heart shared by the Aware-ego and all primary selves fused with the Aware-ego at the moment of penetration. This process of penetrating the Heart and redeeming it allows Christ to prepare a heartfelt dwelling place for the Holy Spirit. That indwelling within the Heart has proven pivotal to the creation of a Christ consciousness process. All of this may be difficult for the reader to appreciate at this juncture. Hopefully, the following chapters will increase an appreciation of the Heart's pivotal centrality in the redemption of conscience. What I can share at this juncture is the observation that when clients allow Christ to finally penetrate their 'Heart' the experience is profound and transformational.

The Christ Conscience Process Defined

Experientially, the Christ conscience process is the felt presence of Jesus Christ abiding serenely within us as a constant, heartfelt, source of forgiveness and guidance in all things spiritual, moral, and ethical. The transformation process allows Christ to become a power for discernment and an ongoing conduit of the Holy Spirit. He does not oppose our thoughts or actions, *but by his presence he continually defines the right thing and lovingly forgives the errors*. No temporal or religious authority - neither church, nor society, nor parents - will exceed the authority of this internal image/voice once conscience is transformed. As discussed earlier, conscience cannot override the free will choices of the Ego. But where Christ becomes a Voice for God, then Christ can become the Ego's constant companion, never far from the Ego's perception and often the focus of its attention.

A Christ conscience process does not drown out other voices or images. It does not suppress the existence of shadow aspects or other archetypal energies, though Christ will have a significant effect on them wherever he is allowed to interact with them imaginatively. Nor is a Christ conscience process the only way Christ's power can heal the Soul, Mind, and Body. Conscience is but one function shaping and energizing our thoughts, feelings, voices, and images. The Soul also empowers images with Temporal and Relational authority (discussed in the next chapter). The Soul can also compromise the Ego's integrity when it allows spiritual infestations or shapes our beliefs with karmic issues. These too are within Christ's power to rectify, but different in kind from issues of conscience.

While conscience does not control the psyche, Freud saw it as pivotal in the client's seeming resistance to getting better; and that remains as true today. When pressed to explain why they are ill, many people with severe or terminal illness are inclined to see the illness as a punishment for their sins. This belief in punishment is also implicit in many books on spiritual healing where unforgiveness is an issue. [106] Belief in the 'Wrath of God' is very old, found throughout the Old Testament and even voiced in the New Testament by Paul. Such beliefs are found throughout the world, [107] not just in the Judeo-Christian traditions, and they all attribute retributive power to an unredeemed conscience or comparable concept. In response to the belief that we are 'punished for our sins,' most therapists and religious point to the value of confession and absolution for easing a guilty conscience. But absolution rituals seem unable to permanently alter, in any significant way, the conscience Freud saw as central to the perpetuation of the most severe personality disorders. In my clinical experience, Freud's observations are valid; only his reluctance to enter active imagination, use the *Light* of willingness, and call upon a higher power able to channel the Holy Spirit, limited his therapeutic outcomes. Where these can be introduced into the therapeutic process, it is possible to transform conscience in a way that ameliorates the symptoms described by him and others.

THE HOLY SPIRIT'S ROLE IN REDEEMING CONSCIENCE

All Christian theology accepts that forgiveness flows from the Holy Spirit and it is asserted here that this power to remit sin is absolutely essential for the redemption of conscience. [108] If the Christ within us lacks the power to channel the Holy Spirit, then he cannot speak as a Voice for God with the power to remit shame. Without exception, the client's Christ image must be able to *baptize* (remit the shame of our falls) with the power of the Holy Spirit. Christ must be able to fill an ego-aspect with the Holy Spirit, thereby remitting the shame inflicted by the Voice-of-conscience and treated by it as enduringly unforgivable. This is a subjective experience of baptism best described as *Interior* baptism. In our contemporary culture, it is generally preceded by the *ritual* baptism of infants or young children – commonly referred to as baptism of water and the Holy Spirit. Ritual baptism is a rite that can be pointed at by an observer. Contrastingly, Interior baptism is the individual's *subjective experience* of the Holy Spirit. Interior baptism is a conscious interior event that *releases* any ego-aspect from the thrall of shame. It is a felt experience of release that the client can immediately observe in the posture and demeanor of any image personifying a Rejected-self. It is argued here that Interior baptism is the necessary requisite for the redemption of conscience however it is received. Though psychotherapy can prepare clients for the transformation of conscience by guiding them through a series of steps, its actual redemption is always treated as a transcendent action of the Holy Spirit consciously and willingly received through the image of Jesus Christ.

(Nearly a decade has past since I wrote the above paragraph. Since then I have clinically proven the thesis. The problem now is that what I say in the remainder of this chapter does not go far enough. In Chapter VIII, I will revisit this whole issue when I introduce the concept of being 'convicted by power of the Holy Spirit.' The effects of that experience are a magnitude greater than Interior baptism. Both are manifestations of the Holy Spirit, but conviction is far more transformative. Conviction has the power to heal any image totally and completely – be it an image of self or other. It does not merely release an image from shame but alters its very being. In what follows, I do not discuss this power of the Holy Spirit to convict, but it follows directly from everything I say below.)

Lacking Interior baptism as an integral part of the liturgy, orthodox theologies have been obliged to treat an unredeemed conscience as the status quo for the better part of seventeen hundred years, even though the ritual equivalents of Interior baptism, i.e. being 'slain in the Spirit' or specific prayers for the indwelling of the Holy Spirit, were offered to every adult entering a Christian community in the early church. In the church's first 200 years, there were three expectations regarding baptism: 1) the individual – always an adult, consciously and wholeheartedly consented to the baptism; 2) the person praying for the initiate asked for a *manifest* indwelling of the Holy Spirit of God through Jesus Christ; and 3) the person, so blessed, received confirmation of the Spirit's indwelling by a *felt* remission of sin often accompanied by an upsurge of positive emotion and consequent gifts of the Spirit.

Being "slain in Spirit" – strongly associated with Pentecostal and Charismatic movements – is seen to have an effect comparable to that experienced by adults in the early church. [109] Interior baptism differs from it in two respects. First, it is the client who makes the request of Christ. In contrast, being slain in Spirit is 'received' when one person prays for it on behalf of the recipient, though the recipient is generally willing or s/he would not be present. Second, *Interior baptism* is offered to specific aspects of the Ego that have been judged *unforgivable* by a Voice-of-conscience. In contrast, being slain in the Spirit is offered to whatever ego-aspect consciously seeks it out; and it is unclear if that self consciously extends it to the Rejected-self, which cannot ask on its own behalf. I suspect that – too often, being slain in the Spirit may actually be sought as a means of "drowning out" the Rejected-self, rather than redeeming it. It really depends on the intent of the recipient. If s/he is truly asking on behalf of the most sinful sense of self, then s/he could very well experience Interior baptism at an altar.

All initiations into Christian churches require a ritual baptism of water and the Holy Spirit, be it sacramental or symbolic, which follows a general form involving the use of water and a formula prayer: "I baptize you in the Name of the Father, the Son, and the Holy Ghost." (All three persons of the trinity must be named, though they can be designated by different names. Thus, an individual could be baptized in the Name of the Creator, Redeemer, and Sustainer.) Persons are not typically baptized a second time by water and the Holy Spirit, unless the second rite is conditional, [110] or the individual makes a significant shift in denominations and the new denomination considers the first baptism invalid. For example, some churches such as the International Church of Christ consider the baptisms of all other Christian churches invalid and insist that new members be re-baptized; the same is true of Roman Catholic church vis-à-vis protestant denominations. But most protestant denominations are more accepting. In those churches, if a person has been baptized as an infant or adult with water and the Holy Spirit, by a proper form of the ritual, then all further 'baptisms' are treated as a renewal, actualization, or quickening of the Holy Spirit already indwelling within the individual through Jesus Christ. So far as I can determine, there is nothing in those rituals that specifically addresses the conscious redemption of a Rejected-self. In most churches, baptism of water and the Holy Spirit is expected to represent *formal* entry into a Christian community without attendant charisms or remission of particular sins. Even St. Paul had to receive a separate baptism for admission to the Christian community of Damascus after being redeemed with the power of the Holy Spirit.

I do consider it noteworthy that being slain in the Spirit has played a pivotal role in the development of Classical Pentecostal churches, which have grown to become the largest Protestant denomination since their inception in 1901. [111] But the *felt experience* of the Holy Spirit is down played in most mainline denominations except in their peripheral Renewal or Charismatic movements. [112] In the early life of the church (first 200 years), Christianity appeared to model itself in significant ways after other mystery religions of that era such as the Elysian mystery sects of the Greeks. [113] Adults seeking to join a Christian community were expected to undergo at least three years of instruction before partaking of the Eucharistic mysteries. [114] But this instruction commenced with their baptism with water and the Holy Spirit, *and it was expected that the indwelling of the Holy Spirit would be manifest by one or more charisms as described by St. Paul and others.* [115] This initiation was seen as modeling Christ's own baptism at the beginning of his ministry. [116] It was after his baptism by John the Baptist, and testing in the desert, that Christ declared: "The spirit of the Lord is on me, for he has anointed me to bring the good news to the afflicted. He has sent me to proclaim liberty to captives, sight to the blind, to let the oppressed go free, to proclaim a year of favor from the Lord (Luke 4:18)."

In the early church, before Christianity became the State religion of the Roman Empire, the Church Fathers [117] most often quoted for that period asserted that adult baptism was expected to both remit sin and impart charisms – manifest gifts of the Holy Spirit, as described by St. Paul. [118] McDonnell and Montague [119] give numerous reasons for the gradual decline of these charisms including heresies surrounding the gift of prophesy [120] and the emerging belief that *infant baptism was necessary and sufficient*. What they only touch on indirectly was the politicizing of the clerical hierarchy – particularly the Bishops, after Christianity became the State religion of the Roman Empire (313 AD). Historically, the Bishops had been the primary administrators of baptism to adult initiates, but that role was eclipsed by the need to baptize great numbers of people. Infant baptism fell to the many priests demanded of a State religion, though Bishops did continue to function as the sacramental administrators of Confirmation. More to the point, in succeeding centuries as the Bishoprics – and most especially the Papacy – became centers of temporal power, the positions were too often filled by persons with less than spiritual aspirations. The consequent waning of spiritual gifts in bishops and initiates led theologians to argue that the gifts were no longer expected of everyone in the church. Interestingly, many of the 'heresies' declared by the church after 313 AD would flow from 'manifestations of the Spirit' that challenged the suppressive temporal authority of Roman clerics who sought to impose dogma, doctrine, and community tithes by force of arms.

The politicization of the Christian church, [121] the emergent belief in infant baptism, and heresies attributed to the gift of prophecy, have all contributed to the suppression of the Holy Spirit as a felt experience in mainline churches. Rather than seeking to be 'slain in the Spirit' – by which I mean a subjective, transformative, experience, such rituals have been actively discouraged, and that is still the case today in most mainline churches. It is argued here that this suppression has inadvertently blocked one of the most significant promises of Christian faith, namely, a new conscience made in the image of Christ, and has forced theologians to accept an unredeemed Ego conscience as the status quo for the better part of two millennia. Insistence on *infant baptism* has institutionalized the unredeemed conscience since infant baptism generally precedes the creation of the dissociative dynamic that sustains an Ego conscience. Unless a Rejected-self can *experience* the felt release offered by the Holy Spirit, there is no way to begin undoing the cumulative adverse effects of an Ego conscience.

Dogmatically, the Holy Spirit already abides within individuals baptized as infants, but not necessarily in any experiential sense, and rarely within their image of Christ as a willing conduit. There is rarely a conscious juxta-positioning of Christ as a conduit of Holy Spirit unless the individual has willingly accepted Christ in an adult ritual sought out for that purpose: a ritual in which Christ becomes the channel of their felt experience of the Holy Spirit's forgiving grace. This opening to the Spirit through Christ can take place in several ways: in Protestant congregations through conversion experiences of being 'saved,' or by any ritual commonly referred to as being slain in the Spirit. [122] Some of the clients I have worked with who were most receptive to the idea of a Christ conscience process had sought out such a baptism of the Spirit in a well-remembered ceremony that each considered life changing. It must be stressed, however, that such rituals are not a prerequisite for Interior baptism. *So long as the client is open to the idea of the Holy Spirit flowing through their image of Christ, that appears to be sufficient for the baptism of a Rejected-self.* Moreover, in my clinical experience, being slain in the Spirit does not by itself insure that aspects of the Rejected-self are baptized. In most cases, the Interior baptism of the Rejected-self and consequent transformation of conscience must still be accomplished through therapy or spiritual direction. I do not know of any rituals that specifically addresses the ego dynamics addressed in this book, except the interventional experiences of Interior baptism and conviction by the Holy Spirit discussed in Chapter VIII.[123]

The reader should not impart a mystical or hysterical aura to this need for Interior baptism. While *external ritualizations* of baptism in the Spirit can be dramatic for participants and observers, it is nonetheless a common and oft repeated experience in Pentecostal and Charismatic renewal movements in the 20th and 21st century. But that said, I will grant that most mainstream churches remain decidedly skeptical at the thought of encouraging baptism in the Spirit. Thankfully, external ritualization is not necessary for the baptism described here.

Rather, if anything, the process is often punctuated by long silences which the client later reports as very peaceful. Ego-aspects can be interiorly baptized without recourse to external rituals. But, whether interiorly imagined or externally ritualized, the image of Christ must be able to claim the power needed to forgive the Rejected-self for its very existence, not to mention its actual sins (be they real or imagined). That power has always flowed from the Holy Spirit. As Jung observed, we are dealing here with psychic truths. [124] Whatever the physical facts of Christ's birth, we must accept that he was mythically and metaphysically conceived in Mary's womb by the Holy Spirit, that he was anointed by the Holy Spirit at the river Jordan, and resurrected by God to channel the forgiving, healing power of that same Spirit to all who ask it in his name. That power must flow now, as then, or his image has not the power to speak for God. My ego can speak of God; only a higher power such as Christ can speak for God.

Experientially, it is possible for any clergy, spiritual director, or therapist to facilitate Interior baptism of the Rejected-self by guiding the client through three internalizations. First, the client must allow Christ to enter his or her imagination. Second, the client must acknowledge that this image of Christ has the power to channel the Holy Spirit if willingly asked to do so. Even if the client was baptized as an infant, s/he must be queried whether the Holy Spirit can manifest through an image of Christ. Surprisingly, many Christians who have only known infant baptism will hesitate to make such a declaration. Their Christ image may be very human, and not perceived as divine in a manner bespeaking the power to channel the Holy Spirit, though the Gospels unequivocally treat Christ as empowered by the Holy Spirit even while he walked the earth. For others, there is a remembered event when they 'accepted Christ,' or were 'saved,' or 'born again,' or 'slain in the Spirit.' For these clients the idea of the Holy Spirit channeled by Christ is quite easy to acknowledge. But however they come to this conclusion, they must come to accept Christ as a willing conduit of the Holy Spirit. [125]

The third condition: the individual's Aware-ego must facilitate the discovery of Rejected-selves and be willing to ask for baptism on their behalf. The felt experience of Interior baptism is always liberating for a Rejected-self. On occasion, clients have reported their image of a Rejected-self being 'consumed by Pentecostal fire.' But however it manifests, there is a distinct sense that the ego-aspect is immediately and permanently released from the bondage of shame. The resulting relationship between the Rejected-self and Christ becomes unconditional, mutually accepting, and loving. I cannot stress enough that change is *never a precondition* of this baptism. The Rejected-self is baptized as s/he is: all 'warts and perversions' fully present and expected to remain. However, where before the Rejected-self would have felt itself living in a state of shame and condemnation, it now experiences itself as forgiven and able to exercise its free will without fear of shameful bondage. Initially, only Christ is seen as extending this forgiveness. At this point, the Voice-of-Conscience and Dominant selves will persist in their shaming, though their perceptions will no longer affect the Rejected-self. Following Interior baptism, primary selves may acknowledge these changes in the Rejected-self while remaining untouched by them. *Only when Ideal-selves open to Christ as a channel of the Holy Spirit and relinquish their power to function as their own conscience will these selves likewise be freed to reconcile with the Rejected-self and participate in the Christ conscience process.* What can occur after Interior baptism of the Rejected-self is a diminishment of the

Voice-of-conscience's power. Following Interior baptism, the Rejected-self can immediately ask Christ to terminate the parental image's Moral authority; and immediately after, the Rejected-self can voluntarily open to Christ as his or her Voice for God. Those acts make it immune to the prideful, shaming, judgments of any self, as it is now guided solely by Christ's discernment and the grace of the Holy Spirit. This redemption of the Rejected-self does not, however, immunize the Body from the self-shaming of a Dominant self, or the defiant shaming of an Ego-in-conflict. Both will continue to generate and accumulate toxic shame. To rectify that state of affairs Christ must now work directly with those aspects. Interventions that facilitate their redemption are described in the clinical chapters.

The process of transforming conscience can begin in earnest once a Rejected-self is freed of shame. [126] At the request of the liberated Rejected-self, Christ can now terminate the parental image's connection to the Empowering archetype. Following this 'dethronement' Christ can now become the Voice for God if the Rejected-self voluntarily opens its Mind to Christ's discernment. The reason why the role of the Rejected-self is so pivotal flows from its willingness to let Christ terminate the power of parental images as the Voice-of-conscience, and to voluntarily accept Christ as a Voice for God, before any other ego-aspect is willing to consider such steps. Without any exception I can think of, the client's Rejected-self has always, unhesitatingly, accepted Christ as its higher power, since this is the same Christ who has freed it from the bondage of shame. But for Christ to abide in the Heart as a Voice for God, other ego-aspects must also come to accept him as their higher power, most especially the Dominant selves that allow him entry to the Heart. Their redemption is by far the most difficult part of the process. It is nearly impossible for ego-aspects that have functioned pridefully, or self-sufficiently, or responsibly, to immediately relinquish their positions of autonomy, if only from fear of being once again vulnerable to dissociation.

The structure of an unredeemed conscience, as I have described it, can be unearthed without the methodologies described in this book. Clients can be asked to self-report their observations of inner-dialogues and proclivities. That is how Freud discerned the effects of conscience in the first place. As Freud observed, the Superego is comprised of a conscience that can be shown to speak with the attributes of a parent, and an Ideal-self, which is essentially a power onto itself (an idol). In turn, conscience and the Ideal-self can be shown, logically and phenomenally, to stand in opposition to a Rejected-self, which functions as the carrier of seemingly unforgivable attributes, actions, and beliefs (what Freud called the id). Even the Rejected-self is discernible without the methodologies described in the following chapters, as books addressing the Jungian Shadow amply demonstrate. [127] But neither of these theories provide for the actual redemption of conscience. [128] So far as I can determine, that can only be accomplished by a higher power channeling the Holy Spirit, and in a Christian context that requires the Holy Spirit incarnate in Jesus Christ. Only by the Holy Spirit's baptism of the Rejected-self is the stage set for Christ to become a Voice for God and begin the process of depotentiating the Ideal-selves. The stone rejected by the builders must first become the cornerstone.

Summary

Conscience has been variously defined depending on the epoch in history, the dominant culture, and the discipline addressing it, e.g. psychological vs. theological. Psychology has tended to overlap with modern Theology but it has not been a perfect fit. In this work, I add to the dialogue by introducing two major re-conceptualizations. The first is the positing of an Empowering archetype that originates in the collective unconscious, and constellates images within the Mind. The images constellated by this archetype are imbued with *a godlike power* relative to the Ego. Parents are the first and most enduring images constellated by this archetype. Early in the child's development the archetype imbues parents with Temporal Authority (described in Chapter VI), which shapes a number of different ego-aspects found to be problematical in psychotherapy. Around the age of seven, a child's cognitive development allows it to internalize the concept of absolute moral opposites. This fosters the development of Ideal-selves as the prideful opposite of a Rejected-self. Working separately but collusively, the Voice-of-conscience and Ideal-selves define perfection and readily shame what cannot achieve that standard, i.e. the Rejected-self and a Dominant self's own shameful core. Dominant selves can seek to preempt the Voice-of-conscience by assuming the power to self-shame and hide the shameful effects within their Heart. Egos-in-conflict can also develop in later childhood and adolescence with the power to defy the Voice-of-conscience. But all of those selves will incur Wrath, as they are inevitably obliged to use socially acceptable or unacceptable behaviors in excess (e.g. alcohol, smoking, overeating, etc.) in order to medicate the tension of their polarized opposites.

The second major re-conceptualization I have introduced is the redemption of conscience by a higher power capable of channeling the Holy Spirit. In support of this thesis I offer a step-by-step process for the redemption of Ego conscience. The primary obstacle to the redemption of conscience is the entrenchment of the reigning Voice-of-conscience and ego-aspects created to accommodate it. These ego-aspects dominate consciousness; and were it not for the fact that the pain of the Rejected-self remains a perpetual thorn, nothing would change. The Voice-of-conscience and Ideal selves repeatedly and painfully condemn the Rejected-self but never heal it. This situation is aptly described by St. Paul in his observation that those who live under the Law are perpetually condemned by the Law. [129] The parentified Voice-of-conscience and Ideal-selves emulating the Voice-of-conscience are the internalized equivalent of the Law.

A redeemed conscience is defined as the discerning, forgiving power of the Holy Spirit flowing through the image of Christ. Jesus Christ's incarnation in the Mind has the power to "liberate the slaves" and terminate the 'lawful' authority of the parents and Dominant selves by supplanting their law with grace, discernment, and forgiveness. The redemption of conscience by Christ is a process rather than a single act. I have already described the necessary steps in general terms. Chapters VII and VIII describe the clinical process in detail.

The redemption of conscience is by no

means a new idea since it is spoken of in scriptures and has remained an 'ideal' of Christian theology since St. Paul. But there does not appear to be any recognized ritual or theology for achieving it in mainstream religions, though it could be argued that it was integral to baptism in the early church. [130] Likewise, the Rejected-self is not new. It can be subsumed by Jung's shadow, Freud's id or St. Paul's 'other.' [131] What may be new is the idea of linking the Ideal-self with the Rejected-self and showing how their reconciliation is integral to Christ becoming a Voice for God.

For several reasons, I have located the clinical chapter on conscience later in the book. First, understanding will be easier when the reader has a fuller grasp of the uses of the *Light* and image of Christ in therapy. Those are provided in chapters III and IV. Chapter V introduces a variety of explorations using both the *Light* and image of Christ that will help the reader better appreciate the connections between Soul, Mind and Body. Chapter VI introduces the reader to the Empowering archetype as a clinical phenomenon and interventions for treating its effects as it manifests in the Temporal Authority of parents. Chapters VII and VIII address the clinical redemption of conscience and the transformation of images governed by Relational authority. Chapter VIII also introduces the clinical application of 'conviction by the Holy Spirit.' Basically, conviction by the Holy Spirit can positively and irreversibly transform any image within the Mind. Anyone who has ever attempted to willfully alter a significant image within the Mind can appreciate the near impossibility of such a feat using the unaided will. But where Christ is allowed to repeatedly convict an image with the power of the Holy Spirit, the transformation is a felt experience that can be judged as total, complete, and enduring without any action of the Ego beyond its willingness.

CHAPTER I ENDNOTES

1 Gula, R. (1991), 'First Response,' in R.E. Smith, Ed., *Catholic Conscience Foundation and Formation*, The Knights of Columbus: New Haven, p.101.

2 Spirit, Soul, Mind, and Body (brain-body) are all capitalized in this work as they name four distinct worlds of being as described by Kabbalah. Heart is capitalized when it describes conscience as the Voice for God and when it refers to the combined effect of the heart chakras of the seven major auric bodies. These distinctions and the reasons for them are discussed at length in Chapters II and V.

3 In this work, Ego is treated as an archetype. Its capitalization is always a reference to its archetypal origin. Within the Mind, Ego manifests as self-images called ego-aspects. Each of us acquires numerous ego-aspects in the course of development. The most common types are identified and addressed throughout the body of this work.

4   In the beginning God created the heavens and the earth. ²Now the earth was formless and empty, darkness was over the surface of the deep, and the Spirit of God was hovering over the waters. ³And God said, "Let there be light," and there was light. ⁴God saw that the light was good, and He separated the light from the darkness. ⁵God called the light "day," and the darkness he called "night." And there was evening, and there was morning—the first day. (Genesis 1: 1-5)

5   According to the Gospels, Jesus Christ was conceived by the Virgin Mary of the Holy Spirit, baptized of by the Holy Spirit at the River Jordon, and resurrected by the Holy Spirit.

6   "But whoever blasphemes against the Holy Spirit will never be forgiven; he is guilty of an eternal sin (Mark 3:29)." "And everyone who speaks a word against the Son of Man will be forgiven, but anyone who blasphemes against the Holy Spirit will not be forgiven (Luke 12:10)." The reason why Christ can be blasphemed against, but not the Holy Spirit, is that the Holy Spirit is the source of forgiveness. When we blaspheme against the Holy Spirit we are cutting ourselves off from the source of forgiveness. In dying on the cross Christ completely subjected himself to will of God and became the perfect channel of the Holy Spirit to all who ask in his name.

7   Freud, S. (1923), 'The Ego and the Id,' in Rickman, J. Editor (1957), *A General Selection from the Works of Sigmund Freud*, Doubleday: New York.

8   Significantly, the parental voice most often used by conscience is the father's. This fact may help to explain not only the perpetuation of patriarchy, but also the reason why patriarchal institutions – including institutional churches, have insisted on the primacy of conscience even in its unredeemed state. By generalization, the authority is passed to other males throughout the individual's life, unless a person can find a way to redeem conscience. Freud was unsuccessful in his own attempts to treat it.

9   This definition is derived from McBrien's definition of a *Christian* conscience. See McBrien, R.P. (1980), *Catholicism*, Vol. II, Winston Press: Oak Grove, pp.999.

10   In theory, other archetypal images such as Quan Yin or Shiva might have the same effect if they are congruent with the individual's beliefs and can demonstrate the power to channel the Holy Spirit.

11   Breasted, J.H. (1933), *The Dawn Of Conscience*, Charles Scribner's Sons: New York.

12   Graves, R. (1960), *The Greek Myths*, Penguin Books: New York, p.424.

13   Wyerl, D.W. (1991), 'The Bishop, Conscience and Moral Teaching,' in R. E. Smith, Editor, *Catholic Conscience Foundation and Formation*, The Knights of Columbus: New Haven, p.127.

14   A notable exception may be the Psychoanalytic literature, which few - outside a small circle of analysts, venture to examine.

15   Freud, S. (1923), 'The Ego and the Id,' in Rickman, J., Editor (1957), op. cit.

16   I am clear in my own mind that Vox Dei always refers to the Holy Spirit channeled by Jesus Christ. But theologians variously, and often obtusely, define it. Harakas, a Greek Orthodox theologian (Harakas, S. (1983), *Toward Transfigured Life*, Light and Life Publishers), asserts that:"...the unique experience of conscience is the profound sense of serious moral obligation and personal responsibility with which the conscience is identified. This imperative character of the conscience is its distinguishing characteristic. And it is in this sense that it is properly referred to as the 'voice of God'...this phrase cannot properly be applied to the conscience if we are primarily referring to the content of the conscience. It is as we focus on the demanding pressure of the conscience upon our being, the profound sense of obligation, that the understanding of the conscience as the voice of God makes sense (p. 110)." According to Harakas, and I would venture, any other theologian, conscience as the *Voice for God* cannot be taken literally: God does not speak to each person telling him or her what is right or wrong. "If that were the case, then there could never be differing ethical perceptions of the same moral situation." (p.111)." (Harakas, S. (1983), *Toward Transfigured Life*, Light and Life Publishers.) Pope John Paul describes it similarly: "...in the depths of their conscience 'individuals discover a law which they do not make for themselves but which they are bound to obey, whose voice, ever summoning them to love and to do what is good and to avoid what is evil, rings in their hearts when necessary with the command: Do this, keep away from that. For inscribed in their hearts by God, human beings have a law whose observance is their dignity and in accordance with which they are to be judged." (R. E. Smith, Editor (1991), *Catholic Conscience Foundation and Formation*, The Knights of Columbus: New Haven, p.2.). To summarize, the Vox Dei or Voice *for God* is always a reference to the felt experience of *authority* of the highest order, very likely Heart conscience.

17   I am very much indebted to Anthony Stevens' explorations of the biological basis of Jung's theory of Archetypes for this perspective and for helping me

to appreciate its value in determining behavior. Stevens, A. (1983), *Archetypes: A Natural History of the Self*, Quill: New York.

18   Jung, C.G. (1958), 'A Psychological View of Conscience,' Hall, R.F.C., Trans., (1970) *The Collected Works of C. G. Jung,* Vol.10, Bollingen Series XX, Princeton University Press: New Jersey, p. 453.

19   In this section of the discussion I generally treat the ego as singular because this is how Freud defined it. But clinically, the ego is invariably fragmented when encountered in active imagination, and then it is more appropriate to speak of *ego-aspects*. Beyond this current discussion, and throughout the remainder of this work, that will be the term of choice when referring to the self-images encountered in active imagination. Whenever 'Ego' is capitalized, it refers to the archetype that generates new ego-aspects demanded by development and circumstances.

20   Freud, S. (1923), 'The Ego and the Id,' in Rickman, J. (1957) Ed., *A General Selection from the Works of Sigmund Freud*, Doubleday: New York, p. 227-228.

21   Hall, C.S. (1954), *A Primer of Freudian Psychology*, The World Publishing Co.: New York, p. 25.

22   Hall, C.S. (1954), op. cit. p. 25-30.

23   Hall, C.S. (1954), op. cit. p. 45.

24   Rand, Ayn (1943), *The Fountainhead*, Signet: New York.

25   Rand, Ayn (1557), *Atlas Shrugged*, Signet: New York.

26   Branden, N. (1994), *The Six Pillars of Self-Esteem*, Bantam: New York.

27   Jung, C.G. (1958), op. cit. p. 446.

28   Freud considered the role of the superego to be central in three personality disorders that to this day remain pervasive and difficult to treat: obsessive-compulsive, hysteria, and depression. see Freud, S. (1923), op. cit. p.229-230 and p.233.

29   Jung, C.G. (1958), op. cit. p. 228-229.

30   "By means of my psychical work I had to overcome a psychical force in the patients which was opposed to the pathogenic ideas becoming conscious

(being remembered). A new understanding seemed to open before my eyes when it occurred to me that this must no doubt be the same psychical force that had played a part in the generating of the hysterical symptom and had at that time prevented the pathogenic idea from becoming conscious. . . . I recognized a universal characteristic of such ideas: they were all of a distressing nature, calculated to arouse the affects of shame, of self-reproach, and of psychical pain, and the feeling of being harmed; they were all of a kind that one would prefer not to have experienced, that one would rather forget. From all this there arose, as it were automatically, the thought of defense. . . . The patient's ego had been approached by an idea which proved to be incompatible, which provoked on the part of the ego a repelling force of which the purpose was defense against this incompatible idea. This defense was in fact successful. The idea in question was forced out of consciousness and out of memory [Breuer and Freud 1895, pp. 268–269]." Quoted from Lansky, M.R., (2005), 'Hidden Shame,' *Journal of American Psychoanalytic Association*, Issue 53/3, pp. 865-890.

31   Lansky, M.R., (2005), 'Hidden Shame,' *Journal of American Psychoanalytic Association*, Issue 53/3, pp. 865-890.

32   Ibid., p. 887

33   Jung, C.G. (1958), op. cit. p. 437-455.

34   Jung, C.G. (1958), op. cit. p.449.

35   Jung, C.G. (1958), op. cit. p.452.

36   The 'psychoid' nature of an archetype is left largely undefined by Jung. Basically, it refers to the idea that the archetype's boundary is open to the world of spirit; that the archetype is permeable or open to the influence of spiritual forces. The best discussion of psychoid that I have come across is by Jeffery Raff. See Raff, J. (2002), *Healing the Wounded God: Finding Your Personal Guide on Your Way to Individuation and Beyond,* Nicolas-Hayes.

37   Jung, C.G. (1958), op. cit. p.453.

38   In his formal statements, Jung treated his theory of Self as a closed system. In effect, the theory did not allow for spiritual influences. The theory, if not its author, was limited to archetypal influences. However, in his memoirs, letters, and post-humus writings, he did allow for those influences. See especially, his memoire: Jung, C.G. & Jaffe, A. (1963), *Dreams, Memories, Reflections,* Vintage Books: NY.

39   Stevens, A. (1983), *Archetypes: A Natural History of the Self*, Quill: New York.

40   Ibid. p.16.

41   Hare, R.D. (1999), *Without Conscience: The Disturbing World of the Psychopaths Among Us*, Guilford Press.

42   "Spitz's (1945,1946) studies of children raised in orphanages and deprived of maternal involvement chronicles the deleterious consequences for children reared in socio-emotional deprivation. Illustrating the extreme in potential outcomes, Spitz documented an infant mortality rate of over 33 percent in a sample of ninety one infants 'in spite of good food and meticulous medical care'." Source: Garbarino, J., Guttman, E. and Seeley, J.W. (1986), *The Psychologically Battered Child*, Jossey-Bass Publishers: San Francisco, p. 14.

43   There may be significant exceptions to this rule. It is true that for infants and children the constellation of archetypal energies is most likely developmental and cultural. However, it is conceivable that constellation of some archetypal energies does require a conscious choice on the part of the individual and only occurs when that choice is made. Shamanistic or ecstatic experiences may well fall into this category.

44   See Jacobi, J. (1959), *Complex, Archetype, and Symbol in the Psychology of C. G. Jung*, Bollingen Series: Princeton, p.25.

45   Ibid. p. 26.

46   The concept of "good enough" is derived from John Bowby's theory of attachment. Bowby, J. (1969), *Attachment and Loss. Volume 1: Attachment*, Hogarth Press and the Institute of Psycho-Analysis: London.

47   Zachman, R. C. (1993), *The Assurance of Faith: Conscience in the Theology of Martin Luther and John Calvin*, Fortress Press: Minneapolis.

48   Job 27:6 - "I hold fast my righteousness, and I will not let it go; my heart does not reproach me for any of my days." In Metzger, B.M. and Murphy, R.E., Eds. (1991), *The New Oxford Annotated Bible with the Apocryphal/ Deuterocanonical Books*, NRSV, Oxford University Press, New York. Unless otherwise noted all biblical verses are taken from this text.

49   A contemporary example is offered by Hugh K. Barber in his book, *A Crisis of Conscience: A Catholic Doctor Speaks Out For Reform*, 1993, Carol Publishing Group: New York.

50   Jung, C.G. (1958), 'A Psychological View of Conscience,' Hall, R.F.C., Trans., (1970) *The Collected Works of C. J. Jung,* Vol.10, Bollingen Series XX, Princeton University Press, p. 454-455.

51   Jung treated a patient who finally got sober after Jung told him he had to experience a conversion – not unlike St. Paul, if he ever hoped to get sober. The patient found a group in England that facilitated the necessary conversion and got him sober. In turn, he was instrumental in getting Bill Wilson sober. Wilson enshrined that series of events in his writing of Alcoholics Anonymous. See Anonymous (1976), *Alcoholics Anonymous: The Story of How Many Thousands of Men and Women Have Recovered From Alcoholism,* Alcoholics Anonymous World Services, 3rd Rev. Edition, pp. 26-27.

52   McBrien, R.P., (1980), *Catholicism*, Vol. II, Winston Press: Oak Grove, p.1000.

53   Ibid. p. 1000.

54   I think it significant that the Old Testament always speaks of conscience in a heart context. It is almost as if the Ego does not exist. Back in the 1970's, Julian Jaynes - a psychologist at Princeton University, put forth the intriguing idea that consciousness and Ego only evolved with the breakdown of tribal nations that forced large groups to move away from their city god centers and the Kings that told them what to do. Until then - as the documents from a variety of sources demonstrate, individuals were guided by the gods, and the gods' earthly representatives, largely without the mediation of an ego. If his thesis is correct, the ancient histories tapped by the Old Testament may be reflecting a people whose sense of self apart from their tribe was very undeveloped, or non-existent, allowing for the unimpeded constellation of gods and kings as Ego conscience. In any case, it is clear from the above biblical quotes that conscience was located in the Heart, not the Mind. In later chapters I will examine the role of Heart more closely. Jaynes' book has remained in print since the 1970's and has even stimulated commentary. I reference the version I read, but there are more recent printings. See Jaynes, J., (1976), *The Origin of Consciousness in the Breakdown of the Bicameral Mind,* Houghton Mifflin Company: NY.

55   The English translation can also be spelled as "suneidesis". See Freedman, D.N., Editor (1992), *Anchor Bible Dictionary*, Doubleday: New York.

56	C. A. Pierce offers a highly technical, exhaustive analysis and exegesis of Syneidesis in the New Testament and Greek culture. He identifies three variants of syneidesis in the Wisdom literature; but notes that the Wisdom literature "... whether written originally in Hebrew or in Greek, represents the meeting place of the Hebrew outlook with the Greek". In effect, the concept as used there is borrowed from the Greek. See Pierce, C. A. (1955), *Conscience in the New Testament*, SCM Press LTD: London, p.58-59.

57	McBrian, R.P. (1980), op. cit. p. 1000.

58	Pierce, C.A. (1955), op. cit. p. 66.

59	Ibid., p. 112.

60	I have relied predominantly on Pierce in examining the scriptural use of syneidesis. At least two other major authorities also reference him and appear to agree with his exegesis in general though differing a little in the details. See Freedman, D.N. Ed. (1992), *Anchor Bible Dictionary*, Doubleday: New York, and Friedrich, G., Editor (1971), *Theological Dictionary of the New Testament*, Trans. and Ed. G.W. Bromiley, W.M.B. Eerdmans Publ. Co.: Grand Rapids, Mich.

61	Pierce, C.A. (1955), op. cit. p.89.

62	Ibid. p.93.

63	Ibid. p.94

64	Ibid. p.126

65	Graves, R. (1960), *The Greek Myths*, Penguin Books: New York, p.431.

66	Pierce, C.A. (1955) op. cit. p.104.

67	Graves, R. (1960), op. cit. p.122.

68	See glosses in Metzger, B.M. and Murphy, R.E., Editors (1991), *The New Oxford Annotated Bible with the Apocryphal/ Deuterocanonical Books*, NRSV, Oxford University Press: New York, p. 324, OT.

69	Metzger, B.M. and Murphy, R. E., Editors (1991), op. cit., glosses, p.320, OT.

70   Freud believed that the superego was directly responsible for much neurosis and especially depression, hysteria and obsessive compulsive behavior; the same can be said for compulsive behaviors used to "medicate" feelings, i.e. chronic use of drugs, alcoholism, pornography, etc. as well as illnesses which the person believes are a kind of punishment for past wrong doing.

71   Pierce, C.A. (1955), op. cit. p.118.

72   Friedrich offers a more detailed etymology of 'conscientia' as used in Latin philosophy and related apocrypha. See Friedrich, G., Editor (1971), *Theological Dictionary of the New Testament*, Trans. and Ed. G. W. Bromiley, W.M.B. Eerdmans Publ. Co.: Grand Rapids, Mich. pp.898-919.

73   The original translation of the Bible from Greek to Latin is attributed to St. Jerome.

74   O'Connell, T.E., "An Understanding of Conscience", In Curran, C.E., Editor (2004), *Conscience: Readings in Moral Theology No. 14,* Paulist Press: New York, p. 25.

75   Ibid. Page 26. "There are not two words in the Greek for conscience, but only one. The distinction between the two concepts may very well be useful, and indeed we shall find it so. But in making that distinction, we must be clear that it is ours, not the Bible's."

76   Two Roman Catholic theologians have argued that such a ritual existed in the early church. In the early church Bishops baptized in the Spirit. But so far as I can determine, that power gradually diminished as Bishoprics became politicized by the Roman Empire. See McDonnell, K. & Montague, G. (1991), *Christian Initiation and Baptism in the Holy Spirit: Evidence from the First Eight Centuries*, Liturgical Press: New York.

77   This aside will probably stimulate no end of debate. It is prompted by the observation that St. Paul spoke of psychic and pneumatic Christians – what contemporary readers refer to as baby vs. mature Christians. Apparently, these distinctions denoted transformations within the person such that the pneumatic Christian lived in grace rather than under the law. The interested reader is referred to Pagels, E.H. (1992) *The Gnostic Paul: Gnostic Exegesis of the Pauline Letters,* Trinity Press International: NY.

78   Harakas, S. (1983), *Toward Transfigured Life*, Light and Life Publishers,

p.101.

79   Philibert, P.(1991), 'The Search For an Adequate Theological Method in the Formation of Conscience,' in R.E. Smith, Editor (1991), *Catholic Conscience Foundation and Formation*, The Knights of Columbus: New Haven, p.88.

80   Ibid., p.88.

81   Ibid., p.87.

82   Wuerl, D.W.(1991), 'The Bishop, Conscience and Moral Teaching,' in R.E. Smith, Ed. (1991), *Catholic Conscience Foundation and Formation*, The Knights of Columbus: New Haven, p.131.

83   Ashley, B. (1991), 'Elements of a Catholic Conscience,' in *Catholic Conscience Foundation and Formation*, The Knights of Columbus: New Haven, p. 49-50.

84   See Ardrey for summation of early ethological studies on territoriality among animals. Ardrey, R. (1966), *The Territorial Imperative,* (reprinted 1997), Kodansha America.

85   Pierce, C.A. (1955), op. cit. p.111.

86   Pierce, C.A. (1955), p.111, footnotes.

87   Anti-depressants may be one of the leading causes of weight gain, as any one who has ever been on an anti-depressant will tell you, which is ironic because it was originally tested as a diet pill. Its other most consistent 'side effect' is a marked reduction in sexual libido.

88   See Jacobi, J. (1959), *Complex, Archetype, and Symbol in the Psychology of C. G. Jung*, Bollingen Series: Princeton, p.26

89   In other writings, Jung recognizes comparable functions in what he calls the persona and shadow, but to the best of my knowledge he does not relate either of those concepts to his definition of conscience.

90   Harakas, S.(1983), op. cit. p.247.

91   The concept of self-love is diametrically opposed to Christ's commandment that we 'love our neighbors as ourselves". Self-love is actually a misnomer;

it is more to be equated with prideful self-absorption than love. Self-love refers to narcissism as a defense against shame, which actively blocks our capacity to love others.

92   Harakas, S. (1983) op. cit. p.247.

93   Exod. 20:1-7: Then God spoke all these words: I am the LORD your God, who brought you out of the land of Egypt, out of the house of slavery; you shall have no other gods before me. You shall not make for yourself an idol, whether in the form of anything that is in heaven above, or that is on the earth beneath, or that is in the water under the earth. You shall not bow down to them or worship them; for I the LORD your God am a jealous God, punishing children for the iniquity of parents, to the third and the fourth generation of those who reject me, but showing steadfast love to the thousandth generation of those who love me and keep my commandments. You shall not make wrongful use of the name of the LORD your God, for the LORD will not acquit anyone who misuses his name.

94   Whitfield, Charles (1987), *Healing the Child Within: Discovery and Recovery for Adult Children of Dysfunctional Families*, Health Communications: Pompano Beach, Fla.

95   Berne, E. (1977), *Intuition and Ego States: the Origin of Transactional Analysis*, TA Press: San Francisco.

96   Two other theorists – R.C. Schwartz and Hal Stone, employ concepts similar to the Rejected-persona, and note the parallels between their concept Jung's shadow. Their work is discussed in some detail in the Chapter IV.

97   Singer, J. (1973), *Boundaries of the Soul: The Practice of Jung's Psychology*, Anchor Books: New York.

98   Jesus said to them, "Have you never read in the scriptures: 'The stone that the builders rejected has become the cornerstone, this was the Lord's doing, and it is amazing in our eyes'? Therefore I tell you, the kingdom of God will be taken away from you and given to a people that produces the fruits of the kingdom. The one who falls on this stone will be broken to pieces; and it will crush anyone on whom it falls." When the chief priests and the Pharisees heard his parables, they realized that he was speaking about them (Matt 21:42-45).

99   The Aware-ego is described in Chapter II and at greater length in succeeding chapters. Essentially, it is the ego-aspect created to accept and use the *Light*, and thereby, to exercise willingness. *Light* methodology is described in Chapter III.

100   The index of Larouses's Mythology is very instructive. Essentially, it lists page after page of gods and goddess, easily numbering in the thousands. There is no culture surviving or extinct which has been without its manifestations of God. See Grimal, P. (1965), *Larousse World Mythology,* Paul Hamlyn: NY.

101   The Roman Catholic Church, among others, offers penance and absolution for all sins identified by a guilty conscience, but has no ritual for the transformation of Ego conscience.

102   Johnson, E.,(1992) *She Who Is: The Mystery of God in Feminist Theological Discourse*, The Crossroad Publishing Co.: New York.

103   Schneiders, S.M., (1986), *Women and the Word: The Gender of God in the New Testament and the Spirituality of Women*, Paulist Press: New York.

104   Peer, E.A., trans. and editor (1959), *Dark Night of the Soul by St. John of the Cross*, Image Books, Doubleday: New York.

105   Palmer, G.E.H., Sherrard, P., and Kallistos, W., trans. and editors (1981), *The Philokalia: The Complete Text Compiled by St. Nikodimos of the Holy Mountain and St. Makarios of Corinth,* Vol. I and II, Faber and Faber: Boston.

106   Often, healing is seen as obstructed by the individual's unwillingness to seek forgiveness. When they extend forgiveness to self or other, dramatic healings often follow. Forgiveness, in Christianity, is the means by which we are released from the burden of a guilty conscience.

107   Karmic law, the underpinning of all reincarnational theologies such as those found in Hinduism and Tibetan Buddhism, presume that all things happen for a purpose and that suffering is recompense for past errors.

108   The Holy Spirit's centrality to the process of forgiveness is reflected in the fact that blasphemy against the Holy Spirit is the only unforgivable sin. Such blasphemy cuts us off from the source of forgiveness. This is recorded in all three synoptic gospels: Therefore I tell you, people will be forgiven for every sin and blasphemy, but blasphemy against the Spirit will not be forgiven. Whoever speaks a word against the Son of Man will be forgiven, but whoever speaks against the Holy Spirit will not be forgiven, either in this age or in the age to come [Matt. 12:31-32]. But whoever blasphemes against the Holy Spirit can never have forgiveness, but is guilty of an eternal sin [Mark 3:29]. And everyone who speaks a word against the Son of Man will be forgiven; but whoever blasphemes against the Holy Spirit will not be forgiven [Luke 12:10].

109   See McDonnell, K. & Montague, G.T. (1994), op. cit.

110   If the first baptism is questionable as to form or intent, then the individual is conditionally baptized by the priest or minister saying: "If you have not been baptized, I baptize you...."

111   See Sienna, V. (1987), *The Twentieth-Century Pentecostal Explosion,* Creation House: Altamonte Springs, Florida.

112   This neglect is recognized even among Catholic theologians. McDonnell and Montague note that: "The element which the Pentecostals have touched on is the one largely neglected in the mainline sacramental churches - that the Spirit received is manifested charismatically and will indeed do so, if one has such an expectation and has not *a priori* excluded it. God, of course, is not limited by our subjective dispositions. But ordinarily God takes us where we are." McDonnell, K. & Montague, G. (1991), Op. cit. p. 89.

113   See Jung, C.G.& Kerenyi, C. (1978), *Essays on a Science of Mythology: the Myth of the Divine Child and the Mysteries of Eleusis,* Bollingen Series XXII, Princeton University Press: Princeton, N.J.

114   See McDonnell, K. & Montague, G. (1991) op. cit.

115   The Library of Congress lists more than a 1000 titles addressing manifestations of the Holy Spirit. One author I have valued for his many references to scripture is: Pytches, D. (1985), *Spiritual Gifts in the Local Church,* Bethany House Publishers: Minneapolis, Minn.

116   All four gospels describe Christ's baptism by John the Baptist. The exegesis on these passages is complex, but essentially, all of them emphasize that it occurred at the beginning of his ministry and was the source of his power - as had always been the case for prophets in the Old Testament; that the baptism was of the Holy Spirit received directly from God; and that John's baptism by water was only the outward sign. I might also note here, that this baptism released him from the authority of his parents. (According to Luke [2:51] he continued to live under his parent's authority until his baptism by John). See McDonnell, K. & Montague, G. (1991), op. cit.

117   McDonnell, K. & Montague, G. (1991), op. cit.

118   McDonnell, K. & Montague, G. (1991), op. cit.

119   McDonnell, K. & Montague, G. (1991), op. cit.

120   Such "heresies" also appeared to be a concern of St. Paul's and addressed so in his letters. See Goulder, M. (1995), *St. Paul Verses St. Peter: A Tale of Two Missions*, Westminster John Knox Press: New York.

121   Walter Wink offers a masterful description of the Christian church compromised by what he calls the Dominator System when it became the official Church of Rome. The Myth of Redemptive Violence governs the Dominator System: the belief that violence can be defeated by violence. Wink sees this myth as upholding a patriarchal, hierarchical, social order that was directly challenged by the teachings of Christ. See Wink, W. (1998), *The Powers That Be: Theology For A New Millennium,* Galilee Doubleday: New York. See Also: Dungan, D.L. (2006), *Constantine's Bible: Politics and the Making of the New Testament*, Augsburg Fortress Publishers.

122   Bennett, D.J. (1970), *Nine O'Clock In The Morning*, Bridge-Logos Publishers.

123   I have recently read an account that might be a notable exception to that conclusion. In his book by the same name, the author describes the experience of Deeksha, which is grounded in the Hindu religion. As he describes it, the experience is more powerful than anything I have described here. A Deeksha is received in much the same way as someone who is 'slain in the Spirit.' It appears to replicate or facilitate many of the transformations described in my work. Of note, the anecdotal reports indicate that all of the people who have experienced it had previously done a great deal of inner work. The experience is expected to be repeated a number of times. In that respect it is very much like being repeatedly convicted of the Holy Spirit; that is to say the effects are said to be cumulative. See Windrider, K. with Sears, G. (2006), *Deeksha: The Fire from Heaven,* New World Library: Novato, CA.

124   Jung makes the following observation regarding the distinction between physical and psychic facts: "The conflict [between religion and science] is due to the strange supposition that a thing is true only if it presents itself as a *physical* fact. Thus some people believe it to be physically true that Christ was born as the son of a virgin, while others deny this as a physical impossibility. Everyone can see that there is no logical solution to this conflict and that one would do better not to get involved in such sterile disputes. Both are right and both are wrong. Yet they could easily reach agreement if only they dropped the word 'physical.' 'Physical' is not the only criterion of truth: there are also *psychic* truths which can neither be explained nor proved nor contested in any physical way....Religious statements are of this type. They refer without exception to things that cannot be established as physical facts....the fact that religious statements frequently conflict with the

observed physical phenomena proves that in contrast to physical perception the spirit is autonomous, and that psychic experience is to a certain extent independent of physical state. Jung, C.G. (1956),"An Answer to Job" in *Psychology and Religion: West and East,* Collected Works, Vol. 11, Bollingen Series XX, Princeton University Press, New Jersey, p. 522-523.

125   Images other than Christ can function as conduits of the Holy Spirit. Channeling the Holy Spirit is not the sole prerogative of Jesus Christ. I accept in principle that other spiritual beings could also function as channels of the Holy Spirit. Clearly, the Holy Spirit inspired the prophets of the Old Testament just as it did the New Testament writers. The necessary prerequisite here seems to be that the Holy Spirit is acknowledged as the source of forgiveness and experienced as such when channeled by the image of a spiritual being.

126   In Chapter VII, I will make a sharp distinction between *being held in bondage to shame and feeling ashamed.* There are two conditions when adults can feel *ashamed*: 1) if the individual is caught in an act considered shameful by self and others; or 2) if the individual identifies with someone who has acted shamefully, for example, a parent who the community identifies as having acted shamefully. In both instances the shame is self-imposed; that is, the individual self-shames in order to evade shaming by the Voice-of-conscience who might otherwise force the dissociation of that sense of self. Any self that exercises the power of self-shame is called a Dominant self. If the shameful act is private - only observed by itself, then the individual is more likely to experience guilt than feel ashamed. Guilt is considered less painful than shame, but painful nonetheless. It does have the advantage of closure. Someone can be made to re-experience shame for a visible action committed ten years ago. In contrast, once 'Mia Cupas' are made, a guilty action is thought to be forgiven. Guilt is felt when an individual has satisfied what s/he considers to be a shameful desire without getting shamed by another. Thus, remorse and feeling ashamed, though often treated as synonyms, are different in degree. Remorse is more akin to the effects guilt, while feeling ashamed is always the result of being caught in or associated with a shameful act. While I do not want to split hairs here, the differences become pertinent when addressing the activity of an Ideal-self. These ego-aspects can experience feeling ashamed if caught in shameful acts, or even feel remorse for their part in treating the Rejected-self as unforgivable. Since they tend to use pride as a primary defense they can also feel ashamed whenever their pride fails them, or they are confronted with their hubristic stance vis-à-vis God and Christ. Even so, *an Ideal-self must willingly ask Christ for the Interior baptism of their shameful core.* The Aware-ego cannot ask on its behalf. Shameful behavior or shame by association – as distinct from a shameful identity, does not paralyze an ego-aspect's will to act. In contrast, the Rejected-self does not merely act shamefully: its very *being* is defined as shameful; and that shame paralyzes

its will to act or ask on its own behalf. It is one thing to satisfy a shameful desire and feel guilty afterward; quite another to be the Rejected-self that embodies that shameful desire.

127   Johnson, R.A. (1993), *Owning Your Own Shadow: Understanding the Dark Side of the Psyche*, Harper: San Francisco.

128   It is conceivable that Jung's theory, especially as it sought to recapitulate Alchemical studies, was capable of transforming conscience. I suspect the necessary elements were present. But to the best of my knowledge nothing like what I am outlining here was ever offered by Jung.

129   See Barclay for an orthodox interpretation of St. Paul's Letter to the Ephesians, which addresses the issue of Law vs. grace. Barclay, W. (2002), *The Letters to the Galatians and Ephesians,* Westminster John Knox Press: Louisville, KY.

130   See McDonnell, K. & Montague, G. (1991), op. cit.

131   St. Paul noted that he did what he would not do, and failed to do what he would do. Implicitly, he acknowledged the existence of more than one self and the 'other' self appears to have its own will and divergent attitudes.

CHAPTER II

THEORETICAL PREMISES AND CONSTRUCTS

OVERVIEW

All of the clinical work described in this book is based on a methodology that involves use of the *Light* and an image of Jesus Christ capable of channeling [1] the Holy Spirit. Both components are described in Chapters III and IV. The *results* of that methodology provide evidence in support of the assertion that conscience – as most people use the term – is a byproduct of the Empowering archetype, which imparts god-like authority to images it constellates. The methodology verifies Freud's assertion that this initial and enduring manifestation of 'conscience' is a *parentified* Voice-of-conscience. More important, this methodology allows clients to terminate the parent's authority and transform the ego-aspects created to cope with that authority such that conscience can become a Voice for God rather than a voice of condemnation.

The methodology offers a good deal more. With practice, the *Light* and image of Christ channeling the Holy Spirit becomes an avenue for the exploration of Mind and the Mind's connection to Soul and Body. Those explorations have led to the discovery of numerous interventions for the treatment of many problems presented in psychotherapy. This chapter supplements the first chapter by providing an overview of the premises and constructs needed to better appreciate the extent of that exploration. Chapters V through VIII describe the actual results.

A general thesis of this book is that archetypal energies – *flowing through parental images* within the Mind [2] – shape and sustain the ego-aspects governing our daily lives. Thus do parents create our sense of self from conception onward. They are the earliest and most enduring creators of ego-aspects. They literally hold the power of life and death for their children, and the children instinctively know this and respond accordingly. If parents are mindful of their power, the child can thrive in their care; if parents abuse this power then the child can languish onto death, or survive and cope. For the past hundred years, psychotherapy has sought to treat the survivors who find themselves ill prepared for adult trials. Most therapies have met with varying degrees of success. This book takes a fresh look at those parental images as they continue to exert their power over adult children; and offers an older wisdom for mediating that power and healing the selves created by it.

Understanding human behavior has been my life's work spanning more than five decades. Despite a rigorous training with Skinner boxes and Learning Theory, my own adult trials have taught me to look much deeper and place God center stage. [3] Not so academia. For the better part of a century, academic psychology has striven to understand human behavior without recourse to any higher power focusing instead on the human brain and observable behavior.

Psychotherapy is another matter. The mature practitioner can walk a fine line between science and metaphysics. Such journeys are rarely walked in ten sessions or less, so I have little to offer therapists striving to meet the demands of managed care. What I can offer is a process whereby adults can come to 'honor' their parents even when the parent's behavior was blatantly rejecting, abusive, or worse. It is not an easy task and never quickly done; but I hope to show it is possible through a therapeutic process willing to draw upon Christ's love and the power of the Holy Spirit.

But why honor parents? Here is the crux of it: the Fourth Commandment is the only one of the Ten that holds a promise. It commands us to: Honor your father and your mother, *so that your days may be long* in the land that the LORD your God is giving you (Exodus 20:12).[4] Other translations would say long and prosperous. Note that the promise is dependent on honoring our parents, and failing to do so we may infer that our days will be less than long and prosperous. The thrust of every commandment concerns what is in the Heart. Therefore, it is not sufficient that we be outwardly civil. We must honor these parents in the secret recesses of our Hearts. This is hard to do given a decent set of parents. But how are we to do this when the father shoots himself in an alcoholic rage in front of the family, after a life of physically and sexually abusing all his children?

The Fourth Commandment is recognition of the power wielded by parents. It is a power that perplexes therapists however often they encounter it in their adult clients. It is understandable for a child to evidence fear of an abusive, shaming parent. But how are we to understand this same fear in adults, now married with children of their own, and many years away from home? Parents seem to rule our psyches whether they live next door, a thousand miles away, or ten years in the grave. It is no wonder we are commanded to establish a right attitude toward them. As Emmet Fox has noted,[5] the commandments are best seen as laws that cannot be broken. Whether we honor or dishonor, our attitude will have a telling effect on our lives. There is a law in Communications Theory to the effect that, 'We cannot not communicate.' Even silence has meaning. Likewise, 'We cannot not have parents.' Even orphans and bastards have biological parents. The psyches of all adopted children are shaped at least as much by the imagined drama of their biological parents as it is by the love and wounds of their adopted parents. Every human being must acknowledge a set of parents at least in their Heart. And the power of the parental images in our Mind and Heart is immense whether we love them or hate them. If we can honestly love and honor them, we are truly blessed. But if we hate them, we will just as surely suffer the reasons for our hating, e.g. incessant anger, impotency, and powerlessness.

The Parental Image

In this work, a crucial distinction is made between parental images in the Mind and Heart and parents as human beings acting in-the-world or long dead. As I'm apt to say to clients: "You have two fathers: an *image* of him in your Mind and another father who is in-the-world, doing something or another, or deceased; and the one in your Mind is by far the most powerful." Most people assume that the image in their head is merely a representation of the real person moving in-the-world, that the image functions much like a photograph. Without question, one of the most significant distinctions I make in this work is that people and *the images of those people* are very different entities. A second distinction of equal import is that these images are comprised of energy and definition, not flesh and blood. Under the right circumstances all images are very amenable to change; and in my work the goal is to change the images as distinct from the people those images represent. This distinction is vital to an appreciation of what I am about here. When I say we must honor our parents, I mean for us to carry an image of them within our Heart and Mind that honors them and ourselves in return.

There are several ways to change the image of a parent in the Mind. One way, which many seek and few attain, is to hope against hope that some day parents will change the way they interact with us; that by some miracle a rejecting, ever critical, parent might become unconditionally loving. It happens, but rarely. Another method of considerable power is for us to set about changing our response to the parent in such a way that the parent changes in turn. Harold Bloomfield, [6] in his book on making peace with parents, describes his own efforts quite poignantly. As his father lay dying from the after affects of a heart attack, Bloomfield decided he must tell his father that he loved him; that he no longer had the luxury of waiting for his father to change and tell his son those blessed words. Bloomfield describes how he made the decision, while flying to his father's bedside, to hug his father each time he entered and left his hospital room, and tell him he loved him. Initially, his father was unresponsive, actually rigid at the contact, but after what seemed like the 100th hug his father could relax and answer his son in kind. Instead of dying in the predicted two weeks, the father and mother returned to California with their son where the father lived for six months longer than the doctors predicted. Family therapy may also serve as a modus operandi for changing parental images as feelings are mutually explored and expressed, often for the first time. But none of these avenues is likely to be effective for parents who are clearly unapproachable in life, long dead, or otherwise lost to all concerned; and often it is the vestiges of those parents that are the most problematic for grown children. But even where the parent might be approachable - if only from the therapist's perspective, it is still the image, rather than the person it represents, that must be changed, and that can happen with or without the parent's actual presence or consent.

A basic premise of this work is that the authority found in parental images exerts immense control over the behavior of their adult children; and this control is so pervasive there is little of much import that is not sustained by those images and the ego-aspects they create. Parental images shape our definition of God and almost always speak as the Voice-of-conscience. They define the authority we assign to others, our ability to be intimate, our choice of spouses, friends and lovers, our raising of children, and our peace of mind. A basic assertion of this work is that those images and the ego-aspects created to cope with them can be profoundly changed. Such changes as I envision are not easy because they must be accomplished without first changing the living parent. But these unilateral changes in parental images have far reaching consequences nonetheless. Altering those images gives the client the power to redefine God, earthly authority, and sense of self; and by altering the perceived relationships between parents, it is also possible to significantly alter our own most intimate relationships with children, spouses, and Self. [7]

Acts of Will

Throughout this work I use 'willingness' and 'willfulness' to designate two distinct expressions of will. The first describes a specific emotion and the second a class of emotions defined by the pride-shame axis. Later in the chapter I discuss the pride-shame axis, which describes the range of emotions most commonly used by an individual's ego-aspects to motivate behavior. That set of emotions is always treated as 'willful.' Willful behavior is generally defined as "having or showing a stubborn and determined intention to do as one wants regardless of the consequences or effects." [8] In contrast to what I will call the 'Soul emotions,' Ego emotions comprising the pride-shame axis always function willfully. In contrast to willfulness, *willingness* embodies the idea of reciprocity: as I seek to change something, I am changed by what I seek to change. Willingness describes the will exercising all higher emotions such as acceptance, forgiveness, and love. Willingness also expresses a primary quality of the *Light* as described in the next chapter: the *Light's* ability to function is solely dependent upon the individual's willingness.

Another basic premise of this work is that willingness and *a higher power* are prerequisites to changing an image. An ego-aspect cannot alter images willfully, nor can it change an image willingly while acting alone. Even if the client's ego-aspect is explicitly *willing* for an image to be altered, actual changes must be implemented by a higher power at the bequest of an ego-aspect's willingness.

Imagine parental images residing in the right brain and the authority embedded in those images residing in the left-brain. Ego-aspects cannot alter the left-brain by force of will. Ego-aspects have no direct power in the left-brain. Think of the left-brain as the subconscious and unconscious spheres of the Self. In Freudian terms, left-brain is the domain of the Id, and in Jungian terms, it is the world of the personal and collective unconscious. The most powerful parental images are constellated by archetypal energies residing in the left-brain. An ego-aspect can rebel against images, or otherwise defend against them in neurotic or psychotic ways, but it cannot change those parental images by forcible acts of will. However, if an ego-aspect is willing to acknowledge 'higher powers' it does have access to significant processes for change, as higher powers such as Christ can effect changes in the left-brain.

Roberto Assagioli devoted much of his professional life to the examination of will. [9] He arrived at conclusions similar to my own regarding the limitations of will directed by the Ego:

> Modern psychology has shown that if the will puts itself in direct opposition to the other psychological forces such as the imagination, emotions, or drives, it will often be overpowered. Yet the limited Victorian conception of the will as force alone prompts us to use our will in just such a direct and often clumsy, or even brutal, way (p.46).... The most effective and satisfactory role of the will is not as a source of direct power or force, but as that function which, being at our command, can stimulate, regulate, and direct all the other functions and forces of our being so that they may lead us to our predetermined goal (p.47). [10]

In sum, the most effective role for the Ego is one of willingness, as distinct from willfulness.

There are two other points regarding free will worth noting. First, the archetypal Ego, as it manifests in the active imagination of Mind, is generally fragmented into numerous ego-aspects as a normal consequence of development. Each of these ego-aspects has a modicum of free will. St. Paul captures this fragmentation aptly when he notes that "I fail to do what I would do, and do what I would not do." [11] The human Mind is often at odds with itself because there are numerous ego-aspects – generated by the Ego in response to trauma and conflict – that have access to a modicum of free will. The existence of these conflicted ego-aspects becomes readily apparent when clients go inside and begin using the *Light*. Second, the Body – as instinct, the Soul – as archetype, and the Spirit – as grace, also exert 'will,' and all of them exert a felt presence within the active imagination defining Mind. While the Ego has some control over the Body's instinctual will, it can only rebel against the higher wills of Soul and Spirit, though never without risk to itself. I will say much more about this throughout the book.

The Power of *Light*

Some years ago, while reading *A Course in Miracles*, [12] I hit upon a method with the power to express and respond only to individual's *willingness*, which has become indispensible to my work with Mind generated images and images constellated by the collective unconscious, i.e. the Soul. My discovery was to all extents and purposes 'an intuitive leap', which I have spent the last twenty years exploring and seeking to explain. I call this method 'using the *Light*'. It has a number of unique properties that I have come to treat as indispensable in my work with clients. All of the explorations and interventions described in this book have flowed, essentially, from use of this *Light* by clients. Chapter III describes a number of protocols that have proven effective in helping just about anyone find and sustain their *Light*. The *Light* is found imaginatively and usually takes the form of a luminous sphere about the size of a softball. One quality of the *Light* that I prize above others is its refusal to do anything that would threaten or attack an ego-aspect. If the client is *unwilling* for the *Light* to act it will not act. *The Light is completely dependent upon the client's willingness.* As a rule, I ask clients to direct all of my suggestions to their *Light* for execution, and generally word the question as such. If clients are threatened in any way by my suggestion, they will either open their eyes (if closed), or the *Light* will simply disappear, or otherwise not respond to the request.

I have observed clients using the *Light* for twenty plus years; and nothing they have encountered in their imaginations has shown itself more powerful than the will expressed by the *Light*, except the *Light's* complete dependence on their willingness. The *Light* demonstrates the absolute power of free will in active imagination in that nothing can overwhelm it. If the client so directs the *Light*, no image or emotion can overwhelm the client's conscious sense of self, however threatening the image or emotion. The *Light* has the power to encircle any image within the human Mind, and thereby contain any attack by any image that threatens the individual's sense of self; but it will also never allow harm or destruction to any image it encircles. The only explanation I can give for this is that the *Light* will not threaten any part of the Mind or Heart, nor allow any part to threaten another part.

The *Light* empowers clients to extend consciousness to every part of the Mind and Heart, provided they are willing. There is nothing in the darkest recesses of the Heart that the *Light* is incapable of reaching, discerning, or retrieving, provided the client is willing. And always, the *Light* will do so safely or not at all. That is its power. Consequently, I will not ask clients to venture any inner work until they have found their *Light*.

The Christ Within

The sense of self that seeks to find and willingly sustain the *Light* is called the Aware-ego. When a client enters active imagination, an Aware-ego will emerge in the midst of any ego-aspect currently dominant for the sole purpose of willingly directing the *Light*. As needed, the Aware-ego can objectify the ego-aspect it is merged with, and offer it a portion of the *Light*, as well as extending portions of the *Light* to any other self-image within the Mind.

Higher powers, such as Jesus Christ, can exercise powers that far exceed what the Aware-ego or other ego-aspects can accomplish even with the *Light*. For one, Christ has the power to move freely between the worlds of Spirit, Soul and Mind, while any manifestation of Ego is limited to Mind. Many of the interventions described in this work do not require a higher power such as Jesus Christ. The recovery of subconscious, suppressed or repressed memory is a good example. An Aware-ego, using the *Light*, can excel in the process of recovering memory. But therapy is far more than the recovery of memories. I am primarily interested in the *healing* of memory and images. In that regard the Aware-ego is limited, with the notable exception that it is always willing to evoke a higher power.

The need of many clients to heal memories was what first prompted me to encourage the evocation of a Christ image. Initially, I only asked clients to work with the *Light*. But the power of the *Light* in recovering repressed material confronted me with a depth of inhumanity that neither my life experiences nor clinical training prepared me to address. There are parents and groups who ritually abuse, murder, and sacrifice children; parents who kill their spouses; parents whose actions publicly shame the entire family; mentally ill parents who terrorize their children; parents who physically, sexually and emotionally abuse their children from infancy onward; parents who commit suicide or otherwise abandon children traumatically, or subject them to constant shaming and rejection. I have never found an easy answer for clients subjected to these childhood traumas. But one day it occurred to me that the image of Jesus Christ might help them find the answers they needed.

I will not permit clients to go inside – to enter the world of active imagination, unless they are willing to use the *Light*. If its presence is a threat, then inner work is not an option until the fear is resolved and they can evoke it. The Christ image is another matter. Without question, his power to heal within active imagination is exponential compared to Ego; but not infrequently, a client will find a Christ image to be threatening. In Western culture, Christ is undoubtedly the most powerful, healing, archetypal image available to us. But his maleness is threatening to some; and his arbitrary association with the condemning judgments of some Christian sects is threatening to others. Consequently, I have never made the evocation of Christ a precondition for inner work. In evoking a Christ image, what I seek for the client is an archetypal image with the power to nurture and heal and which the client can trust unreservedly. To that end, some clients will prefer a female version of Christ (e.g. a Sophia-Christ figure, or the Virgin-Mother, or Black Madonna) or an angel, or Buddha, or spirit guide, even a totem animal. If the client is a nominally practicing Christian, I will always suggest a Christ image, but only as one of several possibilities. I am always interested in knowing the reasons why a client is reluctant to evoke a Christ image, since this will invariably touch on issues needing to be addressed. I have learned, however, to respect their reasons. The majority of my clients have eventually called upon an image of Christ. The most powerful interventions described in this work require Christ or another image with comparable powers to heal and channel the Holy Spirit. In the final analysis, it is the Holy Spirit that forgives and transforms.

Wherever the client is willing to seek assistance from an image of Jesus Christ, the therapist and client can be assured of considerable success. Evoking the Christ image is very much like introducing healing prayer into the therapeutic process. The potential of this image for tapping all the creative resources of the unconscious is immense. I have hardly plumbed its depths in my twenty years of working with the *Light* and Christ image. Each year new layers are revealed as my confidence in the process increases with experience and my clients assert the helpfulness of this process. As the reader proceeds, it will quickly become apparent that I rely heavily on the Christ image in my work, and most especially, the work I focus on in the coming chapters. At least initially, much can be done without recourse to a Christ image, but when we begin to work on issues of parental authority and conscience - which is a primary focus of this book, I find it difficult to do very much without asking the client to evoke an image of Christ. In my experience, it is not possible to redress some of these issues without recourse to a Christ image or comparable manifestation of God. [13]

In some instances, I have found it advisable to acknowledge a feminine, Christ-like image and treat her as synonymous with Christ in her power to heal, forgive and transform. To illustrate, one client - who was severely abused by several nuns and priests, was also taught to identify them as the earthly representatives of Christ. For much of her therapy it was impossible for her to trust a male Christ image. She could tolerate the presence of Christ-as-child, but ultimately, what she discovered within herself was a Christ-like female image willing to suffer for her no less than Christ did on the cross. In willingly sacrificing herself on behalf of the client during the recall of a particularly horrendous memory, this female image was able to offer a healing love comparable to Christ in its power. This image did not claim to be Christ and was quite willing to give way to that image when the client became willing to evoke him some years later. It is almost as if she were standing in for Christ as a surrogate until the client could choose again. Another client participated in a meditation group whose leader channeled a spirit called Teacher. Eventually, her visual image of Teacher became her higher power. Later in therapy, Teacher and Christ 'partnered' with very interesting effects, which I illustrate in the last two chapters.

Discovering the God-like Authority of Parents

To fully appreciate the god-like power embedded in parental images the observer needs a frame of reference. For me, Christ became that gauge when I suggested to a client that Christ intervene, on her behalf, with a parent she was actively imagining. To my surprise, what I discovered was a practicing Christian whose image of her father (a Christian minister) was far more powerful than her image of Christ! She could tell me that Christ was her lord and savior but, when I asked her to envision Christ interacting with her father, her father was seen as far more powerful! This has become such a common occurrence when clients make initial comparisons between their parents and their Christ image that I would consider it an exception to the rule if a client initially described his or her Christ image as more powerful than the parent in question. (An interesting and notable exception is when the client is strongly identified with an Ideal self that is Christ-like. In such instances, the Ideal self sees Christ as a peer, rather than a higher power, and is quite glad to have him to be seen as more powerful than the parent.)

For most clients, entering the world of active imagination for the first time, *there is really no higher authority for them, than the voice/ image of a parent*. For most clients, most of the time, parental voices and images are the most powerful voices and images in their consciousness, if they stop to reflect on it. Almost always, Christ appears as lesser in power and authority. In theory, any acknowledged manifestation of God should be more powerful than parents, but in the inner world of imagination, where these assessments are made, God must manifest as an image, and it is difficult to find an 'image of God' more powerful than the parental images perceived by most clients. That can and does change over time. In fact, bringing about such a change is one of the primary objectives of my inner work with clients. But in the beginning, it is rarely the case that the Christ image exceeds the parent in authority.

Throughout this work, the reader needs to bear in mind that I only generalize to a clinical population that seeks out psychotherapists for the treatment of psychological problems. I have not explored any of the issues addressed here with 'samples of normal people', much less samples from other countries and cultures. I cannot offer, as evidence, any controlled studies involving 'normal people'. But within that limitation, the repeated observation that parental images are initially more powerful than the clients' images of Christ has helped me to finally appreciate the immense power of those parental images. But note, that discovery was dependent upon a juxta-positioning of parental images and the Christ image. If you ask a client to verbally speculate whom s/he thinks is more powerful, most clients would readily give lip service to Jesus Christ. It is only when the Christ image and the parent in question are brought together imaginatively that the distinction is perceived; but given that juxta-positioning, the disparity becomes apparent in a variety of ways. This discovery led me down several paths at once. What, I asked, was the source of this God-like power in parental images? Was it proper for parents to retain this God-like power in the Minds of their adult children even if such authority was unavoidable while the children were physically dependent upon them? Could the power embedded in parental images be removed or transformed? If so, how? These are some of the many questions I seek to answer in this work.

What I have found, using the *Light*, is that clients can discover three different kinds of archetypal authority embedded in parental images. The earliest to emerge developmentally, and the one most directly amenable to change, is *Temporal authority*. This is quite simply the power of an adult to order a child with or without a good reason. The second kind of archetypal authority is the *Moral authority* that generates Ego conscience. At first I thought that each of those authorities was generated by a different archetype. But over time I have concluded that it is the same archetype differentially effecting the child as s/he develops. So far as I can determine, Temporal and Moral authority are both constellated by the same Empowering archetype. The third parental authority is *Relational authority* as constellated by a Gendering archetype, which assigns a gendered composite to all animate images, and most significantly, self-images. The Gendering archetype draws almost exclusively on parental images for its initial constellation of self-images, and in so doing imparts an enduring power to the parental images, that may even exceed what is constellated by the Empowering archetype. The exploration and alteration of these three parental authorities – particularly as they shape and sustain ego-aspects, is the primary focus of this book.

From the outset, I have found it heuristic to distinguish between parental authority and the archetypal energies that constellate it. As I discussed in the first chapter, it is the archetypal energies that give parental images their cumulative authority. These archetypal energies generally 'freeze' the parental images by constellating them; those images, in turn, become the model for self-images, reactively as well as proactively.

In the following sections I describe the three kinds of authority in greater detail. Later chapters will describe specific clinical interventions used to explore and alter each authority.

Temporal Authority

As I define it, the Empowering archetype assigns God-like power to whatever image it constellates. To the best of my knowledge, Jung never identified this archetype as such. I posit it as the best explanation for the Temporal and Moral authority found in parental images. I will leave it to others to debate its efficacy as an explanatory construct.

The parents' Temporal authority is the first to manifest developmentally (birth to age four), and it is more easily observed and transformed in a clinical setting than Moral authority. It seems best described as the absolute power of life and death exercised by a parent. Its power is culturally sanctioned, but clearly, its source is archetypal. The earliest parental images constellated by the Empowering archetype will reflect the absolute power that parents exercise in the raising of children. It is the power to exclusively nurture a child as well as starve or maim it; the power to give or withhold from a child without having to give a reason. Quite literally, it is the power of life and death. Its source appears to be the Empowering archetype, which constellates 'God-like powers' in the human Mind long before the child can make a distinction between God and people. Temporal authority is constellated in the parent by the child's awareness of absolute dependence on something outside itself for its very survival. If there is no suitable person for the archetype to constellate, then the child languishes and dies since the child is literally as well as symbolically dependent upon this manifestation of 'higher power' for its continued existence.

In infancy and early childhood, both parents exercise Temporal authority. From age three onward, however, Temporal authority appears to be most strongly expressed by one parent in the family. This is generally the father, though there are notable exceptions. [14] I think of Temporal authority as a kind of 'primitive, primordial force.' The parental images expressing this power can be relatively benign and even-handed, even loving and compassionate in their exercise of this authority. But when clients seek out these parental images in active imagination, the images are just as likely to be unsympathetically firm, angry, threatening, rageful, cold, aloof, engulfing, devouring, or otherwise intimidating, and exceedingly difficult to approach or reproach. Often, it is an image that appears to not abide any opposition, an image that is difficult for clients to 'stand up to,' challenge, or question. If the client feels the equal of the image, then it is only in his or her ability to go 'toe to toe' without any expectation of overcoming the envisioned parent except by being more like the parent than the parent. These are the images formed when we are youngest and our parents the most powerful. The negative image is not considered universal. Hopefully, many people have images of their parents that are loving and mutually respectful. It is important to reiterate that the experiences described in this book are derived from a clinical population as distinct from a random population sample. But almost without exception, that clinical population appears to share these negative parental images in common. The exception is when the client idealizes the parent, which is equally distorting, and lends itself to equally strong transferences.

Temporal Authority and Transference

I strongly suspect that Temporal authority partially underpins the transference phenomenon addressed by psychoanalysis.[15] Transference is a technical term that refers specifically to the analysand's projection of parental characteristics onto the analyst. Counter-transference refers to analyst's projection of unresolved conflicts onto the analysand. Therapists have known for a hundred years that this 'transference' of parental characteristics to others often governs the interaction between self and other; and that it is by no means restricted to the analytic hour. Freud strove to control this phenomenon in the psychoanalytic setting and, where possible, to use it to effect cures; but controlled or uncontrolled, it appears to be present wherever a role is emotionally or culturally invested with Temporal Authority by parents and culture.

In its broader meaning, transference refers to the generalization of parental authority and its characteristic expressions to classes of adults that are then seen to act like parents. Generalization of the transference phenomenon is said to occur whenever a child, or adult, imbues another adult with characteristics of a parent exercising Temporal authority. Transference is such a ubiquitous phenomenon that it is difficult to appreciate its arbitrary nature. The authority is subconsciously projected into most of the adult roles we encounter as children, e.g. policemen, teachers, preachers, other neighborhood mothers, etc.; and to almost as many roles when we become adults, e.g. army officers, judges, doctors, husbands. Without question, parents and other authority figures (who function in loco parentis) have a rightful claim to Temporal authority so long as the culture makes them accountable for a minor child's behavior and well being. But in just about all contemporary cultures, that power appears to be projected, ad infinitum, to status-roles even after the child becomes an adult. So far as I can determine, this transference continues because there is no ritual whereby the power is stripped from the parental image, even in ritualized rites of passage such as Confirmation or Bar Mitzvah. Consequently, Temporal authority tends to remain firmly embedded in parental images and continually projected into numerous 'parent-child' relationships governing cultural interactions. So far as I can determine, *the only way to ameliorate this authority is to divest the parental images that perpetuate its generalization and provide the individual with the discernment of a higher power.*

It is not merely the failure of culture to terminate Temporal Authority that needs to be emphasized. Equally impressive is the active perpetuation of patriarchal institutions that result from this failure to terminate Temporal Authority when children grow to adulthood. Instead of termination, the authority is simply transferred to other adult males and the institutions they represent, even blatantly so, as when a father gives up his daughter in marriage.[16] This transfer continues to reinforce the status of men at the expense of women.

It is quite possible that the gods and goddesses of most pantheons are constellated by the Empowering archetype, especially if they are empowered to slavishly direct an individual's psyche. 'God the father' is a case in point. More than any other image, this *person* of God – so often confused with the Godhead, reinforces the Temporal and Moral Authority of fathers and males, and they return the favor by insisting he be worshiped as equal to the Godhead, and greater than Christ and the Holy Spirit. Even so, it is possible to remove this constellated authority from any such manifestation of God, if the adult decides that individuation is preferable to continuing enthrallment, and elects to freely choose a higher power. (The interested reader is referred to Appendix II.)

Divesting Parents of Constellated Authority

Christ has no interest in assuming Temporal Authority. Satan is defeated in his efforts to tempt Christ with Temporal authority during Christ's testing in the desert immediately following his baptism by John the Baptist.[17] More to the point, Christ can and will terminate the flow of Temporal Authority in any parental image by simply placing a portion of his own *Light* into the Heart of the parental image. This will immediately produce a change in the image denoting a distinct severing of the archetypal connection. Effectively, the parental image is no longer constellated by the archetype. Once the constellation of authority is terminated, the generalization of the archetypal energy to other adults is greatly diminished, and the affected ego-aspects are free to look elsewhere for guidance. Alternatively, where Temporal Authority is not stripped from a parental image, it will continue to be transferred, ad infinitum, to status-roles in cultural hierarchies.

Some might argue that a method needs to be found for the transfer of Temporal Authority to the child, once the child becomes an adult. But apart from the Self,[18] what part of us can be trusted to exercise it? In this age, Ego represents self for most of us, much of our lives. Ego-aspects have immense power in their control of free will within the Mind, but no control of archetypal processes except repressively, dissociatively, or projectively. That inherent limitation is not altered by an ego-aspect's assumption of an archetypally constellated Temporal Authority. Moreover, direct transfer of that authority to any ego-aspect - rather than having Christ terminate it, is likely to dangerously inflate the ego-aspect. In Chapter VI, I document conditions wherein ego-aspects are likely to be constellated with Temporal authority, and the effects have proven invariably negative from an individuation perspective. Fortunately, I have also discovered simple interventions for releasing ego-aspects from that enthrallment.

Much less frequently, the exercise of Temporal authority will flow primarily through a mother or grandmother, rather than a paternal image. In those cases, a second step is often called for that involves Christ healing or augmenting some portion of the feminine damaged by maternal abuses of that authority. This is not something that needs to be suggested but seems to occur spontaneously, if it happens at all. As women clients have described the process to me, at the point of divesting a maternal image of Temporal authority, another personification of the feminine appears, receives something from Christ, and then disappears again. Often, where divestiture involves a maternal figure, female clients will express a reluctance to allow divestiture until the potential loss of 'feminine empowerment' is discussed. I must stress that feminine empowerment is not something I have interjected into the process. It is, rather, what emerges as the process unfolds. Especially where maternal images have constellated both Temporal and Moral authority, women want to be assured that the authority will not revert to a masculine image when the maternal image is divested; the spontaneous second step offered by Christ appears to be his way of reassuring the woman that the authority will not revert to a male image.

The divestiture of a mother's Temporal Authority – if she was dominant in a household, poses particular difficulties for male clients as well. Males seem to especially fear an intensification of this authority in other anima manifestations, though I have not been able to demonstrate this clinically. Two male clients with clearly dominate mothers both terminated therapy with me while we were addressing the issue of divesting the mother's Temporal authority. Their relationships with women were repetitively contentious, and I strongly suspect – in retrospect, that they feared that divestiture of the mother would further empower the anima energies of women. It is possible that such fears can be offset by first guiding the client through a resolution of Relational authority issues (discussed below).

Often, the Temporal authority of a mother is actually an expression of her own father's authority; that is, the authority of the client's maternal grandfather. Authority derived from a mother's father often manifests as something akin to explosive rages, as if someone has overtaken the mother so she seems like a different person. But however it manifests, such mothers are always seen as the parent in charge of discipline. In such cases where the mother's temper is an issue, I will suggest that the client ask Christ to specifically divest the mother's image of any Temporal authority derived from her father. If the mother is exercising Temporal authority derived from her father, when Christ divests the mother's image by placing a portion of his *Light* in her Heart, there is generally a distinct lightening of the mother's demeanor as if some weight had been lifted from her. Her image will appear calmer, more relaxed, decidedly less judgmental, and much more accepting of her son or daughter's feelings.

Another facet of Temporal Authority that bears noting is what I call disruptions of nurture that create a Pre-moral aspect. Any abuse of Temporal Authority by a parent can severely traumatize a young child. Such abuse appears to be largely responsible for Dissociative disorders originating in early childhood. Object Relationists have long held that such disruptions of nurture are responsible for early ego splitting.[19] I have frequently found this to be the case for clients who exhibit severe psychological symptoms. There are numerous reasons for a severity of symptoms, but one of the most common appears to be a 'disruption of nurture' in very young children. Of note, such disruptions can be unintended as when a child is forcibly taken from a parent in wartime or other catastrophe. But by and large, parents who persistently abuse young children - forcing them to dissociate in order to survive, are the primary cause of most disruptions of nurture. The dissociation can create one or more Pre-moral aspects that become carriers of this painfully felt rejection and abandonment. These ego-aspects are generally hidden, banished to the dark recesses of the Heart; but the ego-aspects that supplant a Pre-moral aspect cannot make the feelings disappear without a trace. Consequently, these disowned selves will be felt in various ways throughout a person's life. Where such aspects are identified in the process of inner work, the therapist can effectively guide the client to provide these abandoned aspects the necessary nurture. That series of interventions is also described in the chapter on Temporal authority.

In sum, I encourage my clients to evoke their Christ for the divestiture of Temporal Authority wherever it is encountered. In no instance have I been willing to suggest that the authority be given to an ego-aspect, other human image, or institution. I treat the Temporal authority embedded in parental images as God-like and therefore likely to corrupt or inflate any merely mortal image or institution. Christ does not appear to be altered by this termination of Temporal authority. Rather, the parental image seems to be diminished in stature. By contrast, of course, Christ seems to gain in power but so too does the client since the resulting parental image is seen as less powerful, with a demeanor more accessible and approachable, or effectively buffered by the Christ image. Also, in many instances, divesting the parent of Temporal authority tends to enhance the client's ability to act willingly.

Might we benefit from a communal ritual that returns Temporal authority to an imageless God? Even if such a ritual existed, it is hard to imagine any institution, currently in existence, implementing it as an integral part of its rites. Much of the authority embedded in any contemporary religious or secular institution is derived from the God-like power first constellated in parental images. If Christ divests parental images of Temporal authority, it would no longer be available to support institutions emulating a parent-child relationship. In effect, the very process would be the undoing of authority held by most patriarchal institutions. There are some rites such as adult baptism that ask the participant to declare Christ as their savior, but none ask for a concomitant divestiture of parental authority. Thus, while the *Light* and Christ image do provide the modus operandi for divestiture, it is difficult to imagine how that process could be institutionalized given the current cultural milieu. For now, divestiture seems limited to psychotherapists and spiritual directors willing to evoke Christ for the purpose of ameliorating the power of parental images acting and speaking with God-like authority.

Moral Authority

The original focus of this book was the study of Moral authority embedded in parental images and experienced by most people as Ego conscience – what I am calling the unredeemed conscience. Using the *Light* and evoking an image of Christ, it is possible to examine the structure of this unredeemed conscience: the Empowering archetype's constellation of parental images and the reactive creation of ego-aspects, particularly Dominant selves that seek to function as their own conscience. Most important, the *Light* and Christ offer the opportunity to profoundly alter this unredeemed conscience whenever the client becomes willing.

I also refer to conscience as the Voice-of-conscience while it remains in the thrall of parental images and ego-aspects that seek to act as their own conscience (i.e. Dominant selves). Essentially, those voices function as Ego conscience in the absence of any reliable conduit for the Holy Spirit's 'still quiet voice.' Conscience is only redeemed when it becomes a Voice for God (vox Dei), which can only happen when ego-aspects accept the power of Christ's discernment and allow the Holy Spirit to move freely through the Heart.

In the first Chapter I provided an historical, psychological, and theological description of the unredeemed conscience, and my understanding of the process needed to redeem it. Chapters VII and VIII will describe the specific clinical interventions used to facilitate a Christ conscience process. Conscience is only redeemed when Christ can (1) terminate the flow of archetypal energy constellating the parentified Voice-of-conscience and its surrogates, (2) instill the power of his discernment in dominant aspects of the Ego, and (3) purify the Heart. All of the clinical interventions offered in Chapters VII and VIII are designed to facilitate that transformation. As previously noted, it is a long-term process, never a single life-changing event.

Except for the past hundred years, Ego conscience has been continuously and exclusively defined by religious traditions and mythology. In all of those traditions, conscience has been assigned the highest moral authority, superordinate to any institutional teaching in the mistaken belief that it expressed the Voice for God. Sigmund Freud was the first theoretician in the 20th century, so far as I can determine, to challenge the claim that Ego conscience expresses the Voice for God. From a psychoanalytic perspective, conscience is treated solely as the internalization of *parental* voices and discipline. In effect, Freud treated conscience as the recapitulation of a parent's use of shame, guilt, and fear to reinforce the beliefs and behavior shaped by those parents. While Freud believed that the Voice-of-conscience was only an internalization of parental behaviors and values, he nonetheless saw it as responsible for the most severe neuroses and, from his perspective, all but intransigent to change. By contrast, Carl Jung treated conscience as an archetypal energy, and something more. As such, it could be constellated in parents but existed a priori, and therefore, was potentially amenable to modification by a higher power. This is a crucial distinction. Jung's perspective allows for the constellation of god-like powers in parental images comparable to Freud's hypotheses; but also allows that psychoid forces, i.e. spiritual energies, could override the authority of that constellation.

In his final analysis, Jung concluded that an archetype could not speak as a Voice for God if it merely reflected the mores of parents and culture (Freud's thesis). Jung believed that 'conscience' had the potential of speaking with the moral imperative of vox Dei, though it was rarely heard in that capacity. In an effort to reconcile and build on the observations of these two theoreticians, I have put forth the thesis that conscience – as most people experience it – is an archetypal energy that assigns God-like authority to parents, institutions, and mythic figures. But I have also asserted that *only the Holy Spirit* can speak as a Voice for God. Finally, I have also argued that an archetypally defined Ego conscience can only speak as a Voice for God when transformed by Christ channeling the Holy Spirit. Without Christological or comparable intervention, Ego conscience is most likely to impede the Voice for God.

For millennium parents and culture have shaped the unredeemed conscience. I suspect it will always be the case that the Empowering archetype will constellate parental images and voices as the initial expression of conscience. In so doing, this initial constellation of conscience is most likely to recapitulate the 'old covenant,' which essentially demands an eye for an eye. It punishes, and it rarely forgives even after it punishes. By contrast, *a redeemed conscience* is a 'new covenant' shaped within the Mind by Christ and the power of the Holy Spirit. The writer of Hebrews describes this new conscience as a gift of the risen Christ:

For if the blood of goats and bulls, with the sprinkling of the ashes of a heifer, sanctifies those who have been defiled so that their flesh is purified, how much more will the blood of Christ, who through the eternal Spirit offered himself without blemish to God, purify our conscience from dead works to worship the living God! For this reason he is the mediator of a new covenant, so that those who are called may receive the promised eternal inheritance, because a death has occurred that redeems them from the transgressions under the first covenant (Hebrews 9:13-15).

The redemption of conscience in psychotherapy and spiritual direction entails a process of numerous steps. First, the client must put a face on the Voice-of-Conscience. Invariably, this face will be that of a parent, most likely, the father. Then the client must seek to identify the primary Ideal selves who seek to evade censor by emulating the parentified voices. As these two components are explored, a third image will eventually emerge that I call the Rejected-self. This aspect will always have qualities comparable to the Freudian Id or Jungian shadow. In most cases, it will appear as a self-image with no socially redeeming value. It will be unmitigatingly rejected by the parentified conscience and all primary ego-aspects in equal measure. *Even so, this self is Christ's primary avenue to the redemption of conscience.* To paraphrase the scriptures: The stone rejected by the builders must become the cornerstone [of a redeemed conscience].[20]

The parentified conscience and Ideal-selves hubristically assume the role of judge and jury. They perceive no need of Christ's saving grace and will actively seek to deny him entry to the true seat of conscience, i.e. the Heart. Only the Rejected-self, the proverbial sinner, has need of Christ and readily permits him to become its Voice for God. Thereafter, Christ can begin challenging the reign of the hubristic selves.

What is at stake here? One rarely hears references to conscience in today's psychological literature. It is almost as if it did not exist or rarely posed a problem. But it is only the word we rarely hear. Its effects are still felt as strongly as ever. Today, we know it as chronic feelings of 'low self-esteem,' or the voice of the inner critic,[21] or the parent in parent-child scripts,[22] or the unseen hand in the shame that binds us.[23] Psychology has sought to secularize the concept – to separate it from its religious tradition and underpinnings, but has yet to find a transformative process equal to Christ that is able to mitigate its power to punish. Rightly formed, conscience may speak the will of God and justifiably claim primacy over any other voice or thought process in the Mind of an adult; but as an unredeemed archetypal complex, the parentified conscience can only impart a *wrathful* Moral authority that is difficult to challenge, even by the still quiet voice of the Holy Spirit. The unredeemed conscience confronts the Ego with a superordinate power that it can deny, defy, or emulate, but never with impunity. While conscience remains unredeemed, it will be felt through a host of negative emotions and psychosomatic illnesses whenever its punishing dictums are aroused. Anything short of its actual redemption will invariably result in our exceeding lawful limits and provoking the 'Wrath of God.' Only a Christ conscience process can ameliorate this state of affairs.

We all would be better off if the initial formation of conscience did speak as the Voice for God and God only. But clearly, parents and surrogates are the initial manifestation of this archetypal power. Ponder this for just a moment: parents speaking with a God-like voice. The 'principalities and powers' of culture enforce the Temporal authority of parents, but the Moral authority of parents is likened to God's own voice. Is it any wonder that parents play so central a role in shaping us?

There are no final solutions in this book, and probably more questions than answers, but I hope this work will at least convey the awesome power of parental images that embody Temporal, Moral, and Relational authority. I have not found, nor ventured to find, any ritual for circumventing the constellation of Temporal and Moral authority during childhood. That is not possible or even advisable while adults are the caretakers of children. However, as children become adults, it behooves them to find more appropriate vessels, particularly if their upbringing left something to be desired. [24] To that end, I can offer interventions for mitigating much of the authority embedded in those images. And those interventions have proven a great help to clients whose parents clearly abused their power during the clients' development.

Sexual Energy and Moral Authority

More often than not, the Rejected-self – so pivotal to the transformation of Ego conscience, is also a primary container of sexual energy because these ego-aspects are quite often the earliest expressers of sexual energy condemned by parental and religious shaming. The more repressive a culture is sexually, the more likely its sexual repressions will be embodied in aspects of the Rejected-self. This is especially true of religious sub-cultures that have traditionally treated "all flesh" as corrupt. Patriarchal Christianity has long sought to control the sexual energy of women and, wherever possible, to restrict it to its reproductive function. To that end it has treated all other expressions pejoratively, e.g. as seductive, sluttish, whorish, shameful, etc. It should not be surprising, therefore, that one finds condemnatory expressions of sexuality embedded in many images of the Rejected-self.

The presence of sexual proclivities in a Rejected-self may pose a conundrum for some Christians, especially denominations that are sexually repressive. Almost without exception, repressive dogma and gender inequality will create ego-aspects perceived by self and others as sexually deviant. Concomitantly, one could expect such individuals to resist even acknowledging the existence of those ego-aspects.[25] Nonetheless, in the transformation of conscience described in this work, Christ is expected to enter into an active relationship with these sexualized self-images without condemnation. Likewise, at some point in the process he will be asked to baptize these ego-aspects. Moreover, these images are not expected to alter their 'deviance' as *a pre-condition of redemptive baptism*. In fact, immediately following their redemption, the only change most likely to manifest is a complete lack of shame regarding their particular mode of sexual expression. Thus, for example, a Rejected-self that exhibits strong masochistic tendencies may continue to do so after it's baptismal transformation by Christ, only now the sexual arousal is clearly pleasurable without being shaming. With further interventions these characteristic tendencies will evolve. In the case of the masochist, for example, rather than being 'forced' to experience pleasurable interactions, s/he will eventually assert a right to them. Stated another way, Christ appears to liberate sexuality from guilt and shame regardless of context, and allow it to seek new channels of expression without condemnation. Initially, these new channels may be expressed sensually and sexually, not unlike the New Testament story of the woman who expresses love for Christ by washing his feet with her tears and drying them with her hair. [26] Christ does not condemn or rebuke her for this; indeed, in the gospels we find him defending her against such accusations:

> Now when the Pharisee who had invited him saw it, he said to himself, "If this man were a prophet, he would have known who and what kind of woman this is who is touching him — that she is a sinner." Jesus spoke up and said to him, "Simon, I have something to say to you." "Teacher," he replied, "Speak." "A certain creditor had two debtors; one owed five hundred denarii, and the other fifty. When they could not pay, he canceled the debts for both of them. Now which of them will love him more?" Simon answered, "I suppose the one for whom he canceled the greater debt." And Jesus said to him, "You have judged rightly." Then turning toward the woman, he said to Simon, "Do you see this woman? I entered your house; you gave me no water for my feet, but she has bathed my feet with her tears and dried them with her hair. You gave me no kiss, but from the time I came in she has not stopped kissing my feet. You did not anoint my head with oil, but she has anointed my feet with ointment. Therefore, I tell you, her sins, which were many, have been forgiven; hence she has shown great love. But the one to whom little is forgiven, loves little." Then he said to her, "Your sins are forgiven." But those who were at the table with him began to say among themselves, "Who is this who even forgives sins?" And he said to the woman, "Your faith has saved you; go in peace (Luke 7:39-50).

And again, in John, Christ rebukes any who would condemn her:

> Mary took a pound of costly perfume made of pure nard, anointed Jesus' feet, and wiped them with her hair. The house was filled with the fragrance of the perfume. But Judas Iscariot, one of his disciples (the one who was about to betray him), said, "Why was this perfume not sold for three hundred denarii and the money given to the poor?" (He said this not because he cared about the poor, but because he was a thief; he kept the common purse and used to steal what was put into it.) Jesus said, "Leave her alone. She bought it so that she might keep it for the day of my burial. You always have the poor with you, but you do not always have me (John 12:3-8). [27]

Sexual expression has always been among the most contentious and repressive issues in Christian churches. But Christ does not condemn it. However deviant, he answers with love, forgiveness and understanding. We do not appreciate the value of this answer because it is so little in evidence in the world around us. But it has tremendous power for those willing to join with him in that context. In this respect Christ's love is like Tantric yoga, which seeks to transform the crudest expressions of sexuality into its most sublime conjunctions. [28] He is always willing to receive our sexual attractions as a first response to his love and transform them with his loving response. We find this to be true in the mystical literature of Judaism, Hinduism, Christianity, Taoism, Sufism, and Buddhism, and no less for our clients.

Dissociative Vs. Repressive Dynamics

Most of the forgoing discussion on Ego conscience is based on a dissociative dynamic. In early childhood development the archetypal Ego fragments in response to shameful trauma. This is called *dissociative* fragmentation. When an ego-aspect is enthralled by shame, a new ego-aspect is created to replace it. When a child reaches the age of reason – age seven or there about – s/he acquires the ability to formulate and internalize absolute opposites, e.g. good/evil, right/wrong, etc. This ability will precipitate the creation of Ideal selves – prideful selves who can do no wrong. Some time later the Ego learns to create a Dominant self. A Dominant self becomes the Ego's primary solution for evading the otherwise painful experience of fragmentation caused by a parentified conscience. It accomplishes this by simultaneously emulating and preempting the parental voice. Essentially, the Dominant self assumes to itself the power to self-shame. In this way it can preemptively feel ashamed, but no longer be subject to the threat of dissociation that would hold it in shameful bondage (which is the fate of all Rejected selves created in dissociative stage of development). The power of self-shaming allows a Dominant self to sustain its identity by *repressing* its shameful experiences within the Heart. While this strategy is generally sufficient to preempt the Voice-of-conscience, it also blocks entry to the Heart and the still quiet Voice for God. Convincing a Dominant self to relinquish its power to self-shame is a major step toward the final redemption of conscience.

While the evolution from dissociative to repressive Ego development is the normal progression found in most clients, it does not preclude further dissociation as a consequence of continuing abuse by parents, other adults, or shock trauma. The Ego of a child needing to survive horrendous, ongoing, abuse throughout childhood is capable of creating hundreds of fragments and alters in a valiant effort to live through the abuse. That Ego can also create alters with the characteristics of a Dominant self whose sole purpose is the denial of abuse by functioning as if it never happened.

The Heart and Conscience

While the Voice-of-conscience persists, and any Dominant self continues to block entry to the Heart by hiding its shame within it, Christ cannot clear the Heart for a revitalized flow of the Holy Spirit into the Mind. But in psycho-imagination, it is possible for Christ to enter the Heart of any self within the Mind, once the client becomes willing. Essentially, Christ enters the Heart auric body of the Aware-ego followed by the Aware-ego and any others involved in the process. The client immediately experiences a shift in perception. Once inside Christ is asked to identify and heal any shameful image or cluster of shameful emotion. Thereafter, Christ and the Aware-ego will frequently return to do more work. It is a 'heartfelt' experience that the client comes to value highly.

Wherever I capitalize Heart in this book, I am referring to the Heart auric body with its interconnecting heart chakras, which culminate in anatomical heart's activity. For thousands of years, Eastern cultures have recognized the existence of at least seven auric bodies, each embedded with the others via comparable sets of chakra energy centers. They are widely recognized by all energy therapists practicing today in the West as well as East. I treat the Heart auric body as the seat of the Soul and proper dwelling place of the Voice for God. The Old Testament also identifies the Heart as the source of conscience (as well as the center of the human being). Conscience - as Vox Dei, must speak *from within the Heart*, i.e. the auric body and its heart chakras. While the parentified conscience and Dominant selves remain dominant, they will inadvertently block Ego consciousness from hearing this center of being except 'through a glass darkly.' Consequently, the client's willingness to enter his or her Heart is a vital step toward the redemption of conscience.

RELATIONAL AUTHORITY

To understand Relational authority, the reader needs to appreciate a particular ability of the *Light*. Very quickly, on going inside, the client can be taught to use the *Light* to draw circles of *Light*. A circle of *Light* can be used to contain anything imaginable within the Mind ranging from the emotions evoked by a butterfly to the powers of an evil spirit; but most often it is used to contain images of self and others. Within the human Mind nothing can gainsay the absolute free will of the *Light*, which it expresses whenever a circle is drawn. That means that whatever is contained within a circle must remain there while it threatens the client in any way. Once this containment strategy is learned, the client can be quickly taught to use *double circles* - one circle of *Light* on top of another. The double circle quickly becomes an indispensable tool for the client and therapist alike. Basically, it can be used to extract anything embedded within an image. Let me illustrate using the image of a client's father. First the *Light* is asked to contain the father's image within a circle of *Light*. Next the *Light* is asked to overlay the first circle with a second circle of *Light*. The *Light* is then asked to separate the two circles thereby extracting whatever is embedded in the father's image. (Remember that images are not flesh and blood, but comprised of energy and myriad definitions. 'Extraction' is the process of separating out one or more definitions hypothesized to be distorting or confabulating an image, including energic images.)

The extraction process just described can be used to illuminate *the gendering process inherent in every sexed-image within the Mind. By sexed-image, I mean any image identifiable as biologically male or female. It is asserted here that every sexed-image within the Mind contains an Inner dyad comprised of one masculine and one feminine aspect. Each aspect can be extracted from a sexed-image using the Light and the process just described*. The demonstrable existence of an Inner dyad in every sexed-image allows me to posit the existence of a Gendering archetype, which begins constellating sexed-images around age three and continues throughout the individual's life span.

Inner dyads come in a large number of variations but all seem to share a number of characteristics in common. First, each aspect will generally manifest as a sexed-image. Most often, the aspects of the Inner dyad are opposite-sexed, but can also be same-sexed. Less frequently, a gender aspect can be amorphous to the point of appearing sexless but still identified as masculine or feminine. Opposite-sexed Inner dyads are considered optimum. Second, Inner dyads are always *complementary* insofar as each aspect serves a function that is indispensable to the sexed-image. Specifically, the masculine-aspect performs an *energic* function and the feminine-aspect provides the *definitional* function. This 'division of labor' attributed to the aspects will hold true regardless of the sex of the sexed-image. The analogy I use most often to describe this complementarity is that of a car comprised of engine and chassis. The masculine-aspect functions as the engine, the feminine-aspect as the chassis. An engine can operate on blocks, but apart from the chassis it has little meaning and no purpose or reason for being. Likewise, a chassis can exist apart from the engine but is unable to function as defined. The feminine aspect always provides the definition even as she may appear to play a subordinate role.

Another characteristic of Inner dyads is a corollary to complementarity: masculine and feminine aspects are *relationally interdependent*. In order to function as a whole, any significant change in one aspect requires a change in the other. This particular quality of Inner dyads is best appreciated when the *Light* is asked to place both aspects in the same circle so they can be observed in relationship. The clinician is likely to observe a wide variety of relationships across clients, but all will reflect a covariant interdependence *that insures some form of connectedness however strong or tenuous*. A stereotypic example would be a dominant masculine-aspect and submissive feminine-aspect. This interdependence is dynamic. If one of the aspects - most often the feminine, is altered in a significant way, then the masculine must also change in order to remain in relationship. Even as a feminine image may appear to be submitting, it is nonetheless defining the relationship. If, for example, the feminine image is altered to act as an empowered peer, then the masculine must accommodate to this new definition in order to maintain a connection. This accommodation is rarely immediate but it is inevitable over time, *provided the newly defined feminine has a transitional source of masculine energy to sustain it*. A transitional source of masculine energy is necessary for otherwise the feminine would have to revert back to its previous form in order to maintain an energetic connection. For this reason, Christ's role is twofold. First, he is asked to heal, or redefine, the feminine as needed. Second, he is asked to sustain this new image with his own masculine energy until the masculine aspect accommodates to the 'new creation' defined by Christ. In practice, Christ is often asked to also facilitate the masculine aspect's accommodation.

Yet another quality of all sexed-images is androgyny. The complementarity and relational interdependence of Inner dyads strongly supports the conclusion that all sexed-images are *androgynous*. Within the Mind, no sexed-image is exclusively male or female. Using the double circle, the *Light* can extract a masculine and feminine aspect from every sexed-image. However 'male' an image may look, the *Light* can extract a feminine aspect from that image reflecting the quality of this "maleness". If such a dyad is altered by Christological intervention then the sexed-image will also change when the dyad is reintegrated with it. I liken these changes to updating a computer with a new version of its operating system. In effect, every image is dependent upon its Inner dyad for its appearance and demeanor. If the Inner dyad is altered by intervention, then the image will also be altered when the Inner dyad is reintegrated back into the image.

Parental images provide the Gendering archetype a prototype for engendering the earliest and most enduring ego-aspects. The Relational authority of parents is predicated on the archetype's use of *their images* – both singly and as a couple. This is deduced from the fact that most inner dyads explicitly or characteristically reflect the parental relationship or the Inner dyad of one parent. In effect, the Gendering archetype uses parental images – sometimes one parent, most often both, to engender all ego-aspects. It goes without saying, that the Inner dyads constellated in ego-aspects are powerful governors of human behavior. Even a cursory exploration of Inner dyads extracted from a client's parental images and self-images will highlight - not only sources of inner tension, but also the reasons for an individual's partner choices and the ways s/he interacts with that partner. It accounts, in no small measure, for the oft-observed phenomenon of daughters marry men like their fathers and sons marry women like their mothers. Generally, parental images are congruent; that is to say, each parent tends to reinforce the Inner dyad of the other parent. However, the congruence is not always favorable to the child. Extreme discord in the marital relationship can result in the creation of Inner dyads within a child that are so painful in their dissonance that death may seem the only way to resolve it. For many clients, survival often requires that they repress any ego-aspects identified with one of the parents to weaken the combined effect of their negative mutual reinforcement. This is likely to lead to bi-polar or dissociative disorders in adult life, not to mention a myriad of other compulsive behaviors. What the client can never do with impunity is attempt to sever the connection between two aspects of an Inner dyad. Depression appears to be the most pervasive effect of any such attempt. In such instances, the feminine-aspect will appear as withdrawing or rigidifying in an attempt to break or resist contact with a negative energic masculine. In such cases, the individual experiences a loss of interest or lack of energy and/or direction; or experiences the inner anger of a feminine aspect rejecting the masculine or a masculine aspect angrily seeking to reinstate contact.

Most discussions of archetypal complexes (e.g. mother complex, father complex, etc.) tend to treat them as islands in the sea. The focus is generally on the particular archetype, such as the mother, without regard for any effect the complex has in conjunction with another archetype.[29] In contrast to that isolation, Relational authority addresses the inherent, demanding, interaction of masculine and feminine aspects. The Gendering archetype is seen as an imperative, archetypal, energy that shapes masculine-feminine interactions at all levels of being; a categorical imperative that strives for the continuing connection of dyadic aspects however painful or sublime the union.

Aspects of an Inner dyad need not be opposite sexed or sexual. By sexed, I mean male vs. female. Clients often describe Inner dyads that are same-sexed but clearly of a masculine and feminine gender, e.g. fem-butch, top-bottom, etc. Nor are Inner dyads normally sexual except in fantasy; and the fact that fantasy dyads are often sexualized has more to do with the untenable connections provided by parental relationships than any inherent need for a sexual connection. *Romantic or pornographic sexual fantasy helps to overcome otherwise untenable relationships such as those reflecting dominant-submissive roles so prevalent in patriarchal cultures.* Without the impetus of sexual attraction, it is likely that many of the female sex would simply and rightly withdraw from all emotional encounters with the male sex. In effect, sexual attraction, at least in fantasy, often serves to offset what would otherwise be a purely shameful encounter. Truly embracing and enduring masculine-feminine dyads must be forged with positive emotions, i.e., acceptance, mutual willingness, love, joy, etc. Any form of dominance-submission likely to generate a shameful, despairing, fearful, or resentful response is counterproductive to the formation of enduring masculine-feminine bonds. Where negative emotions define an individual's relationships, fantasy dyads will be sexualized in order to forge more viable dyads, be they sexually blatant, masturbatory, or disguised as romance. As regards the last, it is interesting to note how often the heroine is strongly attracted to a relationally unsuitable male. In the absence of a 'strong, implicitly sexual, attraction' there would be no romance. At the level of pornography, the role of sadist and masochist, voyeur and exhibitionist - to mention but two examples, also require sexual attraction to sustain an otherwise shaming relationship that would likely be centrifugal in the absence of sexual arousal.

The easiest way to appreciate the effect of Relational authority is *to ask someone for an image of their parents together that seems to characterize their relationship through the years.* If the individual is in therapy, this image will generally reflect a conflictual stance. (Please continue to bear in mind throughout this discussion that I only generalize to a clinical population.) Ideally, we would like to visualize our parents lovingly engaging each other. But this ideal is rarely achieved without Christ's intervention. More often, the images seem to reflect a tension of one form or another between the parents. One or both parents may seem argumentative, even rageful or explosive, while the other seems withdrawing, turned away, sickly, codependent or equally rageful. In other cases, the relational images can be milder but still difficult as in the case of one parent appearing to talk excessively while the other appears quiet and distant. Often, the client is unaware of these images on a day-to-day basis. Though easily brought to Mind, they remain for the most part subliminal. Interestingly, these images often do not reflect the current status of the parents who may in actuality be divorced, deceased or somewhat reconciled in their later years. They appear to be the images most strongly felt in childhood and adolescence, which capture the individual's perception of the parents' relationship as the client contemplated their own relational future.

For many adults, the relational images of parents *will function as active templates shaping the individual's own adult relationships with significant others.* A dyadic template is a stereotypic interaction of parents replicated by one or more of the client's Inner dyads. Further, when the dyadic template of the client's partner is examined it will generally be congruent with the client's dyadic template. Essentially, an individual recapitulates parental interactions in their interactions with significant others; and the controlling mechanism for that recapitulation appears to be the congruent dyadic templates of partners. This can be seen whenever a client is asked to describe their parents' habitual interactions and then later asked to describe interactional issues with a spouse or lover. The overlap is often uncanny, most particularly around marital issues which bring a couple to therapy, or in repetitive patterns of interaction found in two or more successive relationships, e.g. repeatedly marrying spouses who drink in excess.

As a rule, the client will identify with one or the other of their parents, as they are visualized in a typical interaction, and play out this role with the spouse or lover. But significantly, the client may not always identify with the same parent in successive relationships. In one relationship s/he may act out the part of the father, and in the next, the part of the mother. This is most likely to occur where the parental relationship was highly conflicted. It is as if the client was seeking to discern which of the two roles is most powerful or desirable within marriage. Of course, neither is more enviable since the felt experience of the marital tension will manifest regardless of which role is played out. But it does demonstrate that neither role enactment is determined by the sex of the spouse or parent.

An appreciation of Inner dyads is also helpful when a client comes to therapy with a sense of desperation related to the loss of a lover or spouse. I have found it helpful to treat such losses as the feared loss of a contra-sexual connection or tearing of the Inner dyad. Often, clients in the throes of a separation will visualize the lover as turning away from them, or otherwise withdrawing, or with another person. In such cases, I encourage the client to let Christ insert a portion of the *Light* into the Heart of the lover's image, and another portion into their own Heart. This new form of connectedness seems to put the client at ease in the ensuing weeks. Although they will still think about the person, they seem able to get on with their lives in healthy, and often, quite dramatic ways compared to their previous pattern of desperation. The lover's embodiment as an aspect of the masculine or feminine no longer threatens the Inner dyad. Significantly, this new kind of connectedness does not distort their perception of the relationship's current status. If anything, the client will act as if the relationship is over for the foreseeable future and they must look elsewhere for that degree of intimacy. Of note, this intervention is effective for the short term, and should only be treated as a temporary reprieve. Clinically, these obsessions are generally indicative of chronic discord between aspects of the Inner dyads defining parents and self; and that needs to be rectified or the client will simply continue to repeat the pattern.

The above process is also helpful in a general way whenever the client obsesses about another person's behavior, and perhaps even more so, if the other person threatens the client. An example of this would be a spouse in a contested divorce. In such cases, the hardest part of this process is convincing clients that it is truly in their best interest to 're-connect' with the person in question, since in most inner dialogues, the angry or otherwise threatened client has sought to 'vanquish' the image by one means or another. While it is possible to distance ourselves from people in-the-world, attempts to do so in our imagination generally increase the negative energy of the very images we seek to vanquish. The most dreaded images within us are the ones we most need to connect with via the *Light*. This connection is always transformative at both ends of the connection, and always for the better. Again and again, I will repeat: any connection made with the *Light* automatically protects from threat of inner attack since the *Light* now serves as a connective and protective link of communication between Ego and other. All such connections are most effective when made by the client's higher power who can be asked to be the sustaining provider of the connection.

Often, clients who have lost a parent by divorce, death, or abandonment in early childhood have great difficulty believing the spousal relationship can be reconstituted. Even if the surviving parent remarries, the stepparent will rarely serve as an adequate substitute, particularly if the family openly shares the circumstances of the biological parent's loss. Part of the difficulty may involve the client's mistaken belief that it is impossible to reconstitute a relationship involving a living parent and a missing or deceased parent. One client, for example, could envision her father, who died in the Vietnam War when she was a young child; and she could visualize her mother who was still living and remarried. But she could not visualize the two together. She was finally able to do this for the first time when prompted by me to connect them using her *Light*. Such cases validate my basic premise that the in-the-world status of a particular parent is irrelevant. While the physical life-status of parent is pertinent, it is not crucial to desired changes. Those changes seem most easily accomplished if both parents are deceased, and most difficult if both parents are living, and somewhere in between if one parent is deceased. But in all three conditions, change is equally possible. In the first condition, it is clearer that we are only dealing with images of the Mind whereas, when both parents are living, it is as if we were distorting photographic representations of real people. [30] It also helps to emphasize to clients that we are not attempting to change living parents; we are only interested in re-channeling energies interrupted or distorted by their relational images in the Mind. Where the client's Christ image is allowed to alter the Inner dyads of parental images, or the inner template defined by parental images, the client's felt need for change in the actual parents greatly diminishes.

Insofar as parental images act as templates for the Inner dyads of ego-aspects, and in so doing control our interactions with significant others in-the-world, it behooves us to have self-images and parental images whose Relational authority conveys a loving connection. Interventions using Christ and the *Light* have proven immensely successful in providing this type of connection. Of note, no attempt is made in our interventions to remove or lessen the Relational authority contained in parental images. Unlike Temporal and Moral authority – where the intent is to divest the parental image of its power, with Relational authority all efforts are directed at *redeeming* the engenderment embedded in the images. This redemption of parental images seems the best way to honor our parents and claim the promise of the Fourth Commandment.

Early and Later Studies

Relational authority is examined at length in Chapter VIII. That chapter is divided into two major sections. The first section – what I am calling the early studies, elaborate and illustrate all of the findings discussed above, including specific interventions for altering the Inner dyads of the person, parents, and grandparents.

The later studies document the discovery of Christ's willingness to 'convict any image with the power of the Holy Spirit.' Christ is asked to 'convict' any pertinent image until the client is *totally and completely satisfied with its transformation*. Conviction can be asked for repeatedly until the desired goal is achieved. As needed, Christ can also extend the power of conviction to each gender aspect of an Inner dyad. Essentially, Christ is asked to provide each image with the direct experience of the Holy Spirit, as often as necessary, to effect its complete transformation as a manifestation of the grace. In civil law conviction generally refers to guilt, but when the Holy Spirit convicts, the result is an image 'won over' by grace. Ample case studies are provided in the chapters VII and VIII to demonstrate the immense transformational power of this kind of intervention. I appreciate that such assertions may seem highly improbable at this juncture. All I ask is that the reader reserve judgment until s/he has finished reading Chapter VIII. I am hopeful that both the assertions and interventions will become completely tenable by the end of that chapter. Extensive verbatims are offered to that end.

When I began the study of parental authority using the *Light* methodology, I was focused primarily on Temporal and Moral authority. I intuited that something called Relational authority also played a role, but my early attempts to correct those dynamics were only marginally successful. It was not until I discovered the androgynous nature of sexed-images that the real impact of Relational authority became apparent. That discovery, coupled with Christ's role in the healing of Inner dyads and dyadic templates, extends to my clients the greatest power for transformation I can offer them.

LEVELS OF PERCEPTION IN PSYCHO-IMAGINATIVE WORK

While I rely heavily on Jungian Psychology for a theoretical context, there is a metaphysical theory of levels explicit in my work, which I have chosen to treat as superordinate to Jung's stated positions. [31] For many years, I sought a metaphysical perspective capable of encompassing Spirit, Soul, Heart, Mind and Body (brain-body), which could also define their relationship to each other. Eastern thought offers Chakra and Meridian theory, which are experientially demonstrable in their energy therapy applications. I have found both theories helpful in understanding energy dynamics found within active imagination, and rely heavily on those conceptualizations throughout this work. But Jewish Mysticism seems to better serve my overall objective as it offers an explicit theory of levels that has its roots in the Old Testament shared by the three major religions shaping Western and Near-Eastern thought. This Jewish tradition - commonly referred to as the Kabbalah, [32] has at various times been instrumental in guiding the Jewish community worldwide. Since the Renaissance, however, with the exception of Hassidic Judaism, it had fallen into disrepute among most Jews and remained unknown to all but a handful of Christians. [33] Only in the past sixty years, in no small measure due to the scholarship of Gershom Scholem, [34] has it regained some of its lost stature. Indeed, as I write, there are a number of good books describing the theory and practice, and that number is growing each year. [35] The theory can be exceedingly obtuse, and I would only claim a reader's grasp of its basic tenets. It offers many parallels to Jungian theory but goes considerably beyond it in scope. Like Jung's Analytical Psychology, it encompasses what is not visible to the physical senses, and deduces its assertions from the Mind's images and dynamics as experienced in active imagination. I am repeatedly drawn to study it for its promise of offering a coherent understanding of the relationship between Spirit, Soul, Heart, Mind and Body, which is currently beyond the scope of science.[36] (Note that I am capitalizing these words as a way of emphasizing that each can encompass worlds of knowledge and experience distinctly different from the world of Mind and Ego.)

Basically, a theory of levels – as used here, refers to 'worlds' of energy/information dynamics, which effect levels subordinate to them, as well as being affected in turn by those lower worlds. A classic example of level effects would be the sun's effect on the earth, the earth's effect on humankind, and humankind's effect on the individual. Each 'world' (sun, earth, humankind, individual) is completely dependent on the world 'above' it. Spirit *emanating* Soul, Soul *creating* Mind, and Mind *forming* Body (read brain-body) describes a comparable series of levels wherein Spirit is the first cause and Body the final effect.

The current scientific paradigm generally argues for an inverse theory of levels based upon a reductionistic metaphysic. To illustrate: Microbiology determines Physiology, Physiology determines Biology, Biology determines Ethology. In science, in direct contrast to Kabbalah, only parallel or reductionistic disciplines are treated as causal or explanatory. Behavioral psychology is a good example. At the level of individual behavior, one looks to either the environment (a parallel world) or brain physiology (a reductionistic world) for the determinants of behavior. The idea of looking to Mind as a determinant of behavior would be verboten from a Behaviorist's scientific perspective. Most often, Behaviorists would treat Mind as an epiphenomenon, if they considered it at all. The same is also true of Medicine. Even today, it is difficult for physicians to consider the effects of Mind on the Body, the placebo effect notwithstanding. [37] Only parallel physical interventions (e.g. surgery, drugs, nutrition) are acceptable solutions to physical manifestations of bodily disease. This is due in large measure to the reductionistic metaphysic still dominant in much of scientific thought. [38]

A number of influential writers over the past century have asserted that the reductionistic approach offered by science is an inadequate *metaphysical* approach, especially for the study of consciousness. It is not my intention to reiterate their arguments here. [39] In any case, none of them specifically offer constructs comparable to Kabbalah's spiritual theory of levels. But as one reads them side by side with Kabbalistic sources there are major correspondences. I would also note that the resurgent interest in the Kabbalah post-dates many of those authors. Though older by thousands of years, the Kabbalah has remained largely unknown to most of us. Very much like the Tibetan Book of the Dead, which was only translated into English in the 1930's, reputable translations and scholarship on Kabbalistic theory, aside from Scholem's, have only emerged in the last fifty years, which is a small amount of time for arguing a paradigm shift.

The following discourse is a greatly simplified version of Kabbalah, but still likely to be seen as dense and abstract by any reader who has not read on the subject. I suggest the reader absorb what s/he can on first reading and appreciate that none of it is crucial to the method or interventions that follow. It needs to be introduced at some point because it has provided me the most comprehensive and heuristic body of theory I have found to illuminate the relationships between Spirit, Soul, Mind and Body. It illustrates my conviction that Soul activity can be altered via active imagination, but to do so the Ego must become willing to call upon a higher power. (In traditional Judaic understandings of the Kabbalah, angels are seen to function as higher powers.)

Very few psychological theories acknowledge the existence of Soul much less, the exercise of its own will within the psyche. Jung's theory comes closest in his discussions of the Collective unconscious, which implicitly defines Soul as the progenitor of archetypal images. It is asserted here that Soul shapes Mind. Treating Soul as a controlling force in the Mind adds considerable complexity to any theory of psychology. It is very much like adding a third dimension to a chessboard: the levels of complexity with which therapist and client must grapple become exponential. But, hopefully, the added complexity will provide a fuller grasp of the 'world of active imagination' (i.e. the Mind) and an enlarged field of options for discerning interventions on the client's behalf.

To better appreciate what I am about here, the reader must grasp the centrality of active imagination in my work. Clients execute all of the interventions described in this book by entering their active imagination. Active imagination is the arena in which most esoteric religious practices achieve their effects, e.g. all forms of meditation, centering prayer, Alchemy, Shamanism, Kabbalah, etc. When a client engages their active imagination they consciously enter the world of Mind. By working in that world, the client and I anticipate effecting changes that will influence all spheres of being as well as other people. A theory of levels helps to establish the limits and possibilities of working in active imagination wherein it is possible to experience Spirit and Soul as well as Mind and Body.

To begin: the theory of levels offered here is based on the Kabbalistic view of four worlds (levels) manifesting God and derived from the Old Testament. The common English words for describing the primary *activity* of each world are: emanation, creation, formation and action.[40] Each world is seen as superordinate to the one it generates, insofar as it is closer to its godly origin. God *emanates* the world of Spirit, which *creates* the world of Soul, which *forms* the world of Mind, which *enacts* the world of Body (brain-body) in a physical universe. The four worlds correspond to the four aspects of *being* (Spirit, Soul, Mind, Body) that have been used to define human beings throughout our oral and written history.

Generally, Kabbalistic thought is schematized using ten sefirot organized as a Tree of Life. These ten sefirot reflect the ten different names or aspects of God found in Genesis.[41] The twenty-two letters of the Hebrew alphabet comprise the connections between sefirot.[42] Figure 2.1 is an example of a Tree of Life schematic that can be used to illustrate relationships within and between Spirit, Soul, Mind and Body *from the perspective of Mind*. I choose to organize this discussion from the perspective of Mind because that is the domain of Ego and our sense of 'I' and 'me.' But the Tree of Life can be used to visualize many perspectives and subjects, e.g. the human body, the human brain, principalities and powers, the world of angels, etc. There are easily hundreds of different Tree of Life schematics. Each schematic generally illustrates one world, its connections to other parts of that world, as well as the worlds above and below it. Figure 2.1 is an adaptation of this approach designed to illustrate functional connections within the world of Formation (Mind); it also provides a graphic description of conscience in its *unredeemed* state viewed within a Kabbalistic context.

In my work, the focus is on Mind: the exploration and transformation of its emotional contents in active imagination using the *Light* and Christ within us. This is the world where Ego manifests and organizes consciousness. It is called the world of Formation because it is most often likened to blueprints and plans shaping and directing the Body, which is comprised of body and brain functioning in a physical universe. Mind is *the intermediary level* between Soul and Body. Soul creates the Mind by generating a nearly infinite set of opposites, which are the prima materia of images, and then constellating images capable of shaping and directing the Ego. In turn, Mind forms the Body (the world of action), which physically enacts the imaginal blueprints generated by Mind.

In Figure 2.1, the Heart is defined as the seat of Soul – the Soul's primary power for affecting the Mind minute by minute. Not surprising, the Heart has more connections to and from it than any other sefirot in the Tree of Life. The Heart is to Soul as Ego is to Mind. The Heart's centrality reflects the Old Testament assertion that the Heart, not the head (Ego) is the center of being.[43] In my schema, as well as that offered by all Kabbalists, the Heart directs the Mind. In addition to being the conscious expression of the Soul, Heart also has direct connections to the world of Spirit and Divine Being, which also makes it the proper locus of the Voice for God. The connection between Divine Being and the Heart is experienced within the Mind as the grace of God or inspiration of the Holy Spirit.

Ego consciousness will always reflect the matrix created by Soul, Mind, and Body *interacting within the Mind*. The Ego governs interactions between Mind and Body and copes with the varied demands of environment and culture on the Body by its exercise of free will. In much the same way, the Soul directs the Mind's activity via the Heart. In effect, the Ego – directing the Body's activity, and the Heart directing the Mind's activity, both exercise a will of their own. (Concomitantly, *instinct* expresses the Body's exercise of will in the physical world.) While the Ego's primary raison d'être is the direction of the Body, it can also willfully obstruct the Soul's agenda at the risk of evoking Wrath. To safely mitigate the Soul's agenda it must call on a higher power. The Soul's influence can be observed in the Mind's psycho-imaginative process and bodily experiences, but its effects can only be treated palliatively at the level of Body or Mind. Doctoring the Soul is much different from doctoring either the Mind or Body. First and foremost, doctoring the Soul requires willing access to a higher power. The Soul is a superordinate world relative to Mind, which places it well beyond the purview of Ego and its aspects. The Ego can witness the Soul's effects, and suffer them, but its free will is insufficient to change them because the Soul exercises the more powerful will. Change at the level of Soul can only occur when the Ego is willing to allow a higher power to intervene on its behalf.

Some readers may find the idea of 'Soul exercising its own will' a disturbing concept because 'will' is normally treated as the sole prerogative of Ego consciousness. But in striving to understand Soul, one point becomes very clear: the Soul has a will of its own. That will has been cloaked in the concept of *unconsciousness*: the perpetual frustrater of Ego control. Every therapist eventually learns that the primary characteristic of 'unconscious' forces is their power to disrupt and disturb Ego activity and 'frustrate' the best efforts of the therapist. Freud chose to treat that disruption as a function of primitive Id or Superego activity, which he treated as atavistic and unrealistic. Jung, by contrast, insisted that a respectful attitude toward the personal unconscious, and particularly the collective unconscious, was absolutely essential to the individuation process and our wellbeing. Stated another way, he treated the collective unconscious as an operational definition of Soul. These 'unconscious' powers exercise a superordinate will, as measured by their ability to disrupt Ego function and resist all Ego efforts to forcibly curtail the constellations of its archetypal activity. In sum, the exercise of will is not the sole prerogative of Ego consciousness. In fact, I would argue that it is Soul, which most strongly exercises will in its seemingly unilateral effect on the Mind and Body. This may be a novel idea in an egocentric world, but one that must be given increased consideration as we assess the nature of Soul and its effects on the Mind and Body.

Most people tend to treat their 'imagination' as 'a fantasy-making modality' not to be confused with 'the real world of the Ego.' This egocentricity has a similar view of the Soul. Most Christians believe their Soul survives death, and either suffers the pains of hell or the bliss of heaven as a consequence of the Ego's actions. That being so, one might expect the Soul to have a vested interest in the Ego's actions, but most people treat it as a mere passive sojourner rather than an active agent of our affairs (if they think

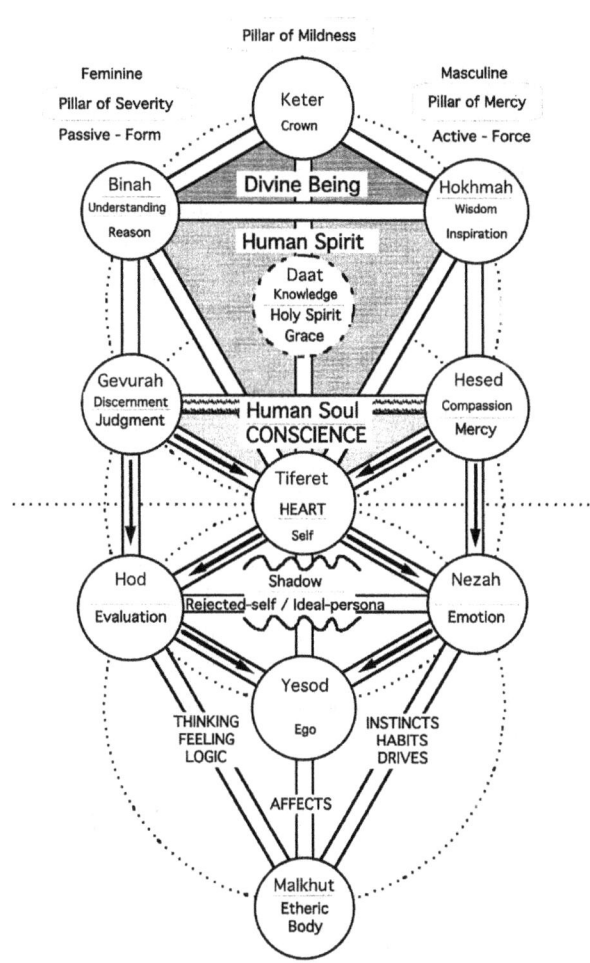

Figure 2.1 – KABBALISTIC TREE OF LIFE

about it at all). In contrast, in my work with clients, I treat the archetypal energies generated by Soul as decisive in their effects on ego-aspects.

One last set of observations regarding the Kabbalah's Tree of Life will prove helpful later on. There are numerous ways of describing the relationships between the different sefirot. One way distinguishes three perpendicular 'pillars' created by the sefirot – see Figure 2.1. The central pillar is described as the pillar of Mildness or Equanimity. It reflects the power of will sequentially exercised by Spirit, Soul, Mind and Body. Ideally, this pillar reconciles the extremes reflected in the other two pillars. It is this pillar which channels the grace of Spirit, the willingness of Soul, the free will of Ego, and finally, the instinctual will of Body. On either side are the pillars of Severity and Mercy. The pillar of Severity is said to embody feminine or yin attributes. It provides structure, definition, form, and limits. As the setter of limits, it precipitates the Wrath of God, but not only that. It is also reason, intellect, judgment, logic, feeling, and thinking. (Note that thinking – an Ego function, is considered by Kabbalists to be a very pale reflection of Reason, which identifies the principles or eternal truths guiding the Soul. Also note that feeling is treated as Jung defined it, as a rational, evaluative, function.) The pillar of Severity can also be thought of as the pillar of form that shapes and limits power and force. Those are defined by the pillar of Mercy, which is identified as masculine or yang in nature. It provides all the energies sustaining the Mind and Body including the affective and emotive energies motivating the Mind and Body. At the highest level, the pillar of Mercy (masculine) embodies wisdom followed by compassion. At the level of Ego it embodies affect, emotion, drives, habits, and desire. The pillars of Severity and Mercy also reflect what is found when feminine and masculine aspects are extracted from sexed-images (reference the discussion on Relational authority). In effect, every animate image reflects the amalgam of the feminine pillar of Severity and the masculine pillar of Mercy.

In this work, I am primarily concerned with the links between Body, Mind, Ego, Heart, and Soul, and the transformative power of the Holy Spirit's grace as channeled by the inner Christ. The Heart, when it functions as an unimpeded conduit of the Holy Spirit, is treated as the fount of a redeemed conscience. The process of redeeming conscience can be thought of as clearing a path between Heart and Ego. Where this path is blocked, generally by the Voice-of-conscience and Dominant selves, conscience will be experienced, quite literally, *in extremis,* rather than through the moderating effect afforded by the Heart. Stated another way, conscience, while unredeemed, must flow through the Pillars of Severity and Mercy rather than being mediated by the Heart. Where that is so, the expression of conscience will be limited to the Body's affects for expression, rather than the higher emotions afforded by the Heart, i.e. discernment, forgiveness and compassion vs. shaming judgment and pain. Further on, I revisit these distinctions is greater detail.

The World of Soul

Thanks to a number of pioneers, a great deal of clinical work has already been done in working with the Soul's effect on the Mind. Soul work is very much like praying for exorcism, but often more effective, and offering a degree of discernment not found in most Christian sources on the subject. In Soul work, identified "dark forces" are treated as a 'second patient' in need of redemption. Thus Soul work contrasts with traditional deliverance prayers, which only evoke Christ to refute, bind, and remove unclean spirits. Such prayer, one imagines, sends the spirit away defeated, yet unrepentant, and quite capable of infesting the individual or someone else at a later date. In the clinical literature of Soul work, that spirit – whatever its nature, is first transformed or redeemed, and then returned to God in its redeemed state. But the clinical and Christian literatures do agree that some form of higher power is always required for the intervention. I cannot stress this point enough. Interventions at this level are exceedingly powerful in terms of the individual's mental and physical well being, but all of them require the manifestation of power greater than anything the Ego can claim for itself. [44]

Without question, one of the most comprehensive books on clinical Soul work that I have studied is by Shakuntala Modi, [45] a psychiatric physician. Her work is remarkable in several ways. First, it is exceedingly comprehensive both in terms of the severity of patient symptoms she treats and the number of interventions she describes. Of note, everything she does can be replicated using the *Light* and an image of Christ without recourse to the hypnosis she uses in her own interventions. In effect, while her methodology differs from mine, I have obtained essentially the same results. It should be noted that most therapists doing clinical Soul work have used some form of hypnosis to intervene whether it be for the purpose of discerning past life influences, the presence of earthbound or demonic entities, negative devices, Soul loss or fragmentation. Where I differ with these authors is in my assertion that none of these interventions require hypnosis. All of them can be accomplished by the client's exercise of *willingness* expressed through the *Light* and their inner Christ, as distinct from relinquishing free will to the hypnotherapist and whoever guides that therapist. But it behooves any reader who would venture into this area to study the works of these pioneers, most especially Modi.

Clearly, an example would be helpful at this point. Consider the following. A client is taught to use the *Light* and evoke an image of Christ. On her initial foray inside to start working on issues, she reports that a grayness appears to surround her *Light*. I direct her to have the *Light* contain it in a circle. She does so, and using the *Light* she identifies it as *doubt,* which she describes as looking like a gray blob in the circle. (Whenever such emotions are encountered, I encourage the client to examine them at length. Quite often they will manifest as dark, almost formless, shapes. A lack of form is always a clear indication that the therapist is dealing with something 'extra-ordinary'.) She owns that she has valued this *doubt* in the past believing it kept her from making bad choices. But what she now begins to appreciate through my respectful questioning is that such *doubt*, of itself, undermines all choices or exercise of free will. In effect, whatever this *doubt* touches becomes doubtful as a choice; doubt can never affirm a choice, only undermine it. Moreover, it appears to feed upon itself. To illuminate this self-feeding, I suggest she release the *doubt* from its circle of containment and give it free reign. Immediately, it begins to fill her Mind with darkness so that everything but her *Light* is obscured. At this point I suggest she ask her Christ image to re-contain it. Immediately, on doing this, she experiences a burst of anger coming from it and sees within the darkness a fearsome face. I suggest she allow Christ, using his *Light*, to turn everything in that circle into pure white light, and return it to the source of light. This is done and the *doubt* completely disappears after being turned into light.

Modi, and not a few Christians, would call the client's *doubt* a demonic Spirit. As a rule, I do not use this kind of nomenclature with clients. I call it, rather, an autonomous emotion. But it should be clear that this is not ordinary emotion. It appears to have a life of its own, seeks to increase its power within the Mind, and would exaggerate ordinary doubt out of all proportion if given the opportunity. Its primary purpose appears to be the undermining of discernment. By discernment I mean the ability to clearly differentiate good from bad choices as distinct from doubting either the goodness or badness of everything it touches. Insofar as such discernment is needed for the proper exercise of free will, the client's doubt would appear to undermine the Ego's judgment. But by whatever name we call this *doubt*, others and I are in agreement on one point: its removal as a force in the Mind always requires a higher power. No amount of Ego exertion can remove such doubt. The Ego can use counter-phobic mechanisms, but such defenses are limited to resisting the *doubt* and require the ego-aspect act *despite* it. And more to the point, those defenses cannot dispel it. One other point: what is true of the Ego is also true of the *Light* when used by the Ego alone. That is, the Ego can use the *Light* to contain anything within the Mind - with the exception of Soul parts belonging to others,[46] but it cannot transform them. In this matter, the *Light* is limited to the Ego's exercise of will. Only when the *Light* is exercised by a higher power such as Christ can it exercise a transforming function. And one final point: *doubt*, as experienced above, is most likely to attach to an ego-aspect that uses denial as a primary defense. That ego-aspect must give up its strong reliance on that defense or risk later infestation by kindred spirits The need to forgo such 'ego powers' in favor of those exercised by a higher power is highlighted in the Gospels.[47] Interventions for addressing 'ego powers' are described in Chapters VII and VIII.

Any sojourn into the realm of Soul, i.e. the Collective unconscious, must eventually address our capacity for evil. I, for one, have come to accept the existence of 'autonomous' forces within the world of the Soul capable of tempting, harassing, and even possessing the Soul - but never the Spirit, and capable of raising great havoc with the Mind and Body. I also accept that wherever these forces of darkness are called to task by forces of light, be it in the form of angels, or Jesus Christ, or any other manifestation of the Godhead, then the evil must give way and relinquish all claim to that Soul or its parts. But always, this relinquishment requires a *willingness* on the part of the individual to effect the intervention, and the recruitment of a higher power to exercise that willingness.

One last thought before addressing the emotions. The Soul can err. Nothing I have read ever placed the Soul on a pedestal. It is fallible. It is the Mind's link to Spirit and God, but it can trip and falter and wander off the path. It is governed by imperatives and a history that we, as Ego, know little of, all the more so when we deny its very presence as an active force in our lives. As Soul is credited with our best, it must also accept responsibility for our worst. Our salvation is in the dialogue. Our path is true only if the Mind and Heart learn to speak with one voice, and even then, only by the *grace* of God are we saved.

THE ROLE AND SCOPE OF AFFECT AND EMOTION

Affect and emotion are integral to everything I address in this work. Psychological theory and research this past half century have increasingly focused on affect and emotion as the underpinning of all motivation. Whether we are speaking of simple pain and pleasure as reinforcers, or the power of shame and forgiveness to guide our behavior, it is clear that affect and emotion guide our thoughts and motivate our behavior. As Nathanson notes, "Despite our view of ourselves as thinking beings, cognition is but a frail craft floating on a sea of emotion."[48] Something becomes the focus of consciousness to the extent it has an affect or emotion attached to it. It is affect and emotion, which makes the world figural. Nowhere is this more evident than with conscience, which is always experienced emotionally or not at all. In its unredeemed state, conscience is experienced as shaming, guilting, fear instilling, or somatically painful. When redeemed it will manifest as discerning, loving and forgiving. To fully appreciate conscience, a therapist must become very conversant with emotions, especially shame. Shame is experienced as taboo (unforgiving) in all cultures. Consequently, most people go to great lengths to hide or deny shame to the extent that they are often unaware of feeling shame, though they name it daily in a number of coded forms. They will tell you that they feel inadequate or inferior, suffer from low self-esteem, are easily embarrassed, are shy in social settings, have their feelings easily hurt, feel self-conscious, blush easily, have difficulty making eye contact, feel inept, stupid, ineffectual, powerless, masochistic, etc. This list could go on for pages. People rarely connect those feelings with shame, but shame is the root of them all.

Guilt infers shame. Some clients, perhaps most, report feeling guilty. Most often, this feeling of guilt is for covert, unobserved, thoughts or actions that, if exposed to the world, would generate shame. In effect, if the actions about which the client feels guilty were actually observed, they would experience the exposure as some gradient of shame, from mild embarrassment to extreme mortification. It is the difference between someone caught binging vs. remembering binging, or someone caught masturbating vs. confessing to it. So long as the actual act remains hidden or unobserved it is only guilting after the fact. Fear provides a similar defense against experiencing shame. When I go into a restaurant, there are hundreds of behaviors I will not enact – from picking my nose to flatulence, for fear of being shamed. Much of our social intercourse is governed by the fear of shame.

In the following discussion, affect, feeling and emotion must be clearly distinguished since these words are often used incorrectly and indiscriminately. Feeling is the Ego's capacity to directly evaluate and name an affect or emotion. It is treated here as Jung defined it: a rational, evaluative function available to the Ego for naming the felt experience of physical (affect) and mental (emotional) events. As Jung noted, this function can be primary for an individual – traditionally women, or woefully undeveloped as in the case of most men, past and present. The feeling function is evaluative rather than evocative. Consequently, affect and emotion can be experienced without our 'feeling' them. If the feeling function is undeveloped, crippled, or suppressed, the individual can have great difficulty naming what is being emoted. Aside from Jung's description of the feeling function in *Psychological Types*,[49] one of the best books I have read on the topic of feeling is by Eugene Gendlin[50] who was a major expositor of Carl Rogers. According to Gendlin, much of Roger's work was aimed at helping people develop their feeling function and using it to resolve psychological conflicts. It was Gendlin's contention that all psychological change was experienced affectively and generally followed on the heels of a client being able to accurately name a felt experience.

Affect is *the body's experience of emotion*. It is genetically programmed and discernible even in infants. Enjoyment, excitement, surprise, anger, desire, fear, distress, dissmell, disgust and shame are the basic affects observed in infants. As a rule, affects are short lived. They are intended as physiological reactions to environmental and proprioceptive stimuli. But internal associations can indefinitely prolong affects. When affects are experienced and/or expressed by the Ego, then they are called emotions. Emotion is always mediated by attributes within the Mind be it memories, archetypal energies, or heartfelt connections. Resentment and smoldering rage are good examples of emotion. Both are *prolonged* experiences of anger (an affect). Resentment is a low intensity response 'nursed' by memories of past slights; and smoldering rage is an extreme form of barely suppressed anger, intensified by remembered associations to shame and/or fear.

My purpose in this section is to compare and contrast two theories of emotion put forward by Silvan Tomkins and David Hawkins, that have shaped my thinking on affect and emotion; and to append both with a Kabbalistic perspective. Tomkins's theory of affect dovetails the one put forth by Hawkins. What sets each theory apart is the methodology used to construct them. To quote one of my own mentors, "method dictates results; change the method and you will likely get different results."[51] The first theory was developed by Silvan Tomkins whose work spanned the last fifty years of the 20th century.[52] (In describing Tomkins's theory, I rely heavily on the work of Donald Nathanson who is a major expositor of Tomkins's work. Nathanson brings a degree of clinical acumen to the discussion lacking in Tomkins discourses and he is definitely more readable.[53]) Tomkins is brilliant but difficult to read. As an academician, writing in an era when the power of emotions was denigrated as a subject of study, he felt obliged to shape his theory within a cognitive/learning model.

Tomkins anchors his theory in the observation of infants, not unlike his contemporary, Jean Piaget, who also relied on the observation of infants to develop his theory of cognitive development.[54] But unlike Piaget, Tomkins was interested in emotional development. To that end, he observed that infants universally express stereotypic, physically observable, behaviors that can be identified as affects. These affects are the strictly biological expression of emotion. Affect is hardwired into the human organism; it is an innate, genetic response, programmed at birth; it is the earliest, visible, form of emotional life, and our first language. Figure 2.2 identifies the nine affects that Tomkins identified as innate. Each is identifiable by characteristic physiological responses that are also described in Figure 2.2.[55]

Tomkins identifies two positive, one neutral, and six negative affects. He uses descriptors that span a range of intensity. The first positive emotion is enjoyment, which becomes joy at its highest intensity. Nathanson and others see enjoyment-joy as the affect used to express what they call healthy pride. Broucek calls this competence pleasure, which is said to occur when competence is tested in an atmosphere of interest-excitement.[56] Nathanson sees pride and shame as forming an axis, or gradient, whose balance creates our sense of self. According to Nathanson, the extremes of this axis are a "hoped-for *personal best* that hovers as an unreachable image within most of us, and the terribly feared *personal worst* that, when revealed, will trigger an avalanche of deadly shame."[57] These extremes correspond with the self-images I have identified as the Ideal-self and Rejected-self. They are also reflected in the components of Freud's superego. In Nathanson's view, healthy pride is the only antidote for shame, though there are also numerous defenses against being shamed or denying shame such as anger-rage. The other positive affect identified by Tomkins is interest-excitement. Both of these positive affects can be interrupted by Shame-humiliation. *It is this power to interrupt ongoing positive affects which makes shame such a painful experience.* The Neutral affect is Surprise-startle, or recognition of the unexpected. Nathanson contends that "the real function of the innate affect, surprise-startle, is to clear the mental apparatus so that the organism can remove attention from whatever else might have been occupying it and focus on whatever startled it."[58] The other six affects are all negative. They are fear-terror, distress-anguish, anger-rage, dissmell, disgust, and shame-humiliation. Dissmell and disgust deserve special mention here because they are similar to shame in their effect. Dissmell basically refers to something smelling bad, and disgust to something tasting bad. According to Nathanson, "a great deal of our personal concept of what is shameful comes from our lifetime response to the affects dissmell and disgust."[59] The final negative affect identified by Tomkins is shame-humiliation. In infants, and adults, the purest bodily expression of shame-humiliation is eyes averted and downcast, neck and shoulders beginning to slump.[60] Other characteristic responses are blushing and turning the head away. This affect is considered painfully aversive because it can interrupt the positive affects. It can stop pleasure, excitement, and enjoyment in its tracks. Phylogenetically, it has a high survival value. In a dangerous world, the ability of a parent to abruptly stop a child's excited activity can mean the difference between life and death. Shame, the affect, serves just this purpose. But its effect is the same whether the excitable activity is dangerous or not. Shaming makes an activity painfully dangerous whether or not it is so.

Tomkins makes two basic assertions regarding his nine, observable, affects. The first, according to Nathanson, is "...Tomkins's idea that the function of any affect is to amplify the highly specific stimulus that set it in motion."[61]

No matter whether that stimulus has come from what the infant has just seen, heard, smelled, tasted, or remembered, if the stimulus triggers an affect, the stimulus will now become important in the way typical of that affect. Affect, says Tomkins, makes good things better and bad things worse...Whenever we are said to be motivated, it is because affect has made us so, and we are motivated in the direction and form characteristic of that affect. Whatever is important to us is made so by affect. Affect is the engine that drives us.[62]

According to Tomkins, affect and memory create emotion. This is his second major assertion. "Swiftly, the growing organism learns to associate the experience of affect with what triggered it, to form the linkages that, as it's powers of memory and higher cognition improve with age, will become adult emotion."[63] To paraphrase with an example: the parent's expression of distaste, in response to a child's particular activity, evokes a shameful affect in the child that then becomes a conditioned response whenever the activity is remembered or reenacted. Shame acts as a negative reinforcer such that even the memory becomes aversive. This definition also provides a description of conscience in its unredeemed state.

Tomkins definition of emotion assumes the classical reductionistic stance of Behaviorism: the *cause* of all emotions *must be reducible* to nine, *observable*, affect clusters coupled with the observable stimuli that triggered them. In effect, all emotion is perceived as shaped by environmental stimuli, e.g. parental actions reinforced by affective responses. Let us grant that *the bodily expression* of emotion is limited to a finite number of affect clusters.[64] This does not require that affect be a necessary cause of all emotion. All it demonstrates is that affect is often a concomitant of emotion. But there are a number of emotions that seem to have only minimal, or no connection, to identifiable affects: courage, willingness, forgiveness, and love come to mind as examples. In fact, arguing from a Kabbalistic perspective, emotions can have causes quite apart from affect. The Kabbalistic theory of levels allows for the Mindful expression of emotion, or even more provocatively, the Soul's expression of emotion. Quite conceivably, it is the Soul – via the Heart, that most adroitly communicates the emotions motivating thinking, feeling, and behavior. Before going there, however, I want to examine David Hawkins ranking of emotions since it introduces a broader range of emotions and provides another context for assessing Tomkins's theory.[65]

Where Tomkins focused on infant behavior in developing his theory of affect, David Hawkins used the physiological responses of adults to a specific kind of test that allowed him to rank order all discernible emotions. Essentially, he used kinesiology to test the *power* of emotions, e.g. how powerful is a particular emotion compared to others? Kinesiology uses muscle testing to assess the relative value of something. This method is based on the pioneering work of George Goodheart, who found that

"...benign physical stimuli – for instance, beneficial nutritional supplements – would increase the strength of certain indicator muscles, whereas inimical stimuli would cause those muscles to suddenly weaken. The implication was that at a level far below conceptual consciousness the body 'knew', and through muscle testing was able to signal, what was good and bad for it. The classic example...is a universally observed weakening of indicator muscles in the presence of a chemical sweetener; the same muscles strengthen in the presence of a healthful natural supplement." [66]

Hawkins uses kinesiology to rank order the power of emotions. Higher numbers reflect exponentially more powerful emotions compared to emotions receiving a lesser value. Hawkins describes the testing procedure thus:

The numerical scale, elicited spontaneously from test subjects, ranges from the value of mere physical existence at 1, to 600, the apex of ordinary consciousness, and then on to 1,000, comprehending advanced states of enlightenment. Responses in the form of simple yes-or-no answers determine the calibration of the subject. For example, "If just being alive is one, then the power of love is over 200?" (Subject goes strong, indicating a yes.)

Figure 2.2 - Typologies of Emotion

	HAWKINS RANKING OF EMOTIONS	TOMKINS INNATE AFFECTS
EMOTIONS EXPRESSING ABUNDANCE	ENLIGHTENMENT (700-1000) PEACE (600) JOY (540) LOVE (500) UNDERSTANDING (400) FORGIVENESS (350) WILLINGNESS (310) TRUST (250)	**ENJOYMENT-JOY** Smile, lips widened and out **INTEREST- EXCITEMENT** Eyebrows down, track, look, listen **SURPRISE-STARTLE** Eyebrows up, eyes blink **ANGER-RAGE** Frown, clenched jaw, red face
	COURAGE (200)	
EGO EMOTIONS EXPRESSING ENTITLEMENT AND LACK	PRIDE (175) ANGER (150) DESIRE (125) FEAR (100) GRIEF (75) DEPRESSION (50) GUILT (30) SHAME (20) MERE EXISTENCE (1) -0-	**FEAR-TERROR** Frozen stare, face pale, cold, sweaty, hair erect **DISTRESS-ANGUISH** Cry, rhythmic sobbing, arched eyebrows, mouth down **DISGUST** Lower lip lowered and protruded, head forward and down **DISSMELL** Upper lip raised, head pulled back **SHAME-HUMILIATION** eyes down, head down and averted, blush

"Love is over 300?" (Subject still goes strong.) "Love is over 400?" (Subject stays strong.) "Love is 500 or over?" (Subject still strong.) In this case love calibrated at 500, and this figure proved reproducible regardless how many test subjects were tested. With repeated testing using individuals or groups of testers with individuals or groups of subjects, a consistent scale emerged which correlates well with human experience, history, and common opinion, as well as the findings of psychology, sociology, psychoanalysis, philosophy and medicine.[67]

A sampling of the emotions tested by Hawkins is given in Figure 2.2. No one, even Hawkins, can tell us why a subject tests weak when a value greater than 20 is assigned to shame, or why the same subject still tests strong when a value of 300 is assigned to willingness, but reportedly, such results are consistent across a large spectrum of subjects. According to Hawkins, all emotions with a value less than 200 are negative. *That is, all such emotions will test weak except where the emotion is tested for a specific value.* What I find significant is that even negative emotions have a range of values, some testing less weak than others and therefore relatively preferable. In effect, the experience of pride, while negative, is still preferable to shame, which is extremely negative. The same could be said of other negative emotions such as anger, fear, desire (craving), grief and apathy: all are preferable to shame, though none of them has the power of any of the positive emotions.

Consider, as an example, the power of responding to a situation courageously rather than despairingly. Certainly, a courageous response would offer the individual a greater range of options than despair. Anger too would offer more options to an individual than responding shamefully, even though both are negative. In many respects, Hawkins ratings are self-evident. It is not difficult to imagine shame as debilitating and love as empowering. The point I consider significant is that none of his positive emotions (200+) are easily reducible to affects as progenitors. It is hard to imagine any of the affects described by Tomkins producing the emotional power assigned to willingness or forgiveness. Yet every book on healing I have ever read will tell you that something called 'forgiveness of self and other' is a major prerequisite to healing. According to Nathanson, the most powerful emotion generated by affects is a healthy form of pride, but in Hawkins topology it is merely the least negative of the negative emotions. Hawkins description of pride might prove helpful here in showing both its power and limitations:

Pride, which calibrates at 175, has enough energy to run the United States Marine Corps. It is the level aspired to by the majority of our kind today. People feel positive as they reach this level, in contrast to the lower energy fields. This rise in self-esteem is a balm to all the pain experienced at lower levels of consciousness. Pride looks good and knows it; it struts its stuff in the parade of life...Pride is at a far remove from Shame, Guilt, or Fear that to rise, for instance, out of the despair of the ghetto to the pride of being a Marine is an enormous jump...The problem, as we all know, is that 'Pride goeth before a fall.' Pride is defensive and vulnerable because it is dependent upon external conditions, without which it can suddenly revert to a lower level. The inflated ego is vulnerable to attack. Pride remains weak because it can be knocked off its pedestal into Shame, which is the threat that fires the fear of loss of pride. [68]

I will discuss pride at greater length throughout the book. What I want to stress here is that Silvan Tomkins's theory of affect identifies pride as the only possible emotion available to the Ego as an anecdote to shame. Hawkins argues otherwise. From his perspective, pride is only the *least* negative of the negative emotions, and even though Nathanson's pride-shame axis accurately describes the level of consciousness for most of us, most of the time, there are many more powerful emotions discerned by Hawkins kinesiology studies. This is graphically illustrated by Hawkins ratings. But even without ratings to bolster the argument, it is clear there is a qualitative difference in emotions. This is not to say that Tomkins theory is in error; only that his theory has a delimited range dictated by its restriction to observable behaviors in infants and children.

Hawkins's ratings divide emotion into two groups. Those scoring less than 200 always tested weak, and those 200 and above always tested strong. This bifurcation is similar to findings published by Abraham Maslow in the 1960's. He found that needs - which he identified as the motivators of behavior, could be grouped as "deficiency needs" or "being needs." [69] I would prefer to embed these groupings in a Kabbalistic context. The Ego moderates between Mind and Body. As such, it needs access to bodily affect, experientially and generatively. It needs this limited range of affective emotions to control the body; the same emotions that Nathanson describes as the pride-shame axis. But what then is the source of the positive emotions? In Kabbalah, those emotions are seen as flowing from the interaction between Soul and Mind and, on rare occasions between Spirit, Soul, and Mind.

Return briefly to Figure 2.1. Notice that in the Tree of Life schema, the Soul is comprised of three sefirot forming a triangle comprised of Tiferet on the central Pillar, Gevurah on the Pillar of Severity, and Hesed on the Pillar of Mercy. Tiferet is the name for Heart – Seat of the Soul. Hesed is said to be the source of Mercy and Compassion, while Gevurah is seen as the source of Judgment and Discernment. Imagine for a moment that these descriptives defined a redeemed conscience. Now consider what happens if the channel from Tiferet to Yesod – the Ego, is blocked, specifically by a Dominant self that shames disowned parts it has hidden in the 'dark recesses of the heart,' e.g. the unconscious. While this blockage is present, the *downward thrust* of Gevurah and Hesed will only be felt by Hod and Nezah respectively rather than moderated through the Heart (Tiferet). Likewise, while blocked, Tiferet can only express itself via Hod and Nezah as well. In effect, one could surmise that the proper sphere of conscience is Heart – as the Old Testament has long claimed, but where the flow of that will is obstructed, the Ego is obliged to experience that Voice for God through the limitation of affective emotions, which are essentially the negative axis of pride-shame. As used here, affective emotions will always refer to emotions that correspond to the nine affective clusters identified by Tomkins.

My own study of conscience has led me to this conclusion: Christ seeks to clear a path between Ego and Heart, by exercising the power of the Holy Spirit within the world of Mind. During the redemption process, the Voice for God channeled through Christ can act directly upon the Ego who can experience it as discerning, forgiving, and finally transformative. But while the Ego is unwilling to call on a higher power, the Heart-to-Ego connection remains blocked and conscience will be forced to manifest as affective emotions, in which case the Ego is forced to experience it as prideful, fearful, or shameful. The Voice-of-conscience constellated by the Empowering archetype initially blocks the flow; later, Dominant selves will exacerbate the blockage. In sum, conscience can rightly claim to speak as a Voice for God when it flows unimpeded from the Soul's Heart or the actions of a higher power such as Christ; but while the Heart connection remains blocked, it can only manifest as affective emotion. Only when the Heart is reinstated as an unimpeded conduit of the Voice for God, can conscience express itself as discerning, forgiving and transformative. As an intermediary step, an ego-aspect's willingness to accept the power of Christ's discernment and his power to channel Holy Spirit, will provide the necessary purification needed to clear the link. For just about everyone raised in our contemporary cultures, unredeemed conscience is almost a certainty, while redemption is only a possibility. Even so, the work of this book suggests it is a viable option and one worth pursuing.

Looking Ahead

Chapter III introduces the reader to various methodologies for finding and using the *Light* that I have found indispensable for examination of an unredeemed conscience and other forms of parental authority. Chapter IV seeks to demonstrate the numerous ways in which the Christ image has proven itself invaluable in work with clients; it also provides a description of other images likely to be encountered on going inside. The last part of that chapter looks at the concept of selves as defined by other theorists. We build on their work by providing a method for reconciling opposites created by the emotional polarization of selves.

Chapter V revisits the whole issue of emotions in the context of duality or pairs of opposites. The structure of Mind demands that everything within it be seen in the context of opposites. By examining opposites it is possible to distinguish levels of activity within the Mind comparable to the Soul, Mind, and Body interactions discussed above. In that chapter I also describe the importance of remediating instinctual rhythms and functional opposites such as feeling/thinking.

The final three chapters focus on clinical interventions and issues. Chapter VI describes interventions for depotentiating the Temporal authority of parents and healing ego-aspects traumatized by that authority. Chapter VII describes interventions for the redemption of conscience. Chapter VIII describes methods for identifying and transforming Relational authority and the final steps needed to redeem conscience. The interventions introduced in chapter VIII – all of them predicated on evoking the Holy Spirit, are by far the most transformational of any in this work. Chapters VII and VIII include extensive, year long, verbatims of work with a small group of clients. Hopefully, they will provide the reader an in-depth look at the actual process of redeeming conscience and transformation of images.

The chapter sequence mirrors the developmental effects of parental authority. Moral authority a primary thrust of this book, but all three forms of parental authority - Temporal, Moral, and Relational, are equally powerful in their effects on the individual. Each is constellated at different points in the child's development, the first two by the Empowering archetype and the last by the Gendering archetype. While Relational authority actually emerges before Moral authority, its full effects are only felt when the individual develops sexually and seeks a mate. For that reason it is treated last.

Another way of thinking about the sequence of chapters is to imagine it as a long series of experiments, which I generally refer to as interventions. Chapters I and II introduce the series. Chapters III and IV define the method. From my perspective, the chapters on method are the most critical since they have dictated the results. Without the *Light* or the Christ within, none of the interventions described in the rest of the chapters would be possible. This is not to say, they are the only way to assess and alter the different authorities embedded in parental images, but that I have not found any way that is equally viable. Chapters V through VIII describe the results of the methodology used in this work, hopefully in a way that is replicable by anyone who employs the method.

There is one other progression in this book, which will become apparent as the reader moves through the chapters. The role of Christ, Christ's *Light*, and the power of the Holy Spirit channeled by Christ, all become demonstrably more powerful as the reader progresses through the chapters. This is due largely to my own 'learning curve.' The more one works with the method, the more powerful it becomes. This work spans a period of nearly twenty years. It reflects both my tentative beginnings and what feels like the first fruits of that labor.

CHAPTER II ENDNOTES

1   'Channeling' has various meanings. Many readers will associate it with psychics who speak on behalf of disincarnate souls or allow spiritual beings to speak through them. As I use the word, it refers to a *Christ image* within the Mind of an individual that is empowered to channel the Holy Spirit to any and all images within the Mind in order to effect changes comparable to those described throughout the Old and New Testaments. Normally, channeling is treated as a paranormal ability manifest in very few people. As I use the concept, an image of Christ in the active imagination of any human being can channel the Holy Spirit as a felt experience within the Mind. What psychics, and human beings who allow Jesus Christ to channel the Holy Spirit, share in common is the conviction that what is being channeled is drawn from the world of Spirit, which is the domain of souls and spiritual beings as well as the Holy Spirit.

2   I capitalize 'Mind' throughout this book to emphasize its existence as a blueprint of the body-brain, as distinct from the more common perception of Mind as a mere epiphenomenon of the brain. The same will be true for Soul, and Spirit and Body. My rationale is given at length further into the chapter.

3   Whatever word we use to name the God of our personal salvation, it is hopefully understood that 'God' per se is neither masculine nor feminine, but rather the source of all manifestations, male and female alike. *Ion Sof* is the word used by Jewish Kabbalists to designate this ineffable, inexpressible, unnamable, experience of God. Tibetan Buddhists prefer the term *Righpa* meaning the unmanifest-ground-of-all-being, while Taoists simply call their understanding the *Way*. In Hinduism it is called *Brahman*, the absolute who is without properties resting

in itself. And in Roman Catholic Theology it is referred to as the *Uncaused Cause* or Godhead. Within all these perspectives, 'God the Father' is only a manifestation of God, i.e. a *person* of God; and to my way of thinking, very likely incomplete without a feminine counterpart.

4	All biblical quotes are taken from the NRSV unless otherwise stated. Metzger, B.M. & Murphy, R.E. (1991), *The New Oxford Annotated Bible with Apocryphal/ Deuterocanonical Books,* New Revised Standard Edition, Oxford University Press: New York.

5	Fox, Emmet (1953), *The Ten Commandments: The Master Key to Life*, Harper and Row: San Francisco.

6	Bloomfield, H.H. (1985), *Making Peace with Your Parents*, Ballantine Books: New York.

7	Where 'Self' is capitalized it is used to distinguish a superordinate quality capable of organizing conscious and unconscious contents. The Ego is always seen as subordinate to this quality. The term is used here as Carl Jung used it in his theory of Analytical Psychology. Throughout this work I also equate Self with Heart, and Heart as the seat of the Soul.

8	McKean, E., Editor (2005), *New Oxford American Dictionary*, 2nd edition, Oxford University Press: USA.

9	See Assagioli, R. (1971), *Psychosynthesis: A Manual of Principles and Techniques*, Penguin Books: New York; and Assagioli, R. (1973), *The Act of Will*, An Esalen Book published by Penguin Books: New York.

10	Assagioli, R. (1973), *op.cit.*

11	Rom. 7:19-23: "For I do not do the good I want, but the evil I do not want is what I do. Now if I do what I do not want, it is no longer I that do it, but sin that dwells within me. So I find it to be a law that when I want to do what is good, evil lies close at hand. For I delight in the law of God in my inmost self, but I see in my members another law at war with the law of my mind, making me captive to the law of sin that dwells in my members."

12	Foundation for Inner Peace (1976), *A Course in Miracles,* Published by the Foundation for Inner Peace: California.

13	It is the Holy Spirit that transforms us. In Western culture Christ is seen to offer the Holy Spirit to any and all who ask. Any person – evoking the name of Jesus Christ can ask for the Holy Spirit's transformative work on behalf of another person. Christ is Christ because he channels the Holy Spirit to any who ask in his name. Others – such as the prophets of the Old Testament, also experienced the Holy Spirit before Christ became historically manifest; and very likely, every major esoteric religion has access to the Holy Spirit by means other than Christ. On rare occasions I have worked with clients whose 'higher powers' were able to evoke the power of the Holy Spirit to achieve all of the goals described in this book. I will leave it to others to debate the theological significance of those observations.

14   On occasion, the mother will be identified as 'head-of-household' or the one who 'wears the pants.' Where this is so, it will have an equally profound effect on all children. I am not speaking of a mother who is head-of-household out of necessity, i.e. the father absent, or deceased, or the parents divorced. In such instances, the father's image can still embody Temporal and Moral authority, or another male implicitly assigned his role, e.g. a grandfather or even an eldest son. What I want to highlight here are those instances when the mother is clearly dominant in the household even if the father is present. In the eyes of her children, she is clearly dominant by her force of will, spirit and accomplishments. In such marriages, the husband is more like a househusband or introverted, quiet, and unassuming, even though he may be a breadwinner. In any case, he will acknowledge her dominance in the marriage. One way she may be dominant is in her rages toward the children that the husband does not challenge even when they are clearly shaming. But this is only an example. Often the dominance, while frequently enacted in terms of disciplining the children, is more apparent in strength of character, high energy, determination and the like. These are powerful women who 'do not take kindly to fools' or tolerate opposition even within the extended family. Their image will be clearly superordinate in the hearts of their children. And she, rather than the father, will define Temporal and Moral authority. In some cases, a paternal grandmother rather than the mother may claim that authority. In that case, the child's father is clearly subordinate to his mother and demands his wife's subordination to her as well.

    In my clinical experience, firstborn sons raised by dominant mothers will seek to stand 'toe to toe' with their mothers. They are very mindful of their mother's power, but tend to focus on events wherein they stood their own ground with her rather than submitting, as they did in childhood. There is, however, a distinct feeling of never being more than equal, and ever a fear of being overwhelmed if they are not continually vigilant. In general, they will seek a higher ground - temporally or morally, whereby they can hold her at bay. This is in sharp contrast to a son whose father is dominant. While the dominant father also demands submission, for most sons it is only temporary. On becoming an adult, a son can generally expect to take his place in a paternalistic world and receive the blessing of paternalistic authority. He becomes like the father and can identify with him. In contrast, the son of a dominant mother cannot identify with that mother without a perpetual feeling of submission and loss of masculine identity vis-à-vis a patriarchal culture. But he also cannot identify with his father without also submitting to the mother, since the father has implicitly acknowledged his wife's authority within the family.

In order for a daughter to resist submitting to her father's authority, she must resist identification with her mother if the mother is herself subordinate. A daughter is most likely to do this only if she is identified with a dominant paternal grandmother or grandfather. But, like the son of a dominant mother, this daughter must live in a constant state of tension. To marry, she must find a man willing to implicitly submit to her authority within the home. She must forgo any strong identity with her sex insofar as they are subordinate to males, unless she plays a clearly dominant role in the relationship. The fact that such relationships occur at all in a paternalistic society is a clear reflection of the immediate family's power in shaping identity. The wider community/culture can reinforce family identity but cannot decisively challenge it except through ostracism and the like.

15   See Bauer, G. P., Editor (1994), *Essential Papers on Transference Analysis*, Jason Aronson; and Goldberg, S. T. (2006), *Using the Transference in Psychotherapy*, Jason Aronson.

16   'Giving away the bride' is an explicit, ritualized example of transference universally found in patriarchies. At the beginning of the ceremony it is still very common for the father to 'give' the bride to her husband-to-be, in effect, 'transferring' his authority to another male.

17   The Gospels tell us that Christ is not tempted by earthly or temporal power: "Again, the devil took him to a very high mountain and showed him all the kingdoms of the world and their splendor; and he said to him, "All these I will give you, if you will fall down and worship me." Jesus said to him, "Away with you, Satan! For it is written, Worship the Lord your God, and serve only him." (Matt. 4:8-10). See also Luke 4:1-13. (I wish I could say the same for the religious leaders who did accept the temporal power of a Roman state religion. It seems prophetic that the last line of Luke's passages reads: When the devil had finished all this tempting, he left him [Christ] until an opportune time (Luke 4:13). While Christ is never tempted, the same cannot be said of those who insist they speak for him.)

18   In his later years, Carl Jung devoted a good deal of reflection to the concept of Self. The Self - capitalized, was seen to encompass the entirety of the person: Body, Mind, Soul and Spirit. Of particular interest to me was Jung's conclusion that the symbols for Self, Christ, and Godhead were seemingly interchangeable.

In theory, each concept was treated as archetypal in origin and therefore distinct, but their symbols - particularly as they manifest in dreams, were overlapping and seemingly interchangeable. In effect, what we call the Christ within can be symbolically equated with Jung's concept of the Self, and the imago Dei imprinted on the human soul. Given that assumption, I have identified the proper locus of Temporal authority in adults as God ineffable, and as a working hypothesis, I have identified Christ as the only image capable of directing us to that source without being corrupted by the process. Since we have no universally accepted image of the Self apart from Christ, he seems the only viable choice to divest parents and culture of Temporal authority and redirect us to its source. For that reason, the Christ image is the only one I have had clients call upon when they become ready to divest their parents of Temporal authority. I have never been specific as to the 'source' of that authority within us. But I am clear that Christ can terminate and re-appropriate it as necessary; and I have come to trust the client's Christ image to act impeccably in this matter. The interested reader is referred to: Jung, C.G. (1961), *Aion: Researches Into the Phenomenology of the Self*, Collected Works, Vol.9, Bollingen Series XX, Princeton University Press, New Jersey; and Jung, C.G. (1963), *Memories, Dreams and Reflections*, Vintage Books, New York.

19   Greenberg, J.R. & Mitchell, S.A. (1983), *Object Relations in Psychoanalytic Theory*, 1st Edition, Harvard University Press.

20   Jesus said to them, "Have you never read in the scriptures: 'The stone that the builders rejected has become the cornerstone, this was the Lord's doing, and it is amazing in our eyes'?" (Matt 21:42). Clearly, this is a reference to Christ himself. Yet, as a metaphor it also aptly describes the Rejected-self; especially in the context of Christ's transformational role.

21   Stone, H. & Stone, S. (1993), *Embracing Your Inner Critic: Turning Self-Criticism into a Creative Asset*, Harper: San Francisco.

22   Berne, E., (1996), *Games People Play: The Psychology of Human Relationships,* (Re-issue Edition), Ballantine Books: New York.

23   Bradshaw, J. (1988), *Healing the Shame That Binds You*, Health Communications: New York.

24   Several of my clients have recently worded a prayer to be offered by a Minister at a healing service: "I ask the Holy Spirit in Christ's name to enter your worst shame, that you may totally, completely, surrender it. I ask the Holy Spirit in Christ's name to release your painful, darkest memories from this bondage of shame that you leave now free and cleansed in the name of Jesus. Go in peace."

25 Sarah Dening, a Jungian therapist, makes a similar observation regarding Old Testament prophets who seemingly went to great lengths to avoid naming the penis out of fear the naming would attract evil. As an example, she quotes Genesis 32:32 - "Therefore the children of Israel eat not of the sinew of the shrank which is upon the hollow of the thigh to this day..." See Dening, S., (1996), *The Mythology of Sex*, MacMillan: New York, p. 133.

26 This is an exceedingly intimate vignette. Only a lover with her beloved would unhesitatingly use her hair to wash the feet of her beloved and kiss them. Anyone other than a beloved would reflexively withdraw from such a self-conscious intimacy.

27 Mark describes a seemingly different event, but makes the same point: (Mark 14:3-9) - "While he was at Bethany in the house of Simon the leper, as he sat at the table, a woman came with an alabaster jar of very costly ointment of nard, and she broke open the jar and poured the ointment on his head. But some were there who said to one another in anger, "Why was the ointment wasted in this way? For this ointment could have been sold for more than three hundred denarii, and the money given to the poor." And they scolded her. But Jesus said, "Let her alone; why do you trouble her? She has performed a good service for me. For you always have the poor with you, and you can show kindness to them whenever you wish; but you will not always have me. She has done what she could; she has anointed my body beforehand for its burial. Truly I tell you, wherever the good news is proclaimed in the whole world, what she has done will be told in remembrance of her."

28 Frost, G. & Frost, Y. (1998), *Tantric Yoga: The Royal Path to Raising Kundalini Power*, Weiser Books: New York.

29 For the reader well versed in Jungian Psychology, and most especially his alchemical studies, Jung clearly attempted to address relational issues in such works as *Mysterium Coniunctionis* (1963, Collected Works, Vol. 14, Princeton University Press: NJ); but on the whole, we still seem to treat archetypes as islands in the sea.

30 One way of getting around the issue of images treated as a 'photographic representation' is to have the client focus on the image of someone in the extended family who is deceased, and after they have done so, to point out that if the image was a 'true' photographic representation the client should have seen the body in a state of death or decomposition or Soul embodiment - which is rarely the case.

31   Jung's theory did not explicitly allow for influences beyond the Self; that is, everything affecting the Self had to be contained within the Self. However, in his Memoirs he did acknowledge the possibility of outside forces as manifested in paranormal phenomena, evil and the like. See Jung, C.G., (1963), *Memories, Dreams, Reflections*, Random House: New York.

32   There is actually considerable correspondence between Jungian theory and Kabbalistic theory. The interested reader is referred to the works of Z'ev ben Shimon Halevi which demonstrate the correspondences in considerable detail, especially his *Adam and the Kabbalistic Tree*, (1974), Samuel Weiser: York Beach, Maine.

33   MacDermot's translation of the *Pistis Sophia* includes a lengthy introduction of Kabbalistic influence on Christian thinkers from the earliest periods of Christian theological development. See MacDermot, V. (2001), *The Fall of Sophia: A Gnostic Text on the Redemption of Universal Consciousness,* Translated with Commentary by Violet MacDermot, Forward by Stephan A, Hoeller, Lindisfarne Books: Great Barrington, MA.

34   Gershom Scholem's writings are extensive. The interested reader is referred to his best-known and earliest translated book: *Major Trends in Jewish Mysticism*, 1941, Schocken: New York.

35   The interested reader is referred to the following books which offer good expositions of the basic tenets of Kabbalah: Cooper, D.A., (1997), *God Is A Verb*, Riverhead Books: New York; Halevi, Z'ev ben Shimon, (1985), *The Work of the Kabbalist*, Samuel Weiser: York Beach, Maine; Kaplan, A. (1997), *Sefer Yetzirah: The Book of Creation In theory and Practice*, Samuel Weiser: York Beach, Maine; Sheinkin, D. (E. Hoffman, Ed.), (1986*), Path of the Kabbalah*, Paragon House: New York; Williams-Heller, A., (1990), *Kabbalah: Your Path to Inner Freedom*, Quest Books: Weaton, IL; Steinsaltz, A. (Hanegbi, Y. Trans.), (1985), *The Thirteen-Petalled Rose*, Basic Books: New York.

36   There are notable exceptions. See, for example Wolf, F.A. (2000), *Mind Into Matter: A New Alchemy of Science and Spirit,* Moment Point Press: New York.

37   See Brody, H. & Brody, D. (2000), *The Placebo Response: How You Can Release the Body's Inner Pharmacy for Better Health*, Cliff Street Books: New York.

38   Most theories of levels are antithetical to the prevailing metaphysic applied

by science that restricts its current scope to a physically objective, reductionistic approach. This view of science, which treats the material and physical as the only 'reality' capable of producing causality, only emerged in the seventeenth century. Willis Harman, a futurist, describes it as "...a declaration of faith in the senses as opposed to the speculative mind, and in the visible world as opposed to the unseen. It emphasized the empirical (as a reaction against the authority of Scholasticism) and the reductionistic (as a better explanation than the medieval 'spiritual forces.')" From Harman, W. (1998), *Global Mind Change: The Promise of the 21st Century*, Barrett-Koehler Publishers, Inc.: San Francisco, p.20.

Reductionism arose out of the Copernican revolution where the idea of man and earth as the center of the universe was decisively turned on its heel. The hallmark of this metaphysic is that 'reality' is only what can be seen and measured. For all practical purposes, this metaphysic makes Spirit, Soul, Mind and Heart epiphenomenon of the brain. When the brain ceases to function, Mind, Heart, Soul and Spirit cease to function; and that is certainly true insofar as the Body is concerned. Empiricism asserts there is no measurable life after death; no conscious existence precedes birth or succeeds death. In psychology, the best known form of this reductionism is Behaviorism, which dominated academic psychology for much of the 20th Century. Psychoanalysis offers a variant of this reductionistic stance by insisting that current behavior be explained by early childhood experiences. But that said, Harman and others insist that we are on the verge of a global mind change, no less dramatic than the Copernican revolution.

39   The interested reader is referred to the following writers: Kuhn, T. (1970), *The Structure of Scientific Revolutions*, University of Chicago Press: Chicago; Bohm, D. (1980), *Wholeness and the Implicate Order*, Routledge & Kegan Paul: New York; Capra, F. (1984), *The Turning Point: Science, Society, and the Rising Culture*, Bantam: New York; Chardin, P.T. (1961), *The Phenomenon of Man*, Harper Torchbooks: New York; Popper, K.R. & Eccles, J.C. 1981), *The Self and Its Brain,* Springer International: New York.

40   According to Z'ev ben Shimon Halevi, "The division into four levels stems from the text of Isaiah 3:7, in which it is said 'Even everyone that is called by my Name: for I have created him for my glory, I have formed him; yea, I have made him." Halevi, Z'ev ben Shimon (1977), *A Kabbalistic Universe,* Samuel Weiser, Inc.: York Beach, Maine, p. 27.

41   Christians tend to treat the names of God found in the Old Testament as all referring to the same God; but Kabbalists see each different Hebrew name as a different manifestation of God; just as Christians would see Father, Son and Holy Spirit as different manifestations of God.

42	To complicate matters further, each letter of the Hebrew alphabet has a meaning. It is not only a sign, but also a symbol such that a single Hebrew *word* in the Old Testament can be assigned both numerical weights and the equivalent meaning of a whole sentence. See for example: Suares, C. (2005), *The Cipher of Genesis: Using the Qabalistic Code to Interpret the First Book of the Bible and Teachings of Jesus*, Weiser Books.

43	See Shackleford, J. (1996), *The Biblical Heart: The Dynamic Union of Flesh and Spirit*, Factor Press: Mobile, AL; also, Bovenmars, J.G. (1991), *Biblical Spirituality of the Heart*, Alba House: New York.

44	The need for a higher power is also asserted in Shamanistic literature that heretofore has had the most to say about the effects of Soul on the individual and how its aberrations are to be treated. Shamans only exercise their powers after they have connected with helping spirits, guardians and/or and power animals. The Shaman never acts alone. See Eliade, M. (1964), *Shamanism: Archaic Techniques of Ecstasy*, Bollingen Series LXXVI, Princeton University Press: NJ; Harner, M. (1980), *The Way of the Shaman,* 3d ed. Harper &Row: San Francisco; Walsh, R. (2007) *The World of Shamanism,* Llewellyn Publications: Woodbury, MA; and Ingerman, S., (1991), *Soul retrieval: Mending the Fragmented Self*, Harper: San Francisco.

45	Modi, S., (1997), *Remarkable Healings: A Psychiatrist Discovers Unsuspected Roots of Mental and Physical Illness*, Hampton Roads: Charlottesville, VA.

46	When the *Light* is used to control anything containing a Soul part the circle will be incomplete, usually on the part of the circumference away from the client's Aware-ego. This incompleteness should always be taken as indicative of a Soul part hidden within whatever is being contained. Christ's *Light* can completely contain a Soul part. The issue is addressed in a later chapter.

47	"When an evil spirit comes out of a man, it goes through arid places seeking rest and does not find it. Then it says, 'I will return to the house I left.' When it arrives, it finds the house unoccupied, swept clean and put in order. Then it goes and takes with it seven other spirits more wicked than itself, and they go in and live there. And the final condition of that man is worse than the first." (Matthew 12:44-45). Christ can remove the evil spirit; but unless the Ego is willing to invite a higher power into the space vacated by that spirit, it is likely to return.

48	Nathanson, D.L. (1992), *Shame and Pride: Affect, Sex, and the Birth of the Self*, Norton: New York, p.47.

49   Jung. C.G. (1971), *Psychological Types*, Collected Works, Vol. 6, Princeton University Press: New Jersey.

50   Gendlin, E. (1981), *Focusing*, Bantam Books: New York

51   William S. Verplank, Ph.D., Professor of Psychology, University of Tennessee, for many years taught a seminar on Operations Analysis. It was his way of getting at the meat of a reported experiment. He cared little for what the experimenter planned to accomplish (introduction) or thought s/he had accomplished (discussion). The method dictated the result and little else mattered. It was a humbling process, but an invaluable lesson, hopefully, well learned; though I suspect he is 'turning over in his grave' given my choice of methods, strict behaviorist that he was. God bless him.

52   Tomkins expounded his theory in three volumes spanning 30 years: Tomkins, S.S., (1962), *Affect/Imagery/Consciousness, Vol. 1: The Positive Affects*, Springer: New York; Tomkins, S.S., (1963), *Affect/Imagery/Consciousness, Vol. 2: The Negative Affects*, Springer: New York; Tomkins, S.S., (1991), *Affect/Imagery/Consciousness, Vol.3: The Negative Affects: Anger and Fear*, Springer: New York.

53   Nathanson, op. cit.

54   Jean Piaget is much better known than Tomkins and there are numerous books by him and others, describing his theory of cognitive development in children. See Piaget, J. (1990), *The child's Conception of the World*, Littlefield Adam: New York.

55   These descriptions are taken from Nathanson, op. cit. p.136.

56   Broucek, F. (1979), 'Efficacy in infancy', *International Journal of Psychoanalysis*, 60:311-16.

57   Nathanson, op. cit. p.20

58   Nathanson, op. cit. p.88

59   Nathanson, op. cit. p.120

60   Individuals with chronically tight shoulders and neck problems could be thought of as exercising a postural defense against shameful affect.

61   Nathanson, op. cit. p.59

62   Nathanson, op. cit. p. 59

63   Nathanson, op. cit. p. 61

64   Ekman, another exponent of Tomkins, provides an excellent description of universally expressed affects, providing extensive pictures for the facial expression of various affects. See Ekman, P. (2003), *Emotions Revealed: Recognizing Faces and Feelings to Improve Communications and Emotional Life,* Henry Holt and Co.: New York.

65   Hawkins, D. (1998), *Power Verses Force: An Anatomy of Consciousness*, Veritas Publishing: Sedona, AZ.

66   Hawkins, op. cit. p.2.

67   Hawkins, op. cit. p.48

68   Hawkins, op. cit. p.66

69   Maslow, A., (1968), *Toward a Psychology of Being*, Van Nostrand Reinhold: New York.

CHAPTER III

A MANUAL FOR USING THE *LIGHT* IN THERAPY

OVERVIEW

The examination of conscience requires an inward focus in order to discern the connections between our felt experience, thoughts, beliefs, and deeds. Over the past hundred years, psychotherapists have developed a number of methodologies for examining these interactions. In my own work, I rely heavily on the interventions described in this book. These approaches involve an inward focus by the client that generally produces a light to medium trance. The word "trance" is bothersome to some people, but, as used here, it is very like our focused absorption when reading a good book. The only real difference is the focus of attention. Instead of entering an imaginary world created by an author, an individual enters the world of his or her own imagination, a world derived from the individual's thoughts, beliefs, felt experience, and whatever the unconscious invariably adds to the equation. As I envision it, the imaginative realm is where conscious volition, experience, and unconscious processes merge; where Soul, Mind, Heart, and Body are joined.

Carl Jung's work remains the pioneering research in active imagination in the 20th century. [1] His self-exploration and conception of the inner world, which he largely derived from dreams, active imagination, and artistic expression, continues to serve as a watermark for students of the Mind. [2] Jung was willing to acknowledge and live with the irrational and numinous. Unlike Freud, who treated the unconscious as atavistic, Jung saw it as a source of God and creativity as well as a source of chaos and evil. His inward journeys were self-admittedly dangerous. For a period of time they threatened his sanity since he lacked the maps he would bring back for us. Jung believed the goal of therapy was the integration of unconscious contents into consciousness and that achieving this goal was a life-long task, now as then. The analyst "equipped" the patient, guided the first series of journeys, and helped to successfully engage his or her first dragons (generally the ones that had driven the patient to seek an analyst in the first place). And that is much the way I envision it. However, there are several significant differences in my approach. Essentially, Jung and his patients entered the world of Mind through active imagination without the use of a *Light* or inner image of Christ (though Jung did acquire his own 'inner guide' that he addressed as Phenemon). By contrast, I always insist that my clients enter this world using their *Light* and proceed only so long as their *Light* remains with them. Wherever they are willing, I also encourage them to evoke an image of Christ or comparable higher power.

This chapter and the next provide the tools needed for entering the imaginative world to a depth necessary for the structural examination of conscience and just about any other psychological phenomenon. The inner world is potentially as awesome and fearsome as anything in the physical world. The *Light* methodology described in this chapter was developed to address those dragons of the Mind that individuals have the greatest difficulty engaging. More important, its particular characteristics will protect the inexperienced counselor and client [3] who invariably encounter difficult issues once they venture inside. If only for that reason, the therapist needs to have the client begin by finding and using the *Light* described in this chapter. Then, if the therapist happens upon some unexpected turn of events, such as those described in this and the following chapters, s/he can either proceed cautiously and trust the limits imposed by the *Light* or safely end the session and refer the client to a more qualified therapist.

The Aware-Ego and Ego Fragmentation

The Aware-ego is that sense of self that exercises *willingness* through use of the *Light*.[4] I treat it as a function of the Ego, but it is very unlike the ego-aspects that surround it, which are generally willful and tend to limit their motive power to the pride-shame axis. Free will is the Ego's power to choose emotional expression. Normally, an ego-aspect will limit itself to those emotions hardwired into the Body, (sic) the pride-shame axis. In sharp contrast, the Aware-ego is only and ever an expression of *willingness* as manifested by the *Light*. The Aware-ego may actually be a manifestation of Soul within the Mind for the explicit purpose of exercising willingness since, as used here, willingness is best thought of as an archetypal energy expressed by a luminous sphere of *Light*. In any case, the Aware-ego is the name given to that sense of self created by the Ego/Soul when the client goes inside for the purpose of exercising willingness as expressed by the *Light*. It is the self that actively seeks the *Light* on going inside.

The Aware-ego's use of the *Light* quickly highlights the phenomenon of Ego fragmentation. The idea of ego fragmentation, or co-existing selves, can be disconcerting when first encountered by some clients. Most people still treat the Ego – their sense of "I" and "me" – as a singular entity. But it is not singular. For anyone willing to go inside, it is quickly and often disturbingly apparent that a variety of ego-aspects are able to affect our thoughts and behavior; and they are often at odds with each other. When active, every ego-aspect has access to one or more emotions, i.e. anger, guilt and the like, as well as other psychodynamic defenses. *And All ego-aspects have access to free will*, which gives each the power to gainsay other ego-aspects. (Rejected selves are the notable exception, as they are essentially stripped of free will by their shameful enthrallment. The same is true, to a lesser degree, of any ego-aspect whose free will is compromised by "undue influences" as discussed in Chapter VII.) The subjective experience of willful conflict is a primary reason for frequently questioning the religious assertion that we exercise free will. If we do, why does it so often feel undermined? The answer is that ego-aspects are often at odds with each other, and each commands a portion of that free will.[5] Dissociative processes, most notable in Multiple Personality Disorders, provide the clearest evidence of opposing selves that function autonomously, and concomitantly as inner voices. Gender dissonance – the experience of self as different from our physical sex – is another example. These examples, while extreme, highlight what all of us experience in milder forms. Our own 'demons' may seem less pronounced, but no less conflictual.

For much of the 20th Century, psychology treated co-existing selves as "cognitive dissonance" or "shifts in mood" or a "chemical imbalance" or "hallucinations" and "schizophrenic voices." This left the ego intact, but just as conflicted. In Jungian psychology, for example, such moods and irrational emotions were generally attributed to archetypes such as Animus, Anima, Shadow and complexes. Those archetypal energies could, on occasion, overwhelm the Ego. Anima possession in a man is an example of being overwhelmed by an archetypal energy. But clinical investigations have repeatedly and reliably demonstrated that, in fact, the Ego also becomes fragmented in its effort to contend with these archetypal energies. All of the research on Object Relations and Dissociative disorders, as well as the Stone's work explored in the next chapter,[6] treats the Ego as fragmented by its effort to contend with developmental experiences. My own clinical experience confirms these findings.

The Development of Willingness

The Aware-ego's willingness must be developed if it is to function in any appreciable way. This self is unique among the cluster of selves created by the Ego since it can perceive and co-exist with all of them. It is created solely to manifest willingness, which is most clearly expressed by use of the *Light*. Until willingness is developed, most people tend to experience Ego consciousness as singular and willful. Whatever ego-aspect is dominant at a particular time is generally able to deny the existence of other ego-aspects while it retains control of conscious volition.

The distinction between willingness and willfulness is vital but difficult to appreciate without reflection. Willingness appears to be an archetypal emotion (i.e. Soul emotion), which makes it more powerful than any emotion in the pride-shame axis. Where willingness is exercised, change is always reciprocal, whereas willful emotions seek to effect change without being affected by it. When functioning willfully, an ego-aspect strives to remain independent of any change it seeks to bring about. In contrast, a degree of reciprocity is always assumed when the *Light* is used. Stated another way: while the Aware-ego uses the *Light*, the Ego functions as an inter-dependent variable rather than an independent variable. Whenever the Aware-ego seeks to make a change via the *Light*, it implicitly accepts that all parts of the Self will be changed by that intervention to some degree; and that they have the 'right' to actively resist that change. It is important to stress here that willful ego-aspects have the power to impede change sought by the Aware-ego, and whenever they make themselves felt, they must be addressed before proceeding. The Aware-ego using the *Light* cannot force another ego-aspect to change. But what it has to offer can strongly encourage those ego-aspects to accept change; and in the interim, it can set limits on willful behavior.

Though subjective, the Aware-ego is operationally definable. The Stones define it as the ego-aspect with the capacity to perceive two or more egos and hold the tension of their co-existence in consciousness.[7] (The Stones' definition of the Aware-ego is discussed at length in the next chapter.) Their understanding is implicit in our definition, but as used here the Aware-ego is primarily defined as the ego-aspect that seeks and uses the *Light* on going inside. When the client goes inside and seeks his or her, s/he is perceived by the therapist to embody the Aware-ego. In effect, the Aware-ego is that *sense of self that exercises willingness through use of the Light.* Its defining characteristic is the emotive power of willingness as defined by the. The Aware-ego is generally not an object of discovery, but rather the explorer.[8] It is that part of us which assumes a conscious control of our faculties when we go inside and exercise willingness. It is responsible for initiating all interventions asked of the and/or the Christ image using his *Light*. It is not alone, however, in its exercise of free will. What makes it more powerful than merely willful self-aspects is the exercise of willingness, which is invariably more powerful than the negative emotions exercised by self-aspects. Of note, any ego-aspect can exercise willingness using the *Light*, and as each ego-aspect is engaged by the Aware-ego, it is encouraged to do so. Use of the *Light* is not the exclusive domain of the Aware-ego. But the Aware-ego is identified as the only ego-aspect created solely for that purpose; it is the self expected to assume conscious control when the client goes inside.

Ego aspects, other than the Aware-ego, are pretty much characterized by their willful use of negative emotions (e.g. pride, anger, fear, desire, sadness, guilt, and shame) to motivate thought and behavior, in contrast to the Aware-ego, which relies exclusively on willingness to express itself.[9] The *habitual* use of negative emotions by most ego-aspects – often as a defense against equally negative parental images and experiences – normally impedes the spontaneous development of an Aware-ego. But the willingness governing the *Light* is more powerful than any of these negative emotions. At the very least, the *Light* can attenuate them through containment. For that reason, the Aware-ego's use of the *Light* will give it an edge wherever it is used. Over time, this advantage tends to be self-reinforcing. The removal of Temporal authority (discussed in Chapters VI), which is by and large a willful authority, appears to strengthen the Aware-ego. Clients who have accomplished this are more willing, thereafter, to explore issues with very negative emotional content. In sum, most clients find it difficult to exercise willingness in the initial phases of therapy primarily from lack of experience with it. Males find it the most difficult, perhaps because they are the most habituated to willfulness. But over time, most clients learn the inordinate power of willingness vis-à-vis the negative emotions.

The Aware-ego is limited in one respect: it has limited resources for transforming images embodying archetypal energies. For that it must rely on higher powers such as Jesus Christ. Most of the interventions described in this chapter do not require a higher power; however, most of the interventions that seek to alter the effects of Temporal, Moral, and Relational authority do require a higher power.

Most important: whenever the client goes inside for the purpose of using the *Light*, the Aware-ego always emerges in the midst of the ego-aspect currently in charge of consciousness (e.g. whoever walked through the therapist's door that particular session). That ego-aspect is often prideful, fearful, angry, despondent, or otherwise negatively aroused. The Aware-ego will feel its emotions without being threatened by them. While holding the *Light*, it experiences itself as perfectly safe since the power of willingness automatically protects it from any negative emotions felt within the Mind. However, the Aware-ego will not carry out any suggestion, if it exacerbates the emotions of the ego-aspect actively co-existing with it. Instead it will simply remain as present as possible until the ego-aspect's emotions are calmed, or the client is asked to execute an intervention that will separate it form the co-conscious ego-aspect.

A Description of the Light Used in Therapy

With your eyes closed it is possible to visualize a luminous sphere about the size of a softball that can rest comfortably in your hand; and within your mind it will do whatever you bid it to do provided your request *does not threaten or attack* any consciously co-existing part of yourself. This *Light* has access to all memory, conscious and unconscious, including memory ordinarily repressed or never previously brought to consciousness. That makes it exceedingly powerful. Nonetheless, the *Light* is completely dependent upon your willingness to act. Nothing in the human Mind exceeds its power except the free will of co-active parts of you, which it never opposes.

Use of the *Light* can be likened to hypnosis in that it can induce a strong inward focus, but this is easily broken if your focus becomes threatening to any conscious part of you. If threatened, you will generally open your eyes or, at the very least, be obliged to stop whatever you are doing since the *Light* disappears as an indication of its refusal to participate. In effect, the *Light*'s presence is always dependent on its ability to provide a safe inner environment to all consciously co-existing parts of you. It cannot respond to any suggestion that will directly result in threatening or attacking an individual's conscious sense of self. I call this inward focus a trance, for on occasion it gives all the appearances of being a trance, occasionally even a deep trance (though a deep trance is never called for and generally counterproductive). But the particular qualities of the *Light* make this 'trance state' very different from what is generally produced by hypnotic induction techniques.[10]

Ordinarily, in hypnotic induction the you are expected to accept the judgment and reality orientation of the therapist. However, when the *Light* is used, the therapist submits to the *Light*, which in turn submits to the your judgment of what is safe or threatening. In effect, use of the *Light* generates an interaction between client and therapist completely opposite to what is sought in most traditional techniques: use of the *Light* requires that the therapist submits to the individual's conscious willingness rather than vice versa.

When I first came upon the idea of using the *Light*, I initially asked clients to visualize any light they felt comfortable imagining: a candle, flashlight, burning torch...whatever s/he was comfortable visualizing. One client initially visualized a bare light bulb in a house, which definitely restricted her movement but otherwise served our immediate purpose. Today, I am very specific: I generally suggest clients visualize the *Light* as a luminous sphere about the size of a tennis ball or softball. I am never exactly sure what they see since each client gives slightly differing reports; but after a little familiarity they report being able to take it comfortably in their hand and move about with ease in their imagination.

What I have discovered is that all my clients have the ability to visualize this *Light* within them. Most of them will take to it immediately without any reservations. Others have difficulty accepting the idea that there is something within them with any degree of autonomy, but this has generally been ameliorated with proofs that it is dependent upon their willingness. In yet other cases, the fear of looking inward, or closing their eyes in the presence of another person, is so threatening that it may be some while before the client is willing to go inside. Even in these instances the *Light* protects, since no inner work is done until a client is able to evoke the *Light*. For all practical purposes the *Light* will only become present to the client when the client is willing to go inside. Some clients are more auditory or kinesthetic than visual;[11] for them the process is more difficult under any conditions. However, even these clients can "sense" the presence of a *Light* and hear, as distinct from visualize, responses to their queries. For one female client visualization was difficult until she imagined her *Light* creating images shaped by sound.

For years, prior to discovering the *Light*, I had used a variety of visualization techniques with clients to access their memories, fears, and conflicts, such as those described by Shorr,[12] Jungian analysts (Hannah,[13] Johnson[14]), Gestalt therapists,[15] NLP,[16] and Eriksonian Hypnotherapy.[17] This was always a tricky business for, not infrequently, it stirred strong emotions that sent both client and therapist scurrying to seal up the breeches.

In my experience, the unconscious is mixed with the 'ground' of imagination; and moving within it, to paraphrase Carl Jung, is much like exploring Africa with a map that only draws the coastline, leaving the interior and underworld largely unmarked. The *Light*'s attributes have proven exceedingly protective of the client in this kind of exploration. Its first and foremost attribute is the *Light*'s refusal to participate in anything perceived as threatening or attacking to any sense of self co-existing with the Aware-ego (i.e. the part of us that finds and holds the *Light* while inside.) Thus, if I suggest to a client that s/he imagine an interaction with someone and s/he becomes fearful upon entertaining that thought, the *Light* will disappear or the client will open his or her eyes. Without the *Light*'s participation the interaction will not occur since, in this therapy, all action is initiated through the *Light*.

The *Light* is dependent upon the therapist for its protective attributes to the extent that s/he can choose not to use it. At any time the therapist can disregard the *Light*. Today, it is hard for me to imagine doing any kind of inner work without the *Light*. But I did, in fact, do therapy for many years before discovering it. Also, at any time it is conceivable that I could tell the client to disregard the *Light* and proceed without it; to proceed as I think s/he 'ought' or 'should' proceed. However, given the nature of the *Light*'s protective attributes, that would put client and therapist at risk for little gain. In fact, I often tell clients that if I should ask them to proceed despite the *Light*'s disappearance, they would do well to simply end the session by leaving. As a matter of course, I simply refuse to let a client work inside without first finding his or her *Light*.

A second attribute of the *Light* is much like the first: the *Light* serves its host; it is dependent upon the *client's willingness*. In the world of Mind the *Light* appears to have unlimited potential; however, all of it is dependent upon the client's willingness, which cannot be coerced. Behavior can be forced, but not willingness. Although, while using the *Light*, clients are in a light to medium trance and open to the suggestions of the therapist, it is the *Light* that executes all suggestions, since all suggestions are worded as suggestions for the *Light* to execute. If for any reason the active sense of self is fearful of the therapist's suggestion, then the *Light* will disappear, or the client will immediately open his or her eyes, or the *Light* will otherwise not respond as requested. Even the client may be surprised by this indication of unwillingness. The reason for this 'bias in favor of the client' is that the *Light* – which is constantly assessing the client's willingness and only that – is also directed to execute all suggestions. In effect, the Aware-ego directs the *Light* to execute the suggestion, which the *Light* will only do if it can do so without threat of attack.

The *Light*'s dependence on the client's willingness is an invaluable asset. Clients often think they *should* do something because the therapist suggests it and will often attempt to bring their behavior into compliance with that *should*. But the *Light* will not do what the client is unwilling to do. The *Light* does not respond to 'shoulds;' this is quickly apparent when the *Light* leaves or fails to respond following a suggestion. If the therapist will honor the *Light* in this, it is often possible to quickly unearth the nature of the resistance regarding a specific issue.

My first experience with the *Light* disappearing is still fresh in my mind. When I started using the *Light* I was often as surprised as the client by the results; this was one of those occasions. Very early, I started using the *Light* to address fears. The method has become more sophisticated over time, but some version of the opening gambit is the same. First the *Light* is used to create a circle of *Light*. Then the *Light* is asked to place the particular fear within the circle. The circle allows the client to examine the fear without being overwhelmed by it. In the example I have in mind, Marty, a doctoral-level graduate student, was fearful of criticism from his dissertation committee; he believed this fear was inhibiting his efforts to finish his research. At face value that made sense, but when it was suggested he ask the *Light* to erase the fear of his doctoral committee, the *Light* left him. I was as surprised as he, for until then this had not happened with a client. I asked him to focus on having the *Light* return, which it did almost immediately. I then had him ask why it disappeared. In response, he became aware of his belief that this fear motivated his behavior. He believed that without this fear of his committee's criticism he would not be motivated to work on his dissertation at all! Thus, removing the fear would have made him fearful of losing a primary source of motivation. The *Light* read this and disappeared to avoid participating in a suggestion that would have made him more fearful. And even though neither he nor I were aware of that consequence when the suggestion was made, the Light was responsive to that knowledge. Throughout the book I offer numerous interventions for safely attenuating or removing such fears that allow the client to find better alternatives.

Willingness Vs. Trying

It is often helpful to discuss *willingness* with clients. There are definite limits to what is possible with free will when it is restricted to the expression of affective emotions – emotions that emulate instinctual affects observable in infants. Motivation regulated by affective emotion is always *willful* and always governed by a sense of lack or separation. In contrast, willingness offers a sense of connection and reciprocity. Willingness is far more powerful than affective emotion in terms of possibilities, though less powerful than love and forgiveness. Unfortunately, most ego-aspects rely predominantly on affective emotions.

A major underlying goal of treatment in this work is dissuading a client from continuing to act willfully. One way of moving toward that goal is to highlight variants of willful motivation such as "should," "ought," "need to," "want," "wish," and the seemingly ubiquitous "try." Compared to willingness, all of these variants are efforts doomed to failure. Basically, it is the difference between merely trying to stand up from a sitting position and deciding to do it. When I "want" something, essentially, I am expressing a state of frustration or deprivation, a desire to have something at some point in the future without the actual expectation of having it now. Only when I become willing to have "something" will that "something" become possible in the present. One indication of the power of willingness is the actual infrequency of its use. People are very selective in what they are willing to have happen, if only because it threatens to throw them into conflict with what they currently believe to be true. Clients will tell you that they "want" something, or "should" do something, or even that they will "try" something, but find themselves reluctant to say, "I will do that very thing." It is helpful to sensitize clients to these distinctions since they are often unaware of the power of willingness; frequently they mistakenly treat such willful variants as equivalent in power.

"I can't" is a variant of unwillingness. It is rarely used in situations where the individual literally cannot accomplish something. Most often, it actually means, "I will not" or "I am afraid to." Unwillingness is not a problem in itself. The difficulty for many clients is their initial lack of awareness of the many self-imposed limitations governing their behavior by limiting their willingness. Many decisions are made at very young ages when clients are unaware of the power those choices will have later in life.[18]

Using the *Light* helps to highlight this process of self-sabotaging willingness and the consequences of doing so.

Willingness that unreflectively infuses belief can be just as self-defeating as willfulness. Will infuses thoughts with the power of belief; it transforms a wish into a mental command. Often, the will must be withdrawn from a particular formulation before it can be used in reformulations. Or the belief governing a particular use of will must be expanded to include its opposite. Throughout the book I will offer interventions that provide clients the opportunity to "choose again." For example, one client discerned that she willingly submitted to the expectations of others, especially her parents. This co-dependence shaped a good deal of her personal and professional life and accounted for her inability to realize many *self-expectations*, such as having a life apart from her parents. She could only express her self-expectations as "wants" or "wishes." Before they could become willing choices, she had to first change previous decisions regarding those significant others.

FINDING THE *LIGHT*

This section describes an induction protocol for therapists that I have found universally applicable in helping clients to discover and begin using the *Light*. Induction is the formal term used in hypnosis to describe methods for inducing a trance state. Any method which asks clients to close their eyes and focus inwardly is potentially trance inducing or hypnogogic. The method for finding and using the *Light* usually induces a light trance in clients. Therefore, I always tell them that what we are doing is like hypnosis, but different from their normal expectations of it. The difference is that the *Light* will guide us both; that I, as well as they, will be bound by the *Light* while they are inside. In effect, the work in progress will be dependent upon the presence of the *Light*, and the *Light* will not enact any suggestion experienced by the client as threatening. Further, should the *Light* disappear, for whatever reason, one of two things will happen: they will open their eyes or they will report that it has left and we will stop whatever we are doing until we discern and correct whatever is threatening. If the *Light* leaves, and invariably it will from time to time, it is always understood to mean that the client feels threatened or attacked, and all agendas must be set aside till s/he is protected and his or her inner safety assured. The *Light* is, first and foremost, the guardian of the first principle of healing: *namely, that we do no harm!* Provided the therapist also submits to the *Light*, no harm will come.

An analogy I use to contrast *Light* therapy with hypnosis is to compare it to the self-induced trances many individuals have experienced while driving or daydreaming. Most of us have experienced the phenomenon of driving on "automatic pilot." This is particularly likely on sparsely traveled stretches of an interstate highway. The trance one enters when using the *Light* can be likened to such a trance. On those occasions anything unexpected is likely to startle us into full conscious awareness, as for example, a car pulling unexpectedly in front of us. In contrast, in a hypnotic trance that kind of event would not automatically startle us. In effect, the trance in *Light* therapy is self-induced as distinct from other-induced and consequently all volitional control and responsibility remain with the client.

Usually, I introduce the concept of the *Light* one or two sessions before we actually use it. Like Erickson,[19] I "plant the seed" for it by saying a little about it whenever the opportunity arises, telling stories about its use, making reference to its use with others, etc. In fact, I may not use it with a particular client for some time, but since a day rarely passes when I don't use it in my practice, I am always conscious of its potential for examining the issues a client is addressing. I often say to clients, "We can sit here and speculate or second guess about what might be going on, or when you're ready, we can go inside and find out." And that's the truth: however good I am at guessing, it is the client who knows and that knowing is within him or her if s/he can find a safe way to look.

On rare occasions I have used the *Light* with very little preparation; the client is asked to close his or her eyes, and I proceed with the induction procedure described below or even one more abbreviated. As might be surmised, the client has to be in acute distress to prompt me to this. On such occasions the *Light* appears to exhibit all the characteristics I have attributed to it, even though I have not spelled these out to the client beforehand.

I use the *Light* with most of clients if I see them for more than a few sessions, but I do not use it all of the time, and rarely more than 30 minutes in any hour. Both therapist and client are highly focused when the client is using the *Light*. The experience is rewarding in that both are very much "in" the experience rather than talking about it, discovering as distinct from speculating. But it is definitely a focused effort; the therapist cannot get by with encouraging monosyllables. Even during periods of silence there is a need to stay focused on the client's body movement and facial expressions for a sign indicating s/he has become conscious of a thought, memory, or image. In effect, the frequency of use is as dependent on my readiness to exert a focused effort as it is on the client's willingness. Using the *Light* has the quality of shared participation in an intense drama that, at critical points, calls for impromptu coaching, confidence, and direction from the therapist. Fortunately, there is always the *Light*: It will protect in any situation I have encountered. Even so, "being there" with the client will frequently test the therapist's inspirational and intuitive reserves. Finally, I would encourage the therapist using this process to take notes during the session. I always write my clinical notes during the session as distinct from writing them afterward. Most of my notes are verbatim statements of questions and answers while the client is inside. The inward focus generates a great deal of detail, which is nearly impossible to remember from session to session if it is not recorded as it occurs.

The client's willingness is also a significant variable. I have worked with some clients for upwards to a year before using the *Light* to any extent. One group of clients that is likely to experience initial difficulty will be found to suffer from repressed trauma. Many children use dissociative states (self-induced trances) to cope with assaultive abuse. The recall of those memories is most likely in a trance state. Conceptually, the recall of repressed memories is considered state dependent; [20] that is, it is most likely to be recovered in the state in which it was "learned." In some cases, the resistance to hypnotic techniques is a fear of remembering trauma experienced in a dissociative state. But upwards to a year is an extreme; most clients are prepared to go inside within the two or three sessions. If the client is in acute crisis, s/he may be willing to go inside in the first session.

Clients will generally express their fear of the *Light* through an inability to find it or sustain it. I take this to mean that the therapeutic relationship must develop further before they will trust me with this aspect of themselves. Under no conditions will I ask them to disregard its use for another method of intervention, e.g. other methods of hypno-analysis. The *Light* affords the client a protection in inner work that I have not found with other methods. If the client is unable to find the *Light*, I simply assume they do not yet feel safe enough to go inside under any condition; I will respect that for however long it takes them to gain that trust.

Sometimes the initial fear of using the *Light* is caused by the clients' self-consciousness at closing their eyes. In such cases I note that it is not necessary to close the eyes, that they can access the *Light* with the eyes open, directing queries to their sensed presence of it. Bandler and Grinder observed this phenomenon [21] some years ago. I had one client who initially kept her eyes open. After several weeks she then began to close her eyes to access the *Light* and then opened them for the rest of the session to indicate that she had the *Light*. In her case, opening her eyes also indicated a trance state: she was no longer aware of her surroundings and would not be until she closed and opened her eyes again. It is not uncommon for people to be in a trance with their eyes open. Other clients seem to use a "quick look" routine, at least initially. With their eyes open they visually access a sensed *Light* to which they direct their questions. The latter method seems particularly helpful for clients who are more auditory than visual and are essentially "reading" patterns of sound.

Although a few clients will spontaneously enter medium or deep trances, I do not encourage it. I envision the process as an ongoing conversation between the client and myself with his or her eyes closed and focused inward. If a client is silent for a prolonged time, even if s/he seems to be working on something, I nonetheless generally encourage the client by asking if s/he will "please stay in touch" or "please share what is happening." [22] I cannot read a client's mind and can only know what s/he shares with me. Also, I treat any changes in facial expression or posture as indicative of something happening inside, and I am likely to encourage/query the client with monosyllables such as "yes...?", or some other comment that conveys that I am aware of his or her nonverbal communication. But I might note here that you must also be sensitive to the client's need to not be interrupted at critical intervals. If the client is very focused on what is happening, particularly if you have given a task, s/he may convey that your voice is distracting by nodding or moving the hand in such a way as to answer but also to let you know s/he is too focused at the moment to talk. Going inside requires and elicits intense concentration on the part of the client. As noted, I generally record almost verbatim whatever a client says while inside. This is easy to do since s/he speaks more slowly. These verbatims prove exceedingly helpful as a review for the next session. When you do this work several times a day, it is difficult to remember who did what the following week. Detailed notes allow you to pick up where you left off. Often, the client can be equally forgetful until s/he goes back inside.

The following protocol was formulated in the early period of my use of the *Light*. Today, I do it differently if clients have access to the Internet. Essentially, I send them a copy of this manual, which describes the following protocol. Reading it provides them with a chance to "rehearse" before they even go inside for the first time. When I was in Officer Training in the Army an instructor made a lasting impression on me when he said: "First, I'm going to tell you what I will teach you, then I will teach it to you, and finally I will tell you what I have taught you. By the third time you will have it down pat." It is nearly impossible to read this manual without actually experimenting with the process in your mind.

Also, the whole process can be greatly facilitated if the client is willing to evoke a higher power such as Christ the first time they go inside, or in some cases one of their children, if the client is a parent. These figures are highly trusted. Once visualized, the image is asked by the client to reach behind his or her back and bring forth the *Light* as if by magic. Those particular approaches notwithstanding, I strongly encourage the beginning therapist to walk through the following protocol with their first few clients.

Finding a Safe Place

As a rule, the first thing I do is ask the client to imagine a place where s/he has a sense of privacy and peace, a safe place where s/he is not likely to be interrupted. This can be a place the client has actually visited in the past or an imagined place. It can be as close as the client's back yard or as far as the most distant island or mountaintop. When the client has decided on a place, I ask them to go there in his or her mind and describe it to me so I can also have a sense of it. On rare occasions this safe place may be simply a dark, formless background. Such a place cannot be used for the following protocol but may be used in later sessions. On occasion, I will show clients a book cover that pictures two hands holding a light. If the client can use this suggestion without any difficulty, then entering a formless space is not problematical.

If possible, I will have clients do most of their inner work 'out of doors,' e.g. on a beach, in a vale, on a hill top, because I have found it is easiest for clients *to find the Light among the first stars of the evening*. For this reason I generally suggest they find an 'out door' place; but I'm also a firm believer in Erickson's suggestion that you start where the client directs you. One client, for example, could only visualize her *Light* on the altar of a small church remembered from childhood. Another client, who used hypnosis, had an underground workshop in a forest where she went during self-hypnosis; she always found her *Light* there. Still another needed to be in a closet, which was the only place she had felt safe as a child. After a client has developed the facility for holding the *Light* and moving about with it, s/he can easily move out of doors or have the *Light* transport him or her somewhere else.

I tend to think of the client's 'place' as an inner signature which both of us quickly come to recognize as unique to the client. Over repeated sessions this place may acquire a number of unique features. Often, if appropriate the place can acquire a house, which may in time be peopled with helpers. For example, one method I have found useful in connection with the recall of traumatic events is the rescue of the 'child' who suffered the event. It is helpful to have a place where this child can be brought for healing. I have found this particularly helpful with MPD clients who have to recover the memories of many alter fragments.

Over an extended series of sessions the client may choose a new place or add on to an existing landscape. For example, one client originally chose a large rock in the woods. Later she would go to the front porch of a house originally seen in a dream. The house symbolized the 'many rooms' of childhood memories and her personality. Several clients continued to find their *Light* in the same place, but felt the need to have a cave nearby where they would go to actually work on issues.

It can also be helpful to have clients describe their surroundings upon going inside even if the place is familiar, since it may change in significant details that are diagnostic, e.g. a beach may be rainy, pleasant, dark, "trashy" from a storm, cold or warm, etc. Allowing the inner landscape to remain fluid increases the likelihood of unconscious processes using it for communication. One client always went into an adobe house in the desert to get his *Light*. Frequently, there would be something on a table in the main room suggestive of the direction we could take in addressing an issue.

Finding a Sacred Space

Asking the client to imagine a sacred place is a variation on the above theme. Almost always what the client envisions is out-of-doors. Frequently, it will have a dark glade appearance with a distinct sense of peace and safety. Less frequently it will be in the open, but then almost always in the desert. If indoors, it will be something like a chapel. Not surprising, for most people, a "sacred" place is set apart from our civilized daily lives. When clients evoke sacred spaces they are also quite willing to envision their *Light* within that place without having to use the protocol described below. However, I would encourage everyone to learn following protocol before using this variation.

Locating and Making Contact With the Light

By the time a client has closed his or her eyes in search of a safe place, I have already made a number of suggestions on how to proceed. First, if possible, I have suggested s/he imagine a place outside; and second, that s/he imagine being there while it is still daylight, but just as the sun is about to set. After s/he has described to me where s/he is, I ask the client to focus on the eastern sky *where s/he can just barely see the first stars of the evening.* It is there s/he will find the *Light*, among those first stars.

Essentially, the therapist makes suggestions that strengthen and sustain the inner focus of the client. Asking clients to be aware of and describe the details of their chosen place strengthens that focus. Looking for the first stars of the evening in a still lighted sky will further strengthen that inner focus.

Long before the client begins to visualize a place, I have already suggested that the *Light* is most easily visualized as a *luminous sphere about the size of a tennis ball.* (I might also use the analogy that it is like Tinker Bell in Peter Pan since just about everyone knows this story and it may very aptly describe a client's initial experience of the *Light*.) Having focused attention on the first stars of the eastern sky, I then suggest that, *if s/he is willing*, s/he can actually *sense the presence of the Light among those stars*. The client might not be able to actually see it yet, but s/he can sense its presence if s/he wants to. If s/he chooses, s/he can even point at it with a finger, just as s/he might use a finger to guide someone's attention to a far object.

As soon as the client has *noted the presence* of the *Light*, I ask the client to direct it to a point on the ground a *comfortable distance away* and to tell me as soon as it is there. I suggest that s/he point at the *Light* with a finger and direct it to a place on the ground where s/he wants it to settle, just as a car attendant might direct traffic on an open field being used for parking, or an usher might direct someone to a seat in an auditorium. Of note, some clients may physically enact this suggestion by actually pointing with their finger. Initially, I do not say anything since it might break their focus, but when I think it appropriate I will gently suggest that it is only necessary for the internal sense of self to do the pointing. However, on rare occasions a client may persist in physically enacting a suggestion, such as holding out his or her hand as if s/he was physically holding the *Light* even after the suggestion to internalize it. If so, then I might only suggest s/he rest that hand on the knee so as to reduce any strain.

As soon as a client reports that the *Light* has settled on the ground, I immediately direct the client to tell it to leave, to direct it back where it came from. My purpose in doing this is to teach clients from the outset that the *Light* serves them, that it is dependent upon their will. Initially, some clients may want to impute autonomy to the *Light*, not wanting to believe that it is indeed dependent on their willingness. Thus, this first directive ordering its withdrawal and the suggestions that follow, all serve to reinforce the fact that the *Light* is dependent upon their willingness. It also serves as a safe, initial interaction since everything takes place at a comfortable distance.

Once the *Light* has left, I will tell the client, "Now, *ask* it to return." Note that up to this point the client has directed the *Light* kinetically (e.g. pointing); now I am asking the client to direct it with thoughts. When the *Light* has returned I then ask the client to, "*Tell it to go straight up in the air*...(pause) *and return*." Next: "Now have it go off to the right...(pause) and return." And finally: "*Now have it go off to the left*...(pause) *and return*." By this very simple process the client quickly acquires the ability to direct the *Light*'s movements.

Next, the client is directed: "Now ask the *Light* to raise off the ground about three feet (or waist high) and remain absolutely still." Then I say, "Now when you are ready I want you to begin walking completely around the *Light*." In effect, I am directing the client to begin an approach to the *Light*, which will hopefully lead to the client's taking it in hand. When I sense the client has walked around it somewhat, I suggest: "Now just reach out and probe the *Light* with your fingers...be tentative if you want... just get a feel for it." I might then ask, "Is it warm? What does it feel like?" I then suggest the client recommence walking in a circle and pausing to reach out and touch it yet a second or third time. Finally, when I have a sense the client is comfortable with this degree of interaction, I suggest: "Now, if you are willing, I want you to reach out and take it into your hand...just cup your hand as if you were going to scoop up water from the ocean or a stream ...and once you have it in your hand, just begin to walk with it."

Using the Light to Answer Yes/No Questions

Once a client has mastered holding the *Light* in hand, I immediately begin teaching basic skills. The first of these is the *Light*'s capacity to answer yes/no questions. The process is similar to the ideomotor technique described by Rossi and Cretch [23] wherein fingers of the hand are used to permit the 'unconscious' to answer yes/no questions. As noted earlier, the *Light* has the capacity to access all memory, including physiological and preverbal memory. Training clients to ask it yes/no questions is a simple way of introducing them to this capacity of the *Light*.

I explain to clients that the *Light* generally answers such questions by momentarily brightening if the answer is "yes," and momentarily dimming if the answer is "no." (In practice, many clients report seeing a sort of on/off flickering rather than a dimming.) I explain further that, while most clients see the *Light* as brightening or dimming, for each client it can be different. One client, for example, reported seeing a black band around his *Light* indicating "no" and a white band around his *Light* indicating "yes." Another client saw her *Light* write "yes" and "no" in neon, while yet another saw it turn different colors indicative of "yes" and "no." (In this work there is no rule without exception.) For these reasons, I encourage clients to be curious about how their *Light* will answer "yes" and "no," even though most clients will see the *Light* as brightening or dimming. I also tell them that if the question is threatening, the *Light* will either:

    a) not respond (its intensity will stay constant); or

    b) leave altogether; or

    c) on occasion, change colors to indicate that it knows the answer, but the client is not yet ready to assimilate it (this last option is rare in practice).

After explaining to clients the responses they are most likely to encounter, I tell them that I am going to have them ask their *Light* a series of questions for which they already know the answer, and that I am doing this so they can become familiar with how the *Light* will answer them. Since they know ahead of time whether the answer will be yes or no, how the *Light* responds will correspond to the answer. The first question I always ask is: *Is your name _____ (the client's first name)?* Followed by: *How did the Light respond?* Next, I may ask: *Have you ever been to the Antarctic?* In effect, I will ask them if they have ever visited a place that is likely to elicit a "no" response, e.g. the top of Mount Everest. (I did have one client answer "yes" to the Antarctic question, and indeed she had been there; but she was the only one of hundreds, so I continue to ask expecting the answer to be "no.") I will continue to ask such questions, e.g. names of children and/or spouse, occupation, places visited or not, until I sense that the client has acquired some confidence in reading and reporting the *Light*'s responses.

It is important to remember that some clients are more auditory than visual. In such cases they can generally "sense" the presence of the *Light* but may have difficulty visualizing it. For such clients, it is helpful to allow them to hear the response rather than visualize it. Also, at least initially, some clients (though otherwise very visual) may not be able to see the *Light* brighten or dim. If there is a lack of responsiveness after a series of questions, I generally proceed to the next task of learning to draw a circle. A lack of responsiveness to yes/no questions generally indicates that the individual is threatened by the idea of the *Light* being able to respond in such a matter. This fear generally abates with familiarity; consequently, the therapist should continue to test for it in successive sessions.

On occasion, even clients who are facile at discerning the *Light*'s yes/no responses may have difficulty perceiving a particular response. This is true if the question is potentially threatening, such as: "are there any more significant memories in need of recall at this time?" Such questions might border on being threatening, thereby producing no response. On such occasions I might suggest to the client that they write "yes" and "no" on the ground in front of them and direct the *Light* to move to one or the other by way of answering. This method is also helpful with clients who normally have difficulty discerning visual changes since it relies more on a kinetic response. But let me stress, again, if the *Light* fails to respond, I generally take this to mean that the client feels threatened by the question. At such times, I ask the client to rejoin me so we can discuss possible causes. As a rule, I do not like to discuss "possible causes" while a client is inside. Also, bringing clients back and then having them go back inside facilitates their ability to move back and forth with comfort.

Over the years I have encountered a number of clients whose *Light* initially fails to give a "no" response. It will clearly brighten for a "yes" response, but maintains a steady state rather than dimming or going out when the answer would obviously be "no." Since teaching clients to evoke yes/no responses is among the first tasks I give them after finding their *Light*, I initially thought the problem was simply one of lack of familiarity with the process. Frankly, it did not occur to me that "no" might be a fearful response for some people under almost any condition. But in fact some clients seem unable to tolerate "no" without discomfort; consequently the *Light* remains unresponsive. Today, when I encounter this situation I generally stop the protocol and ask the client to return to me so we can discuss his or her feelings to hearing the word "no." As with much else that goes on inside, the unexpected is often the most fruitful. While it may not be possible to immediately desensitize the client, it will generally prove enlightening if some consensus can be reached about what is prompting the fearful response to "no." In any case, if the client can clearly discern a "yes" response, the therapist needs to rule out whether "no" is a fearful response.

The ability to ask yes/no questions at any juncture is an invaluable resource. For example, before asking clients to undertake what might be a threatening task, I will have the client ask the *Light*, if s/he is *willing* to undertake the task? Yes or no? If the answer is yes then both the client and myself are confident of proceeding. If the answer is no, then we must first ascertain the source of fear or reluctance and address that before proceeding further. Methods for doing so are described further on. It is also helpful to confirm if a suggested task or question was threatening, i.e. generally indicated by loss of the *Light*. First I will ask the client to ask the *Light* to return, and then I will have the client ask the *Light* if the previous question or task was in any way threatening? Almost without exception the *Light* will brighten momentarily. I would then proceed to identify and contain the source of the client's fear or unwillingness and address it as the focus of therapy.

Drawing A Circle

The circle of *Light* quickly becomes an indispensable element of *Light* work. There are a number of ways to visualize or imagine it. I describe it as a kind of force field created by the *Light* to contain whatever the *Light* is directed to place within it. I always suggest that the circle be drawn on the ground. Metaphorically speaking, this ground is the "ground of consciousness" and the circle permits "below ground, unconscious material" to become conscious without overwhelming or flooding consciousness. In effect, the circle provides a safely contained access to otherwise threatening elements.

I generally use the following protocol to teach clients to draw a circle. First, I ask them to bend down and draw a circle on the ground with the empty hand while continuing to hold the *Light* in the other hand. Then I ask them to touch the *Light* to the edge of the drawn circle as if using a light to ignite a gas stove. It is helpful here to tell the client what to expect before asking them to actually do it. When told what they might expect to see, no client has ever failed to execute this task the first time, quite possibly because the image of a gas burner is such a common experience. Once the circle has been created, I then direct the client to ask the *Light* to dissolve the circle, to make it disappear.

After the first circle has been dissolved, I will have them direct the *Light* to create a new circle without first drawing it on the ground. I tell them to imagine the *Light* leaving the hand, drawing a circle on the ground and immediately returning to the hand. Drawing a circle is quickly learned, and once learned, is always available. In practice, asking clients to "contain" something (e.g. a feeling or image) is always equivalent to having the *Light* to draw a circle around it.

When the client has successfully directed the *Light* to create circles, I set up tasks to begin testing the power of those circles. I begin by asking the client to imagine a person s/he does not like. S/he chooses the person; I give no suggestions here. When s/he has identified a person, I ask the client to have the *Light* draw a circle and then direct the *Light* to contain the image of that person within the circle. I then suggest s/he try to break through the circle and kick the person. Invariably, client reports being unable to penetrate the circle. I point out that, similarly, the person within the circle cannot reach client in any threatening or attacking way.

Once the client discovers s/he cannot penetrate the circle in a threatening way, I suggest s/he ask the *Light* to send the person and circle far away. I then suggest, if s/he is willing, to ask the *Light* to go to the place in the mind where the *Light* sent the encircled person. The first client who did this went to a meadow on top of a mountain. The *Light* sent the circle and disliked person to another mountaintop. I then suggested he have the *Light* return him to the place of greatest security. This simple exercise teaches the client another attribute of the *Light*; namely, its ability to transport the client to different 'places' within the mind. The whole exercise is also helpful in reducing fear of the object.

A word of caution at this juncture: usually, the above protocol works as described. But on one occasion when I directed a male client to kick the circle, which contained his boss, everything went black, i.e. his *Light* left him. It returned on request and we very quickly learned that this client was afraid of his anger; consequently any expression was threatening. Another male client projected a woman into the drawn circle, whom he disliked because she lied. However, as he continued to describe her, he became aware that his whole life threatened to become like hers. In both instances, what started as a demonstration very quickly evolved into therapy proper. The inexperienced therapist might be taken aback by having to so quickly address issues not anticipated. One way of buying time is to ask the *Light* to place the circle at a safe distance from where the individual is standing with the understanding that it will be dealt with after further discussion. Then, ask the client to rejoin you (open his or her eyes), discuss the issue evoked, make a plan, and go back inside.

The *Light*'s power to contain within a circle is absolute. To date, I have found nothing in the mind that exceeds the *Light*'s power in this respect. In my experience with various clients, the *Light* has successfully contained the alter personalities of individuals with multiple personality disorder, 'evil spirits,' disincarnate spirits and 'spirit guides,' and the most extreme feelings of fear, shame, panic, rage, sexual energy, and body memory. Essentially, a circle functions just like the *Light* in its power to protect from threat or attack. That is not to say clients never experience the feelings contained by a circle when they go inside; only that the *Light* has the power to contain emotion within a circle when directed so that the emotions are attenuated to a point where the feeling is not overwhelming. It is conceivable that the *Light* could effectively block all feeling, but this would generally be counter-productive since clients are likely to distrust the authenticity of a memory or image if there is no feeling attached to it. In addition, very often the focus on feeling is instrumental to the retrieval of memories and images. The optimum is sufficient feeling to validate without overwhelming the client. This is particularly true of traumatic memory. I frequently emphasize to clients that it is only necessary to *remember* a memory, not to relive it. Throughout the book, I offer a number of interventions for attenuating fear of emotion.

Once the client has permitted the *Light* to draw the first circle, the process quickly becomes instantaneous; that is, the client has only to think it and it is done. As a rule, the *Light* is also directed to determine the size of the circle; generally, I suggest the client let the *Light* draw a circle *large enough* to contain whatever we are addressing. Also, with very little practice, the client quickly learns to use several circles at once if the situation calls for it.

The *Light* can also be asked to create a dome of *Light*. This dome can be opaqued so that only a *presence can be felt*. The concept of a dome is reassuring to many clients so I suggest it often when helping them to first identify a fearful or disowned self. The dome can be made more transparent as the Aware-ego approaches the dome. I discuss its use at length in the next two chapters.

A Circle of Protection for the Client

Typically, clients use the circle to contain feelings, images and memories that might otherwise overwhelm them when initially brought to full consciousness. However there are occasions when clients need their own circle of protection. This type of circle may be particularly helpful if the client is having difficulty going inside, i.e. to the place where he or she generally goes to meet the *Light*. This type of difficulty generally manifests itself when the individual is anxious about the prospect of going inside, typically because of some foreknowledge of what must confronted once s/he is inside, e.g. a repressed memory or disowned self. On such occasions clients will report difficulty in visualizing their "place" or clearly visualizing their *Light*. The following procedure is generally effective in such cases.

Once a client has visualized the *Light*, it is always possible to sense its presence even if s/he cannot see it clearly. Consequently, I first instruct client to sense the presence of the *Light* (which can even be done with the eyes open) and – using that felt experience of contact – direct the *Light* to draw a small circle inside. When s/he goes back inside the client can go directly into that circle of protection. I explain to the client that this intervention will automatically place the source of fear *outside the circle*; in effect, the *Light* is instructed to create an island of safety amidst the feeling of disquiet. When s/he goes back inside, I might then suggest s/he ask the *Light* to increase the size of the circle, thereby giving the client 'more air to breathe' or 'more space to move in' or a 'beach head.' This procedure is quite effective in giving the client access to the *Light*.

Having successfully created an island of safety, I will then suggest to the client that s/he direct the *Light* to draw a second circle outside the circle of protection, and direct the *Light* to contain whatever thought, memory, image, belief or emotion was making the client fearful. A dome can also be used for this purpose. Note, it is not necessary that the client to actually know what threatens before containing it. The *Light* will know what the person finds intolerable and place it in the circle in a form acceptable to the client. Thus, in only a few moments what was obstructing entry can become the object of inquiry. The client is now in a position to begin exploring this threat to his or her inner space.

Note that the *Light* can also be asked to draw a circle of protection around the client at any time after the client is inside. Some clients seem to feel more secure with a circle around them, while others feel most secure in containing whatever threatens them. Once inside, the request for any type of circle is answered instantly. The client has only to think it and it is made, be it to protect the client or contain whatever threatens the client. With use, clients will do this spontaneously without my even suggesting it. Any time the client seems threatened by what is contained in a circle, I generally suggest s/he take a moment to refocus on the circle itself and ask the *Light* to strengthen it; or that s/he asks the *Light* to move the circle away from him or her, which invariably lessens the threat. A third alternative is to have the *Light* weave the source of threat with *Light* as if wrapping it like a cocoon, and to allow the *Light* to continue this wrapping till the client is satisfied the threat is contained. Another aid is to simply have the client focus completely on the *Light* to the exclusion of anything else. Actually, that may happen spontaneously without my suggesting it, as a way of blocking unwanted thoughts or intensity. In fact, on occasion, the client may report that all s/he can see is *Light*. I always assume this is the *Light*'s protective response to some threat. At such junctures, the therapist can ask the client to provide a circle of protection or temporarily return and discuss the situation s/he has encountered. Let me stress here that there is nothing sacrosanct about the inward focus. I frequently ask the client to break off the inward focus so we can discuss what is happening or how we might proceed with information already gained.

Containing Others in a Circle

When I first started using circles of *Light* in therapy I was reluctant to have the client use them to contain the images of others. Initially, I only used circles to contain feelings, particularly fears. Today I generally suggest that anyone who is in any way threatening to the individual be contained in a circle while we are working with that image. At first, I thought this might interfere with how the client felt about the contained image. In fact it generally puts them in better touch with their feelings since they can frequently experience those feelings without fear of retaliation. It should be stressed that the *Light* protects in *both* directions. It protects the person imaged within the circle as well as the client. As such, the contained image cannot be attacked by the client's negative feelings and vise versa.

Image containment is helpful in another way: on occasion all of us find ourselves verbally attacking someone we care about, e.g. spouse, sibling, child. If we are willing to have the *Light* draw a circle around that image, our anger is then essentially deflected. Often this is helpful in allowing a client to examine negative feelings without feeling guilty about having them. I also ask the client to contain self-images, such as images of the Rejected-self or images of themselves that have been traumatized. This is particularly helpful for clients who experience strong body memory of abuse. Before recovering the memory I will ask them to contain the child who experienced the memory; this approach coupled with other containment strategies greatly diminishes the client's need to over-identify with the abuse experience. I always tell clients it is only necessary to remember the memory; they are not obliged to relive it. The containment of self-aspects is also helpful when first encountering 'shadow children' or rejected aspects. An example from my practice was a client whose worst fear was the image of a child who seemed deprived of all childhood stimulation: withered, hollow eyed, empty hearted, near death. She was able to face this aspect of herself only after first containing it in a circle.

The Double Circle

The double circle has emerged as one of the more powerful interventions possible with the *Light*. The two circles of *Light* can be concentric or overlapping. Concentric circles are used to help the Aware-ego separate from a co-existing sense-of-self. It consists of a small circle – containing the Aware-ego surrounded by a much larger circle that contains the co-existing ego-aspect. Overlapping circles are two circles of the same size, one on top of the other. For those readers familiar with a basic paradigm of logic, the double circle emulates Venn diagrams. Overlapping circles are used to tease out energies contained or hidden within an image or to extract projections hidden in another image. Essentially, overlapping circles of are superimposed around an image, one on top of the other. This can be a self-image or image of another, e.g. lover, spouse, sibling, co-worker, parent, etc. Consider, for example, a client who reports feeling very hostile toward someone without provocation. A double circle would be used to separate out whatever might be provoking the hostility. This could, literally, be anything - an image of a parent, a disowned self-image, or a suppressed memory. In effect, overlapping double circles can be used to unearth projections and transference as well as a host of archetypal and/or "spiritual" energies.

Concentric Double Circle

In a previous section I described how a circle of protection is used to help clients go inside when they were having difficulty finding their or felt threatened in some way by the prospect of going inside. The concentric double circle is actually the next step in separating from, and discerning, the source of that difficulty. Basically the client is asked to have his or her draw a small circle around the Aware-ego and a larger circle around whatever surrounds him or her. The 'surround' is generally expected to be a co-existing ego-aspect who is dominating consciousness, and generating a strong feeling, somatization, or preoccupation. Consider, for example, a client who comes in and reports that s/he is feeling "very sad." The therapist would suggest that s/he go inside and draw a small circle around the sense of herself holding the *Light*. Next, s/he is instructed to draw a larger circle around the first circle, large enough to contain the source of sadness that seems to surround and envelope her. Ideally, if the Christ image is evoked, he is generally the one who is asked to draw the second larger circle using his own *Light*. But the separation process is possible even without Christ's assistance. Before separating from the larger circle, the client is asked to divide the *Light* into two equal parts and place one part outside of the little circle into the larger circle. (If the client holds the *Light* in both hands and separates the hands, the will divide into two equal parts. This process never diminishes the *Light*.) Next, the client is asked to have the Aware-ego – in the small circle – move from the center of the larger circle to the inner edge of the larger circle. The small circle is expected to stay centered on the Aware-ego as s/he moves. From there, the Aware-ego is asked to gently push through the edge of the larger circle till both circles are separate, and go stand by Christ, if he is a participant in the process. When the two circles have separated, the client (sic) Aware-ego is asked to look back into the larger circle and describe what is there.

The *Light* of willingness exercised by the Aware-ego can be infinitely divided without being in any way diminished. Whenever a client holds the *Light* in both hands and then separates the hands, the *Light* will divide into two parts. The new portion of *Light* can serve a number of purposes. Almost without exception, whenever a client identifies a new sense-of-self, I will immediately suggest that s/he extend a portion of the *Light* to this new aspect. That aspect, in turn, can use its portion of the *Light* in any of the ways discussed in this work. Normally, it will limit itself to the suggestions made in therapy, but in theory it can exercise its own willingness in any way it sees fit. However, since most ego-aspects tend to function willfully, they normally have difficulty functioning willingly aside from specific suggestions that they perceive to be in their best interest.

As regards the process of separating from a co-existing self, it is important to stress to the client, and bear in mind as the therapist, that this separation process only personifies the ego-aspect. In no way does it hold the separated self 'captive.' The moment a client leaves the therapist's office this self will reassert its dominance, even as it may be more reflective as a result of what it learned in the therapist's office. As will be demonstrated in the later chapters, a Dominant self can be dramatically transformed to the extent it is willing, but until then it remains willful and conditioned by its past history. Thus, even though it becomes a distinct entity inside, it retains its power to dominate consciousness once the client is focused again on the physical world, particularly as the Aware-ego tends to lose its power when the client is focused outside. Treat such selves respectfully or they will sabotage the therapeutic process.

In later chapters, I will examine co-existing ego-aspects in depth. These are the self-images that embody the motivations controlling our problematic daily behaviors. Often, the client fails to identify these aspects as distinct selves: most often they are experienced as something that happens to the client, i.e. blushing, migraines, temper outbursts, etc. But any characteristic physiological behavior is likely to reflect the presence of a co-existing self, e.g. eyes rolling back in the head, frequent tilting of the head, nasal gestures of disgust, blushing, headaches, severe chronic ailments, and the like. The concentric double circle is an ideal intervention for personifying these self-aspects; that is, for separating them from the Aware-ego. This is best done by a Christ image. Where Christ is evoked, the client asks the *Light* to draw a small circle around the part holding the *Light*. Then s/he asks Christ to draw a second circle large enough to contain the self expressing the behavior in question. The following case illustrates the use of concentric circles in practice and the initial process of discovery.

Michelle. This client, 27, is the oldest of four siblings. I have worked with the family and she has seen me before in that context. She suffers from severe neurological and dermatological problems that began very soon after her stepfather's death. In this session, she is introduced to the *Light* and its basic functions and finds her image of Christ, which most of my clients evoke on going inside. Her somatic problems are severe and chronic and affect her joints, skin, and muscles. She is chronically tired and achy. She has rashes, numbness in her hands and toes, extreme temperature changes, and painful joints, particularly her knees. In her mind, the symptoms seem to have started immediately following her stepfather's death, though there were some milder manifestations while he was still alive. The concept of the concentric double circle is explained. She uses it to separate from the part of herself that personifies her illness, which she experiences as all pervasive. Almost immediately she begins describing it: "It is ugly...tearful...it looks tired, emaciated...a lot of things on it physically...knots, rickety, crippled... looks sick, older than me." I suggest she let Christ touch it on the lips with his *Light* so it can answer her questions. I ask if the image remembers her stepfather? Instead of answering directly she proceeds to describe her image's emotions. She says the image is "evil, mean, intentionally forceful, physically and emotionally." Then she says that the image remembers him, "He was mean to her...they are connected in a bad way... they are a lot alike...he intentionally did a lot of stuff to hurt people...they clashed and yet are alike in that sense." (In Chapter VI, this kind of self is identified as a Mirror aspect.) I ask for an early memory of his hurting her. She remembers first being spanked by him at age eleven even before he married her mother. "He spanked me often after the marriage...age 12-13...and even more after he went into drug treatment...I was the target of his anger...he stayed on my back about everything...a few times he used a paddle... he was full of rage when he did it...then I started hitting him back...biting, punching, hitting...to get him off my back...my mom was always on my side, but she could not stop him...there were times when I was ready to give up everything to kill him." At this point, the session is nearly over. I have her ask Christ to contain her stepfather in a separate circle and then ask Christ to stand between him and her seemingly murderous self-image until we meet again. In the next session we will begin resolving a number of the issues surrounding this relationship and the illnesses sustained by it.

Of note, I rarely move so quickly in terms of helping a client find the *Light*, image of Christ, and the reason for symptoms. The rare exceptions are when physical symptoms are present, chronic, and severe. Also, in the above case, I had previously worked with the entire family, was familiar with the family background, and was trusted by the client's mother and other siblings.

Transference and Projection

An overlapping double circle is particularly valuable for the exploration of transference and projection. These will be addressed in detail in Chapter V. Transference is the technical term originally used to describe the unconscious attribution of parental qualities to a therapist. Clients will invariably *transfer parental attributes* to their therapist, an observation first noted by Freud. This "transference" from parent to therapist is called negative transference if the client perceives the therapist as having qualities of the parent that made parent-child interaction conflictual, such as threatened abandonment by the parent. Positive transference occurs when the client idealizes the therapist. The analysis of transference is central in psychoanalytic work and the interested reader can find a large number of references describing it.[24] However – and of special interest here, the transference phenomenon is by no means restricted to therapists. *Children, spouses and significant others are also universal recipients of transference and the double circle is exceedingly helpful in discerning this*. When explored, the images of significant others are often found to be imbued with negative characteristics of the client's parents. The double circle can be used to tease out these characteristics. Whenever the client appears to be overreacting to a particular person in the client's life, e.g. spouse, employer, stranger, it is helpful to have him or her contain the image of that person in a double circle and ask the *Light* to separate the circles extracting anything that might be contributing to the strong reactivity. Often an image of a parent emerges in the second circle, in which case the issue is one of transference. Not infrequently, however, it can be a projected, negative, (sic) disowned self-image, in which case the therapist needs to address issues of projection.

As a rule, I *discourage* the use overlapping double circles for the exploration of transference toward myself as the therapist. The therapist needs to remain "outside" the world of imagination, insofar as s/he has control of the process. Especially as regard this kind of inner work, the therapist needs to be someone the client "returns to" in the session. Encouraging the client to imagine the therapist opens too many doors for counter-transference and is probably idolatrous given the availability of other inner helpers such as Christ or comparable archetypal figure (e.g. an angel). Transference issues between client and therapist are best dealt with in a face-to-face dialogue.

Projection refers to the individual's ability to shift unacceptable or denied qualities of the self onto other people, i.e. what I am not willing to see in myself, I am quick to see in others. Thus, technically speaking, transference refers to imbuing others with *parental attributes* while projection refers to the unconscious transference of *unacceptable self-attributes* to others. Positive attributes can also be transferred and projected. The mental operations used to enact transference and projections are probably the same. What distinguishes the processes is the source of the attributes: parental attributes vs. self-attributes. Transference helps us to understand how adults other than parents seem able to speak with parental authority or the Voice-of-conscience. Likewise, the projection process helps to explain how it may be possible to hide our shadow qualities in others. Often, a combination of the two will account for obsessive, unhealthy attachments, e.g. staying married to an abusive husband. The image of the husband will often be found to embody not only images of an abusive parent, but also disowned parts of the self that would act like the parent if allowed into consciousness.

Projection was not discovered by psychology.[25] Finding "the speck in a neighbor's eye and missing the log in our own" is a classic example of projection. But its seeming agelessness notwithstanding, for many years I had a problem imagining how my mind "projected" the attributes from me to the other person. That difficulty was resolved when I finally learned to distinguish between the person-in-the-world and the *image* of the person created by Mind, e.g. that seemingly photographic representation of the person in my imagination. We are raised to believe that the person-in-the-world and the person's image are identical, equal, and accurate in all respects. In truth, the images are never identical and should always be treated as distinct and separate entities. It is the mental representation, the *image* of the person-in-the-world, that is imbued with the qualities of a parent or rejected part of the self; and it is this *image*, in turn, which controls our responses to that person-in-the-world. There are many examples to illustrate this, but by far the most common is the phenomenon of falling *in* and *out* of love – an experience most of us have had at least once since adolescence.[26] It is not the person-in-the-world that controls our many moods, sacrifices, and commitments while 'in love,' but rather the image of that person imbued with lovable qualities and all the lures of Anima or Animus. When I fall *out of love*, any objective assessment would tell me that the physical person-in-the-world that I previously loved remains essentially unaltered. What changed is something within me. The person-in-the-world remains as s/he is. It is the *image* of the person, or my inner response to the *image*, that is drastically altered. Another example is the image of someone who has been deceased for some years. If the *image* of the deceased was a true and accurate representation of a person-in-the-world, then we would have to see the person as skull and bones, or ashes - which I have only encountered once in doing thousands of hours of psycho-imaginative therapy.

All mental images are shaped and felt in an imaginative context; within that domain, they are always susceptible to unconscious influence despite our conscious intention to be objective. Imagination is the arena where conscious and unconscious are joined. It is possible to discern this confluence or confabulation of conscious and unconscious agendas using a double circle, but only if one appreciates that confabulation is a possible and frequent occurrence.

The double circle is particularly helpful in situations where parents seem consistently negative toward their children. Such children are often the repository of attributes originally belonging to grandparents or the rejected parts of the parents. The double circle is often the most effective way of teasing out these transferences and projections from the parents. The protocol for helping the client to discern this kind of transference or projection is essentially the same as described above. First the client is asked to encircle the image of the son or daughter whom the therapist suspects may be a container of projected or transference attributes. A second circle is then drawn atop that one and the *Light* is asked to separate the two in order *to draw out any other image that might share in the bothersome qualities identified in the first image.* In effect, the double circle is used to tease out attributes of the self, parents, or grandparents that the client has transferred or projected onto the son or daughter contained in the circle. As a general rule, wherever this is done the client becomes less reactive to the person contained in the circle, and the relationship is likely to change discernibly.

When A Circle Fails to Close

The failure of a circle to close when the *Light* is asked to contain something is rare, but always significant. Imagine that the client seeks to contain a ubiquitous emotion, or a more or less formless color such as 'blackness.' The *Light* responds, but the client describes the circle as partial. In such instances, the client senses that the circle is shielding them, but also that the circle is incomplete at the point farthest from the client. When I initially encountered this phenomenon, it was almost as if the situation was saying that whatever we were attempting to contain was infinite and therefore uncontainable. I have since learned otherwise. Now, I always interpret this phenomenon to mean that a part of us is hidden in the 'darkness,' held in bondage by it. Essentially, the *Light* is containing the 'formlessness' without cutting us off from that part of us. By this means it seems to distinguish between self and not self. It does not really matter if we call it a Soul part or ego-aspect. What is important is to appreciate that within that 'darkness' is something that belongs to us whether at the level of Mind or Soul, and extracting it can prove this. Once extracted, the *Light* will completely enclose the 'darkness.' The safest way I have found to extract these disowned parts is to give a portion of the *Light* to Christ, ask him to enter the darkness,' and retrieve the part hidden there. Once that is done, the 'darkness' can be named, if necessary, and/or simply transformed into pure white light by Christ and returned to the source of all Light.

I have drawn from the work of Modi[27] in my suggestion that a negative emotion be turned into "pure white light and returned to the source of Light." The *Light* will not destroy anything, but it can always be asked to transform an emotion into its best possible form. As I have noted elsewhere, it is difficult to tell what is the true nature of some emotions. The bottom line is not the nature of the emotion, but rather the client's willingness to allow transformation to a higher vibratory state. As a rule, clients are generally willing to do so, but only after whatever has been held in darkness has been extracted and provided a circle of protection.

Drawing A Portal

A portal is a circle of *Light* stood on its edge. It can be any size. I imagine it at least six feet in diameter, or tall enough to contain the image of a person on the other side; but at least one client wanted her portal relatively small so as to give her a view of the person but make it impossible for him to physically get through. I call it a portal because, initially, I envisioned it as analogous to a boat port, wherein you can look out into the sea without getting wet. Another analog might be a circular doorway filled with a shimmering light field.

The primary distinction between a circle and a portal is this: a circle is used to *contain or separate* an image so it does not overwhelm consciousness, while a portal is used to *facilitate contact* with an image or different dimension. The distinction is somewhat arbitrary since both circle and portal can achieve the same effects. For example, I sometimes encourage clients to imagine a drawn circle as cylindrical and suggest they approach it and place their hands on the outside as a way of getting in closer touch with whatever is contained within. However, since the circle is most often used to separate, contain, and protect, it is hard for most of us to also imagine it simultaneously facilitating contact (though this is exactly what it does). Psychologically, it seems easier for a circle on the ground to perform one set of functions and a portal to perform another set. In any case this is how it has evolved in my practice.

The portal was initially designed to provide a modus operandi for making safe contact with images that have negative characteristics for the client. As a way of reinforcing the safe aspect, I often encourage clients to have their Christ image create and hold the portal using his *Light*. As I envision it, Christ stands between the image and the client's inner sense of self, holding the portal between them. This configuration seems especially helpful when exploring particular feelings associated with an image. For example, one client found her mother 'draining.' In this instance, Christ was asked to use the portal like a polarizing filter that could be rotated until the 'drained' feeling was filtered out. This simple process appeared to have a lasting, positive effect on her interactions with her mother.

A portal can also be used to provide entry to past lives. Any therapist who does a lot of inner work with clients will eventually encounter spontaneous regressions to previous lives in response to symptom exploration. For many years I was reluctant to explore this phenomenon systematically because I could not discern an intervention that allowed clients to take their *Light* and Christ with them. Recently, I came across a book by J.H. Slate that describes a self-hypnosis technique for accessing past lives.[28] The client is asked to imagine being in a corridor having a number of doors on either side. The doors can be of any shape or size. If the client enters the corridor with a specific question in mind then s/he is directed to approach the door that stands out, that being the door to the most relevant past life. I have modified this method so that clients can use both their *Light* and Christ image when entering the corridor. Christ is asked to draw a portal that will take them directly to the corridor. Taking his hand, the client and Christ step through the portal directly into the corridor. Christ is then asked to direct the client to the most relevant door. Once the door is opened, the client can merely look in or actively enter into the past life.

Reincarnation is a contentious issue. I will not debate it here. But past life regression therapy is definitely helpful in discerning the meaning and healing of symptoms that have defied all other attempts at intervention. Once a client has identified a 'reason' for such symptoms in a past-life context, the symptoms generally abate. This has been documented time and again by past-life regression therapists. From my perspective, it does not really matter whether we are accessing actual past lives, spiritual connections, or deeply repressed fantasy-memory. If the symptom abates as a consequence of recovery, that seems sufficient, particularly when all else has failed.

Circle of Effect

I use this type of circle sparingly, but there are times when it has seemed necessary. Wherever possible I have asked that Christ create this kind of circle using his *Light*. Basically, an image of someone other than the client, most often a parent, is contained within a special circle of effect, *which reflects back to the contained image the effect that the image's behavior has on another*. The therapist needs to be very discerning in evoking it. It assuages pain but does not heal it. Basically, a circle of effect obliges the offending image to experience the *effects* of his or her actions and thoughts. Imagine a father whose rages are frequent and abusive. It is possible to ask the *Light* to place a circle of effect around this image such that the father is now obliged to experience the effects of his rage on the client or child. Very quickly the father stops raging, or his rage is quickly followed by a deep sense of pain and bewilderment, or a rapid oscillation between these two emotions. In sum, the circle of effect obliges the father to experience whatever the child experienced when the father raged; it is one trial learning with highly amplified negative feedback. Evoking this circle is quite simple. The therapist describes it to the client by pointing out that when someone is contained in a circle of effect, s/he will be obliged to feel whatever the client has felt in response to that person's behavior. It is important to always designate it as a *circle of effect* and distinguish it from others, such as circles of protection or containment. As a rule, it is best thought of as a second circle imposed on an earlier circle used to contain the image.

On very rare occasions, I have suggested that the alter personalities of an MPD client place a particular alter into a circle of effect. In such instances, I always insist that more than one alter be willing to enact this intervention. Generally, this is only done if a particular alter is acting out in a way that endangers the others, as when a particular alter engages in dangerous sexual solicitations. Please note that there are real limitations to this usage. As a rule, alters are not interminably contained by a circle of effect as is the case for parental images. They can still come out, i.e. take over conscious control of the body. But the circle insures that they experience all the consequences of their behavior, its effects on the body, as well as the trauma caused to other alters, especially those who take the alter's place when the experience becomes too painful for the alter who initiated it. Whenever a circle of effect is used with an alter, afterward a concerted effort must be made to work with that alter to recover and heal the memories motivating the behavior.

On the whole, this intervention seems most appropriate for abusers of children, be it parents or others, where the abuse is so severe that the therapist is close to suggesting the worst revenge. Any therapist who has worked with severely abused clients has had to work through such feelings. The circle of effect creates a kind of hell for such people since they are now obliged to suffer all the consequences of their thoughts and actions. In time, an effort must be made to redeem these images, but as the Linns note, it is not always wise to forgive too soon.[29]

The Capturing Circle

I intuited this kind of circle very late in the process of writing my book. I first had to grasp the fact that unexpressed emotions accumulate in the Mind/Body. For example, if there is a Dominant self that constantly seeks to control *fear*, that fear will accumulate in the Mind/Body, such that everything seems to become fearful for particular selves. Use of the Capturing circle requires a higher power such as Jesus Christ. The internalized image of Christ is asked to both define and draw the circle with his *Light*. The circle is placed between the Aware-ego and Christ. Then the Aware-ego walks into the circle and exits on the side closest to Christ. In this intervention, the request is generally emotion specific. Christ is asked to draw a circle that will 'capture' a particular emotion. For example, Christ can be asked to capture all accumulated unexpressed shame. Essentially, as the Aware-ego leaves the circle, the self will be separated from that emotion. After examining whatever is in the circle, Christ is then asked to completely absorb it with his *Light*. This intervention does not remove the self's capacity to generate more of the emotion, only its unexpressed accumulation in the Mind/Body. Whatever this process discovers can be quite dramatic in two respects.

First, it strongly encourages the self to *stop using* whatever defense strategy is generating the emotion, which is always decidedly ugly; and equally important, it appears to remove the toxicity from the Mind/Body. The circle is illustrated in a number of verbatims in Chapters VII and VIII of the book.

Extending a Portion of Light to Other Aspects of the Self

Consider that the Rejected-Self is initially unattractive, even potentially threatening, to Dominant selves; and it is their willfulness that is most likely to block the *Light*. This Rejected-self is a part of the Ego. The same is true of alter personalities found in Multiple Personality Disorders [30] and images of ourselves as children experienced in the context of traumatic memories. They are all aspects of the Ego even though the context in which they are discovered is often very threatening to primary selves. The *Light* can be used to establish a safe connection with these initially threatening aspects of the Ego by having the client extend a portion of the *Light* to that self-aspect. I have already described the protocol. It is quite simple. Ask the client to visualize holding the *Light* in both hands and then separating the two hands. The *Light* will divide into two equal parts and one of those parts – either one – can be extended to the self-aspect that is the focus of attention. Generally, that image has already been contained in circle. The designated portion of the *Light* can enter the circle on its own, the Christ image can carry it in, or the client can pass it directly to the image, whatever seems most comfortable at that moment.

Dividing the *Light* and extending a portion of it serves several purposes. First, it establishes a safe link for communication between the self co-existent with Aware-ego and the self-aspect that is the focus of attention. Even more important, it begins the process of reconciling the Ego with its disowned aspect. Extending a portion of the *Light* is tantamount to acknowledging a personal relation to it. In many respects, these self-aspects can be likened to manifestations of the Shadow, [31, 32] which contain all those qualities we seek to deny in ourselves; the therapist needs to encourage every effort to acknowledge them. This is necessary to attenuate their negative effects on consciousness. Extending a portion of the *Light* is one of the safest ways to initiate contact with these disowned parts of our selves.

The *Light* will contain these dissident parts of the Ego, as when we use it to create a circle, but its ability to safely reconnect us to these disowned parts is a far more powerful attribute. Initially, I emphasize containment since it helps the client master his or her fear of the inner world, but ultimately, the goal is connection and transformation. Using the *Light* to connect discordant parts effectively begins a process of reconciliation and redemption.

Ending a Session When Using the Light

In using the *Light* I always make a clear distinction between 'going inside' and the idea of returning. Conceptually, the distinction is between an inward focus vs. the ordinary waking focus on physical surroundings and interpersonal space. Without exception, I anchor myself in the interpersonal space to which the client returns. Generally, I say to the client when it is time to end an exploration: "Please ask the *Light* to return you here to me when you are ready." Often, the return is as simple as that, though it may take some clients a little time to open their eyes. The counselor must allow some time to elapse before expecting clients to be fully reoriented, particularly if the inward focus has been prolonged and intense. The suggestion to return can be repeated, but clients should never be hurried or they will come back disoriented and still require time to comfortably readapt to their interpersonal space.

If the session needs to be brought to a close while there is a sense of 'unfinished business' – generally because of time constraints – I will make suggestions that allow for safety and continuity. For example, if the client has recovered some portion of a memory I am always mindful of the child of that memory – the image of the client at the age when the memory occurred – and take steps to insure that even while s/he will break contact with that image by returning to an interpersonal space, the child is nonetheless looked after and not abandoned. This generally includes extending a portion of the *Light* to the child as described above; however, in addition I will always seek to leave the child with a helper. The Christ image is ideal for this, but if the client is unwilling to elicit him for any reason then I will have the client seek someone else who is nurturing and able to protect from any further harm. The list of possibilities can range from a remembered nanny or grandmother to angels or Virgin Mother. As a rule such an entity would be identified and present before I undertook to help the client recover any traumatized selves.

Sometimes it is also advisable to bring the client back in the midst of a session. There are times when the exploration has posed a conundrum for the client and therapist alike, and I do not like to discuss options with clients when they are inside. In this work, counselors will invariably encounter situations that have no ready answer and truly require a creative solution. At such times I will ask the client to have the *Light* return them to me so we can discuss it. Essentially, everything is put on hold so we can discuss the issue as 'an aside' or 'outside the frame.'[33] If an exploration is interrupted in this fashion it is generally advisable to go in at least one more time, if only briefly, to put some closure on whatever was ongoing. This can be something as simple as asking the *Light* to contain whatever is at issue in a safe place until it can be explored further in the next session. As a rule, it is very easy for the client to return to the place where s/he left off. Generally, just re-closing the eyes is sufficient.

In this process of inner work the therapist needs to walk with humility and assurance in the *Light*. All the years I have used this process notwithstanding, occasions still arise – weekly if not daily – when I am not sure how to proceed. At such times, I am always reminded of the saying: The saints smile when the situation is clearly impossible because then they can look to God to take a hand. Whenever in doubt, ask clients to ask the *Light* and/or their image of Christ for suggestions and assistance. Very often, these are the source of greatest creativity.

USES OF THE *LIGHT*

It is beyond the scope of this book to describe all possible applications of the *Light*. Most psycho-imaginative techniques can be adapted for use by the *Light* provided they do not threaten or attack the client or any object of the client's focus. The following sections describe some of the most common uses of this method. All are expanded upon in the book chapters.

Manifesting the Law of Connection

The Law of Connection overarches most of methods of discovery. This law of the Mind distinguishes it from the physical world. Nothing imagined is ever separate or isolated from everything else, even though a willful ego-aspect would have us think otherwise. In the physical world a wall can separate us from whatever is on the other side. In the Mind that wall connects us to whatever is on the other side. Everything is connected. If a client experiences a strong emotion, my first question is to have them ask the *Light* what that emotion is connected to, or even more likely, to whom the emotion is most connected. Often, clients are mystified by feelings and sensations. This is particularly true of somatic complaints, i.e. a tense jaw, tightness in the chest, a crick in the neck, a churning stomach, etc. I will have them imagine placing the *Light* on the place of this discomfort and ask it to trace the feeling to its source and then contain it. Alternatively, a concentric double circle can be used to separate and personify the emotion. In the inner world of the imagination *nothing exists in isolation; everything is connected*. Soul, Mind and Body are connected and interactive. The Therapist's role is to facilitate a conscious awareness of those connections. Much of what the client is asked to do with the *Light* involves tracing those connections from one form to another. This concept of connectivity cannot be overstated. In the world of imagination everything is linked to something else. The question is not whether, but to whom or what.

Examination of Feelings and Emotions

Clients often report vague feelings without a particular referent; for example, feeling 'restless' or 'moody' or 'agitated.' These feelings can be placed in a circle. It is then easy to apply discovery techniques such as those described by Gendlin,[34] Hendricks,[35] and Shorr.[36] Feelings and somatic complaints often provide the entree to a great deal of inner work with clients. Each is addressed at length in chapters of the book. Often, I describe them as the buoy on top of the water that functions as a conscious connection to unconscious contents. By way of illustration, a woman came to a session with a long list of preoccupations: self, relationships, work, and financial concerns. I suggested we place them all in a circle, one by one, to ascertain if they had a common denominator. Almost immediately there appeared an image of her deceased father. Discussion of that image led to identification of the *fear* that prevented her from knowing what so disturbed her about her father. A second circle was created to contain that fear and the remainder of the session was devoted to its resolution.

I am very careful to always listen for expressions of feeling and emotion. Fear, guilt, and shame play a dominant role in the lives of most people seeking therapy and are often the defining characteristic of particular ego-aspects. The *Light* is very helpful in containing such feelings and the ego-aspects exercising them, so the client can examine them without being overwhelmed. If the client has difficulty separating his or her Aware-ego from the feeling that is the object of focus, that is an appropriate time to introduce the concept of concentric double circles. But I need to caution therapists to expect the unexpected when using this approach. The first time I did this the client felt she had separated herself from two demons that had been with her since she was born. Since other therapists have reported similar experiences,[37] I am inclined to accept such pronouncements and explore them rather than challenge or denigrate them, especially since the Christ image can easily exorcise[38] them at any time in the process if they are found to be something more than shadow aspects.

Exploration of Somatic Complaints

Throughout this work, I explore the hypothesis that repressed memories, mental conflicts, beliefs, negative emotions, and issues of conscience significantly contribute to physical dis-ease, injury, and illnesses; that the Body does not have a mind of its own. Mind and Soul – as higher order realities – effect brain-body function. Brain-body is the microcosm and Spirit-Soul-Mind is the macrocosm. The work of researchers such as Brigham,[39] Rossi,[40] Siegel,[41] Mindell,[42] Lowen[43] and Perls[44] support this hypothesis. Given the thesis that the Mind is instrumental in generating or aggravating a physical symptom, then purely physical solutions for symptoms will be followed by a reoccurrence of the symptom or psychologically comparable symptoms at some point in the future. In sum, the Body mirrors the Mind; and if mental conflict is left unresolved the conflict will continue to express itself in physical symptoms until the conflict is resolved.

I am well aware that the mind-body connection remains an issue of debate: am I, or am I not, responsible for my dis-ease, injury, and ultimately, my death? By way of an answer, I would hold to the dictum that in physical matters, a cause must be both necessary and sufficient to be the *sole* cause of an effect. Increasing evidence supports the hypothesis that many illnesses are psychosomatic; that what takes place in the Mind is often a sufficient cause of disease.

But to the best of my knowledge, no psychological component is both a necessary *and* sufficient cause of illness/death. For example, excessive unremitting stress will be a significant factor in compromising the immune system, but that is only an issue if there is a microbiological organism attacking the body. Pathogens kill, but only if the immune system is first compromised or overwhelmed. All of us will die. The breath of life will leave our bodies, and our bodies will return to dust. Nothing I can do will alter the ultimate death of my body. But to the best of my knowledge, no pathogen or injury inevitably and automatically results in death. Miracles and prayerful healings are a continuing fact of life.[45] Likewise, and perhaps far more common, the conscious resolution of unconscious conflicts and self-destructive beliefs can often have an immediate and dramatic healing effect.[46]

Whenever clients report acute or chronic conditions, I strongly encourage them to examine their symptoms with the *Light*. The process of discovery can be quite straightforward as when a double circle is used. Throughout this book, I describe even more effective interventions. One is to have the client envision a physical template of the body, draw a circle at the site of the injury or symptom, and spin the *Light* so as to draw the body sensation into the circle as an image, thought, or memory. Originally, I just suggested that the client place the *Light* on the site of the symptom; the notion of spinning is an elaboration that has proven more effective. A variant is to have Christ place his *Light* on the site of the symptom and spin it while the client is asked to simply attend to whatever comes to mind. Alternatively, I might suggest that the client stand in the circle, extend the *Light* over his or her head and direct it to 'wash' the sensation of the symptom. When clients have a sense of having shed some of or the entire symptom, they are then directed to step out of the circle, at which point they can become aware of the symbolic meaning of what they have shed. The latter method also works with generalized feelings of fatigue.

The most effective method I have found for addressing sensation is the Well of Pure Sensation described in Chapter V. I note the other methods in the preceding paragraph to emphasize that any number of interventions are possible; the therapist is encouraged to expand his or her repertoire borrowing from any other therapists that provide psychosomatic interventions. I have done so repeatedly and that is reflected in many of the interventions described in this book. The issue of somatic symptoms is taken up again in Chapter V at greater depth.

Essentially, every psychological and physical symptom is treated as connected to a conflicted belief, memory, denied aspect of the Self, Soul issues, disincarnate spirits, or misplaced archetypal energy. In almost every case I have examined, recurring chronic conditions such as painful menses, migraines, sinus conditions, abdominal pains, lower back pain and the like appear to be physiological manifestations of unconscious conflict or disowned parts of the Self. In all such instances the *Light* can function as a conduit for the release of that memory into a portion of consciousness protected by a circle. The *Light* can also be used to evoke the Inner Physician described by Upledger [47] or the Inner Christ described in Chapter IV, and these figures can be used not only to diagnose, but to heal as well. Of note, the *Light* can also be used to recover the symbolic significance of childhood illnesses that stand out in the client's Mind as an adult. Often such illnesses have been found to precede or follow a traumatic event otherwise repressed. Let me stress that I never offer these interventions in lieu of referring clients to their physician. Quite the contrary, clients are always encouraged to seek the services of a physician first wherever the problem is acute and has not been diagnosed by a physician. This approach is only offered as an adjunct to medical treatment or when the physician has little to offer other than palliative measures.

Working With Images

An image is the internalized representation of any person, animal or object in the physical world, e.g. a spouse, parent, child, friend, lover, family pet, devil, angel, house, sculpture, etc. For example, when a client is fearful of 'hurting' a parent's feelings, s/he has in Mind an image of a parent that is capable of being hurt by the client and is equally capable of hurting the client in return. Most people underestimate the power of these images. In my work with clients, I have found the images to be instrumental in controlling our sense of self and others. If I teach clients anything it is, hopefully, to distinguish between these images and objects-in-the-world and to appreciate that the inner image is by far the more powerful in guiding perceptions and behavior. I have already touched on this power of the image in my brief discussion of transference and projection, but it is worth reiterating here. Images are the modus operandi or 'containers' of such phenomena as projection, transference, displacement, depersonalization, archetypal energies, alter personalities as in Dissociative Identity Disorder, and other defenses described in classical texts on psychodynamics and object relations. The defense mechanism distorts the image, which in turn shapes our perception of the person-in-the-world. For example, transference is said to occur when the client appears to treat the therapist like a parent. The client does this by unconsciously merging his or her image of the therapist with qualities of the parent. In the physical world this would be not be possible, but in the world of Mind two objects can occupy the same space. The *Light* can be used to discern this type of confabulation as well as the effects of other psychological defenses.

To work effectively with images a major fallacy must be addressed with each client: namely, the assumption that any image is an accurate reflection of the individual it represents. An image should never be treated as identical with the person it is seen to represent even as it is imbued with the qualities attributed to the individual. These images are no more the absolute truth than a photograph is the absolute truth. Consider the following series of photographs: an adult as a child, the same adult as an adolescent, the same adult as an adult looking very angry, the same adult looking smilingly at an infant, the same adult deceased and lying in a coffin. Which of these images bespeaks the absolute truth about the person that any one image is thought to represent? All images in the Mind are creations sustained by the Mind, but amenable to change under special circumstances.

Images are very enduring and exceedingly powerful in shaping how the individual perceives the flesh-and-blood-person; and it generally dictates the client's relationship to that person. When the Mind has shaped such images, they become the guiding truth ordering our perceptions and actions. Images only seem to represent actual people because they guide our interactions with those people. That is their power: they shape our behavior and interactions toward the significant others in our lives. As a consequence we believe them to be identical with the persons they represent. The fallacy is discerned when we can realize that the flesh-and-blood-person – the person-in-the-world – may not have changed at all even though our perceptual image of them has changed significantly (sic) lover vs. ex-lover. In sum, no image is the same as the person it represents; if anything, an image should be seen as more powerful than the flesh-and-blood-person it represents given its power to govern and shape our responses to that person. But all that notwithstanding, also bear in mind that those images can be changed even as the flesh-and-blood-person remains unchanged or unavailable due to death, estrangement, or physical dangerousness. Even though a flesh-and-blood person remains unchanged, it is possible to alter the image of him or her and thereby alter our affective and behavioral responses. And quite often, altering our image of a person can have a decidedly positive effect on the person-in-the-world.

Recovery, Exploration and Reworking of Dream and Fantasy Contents

My own work supports the observations made by Rossi and Creech[47] and Mindell[49] that physical symptoms can result from unresolved dream conflicts that are suppressed or not addressed upon awaking. To illustrate, one client reported heavy menstrual bleeding over a three-day period, which was very atypical for her. The *Light* was asked to take her back to the onset of the symptom. Her menses started shortly after waking three days previously. This led to her gradual recall of a dream in which the members of her family were on a bus being driven down a winding mountain road by her father. In the dream, her father was not paying attention to the driving, thereby placing everyone at risk. The feeling associated with his driving was that the situation was out of control. Using the *Light*, the client reentered the dream, demanded that her father stop the bus, and relinquish the driver's seat to her. She then visualized herself driving the bus competently down the mountain. She reported that shortly after leaving the session her menstrual bleeding stopped.

As the above incident illustrates, once a dream is recovered, its conscious reworking is always advisable, particularly if there are physical symptoms or disturbing feelings associated with it. Strategies for entering and altering dreams are not unique to *Light* therapy. They have been variously described by Jungians using active imagination [50] and dream therapists such as Delaney.[51] Researchers of lucid dreaming also describe similar methods of intervention.[52] Most of the interventions suggested by these clinicians can be adapted to interventions using the *Light*. But the *Light*, particularly in conjunction with the evocation of Christ, offers safety and power that is not automatically available with those methods.

The *Light* can also be invaluable in the interpretation of dreams. After client has reported the dream in its entirety, s/he is encouraged to 'walk through it' again, this time with the *Light*. Wherever s/he or the therapist want to know the symbolic meaning of a particular content, the Aware-ego is instructed to touch it with the *Light*, or focus the *Light* on it, or contain it, and enter into a dialogue with the image. As a rule this is far more powerful than any interpretation the therapist could render since the answers come from the client. The above methods are particularly useful in working with recurrent childhood dreams that the client remembers as an adult. Reentering those dreams will often bring repressed events to the surface.

Though I do not ordinarily offer dream analysis, I do encourage my clients to share their dreams with me. Recurring dreams tend to highlight current or chronic conflicts, and I have found it fruitful to explore them for potent images. These are generally contra-sexual in nature (i.e. Animus and Anima images). Wherever these occur I will encourage clients to engage these images, first by containing them in a circle, then by extending a portion of the

Light to them and proceeding to engage in a dialogue. Where clients are willing to share their sexual fantasies I will do much the same with the contra-sexual images in the fantasy. These are powerful figures that can have a significant effect on clients' dynamics. Discerning these images and entering into a dialogue with them has invariably proven pivotal in therapy. Several of the longer verbatims in the book illustrate these interventions.

Recovery of Repressed Trauma

By repressed I mean not accessible to consciousness as an explanation for current experience, as when a person acts obsessively or compulsively, or when they experience feelings of panic for no discernible reason. It is Rossi's[53] contention that events are 'repressed' because they are first experienced in a trance state, dissociative state, or preverbal state such as infancy and will not be normally recoverable without reentering that state. Individuals generate dissociative states when confronted with traumatic events by dissociating from the ego-aspect traumatized by the event. In my experience, such events are generally associated with extreme fear, shame, and/or pain. Repressed experiences of sex abuse and/or physical abuse in infancy and early childhood are examples of this kind of trauma. The *Light*'s protective quality makes it exceedingly helpful in the recovery of these memories. Unfortunately, using the *Light*, I have also found repressed childhood abuse to be an all too common occurrence in clients seeking therapy.

Light therapy is very effective in recovering traumatic memory. It is the response demanded by those memories that often proves the most problematical. What I have in mind here are not singular events, such as being molested one time by an uncle – as unconscionable as that is, but horrific memories such as being obliged to witness and participate in the sacrifice of infants when the client was, herself, little more than a child. Cultic abuse is regrettably very real, horrific, and beyond the imagination of most of us. The healing of these memories is the work of therapy, but in my experience, the therapist is hard pressed to attempt such healing without the help of higher powers. The greatest difficulty with repressed memory is the client and therapist's emotional reactions to the memory. Such memories evoke strong emotions in therapist and client alike: shame, fear, disgust, despair, rage, and horror, and all of them must be mitigated. Attempts at catharsis are often blocked by competing emotions. Clients must be offered the means of healing all of their negative emotions and self-judgments. In my clinical experience, this can only be done satisfactorily where the therapist is willing to call on higher powers such as the Christ within each of us. This issue is addressed at length in Chapter IV and the remainder of the book.

Repression is an active force that is likely to manifest throughout the therapy process. The therapist encounters it most blatantly when a client reports almost complete amnesia for whatever occurred in a previous session. The therapist may have ended the previous session with a sense of great progress only to discover in the following session that the client has no memory of what transpired. Often, this amnesia is erased when the client goes inside, though equally often special interventions may be needed – such as a circle of protection, to get inside. Basically, what the therapist is 'experiencing' is a Dominant self that has completely repressed the events of the previous session by consciously shaming it. Once inside, the client can begin the process of separating from that self for the purpose of discerning the reasons for its repression.

Depersonalization and Dissociation

As a rule of thumb, when the client goes inside his or her sense of self will reside within a sense of the body; that is, s/he will have the same sense of self normally experienced in the physical world. This means s/he is looking out through the eyes, and sees the hands in front, and it is these hands that receive the *Light*. Normally, s/he is not looking at a body receiving and holding the *Light*, as if s/he was seeing it all from an observer's perspective. Even when the Aware-ego separates from an ego-aspect, it continues to organize consciousness by looking through the inner eye and perceiving the hand holding the *Light*. If the therapist suspects it is otherwise, the best way to ascertain this is to ask the client: "When inside, are you seeing the *Light* through your eyes, or looking at an image of your body holding the *Light*?" Initially, the client may be totally unaware of being 'out of touch' with his or her body sense. This 'out-of-touchness' will be reported as the experience of seeing a self-image holding the *Light* from the side, or from slightly above, or from behind – all of which are visual analogs of body depersonalization.

Depersonalization is relatively easy to describe phenomenally. It is harder to explain conceptually, particularly in the context of the Aware-ego. It is the only condition I have encountered in which the Aware-ego is the object of perception rather than the perceiver.

Depersonalization appears to occur frequently during traumatic episodes. Often the client will report its repetition during the recall of a traumatic event. At some point s/he will report 'looking down' on the event, and that the body seems relatively lifeless or acting differently. This is also a common report of people who report 'out of body' near-death experiences. Depersonalization appears to be the visual analogue of shock. Essentially, an ego-aspect becomes a witness to the event rather than a participant. In some way the ego-aspect is able to sever its connection to its sensed body, generally in response to intense pain or emotional trauma. It is an incomplete form of dissociation. Basically, the ego-aspect separates from its body sense while retaining consciousness within the mental state that previously organized the body sense. In dissociation proper, *a new mental state with the free will to exercise of a new body sense will supplant the control previously exercised by a failed ego-aspect*. (All these distinctions are addressed in greater detail in the book chapters.)

The most frequently encountered form of depersonalization is what I would call *traumatic* depersonalization. Out of body experiences (OBE) may fall into this category since they most often occur following trauma to the body. But I have no way of demonstrating that clinically. What can be observed with some regularity is the traumatic depersonalization often reported in the recall of severe childhood abuse. At some point during the experience, the client reports leaving the body sense defining the body image. The depersonalization appears to correlate with that point in the recall when just about anyone would find the abuse physically intolerable.

In working with depersonalizing memories the therapist needs to be mindful that the mental state of awareness and the body sense need to be reconciled following the recall.[54] First, Christ needs to be asked to heal the body sense – or whatever aspect of the personality was left to endure the rest of the abuse. Then Christ is asked to gently assist the mental aspect's return to his or her healed body sense. Often, this reconciliation is overlooked in therapy even though it is directly responsible for numerous somatic complaints. One reason is that other ego-aspects may have been created to take control of the

Body, and they are the ones 'left standing' at the end of the experience. This is most likely to be observed in MPD clients who report the most severe and extensive abuse experiences, often requiring the creation of numerous fragments and alter personalities.

Another form of depersonalization is what I call *habitual* depersonalization. This is the condition in which the client, on going inside, self-describes as an observer rather than the participant. In effect, s/he observes a self-image holding the *Light*. This generally appears to occur as an intermittent or habitual response to inner work.[55] The client copes with suggestions made to the *Light* by "mentally" separating from the experience. Whereas traumatic depersonalization is seen as a remembered *reaction to actual abuse*, habitual depersonalization is considered to occur in the present tense *as a defense against remembering abuse or painful memories*. When encountered, this is where the therapist needs to begin; that is, to begin the work by helping the client rejoin with the image of his or her body. But be warned: clients do not habitually depersonalize without cause. Once the connection is made, the therapist needs to be prepared to assist the client with whatever is brought to consciousness by this reconnection. An illustration will help here. The client – Jonathan – experienced a depersonalized response while seeking to engage an image of his wife who appeared to him with Anima-like qualities. Prior to the session he was reading Robert Johnson's book describing the Anima,[56] which undoubtedly embellished his image of her. On going inside he evokes an image of his wife that has a priestess quality: she is wearing a robe with a hood over her head that places her face in shadow, giving her an Anima-like quality. Confronted by this image, he is unable to 'join' with his body; he can only experience the scene from above. He can see the *Light*, but he is not holding it. At my suggestion, he asks the *Light* if there is any memory contributing to his difficulty. In response he sees an image of himself as a toddler with his mother screaming at him, and he is turning his back on her. At my suggestion he asks Christ to intervene in the memory. When Christ joins with the mother and child of the memory, the 'bad' mother abruptly begins nurturing the child. (Of note, Jonathan is familiar with Neurolinguistic techniques and these seem to shape that particular response.) Following this intervention, he is able to rejoin with his body sense and interact with the image of his wife.

In any situation where Christ is present, he can be asked to intervene. For that reason, I normally ask the client to evoke the Christ image whenever s/he goes inside regardless of what we intend to do.

Habitual depersonalization appears to separate the observing self from its embodied self-image, and the Aware-ego appears to be co-present with the observing self as the only non-threatening way for the *Light* to be present. The habitual depersonalization response is generally subconscious. Often, the client only becomes aware of it when asked. I recall working for two months with a client before realizing she was seeing herself from behind and above her body. Efforts to bring her back in touch with her body resulted in a long series of traumatic recalls and significant issues regarding her feelings and sexuality. This experience taught me to periodically check with clients as to where they are with regard to their body. I suspect my asking also sensitizes the client to such changes. Today, I routinely check with new clients. Whenever a client reports body depersonalization, s/he can begin the process of reintegration by asking the Aware-ego to contain the observer and place a portion of the *Light* into that circle. This introduces a safe connection for ongoing dialogue.

But the observer only becomes body-connected when the sense of self is joined with the body sense: when the client is looking out through the eyes and can see the hands holding the *Light*.

Habitual depersonalization is one way an ego-aspect can cope with the fear of stressful repetition. It appears to mimic dissociation without going to that extreme. Unfortunately, it is also the defense most likely to precipitate repressive somatization and projection, both of which are discussed at length in Chapter V of the book. Dissociation is the Ego's primary coping response to severe stress, whereas repression and depersonalization are primary defenses of ego-aspects, which are created by the Ego. Depersonalization separates an ego-aspect's mental construct from its somatic presence, whereas with dissociation the archetypal Ego's strategy is *to create a new ego-aspect able to supplant* the ego-aspect overwhelmed by the stress. The preexisting ego-aspect continues to exist, but remains the 'weaker' while unhealed. Over time, it will also become the lesser developed as the supplanting ego-aspect grows older. Dissociation can also occur whenever a developmental epoch threatens the sense of self, as is too often the case with budding sexuality.

Historically, dissociation was treated as a rare occurrence. It was seen as the Ego's unique response to the *most severe* abuse scenarios. Even today, most therapists still treat the Ego as a unitary phenomenon except in the case of diagnosed dissociative disorders, which are considered rare. In fact, however, most people have dissociated selves, but their existence is generally attributed to other causes such as 'mood shifts,' cognitive dissonance, or 'bipolar' disorder.

As an Aware-ego, the client can ask the *Light* to contain and objectify any set of discernible qualities, i.e. mood, body memory, strong emotion, physical symptom, etc. Without any exception I can think of, *this containment is the safest way to initially recall traumatic memories*. If the particular symptoms suggest abuse, then the *Light* is asked to contain an image of the self *at the time of the abuse*. Most often, however, I word the suggestion more generally, such as asking the *Light* to contain the self expressing the mood, or symptom, etc. When this is done, the Aware-ego essentially becomes an empathic observer-participant. The client will "feel" this contained self, but still be sufficiently disengaged so as not to be overwhelmed.

Think of dissociation as the primary process by which the Ego is fragmented, and depersonalization as the process by which an ego-aspect mimics dissociation. Depersonalization generally occurs in the throes of trauma. It is a response to shock. Dissociation is the process whereby the archetypal Ego creates an ego-aspect to actually supplant another ego-aspect. While in the psychiatric literature, dissociation is generally associated with severe trauma, it is in fact a nearly universal occurrence in human beings in the earliest stages of development. Only repeated severe trauma over a period of months and years is likely to result in the creation of a Dissociative Identity Disorder, e.g. Multiple Personality Disorder. This disorder can be marked by the creation of literally hundreds of fragments and numerous alters. (A fragment is a self created to hold one or more memories. Its active life is generally short and two dimensional.) But some form of dissociation is a nearly universally characteristic of the inner lives of most people. The numerous self-aspects of the Ego described throughout the book are the product of dissociation. Whenever we envision a distinctly different image of the Ego, which has the power to exercise free will in active imagination, we are perceiving a dissociated part of Ego. For that reason, it is helpful to distinguish the motivation of a dissociative act. In active imagination, the process is described as *intentional* if the Ego archetype generates successive aspects to cope with instinctual or archetypal demands. Such creations are always willful and, frequently, antagonistic opposites. Dissociation is described as *traumatic* when depersonalization precedes dissociation. Depersonalization can be an habitual defense employed by an ego-aspect, as illustrated in the example above. Where that depersonalization fails (sic) the abuse persists, then the Ego is likely to dissociate and create a new ego-aspect.

While all people can be expected to dissociate during early development (before age seven), traumatic dissociation is comparatively rare. In situations where there is only one abuser, it is likely to generate bipolar or borderline disorders; where there are a number of abusers and the abuse extends over a period of years, the abuse can force the creation of hundreds of fragments and several major personalities (i.e. alters), all created to cope with the horrendous abuse. The alters will be of two types: those that deny the existence of the abuse and seek to imitate a 'normal' life and those created to cope with the myriad repetitions of abuse.

Finally, I would note that once the client begins working with dissociated parts of the Ego, new self-aspects are likely to make themselves felt from week to week through body memories and moods. That is, in weeks following the client's awareness of multiple selves, the client may come in with a report of having felt a particular way during the week, e.g. tearful, depressed, irritable, frightened, etc. I will always ask if there are environmental stressors that could account for the mood, and if there is nothing obvious, I begin to suspect the presence of disowned or reactive self-aspects. Often, these ego-aspects are readily accessible. On going inside the client is simply asked to separate from the feeling and its source, using concentric circles. As part of the separation, a portion of the *Light* is always extended to these self-aspects as the safest way to set up a link of communication. If the aspect is a young child, it is always advisable to leave it with a caregiver before the client ends the session.

Alter Personalities

The dissociative process is likely to occur in response to any trauma where there is no opportunity for catharsis,[57] which is very often the case in childhood abuse and many instances of rape. If the event occurs only once, is comparatively mild, of short duration, or simply repetitive, then the 'memory' – if repressed – is most often embedded in somatic and psychological symptoms, dreams, and/or fantasy. But where the abuse is severe (i.e. horrific or unbelievable to most people) and prolonged (i.e. daily, weekly, lasting for weeks, ongoing for years), then the consequences are likely to manifest as severe, often terminal, illnesses and/or the creation of alter personalities of the kind found in Multiple Personality Disorder. Very likely, the ability to create alters is a genetically determined propensity, and, without it, the client would not have survived the abuse. In these cases, the psyche spontaneously creates new personalities (i.e. alter personalities) and even more numerous fragmented personalities (i.e. fragments) in a valiant effort to endure and survive the abuse. The process is truly heroic given the severity and duration of the abuse, which may have to be endured from infancy into adulthood. The clinical discovery of alter personalities is comparatively rare, if only because few therapists have any experience with the phenomenon, and even the alters who come for therapy may be unaware of or in denial about the nature of their disorder. The basic strategy in MPD is to create one set of alters who cope with the abuse and a second set that deny the existence of the abuse and attempt to live a 'normal' life. Consequently, unless the client and therapist are able to acknowledge the existence of alter personalities, they may not be discerned; instead, the client will be given increasingly severe diagnoses (i.e. schizophrenic, borderline, manic-depressive, etc.) that fail to reach the mark. The presence of alter personalities is always indicative of Multiple Personality Disorder (MPD) [58] and portends a history of the severest childhood abuse or trauma.

Essentially, alters are aspects of the Self *capable of instantly assuming complete control of the body's conscious and unconscious functions.* They are likely to remain hidden when the client goes inside unless client and therapist can deduce their existence from discrepancies in the client's behavior. I worked with my first MPD client for two years without any hint that she was MPD, and we regularly used the *Light*. In retrospect, I should have suspected something given the severity of her symptoms and the relative *absence of any memories or life experiences to account for them*; however such is the denial within our culture, including academia and professional training programs, that nothing in my training had prepared me for this degree of dissociation or abuse.[59] Since one of the primary functions of this disorder is to keep the unaffected alters in ignorance of the abuse, it is possible for client and therapist alike to remain mystified. Normally, a therapist must discern MPD by abrupt changes in the client's demeanor either within a session or between sessions. This switching finally penetrated my own denial when a five year old alter took over the client in the session and asked, in a child-like voice, if she could play with some toys in the corner of my office. Within a few minutes, the alter normally present for therapy (with strong direction from me) was able to contain that alter in a circle of *Light* and reassert control of consciousness. (Two alters can struggle for control of consciousness. Such struggles are most likely to manifest, literally, as headaches or a strong desire to sleep.) In the five years that followed the discovery of alters in this client, I would interact with a dozen plus alters and hundreds of fragments (two-dimensional personalities whose primary function is to encapsulate specific memories). MPD clients are among the most difficult to diagnose and treat; however, they are also among the most challenging and rewarding teachers I have encountered, bar none, and they have taught me more about the psyche, the redeeming power of Christ, and the *Light*, than has any teacher or book.

As a rule, one does not 'encounter' alters on going inside unless the diagnosis has already been made. The therapist is more likely to discern them because the client 'switches,' i.e. another alter takes control during the session, or the alter who is out dialogues with 'inner voices' that the alter can describe and report upon. In working with MPD clients, where client and therapist have agreed on the diagnosis, much of the work will consist of one or two alters, co-existing with the Aware-ego, engaging fragments which generally make themselves felt through dreams, somatic complaints, or life triggers associated with abuse memories. In this respect, the process is not much different from working with ego-aspects. The complexity lies in reconciling alter personalities who are in denial, working with alters who may themselves have become perpetrators in order to survive, or are self-abusive in their role as protectors. What also makes these cases exceedingly difficult is the severity of the abuse, which most people simply find unbelievable. I have worked successfully with a number of these clients only after working through my own denial that such abuse is possible. But I hasten to add that beyond all that, any success is largely attributable to their use of the *Light* and willingness to call upon an image of Christ or comparable Inner Self Helper. Working with MPD clients teaches you humility. The true therapists in this process are their own higher powers.

Clear distinctions can be made between 'alters' and 'ego-aspects.' First and foremost, the occurrence of MPD and alter personalities is rare, while the presence of ego-aspects is always to be expected, and actively sought out, on going inside. An ego-aspect is a self-image, though it can be a very negatively charged self-image, as when we encounter shadow images of the Ego. The Rejected-self and Ideal-persona, as well as all child and adolescent images of Ego, are examples of ego-aspects. As an Aware-ego, the client can feel the ego-aspects and be greatly affected by their moods, willfulness, and characteristic stances; but in MPD, the Aware-ego is more likely to simply be displaced by the emergence of a new alter. The newly conscious alter assumes total control of consciousness and bodily functions, though often with lapses in memory regarding recent events.[60] In the space of a few seconds, or while excused to use the bathroom, an MPD client can go from being a mature adult to a rebellious adolescent.[61] As a matter of course, the *Light* is extended to every identified alter and fragment. Once the diagnosis of MPD is made, I encourage the client, as Aware-ego, to contain alters and fragments, extend a portion of the *Light* to each, and work with them interiorly.

Ego-aspects can serve a function comparable to MPD fragments, as for example, when child ego-aspects embody memories. But, normally, ego-aspects co-exist with the Aware-ego, they do not assume the power of 'I.' If an ego-aspect is exceedingly fearful, it may temporarily block the Aware-ego from emerging, but this fear can generally be contained. Containing ego-aspects in a circle of *Light* is the best method I know of for attenuating their negative effect while a memory is being cathected, or they are otherwise engaged by the Aware-ego. If the client is willing to evoke Christ, then more elaborate and effective procedures can be used as described throughout the book. Fortunately, the *Light* can contain most fragments, preventing them from taking control of the Body. This allows the client to retrieve the fragment's memories without the fragment having to take conscious control of the client. For a limited time, some alters can also be contained, thereby preventing their resumption of conscious control. However, this is generally only possible if the alter is a child contained by an adult alter co-existing with the Aware-ego, or when several alters work in concert with their *Light*s to contain another strong alter, typically, an abusive protector (see the discussion below on protectors).

I have worked intensely with hundreds of clients; however, less than twenty of them clearly exhibited alter personalities. Very likely there were more that I failed to assess from lack of experience or sufficient opportunity to work with them. Counselors are unlikely to encounter them in their work unless they are willing to court the kiss of death from Managed Care panels and work with clients for extended periods. But if you see enough clients, for sufficiently long periods of time, and you ask them to go inside, you will encounter this disorder and become thankful you and they can call upon higher powers such as the *Light* and Christ.

In my current work I generally rely on a higher power to contain the multiple selves that are created to cope with the traumatic memories of a Dissociative Disorder. Most of my interventions now assume the use of a higher power. I typically ask the client to seek a Christ image or other higher power very quickly after learning to use the *Light*. From then on, I encourage the client to rely on Christ or a comparable higher power. The Christ image is expected to use his *Light* to enact specific interventions. Thus, for example, Christ is asked to use his *Light* to contain any self-aspect that makes itself felt in the process of recovering a memory; this is generally identified by new symptoms or headache. The client then extends a portion of the Aware-ego's *Light* to it. The *Light*, in turn, provides a safe link of communication between the newly emerged ego-aspect and the Aware-ego. These alters or fragments have generally endured horrific feelings of pain, abandonment, and/or shameful arousal. They can come in all ages, sexes, and demeanors – some may be masculine toughs or bullies, others detached or completely numbed; whatever the client's imagination can conger up to get through the experience. But whatever the client's affect or strategy, he or she must acknowledge the part each ego-aspect has played in the memory by recovering all the fragments and what each had to endure. Often, it is helpful to have Christ lessen the accumulated unexpressed pain and/or emotions associated with the memory even before it is recalled. Methods for doing so are described throughout the book.

Characterological Issues

Character traits refer to qualities we attribute to ourselves which, on reflection, can be problematical because of their compulsive, pervasive quality. Persons who are 'self-conscious' in most group settings, or a person who has 'angry outbursts' most days, or someone who is 'competitive' in just about every situation are common examples of characterological issues. Also in this category would be negative thought processes, such as bitterness, worry, analytical distancing or skepticism, which permeates a person's thinking or feeling, and also sexual deviations.

Once the trait is identified, the *Light* can be asked to place an image of the client exhibiting that behavior into a circle where it can be examined in a variety of ways so as to assist the client in forgoing the behavior as a compulsive response. More often than not, such behaviors will be found to model behaviors attributed to a parent; changing the behavior will generally require a change in the parental image or the person's relationship to the parental image. When characterological behaviors mirror a parent, their intent is the defeat of the parent's mirrored behavior. If, for example, the parent was frequently angry in the client's childhood, then the client may exhibit a similar, characterological anger. No attempt should be made to remove this without first addressing the parental anger or the client will become unnecessarily fearful since s/he is now devoid of a comparable defense in response to parental images of anger. But, note, such 'characterological' traits can also be sustained or aggravated by 'autonomous emotions.' Emotions such as the chronic use of doubt and fear seem to feed on the energy produced by their obsessive use. Often, when contained, they will take on a malevolent aspect. Some might call them spirit energies. But whatever their nature, they are easily transformed into pure white light. Transforming an autonomous emotion does not release a client from the character defect that seemed to attract the 'self-perpetuating' emotion, but it does give the client a strong incentive to do something about it or risk a reoccurrence.

Another major source of characterological issues are projections and past lives. Projections, particularly those imposed by authority, are addressed in Chapter V. The next section addresses past lives.

Past Life Regression

Past-life regression therapy is recommended for long-standing, chronic symptoms that are seemingly resistant to all other more conventional forms of intervention. It is certainly not the first treatment of choice for most of the clients I see who have grown up in a culture that theologically rejects the concept of reincarnation. Even when I suggest it I tend to downplay its implications. Some scholars have found support for reincarnational beliefs within the Bible, but their work is neither widely known nor accepted.[62] I tend to emphasize the 'curative' effect. Appreciating a symptom in the context of a past-life, whether real or merely imagined, is often sufficient to abate the symptom. Likewise, in my use of Slate's method for visiting past lives (previously described), the client is always escorted through the process by the client's higher power, which is almost always a Christ image. It is Christ who is asked to draw the portal and walk the client through to the corridor where he points out the life-door to be addressed. Given the security of his presence, most clients have readily embarked on this process of discovery. Often, Christ's presence is instrumental in other ways as well, as is illustrated by the following case.

Pearl. I had worked on a variety of issues with Pearl for four plus years. She began her therapeutic work with me in her mid forties. During this time she was essentially asexual in all aspects of her life. Prior to beginning therapy, her dating history consisted of two relationships, the first with a woman and the second with a married man. The heterosexual relationship was the more fulfilling of the two, but both left a lot to be desired. Pearl rarely masturbated. For most of her life, her parents functioned as her primary relationships. She is an only child. I repeatedly focused on her lack of sexual desire for several reasons. For one, it seemed to keep her emotionally isolated; and second, I suspected that some of her chronic weight and depression issues were tied to this suppression of sexual energy. Despite many interventions seeking to rectify this lack of sexual interest, I was singularly unsuccessful in helping her to become more sexual. I seriously began to think she was one of those people whose libido was constitutionally low. But then we had what seemed like a major breakthrough while examining projections imposed by her parents. Pearl observed that when she was beginning to develop sexually there was a period of time when she felt "special," desirable, and desiring. This was quickly squashed by her father's unenviable comparison of her body to other girls her age. It was this observation that made me think that projections imposed by her parents were the root cause of her asexual attitude. But when I suggested that she contemplate having these projections removed she balked. She saw her parents' projections as giving her grace and refinement. She was afraid that if we sought to remove the projections suppressing her sexuality all of her other projections would be removed as well, and there would be nothing left of her! Her fear was understandable given that she had never stopped cleaving to her parents, and remained closely bound to them as their primary caretaker. In effect, she had little opportunity, and seemingly little desire to develop other roles such as lover, mother, and/or spouse that might have mitigated her seeming lack of sexual desire. She did have a successful professional persona.

Following our initial discussion about removing projections, Pearl returned the following week having reflected on her reluctance. She believed her parents treated her as a hothouse artificial flower. In contrast she saw herself as a Shasta daisy, scruffy, hearty, adequate. I asked how she imagined herself as an animal? "Like a lizard. My parents would have seen me as like a dog, tractable, and controllable." At this point Pearl seemed willing to let Christ extract the projections imposed on her self-image by her parents, even though she believed it would require a gigantic shift in her self-image. But, suddenly, it is I who am most hesitant. Call it an intuitive leap, but I have the sudden thought that this client has reincarnationally 'chosen' her parents to insure she would be raised as an asexual person; that is, that she has 'chosen' her parents for karmic reasons. Their upbringing is expected to insure she remains essentially, and safely, asexual. For whatever reasons, she has needed to live an asexual life, one where even masturbation does not interest her. I confess the thought caught me off guard as it did her when I voiced it. But surprisingly, she was quite willing to explore it, so I explained the protocol of using a portal to enter a corridor filled with doors. She and Christ were to step through the portal and he would point out any door that might shed light on her asexual behavior in this life. The client stepped through the portal. Christ was on her left. The hallway was dark, but she was immediately aware of a door just to her right. "I can see the highlighted door; it is very bright, almost blinding. It is uncomfortably bright as I approach it. Christ beside me seems to balance the brightness, making it bearable, approachable. The door opens in…the visual sensations are too intense. It is impossible to imagine anything living in there. They would be burned." All this was unclear to me, but I suspected there was a lot she was leaving unsaid. All I could do was to remind Pearl that she needed to learn how all of this informed her current asexual reality. "It speaks to me of punishment, shameful exposure. At some point I was stripped naked and exposed to public ridicule. It is too bright as if I was in some kind of stock or being burned alive. I scandalized the community by my behavior. First there was punishment for scandalous sexual activity, then I think I may have been burned at the stake, or something like it." As I listened to her share what she was experiencing, and anguish with her, the thought that comes to me is 'crucified with Christ.' I have Pearl return to me as I struggle to formulate what I am thinking and feeling. I have the very real sense that Pearl – whether she is merely imagining it, or actually reliving a past life – is experiencing a mortifying sense of shame, which has left her utterly defenseless and 'justifiably' denied her all access to love and forgiveness. This is what we might imagine was intended for Christ to feel on the cross, but did not. Unlike Pearl, *Christ was not crushed by the shame imposed by others*. As Christ said to the sinners on each side of him, "Believe in me and this day you will be with me in heaven." To be crucified alone, without recourse to a higher power, is to be crushed by shame. But to be 'crucified with Christ' defeats all the institutions and mores that seek to control us with shame. This understanding is opposite to what I was taught as a child. Then I was told that being crucified with Christ meant suffering as he suffered on the cross. But now I understood this much differently. Christ does not ask us to suffer as he did, but rather, to let him be present when we feel crucified (shamed) that he may help us live through it without being crushed by the shame. With all this in mind, I strongly encouraged Pearl to return to the scene of her ignoble shaming and ask Christ to shield her suffering self. This done, we quickly ended the session as we were running well over. Her parting comment was the thought that she would be forever changed by this recall.

Between sessions Pearl revisited this past life and learned more about it. Essentially, she was a beautifully developed woman who took pleasure in men lusting after her. She was not a prostitute, but aroused by the sensations of her own body being desired by others. She ended that life deeply shamed by the community and finally burned naked. Pearl felt purified by Christ's presence as if he walked her out of the flames, out of hell, into the light. At our next session she expressed a strong desire to integrate everything she had learned and to no longer be afraid of repetition. In the ensuing months she did not become more sexual; but she did become more interested in meeting others. Later in therapy she would also become more sexual. The interested reader is referred to Pearl's verbatim in Chapter VII.

Most therapists practicing past-life regression therapy would not see Christ's involvement as necessary. But frankly, what was most memorable for me about this session was my own newfound appreciation of what it means to be 'crucified with Christ.' This has become a teaching story for me, one I have shared with others with the client's permission. This client's whole life had been shaped by the conviction that her behavior was shamefully unforgivable and punishable onto death. Christ altered all of that. He helped her to bear the recall, to die and live with a love and forgiveness more powerful than any shame. Over the ensuing months, the power of her Christ consciousness became quite profound.

Other Uses of the Light

The list of applications described above is merely illustrative of the *Light*'s many uses. Other applications are described throughout the book in conjunction with evoking the Christ image and the exploration of different kinds of authority. I trust readers are already contemplating ways of applying the *Light* in the context of their own theoretical and methodological approaches. Just about any kind of inner work can be accomplished using the *Light*. Trance states, inherent in all forms of active imagination, may be the only effective, consciously directed, way of altering images, feelings, and beliefs that have their roots in the unconscious (aside from lucid dreaming). The *Light* appears to offer the individual a safe way of entering that state without foregoing conscious volition or being overwhelmed by unconscious content.

The Breath of Life

I frequently teach my clients basic breathing techniques in conjunction with using the *Light*. Several years ago I finally discovered what it means to breathe properly. When we inhale, the center of that breath needs to be about one inch below our belly button. For most people it is habitually located at the center of the chest or just below the sternum. We are a nation that seems to follow the drill sergeant's admonition of "stomach in, chest out!" But to the extent that we insist on following that admonition we are much more prone to anxiety, fear, shallow breathing, and a lot of unnecessary symptoms in old age.[63] Several authors, notably Hendricks,[64] Kabat-Zinn,[65] and Hanna,[66] have popularized the power of proper breathing. Their writings clearly describe methods for shifting from shallow chest breathing to abdominal breathing. I strongly encourage interested readers to review these texts. I mention them here because I have found abdominal breathing a valuable adjunct when using the *Light*. If a client habitually breathes from the chest rather than using his or her abdominal muscles, I will strongly encourage them to practice the exercises offered by Hendricks, Kabat-Zinn, or Hanna. In addition, whenever clients go inside I pay special attention to their breathing. During periods when they are likely grappling with difficult issues, I repeatedly have them focus on proper breathing as a way of calming themselves.

CHAPTER III ENDNOTES

1	Jung, C. G., Edited by H. Read, M. Fordham and G. Adler, *The Collected Works of C. G. Jung, 1967-1978*, Princeton: New Jersey.

2	The flavor of this journey is captured in his autobiography. Jung, .C. G. (1963), *Memories, Dreams and Reflections*, recorded and edited by Aniela Jaffe, Winston R. & Winston C. (trans.), Vintage Books: NY.

3	For the grammarians among my readers: I use the term 'client' to designate an individual seen in psychotherapy and also to designate the group of *all* clients. Sometimes, I switch from one to the other within a paragraph. I know that is verboten, but hopefully intelligible. The same rule applies for terms such as 'counselor' and 'therapist'.

4	The term 'Aware-ego' is borrowed from the work of Hal and Sidra Stone. The Stones see the Aware-ego as developing when the individual begins to separate from their primary selves, See Stone, H. & Stone, S. (1993), *Embracing Your Inner Critic: Turning Self-Criticism into a Creative Asset*, Harper: San Francisco.

5	Note, free will is an Ego function. Bear in mind that within the Mind, Ego must also contend with Instinctual will and the Soul's will, i.e. the collective and personal unconscious, as well as ego-aspects at odds with one another.

6	Stone H. & Stone S., 1993, op. cit.

7	Stone H. & Stone S., 1993, op. cit.

8	The exception to this rule is when the Aware-ego is dissociated from the body sense as a defense against experiencing emotions associated with the body. Then, the therapist is encouraged, as described in Chapter IV, to facilitate a reconnection of the two.

9	Hawkins' research using kinesiology has found that emotions can be ranked as negative or positive and as more or less powerful than other emotions. Willingness is ranked very high, but less than forgiveness and love. It is seen as more powerful than any of the negative emotions, which may account for the *Light's* ability to contain images that rely on negative emotions such as pride, fear, anger, guilt and shame.

10   Erickson, M.H. and Rossi, E.L.(1979), *Hypnotherapy: An Exploratory Casebook*, Irvington Publishers, Inc: New York.

11   The interested reader is referred to Bandler and Grinder for a description of these differences and how to assess them. Bandler, R. & Grinder, J. (1979), *Frogs Into Princes*, Real People Press: California.

12   Shorr, J.(1972), *Psycho-imaginative Therapy*, Intercontinental Medical Book Corp: New York.

13   Hannah, B. (1981), *Encounters with the Soul: Active Imagination as Developed by C.J. Jung*, Sigo Press: Boston.

14   Johnson, R.A. (1986), *Inner Work: Using Dreams and Active Imagination for Personal Growth,* Harper & Row: San Francisco.

15   Perls, F.S. (1969), *Gestalt Therapy Verbatim*, Real People Press: California.

16   Bandler, R. & Grinder. J. (1975), *The Structure of Magic: a Book About Language and Therapy*, Science & Behavior Books: Palo Alto, Calif.

17   See Haley J. (1973), *Uncommon Therapy: The Psychiatric Techniques of Milton H. Erikson*, M.D., Ballantine Books, New York; and Rossi, E.L. and Cheek, D.(1988), *Mind-Body Therapy: Method of Ideodynamic Healing in Hypnosis*, W.W. Norton & Co: New York.

18   I once heard a dentist comment on the *audacity* of his eighteen-year-old self deciding to become a dentist, which decision had governed much of his adult life; and yet as children and adolescents we make many such decisions that significantly shape the rest of our lives.

19   See Haley J. (1973), *op.cit.*

20   Rossi, E.L. (1986), *The Psychobiology of Mind-Body Healing: New Concepts of Therapeutic Hypnosis*, W.W. Norton & Co: New York.

21   Bandler, R., & Grinder, J. (1979), *Frogs Into Princes*, Real People Press: Calif.

22   In Chapter VIII I discuss a notable exception to this rule. Often, when some part of a client's self is convicted with the power of the Holy Spirit, I find it

advisable to give the experience a respectful space of time.

23   Rossi, E.L. & Cheek, D. (1988), *Mind-Body Therapy: Methods of Ideodynamic Healing in Hypnosis*. W.W. Norton & Co.: New York.

24   The following sources will introduce the reader to basic concepts of transference and counter-transference: Hall, C.S. (1954), *A Primer of Freudian Psychology*, The World Publishing Company: New York; and Leites, N. (1979), *Interpreting Transference*, Norton: New York.

25   See Matt. 7:3-5: "Why do you see the speck in your neighbor's eye, but do not notice the log in your own eye? Or how can you say to your neighbor, 'Let me take the speck out of your eye', while the log is in your own eye? You hypocrite, first take the log out of your own eye, and then you will see clearly to take the speck out of your neighbor's eye."

26   Robert Johnson offers one of the more sensitive descriptions of this process and the role played by animus and anima - the masculine and feminine principles, which Jung considered central to the process. See Johnson, R. (1983), *We: Understanding The Psychology of Romantic Love*, Harper & Row: San Francisco.

27   Modi, S. (1997), *Remarkable Healings: A Psychiatrist Discovers Unsuspected Roots of Mental and Physical Illness*, Hampton Roads: Charlottesville, VA.

28   Slate, J.H. (2005), *Beyond Reincarnation: Experience Your Past Lives and Lives Between Lives*, Llewellyn Publications: Woodbury, MI.

29   Linn, D., Linn, S., & Linn, M. (1997), *Don't Forgive Too Soon: Extending the Two Hands That Heal*, Paulist Press: New York.

30   This process described here was originally developed to contain and access alter personalities. First the alter is contained in a circle and then a portion of the *Light* is extended to it. This protocol greatly reduces the incidences of alters overwhelming the primary personality since it provides a process for communication that does not require their "coming out".

31   Sanford, J.A. (1981), *Evil: The Shadow Side of Reality*, Crossroad: New York.

32   Johnson, R.A. (1991), *Owning Your Own Shadow: Understanding the Dark Side of the Psyche*, Harper & Row: San Francisco.

33   Note, the counselor should never interrupt a cathartic memory unless they are working with a multiple personality and sense that the recall may involve several alters over a prolonged period of time. In that case it may well take several sessions to recover all parts of the memory even if most of each session is spent in active recovery.

34   Gendlin, E.T. (1981), *Focusing*, Bantam Books: New York.

35   Hendricks, G. & Hendricks, K. (1993), *At the Speed of Life: a New Approach to Personal Change Through Body-Centered Therapy*, Bantam: New York.

36   Shorr, J. (1972), *Psycho-imaginative Therapy*, Intercontinental Medical Book Corp: New York.

37   Crabtree, A. (1985), *Multiple Man*, Praeger: New York.

38   In the early days of this work I had the client ask Christ to bind and remove such autonomous emotions. Today, I simply ask him to turn them into pure white light and return them to the source of light.

39   Brigham, D.D. (1994), *Imagery for Getting Well: Clinical Applications of Behavioral Medicine*, W.W. Norton & Co: New York.

40   Rossi, E.L. (1986), *The Psychobiology of Mind-Body Healing: New Concepts of Therapeutic Hypnosis,* W.W. Norton & Co: New York.

41   Siegel, B. (1989), *Peace, Love and Healing: Bodymind Communication and the Path to Self-Healing: An Exploration*, Harper & Row, New York.

42   Mindell, A. (1982), *Dreambody: The Body's Role in Revealing the Self*, Sigo Press: Boston.

43   Lowen, A. (1980), *Fear of Life*, MacMillan: New York.

44   Perls, F.S. (1969), *Gestalt Therapy Verbatim*. Real People Press: California.

45   Dossey, L. (1993), *Healing Words: The Power of Prayer and the Practice of Medicine*, Harper: San Francisco.

46   Rossi, E.L. and Cheek, D. (1988), *Mind-Body Therapy: Method of Ideodynamic Healing in Hypnosis*, W.W. Norton & Co., New York.

47   Upledger, J.E. (1991), *Your Inner Physician and You: Cranio-Sacral Therapy and Somato Emotional Release*, North Atlantic Books: Berkeley, Calif.

48   Rossi, E.L. and Cheek, D. (1988), *Mind-Body Therapy: Method of Ideodynamic Healing in Hypnosis*, W.W. Norton & Co., New York.

49   Mindell, A. (1982), *Dreambody: The Body's Role in Revealing the Self*, Sigo Press, Boston.

50   Hannah, B. (1981), *Encounters with the Soul: Active Imagination as Developed by C.J. Jung*, Sigo Press, Boston.

51   Delaney, G. (1988), *Living Your Dreams*, Harper & Row: San Francisco.

52   LaBerge, S. (1985), *Lucid Dreaming*, Ballantine Books: New York.

53   Rossi, E.L. (1986), *The Psychobiology of Mind-Body Healing: New Concepts of Therapeutic Hypnosis,* W.W. Norton & Co: New York.

54   In Chapters VII and VIII I examine the work of Peter Levine, a body therapist, who has developed a very workable thesis addressing what he calls *shock trauma.* See Levine, P.A. & Frederick, A. (1997), *Waking the Tiger*, North Atlantic Books.

55   I have worked extensively with a client diagnosed with Asperger's Syndrome. We finally identified a self called the Observer – a disembodied presence that effectively resisted all my efforts to reconnect it with a sensate body. The Observer appeared to be a characterological function rather than the result of a traumatic event. But he is a notable exception. With just about anyone else, depersonalization seems to be the result of trauma and it is possible to reintegrate a depersonalized self with their sensate body.

56   Johnson, R. (1985), *We: Understanding The Psychology of Romantic Love*, Harper: San Francisco.

57   This is a good word but not frequently used. Its meaning is very apropos of the idea that emotions generate and sustain trauma:. Initially it referred to purgation or vomiting as a way of dispelling noxious emotion, feelings, smells, etc. Eventually it evolved to mean a purification or purgation of the emotions (as pity and fear) primarily through art; it can also refer to a purification or purgation that brings about spiritual renewal or release from tension; and finally it refers to the elimination of a complex - an emotionally charged memory, by bringing it to

consciousness and affording it expression.

58   This disorder is now identified as the Dissociative Personality Disorder. See DSM-IV. I continue to use the older nomenclature because it is still more commonly associated with the characteristics of the disorder; and because, frankly, I am concerned that the name changes are an effort to stick this phenomenon under the rug as was the case at the turn of the last century.

59   Dr. Alice Miller, a German analyst has amply described cultural denial in several of her books. See Miller, A. (1991), *Banished Knowledge*, Anchor Books/Doubleday: New York.

60   Under hypnosis it is possible for ego-aspects to assume alter-like qualities if they are asked to respond in the first person. However, in *Light* therapy that is rarely the case since the alter is generally contained and what they say is reported by the alter who has contained them. The reader is referred to the inner dialogue technique used by Hal and Sidra Stone, which does encourage first person dialogues with various aspects. See Stone, H. & Stone, S. (1993), *Embracing Your Inner Critic: Turning Self-criticisms into a Creative Asset*, Harper: San Francisco.

61   The only other cases of abuse that I have encountered, that approximate the severity of MPD, have been clients with severe, multiple, chronic illnesses and somatic complaints which appear to function as 'containers' of the abuse.

62   See MacGregor, G. (1978), *Reincarnation in Christianity: A New Vision of the Role of Rebirth in Christian Thought,* The Theosophical Publishing House: Wheaton, IL.

63   Without question Thomas Hanna has written one of the best books on this subject for people over 40. See Hanna, T. (1988), *Somatics*, Addison-Wesley Publishing Co.: New York.

64   Hendricks, G. & Hendricks, K. (1993), *At the Speed of Life*, Bantam: New York.

65   Kabat-Zinn, J. (1990), *Full Catastrophe Living*, Dell Publishing: New York.

66   Hanna, T, (1988), op. cit.

CHAPTER IV
THE CHRIST WITHIN US

> *Jesus Christ revealed to us not only God but also the human person. He showed us who God is and He has shown us who we are.*
> *- John Hass*[1]

INTRODUCTION

Let me be clear at the outset that the Christ envisioned in this chapter is Jesus Christ, begotten of the Virgin Mary by the Holy Spirit and reborn in the Spirit following his baptism by John the Baptist. He died on the cross for humankind and was resurrected by God on the third day, that all of us may receive the grace of the Holy Spirit evermore. His death lovingly redeems God and us. Through him I can seek the Ineffable Source of all being and nonbeing.

My relationship with Christ has changed dramatically over the years. For too long, I saw him as ineffectual. Today, I see him as a singular source of salvation for me, and a superordinate source of love and forgiveness within the human psyche through his willingness to channel the Holy Spirit unceasingly to all who ask. I also accept that through him I can know the God he lovingly called Abba.[2] But whatever my relationship, in my mind he has always been Jesus Christ, the Christ of the Old and New Testament.[3] I stress this because there are a number of 'Christ's' in the world today vying for the allegiance of people's hearts and minds. To mention but a few: the Christ channeled in *The Course in Miracles* by Helen Shutchman,[4] the 'Himalayan' Christ described by Spalding,[5] the Gnostic Christ,[6] and the Christ of the Church of Latter Day Saints (Mormons)[7] who purportedly appeared in the Americas following the resurrection of the historical Christ. These are but a small sample. A complete list would be quite long and, to my thinking, indicative of *Christ's* immense power to nurture the world's hope. While each of those authors refers to the New Testament, their understanding of Christ is nonetheless their own inspired or channeled experience, which seeks to supplement the gospels and epistles in significant ways. The Dead Sea Scrolls,[8] Nag Hammadi Library,[9] and other Apocrypha[10] would also fall into the category of addendum to the New Testament. At different times, I have found all such writings helpful in deepening my own sense of Christ, but for the purposes of this work the Old Testament and the canonical books and epistles of the New Testament are sufficient to define the Christ of my understanding.[11]

Channeled voices – such as Helen Shutchman's, can speak with great love and compassion; and I must confess that my first encounter with the saving power of Jesus Christ was in a channeling context, though I am not sure that was the intent of the channel. Some years ago,

I read extensively about channeling phenomena in an effort to understand what those observers meant by a spirit world, and attended a workshop to better understand the process. [12] At that point in my journey, I would have described myself as an agnostic Christian seeking a spiritual path. The workshop focused on the power of love vs. fear. Each participant was asked to consider how s/he had inadvertently made contracts with fear – instead of love, as a motivator of behavior. A common example is the idea of using a 'fear of failure' to motivate success. After a night of reflection, we were asked to share our 'contracts' with the group. As each person shared, we were all asked to extend loving support to the person speaking, as the process was self-disclosing. In my mind, I imagined a very warm feeling of positive regard reaching out and supporting each participant in their effort to share honestly with the group. I had no difficulty sustaining this as the first four people shared their contracts, but then found myself unexpectedly blocked when a woman behind me began sharing her contract. Something – the tone of her voice, the turn of her thoughts, I don't know what, started to grate on me so that I grew increasingly irritated with her and anything but loving. The conflict within me grew intense as she continued to speak. A part of me wanted her to shut up just as strongly as another part of me wanted to extend a feeling of love toward her. I simply could not break through my irrational but very real hostility. Then, completely out of context, both in terms of the workshop and my own frame of reference at that time, the thought came to me that Jesus Christ would not be conflicted in this situation. Almost immediately, I imagined in my mind a 'Sunday school' image of Jesus Christ, first standing in front of me as if awaiting my willingness for him to act, and then moving to stand next to the woman who was speaking, and gently placing his hand on her shoulder. As he continued to maintain contact with her my anger began to abate. By the time she completed her story my feeling toward her had gone from hostile to neutral-positive.

As a purely psychological matter, a number of explanations can be given for my shift in feeling on that occasion, and none of them require the existence of an historical, resurrected, living Christ. Neurolinguistic Programming [13] can offer a number of techniques for rapidly transforming a strong negative feeling by juxta-positioning it with a competing image. A Christ figure easily meets the criteria of a competing image, but so might an image of the Buddhists' Tara, [14] images of Sophia Christ, [15] or one of the living Hindu saints of India [16] for anyone who believes in those manifestations. What struck me as significant about this experience was *the power of that image to accomplish what I seemed unable to do with my own unaided will*. Even as I was actively blocked in my effort to extend loving support to that woman, there was nonetheless something within me with the power to accept and love her and thereby neutralize the hostility from which I truly wanted to be free. In effect, my image of Jesus Christ was able to tap a power that my unaided will was unable to tap without recourse to that image. A good while later, it occurred to me that this power potentially resided in my clients as well, and might prove helpful if ways could be found to evoke it. Conceivably, such images had the power to effect transformations inaccessible to the individual relying solely on an autonomous, self-sufficient sense of self, i.e. the ego's unaided will.

As I reflected further on my conference experience, the thought came to me that this Christ figure, in Western culture, had a greater potential for healing in active imagination than any other inner image I had encountered. Reading on the subject of Christ imagery

I discovered a number of books written by practitioners of spiritual healing that encourages the believer to evoke an image of Christ in the mind and ask him to heal the focus of concern. The techniques described by those authors [17] are as sophisticated as anything described by Neurolinguistic Programmers [18] or Eriksonian practitioners.[19] But what may be the more significant observation is that the power to bring about these changes resides in an image of Christ *within the individual* rather than in the person of the psychotherapist (which is generally the case in standard hypnotic induction); and, as I hope to demonstrate throughout the remainder of this work, the image of Christ has considerably more power than anything those disciplines can offer, if the client is willing to internalize an image of Christ with the power to channel the Holy Spirit.

Academic psychology, in its concerted effort to be scientifically respectful, has all but divorced itself from the spiritual/ religious/ mythical universe of its origin, i.e. the study of the Soul. Academia would be, most decidedly, uncomfortable with the idea of evoking a Christ image in therapy. But in my own practice, I have come to see it as the single most powerful intervention I can encourage a client to undertake provided the client is willing to espouse even a modicum of faith in Christianity. Much of this chapter is devoted to illustrating how a Christ figure can be introduced and asked to provide guidance, alleviate guilt, remove shame, provide insight and transformation, exorcise felt experiences of evil, and heal the most painful and traumatic memories imaginable. That is also true of the chapters to follow. This book describes a Christ image with ever increasing powers to heal. In my fifty plus years of psychological training and clinical experience, I have never encountered another image – when used in conjunction with the *Light* – that provides such a consistent, unmitigated, power to heal the Mind, Heart, and Soul.

The *Light* has whatever power and protection the client requires when s/he goes inside. It is an instrument of inordinate power and peaceful security and, though it cannot assume the image and likeness of a human companion to accompany the client, it can readily evoke one. As clients progress in their inner work a need invariably arises for inner helpers / companions / guides. What I have come to appreciate is that the incarnate Christ has the potential to meet this need better than any other inner object, particularly in terms of its cultural power to function as a trusted guide and archetypal image of spiritual and psychological healing.

The inner world of imagination can be as awesome, mysterious, and dangerous as anything in the physical world; and it is often filled with fearsome images and traumatizing, paralyzing memories. As John Sanford [20] persuasively demonstrates, the 'Kingdom of God,' and all that infers, is within us as well as in the heavens. So too are the principalities and powers referred to by Peter and Paul. [21] Christ seems uniquely qualified to enter this realm and transform it on behalf of the willing Ego. The Christ figure is unique in symbolizing both human and divine nature. As distinct from other, purely human figures, the archetypal Christ has human understanding and divine resources. He willingly channels the Holy Spirit to all who ask and this is probably the most powerful antidote to shame available to the human Mind. Of all the mythological gods and goddesses of whatever pantheon, the figure of Jesus Christ seems by far the most trustworthy and most capable of healing within a Western perspective. Without question he is archetypal and mythical in aspect; he and his mother are the modern incarnation of all mother-son pairs in mythology. [22] But he is unique – mythologically – in having been born into human history as a human being for the sole purpose of redeeming humankind with the Holy Spirit's power of love and forgiveness. [23] God incarnates in a new way through Jesus Christ.[24] We call him the only begotten Son of God because he is seen as the model most worthy of emulation by the Heart and destined to bring God to all the nations of the World.

There are occasions when other images such as the Black Madonna, Virgin-Mother, even Mary Magdalene, or a Sophia-Christ figure can enact a healing role for some clients, particularly if they are fearful of internalized male figures. Such images are all derived from the historical figures of Mary or Christ. [25] I would caution, however, that the efficacy of such images is limited if the client cannot perceive the image as capable of channeling the Holy Spirit. A Madonna figure can channel the Holy Spirit by evoking it in the name of Jesus, just as human beings can prayerfully evoke the Holy Spirit in the name of the Father, Son, and Holy Spirit. But under no circumstances would I encourage the use of an ego-aspect, or the image of a human being that merely acted in a Christ-like manner. Such images are invariably hubristic. In my clinical experience all idealized self-images that seek to be Christ-like are surreptitiously seeking to supplant him. This can generally be ascertained by having the client query such an image to determine if it is prepared to *accept* Christ as its higher power. Invariably the answer is "no" – that it is essentially perfect and has no need to relate to him as a higher power. This type of ego-aspect is by any other name an idol. No ego-aspect can claim parity with a higher power, though not from lack of trying. When it does so it becomes – in effect – an Ideal-persona, an ego-aspect inflated by archetypal authority.

Also, while I unhesitatingly support Christ images that have been screened by the *Light*, I actively discourage clients from evoking any 'image' of God the Father. Unlike Christ and Mary, that image has no historical incarnations within the Gospels – other than a disembodied voice heard by Christ and John the Baptist [26] – and that leaves it too susceptible to gross distortions within the Mind. Though the Nicaean Creed declares the 'Father' a *person* of God, and therefore susceptible to personification, he is too easily misperceived as synonymous with the Godhead. [27] More to the point, in a patriarchal culture, a shaming, angry father is likely to imbue any 'God the Father' image with the worst attributes found in the Old Testament since there is no historical incarnation of *Abba* apart from Jesus Christ. Without the historical anchor of Christ, clients are too often forced to contend with contaminated 'God the Father' images that too often deny God's loving forgiveness and literally create idols made in the image and likeness of the client's father. While a Christ image can also be contaminated, those distortions can be corrected by referring back to the gospels' descriptions of Christ or by having the image re-screened by the *Light*. Referring back to the Old Testament for attributes of 'God the Father' is likely as not to reinforce negative distortions. For that reason, I discourage any use of father-God images. If the client insisted on such an image I would certainly not gainsay that choice, but I would encourage the client to explore his or her desire for a father image over a Christ image.[28]

The concept of 'God the Father' is contentious on a number of levels. I seek to address some of those issues in Appendix II. It is problematic because many clients unconsciously equate 'God the Father' with God Ineffable despite the fact that no theology – I am aware of – supports such an equation. What I have discovered is that the idea of 'God the Father' is frequently constellated with *Animus* energies that unconsciously bind individuals to this sense of God as their 'highest power,' even though they turn to Christ in all matters psychological and spiritual. It is very difficult to work directly with Animus/Anima archetypal energies. They are easily extracted from an image or even someone's sense of 'God the Father,' but the individual must then be provided an appropriate alternative. Only another archetypal image such as Christ will suffice. The series of interventions able to effect that kind of transformation are described in the last chapter.

The therapist should never assume that any particular image will automatically hold a positive value for the client. Even if the client attends a Christian church and has sought me out as a 'Christian counselor,' I am careful about suggesting the use of a Christ image in a therapy setting. At some point during inner work with the *Light* – when it seems appropriate, I will invite clients to use their *Light* to evoke an image that can intervene on their behalf in a given situation. By way of orientation, I might list a number of potential images, e.g. an image of Christ, a guardian angel, Quan Yin, the Blessed Virgin, etc. I will never suggest images that are likely to respond in a situation by a show of force. Also, I actively discourage clients from evoking an inner image of me (the sole exception being the examination of myself in their dreams, and that is very rare). Every religion and culture has images with inherent power to heal. But whatever the image, it is vital that the therapist never assume what will best serve the client. This is less likely to be an issue if the *Light* is used to evoke the image because the *Light* will not permit a forced fit. A 'forced' image will disappear when screened (see below for screening procedure).

Generally, if the client has been raised in a Christian denomination, the Christ image will be the first choice. But one of my clients, a married, practicing Catholic, terminated therapy for two years following my suggestion that she evoke a Christ image. When she returned two years and two therapists later she told me that the idea of *any male image in her mind*, even a Christ figure, was too threatening to her at the time I suggested it (although she was comfortable using only the *Light*). Similarly, the life experiences of some clients have instilled images of a judgmental, condemning or ineffectual Christ that alienates them from the idea of a powerfully loving and ever-forgiving image. Finally, it should be noted that many people imagine God/Christ as 'outside' of them, and they can be very fearful of any sense of presence within, particularly if they consciously struggle with shame and low self-esteem. In sum, the therapist is always encouraged to invite the client to evoke an inner image of Christ, but should never assume the client will be at ease with that image; and for that reason a lesser image may be more desirable at the outset. Many clients – including people of other faiths such as Islam or Judaism, are very comfortable evoking images of the Virgin Mary, a guardian angel, an Inner Self Helper [29] or Guide; [30] and those images can often demonstrate many healing behaviors. One crucial variable is the image's ability to channel the Holy Spirit. This is not requisite for most interventions, but as I stressed in the Chapter II, it seems crucial to issues of conscience and other issues of authority.

Even if male images per se are not a threat, the early experiences of some clients can deeply scar their formative image of Christ. My early work with one client in particular made me ponder whether Christ can incarnate by other names and gender when the formative images were traumatizing. This client was repeatedly abused by several Roman Catholic priests and nuns as well as her parents and others. She grew up in a city slum area and attended parochial grade schools. All of these adults made her responsible for their actions. It was impossible for her to evoke even a child Christ because of its strong negative association with the priests who taught her to believe they were the earthly representatives of Christ.[31] In early recovery from some of her memories this client sometimes relied on an image that she called the Loving Voice. While helpful, her Loving Voice seemed to lack Christ's power to heal and forgive. That seemed to change following a memory that actually involved her being tied to a large gold cross by one of the priests who then proceeded to rape the client's sister. In the midst of this particular recall, in which she saw herself as a child tied naked to a cross, the Loving Voice offered to take the child's place on the cross. It was one of the most Christ inspired experiences I have encountered. Let me stress that at no time – then or later, did this Loving Voice see herself as Christ. She was, in fact, quite willing to advocate for Christ and step aside as and when the client was prepared to trust an image of Christ. But after her 'crucifixion,' this Loving Voice began to function as a singular voice of love and forgiveness. For all practical purposes, she became a Sophia-Christ incarnation.[32] Another client, who also suffered from Multiple Personality Disorder (MPD), could not evoke a Christ image because of its strong associations with her abusing father, a Baptist minister. In that case, the *Light* was able to serve a healing, forgiving, function when used by other alters working in concert. Later in treatment she also began to rely on an Inner Self Helper who could definitely function in a loving manner. Both of these cases highlight the idea that an image by any other name may nonetheless function in a compassionate way. But the therapist needs to be discerning in such instances. It would be counter-productive to encourage *any self-image* that acts in a Christ-like manner. The Inner Self Helpers that I have encountered in working with MPD clients have all been 'other-than-self.' The client does not consider them another alter or fragment. They can function like Christ in many respects, but do not seek to supplant him in any way, as distinct from images of the Ideal-self, which do seek to supplant and thereby obviate the need for Christ. Any ego-aspect that offers itself as Christ-like is best treated as a persona of the Ideal-self much in need of redemption. The therapist should only encourage images that the client can clearly identify as not an aspect of the Ego. If the client cannot evoke a Christ image, then images other than ego-aspects can be helpful. As a rule of thumb, these images will be mythological in aspect, otherworldly, and clearly spiritual.

The efficacy and power of the Christ image in therapy is to some extent determined by the therapist. The image will have its greatest power for the client when the therapist can accept Christ as a *living presence* in the world of Mind, as a source of complete forgiveness for all our own misdeeds, as a source of healing for all misdeeds against us, and always sufficient in addressing any shadow or evil within us. The Christ image is not hampered by time or space. Christ can be everywhere at once – temporally as well as spatially, undoing the past as well as transforming the present. As a way of conceptualizing Christ's presence everywhere-at-once, I often use the illustration of holographic pictures. When a holographic negative is shattered each piece contains an image of the whole. Temporally, Christ cannot enter a memory and prevent it from happening; but he can enter the memory and undo its effects, and in that way he can go backwards in time. All memories in need of healing are painful now and therefore accessible to healing in the present. What Christ accomplishes in his regard is the transformation of emotions from negative to neutral-positive and the alteration of beliefs.

Some clients can become very angry

when the Christ image is evoked for the first time following the recall of a traumatic event. I have generally found this to be the case where parents were outwardly religious and actively involved with a church, perhaps even part of the ministry, but nonetheless physically, emotionally and/or sexually abusive toward their children. The client's anger appears to express a fear that since Christ/God is all-powerful he chose not to help: "Where was Christ when I needed him? If he is who they said he is, why did he allow this to happen?" This should not be *light*ly dismissed as an infantile expectation. When Christ seemingly failed to intervene, his absence reinforced the idea that whatever happened to the child was the child's fault. Abusive parents very often make the child responsible for the parents' actions: 'you are no good,' 'you are a slut, a whore,' 'you are shameful,' 'this is your fault,' 'you brought this on yourself.' Christ's failure to intervene – especially if the child prayed for his intervention – would seem to support the parent's judgments. Moreover, in order for catharsis to be complete, a Christ image is never asked to intervene in the midst of a recall (though spontaneous interventions should not be stopped). All must suffer the recall – client, counselor, and Christ – until it is completely remembered. Consequently, the first offer of a Christ intervention at the end of a recall may be met with anger and disbelief by the client. The Christ image – if it is present, willing suffers these recriminations and the counselor should permit the client to ventilate against Christ till the emotion is spent. Only afterward is it appropriate for the counselor to gently help the client make distinctions. In my experience, Christ is never harmed or put off by a client's need to vent in his presence.

Eventually, the client must be helped to understand that Christ's power is within the Heart and Mind. Christ endured his own suffering on the cross. The child is blameless, as Christ was blameless, for the abuse they both endured – his on the cross, the client in the recall. But the client still suffers the effects of that memory and s/he is encouraged to seek Christ *now* for his power to release the client from present suffering. He can release the child from the closed-loop repetition of abuse that the mind appears to compulsively repeat till it is brought to consciousness and resolved. Within the mind of the client, Christ can quicken the conscience of adults who inflicted the abuse.[33] He can forgive the client whatever s/he believed unforgivable;[34] and help the client identify and resolve long-standing resentments toward the abusers. Above all, he can be a source of unconditional love and protection against further harm. But a distinction must be made between the Body and Heart-Mind. The Body can be hurt, even destroyed. *Christ's power lies in healing whatever consequences, thoughts, feelings, beliefs, and images persist beyond the abusive act.*[35] Christ has the power to heal body memory, active imagination, nightmares, a persecuting conscience, and traumatizing authority. He can put an end to self-abuse and the compulsive reenactment of suffering, but for the original suffering, he can only offer up his own passion and crucifixion as proof that parents and culture can seek to shame and hurt the innocent and blameless.

THE INITIAL SCREENING OF ANY POSITIVE IMAGE

Whenever a healing, protective image is evoked for the first time – and most especially the Christ image, I generally ask that it be screened with the *Light* to insure it is a safe presence for the client. As a rule, I instruct the client in this procedure prior to evoking the image. Once the image appears within a circle drawn for that purpose, I tell the client *to enter the circle and touch the Light to the forehead, base of the throat, and chest of the image*. This ritual is not absolutely necessary. The image could be touched *anywhere* by the *Light*. I suggest the ritual because it has a nice feel to it, but the merest contact of *Light* and image is sufficient for screening. Infrequently – but with sufficient frequency to warrant the procedure, the image will disappear when screened in this manner. I do not know why. For some reason the image has posed a threat; or perhaps the client needs to be reassured that the image is subordinate to the *Light* and his or her free will. Whatever the reason, I simply accept that it happens and ask the client to once more ask the *Light* to evoke the chosen image and again screen it using the *Light*. I cannot recall an instance where a Christ image failed this screening on the second pass. In general, the procedure is only needed the first time an image is evoked; thereafter, the image acquires an identity for the client that is unmistakable. *However, it is always advisable to re-screen the image if the client reports that it has changed in some significant way*. An example of this is given further on. Of note, this procedure can be used to screen any image, not just images of Christ.

There is a notable exception to the above procedure. *Today, I frequently use the Christ image to introduce the Light.* [36] If the client says s/he is comfortable evoking a Christ image, then I will have Christ find and give the *Light* to the client. For some clients this actually works better than having them seek out the *Light* using the protocol described in the previous chapter. Some clients have difficulty imaging a seemingly autonomous *Light*, but are quite willing to receive it if handed to them by a Christ image. In that situation, after finding a safe place, I will suggest that Christ come to them with the *Light* in his hand and give it to them. Or, I have them ask Christ to reach behind his back with his hand, and bring the *Light* out from behind his back. In effect, the Christ image and the *Light* appear simultaneously such that the *Light* has screened the Christ image by virtue of his holding it. [37] Once the client has accepted the *Light* from Christ, I then walk him or her through the remainder of the protocol used to introduce the *Light*, as described in the previous chapter. Christian counselors such as the Linns[38] have used the Christ image for years without recourse to the *Light*. However, I am frankly reticent to do any inner work without it other than the preparatory work needed by the client to access it. In my clinical practice, use of the Christ image remains optional since I work with clients of many different faiths and belief orientations, but I will not embark on any inner work without the *Light*.

The appearance of a Christ figure is rarely extraordinary. He generally appears in a robe and sandals and of average height. One client visualized him informally dressed in a shirt and jeans. On rare occasions, he has appeared as a *light*-form. This latter image appears to represent Christ resurrected, while the 'robe and sandal' Christ seems to represent an historical Christ or Sunday school Christ. I always ask the client regarding his appearance and accept whatever image is conveyed – provided it passes the screening. Typically, clients do not have a clear image of the face. On rare occasions, there may be eye contact between Christ and the client. Invariably, the contact is described as conveying unconditional love that visibly moves the client.

As noted earlier, Christ's appearance will remain constant in successive sessions. On rare occasions the image may change. Whenever that happens something powerful within the Mind has taken possession of the image. The client should be cautioned of this possibility, even though its occurrence is rare, and asked to immediately report any such change. In turn, the therapist should immediately instruct the client to contain that altered image within a circle, or screen it again with the *Light*. Not all such alterations are considered harmful. In several instances they were found to represent the emergence of a more vital Christ image. The caution is given for those instances where other images seek to act with a Christ-like authority by superimposing themselves upon the Christ image. In all such instances, the client is aware of a distinct difference. If the shift is positive, the new image will not object to submitting to the *Light*'s scrutiny; if negative, it will actively resist re-screening.

OTHER HEALING AND NURTURING FIGURES

Very often, particularly in cases of severe childhood abuse where there may be extensive recalls, I encourage the client to let the *Light* create a house or pastoral setting to shelter any children encountered during inner work.[39] This is especially helpful in working with MPD clients whose repeated trauma has forced them to create numerous – often childlike, alters and fragments. Since the client *returns to me* at the end of any inner work there is sometimes the sense of leaving a child self behind and unattended. To offset any further sense of abandonment, the *Light* can be asked to evoke a nurturing 'mother' or caretaker, someone who always remains in a created shelter to care for whomever is brought there. Whenever a caretaking image is evoked for the first time I ask that it also be screened by the *Light* in the manner described above; and to give us a name by which it will be known. On occasion this might be a given name; often it is simply referred to as "mother" – obviously an idealized mother, and frequently a Mother-of-Christ or Demeter-like mother. These caretakers are not evoked in lieu of Christ but in addition to him. If the client was unwilling to evoke a Christ figure I would still invite him or her to evoke any figure that extended a nurturing love and protection to the child including real people such as grandmothers living or deceased. Of note, clients who are unwilling to evoke a Christ figure may nonetheless be willing to evoke a guardian angel. A number of people who are otherwise agnostic have reported experiences of angelic intervention. One client, who considered himself a Jewish atheist, selected Mother Teresa of Calcutta, in a time of need, to good effect. I would also note that some women, especially, might need a feminine figure such as the Great Mother, Earth Mother, Virgin Mother, or a Goddess, as integral to their healing. [40] Such images generally evolve later in therapy. Invariably, wherever I have assisted clients in identifying and using these images, they are compatible (sic) non-competitive with the Christ image. Often, the two images work in tandem with each other.

In the chapter on Temporal authority, I explore at some length the search for a mother who can satisfy the needs of a Pre-moral aspect. These are very young ego-aspects that have been abandoned or severely neglected. Their existence often accounts for schizoid tendencies and other problems identified by Object Relationists. Christ can play an instrumental role in finding a mother capable of meeting the needs of such images. Christ can also serve as a transition object in such cases. He is particularly helpful where the client identifies a particular image – such as the Rejected-aspect or Pre-moral aspect, but is initially unwilling to connect with it, even while appreciating that the image in question may be vital to his or her well being. On such occasions the Christ figure will readily hold and care for that rejected but vital aspect of the client. For one client, the Christ figure carried a sleeping infant for several months, nurturing it till the client was ready to take responsibility for it's care and eventual integration (it represented the core personality of a woman with multiple personalities). In another case, he carried the 'child-abandoned-by-the-mother' who had also been abandoned by the client when she became a teen-ager. In still another instance, he carried a small witch-like creature about the size of an infant till the client was ready to address it's meaning: it represented the initial fervor of her spirituality that had sprung up but was then squelched in adolescence.

IMAGES ENCOUNTERED ON GOING INSIDE

When our gaze turns inward everything is possible. Every creation of humankind, sacred or profane, flows from the inner world. Christ is but one image, albeit crucial to our work. In this section, I want to briefly describe some of the images a client and therapist may encounter on going inside. Some are common to most people and some are quite rare as in the case of alter personalities and 'other lights.' The following descriptions are offered, first, as a way of providing a context for further discussion of the Christ figure and reasons for his involvement in the inner work. Beyond that, it will apprise the counselor of potentially unplanned-for-encounters that can occur when the client goes inside. The unconscious is always active and does not ask our permission before making its self felt. I rarely go inside without an agenda, but the 'powers' residing in the unconscious also have agendas and when the client turns inward our two worlds are joined. At such times, it is good to remember that the client is never without the *Light* in time of need. It has never failed to provide a circle of protection or circle of containment. Indeed, most of the images described below are usually encountered only after a circle has been drawn to contain the client's felt experience of the image. Finally, none of the categories used here should be treated as inviolate or ironclad. The unconscious is an emergent function: it creates and recreates anew. Just know that whenever someone goes inside all things are possible. What I am describing here are only some of the possibilities, most of which correlate with Jungian archetypes.

By far, the most common images encountered on going inside are images of the self: ego-aspects, which I also refer to as self-aspects. (Later in the chapter, I will discuss the work of R.C. Schwartz who advocates alternative methods of working with this multiplicity of selves. He calls them 'parts' of the self.) Anyone who engages in this work will quickly confirm this multiplicity phenomenon: the Ego is not singular except as an archetypal energy. The pretence of singularity can be maintained in a didactic setting but is quickly dispelled the moment one goes inside. Without exception, all clients will exhibit Ego fragmentation.

Aspects of the Ego are frequently at odds with each other. This is inevitable since in most cases new ego-aspects are created to cope with situations that previously dominant ego-aspects were unable to manage. In addition to being normally polarized, ego-aspects – as well as images of others, are also susceptible to instinctual (Body) and archetypal (Soul) influences. Within the context of those myriad influences and conflicts, the role of the *Aware-ego* is unique. It is the only ego-aspect influenced solely and *consciously* by the archetypal authority governing the *Light*. It is not the purest expression of that authority. Christ can use his own *Light* when called upon to do so, and in principle that is considered a more powerful or purer manifestation. But phenomenally, the Aware-ego is the first ego-aspect called into conscious existence to receive the *Light* and use it. In this it is distinctly different from other ego-aspects created to contend with each other or unconsciously enthralled by bodily instinct or soulful authority. More to the point, if the client is asked to go inside for the purpose of finding the *Light*, the Aware-ego normally becomes the first ego-aspect encountered on going inside.

Self-Images

Other theorist-clinicians use different names to categorize ego-aspects. For example, the Stones – whose work is discussed later in the chapter, categorize ego-aspects as primary or disowned selves. R.C. Schwartz, also discussed later in the chapter, identifies three major categories of ego-aspects: managers/protectors, exiles, and firefighters. He refers to them as 'parts' rather than selves or ego-aspects. In this work the term 'ego-aspect' is comparable to the 'selves' and 'parts' nomenclature used by those other authors. My term highlights the self's archetypal origin. As an archetypal energy Ego is seen to constellate numerous aspects of itself. What manifests in the Mind are constellations of the Ego, or more simply, ego-aspects. Ego-aspects are further identified in this work by the archetypal energies shaping them, i.e. Temporal, Moral and Relational authority. Thus, for example, in the Chapter addressing Temporal authority, I identify several categories of ego-aspects shaped by that authority, such as the Coping aspect, the Pre-moral aspect and the Temporal-persona. In the chapter addressing Moral authority, I identify four more major categories: Ideal-self, Rejected-self, Ego-in-conflict, and Dominant selves. It needs to be stressed that these are types, not a specific ego-aspect. Within an individual, for example, there can be several different Rejected-selves. What they would all share in common is their bondage to shame; but the specific motivation of each ego-aspect will be determined by the polarity of a specific set of opposites, e.g. masculine/feminine, weak/strong, positive/negative, feeling/thinking, etc. Polarity is discussed in the next chapter.

Throughout this work, I frequently use the nomenclatures offered by R.C. Schwartz and the Stones in referring to ego images. Primary selves, protectors/managers, and Dominant selves are seen to co-exist with the Aware-ego. These are the ego-aspects that generally assume responsibility for governing the client's daily behavior. They – not the Aware-ego, are generally in charge when the client is going about his or her daily business. When inside, the primary self or protector co-conscious with an Aware-ego will vigilantly monitor the Aware-ego's actions and be ready to interfere or make its presence felt if what the Aware-ego is asked to do threatens it. Any suggestions made to the Aware-ego will not pose a threat to it because the Aware-ego is 'constitutionally' willing to engage any part of the psyche however abhorrent to the other parts. It is the primary selves, aptly called the Manager, Controller, Problem Solver, etc., who will most strongly object to suggestions put to the Aware-ego. As regards the treatment of these selves, therapy consists in first helping the Aware-ego contain and separate from these primary selves, extending protections to them, and then asking them to identify their disowned opposites. This is discussed in greater detail later in this chapter, and more extensively in all later chapters. (Of note, when working with clients, I generally 'personalize' these selves by assigning them attribute names which the client and I have agreed upon, e.g. Controller, Pouty, Rigid, Critic, Doubter, etc. Of further note, those names are likely to 'evolve' as the ego-aspect is healed.)

Finally, there is a special class of ego-aspects that have the power to assume total control of consciousness for limited periods of time. These are the self-aspects called alters as defined by Dissociative Identity Disorder (also called MPD or Multiple Personality Disorder). Each alter strives to function as a total personality and may in fact have several ego-aspects co-existing as components of that personality.

When an alter is in control of consciousness, it generally denies awareness of other alters until treatment reveals their existence. This 'amnesia' regarding other alters is the MPD's primary defense. It allows certain alters to function as if there was no history of abuse. Such denial can persist despite years of therapy and the revelation of horrendous memories by other alters. [41]

The Aware-ego is capable of containing any and all alter personalities. The Aware-ego is capable of co-existing with any alter personality. While working with MPD clients can be exceedingly complex and trying, the protocol remains the same. The Aware-ego assumes responsibility whenever the client goes inside. I have worked with a wide range of MPD clients over the years and this methodology has proven to be both effective and advantageous in all cases. In many instances, it is actually the process by which alter personalities are first identified.

In contrast to the exclusionary quality of alter personalities, the ego-aspects of most people *co-exist* in consciousness. The work of R. C. Schwartz and Hal and Sidra Stone described later in the chapter completely support this conclusion. Ego-aspects function much like a group of individuals, though more often like a family group than a democratic group. As with some families, there can be considerable estrangement, even cutoffs, among these co-existing self-aspects, but none can claim the power to completely control consciousness even while they may seek to dominate it. I have yet to work with a client who did not exhibit the existence of several co-existing ego-aspects. Treatment seeks to foster a harmonious co-existence among these ego-aspects by altering their inner dynamics and asking them to become open to Christ's higher authority. For all practical purposes this requires that the ego-aspects learn to exercise willingness and acceptance among themselves. Where therapy with MPD clients is successful, they too will have learned to function as co-existing self-aspects that exercise willingness rather than willfulness.

Appreciating the co-existence of ego-aspects in consciousness is critical to understanding an individual's inner dynamics. All ego-aspects have the ability to influence physiology, mood, and behavior since each exerts a modicum of free will. This observation does not gainsay the traditional Christian view of free will as all-powerful. But where every ego-aspect has a modicum of free will, it is understandable how free will can appear to be thwarted, as each fragmented ego-aspect seeks to dominate others or express a conflicting view. To quote St. Paul's famous dictum: "I do not do the good I want, but the evil I do not want is what I do (Rom. 7:19)." Again, therapy seeks to teach each of these ego-aspects the power of acting willingly rather than willfully. The Aware-ego models this activity and extends the opportunity for it to every ego-aspect contained by the *Light*.

What distinguishes ego-aspects – not otherwise enthralled by the Body or Soul, is their preference for specific emotions and/or defense mechanisms in response to internal and external stress.[42] In general, defense mechanisms manifest as disruptions of thinking and feeling, projection of disowned qualities, somatic dissociation and/or the expression of specific emotional states. If a client begins expressing uncharacteristic emotions such as paranoia, or despondency, or acute somatic symptoms, e.g. headache, sinus problems, stomach upset, etc., or making globally negative or positive statements, or precipitously shifting moods, it is generally because consciousness is being dominated by a particular ego-aspect that is seeking to hold the Aware-ego in check and control the individual's perception and behavior. These self-aspects can be contained when discerned, their dominance notwithstanding. It does help on such occasions to have Christ's help. One method I have found to work with them is the *contain and invest* intervention described later in the chapter. Essentially, that intervention delimits the activity of a willful self-aspect while simultaneously offering it willingness options and protections. No willful self-aspect can exert greater power than the Aware-ego exercising the *Light*'s willingness. Only willingness can achieve penultimate expressions of free will within the Mind. Clients may doubt this initially because particular self-aspects will have been willfully dominant for much of their lives. But once the client and/or therapist have identified the characteristic responses of a particular ego-aspect, it is always possible to ask the *Light* to contain and separate the ego-aspect from the Aware-ego by the exercise of willingness.

Protectors

I will frequently refer to a primary self as a protector. R.C. Schwartz identifies his primary selves as protectors and managers.[43] Most clients will manifest a number of protectors. But the term is also used in MPD literature, and though there is much overlaps between these two uses, there are notable differences. I first encountered protectors while working with MPD clients. They are commonly referred to by that name in the MPD literature. They are alters who seem to take on the personality characteristics of a perpetrator such as an abusing parent, for the purpose of keeping other alters quiet and incognito. In MPD there are generally a group of alters who are children. The 'protector,' often male, will be tyrannically and emotionally abusive to these children to keep them from sharing the truth of their abuse with others. The intent is to protect the client from exposure and possible retaliation. These alters, because they are often male, have a macho attitude and may even pretend to like some forms of abuse such as sodomy. When encountered, the *Light* can contain them. In such instances it is always helpful to use a double circle since protectors often assume personas - like the wizard of Oz, as a means of reinforcing their dictates. Protectors who assume a disguise are generally revealed to be children themselves, often about the same age as the children they are attempting to keep silent. Generally, protectors also have abuse memories. It is vital that protectors be helped to share their memories for only then can they become more empathic and positively support the other children.

While MPD and their concomitant protectors are rare, there are several kinds of protector images discernible in most clients. The most common are self-images. But others can assume an image that is other-than-self. Those images will function as 'firewalls' that allow ego-aspects to separate from unacceptable impulses, and the events that generated them, but nonetheless have access to some aspect of the experience such as sexual arousal. I first discovered this phenomenon during the exploration of a client's recurring sexual fantasy. In this particular fantasy the client was always required to submit in a humiliating way to the dictates of an older man. While always humiliating, this fantasy was one of the few ways she could sexually arouse herself and use that desire to escape severe bouts of depression. The older man in this fantasy seemed very much like her father who, in real life, severely and repeatedly shamed all of his children, battered his wife, then used her sexually, and very likely had sex with at least one of his daughters. At one point, I decided to have her challenge the older man's authority. She did this, first, by containing his image in a circle and transporting them both to a sunny secluded beach where she remembered feeling very relaxed. This change of scene introduced a parity, both of them sitting at ease in chairs outdoors. I then had her ask him questions concerning another issue we had been talking about earlier. When she refused to accept his evasions, he suddenly became cooperative and very revealing! Basically, what he conveyed was the fact that he protected her from many of her abuse memories, particularly shameful sexual memories. Essentially, in his role as the older man who dominated her, he took full responsibility for her sexual impulses. Since many of her earliest memories involved shameful situations he allowed her to recapitulate their arousal without being responsible for it. But more importantly, he kept the memories a secret from her; in effect, he functioned as a wall between her and the memories, protecting her from conscious knowledge of them. This was born out in the following weeks when, through continuing dialogue, he revealed crucial parts of several memories. Significantly, as this dialogue continued, his demeanor also changed. He continued to function as her protector, but now quite openly and in new and often powerful ways. For one thing, it was he – rather than Christ – who would be instrumental in initially altering the Relational authority of the parents; though whenever this client felt particularly threatened she was quick to call on her image of Christ.

Sexual fantasy is discussed further in the chapter on Relational authority. Suffice to say, it often serves a multivariate role. As in the case above, recurrent sexual fantasy, or acting out, serves to 'manage' sexual impulses, which most people must contend with in some way, more or less, on a daily basis. If great shame is associated with sexual desire, then the Ego must find ways of coping with the body's instinct that allows it some form of expression while simultaneously curtailing the threat of shame. A masochistic stance serves this purpose. For example, a client who habitually has rape fantasies is using that particular setting to experience sexuality without being responsible for the actions needed to arouse her. Of note, sexual fantasy may also be serving an even more vital purpose of temporarily overcoming discordant gender aspects. That issue is also addressed in the chapter on Relational authority.

Particular setting conditions can also function in a protector role by hiding or shadowing disowned/dissociated aspects. When actively seeking to identify self-aspects, some clients will find themselves confronted with areas of seemingly impenetrable darkness or other kinds of 'walls' or invisibility (denial) that serve the purpose of a firewall. As a rule, the client finds it nearly impossible to penetrate these dark places even with the *Light*. There are several ways to address this 'resistance.' The most effective way I have found is to first separate the aspect that is fearful of this darkness from the Aware-ego. Next provide the separated aspect with a portion of the *Light* and encourage it to use the *Light* to create a garment of protection for itself that will allow it to fearlessly approach whatever is in the darkness or behind the wall. Examples of this intervention are given further in the chapter.

In general, all protectors mirror the Law of Connection described in the first chapter – the idea that in the Mind nothing is actually separate; every image potentially functions like a wall connecting us to whatever is on the other side. In effect, every protector implicitly points to another self in need of protection. For example, there is no way to completely suppress our sexual impulses though many of them are made frightful, negative and conflictual by cultural mores. Protectors appear to function as 'walls' between those impulses that conflict with an Ideal-self. Protectors that assume the identity of other people are most often found in masturbatory fantasy, but by no means restricted to it. In such cases, the protector in the fantasy (e.g. 'the slut') is the active participant expressing the sexuality, however deviant, thereby freeing an ego-aspect from responsibility for the deviance. Identifying protectors is often one of the best ways to help the client begin to get in touch with a Rejected-self, which often contains a strong sexual component. Historically, Christianity has acted repressively toward all expressions of sexuality except the procreative function within marriage. The more fundamentalist the client's parents, the more likely sex will be developmentally associated with the shame, fear, and the punishment of an unredeemed conscience. Consequently, the client must often contend with a Rejected-self that is deeply sensual and sexual but walled behind 'pornographic' protectors.

I address a third group of protectors in the chapter on Temporal authority where I discuss the creation of Mirror aspects. These are ego-aspects that emulate the behavior of an abusive parent. Essentially, they mirror the problematical behavior of the parent – most often anger. This mirroring allows them to go toe-to-toe with the parent, at least in their imagination. Mirror aspects are frequently responsible for characterological anger found in adults.

Images of People Known to the Client

Aside from ego-aspects, images of other people are the most commonly encountered images addressed in therapy. These are the mind's created representations of people in the physical world, e.g. mother, father, spouse, sibling, friend, neighbor, etc. The power and authority embedded in these images is a major focus of this work. In therapy, every effort is made to distinguish these images from the people they are said to represent. Wherever possible I remind the client: "There are two of each person: there is the person-out-in-the-world going about his or her daily business (or dead and buried), and then there is the image of that person in your Mind. It is the image within that guides much of your behavior. Change that internal image, or how you relate to it, and your responses to that person-out-in-the-world will also change." Initially, this distinction is difficult for many people to grasp since they are inclined to equate the image representing a person with the person-out-in-the-world. The two are not the same, and the inner image is by far the most powerful. The 'face of conscience' is a case in point. Any image that speaks for conscience is exceedingly powerful and the client will initially equate it with a person-out-in-the-world, which effectively binds the client to that person's authority. Every effort must be made to help the client distinguish these two realities: the world of physical bodies and the interior world governed by Spirit, Soul and Mind, and the Mind's experience of Body.

When going inside, images of others rarely appear in the inner landscape without being actively evoked and, if protocol has been followed, they are generally evoked within a circle. As a rule, the client simply directs the *Light* to draw a circle and place the image of the person within it. Whenever an image appears unannounced, which is rare, I immediately suggest it be contained by a circle of *Light*. For example, as one client was preparing to explore symptoms suggesting early sexual trauma, the images of her father and mother spontaneously appeared. She contained them, but immediately sensed they were present to support and encourage her effort. She experienced their presence as a relief since it indicated she was not likely to discover them as one of her abusers. The unevoked presence of an image is rare and it generally comes as a show of support; but it only takes an instant to have a circle drawn by the *Light*. *Images can change.* All images are comprised of psychic energy that can be altered by unconscious operations as well as consciously altered by interventions using the *Light* and/or Christ image. But short of intervention or unconscious actuation, images of people-out-in-the-world tend to be stable over time.

The constellation of images by Anima and Animus energies is a frequent cause of conflict and distortion. Such constellations can occur early in a client's life such that they become an inherent part of an image whether it is a self-image or image of another. The individual has little control over such constellations as they are dictated by the archetype not the Ego. Jung devoted considerable reflection to these constellations. They are touched upon in most of his Collected Works. His initial therapeutic efforts generally focused on addressing Shadow issues, but the greater part of his therapy focused on Animus and Anima complexes. I address the issue of the unconscious constellations of both self and other in the last chapter, which specifically addresses anima/animus issues.

Animals

I have had relatively little experience with animals. Early on, before I began actively encouraging the use of the Christ figure, I might occasionally suggest that the client ask the *Light* to bring an animal that could act as a guardian companion. If the animal was chosen by the *Light*, it never failed to function in that role. I still use this intervention if the client suggests it or is unable to evoke a higher power.

In my experience, whenever animals are encountered, it is generally helpful to examine them for their symbolic meaning. For example, one client was strongly identified with a horse she had as a teenager; she generally found her *Light* in the barn where the horse was kept. One day I suggested that she imagine riding the horse bareback without saddle or bridle since she had ridden horses for many years. She immediately replied that she could not, that she did not have the balance, composure, or freedom to do so. Later in that same session, while discussing her role in the family, she identified herself as being like the pet dog. She was encouraged to examine the dog through the *Light* for its symbolic meaning. The dog was identified as devoted, loyal, responsive, and easily shamed if it failed to be attentive. When asked to contrast the dog with her horse the first thing that came to her was that the horse could not be shamed since it is hard to shame an animal when you are looking up to it. Also, it was more "its own person." It was obvious she would be a much different person in her family if she could be more like a horse in their midst. For the reader interested in pursuing this topic, I would note that Gallegos [44] has worked extensively with 'inner animals' as representative of our selves and as correlates of chakra energies.

OTHER LIGHTS, CHRIST LIGHT, FORMS, AND IMAGES OF OTHERS

Other *light*s are perhaps the strangest, and rarest, phenomena I have had to address in thousands of hours of inner work. My first encounter with this phenomenon occurred while working with a client diagnosed as MPD. In the process of discovering and containing a very young alter, the client identified the presence of a "sickly green *light*," which her *Light* was able to contain on request. She described this *light* as a "presence," distinctly different from the images she normally saw inside and basically formless, much like her own *Light* but sickly green in color. It was eventually identified as the presence of her deceased grandmother. Of note, her grandfather was one of the client's primary abusers in early infancy and childhood, often using her as a substitute for his deceased wife (with the parents' collusion). The client was certain that this "other *light*" was not an alter, though it was closely identified with a particular alter who felt befriended by it; and it was that alter who carried the memories of the grandfather's early abuse. After several exploratory sessions it was decided to give this *light* to Christ for deposition. The actual process was quite simple since the client generally had Christ with her whenever she went inside. She asked her *Light* to bind the sickly green *light* in the name of Jesus and commanded it to go with Him.

Another early experience with this phenomenon involved a woman who was very interested in Native American spirituality and had been actively seeking an Indian spirit guide before coming into therapy. Concurrently, she was also involved in a study of *The Course In Miracles*, which seemingly conflicted with her first interest since it advocates Christ and the Holy Spirit as guide. What happened surprised us both. She was very adept at finding and learning to use her *Light*; and *the very first time* she went inside she found herself in the presence of another *light* which her *Light* was able to contain in a circle. When asked, her *Light* identified the other *light* as a Native American spirit guide named Running Deer Woman. She decided to keep the Indian spirit contained till she could resolve whom she wanted as her guide. She deliberated over several sessions – which also involved getting in touch with her inner image of Christ (who appeared to her as an image, not another *light*). I had her contain this presence only because it presented itself as another *light*, not because it purported to be a spirit or guide. Frankly, I was being cautious having never previously encountered another *light* claiming to be a disincarnate spirit. Finally, after several sessions and what I suspect was considerable deliberation, the client chose Christ as her guide. He, in turn, was given the task of removing Running Deer Woman who – according to the client – went quite unwillingly, but was nonetheless obliged to go. I might note here that much later in therapy this client would use the *Light* to get in touch with an image of her great-grandfather, a Native American Indian; and apparently it was her desire to link with him that had motivated her to study Indian lore in the first place.

The discovery of 'other *light*s' is comparatively rare. What seems to distinguish them from images is their lack of bodily form: they appear to be experienced by the client as a formless, *light*-like presence rather than an image. The clients' descriptions have generally conveyed to me an otherworldly presence attached to the individual's psyche rather than an inherent part of it. The difficulty they pose for the therapist is in the nature of the beast: what are they, what do they represent? I have yet to read a description elsewhere that specifically describes the presence of other *light*s other than those described by people reporting near-death experiences. However, to the best of my knowledge, no one uses the *Light* as described in this book; and the method may account for this particular manifestation. In practice, wherever the client identifies another *light* as the spirit of a deceased person, I have decided to treat them as just that. This necessitates positing a world of Spirit, which most of academia would treat as an unacceptable assumption. From my perspective the operable word is *belief*. If someone believes in spirits then that belief has the power to affect a person's life for good or ill. However, naming the phenomenon may be less important than the fact that it can be contained by the *Light* on request, and whether real or imagined, it can be redeemed and removed by the client's image of Christ. As a rule, I am generally inclined to recommend removal since the spirits do not appear to be an inherent part of the psyche, and according to other authors, the client may experience symptoms associated with the spirit. [45] I have found that to be the case for several clients who I describe later in the book. Of note, none of my clients have had to 'exorcise' these other *light*s without the assistance of a Christ image; however, it is possible to do so without a Christ image or the *Light* by using the methodologies described by Fiori [46] and Modi. [47]

The Christ Light

My first encounter with Christ *Light* was via a Christ intervention of a client's dream. Until then, I had been essentially oblivious to the possibility of Christ having his own *Light*. On the first occasion I encountered this, the client dreamed a house that seemed symbolic of her Self (the proverbial mansion of many rooms). The house had a porch that did not fit the rest of the house in that it was fortress-like. The *Light* identified it as providing a false sense of security. When I suggested that she seek an inner source of strength to replace this false exterior her Christ image took her to the basement of the house. Interestingly, the cellar was actually described as larger than the house as it had many passages, all leading to the left; paradoxically, Christ led her to the right hand corner – the darkest corner. In that corner he unearthed a *light* and handed it to her - it was bigger than the *Light* she carried, and brighter, "more Christ's than mine."

She then reflected on the idea that lots of people thought Christ was weak, but his sense of Self did not require the approval of others. From this she gained the insight that she did not have to be the image she believed others demanded of her. At that point, Christ put the *light* he had been holding back into the corner; and she returned to the outside of the house to find the porch transformed: "The same concrete base... but not hard and rigid... the rail is softer... ivy growing around it... inviting." I no time during the session did I feel the need to contain that particular *light*.

Beginning with that client's particular experience, I became increasingly comfortable suggesting to clients that they ask their image of Christ to use his *Light* in many situations. For example, today I would encourage the client to ask Christ to use his *Light* whenever there is need for healing; and all of the energy work described in later chapters is predicated on Christ's use of his *Light* to draw circles, terminate undue influences, convict with the power of the Holy Spirit, and much more.

Sometimes, the Christ *Light* is the only viable solution through an impasse. One male client was very good at visualization until it was decided that he and Christ would enter a cave on the heels of two images representing his feminine. He did not enter during that session and for the next several months his ability to concentrate and visualize diminished dramatically. During this period, I attempted to have him work on a variety of issues, all to little or no effect. Finally, I encouraged him to return to the cave near the end of a session. As he sought to approach the entrance, a "wind" blew out his *Light*; actually, as he described it later, a big fart! And he sensed a disdainful laughter from the fart-maker from somewhere within the cave. In the next session, we returned to the cave entrance. Essentially, my objective was to have him contain the fart-maker with his *Light*. No success. I asked him to imagine what was in the cave that was draining his willingness, snuffing it out. He began to speculate about having to encounter his "true self" and being damned by it. At this point, I suggested he ask Christ to contain the cave guardian with Christ's *Light*. Almost immediately, Christ contained darkness within a circle. When I asked him to have Christ transform the darkness into *light*, the whole cave lit up and the client got a glimpse of himself as a miniscule male in an immense cave symbolizing a vaginal, feminine, cosmos. He did not feel threatened at this point, he was, rather, in awe of it, and overwhelmed by its incomprehensibility. When I asked about the role of the masculine in this universe, a voice replied that its only purpose was to produce sperm so the feminine could procreate. The dialogue evolved over a number of sessions, and as one might suspect, the client's appreciation of the feminine was greatly altered. But that is another story. What I want to stress here is the role of Christ's *Light*. If the client is willing, Christ can bring him or her into situations, so archetypal in their power, that our mortal willingness seems insufficient to approach it.

Distinguishing Ego-Aspects and Light Forms

As the forgoing discussion makes clear, the therapist needs to distinguish between 'other *light*s' and aspects of the self. There are many "prayer warrior" Christians intent on exorcising anything not acceptable within the narrow confines of fundamentalist behavior. I have encountered very, very little in the human Mind in need of exorcism, but a great deal in need of redemption and transformation. As Pogo said, "We have met the enemy and it is us'uns." Nothing in the human Mind can be destroyed. I do not know what happens when a light form is given to

Christ. I know he does not destroy it. From my perspective, it is much the same as when I commend spirits of the departed to his eternal care. The only time I have employed an exorcising formula, such as that described by the Linns,[48] has been in those few instances where the client seemed to be experiencing a distinctly evil presence. On one occasion, the client described a palpable sense of evil evoked in the context of recovering a memory of ritual abuse, and then I did fervently, but silently, say a prayer of exorcism till the presence was visually contained and remanded to her Christ image. But even in such instances, I have modified the prayer to ask Christ to transform whatever has been contained into pure white light, and return it to the source of all *Light*. [49]

The best procedure, whenever something unexpected is encountered, is to begin by having the *Light* contain whatever has become the focus of attention. There are aspects of the Ego very like the Wizard of Oz who would have you believe they have powers well beyond their ken. Often, the use of a double circle enables the client to extract that ego-aspect from its fantasy distortion. Remember too, that one objective of this work is the engagement and transformation of the Rejected-self. That aspect can be extremely abhorrent to primary ego-aspects when first encountered; as can other ego-aspects with strong shadow qualities or the darker aspects of anima and animus. Inevitably, if you go inside often enough, you will encounter the palpably daunting. But with willingness, the *Light* and image of Christ will answer with loving, unflinching, assurances of safety and resolution.

In my practice, I have never encountered anything approximating *possession* by an evil spirit but were I to do so, based on what I have read, [50] I would never attempt an exorcism. I would be willing to document the need and refer the client to a priest or minister. It should be noted, however, that most theologies that address this issue recognize that spirits can affect people without possessing them. That is, a spirit can be said to tempt or harass an individual as well as possess them. In Roman Catholic theology, a prayer of deliverance said by any believing person has the power to free the individual from the bondage of the temptation/harassment, even if the prayer is said silently and without the client's awareness. [51] I have encountered clients who appeared to be tempted and/or harassed by such spirits – all of them containable by their *Light*. On occasion these spirits are described as having a light quality in appearance with names such as 'control' or 'lust' or 'fear.' What makes them distinctive is the conjoining of *light* and image such that the light is identified with a shape rather than constituting the shape. Again, I believe we are dealing here with an issue of belief governing perception. From my perspective, the important thing is the existence of a viable solution in calling upon the Christ image. As a rule, I would first employ a double-circle to extract any self-aspect hidden within or attached to such an image. If none are found, I would then suggest to the client that s/he ask the Christ image to transform the image into pure white light and return it to the source of all light. If there is a sense that the light presence is the disincarnate soul of a deceased person, then I would simple remand it to Christ's eternal care.

I am inclined to identify 'other lights' as spirits, though I generally refer to them as 'autonomous emotions.' But however defined, the phenomenon is containable by the *Light* and that seems the decisive factor. If therapist and client accept that what has been contained is a spirit, then they can address a prayer of deliverance to Christ. I have not had to deal with one of these 'spirits' without the Christ figure. I have already noted that Fiori [52] describes a technique for exorcising the spirits of deceased persons which does not require the presence of a Christ figure, but does require a belief in an after-life and the near-death literature; however, her procedure is only applicable to disincarnate spirits, i.e. spirits of deceased persons, not to spirits of evil. Crabtree [53] also describes a methodology for dealing with infestations from living people and spirits. Kenneth McAll describes another effective method that I have frequently used.[54] It involves the client receiving Eucharist on behalf of the deceased person – a method that I have found particularly helpful in removing any vestiges of guilt concerning abortions, stillbirths or miscarriages. But again, this solution requires belief in the power of Christ and the Eucharist.

All of the world's religions and shamanistic beliefs [55] have rituals for the exorcism of spirits so if they are merely a 'figment of the imagination' they are not merely a figment of the Christian imagination! Finally, it must be noted that just about every deliverance-type of intervention emphasizes the need for further work following an actual deliverance; in particular, the healing of whatever psychological emotion/wound/memory allowed the spirit's admission in the first place. The Rejected-self and other aspects commonly referred to as shadow images are clearly vulnerable to such infestations. The Ideal-self is also vulnerable through pride and hubris. But, generally, it is the denial of selves that leaves us most vulnerable to attack by spirits and beliefs. [56]

Lastly, let me reiterate that *shapes*, other than lights, can manifest in the active imagination of a client. These too can have a spirit-like quality. They are generally identified as dark formless shapes such as 'blobs' that are associated with particular feelings such as doubt and fear. When the client is asked to contain these feelings using the *Light*, s/he may initially report that there is nothing in the circle. If so, I encourage the client to check whether the coloring in the circle is any different from the coloring outside the circle. If there is a distinct difference in coloring or shading, then I generally conclude that the *Light* has contained a presence. Shakuntala Modi describes these presences at length. [57] Her approach to these 'spirits' is distinctly different from that offered by many exorcists. She sees such spirits as evil and in need of removal, but not 'casting out.' That is, she believes the spirits are as much in need of redemption as any Soul. In fact, she identifies most of them as souls or soul parts. Her strategy is to ask that all such presences be turned into pure white light and returned to the source of light. I evoke a similar approach when commending such forms to Christ's care and redemption. Today, I am apt to use Modi's formulation whenever the client contains formless shapes. After carefully examining them, I generally have the client ask Christ to transform them into pure white light and return them to the source of light. What is important to remember is that some ego-aspects may be hiding within a darkness. Thus, as a matter of protocol, I always ask Christ to use a double circle to extract any ego-aspect hiding within, before asking him to turn the 'darkness' into pure white light and return it to the source of light.

THE CHRIST WITHIN US

Once the client has comfortably learned to call upon a Christ figure, I encourage the habit of evoking Christ immediately after s/he finds the *Light*. Often the client will do this without my even suggesting it. Some clients will use Christ to bring the *Light* to them. Very quickly client and therapist learn to use the *Light* and Christ figure interactively. In this section I want to illustrate some of the numerous possibilities for interaction. This group of interventions is only a beginning. In successive chapters the role of Christ becomes ever more central and, for all practical purposes, indispensable. Much of the work described in this book is predicated upon the client's willingness to evoke Christ within the Mind.

Support and Discovery

First and foremost, the Christ image extends a reassuring presence and support. The client is no longer alone when going inside to face whatever dragons s/he must engage. Despite the absolute power of the *Light* within the mind, the presence of Christ in human garb is like having a friend, healer, guide, leader and beloved all in one image. Very often, in the midst of a trying experience, clients will note that Christ has his arm around their shoulder, or is holding their hand, or hugs them to his chest as they cry, or is simply walking beside them or gently leading. If our focus is on a child aspect then Christ may spontaneously carry the child or hold it in his lap.

In therapy, I have always made it a rule that there be no physical contact between the client and myself. Over the years my dilemma has been that there are many times when their pain cried out for reassuring touch. The Christ figure can meet this need while the client is focused within. Quite often it will happen spontaneously without my even suggesting it. The following session highlights this support role. For some months, the client has been using the *Light* to uncover memories of severe childhood abuse. On this occasion, she has been getting flashbacks of the memory before coming into the session and was justifiably anticipating a frightful recall. This client always went first to a particular beach to get her *Light* and then join with Christ who would take her to a cave where she would do the actual work of recall. When she went inside I suggested at the outset that she let the *Light* and Christ set up the situation so the memory could be remembered safely. She reported the following over the next several minutes: "Christ gives me a portion of the *Light* and he takes the rest and goes through a door to prepare a place for me. He blesses me when he returns... holds me real tight...says no matter what I see he will stand beside me...I'm kind of numb...its how I've gotten through this whole day... how I've been able to act as if everything was OK. We enter a dark, torch filled room...He has me sit in a chair...like I'm going to watch something...He has a chair next to me and holds my hand and he blesses me again...and says I'm here... and He tells me to look at the pictures now." She then proceeded to describe the memory without being overwhelmed by it. Christ and the client spontaneously arranged all of this. For much of the session I did little more than initiate the process and take notes. It was a horrendous memory of cultic abuse.

The discovery aspect essentially involves the interchangeable use of the *Light* and the Christ to help the client clarify or uncover the issue at hand. Instead of having the client pose questions only to the *Light*, s/he can also be asked to pose a question to Christ regarding any facet of an event. Often, I will suggest that Christ lead clients "to the place in your mind where a particular ego-aspect abides." For example, in working with a woman with Multiple Personalities we very quickly developed a ritual for their containment. Whenever she identified that an alter or fragment was the cause of a particular feeling or difficulty she would immediately ask the *Light* to contain it in a circle and name it. Then she would ask her Christ to either take her to wherever the circle was – if there was time to engage the alter, or she would have her Christ take a portion of her *Light* to the alter and plan to address it in the next session.

If you ask a client to hold the *Light* in both hands and then separate the hands, the *Light* will split into two equal portions. One of these portions can be extended to an alter or ego-aspect in recognition that it is a part of the Self – often a vital part. More important, these portions of the *Light* will safely link the client with that aspect. The *Light* will not permit communication that threatens to attack or overwhelm the client. Christ is very helpful in this since he can enter the circle and extend the *Light* to the alter/aspect without threat to either. Of note, Christ can also be asked to take the client into a remembered dream so that he can alter it at the client's direction. Further on, I will give several examples of how Christ is asked to enter a memory/dream and significantly alter its outcome.

Christ can also be asked to intervene when the client and therapist are confronted with time pressures. Often, crucial images are discovered late in a session when there is relatively little time to explore their implication and meaning, and the discovery is obviously upsetting to the client. When these ego-aspects have been contained within a circle, I will then suggest that the client permit Christ to enter that circle and stay with the aspect throughout the week until s/he returns for the next session. I am most likely to suggest this if the ego-aspect is a small child. On the other hand, if whatever is contained in the circle is particularly threatening to the client, I will suggest that Christ stand as a buffer between the client and whatever is in the circle, shielding him or her from its effects, until we have an opportunity to address the aspect's issue/memory at our next scheduled meeting. These 'safety' precautions can be further strengthened by asking Christ to place an opaqued dome of *Light* over the circle and anchoring it in place. In theory, only a circle is needed, but clients feel more secure with these further precautions in place.

Reaching Into Our Hearts

This is a very specific kind of discovery. Throughout this book methods are suggested for uncovering reasons why a person resists change. One effective method involves asking Christ to look within or reach within a person's heart for the resistance to change. The method is powerful because the archetype of Christ has the power to read the deepest recesses of the heart and that is often where our 'darkest' (i.e. shameful) secrets are kept. If the client is willing – always and only if the client is willing, I will suggest s/he stand before Christ and permit him to reach into the heart for the resistance to change on a particular issue. Often, he will quite literally reach into the chest and draw out something symbolic of the issue. [58] For example, one client was struggling with the issue of sugar abstinence. When she asked Christ to reach into her heart for the source of her resistance he drew out a ruler, which she immediately identified as "a measure of control." As she understood this symbol, sugar provided her with a measure of control over her feelings. Of note, while I had very little idea what the ruler might have symbolized its meaning was quickly accessible to the client, and I have found this to be generally the case. If the meaning is not readily accessible I will have the client ask the *Light* or Christ for the meaning.

Another client had a deeply felt desire to be taken care of by others, which she strongly resisted. When she permitted Christ to reach within her heart for the source of resistance he drew out two dolls symbolizing her role as a supervisor and minister. She believed it would be necessary to forgo her prideful identification with both roles in order to be cared for. As this particular case illustrates, the process can quickly clarify the conflict but does not automatically lead to resolution. Most often what happens is that the client is confronted – quite literally, with the dark recesses of the heart (sic) the price we pay for pride, control, passions and the like. Giving them up is quite another matter. Rarely, will the client just tell the *Light* to remove the obstacle. More often, s/he is obliged to acknowledge that the obstacle has been more valued than the change s/he thought was valued. However, as and when the client is prepared to let go of an obstacle the process is very simple. The therapist directs the client to ask Christ to take the obstacle to himself and to heal the wound in client's heart. I should note that this does not always result immediately in the desired change since there may be other obstacles, but it strengthens the desire for that change and the belief that it can be accomplished; moreover, it is generally the case that no change can take place until the client is willing to forgo attachment to the obstacle in question, and that generally requires that a Dominant self open the heart to Christ.

The process described above is essentially the same as that described in Steps six and seven of the 12 steps of Alcoholics Anonymous.

Step six: "We became *entirely* ready to have God remove this defect;" and Step seven: "We humbly asked God to remove this shortcoming." What I tell clients is that what is required of us is that instant of willingness. We must be willing to ask. Christ will not act against our will. Very few therapies tend to high*light* this fact as clearly as the *Light*. From my perspective, the therapist's role is one of showing the client the advantages of becoming willing and the disadvantages of remaining unwilling or willful, and never doubting that change is always dependent upon the client's willingness.

The source of most resistance is the power of emotions controlling our thoughts and behavior. David Hawkins has used Kinesiology to explore the relative strength of emotions. [59] I discussed his theory of emotion in the Chapter II. Essentially, Hawkins' methodology has allowed him to rank emotions as relatively stronger or weaker than others in their power to cancel each other's effect. His ranking has an inherent logic. For example, anger is more powerful than shame or fear since it can hold these two emotions at bay or galvanize the person to fight rather than f*light*. But anger also has its limits since it can only push away or destroy; it has no power of itself to creatively alter the situation. Strength can hide weakness, but cannot heal it. As a rule, anger begets anger in a never ending spiral of violence. [60] As a culture, we appear to be motivated by emotions (shame, guilt, apathy, grief, fear, desire, anger and pride) that Hawkins describes as progressively more powerful but essentially negative. While those are the primary emotions shaping much of our cultural exchanges, Hawkins argues that there are far more empowering positive emotions. Courage is the first emotion he identifies with this capacity. In effect, we have emotional options. We can, for example, respond fearfully in a given situation or courageously. Not surprising, 'willingness' is given a high ranking, less than 'acceptance' and 'love,' but considerably stronger than 'courage.'

The *Light* can be helpful in showing the client the limits of certain emotions. Simply have the client ask the *Light* to show him or her the consequences of continuing to be motivated by a particular emotion. Very often this request will evoke images of the pain that the emotion inflicts. For example the *fear* of change is just that: the abiding experience of fear. In the case described above of the woman seeking to be cared for, she saw herself as obliged to move through life "fearing the care" of others as a threat to prideful images of self. Again, such awareness does not often result in an immediate willingness to change, but it definitely high*light*s the price of putting off change, and clearly emphasizes that the resistance is *within* the client. In effect, it is not the world that withholds the caring, but the client who holds the world at arm's length from a self-sabotaging sense of pride.

In the chapter on Moral authority entering the Heart is seen as pivotal to the creation of a Christ conscience. In that intervention, which is actually the culmination of a series of interventions, Christ will literally enter the Heart of the client and baptize the shameful core residing there. Thereafter, a portion of his *Light* is expected to reside there on a daily basis exercising love, discernment, and forgiveness.

Dispelling Evil Actions

On occasion, several of my clients have recalled particularly heinous memories of forced participation in Satanic rituals during childhood.[61] The probability of encountering such memories is quite high in most cases of severe dissociative disorders. On several occasions their recalls have included participation in the sacrifice of infants, sadistic torture, blood rituals and cannibalism; also, rapes in which they believed they were impregnated with semen capable of giving birth to Satan. All such events are designed to convince the client s/he has been made a minion of Satan against his or her will. Again, I would stress that we are dealing here with the power of belief. I have no way of proving or disproving such events. I know that the existence of cult rituals is treated by some groups as debatable. Personally, I accept their existence. More than 900,000 children were reported missing in 1997 alone. If only one percent of those children became cult victims that is 9000 children. Quite frankly, the first time I encountered this situation I was at a loss what to do. Nothing in my experience had prepared me to respond to this degree of malevolence. But I could feel the hold it had on the client. I honestly said a silent prayer that first time: and what I discovered was that Christ could be asked to enter the scene at any point and provide rites of purification or undoing. Today, it is hard for me to imagine any other response. An example of the undoing or purification process is provided in the next section in conjunction with another intervention called empowering the loving body.

The Loving Body

The idea for this intervention came from an account described by Spalding [62] in which a Christ-like Master confronts a horde of thieves with the radiance of heavenly love. This energy has the power to reflect back to the thieves the effects of their intentions. This mirroring results in their turning on themselves in fear and terror. As best I can describe it, the abuser, when confronted by a potential victim whose body radiates love, acts as if the victim is exposing them to the deepest recesses of his or her own heart and the unavoidable judgment of his or her actions. This judgment is not condemning but experiential: the abuser is obliged to experience the *effect* of his or her actions as distinct from the desires that motivated them. Invariably, abusers seem to fall back in dismay and horror. It makes me mindful of the near-death experiences (NDE) described by several researchers.[63] A number of individuals who have experienced NDE have reported that at some point they are asked to review their lives from the perspective of how others experienced their actions. Thus, for example, if I forcibly took a toy from my younger brother to play with by myself, I would re-experience that memory, not as pleasurable, but rather in terms of my younger brother's painful reaction. And this appears to be what happens when Christ is asked to empower the victim of an abuse memory with a radiant loving body. Not only is the victim no longer accessible to their abuser(s), but the abusers appear to fall back in fear and dismay in response to the pain they would inflict. The loving radiant body appears to function as a perfect shield toward any who would threaten or attack.

The following clinical intervention illustrates both the power of the loving body as well as Christ's power to dispel and undo the effects of a client's forced participation in ritual acts. In this recall, the client had been "kidnapped" at age 14 by a Satanic coven (she had previously voluntarily involved herself with group members). In the ensuing rituals her mind and body were desecrated in just about every way imaginable; she was drugged, forced to perform sex acts on very young children, to witness animal sacrifice, threats to her own life, and finally made to believe that she had been impregnated by and for Satan and made his minion against her will. (This is a type of recall that I cannot imagine addressing without recourse to Christ. Whether such events are true or not, the client most certainly believed them, and could only cope, up to that point, by multiply dissociating.)

Immediately following this recall, I had the client reorient her focus to the *Light* and the presence of the Christ who had been beside her during all the preparations for this recall. I asked her to tell him how they had desecrated her body and placed a curse on it. I then asked her to have Christ enter the memory and empower her adolescent self with a loving radiant body. Her immediate response to this suggestion was: "Do I have to stay naked?" She was obviously experiencing great shame at this point. I told her that she – the adult self, had only to go as a witness – not as a participant. She then described the following:

"Christ has gone into the room ... it is filled with *light* ... now they look like ugly witches ... he is firm with them ... he commands them to stand in the same spot ... and they do ... he comes to me ... he has this white cloth... he slowly wipes it over my body ... there is a glow ... my body is clean ... it glows ... he puts the cloth in my mouth ... and he takes out all the awful taste ... he tells me he will do the same thing between my legs ... I'm not to be afraid ... he will clean me ... he lays the cloth over me between my legs ... I was scared he would touch me but he does not ... he tells me to look at my body ... I have a hard time looking at myself ... he tells me to go over each part of myself and realize it is clean ... my disgust is so strong ... I can't do it ... he takes my face and looks at me ... it is very tender... he tells me it is OK ... he has given me a new body ... all healed ... he takes me to these people and tells them I am covered with his glory ... nothing can penetrate it ... and they are really scared ... they are as scared as I was on the table ... he is not being ugly ... just showing them my new body and they are terrified ... then he commands them to leave ... he puts this blessing on each one ... it freaks them out ... he takes me back to the table room ... and hands me the cloth and directs me to the two children

... he brings them one at a time and holds them while I wipe the cloth over them ... just the way he did to me ... then he also does it ... they glow too ... he blesses them and wipes this memory from them ... I thank him for what he has done ... but I feel guilty because I still don't feel good about myself."

When I ask why, she replies: "He has cleaned my body but not my soul ... he looks at me ... tells me he cannot take the memory away, but he has healed it and I have to trust him ... I have to embrace my body ... he says he knows that it will not be easy, but I need to do it every day and it will become a part of me ... the pain is gone (she had been experiencing considerable cramping prior to and throughout the session)."

Her comment near the end of this intervention to the effect that, "He has cleaned my body but not my soul" is a telling one. In the next session she will remember that a part of her responded sexually to the assaults and in the months immediately following the incident she voluntarily returned to the house where the events occurred. But Christ's response appears to speak to these issues as well though neither of us are aware of it during the session. I think it is important to note here – as this particular intervention so well illustrates, that for this kind of trauma the recall and intervention are rarely accomplished in one session. This particular recall involved several sessions of discovery and will require several more to satisfactorily resolve it. And between sessions the client will also avail herself of prayers for healing from her minister and the support of other incest survivors. The real power of the Christ figure is not in any particular intervention – though his actions are often more elegant than any I could devise, but his abiding presence and support whatever the issue. No matter what is happening, or what the client has done, Christ will never shame or abandon.

In a number of incidents involving memories of abuse, I have suggested to clients that they permit Christ to imbue them with a loving body. In no instance have I told them beforehand what I might expect to be the consequence of this action. When they report that it is done I suggest they allow the ego-aspect of the memory – now with a loving body, to confront the abuser(s). Invariably, this new body appears to have the power to perfectly shield the aspect and transform it from victim to victor.

At this juncture it may be hard for the reader to discern what is fact and what is fiction. The above intervention is an extreme example and not likely to be encountered by most therapists. But step back a moment. Accept that someday someone comes into your office and over a period of months or years reports life experiences that put him or her outside the pale of your experience of human behavior. From your safe perspective, it all seems so untenable. But measured by symptoms and demeanor it is obvious the client has lived something – that if only the smallest portion were true – leaves you at a loss of how to respond, how to offer healing and support, how to undo the terrible wrongs s/he has born, and of which you are now a witness. How does s/he live with it in your presence and when s/he is alone again after the session? The therapist is not God and has not the power to undo these terrible wrongs and forgive them. I would be like Christ: without blame or condemnation. But we both know I am only human and have not the power of his divinity to undo and forgive. What I do have is a willingness to evoke Christ at such moments and implicitly trust his actions, which have never yet failed to meet a client's need for healing. In so doing, I ask her to accept his perceptions and actions regarding her experience – which have always proved lovingly sufficient, and more than I could ever offer on my own authority.

Connecting Abused and Abuser

On other occasions, I have used a method similar to the loving body to dramatically alter the outcome of a memory. It has proven especially helpful for clients dealing with one-on-one abuse found in incestuous situations. In this intervention, Christ is asked to connect the ego-aspect with the abuser in such a way that the abuser is obliged to experience the abuse as it affects the ego-aspect. This can be done by Christ touching both at the same time, or using his *Light* to connect them or using the client's *Light* to connect them. This invariably has the effect of stopping the abuser from further abuse and stepping away dismayed. In effect, the abuser must now feel what the child was feeling rather than feeling the lust/anger that motivated the abuser's behavior. Please note, again, that such interventions should only be enacted after the client has fully recovered the memory.

The above intervention is particularly helpful where the client seems to compulsively revisit or reenact the memory because it is pivotal developmentally. An example would be a client whose relative forced the client sexually in early adolescence when the client was becoming sexually aware. Be aware that this intervention is different from the one employing a loving body and can evoke quite different responses. Consider, for example, the response of one client who asked Christ to forge this connection: "I can see him having to experience all those emotions...makes me uncomfortable...I have to remember them [the emotions she felt]...fear at first...anger...shame." I ask, does he persist? "He recoils in self-hatred...and I am really pissed... enraged...he betrayed his trust...I'm furious ...can feel it in my stomach...I can see what the situation deserves...he cowers....not one thing he can say in defense of his behavior....I have never fully appreciated how angry I was." This intervention can provoke retributive qualities as when the father is seen to cower in response to her growing anger. It provides a reciprocal mirroring of cause and effect unmediated by Christ's love and forgiveness. In that sense it is more powerful than the one provided by the loving body since it is not mediated by Christ and therefore puts the client in touch with pure ego emotions - which in her case, had long been suppressed. Which intervention the therapist suggests may be dependent on the situation addressed. The loving body intervention seems better suited to situations where the client must deal with horrendous abuse and/or confront a group of people or strangers as in the case of cultic abuse. But in one-on-one situations, the unmediated connection offers the client an opportunity to de-cathect long suppressed ego emotions which may be necessary before s/he can move toward forgiveness.

Christ's Power to Heal

In Western culture there is no figure – historical or contemporary, with greater power for healing than Jesus Christ. Nearly one third of the New Testament is devoted to Christ's healing ministry. There is a saying: the saints smile when the situation is clearly impossible because then only God can take a hand in the outcome. Very often, as a therapist, I am faced with situations that seem to require the power of God for resolution. Shameful experiences leave a mark that psychology simply cannot erase without recourse to grace, forgiveness and a Higher Power. In the world of Heart, Mind and Soul the Christ image appears to have infinite power if therapist and client are willing. The needs of my clients have taught me to be willing. There is no sin, no shame, no guilt, no fear that Christ cannot forgive (erase) and heal in the mind of anyone who is willing to evoke him.

All of the interventions described in the forgoing sections come under the rubric of prayerful healing. If the client is willing to evoke the Christ image then invariably I will encourage him or her to turn to that image for the healing of memories, relationships, feelings and compulsions. One of my very first experiences in asking Christ to intervene remains one of the most poignant for me. A client related a recurring nightmare of her childhood. In the dream she is participating in a grade school Christmas pageant in which she plays a simple musical instrument. In this dream she is very poor – which was also her real life experience as a child. Her mother has promised her a dress for the pageant; but fails to complete it on time. Consequently she is obliged to stand on stage in a dress little better than a flour sack – which she also wore in real life. Because she appears so out of place, a spotlight is placed on her by the teacher, which accentuates her shame. How do you tell a person who has been ashamed of her poverty all of her life that it need not be? At that moment all I could suggest was that she permit Christ to enter the nightmare with her. She went inside and imagined that Christ and her adult-self were sitting in the audience. When the performance is over, and the child is about to be shamed, Christ's response is to join the child on stage, gently take the instrument she has been playing so he can hold her hand, and then *bow with her sharing the spotlight*. That is all he did. But no action has ever spoken louder to me of how secure we stand in his presence, how perfectly shielded. Once the client is willing to evoke the Christ he will provide an answer, whatever the need, and with greater power and authority than anything the therapist can offer. I can want a client healed with all my heart, but only the Christ within has the power to forgive and heal the client's heart.

The remainder of this book is devoted to an exploration of Mind, Heart, Soul, and Body using the *Light* and image of Christ. That image becomes increasingly indispensable as the work progresses. But there are two other clinician-theorists who also work with multiple ego-aspects; and neither uses the *Light* or image of Christ. I would like to devote the remainder of this chapter to an exposition of their work. Each has a method for exploring, defining and working with selves different from the one described in this book. Both limit themselves to the power of the Ego when functioning willingly. Their work is important for several reasons. First, they strongly support my own finding of multiple selves in all of us. Second, they offer alternative approaches to uncovering and working with these selves. The Stone's approach is particularly helpful for clients who have difficulty visualizing, or who tend to treat other selves as merely figments of their imagination, since it uses an auditory rather than visual method that has a powerful impact on the client's awareness. Neither of the theorists requires access to a Christ image or other higher power and, in my opinion, this places considerable limits on what they can accomplish, but their methods do provide options for clients who are unwilling to evoke a higher power, and all of their methods and theoretical constructs are easily incorporated when using the *Light*.

The Work of R. C. Schwartz [64]

The work of R.C.Schwartz parallels my own in many respects with the notable exception that he does not evoke a *Light* or higher power. But he is quite successful in many of his interventions. Readers would do well to familiarize themselves with his work. He provides a good entrée for working with active imagination. His system of conceptualization is relatively simple but effective in working with a number of difficult symptoms. I will leave it to the reader to decide which system is ultimately more viable. His work also parallels that of Hal and Sidra Stone. [65] Their work is discussed later in the chapter. Their respective systems are contrasted by the different modalities they emphasize. Schwartz, like me, relies heavily on visual interventions, while the Stones rely on an auditory-kinesthetic intervention they call Voice Dialogue. All three systems – Schwartz, the Stones, and my own – replicate the finding of numerous selves in each of us. The major difference is that my interventions rely on the *Light* and Christ image while theirs are primarily limited to ego-ego interventions (the Stones do address archetypal antagonists). I believe that a willingness to call on a higher power offers the therapist and client more options, greater safety, and a broader reach, but I will leave that judgment to the reader. Here I want to give a fair description of these other systems, which replicate my own findings and provide valuable, alternative interventions. In the following sections I also give examples for the integration of their systems within *Light* therapy and the evocation of a Christ image.

R.C.Schwartz was initially trained as family therapist. In search of more effective interventions, he journeyed inward with his patients and used family systems theory to conceptualize what he found. Like Jung, the Stones, [66] Fritz Perls, [67] and others, he sees the psyche as comprised of a multiplicity of ego-aspects, which he calls 'parts.' All of these theories come together in this shared focus on active imagination and the Ego dynamics observed from that inner perspective. Essentially, Schwartz has attempted to internalize family systems theory while others – including myself, have relied primarily on a psychodynamic orientation. Schwartz does acknowledge the work of those theorists, most notably Carl Jung. The multiplicity of selves and the use of active imagination were both developed by Jung. To quote Schwartz, quoting Jung:

> In 1935, Jung described a complex as having the "tendency to form a little personality of itself. It has a sort of body, a certain amount of its own physiology. It can upset the stomach, it upsets the breathing, it disturbs the heart – in short, it behaves like a partial personality…I hold that our personal unconscious, as well as the collective unconscious, consists of an indefinite, because unknown, number of complexes or fragmentary personalities." [68]

Schwartz's work provides a simplified model for inner work. It is also quite secular, meaning that it proceeds – for the most part, without recourse to a world beyond the ego or the safeguards and options provided by the *Light* and a Christ image. [69] Even so, I would recommend it to therapists as a viable, alternative approach for addressing many of the symptoms addressed in the psychiatric literature, if those therapists are unwilling to evoke higher powers in a therapeutic context. His methods have proven effective in working with bulimia and anorexia. While all of Schwartz's interventions and thinking are easily integrated into *Light* therapy, Schwartz might consider its use superfluous. He would argue that a clinician could use his methodology and interventions without evoking a higher power or *Light*. Schwartz does note that there are dangers to his approach – a good indication of its power, but only if the clinician disregards his cautions.

Basically, Schwartz views the psyche as a system of interactional roles that he calls 'parts.' Ideally, these parts can work harmoniously, but in a clinical population the parts are most often polarized or enmeshed, and often leaderless, much like a dysfunctional family. Schwartz identifies three different kinds of parts: managers/protectors, firefighters, and exiles. These three are often triangulated by positive feedback loops, which forces them to enact extreme positions. There is a fourth category which is singular: the core 'Self.' While there can be numerous managers/protectors, firefighters and exiles, there is typically only one core Self. It is important to note that this Self is capitalized in Schwartz's nomenclature. He equates it with the Jung's sense of Self (which Jung also capitalized). But where Jung intended the Self to represent the total psyche, including the contents of the collective unconscious, Schwartz uses the term to designate an ego-aspect that is compassionate, nonjudgmental, and potentially capable of providing a leadership role – not unlike my description of the Aware-ego. This core self comes as close to a higher power as Schwartz's system will allow. In my own work, I identify the Self as an expression of the total person inclusive of conscious and unconscious contents in the way that Jung used the term. For that reason, I refrain from capitalizing Schwartz's core self.

In my system of thought, the Aware-ego is the ego-aspect most like Schwartz's core self when the latter is functioning optimally. But the two are distinguishable in significant ways. First, the Aware-ego, that part of us that assumes the *Light* on going inside, is invariant in its function. It exercises the willingness expressed by the *Light*, and extends the power of that function to other ego-aspects. In contrast, the function of the core self in Schwartz's system tends to wax and wane dependent upon its history. Optimally, it is expected to function as the equivalent of an executive ego capable of reconciling the disparate managers/protectors, firefighters and exiles. But as Schwartz notes, it may be largely ineffective at the outset as a result of trauma. According to Schwartz: "...[I]n the case where the Self is impotent to protect the system and not allowed to help those most traumatized afterward, [other] parts lose trust in the Self's leadership and become overprotective of the Self and of the parts who were hurt. Such people become dominated by their protectors and often report feeling no sense of Self." [70]

The following case example illustrates the abdication of a core self. As this case also illustrates, the core self is generally easy to access when the Aware-ego is asked to identify it as well as highlighting the problem of expecting it to function executively from the outset of therapy. When this client's *Light* takes her to her core self, which she immediately experiences being happy and peaceful, I ask her to have her *Light* place a circle of protection around this part. When I suggested this part could be a leader, the client immediately expresses reservations: "It is silly, I do a lot of silly things when I am with grandma (a primary caretaker). I am childlike, I like to dress up like a queen." I ask if she is little because she has had to stay locked away? She replies: "At age 7 or 8 I realized that the world was a horrible place, my eyes went bad too, I could look right at something threatening and not see it anymore." I ask if there was a part of her who took responsibility for blurring her vision. In reply, she said she became Durga.[71] I ask her to contain Durga. Once contained, Durga becomes calm; before she was contained the client saw her as ranting and raving. I ask why it is necessary for Durga to protect this core self. "I did not want to participate in my family's drama anymore, particularly my grandmother. I was happy to be with her but she was always unhappy. I could not make her happy. My mom too was always unhappy. My father would say crushing things. Getting mad seems preferable to giving in to all that sadness. (Earlier in the session we were talking about an aspect she calls the Crier; so now I ask her about this part.) "I remember standing in front of the mirror after I was crying. My eyes were red with a green iris, my face was red, and I looked like a demon, a green eyed, bloodshot demon. No one would listen to me. I could not wait to grow up and get away from there." (This client is unwilling at this point in the therapy to evoke a Christ image but is quite comfortable with the Virgin Mary. In a previous session the Virgin Mary has taken the ghost of her deceased mother to herself so that the two seemed to merge.) I now suggest that she take the Crier to her Virgin Mary. She says that is what the Crier wants, to be comforted by her mother and grandmother. Durga now sees her as fulfilled in the presence of the Virgin Mary. But then she immediately identifies another problem – her Durga habit of getting mad. I ask how the Durga would be around the Crier and the Virgin Mary. She immediately saw that the Durga could be comfortable with the child in the presence of the Virgin Mary.

As the above case illustrates, Christ or the *Light* can quickly identify and take the Aware-ego to the place where the client's sense of a core self resides. Too often, however – as Schwartz notes, this self appears to abdicate responsibilities in the face of childhood trauma.

It is also possible to confuse manifestations of the Ideal-self with Schwartz's core self. Not infrequently, an Ideal-self will seek to emulate Christ in an idolatrous way; and in that mode it can seem to act very compassionately. Schwartz' system has no frame of reference for testing this possibility. As a rule, I do not seek out 'core selves.' Instead, I rely on the Aware-ego to function in that capacity.

In Schwartz's system, all parts excepting the core self are assigned to one of three roles: manager/protector, firefighter or exile. According to Schwartz:

> One group tends to be highly protective, strategic, and interested in controlling the environment to keep things safe. In an internal family, the members of this group are called the "managers." Another group contains the most sensitive members of the system. When injured or outraged, the members of this group will be imprisoned by the managers for their own and the larger system's protection; they become the "exiles." A third group reacts powerfully and automatically when the exiles are upset, to try to stifle or soothe those feelings. Its members are called the "firefighters." In many internal systems, polarizations exist among these three groups and also within them…. The more the hurt, rageful, or sexually charged exiles are shut out, the more extreme they become, and the more the managers and firefighters legitimately fear their release. So they resort to more extreme methods of suppression. The more the exiles are suppressed, the more they try to break out, and all three groups become victims of an escalating vicious circle.[72]

Schwartz's terminology is helpful in

highlighting the interplay between different aspects of the Ego. Ego-aspects never function alone. Managers always point, implicitly, to the existence of exiles, and the likelihood of collusive firefighters. This triangled grouping is nearly universal. But Schwartz does not treat his tripartite system as archetypal despite God-only-knows how many similar systems have been advocated by other theorists to describe similar phenomena, e.g. Freud, [73] Eric Berne, [74] Stone.[75] Schwartz dismisses the idea of an archetypal configuration determining his tripartite system. Instead, like Freud, he favors treating the world of Mind as a blank slate where aspects merely emulate dysfunctional family members. This is all he can allow since his system is restricted to manifestations of Ego.

Finally, and surprisingly for a family therapist, Schwartz's theory does not acknowledge the existence of internalized parental images, much less the archetypal energies that often shape those images. He only allows a dynamic interplay between parts of the Ego. These parts can emulate a parental figure – as is often the case with his managers, but his theory neither recognizes nor contends with parental images. [76] It is as if, parents can only exist in an extroverted context, i.e. as a person-in-the-world. Even so, the authority and intransigence exhibited by certain managers, points to the existence of archetypal authority. Schwartz's confabulation of parent and managers does accentuate the need to identify any ego-aspect that is emulating a parent since that aspect is likely using parental authority to justify willful actions, and s/he will actively resist having that authority removed from a parent. That issue is taken up in Chapter VI where I identify the Temporal persona, and in Chapter VII where I address the Dominant self.

The above considerations notwithstanding, Schwartz's methodology and interventions provide valuable insights that are easily integrated into the framework of *Light* therapy. I strongly encourage therapists to review his work and use whatever they find applicable. What I have come to value most is his consistent treatment of all ego-aspects (sic) 'parts' as redeemable from their extreme positions, and as capable of harmonious, cooperative interaction. The two interventions described in the following section provide a way of consistently applying that perspective.

CONTAIN-INVEST AND A GARMENT OF PROTECTION

When Schwartz has his clients go inside he is most concerned about blending and reactivity. Blending is "when the feelings and beliefs of one part merge with another part of the Self."[77] This blending with other parts allows an exile to permeate the system with its feelings. What Schwartz is most concerned about in the early phases of therapy is that the therapist will inadvertently trigger a flood of feeling from an exile that would in turn provoke firefighters to correct the imbalance in symptomatic ways.

"What the managers and firefighters fear is flooding of the exiles' feelings, thoughts, or sensations, so that they blend with the person's Self or permeate the entire system. That is, if given an opportunity, parts have the ability to erase the boundary separating them from other parts or the Self. When a part infuses its feelings into the Self, it obscures the Self's resources and, in a sense, merges with the Self or takes control of the system [sic, consciousness].... Finally, child-like exiles are often surrounded by firefighters who react powerfully to any sign that the children are upset. In some cases then, managers are not afraid of the child-like exiles per se, but instead fear the release of firefighters who use rash, destructive methods to "help" the exiles....All these firefighters lurk like hidden bombs that can be triggered by opening the door to the exiles prematurely. Rightfully, managers resist the efforts of well-meaning therapists to pry the door open until these bombs have been defused [brackets added]." [78]

When going inside it is difficult to determine right off 'who is who' in terms of roles being played. But as a rule of thumb the interplay described by Schwartz is helpful in reminding the therapist to always anticipate relational dynamics, to assume that, if some aspect of the self is angry or fearful, it is most likely angry or fearful vis-à-vis another image, be it another ego-aspect, parent, or person. The presence of one aspect expressing strong negative feeling implicitly points to the existence of a countermanding second presence, and often a third. Once the first aspect has been contained, the others can be identified and contained in turn. But quite often more than mere containment is called for whenever ego-aspects are involved; they must also be worked with before proceeding. As a general rule, it is always advisable to provide an ego-aspect with its own portion of the *Light* and equal access to Christ. This is what I call 'contain and invest.'

When Christ or the client is asked to contain an ego-aspect, I generally recommend that the aspect be immediately invested with all of the power available to the Aware-ego: specifically, use of the *Light* and access to Christ. In effect, all aspects of the Ego, regardless of their relationship to each other are eventually granted equal access to the *Light* and Christ. With their own *Light*, they can contain any other aspect that threatens them or ask Christ to contain any other aspect that is perceived to be a threat to them. Insofar as an aspect is prepared to act willingly, as distinct from willfully, the *Light* empowers it to act just as the Aware-ego acts. The newly invested aspect can evoke Christ and, extending a portion of its own *Light*, ask Christ to contain any other image that is threatening to it. Sequential containment and investment is particularly helpful in working with the alters and fragments of someone suffering from MPD. Often, MPD clients will have a number of alters/fragments involved in the recall of a memory. Their memories can be exceedingly horrendous and prolonged. The client may have switch numerous times in an effort to survive, generating a number of fragments specifically created to compartmentalize and cope with a particular memory. [79] The general protocol is to have whoever is out give a portion of their *Light* to Christ and ask him to contain whoever is pushing to come out and invest them as well with a portion of the *Light* so they can add their memory to the whole without overwhelming the others. Note that, while all ego-aspects are offered a portion of the *Light*, they need not accept it, but while they remain unwilling to accept it, they are contained by it, and only released if they do not threaten other aspects also holding the *Light*.

Also, it is not necessary, or even advisable to attempt to contain all ego-aspects. In the next section I examine the Stone's work. They identify some ego-aspects such as the Rational mind, which are best not contained until they can recognize their own limitations.

The 'shielding garment' is an ancillary intervention that I will offer any ego-aspect who is *fearful* of being overwhelmed or otherwise threatened by another ego-aspect or parental representation. Essentially, any ego-aspect with access to the *Light* can ask the *Light* to forge a garment of protection that will shield it against *fearful* emotions or acts expressed by other ego-aspects. This is not unlike the loving body described earlier. Shielding will not solve the relational problem. A shameful exile would still be the bearer of shame, but another ego-aspect, now shielded, would not have to be fearful of guilt by association, or of having that fear provoke a firefighter into action. The garment of protection is also helpful in placating angry aspects by allowing them to refrain from anger once they are shielded from fear. In therapy, I am the one who identifies the need for a garment and suggests it to the client. After a self in need has asked the *Light* to create a garment of protection, I ask the client to describe the kind of garment that has been created. Over the years I have encountered a wide range of garments. They all seem to work.

Negative emotions range from shame – the most severe, to pride – the least severe. Between these extremes are negative emotions such as anger, fear, desire, despair, and guilt. Fear, desire, and anger are the three emotions most frequently used to guard against worse emotions such as despair, guilt and shame. (They are discussed at length in the next chapter.) A shield of protection is automatically extended to any aspect manifesting anxiety or fear. Once a client can appreciate that most anger is primarily a defense against an object of fear, I encourage them to offer it to angry aspects as well. A number of examples are given below.

The following clinical example illustrates the *contain and invest* intervention and use of *the garment of protection*. It is a continuation of the case described above: the client with an angry protector called Durga, who is highly antagonistic toward the Christ image. Previously, the client has trustingly used Mary to assist her when inside. Therefore, I encourage her to extend a portion of her *Light* to Mary who will use it to contain both Christ and Durga. Then Mary is asked to give a portion of her *Light* to Durga who can now use it however she chooses. At first, the client smiles to herself. When asked why, she reports that Durga feels inappropriately attired in her body armor since Christ is clearly a noncombatant. So Durga first uses of her *Light* to dissolve both of the circles. I now suggest that, should she choose to take off her body armor, Durga could ask her *Light* to provide another garment to shield her from the negative emotions of others. (I am assuming here that Durga's anger is defensive.) Durga appears willing. Very quickly after Durga responds, the client describes her as wearing a white veil. Shortly afterward, the client becomes tearful. When I ask why, she reports that Durga is laying her head on Christ's shoulder. In a very few minutes, the aspect has gone from angrily antagonistic to Christ to seeking his supportive strength. This transformation will also allow him to play a more central role in the therapy thereafter. Extending a portion of the *Light* to the Durga aspect, and encouraging her to let it forge a garment that protects her against the negative emotions of others, has facilitated this transformation.

This next example represents a more complex interaction. The client has a manager called the "controller." This aspect is very successful, charismatic, task oriented, focused, on top of things. Its counterpart is an exile called "weak" that is described as noncommittal, unassertive, indecisive, very emotional, and pasty in complexion. The client is being seen by me to help him deal with a wide range of addictive 'firefighting' activities that threaten his career and marriage (gambling, drinking, etc.). In this particular session, the Controller is complaining about a lack of focus, primarily as a result of the client's emerging grief over the death of his mother. I ask the client what emotions are most threatening to the Controller, and most likely to prod his addictive 'firefighters' into activity. He names them in quick succession: guilt, sadness, loneliness, regret, sorrow, and fear. I suggest he ask Christ to extend a portion of the *Light* to the Controller who can then use it to furnish a garment that will protect him from the fear of being overwhelmed by those emotions. I tell him that the objective here is for the Controller to be able to stand beside the "weak" aspect without being overwhelmed so that Christ can then work with the "weak" aspect. Almost immediately, the client describes the Controller as wearing a white aura that allows him to approach Weak without adverse affects. At this juncture I have the client ask Christ to baptize Weak. The client reports that the Controller seems to tolerate this, even accept it, and almost immediately he describes Weak's color as warmer and normal, not pasty anymore, and expressing emotions of relief, gladness and satisfaction, as if he has been released from something. Significantly, Weak will play an increasingly important role in the client's life as therapy progresses. It will be the part of him that most often comes to therapy since that is one of the few places he can emerge until integrated fully with the Controller.

Contain-invest and *garment shielding* interventions are further illustrated in successive chapters. As a rule, they are always offered to primary selves prior to seeking disowned selves.

VOICE DIALOGUE

Hal and Sidra Stone developed voice Dialogue in the 1970's. [80] It has a number of antecedents, most particularly: the Jungian concept of selves, Gestalt Therapy's famous "hot seat" developed by Fritz Perls, [81] and Moreno's Psychodrama. [82] In recent years it has eclipsed those sources to evolve into a powerful, theoretical and dynamic psychotherapy in its own right.

The Stones concept of the Aware-ego comes closest to my own and clearly precedes it in terms of theoretical development. They, as well as R. C. Schwartz and myself, focus on the seeming plethora of selves comprising the Ego. What sets their therapy apart is their method for accessing these selves. It is predominantly auditory and kinesthetic rather than visual. Their method – which they call Voice Dialogue, provides the client with a very powerful, direct, experience of their sub-personalities. To some extent, this is also a limitation of the method: it generally requires that selves be worked with sequentially rather than relationally. Also, Voice Dialogue is not considered a good method for working with Dissociative disorders or severe personality disorders, schizophrenics, etc. But that limitation aside, it is an excellent process for introducing clients to their inner selves, and augmenting treatment with clients who have difficulty visualizing. For many clients it can be used as a stand-alone method without recourse to any other kind of psychotherapy. It is considered spiritual by some practitioners because it offers clients access to meditative and Zen-like experiences. [83]

According to Marian Dyak, a Voice Dialogue facilitator, the Stones base their method on a consciousness model comprised of three interactive, interdependent, levels of awareness:

"The awareness level which stands outside of us observing the selves and does not take action; the selves which are immersed in living, the level on which we experience life; and the Aware-ego which stands between the opposites, makes choices based on information from the awareness level, and calls in the appropriate selves or energies in each situation. (The Stones compare the Aware-ego to a symphony orchestra conductor who knows all the parts and calls on each instrument to play at the appropriate moment in the performance.)" [84]

Probably the best way to appreciate this model is by examining the protocol for accessing all selves in Voice Dialogue facilitation. The process begins when therapist and client have identified one of the client's primary selves. Common examples are the Inner Critic, the Rational mind, the Pusher, the Doer, or Pleaser.[85] Wherever the client is *initially sitting* is designated the ego space. In time, this physical location will become the Aware-ego's space as well. Once a primary self has been identified, the client is asked *to move to a different physical space (i.e. another chair, another portion of the couch, or to move their chair to a different space)*. All selves, other than the Aware-ego are accessed from a physical space different from where the client normally sits. Essentially, in the process of changing their seat, the client is seen to become the self that has been identified since s/he moves there for the specific purpose of entering that role and expressing the views of that sub-personality. The facilitator, in turn, interviews the client in this new physical space in such a way that the client can easily become that sub-personality. The facilitator is trained to be very sensitive to physical changes in demeanor, posture and the like. Both s/he and the client should feel the visceral effects of the client assuming the role characteristic of the self to be interviewed. The facilitator then proceeds to interview this self. (Marian Dyak provides excellent, in-depth, descriptions of this interview process.[86]) If another self begins to emerge after an appropriate period of interviewing the first self, that new self can also be interviewed by having the client move to yet another place. (Voice Dialogue facilitators tend to do therapy in chairs that are easily moved.) When the facilitator senses that the self's repertoire of behaviors has been adequately examined, s/he asks the client to return to the original seat which, de facto, creates the Aware-ego.

The creation and nurture of the Aware-ego is the pièce de résistance for Voice Dialogue. Basically, it comes into being when the client has sufficiently separated from a self so as to sense-feel-appreciate its distinctive characteristics. It is the Aware-ego who recognizes that no particular self represents the totality of Self. It has the capacity to experience two, or more, ego-aspects simultaneously without attachment to any of them, and with practice, to govern their energy and relationships. Of note, the client must use active imagination to enact this part of the process. The Aware-ego is not, normally, expected to exist at the beginning of the Voice Dialogue process. S/he only comes into being with the client's recognition of an ego-aspect as separate and distinct, which follows the interview process when the client returns to the original seat. I would note here, by way of contrast, that when using the *Light*, the Aware-ego is the *first* ego-aspect encountered on going inside since it is the one that willingly receives the *Light* and uses it to engage all other images. Also, the Voice Dialogue method is easily integrated into any session using *Light* therapy. The only difference is that when the client returns to the original seat, s/he is asked to become the self "who holds the *Light*."

The third level of awareness is seen as pure witnessing. (The first two levels are [1] selves acting unreflectively followed by the emergence of [2] the Aware-ego, which can perceive them imaginatively.) For all practical purposes this is selfless awareness, though integral to the Voice Dialogue process. After the client has been asked to return to the original seat he or she may then be asked to stand near the facilitator, or sit in yet another seat while the facilitator describes and anchors each of the selves *including the Aware-ego*. This is done by having the client *imagine* each of the selves in their separate seats as the facilitator describes their characteristics including the client's reported body sense and attributes learned from the interviewing process. This witnessing is not done in every session, but is repeated to help the client distinguish from pure awareness – which only witnesses, and selves that act in the world of Mind. The concept of pure awareness makes more sense if the reader can appreciate that Voice dialogue can unearth a considerable number of selves.

In addition to the protocol described thus far, the client is taught strategies for relying more and more on the Aware-ego to govern behavior and inner life. Aside from the separation process and revelations derived from it, these additional strategies are the primary interventions. No attempt is made to alter selves be they primary, disowned, or archetypal. Essentially, the client learns to detached from the intensity of polarized selves via the Aware-ego, to modulate that intensity, and hold the tension of the co-existence of various selves in consciousness. The modulation of intensity by the Aware-ego appears to eliminate the more onerous aspects of a self, e.g. turns critical judges into discerning aspects. The Stones do not normally address interactions between selves and other images in the Mind. This is partially a consequence of the method, which focuses on the sequential enactment of selves. This is both a strength and limitation of the method. On the one hand, auditory-kinesthetic enactment makes a self powerfully and consciously figural. While some clients will initially distrust the visual process as "merely imaginative," they are hard pressed to deny the existence of a self once Voice Dialogue has separated it. On the other hand, this auditory-kinesthetic method does not work easily with imaginative interaction unless it is first made subordinate to it. In Voice Dialogue as generally described, the imaginative element is pertinent (1) at the level of pure awareness (which allows for witnessing but no interaction), (2) when the Aware-ego is asked to modulate polarized opposites, and (3) when interacting with archetypal images. The latter are discussed below.

Voice Dialogue demonstrates that with increased awareness individuals can attenuate the positive amplification of polarized selves, *but remain unable to alter the tension of irreconcilability*. I stress this limitation because I think it is possible to reconcile opposites using the *Light* and Christ image. The Stones' theoretical framework does not allow for this, but in the next section I take up the proposition that most, if not all polarized opposites, are created and sustained by bifurcating forces which can be identified and removed. By *polarized* I mean opposites whose extremes are seemingly irreconcilable as a result of splitting. Unlike triangulation, where a third person or force is used by two people defuse the tension in their relationship, in polarization a third person or force has split the relationship into seemingly irreconcilable halves. In the Stones conceptual framework, the Aware-ego essentially fosters a form of positive triangulation. Interestingly, it is a basic precept of family therapy that triangles are the most stable relationships because of their ability to defuse tension between any two parties; but that function is insufficient, of itself, to heal the discord.

Finally, I would note that the Stones do emphasize the role played by archetypes in the creation of primary and disowned selves. All facilitators are encouraged to draw upon archetypal dream images for self-enactment and discovery,[87] and all selves are treated as having an archetypal core, which they will evolve if treated respectfully. This acceptance and respect is seen as the transforming power that abates the negativity and polarized intensity of selves.[88] Sidra Stone has written a book describing her discovery of an Inner Patriarch in women (and his aphoristic counterpart), which unconsciously reinforces patriarchy by consistent devaluation of feminine qualities.[89] In her treatment of this archetypal energy, conscious separation and positive regard for the archetype is seen as the primary transformational power mitigating its negative effects. It reminds me of Christ's counsel that we "resist not evil." No other effort is made to change the Inner Patriarch beyond limiting its conscious involvement via the Aware-ego. The Stones' theoretical framework also recognizes other archetypal images that seem to approximate spiritual selves. Those findings are discussed later in the chapter.

BIFURCATING FORCES AND BILATERAL ASSIMILATION

The methodology described in this book differs from the Stones' approach in several major respects. First, in my work, the client focuses using active imagination rather than relying primarily on an auditory-kinesthetic process. In the Stone's work, visual imagery is used secondarily, though seen as crucial in several respects. Their strong reliance on the auditory method emphasizes the interaction between client and therapist, as distinct from inner interactions between selves. A second crucial difference is that with *Light* therapy the client nearly always functions from the perspective of an Aware-ego utilizing the *Light* to engage all other ego-aspects, images, and felt experiences. For the Stones this is a goal of therapy; for me it is the modus operandi for doing therapy. What makes that possible is the conscious assumption of the *Light* when going inside. Second, in much of my work, the client is encouraged to call upon a higher power such a Christ, to facilitate healing and change, and perform operations beyond an ego-aspect's purview. While the Stones' theoretical framework allows for the emergence of spiritual selves and mythological archetypes capable of dispensing very good advice and altering states of consciousness, it has yet to allow for active interventions by a higher power. In principle, such interventions would appear to violate the preeminence given to the Aware-ego.

Theirs is a psychology of the Ego rather than a psychology of Self. By contrast, a psychology of Self allows for interactions between Spirit, Soul, Body and Mind. The Stones can work with ego-aspects created by parental authority, but not directly address the arbitrary nature of parentified authority, or the splits caused and partially sustained by parental authority. Thus, in the Ego dominated 'world view' created by Voice Dialogue, selves are allowed to co-exist, but unable to reconcile. It is this limitation that I want to address now.

The issue of polarization is an oft-repeated observation of inner work. It is focal to the Stone's work since most primary selves are seen as having polarized opposites. In some cases they are simply other primary selves found to be in conscious conflict, i.e. controlling vs. easygoing, doing vs. being, inner critic vs. rebel, personal vs. impersonal, responsible vs. irresponsible, etc. [90] But the most severe dichotomies are created by a primary self and a disowned self that has been repressed, projected or dissociated. A self with the characteristics of a Slut or Berserker easily personify a disowned self. It does not take much imagination to sense their irreconcilability with primary selves characterized as Virtuous and Civil. I strongly suspect this irreconcilability is a consequence of mistakenly treating all polarized opposites as immutable archetypal opposites rather than recognizing their common cores within the Mind, i.e. that they are flip sides of the same coin. In the physical world – which includes the brain and body, the separation of objects appears hard and fast. But in the Mind, the energy patterns defining images are quite malleable under certain conditions. They are particularly amenable to interventions by higher powers. In the same way that a male can comfortably exhibit both masculine and feminine characteristics within the same male body, it is possible to reconcile polarized opposites within the Mind, if one can address the bifurcating forces polarizing them. Bifurcating force literally means the power to separate one into two. Every image can be thought of as a complementary energy pattern held together with a positive and negative valence – like a combination of neutrons and protons, or comparable to the yin and yang of Tao. Bifurcating forces can separate these charges and sustain the separation until removed (like splitting off electrons from a proton). Just as opposites are said to attract as in the selection of mates, so too inner opposites have an inherent active force for reconnection, once the bifurcating force keeping them apart is removed.

For too long, the culture has polarized ego-aspects into immutable opposites with concomitant adverse effects on Body, Mind and Soul. The reversal of that process is explored at length in successive chapters, but it seems worthwhile to anticipate it here given the centrality of seemingly immutable opposites in the Stone's theoretical framework. In this section, I want to outline a strategy for depolarizing primary and disowned selves. Of note, R. C. Schwartz identifies these polarities as protector/manager vs. exiled parts. Where I have identified such dichotomies in my own work, I have generally labeled them to reflect the forces creating the bifurcation: the Rejected-persona and Ideal-persona created by Moral authority, Coping-aspects and Pre-moral aspects created by Temporal authority, etc. The same strategy outlined below works for all three theoretical positions and is recommended wherever the therapist and client encounter seemingly immutable polarizations. As a practical matter, it is impossible to identify a willful self that does not have a polarized opposite. Every *willful* self is created to contend with a polarized opposite.

What makes the reunification of polarized selves possible is the willingness of the

Aware-ego to call upon Christ or a comparable higher power. Left to its own devices, the Aware-ego is limited to the role played in the Stones' scenario – which is considerable, but still limited to modulating seemingly immutable opposites. That same limitation is also true for the theoretical position put forth by R. C. Schwartz. Only an archetypal power such as Christ appears to have the wherewithal to reunite opposites into a dynamic harmony.

Of note, the Stones do not make a distinction between protectors/managers and firefighters as defined by R. C. Schwartz. They encounter these ego-aspects, but do not appear to appreciate their distinctive role in coping with bifurcated opposites. The function of firefighters is to cope with the tension created by bifurcated primary and disowned selves. In my work, firefighters are called Egos-in-conflict or Dominant selves. An Ego-in-conflict is a dissociated self created to address extremes created by the Rejected-self and Ideal-self. An Ego-in-conflict generally manifests socially unacceptable behavior such as alcohol and drug abuse. In contrast, the Dominant self manifests a repressive dynamic wherein the shameful core is hidden within the Heart rather than dissociated. The Dominant self copes with that repression by then using socially acceptable behaviors in excess. Eating and smoking are the two most common examples found in our culture. Numerous forms of somatic complaints, and all forms of addictive behavior, as well as most psychological defenses, are characteristics of the Ego-in-conflict and Dominant selves. They might best be thought of as countermanding selves that seek to offset the bifurcating forces creating an opposing pair. It is unclear to me why the Stones do not include a firefighter category in their grouping of selves. It may be that visual methodologies lend themselves more easily to the discovery of interactive triumvirates. Or, it could be that the family systems background shared by Schwartz and myself make us more sensitive to the benefits and pitfalls of triangulation. But whatever the reason, these functional distinctions need to be made. The Ego-in-conflict and Dominant self (a.k.a. firefighters) are the bogy-men of inner work. I have discovered that the best way to work with them is to actively elicit their assistance rather than fearing them. Their role in the life of the client is definitely pivotal, especially in the case of the Dominant self.

Polarization

Bifurcation is a primary source of polarization, which is invariably precipitated by some form of shaming behavior on the part of parents or surrogates. There are two sources of bifurcation, both of them consequent to the initial bifurcation. When shame strips an ego-aspect of free will new selves are created by the Ego to cope with that experience. The most common form of creation are selves designed to *fear* a repetition of the shaming. They are organized around the mission of *evading and avoiding the repetition*. When they fail more drastic ego-aspect are created to suppress the *fear* of shaming. Those are the firefighters, what I call Egos-in-conflict. Basically, all of less negative ego emotions serve to evade shameful repetition in one way or another; and consequently, all of them are polarizing. The third form of polarization is the power of shaming exercised by a Dominant self coupled with pride and anger. The power of self-shaming *represses* a shameful event, which saves the Dominant self from dissociation. The Dominant self shames the event in question in an effort to evade the shaming of a parentified conscience. The following case example illustrates the first two conditions. Work with the Dominant self is illustrated in Chapters VII and

VIII.
A Clinical Illustration

(This is a long case that illustrates a number of variables in addition to polarization and the resolution of bifurcation. I will attempt to highlight and summarize them at the end of the verbatim.)

Micah, is a 44-year-old male, married for 24 years. He has a 22-year-old son who was born three months premature and has required complete custodial care since birth. The son is spastic muscularly, has never been able to speak or do much of anything for himself. The client's wife was the son's primary caretaker for most of his life. Micah augments her care when at home. Basically, their whole married life has been organized around his care. Micah, though he only has a high school education, has worked much of his adult life at a law firm performing quasi-legal duties. The couple's extended families have rarely if ever assisted them with their son. The wife's family lives a good day's drive away. Most of the Micah's extended family lives in his community located in rural east Tennessee.

In my first session with Micah, he described his father as a "punishing god." His mother he saw as an exceedingly needy person, who could never make a decision. The father was "the general of the family, he ruled the roost." The father always worked, never drank, and religiously took his family to church several times a week. His father had tried to teach the mother to drive, but "she drove up a bank that first time so after that he drove her everywhere she needed to go." While growing up, his family lived practically next door to the MGM and most of the mother's siblings. Micah said he always wanted his father's respect, but then added: "I'm proud of myself, it doesn't matter." In recent years his father has admitted he was afraid of the grandson and the care he required. But Micah minimized this by saying that even he was afraid of his son when he was a child. His oldest sister's husband was a preacher who said the son was defective because Micah and his wife had sex before marriage. According to Micah, he and his wife have never been alone together (out of the house) since the son's birth. Their sexual relations were unsatisfactory. When I first saw him the couple had not had sex for six months. But in the past they had been abstinent for as long as two years. They slept in separate beds. She complained the nicotine odor from his two-pack a day cigarette habit was too much.

Micah's wife has been in therapy for several years with another therapist. When he first came to see me, she had progressed to the point where she was finally able to take a vacation away from home for a couple of days. This was the reason why Micah has come to see me. He describes himself as a worrier. All he could do – those couple of days she was at the beach – was worry about her. He just knew she would need him; that she would get hurt, maybe have a car wreck. So he sat by the phone fearful of missing her call. He has never, himself, taken a vacation. Micah's focus on marital estrangement, familial obligations, and general guardedness ("If I let my guard down and something screws up, I only have myself to blame") dominated the sessions for several weeks. I began intervening slowly. First, I discussed the idea of learning to breathe from the stomach since I have some tapes he could listen to in the car as he has to travel over an hour to my office. I told him such breathing might help the Worrier to relax a little. We began talking about the idea of him and his wife getting out one night a week. I suggested he only smoke out on the porch at home and take a shower before he approached her for lovemaking. In a similar vein I suggested they just lie together for a few minutes each night even if they did not make love, etc. I deliberately avoided talking about separation issues, since these only seemed to increase his worry. In the sixth session I introduced the *Light* in the context of helping to ease his fears concerning his son.

Micah's greatest fear was life without his son. "What am I without him? I don't have to prove myself to him, he accepts me good or bad, does not question my love." I had him contain his son in a circle of *Light* and to extend a portion of the *Light* to him as a further protection. Unspoken was my clinical sense that a very significant part of Micah was projected into this image of his son. Clearly, he could not accept any weakness of his own that would identify him with his mother rather than father. He loves his son but detested his mother for her neediness. His son seemed to provide an acceptable vessel for this detested part of himself because the son's 'weakness' was clearly outside of the son's control. Previously, his wife served as a partial vessel of his 'weakness' (which we would initially identify as 'deep sadness'), but as her own therapy progresses she seems less and less suitable. Over the next four months I offer a number of interventions to access Needy, that weak part of him hidden in his son and detested in his mother. I am able to diminish his father's Temporal authority – discussed in Chapter VI, and the marital relationship improves, but I cannot get him to identify Needy. Invariably, a feeling washes over him that brings him to the verge of tears and his *Light* breaks contact. He stops coming to see me after four months of therapy and I do not see him again for another fourteen months. To be honest, at this point I have yet to develop the interventions for reconciliation; and the interventions I can offer do not afford enough protection. (Sometimes, I think clients quit and then return later to see if I have figured out what they need.)

Micah returns with the same precipitating event as previously, and more ready to work on it. It is this phase of the therapy that high*light*s the steps described above. This time, his wife and her daughter go to visit her mother in a nursing home in another state. He begins obsessing about her the moment she leaves. He worries she will get up there and need him. He paces and paces to quell his anxiety. "I'm only good when she is bad off. I did not sleep. I want her to be needy and she was managing on her own." I suggest we allow Christ to separate him from this Pacer. This done, he immediately recalls how he use to care for his MGM as a boy when she had coughing spells. He would go down to the house and rub turpentine on her throat. It gave him a sense of power. He then remembers being left with the other grandmother, found crying, and being severely chastised by his father. He remembers feeling needy and being afraid to ask for help, "The Pacer is a chicken shit if he asks for help, but he feels the need in his throat" (which feeling is partially suppressed by chain smoking). When I suggest that the Needy part be contained and given a portion of the *Light* all contact is broken immediately. After reorienting to me, he addresses yet another issue: his feeling that Christ will chastise him like his father. I reassure him with numerous examples from the gospels that Christ seeks to forgive, not chastise.

In the next session, we begin again with the Pacer, a.k.a. the worrier. I identify him as a firefighter who comes out whenever he cannot be in his primary role as a caretaker of others. This time, I also suggest a new intervention. Micah will let Christ go to whatever self agitates the Pacer. Christ will contain it, give it a portion of the Micah's *Light*, anchor it so it cannot move about, and place an opaqued dome over it so it cannot be seen. Micah will only be able to sense it, and only then to the extent he approaches the area where it is contained in his Mind. Micah allows Christ to do all of this and then reports feeling a "deep sadness" that precipitates the recall of several memories: the death of a childhood friend and the death of his mother. (This "deep sadness" appears to be another manifestation of Needy who will go through yet another transition to 'Weak' further into the therapy.) He remembers that the only time he ever saw his father cry was at his mother's funeral. We talk about his visiting these graves, which he has never done. He reflects that his mother always seemed sad and pitiful to him. He begins to appreciate that he has often felt this feeling of "deep sadness" but could not name it before now. Then he becomes agitated, complaining about people who are self-pitying. I ask him if the feeling of Deep Sadness upsets the Pacer? "Yes." I suggest that he have the Pacer use the *Light* to create a shield of protection against this fearful feeling. The *Light* creates "a flowing that covers the whole image" of the Pacer so that he seems relaxed for the first time.

It may be helpful to note here that "deep sadness" is an expression of grief that, while painful, is still preferable to the shame that will be identified with Weak. The reader is referred back to Chapter II and my discussion of David Hawkins's ranking of Ego emotions from least negative to most negative: pride, anger, fear, desire, grief, apathy, guilt, and shame in descending order.91 As Micah moves toward the disowned self that will be identified as Weak and shameful, he first moves from fear to grief in closing the distance.

In the next session, Micah begins by reflecting that over the years he has lost his spirituality. The Caretaker and Pacer have to do it all, much like his father. He notes in passing, that the Pacer seemed more relaxed following the last session; that the garment created with the *Light* seems to help. He says that following the last session he sensed Deep Sadness a lot "Because it was raw and on the surface," but felt it was OK to feel it. Also, "If I shut it off I become more like my dad." He can also own that he felt this deep sadness in his wife, and whenever she rejects it, the Pacer comes out. (Throughout the therapy I was continuously impressed with Micah's perceptivity.) I suggest he allow Christ to walk him a little closer to the source of Deep Sadness contained in the dome. In reply, he notes that he has not had Christ as a buffer for years, but felt this process was giving him back some of his spirituality. I suggest he ask Christ for the courage (the weakest of Hawkins positive emotions) to move into sight of the image within the dome. Initially, nothing happens; then he reports feeling an awareness of its being. Micah then reports that the sense of sadness has left the image. This, he attributes to Christ entering the circle and embracing whoever is in there. It is a good feeling as if the image were saying, "Where have you been all this time?" Micah reiterates that he was very religious growing up, but his father was the real boss, that God was always seen as chastising, and he – Micah, was always "screwing up." I surmise that Deep Sadness is the screw-up. At this juncture, I suggest a healing intervention: "Ask Christ to put his sign on Deep Sadness, to make him a permanent dwelling for the Holy Spirit. Let Christ baptize him." Immediately, he reports seeing a glowing *light* in his being that "Feels good, comforting, warm, secure, very comforting to the mind" (all his words). Next, I suggest that he bring together an image of his father and this new sense of Deep Sadness. He envisions Deep Sadness as a little boy looking up to his father. I then suggest that he allow Christ to remove his father's authority to punish this little boy, but at this the client bulks. "I don't want to see my father as weak or myself as weak." It is suddenly clear to me that Micah has self-protected from weakness by strongly identifying with his father, and he is understandably wary of letting Christ do anything that will diminish the parental authority that sustains both of them. Nonetheless, in this session, two steps and a new awareness are gained. A disowned self – Deep Sadness, is clearly identified and Christ is allowed to extend healing in the form of baptism. The new awareness is Micah's strong identification with his father and the fear that removing the father's authority will leave them both weak.

In the next bi-weekly session, we get closer to Weak. I can now ask Micah if he is willing to let Christ identify the Weak part of himself. When he asks this of Christ, he is reminded of the four year old image of himself needing his mother, hiding under a sink, and being spanked by an aunt for being so childish. When I ask what part of him is most upset by this Weak part, he immediately identifies his father. I then have him ask Christ who took Weak's place? At first, he thinks it was Deep Sadness, but then reflects that it may have been himself. "Maybe, I took dad's place, my mother was not there for us emotionally." Again, I ask who took Weak's place? This time he identifies himself as the Caregiver. How, I ask, does the Caregiver react to Weak? Micah replies that as the Caregiver he has no clue what to do with him. At this point, he hears his father saying, "Don't make me weak, boy." In order to protect the father and the Caregiver, I suggest that Micah allow Christ to place *any image* in his mind that is identified with weakness within a cylinder of *Light*. Christ immediately identifies the client's son, who terrifies the father, followed by the client's wife, and deceased mother. I then suggest that the only one who can enter that cylinder – for now – is Christ; that Micah cannot enter it for the foreseeable future. The goal here, as ever, is to protect the primary selves from their polarized opposites until polarization can be resolved.

In this next session, we identify his mother as a bifurcating force. Micah begins with a complaint. As a rule, at the beginning of each session I ask clients how they are doing vis-à-vis significant others. When I ask how he and his wife are doing, he says that she does not like it when he persists in speaking up for himself. She says he is acting childish. He goes on to say that, in the past, he let her opinion reverse his thinking, that he always needed her approval. I suggest he go inside and separate out the part that needs her approval. When this is done, I next suggest he allow Christ to contain and identify the part that *does not need her approval*. He envisions a dark figure in the shadows that looks like his father inspecting him. For the first time, he is almost able to separate the part of him that is so like his father. I ask what it is the father is looking for? "Weakness. When he cannot see it, it is not painful, not threatening." (Clearly, the cylinder created the previous session is having an effect on his inner dynamics.) "We were not allowed to cry, not allowed to show weakness around him. He beat us up for acting weak, childish, around him…but my mother would try to get in the middle of it when he whipped us." I ask if there is a part of him that agrees with his father, a part of him that he is hiding in his father, a part that did not take his mother's side? In response he can say, "I admired the man…he went to work everyday and came home to a woman who left a lot to be desired." He then adds that weakness has to ask rather than demand, weakness risks rejection. When I ask his frame of reference, he replies that his wife is a hard person, hard to accept affection, *like his mother*. "Daddy tried to please her, but always fell short. It was mother who made us hard."

In the next session, my intent is to remove the parents as a bifurcating force polarizing Weak and Strong. (Understand that Weak and Strong are abstractions encompassing a number of primary and disowned selves identified in the process of discovery.) I set this up by having the Micah ask Christ to draw three circles, one each for Strong and Weak, and a third between them containing his parents. Next I have him ask Christ to step into the circle containing his parents and use his *Light* to absorb the authority keeping Strong and Weak separate. Initially, he sees his parents as standing apart, but afterward they appear almost childlike, no longer at odds, no animosity. Now I have him ask Christ to place a portion of Christ's *Light* in yet another circle that will draw Weak and Strong together in an unthreatening way. He immediately reports feeling a rush of energy, intense but too good to be frightening, "A strong wholeness…more awareness of surroundings…something has come home…back in sync…don't want them to be separate again…neither one of them is bad even together…almost spiritual…I just feel awareness…I suspect I'll let go of fear of certain things…how people perceive me…will be less effected by their perception." In the session following this one the Micah will share with me that he cried from a feeling of fullness all the way home. In the weeks following he will reflect that much of his life had been guided by his father's "hardness" and unrelenting sense of duty. He makes plans to take his first ever vacation with his wife, trusting his son to other caretakers for the first time.

The above vignettes covers a two year period where I met with the Micah every two weeks for a period of months, and he furloughed himself for a year between the first and second phase. Even where clients are prepared to stay with it on a weekly basis, the process can take a number of months. Reconciling polarized pairs of opposites is no mean feat where family and culture treat them as immutable. What makes it all possible is permitting Christ to intervene at critical intervals. He provides protection for the primary selves, heals disowned selves as necessary, and removes the bifurcating forces separating them. What takes the most time, however, is not so much Christ's interventions, but the client's willingness to accede to them. Micah, for example, had been raised in a Christology that was anything but forgiving. He first needed to separate Christ from his father's 'punishing God' in order to finally make the strides he did.

The process of depolarizing a client's selves begins by identifying a primary self and/or firefighter. In Micah's case, the 'presenting symptom' is attributed to a Responsible Primary self called the Pacer (a worrier par excellence) who has to cope with another primary self called the Caregiver (a manager with many of his father's qualities) and a disowned self identified as the Weakling (an exile with many of his mother's qualities). Since the Pacer is so closely aligned with the primary caregiving self, the two were initially difficult to distinguish. Quite often I use physical and/or behavioral symptoms to identify a currently active self, so the Pacer was an obvious first choice to begin the work. The first self is separated out – generally using concentric circles, which automatically insures that it has a portion of the *Light*. The fears or angers of this primary self are then seriously examined, particularly as regards other selves. When the therapist and client are ready to contain a disowned self – the object of the primary's fear, the primary self is offered several options. As a first choice, it is always encouraged to use the *Light* to create a garment of protection. A second option, often used in tandem, is to have Christ contain the disowned part within an opaqued dome of *Light* that is anchored in such a way that whatever is in the dome cannot be seen, escape or move around. By this process, the client is further reassured that the disowned self is safely contained and will not overwhelm the consciousness of other ego-aspects. The anchoring by Christ keeps it in place, providing the primary self, via the Aware-ego, with optimum control. The opaquing allows the disowned self into consciousness as a minimally felt presence so the client does not have to focus too clearly on it. Anchoring allows the Aware-ego to modulate the intensity of that felt presence. The closer the client approaches the contained disowned self the more it is felt by the Aware-ego, a.k.a. the client. By controlling the rate of approach, the Aware-ego can control conscious awareness. At any time, the Aware-ego can back off, as well as establish a comfortable distance between sessions. It should be stressed that this process can take a number of sessions. It is rarely done quickly. Of further note, this progressive desensitization is often accompanied by the client having recalls of the events that resulted in the disowning of a particular self.

Quickly, or slowly, as the client can tolerate, the disowned self is visualized and owned as a self-aspect. As the client approaches fuller acceptance of the nature of this aspect, s/he will often recover a number of events surrounding its creation, which can have the quality of confession. For my part, I am most concerned with the attributes that have forced it into exile. In most instances, the bifurcating force has devalued the qualities that are figural for this disowned self. Almost always, there is shame associated with the disowned ego-aspect. Where that is so, Christ is asked to remove all vestiges of shame. This is done by filling it with the Holy Spirit, i.e. Interior baptism.

Primary selves always experience negative emotions such as fear, anger or guilt in relation to the disowned self. In therapy, those emotions can generally be used to point to the disowned opposite self. This is especially true of fear, which always has an object. I will repeatedly encourage my clients to identify the object of fear. What is the primary self afraid of? Once that the object of fear is contained in a dome, the therapist then wants to assist the primary self in dispelling the defensive emotion. Numerous interventions are described throughout the book for accomplishing this.

When the primary self is freed of its negative emotional defenses, and the disowned self is freed of shame, the client and therapist can proceed to an examination of the bifurcating force responsible for the creation of this polarized pair of opposites. I generally introduce this step with the concept of a wedge that has the power to separate these two parts of the self, making each one a negatively repellent charge. In the process of separation one part – a primary self, is negatively weighted by making it fearful, and the other is strongly unbalanced by shaming it. In essence, the bifurcating force has the power to negatively charge both sides of the same coin. When the two selves have been identified, Christ is enlisted to help identify this force and defuse it. This is done by first bringing the polarized primary and disowned selves into close proximity, each in its own circle. Christ is then asked to draw a third circle between them and contain the force which has been keeping the two selves polarized, immutable, estranged. Without any exception I can think of, the bifurcating force will be identified as a parental image – mother or father, often both parents. Regardless of whom it is, in each case Christ is asked to enter the circle and use his *Light* to remove/absorb the authority that has been sustaining the polarization. Immediately thereafter, Christ is asked to create yet another circle in which he places a portion of his own *Light*. This circle is used to reunite the polarized pair via Christ's *Light* in way that is not threatening to the client. In some instances, this step is unnecessary. Some clients report the collapse of both circles into one immediately following the removal of authority from the bifurcating force, i.e. the parent. When the step is complete, whether spontaneously or as a planned action, the client will report feeling a new sense of self. It is as if the primary and disowned selves have blended into each other harmoniously. Of note, clients are often reluctant to take this last step in the session it is first offered. I encourage them to go home and reflect on it. Not infrequently, they take the step between sessions, and spend the next session telling me about the changes they have experienced. More often, however, there are power issues that must be addressed. This is especially true for Dominant selves, which I examine in Chapters VII and VIII.

It is rarely as simple as I have just described it – and even that is not simple. But the steps are accurate as broad strokes. In successive chapters I hone the process in significant ways. Micah's case describes my earliest approaches in reconciling polarized selves, including a number of missteps. The client and I were nonetheless successful because I implicitly trusted the *Light* and Christ image to lead.

USING VOICE DIALOGUE WHEN THE AWARE-EGO IS BLOCKED

This section is out of place. It rightly belongs with my previous discussion of the Aware-ego. But the case examples offered here require an appreciation of Voice Dialogue, so I have left off the discussion till now. What I want to address is an important observation regarding inner work, namely, that the client rarely, if ever, comes to therapy as an Aware-ego, even after functioning as an Aware-ego in therapy for some length of time. The self or selves – generally Dominant selves – who bring the client to therapy in the first place, are likely to continue in that task. These selves will allow therapy to commence until threatened with the uncovering of a particular self. This can be very early in the process. Some selves are even threatened by the prospect of going inside under any circumstances and will actively block the process from the outset. But at whatever point they are upset by the process, they will make themselves felt. At that juncture the client will report difficulties. Clients who could visualize stop being able to do so; or they will report that they are dissociating, i.e. observing an image of themselves holding the *Light*. When this occurs, the therapist needs to focus on the self whose fears have been aroused. I would note that this usurpation does not normally occur on initially going inside. If it does occur at the outset – and the client is unable to contain the self who is resisting inner work, then Voice Dialogue may provide a viable alternative. Essentially, the therapist asks – using a Voice Dialogue protocol – "to speak to the part that most objects to the inner work." If some inner work has already been done, and the client has accepted the concept of multiple selves, it is best to speak to this new self as another part of the client. In that case the part is not identified by the client's name but as "the part of you that objects to the client's continuing."

Renee. The following case illustrates how a self can complicate the process of going inside. The client, Renee, has sufficient experience using the *Light* to report that she is dissociating. She sees herself watching the part of her "with the *Light*" approach a fearful part of herself. I ask if I can dialogue with whoever is observing this. When she agrees I have her move to another chair and go back inside. She identifies herself as the Intellect, the primary self that had brought Renee to therapy to understand why she is having problems. (This part is very much like the Rational Mind described by the Stones.) She has been a co-conscious observer of the process until this session, observing as other parts were separated out and given portions of the *Light*. I ask what "fear" obliged her to take control at this juncture? She tells me that the Aware-ego was given the specific task of getting closer to an aspect identified as Weak. Before approaching this weak aspect, several selves — identified as the People Pleaser, Procrastinator, and Panic, have all been contained within an opaqued circle so they will not be upset by the task of approaching Weak. *As a further precaution*, the Aware-ego was instructed to ask Christ that only the Aware-ego and Christ be able to see Weak. It was that condition that upset the Intellect. Among other disclosures, she tells me that she cannot see anything in the anchored dome, that it is black. The *Light* was restricting what she could see. This is very likely why she assumed control of consciousness. She could no longer follow what was being done. In such instances, the best strategy is to give a portion of the *Light* to this newly identified ego-aspect and assist it in whatever need it expresses.

THE SPIRITUAL SELVES

Near the end of their manual for doing Voice Dialogue, the Stones describe a number of 'spiritual' selves they have sought out or encountered. These selves fall into three categories: 1) altered states of consciousness, 2) images from visions and dreams, and 3) archetypal energies, specifically the "higher mind." In working with these selves the Stones are clear that Voice Dialogue is often insufficient to engage them; that more is needed in the way of visualization and meditative techniques. [92] The Stones are both cautionary and encouraging in this matter of spiritual selves. On the cautionary side they argue, with excellent case examples, that primary selves can masquerade as spiritual guides that are judgmental, critical, and unrelenting — very much like the unredeemed conscience created by parentified Moral authority or Dominant selves. In fact, from the Stone's perspective, the primary selves generally function much like Freud's superego. The Stones also caution that spiritual experiences can be limiting if they disengage the individual from instinctual and disowned aspects. "The danger to an individual when these spiritual energies are first experienced is the potential split between spirit and matter. These energies are so seductive that many spiritually identified people lose their connection to earth, to instinct, to their physical bodies. Our challenge is to learn how to live in spirit on the earth and avoid splitting spiritual energies away from life." [93] This is a basic tenet of Kabbalah as well. But that said, I agree with them that there is undoubted value in eliciting voices of a spiritual nature. "The voice of the spirit, whether it speaks in dreams, visions, or Voice Dialogue, always has a very special energy connected to it – it is uplifting and non-judgmental. Things may be pointed out to us, but we are never admonished. It as though we are taken to another level to view the personal issues with which we are wrestling."

The Stones introduce their sense of spirituality with an examination of doing vs. being. They rightly note that most of the primary selves identified by Voice Dialogue are focused on doing and action: "Western civilization in general focuses upon doing and action, and much of the impetus for the heavyweight selves is derived from this focus." [95] Using Voice Dialogue they describe a process for accessing the polarized opposite of all this doing, a self that abides in the present moment:

> In Voice Dialogue we can contact another self – a self that can open us to our spiritual selves. This self is more concerned with being than with doing. When we experience this "being" energy, there is no goal and no task; there is nothing. We sometimes refer to this self as the "nothingness" voice. It is not a child state, though sometimes the feelings of the vulnerable child come out in its presence. To facilitate being energy, the facilitator first asks to make contact with the doing or action side. This is in line with our basic viewpoint that the primary selves, the selves with which the ego is identified, should be approached first. This action self will often be very closely aligned with the pusher and power selves. We don't worry about that. We simply focus on what the action self likes to do and how it likes to keep busy. Once we have talked to this part, we then move towards the being self....This particular energy brings with it a feeling of great peace and quiet, a sense of being centered and grounded. [96]

The Stone's process for identifying 'doing and being' selves is illustrated in the following case example. In this case, doing and being were treated as selves that have been polarized by a bifurcating force. The resolution of that bifurcation is also illustrated. It is possible that my method has confabulated the Stone's understanding of the 'being' self with what they refer to as a meditative or fantasy self.[97] Of note, the being state - as the Stones understand it, is predominantly a non-verbal I-Thou connection between client and facilitator. This is a distinct consequence of using Voice Dialogue to evoke it. In active imagination, the being state is always interior, but as the client in the following case describes it, it is almost identical to what the Stones experience in Voice Dialogue. Lastly, this case is also noteworthy because the client – Lee – calls on a higher power other than Christ. Lee was raised in the Catholic church but experienced it as judgmental and punitive. For several years she has been an active member of a group whose leader channels a spirit calling himself Teacher. Lee elected to envision Teacher as her higher power. For my part, I confess I often imagined her image of Teacher as Christ by another name. But that is not the case as he is distinctly different from Christ. Years later she will work with both of them in the same session! In any case, his interventions on her behalf are quite effective.

Lee. Lee is a very competent nurse, divorced, no children, middle aged. She is an active meditator and very good at visualizing. Two weeks earlier Lee came to therapy distraught over an incident that occurred in the work place. When working, she feels as if she has to do it all and often extends herself to the point of exhaustion. I encouraged her to set better limits on herself. In fact, I have repeatedly encouraged this, as her over-extension is a chronic problem. But as one of my mentors said: you give good advice with the foreknowledge it will not be followed, and then proceed to discover the source of resistance. So not surprisingly, she returns with the same complaints. I suggest we examine this "pusher-driver" that she and her coworkers so highly value, and that only her depressions and sporadic love interests seemed able to hold in check. At her request, Teacher separates this part of her using a double circle and then gives it a portion of her *Light*. Lee describes what she senses within the circle as lacking form, a moving energy, almost transparent, swirling. In a few moments it seems to settle down but remains shadowy. "What I sense is intensity, hell bent on getting everything done, not anger or rage, but driven." I ask what complex of emotions seems to drive her? "Get off your lazy ass – from Mom." Also, "You are going to fail. The Driver's determination is to prove that one wrong." I ask if there is a part of her prone to failure? Here I am attempting to get at the disowned self that has been polarized. But she is not able to make this leap yet. Instead, she continues to ascribe motivations to the felt intensity. "The message is universal. It's the same message from school mates and teachers – you are not good enough, did not do it right, or you did it half ass." At this point I ask if there is a part of her that is a threat to the Driver. To this she replies that, "The Driver has a hard time with me not getting things done. Yes, there may be a part that interferes with task completion. She does not value playfulness." I suggest that Teacher contain the part that is the greatest threat, but keep it invisible to the Driver so as not to push her into overdrive. Her response is quite unexpected for both of us: "The Driver just faded… she did not go away…she is wrapped in a protective cloud…I can no longer see her dark silhouette. Immediately after, this threatening part emerged in her own circle…I felt this incredible *softness* – not a form but a feeling, no beginning and no end…without limit…in the moment…no sense of time…time is unimportant to her." I ask if there are times when this part is strong in her? What are her assets, strengths, what would Lee value in her? "She seems to live in the moment, to be exactly where she is…she has the ability to be amazed...playful…not worried about moving along…she could care less whether something gets done or not." Lee goes on to describe how this ego-aspect seems to be eternal, to live outside of time. Lee definitely values the feeling of it, but also recognizes it would be ultimately self-destructive to exclusively seek this state of being. At this point, I suggest she ask Teacher to use a third circle to contain the bifurcating force that keeps these two selves separate and a threat to the Driver. Without hesitation she says, "Mother, mother, mother." I ask when did her mother initiate the process and by what authority? "I was young, but not at birth. After my father died at age seven, and again when I was in adolescence." Finally, I ask if she is willing for Teacher to remove the authority from her mother that is preventing these two selves from rejoining and functioning in concert. Not yet. She wants to reflect on it more.

When Lee returns two weeks later, she seems much more peaceful and energized. She reports having spent more time doing things for herself. But she has not attempted to reconcile the Driver with the profound sense of softness she experienced in the previous session. On reflection, she decides to identify the softness as a playful child, and after some discussion of exactly how we might proceed, she elects to let Teacher remove the authority from her mother using his *Light*. Before she goes inside, I describe how Teacher will contain the mother image exercising her authority to keep the two ego-aspects separate, which keeps them polarized, and how he will be expected to remove that authority with his *Light*. Immediately on going inside and visualizing the three circles it is done. She has allowed it to happen even as I was setting it up. "Hard to explain what happened, it just happened so quickly, the three circles just collapsed, the separateness is no longer there." I asked if she is aware of any difference? In reply, she notes that previously when I used the phrase "mother's authority" it brought tears to her eyes, but no longer.

In my clinical experience it is best to treat such interventions as emergent functions. The effects can only be measured in retrospect by what the client perceives as different in the weeks following the intervention. It is a totally new experience. For Lee, in the weeks that follow she acquires a new kind of perception. Basically, she becomes aware of the ability to step back and assess ongoing activity: to simply be present amidst the doing, to be simultaneously anxious and not anxious, to more clearly assess the fearful parts of herself and the reasons for their existence, and to actively assist in developing strategies for reconciling other polarized aspects. Archetypal "being" appears to have constellated itself in the felt experience of a child playing "in the moment." It is that energy which appears to have been reintegrated with the Driver.

The Higher Self Verses a Higher Power

In addition to facilitating being vs. doing, the Stones also seek to evoke the client's higher self. The Stones assert that:

"Voice Dialogue creates the possibility of directly connecting with spiritual energies. A facilitator can ask directly to talk to the higher mind, or the subject can be led into the higher mind through a meditative procedure followed by a shift to Voice Dialogue." [98]

For the most part, this higher mind appears to be imagined before it is engaged via Voice Dialogue. Often, it seems to take the form of archetypal images such as a Sage, Hermit, Crone or Wise Old Woman. The Stones repeatedly stress that, "It is very important in dealing with the higher mind to discriminate between an orthodox patriarchal father/pusher/critic and a genuine spiritual energy." [99] As a rule, this can only be done after the fact. The higher mind is only considered genuine if it does not act like an unredeemed superego. I am reminded here of the oft observed second personality described by the early hypnotists which seemed to function as an objective witness, or the Inner Self Helper identified in MPD literature. [100] In general, the higher mind is seen as a source of detached wisdom which the client can accept or not, that is free of any negative judgment. It is not envisioned to be god-like, as would be the case for a Christ image, and this higher self is not expected to directly intervene with other selves on the client's behalf. With a few notable exceptions, I do not deliberately evoke such images with my clients. The Christ image or a comparable higher power has proven more than sufficient. In the chapter on Temporal authority, I do describe situations where Christ is asked to seek out a mother who can meet the needs of a Pre-moral aspect. In all instances where this has occurred the found image generally has a numinous quality denoting an archetypal nature. Also, there are occasions when clients – particularly women, will want to seek out a goddess-like feminine image to serve some particular purpose. As a rule, if the image passes screening using the *Light*, then I am quite content to evoke such an image and let it be used to make therapeutic interventions.

It may be helpful to note here that the Stones developed their theoretical framework within a Jungian context. Jung's psychology – long considered exponentially more spiritual than any other theory of his times, was nonetheless bound to the closed system of the Self comprising consciousness, personal unconscious, and collective unconscious. The ego could submit or rebel against this Self, but never really know it or strive to be dominant without destroying itself. Jung asserted that the Self is ever beyond the reach of the ego's compass. This sense of Self also exceeds the numerous of archetypal energies it generates that manifest as hero, sage, warrior, hermit, hierophant and the like. It was Jung's contention that the symbols for Self, Christ, and God were essentially interchangeable, and distinctly different from Self's archetypal manifestations. In sum, Jesus Christ and comparable higher powers are not archetypal constellations. Even the gods in the pantheons of ancient Greece and Rome are a step above the Self's personal archetypes.

SUMMARY

In some respects this chapter has been less about Christ and more about the various ego-aspects, images and entities that a therapist and client are likely to encounter on going inside. These are the 'problem children,' the reason for calling on a *Light* and Christ. As the reader progresses through the remaining chapters it will be readily apparent that Christ is instrumental in just about all of the explorations and indispensable for most of the interventions. I have noted the works of R. C. Schwartz and the Stones as frames of reference for what is possible without use of the *Light* and Christ; and because they support my finding that all of us live with co-existing selves. From my perspective, the reach of their interventions is somewhat limited. But that said, all of their observations and interventions are easily integrated into the methodologies used here. Moreover, Schwartz's internalization of family systems offers therapists with that orientation a wonderful entrée into active imagination; while the Stone's work offers clients who have difficulty visualizing another entrée to the inner world of ego-aspects. As demonstrated, voice dialogue can also be integrated into active imagination and a sensed presence of the *Light* and Christ.

Most of the issues described in this book are explored by a tripartite system comprised of the Aware-ego, *Light*, and image of Christ, or a comparable higher power. In most instances, it is the higher power afforded by Christ which makes the crucial difference, particularly when he is permitted his own *Light* and allowed to channel the Holy Spirit.. When the Christ energy is provided an imaginal vessel within the Mind, it will facilitate the healing of most psychological and many physical problems, as well as providing an avenue for the healing of Soul.

CHAPTER IV ENDNOTES

1   Hass, J. (1991), 'Second Response', in Smith, R.W., Editor, (1991) *Catholic*

Conscience Foundation and Formation, The Knights of Columbus, New Haven, p.110.

2   The Gospels are very clear that we can only know the Father through Christ. Both Matthew and Luke assert this: "All things have been handed over to Me by My Father; and no one knows the Son except the Father, and no one knows the Father except the Son and anyone to whom the Son chooses to reveal Him (Matthew 11:27; Luke 10:22)." The nuances of this assertion are addressed in Appendix II.

3   Unless otherwise specified, all bible references are taken from: Metzger, B.M, & Murphy, R.E., Editors (1991), *The New Oxford Annotated Bible with the Apocryphal/Deuterocanonical Books: New Revised Standard Version*, Oxford University Press: New York.

4   *Course In Miracles*, (1992), Combined Volume, 2nd Edition, Foundation for Inner Peace: Glen Cove, California.

5   Spalding, B. (1924), *Life and Teaching of the Masters of the Far East*, California Press: San Francisco.

6   See Freke, T. &Gandy, P. (2001), *Jesus and the Lost Goddess: The Secret Teachings of the Original Christians*, Harmony Books: New York

7   Smith, Joseph (1989)*The Book of Mormon: Another Testament of Jesus Christ*, The Church of Jesus Christ of Latter-day Saints, Salt Lake City, Utah.

8   Campbell, J. (1998), *Dead Sea Scrolls: The Complete Story*, Ulysses Press: Berkley, CA.

9   Robinson, J.M., General Editor (1988), *The Nag Hammadi Library in English*, Harper: San Francisco.

10   Barnstone, W., Editor, (1984), *The Other Bible*, Harper & Row Publishers: San Francisco.

11   Most exegeses would insist - and I concur, that the New Testament can only be fully understood in the midrashic context of the Old Testament. It is not argued here that one can solely understand Christ through the New Testament, but rather, that those books are a sufficient midrashic continuation and culmination of biblical Christology.

12   The particular workshop described in this paragraph was led by Pat Rodegast who channels Emmanuel. See Rodegast, P. (1985), *Emmanuel's Book*, Bantam Books: New York.

13 Bandler, R. & Grinder, J. (1975), *The Structure of Magic: a Book About Language and Therapy*, Science & Behavior Books: Palo Alto, Calif.

14   Galland, C. (1990), *Longing For Darkness: Tara and the Black Madonna*, Penguin Books: New York.

15   Schaup, S.(1997), *Sophia: Aspects of the Divine Feminine*, Nicolas-Hays, Inc.: York Beach, Maine.

16   Johnsen, L. (1994), *Daughters of the Goddess: The Women Saints of India*, Yes International Publishers: St. Paul, Minnesota.

17   See for examples: Linn, D., Linn, M. & Fabricant, S. (1984), *Praying With Another for Healing*, Paulist Press: New York; also, Linn, D. & Linn, M. (1978), *Healing Life's Hurts: Healing Memories Through the Five Stages of Forgiveness*, Paulist Press: New York.

18   Bandler, R., & Grinder, J. (1969), *Patterns of the Hypnotic Techniques of Milton H. Erickson, M.D.*, Vol. 1, Meta Publications: Cupertino, Calif.

19   Erickson, M. & Rossi, E.L., (1979), *Hypnotherapy: An Exploratory Casebook*, Irvington Publishers, Inc.: New York; see also: Haley, J. (1973), *Uncommon Therapy*, Norton: New York.

20   Sanford, J., (1987), *The Kingdom Within: the Inner Meaning of Jesus' Sayings*, Harper & Row: San Francisco.

21   See Wink for a definitive description of principalities and powers: Wink, W. (1992), *Engaging the Powers: Discernment and Resistance in a World of Domination*, Fortress Press: Minneapolis.

22   See Harpur, T. (2004), *The Pagan Christ: Recovering the Lost Light,* Walker & Co.: NY.

23   Even in the 21st century there continues to be heated controversy over the historicity of Jesus Christ. See, for example, Freke, T. & Gandy, P. (1999), *The Jesus Mysteries: Was the 'Original Jesus' a Pagan God?*, Thorsons: New York. Even if the only valid historical Christ is a biblical one – a man-god described in

the gospels, he has manifest in history. Our faith and understanding is predicated upon those gospels – which are an historical fact, and his healing power in our lives. See also Schweitzer, A. (2005), *The Quest of the Historical Jesus*, Dover Publications (originally published in 1910).

24 Richard Bauckham argues quite persuasively that the highest Christology found in the New Testament treats Christ as the evolutionary or eschatological incarnation of YHVH; that Jewish exegetes had fully developed a high Christology in the New Testament that in no way conflicted with Jewish monotheism. See Bauckham, R. (2008), *Jesus and the God of Israel: God Crucified and Other Studies on the New Testament's Christology of Divine Identity,* William B. Eerdmans Publishing Co: Grand Rapids, MI.

25 As Johnson notes, many of the attributes attributed to Christ in the Gospel of John are derived from those attributed to Wisdom or Sophia. Johnson, E.A. (1994), *She Who Is: the Mystery of God in Feminist Theological Discourse,* Crossroad: New York.

26 God the father is only said to have spoken one time in the gospels. That is when Christ is baptized by John the Baptist, and then only to Christ and – possibly – John the Baptist. "As soon as Jesus was baptized, he went up out of the water. At that moment heaven was opened, and he saw the Spirit of God descending like a dove and *light*ing on him. And a voice from heaven said, "This is my Son, whom I love; with him I am well pleased (Matthew 3:16).""

27 The Nicaean declaration has become a point of contention among theologians. The Nicaean Creed declares that 'God the Father' is a person of God, but it is a hard to support this thesis when one considers that "Rebbe Jesus" and the Jews who wrote the Gospels could not have tolerated the idea of YHVH being relegated to a mere person of God. From their perspective, the title of 'Abba' was considered Jesus' preferred name for YHVH comparable to 'Adoni,' 'The Holy One, Blessed be He,' or G-d. See Bauckham, R. (2008) op. cit.

28 I have only had one client insist on using a Father-God image. The image was essentially unforgiving. The client expected that this 'father' would be forgiving in the short run but not on the final day of judgment.

29 Invariably in working with clients who suffer from severe Dissociative Identity disorders a voice-image can be discerned that has repeatedly made itself felt to the client at moments of severe stress. Often, they think of it as another alter, but when more closely examined, recognize that it is different from other alters. In the MPD literature this 'other' has come to be called the ISH or Inner Self Helper. See Putnam, F.W. (1989) *Diagnosis and Treatment of Multiple Personality*

Disorder, The Guildford Press: New York. See also Freisen for a Christian perspective on MPD: Friesen, J.G. (1991), *Uncovering the Mystery of MPD*, Here's Life Publishers: San Bernardino, CA.

30   In New Age literature, especially that addressing near-death and after-death experiences, common reference is made to a Guide, which is always available to the individual if called. See, for example, Newton, M. (1999), *Journey of Souls: Case Studies of Life between Lives*, Llewellyn Publications: St. Paul.

31   The Catholic Church's insistence that their priests be seen as "the earthly representatives of Christ" tends to create a conundrum for some Catholics. It obliges them to envision Christ as outside of them and faraway. Were it otherwise, an earthly representative would be unnecessary. Similarly, many Catholics have been raised to believe that Christ can only dwell within while the individual is free of sin. As soon as they have sinned, the 'temple' becomes too impure for the pure Christ. This is somewhat at odds with the Christ of the Gospels who appears to actively seek out sinners in order to offer them his saving grace.

32   Johnson provides theological arguments for a number of Sophia-Christ images. Johnson E.A., (1994), op. cit.

33   This is a very helpful strategy. Essentially, Christ is asked to use the *Light* to connect the perpetrator with the self-aspect experiencing the memory in such a way that the perpetrator is obliged to feel whatever emotion the child is feeling as a result of the abuse. Almost without exception, the perpetrator will cease what they are doing because it now inflicts pain on them as they are now obliged to experience the effects of their attack.

34   Where abuse is extensive - that is lasting over a period of months or years, it is quite likely that there will be episodes when the client actively participated in some way as distinct from being a victim, though it must be stressed that the client is unlikely to have participated if acts were not initiated by the perpetrator. In any case, while early memories show the client as a victim, later memories may show the client as taking more initiative, which invariably produces much guilt and the conviction they are unforgivable.

35   I do not mean to infer here that it is beyond the power of Christ to heal the body. To my way of thinking the body is controlled by the Mind. As the Mind is healed I think it reasonable to expect comparable healing from the body. Often, the greatest obstacles to physical healing are persistent emotions such as vengeful anger and unforgiveness.

36   Because most of my clients now have computers, I normally arrange to send them a copy of my '*Light* Therapy Manual,' which describes much of what is contained in Chapter III. I ask them to read the first dozen pages so as to get a feel for the *Light*, how it works, etc. When anyone reads the manual, I assume they are also role-playing what it will be like. So in one sense they have already been inside before I formally take them inside in a later session.

37   Images of children known to the client can serve the same purpose as a Christ image where the client has difficulty with the idea of finding their *Light*. In such instances, I have the client imagine a child, often one of their own or a close relative's, who reaches behind their back and brings forth their *Light*.

38   See for examples: Linn, D., Linn, M. & Fabricant, S. (1984), *Praying With Another for Healing*, Paulist Press: New York.

39   For some clients such a place already exists and if they are willing to acknowledge its existence to the therapist then this would be an ideal choice. One client, who had been severely abused, had created what she called a Womb room - a place that felt warm, completely contained and insulated from the outside world.

40   See, for example, the work of Carlson. Carlson, K. (1990), *In Her Image: the Unhealed Daughter's Search for Her Mother*, Shambhala: Boston.

41   One MPD client had an alter personality who was able to acknowledge that "something" had happened but was then able to "erase" it from her mind such that whatever had happened had not happened to her. This repression allowed her to function as if she had not been abused. She was only able to work through this denial when she became willing to identify the recipient of all these erasures, essentially an alter-ego in every sense of the word. When working with alter personalities, the therapist should always bear in mind that these ego manifestations are three-dimensional. They can and do exercise all of the defense mechanisms available to other people including dissociation, repression, denial, projection, and depersonalization and paranoia.

42   The reader is referred back to Chapter I and my discussion of emotion. Pride, anger, fear, desire, despair, guilt and shame are all considered negative emotions even though some of them are valued by culture.

43   Schwartz's work is examined later in the chapter. Schwartz, R.C. (1995), *Internal Family Systems Therapy*, Guilford Press: New York.

44   Gallegos, E.S. (1990), *The Personal Totem Pole: Animal Imagery, The*

Chakras, and Psychotherapy, Moon Bear Press: Santa Fe, NM.

45   Fiori, E. (1988), *The Unquiet Dead*, Doubleday: New York.

46   Fiori, E., op. cit.

47   Modi, S. (1997), *Remarkable Healings: A Psychiatrist Discovers Unsuspected Roots of Mental and Physical Illness*, Hampton Roads: Charlottesville, VA.

48   Linn, Matthew, Editor (1981) *Deliverance Prayer: Experiential, Psychological and Theological Approaches*, Paulist Press: New York.

49   his ritual response is different from the traditional prayer of exorcism: "I rebuke thee in the name of Christ, I bind thee in the name of Christ, and I command thee to leave in the name of Christ." Today, I approach all potential entities as redeemable and use a method similar to the one described by Modi (op. cit.). I ask Christ – using his *Light*, to transform whatever is contained in circle into pure white *light* and to return it to the source of all *light*. I find this far preferable to merely "casting out devils" that will continue to roam and re-attach themselves to the unsuspecting.

50   See Crabtree, A. (1985), *The Multiple Man: Explorations in Possession and Multiple Personality*, Pragaer: New York; see also Martin, M. (1992), *Hostage to the Devil: The Possession and Exorcism of Five Americans*, Harper: San Francisco; see also Peck, M.S. (1983), *People of the Lie: The Hope for Healing Human Evil*, Simon & Schuster, Inc.: New York.

51   Linn, Matthew, Editor (1981) , op. cit.

52   Fiori, E., op. cit

53   Crabtree, A. (1985), *op.cit.*

54   McAll, K. (1982), *Healing the Family Tree*, Sheldon Press: London.

55   See Harner, M. (1982), *The Way of the Shaman: A Guide to Power and Healing*, Bantam Books, New York.

56   We do well to never underestimate the power of *belief*. One of the most thought provoking books I have ever read on this subject is still in print: Pearce, J.C. (1971), *The Crack in the Cosmic Egg: Challenging Constructs of Mind and*

Reality, Julian Press: San Francisco.

57   Modi, S. (1997), *op.cit.*

58   As a rule, I instruct my clients in the concept of chakras before asking them to let Christ 'enter' their heart. The heart chakra is seen as the blueprint of the physical heart as well as the most direct link to the Soul. From an energy perspective, the chakra heart is actually one of seven hearts, one for each of the seven main chakra bodies, each nested within the other. Stated another way, the heart chakra is seen as the link between the three chakra templates of the soul and the three chakras of the Mind – mental (solar plexus), emotional (abdominal), and etheric (root).

59   Hawkins, D.R. (1998), *Power Versus Force: An anatomy of Consciousness and The Hidden Determinants of Human Behavior*, Veritas Publishing, Sedona, Arizona.

60   See Wink's penetrating analysis of the myth of redemptive violence, which permeates our culture. Wink, W. (1992), *Engaging the Powers: Discernment and Resistance in a World of Domination*, Fortress Press, Minneapolis, Minnesota.

61   The veracity of such reports is not an issue here. I have never sought to verify such reports or encouraged my clients to seek legal recourse unless their abuser was a therapist or similar professional. I do accept that something like their memories occurred. Without question, the patient experiencing the recall believes the events happened. Even if the memory were a complete fabrication, which I seriously doubt, it would still need to be healed.

62   Spalding, B. (1924), *Life and Teaching of the Masters of the Far East*, California Press: San Francisco.

63   Moody, R.(1987), *Life After Life: The Investigation of a Phenomenon - Survival of Bodily Death*, Phoenix Press: New York

64   Schwartz, R.C. (1995), *Internal Family Systems Therapy,* Guilford Press: New York.

65   Stone, H. & Stone. S., (1993), *Embracing Your Inner Critic,* Harper-Collins: San Francisco.

66   Stone, H. & Stone. S., (1993), op. cit.

67   Perls, F., (1969), *Gestalt Therapy Verbatim*, Real People Press: Moab, UT

68   Taken from Schwartz, R.C., op. cit. Quote taken from Jung, C.G., (1968), *Analytical Psychology: Its Theory and Practice – The Tavistock Lectures,* London: Routledge and Kegan Paul, p.p. 80-81.

69   In personal communication with Dr. Schwartz he has acknowledged the existence of "critters" and the need for guides, particularly in his work with multiple personality disorders. This would seem to indicate the existence of spiritual realms. But I cannot reference that in the work cited here or be more specific than to note his verbal reference to such phenomena.

70   Schwartz, R.C. (1995), op. cit., p. 46.

71   This client is a highly intelligent, largely self-educated, young woman who has read extensively in metaphysics and world religions. She has named this self 'Durga', after the Hindu goddess, who took up arms against an abusive patriarchy.

72   Schwartz, R.C. (1995), op. cit., p. 46.

73   Freud's tripartite system comprised of Superego, Ego, and Id is a prime example.

74   Berne, E. (1961), *Transactional Analysis in Psychotherapy*, Grove Press: New York.

75   Stone, H. & Stone. S., (1993), op. cit.

76   There may be a notable exception to this observation. In a number of instances, Schwarz has his clients role-play interactions with parents in active imagination. At such times, the parental figure is obviously internalized. This is done so as to coach the various parts into envisioning a different outcome in an interaction between the client and the parent. But aside from this particular intervention, Schwartz does not appear to focus on the parental image.

77   Schwartz, R.C. (1995), op. cit., p. 231.

78   Schwartz, R.C. (1995), op.cit., pp. 96-97

79   A number of MPD clients have reported being in a torturing situation for days and weeks. Such a duration can generate a large number of fragments as the individual seeks to endure the myriad feelings generated by the event.

80   Stone, H. & Stone, S., (1989), *Embracing Our Selves: The Voice Dialogue Training Manual,* Nataraj Publishing/New World Library: Novato, CA.

81   Perls, F., (1969), *Gestalt Therapy Verbatim,* Real People Press: CA.

82   Dayton, T., & Moreno, Z. (2004), *The Living Stage: A Step-by-Step Guide to Psychodrama, Sociometry, and Group Psychotherapy*, HCI: New York.

83   See Stamboliev for an excellent discussion of energy patterns encountered in the Voice Dialogue process. Stanboliev, R., (1992), *The Energetics of Voice Dialogue: An In-Depth Exploration of the Energetic Aspects of Transformational Psychology,* Life Rhythm: Mendocino, CA.

84   Dyak, M. (1999), *The Voice Dialogue Facilitator's Handbook: Part I,* L.I.F.E. Energy Press: Seattle, WA., p. 9.

85   See the Stone's manual describing their process which identifies many selves seen as common to American and European societies: Stone, H. & Stone, S., (1989), *Embracing Our Selves: The Voice Dialogue Method*, New World Library: Novato, CA.

86   Dyak, M. (1999), op. cit.

87   Dyak, M. (1999), op. cit.

88   Stamboliev, Opt. Cit., p.63.

89   Stone, S., (1997), *The Shadow King: The Invisible Force That Holds Women Back,* Nataraj Publishing/New World Library: Novato, CA.

90   Stone, H. & Stone, S., 1989, Opt. Cit.

91   Stone, H. & Stone, S., 1989, Opt. Cit.

92   "Voice Dialogue can be used to reach a certain level of these energies; however, used alone, it can only go so far. Other approaches must also be utilized." Stone, H. & Stone, S., 1989, Opt. Cit., p. 234. Basically, they are referring here to the use of active imagination evoking visionary experiences as well as developing motifs found in dreams.

93   Stone, H. & Stone, S., 1989, op. cit., p. 228.

94 Stone, H. & Stone, S., 1989, op. cit., p. 229.

95 Stone, H. & Stone, S., 1989, op. cit., p. 218.

96 Stone, H. & Stone, S., 1989, op. cit., p. 219.

97 "Sometimes the facilitator might observe that the subject is spacing or seems to be in a meditative state, even though he or she is supposedly with the facilitator in being energy. A spacing subject has become lost in fantasy or day-dreams, or has simply disappeared within. As with all other selves, we do not judge this state. We simply recognize it as a different self and move the person over so that the Aware-ego can gradually learn the difference between the being energy in contact with another and the being energy that leads people within, away from contact with others."(Stone, H. & Stone, S., 1989, op. cit., p. 221)

98 Stone, H. & Stone, S., 1989, op. cit., p. 234.

99 Stone, H. & Stone, S., 1989, op. cit., p. 237

100 See Crabtree, A.,(1985), *The Multiple Man: Explorations in Possession and Multiple Personality*, Pragaer: New York

CHAPTER V

EXPLORING MIND: EMOTIONAL SELVES IN THE CONTEXT OF OPPOSITES

"When duality is not fun we call it neurosis – a condition in which two opposing forces are at war within the same individual. We set them at war with each other by judging one as good and the other as bad. We then identify ourselves with the one that is judged as good, and pretend that the other doesn't exist (except in someone else)." [1]

When confronted with an either/or situation choose the third alternative.
-Anonymous

THEORETICAL OVERVIEW

In this chapter, my goal is your *conscious* introduction to the world of Mind. As Ego, we live in the Mind every day of our lives; but without reflection it can seem strange when first encountered. It will also seem oddly familiar. So persevere: it is worth the effort.

The world of Mind is analogous to the physical world of air, water, and earth. A primary difference is that *emotion* – rather than air and water – is the medium used by mental constructs such as ego-aspects to communicate with each other. Similarly, in the world of Mind, *thought, feeling, sensation and intuition* replace the eyes, ears, and other sensory organs. Finally, instead of earth's Periodic Table of Elements and DNA structures, a nearly infinite *set of opposites* provides the building blocks for all inhabitants within the Mind.

Basically, Mind is comprised of a nearly infinite set of dualities established by the Soul, which shape and constrain the Mind, the Ego, and the Body. All facets of imagination require these dualities to define its images and spaces. Even the very images we think of as singular require complementary opposites to animate them. All activity in the Mind and Body takes place in a duality context, whether we are talking about left and right hands or figure and ground. Imagination is the conscious experience of Mind and it is made possible by a nearly infinite set of opposites.

Emotion communicates the *free will* of images within the Mind. Emotion also communicates the distinctly different wills of Body and Soul as experienced by the Mind. Stated another way, emotion communicates the *intent and belief* of every ego-aspect within the Mind to every other image within the Mind; and via the Body, to observers in the world. Likewise, emotion conveys the *impact* that an image has on itself, its relationship to other images, and its effect on the Body and Soul. In contrast, the Body (brain-body) uses *affect* to communicate to itself, the world at large, and the Mind and Soul. *Affect becomes emotion* when experienced *within* the Mind. Emotion is an experience of Mind; affect is an experience of the Body. Soul also communicates with the Mind using emotion, which accounts for a range of emotions far exceeding the repertoire of Body affects. The emotions most like instinctual affects are called *affective emotions* in this work. These are the emotions most commonly employed by the Ego to direct itself and the Body. Left to its own devises, the Ego generally restricts its emotional expression to the pride-shame axis, which defines the range of affective emotion. The Ego is capable of communicating, receiving, and responding to a far greater range of emotion, which the culture values in the abstract but rarely draws upon in day-to-day living.

Emotional Confusion

Emotion is a subject very much in the public domain whose definition is often contested by differing perspectives. We all experience it and many disciplines have sought to understand it: philosophers, neurologists, endocrinologists, psychologists, psychotherapists, and journalists, to mention but a few. Most individuals are able to differentiate affective emotions, but might be hard pressed to define emotion per se in a way agreeable to other students of emotion. As one dictionary of psychology notes: "Historically this term has proven utterly refractory to definitional efforts; probably no other term in psychology shares its combination of nondefinability and frequency of use." Greenberg, a noted researcher, makes much the same observation regarding terms such as affect, emotion and feeling: "In the history of scholarship concerning the concepts of affect, emotion, and feeling, no clear demarcation has been formulated about the use of the terms "affect," "emotion," and "feeling" themselves…."

20th Century Behaviorists have insisted that emotion be treated solely as an observable feature of the body-brain, which may account for much of the current ambiguity surrounding emotion. Those researchers have sought to build their concepts of emotion on the observation of a limited number of bodily affects, such as those identified by Silvan Tomkins in infants (See Fig 2.2 in Chapter II). Without question, Mind generated emotions, such as fear, can evoke affective responses in the Body, but the Mind's range of emotions vastly exceeds the Body's genetically programmed ability for affective communication. Forgiveness, acceptance, and trust are emotions, as are shame, anger and sadness. But whereas the shame, anger, and sadness have clearly observable and consensual affective expressions via the Body, the former do not. Yet forgiveness, acceptance, and trust are, if anything, more highly valued and sought after by the individual, while affective emotions are generally to be avoided.

In my work, the term 'affect' will distinguish objective observation from subjective emotional experience. *Affect is what an observer can see; emotion is what the subject experiences*. Affect describes what an observer can discern, primarily from a person's face, body posture, and voice. Similarly, *affective emotion* is emotion that can be consensually described by an observer watching the subject. Affective emotions are generally limited to what is commonly referred to as the pride-shame axis. Most emotions cannot be easily read from Body affects, if at all. The Ego is capable of experiencing and acting upon many more emotions than allowed for by the Body's primary repertoire of instinctive affects; and even those can be feigned. Individuals can become quite adroit at hiding affective emotions or feigning them. Affect is our earliest language, which we share universally with our species and, in some measure, with other mammalian species. Even as infants, our species can generate meaningful affects. But most emotions will not have an easily recognizable or distinguishable expressive component. Emotion can evoke affects, and affects can evoke emotions within the Mind, *but emotions represent a higher order of expression,* i.e. imaginal communication as distinct from Body communication. Affect is biochemical and physiological in nature. Emotion is the Mind's medium for communicating intent and belief within a range of nearly infinite opposite poles.

Behavioral researchers prefer to study *affective emotion* because it is more readily consensual or objective. But that limited objectivity aside, *emotion* is a private, internal, event that we can only collaborate with others by describing the experience with words of sensation and feeling, or by what we think about it. The emotions of poetry, religious experience, love, and anguish are primarily internal, subjective, events.

Objective and subjective perspectives definitely overlap given that all observable affects will stimulate subjective emotions; and affective emotions generated by an ego-aspect can stimulate sensation and Body affects. But aside from affective emotions – which others can point to, any meaningful definition of emotion is really dependent upon descriptions of subjective experience. There are just too few instinctual affects to accommodate the vast set of all emotions. Historically, the distinction was correctly made by using *affect* to designate the objective, external, observation of concomitant emotion. But in limiting observation *exclusively* to Body affect, contemporary researchers have frequently lost or confused the distinction between objective observation of affect and the subjective, concomitant, experience of emotion. If the observation of emotion is restricted to subjective experience, and 'affect' is reserved for the objective observation of facial and gesture behaviors, then I believe there will be considerably less confusion. In sum, while there is often a clear causal connection between emotion and affect, emotion should not be limited to what the Body can express. Affective emotions are a powerful, but very limited, form of communication that hardly begins to express the full breadth of subjectively experienced emotion. That said, the most problematical emotions for most people are affective emotions, i.e. fear, shame, anger, etc. As a species, too much of our behavior is still governed by these affective emotions; and, very often, affective emotions are at the root of mental and physical illness. By and large, the healthy emotions seem less potent because they are less visible affectively. But they are only less visible to the untrained eye: healthy emotions are very definitely *felt experiences* with discernible effects on the Body. Without healthy emotions, there is little chance of reversing traumatic experiences.

The Heart's Centrality in Communicating Emotion

The Heart *governs* the communication of emotion between Body, Mind, and Soul. To appreciate this assertion the reader needs a basic understanding of chakra energies. In Near and Far Eastern cultures, chakra energies have been accepted for several thousand years as the primal energies underpinning animate beings.

Most books addressing chakra energies identify seven major chakras sustaining a human being's energy field, which in turn sustains the Body. Each of the seven major chakra energy centers sustains a specific auric body, which is described as structured or amorphous. There are four structured auric bodies interspersed with three amorphous auric bodies. *Each auric body* has its own set of seven chakra centers, which allow it to connect with the other six auric bodies. *The Heart* continuously communicates the minute-by-minute activity of all seven auric bodies to the physical body via the physical heart.

Where *Heart* is capitalized in this work, it always refers to *the heart auric body, the six heart chakras connecting it to the other auric bodies, and the heart chakra's connection to the physical heart*. The heart auric body communicates emotion generated within the Mind as well as well as emotion communicated between the Soul, Mind, and Body. It is 'nested' between three auric bodies defining the world of Body and three auric bodies defining the world of Soul. This is why the Heart is assigned a central role in all esoteric systems. This centrality of the Heart is stressed in all Kabbalistic texts as well as the Old Testament. In both Kabbalah and Chakra theory the Heart communicates emotional vibrations from one auric body to the next and back again. Significantly, the Heart chakras provide *the most direct and immediate* emotional communication to the Body (body-brain) via the physical heart. (Emotion can also be communicated between Mind and Body via sensation, which is discussed further on.)

In Chakra theory, the world of *Mind* is defined as a triad comprised of three auric bodies – mental, emotional, and etheric – corresponding to the first three chakras associated with three distinct body locations: the solar plexus, abdomen, and root. The world of *Soul* is defined by a second triad of three auric bodies corresponding to three chakras whose body locations are the crown, brow and throat. That triad is seen to function as the *template* for the Mind's triad. From the perspective of Chakra theory, these two triads create the entities we call Soul and Mind. Each triad is comprised of two 'structured' auric bodies with one 'amorphous' auric body between them. Between those two triads is the auric body of the heart chakra; it too is amorphous, unstructured.

Lastly, I would note that most of the human body is comprised of water, which makes it a perfect medium for transmitting *second by second changes in the Heartbeat*. Variations in rhythm, strength, and rate can differentiate specific emotions, which the physical heart instantly communicates to all parts of the body including the brain. Research done by the HeartMath group has shown that the physical heart actually precedes the brain by a full second or more in the subliminal perception of arousing events. Few people are aware of the emotional control exercised by the physical heart. Nonetheless, extensive research by the HeartMath group has demonstrated its normal predominance over other sensorimotor and endocrine systems in communicating emotion. I will revisit their conclusions throughout the chapter.

The Etheric Body and Sensation

The observations of psychics – perceivers of paranormal phenomenon – are normally excluded from the Behavioral sciences because most observers cannot validate their perceptions. But I have found their subjective observations *conceptually* helpful, since we are both addressing the same domain, namely, the world of Mind. Drawing on the formulations of psychic healers such as Brennan and Bruyere, I envision the Mind as comprised of three interactive fields of auric body activity – mental, emotional and etheric – corresponding to the attributes parapsychologists generally assign to the first three auric bodies (the Mind triad). In this conception, the mental and emotional auric bodies provide the *Mind its form and medium of communication*. Ego-aspects are constellated in the mental auric body and use the second – the emotional auric body – to communicate with the physical heart and etheric auric body. In this schema, the etheric auric body (root chakra) connects the Ego to the Body (body-brain). The etheric body is perceptible as measurable chakra energy centers, meridian currents (acupuncture points), and polarities, but for most of us it is simply experienced as a 'felt sense of being' or sensation.

The Mind's *sensation function* provides the Ego its conscious, experiential, connection with the etheric auric body (i.e. root chakra). Sensation is the Mind's guidance system for directing the physical brain and body. Sensation provides *feedback* regarding all voluntary actions initiated by Ego, and involuntary responses executed by the Body. Various disciplines have developed measuring techniques for studying and altering this 'esoteric' etheric body. Homeopathy, Kinesiology, and Acupuncture are examples of three such disciplines. But there are also medically sanctioned physical monitoring instruments such as those used in the Rolf Study described by Bruyere and the HeartMath research group. A major hurdle to understanding the Mind's etheric body is the required paradigm shift, which asserts that the etheric body being measured by these various disciplines not only enervates the brain-body but also directs it.

This new paradigm asserts that the emotional auric body allows created mental structures such as ego-aspects to communicate their intent and beliefs to the physical body *via the etheric body and physical heart*. In sum, emotion's effect on the physical heart and etheric body affords every ego-aspect the ability to communicate with and direct the Body emotionally, as well as communicating with other images within the Mind.

The Body (brain-body) does not differentiate between real – occurring in the world, and imagined events. As I frequently tell clients, "the Body does not have a Mind of its own." The intent and beliefs held by ego-aspects can generate the same intensely felt affective emotions, as would an actual event. Panic Disorders are a prime example. They are sustained by the Mind, not the immediate environment, but nonetheless exercise a powerful control over the physical body. In the Mind, the etheric body and Heart can respond to imagined events as if they were real, thereby stimulating Body affect, sensory-motor, and endocrinological responses. "That hurt!" might reflect an actual event experienced by the brain-body and affectively communicated to the etheric body and Heart. But, to a greater or lesser degree, the etheric body can also respond to an ego-aspect's terrifying supposition that "it will hurt if it happens again," though its happening again is *only imagined*. For example, when someone tells me about a falling injury I often experience a sharp sensation in my perineum, which is also the physical location of the root chakra (the etheric body). Affective emotion can be generated by both actual physical events and imagined events, i.e. events remembered as well as events anticipated in a future context. Whether real or imagined, the event is similarly experienced by the brain-body. Most often the Body experiences imagined events less intensely, but sometimes even more intensely than the actual event. An ego-aspect experiencing fear verging on panic will evoke a body response regardless of the fear's source. This lack of differentiation is what makes emotional states so problematical for the individual. Compulsive stimulation of the most negative emotions, such as shame, is invariably detrimental as the emotions accumulate in the emotional fields of the Heart and etheric body rather than being discharged. This accumulation is hypothesized to be a necessary and sufficient cause of much 'stress' and chronic disease.

The Four Functions

Emotion can be read by each of the four functions described by Carl Jung: feeling, thinking, sensation, and intuition. Each function registers a different aspect of emotion. Figure 5.1 attempts to pictorially capture all the concepts delineated by the following discussion of the four functions.

Thinking and Feeling. All ego-aspects can evaluate a mental image with thinking and/or feeling – if they choose. Thinking is a rational function available to all ego-aspects. It can *deduce or at least speculate about the thought structure of an image*, including its motivation. Feeling is the rational function that can register the direct *emotional impact* of an image's intent or belief. Feeling insures that all selves – not just the emoting self, have access to the information being sent through the emotional auric body to the Heart and etheric body. Feeling is not the purview of any particular self. The feeling function provides any ego-aspect the wherewithal to identify a specific emotion compared to all other possible emotions. Emotions can occur, and often do, without an ego-aspect's conscious feeling evaluation, but it is difficult to compare or change them until felt.

Thinking can deduce an image's motivation by evaluating the thought structure of the ego-aspect generating the emotion. Thinking evaluates images. It evaluates pictorial changes as a function of time and assigns value (belief and intent) to those changes. Feeling tells us the emotional impact of those changes on the Ego and Body. A thinking ego-aspect can block the feeling function or use it in tandem. But blocking the feeling function does not block emotion; it only blocks the feeling evaluation of emotion. Even if an ego-aspect blocks feeling, the Body, Soul, and other aspects of the Mind will experience the emotion. The same is true of an ego-aspect that relies primarily on feeling. It too can use thinking in tandem or block it. (Of note, an ego-aspect can block the sensation of an emotion as well as the feeling of it. An ego-aspect is only likely to block both functions if the Body has been unendurably stimulated or shamed. Such extreme blocking generally produces the imaginal equivalent of an out-of-body experience or depersonalization.)

Many dominant ego-aspects rely predominantly on thinking to avoid feeling the painfully perceived existence of another ego-aspect or archetypal authority. The 'Rational Mind' – a common primary self – can use thinking to minimize the felt experience of an unremittingly shaming conscience. Later in this chapter I further elaborate on these two functions and offer several interventions for addressing disruptions of their duality.

Intuition and Sensation. Human images are the most complex forms created within the Mind. Self-images are collectively referred to as the Ego. Any ego-aspect created by Ego can read emotion from the perspective of intuition and sensation as well as feeling and thinking. Intuition is different from the other three in terms of its orientation, which is the Soul. Intuition registers emotion and thought *originating from and defined by the Soul*, and communicated via the Heart. The 5th, 6th and

FIGURE 5.1 - EGO IN THE CONTEXT OF SOUL-MIND-BODY

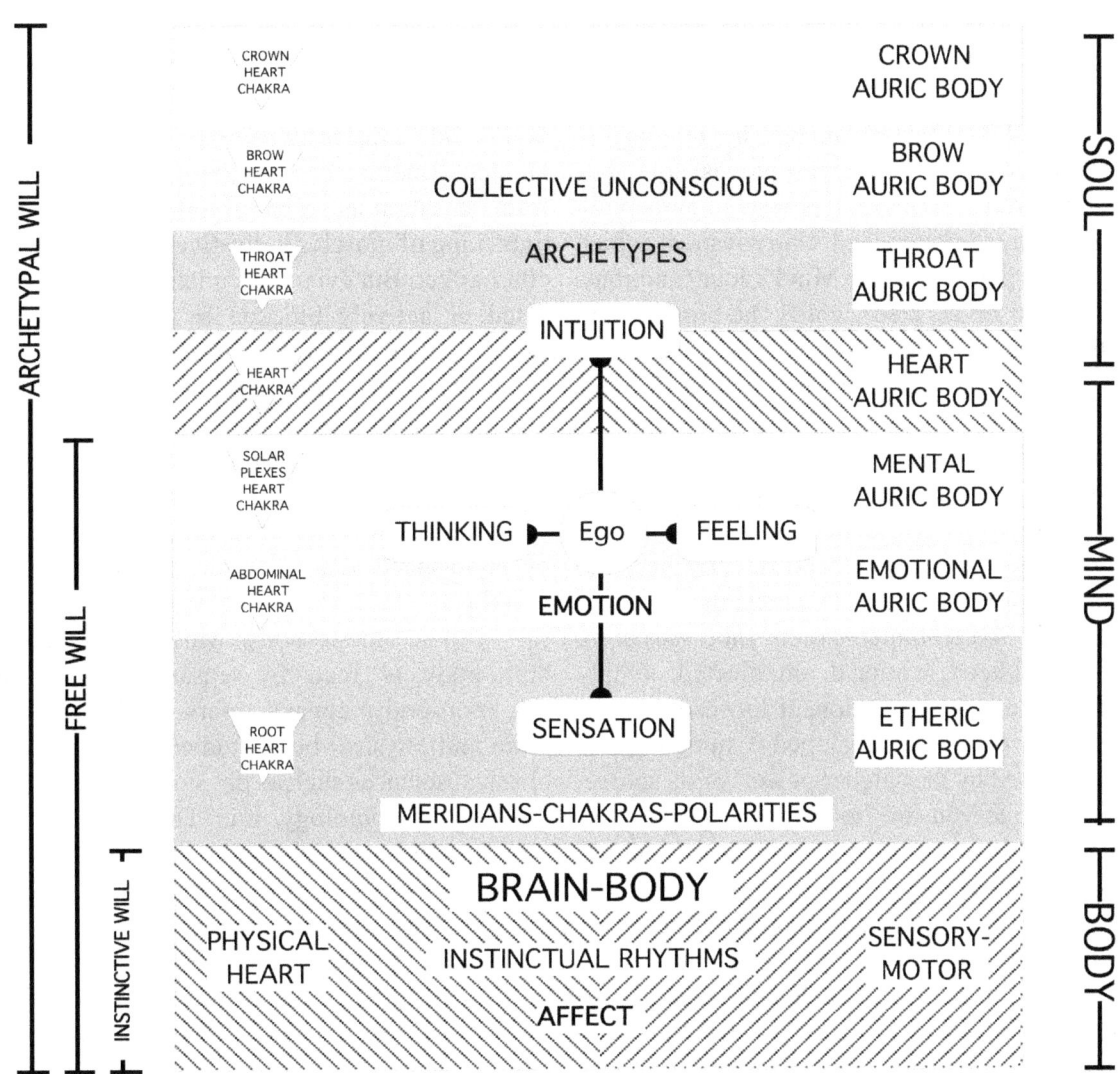

7th chakras define the Soul. The 5th chakra, also called the Throat chakra, or 'voice,' is the Soul's counterpart to the Mind's etheric body. It brings into being by 'naming' (i.e. generating specific thought forms and concomitant emotions), in much the same way as the etheric body initiates the Body's actions. Likewise, the 6th chakra – also called the brow chakra or 'third eye,' is comparable to the emotional auric body. Both are amorphous, unstructured. The 6th chakra has long been associated with parapsychic ability – the Soul's paranormal powers of perception such as precognition and clairvoyance, which have their parallels to the Mind's four functions. Psychic observers also identify the brow chakra as the 'source' of intuition.

Intuition provides Soul its most direct means of communicating with the Ego. Where intuition is blocked by the Ego, the Soul can express itself via dreams and other archetypally charged images. Stated another way, intuition is the Ego's capacity to directly hear the Soul's 'voice.' It is the Ego's most direct 'experience' of Soul communication. Like sensation, it is considered irrational, unreflected, simply 'given.' And like sensation, it too can be suppressed or remain undeveloped if an ego-aspect is threatened by the 'higher power' of its source. (Feeling like you are 'in a fog' is generally a good indication of actively blocked intuition; ditto for chronic sinus conditions.) I am probably going out on a limb asserting intuition's connection to the Soul. Where intuition is studied in academic circles, it is not generally attributed to the Soul. But if Soul is granted the status of an active force within the Mind, then it must have a direct means of communication beyond dreams, the voices of our 'gods,' and other archetypal constellations.

The Ego's ability to obstruct any particular function precipitates many psychological dysfunctions: dissociation, denial, depersonalization, projection, and hysterical conversion reactions, to name but a few. If thinking, feeling, sensation, or intuition, are considered 'painful' to an ego-aspect, it can generate mental or emotional activity that effectively blocks the painfully experienced function. Thus, even though feeling can provide an ego-aspect with the most precise method for evaluating emotion, it can nonetheless be blunted, if emotion is too persistently painful. Where feeling is blunted, emotion can be thoughtfully deduced from sensation as when an individual reports a tightening of muscles indicative of fear, anger or other affect. But even that function can be attenuated or actively blocked by Dominant ego-aspects. Such blockage will become problematical for the client. Blocking of sensation causes a relative numbness, which can have adverse psychosomatic effects on the body. Intuition is probably the function most commonly blocked, minimized, or distrusted by the Ego, most often by ego-aspects that over rely on the thinking function.

The etheric body, which enervates the brain-body, is 'read' by sensation. The Body, i.e. brain-body, always refers to the physical brain and physical body studied by the various physical sciences such as physiology, neurology, biology, microbiology, etc. The etheric body provides the auric underpinning of the Body. It shapes and sustains the physical brain-body. Stated another way, the etheric body continually 'blueprints' the brain-body moment by moment. To use a computer analogy, the Mind continuously *refreshes* the Body image on the computer screen, effectively altering and moving physical matter via the etheric body. The etheric body is observable via acupuncture points, physical polarity releases, and Kinesiology. In Kabbalah, the etheric body is generally referred to as Malkhut. In Chakra theory, the etheric body is always identified as the root chakra auric body or 1st chakra. The Ego exercises its emotional control of the physical brain and body via the Heart and etheric body. Sensation reports the effects of Mind on Body and vise versa. Finally, the etheric body expresses the will to act whether will is stimulated by instinct, an ego-aspect's free will, or the will of the archetypes. Each is experienced as sensation as regards their effect on the Body. The three wills are discussed and elaborated upon throughout the chapter. Initially, some of these distinctions will be difficult to appreciate because we mistakenly believe ourselves to live in the Body. In fact, as Ego, *we live in Mind intimately connected to the Body via the etheric body and Heart.*

The Singularity of God and the Duality of Mind

Opposites literally define our worldview at all levels of experience. Even God can only be said to be singular at the level of Intellect, which Kabbalah treats as a function of the world of Spirit. *At that level, God can be said to have no opposite. The Course in Miracles* attempts to capture this in its briefest of Introductions: "The opposite of love is fear, but what is all-encompassing can have no opposite. This course can therefore be summed up very simply in this way: Nothing real can be threatened. Nothing unreal exists. Herein lies the peace of God." Like all opposites this is paradoxical, and studying The Course makes it hardly less so. Yet all major religions point to the same inexpressible awareness of this oneness. Orthodox Christians call this oneness the Godhead or Uncaused Cause. Gnostic Christians call it the Mystery from which emerged the primal syzygy. Taoists call it The Way encompassing the Yin and Yang of the 10,000 things. Hindus call it Brahma, the Supreme Principle, container of Vishnu, the Preserver of Things and Siva, the Destroyer of Things. Buddhists call it Righpa, 'the ground of all being,' while Kabbalists call it Ion-Sof or 'no-thing.' Last, I would mention Hermeticism, which calls it 'the All' as distinct from the many. All of these perspectives would argue that the singularity of God is the foundation of duality. The 'two' of every duality is a homeostatic path divided into its complements, which comprise differing degrees of energy and form – each attracting the other to manifest as an image.

The inherent affinity of each pole in a duality dictates the existence of the other and no other. Consider that light and dark are opposites as are masculine and feminine. But light and feminine or dark and masculine – while possibly descriptive, are not categorical imperatives. The inherent affinity of two poles is what dictates the underlying singularity. Or the inverse: each singularity in the Mind is archetypally governed by opposite poles with inherent affinities. That assertion is extensively illustrated in last later chapter addressing Relational authority where I describe the Gendering archetype. In that chapter I demonstrate that all human images embody a masculine-feminine polarity that categorically defines the image. Each pole of that duality can also be demonstrated to function differently wherein one pole provides a *preponderance* of mental structure or definition, and the other its replenishing energy, making both absolutely essential for the manifestation of any human image. Hermeticists refer to this appearance of singularity in the Mind as the *polarity of opposites*, the *ying and yang* of the 10,000 things. In sum, complementary pairs of opposites demand each other in order to generate a singularity. The Mind requires complementary poles for the creation of every image within the Mind. Even the singularity of God is subject to this duality of Mind. Thinking requires that God be both being and non-being, immanent as well as transcendent, the first cause as well as the uncaused cause, the one and the zero, the alpha and omega; only the Intellect of Spirit can envision God as singular.

Hermeticism – said to be one of the oldest esoteric disciplines, may be the work most accessible to students seeking to understand opposites. According to Hermetic philosophy: "Everything is dual; everything has poles; everything has its pair of opposites; like and unlike are the same; opposites are identical in nature, but different in degree; extremes meet; all truths are but half-truths; all paradoxes may be reconciled." All of these assertions are thought provoking and demonstrable in Hermetic philosophy, but it is that last assertion that most concerns me in this chapter: the idea that opposites can be reconciled; that all *polarizations* defined by pairs of opposites can be reconciled. In the previous chapter, I sought to demonstrate the reconciliation of opposing selves using Christ and the *Light*. In doing so, I went beyond the work of R.C.Schwartz and the Stones, but clearly, I am not alone in my assertion that it is possible to reconcile seeming opposites. Hermetic philosophy has been insisting on it for three thousand plus years. And more recently, Jung has offered similar arguments from alchemy, as do Kabbalists, Zen Buddhists, and modern day Alchemists.

The basic premise of this chapter is that Mind is defined by a nearly infinite set of opposites whose dynamic interaction is the underpinning of all mental images created in active imagination. In Chapter II, I made a distinction between a person-in-the-world and *images* of that person. I focus on the *image* in the conviction that it has far more effect on a client's behavior than the person-in-the-world, who may be many years deceased, a thousand miles away, or sitting next to us. But successful healing requires yet another distinction. In working with the *image* of any person-in-the-world, a major hurdle in healing that image is the erroneous assumption that the image is a flesh and blood person. In fact, every image is a thought-form animated with psychic energy. Images are comprised of myriad dualities sustained by will within a medium of emotion. They are not made of flesh and blood, or brain cells and bone, even when imagined as such. Even so, they exercise the *power* to regulate and control the human body through their impact on the emotional and etheric fields. Yet they are also very malleable and easily altered, if the Aware-ego is willing. Therapists and clients need to continually make this distinction. The physical body normally takes days and weeks to self-repair only because human images inadvertently sustain that belief. (As one sage put it: We grow old and die because we watch others growing old and dying.) But change the Mind and the Body will follow; it has no Mind of its own. Christ taught this to his followers time and again. When let into the Mind, Christ has the power to heal the Body as well as the Mind and Soul. Where Soul and Mind are treated as superordinate to Body they contain the necessary and sufficient power to heal the Body with much fewer constraints than are placed on it by the Physical sciences acting alone.

The Homeostatic Balance, Desire, and Instinctual Rhythms

Homeostasis is generally defined as the tendency toward a relatively stable equilibrium between interdependent elements, maintained by physiological processes. The term was coined in the 1930's by Walter Cannon to describe steady states, which the physical body seeks to sustain at any particular moment. It is argued here that *every duality creates a polarity generating a homeostatic path –a steady state, between opposite poles*. This path is the Soul's way of directing the Ego (though not the only way).

Desire reflects deviations from a homeostatic path. Whenever an ego-aspect deviates from a homeostatic path, or center, the waning pole will pull it to return (sic) by generating compensatory desire. Desire always points to a sense of lack. As regards any set of opposites, lack can be defined as the need to return to the homeostatic path, to swing back toward the complementary pole. Emotion communicates the experience of homeostatic governance as the Ego ranges between the poles defining a homeostatic path. For example, one of the most persistently active sets of poles is the pleasure/pain duality since it serves as a primary guidance system for the brain-body. Movement from the homeostatic center of this duality creates pleasure or pain depending on the direction of movement. But whatever the direction, either sensation will sequentially become the other experientially. The more intense the pleasure, the more painful its inevitable loss; the more intense the pain, the more pleasurable its cessation. If pleasure is too intense it becomes painful; when pain becomes unbearable it suddenly creates the pleasure of dissociation.

Deviations from homeostatic centers are inevitable in the case of the Body, which is continually depleting and needing to refurbish its supply of energy and structure. Counter-deviation is necessary for the successful balancing of an organism's biological systems, as when an animal seeks warmth in cold weather. But deviation can also be arbitrary as when the Ego seeks to actively avoid certain poles of opposites in compliance with the dictates of culture and parents. Persistent deviation toward one pole, without allowance for rhythmic swings back toward the other, will provoke acute and chronic desire for the opposite pole. The most persistent form of chronic desire is shameful desire because an ego-aspect held in the thrall of shame cannot release itself; and any time it is temporarily released by other ego-aspects it will inject further shame into the Mind's emotional field.

The Ego is generally quick to respond to the obstruction of instinctual opposites such as hunger/satisfaction, filling/excreting, waking/sleeping, arousal/release, fight/flight, and inhaling/exhaling. These polarities are best thought of as *instinctual rhythms*. The regular depletion of energy and matter required to sustain the Body dictates that the Ego be able to move to and fro between poles defining instinctual rhythms. Any prolonged disruption of this movement will result in pathology if not death. The density of matter shaping our bodies requires a great amount of sustaining energy as well as regeneration of definition. In the case of humans, the need for replenishment can be measured in seconds, minutes and hours. Consider that the average Heart rate is 60 beats per minute, inhalation ten to fifteen times per minute, sleep several hours a day, water a daily requirement, etc. The more physical or "mattered" a set of opposites, the greater will be the requirement for energy and definitional replenishment as a function of time. In later sections, I examine these instinctual rhythms in greater depth. A primary task of the Ego is the satisfactory regulation of these instinctual rhythms, but all too often parents and culture espouse disruption, rather than regulation, at the expense of the Body, which is dependent upon adequate regulation for its well being.

Selves Are the Psychiatric Problem

The reconciliation of opposites is a misnomer. It is selves – not the governing dualities – that require reconciliation. The homeostatic path reconciles any pair of opposites. It is an ego-aspect who becomes polarized when blocked from ranging equidistant between opposite poles. The reader needs to distinguish between polarization and polarity. *The reconciliation of selves - their depolarization, is the major thrust of this work.*

Hypothetically, only one self is ever needed to range between dualities. But inevitably, in the course of development, as the Ego seeks to traverse the homeostatic path laid down by rhythmic opposites, it is fragmented by parental, cultural, or fateful demands. It is the Ego's fragmentation into multiple aspects that needs reconciliation. The primary cause of fragmentation is the creation of beliefs that continually regenerate polarizing emotions such as fear and shame. *Most psychological and psychosomatic symptoms are the byproduct of fragmented selves polarized by affective emotions.* Hopefully, I can demonstrate this by showing how the reconciliation of emotionally polarized selves consistently ameliorates those symptoms.

Another common misunderstanding is the notion that the client is the source of all the emotions s/he feels. The 'client' is merely a primary self among selves. S/he needs to learn that emotions have many sources, not just the self that is consciously registering the emotion s/he is reporting. Some therapists refer to these received emotions as ego-dystonic, which is another misnomer. The emotion may be dystonic from the perspective of a primary self, but it is still, in all likelihood, being generated by an ego-aspect who perceives it as central to its own needs and identity. In the early stages of therapy it is helpful to keep reminding the client that all ego-aspects have a modicum of free will and are capable of emoting. Even a Rejected-self will emote the pain of its shameful bondage. On many occasions, the client is *receiving* emotions rather than generating them, and the task is to contain the emoting ego-aspect within a circle. Some ego-aspects can generate very strong emotions, but once the ego-aspect is objectified, interventions involving the *Light* and Christ image can be used attenuate the emotion so it is no longer overwhelming.

Affective Emotion in a Duality Context

Ego-aspects can use affective emotions to stimulate types of movement relative to any set of poles. The affective emotion with the greatest power to *restrict* movement is called 'shame,' which can freeze the activity of an ego-aspect as it moves toward either pole of a duality, *thereby blocking the ego-aspect's movement back to center*. If the Ego then dissociates the ego-aspect, preparatory to creating a new self capable of moving back toward the center, the now dissociated, shamed, aspect will effectively block further movement toward that pole. This creates a polarized state within the Mind. First off, any desire to reach the shamed pole becomes an additional source of shaming, which is either experienced or posited within the emotional fields of the Heart and/or etheric Body. Therefore, the Ego is most likely to create a new ego-aspect that is fearful of that pole and will seek to avoid a repetition of the shameful restriction by withdrawing as far as possible from it. If, for example, the shamed pole represented some form of 'connection,' then the fearful aspect will seek 'isolation.' This strategy may avoid shameful repetition, but over time the desire for 'connection' will reassert itself; that is a law of opposites. An ego-aspect can temporarily override its fear of the shameful desire by inducing affective desire, which is the Body's experience of a sense of lack. In effect, physical desire can generate a sense of lack within the Mind and Body powerful enough to temporally block the sensate fear of the shamed pole, which allows the ego-aspect to temporarily access the shamed pole. This is correctly called 'shameful behavior' as it will generate further shame even as it also allows the ego-aspect to satisfy its desire for the pole blocked by a shame enthralled self. But once the physical desire is satisfied, the centrifugal force of the polarizing emotions (e.g. fearful isolation and shamed connection) will reassert, often with a vengeance. Consequently, the *physical desire* must be re-stimulated as soon as possible to reinstate any semblance of homeostasis. (Addictive selves, described at length in the chapters on Moral and Relational authority, exercise physical desire to the nth degree for the purpose of repeatedly overcoming polarization. But so too, does the Dominant self, which is also described in those chapters.) 'Anger' – which is even more powerful than desire, can energize an ego-aspect to temporarily overwhelm any ego-aspect that threatens to shame it. The use of anger can also become chronic as in the case of chronic resentment, simmering anger, road rage, etc.

It is important to note that what I have just described are *affective* emotional states generated by ego-aspects. Both Mind and Ego are capable of a much greater range of emotion than those expressed by the Body's affective range. But that said, the Body's distinguishable affects play a daily role in the lives of most people, most notably, in the Ego's use of them to regulate the Mind's activity. In effect, the Ego seeks to emulate the Body's affects in the mistaken belief that they can most effectively control other images within the Mind. The difficulty is that none of these affective emotions has the power to heal shameful accretions. Therefore, the ego-aspect must continue to evoke those coping emotions despite the deleterious effects of long-term use of affective emotions.

The Governance of Selves by Opposite Poles

Dualities govern the activity of selves, not vice versa. The homeostatic path created by a duality guides an ego-aspect ranging between a pair of opposites. Whenever a self moves away from the homeostatic path of least resistance, desire generates a feeable tension within the self for countermanding movement. The Body's *experience* of duality is best treated as a gestalt of sensations rather than a single sensory association or duality. Some observers see this plethora of sensation as delusionally binding the Ego to the Body, as if the Body were the sole source of the Ego's experience. In fact, however, the Ego must also contend with other dualities within the Mind involving relations with other ego-aspects and images of others, as well as obliging it to deal with opposites governing Soul-Mind interactions (archetypes). In effect, the Ego is constantly engaged by the dualities of *three domains* – Body, Mind, and Soul. Even so, in therapy the focus will generally be on one specific duality at a time, whichever one appears to be exerting inordinate influence over the currently dominating ego-aspect.

Emotion describes the ego-aspect's *relationship* to any set of opposites actively governing its movement. Where positive emotions such as willingness, acceptance, and love, govern an ego-aspect, there is really no restriction on the ego-aspect's ability to range between opposite poles. But negative emotions – as defined by the pride/shame axis – are always considered restrictive; and for most of us, much of the time, they define our movement within significant pairs of opposites. The pride-shame axis largely shapes our culture's response to opposites, but even apart from culture, those affective emotions would likely be encountered as a consequence of testing the limits of living on earth.

Affective emotions become a clinical problem when they are the raison d'être for an ego-aspect. For example, a Responsible primary – described in the next section, is generally created to *avoid* behavior that results in shame; and it does so by *fearing* movement toward a particular pole. *Fear* dictates its behavior, which forces it to exist in a chronic state of tension as a result of its inability to move toward a particular pole. So long as it remains fearful, it cannot approach the object of its fear, i.e. the shamed pole. Fear avoids; it never willingly approaches.

'Emotionality' is a consequence of 'stuckness' within a range of opposites; the 'stuck' self is unable to return to homeostasis without stimulating more duress. Insofar as the Body feels this tension and amplifies it back to the Mind, physical desire can provide temporary relief because it is more powerful than fear. Unfortunately, the chronic use of physical desire will generate more shame; though it will not be felt at the time because physical desire will suppress the conscious experience of that consequence. The Ego-in-conflict and Dominant self – described in Chapter VII – both use physical desires to blunt the fear and angst of shame, which allows them to move toward homeostasis. The Ego-in-conflict can even use it to approach the shamed pole. Since the 'desire' of an Ego-in-conflict is often for *mind-altering* substances, their potency will frequently allow for 'shameful expression.' Most primary selves are temporarily liberated from fear by the machinations of an Ego-in-conflict, which allows them to express in a 'shameful' manner. This generally leaves the individual feeling guilty after the fact, provided the shameful desire goes undetected by others. But either way, the result will be a further accumulation of shame in an individual's emotional field. A Dominant self can use socially acceptable behaviors in excess – such as eating, smoking, or adrenalin rushes, to reduce chronic, fearful, tension. Such behaviors provide a temporary reduction of the pain of ongoing fear and shame, but do not allow for the overt expression of a disowned opposite, except for the shaming quality expressed by the excess. So even a Dominant self is likely to require the activation of an Ego-in-conflict from time to time. Of note, both selves can use fear fused with anger to produce adrenalin rushes. People who use this strategy report that it energizes them. Many popular video and computer games, action movies, outdoor adventures, and the like can generate this adrenalin effect.

Can a Rejected-self be liberated temporarily by the machinations of an Ego-in-conflict or Dominant-self? Not so far as I can determine. The addictive behaviors employed by these two selves allow for a temporary ranging toward the shamed pole and/or a temporary reduction in the angst of not being able to access the shamed pole. The only strategy able to resolve polarization is the liberation of the shamed self from its enthrallment so it can freely range back toward homeostasis and beyond. This will require its permanent liberation and reconciliation with any self that supplanted it. To accomplish this, the primary self that took the place of the Rejected-self must be freed of its fear so it can comfortably ranged toward the previously shamed pole while allowing the Rejected-self a comparable freedom to move toward homeostasis. In effect, each must be reconciled with the other.

In theory, only one ego-aspect is ever needed to span the range defined by a pair of opposites. If that one self becomes insufficient, it is hypothesized that sufficient selves will be created to span the range defined by the pair of opposites. I call this the *Rule of Sufficient Numbers hypothesis*. Basically, the rule stipulates that the Ego will create ego-aspects sufficient in number to span the range defined by any duality. For example, teaching the Ego to associate a particular pole with 'shameful badness' will necessitate the creation of at least two ego-aspects, one forced to experience the 'badness' shamefully (i.e. a Rejected-self) and another that is fearful of badness, forcing it to move in a direction opposite the shamed pole. Those two, in turn, will generally necessitate the creation of a third ego-aspect that seeks to reduce the tension created by these seemingly irreconcilable extremes, (i.e. Dominant self and, likely, a an Ego-in-conflict). Of note, a Dominant self seeks 'pseudo' reconciliation when it actively uses shame to suppress its ranging toward the forbidden pole, while concomitantly using socially acceptable behaviors in excess to blunt the chronic tension.

When all ego-aspects active within a duality have been released from their negative emotional states, it is hypothesized that they can be reintegrated into a functional singularity governed by one or more positive emotions such as acceptance, willingness, or forgiveness. This allows the 'reintegrated singularity' to move freely between the two poles.

Levels of Duality

Specific dualities differentiate levels of being, i.e. Spirit, Soul, Mind, and Body. Consider that hunger/satisfaction (Body) is different in kind from thinking/feeling (Mind), as the latter is different from mortal/immortal (Soul). Each can be said to represent a different level of functioning. Dualities can be identified for each level that are likely to be problematical in a therapy context.

All *sensory* dualities are treated as brain-body dualities. Dualities within this group are those defining sensory modalities such as vision, sound, smell, taste, and tactile organs, e.g. light/dark, loud/quiet, putrid/aromatic, sweet/sour, and hard/soft. Another set of brain-body dualities addressed in therapy are instinctual rhythms. Those are hunger/satisfaction, filling/excreting, arousal/release (sex), inhaling/exhaling, and waking/ sleeping. Pain/pleasure, along with fight/flight, are treated as survival rhythms, which are considered a subgroup of the instinctual rhythms. The largest single group of brain-body dualities addressed in therapy are those describing physical dis-ease.

Among the dualities attributed to Mind, two pairs of opposites are crucial to the Ego's guidance and feedback: thinking/feeling, and intuition/sensation. The Ego must rely on these four functions to provide feedback and planning regarding its activity. Many clients exhibit issues around the use of feeling/thinking, the most prevalent being the suppression of one or the other. Feeling and thinking function very much like vision. When only one eye is used, perception is two-dimensional. While either eye can see, both eyes must be used to achieve stereoscopic vision. An ego-aspect can rely heavily on one function, and use pride/shame, anger or fear to suppress the activity of any dissociated self strongly identified with the other function, but always to its detriment, as it must then function with one 'blind eye'.

Sensation provides every ego-aspect the sensate body needed to experience and direct the brain-body. The Ego can exile an ego-aspect from relational consciousness by dissociation, or the sensate body of an ego-aspect can be dissociated by traumatic separation. (When the latter happens, the ego-aspect's mental component remains conscious, but its sensate body is repressed resulting in depersonalization.) But even repressed, a sensate component will remain painfully active and communicate the trauma that forced it out of relational consciousness. The sensate perseveration of a dissociated ego-aspect or sensate component of an ego-aspect probably accounts for most of the symptoms identified with Post-Traumatic Stress Disorder.

Intuition provides the Ego direct access to the Soul's feedback via the Heart. The Ego can suppress the intuitive connection – often by stimulating somatic interference such as sinus headaches, or by creating selves that become enthralled to sensation. One example is the Ego-in-conflict, which is almost purely sensate in function. The reconciliation of the intuition/sensation duality can be quite complex, often requiring the rehabilitation of undeveloped selves, and considerable assistance from a higher power.

Another group of dualities that often need to be addressed in therapy are imaginal *relationships* between selves, and selves and others. This is a potent set of dualities that include strong/weak, dominance/submission, lead/follow, approach/avoid, connection/isolation, and self/other. Self/other discord generally occurs as a consequence of projection and/or constellation by archetypal authority. The projection of disowned selves can raise all kinds of havoc in the interpersonal lives of clients and their spouses, children, or peers. I address this in the section on projection later in the chapter. Parents and other authority figures are the images most frequently constellated by archetypal energies. Constellated authority will manifest as Temporal authority (experienced by the client as dominance/submission), Moral authority (right/wrong) and Relational authority (masculine/ feminine). (Note that right/wrong is not the same as good/evil. The latter is best seen as a Soul level duality since it addresses the influence of 'spirits.')

All dualities are manifestations of Soul insofar as Soul is superordinate to the Mind. But as a practical matter, there are a number of dualities encountered within the Mind that point to the Soul's *active* role within the Mind. Mortality/immortality is clearly a duality demanding the existence of Soul and Body, and a Mind needing to reconcile both. Anima/animus is also a Soul duality, as distinct from male/female images reflecting the world of Body. And all dualities that distinguish conscious/unconscious processes refer back to Soul insofar as 'unconscious forces' bespeak a will more powerful than the free will of Ego functioning in the Mind.

Homeostasis

For as long as I can remember, I have heard and accepted as true the assertion that opposites attract. The most common illustration of this is magnetism where positive and negative attract and like poles repel. But why is that so: why do opposites attract? Any attribution of ultimate cause has to be speculative, but the homeostasis resulting from this attraction appears to be an inherent aspect of all pairs of opposites. It is as if all reality was simultaneously dualistic (as exemplified by Quantum Physics) and concomitantly striving toward singularity, as if duality expresses the world while simultaneously pointing to the underlying singularity from which it derives. This mutual attraction generated by a pair of opposites has a profound governing effect on the behavior of selves. The homeostatic mandate exercised by opposites insures that a person will experience tension whenever an ego-aspect veers from the homeostatic balance defined by a set of opposites and is not able to reassert that balance. Stated another way, homeostatic demands will press the ego-aspect to return to the straight and narrow whenever it deviates from the path. Consider, as an example, the poles defined by introversion and extroversion. Homeostasis would dictate a balance between the two. Most people seem to be more one than the other. Yet even the most extroverted people are forced into introverted interludes by the need for sleep, by drugs and alcohol, and their seemingly inevitable attraction to introverted mates. And Jung made much of the observation that if you were extroverted in youth, you had to become more introverted from midlife onward, or risk psychosomatic or neurotic ill health. (Note that not all opposites dictate pendulum swings of short duration. Instinctual rhythms such as breathing and thirst are on a short leash, but others such as doing vs. being or introversion vs. extroversion can have pendulum swings measured in years, even decades.)

In his book on the *Alchemy of Opposites*, Scarfalloto does not differentiate between pairs of opposites and the ego-aspects constelled to span their range, but he nonetheless captures the consequences of conflict and reconciliation, and the homeostatic tensions underlying both. He calls it the big joke:

> The big joke is this: *In any form of duality, the one we have judged as inferior is the one that rules us*. Likewise, the moment that we recognize each set of opposing forces, and genuinely give equal value to both sides, the neurosis dies. But, it does not die as a soldier on the battlefield. It dies as a seed dies when it breaks its skin, and gives way to the sprout. The sprout is the beginning of life beyond the war of opposing forces. In other words, seeing beauty in the world of *duality* awakens us to *singularity* [italics added].

Scarfalloto's observations highlight a recurrent problem regarding the discussion of opposites. He treats the Ego as singular. He fails to apprehend Ego fragmentation and thereby confabulates poles and selves. I did the same for a long time. It is vital to appreciate that dualities and selves are *both in play, but only a self can treat a pole as inferior*. Dualities are the modus operandi by which the Soul *strives* to homeostatically direct Ego activity. But the Ego must also contend with 'life experiences,' which too often associate one pole with shame or physical pain. This generally results in fragmentation. Parents exercising archetypal authority are most often responsible for this fragmentation (though many are only teaching the norms of their culture). In effect, fragmentation is caused by the simultaneous demands for homeostasis and normative parental-societal demands that negatively and/or positively reinforce only one pole of a duality. Note here that both physical pain and affective emotion can play a role in fragmentation. Operant conditioning by the world (parents, culture, etc.) can selectively reinforce with physical pain as well as with affective emotions that express disdain, anger, disgust, and shame.

Rephrasing the quote by Scarfalloto helps to distinguish the different roles played by selves and dualities. Dualities rule us by defining the range of behaviors we are obliged to engage. A self can be negatively reinforced in its effort to span that range of behavior, and the resulting fragmentation will also rule us. It is not only a duality – such as connection vs. isolation, that rules us, but equally so the self that is repeatedly shamed for attempting to homeostaticly traverse both poles of the duality.

The Rule of Sufficient Numbers

The Rule of Sufficient Numbers hypothesizes that the Ego will always create a sufficient number of selves to span a range of opposites. A range is defined as degrees of noticeable difference spanning two poles of a duality. A dichotomy would be the simplest definition of a range. But feeling, thought and sensation generally allow for a larger number of increments. If, for example the opposites were hot and cold, then the range could contain degrees measuring cooler to warmer. *Basically, the Rule of Sufficient Numbers asserts that either a single ego-aspect is able to experience the entire range of a set of opposites, or the archetypal Ego will generate more ego-aspects of sufficient number to span the range. Stated another way, whenever an ego-aspect is restricted by an emotionally polarizing state such as shame, the archetypal Ego will create additional ego-aspects sufficient in number to span the remaining range.* It is further hypothesized that the Ego will also generate aspects capable of temporarily reducing the angst of polarization if it cannot reconcile polarized ego-aspects.

A *fearful* ego-aspect is a prime example of an emotionally polarized state. It can only react fearfully, obliging it to move away from the object of its fear, which is always an opposite pole. Because a fearful ego-aspect always operates within a duality, it is generally possible to quickly identify the polarized 'inferior' pole and ego-aspect shamefully bound to it. If, for example, an ego-aspect is *fearful of connecting* with others, then it will hover around a pole defining *isolation*, and 'painful connection' will define the object of its fear. In effect, *the object of fear is always definable by its duality context and the emotion or belief that makes it fearful.*

Movement away from homeostasis automatically generates a compensatory pull generally experienced as a tension or sense of lack. *Emotionality* is generated when an ego-aspect is unable to accede to that counterforce and return to homeostasis. Emotionality can also be thought of as excessive tension created by frustrating the Soul's demand for return to homeostasis. Emotionality can be temporary, as when an infant cries in hungry frustration. Or, emotionality can become an *emotional state* wherein a self is largely bound to the expression of one emotion, which limits its movement within a duality. In this chapter, I am primarily concerned with the latter. *Emotional states are what necessitate the creation of multiple selves needed to span the range of a duality.* As such, emotional states are always treated as situational: their definition always requires a contextual duality. For example, a 'strong self' disdains (i.e. pridefully rejects) any self weakened by shame. Disdain (pride) is an emotional state that makes an ego-aspect strong with respect to a weak (shamed) self. While 'strong' disdains 'weak' it remains polarized around the 'strong' pole and unable to return to homeostasis, much less swing to the 'weak' pole. Of note, the shameful anchoring of a self to the 'weak' pole will generally precede the creation of a strong self. Also note that a strong/weak duality generally needs to be further elaborated before it can be effectively reworked. We do not yet know what is strong and weak. The duality governing strong/weak still needs to be identified. Often, for example, it could be an attitude toward perceptual functions such as feeling vs. thinking, wherein thinking is identified as strong, and feeling as weak. Even more often, strong and weak will express polarizations between masculine vs. feminine selves, or sexual proclivities. Strong/weak is one of the most difficult dualities to work with because of the prideful quality identified with the strong pole.

Any ego-aspect in the thrall of an emotional state is considered willful and fragmented. As used here, willfulness is always seen to be the consequence of an ego-aspect's predominant expression of one affective emotion such as fear, desire, anger, or shame. An ego-aspect's will is only considered truly free when it can experience the entire range defined by a duality. Two emotions – willingness and acceptance, generally provide an ego-aspect with access to an entire range of experience whereas any emotion along the pride-shame axis bespeaks willfulness. With reconciliation, selves can regain the ability to span a range of opposites as a singularity. They can, in the parlance of dissociative disorders, be reintegrated. But short of reconciliation, the very existence of primary and disowned selves points to a fragmentation of selves governed by a willful restriction to the pride-shame axis. Many pairs of opposites can be spanned, without strain, by a single ego-aspect. I am only concerned here with pairs of opposites where the Rule of Sufficient Numbers has necessitated the generation of more than one ego-aspect to span the range. Common pairs of opposites likely to require multiple ego-aspects are good/bad, doing/being, masculine/feminine, selfless/selfish, isolation/connection, pain/pleasure, strong/weak, hunger/satisfaction, and sexual arousal/release.

Everything in this chapter highlights the distinction between polarized selves and pairs of opposites. The presence of a constricted self, such as a chronically *fearful* self, is always indicative of polarization. Any self restricted to variants of one emotion such as fear – a proverbial one-track railroad, reflects polarization. When constricted selves are freed from their arbitrary emotional attachments by reconciliation, they generally reintegrate into a single self vis-à-vis their contextual duality. Remember, it is not the opposites, but rather the polarized selves that need to be reconciled. Multiple selves tend to function centrifugally by pushing against each other and the homeostatic attraction created by the duality. Any self-image tasked with spanning a pair of opposites will optimally strive for homeostasis. Even as it may rhythmically ebb and flow, the self will seek to align with the homeostatic path laid down by opposite poles. As such, a pair of opposites is never the issue per se. As I recall, (but cannot site the source) it was the poet, Rumi, who said, "God gives us one feeling and then its opposite so we can learn to fly with two wings, not one." A fragmented ego-aspect attempts to fly with one wing.

Shame is the emotion most often responsible for ego fragmentation. Imagine a self deeply shamed by efforts to *connect* with significant others. This aversive conditioning creates a self that experiences shame whenever connection is sought or offered. Shame anchors the Rejected-self closest to the 'connection' pole of the isolation/connection duality by essentially 'freezing' its movement – stripping it of its free will to return to homeostasis. The Rejected-self's shameful enthrallment identifies 'connection' as a desire to be avoided on pain of further shaming. It also necessitates the creation of self that is both fearful of shameful 'connection' and only able to comfortably ranged toward the pole defining 'isolation.' Likely, such a self will be characteristically shy. If polarization is severe – generally the case where the individual is repeatedly shamed – then a third self-image will be created to foster conditions capable of temporarily abating the tension between isolation and connection. An Ego-in-conflict exemplifies this third kind of self. It has the ability to reverse polarization at *the Body level* while desire is active, which is what gives it so much power in people's lives. Thus, for example, shy people can become sociable under the influence of alcohol, but will once again revert to their shy stance when the effect wears off. The Ego-in-conflict is prevalent in all cultures, though the set of opposites it addresses will vary from individual to individual. In most cultures, the Ego will eventually create a Dominant self that can incorporate the functions all three of the selves just described. The intent is to protect the Ego from further fragmentation, but the strategy cannot reconcile the younger selves who continue to experience the painful tension; and more crucially, the solution offered by a Dominant self also accumulates more and more shame in the its emotional fields.

An ego-aspect needs to be equally receptive and responsive to all emotions without becoming enthralled by them. It needs to experience them as well as effecting them, since they are the modus operandi for regulating body behavior in the environment. This includes affective shame, which has the power to momentarily freeze the Body in its tracks. Stated another way, an ego-aspect's functionality becomes disordered when it constantly relies on one affective emotion such as fear or shame. A constricted ego-aspect interferes with environmental adaptation by lock stepping behavior with its dominant emotion. Note, however, that what determines its activity is not just the emotion, but equally the context defined by a specific pair of opposites. An ego-aspect fearful of connecting to others may only be active in that context. It will be least fearful when the person is alone, on a high hill, in the middle of winter; in that situation it could safely *long for connectedness*. To be properly understood, any definition of emotionality needs to tied to its duality context.

Finally, I want to stress that the Rule of Sufficient Numbers refers to the creation of *selves*. It has nothing to do with the creation of opposites. Those are dictated by the Soul. The rule only asserts that sufficient selves will be created to span a range dictated by a duality. Ideally, one self could serve that purpose and, hypothetically, the Aware-ego could provide that breadth. But when the Aware-ego emerges into being during therapy it is never alone; nor is it generally connected to the etheric body. In every case, it has been preceded by the creation of numerous selves needing reconciliation. Those hurdles notwithstanding, the Aware-ego is strengthened any time a set of opposing selves is reconciled until finally it can become the central focus of consciousness relating to a higher power and the Body.

Three Kinds of Will Experienced Within the Mind

To understand the import of what I want to address in this section, it is important to maintain a 'mindful' perspective, literally and figuratively. Mind – the habitat of ego-aspects, is the center of focus throughout this book. Within the Mind, Ego consciousness, Body consciousness, and Soul consciousness, manifest as three distinct expressions of will. The Soul expresses its superordinate will through the homeostatic force of opposites, archetypal constellations, intuition, paranormal powers, and dreams. The set of all opposites constitutes the structural building blocks of Mind. When a single ego-aspect strives to homeostaticly span a range defined by a pair of opposites, it is conforming to the Soul's will. Likewise, when an ego-aspect seeks to accommodate to instinctual rhythms it is responding to the Body's will. Whenever an ego-aspect seeks to *disrupt* those instinctual rhythms or control them, then it is seen to exert its own free will. The Ego's free will is also in play when an ego-aspect seeks to disrupt or deny a Soul duality such as doing/being, or disrupt one of its own dualities such as feeling/thinking.

The Soul's will is expressed whenever a *duality* – at whatever level, motivates an image; and is further expressed whenever an image is constellated by an archetypal authority. Within the Mind, *emotion* communicates the Soul's will. Similarly, affective emotions communicate the Body's success (i.e. instinctual will) in regulating instinctual rhythms and sensory-motor actions. Lastly, free will expresses the Ego's will. *These three wills can act in concert or at odds with one another*. As a rule, instinctual affect is expected to be short-lived, abating soon after the internal or environmental stimulus that provoked it ceases. But ego-aspects can indefinitely prolong affective emotions and thereby disrupt instinctual rhythms, as when an ego-aspect frustrates the body's need for sleep, or a dominant fearful aspect chronically blunts sexual desire. An ego-aspect's free will is said to act congruently with archetype and instinct when it seeks to reinstate homeostatic balance at the level of Body, Mind, and Soul. But an ego-aspect's free will can also oppose homeostasis indefinitely. Such opposition is inevitable whenever the created nature of an ego-aspect binds it to a limited range of emotion such as fear, anger, or sense of lack (desire).

Few people appreciate that, within the Mind, any definition of free will must consider an ego-aspect's nature and concomitant freedom to choose. By 'nature' I mean an ego-aspect's created beliefs relative to a set of opposites; by 'choice,' I mean the potential range of movement either limited or augmented by that belief. An example of limiting belief would be an ego-aspect who *fearfully avoids* particular kinds of sexual expression that previously shamed and enthralled another ego-aspect. Intense shame will force a child's Ego to dissociate and create a fearful ego-aspect that compulsively avoids comparable expressions of sexuality. *The most common restriction on choice, and thereby free will, is a created nature that blocks a homeostatic rhythm*, which is the sum effect of most affective emotions. This limitation is characteristic of most ego-aspects when first identified. An ego-aspect's limiting beliefs can be altered in a variety of ways. *Those beliefs are most effectively altered by the willing intervention of a higher power promoting the reconciliation of all ego-aspects ranging between a set of poles*. But short of that, or preparatory to it, providing an ego-aspect with a new range of felt experience can extend its free will. Christ will do this whenever he is asked. Those interventions are illustrated throughout the book, but particularly in the chapters VII and VIII.

Most Ego-aspects fail to appreciate the changeability of their natures. Almost without exception, they are created believing their nature is 'fixed' by the belief(s) that created them. An example is the Mirror-aspect phenomenon discussed in Chapter VI. Mirror-aspects are created to stand toe-to-toe with an abusive parental image or surrogate. The Mirror-aspect seeks to be more like the parent than the parent, more intensely so, or more competitively so, more angry, more driven, etc. It does so in order to protect itself from further attack by a parental image or parental surrogate. Essentially, the Mirror aspect becomes a cartoon or exaggeration of the parental characteristics that wounded the child. Such an ego-aspect perceives its choices within the proscribed limits of this 'nature,' which is its raison d'être. It does not believe it can change its nature, i.e. walk free of the struggle. But it is possible for Christ to alter its 'nature' by extending its range of choices, i.e. by altering its beliefs and/or extending its range of felt experiences. Imagine, for example, an ego-aspect created to contend with a parent's bullying anger. It will have a very limited emotional range. Basically, this aspect will model the parent's anger upping it one or more notches in intensity in order to defeat the parent or at least hold the parent at bay. Christ can give this Mirror-aspect experiential access to an extended range of emotions. Where this is done, the Mirror-aspect could still respond in anger, but can now also respond with courage, acceptance, a willingness to change, an openness to alternatives, etc.

In a matter of speaking, all of the clinical interventions in this book describe efforts to extend an ego-aspect's effective range of free will. For example, freeing a particular ego-aspect from shame by baptism releases it to potentially experience the entire range of emotional expression defined by a set of opposites as well as assuring it will never again be permanently immobilized by shame. Its nature is no longer 'fixed' by shame. A baptized ego-aspect will still be susceptible to the felt experience of *affective shame*, but now it has the wherewithal to respond with an extended range of emotion (sic) anger, courage, neutrality, willingness, acceptance, forgiveness etc., in response to shaming from others; and self-correction, if the shame is stimulated by an action that induces guilt.

Incorporating a specific felt experience into an ego-aspect's repertoire of potential responses can alter its nature dramatically, if the new emotion allows it to span a range of opposites. As a rule, *experience trumps belief.* Consider, for example, the ego-aspect created to avoid the shame of rejection. It can *want* acceptance, but its fear will prevent it from actually experiencing it. In such a case, Christ can stimulate an emotional experience of acceptance equal in power to any experience of rejection. Over time this will allow the self to have experiences of acceptance beginning with acceptance by Christ. Note, that the introduction of acceptance into the ego-aspect's repertoire does not negate its experience of rejection. But it does provide considerably more than the mere desire for acceptance. With Christ's help an ego-aspect can actually *experience* acceptance, and seek it again as far preferable to merely wanting it. Alcoholics Anonymous captures this shift in one of their sayings about people who have had a taste of sobriety: "Anytime you want to go out and drink again, we will be glad to refund your misery." In effect, AA sees itself as extending the individual's choice to include the rewards of sobriety.

A higher power is generally required for any alteration of an ego-aspect's created nature. In General Systems Theory such alterations in belief are defined as 'second order change,' meaning the reorganization of a system by powers outside the system. First order change refers to corrections within a system, as when you raise or lower a thermostat regulating a heating unit. Second order change would involve creation of a thermostat with a much greater range, such as one capable of regulating an air conditioning unit as well as a heating unit. Most of the interventions in this book aim for second order change, which can only take place from outside the system, (i.e. outside the created nature of an ego-aspect) and this generally requires the intervention of a higher power.

The Superordinate Power of Belief

In the early 1970's, Chilton Pearce wrote a thought-provoking book on the power of belief called *The Crack in the Cosmic Egg.* He compiled the material for that book in an effort to convince his wife that her breast cancer need not be fatal: that her fatalistic belief was undermining her power to heal. Four years previous, his wife's mother had died of breast cancer. Two years previous her sister had died of breast cancer. Pierce was convinced that these tragic antecedents, coupled with the cultural stigmas that still surrounded cancer at the time, all fed his wife's belief that she would also die of cancer. Pierce collected a large body of evidence showing how a change of belief could dramatically alter otherwise fatal outcomes. Everyday, he read to her what he researched and with treatment she went into remission. One of the examples he reports in his book has always stood out in my mind. He describes a Far Eastern culture whose inhabitants had long practiced walking a gauntlet of hot coals without burning their feet. Since the first publication of Pearce's book in 1971 a number of people at various sites in America have also done this without burning their bare feet on coals hot enough to inflict third degree burns. A change in belief allows them to do this. What I am suggesting here is a change in belief of equal power: the treatment of human images as thought-forms and energy actuated by will and sustained by belief. These thought-forms are *images* expressing belief. Alter the image and its sustaining energy, and you have altered a belief regulating the Mind and Body. Of most interest are those beliefs that fatefully impede healing the body, or establish very restrictive conditions for healing such as time determinants or very low probabilities.

Delimiting belief is comparable to the Zen Buddhist view regarding obstacles to Satori, or enlightenment. In their perspective, the perpetual attachment of self to desire, or the fear of desire, or ambivalence about desire is treated as the root of problems. One author refers to this thesis as the Theory of Root Relations.

> The theory of root relations states that all dukkha (mental suffering) can be traced back to three bitter roots, greed, hate and delusion, and that all wholesome states can be traced back to three sweet roots which are the opposites of the bitter ones....We may feel overly attached to things and have distress separating from them. This is called lobha, roughly 'greed.' Or we may feel overly detached, separated, alienated, and experience distress when we have to connect with them. This is dosa, roughly 'hate' or 'aversion.' Or, again, we may be in the grip of fixed ideas, prejudice, or confusion, which paralyze our better nature. This is moha, variously translated as delusion, confusion, or dullness…The Buddha says that the unfortunate consequences of lobha [greed] are mild but last a long time, those of dosa [hate] are severe but do not last so long, while those of moha [delusion] are both severe and long-lasting [brackets added].

In effect, beliefs governing emotions are a major factor in creating the perpetual tension obstructing the clear mind. Attachment is the operative word here. Emotion per se is not the culprit. Zen Buddhist enlightenment does not preclude the experience of emotion. Anything but. The concern is with the perpetual attachment of an ego-aspect to beliefs that perpetuate an emotional state or mood within the Mind whenever the ego-aspect is active and for however long it is active. (This should not be hard to imagine. Our culture is said to be driven by fear and greed.) A common example would be a self that is *perpetually fearful*. Whenever a fearful self is active it will enact and communicate that state of mind to the exclusion of other possibilities, and cloud the perceptions of other selves co-existing with it. A fearful self perpetually generates an emotional state that restricts its movement within a duality. It will fear or hate movement toward a prohibited pole. Most selves that act willfully are fixated by their belief driven nature. Their belief generated emotional states are what actively sustain conflict with other willful selves – since the dominant emotion generally precludes reconciliation. Thus, releasing an ego-aspect from its attachment to a particular emotional state is an integral step toward the reconciliation of opposing selves, and that seems best achieved by altering its belief system.

Because attachment to particular beliefs is such a pervasive problem in therapy, considerable space is given in further sections to examining the belief systems underpinning the most common emotions: fear, anger and desire. (Pride, sadness, guilt and shame will be addressed in the chapters on Moral and Relational Authority.) Fear/anger are Ego emotions, which the Body experiences as the fight/flight reflex, and the Soul expresses as approach/withdraw.

While the focus of this chapter is on opposites and emotion, belief is the superordinate power governing most emotions generated by ego-aspects. In this work, I often use the terms *intent* and *belief* interchangeably. Intent bespeaks an objective sought after or to be avoided. Belief describes the raison d'être, usually based on the past experience of self or others, for achieving intent. The dictionary defines *belief* as having confidence in the truth, existence, or reliability of something without absolute proof that one is right in doing so; it is a primary source of pride for most people, particularly as manifest in the belief that, 'my judgment is the right one.' From the perspective of this work, belief is seen as validating itself by setting limits on what is possible. Belief sustains the emotional field surrounding a self and this is why it is considered superordinate. Alter the belief and the surrounding emotional field is causally changed.

The only way to appreciate the *prideful* aspect of belief is to compare it with Christ's discernment or the Holy Spirit's knowing. This is difficult to do while we only accept parental judgments and our own judgments of the world. Until we become open to the discernment of Christ and the knowing of the Holy Spirit we are obliged to trust our judgment (pride), even if it shames us, which it often does. Prideful judgment is addressed at length in Chapters VII and VIII.

The binding of will to a thought is always arbitrary even though the belief it creates may be held in common by a number of selves and the individual's community. When belief sustains an affective emotional state, it aligns the ego-aspect with the pole most accessible to that state, and concomitantly devalues the other pole. Affective emotions reinforce beliefs by blocking movement toward an opposite pole thereby creating a negatively amplifying viscous circle. Consider, for example, the duality expressing isolation/intimacy. Any self that treats intimacy as *fearful* will avoid intimate connections; and repeated avoidance will increase fear of connection. Some beliefs can be relatively insignificant in the scheme of things such as believing that cauliflower smells bad while cooking. But what George Kelly – the author of Personal Construct theory, called superordinate constructs can shape a significant number of subordinate beliefs dictating behavior. For example, a strong belief in 'good etiquette' can dictate the observance of *many do's and don'ts*. Likewise, a strong belief in a specific religious sect can dictate beliefs about many other religious sects ranging from neutral to negative.

In later sections I describe interventions for altering an ego-aspect's core beliefs in a way that allows the ego-aspect to value both poles of a set of opposites. The interventions – which are always implemented by a higher power, are intended to balance a belief system so the ego-aspect can approach as well as avoid either pole of a set of opposites.

Projection and Repressive Somatization

The last section of this chapter will address projection and repressive somatization. These are two primary Ego defenses that perpetuate trauma in the lives of many people. They are the two most common consequences of Ego polarization encountered in psychotherapy. When the Ego is punished for activity at one pole sufficient to force its dissociation, the Ego will create another ego-aspect to function at the opposite pole. The second ego-aspect will express *fearfully*, which empowers it to avoid conscious awareness of the ego-aspect now strongly associated with a less powerful emotion such as shame, guilt or despair. An ego-aspect in the thrall of shame is effectively repressed. It is stripped of its free will and thereby deprived of the power to move back toward homeostasis. *But even though unable to function homeostatically, the enthralled ego-aspect will still be felt somatically; that is, it will still be felt as a sensation that captures its shameful state in the context of whatever pole it cannot break free of or express.* This form of repression can be undone and that is what allows us to presume what has happened. In repressive somatization, the shamed ego-aspect is reduced to painful somatic *sensation*, which can manifest as any one of a legion of 'physical diseases.' The 'symptoms' of the disease will point to a shamed aspect: they can be examined as pure sensation and used by Christ to recover and redeem the ego-aspect from shameful bondage.

In projection, the ego-aspect is likewise stripped of its ability to range freely, but instead of being somaticized it reemerges in other images. How the Ego comes to rely on one defense and not the other is not clear to me, but the projection is easily demonstrated using the *Light*. Using a double circle of *Light* it is easy to extract Ego projections from other images. The 'projective solution' appears to reduce adverse somatic effects on the Body but increases relational turmoil with its own iatrogenic effects. Interventions are described later in the chapter for undoing repressive somatization and projection. The corrective effects of these interventions are often quite dramatic.

THE RESPONSIBLE PRIMARY

The remainder of this chapter addresses clinical issues and interventions. Hopefully, the forgoing theoretical framework provides a container for them, but the interventions are not dependent upon it. They are dependent upon the methodologies described in Chapters III and IV, specifically, the use of the *Light* and image of Christ.

Generally, one of two kinds of selves will bring a client into psychotherapy. The Responsible primary is one of those selves. The other would be a Dominant self, which I discuss and illustrate at length in Chapter VII. The Responsible primary is the ego-aspect that assumes primary responsibility for controlling or managing a client's behavior by *avoiding behaviors* associated with a disowned self. But most often the client is unaware that its primary function is avoidance of further shaming. Rather, s/he will generally view this sense of self as acting responsibly.

A Responsible primary is created to cope with the adverse effects of Temporal authority exercised by parents. It does this by *avoiding* behavior that provokes the parents' ire. This avoidance will generalize to other authority figures. Consequently, the Responsible primary is likely to imbue any therapist with Temporal authority. The generalization of that authority is largely responsible for the *transference* phenomenon described by Freud.

When described by a client, the Responsible primary is most often pictured as a juvenile. In contrast, a Dominant self will be seen as older. In addition, a Dominant self will rely on repression and the excessive use of socially acceptable behaviors to maintain a strained homeostasis rather than mere avoidance, which is the primary defense of a Responsible primary. Once the Ego has created a Dominant self, that self tends to supersede the Responsible primary in daily life. The Responsible primary is most likely to take charge when the individual enters a 'parent-child' relationship with an authority figure, or when Christ redeems a Dominant self.

The Responsible primary is 'weaker'

than a Dominant self in terms of defenses and for that reason seems to be the one most threatened when faced with the prospect of going inside. A Responsible primary is also likely to come to the fore following successful work with a Dominant self, but then it is best described as a Regressive dominant. All of these distinctions are addressed at length in Chapter VII. Here, I just want to emphasize that the Responsible primary may be one of the first selves encountered in therapy, that it can serve as a prototype for a Dominant self, and is the self most likely to resist going inside at the outset.

The Responsible primary is a client's first defense against the recurrence of a traumatic experience. If a child or adult is unable to discharge the negative energies of a traumatic event soon after the event, a Responsible primary will be created to avoid aggravating the negative energies trapped in the client's emotional field. This avoidance strategy is frequently responsible for post-traumatic symptoms, which symptoms generally infer the entrapment of negative energies and contents. Often, it is difficult to know whether the client is dealing with the symptoms of shock trauma caused by an environmental event or the shame of an enthralled self. Resolution is probably the only way to make a determination. If the therapeutic process discovers a disowned self then at least part of the trauma was shame-induced. If it only elicits negative energies such as pain and fear, then it is likely the consequence of environmental trauma such as an auto accident, surgery, tornado or the like. Either way, a Responsible primary is created to cope with trauma by avoiding the festering wound of that trauma. Its short-coming, aside from not being able to heal the trauma, is that it seeks to move as far away as possible from the pole associated with the trauma. But simple avoidance invariably stimulates a concomitant desire to return to homeostasis, which generally stimulates more fear. In contrast, a Dominant self can achieve a degree of strained homeostasis, though it pays a far more toxic price in the long run.

The Responsible primary and Dominant self are so ubiquitous in the lives of clients that it is difficult for client or therapist to see them as separate and distinct from the 'totality' of the person. A Responsible primary is generally responsible for bringing a client to therapy insofar as it is most easily stressed by life's vicissitudes and its own avoidance strategy. Unlike a Dominant self, a Responsible primary can only strive to avoid stressful situations. Unfortunately, this is also true in psychotherapy. Its desire to avoid is likely to interfere with going inside. Even so, if it is not treated with the utmost respect, it will sabotage therapy, and quite often the client's well being. (It does not do this directly, but when inordinately stressed it will precipitate the activity of other selves that will react somatically, projectively, or addictively.)

The strategy for working with a Responsible primary involves separating it from the Aware-ego and *using its overriding sense of responsibility* to elicit its cooperation. This strategy is dependent on a higher power who negotiates a contractual arrangement based on *responsibility and commensurate authority*. To fully appreciate the role of responsibility the client must come to understand its relationship to authority, i.e. the power to actually accomplish a given task. Initially, I emphasize the positive aspect of responsibility, but then I note that it is limited if there is not commensurate authority. I first encountered this distinction in the Army and it has proven invaluable ever since. In all Armed Services, the rule is "responsibility commensurate with authority." Basically, you do not give an enlisted person responsibility for a mission that includes ordering a lieutenant. The enlisted person does not have the authority to order a lieutenant. If a mission or task requires the authority to order a lieutenant, then the mission must be given to someone of superior rank to the lieutenant.

A Responsible primary quickly becomes a valuable asset to a young child negotiating daily life but lacks the power to *change* the behavior of a disowned self, i.e. to decouple it from shame. It *lacks* the authority to dispel the shame, despair, or pain borne by the disowned ego-aspect, even as it has the responsibility to avoid a repetition of the behavior. If a Responsible primary had the authority, it would not be obliged to merely avoid the onerous pole. Most clients fail to appreciate the limitations of the Responsible primary, in part because they are unaware of its relationship to the disowned self or negative charge of shock trauma. Most often, they perceive their locus of control as outside, in the environment. They focus their 'responsibility' on the management of other people, especially parents, or their spouse and children, or employers, or even their own body (if they suffer from chronic physical problems) or their brain (if they suffer from diagnosed psychiatric problems).

While the Responsible primary generally fails to consciously identify the impetus for its creation, it is well aware of its 'overly controlling nature,' its constant need for vigilance. Most clients will verbally identify with the particular responsibilities of a Responsible primary. Often this identification is voiced as an admission that others find him or her too responsible in terms of a particular trait (sic) overly controlling, obsessive, worrying, or working to the point of being a workaholic, etc. Self declared 'worriers' are Responsible primaries par excellence. But even as these clients willingly admit that others sometimes fault them for excess, they are hard pressed to understand how it could be different for them, because the consequences of being '*irresponsible*' would be unbearable. This quandary is easily assessed. The therapist has only to ask the client to name *the opposite of control*, or successful management, or responsibility (a question that comes readily to mind once the therapist is attuned to the world of opposites). For one client, the opposite of control was *chaos* and all the fear that evoked. Given a choice between control and perceived chaos, it is clear why someone would desperately cleave to control at all costs. Unfortunately, this solution generates a treadmill existence with its own adverse consequences. It does not allow for change, it inevitably reinforces fear of the exile, and over the long term the subconscious object of fear will manifest psychosomatically, addictively, or compulsively.

The Responsible primary is most effectively worked with when it can be convinced to delegate its responsibility to a higher power. I have developed several interventions for negotiating the delegation of this responsibility to Christ, who can then heal the disowned self and reconcile it with the Responsible primary; or, if the issue is environmental trauma, Christ can safely discharge the accumulated negative charge associated with the trauma (generally fear, pain, or a combination of the two.) This delegation is necessary because the Responsible primary has insufficient authority for the mission it seeks to accomplish. But without a perceived alternative it is obliged to press on until *chronically depleted*. (It is amazing how often these images – once separated and personified, are seen as ravished or exhausted by their labors.) *Light therapy* – in its offer of Christological solutions, can provide a viable alternative. The basic stratagem is to encourage a Responsible primary to recognize its *limited authority* for change and to negotiate its release from responsibility by delegating it to Christ, who is perceived as having sufficient *authority* to bring about the desired change. In effect, Christ is treated as having the authority but lacking the necessary responsibility to act, while the Responsible primary is seen as having the responsibility but lacking the authority needed to bring about change. Christ can only act if he has responsibility commensurate with his authority. The Responsible primary must freely give him that responsibility.

The intervention is relatively straightforward. First, the client is taught how to separate from the Responsible primary using concentric circles and Christ's assistance in such a way as to not threaten or diminish the Responsible primary's ability to act. Next, the client, as Aware-ego, is asked to describe and question the separated Responsible primary. Initially, attention is paid to the emotions experienced and used by the Responsible primary in the exercise of its responsibility, e.g. pride, sense of control, fear, anger, etc. Also, at some point, the Responsible primary is asked to identify its disowned opposite or the negative charge that is the reason for its control. As a rule, the disowned self or negative energy is only identified *after* the Responsible primary is shielded from fear using a garment of protection, and becomes willing to use the *Light* to contain and anchor the disowned self or traumatizing energy. The case examples described below include a session where these requisites *were not in place*. The client's *reactivity* is quite noticeable. Finally, the Responsible primary is encouraged to turn its responsibility over to Christ. This is a contractual obligation that is understood to be non-binding for the Responsible primary. That is, s/he enters into the contract with Christ, but s/he is free to take back the responsibility any time s/he feels threatened by the process. The contractual obligation is 'sealed' by giving a portion of the *Light* to Christ. If Christ accepts it – and he always has, this is tantamount to his accepting the responsibility. The work then focuses on healing the exiled self and reconciling it with the Responsible primary. Two client verbatims are offered below by way of illustrating the process. Later in this chapter I will describe another intervention called 'the well of sensation,' which is particularly effective in identifying and dissolving negatively charged trauma energies, as well as selves bound to them.

Charlene. The client – Charlene, is a woman in her thirties. She has two grade school children and an infant, all by different men. Her husband – the father of the infant, is passive-aggressive, moody, and explosive. She likens him to having another child in the home. She is very intelligent, but has had limited educational opportunities. She is attempting to raise three children and create a work-at-home business to support her family, without support from her extended family and very limited assistance from her current husband or the other children's fathers. *She is very responsible*. Her sexual fantasies suggest she has had considerable difficulty with her own sexuality and physical intimacy. Historically, these inhibitions were mitigated by excessive drug and alcohol usage, which played a role in each of her pregnancies. For several weeks we have focused on altering her sexual fantasies, which were strongly dominant/submissive in nature. In the previous session she reported masturbatory fantasies that – for the first time – did not involve the use of force. "Recently, the images are more consensual…the male is not dominant…happened twice…afterward I cried…happy and thankful…I had never thought that way before…the other way was a source of guilt because the fantasies bordered on the extreme." I note all this because it has also provided Charlene with a growing awareness that her sense of responsibility has a strong *masculine* overlay, not unlike the dominant males in her sexual fantasies. This leads us into a general discussion of her 'Responsible self.' Inside, I have her ask the *Light* to identify her earliest motivations for being so responsible. She remembers hearing very clearly as a child, "to not be a burden on the family." For Charlene the opposite of responsible is 'being a burden.'

In the next session, I look for an opportunity to return to the theme of responsible vs. burden. It quickly emerges as she complains about her husband being a burden, like having a fourth child rather than a helpmate. I ask her again about the sense of 'burdensomeness' as she understood it in her extended family. She remembers a grandfather telling her: "If you do not take care of yourself, you leave it up to us to take care of you." She feels a strong need to protect the family from any burdening by her. I ask her what makes something burdensome to the 'Responsible self'? "Being irresponsible," she replies. I ask for synonyms. "Procrastination, evading, avoiding, spending money without thinking, thoughtlessness, not thinking of the kids needs, not taking care of the kids first, things that are avoidable if you think ahead…I have a lot of contempt for anyone not caring for the little ones first…I think it is selfish." Having gotten this very good description of what it means to be a burden, I now ask if she ever worries that there is a thoughtless, selfish, part in her? Yes. But then she quickly adds, "I will not stop for myself (at a store), but I will do it for one of the children." I move away from further focus on the burdensome self by asking what feelings the responsible part is most likely to experience? Surprisingly, she is quick to say that she experiences responsibility with a sense of pride; that the responsible part of her is pleased to do the right thing, and feels guilt for not doing what she needs to be doing. (Pride is a common emotion associated with the Responsible primary but it is not always present.) Charlene then adds that she has to say "no" to herself a lot, often out loud. When asked to elaborate, she gives examples: "no, it is not right…no, you do not want that." *And here is where I make a telling mistake*. Without first negotiating with the 'Responsible self' about how to safely discover her disowned self, I ask Charlene if "no" is still around, meaning the part of her she has to so frequently admonish. Charlene says she has difficulty focusing but can sense a presence. She sees the relatively unformed image of a person looking down with a hood over her. This description identifies the image with something shameful but for no clear reason. I have her ask Christ to give this image a portion of the *Light*. He places it in front of her but she is unwilling to pick it up. The image has long hair in here face and is crying. Christ is standing behind her. When I suggest he come around and stand facing her, she falls to his feet. In other sessions, Charlene has had Christ baptize disowned selves so she is not surprised when I ask her to let him do this again. At this point Charlene becomes very tearful but is unable to let Christ baptize. "Not yet" but no explanation as to why. At this point we are well over our session time so I respectfully bring her back and we quickly end the session.

In the above session, the Responsible primary was inadvertently by-passed. No effort was made to protect it with a garment of protection or release it from the responsibility of managing its burdensome part. Without preparation, I encouraged the emergence of 'Burdensome' into consciousness and even went so far as to suggest that Christ baptize her, which would have completely liberated the self. It is not clear who decided "not yet." The burdensome self has no real power in this matter. The 'Responsible one' has to be willing, but is undoubtedly threatened by the whole process at this juncture, as the following reports will make very clear. I honestly suspect it was Christ who said "not yet" because to act without being given the responsibility would have been tantamount to running rough shod over the Responsible one's overwhelming sense of responsibility. Such an action would be like the State capriciously stepping in and taking responsibility for a parent's child. In no uncertain terms, the 'Responsible one' lets me know in the next session that I was stepping on her toes and definitely upsetting the apple cart. I am told two things: one at the beginning of the session and one near the end. First, Charlene tells me that during the week she decided to file for divorce, that she is fed up with having *to carry the burden* of a husband who is so irresponsible. And at the end of the session she also admits that the previous week was a struggle. When I ask for specifics, she belatedly tells me that on Friday night she got drunk…for the first time in two years. Charlene has a long history of drug and alcohol abuse so getting drunk even once is a very dangerous thing, particularly as she also contemplates divorcing one of her few sources of support. Of note, I did not see the drinking as instigated by the Responsible Primary. Rather, her Ego-in-conflict stepped into the breech to quell the rising panic of the Responsible Primary over 'burdensome' issues and give her a temporary respite. What all this told me is that I better give the Responsible primary my undivided attention and support, and not propose any more interventions without her voluntary consent. So, basically, I spend this session doing what I should have done in the previous session.

First, I have Charlene go back inside for the explicit purpose of shoring up her Responsible self. I tell her that it is clear to me, if not to her, that her Responsible self has been greatly upset by the work we did the previous week. I note the parallels between the burden of the husband and the burden she identified in herself. Not surprising, Charlene has forgotten all about that part of the previous session until I mention it. I then encourage Charlene to separate from her Responsible self so we can dialogue with her and respond 'responsibly' to her needs. The protocol I use is very typical of what I now offer most clients. First, with her eyes open, I have Charlene sense the presence of her *Light* and ask it to draw a very small circle, which she will enter when she goes inside. Having established this very small beachhead, I then have Charlene invite Christ to draw a second circle *large enough* to contain the Responsible primary who is surrounding her. I emphasize the largeness of this second circle and the fact that Christ will draw it using his own *Light*. No matter how important a particular self is to the client's dynamics, it is finite, and can be contained within a circle of *Light*. Next, I have Charlene divide her *Light* in two and place one portion outside the small circle into the circle drawn to contain the Responsible primary. At this point I emphasize that although the Aware-ego will soon separate from the Responsible primary, the latter's power will in no way be diminished. With her own portion of the *Light* the Responsible primary can accomplish whatever the Aware-ego is accomplishing. She can even dissolve the circle surrounding her once the Aware-ego has separated, provided she is *willing* to do so without threatening other selves. Implicitly, I am encouraging the Responsible Primary to act willingly rather than willfully, but simultaneously reassuring her that her limited authority will not be diminished while she chooses to retain her responsibility and – really – not even then. (As a practical matter, this self will reassume control of Charlene's behavior the moment she leaves the office. The self is only objectified. It may be a little more reflective after this session, but essentially unaltered until reconciled with her disowned self.) Next, I ask Charlene's Aware-ego to move toward the Christ image. I suggest this in two steps. First she moves to the inner edge of the larger circle.

Once there, I have her push gently through it until *the two circles are completely separated*, and then go and stand beside Christ. (Her small circle is expected to stay centered on her and move with her, so it is actually the small circle that first pushes through the larger circle.) Once the Aware-ego is completely separated from the larger circle and standing beside Christ, I have her turn around and describe who she sees in the larger circle. I emphasize that she is now *separated* from the circle containing the Responsible primary, which will allow her to see it personified. Since most clients are strongly identified with this Responsible primary, the image they see will look much like them, and I will even suggest this on occasion. Significantly, in this instance, Charlene reports *also seeing* an image of the longhaired 'burdensome self.' I immediately suggest that she let Christ draw a circle around the 'burdensome self' and separate her from the Responsible one. This has an immediate effect. The Responsible one was seen as extremely agitated, but begins to settle down once Burdensome is separated from her. I ask Charlene if the Responsible one has felt specifically responsible for this burdensome self? "Yes, of course." I suggest that the Responsible one can use her *Light* to anchor Burdensome in place and opaque the circle if it continues to bother her. She does this and then proceeds to tell me of her struggle the previous week that culminated in the drinking. In turn, I tell her that Christ can accept responsibility for this 'burdensome self' if the Responsible Primary wishes him to do so at some point in the future. But at this point we are again over time, so that intervention must wait until the following session.

The next session is two weeks later. Charlene tells me at the outset that, "She is working hard, putting up with her husband, and raising three kids." She follows this up by telling me that she has canceled her appointment with the divorce lawyer but still plans to keep it at some point in the future, and that she is scared to death at the prospect of having to raise three kids alone. I sympathize with her plight, which is definitely real, but also wonder aloud if perhaps the Responsible primary is having to cope with internal stresses that are making her situation even more burdensome. She agrees to look inside. I ask if the Responsible primary is still contained? "Yes, she is in her own circle and has her own portion of the *Light*." Charlene comments that she looks a lot like her. I question how it could be otherwise since this part plays such an active role in her life given all of her responsibilities. I ask if the Responsible primary is aware of how upset she was two weeks ago? Again, yes, "She is aware of the need to divorce her husband… hating his abusive moods and threats… but she also resents the overwhelming responsibility of raising three kids without support, and fears she will not be able to handle it alone…that is why she gave the drinker permission to numb her for awhile. The drinking was a way to pop the tension that had built so unbearably, so she could start over." I ask if she is aware of any part inside of her that is threatening? "Guilt comes to mind for *resenting the responsibility* demanded by my husband's failure to pull his own weight." Again, I stress the idea of a part inside of her that may be aggravating the situation, some part for which she feels responsible but powerless to change? "Yes", she says, "but it is so big and it makes her fearful to acknowledge it." I immediately suggest that she use the *Light* to create a garment of protection. Charlene now sees the Responsible primary with a cape of *Light* and a sense of detachment. Next I have Charlene ask Christ to provide a double circle that will separate from the Responsible primary whatever has been the object of fear. Significantly, she identifies three images: a part that lacks self-control (I suspect this is the drinker), one that limits physical intimacy with others, and a third that is self-defeated and overwhelmed. She feels responsible for all three but owns she cannot change them, not by herself. The responsibility for them creates a "locked-in feeling." I explain to her in detail that it would be possible to give over her responsibility to Christ – who might have the authority (power) to change these parts – but only if he is given the responsibility to act. She could turn it over for one part at a time. I also emphasize that the Responsible primary could take back the responsibility if she did not like how Christ was proceeding with it. Interestingly, she gives Christ a portion of the *Light* and then they exchange it back and forth several times as a way of assuring her that she could in fact reassume the responsibility if she chose.

I suggest that Christ be allowed to extend a portion of the *Light* to the self-defeated part and everyone examine her more closely. Charlene reports that, "She shows fear and a distorted face; she is jumping around the *Light*. The face is a horror face. The fear is inside of her... lack of performance, lack of self-esteem, inadequacy, failure, lack of control. She cannot create value." All of these are shame words, though Charlene cannot identify them as such. I suggest that she let Christ extract all these negative emotions from 'Self-defeated' and place them in a separate circle. When this occurs Charlene can comment that, "She is standing by herself, no longer jumping around... I don't see her clearly, but she is not dark anymore." She describes the circle containing the extracted qualities as tightly packed with little blobs. I suggest that Christ can turn these into pure white light and return them to the source of *Light*. (Because of their non-human shape, I am choosing to treat them as autonomous emotions.) When he does this, they all coalesce into one shape but remain in the circle, which puzzles me. I rephrase the suggestion by asking if we need to retain this shape for Self-defeated, or can Christ send it into the universe? Christ assures us that she does not need it, then he takes it into himself and it dissolves.

Next, I suggest that Christ can fill the empty space left by the blobs with the Holy Spirit. Charlene reports that the Self-defeated part breathes it in but does not seem changed by it, except that she is not overwhelmed. Since we are running out of time, I ask if the responsible part wants to undo anything that Christ has done. The first answer is a firm "No," but then she reports being tempted. "A little part of her wants to take it back, but not really. The white shape is back (the part Christ had absorbed into himself) but it does not make contact with the Self-defeated part." We leave it there. I have Charlene return to me and we end the session. Her last observation helps to explain the failure of the single white shape to leave. While the Self-defeated part seems quite willing to be free of it, the Responsible primary remains ambivalent. Quite possibly, the white blobs were characteristics, which the Responsible primary fears she could no longer evade in herself, if they are removed from the Self-defeated part.

The following week I expect to pick up where we left off by examining the white shape that returned at the end of the last session, but events seemingly dictate otherwise. Charlene comes in with a very bad case of hives, which broke out the evening before our session. This is a good example of repressive somaticization. She had spent a really pleasant weekend by herself. Her husband took their son to visit his parents and her young daughters went to stay with an ex-husband and his second wife. She does not act out. She has taken time to reflect on her Responsible primary. One insight is the realization that she has chosen partners who "stroked" her sense of responsibility, complimenting her highly on her ability to succeed. But, as she wryly notes, they also provided a ripe environment for responsible caring. She also notes that for her, and her parents and grandparents, the ultimate test of responsibility was taking care of children, not just yourself. She traces the onset of the hives to her husband's return the previous evening…and a planned meeting with an attorney following our session. The latter is probably the most significant. Later she can tell me that she imagines it as signing the death warrant to her dream of turning around the marriage.

As soon as possible, I have her go inside to address the hives. She is asked to use an intervention identical to the one we used to separate from the Responsible primary. She enters a very small circle; Christ draws a larger circle around her sufficient to contain the "Hiver." She divides her *Light* and, leaving one portion for the Hiver, she then separates from the larger circle and joins Christ. She describes seeing an image very much like the Self-defeated part we worked with in the previous session. She is kneeling before the *Light*, shrouded in darkness. I ask what emotion she is expressing? Fear. But why via the hives specifically? "They are letting heat out…anger too…she has also been generating a lot of low back pain…she is also expressing some of the Responsible Primary's anger, and *hurt* from the person inside of me that is feeling neglected…she is a soft person…a lot of emotions…hurt is there because I am coming to the death of the hope that things will turn around with my marriage." (While I do not say so, this 'hurt' is likely shaming to her.) At this point I am feeling a need to intervene, to give this part some relief from the grip of all of these negative emotions. I have Charlene focus on her Heart. I first ask how the anger is affecting her Heart? "Like poison…like a green fluid." Next, I ask what is her responsibility toward these emotions? (This is a significant question that becomes pivotal to the rest of the session. Basically, I intuit that this ego-aspect also has a responsibility, though clearly one that is exceeding her authority to accomplish her mission.) "Her responsibility is to hold the anger, especially the hurt that turns into anger." Why is the anger inexpressible? "It would be destructive…it would lash out." What is the anger telling you? "To be afraid… that I will be alone again with even more responsibility…I did not want this." At this point I am feeling the need to give this ego-aspect charged with holding so much emotion a breather, and I use exactly those words. Could Christ give her a breather? Here I am imagining his placing his hand on her Heart and stimulating it with his love to help her relax. Interestingly, Charlene wants me to know that she now sees the Mother of God standing beside Christ. She has never seen this before. I do not focus on her except to ask what she is doing while Christ does whatever he is doing. At first nothing seems to happen other than Christ putting his hand on her Heart. "I don't see anything more than his trying…he places his hand on her chest…she does not respond...but she is not resisting…the Mother of God has her arm around her…like the white cape that the Responsible Primary is wearing…it is getting better…she stands up… the hood comes off…her hair is messy…she is facing Christ…and she is going into his arms… she is so ill-formed…black spiky hair…going into him is kind of an unveiling." (Apparently, the Mother of God image is functioning like a garment of protection.)

At this point I redirect Charlene by suggesting that perhaps the problem is with the Hiver's belief system. I suggest she ask Christ to read it. Immediately, she starts sharing what she is hearing. "A traffic jam of junk that is overwhelming…can never be sorted…she was formed because my life was formed to function like a ball in a pin ball machine…hitting and rebounding…shot out again and again hitting and rebounding…she takes it all and holds it… she thrashes around, with teeth and messed up hair and a horrified face all crouched down…all very tightly compact...something about forgiveness of myself…I made a lot of bad choices…this is my way of taking responsibility for those choices." This seems very significant. I ask if some part would feel irresponsible for letting go of these held in emotions? "It would be like not accepting accountability for my actions." I ask if she has the authority to alter whoever is making the choices? "No, I do not see her with that strength. She is mainly an internalizer." I point out the incongruity between authority and responsibility, that even though she does not have the strength (authority) to change things she is nonetheless responsible for the hives and low back pain, etc. To this interpretation, Charlene makes a very interesting observation. "Her cup is full to overflowing, the hives are providing a form of release."

We are nearing the end of our session. I make a suggestion that she allow this part to be yoked to Christ, that she allow him to share the burden of all these unexpressed feelings, that he could stimulate her Heart with love to the extent she gives him some of her internalized emotions. She immediately imagines handing him a basket of 'yuk' in exchange for warm bubbles. For the first time she smiles. I suggest a more formal yoking. They touch *Lights*, and this creates a barbell connecting both *Lights*.

The preceding session is interesting in a number of respects. First, it highlights the dark side of accepting responsibility with insufficient authority. It obliges the Ego to create an aspect that internalizes all the negative emotions associated with poor choices because it feels responsible for whoever made those choices. This internalization is actually quite common, though more often experienced as empathic selves who absorb or assimilate painful emotions from others. In the above case, the reason is an overriding sense of responsibility. More often, the empathic self is a young child who seeks to take on the pain of a hurting adult in an attempt to alleviate it. Such selves can become very vulnerable to everyone's pain thereafter, to the point that it cripples the client in adulthood, or even earlier, with unremitting painful conditions such as migraines, shingles, arthritis, etc.

In the next session, Charlene reports that her hives cleared up shortly after leaving the office. Also, that she has met with the lawyer and deferred any decision till later. In the following weeks we will go inside and finally reconcile the Responsible primary with her Self-defeated part. Very likely, some portion of her Self-defeated part was also projected into her husband's image, though not addressed as such in therapy. As a consequence of owning and healing the Self-defeated part, the projection could be expected to gradually diminish in strength as well as her need to stay with him. The couple separated a year later.

Bella. This second case is briefer. In addition to working with the Responsible primary, it also illustrates a particular intervention for addressing issues of pain. The client – Bella, came to see me after getting out of a treatment center for pain-pill addiction. Bella started taking pain pills four years earlier following surgery for lymphatic cancer. She is currently free of all medication and actively committed to working an AA program, but still experiencing a lot of pain on her left side, left hip, left knee, and headaches. In the previous session we identify a part of her that I call the Doer. In this session I suggest she go inside and separate from the part of her *most threatened* by the pain on her 'left side.' Bella separates from this part and identifies it as the Doer: "Skinny, rigid, austere, unforgiving, fearful of everything, but capable. She is strongly motivated by fear of the known and unknown, fear of not being right, fear of being exposed for things done secretly, or thought secretly. The Doer can forgive what shows to the world but not the inner part, the real part." I ask if the Doer part suspects another part of causing the pain? "No. The pain is physical." This is a significant answer, and not surprising given that Bella is a nurse. The Doer is responsible for the body's function, that is, it is strongly identified with the physical body. The Doer has not allowed for the possibility that pain could be caused by another self. In her mind pain has always had a purely physical explanation. I ask her if the Doer can acknowledge the existence of other parts, and then ask if she could imagine whether another part might be pained by the Doer's suppression of it? Is it possible, I suggest, that a particular part might be expressing its dissatisfaction through bodily pain because this is the only avenue of awareness available to it? Bella owns that it might be possible though the idea is new to her. I ask if the Doer is afraid of being overwhelmed by pain? Bella feels this might be the case. I suggest that the Doer could ask the *Light* to provide it with a garment of protection against the fear of overwhelming pain. It would be a garment completely dependent on her willingness which she could withdraw the instant it no longer suited her. The Doer immediately requests this and is clothed in a white, satin, gown with a big collar, lined with soft, cottony, blanket-like lining. "She feels very royal and comforted, and protected; things can roll off the satin. She feels like she could walk through life with ease and grace." The Doer now becomes willing for her *Light* to contain, in an opaqued circle, any part of her capable of generating pain on her left side. When this is done Bella immediately begins complaining of various pains on the left side her body. It is here that Christ is asked to intervene in a special way. I have Bella ask Christ to enter the opaqued circle and use his *Light* to ease the pain of the self who is *emerging into consciousness within the circle*. (This particular intervention is comparable to the 'well of sensation' intervention described later in the chapter.) I explain to Bella that this painful self has a strong negative charge as a result of having been so long suppressed, but that Christ can absorb this, and that is what happens. Very quickly her sense of pain abates. Bella says that the opaqued circle is very radiant as if there is a lot of light inside, and that the various parts of her left side no longer hurt. I now ask about the Doer. "She is OK, not agitated, not frightened." Bella then goes on to report an insight into the Doer's fear. "The fear is an illusion. The Doer does not have to be frightened of her abilities. She is capable." I ask if she can appreciate that working with Christ has benefits? "Yes. She is aware that all during the session the *Light* has had purple in it which she identifies with Christ." I suggest that the Doer begin walking toward the dome and that as she gets closer the dome will get less opaque. But this does not happen. "It has all stopped. I got to the dome. I can sense a presence inside of it. The Doer is very aware of being in her garment. The dome is very thick. No cracks." Obviously, the Doer is not ready for more at this time. We end the session here. In a series of later sessions several selves will emerge that have had to carry severe psychic pain for years. I will pick up on Bella's case again when I revisit the issue of pain later in the chapter.

Of note, many clients have selves that are strongly identified with the physical body as a way of blocking the awareness of other selves. If the denying self is dominant, and s/he generally is, s/he can deny relational consciousness to other selves by focusing on sensate consciousness. One way to conceptualize the difference between relational and sensate consciousness is to recall the three auric bodies comprising

Mind – mental, emotional and etheric. In that context, relational consciousness can be defined as a mental-emotional-etheric connection while sensate consciousness can be defined as a mental-etheric connection. Blocking the emotional component can suppress awareness of another self, but the other self's etheric connection will continue to "communicate" its painful existence via bodily sensation. In effect, the denied self will manifest as one or more physical symptoms. In the case of pain, blocking the emotional component that would identify the pain as an emotion generally stems from the fear that the pain will increase exponentially if the sensate self is allowed back into relational consciousness. And there is a kernel of truth in that belief. Letting Christ enter an opaqued dome to absorb the negative charge with his *Light* will obviate the charge and concomitant fear. In sum, the therapist needs to anticipate the client's fear of being overwhelmed by negative emotions when a self is allowed to remerge into relational consciousness, even in an opaqued dome, and plan for Christ to intervene during the process of emergence.

Later in the chapter I elaborate on the concept of the somaticized selves. These are ego-aspects that have been repressed, dissociated, or suppressed in such a way that their banishment relegates them to pure sensation. The ego-aspect is not literally exiled to sensation; rather, it is blocked from relational consciousness. This can be demonstrated by the presence of somaticized selves in clients with acute and chronic physical problems, and interventions for bringing them into relational consciousness where they can consciously express with emotion as well as sensation. Sometimes, the somatization can be the result of environmental trauma in which case it is the negatively charged emotion, rather than a self, that must be addressed. But once a somaticized self or emotion is allowed a self-image in active imagination it can be healed and the physical problems expected to abate. Actually, there is often a lessoning of symptoms even before the healing if Christ is allowed to provide triage interventions such as absorbing accumulated unexpressed anger or pain.

To summarize the foregoing: when going inside, the therapist needs to identify any Responsible primary as soon as possible and work with it. Sometimes this is easy and even unavoidable, if the therapist is willing to address physical problems. The Responsible primary will generally make itself felt in order to object to focusing on a disowned self before protections are in place. The exploration of any physical symptom is likely to evoke such objections, since the symptoms invariably point to a self that is being blocked from relational consciousness.

The Responsible primary relies on fear to avoid repetitions of abusive or traumatic events. When fear fails to evade the source of fear, other selves will reactively emerge to help reinstate its avoidance strategy. If highly reactive, the client is likely to miss the next session or even terminate therapy. Assuming s/he does return, s/he is likely to have little or no recall of the previous session. If amnesia is insufficient to "soothe" the client then other ego-aspects – an Ego-in-conflict or Dominant self, will become active in an effort to reinstate the status quo. Before working with any disowned self, the therapist must elicit the Responsible primary's cooperation. If a Responsible Primary is by-passed, even inadvertently, its reactivity will sabotage treatment. Even if an Ego-in-conflict or Dominant self is not the focus, remember that they work in collusion with a Responsible primary. Whenever the symptoms of a disowned self threaten a Responsible primary, the Responsible primary's agitation will provoke an Ego-in-conflict, Dominant self or Coping aspect (discussed in the next chapter).

Lastly, I need to emphasize that it is often impossible to distinguish between a Dominant self and Responsible primary. The latter is created earlier and tends to be younger when personified. I only 'discovered' the Dominant self some years after I had learned to identify the Responsible primary. Both will function responsibly. What sets the Dominant self apart is its power to self-shame. Repressive somatization and observed amnesia between sessions, which I have identified in both of the above cases, is most likely the result of self-shaming. It may be, in the final analysis, that the two selves are indistinguishable. What makes me think otherwise is that often, after successfully working with a Dominant self, the therapist will be confronted with what I have come to call a Regressive Dominant, which has most of the characteristics of a Responsible primary. But however it is defined, either Ego manifestation must be treated respectfully or their fear of the therapist disrupting the status quo will exacerbate a client's symptoms and/or push the client to terminate therapy; and be assured one of these selves is always present when the client is therapeutically engaged.

Opposites Governing the Ego Mind: Feeling and Thinking

Jung defined feeling and thinking as the two *rational* functions available to Ego for apprehending the Mind's activity. In contrast, he defined sensation and intuition as *irrational* functions. By rational, Jung meant reflective and evaluative as distinct from data directly sensed and received. Jung observed that a person who relies primarily on feeling is likely to treat thinking as inferior, meaning undeveloped and untrustworthy. The same is true for someone who relies primarily on thinking. For them feeling will be the inferior undeveloped function. The modern variant of this lopsidedness is the idea that women are from Venus and men are from Mars. But Jung also asserted that the inferior function will press to become equal in value during midlife, and if the individual fails to integrate its emergent perspective, the function's persistence will overwhelm the individual in a negative way.

In my work, feeling and thinking are treated as a duality. Both functions are considered indispensable for the Ego's adequate processing of the worlds of Mind, Body, Soul and Spirit. Thinking is needed to evaluate thought-forms and feeling is needed to evaluate emotion generated by thought-forms. Put another way, feeling is needed to evaluate the quality of emotion generated by structure, and thinking is needed to evaluate the kind of structure (e.g. belief) generating emotion. If used concomitantly, the two provide a stereoscopic gestalt of the Mind's activity and structure, while reliance on only one restricts understanding to a one-sided perspective. It is the difference between seeing the world with only one eye or both eyes. Ideally, the Ego needs to move back and forth between these two poles of evaluation defined as feeling and thinking. Feeling also evaluates the effects of an ego-aspect's thinking and vice versa. For example, if the thinking only generates negative feelings such as anger and frustration, then thinking needs to take a different direction. Likewise, if feeling has no way of addressing a high degree of emotionality, then the client needs to look to thinking and intuition for answers. Typically, the dominant ego-aspect of most individuals only relies on one of these two functions and dis-identifies with selves that seek to use the other function. In most cases, this preference is easily discerned by simply asking a contained ego-aspect if it favors one or the other function. (Rarely will it favor both.)

While thinking or feeling can be strongly identified with a particular ego-aspect it is never the exclusive prerogative of that self. Every self has equal access to all four functions. They are functions of the Mind, not the Ego. But a self is necessary for the conscious experience and development of any function. If an ego-aspect is punished for exercising any of these four functions, it will learn to rely exclusively on its opposite if possible. Historically, Western cultures have tended to denigrate women who presume to think, and shame men who rely on feeling.

Often, 'emotion' and 'feeling' are used interchangeably as if they were synonyms. Feeling 'names' the conscious experience of emotion, so in that way they are alike. But emotion is ongoing whether or not it is consciously felt. Feeling *evaluates* emotion, but is not itself the emotion. Emotion can occur without its conscious apperception by feeling. A self that relies on feeling will be rationally guided by the evaluation of emotions, i.e. assign values to them. In contrast, the *thinking function* does not focus directly on emotion, but rather on the structures generating emotion, i.e. images, motivations, and beliefs. Though emotion is not its focus, a *thinking self* will, nonetheless, generate emotion as a consequence of its evaluation. A thinking self will also express any emotion instrumental to its creation such as fear or anger. Even an ego-aspect identified as the "Rational mind" can be strongly motivated by a specific emotion such as fear. This may not be self-obvious (since a predominantly thinking self normally eschews the feeling process), but it can become apparent with sensitive questioning regarding what motivates that self. Most selves are motivated by the need to cope with dissident emotions impinging on their structure. For example, an exclusively thinking self will likely fear a feeling self that keeps identifying overwhelming negative emotions. The thinking self will block the feeling self as much as possible, and lacking access to feeling, it will simultaneously blind itself to the emotional energy guiding its own activity. All selves must use emotion to communicate their willed intent, but they can do so without feeling what they emote. Without feeling, a self will have considerable difficulty evaluating the emotions motivating it or those it generates. Without a modicum of thinking, a self cannot evaluate the structures producing emotions, particularly beliefs and intent.

Both thinking and feeling selves *can use sensation* to deduce affective emotions. But the Ego can block that function as well by severing the connection to sensation. Depersonalization occurs when a thinking self severs its emotional connection to its sensate body. It is something akin to dissociation, but phenomenally different in that the depersonalized self can imaginatively observe the sensate body, but rejects ownership of it. It apperceives from a purely mental perspective. Generally, the body it observes will embody conscious sensation. In contrast, dissociation denotes the simultaneous repression of all thinking, feeling, and sensation connections, generally as a result of mental thought being overwhelmed by emotion and sensation. When that happens, the Ego constellates a new ego-aspect to organize consciousness with emotional strengths sufficient to push away from the severed ego-aspect bound up in the unbearable pain.

Another strategy that the Ego can employ is to dissociate itself specifically from ego-aspects that rely on feeling to read emotions. Though effective in the short term, the latter is a dangerous strategy. Lacking access to the feeling function, an ego-aspect greatly handicaps its ability to evaluate persistent negative emotional energy, except by sensation or intuition, which it can also block. In the short term, a thinking ego-aspect can believe "out of sight, out of Mind." But the Body experiences affective emotions whether or not they are consciously experienced by an ego-aspect; and the repetitive generation of negative emotions is a primary cause of 'stress,' that all encompassing rubric for the ills of modern man, and likely the primary cause of most chronic physical problems.

Unidentified accumulated shame, fear, anger, and pain is a common result of exiling ego-aspects that either generate those emotions or could identify their presence. On numerous occasions, I have found it helpful to have the client allow Christ to scan and absorb accumulated anger and/or fear stored in the sensate body mirroring the brain-body. The client is often amazed by both the *extent* of this accumulation, its *correspondence* to sites of recurring physical problems, and the *memories* it releases, as it is absorbed/removed by Christ. In all such instances, I emphasize that allowing Christ to absorb the negative emotion with his *Light* does not removed the self's capacity to communicate with that emotion; nor will it preclude further accumulation. To prevent further accumulation, the client must become willing to identify who is generating the negative emotion and why. But removing accumulated, unexpressed, emotion does help the client become proactive since, before the intervention, s/he was fearful that any expression would precipitate an avalanche or deluge. As one client said, "If I allowed myself to be angry, I would kill someone."

Where feeling and thinking are addressed in therapy, I describe them to the client as two processes of the Mind that assist us in knowing our thoughts and emotions; and further, that access to them is generally controlled by one or two ego-aspects. A basic intervention for addressing these functions is to have Christ draw two circles that capture the flow of each one. When this is done the client is simply asked to describe what they see. This is a deliberately vague directive, but surprisingly, very few clients have difficulty allowing Christ to contain their understanding of feeling and thinking. For each client it is something different but nonetheless distinguishable as thinking or feeling. What is contained generally provides a representation of the relative value assigned to each. (A Dominant self or Responsible primary is always active in this process and likely to be biased regarding what is seen.) If either of the processes seems damaged, my initial suggestions will be directed at healing them. A distinction needs to be made here between the function itself, and selves associated with the function. Sometimes, it is the function that is in need of work (a chakra issue), but most often it is a self that has been punished for using the function that is most in need of work. This intervention often requires uncovering disowned selves adversely affected by association with a particular function. For example, a disowned self can be seen as strongly reliant on the feeling function, and profoundly shamed for being associated with it. A disowned self can also be dissociated for merely expressing particular emotions such as anger, which is tantamount to its becoming a magnet that accumulates that particular emotion. Whatever the case, the initial examination of the thinking/feeling poles will generate significant insights into the client's dynamics for both the client and therapist. Below, I give three case examples illustrating this kind of intervention and resulting discoveries.

Of note, in these interventions I do not ask Christ or the client to contain the ego-aspects that most strongly rely on feeling or thinking. Asking that both kinds of ego-aspects be contained at the same time is likely to evoke a high degree of resistance, particularly, if an ego-aspect associated with one of the functions has been dissociated. Wording the suggestion as a request to study the functions opens the possibility of discovering such selves by inference, without threatening the primary self whose perspective is being studied.

Case Examples

Juanita. Juanita has been seen for several years for a bipolar disorder related to posttraumatic stress in childhood. She was raised in a highly intelligent, explosive, incestuous family. As a result of therapy she has made considerable progress in all walks of her life. She came back into therapy for the explicit purpose of having me monitor her gradual withdrawal from seizure medication prescribed for her bipolar disorder. She understood the medication could be suppressing unaddressed psychiatric issues and wanted me to work with her through the withdrawal process. Her doctor was providing the withdrawal regimen. Juanita is highly intelligent, a gifted musician, and very visual, imaginatively and symbolically. Whenever she goes inside, she is very active in the sense that she will often pose her own questions to whoever is contained. Consequently, there is a lot of movement in these sessions as Juanita greatly augments my questions with unspoken questions of her own. It may also be helpful to note that Juanita is very active in twelve step programs and in the process of converting to Catholicism, her husband's faith. In this particular session, prior to going inside, she identifies experiencing some pain in her shoulder and elbow. While my primary objective is to simply have her examine the process of thinking and feeling, I hope to use them both to examine her physical symptoms. At my suggestion, Juanita asks Christ to draw two circles: one to hold the energy flow of feeling and the other the energy flow of thinking. When this was done she spontaneously visualizes a symbol for each. For thinking it is a question mark and for feeling it is a Heart. She then adds that she imagines a DNA strand going up through the thinking process. To this she adds the idea that this is God, as we understood him, the energy that draws the universe. I ask if she can identify a part of herself most identified with thinking. She immediately identifies "Juanita, the learner." She adds, "It is why I like Bach. Thinking is the analytical part of my musical ability." At this point she spontaneously reiterates that she is feeling pain in her left shoulder, which she attributes to playing a particular musical instrument in the past. I suggest she allow Christ to reconcile the thinking and feeling circles, using his *Light* to connect them to a third circle, which I identify as a circle of reconciliation. Then I ask her to join Christ in the circle and listen to what her shoulder is saying to her. She immediately envisions "another gremlin" digging his claws into the shoulder. (She has previously envisioned an animal-like creature in another session, which was perceived as communicating to her somatically.) I have her ask Christ to extract it from her shoulder and encapsulate it in a bubble of *Light*. It is described as an irritant that wants to get her attention. "It wants to play music for the fun of it, for the enjoyment of it – which I rarely do." Next she reports that her left elbow is also feeling irritated, and that often the fingers of that hand are numb. The gremlin identifies this as his twin brother. Christ is asked to extract and encapsulate this one as well. I then suggest that Christ be allowed to fill these bubbles with loving energy. She envisions them glowing blue, pink and white. She then identifies a third gremlin. This one, she says, is not so easily placated. It likes being crotchety and irritating, "A little irritation is good for the soul." Then she hears somebody saying that she has no backbone. She identifies the source as being between her shoulder blades. But then she hears, "Don't have to get bent out of shape over this, embrace the light, don't fight it, surrender your will and I will give it back a hundred fold." (That last statement comes in response of an inner ongoing dialogue with Christ, which she had not reported till now.) I note to her that the place she identifies in her back is considered the Heart chakra's expression of will. I suggest that perhaps she can ask Christ to place his seal on that center. She reports feeling as if she has been given a form fitting leather jacket, a corset with a spine built into it, an armor of God.

In the next session, Juanita returns with an upper respiratory infection. I assume it is psychosomatic and wonder if anything in the previous session has precipitated it. She thinks she has gotten it from her husband who is a schoolteacher; that she has been doing too much and is rundown. She and her husband are in the process of selling their house. They are hopeful of moving closer to his family, but as yet he has no job prospects. It is a stressful time. But most significantly, they are planning to move into her parent's home after they sell their house, till they either move or decide to stay and buy a better home. Her father is very controlling, easily angered, and has been a major source of her psychiatric problems, including sexual abuse issues. The previous weekend, although I do not know this when she goes inside, he discussed their moving into the house and insisted that his granddaughter sleep in his room (he would sleep elsewhere). Her parents sleep in separate rooms. She has not told him this is unacceptable. I mention all of this as it clearly becomes an issue as she explores her respiratory infection within the circle of reconciliation for feeling and thinking. When she goes inside, I suggest she step back into that circle and ask her *Light* to contain whoever was expressing through the infection. She immediately identifies a 12-year-old self, who we have worked with before, with whom she immediately begins a self-dialogue. "She wants to breathe." I suggest she have Christ extract whatever is blocking her breath. "He pulls out an oversized green gunk, like the phlegm she has been coughing up." The 12-year-old immediately feels better. Christ has contained the gunk in a circle without our even asking. It is described as not alive, but bubbling, alive like a germ. When she asks Christ what it is, he encourages her to ask it. It does not talk but a cartoon balloon appears over it to say it is the ghost of Christmas past. She asks when she was choking in a past Christmas. She immediately sees a picture of herself around age four sitting on the floor with her mother and teen-age half sister standing around her. Their breathing is labored. She understands that, "He (her father) has been spewing forth for weeks and that is why the air was so bad up there." By this she means her father's constant rages, which do not seem to affect her till later in her development. At age 12 she becomes old enough to breath the Dad air. She then observes that, until this week, this has been one of her best years in terms of no illness. I ask her to have the *Light* tell us more about the bad air. "It is a soul sickness, sin...not self-righteous anger...the sin of self-destruction...why my mother slit her wrists, why my sister overeats...they are infected with the sin from my father...and I will be too if I do not put a stop to it." A stop to what, I ask? Christ answers the question very directly: "You can't move in with them." It is now that she tells me about her father's proposed living arrangements for her eleven-year old daughter. I don't have to add anything. It is now all too clear to the Juanita that moving in with her parents is not an option.

In the above case, very little was done with feeling and thinking per se beyond providing a circle of reconciliation. What it does illustrate is the intervention's power – via the circle of reconciliation, in identifying thoughts and feelings regarding a client's aches and pains.

Tory. This is a married woman in her fifties. She is highly fused with both her mother and only daughter. Therapy has been aimed at helping her separate from both. In the past, she has talked to each of them daily, sometimes several times a day. The mother lives close by while the daughter lives a 1000 miles away in a distant state. But that has not deterred either of them from frequent, though often contentious, cell phone calls. In the previous several sessions, Tory has identified a primary-self, which we call the Manager and also a disowned ego-aspect identified as "flawed" but as yet uncontained. Tory is very intelligent, intuitive, and very good at visualization. In this session she tells me about a number of somatic problems. She is suffering from tinnitus. In addition, her doctor has told her that her hearing in her right ear is weak. Finally, her eye doctor has told her that her right eye is also weak. I ask in passing whether she thinks her Manager is a thinker or feeler. She is quite certain that it relies on thinking. I suggest that perhaps it might be helpful to examine thinking and feeling to see what they can tell her about her symptoms. (What goes unspoken here is the hypothesis that the Manager will equate with thinking, and the 'physical weaknesses' with the feeling function.) I explain that she needs to allow Christ to draw two circles. One will contain the flow of thinking and the other feeling. I ask her to identify clearly which is which.

She immediately identifies the one on her right as thinking. She sees a square dark red column within the circle. There is very little movement in it, but it is really tall. It has nicks in it. The feeling circle is round and fluid. It has gold flowing in it or something shiny almost like gold. The thinking column feels cold and sharp; the red is intense. In contrast, she notes, the feeling column is something you want to watch, the gold is bright and reflective, almost like a prism. The images seem paradoxical given how much she seems to value thinking.

At this point I suggest to Tory that she allow Christ to reconcile the two of them so she can step inside and use both to examine her physical symptoms. Interestingly, she says that she is unable to connect the circle of reconciliation with the thinking circle. "I can't get the *Light* to the square column," she says. I reiterate that Christ is to do it. When she lets him, he is able to connect to the column, but via the top of it. I invite her to join Christ within the circle of reconciliation so she can better evaluate her symptoms. When I ask her what is responsible for the tinnitus and weak right eye, she identifies the thinking part of her as creating the imbalance. The process is helping her to realize that thinking alone is not working. I have her ask about the redness covering the thinking column? Tory says it is a dark red, almost as if it has faded or dried out. I have her ask Christ what is wrong with it? He says it has faded because there is a lot of heat and light in it. It is cracked, like alligator skin, baked and parched. The bottom of the square column is most affected, less so at the top where the *Light* is connected to it. I ask what makes the bottom the way it is? Tory replies that it is that way because of old beliefs, old trust, and old ways of doing things. I decide not to pursue this further at this point, but shift her attention to the tinnitus. But this time, when she asks Christ to read its meaning, she gets no answer.

So instead, I suggest she allow Christ to extract it from her and place it in a circle, thinking that it is being produced by an emotion. Christ does this immediately. What Tory sees is a stiff rod taken from her left ear and now encapsulated in *Light*; her left ear is the one most affected by the tinnitus. I have her ask her *Light* if it belongs to her, is it a part of herself? (It reminds me of Modi's observation about spirit entities, which reportedly can manifest as rods or triangles or other shapes.) She is puzzled that I ask the question, and even more when she hears the answer, "No, it does not belong to me; it got into me but it does not belong to me." I have her ask Christ to turn it into pure white light and return it to the source of all light. She sees it washed away. Next, I have her ask Christ to place a small portion of his *Light* into the place where the stiff rod was lodged. She experiences it as a warm feeling that seems to mesh with everything in her ear. At this point, I quickly end the session without explanation as we are well over time. (In future sessions, she no longer experiences the tinnitus in her left ear, but it does persist in the right ear until other issues are addressed.)

In the next session, Tory owns that she has not gone inside to look at the circles, and has given the previous session little thought. But when I suggest we return to the two circles she is reminded that she knows something about the thinking circle that she has not previously mentioned, namely, that the red color suggests to her a clear connection between thinking and anger. I ask her if there is a self that has fused anger with thinking? Her immediate answer is "intensity," which seems ambiguous, but then she goes on to explain that, "Thinking adds intensity to the anger." I ask if she would be willing to separate the thinking from the anger? When she says "Yes," I ask her to give Christ a portion of her *Light* as an expression of her willingness to have him separate the two. According to Tory, Christ's *Light* dramatically took over the column of thinking, "the cracked red flexed off, there is a stainless steel-like material underneath, not hard but refined, pure, shiny." I ask her if he can tell us how the anger got fused with the thinking? She replies that, "it is a way to fight back, a survival technique."

Though I have Tory focused on thinking and feeling, I remain aware that for the past several sessions my therapeutic objective has been to help her separate from a primary self, which we have named the Manager. Given Tory's description of thinking fused with anger as a survival technique, "a way of fighting back," I wonder out loud if by separating the two, we have deprived some part of her of that option, and could we offer it a better option? She immediately identifies thinking with her Manager, "It is what she generally does." As she imagines this from the Manager's perspective, she begins to see the anger as a reaction, or resentment. "The Manager always has to be thinking, planning, saying 'what if.' The anger expresses resentment at having to be ever vigilant. A perfect example was talking to my mother last night. I always feel a need to keep her pleasant and talkative." Tory is intellectually aware that the Manager protects a part of her as yet unidentified. At this point I suggest that if that part could be identified and responsibility for it given over to Christ, then the Manager would no longer have to manage her mother's moods, which she feels obliged to do as long as she is protecting that part. At this point the Manager seems agreeable to separating. I am very careful in this process. This is a major self for Tory, one who has directed much of her professional and social life. I make it very clear that the process of separation will include ample safeties for the Manager including her receiving a portion of the *Light* prior to separation so that the separation in no way isolates her from the ongoing process.

We proceed with the separation in the following session and then identify and work with a flawed self over a number of sessions.

Tory's case is interesting because it shows how working with feeling and thinking can dovetail into other critical issues. In this case, it allowed Christ to help her identify the anger generated by her Manager's thinking and remove its accumulation. It also served to show Tory and her Responsible primary the limitations of relying exclusively on one function, as well as making her aware that ego-aspects emote whether or not they access the feeling function to evaluate their emotions.

Leona. This case provides a number of surprising responses to the request that Christ contain her thinking and feeling processes. Initially, each circle is only distinguished by the word designating the process, i.e. 'thinking,' and 'feeling.' Her first comment about 'thinking' is that she does not like the circle. "It keeps changing. Now it is elongated, elliptical, the edges move." (This has never happened to her before and she has been inside many times.) I ask what it signifies? "It is a self that, instead of staying in the circle, keeps bumping around and changing the shape of it...opposing thoughts create agitation and reactivity." I suggest she separate this self from the thinking process. This separation stimulates her to remember a description of conscience wherein 'the devil is in the thinking and an angel is in the feeling.' The separated self is envisioned as having a devil on her shoulder. I suggest to Leona that she allow Christ to encapsulate 'the devil.' Immediately the image of herself changes. Before it was quite small, lost in the circle. "Now, I see a full sized self who is calm." I suggest she allow Christ to transform 'the devil' into pure white light and return it to the source of all light. She now reports seeing the thinking part as logical, down to earth, responsible, a self that manages activities and makes decisions. I ask if it has any assistance from feeling? "Feeling is an aggravation. When my kids were young I remember feeling overwhelmed and looking to my husband for help. His response was to tell me he was sick of my GD feelings and me. I stopped sharing my feelings, but it depresses me to be limited to thinking. It would be better, easier, if I had other tools, but I'm told that the other tools are worthless." I ask her to focus on the feeling circle. "Feeling is screaming to get out, to be heard...my husband was deaf to my feelings. There is a white bird sitting on the shoulder of the feeling self. It feels important, appears important." I suggest that she ask Christ to encapsulate the bird. (I intuit it needs to be treated like 'the devil' addressed earlier.) Immediately, the feeling self is described as standing up and getting larger. "The white bird felt like conscience telling me what my feelings ought to be." I ask her to have Christ contain the authority that created this bird. She sees her parents and her deceased husband. "My parents reinforced my husband's authority."

I shift focus to the parental authority that seems to be suppressing the feeling function. I suggest that Leona consider letting Christ terminate the parental authority to shame feeling. For this to happen all three – the Aware-ego, feeling self and thinking self, must give Christ a portion of their *Light* as an expression of their willingness for him to terminate this authority. When they do this Christ immediately enters the circle and lays hands on each of the authority figures. "They shrink in stature, he gets larger but there is no other change in his demeanor. I see him mostly as light and that has not changed." I ask how thinking and feeling appear? "They remain the same - same size, same shape." I now suggest that she consider reconciling feeling and thinking using a circle of reconciliation. Each self is expected to give Christ a portion of its *Light*, which he will then mix with his own *Light*. When Leona came to this session she complained of feeling torn and depressed. Now I ask her to consider that feeling in the context of what we have done. "I see an argument of conflicting thoughts and feelings. They are antagonized by each other. They are not congruent." I suggest that she allow Christ to create a conduit between them, directly connecting them with a band of his *Light*. "Now, energy is flowing into the circle of reconciliation, but I am separate from the flow, cut off in some way." The cut off appears to be momentary as something happens inside, but what exactly remains unclear to me. Christ has instigated it. The effect changes the flow of energies in a way that allows her to connect with feeling and thinking. I ask if it would be helpful to bring the selves together into the same circle. She says that it does not matter, but it would be more whole and they are willing. Her last comment is, "I guess we will see. Over the next several weeks she makes and acts upon two major decisions that she has been struggling with for months. She reported feeling much better, "Not so trapped, and definitely not torn or depressed." She is looking forward to a new phase of her life.

Further Observations about Thinking and Feeling

The processes of thinking and feeling are so complex and varied in their manifestations, that I can only suggest the most tentative of guidelines. First and foremost, facilitating their equal viability in the life of the client seems the best goal of treatment. Once the two processes are healed to the point where they become equal in stature, they can be connected by Christ to a circle of reconciliation and used to evaluate any number of issues, provided an ego-aspect is willing to enter the circle. Often, this healing requires working with ego-aspects controlling the conscious awareness of one function at the expense of the other. It is frequently the case that a primary self, likely more than one, will be strongly identified with one of these functions. Where that is the case, the other function will be undeveloped or strongly associated with a disowned self. The selves need to be reconciled so they have equal access to both functions via the circle of reconciliation. It is difficult to be more specific. As the above cases illustrate, once engaged, this intervention quickly takes on a life of its own leading in any number of directions.

I would also note that Bandler and Grinder, the creators of Neuro-linguistic programming, made much of the fact that individuals show a decided preference for modes of perception: visual/auditory/kinesthetic. They encouraged the therapist to listen carefully to the client's choice of words in describing their experiences and to mirror those choices in framing interventions. For example, if a client uses a lot of visual words in describing experiences, s/he will likely have difficulty with interventions framed in auditory descriptions. The same seems true for thinking and feeling. Some clients can be balanced in their use of both, but most will show a decided preference. This is particularly true of ego-aspects such as the Responsible primary. To speak in the language of feeling to an ego-aspect that relies almost exclusively on thinking will disconcert it, to say the least, until it is reconciled with the feeling ego-aspect it has long sought to suppress or disregard. So even if the therapist chooses to not address issues of feeling and thinking, s/he would do well to be sensitive to the client's preferences.

Without question, a Dominant self or Responsible primary that relies on thinking must eventually be separated and helped to identify the *emotional effects* of its thinking, which are invariably negative and controlling. Beyond that, it is generally helpful to examine thinking and feeling as functions. For one, the circle of reconciliation can greatly facilitate the examination of somatic symptoms. Likewise, the process can bring to light the need to reconcile with disowned selves that embody the opposite function. If not addressed, they will eventually make themselves felt in a variety of negative ways.

Jung, for example, made much of the idea that strong opinions were the result of undeveloped thinking in someone who relied predominantly on the feeling function and resisted the development of their thinking function. (He considered feeling and intuition his own strong suits.)

OPPOSITES GOVERNING THE EGO MIND: INTUITION AND SENSATION

Overview

From the outset, I want to acknowledge my reliance on intuition for most of the therapeutic interventions described in this book. Whenever a client goes inside, I devote one ear to what they are telling me, and the other to hearing my 'inner thoughts.' I am always *listening* quite intently for suggestions on how to proceed. Generally, these 'suggestions' come in the form of questions that I ask the client, particularly when they are inside. I honestly cannot identify the source of those questions or suggestions. But over the years I have come to trust the source implicitly. One reason for this trust is that all of my questions and suggestions will involve the *Light* and image of Christ. If any question or suggestion threatens the client, I trust the *Light* or Christ to immediately tell us both. Also, I assume that something comparable is going on in the Mind of the client. To some extent, they too are listening to 'intuitive' sources of information via the actions of their Christ image and the *Light*. On reflection, I subject my intuition to the cross validation provided by thinking, feeling and sensation; but that said, intuition remains the primary source of datum for my questions, hypotheses, and experimental interventions.

In this work, sensation and intuition are treated as opposites, but more extreme than feeling and thinking in terms of their poles. If one imagines a Celtic cross, feeling and thinking form the horizontal bar, both poles resting firmly within the Mind. In contrast, intuition aptly points to the heavens while sensation grounds us in the earth. Intuition and sensation provide the 'facts' addressed by feeling and thinking. Neither intuition nor sensation is considered rational since the datum they provide is unreflected; it simply is. It comes to us and we simply accept or reject it. In the case of sensation, the datum is usually treated as flowing from our sense organs, which we implicitly trust to provide us the most verifiable facts. In the case of intuition, the source is harder to name, but the information is no less valued, if it is used. It is my own conclusion that intuition receives its input from the three chakras defining the Soul. Thus, while both functions provide the Mind its 'facts,' the sources of those facts represent diametrically opposite spheres. Sensation provides the bridge between Mind and Body, while intuition provides our most direct access to the Soul's input. In effect, I am arguing here that intuition is the function whereby Mind hears the Soul. Thinking and feeling create rational paths for getting from point A to point B. Sensation most often defines point A. Intuition takes us to B as a sudden insight without having first traversed a path from point A. Only afterward, do we rationally construct a path that others can follow.

I have yet to encounter an ego-aspect that claims to rely on intuition as its primary function in the way that other ego-aspects rely predominantly on feeling, thinking or sensation. To the extent that intuition is imagined, it seems to be experienced as a 'presence' essentially without form. It is *felt or heard* rather than seen. On occasion, clients have reported a presence in a space such as a cave that spoke with the power of a categorical imperative. Images embodying a higher power can definitely function as conduits of intuition. The *Light* and Christ image are prime examples. But so far, I have not discerned any self-images that function as conduits of intuition. All self-images seem capable of 'hearing' or 'sensing' intuition, though most are likely to disregard or denigrate its input. But no ego-aspect I have encountered has claimed to be oracular. Intuition is something 'received' by an ego-aspect rather than something embodied. In contrast, most ego-aspects will claim thinking or feeling, and less often sensation, as a primary function. Parental images do not speak intuitively, but they can embody Temporal and Moral authority, and in so doing they can speak with a voice that is difficult to gainsay until that authority is removed. In that sense they can be seen as 'speaking with the Soul's authority,' but not intuitively.

Ego-aspects frequently dismiss or denigrate their intuitive insight. In sharp contrast, most selves maintain an active connection with the sensate body that personifies sensation. All ego-aspects have ongoing access to the Body via the sensate body. Sensation is the modus operandi by which the Ego and Body exercise their reciprocal relationship; and that relationship is the primary reason for Ego creations. By and large, it is Ego that exercises voluntary control of the Body. The Body can give the Ego feedback that it is exceeding the Body's limits, but must otherwise accede to its demands. It is actually quite common for ego-aspects to disregard real time negative feedback (actual pain in-the-moment). Most people past the age of forty begin the long journey of ignoring their aches and pains.

The Ego can partially block the conscious awareness of *negative experiences* by dissociating any ego-aspect that carries the memory and creating a new ego-aspect to supplant it. An ego-aspect can do something comparable by depersonalizing. Unfortunately, banishing or attenuating memory in this way is never complete because the sensate awareness remains intact in whatever is disowned. Dissociation allows the supplanting a disowned aspect that has lost its access to free will with a new ego-aspect, but the exiled aspect remains viable as sensation that can be stimulated by memory and/or affect. In sum, the sensate component of an ego-aspect remains connected with the Body whether the ego-aspect is conscious, repressed, projected, or fragmented. While some disowned selves can find alternative embodiments in the images of others (projection), most will simply persist as Repressive somatization, which means they will be sensed somatically if re-stimulated by mental or emotional triggers. Repressive somatization – the somatic expression of banished ego-aspects, is one of the most common consequences of Ego dissociation and repression. Repressive somatization and projection are described and illustrated later in the chapter.

When a client actively imagines the *Light*, the Aware-ego emerges as *the self least tied to sensation and most receptive to intuition and pure awareness*. It is also the ego-aspect most receptive to higher powers, beginning with the *Light*. Unlike other ego-aspects, which can be visualized once they are separated, the Aware-ego is almost always experienced in the first person as holding the *Light* and hearing, visualizing, or sensing whatever is happening in active imagination. The client embodies the Aware-ego, looking out of its eyes, hearing with its ears, holding the *Light* in its hands. But without any exception I can think of, the Aware-ego always emerges in the midst of a co-existing ego-aspect. Once and ego-aspect is separated from the Aware-ego and contained it can be visualized or sensed because its mental/emotional state and/or connection to the sensate body 'fleshes' it out. The Aware-ego is expected to organize consciousness while the client remains inside. But for most clients, the Aware-ego's perspective is generally limited to therapy sessions, unless the client consciously evokes it between sessions; and few clients are willing to evoke their Aware-ego between sessions until they have successfully entered their Heart; or are prompted by me (telephone, e-mail) because they are functioning under duress. Thus, primary selves are generally expected to reassert dominance once the client leaves the office, even though separated from the Aware-ego during a session. Separation is a process of personification or objectification; it does not automatically alter an ego-aspect's viability in the life of a client except as it gains insight or is transformed by Christ. That is one of several reasons why separated ego-aspects need to be treated respectfully. A Dominant ego that is separated and then minimized will sabotage therapy if threatened by the process. As a rule, it is safe to assume that the Aware-ego always emerges in the midst of a co-existing ego-aspect; and whenever an ego-aspect is separated from the Aware-ego another will emerge to take its place. As frequently as not, *I will ignore the fact that another self has stepped in* as long as the newly merged ego-aspect is not interfering with the work. But ideally, all merged ego-aspects must eventually be identified and worked with, either in the first person or as personifications, if their dominance adversely affects the client's ability to function or call upon a higher power in time of need.

I have never attempted to contain sensation and intuition in two circles in the way described above for thinking and feeling. Thus far, I have only explored sensation as a 'well of sensation' or as a sensate body. As for intuition, I do not focus on it unless it appears to be blocked, which is almost always the case with an Ego-in-conflict. The first several times I encountered 'intuition' in active imagination, I did not know quite what to make of it. I only suspected its role because it seemed to repeatedly present *as a presence* rather than an image. As noted, intuition is hypothesized to be the 'conscious bridge' between Soul and Mind. Any constellation that 'speaks' intuitively has thus far reflected this confluence by manifesting as a presence rather than an image. These observations are offered as hypotheses. I have not had a great deal of opportunity to explore them in a clinical setting, unless there is a disturbance of the intuitive function that directly impinges on the client's cognitive ability. What I have discovered is that intuition is often blocked by ego-aspects. When this occurs, the client generally experiences the blockage as symptoms focused on the brow chakra – the area between the eyes. They may complain of 'being in a fog' or more commonly, they will complain of sinus headaches and 'allergies.' This is illustrated in the next section on intuition.

Intuition

Over the years, I have occasionally felt an overwhelming desire to close my eyes during a therapy session. I remember Carl Whitaker having a similar problem though he would simply give into it and briefly fall asleep in the therapy session; and then wake up with a sudden insight. I rarely feel this desire to close my eyes outside of therapy sessions. If I can get the client to go inside then it seems to abate quickly. Even so, for the longest time I thought it might be a blood sugar problem or biorhythm problem, since it seemed to happen primarily in the afternoon. But then I also started experiencing it in the morning, on what I have always considered my most alert time. One day I had an insight: maybe it was a different kind of energy problem. I am very intuitive. I know that. Maybe, I thought, my brow chakra – long associated with intuition, was closing down. I suddenly conjectured that my clients were directly *closing down their brow chakra out of fear* and some form of entrainment was affecting my own brow chakra. (This is different from a client whose intuition is being somatically blocked, which most often manifests as a sinus condition. Generally, somatically blocked clients do not rely heavily on intuition as a matter of course. The type of 'closing down' I am speaking of seems to emanate from a self that is actively blocking intuitive activity in a client who normally relies on it. I have most often encountered it with MPD clients.) If, hypothetically, intuition does manifest through the brow chakra, which embodies the emotional field at the level of Soul, then closing it down would interfere with the activity of that function, and concomitantly affect the eyes. It could also interfere, inadvertently, with my being able to connect with the client in this way. Several observations finally convinced me of this possibility. The first came from resisting the urge to close my eyes in order to more closely study the sensations being generated by the urge. I felt the source of my drowsiness as noticeably present between, and slightly above, my eyes. I can only describe it as a dissonant, buzzing, ache accompanying a desire to close my eyes. The first time I identified that 'feeling' I challenged the client by asking what she was feeling afraid of just then. I did not ask it as a question, but rather as a declaratory conclusion about what was going on with her at that moment. And it prompted a quick reply describing the fear she was experiencing in the session. Once we could focus on the fear my drowsiness began to abate. Since that first time, I have become very sensitive to that 'buzzing ache' and concomitant desire to close my eyes. When it occurs I now associate it with a client attempting to block the intuitive function. The following case exemplifies this in several ways.

Zelda. Zelda is a highly intuitive MPD client. When she goes inside – which happens most sessions, her perceptions are like somebody being presented with fact, after fact, after fact. She is very good at reading her dreams and the dreams of others. I have often thought she relies too much on her intuition. It is very hard to give her suggestions when she is inside. Christ is completely in charge. She hears my suggestions easily enough but still persists in wanting to follow her own intuitive sense of direction, which is usually provided by her Christ image. In recent months she has established a routine of daily shamanic journeys between sessions. In this session, however, she complains of being 'dry.' She has nothing to work on, which is highly unusual for her. Shamanic journeying has seemed impossible for her over the two previous days, and likewise, her dreaming seems almost nonexistent. She can tell me of some interesting events in her life, that she feels are important, but she cannot tease out the significance. As she relates all of this I became increasingly drowsy. In the past I would have dismissed the feeling and attempted to "push through" with shear willpower. But it is mid-morning when I am generally at my best, and Zelda is complaining of being cut off from her normal sense of intuitive functioning. I decide the problem is a self that is *actively blocking* her intuitive function. Zelda is also complaining of a sore shoulder, a recurring problem, which we have attempted to work with in the past. The doctor says it is the result of a torn ligament, but the felt pain is episodic. I suggest she go inside and address it. Once inside, I will suggest that she draw three circles: a small one for the Aware-ego, a second larger one for the self sensed by the sore shoulder, and a third, overlapping the second, for the ego-aspect that is attempting to *banish* 'sore shoulder' to pure sensation. The latter is an intuitive leap on my part. I also suspect this third ego-aspect is deliberately or inadvertently blocking Zelda's intuition.

When Zelda goes inside, I first have her separate from 'Sore Shoulder' and then from the self responsible for exiling 'Sore Shoulder.' She quickly identifies the self experienced as a Sore Shoulder: "I get the number seven which could mean seven years old, but no image yet." I suggest that she ask Christ to compress the circle till an image appears. "What I get with the compression is the image of an arm in a sling and a voice saying, 'no excuse for what happened to them,' and a sense of despair, brokenness, disintegration, gloom and doom." I have Zelda ask Christ for assistance in working with the part that is blocking awareness of the seven-year-old. "There is no movement from anyone." I have her ask Christ what is closed down? "He points to my eyes, Heart, abdomen and feet." I ask if the seven-year-old controls these centers? "The closing is generated by fear." I ask if Christ can sever the psychic connection between the eyes and Heart (mental and emotional)? "The circle with the invisible Banishing part now looks like a Petri dish. Christ has put a drop of something in it and all kinds of things seem to be sprouting up. Now I am remembering being in the basement of the cult house with the men. They expect me to know something. They are pushing me around for not knowing. This is really hard. Christ puts his hand on my brow and is holding my head to his chest (at this point Zelda seems to be identified with the seven-year-old Sore Shoulder and speaking form that perspective). It was just horrible. They took the boy away." I should note here that Zelda suffered extreme cultic abuse as a child, which ended, for the most part, at age eleven with the death of her grandfather who was her link to the cult. Christ appears to be shielding her intuition by holding his hand over her brow and holding her head to his chest.

Between sessions Zelda begins recovering the memory. It is a terrible memory involving her grandfather and a cult member dismembering the dead body of a young boy. An alter personality was expected to stand in the corner and watch. If she said anything there was the real fear they would do something similar to her. I have her go inside and draw a circle containing Ruth, the alter with the memory. "I am getting a headache, a dull ache in the center of my forehead, like a pressure or a palm pressing in, holding down, holding back, blotting out, not seeing. Ruth seems to be coping by not seeing. It feels like being knocked out; I feel powerless. She is doing it for herself but attempting to protect the little ones as well." I have Zelda ask Christ about the emotions that Ruth is struggling against. "I see the emotions being put into a circle: repulsion, sex acts and sexual response, shame, men on top of me." I ask her to have Christ enter the circle and dispel these emotions. "He places his hand in the circle. The memory was creating a lot of sexual energy, pulling me in. Another alter is feeling the sexual energy. All the senses have been engaged by this experience, the eyes, ears, tasting, eating. The body feels frozen. Different alter personalities are attempting to do cleaning in order to distract from the experience. I see Harriet – another alter, doing laundry. Harriet wants to keep things clean. Christ asks why? I see him on the cross, not neat or tidy. I see his bruised and torn flesh. It does not need to be tidy. I am trying to keep my sexuality neat and tidy. What happens if I let go of it and it creates a disaster? He says it may." I suggest an intervention that involves separating sexual energy and negative emotions from Harriet's memory. (This intervention is described in Appendix I.) "I see Harriet's laundry. The terrible emotions are like dirty laundry under clean laundry. Christ needs to empty the basket of both. He dumps it out. Underneath is old garbage. He washes out the basket." I ask about the sexual energy, is it healthy and vibrant? "I see little pops of energy, like pop-pop, what I called my grandfather." I have her ask Christ to enter the circle and heal the energy. "I see him doing that. Now it is exploding in a different configuration. Not so dark. The colors are reds, purples, pinks, greens and whites." Is Harriet any different? "I see her as a woman out in the sun, saying she is glad that job is over, meaning having to always keep the laundry so clean to hide the dirty garbage. Now she is setting on a porch resting." We are over our time. I suggest that between sessions she can extend this same intervention to the others. She is not able to do that, but when she returns she can report that her intuitive functions appear to have returned intact.

I have described this case to illustrate the power an ego-aspect can exert in the suppression of intuition. In this particular case the intent was the blocking of a sexually charged recall. As Zelda relies heavily on intuition for recall, she is very sensitive to any blocking of that function. Extrapolating from my own experience, a client relies on intuition, then it's active blocking – for whatever reason – may be experienced by the therapist as a buzzing ache and desire to close the eyes. The client will feel the block as a dearth of symbolic connections, and an uncommon lack of connection between events. The blocking of intuition by a client may also manifest as a headache or general sense of tiredness. Headaches are a common experience of MPD clients when they are struggling to keep an alter from consciousness. But that kind of somatic blocking somatic blocking is distinctly different from an ego-aspect that is actively attempting to close down a Brow chakra's function. I have not experienced the 'buzzing ache' when clients somaticize in an effort to block intuition, i.e present with sinus conditions, allergies, colds, and the like.

There is so much more to discover about intuition, and I hope others will have the opportunity to explore it in greater depth, particularly, its connection to the Soul. But sensation duly demands most of my attention, as it is by far the most problematic in a psychotherapeutic setting.

Sensation

In this work I treat the Mind as superordinate to the Body, and sensation as the *reciprocal experience* of the Mind's ego-aspects directing the Body and the Body's feedback. The *conscious* experience of this process is called the 'felt sense' of something. A great deal of that experience can go on subliminally. Neurologically, here is no distinctive cerebral substrate that can account for sensation, unless you consider the whole brain and body as serving that function, and then you are obliged to ask: what is the 'conscious' recipient of all that datum? A theoretical perspective offered in this work identifies the Root chakra's auric body – also called the etheric body, as the source of sensation within the Mind. (Recall that Mind is defined as the coordinated function of the mental, emotional, and etheric auric bodies and their related chakras.) *The sensate body* – described below, is the *visual* analogue of sensation within the Mind, which is consciously experienced by an ego-aspect as its felt sense of being.

Let me quickly acknowledge that the current scientific paradigm considers the foregoing assertions untenable. If anything, academic psychology, physiology, and neurology would assert the opposite: that Mind is an epiphenomenon of the brain and body. Notable exceptions are Candace Pert's work in psychoneuroimmunology and Bruce Lipton's work in biology. But the assertions of academicians notwithstanding, I will maintain, as I have throughout this work, that the Mind blueprints the Body, not vice versa, and that *sensation is a function of the Mind, which the Ego embodies, reads, directs, and uses, to consciously blueprint our sense of being moment by moment*. I use 'blueprinting' in the same way that, analogously, a computer refreshes a monitor screen, millisecond by millisecond. Such assumptions can be neither proven nor disproven, so rather than argue them, allow me to just focus on exploring the role of sensation in a psychotherapy that uses the *Light* and image of Christ, and demonstrate the heuristic value of my assertions as hypotheses.

For beginners, I would note that the sensation function is easily manipulated by Ego, which would not be the case if it were a hard-wired aspect of the brain. For example, a dominant, active, ego-aspect can become hysterically blind, even as the brain's visual centers remain functional as measured by instruments that record the activity of the eye and visual cortex. Today's conversion reactions are more sophisticated than the glove anesthesia of yesteryear, but they still occur. Hypnotic suggestion has long demonstrated the power of belief in short circuiting all forms of sensory function. In sum, the Ego both perceives and controls the conscious experience of sensations generated by the Root chakra's auric body. It uses the sensate body to both direct the Body and embody its particular beliefs. Left to its own devices – sans Ego, sensation's control of the brain-body would probably function much like it does in animals. It would be the primary source of learning, a la Skinner and Pavlov. But Ego can override those learning principles, though most often it simply accepts them as 'true' and copes.

My general thesis that Ego controls sensate experience is collaborated by Peter Levine, who asserts that the Ego often impedes the resolution of shock trauma by interfering with the Body's innate ability to resolve trauma; and this active blocking is seen by him as responsible for our failure to resolve many symptoms related to Post Traumatic Stress disorder (PTSD). As he notes, animals have an innate capacity to 'shake off' the effects of 'freezing,' i.e. feigning death as a last ditch attempt to evade a predator. The intense energies generated by a fight/flight response are instantly blocked by this instinctual tendency to 'freeze.' To mitigate this shock to the energy system, the blocked energy must be discharged immediately or soon after the event; otherwise it will itself be blocked by fear, which leaves it undischarged in the emotional fields of the auric bodies. Levine offers a bodywork solution to this problem and has successfully treated several hundred clients in relatively short periods of time with interventions based on his conceptual work. The work in this book offers comparable solutions. Basically, the client is given the tools via Christ to reconnect with and decathect the undischarged energy of early trauma, particularly trauma generated by shame as well as the environmental traumas described by Levine. Both instinct and shame generate the same 'freezing' response so they are really indistinguishable at the level of sensation.

The Sensate Body

When the Ego constellates an ego-aspect, that self-image automatically acquires a sensate body as part of its constellation. The sensate body empowers it to control the Body, which is every ego-aspect's raison d'être. The sensate body is the visual analogue of the etheric auric body, so it will also embody the *instinctual will* that regulates Body homeostasis, making it a semi-autonomous component of the ego-aspect. Concomitantly, the mental auric body imbues every ego-aspect with the free will necessary for *voluntary control* of the Body. Both wills exercise their reciprocal control via the emotional auric body. The instinctual will sustaining a sensate body sets limits on what the mental auric body can generally accomplish with free will. But most important to this discussion, as the sensate body is sustained by the instinctual will of the etheric auric body, it can exist independent of the mental auric body. So even though the sensate body is an integral part of an ego-aspect, it will continue to exist even if separated from its free-willed component.

Connections between the three auric bodies can be severed, if the emotional connection becomes overwhelming to the mental auric body or physical body. The severing can happen in three ways: dissociation, depersonalization or repression. Dissociation occurs when the parental exercise of authority or shock trauma generates overwhelming or 'global' shame that effectively obliges the Ego to 'abandon' an ego-aspect and create a new one to replace it. This will only happen if an ego-aspect is so overwhelmed by shame that it can no longer range between a set of opposites. The abandonment effectively strips an ego-aspect of its free will by leaving it in the thrall of shame. But its sensate body and instinctive will remain intact. Consequently, the enthralled ego-aspect will continue to broadcast its blight as a physical disturbance that can progressively range in severity from heartburn to a heart attack, and every known disease in between, most of which result from a compromised immune system.

Authority figures constellated by the Empowering archetype have the power to force the Ego to abandon an ego-aspect. Severely traumatizing physical and environmental events can have a comparable effect. Authority figures can to repress an ego-aspect's free will, which forces the Ego to 'abandon' that particular self and create another ego-aspect. But a shamefully enthralled self still retains sensate consciousness by virtue of its instinctive will. And if it is not released, the particulars of that shameful servitude will eventually manifest as mental or physical dis-ease demanding the attention of a physician. Unfortunately, attempts to treat those dis-eases on a purely physical level will only mask the troubling sensations or only temporarily generate a remission of symptoms. The only way to effectively treat a dissociated ego-aspect is to end its enthrallment and reconcile it with the self that governs access to the opposite pole.

In depersonalization, *the mental component of an ego-aspect exercises its free will to sever the connection with its sensate body (aka etheric body)*. This can be the direct consequence of severe shaming by an authority figure or in response to some form of shock trauma that results in a sensation overload. This appears to be a self-induced response, but for all practical purposes almost reflexive, as if verging on the instinctual. But bear in mind that both components have access to a manifestation of will: free will in the case of the mental component and instinctual will in the case of the sensate component. So even when a sensate component is emotionally severed – for whatever reason – it still retains the capacity to react. Though both components exercise a form of will, I assume that the mental component is generally responsible for initiating the emotional severance, but have not been able to clinically determine that at this writing. In any case, depersonalization reduces the ego-aspect to the status of an observer.

In Chapter VII, I will hypothesize that depersonalization may be the root cause of addictions. In that scenario, the mental component will experience an insatiable desire to reconcile with its sensate component after the severance. Unfortunately, once done, the severance can become very difficult to undo. Depersonalization can stop the immediate pain, but it is not a good strategy for more than a brief period of time. If the mental component fails to regain access to its sensate component in a relatively short period of time, the Ego will be obliged to constellate a new ego-aspect able to exercise voluntary control of the sensate body.

Depersonalization is generally experienced as a sense of numbness intended to protect the observer from the overwhelming affective emotions or sensations that caused the split. If the split cannot be reconciled, the sensate component will continue to fester and remain reactive in the etheric auric body until the negative energies are fully discharged and the two components can be reconciled. But any ego-aspect created to replace the disabled 'observer' is most likely to act *fearfully* in a way that now makes it much more difficult for the mental component to rejoin with its sensate component and discharge those energies. This prolonged avoidance invariably generates an 'energy cyst' that eventually becomes the 'symptoms' of post-traumatic stress, e.g. nightmares, hyper-vigilance, compulsive behaviors including addictions, dangerous acting out, etc., all reflecting a failure to discharge the festering energy. ,

Repression is a 'normal consequence' of the Ego's constellation of a Dominant self in childhood. Repression occurs when the child becomes old enough for the Ego to create a Dominant self that is able to assume the power to self-shame and thereby preempt a Voice-of-conscience. (In contrast, Depersonalization can occur at any age. It can be equally the result of developmental trauma and environmental trauma.) In repression, the ego-aspect shames *events* (i.e. mental contents and their concomitant emotions) which effectively hides them in the emotional auric bodies, most frequently the heart and abdominal auric bodies. Repression can protect an ego-aspect from being dissociated by the Voice-of-conscience or from having to sever its functional connection with the sensate body. But there is a very real downside to this strategy as well: every time a Dominant self shames itself, it injects more shame into the emotional auric bodies. And this accumulation is seen as a significant player in the generation of all chronic disease.

Environmental shock trauma that does not force depersonalization – such as surgery or a serious auto accident, may nonetheless generate energies that will somaticize the Body if left undischarged. A voluntary or reflexive 'freezing' response to the anticipation of trauma will block the discharge of fight/flight energies. If that blockage is not 'thawed,' and the energies allowed to discharge in a reasonable time after the event, the ego-aspect will develop a fear of the discharge, which eventually results in the development of post-traumatic stress symptoms. In those cases as well, the goal of treatment is to facilitate discharge of the negative energies. These negative energies can manifest as a self-image of the person at the time of the original traumatizing event or, just as likely, as a disturbing 'felt sense' of the need for physical release.

Since an ego-aspect is first and foremost a function of the mental auric body and it's exercise of free will, it could not reduce itself to pure sensate consciousness even if it wanted to do so. If sufficiently stressed, it can dissociate its sensate body (i.e. depersonalize it) or repress a shameful event. Depersonalization is always an exercise of free will wherein an ego-aspect *strips itself* of the ability to act on the Body by severing its emotional connection to the sensate body. Likewise, when a Dominant self assumes the power to self-shame, it can repress events thereby pre-empting parentified authority. That pre-emption protects it from being stripped of its free will or the need to depersonalize, but generates an ongoing accumulation of shame in the emotional fields of the auric bodies, particularly the heart and abdominal chakras.

In sum, if a mental component is shamed, the effect will be a dissociation of the ego-aspect; if a sensate component is shamed, the effect will be depersonalization; and if an event (imaginal contents and associated emotions) is shamed, the effect will be repression.

Finally, I would postulate one other cause of depersonalization that may be testable if the setting conditions were met. This would be the sensate component's instinctive withdrawal from its mental component. Bear in mind that the sensate component is intimately connected with body sensation and the brain-body's instinctual will. If the Body attributed a sensate overload – such as severe shaming – as threatening a vital function, then it might reflexively withdraw from the mental component thereby leaving the mental component in a depersonalized observer state. This would seem to be most likely, if the sensate component was fulfilling a vital function that parental authority or the mental component sought to repress. This kind of depersonalization would be considered a 'instinctual response' of the brain-body to its mental connection in the Mind. The suppression of ongoing sexual arousal with a powerful shaming response by the mental component might cause such a depersonalization. Another cause might be the attempt to repress the sensation function. If the authority figure that precipitated the shame went unchallenged, or the mental component was unable to mitigate its own belief system, the resulting standoff could result in ongoing depersonalization from the vital function.

Well of Pure Sensation

The 'bottom line' in the foregoing discussion is the persistence of a sensate body once it is created by the Ego's constellation of an ego-aspect. Even if dissociated, depersonalized or repressed, the ongoing experience of a sensate body will continue to generate sensations and affective emotions however painful or pleasurable they may be. Remember, the sensate body of an ego-aspect is sustained by instinctual well. The ego-aspect only *directs* it with free will and even then, only within general limits whose extremes are dictated by physical limits. Ego-aspects and archetypal authority can 'banish' the sensate body from relational consciousness; but neither one can silence its continuing generation of sensation and affective emotion. Without healing intervention, the unexpressed emotional accumulation will become increasingly painful. All of the ego defenses used to cope with those repressions only add to the accumulation of toxic emotion. As regards the range of symptoms generated by a banished sensate body, any good medical dictionary will give you the complete list of possibilities.

I have experimented with a variety of interventions designed to unearth somaticizing sensate bodies and undischarged negative emotions. The most effective method I have found to date is the 'well of pure sensation.' This intervention works on a number of levels, which is probably why it has proven to be widely applicable. The client is given to understand that we are seeking to bring into consciousness a self or emotion *that is currently experienced only as sensation*. Most often, the sensations in question are physical symptoms. The dizziness of high blood pressure, the pain of arthritis, the stuffiness of a cold, the anxiety of a panic attack, or the cramping of PMS are all examples of sensation experienced as physical symptoms. Literally any felt sense of 'dis-ease' that has disturbed the client on a recurring basis or even just for the first time can be treated as a troubling sensation. The intervention for remediating these problematical sensations is rarely completed in one session as it involves working simultaneously with a banished somaticized self or negative affective emotion, and *any primary selves that are threatened by its release*. The initial strategy for this intervention involves setting up strong protections for the primary selves most threatened by the banished ego-aspects /or undischarged negative emotions.

In working with a troubling sensation, no initial attempt is made to first separate out the ego-aspect co-present with the Aware-ego. The client is told that once inside s/he can use the *Light* to provide a circle of protection and a garment of protection if that would be helpful, but both are optional. The most significant protections will come from Christ. First, *Christ is asked to use his Light to create a well of pure sensation*. He does this by drawing a circle within a dome. He will use the inner 'circle' to drill a well down through sensation to wherever the problematical sensate self or energy is lodged. This is always experienced as below the 'ground' on which the Aware-ego and others are standing. The drilled well of pure sensation is what allows the troubling sensation to emerge into relational consciousness, which is always 'above the ground' where Christ and the Aware-ego are standing. ('Imaginal' and 'relational' are synonyms for conscious awareness and conscious movement in active imagination.) As noted, before Christ drills the well of pure sensation, he is asked to place an opaqued dome of *Light* over the circle that contains the well. With the opaqued dome in place, whatever emerges can be sensed, but not seen as long as the dome is opaqued. Finally Christ is asked to place a portion of his *Light* in the center of the opaqued dome near the ceiling. Christ *directs this Light to absorb whatever negative charge is asked of it*. When sensations emerge, it is always assumed they will initially manifest as some kind of *accumulated, unexpressed, negative emotional energy*. It is the negative energy – usually some form of pain, anger, fear, or shame, which is so threatening to the conscious Ego. Basically, this intervention is designed to depotentiate the strong negative charge(s) associated with the energy or somaticized-self. All of this is explained to the client at least once before s/he actually goes inside. On occasion, I have outlined the process repeatedly over several sessions. I have used this intervention effectively with all kinds of anger, fear, pain and shame. It appears to be most effective – or most called for, in cases of somaticized emotional pain, i.e. the pain of early childhood abuse or trauma.

The following case illustrates the process of facilitating the emergence of a somaticizing self; but not the well of pure sensation per se. Several case examples are given later in the chapter when I examine fight/flight and pain/pleasure, which do call for the use of a well of pure sensation. And that particular intervention is also illustrated in a number of verbatims in the later chapters.

Lee. Lee, a nurse, has been single for a

number of years. Recently, she invited a close woman friend to move into her house while the friend recovered from a broken foot. When I see her in this session she seems a little 'worn.' Working her job and also caring for her friend's needs seems to be taking a toll. She complains of feeling 'congested.' I suggest she go inside and let her higher power, called Teacher, create a well of pure sensation with an opaqued dome over it. Whoever is 'congesting' her can safely emerge so Lee can sense her presence and assess her own attitude toward the emerging self. (Since the 'congestion' is acute and not severe, I do not suggest that Teacher also include a portion of his *Light* within the dome.) Very quickly, Lee begins to describe her sense of the emerging self: "She is a shy little girl, afraid to speak up, quiet, bashful, withdrawn, fearful. No one will pay attention to her, she is overlooked; they will not hear her." I ask how it feels to not be heard? "That nobody cares. My sense of her is that she is a little jealous because she is not getting attention." How, I ask, has she been silenced in the past? "Not supposed to be selfish, not supposed to ask for anything." Is she shamed for doing things labeled selfish? "She was taught it was rude to ask for things, it inconveniences others." At this point I suggest that perhaps Teacher could release the shy little girl from shame, and Lee from *her fear of being shamed*. In effect, I suggest that Teacher be allowed to simultaneously baptize the shy little girl in the dome and alter Lee's belief system. Lee is agreeable so I suggest she allow Teacher to baptize the child first. What follows is at first a little confusing because Lee only shares afterward that when Teacher baptized the little girl in the dome, she immediately came out of the dome and Lee is actually embracing her as she describes her. "Kind of funny. I have this sense of what she is feeling. She has to fix dinner only because my friend is hungry. She came out of the dome when I said it was OK for her to be angry for having to fix my friend's supper. Then I saw me sitting and holding her in my lap. I was laughing with her. I stood and held her hand. We are in this together. I feel like there is a release from the shame. I don't feel any kind of congestion." I might note here that this is not the first time Lee and I have addressed self/other issues. I will revisit Lee's case in Chapters VII and VIII because she is one of the few clients who consistently called on a higher power other than Christ.

In the above example, the intervention by Teacher is two-pronged. Lee has an angry somaticized self that is in the thrall of shame for having selfish impulses. A Responsible primary experiences her as 'congestion.' Basically, the Responsible primary has blocked the angry 'voice' of the little girl and the anger has accumulated in the Heart's auric body as congestion. Teacher is asked to work with both parts simultaneously, to free the child in the dome from shame, and release Lee from her fear of shame for harboring selfish feelings. He appears to do this by helping Lee become empathetic of the child's needs – something her mother failed to do, and in that way alters her belief that the child's feelings are purely selfish. To be most effective, the therapist needs to be concerned for all the selves, not just the one bearing the shame. *Fear of shame* is a powerful motivator of behavior and it controls most primary selves charged with governing the client's behavior in the world, so it is always important to address the needs of the primary ego-aspect as well as the disowned self with whom it is coping. In most cases, the reconciliation of the two selves is generally the most difficult. Teacher seems able to abate that resistance by planting the thought that it is OK for the child to be angry at having to cook for another without regard for her own needs. Very likely, in early childhood, the mother soundly shamed Lee for expressing her need to eat when it was not convenient for the mother.

The Sensate Body of the Aware-ego

In active imagination, the Ego experiences the sensate body as sensation. A sensate body is the sensory template of the physical body complete with instinctual will. It is constellated in every ego-aspect created by the Ego, which empowers each one of them to direct the Body's actions. Quite often, the client confuses the sensate body with the actual physical body. But in active imagination, the sensate body can be personified move even when the physical body is still. In my discussion with clients I refer to this inner experience of the Body by a variety a names: the sensate body, the sensed-body, even as the 'body that holds the *Light* and looks out the eyes' (i.e. the Aware ego). The Aware-ego ideally embodies a purified form of the sensate body, while *all other ego-aspects* will experience a sensate body that reflects their particular attributes and limitations. Shared access to the etheric auric body is what allows any ego-aspect to inadvertently 'abuse' the physical body with its beliefs or trauma history. But a sensate body can also be a conduit for healing, particularly when embodied by the Aware-ego.

To effect healing with the sensate body, the client must be 'in' their felt sense of the sensate body. This is most easily accomplished when consciousness is focused by the Aware-ego. Most ego-aspects are so strongly identified with the body that they cannot envision a separate existence (sic) moving without the body actually moving, unless they have severed their connection to the sensate body. Healing via the sensate body is accomplished by having the healing take place in active imagination while the client remains in the 'body' to be healed – rather than separating from it. For that reason, I often refer to this kind of healing as a first person experience of the sensate body. Christ, or a comparable higher power, functions as the healer of the sensate. Essentially, Christ works directly with the Aware-ego and *any ego-aspect that remains merged with it*. The goal of this intervention is to clear the sensate body's emotional field of accumulated unexpressed emotions likely to have a negative impact on the Body. To accomplish this the Aware-ego must experience itself as separate from the physical body. If the client imagines lying on a massage table, then s/he must imagine lying horizontal even if actually sitting. S/he cannot 'see' herself lying on the table from the perspective of someone standing or sitting. This is always a 'first person' experience. I stress this to the client because many of the strategies offered in this work actually call for some form of separation, but in this instance just the opposite is required. At all times, the client must imagine embodying a felt sense of the Body. In my clinical experience, this is best accomplished as an Aware-ego holding the *Light*.

Healing the sensate body will generally require separation from any selves opposed to the healing. As I have repeatedly asserted, most chronic disease is sustained, and accidents instigated, by selves *opposed to symptom clearing*. Those selves must be separated from the Aware-ego embodying the sensate body, and reconciled to the healing, or they will sabotage the work. The easiest way to discern these selves is to proceed as if they did not exist. They will quickly obstruct the process. The client will become blocked in some fashion: the client will not be able to access the *Light*, or a felt sense of the body, or Christ, or s/he will be distracted, or otherwise obstructed from the goal of the session which is some form of healing. Any separation processes so far described will be sufficient to contain and identify these opposing selves. Oppositional selves must be treated respectfully, but firmly, similar to working with Responsible primary-selves. These selves do not self-perceive that they are obstructing healing. Rather, they perceive symptom clearing as a threat to their control, and act to defend the Body as if it were solely their own. And generally, they are the ones exercising conscious control of the Body via their sensate body so their claim is not without merit, in the sense that possession is 9/10's of the law.

Tory. The following case example illustrates working with the sensate body of the Aware-ego. In this example, much of the work was already done in prior sessions. Tory broke her arm some weeks previous and was able to identify interpersonal reasons for this 'accident.' The break appears to signify and augment an emotional breaking of the fusion with her mother. This process of separating from the mother has been a recurring focus of therapy during the preceding months. Tory calls me earlier in the week to change her appointment time because she has started physical therapy for her broken arm. Over the phone she complains that the physical therapy leaves her in excruciating pain. I suggest over the phone that she allow Christ to work with the arm after each physical therapy session using his *Light* to facilitate healing of the muscles. When she comes in to see me two days later, she reports having done what I suggested and that the pain eased between physical therapy sessions, but she still feels great pain in her efforts to do the required exercises. The pain is so severe it makes her nauseous. I ask her to make a fist. She can feel muscle tension to her elbow but not for muscles in the shoulder or upper arm – where the break had occurred. Tory and I have previously discussed how this break has served her in terms of getting more attention for herself and putting distance between her and her mother. I ask if she can think of any other reasons for keeping this arm 'broken.' "I took care of the last problem this morning. I canceled a job I did not want to do. I can't see anymore need for this broken arm." At this point I discuss the idea of Christ reconnecting any broken connections between her elbow and shoulder. We also discuss the idea of dissolving the 'glue' that had been holding muscle fascia in contraction, keeping the bone and shoulder from being moved. These are suggestions only; and while they may have been helpful it will be clear from Tory's report that the necessary healing was primarily a product of her and Christ working together. "I am on a massage table. I have given him a portion of my *Light* to mix with a portion of his own *Light*. He does the reconstruction first. It is like a web of thread which he is sewing back together between my shoulder and elbow." At this point I ask if there is anyone who objects to his completely healing her? "No one seems to be objecting. I feel ready for him to continue." I ask Tory if Christ is dissolving the glue that is binding the muscles? "That is not what he is doing. A liquid is being poured over the upper arm and rubbed in. It feels smooth, like rubbing out a knot. It feels done." I ask if there is anything else we need to give him the opportunity to do? "The arm needs some strength." How does one acquire that? "The arm is being wrapped, but I don't know with what. Something is definitely being wrapped around it. Now he is wrapping it around the shoulder. It is finished. Once it was wrapped everything seemed to relax." I speculate that maybe it took the place of an inner guardedness. "Maybe, it feels different, far more relaxed, especially the shoulder. I have not felt my shoulder till right now. I can actually feel it and move it. I have not done that since it was broken." Does it hurt to move it? "No, it feels freeing." By the following week, Tory can report considerable change in her ability to exercise and move her arm free of pain.

For many years, I have followed the

evolution of alternative therapies that work with the physical body. Many of them are reportedly quite effective in easing or ameliorating painful acute and chronic conditions. What has impressed me – aside from the results, is that often the 'manipulation' is little more than the placement of a fulcrum on a bone, or the gentle placement of fingers that purportedly alter Body polarity. These therapists appear to be manipulating a system that is simply overlooked by allopathic medicine. I suspect they are communicating with their client's sensed body and offering it a remediative awareness. Christ appears to be doing much the same thing when he works directly with the sensed-body.

When Sensation Becomes a Defense Mechanism

I have worked with very few clients whose sensation function was dominant. Like any other function this has its strengths and liabilities. Ego-aspects that are sensation dominant tend to focus on details. They seem to perform very well in any occupation requiring detail and/or the senses: house painters, accountants, carpenters, fashion consultants, dental hygienists, etc. But they also tend to be poor candidates for long-term therapy as they normally lack the inclination to pursue what is decidedly a reflective activity. Nonetheless, the sensation function can become quite problematical, especially when it functions as a defense mechanism – as well as a natural propensity. When that occurs it *actively suppresses* other functions such as intuition and feeling. Sensation is the 'survival function' and, therefore, will almost always take priority while dominant. This is illustrated by the following case.

Eduardo. This client is married to a woman who is highly intuitive, but often numb to bodily sensation. Eduardo is more sensation oriented than anyone I have worked with to date. Clearly, their marriage is an attraction of opposites. Early in therapy, Eduardo is able to separate from a Dominant self we quickly identify as the "Worker Bee." It dominates and directs Eduardo's life to the exclusion of any other self I can identify. Even when Eduardo is able to separate from this self in sessions, I cannot identify any other selves able to come to the fore and balance the Worker Bee. Eduardo is a life long Christian who devotes many hours to his church in his role as a Worker Bee. That self, however, sees Christ more as a peer than a Savior. The Worker Bee invests much effort to impress others with his self-worth. Eduardo is the oldest of four children. His father was a youngest, and a life long alcoholic, who provided minimal support to the family, which included the maternal grandmother. He did not beat his wife or kids or womanize. He just drank at home after work and through the winter when he could not find work. He did have a bad temper if crossed. The Worker Bee appears to have emerged in early adolescence. Eduardo learned to earn money working at odd jobs, which he used to paint the family home, lay new linoleum floors, and buy the family its first color TV. In childhood and adolescence, church participation was the mainstay of his social life. He was very, very, responsible, but also generally insensitive to nuances in social relations other than being polite to everyone. He has managed to completely estrange himself from the adult children born of his first marriage, mostly by benign neglect since they do not live close by so he cannot 'do' for them. I had seen Eduardo in therapy ten years before for work, family, and marriage related issues. He returned for treatment when his family doctor diagnosed him as suffering from early stage Alzheimer's. I questioned the diagnosis and had him seen by a specialist who agreed he was not. Eduardo has been 'forgetful' much of his adult life. The stress of change increases his forgetfulness. After several months, Eduardo dropped out of therapy. I continued to work with his wife individually. He returned when she became strong enough to tell him she was ready to leave if he did not change his continuous 'thoughtlessness' regarding her needs. Eduardo was willing to change. He simply had no notion as to how. He realized that the Worker Bee had become a liability but could not imagine being without him or what would take his place.

In this first session of the verbatim, Eduardo has decided he is in spiritual warfare with the Worker Bee; that the Worker Bee is an addiction. I decide on a drastic measure insofar as it seems to go against my own rule about keeping a dominant ego-aspect respectfully involved in the treatment. I decide to temporarily isolate the Worker Bee as a way of 'protecting' him *while Eduardo (aka Aware-ego) seeks out its opposite*, the self who might be in need of Christ, unlike the Worker Bee. Eduardo willingly separates from the Worker Bee and allows Christ to opaque his circle, to 'protect' him while Christ then searches out the Worker Bee's opposite. This is easier than I expected. Since the Worker Bee – by his own estimate, has no one to protect but himself, he has no objections. Note, the Worker Bee is given a portion of the *Light* beforehand, that being a part of the separation process, so he does have the wherewithal to dissolve the circle. The search proceeds quickly and I am frankly surprised by what is found. I have suggested to Eduardo that he allow Christ to identify where the opposite self will be found. Immediately, Eduardo replies that, "It is an inner most self within the Soul – which is a comment totally unlike any I have heard previously from Eduardo. I ask if Christ can take him to the place of this Soul self? Eduardo takes Christ's hand and lets him lead to that place. "It is a beautiful garden, a bright light overhead. Sounds of music playing (Eduardo plays the piano well), a big choir, warm and pleasant, grass and fields, different wild flowers, some small animals, a stream there too. (Notice the detail. Even without the Worker Bee sensation still plays a strong role.) Christ takes me to a large tree. There is another self there who is in his 30's or 40's, muscular, tanned, looks like he lives here. Casual dress. Christ says that he knows about the Worker Bee." I ask how he is different from the Worker Bee? "He is not geared to *worry* about time schedules. (This is my first clue to the significance of worry in the activity of the Worker Bee.) He is flexible. He loves people, nature, and animals. He likes to sing, he likes music, and he likes being with people (in contrast to many of Eduardo's activities, which are by their nature solitary). He loves God. He has a daily relationship with Christ and God." I ask how it was that he and the Worker Bee became split apart? "When I was young, things happened that caused my life to be so fragmented that the part like my soul was compromised. There was disarray and chaos in the house. I substituted work activities for soul activities. I never allowed the soul elements to become strong where there could be a balance. I allowed the work system to take over. As the house got more chaotic I looked to work for order. The soul part was suppressed; it was there, but very removed." I suggest that he give this soul part a portion of *Light* and have Christ teach it how to create a garment of protection, and then bring Eduardo (Aware-ego) and the Soul part back to the circle containing the Worker Bee. Eduardo does all of this but also makes the observation that, "The Soul part seems a little insecure." (In fact, it is not the Soul self, but another self that has emerged and is co-existing with the Aware-ego. But that does not become clear till later.) At this point what I am looking to do is identify the bifurcating force that has split the two apart by bringing the two into closer proximity. I suggest that Eduardo have Christ draw a third circle and use it to identify the force that is splitting the two selves. "I don't see anything. There is a mist or cloud in the circle. It is intermingled with a lot of emotions, most strongly anger." I ask who is generating the anger? "Over the years I have repressed anger. I have stored it up against my family, especially, my parents, my father. He did not help me to grow up and learn things. My mother was a non-entity who always deferred to her mother. It just destroyed the family. No structure. My grandmother was the only stabilizing force. I am angry toward both of my parents for withholding so much from me." I suggest that he ask Christ to absorb the accumulated, unexpressed anger with his Christ *Light*. "There is only a little cloud left." Can you see the angry part? "The Soul part was angry, but he did not interfere with my life or try to change the quality of it. I think he thought he could, but there was too much going on for him to break through it all." The session ends here.

What have we learned? Parents are the bifurcating force, and the Soul part supposedly has some strong emotions held in check by the Worker Bee. But as the next session will show, it is really not clear whose anger has been addressed. There is another ego-aspect yet to be identified, who has emerged co-existent with the Aware-ego following the containment of the Worker Bee; and it makes sense that another ego-aspect would replace the Worker Bee, as he has normally functioned as the Dominant self.

The next session picks up where we left off, except now the focus is equally on the Worker Bee and Soul part. But significantly, once inside, the part that begins speaking on behalf of Eduardo is neither the Worker Bee nor the Soul part, but someone who feels able to speak for both. I mistakenly assume that it is the Aware-ego that is speaking, but that turns out to not be the case. This is what the new self tells us: "The Worker Bee knows about the Soul part's anger and can even share it. It started early, living in a home with no real structure. I almost had to be the father figure, but never felt close to my sibs. I had no wheels, a limited choice of friends. No bike till high school. I was angry all through childhood. It was chaos. I made structure for myself. Got jobs. Tried to fix the house. Dad never did anything to the house. One time he fixed the porch before it fell down. I painted the whole house, fixed the roof. That's when the Worker Bee gained in strength." I ask how the Soul part coped during that time? "He was hurt, unfulfilled, disjointed. There were no close friends, not able to be sociable except in church. The church friendships were superficial. I liked music, chorus, plays." What did the Soul miss most? "Acceptance. *I felt inferior as a person.*" Did the Soul know that feeling of inferiority? "No. He never had that feeling. The Soul was protected from the brutal feelings." Who had to take the brunt of the brutal feelings? "The Worker Bee and Soul part both know about that part. They just don't let it surface. I had God, don't know what I would have done without Him." I ask if either the Soul part or Worker Bee feels responsible for the inferior part? "No. It is out there on its own." If Christ wanted to claim it would they object? "No. But he can't claim it. *I am responsible for that part.*" It is at this point that I become aware of yet another part unobtrusively co-existing with the Aware-ego. The dialogue has uncovered two new ego-aspects: the unworthy part and the other who accepts responsibility for it. Essentially, the Worker Bee has been standing in for a Responsible primary that preceded it developmentally. While inside, the Worker Bee remains contained so the Responsible primary has reemerged to organize consciousness.

In the next session I ask Eduardo to

separate from the responsible part so we can dialogue with it. Early in adolescence, it seems to have relinquished dominance to the Worker Bee, who acts like a Dominant self that does not feel responsible for anyone other than himself. Of note, this Responsible primary has only emerged with the containment of the Worker Bee, and identification of the Soul part. The resulting diminishment of the Worker Bee's dominance appears to have thrust the Responsible primary back into the limelight by default. Significantly, Eduardo can also say of this Responsible primary: "If the Inferior part was not there, I might have more strength to deal with the Worker Bee."

I suspect the Responsible primary is weakened by identity with his father though this is not immediately apparent. Eduardo goes inside and I walk him through the process of separating from the Responsible primary. "I don't see anything yet." I suggest that he ask Christ to compress the circle until something emerges. "It does not look like me. It looks almost like my dad – partly bald, a lot like dad when he was in his 50's, muscular, not as tall as me, a good looking guy." Is this a part of you that identified with your father? "This is the part of me that identified with him when I was young. I always admired him for his knowledge. He could do anything with carpentry, and he had a great knowledge of history and the Bible. Nobody could trip him up on the Bible. He could have gone to college if he chose. He did not have the drive to achieve goals. He did not plan, he just let things happen." (In other words he was also sensation dominant.) I ask Eduardo if he could evoke an image of his father free of alcohol? "He had a brilliant mind; alcohol squelched his ambition and drive. The other barrier was mother. She did not support his rehabilitation when he did try going to AA. She reveled in being seen as suffering a hard life. She ate it up.

Mom would not participate the one time dad got involved with AA. Nanny and Mom allowed him to drink." We are near the end the session. I shift the focus and ask if the Responsible part is aware of the Inferior part, and if so, can he contain it and opaque its circle? Eduardo does this and then we end the session. In the following weeks, therapy will proceed along the lines described in the chapter on Moral authority.

Eduardo's case illustrates a unique permutation of sensation wherein a Dominant self uses sensation as a defense mechanism. Eduardo's sensation function appears to be naturally dominant. But as it manifests in the Worker Bee, it functions much as it would in a Dominant self that uses sensate behavior in excess. It trumps his Responsible primary; and characteristically, the Responsible Primary accepts the subordinate role. A partial reason for acquiescing appears to be the Responsible Primary's strong identification with a father he could no longer admire; and a further identification with a paternal uncle who he began to see as 'effeminate' in adolescence. All this came out later in the therapy. When the Inferior self was finally identified, it was seen as very effeminate – like the father's brother, and a sharp contrast to Eduardo's conscious sense of himself as manly and muscular. Later, Eduardo would also identify yet another self, the Worrier, who actively controlled much of his social interactions. Suffice to say, the Worker Bee was coping with a number of dysfunctional ego-aspects. This case illustrates the occasional necessity of isolating a primary self that is strongly sensation oriented; and seeking out its opposite as a way of neutralizing its dominance of the personality. What is likely to emerge, as in this case, is a kind of collusion between the sensation-dominated self and other primary selves.

This case also highlights a strategy based on the universality of opposites. Every ego aspect, however dominant, has an opposite. That opposite can be undeveloped, nascent, little more than a thought, but it will exist, and Christ can find and contain it if the client is willing. The opposite self is illustrated in this case by the part found 'in the Soul' that, very likely, also manifested as a projection in his wife's image, as she is highly intuitive.

Since working with Eduardo, I have used the isolation-protection approach with several other clients *whose ego-aspects claim no responsibility* for any other selves. Identifying the opposite helps to neutralize their dominance by allowing for the emergence of opposite selves, who in turn precipitate the emergence of still other selves that underpin their shared bifurcation.

Normally, the most common sensation-dominant selves will be Egos-in-conflict. (The Ego-in-conflict is described in the chapter on Moral authority, as it is most likely to emerge in that context.) In my clinical experience, Eduardo's Worker Bee is a rare occurrence. I suspect it only came into prominence because his Responsible primary was greatly weakened by his need to disidentify with his father and paternal uncle in adolescence. Finally, I would note that compared to 'thinkers and feelers,' sensation-dominant selves rarely persist in long term therapy, unless – as in Eduardo's case – their feet are kept to the fire by an intuitive spouse.

INSTINCTUAL RHYTHMS

Waking/sleeping, ingesting/excreting, inhaling/exhaling are all examples of instinctual rhythms. Every duality reflects this principle of rhythm, which Hermeticists insist is integral to all activity envisioned by the Mind. The principle of rhythm is repeatedly and dramatically illustrated in Jesus' life. Baptized by John, he becomes the anointed of God. Immediately afterward he is driven into the desert where he must contend with Satan. Embodied as the perfect good he must now contend with the world's evil. The pendulum has swung from the pole where Christ becomes the incarnation of Spirit to the pole where Satan is seen to rule the world. Nor is Satan defeated by Christ's refusal to be tempted; he simply leaves to come again at a more opportune time, at the next swing of the pendulum. Again, at Passover, the pendulum swings as we see Christ entering Jerusalem triumphant, only to be crucified the next day. Two contemporary writers on matters spiritual also illustrate this swing from good to evil and back. In the 1980's Scott Peck wrote *The Road Less Traveled* that strongly advocates for the value of a spiritual life. Then, in 1998 he wrote the *People of the Lie*, a book that focused on the existence of evil in the lives of seemingly ordinary people. The latter focus was clearly a swing of the pendulum. Thomas Moore, author of *Care of the Soul*, replicated this swing of the pendulum with an equally dramatic shift of focus. A year later he published *Dark Eros: the Imagination of Sadism*, a treatise on the writings of Marquis de Sade. Anyone who would focus on the good is invariably led to address the evil. As Kahlil Gibran said in *The Prophet*, joy and sorrow spring from the same well; we cannot drink of one without drinking of the other. This seems true of all pairs of opposites, at whatever level, but especially so at the level of Body. Moving toward one inevitably necessitates movement back toward the other.

The Body's will is traditionally defined as *instinctive drive* to distinguish it from free will. But instinctual drive is not linear; it is actually rhythmic. It is also *complementary* and insistent that each pole be equally valued. The Body's instinctual will compels it to rhythmically fluctuate between opposite poles. This understanding of instinct is described in Hermeticism's principle of rhythm. "Everything flows out and in; everything has its tides; all things rise and fall; the pendulum-swing manifests in everything; the measure of the swing to the right, is the measure of the swing to the left; rhythm compensates." Hermeticism argues that, "The [rhythm] principle manifests in the creation and destruction of worlds; in the rise and fall of nations; in the life history of all things; and finally in the mental states of Man." As regards instinctual rhythms, the brain-body must have equal access to both poles in order to sustain a healthy Body. Wherever instinctual rhythms are disrupted, the Body must reinstate homeostasis or die. This innate striving notwithstanding, the Temporal and Moral authority of parents and cultures invariably disrupts these rhythms in their efforts to regulate children and members of the community; and where instinctual rhythms are polarized by fragmentation of the Ego the physical body is placed at risk. A classic example is splitting hunger from satisfaction, wherein hunger becomes valued and normal satisfaction is devalued, i.e. the anorexic condition. That seems an absurd split at first blush, but when we consider the value placed on self-denial and deferred gratification in many cultures, it is not so very strange that some individuals will carry it to extreme if inadvertently conditioned to do so by parents and culture. Traditionally, cultures have valued regular fasting, and only intermittently valued feasting; and valued sexual abstinence even more, while concomitantly shaming sexual satisfaction. (Today, fasting has been replaced by work, and feasting replaced by relaxation. And while relaxation is valued, it is often shamed as 'lazy' if given an equal value with work.)

Instinctual rhythms become *polarized* when their rhythm is disrupted; when one pole is devalued by repetitive pairing with one or more negative emotions. The most common negative emotions are pain or shame exercised by a devaluing parent or equally powerful figure. That bifurcating force is the most frequent cause of polarized rhythms. Most often, a *fearful* self will be created to cope with this bifurcation. An example would be the bifurcation of "sexual arousal and satisfaction" which splits the rhythm into two parts, one valued and one denigrated. The fearful self learns to avoid one or the other. But instinctual rhythms cannot be blocked with impunity. Wherever such splits occur, a disowned self will eventually produce countermanding forces capable of demanding some form of homeostasis even if it results in an accumulation of shame in the auric bodies. In effect, the brain-body's demand for homeostasis will oblige the Ego to create aspects capable of reestablishing that homeostasis, if only intermittently on a physical basis. The Ego-in-conflict is created to serve just that purpose. The most common manifestation of the Ego-in-conflict is addictive, mind-altering, behavior. Unfortunately, that particular solution, while prevalent in every culture, invariably results in the wrath of God if not corrected. It is described at length in the chapter on Moral authority.

An biological organism's energy and structure require the replenishment provided by rhythm; it is not enough to hover in the still point of homeostasis. Inhaling/exhaling is the most obvious expression of rhythm in our lives. Each requires the other for the continuation of life. The more we inhale the more we must exhale. The same is true of the other most commonly addressed instinctual rhythms: eating (ingesting/eliminating), sleeping/waking, and sexuality (desire and satisfaction). These are the instinctual rhythms most frequently disrupted by ego-aspects. Although the Ego can disrupt them, it can never do so with impunity. One way or another, the rhythm must eventually correct by swinging to the suppressed pole, or the Body will adversely suffer the effects of that failure.

There is a second category of instinctual rhythms that I call survival dualities. The best-known dualities in this category are pain/pleasure and fight/flight. They could be grouped with the instinctual rhythms. I separate them only because they seem to function as components of the *sympathetic nervous system* rather than parasympathetic nervous system. They act in close concert with instinctual rhythms, and are frequently problematic for the client because of inadvertent overuse or abuse. Pain/pleasure and fight/flight both have organic correlates in the oldest parts of the brain; and both appear to serve a survival function. Pain/pleasure reinforces concomitant events in the internal or external environment that will consequently be avoided or repeated (the basic stuff of Operant and Pavlovian conditioning). That duality can also evoke the fight/flight reflex. The fight/flight 'reflex' accelerates defensive actions. It is meant to be reflexive and short lived since it puts considerable strain on the Body by suppressing instinctual rhythmic activity associated with the parasympathetic nervous system. Unfortunately its physiological concomitants can also be activated by the Ego's use of fear and anger, the two most common emotions expressed by dominant ego-aspects. The survival dualities are addressed at length in the next section.

The major instinctual rhythms are frequent foci of concern in psychotherapy. I address each, briefly, in the following subsections by way of acknowledging their importance, but in the remainder of this chapter my primary focus will be on the Survival rhythms given their pervasive role in the life of just about everyone seen in psychotherapy.

Eating

As I complete this book in the early part of the 21st century, eating has become America's new drug of choice after successfully supplanting nicotine. Instead of dying from related lung diseases we now face the likelihood of dying from complications of obesity such as diabetes. Very likely this epidemic of obesity will only be "cured" when we have found other drugs of choice, legal and illegal. The underlying problem has yet to be addressed: namely, the implicit need to manage seemingly irreconcilable emotions or painful affects temporarily medicated by nicotine, sugars, alcohol, street drugs, etc. There are actually many management options at the physical level: any mind-altering drug will suffice, even pain and pleasure. Currently, eating is the most accessible and culturally permissible. But the human mind is endlessly inventive. Replacements will be found. I frequently address eating issues with clients as a way of engaging the Dominant self discussed in Chapters VII and VIII. I tend to treat all eating disorders as strategies for coping with shame. If an addiction is life threatening, as is often the case for alcohol and drug addiction, I make its remission a primary focus of therapy. As I am apt to tell a client, "Dealing with their drug addiction is not a pre-condition for continuing to see me, but it will remain a primary focus of therapy as long as you are actively using." I am a firm believer in the AA adage that there is nothing so bad that alcohol – or any other mind-altering substance, does not make worse. I am more tolerant of overeating and smoking. As one recovering alcoholic noted: alcohol will kill you in five years, cigarettes in 20. With eating and cigarettes we have more time to address the issue, but the underlying conflicts must be addressed at some point or they will just as surely affect the quality of life and hasten life's ending.

Eating rhythms can be disrupted for many reasons. I tend to treat the disruptions as issues of desire. That emotion is more powerful than fear, guilt or shame. *The anticipation of satisfying desire* (whatever the object of desire) can be a powerful suppressor of, or distraction from, those more negative emotions *while desire is active*. Between anticipating eating and actually eating, we can keep desire alive for much of the day and evening, and thereby suppress the emotional object of our fears. This is particularly true of sensate desire The real problem is when desire for food is obliged to do double duty, as when it is also used as a substitute for sexually tabooed activity or a dysfunctional sensation function, in addition to its suppression of negative emotion. Then we are likely to eat even more. Another complication is when desire itself becomes an object of shame, be it a desire for food or something food is meant to substitute for, such as sex, or the simplest of all needs – human touch. Then, I think, we are looking at the underpinnings of most severe eating disorders such as bulimia and anorexia.

The primary difficulty with the use of desire to satisfy urges perceived as shameful is its failure to prevent repercussions. While desire is active it can *suppress awareness* of the shame being inflicted on our auric bodies, but it cannot prevent the accumulation of that shame in the emotional fields of our auric bodies. Desire can block awareness of that accumulation while we act 'shamelessly' insofar as desire is more powerful than the shame; but it cannot prevent the toxicity of shame from being injected into the emotional field. In effect, desire can function as white noise, which drowns out other 'obnoxious' sounds, but it cannot prevent those sounds from occurring or eradicate their presence in the atmosphere. The accumulation of toxic shame in the individual's emotional fields is the source of much Wrath experienced by the individual, not to mention the wrathful physical effects such as obesity. Shame is exceedingly difficult to acknowledge, even when we do it to ourselves. And the secular culture has yet to offer individuals a viable way of discharging shame injected into the emotional fields of our auric bodies – excepting abstinence. In Chapters VII and VIII, I will revisit this thesis at length. I have come to treat this inadvertent accumulation of shame in the auric bodies as the primary cause of most chronic and life threatening diseases.

Breathing

We are a nation of shallow breathers who seem to live by the mantra "stomach in, chest out." It may be a legacy from the days when everyone smoked or had to endure someone else's smoking, or it may be a simple reflection of how fearfully we live. When the body responds to fear the abdominal muscles tighten involuntarily. This prevents the diaphragm from drawing completely. To breathe deeply the abdominal muscles have to relax so the intestines can get out of the way as the diaphragm is pulled toward the groin. This is what allows the lower lobes of the lungs to fill completely. When this is allowed to happen the center of breath becomes felt about one inch below the belly button, rather than centered in the chest. It feels as if you are breathing into the pelvis, which is the feeling of the diaphragm compressing the stomach and intestines. The 'stomach' feels as if it is being pushed out rather than held in. That is actually the reverse of how most people breath. But with each in-breath you take in twice as much oxygen when breathing abdominally. Equally significant is a second benefit: you regain control of your abdominal muscles. I finally came to appreciate the value of that after reading Gay and Kathlyn Hendricks' book *At The Speed of Life*. Their basic assertion is that regaining voluntary control your abdominal muscles allows you to dispel gripping feelings of fear and other negative emotions. By bringing the abdominal muscles under voluntary control you can countermand the usually involuntary, physiological, responses of the fight-flight reflex. (I will talk about this again in the sections on fear and anger.) The Hendricks provide a variety of exercises for learning to breathe abdominally, as do a number of other authors addressing this from different perspectives. Another book of this subject, which has remained consistently in print, is *Somatics* by Thomas Hanna. I have often recommended it to my clients. It is one of the best books I have read for anyone over forty as it points out how *not addressing* the effects of the fight-flight reflex greatly contributes to our physical debilitation as we grow older by greatly compromising our ability to breathe. Finally, I would mention *Unwinding the Belly* by Post and Cavaliere, which also helps the reader work with muscles and emotions that interfere with learning to breath abdominally.

What the above references all make clear is that abdominal breathing can be relearned. It is the natural way of breathing observed in newborns and animals. Recovering that natural state will have easily discernible, positive, effects on physiology generally and the individual's control of negative emotions specifically. With all of my clients, I emphasize the need to make this shift. Basically, fear inhibits breathing. Regaining voluntary control of abdominal muscles allows the individual to know that the fight-flight reflex is active since part of the reflexive response is the inhibition of abdominal breathing. But the individual who relearns to breathe abdominally will be aware of that interference and can reassert voluntary control, thereby 'breathing through' and effectively dispelling the emotion's hold over the body's physiology. All of the authors referenced here give numerous examples of the causes of breathing disruptions and their correction. I cannot do better than refer the reader to them. Whenever a client goes inside, I am constantly monitoring their breathing and reminding them to breathe whenever I observe them holding their breath, or directing them to focus on their breathing as a way of further dispelling the negative emotions being addressed. While I do not consider these suggestions critical to the success of inner work, they have proven helpful to my clients who have acted on them; and I have definitely benefited on a personal level.

While my own interest has focused on breathing in its capacity as a physical regulator of emotions, it is even more noteworthy that all religions emphasize the centrality of breath in the healing of Body, Mind and Soul. It is comparable to the Heart's centrality as a sustainer of life. Breath is the word of God made flesh. "God breathed the breath of life into man's nostrils, and man became a living soul (Genesis 2:7)." Most religions, including the Torah, treat breath as two breaths, the physical breathing of oxygen and the simultaneous breathing of the breath of God, which is variously called Prana, Chi, Ruah, Ki, or Tao. These are the energies cultivated and directed by various disciplines for healing the body. Caponigro, whose book describes many breathing exercises, also addresses these more esoteric aspects of breath. The thrust of his assertions is aptly captured in a quote from the *Tao Te Ching*: "Tao is the breath that never dies. It is the mother of all creation." Disrupting the rhythm of our breath jeopardizes our health; uniting with its fullness brings health.

Sleeping/Waking

An occasional sleepless night will leave us tired the next day, but normally, we sleep more easily the following night. If sleeplessness persists, or we are awakened nightly in the early hours and unable to get back to sleep, this can quickly take a toll on an individual's ability to function during the day. Given all the drugs and sleep aids sold in America, not to mention all the doctors who study our sleepless nights or dangerous sleep (sleep apnea), a good night's sleep is clearly a problem for many people. Whenever a client reports sleep disturbances, I make it a priority of treatment because I know it is adversely affecting the waking hours.

Regardless of what descriptive name is given to the sleep disturbance by physical medicine, I treat all sleep disturbances as a struggle precipitated by primary selves seeking to maintain control of disowned selves. I have no problem referring the client to a physician for whatever treatment s/he can offer. But the long-term treatment of sleep disturbance with drugs – while it may 'drown out' the inner struggle, does nothing to heal it and is likely to become iatrogenic; and it is relatively easy to discover sleep-disrupting selves and work with them. Basically, the client goes inside and imagines being in bed *trying* to go to sleep. Christ is asked to hold the hand of the self that is keeping the client awake with its thoughts (sic) ruminations, lists of things to do, plans, regrets, etc. While holding the hand of that self, Christ is asked to place a double circle around the bed and separate whoever is being suppressed by the forced wakefulness of a primary self. It is best if Christ opaques the second circle so that only a presence is experienced initially. Christ can locate the second circle at the foot of the bed or further away. At this point the client is asked to begin a dialogue with the presence, and the therapist begins to work with whatever is related. The goal of this intervention is always straightforward: a good night's sleep without medication. Whatever self is keeping the client awake is addressed and worked with until that goal is achieved. As needed, other interventions can be developed but the paradigm remains the same: address whatever is being fearfully suppressed by the hyper-vigilance. In the last chapter, I provide verbatims describing a lengthy series of sessions with a client – Leigh – who is diagnosed as bi-polar and chronically sleep deprived.

Sexuality

For most mammalian species the instinctual rhythm of sexuality is controlled by 'chemistry,' i.e. instinct. When a female mammal is in heat – for very delimited seasons of the year, the desire created in both sexes is more powerful than most other activities including eating and personal survival. The aroused desire so disrupts homeostasis that the animal is driven toward compensatory satisfaction, to the exclusion of much else. But humans have the evolutionary 'advantage' of being aroused throughout the year. Most adult females are 'in heat' at least one week out of every month; and where large numbers are congregated, female menstrual cycles will vary sufficiently such that some portion of the female population will be 'in heat' every day of the month. Consequently, the male could be aroused just about all of the time, *if instinct and phonemes were the only factors in play*. Since unmitigated sexual arousal is not in the best interest of the species, the Ego's ability to defer gratification has long been a necessity. But note that deferral is not the same as denial or abstinence. The Ego has the wherewithal to defer gratification for long periods, even redirect it, but not to permanently repress it with impunity.

No culture that I am aware of has been able to develop customs for the regulation of sexuality that do not involve shame. To a greater or lesser degree, the mores of most cultures seek to shame all but a narrow expression of sexual behavior, at considerable expense to one or both sexes, in an effort to control sexual activity.

In my clinical practice, I treat sexuality as *sexual energy*. At the level of Mind, sexual energy can be separated from ego-aspects. I have found this exceedingly helpful in two regards. First, in *clinical populations* many ego-aspects have experienced early sexual events that were painful and/or shameful. Thereafter, whenever sexual energy is aroused, it evokes the concomitant negative emotions remembered by the ego-aspects that suffered the abuse, even if the current situation arousing the sexual energy is unmitigatingly pleasurable. Fortunately, both the negative emotions and the sexual energy can be separated from those ego-aspect(s), who are often undeveloped children in stature. Christ can dispel the negative emotions, and make sexuality a choice rather than a compulsion. Once the ego-aspect is separated from sexual energy it can remain separated from that energy, or reconnect to it using the *Light* or by self-arousal. Ego-aspects can also suppress sexual energy in a prideful need to control it, which denies its conscious access to other ego-aspects. These conditions are harder to work with but doable. These and a number of other issues are addressed in later chapters and in Appendix I.

The sexual instinct is the most obvious example of a culturally disrupted instinctual rhythm. The history of hysteria amply describes the de facto effects of arousing sexual energy in women while denying them satisfaction. But eating, drinking, sleep cycles, even breathing, are equally susceptible to disruptions by the Ego. Even as different types of yoga can demonstrate the many benefits of optimum breathing techniques, cultures persist in disrupting breathing by incessantly stimulating fight-flight reflexes and encouraging shallow breathing with such clichés as "stomach in, chest out." In sum, the Ego is capable of disrupting most instinctual rhythms. Sometimes, this is life saving as when we hold our breath underwater, but in the case of chronic shallow breathing it is clearly a detriment, and the same appears to be true when sexual energy is blocked by pride and shame. The major problem with blocking sexual energy is that it creates an unremitting desire (sic) arousal, which the Ego then seeks to satisfy with substitutes such as food, compulsive exercise or other addictions. The individual, if not the culture, needs to learn how to direct sexual energy, not block it.

The Survival Rhythms:
Anger and Fear

Overview

Three sets of opposites help to put anger and fear in perspective: expansion/contraction, approach/withdraw, and fight/flight. Anger expands *quickly*, fear contracts *quickly*. Anger approaches *quickly*, fear withdraws *quickly*. In effect, anger and fear *copy* the action of the Body's fight/flight reflex by accelerating the speed of response. They are not merely an approach or avoidance action; rather, they generate *intense* reactions similar to the Body's reaction when startled. Basically, anger and fear are knee jerk reflexes at the level of Mind. But unlike the fight/flight response, which is a nearly involuntary body reaction to environmental stimuli, fear and anger are always stimulated by an *internal sense of threat* precipitated by expectation and belief, even though the Body is obliged to respond as if the threat was external and immediate.

Expand/contract is the same rhythm that describes breathing, the cardio-rhythm, and the craniosacral rhythm.[99] Those rhythms need to be measured and balanced overall. Expand/contract describes the normal state of affairs. Anger and fear describe an intense acceleration of those rhythms ranging from mild to very intense. When someone is 'angry,' s/he expands/approaches with degrees of force, e.g. irritated, mad, raging, berserk. When fearful, s/he withdraws/contracts with degrees of force, e.g. anxious, fearful, panic, emotional paralysis, catatonia, etc. And it cannot be stressed enough that these are always the responses of anger/fear. If fear approaches it is with trepidation; if anger retreats it is with resentment and thoughts of revenge.

Anger/fear are not the same as fight/flight, though they are comparable in action and effect. Fight/flight refers to the Body's physiological response to being startled or threatened. It is reflexive. The complete physiological response occurs in milliseconds and evokes very specific muscular systems depending on whether the response is approach or withdrawal.[100] Fight/flight is a reflexive action akin to anger/fear in terms of approach/avoid and expand/contract, but fight/flight is generally the *most intense measure* of those reactions and relatively unmediated. However, anger/fear will stimulate physiological reactions comparable to those observed in the fight/flight reflex. Fight/flight is the Body's reflexive reaction to immediate environmental threats; anger/fear are the Mind's reactions to internal threats even when perceived as coming from the environment. The two overlap in their effect on the sensate body, and in their reciprocal effects on the Body and Mind.

Peter Levine hypothesizes that the 'collapse' of the fight/flight reflex is responsible for post-traumatic symptoms.[101] Collapse occurs when neither fight nor flight is any longer a viable solution for the organism. At that moment, the organism freezes its choice – be it fight or flight, and becomes immobile or plays dead. This capacity to 'freeze' an intense reflexive action is comparable to what happens when an archetypal authority shames an ego-aspect stripping its power to exercise free will. If this 'collapsing' survival strategy works, then the organism must afterward 'shake off' the energy blocked by the freezing response. Animals can do this instinctively. Many humans appear to impede the discharge; that is, having severed the connection, they become too fearful to make the necessary reconnection. Levine asserts that this inability to reconnect with the energy and discharge it eventually generates post-traumatic symptoms. He offers remediation techniques for discharging the energy, especially, in young children.

Another practitioner, Thomas Hanna, has treated the adverse effects of anger/fear on the human body for the past 30 years. He focuses on the trauma caused by the chronic *overuse* of the fight/flight reflexes. His observations and remediations go a long way toward understanding and alleviating many of the physical problems suffered by an aging population who have chronically stimulated the fight/flight reflexes. It is difficult to discern whether the effects he documents are the result of the chronic re-enactment of shock trauma or the effect of chronically stimulating the fight/flight reflex with affective emotion; shock trauma could account for both. While, he does not make a distinction, his observations clearly delineate the adverse effects of chronic stimulation in older adults. For years, I have introduced his work to clients by telling them that he has written one of the best books I have read for people over forty.[102] His book – *Somatics*, describes the debilitating effects that anger/fear have on the human body and offers a specific set of exercises for remediation.

Somatics

While Hanna's work addresses a wide range of clinical topics, he emphasizes the effects of two neurophysiological responses that he calls the Red Light reflex and Green Light reflex:

What I have found is that the neuromuscular system has two basic responses to stress, both of which have their focus in the middle of the human body, at its center of gravity. These two basic responses differ from one another because they are two very different forms of stress – what Selye [103] would distinguish as "distress" and "eustress".... The neuromuscular adaptation to sustained negative stress ("distress") is the withdrawal response, which occurs primarily in the front of the body. The neuromuscular adaptation to sustained positive stress ("eustress") is the action response, which occurs in the back of the body. It is easier to think of the withdrawal response as the Red Light reflex. The action response may be thought of as the Green Light reflex.[104]

Basically, these two responses are antagonists. One propels us forward and the other contracts us, both quickly. Hanna notes that for many decades neurobiologists have been particularly fascinated with the Red Light reflex because it occurs throughout the entire animal kingdom.

It is sometimes referred to as the "startle response;" at other times it is referred to as the "escape response," because it aids the animal in avoiding or evading a threat. It is a primitive reflex of survival. Its action in the central nervous system is usually mediated by "giant" nerve fibers large enough to allow the nerve impulse to travel more quickly. It is a "rapid motor act" that is built into the circuitry of even very simple organisms....The mechanism of this reflex lies deep beneath the control of the [human] forebrain where conscious, voluntary actions originate.

Not only is the withdrawal reflex more primitive than our voluntary actions, it is much faster. It happens before we can consciously perceive it or inhibit it. It is our primitive protector, whose motto is "Withdraw now, and think about it later." [105]

Hanna argues that this reflex can become habituated, which he describes as "a slow relentless adaptive act, which ingrains itself into the functional patterns of the central nervous system." [106] This habitual response will occur not only when stimulated by an actual threat, but on a lesser scale whenever we respond fearfully. Quoting research done in Canada, he notes that, "It was found that EMG [electromyogram] tension rose when a person was engaged in any challenging task involving fear of failure. When the task was completed EMG tension fell back to normal levels." [107]

In contrast to the Red Light reflex, the Green Light reflex is treated as a positive reaction, though its habituation is seen as largely responsible for low back pain.

The Green Light reflex is the opposite of the Red Light reflex, as both a muscular activity and an adaptational function. The Red Light reflex contracts the anterior flexor muscles, curling the body forward; the Green Light reflex contracts the posterior extensor muscles, lifting and arching the back in the opposite direction. The adaptational function of the Red Light reflex is protective; it is a withdrawal from the world. The Green Light reflect is assertive; its function is action, and it too is adaptational. One makes us stop, the other makes us go. They are in balance, and are both necessary for our survival. [108]

Hanna sees the habituation of the Green Light reflex as largely responsible for the high frequency and chronicity of low back pain. John Sarno, a specialist in rehabilitative medicine, would concur, but emphasizes that the underlying issue is unexpressed anger. [109] Sarno argues that unexpressed anger can also chronically stimulate the Green Light reflex. This results in inordinate and prolonged tightness of the back's neuromuscular system, which produces the pain response.

Hanna argues that it is the combined habituation of both reflexes – Red and Green that is responsible for what he calls the 'dark vise,' the senile posture responsible for so many chronic problems in older people. The habituation results in what he calls muscular amnesia. The patient comes to accept a body posture generated by a stress reaction as the normal posture. "Gradually, the Red Light and Green Light reflexes interfere with one another. When one is partially contracted, the other cannot contract fully… generating a state of muscular immobility caused by the gradual buildup of chronically opposing contractions." [110] Much of Hanna's book is devoted to very specific exercises for identifying the presence of these reflexes and helping the reader regain a conscious awareness of a relaxed vs. stressed posture.

While Hanna draws numerous connections between anger and fear and the actions of the Red and Green Light reflexes, his focus is at a neuromuscular level, both in description and remedy. My own focus is on the anger and fear underlying those processes, which is more in line with the work of John Sarno. What Hanna demonstrates is a clear connection between those emotions and Body specific responses that become detrimental when habituated. We cannot be habitually angry or fearful with impunity. The Red and Green reflexes are meant to be just that: intense, rapid, but *short-lived* actions. When the reflexes are chronically stimulated, the body adapts to them as an habituated response with all the predictable adverse effects described by Hanna. This habituation drives home my oft-repeated assertion that the body-brain does not have a Mind of its own. It adapts to the Mind's demands even if the demands eventually result in the Wrath of God. Over time, the Body even loses its capacity to provide negative feedback to the Mind via sensation, unless the individual can be helped to consciously refocus on these amnesic areas.

Anger and fear are easily identified as affects. However, without a context it is difficult to determine whether Mind or environment is primarily responsible for an affect's stimulation. For example, if you press baby's arms of against its body s/he will begin to cry and attempt to break free in a way characteristic of angry frustration. This could be described as reflexive anger or unmediated affective anger. But then, even as a toddler, the child can learn to express anger as a temper tantrum when a self-perceived need is denied. That is emotional anger, a learned reaction, operantly reinforced. The Ego quickly learns the short-term efficacy of anger and fear in controlling itself and coping with its environment. In doing so, it is simply mimicking the culture at large, which seems to be driven primarily by fear, greed, and anger. Of those three, fear appears to be the most socially acceptable, particularly fear of shame and guilt.

The forgoing begs the question: how do we address these two emotions given their socially sanctioned and pervasive presence in our lives? Notwithstanding Christ's repeated challenge to 'fear not,' is it even desirable to strive for the elimination of fear/anger responses given their cultural approbation? Clearly, the answer is yes. It puts inordinate strain on the human body to maintain a fearful or angry vigilance. The Body is not designed to sustain long-term affective reactions, be it fear or anger. Nor are the problems associated with prolonged affective reactions limited to the physiological effect on specific neuromuscular and endocrine systems. Anger always places us at risk of retaliation. It is most likely to evoke 'an eye for an eye' reaction even if the recipient does not express it overtly. And if anger is directed inward – what some have defined as the precursor of depression, then that locus of the anger will also become toxic. Attacking our selves has real consequences. When an ego-aspect becomes sufficiently bruised by repeated attacks, that wounding will manifest in the Body as some form of physical dis-ease or psychological despair capable of stimulating suicidal or homicidal ideation.

Treating Anger/Fear as Opposites

Anger and fear are treated as opposites because they evoke diametrically opposite responses in both the Body and Mind. As Hanna and Selye both demonstrate, these two emotions evoke opposing responses in the human body, one serving forceful approach the other retreat. Similarly, in the Mind, ego-aspects use anger to suppress and overwhelm, and use fear to avoid being overwhelmed. Another reason for treating them as opposites is their cyclic nature. Most often, fear appears to precede anger, though the precedence is probably measured in milliseconds. *Affective anger is a response to perceived threat*, a response to the fear of something happening, e.g. the fear of being shamed. In the absence of threat, one can approach without anger. One can approach, as it were, with ease, or determination, or confidence, to offer just a few possibilities. In sum, *anger requires both a measure of intensity and a preceding fearful response*. The intensity serves to overwhelm the object of fear by actively pushing it away or seeking to wound it. But anger can also stimulate fear, particularly the fear of retaliation. When the fear is dominant, the object of its fear (a force perceived as more powerful than its own anger) will suppress the active expression of anger. An image or voice embodying parental retaliation is a classic example of a fearful object able to suppress the expression of anger. In such instances, the angry self is likely to be repressively somaticized and/or projected, or become the carrier of abiding resentment or hate (i.e. impotent anger). In sum, anger and fear appear to cycle, each aspect stimulating the other. Thus, as a working hypothesis, I always assume that expressions of anger are a response to fear, and that at least some fear is precipitated by a fear of retaliatory anger.

A classic example that I offer to clients, by way of showing the intimate relationship between anger and fear, is a parent's response to a child running into the road without looking and nearly getting hit by a car. The parent's first response will be relief that the child is not hurt, quickly followed by anger at the child for having scared the hell out of them. This is a classic example of fear precipitating an angry response.

When I see a client with 'anger issues' the initial goal of therapy is to understand the underlying fears and address those. *Anger seeks to control fear by suppressing the object of fear.* Helping the client identify their fear is one of the best ways I have found to address anger. Once the client can intellectually identify the fear underlying the anger, s/he then needs to identify the *object* of fear, i.e. the disowned self evoking the fearful response. This is never an easy process. As one client said, "I've never been angry without good reason." In my experience, unless an angry client is under some form of external duress, e.g. spouse threatening to leave or court ordered therapy, s/he is unlikely to remain in therapy long enough to address issues of chronic anger.

David Hawkins – whose work was discussed in Chapter I, does not address opposites. He treats fear and anger as hierarchical. Anger is seen as more powerful, less negative, than fear. In Hawkins' hierarchy, anger and fear are separated by *desire*; meaning desire is more powerful than fear and less powerful than anger. Because anger is physically draining if continuously evoked, and automatically reinforces the *fear* of retaliation, desire is generally the culturally preferred response for containing fear.[111] Often, the Ego will create an Ego-in-conflict or Dominant self for the purpose of using desire to cope with fear. Both kinds of ego-aspects use physical desire to cope with these seemingly irreconcilable opposites. I describe the dynamics of both ego-aspects in the chapter on Moral authority.

A common *fear* of clients is their *accumulated unexpressed anger.* It is this unexpressed anger that Sarno argues is the root cause of most chronic back pain. In these cases the client fears that if they ever became really angry, the emotion would overtake them and wreak havoc. The extreme variant of this fear is catatonia. Further on, I also offer clinical examples illustrating situations where fear, or anger, is blocked or fused, thereby creating a situation where each reinforces the other in the cyclic fashion expected of rhythmic opposites.

Release From Fear

I have learned to apply a general rule of thumb in working with Ego emotions: when pride fails anger arises; when anger fails, there is generally a fall into a fear of shame that must then be assuaged with desire. Where neither pride nor anger is evoked, the emotions of choice for coping with shame will be desire (addictive and compulsive behavior) and/or fear and/or fear of shame (avoidance). Guilt can also serve if the desire is shameful, but goes undetected. Guilt is always experienced after the fact, with 'the fact' being the undetected satisfaction of a shameful desire. All of these emotions are employed *to avoid* a repetition of shameful experiences, and in that regard fear is pivotal. Pride, anger, and desire all serve to distance from, suppress, or distract from fear, which is generally the primary defense against shameful repetition. This regressive hierarchy illustrates why fear is both tenacious and pivotal.

Often, the individual is unaware that s/he is experiencing fear. Panic attacks are frequently misperceived – at least initially, as heart problems, which is quite understandable given that panic is experienced as a racing heart and tightening of the chest, which makes for difficult breathing in shallow breathers. The surest indication of anxiety is a disruption of abdominal breathing. But most adults have lost that awareness. In our culture most individuals become habituated to the chronic tightening of their abdominal muscles and consequent shallow breathing. In therapy sessions, I frequently observe clients' yawning, indicating a fearful tightening of the chest making it difficult to breathe easily. Other common signs of fear are a painful tightness of the stomach (the proverbial knot) and sweaty palms.[112]

The *garment of protection* is one of the best strategies I have found for initially addressing an ego-aspect's fear. It effectively blocks the threat of attack from another ego-aspect or unresolved shock trauma that is the object of fear. As I tell the client, this garment will not protect from *actual* attacks in-the-world, but does provide respite from the constant *fear* of attack. Basically, a fearful ego-aspect is contained and given a portion of the *Light*. The Aware-ego or Christ is asked to instruct the fearful ego-aspect in using the *Light* to create a garment of protection, which will shield it from fear. The garment can assume any shape that satisfies the ego-aspect. The intervention is successful when the ego-aspect self-reports an experience of relief. It loses its fear of the object of fear.[113] Generally, this intervention is offered in the context of also containing the object of fear. As a rule, ego-aspects are fearful of other images within the Mind. Most people do not appreciate the fact that we are most vigilant against other selves, particularly selves that have been wounded and made vulnerable to shame. After the disowned object of fear has been identified and healed, it needs to be reconciled with the fearful aspect. This may require several kinds of interventions. Christ can be asked to alter the belief system of the fearful aspect by injecting – with its permission, emotional *acceptance* to counterbalance the fearful avoidance. Christ can be asked to actively reconcile the two in other ways as well, which I describe throughout this and further chapters.

The Fear of Repetition Vs. Actual Experience

Fear is a major force in creating bifurcation. Fear allows the Ego to avoid a repetition of painful, emotional, experiences. The ego-aspect that is fearful of repeating a painful event can become very powerful, particularly if parental authority has precipitated the fear. What gives fear its power is its ability to avoid the more painful emotions experienced by the disowned parts racked with despair, guilt, or shame. The Ego cannot heal these ego-aspects on its own, so dissociation and the creation of a *fearful* ego-aspect is often the best defense for avoiding a repetition of the experience. The disowned part holds the memory – the actuality of the experience, while the newly created primary self directs voluntary behavior that is *fearful* of any repetition of that actuality. *In effect, most managers, protectors, and primary selves are governed by fear.* They will seek to avoid a repetition of the experience identified with the disowned aspect. Unfortunately, fear cannot heal the experience; so the fear becomes self-perpetuating once enacted. To remove the fear, the fearful aspect must be shielded from further fear, and then the ego-aspect who actually experienced the trauma must be identified and healed by Christ. As necessary, Christ can then be asked to remove the bifurcating authority that obliged the dissociation or sustains it, and reconcile the two ego-aspects if that does not occur spontaneously.

It is helpful to distinguish between disowned ego-aspects that have *experienced* an event and primary ego-aspects that are *fearful* of its repetition. The therapist can offer examples to help the client make this distinction. The most common are experiences of pain that precipitates a fear of repetition. Falling off a roof or out of a tree are classic examples. Such events often leave the person fearful of being on roofs or in trees and most people can relate to their fear. Making a distinction between the *actual* past experience and *fear of future* experiences can be helpful in pointing to the existence of a disowned self. Generally, a disowned ego-aspect's *actual* experience is the basis of the fear. Any fear of future experience will implicitly point to the existence of a disowned aspect or residual energy cyst associated with shock trauma. To continue our example, most clients can appreciate that a *respect* for precarious heights is probably healthy, but a *fear* that generalizes to all high places is probably not. The *experience* of shame is also subject to this kind of fearful generalization, but it is more insidious than a fear of falling off roofs. Shameful experiences are an inherent possibility in most relationships, particularly those involving authority; and entering into relationships is far more likely than having to cope with precarious heights. If a disowned aspect is making the individual fearful in relationships, it behooves the client to find ways to identify and heal that ego-aspect.

Fear Within, FearWithout, Fear Projected

Once a fearful ego-aspect such as a Responsible primary has been contained and protected, the next step is to identify the object of its fear. Usually, the fearful self will identify the object of fear as outside the contained sense of self. But it is always good to ask the fearful aspect if s/he fears something within. If identified as within the fearful self, the client is likely to point to the stomach or heart. Where this is the case, the client is asked to divide the *Light* in two, and give one portion to Christ who uses it to draw a second circle, which will contain the object of fear. Next, the fearful ego-aspect is asked to hold its *Light* on the part of the body holding the object of fear, and simultaneously, to ask Christ to draw the object of fear into the circle he has prepared for it. Another method of extraction is to have Christ draw a double circle around the fearful ego-aspect and separate it from the fearful self. A third method is to have Christ draw a capturing circle and walk the ego-aspect through it. All three interventions have proven equally effective. Very likely, a Dominant self will identify the object of fear as being within, while a Responsible primary is likely to perceive it as without. Either way it is possible to extract and/or contain the fearful object.

Occasionally, when the fearful aspect is asked to contain the object of fear, the first image contained is the image of a parent who the client dreads being like. Where this is the case, it can be assumed that the object of fear is likely a self that is closely identified with the parent.

(This is illustrated in a case example below.) That self is likely to be part of a Not-me complex described in the next chapter. If the client is willing, a double circle can be used to separate this projection. Alternatively, Christ can be asked to use his *Light* to draw a second circle, which he uses to *lift the parental image* off of the self-image hidden within it. Detailed interventions for working with projections are described later in the chapter.

Most often, the fearful ego-aspect will perceive the object of its fear as outside of its self. Where this is the case, the most effective course is to ask the fearful self to direct its *Light* to contain the disowned self – wherever it is – and anchor the circle to that spot in the Mind. Next, have the *Light* place an opaqued dome over the circle so the disowned self can be sensed but not seen. The Aware-ego and Christ are then asked to approach the dome. The shielded fearful self is given the option of coming with them or staying behind. Since the fearful ego-aspect has already been given a garment of protection, it can approach the dome without fear, and often does follow Christ and the Aware-ego. By requiring that Christ and the Aware-ego *approach the dome* – rather than having the *Light* bring it to them, everyone can better pace the movement toward disclosure. Also, I am likely to suggest that clarity be a function of approach so that whatever is in the dome will only become clear as the group approaches it. This allows for what I might call 'dawning awareness.' The approach can require more than one session. This process cannot be pushed. Often, a client's psyche needs a week or more to acclimate to the discovery of a disowned self within the Mind, especially, if this is the first round of discovery.

Various Expressions of Anger

It is difficult to assess anger out of context. Just as there can be many objects of fear, anger too can have a variety of objects or contexts. I want to mention just two here that seem to play a role for many clients. The first is what I will call identity related anger. Many clients harbor longstanding anger and/or resentment toward a family member, often a mother or father. This is likely the result of a strong identity with that person which the client has disowned. It is often expressed as a concerted desire to be *not like the person*. This attitude is by no means restricted to parents. For example, one client and husband both saw a strong similarity between the wife and the husband's mother. In these cases, the client's anger is an attempt to distance from the perceived identity, whatever it is that the two share in common. I address this issue in the next chapter and revisit it again in the last chapter where I explore Christ's power to convict with the power of the Holy Spirit. That intervention is particularly helpful in resolving conflicted identity issues as it provides a means of simultaneously changing both selves.

Another form of anger in psychotherapy has become quite pervasive in our culture. This is the anger expressed in video games where players attack other combatants, aliens, or the like. Several of my clients have confessed to spending many hours at a time participating in these games. My question to them is "who is the internal recipient of this anger. I suggest that they first identify the 'shooter' and then identify who is being repeatedly shot. The effects of this type of intervention are too varied to synthesize, except to say that shame is generally at the root. But when the two selves are successfully reconciled the amount of time on the computer generally abates.

The foregoing are but two examples of the numerous manifestations of anger. Really, every culture seems to have too many reasons for anger. Some cultures and countries are dominated by anger, often as the result of repetitive war trauma, widespread poverty, or dominator systems. Even in America, which seems less inflicted by culture-wide trauma issues, we are constantly being aroused by fear and anger stimulating newscasts. Suffice to say, finding a modicum of peace among all the fear and anger generated by most cultures is no mean feat.

Removing Accumulated Unexpressed Anger

Many clients are afraid to express anger. One reason is the *fear* that their anger will get out of control, consume them, or destroy them or others with its intensity. Psychics describe the accumulation of anger in the emotional body as a major contributor of disease and discomfort. I have found it helpful to have Christ remove any accumulated unexpressed anger. When offering this to clients, I make the distinction between *accumulated unexpressed* anger and the *capacity to express* anger. The client retains the capacity to generate and express anger but will no longer have to fear it's turning into uncontrolled rage as a result of releasing fearful blocks to its expression. I also tell the client it will be necessary to work with the ego-aspects who accumulated the anger helping them to find appropriate ways to acknowledge and express it. The following case illustrates a process for removing accumulated unexpressed anger.

Tory. In a preceding session, Tory worked with a self strongly identified with both the feeling function and suppressed anger. This self was named the Isolate. Tory describes this image as a grotesque little girl, squarely built with very sharp corners. In the intervening week, Tory has come to the realization that the Isolate's sharpness symbolizes real enragement at her mother for all the hurtful things she has done to Tory throughout her life. Tory identifies the opposite of the Isolate as the Gingerbread girl.[114] That self is very detached from feelings and superficially attached to the mother. The attachment is symbolized by a connection with her mother at the tips of the toes and hands and head. The Gingerbread self has a hole where the body is supposed to be. According to Tory, "I can talk about the Gingerbread girl with detachment, but I can't talk about the Isolate with detachment. I feel things boiling." I suggest she allow Christ to scan and remove any *unexpressed accumulated anger*. My suggestion turns into a lengthy process. Christ works with her Sensed-body. Tory imagines lying down on a massage table looking up at Christ. She is instructed to hand Christ a portion of her *Light*, which he will use to absorb any accumulated unexpressed anger found in her body. Before the process is complete she will actually hand him several portions of her *Light*. Tory describes the process as 'lightening.' Interestingly, as Christ moves toward her solar plexus, Tory reflects that there is a lot there, "I know there is a lot in my stomach and abdomen, and I know it is like an infection or pus, really putrid." Since we are well over the session time, I strongly encourage Tory to let Christ continue the process at home.[115]

When Tory returns she has a great deal to report. First, she relates that she knew this was going to be big when she asked Christ to remove the accumulated anger, because she believes the anger is a major reason for her overeating. In support of that contention she reports that in the previous week, as a seeming result of all her work, she lost 8 lbs., though she could not observe any changes in her eating habits. Her chiropractor gave her an incentive to continue working on her own. In his examination he noted an improvement, but when she worked with his assistant she found her back unbearably sore. The doctor attributed this to 'toxins.' This motivated her to go home and continue the process of allowing Christ to draw out the accumulated anger. "I could feel Christ drawing it out, I could feel the sensation of drawing; by yesterday I felt sore all over my back. Today, I can barely sit back in your couch." The soreness notwithstanding she remains elated about the weight loss. She has also observed a shift in the relationship with her mother who came for dinner over the weekend. "There was no pressure. It was like I was visiting with someone who was not my mother. All the pressure seemed to be on her to say nice things and show appreciation." Tory makes one other observation before going inside: "The Isolate is not square any more, and she has gotten older; she is no longer a child. Despite my soreness, she has a real sense of freedom."

While I am frankly impressed with all the changes, my primary concern is Tory's generalized soreness. I ask if the Isolate is feeling the soreness. "No, clearly, the pain is mine (meaning another self). The Isolate has a real sense of freedom and no pain." I tell Tory that I think it would be helpful if she could enter *a dome of sensation* and allow Christ to work with the etheric body she finds there. (Tory is already familiar with the concept of an etheric body.) I describe this intervention to her in general terms and invite her to go inside. Christ takes her to a dome that is like cut glass, lots of facets, a crystalline structure. "We enter the dome. An image of me is standing in it. There are lots of light rays in this dome, but you can still see the light of the body." I ask if the rays are connected to the body? "No. The rays are in movement, they are related to the dome." I ask what is their meaning? "They have color, some are red and orange and others are white, but I don't know what the colors mean." I hypothesize that the etheric body has been damaged and is responsible for her soreness. But my train of thought confuses Tory because she perceives the etheric body in the dome as a healthy sense of self. "The body seems good, whole, healthily energized…Christ is not doing anything to change it." I ask if this body is the source of her soreness? "It is the goal, not the source…Christ says I need to walk into this body…I have a strong sense that I am supposed to walk into it." All I can do is stand corrected and encourage her to follow Christ's direction. "When I walk into it, the body stays in me, it has become a part of me….when we started doing this I could hardly sit back on the couch, my back was hurting so much…when I walked into that body, I felt a stretching out, a lifting up and stretching out as if somebody was pulling my feet and pulling my hands over my head. Now my back feels much better, I'm fine. When I started through the body of light it became enmeshed with something inside of me. I can't see it anymore. There are no rays in the dome now, just light" I ask if the body was there before we worked with the Isolate's anger? No, it was not there, it is a new thing, a new creation." Was it hidden by anger? "No, it could not exist until this work was done, the work with the Isolate." What does this inner body symbolize? "Strength and openness, it gives me a backbone, not rigid or hard, but it is an opportunity to stand straight."

Tory's case is a good illustration of how the removal of accumulated unexpressed anger can precipitate a number of changes; but it also precipitates a number of consequences that I cannot explain. I don't feel I can make any generalized statements here. It is possible that what Tory experiences is a reconciliation of the Gingerbread Girl and the Isolate via the etheric body; that the Isolate's healing makes it available to the Gingerbread girl. Seeking out the "etheric body in a dome of sensation" was an intuitive prompt on my part; it was the first time I used that particular intervention; and when I proposed it, I was thinking primarily of a healing setting for the etheric body. But some self, now freed from the fear of anger (very likely the Gingerbread girl), appears to experience the lack of sensation as a generalized sense of soreness, and once she can connect with sensation – apparently as a 'new creation,' the soreness immediately leaves her. I think the image of the Gingerbread girl prompted me to suggest this intervention as that image appeared all but severed from sensation; but it is not clear that she was the actual beneficiary. I have come to accept such ambiguities in the therapy process. I simply assume that whatever is most in need of healing or transformation will emerge and re-emerge until the appropriate combination of need and solution offers closure.

The etheric body in a dome of sensation appears to be nominally different from the sensate body. It is actually a chakra and it is quite possible that by entering that body Tory was opening her root chakra or allowing the Gingerbread girl and Isolate to do so. But again this is speculation. I was intuitively prompted to offer this intervention; and I have not had the opportunity to use it with others.

Worry

Worry is a unique expression of projected anger. On the surface it appears to be a fearful response. In fact, however, it is the sum of owned fear and projected anger. The fear is expressed as *concern* and the anger is projected into a 'shadowy' other. To illustrate: a wife worries when her husband fails to come home when expected. She envisions him lying hurt in some hospital, or dead on the side of the road as a result of an auto accident. She is not angry at him, only fearful for his wellbeing. But who caused the accident *in her mind*? Who drove the other car that broadsided him? The person who worries owns the fear and projects the anger. Such people fear the consequences of their own anger, and so must project it into a world they perceive as hostile. The extreme form of worry is paranoia. The price of worry is a sense of powerlessness in the face of a seemingly hostile world.

Eduardo. This case is a complex example of worry. Very quickly, Eduardo will identify a *disincarnate soul* as the primary agent of his worry. He will not name it as such, but it is clearly not a self-image. To further complicate matters, *I repeatedly fail* to address this facet of his worry. Dealing with disincarnate souls is not a big deal if the therapist is willing to let the client evoke the *Light* and a higher power. If a therapist is unwilling for the client to call on a higher power such as Christ, s/he is likely to miss this 'facet' altogether, which makes whatever issue the client is addressing difficult to resolve. Ordinarily, the therapist will not have to address disincarnate souls when addressing worry. But disincarnate souls can manifest in any situation that is a chronic problem for a client, so hopefully this case will provide the therapist with another heads up on the need to be sensitive to this issue. The second 'complexity' in this case was my persistent *forgetfulness* despite numerous – and retrospectively glaring – clues that a spiritual level intervention was needed. For reasons I cannot explain, I kept getting sidetracked. It took me a full two months from the time the disincarnate soul is first identified to finally suggest an intervention. There was a lot of movement in each session after the soul was identified, particularly around issues of anger. Anger issues can become forcefully figural when finally addressed. But honestly, I also think something was blindsiding me. Thankfully,

Eduardo's Christ image kept conveying a clear sense of the soul issue and actually seemed to address it without our asking him to do so.

Eduardo's case will make more sense if the reader appreciates that I confabulated two distinct entities for at least two months. The first one I will call the Worrying self. This is a self-image of Eduardo. The second image – the Worrier – is not a self-image. Keep in mind that I continued to treat both images as one and the same for two months; I am only able to distinguish the two in retrospect. Very likely, since Eduardo never visualized either construct before, he was equally in the dark. Few people are comfortable with the idea having a disincarnate soul attached to an ego-aspect, so most tend to look for other explanations. And normally, a disincarnate soul such as the Worrier will attach itself to a like-minded ego-aspect in such a way that the two would be normally indistinguishable to anyone but a strongly sensate person such as Eduardo; and even then, only if an effort is made to seek out the like-minded self in active imagination.

This series of sessions actually begins with Christ helping to identify a self called the Artist. I was attempting to find a self within Eduardo who could be more spontaneous. After Christ highlights the existence of the Artist – a spontaneous self, I ask Eduardo to identify the self most threatened by the Artist. He immediately identifies the Worrier. According to Eduardo, the Worrier is afraid of losing control of his emotions – as distinct from expressing them, as would the Artist. "The Worrier really values fear about the future. It is the only way he can imagine approaching the future. He worries about finances, his health, the future, the family, friendships." I ask Eduardo to contain the Worrier expecting him to contain a self-image. "He is a blur. He does not look like me. Somebody younger. An omnipresent force." At this point I am not sure what we are dealing with here. Eduardo is very detailed in his visual imaging. He has been inside numerous times. He is describing someone other than himself. I suggest that he have Christ contain the image with Christ's own *Light* and absorb all the anger-fear emanating from the image. "The whole thing is light now. I can't see the man. Now he is coming back little by little. The man looks younger." I ask how it is the man came to be 'attached' to him? (At this point I have decided to treat it as a disincarnate soul.) "Growing up at an early age; his energy intertwined with my worry. I had experiences that frightened me, and no assurance from adults that things would be OK. Mother never held me. No one to assure me I could cope. At age nine I almost stepped on a Copperhead. A miracle I did not get killed a dozen times."

In the next session I ask Eduardo to again describe the Worrier. Again, he describes someone distinctly not like him in appearance. When asked, Christ says that the identified Worrier is a distinct entity with a soul separate from Eduardo. Apparently, it structures the activities of the self that worries. Eduardo is unable to identify a self-image in this session. In the session that follows, Eduardo identifies the part most strongly identified with the Worrier. "I see me in my early 20's, deep in thought, strung out in space, deep wrinkles in my forehead, in the military – first time away from home – worried about how things were going at home, my dad's alcoholic binges. I was worried to be on my own. I would not go with the guys to the bars. Afraid of getting drunk and beat up. How was I going to make a life for myself? I most worried about becoming like my dad. If I started drinking I might not stop." I ask if he knows where that part of him is hidden – the part like his father? (Instead of addressing the soul issue, I get sidetracked by the identity issue.) "In my memory, my subconscious. I always felt uneasy in complaining about my younger brother (an alcoholic)." Eduardo has intuited that a part of him is like his younger brother. I suggest that he have Christ contain this hidden part in an opaqued circle. I then ask Eduardo to speculate what might push him to drink if this hidden part took over? "Being constantly told to do stuff, isolated by himself, no friends, no support, loneliness, being constantly manipulated and lied too." I ask Eduardo why he believes this part feels so alone? "No one acknowledges his existence, no guidance, no structure, no limits, lack of inner guidance, afraid of making social mistakes."

The above session has taken a number of unexpected twists and turns. First, I anticipated dealing with the disincarnated soul when Eduardo went inside. Instead, Eduardo identifies his self-image of worry – the Worrying self – and then the source of his worry: a self-image like his alcoholic father. The disincarnate soul is all but forgotten, and will remain forgotten during the next two sessions while we address these other self-images.

When Eduardo returns he recalls the self-image that worries, but not what is in the opaqued circle (the projected self so like his father). I suggest that he go inside and separate from whatever is blocking his inner vision. All he can see in the separated circle is darkness. I suggest that he have Christ add more darkness. (This is a paradoxical technique. Whatever it is that Christ does with this kind of suggestion, the 'added darkness' seems to illuminate what is in the new circle.) "I see the dark area. It is fear and foreboding, a dark cloud about ready to rain." Now I ask him to have Christ dispel the darkness and reveal the figure. Again, he does not see a figure but this time Christ identifies the source symbolized by the dark cloud. "The darkness is tied up with experiences (shock trauma) I had in childhood that left scars that resulted in fear, extreme fear, more than normal. It is also tied up with feelings about my dad, and his relationship to my mother, which was argumentative and strained." Eduardo goes on to describe his father's unpredictable behavior when drunk, and a particular incident as a teenager when he had to restrain his father from hitting his mother, and in the process broke several of the father's ribs. (This was no mean feat from Eduardo's perspective as the father was a golden gloves boxer in his own youth.) Most of this session is devoted to Eduardo sharing conflicting feelings about his father, as well as fear of his father, coupled with shame and anger at the father's failure to provide a role model for him as the eldest child. Near the end of the session he can identify the self in the opaqued circle as most like his father. *It is this self that has long held the anger underpinning the worry.* But again, I have failed to address the issue of the disincarnate soul.

In the next session there is a dramatic shift in focus, partially as a consequence of having more fully identified the angry drinker in the opaqued circle, and partially as a result of my suggestions. I again ask Christ to contain the Worrying self preparatory to safeguarding it and moving on to deal with the angry drinker in the opaqued circle. But Eduardo can identify nothing, hears nothing, which is uncharacteristic of his inner work. I suggest that he ask Christ to identify the part most fearful to the Worrying self. "Christ says there is another entire part of my personality that holds the potential for me to be a much different kind of person, more dynamic, settled, consistent, focused, on track. I experience parts of it now, but it is not well rounded." I ask if Christ can identify it? "There are elements in the unconscious, but they are not obvious. I ask what blurs them? "Stress and anxiety, my preoccupation with fear, occasionally anger, but mostly anxiety, fear, and stress.

Christ says the Worrier is a parasite, a leech, that does not contribute anything positive." These negative descriptions are unlike Christ. In my experience, the Christ image does not describe self-images in a derogatory way. But I am confusing the Worrier with a self-image. In fact, Christ is encouraging us to address a disincarnate soul. As for the positive attributes in the unconscious, Christ seems to be providing a contrast to the activity of the Worrier. My intuition prompts me to wonder out loud what sustains the Worrier, and ask if Christ can identify the energy source that sustains him. Christ uses his *Light* to quickly separate the Worrier's essence and Eduardo describes it: "All I see is electricity, sparks, streams of light." I wonder what would happen to the Worrier if this energy was transformed, but save the thought till the next session. (In this session I continue to confabulate the Worrier with the Worrying-self. Christ appears to be talking about the Worrier, and in that context his comments about its being a parasite makes sense. I pick up on the dissonance in the descriptions but not the reason for it. In this session I have completely forgotten about the Worrier.)

As a rule, I always ask the client how things have been between sessions. Interestingly, Eduardo seems to be improving on several fronts. He is working much less compulsively, has become more attuned to his wife's needs, and his own creative needs, and less fearful of trying new things. Whatever we are doing – and it is hard to tell when I review the sessions of the past month, it seems to be working. In this session I focus on the energy that we have separated from the Worrier in the previous session (once again thinking it belongs to the Worrying self). In the intervening weeks I have forgotten about the Worrier, the image of a man who is unlike Eduardo and actually identified as a disincarnate soul by both Christ and Eduardo. Nor do I remember him in this session. No effort is made to have Christ remove him, and his continuing presence confabulates my understanding of this session as well. Even so, Christ is clearly doing something. Eduardo remembers identifying the energy associated with the Worrier. I suggest that both he and Christ describe the energy. "It is a kinetic energy, like electricity, it permeates the Worrier. A cloud is intermingled with the electrical force, like the two are living together, they seem to be part and parcel." (This is bar none, as good a description of a disincarnate soul as any I have heard, but again I miss the boat, at least consciously.) I ask how the Worrier appears when the energy is separated? "He seems less active, less focused, not into anything. It is like the energy takes him over, effects him negatively. It does not enhance his skills at all." I suggest to Eduardo that he ask Christ to recombine the energy and Worrier. "He still looks like an older man, but less worried when the energy is a part of him." Again, Eduardo is describing someone other than himself, but I fail to pick up on it. I am confused because the sequence seems paradoxical: when the Worrier is separated from its energy, he seems less reactive but more worried. At this point I suggest another intervention: Eduardo will ask Christ to channel the energy through Christ's Heart and back to the Worrier. This action seems to alter the Worrier. "His attitude and demeanor are different. He does not have the frown on his face. He seems happier, more content." Now I ask Eduardo to have Christ again separate the energy into a second circle. I am curious to learn what happens if Christ separates the cloud from the kinetic energy. "When the cloud is separated it seems small and misty, real thin, no depth, not large. The kinetic energy is all but invisible, sparks occasionally, more intense when the two are together." At this point, I suggest that he recombine the two circles containing the cloud and energy, and stand them on edge so as to create a portal. I am frankly mystified by this 'energy' and cloud and setting up interventions in an effort to understand it. "The portal looks brighter, more like an opaqued cloud, white with some gray sparks occasionally, not a lot." I ask him to approach this 'portal' and touch it with his *Light*. "It turns bright." I suggest that he take Christ's hand and step through the portal. "It is a plume of white light. I don't see kinetic energy, maybe a little bit, the plume goes into space." At this point I suggest that he have Christ return him to me. (God only knows what has prompted me to suggest this set of interventions. Separating the energy and cloud from the Worrier, and having Christ channel it through his Heart, frees the Worrier from something. Eduardo is clear that this has a positive effect on the Worrier. The idea of having Christ create a portal comprised of the energy and cloud came to me as a result of work I was doing with another client. In this instance, what it seems to demonstrate, unbeknownst to me, is that – once again, we are dealing with a disincarnate soul. When Christ and the client step through the portal they find themselves in a plume that goes into space!

I have complicated the whole process of working with worry by *forgetting* about the initially identified Worrier, which appears to be a disincarnate soul attached to the Worrying self. It will be another month before I remember, and only then because I finally take the time to review all my notes on this series of interventions. Christ and Eduardo have continued to give me clues. But after Eduardo identifies his Worrying self, his self-references are to that self, not the disincarnate soul. And who can blame him for being as 'forgetful' as his therapist. Fortunately – whether of Christ, intuition, or providence – I am able to suggest a series of interventions that effectively allows Christ to isolate the Worrier soul and at least diminish its hold on the Worrying self. Two months after the initial discovery of the Worrier, and reviewing my notes yet again, I can finally remind Eduardo of the image that does not look like him. I tell him my surmise that this is probably a disincarnate soul that needs to be remanded to Christ's care. He goes inside and does this in quick order. After providing himself a small circle of protection, and providing a similar circle for the Worrying self, Eduardo observes a "cloud" around the second circle. Almost immediately, Christ transforms it into pure white light and it disappears. I ask if there are any more clouds in his Mind like that one? "Not at this time. The Worrying self seems at ease; not pre-occupied or depressed." When I ask Eduardo to provide Christ's assessment, he replies that, "Christ says it was a spirit. It was interfering with my Mind's thoughts; it may have affected me for a long time. My worry has been an almost constant state of mind. I really don't have that sense of worry now – the intensity of it. I have not had it for some weeks. I plan but I am not worried of making a mistake. I am not obsessed with things like I used to be. Another thing, for a long time I have had difficulty sleeping, now I am able to sleep through the night." This final intervention appears to make him aware of how much has changed. Unbeknownst to both of us, Christ has been executing changes throughout the process.

Most cases of worrying selves are not so complicated, though few cases are ever straightforward. In each instance, the general objective is the same. Once the worrying self is separated and engaged in dialogue, s/he is encouraged to self-protect using a portion of the *Light*, and then asked to identify the source of fear, the disowned self that threatens. This disowned self is generally another self-image. If the image is someone else, e.g. a parent, then very likely that image is carrying a disowned self that is like the person/parent. The client will give you clues.

In the above case Eduardo describes himself as worrying (sic) fearing a lot about being like his alcoholic father (deceased) or his younger brother who is in frequent medical crises precipitated by alcohol abuse. The most difficult part of this process is separating the disowned self-image from the image holding the projection. The disowned self will be a threat in a way that is frightening to the worrying-self. That is why it was exiled in the first place and obliged to re-emerge in a projected image. Often, the anger is associated with a parental figure who was frighteningly angry, and whom the client desires to be *not like*. In Eduardo's case, that self was identified as the Drinker. Eduardo did not drink, but was ever fearful that if he did drink he would become angry like his father and get into fights.

In Chapters VI and VIII, I revisit this issue of not being like someone. It invariably refers to a sense of identity that the self considers shameful. Often, it is hidden the client's image of a parent.

Reconciling Fear and Anger

Fear and anger are revisited throughout the chapters of this book. Aside from desire, these two emotions are the most common sources of motivation governing the activity of primary ego-aspects. We live in a fearful, angry, world because that is what the culture models. Walter Wink describes it as the myth of redemptive violence, the belief that the violence of the 'just' can be used to defeat the violence of the 'unjust.'[116] To an ego-aspect perceiving itself as standing alone, it makes sense to treat the world with fear and anger. But neither fear nor anger can heal the disowned self that a primary self seeks to protect or evade. So the selves governed by fear and anger, once created, seem doomed to a lifelong perpetuation of those emotions. The only way to break this cycle is to contain the fearful aspect, shield it from the object of its fear (which is always internal – even when projected into others), identify that object of fear, and heal it. It is as Christ says time and again in the Gospels: 'fear not' and 'resist not evil.' Healing is beyond the ability of any ego-aspect that remains fearful. But all is possible once a fearful willfulness is exchanged for willingness. In therapy, I strive at every turn to help ego-aspects reflect on the limitations of anger and fear, and provide them access to a higher power that can provide the necessary healing.

On occasion, *the object of fear is anger.* That is always the case with worry but the fear may also manifest in other forms. In such instances the angry self has been repressed, somaticized and/or projected; and thereby cutoff from the other pole of its natural rhythm. If projected, it is likely to be found in someone close to the client. The major problem in reconciling a fearful self with its disowned angry self is the nature of fear and anger. While it is important for the client to have access to anger, neither fear nor anger is an ideal response, particularly in relationships. Emotionally speaking, the client may have already learned this and seeks to avoid angry responses as a result. However, anger and fear also function as affects, and this fact of life cannot be denied with impunity. Unexpressed fight reactions accumulate toxic effects. Likewise, unexpressed fear affects, long suppressed by overt anger, will also accumulate. Both will have somatic consequences over time, as reflected in the somatically debilitating postures described earlier in Hanna's work. Alternatively, if projected, the client is obliged to live with an angry or very fearful mate. It is a no-win situation either way. Expressing anger and fear can be as problematical as suppressing or projecting either of them. Either road leads to battering, alienation, and/or co-dependence. So what is the solution?

Anger and fear need to be reconciled and available to one ego-aspect rather than being polarized in two selves, one primary and the other disowned. The two must be remerged into one. But without further intervention, the 'reconciliation' of anger and fear is little better than their polarization. The self created by reconciliation is best served if it can be further encouraged to accept Christ's discernment. It is a complex set of interventions, which I will illustrate in a later section on projection. The crux of those interventions is awakening the reconciled ego-aspect to a greater range of choices once the angry and fearful selves have been merged. Conceptually, the merged self must be helped to understand that anger and fear are *extremes*. Their homeopathic center is a *non-anxious presence*: alert, attuned, and aware without being angry or fearful. This sounds good in the abstract, but how is it achieved in the face of anger from others? The client can, of course, respond in kind, and more effectively so if anger and fear have been reconciled within a single ego-aspect. The challenge is a third alternative: the non-anxious presence.

Some years ago I came across a book by Thomas Crum called *The Magic of Conflict*.[117] In this book Crum introduces the principles of Aikido – a martial art, for resolving conflicted relationships *off the mat*. Essentially, Aikido teaches the practitioner how to use the aggression (anger) of another to defeat the aggressor. The aggressor's anger is directed in such a way that it actually defeats the aggressor. Aikido is a purely defensive art. It only comes into play when someone attacks you. I illustrate it to the client by miming with my fists. Two fists clashing is the normal expression of conflict. But when an opponent is defeated in this way s/he will often seek revenge, or a rematch, or a more opportune time to attack. In contrast, with Aikido, the practitioner moves out of the way when attacked, in a circular movement, which off-balances the aggressor; and then s/he accentuates the aggressor's off-balanced movement by adding to the direction of its force, which completely unbalances the aggressor leaving him or her floored and bruised. Once the principles of Aikido are learned, practitioners quickly grasp that the principles can be used against them if they become the aggressor; so it tends to mitigate their aggression as well. Any bookstore will offer a number of books on Aikido in the Martial Arts section. *The significance of Aikido principles, for me, is that the individual can use them to defeat anger without using anger*. Obviously, doing so with any consistency would amount to a paradigm shift in most of us. But the first step is knowing it is even possible. Crum and other Aikido masters teach us that it is. Clients can be encouraged to imagine this paradigm and seek Aikido solutions from Christ. Christ taught it 2000 years ago; and both Gandhi and Martin Luther King taught it to us this past century.[118]

At some point in the reconciliation of anger and fear I will introduce the ideas found in the practice of Aikido. But I do not expect the client to become a practitioner. Rather I ask that their reconciled ego-aspect become open to Christ's teaching by asking him to increase their emotional options. All this is illustrated in a later section that also addresses projections imposed by authority.

THE SURVIVAL RHYTHMS: PAIN AND PLEASURE

The pain/pleasure duality provides the Body its capacity to distinguish degrees of deviation from a homeostatic path that is best described as 'feeling good.' The duality is a measure of intensity. Alexander Lowen, a noted analyst, defines the pleasure closest to the homeostatic path as 'feeling good.'[119] According to Lowen, "Good feelings represent a state of ease and relaxation in the body manifested by quiet and harmonious movements. This is the basic pleasure state expressed in the remark 'I feel good.'[120] He goes on to define degrees of increase from the basic state of feeling good: pleasure proper, joy, and ecstasy.[121] As much as I would like to focus on the pleasure side of this duality, it is pain that is normally figural in therapy, both actual pain and the *memory* of physical and emotional pain.

For good reason, pain receptors are found throughout the body.[122] They serve as a primary negative feedback system for reporting injury. But much of our pain is chronic rather than acute; and chronic pain is most likely caused by a *failure to heal* from trauma. It is hypothesized that most of that pain is the result of emotionally traumatized selves exiled to sensation; or undischarged reflex energy trapped in the emotional or sensate fields. Unresolved pain can be the result of actual physical trauma or emotional experiences such as terror, shame, despair, abandonment, and overwhelming stimulation. What produces the iatrogenic effects of unhealed trauma is the characterological constriction of muscle groups, which point to a shielding against further pain; or the inordinate accumulation of negative unexpressed emotion.[123] When an ego-aspect is exiled to sensation, it remains in a traumatized state and that state will constrict muscle groups, sensory modalities symbolic of the exile's mental status.[124] Unhealed trauma can also manifest as a blocking fear of certain emotions or energies, e.g. fear of expressing anger or fear of expressing sexuality, which accumulate as a result of their blocked expression.

The entire body, excepting the brain, is permeated with pain receptors. The brain has no pain receptors of its own, but registers pain from everywhere else when impulses converge in the sensory cortex. Problems with the brain are registered as functional disruptions of the brain. In sharp contrast, the brain does have a pleasure center. When some animals are given unlimited access to this center they will stimulate it to the exclusion of much else including sleep, food, and sex.[125] Similar experiments on humans have produced equally profound, though short lived, results.[126] There is also pleasure that results from a cessation of pain. The lessoning of pain can actually cross over the homeostatic line into active pleasure. It is important to make clients aware of this; that is, to emphasize that the goal here is not just the alleviation of pain but the active experience of pleasure as well.

Ideally, the Ego is expected to evade dangerous situations and repeat experiences of pleasure. In fact, however, most primary ego-aspects seek *to avoid further pain* in an effort to protect the selves that have suffered unresolved trauma. The notable exception is an Ego-in-conflict, which will use the satisfaction of *physical desires* to modulate tensions created by those polarized selves. There are few 'hedonists' in the pantheon of ego-aspects found in most clients; few selves have sufficient power within the Mind to actually take the time to 'smell the roses.' Most selves are geared to *defer* gratification, most often, out of fear of painful repercussions should they actually seek gratification.

There is a genre of psychotherapy first introduced by Wilhelm Reich, which argues that Ego constrictions, i.e. character armor, restrict physical movement and thereby interfere with physical wellbeing.[127] Something similar is being argued here: healing traumatized ego-aspects and reconciling their protectors and managers reverses the painful effects experienced as sensation and Body somaticization. The reversal of trauma at the level of Mind has a concomitant, positive, effect on the Body. Traumatized selves can be healed if the Ego is willing to evoke a higher power that can release the traumatized self from its enthrallment. The basic intervention is a well of pure sensation created by Christ coupled with the use of his *Light* to absorb actual, and accumulated, unexpressed pain; further augmented by the idea that giving up remembered pain will eventually result in actual pleasure. Once an exiled self has been raised to consciousness, Christ is asked to actively work with it, including the offer of baptism. Concomitantly, Christ is asked to work with other selves fearful of this traumatized self. Of note, this process often becomes merely the first act. Other selves quickly emerge who are also sources of pain.

Of further note, undischarged energies following shock trauma can also be a dramatic source of pain. Work with such energies is similar to the protocol described here with the notable exception that often it is just the energy rather than a self that is brought to the surface by a well of sensation. In many cases it is difficult to distinguish the two at the outset of an intervention. The following case illustrates the protocol I have developed for working with 'pain.'

Kristen. In this case, I have no expectation of encountering a self that holds pain when the client goes inside at the beginning of the session. So I begin with a completely different intervention, which is set up to address a sense of hyper-vigilance experienced by a primary self called the 14 Year Old. Kristen was severely physically abused as an infant, taken from her birthparents and placed in the care of an aunt and uncle who were emotionally abusive. She challenged them when she was 14 years old, which resulted in her being forced to leave their care and live temporarily with her oldest sister. In this first session, Kristen goes inside to address a pervasive sense of hyper-vigilance, which she had felt since early adolescence. In this session Christ is asked to create a portal of sensation (as distinct from a well), which the 14 Year Old is asked to walk through. It is hypothesized that walking through this portal will separate Kristen from 'hyper-vigilance.' Basically, Christ is asked to create a portal that will filter sensation. Once the 14 Year Old steps through it she will be separated from extreme emotions created by the sensation of hyper-vigilance. The 14 Year Old has always valued being in 'full alert mode.' As Kristen notes, "I think I have lived my whole life there." For that reason it is stressed that the process is reversible, and that she can step back through at any time. I point out to Kristen that, once through, she is expected to address the emotions that necessitated the hyper-vigilance, but that the emotions will be manageable. Kristen reports a thought in response to what I am saying: "I will finally get to face the pain of losing my twin, that other part of me." I am not clear what she means by this, but with that thought Kristen steps through the portal. "Wow, I'm glowing, yellow, silver blue, all in the *Light*. Before I stepped through, I felt pursued by all of these energy forms, dark stuff. I had to let go of the 14 Year Old's hand; she had to step through on her own. She is within me. We are through. She has a *Light*. There are other parts of me with us. We sit in a circle. I don't want to identify the others. They do not want to show them selves to you. Their energy is gentle. One feels like a five year old who broke her arm. There are others much younger, the age when my father died. The 14 Year Old is quiet, not her usual self. She knows that she is protected, but does not know what to do. She feels almost empty. She is aware, she feels very vulnerable; she feels like she is in intensive care. She is searching, and she finds a faint pink Heart. She is feeling her heartbeat, she is feeling her body." This ends the first session. Since I have never used this particular intervention before, I am not sure what exactly as transpired even after the fact. The 14 Year Old is clearly a protector who has joined with or taken with her a number of younger selves when she steps through the portal. Stepping through the portal has apparently created a safe space for them all. My impression is that stepping through the portal has actually separated these selves from a lot of painful sensation. I deduce this from what occurs in the next session.

Kristen returns five days later and reports the following symptoms: "I feel sick, my 'sinuses' are acting up, my throat is sore, I feel like I am facing a black wall." All of these symptoms suggest blockage of her intuition, her third eye, and the power to give voice to what it tells her. Kristen is vaguely aware of this and speaks to it when I suggest it. She believes that, "Someone is blocking inner sight. What I can't get to was done early. No words. I was not wanted. It is *dark* and I don't need to know about it. 'It shuts down' and the 14 Year Old has to be hyper-vigilant." I have Kristen go inside and have Christ draw concentric circles which will help her separate from the 'darkness.' Before separation, she divides her *Light* in two and leaves a portion for Darkness. Once separated, she observes that Darkness has pushed the light to the very edge of the circle, as if to rid her self of it. I suggest that Christ create a dome of protection for Darkness. "She does not like any of your suggestions. She does not trust the *Light*. She does not want to be disturbed. She has kept my ass alive and functioning this long without help. A strong essence, a sense of not losing it, of holding myself together. She believes she holds me together. Otherwise, I'd be like everyone else in the family – drug addicts, alcoholics. She holds me separate from them."

It is at this point that I make a suggestion prompted by her reference to drugs and alcohol, which are often used to medicate emotional pain. I suggest that Christ needs to absorb the pain of whoever was abused by the parents. Kristen's response to this suggestion reveals the nature of Darkness: "That is her job, she holds in the pain. Later I used my anorexia, then later my obsession with exercise, and now I store it with eating and activity. I never stopped." I note that she absorbs the pain but is not its source. In reply Kristen observes that, "Darkness is afraid of being exposed, afraid of losing her purpose. She holds the pain of not having anyone who loves her, anyone who cares. She holds the void." The session ends here. We are over time, but frankly, I am also not sure how to proceed at this point. (I must confess this 'not knowing' is more common than I care to admit. It is counterbalanced by my implicit trust in Christ's ability to see us through – the client as well as myself. In Kristen's case she will find a 'solution' by evoking an archetypal feminine image. Other female clients have spontaneously used the same stratagem.)

Between sessions, Kristen has re-evoked the image of Indian Woman, an archetypal figure, which she has called upon in the past. "I brought up the old Indian Woman. Darkness felt safe with the Indian Woman.

Darkness gave the Indian Woman some of her *Light* and she mixed it with her own and made a cocoon of *Light* around them. Darkness also gave the Indian Woman a little of her pain so she could feel a little less of it." At this point I tell Kristen the hypothesis I have formulated in response to Darkness: pleasure is the opposite of pain; the goal is to integrate the two opposites; to incrementally reduce the pain and increase the pleasure. Kristen expresses the belief that there are multiple sources of pain. I suggest that Kristen ask the Indian Woman to use her *Light* to absorb the accumulated pain and help Kristen to identify the multiple sources of this pain, and then teach them to integrate pain with pleasure. I emphasize this by suggesting that integrating pain with pleasure could become a new purpose for Darkness, a new reason for being. Darkness gives the Indian Woman more of her *Light*. The Indian Woman uses this to create a cradle into which she places a portion of Darkness' pain. Darkness accepts the idea that it will only be a lessoning of pain in the beginning. The Indian Woman has handed Kristen a fluffy ball of *Light* to place in Darkness' circle. She gets the sense that, "Yes, Darkness can sit with this, tolerate it." Now Kristen complains of a sore throat. I ask if this is coming from Darkness or someone else? In response, Kristen hears the statement-question, "What does it matter." This new sense of self prompts me to suggest to Kristen that she have Christ create a well of sensation and place a dome over it to allow the sensation of the sore throat to emerge into relational consciousness. "The raw throat feels like chaos, a child being yelled at, she just wants it to stop, be safe, enjoy peace, but she is very scared." I suggest that she let Christ enter the dome and that the Indian Woman can join him there too if Kristen feels she can help. Kristen identifies the sore throat as a little child known to the Indian Woman. The session is near over. The Indian Woman agrees to stay with the sore-throated child in the dome.

At the next session, Kristen reports that after the last session she had terrible anxiety, and her wrists, jaw and chest hurt. (I cannot stress enough how important it is to 'follow the symptom,' whether it is terrible anxiety, a sore throat, or hyper-vigilance. The therapist needs to focus upon, or at least bear in mind, whatever the client reports as figural at the outset of each new session.) When Kristen goes inside the anxiety is identified as belonging to the 14 Year Old. Christ provides her with a dome of protection and a garment of protection. Then I ask Kristen to identify the source of the anxiety. She can trace it to an experience of the past week that reminded her of her aunt. "She was always out of control. If the 14 Year Old tells the truth again she will get hurt (the first time resulted in the aunt beating her and forcing her to leave home). Apparently, the 14 Year Old was traumatized by those events, which largely accounts for the resultant hyper-vigilance. Kristen goes on to describe subsequent experiences where she felt the 14 Year Old would have done most anything to avoid a repetition. The 14 Year Old is deathly afraid she will be betrayed by anyone she trusts. I ask what she trusted that got her betrayed? "Fun, love, sexual feelings" – all referring to infatuation with a boy at age 14, which precipitated the aunt's abusive, abandoning, behavior.

Kristen will return to these themes time and again in the following sessions till they are resolved by Christ helping to correct the 14 Year Old's belief system as well as helping Darkness give up her pain in favor of pleasurable alternatives. Unlike accumulated unexpressed anger, pain generally refers to deep emotional pain suffered at a young age that needs to be healed at several levels. What the above case illustrates are ways of approaching it, identifying the 'holders of pain' and the selves they are protecting. Generally, selves that hold pain see themselves as acting responsibly as do selves that hold anger and fear.

The primary concern of selves that protect from pain is the fear of being overwhelmed by pain, i.e. a resurgence of remembered trauma. Those selves need to be protected before asking Christ to provide a well of sensation, a dome, and a portion of his *Light* to *absorb accumulated unexpressed pain*. Then, the pain-holding self needs to be unburdened of its responsibility and eventually convinced to assume the new purpose of lessoning pain and seeking pleasure and thereby achieve a sense of wellbeing. Beyond that, Christ must be given the opportunity to begin working with the selves that actually experienced the trauma. In Kristen's case, those were the selves, like the five year old with the broken arm, who came through the portal of sensation, but did not want to be known to the therapist. I appreciate that all I have covered in this case could be overwhelmingly complex to an inexperienced therapist. But there is a rule for working with the complexity: the goal of treatment is always the abatement of pain. As long as the client continues to report painful symptoms, however much has been accomplished, the first order of business will be the discharge of that negativity from the emotional field and the reconciliation of the pertinent selves.

Repressive Somatization and Projection

Repressive somatization and projection are the two most common manifestations of Ego polarization encountered in psychotherapy. When a child's Ego is shamefully punished for activity at one pole it will fragment and the Ego will create other ego-aspects to span the poles. (This kind of fragmentation is less likely to occur in later development when the Ego can create a Dominant self.) The Ego's reaction to painful enthrallment is the creation of a second ego-aspect that expresses *fearfully*. The new ego-aspect supplants the aspect in the thrall of shame thereby sustaining the repression (i.e. loss of free will). In effect, repression is the combined result of parentified authority stripping an ego-aspect of its free will, and the Ego's subsequent creation of a new ego-aspect to replace it. Repression is relatively easy to sustain because the enthralled ego-aspect lacks the will to sustain itself in relational consciousness and a new ego-aspect is easily constellated by the Ego.

Repressive somatization is the iatrogenic effect of reducing an ego-aspect to pure sensation. A repressed self will eventually manifest as a bodily somatization: a physical problem. The alternative outcome is projection. In that case, the exiled self reenters relational consciousness by blending with a powerful image that is seemingly irrepressible, e.g. a parental image or comparable image. The 'projective solution' appears to reduce the repressed ego-aspect's somatic effects on the Body but increases relational turmoil exponentially.

I suspect the factor determining whether an ego-aspect is projected vs. somaticized is the power of the emotion most strongly associated with the disowned ego-aspect. Emotions such as despair, guilt, and shame that are less powerful than fear will be somaticized. Emotions such as desire and anger, that are stronger than fear, will be projected. This is merely a deduction based on the power of the emotions most likely associated with a disowned self; and while it may hold true generally, there will be notable exceptions.

In both repressive somatization and projection the disowned self is still experienced, but as something foreign and distinctly 'not me' from a conscious perspective. Shame appears to be the bifurcating force whether it is exercised by authority figures or a Dominant self using the power of self-shame. The shamed self no longer has the will to act, but it cannot be silenced. In the case of repressive somatization, it is experienced as some form of 'dis-ease' that captures the cumulative intensity and circumstance of the shaming; in the case of projection, it is experienced via the 'unacceptable' behaviors of another person, most often someone in a close, ongoing, relationship with the client such as a parent, spouse, lover, or child. (Prejudice is projection of 'the unacceptable' into a *group or class*, which the individual cannot envision joining because they are ethnically, religiously, or culturally different; and therefore a safe repository of 'the unacceptable.')

Projection and repressive somatization are deduced from the ability of the *Light and Christ* to *undo the process*. In the case of repressive somatization, the somaticized-self is most effectively returned to consciousness by having Christ create a well of sensation, as described in previous interventions. In the case of projection, since the self is hidden in the image of another, any number of separation interventions can be used such as a double circle, or drawing/lifting a disowned self out of the image in which it is embedded. The therapeutic 'art' is more in the preparation and wording than in the actual intervention. When a disowned self is allowed reemerge into relational consciousness, the client's sensation and the images of others are released from the burden and permitted to heal. The challenge is convincing fearful, angry, selves that it is in their best interest to allow that recovery.

The rest of this section is devoted to a further discussion and illustrations of repressive somatization. As I have already illustrated throughout this chapter, repressive somatization is a common occurrence, and often an excellent entrée to Ego dynamics. But projection is even more problematical, pervasive, and complex. I address it at length in the next section.

Repressive Somatization

Repression is the classic Ego defense defined by Freudian psychoanalysis. Historically, repression was based on a construct that treated Ego as a single entity coping with the contents of the unconscious. Ego defenses were seen as strategies available to the Ego for coping with the most painful emotions generated by conflicts between Id, Ego and Superego. The theoretical perspective offered in this work treats the Ego as archetypal and thereby capable of constellating numerous images of the self all imbued with free will. That is also the basic assumption of the theoretical models delineated by the Stones and R.C.Schwartz. The distinction between singularity and multiplicity is vital to understanding my definition of repressive somatization. Freud thought of repression as the Ego's primary defense against overwhelming anxiety, which could arise from a variety of sources, e.g. the environment, instincts, superego and the universal condition of birth, which Freud considered traumatic. The individual coped with these contents by 'repressing' associations likely to evoke them. Cofer and Apply capture the flavor of the Freudian construction in their 1966 work on motivation:

> *Repression and Defense.* It is clear that that against which the ego must defend itself is the outbreak of uncontrollable anxiety. If its integrity is threatened from the outside, the ego can either flee or attempt effective motor action to remove the danger. If it is threatened from the inside, however, the defenses of the ego must take another course. Here the primary weapon is exclusion from consciousness. We will remember that the ego controls both access to consciousness and access to action. When the instinctual impulse that would endanger the organism becomes strong, the ego attempts to isolate the instinctual energy by forming an anticathexis around it. That is, the ego "blocks" the energy of the instinct with an equal amount of energy so that it cannot force its way into consciousness. This mechanism is known as *repression*. A dangerous thought or idea is forced out of consciousness as a result of giving rise to the "alarm" signal of anxiety.[128]

As the above quote illustrates, the Ego is seen as singular and working alone. The concept of dissociation was not appreciated in 1966 because the Ego was always treated as singular in psychodynamic models. One body equaled one Ego, as if the Ego was made of the same flesh and blood as the body.[129] Also, the Ego is seen as coping primarily with anxiety (fear) and guilt, rather than shame. Of course, if one treats guilt as following on the heels of satisfying a shameful desire, then shame was never far removed. But for reasons that escape me, Freud avoided the use of shame as a primary construct, though it is clearly the antecedent of most fear and all guilt. When shame and dissociation are introduced into the equation, the idea of repression is still viable but in need of redefinition. First off, dissociation rather than repression becomes the primary defense until the Ego is mature enough to create ego-aspects with the power to self-shame. Until then, anxiety – the experience of *fearful* ego-aspects, remains the primary guardian against the unacceptable. In early development, it is dissociation that most effectively 'represses' an ego-aspect.

The consequences of forcibly shaming an ego-aspect can manifest in a variety of forms: *regression* (the temporary resurgence of activity by younger selves when an older self is temporarily overwhelmed with shame), *reaction formation* (the severing of specific sensory pathways as in the case of hysterical blindness), *depersonalization* (the global severing of ties with sensation while retaining a mental, imaginal, image of self), *projection* (the blending of disowned self-images with the images of irrepressible others) and finally *repressive somatization* (restricting an ego-aspect to sensation by stripping it of its will to act). In this work, repressive somatization is seen to be a consequence of either dissociation or the repressive action of a Dominant self. The disowned aspect or event is exiled from relational consciousness by being stripped of its free-will. Thereafter it can only be experienced via sensation. But bare in mind that sensation can express affectively as well as somatically.

The emotionally charged nature of a disowned ego-aspect, which necessitated its exile in the first place, will eventually produce a physical dis-ease and/or recurrent emotional state symbolic of the trauma. A disowned ego-aspect's chronic stimulation of the etheric body – if not addressed, will eventually result in some form of body dysfunction. The alternative to this exile into sensation is actual projection into another imaginal image closely connected to the client but not an actual self. In some ways this might seem preferable to the extent it alleviates pressure on the physical body; but projection is just as likely to place the Body in harm's way via prejudicial, violent, or otherwise dysfunctional relationships. Repressive somatization is amply demonstrated by the findings of psychosomatic medicine, stress disorders, and psychoneuroimmunology, but goes well beyond those in scope. Essentially, this construct hypothesizes that most, if not all, physical symptoms have a spiritual or psychological antecedent and sustaining cause.

Repressive somatization can manifest in two different ways. The disowned ego-aspect can make itself felt as an emotion. Often, clients come in with strong feelings such as guilt, fear, anger, unremitting sadness, or general angst without being able to identify a source or reason.[130] Alternatively, and just as frequently, it will manifest as one or more physical symptoms.[131] The symptoms are real, there is nothing imaginary about them. For my part, I have come to accept as a working hypothesis that all physical dis-ease, particularly of a chronic nature, is the result of the repressive somatization of disowned selves, or something to do with the Soul.[132] I have already illustrated this in a number of case examples, and will continue to do so throughout this work. Working with physical symptoms is one of the quickest ways to unearth disowned ego-aspects that are clearly problematic to the client. In any case, the client does not normally report physical symptoms unless they are a cause of ongoing concern, and the client is likely to be distracted while they are not addressed. Everything considered, focusing on physical symptoms will generally prove helpful on several levels and after twenty years of working with the *Light,* I am prepared to treat any physical symptom as psychosomatic.[133] I allow that all such symptoms have concomitant physical causes but believe there is generally an antecedent and contributory psychological or spiritual reason for the physical cause. For that reason I am always willing to seek the Mind's input whenever a client tells me they are experiencing a physical symptom.[134]

Over the years I have developed a number of interventions for accessing somaticized selves. By far the best intervention is the *well of sensation* described earlier in the chapter. It affords the greatest protections for the selves most likely to sabotage the process. But there are other ways. The following case illustrates another approach, which I used prior to developing the *well of sensation* intervention.

Lorna. I have seen Lorna periodically over the years for a variety of personal and relational problems. She is the oldest of four siblings and the mother of three grown boys. Her father, a physician, has abused alcohol most her life. She has been widowed for the past five years. She has had a long-term relationship with a married man who recently divorced and now wants to marry her. She is in her early 50's. For the past six months she has had menses bleeding every three or four days. An exhaustive medical exam found nothing to account for it, aside from fibroid tumors. Lorna has been using self-hypnosis to reduce the tumors. She is under the care of a highly reputable group of gynecologists who prescribe for post-menopausal women. Since Lorna was quite familiar with the *Light* and very comfortable calling on her Christ image, the intervention is straightforward. I have Lorna ask Christ about the bleeding. What she hears is that, "The bleeding is the way it is suppose to be. Her male friend is sucking her life away." Further questioning reveals that the paramour is possessive and very jealous of any activity that does not involve him. He is strongly identified with her father. I suggest she have Christ use his *Light* to draw two circles, one for her father/male suitor, and a second for the 'Bleeder.' Lorna is quite comfortable with the idea of personifying selves so it is not necessary in this case to go through a more elaborate process. She immediately visualizes the Bleeder. "She is bleeding all over, there are numerous holes poked into her. She is pale, listless." I ask if she can identify the nature of the wounds? "I imagine a little bitty girl, Dad saying that you can't cry, that it made him feel bad. The Bleeder is leaking femininity, sexual energy, and a vital energy." I suggest that she let Christ taste it and that she also taste it. "It is a sweet taste that seems to correspond to something like joy. According to these men the energy can only be expressed sexually." I suggest that she let Christ remove the authority from the men and transfer it to her, that she be given the authority to redefine herself until the image alters to her satisfaction. "The energy goes around Christ's Heart and back out to her. She is not bleeding, she is no longer pale and listless. There is no change in the men except they are no longer animated." I encourage her to pay close attention to the relationship between Christ and the Bleeder. "She approaches him as a free agent."

When I see Lorna three weeks later she reports that the bleeding has all but stopped. She has also been refusing to have sexual relations with her male friend until he becomes more sensitive to her needs. I have her go back inside and revisit with the Bleeder. "She is wearing a yellow dress, cool and clean. Not something you would wear if you were worried about bleeding." I have her ask the Bleeder about the spotting? "I am not thru having periods. It is normal." I have her ask if there is anything she needs from Lorna? "I need to go back to my regular exercise program." I ask if setting limits on your male friend has been helpful? "Yes. He was not listening to me." Is any part of her body still vulnerable to male authority? "No. She only answers to Christ's authority." I suggest that she let Christ regulate her menses, give it a 'moon rhythm,' noting that it is supposed to be a lunar cycle. "She agrees. It got messed up listening to those others."

I note the above case because dysmenorrhea is a common problem among women. Today, I would probably approach this using a well of sensation. I will not offer any other examples of repressive somatization since it has already been illlustrated in previous sections and further examples will be given in later chapters. Let me turn now to projection, which is the cause of so many dysfunctional relationships. Of note, the dysmenorrhea described above might have also been approached as a *projection imposed by authority* as defined below.

PROJECTION

I have already illustrated projection in some earlier examples. The section on *worry* is particularly noteworthy since it illustrates projection of self-images into a sibling and parent. Here I want to illustrate projections into a spouse/lover, children, and co-workers. The projection of a self-image into a child is likely the process by which the 'sins of the fathers are visited on the sons for three onto four generations.' Lastly, I will take up the topic of *projection imposed by authority*. Many selves exhibiting character issues that present from childhood onward can be attributed to *projections imposed by authority*.

Projection Into a spouse

Projection takes its name from the insertion of disowned behavioral characteristics into another person. Basically, it functions on the principle of like-attracts-like. In this and following sections, I give examples of projection into a spouse, a child, a co-worker and, lastly, the self. As the following cases illustrate projection is often the result of very strong emotions, such as hatefulness or sexual passion that are too ego-dystonic for the client to bear consciously. In most instances, the projections have a disowned ego-aspect as their source. But, as in the following case, sometimes it is helpful to focus on the emotional aspect rather than asserting that what is being projected is a disowned self.

Carmelita. The projection of a very strong emotion into another person is likely to evoke and equally strong emotion in the client, in this particular case a *fear* of other's anger. Carmelita's ex-husband is a paranoid schizophrenic. Because she has three children by him, their lives keep crossing. She is very afraid of him and at one level her fear is understandable. He does a lot of things that make him fearful to her and others. But I finally begin to suspect she had projected something into his image that makes him even worse in her mind. In the session described here, I develop a new intervention that helps us identify the part of her projected into him. First, she has Christ contain the image of her ex-husband. Then she has Christ *draw a circle behind her and Christ* (who stands beside her), while she continues facing the circle containing her ex-husband. Then, she asks Christ to use his *light* to create an arc over them connecting the two circles. Then I tell Carmelita, that when she turns around, she will see the part of herself *most attached* to her ex-husband. "I see me at 14-15 years old, before I knew my ex-husband. We are bonded by hate. I am full of hate the way he is full of hate." How, I ask, did she come to be so full of hate? "Her life is horrible, a situation she hates…toward her mother, her situation." Has she been hiding in your ex-husband? "Don't know." Does she also fear your mother? "No, she is willing to fight her. She does not fear anything." I am reminded of an incident Carmelita has shared in another session about chasing someone with a butcher knife when she was an adolescent. I ask if this part of her knows anything about the incident? "She remembers it but not why. She was full of rage, but did not want to hurt anyone." At this point I suggest that she give the adolescent a portion of her *Light*. Immediately, the adolescent sits down with the *Light* and starts crying. I suggest that she allow Christ to absorb the adolescent's unexpressed anger. This stimulates her to say: "I have this total unexpressed rage toward him, but I have been afraid of him as well. I would like to get into his face and tell him." At this point I am feeling a strong need to help the adolescent self work free of her rage. I suggest that she allow Christ to give her adolescent a mirror that would reflect back to her ex-husband the effect his anger has on others. I suggest that the adolescent stand in front of him so he will reap what he sows. In reply, Carmelita reports that, "I sense a darkness descending on him, a cape over him, dark and soft, I can't see him above the waist." I ask what the cape symbolizes? "Christ is saying that he is one of his dark souls. Christ is clearly sad about his situation." I ask if there is anything that the teenager can do to redeem him. "She can't redeem him, but she can have the willingness for Christ to *redeem him in her heart*, and also for Christ to forgive the teenager for her hate. Christ lays the teenager down flat and now he is scanning her. He takes out a bowling ball of hate from her chest, makes it gold colored and weightless so she can throw it away. Now she wants to sleep."

In the following weeks Carmelita reports feeling little fear of her ex-husband, but interestingly, she has little recall of this session. Instead, she becomes pre-occupied with low back pains (repressive somatization), which place her in continuing contact with the angry teen and issues that revolve around guilt about sex and depersonalization of the Body.

Most projections will be to a lover or spouse. Such projections simultaneously disrupt the relationship on a recurring basis while also providing a major reason for its endurance. It is paradoxical to say the least. In many instances, the relationship can only be ended if another 'vessel' is waiting in the wings to receive the unacceptable. It is hard for the therapist not to take sides in these situations since the client is generally seen as legitimately aggrieved. But taking sides most often leads to naught, because the 'victim' continues to need the partner until s/he can re-own and integrate the projection.

I do not advise addressing projections in the first several sessions, before the client has gained some familiarity with the multiplicity of selves and the idea of opposites. At the outset, only the most sophisticated of clients can grasp the idea of projecting disowned parts. Ideally, a discussion of projection with the client needs to precede any interventions. In such a discussion, I stress the idea that there is a part of us reacting very strongly to the partner, and whatever s/he is reacting too may also be a part of ourselves. The disowned part can be likened to our Shadow – a Jungian concept familiar to some clients. The projected part is described as a part of ourselves with the characteristics of our partner that we most dislike or that are most likely to lead to quarrels. For that reason, we do not want to accept it as a part of our selves but find we are repeatedly attracted to people with these characteristics. (The astute therapist will have already noted parallels between the current partner and other people in the client's history, especially parents or earlier intimate relationships. Once the client has some understanding of projection the therapist needs to shift their emphasis to protection and security. Any interventions regarding projection must involve the ego-aspect who has the most difficulty with the partner holding the projection. The therapist's stance is similar to the one taken with the Responsible primary. The ego-aspect who has the most problem with a partner's unacceptable characteristics must be addressed first. Only when that part is identified and fully protected will Christ be asked to extract the projected, disowned part. Because protection is so important it is emphasized in the next case example.

Lorna. This is a continuation of Lorna's case. Lorna has determined she needs to end her long time relationship with a man who is very possessive, jealous, and prone to episodic drinking during which he was likely to threaten her. She has followed some of my suggestions for ending the relationship, but when all is said and done she cannot bring herself to tell him it is over. She understands the idea of projection and is willing to pursue this avenue as an explanation for her reluctance to end the relationship. I note that she is feeling afraid of him, and ask her to imagine this fear of him. She immediately identifies it as feeling 'trapped and angry.' With those characteristics in mind, I have her go inside, draw a small circle around herself, and then have Christ draw a second circle containing the boyfriend. Then I have her ask Christ to draw a second larger circle around her to contain "whoever is most afraid of her boyfriend." She is then instructed to leave a portion of her *Light* in the larger circle and move toward Christ staying within her smaller circle. When she completely separates from the larger circle, she is instructed to turn around and visually engage whomever she sees in the larger circle. "It is me as a teenager. She equates my current boyfriend with my father and the man who will be her future father-in-law (at 17 she was dating her future husband). She is feeling rebellious, resentful, angry, and resistant. They (including the current boyfriend) have all been keeping her from growing. They have authority. They rule their kingdom and everything in it. She deals with them by withdrawing from them." I now suggest that she offer this teen a garment of protection. This will shield her from any fear of the boyfriend and whatever is being hidden within him. I stress that the teenager must be willing for Christ to extract any projection and that he will only proceed when she gives him a portion of her *Light* expressing explicit willingness. "She is willing." I offer two suggestions: Christ can create yet another circle behind them and use his *Light* to arc from the current boyfriend to that circle (like the intervention described above), or Christ can use his *Light* to draw a double circle around the boyfriend and separate the projected part in that way. As it turns out, neither suggestion works. Both are tried but the resulting circles remain empty. I have her ask Christ if the projected part is *in the teenager* as opposed to being in the males. "Yes." Lorna then asks Christ to arc it out of the teenager into the circle behind her. This time she senses strong emotion in the arced circle. "I can sense anger in the circle, but no visual. The teen feels more relaxed and freer. There is something in this about being the oldest child. I think it is masculine (I have just asked if it had a masculine or feminine presence). It is masculine and angry." I asked if it is *her* masculine? "Yes. It is angry at being ignored, not recognized. *I am not supposed to have it* (even though, as the oldest child, she would be the most strongly identified with her father and her grandfather)." I suggest to her that her difficulty is between her masculine and this teenager, who could not integrate the masculine into her sense of self, and has to project it into the significant men in her life, all of them like her father. I suggest an intervention that might begin a process of integration. If the teenager is willing, she can have her circle overlap with that of the masculine energy. Christ can enter the overlap and create an "equitable, safe, connection between the teenager, defining the feminine, and the masculine energy in the other circle. Her first image is that of a milkshake. "Once it is blended you can't take it apart." I tell her that the milkshake makes sense as a symbol, but to be viable she must eventually have a self-image capable of integrating the two. The session ends with her telling me that one of her screen names on the Internet has Zena (the warrior princess) as part of the name. In later sessions this process of integrating the masculine will evolve beyond mythical figures to a greater comfort with the masculine as an integral part of her self.

It was Jung's contention that in first phase of therapy the client is obliged to address Shadow issues, i.e. the disowned selves. If integration of the shadow aspects is successful, then later therapy was to address the contra-sexual aspects in ourselves: the Animus (masculine) in women, and the anima (feminine) in men. Insofar as the individual consciously rejects a contra-sexual aspect, it will be projected into images of others. This kind of projection can definitely complicate any understanding of projection. Animus and anima are treated as archetypal by Jungians. As such, any manifestation is not merely a disowned self, but a disowned archetypal energy. Anima and animus are 'godmakers' in the sense that they give great power to whatever image is constellated by the energy. (Anima is the Latin word for Soul while animus is the Latin word for Spirit.) In many cultures, gods and goddesses are identified as worthy vessels of this projection. Unfortunately, in Western

Culture there is a dearth, especially, of feminine vessels. As a consequence, human images such as parents and lovers often fall under the sway of these archetypal energies. Elsewhere, I have noted that Robert Johnson's works provide excellent expositions of this phenomenon.[135] Chapter VIII is devoted to a further exploration of masculine and feminine energies.

Most of the projections into intimate others appear to involve ego-aspects or energies that emerge in adolescence. Adolescence is the period during which the individual is expected to integrate masculine/feminine issues. Basically, they need to achieve an identity that allows for the comfortable integration of the masculine and feminine within themselves. This can be exceedingly difficult if the parents' marriage is fraught with difficulties, or the relationship with the opposite-sexed parent is contentious, or there is a distinct absence of one sex or the other in the household. These issues are taken up at length in the last chapter on Relational authority. Here, I only want to demonstrate the existence of projections that result from the failure to integrate contrasexual energies.

Projections Involving Children

Kristen. This example continues the case of Kristen. She has a grown daughter who she describes as single, intelligent, attractive, and bi-polar. The daughter lives in another city holding down a good job in her profession. She has recently broken up with her boyfriend. The mother claims her daughter is very needy, cannot tolerate living alone, and may be suicidal. I have already done some inner work with Kristen. We have identified a Responsible primary who she calls Athena, after the goddess Athena. It is a fitting name. Athena was born from the head of her father Zeus, a warrior-like, self-sufficient type. Kristen has been self-sufficient most of her life. She was removed from the home of her biological parents at age three, lived with an aunt who exploited her looks, defied the aunt at age fourteen and was forced to leave that home to live with an older friend of her older sister till she was eighteen. She has had a career that many would call both adventuresome and successful, and raised two children in the process. In this session, I suggest that Kristen may be projecting something into her daughter that is making it difficult for the daughter to live alone, and also contributing to the daughter's suicidal ideation. Kristen has a basic understanding of the concept of projection and is willing to examine her daughter for any projections. She goes inside and invites Athena (the Responsible primary), Christ, and Mary (Christ's mother) to join her. She has Christ draw a circle containing her daughter. I tell her that Christ will extract any projected selves provided she and Athena are willing. I have each of them give Christ a portion of their *Light* as an explicit expression of willingness. He uses a double circle to extract the projected part. "I see a light filled image of my daughter. She looks a lot like me at fourteen years old. I have always imagined myself as carrying a light." I ask why she has projected this fourteen year old with light into her daughter? "I always wanted her to know I was there for her." I ask how her daughter appears without the light and fourteen year old? "She seems meditative and quiet. She looks peaceful. She stands up, looks at me. She is OK. She seems to be saying that "now there is room inside of me." I suggest that perhaps Christ or Mary could take the place of this fourteen year old projection in the life of her daughter. "Athena says it has to be Mary as well as Christ. My daughter seems relieved that it will no longer be me." I suggest that Christ offer her daughter a portion of his *Light*, which she can place in her Heart, but he will remain separate from her. "I feel there are fireworks coming out of her head. This feels good to her." I now decide to focus on the fourteen year old extracted from the daughter and do this by asking Kristen to give her a portion of her own *Light*. "She wants me to give it to Mary and for Mary to give it to her. She accepts it from Mary." I ask Kristen if she can discover the meaning of the light emanating from the fourteen year old. "She feels terribly lost, no sense of belonging. Fourteen was the year I overdosed on pills." The session ends here.

Over the ensuing weeks Kristen's daughter becomes quite unlike herself: much less demanding of her mother, offering to actually help her mother, more stable in her relationships with others, particularly males, and making serious plans to move to a larger city where she has more opportunities in her chosen profession. Kristen, for her part, stays focused on the needs of her 14 Year Old.

Darla. Darla has been a single mother for much of her children's lives. Her unwed daughter and young grandson moved back into the home some months ago while Darla was recuperating from heart surgery, ostensibly to help her mother. She also has a teenage son still at home. Darla is a very responsible professional who came to me with heart problems clearly related to the stresses of her job and family, and further aggravated by smoking. Early on we worked with all of these issues. Increasingly, the focus of therapy has been on her daughter's seemingly irresponsible behavior. I strongly suspect that part of the daughter's problem is a projection from her mother. The mother owns that her daughter is a good mother and responsible *outside of the home*, but the height of irresponsibility and insensitivity in the home. "Nobody is safe from her emotional attacks. She hates her brother. She is not loyal to anybody if they make her mad. She is driving me crazy; she is driving her brother out of the home. She manipulates me, takes advantage of me. I have learned to give in or she keeps on till she gets her way." I sense a strong projection in all this, but before it can be addressed, Darla will need to separate from her Responsible primary. In the first session of this series, Darla is able to separate from the Responsible part and dialogue with it. In the next session, the Responsible primary is again separated and then opaqued for its safety while Christ identifies its opposite, which the Aware-ego can approach without judgment. Darla describes it as happy, younger, and carefree. I asked what allows it to be that way? "It is not worried, not guided by worry, actually she is worry free. She is not responsible for others, not even herself. Others will care for me. My mother would care for me, my sisters, friends, even my co-workers." I ask how such a self can live in the world? "She takes what others give her. She is a taker. She will crash and burn when not cared for anymore. She is peaceful and happy. She lives in the moment. But it is impossible to be worry free if you care for someone. You must remain fearful on their behalf." I ask what would happen if she – the Responsible primary, were less fearful on behalf of her children? "I have had to take their father's part as well as my own responsibilities. If he had acted responsibly I would have gotten a break from time to time. He gave no guidance, no loyalty, and no love. Sometimes I went overboard and spoiled them." Darla's own father was responsible early in her life but after recovering from a stroke he became a binge alcoholic. It is really unclear in the above descriptions of her ex-husband who she is talking about. When I comment on the similarities, Darla replies that, "My ex was totally irresponsible. My father was there in body, he woke up from time to time." All these remarks became particularly pertinent when we began to look closely at her daughter in the next session. Before I have Darla return to me, I have her refocus on the Responsible primary so she can be taught to create a garment of protection that will shield her from fear (i.e. worries). The Responsible primary is able to do this and there is a felt difference in her demeanor according to Darla, though she still retains a strong sense of responsibility.

In next session I tell Darla my hypothesis that she is projecting some part of herself into her daughter. The projection occurs because this part of her is totally unacceptable to the Responsible part. Darla cannot really accept this but is willing to at least go inside and let Christ work with the daughter's image. I emphasize that the Responsible part must be protected before Christ works to extract the projection. When Darla goes inside her first task is to separate from the Responsible part and let Christ opaque its circle, so it is not threatened by what we will do. I also remind Darla that previously the Responsible part learned to create a garment of protection and needs to be encouraged to reinforce that after separation. Next Christ is asked to contain an image of her daughter, which Darla proceeds to describe. "She looks like my daughter: stubborn, determined, lazy, outspoken. These qualities could be from her father or from me. Her father does not drink but he does smoke like her and me. These qualities seem to overpower her when she is around me. I want to run away. I want her to go away. She is irrational, disloyal, mean, and unrelenting." I suggest that she have Christ draw a second circle *behind them*, and separate all those characteristics from her daughter, arcing them out of her circle and into the circle behind them. "I see her happier, working, responsible and picking friends that are decent." I ask her what she sees in the other circle? "Hateful looks, mean, hollering." Does it remind her of anybody besides your daughter? "Of myself, my dad, my ex-husband. Myself taken to the nth degree." When did she learn that behavior? "In the 8th grade. I learned how to be sarcastic, cutting. She is the worst in me, me screaming, leaving, wanting to smoke. I feel trapped, I want to tear my hair out. I am not tolerant, not understanding it. She is always correcting me. Critical." Does she mirror you (referring to her daughter)? "No she hates me. She will take from me for as long as she can. If it were not for my grandson I would have kicked her to the curb. My mother is appalled at her behavior. She is just like her dad." We are nearing the end of the session. I suggest to her that she have Christ "quarantine" the image of her daughter that is like her, her father, and her ex-husband (the daughter's father). I suggest she have Christ enter the circle and work with the image between sessions extending whatever healing is possible. When Darla refocuses on me she remembers an event from years ago. She was in a store with her daughter and a woman complimented her on how in rapport she seemed to be with her young daughter. It is a brief moment of positive connection. Very quickly, however, the Responsible part reasserts herself and insists that all of her daughter's issues are Darla's fault. I agree, but also stress the idea that if we claim fault we can retain the power to change the situation in a positive direction. She can exercise that power by allowing Christ to intervene with her daughter's image, to enter the circle everyday and heal her.

In the above case both mother and daughter are oldest children. Each has been strongly identified with their respective fathers.[136] Darla's daughter has become a vessel, not only of the mother's disowned self, but of all the abhorrent characteristics she could not own in her own father and had projected into her ex-husband. Darla has split her father's image in two, assimilating the part that acted responsibly and exiling the irresponsible binge drinker first in her ex-husband and now in her daughter. In effect, as the oldest child most identified with her own father, Darla's daughter has been delegated to carry shadow aspects of her mother, the mother's deceased father, and the daughter's own father. It is no wonder she is a constant source of anger for her mother.

Many projections become 'over-determined' by serving as vessels for more than just a self of the client. But initially, most clients will identify the projection as a disowned ego-aspect. Later, it may come to light that the disowned aspect has characteristics of a parent with whom the client is also conflicted. It is easier to work with extractions that are clearly self-images. In the above case, Darla could not yet tolerate the idea that she was solely responsible for the projection, or that her disowned ego-aspect was sufficient to account the daughter's behavior. The ex-husband – the daughter's father, had also acted irresponsibly, and continued to be seen as equally 'responsible' for the daughter's problematic behavior. But so long as Darla remains willing for Christ to heal the over-determined effect on her daughter, I remain hopeful of positive change in their relationship.

In successive weeks the focus will shift to Darla's physical problems – particularly her high blood pressure, which she sees as the cause of her father's stroke. This leads to identifying several selves whose belief systems are altered by Christ. Concomitantly, Darla will report significant changes regarding her daughter: she decides to move out of the house and is seemingly more thoughtful of her mother, etc.

Projections In The Workplace

Murray Bowen,[137] a family therapy theoretician, was one of the first therapists to describe projection in the workplace. Edwin Friedman[138] – a far more readable exponent of Bowen's theory, illustrated Bowen's projective replication of family triangles in church and synagogue. It is a must read for ministers seeking to survive in their congregations. But it is psychoanalysts who have identified 'transference and counter-transference' as the most ubiquitous of all 'workplace' projections. Transference is the projection of parental characteristics onto the therapist; and counter transference describes the therapist's reciprocity if s/he is poorly trained. Transference is a nearly universal phenomenon; and this projection of parental authority is likely responsible for the perpetuation of patriarchy. All told, it is hard to escape this kind of projection in therapy or the world at large, whether as actor or recipient. But it is also possible to defuse it by extracting the projection and healing the selves perpetuating it. A case of projection in the workplace is offered below by way of illustration.

Darcy. In addition to illustrating projection in the workplace, Darcy's case further illustrates that the projection is not always a self, but instead an authority figure that remains problematical for one of the client's selves. This is also an example of projection imposed by authority discussed in the next section. Darcy reports difficulties with a supervisor at her workplace. She has a good relationship with her own supervisor who previously dated the problematic supervisor. Interestingly, some of work on this projection was actually done by Darcy before coming to the session. At work she had felt a strong need to cry, "An awful feeling in the chest which I did not feel I could release." She used her *Light* to contain the self that was feeling this and that prompted her to reflect on the source of her feelings about the female supervisor. "She picks on me, she seems jealous of my relationship with my supervisor, she reminds me of my mother." I suggest that she contain the female supervisor in a circle and have Christ separate whoever has been projected into that image. *She identifies her mother and several schoolteachers.* I now suggest that she have Christ draw a new circle and contain the part obliged to cope with these women. "It is a part of me that feels powerless. I see her at two ages, at 5-6 and 14-15. I now suggest that she let Christ terminate the authority these women exercise over this self. "He moves through all of them in the circle. They acted as if they owned me, that they could tell me what to feel and how to feel." I suggest that, if the fifteen year old is willing, she can ask Christ to raise her to adulthood. She is to express her willingness by giving Christ a portion of her *Light,* which he then blesses and places in her heart. "It feels like a healing fire. My mom broke my heart when she spanked me." We are well over the session so I am obliged to end here. In successive weeks we look more directly at the relationship with her mother and the dysfunctional selves created to cope with her.

Projection Imposed by Authority

In this section I come full circle. A basic premise of this work is that the authority exercised by parents' shapes many of the selves that control the daily activity of persons seeking therapy. But for most of this chapter I have focused on selves created to cope with duality and emotion, as if the input of parents was minimal compared to those demands. In truth, all three have a role to play and nowhere is this clearer than in the projections imposed by authority. In previous sections, I examined projection from the perspective of the person doing the projecting; and how withdrawing projections from children, spouses and co-workers positively alters both the recipient and the relationship. In this section, I want to begin examining how projection imposed by authority affects the recipient, how it shapes the selves controlling a recipient's behavior, including their own projections. Or stated another way, how the client's behavior is governed by projections imposed by a parent. I will not spend a lot of space addressing this since much of the next three chapters describe the effects in detail, but I do want to introduce the basic paradigm for removing the projections when encountered in therapy. These projections are a pervasive finding in therapy, capable of controlling the client in myriad ways, and exceedingly difficult to remove without access to a higher power.

Projection is not the only consequence of parent-child interactions, but it is a major player, particularly in terms of its power to inculcate character defects as well as strengths. Parents often use their authority to project character definitions onto a child, which the child unconsciously *accepts* as true. Often, the experience seems equally unconscious for both parties, child and parent alike. Even so, parental authority appears to have the power to project character definitions, which the child unquestioningly accepts. Most of these projections appear to occur before the child has the critical faculty to challenge them. The client believes the projection as if it were their own assessment of themselves confirmed by others in the family and community. These projections appear to 'solidify' or shape the self-image, to constellate it as an archetype is said to constellate an image. It is hard to appreciate how much so until the projection is removed.

Eileen. I have chosen a case example that illustrates the effects of *disowned* anger in its numerous guises: imposed, disowned, projected, and somaticized. Eileen's mother disowns anger toward her own father – an alcoholic who abandoned the family. Her disowned anger appears to be projected into her husband whose family legacy includes a well-known temper. The mother also insists that her children disown their anger. As the oldest child, Eileen is obliged to accept her father's legacy but disown it in face of the mother's ire. She also seems obliged to carry the anger that the mother denies toward the abandoning grandfather. Eileen married an alcoholic who entered recovery prior to their marriage, and has remained sober of alcohol, but becomes episodically addicted to smoking, prescription drugs, and motivational gurus; and is constantly and irritatingly critical of others. Over the years Eileen has been very tolerant of his behaviors. She is a stay-at-home mom devoted to her adolescent sons who are high achievers. The younger one is OCD, but after years of individual therapy may be better adjusted then the rest of his family. Eileen was trained as a nurse but has not worked since her wedding. Both husband and wife were seen previously in marital therapy. They both stopped coming after several months. During that period the husband went inside several times, but not Eileen.

The following series of sessions extends over several months. Eileen has reentered therapy after being placed on blood pressure medication. She is pretty well convinced it has a psychological component. I suggest she purchase the HeartMath feedback program and this proves helpful; after several weeks the calming effect of its practice helps her to be more aware of her own negative feelings, particularly toward her husband.[139] Eileen quickly learns to go inside and is taught to use a circle containing a well of pure sensation, which allows Christ to bring into consciousness the ego-aspect responsible for raising her blood pressure. It is identified as an angry self. This self is particularly angry with her husband and mother, but feels obliged to suppress this emotion in their presence. Eileen is very clear that she should not be angry in her mother's presence. Likewise, she is aware that any overt anger at her husband is likely to make him pouty and passive aggressive. As a child, her mother shamed her for being angry. The only spanking she ever remembers was her younger brother getting spanked for a display of anger. I suggest to Eileen that she go back inside, contain an image of her mother in one circle and an image of herself with her *suppressed anger* in a second circle. Then I have her ask Christ to place yet another circle around her image and extract from it whatever her mother has projected into her, *and she has accepted*. What she 'sees' is her mother's disowned anger toward the maternal grandfather (the client's MGF abandoned his family and died of alcohol abuse). Simultaneously, she sees the image of herself – now free of the projection, as floating, feet off the ground, elevated, free, liberated.

It is not clear at this point what is the source of the imposed projection. Remember that Eileen is the oldest child, the one most identified with her father. Given her father's family legacy of a fine temper, the projection could be from him as well. In fact, it could be a combination of family legacy and the mother's projection of her own disowned temper into her husband. Basically, Eileen is getting it from both sides. She has been asked to carry her mother's disowned anger toward Eileen's maternal grandfather as well as the temper inherent in the father's family legacy. (As an aside, the mother is not without her own displacements: she is an avid collector of guns and pit bulldogs.) Having separated the mother's projected, disowned, anger from Eileen, the next question is what to do with it. I ask what would happen if her mother had to withdraw all of her projections from her siblings and their father? Eileen's response is telling. "When I imagine that her image appears to be charged with electricity. It does not hurt her but it will arc to me if I come close, or to anyone who touches her." At this point, I suggest that Christ baptize that part of Eileen that has had to carry her mother's anger, so she can no longer be shamed into silence for expressing anger, since anger is instinctual not just a projection. I also suggest that she let Christ place a portion of his *Light* into her mother's circle where it can begin absorbing her unexpressed anger so it does not overwhelm Eileen when she is near it. Eileen allows both to happen and we quickly end the session.

In the next session Eileen reports that she has begun taking a different blood pressure medicine with fewer side effects; her blood pressure is lower and her Heart rate is "really well." Her husband is being nicer. She told him to stop correcting her grammar. Her blood pressure is more stable around him (she could previously feel it rising when he was around); he seems to be less of an irritant to her. Her mother called recently, expressing an interest in Eileen's family in more than a perfunctory way, which is very unusual for her. (These positive changes will continue in the following months.) Eileen reports that she is reading *Healing the Family Tree* by Kenneth McAll – at my suggestion. She feels there are a lot of deceased relatives in need of healing. (Over the coming weeks she attends several healing sessions at an Episcopal church to specifically ask for prayers for healing for her maternal grandfather.) Since her life is on the upswing and there are no physical complaints, I suggest we look more carefully at the *relationship between* her parents. I have her envision her mother and father in the same circle. She observes that Christ's absorption of her mother's anger appears to be working. Her mother seems puzzled by the effect but not unhappy with it. I ask her to pay close attention to how the parents appear together. "There is a distance between them, a sense of each repelling the other, but not strong. The center is yellow."

(Eileen sees auric colors around people.) I have her ask Christ to identify the reason for the repelling by raising another circle over their head, which extracts core beliefs about the relationship. (This is described in a later section that addresses belief.) "It is related to a power struggle and control. Mom needs control. When she was little she had no control. She was left alone a lot as a child. She can be hard to please. She does not like touch. Makes her fear out-of-control to be touched. Hard to give her a gift." I suggest that she allow Christ to inject an equally potent belief in the *pleasure* of touch into this relationship. I also suggest that Christ give her mother a garment of protection that will permanently shield her from the *fear* of touch. Finally, I have her lower down the circle containing the extracted beliefs and observe any changes. "My mother looks puzzled. Dad is closer, holding her hand. There is a blue color around them, calmer. My dad looks like dad, not puzzled." I ask what happens if Eileen enters their circle? "Much brighter, they are smiling, still holding hands in my presence." I ask if she can touch each of their shoulders? "Yes. Mother permits it. She got bigger, brighter, not as shrunken, not as fearful." I encourage Eileen to take each of their hands. "Each becomes the same size. The colors are not as bright. We are all just present together."

I don't see Eileen again for several weeks. She goes on an extended vacation with her husband and sons. She returns to report that it was difficult at times because of her husband's irritating need to control everyone or be angry. During the vacation she developed 'sinus problems' that resulted in her coughing a great deal, especially around her husband and his family, frequently requiring that she leave the room. I would remind the reader at this point, that the angry self has yet to be consciously owned and integrated with her fear of it. Though it has been baptize and released from the projections imposed by the mother, it remains domed. The dynamics have shifted, but the tension of polarization still remains. What is new are the coughing fits, which strongly identify her with her father and his temper. The coughing fits are a characteristic of her father, though I do not learn of this till later. He is a minister, who seems truly dedicated, forbearing, and generally even tempered despite his legacy. His 'coughing' fits are quite pronounced when they occur, and *effectively end whatever is being discussed*. In this session I focus on Eileen's coughing because this is what she presents. She goes inside and has Christ create a well of sensation to bring the Cougher to the surface so she can dialogue with it. "The coughing feels like a lack of control, like coughing in church." I ask if there is any part of her anxious about its coming to the surface. "Not particularly. There is a sense of uncertainty, inability to control the situation, especially when we are around my husband's family. His 'addictions' seem to kick into high gear then. I imagine bad things happening to him, that he might slip and start drinking again. He has started leaving little notes around for people to do things; it really irritates me because I am generally on top of things anyway." I ask if he attacks her 'perfectionism' by these notes? Can she identify the opposite of perfectionism? "Apathy, laziness, don't care." This leads her to reflect that she is unable to control her husband's addictive behaviors, but if she says anything (angry) it will just cause a scene. Then out of the blue she observes that, "My father would not want me to voice my anger. Anger is not perfect. My anger is not right. The hacking and swallowing of the gunk it produces seem to me like having to swallow my anger." We leave it at that for this session.

    Eileen's husband is constantly irritated by lack of performance in others; Eileen is not, but strives to do well in everything she undertakes. I suspect that, for many years, Eileen's disowned anger has been projected into her husband, who is constantly on somebody's case in the home, be it his wife, two adolescent sons, or the world at large. At this point in the process, Eileen can cede the very real possibility of projection (when I hypothesize it), and agrees to go inside and have Christ extract any projections from her husband's image. The projection is removed using an arc and opaqued dome. Christ first contains the husband in a circle looking angry. Next, he draws a domed circle *behind* Eileen. Finally, he uses his *Light* to draw the projected self out of the husband in an arc over her head and into the circle behind them. Before turning to face the extracted self in the opaqued dome behind her, I have Eileen examine her husband's image to assess any change as a result of extracting the projection. She observes that he seems *less* angry than before. I note that he would not have been a good container for her anger if he did not have some of his own. Now I have her turn toward the domed circle. Before she and Christ are asked to approach the opaqued dome, I have Eileen draw yet another circle close to where they are standing, and ask her *Light* to place in that circle *any self strongly reactive to the presence of the angry self*. "I hear acceptance, the fear of not being accepted, not being loved, not being good." I ask her to be more specific, to name a quality rather than what it is not. "It is the fear of rejection. When not fearful of rejection this self is pleasant." I have her extend a portion of the *Light* to Pleasant and teach her how to create a garment of protection. Pleasant is then given the option of also creating a dome for herself or staying with the Eileen and Christ as they proceed toward the opaqued dome. In sum, everything possible is done to protect Pleasant from her fear of the angry self. Eileen is now asked to move toward the angry self with the understanding that, as she and Christ get closer, the image and qualities will become clearer. She quickly begins describing what she sees. "She is just standing there red in the face, not at all pleasant. She seems self-righteous. She thinks she is right – righteous indignation. Definitely reminds me of my husband." I ask if this image scared her mother when younger? (Eileen has previously shared that her mother is intolerant of anger in any family member.) "Oh yes. I remember my little brother having a temper tantrum. She gave him a spanking; the only time I remember her hitting either of us. I remember her saying that 'it broke him of that tendency.' I also remember now that my dad coughs." (The coughing is a reference to a Somaticized-self we worked with in the previous session, which was finally identified as produced by having to swallow her anger.) She goes on to note that, "Expressing anger toward my husband only makes it worse. Then he will pout and become passive aggressive."

At this point I have Eileen return to me so we can discuss the dilemma posed by fear/anger; and I share some of the solutions offered by Aikido and Christ. I observe to Eileen that individuals need to have easy access to fear and anger since the two qualities can tell them when something is a threat, and respond quickly if it is a physical threat. The difficulty is that anger is rarely the best response to perceived *relational* threats. It is more likely to alienate, unnecessarily harm, or provoke retaliation, e.g. an equally angry retort or passive-aggression. I suggest that she allow Christ to baptize this angry self, and waken in her the insight "to direct the forces of anger constructively in her self and others." The Angry self permits this. Next, I have her contain images of her parents in a circle between the now baptized, discerning, Angry self and the previously identified 'Pleasant' self. Christ is asked to enter that circle and remove from the parents their authority to keep the two selves polarized. Eileen shares that the parents seem relieved.

Finally, Christ is asked to draw yet another circle between the two selves, which I call the Circle of Reconciliation. Eileen experiences the two selves merging into one within this circle: "Pleasant is satisfied because Angry is no longer violent. Angry seems relieved to be alive without having to fight so hard." Finally, I ask Eileen about old anger. I ask if she can identify where it is held. She points to her head. I suggest that she give Christ as many portions of her *Light* as he needs to absorb it while she imagines herself resting on a massage table. Since we are well over the session time I suggest that she continue doing this through the week.

The above case illustrates a number of the interventions already discussed in this chapter such as the *well of sensation* and *garment of protection*. Working with belief is discussed in the next section. Projection plays a crucial role in this case. It appears to be the raison d'être for Eileen's steady rise in blood pressure, which finally necessitated her being placed on medication and reentering therapy. The primary projection is a chronic anger disowned by Eileen's mother and projected into her daughter's image. This is what I mean by projection imposed by authority, in this case the mother's authority. The anger was suppressed by the mother's threat of fearsome retaliation if it was expressed, and the father's attempts to hold his own familial anger in check (and expecting the same of his daughter). Extracting the projection from Eileen becomes quite freeing for her and her mother. In this series of sessions, I also focus on the *relationship* between the mother and father, in the conviction that their relationship strongly influences the client's relationship with her husband. The role of such interventions is discussed more fully in the chapter on Relational authority. Lastly, we examined the projection of her inexpressible anger into her husband's image and the process for liberating both of them from the disowned angry self.

I would speculate that the blood pressure increase did not just happen. I worked with Eileen and her husband, individually and as a couple, during the previous year. The husband stopped therapy when we started working with an ego-aspect he was not willing to address at the time. Thereafter Eileen also stopped coming. I suspect that the tension of their unresolved issues contributed to pushing her blood pressure over the edge, which prompted her to reenter therapy. In the weeks following the sessions described above the husband also resumed therapy and began addressing the effects of a very willful ego-aspect.

The Projection of Family System Dynamics

Family systems theory trains the practitioner to attend to roles assigned by families and culture. 'Oldest' and 'youngest' come immediately to mind, as well as less common roles such as 'black sheep' and 'family hero.' Another role observed in single parent families is 'parent surrogate,' the expectation that a son or daughter replace a deceased or absent spouse or grandparent. All of these roles are essentially projections imposed on a family member by parental authority, generally reinforced by siblings, grandparents, aunts, uncles and the wider culture. This set of projections can be difficult to address, until the therapist challenges his or her own belief that such roles are essentially inalterable, particularly the roles of youngest and oldest. While familial roles are among the strongest reinforced within the family and culture they can nevertheless be treated as projections, which Christ can be asked to extract from a client's sense of identity. The role of 'youngest' can become particularly handicapping when the child becomes an adult, as illustrated in the following case example.

Marion. Marion belongs to a religious order that has allowed her to be a 'follower' all of her life. Her role as a youngest only becomes an issue when she is required to assume a leadership role outside of the institution in order to maintain her livelihood. She is very comfortable in the role of youngest and, were it not for this crisis, she would be hard pressed to relinquish it. She is mindful (with the help of numerous observations from me), that her preferred role as a youngest has prevented her from filling supervisory positions in the past, and kept her in unsatisfying, dependent, relationships with others. All told, she is not well served by the role of youngest, even as it gave her a false assurance of always being looked after. For several sessions Marion resists asking Christ to remove the projection. This is typical of her. Her response to most change is an initial, and sometimes prolonged, anger directed at Christ, herself, or myself. But in the past she has often, and successfully, enacted changes *between* sessions during one of her daily prayer-meditation periods, which she adheres to quite religiously. So when she returns after a particularly testy session reporting that she has given up her role as youngest, I assume she has followed through with the protocol. (The protocol in her case calls for Christ to separate the projection from an ego-aspect personifying her role as youngest, baptize the freed self, and invite it to seek Christ's discernment in lieu of being guided by her role.) However, as Marion goes on to talk about events surrounding her estrangement from a long-standing relationship, I began to have second thoughts. "I gave it up – my role as youngest, but now I am aware of having to choose my roles. I wanted it to go away but it is still an option for me. Little sister would do it one way; older sister would do it another way. I am aware of both now and chose to act as a big sister toward my friend. At least before I did not have to go back and forth about this stuff. Easier being the little sister. Now it is like having a split personality." As she goes on in this vein, I began to suspect that she had done "something," but not the intervention I gave her the previous week. And whatever she has done now leaves her betwixt and between, which is not at all typical when Christ removes a projection and begins to provide internal guidance. I ask her to describe exactly what transpired during her prayer session. "I threw the projection down at Christ's feet and left the circle, not in anger, more like independence. I was not going to be that way anymore." In effect she goes off on her own after *disowning* her sense of self as a youngest. "I don't know how to need people a little bit. I have not had a relationship with Christ. Now that I am desperate it seems hypocritical to seek one with him." I confess Marion can be exasperating at times. I bite my tongue for several minutes, till I can find the words to move the session forward. I say to her: "I think this will all go more *smoothly* if you go back into the circle, and ask Christ to send the projection back to your father, brother, and the universe. Instead of you leaving the circle, you need to ask Christ to remove it from the self in the circle." Marion reports a kind of paralysis in response to my suggestion. In her mind she is in the circle, but feels like she is "standing there desperate, asking for help, what youngest do (she has assumed the projection once again). If I grow up in that circle, I know that I will be calmer, but I don't have your faith." I suggest it is not a matter of faith, but of choice; that the only difference between her and me is that I choose to *live* in the circle without the projection, and then I pose the question: how many *minutes* of your 60 years have you consciously chosen to be in this circle with Christ free of the projection? We are well over the session time, so I bring her back and arrange to meet her the following week. Marion leaves with her projection intact.

Marion has made two significant observations, at least from my perspective. First, despite years of prayer, she has no real relationship with Christ. Her role as youngest appears to preclude it, since the role she so strongly cleaves to requires that the family be her primary authority and source of support. Second, she understands intellectually that giving up the role will allow her to be calmer, more centered. These insights appear to have a telling effect on her. In the next session she is observably different. During one of her daily prayer times she asked Christ to intervene in a different way. She finally realizes she can have a relationship with him and ask *his* help. He removes the projection and remands it to her father. He takes the 'youngest self,' to join a group of other selves that have been baptized during previous interventions. In my office Marion reflects that she can still be fearful, that she does not yet know how to be 'mature,' but she is willing to let be what will be. "Christ will help me to do what needs to be done. Now, when I get upset – angry, I stop myself and think about living with the Spirit as Christ did. I never ever thought of that before, a connection between Christ's' way of living and me." Marion then relates that she has visited a priest. This is significant since Marion has wanted nothing to do with priests for some years. Significantly, the priest supports her "independent" search for God apart from the church. In the following weeks another theme will emerge around the strong/weak duality. This is a significant duality because its resolution is often critical to the redemption of conscience.

The Psychoid Dimension

Raff and Vacatura [140] use the term 'psychoid' to identify the realm that borders the collective unconscious and merges with the world of Spirit. They suggest this dimension can affect the Mind in a non-local way, i.e. without *observable* behavioral precursors. That is to say, other people appear to change – often dramatically, when a projection is removed from their image, and when there is really no other explanation for the change in their behavior. Some aspect of projection appears to exercise a psychoid influence. Very often, in my work with clients, there is a significant effect on *the recipient* of the projection once the projection is removed. The recipient changes, generally for the better. The changes appear to take place even when the client has no ongoing contact with the recipient. For example, I recently worked with a client who was estranged from her son for some years. We extracted a disowned self from his image that she negatively identified with her father and ex-husband. Two weeks later the son called her 'out of the blue' to apologize for his estrangement and hopeful they could start with a clean slate. It is difficult to account for such changes in a rational way, despite their consistent occurrence. Whenever a projection is withdrawn and successfully worked with, the relationship between the client and recipient is frequently altered even though the recipient is in no way directly involved with the process. What makes the change noteworthy, aside from its predictability, is the quickness of it all. The change appears to occur without preamble or discussion between the principals, as if the withdrawal has affected a *psychic* connection between them. Ultimately, our understanding of the power of projection may require the admission of this psychoid dimension into the equation.

Summary

In therapy, projection takes two general forms. In the first instance, *the client is the recipient of projection from parents or significant others*; this is called projection imposed by authority. For example, a parent can unconsciously project his or her anima or animus into a child's image, which can often result in emotional, if not actual, incest. This in turn can result in the client projecting his or her own contrasexual aspect into persons of the opposite sex. A far more frequent projection from parents to children is the projection of family legacies, wherein the child is given the identity of a particular grandparent. A recent example comes to mind. The client was a very nice person, attractive to women, and in denial of his alcoholism. When drinking he often blacked out and became a mean drunk. In a joint session, his mother could own that he was very like his maternal grandmother, who never admitted to the grandfather's alcoholism, as well as being *like the grandfather*, who was a mean drunk and a womanizer. In this instance the son seems obliged to carry the legacies of both maternal grandparents. By way of compensation, his mother's efforts to care for him were endless. Lastly, almost every client will receive the imprint of the parents' masculine and feminine identities. This is the effect of Relational authority and the subject of Chapter VIII.

In the second kind of projection, *the client is projecting his or her own disowned parts into others*. In therapy, we are likely to encounter both kinds of projection in the same client. Any relationship that is described by the client as intensely conflictual likely involves some form of projection. The problem for the therapist is teasing it out without alienating the client. Never forget that there is some truth in the client's descriptions of the other. In cases of voluntary association, the other was likely selected for the characteristics that justify the projection, i.e. a paranoid schizophrenic husband is an ideal vessel for hate. In many cases, "project-ability" may be a primary reason for mate selection. This is a major reason why dysfunctional relationships so often endure, even in work relationships.

As a general rule, it is always advisable to identify the self most consciously affected by the projection; that is, the self that finds the idea of being 'like the projection' reprehensible or intolerable, but is seemingly unable to escape it in 'others.' That self – often a Responsible primary, must be protected and their cooperation elicited; otherwise, they will surely sabotage therapy. Christ must provide the Responsible primary with a garment of protection and only proceed to extract the disowned self from the other person when the Responsible Primary expresses an explicit willingness for him to do so. If the disowned self has little potential for successfully interacting in the world (from a conscious perspective), then it has a very high probability of being projected as its only means of expression. Ultimately, these two selves must be reconciled. In effect, the client must come to understand that neither is healthy when the other is excluded.

BELIEF'S EFFECT ON THE EMOTIONAL AURIC BODY

Up to now, I have focused on the ego-aspects generating emotional states such as fear, anger, worry, shame and the like. Now I want to introduce a 'new' level of intervention: the direct alteration of emotional states sustained by core beliefs. Once an image has been identified, it is possible to extract its *core beliefs*, as well as the *energy field* sustaining those beliefs, and the *emotional field* generated by those beliefs; and finally, to ask Christ to alter each. (The *energy field* of the mental auric body sustains belief, and the belief – in turn – is responsible for sustaining the image's emotional communication as experienced by Body, Soul, and other images.) Altering belief greatly facilitates the reconciliation of opposites. In changing beliefs, the goal is not to negate what an ego-aspect believes but to expand its belief so it can *experientially* range between both poles of a set of opposites, which gives the ego-aspect the power to grow beyond choices delimited by the original nature of its creation. To illustrate, imagine a self created to fear intimacy, perhaps as a result of another self shamed for seeking intimacy. The fearful self can only range between isolation and fear of intimacy, which effectively blocks the experience of intimacy. In effect, the ego-aspect is reduced to fully *experiencing* isolation and holding a *belief* regarding intimacy, which blocks its full experience of intimacy. The goal of treatment is to provide it with an experience of intimacy equal to its experience of isolation so it is freer to range between the two. Experience is a stronger motivator of behavior because it can normally trump limiting fearful beliefs to the contrary.

Quite often an ego-aspect lacks the experience that can challenge a self-defeating belief. Belief is very powerful in the absence of experience or a belief to the contrary.[141] In this section, I offer the therapist a specific method for exploring and altering an ego-aspect's belief system. The basic intervention is quite simple.

Christ is asked to place one or two circles around the ego-aspect. Christ is then asked to extract the ego-aspect's core belief by raising the circle(s) over the head of the ego-aspect. This part of the process does not need the ego-aspect's willingness since the process alters nothing; it only serves to provide reflection and differentiation. The first circle raised over the head of the ego-aspect *extracts* the core beliefs; the second circle, if used, extracts either 1) the energy sustaining a belief or 2) the emotional field being generated by the belief. If two circles are raised, they are immediately separated. The second circle containing either the sustaining energy or emotional field is adjunctive. It is not necessary but sometimes proves helpful. Often as not, I only ask that Christ be allowed to extract (raise up) the core belief. In the verbatim that follows this introduction, the two circle method is accidentally used in the two different ways, which allowed me to discover the difference between sustaining energy and emotional field. I 'mistakenly' used the phrase 'sustaining energy field' when I meant to say, 'emotional field' the first time I used this intervention with the client. A sustaining energy field can be thought of as causal in that it contributes to the resultant emotional field generated by the core belief of an ego-aspect. Sustaining energy is very likely the effect of exercising free will or providing the energy needed to 'voice' a belief. Frankly, I have not explored these interactions enough to say much more on the matter. Clearly, in the case described below there were significant differences in terms of what Christ does and how it affects the client.

The vertical extraction process for core beliefs is the only time I have used circles in this way. The 'raising up' appears to be symbolic of working on a higher plane, i.e. mental plane. Typically, clients do not perceive images within the raised circle but they can readily "read" the ego-aspect's core beliefs after the circle has been raised. The emotional field, when identified, is described as dynamic but without much form. That is also true of a sustaining energy field if that is identified. Identifying an ego-aspect's core beliefs is often the first time the client has reflected on what its values are. With any degree of reflection, these beliefs are usually found to be lacking, restricting, unmitigatingly negative, or otherwise limiting. At that point, the ego-aspect becomes more open to reason and logic, and willing to consider a wider range of choices. This "cognitive persuasion" is vital because, although Christ can extract the belief system without the ego-aspect's willing involvement, he cannot alter it without the ego-aspect's explicit willingness. The ego-aspect must express that willingness or no change will occur. Often, the ego-aspect despairs of making a change in the mistaken belief that change will mean its demise, or loss of usefulness and meaning. The ego-aspect can be reassured that quite the opposite will occur. In every case, Christ only intends a broadening of choices and a resulting power of discernment. In effect, the ego-aspect acquires a new belief system that allows it to approach as well as avoid each pole of a duality, and a discriminating power to chose the most appropriate course of action in each instance.

I would note here that this is not the only way to access an ego-aspect's belief system. It is possible to do so by having the client dialogue with the ego-aspect or having the client address questions to the *Light*. The most common question would be "What *motivates* the ego-aspect to do such and such?" If for example, a particular ego-aspect shows a lot of anger then it can be asked what makes it the *most* angry or *least* angry? The advantage of examining the belief system directly is that it allows for discovery without provoking the emotions, and even more valuable, it provides a ready context for altering the belief. Some clients will begin describing the core belief even before the circle is drawn or raised. Even so, it is always advisable to proceed with this intervention as described because Christ needs to work with the *extracted* core. Essentially, when asked to do so, Christ injects a new belief into the extracted belief core. Often as not, what he injects goes unseen except as a difference felt by the ego-aspect and client. The felt differences are generally immediate and also observable over several weeks. The following case illustrates the protocol for working with core beliefs, as will as the use of other interventions already described in this chapter, and reconciliation techniques described in the last section of this chapter.

Leigh. Leigh comes in expressing exhaustion attributed to her work. "I am freaked out – if I go inside I am likely to just fall asleep." This is a chronic problem for Leigh. She regularly pushes herself to exhaustion; and nothing we have worked on so far has made much of a difference. (Leigh has been treated, and heavily medicated, for a number of years by a psychiatrist, who has diagnosed her as suffering from a severe bi-polar disorder. It could be argued that, during the period of these sessions, she is coping with both the manic phase of her disorder and the medications used to control it. Equally, it could be argued that she is struggling to function in a demanding profession while severely handicapped by the effects of powerful psychotropics and a belief system and dynamics that drive her to exhaustion as well as mania. I opt for the power of belief, but in the final analysis it may be impossible to tease out the independent variables.) I suggest she go inside and have Christ put a circle around her that will include the 'exhausted' part of her, then two additional circles that will be used to extract its core beliefs and the energy sustaining them. (Note, the *first* circle only holds the Aware-ego and 'exhausted part' in place. The *second* and *third* circles extract the core beliefs and energy field. Also, in this instance no effort is made to first separate the Exhausted self from the Aware-self. Quite often, I will have the client first separate the Aware-ego from the problematic ego-aspect, but in this instance I choose to leave the Exhausted part co-existent with the Aware-ego.) When the circles are in place Christ is asked to lift the two circles containing the core belief and sustaining energy. Leigh shares her thoughts as this happens: "As the circles move up my legs it feels uncomfortable letting go of being exhausted. It feels like it is ripping the skin off my legs.[142] I'm getting something valuable from this part of me, but trying to do it all myself is exhausting. It is up above me now." (Leigh appears to be experiencing the Exhausted self – or the energy sustaining her – being separated from the Aware-ego.) I have her *look up* in her imagination and identify the beliefs. "I can't make it work [be successful] unless I work as hard as I can. *I must be exhausted to be successful.*" I have her ask Christ if that premise is true? "He says it is not true, that I work better when I don't work to a frazzle." I now suggest that she have Christ separate the energy that sustains the belief. "First it was a black smoky cloud with silver sparks in it. It looks dangerous, makes me think of a nervous breakdown. (For years Leigh has been deathly afraid of having a nervous breakdown.)" I ask Leigh to identify the part of her body obliged to hold that energy. "My hips, they have been bothering me; and my stomach has been bothering me." Next, I ask who taught her that this belief was gospel? "My father." Finally, I ask her what does Christ need to reframe her belief? After several minutes she comes up with a surprising answer. "I can do *his* work well here today," meaning I can do Christ's work as I do my work. I ask her to let Christ insert that thought into the dangerous energy field sustaining the core belief. "The circle has cleared. There is a feeling of timelessness, no rush, flowers blooming in their seasons." The session ends here.

Frankly, I am not sure what has prompted me to have Christ work with the energy field sustaining the core belief, rather than the belief per se, or even for that matter, what prompted me to ask Leigh to contain the energy field rather than the emotional field, which I would normally do. I attribute the choice to intuitive guidance. Clearly there was something in the energy field that was very negative and filled the client with fear of a nervous breakdown. It could be spiritual, but I don't have to accept or reject that conclusion in order to correct it. The suggestion that "I can do his work well here today" is synonymous with injecting Christ into that energy field. When that is done it clears immediately. But the core belief remains essentially unaltered, and while no longer compulsively driven it will remain a problem for Leigh till treated directly, as the next session indicates.

Leigh comes in reporting that her work performance the previous month was outstanding. She still feels exhausted by work, but less so. She has been daily repeating the thought, "I can do his work well here today." Aware that we have yet to address her core belief, I have her ask Christ what belief he could inject into her core that would alter the emotional field in a positive direction. (This suggestion shifts the focus from the energy that was feeding the belief to the emotional field generated by the belief.) Without my asking she immediately tells me about the emotional field being generated by the core belief: "I feel like a rabbit caught between two headlights, immobilized by fear. It keeps me up at night." I ask her to consider letting Christ inject himself into that belief system? After several minutes of inward reflection she replies: "A lot more comforting images. An image of him carrying me and saying to me, 'I never meant for you to live like this, to hate life like this, to not see beauty and joy.' I have an image of myself being held and sobbing. I see a spring coming out of my body, a springing back. I need beauty around me, pleasure in my life." I ask if she has let Christ inject himself into her belief system? "I get a clear message. A sunset and a sense that he will carry me if I let him." I take this to mean, he is asking to be let in, giving her a sense of the effect, but she has not yet committed to it. Again, I suggest that she let Christ inject himself directly into the belief system, adding that how he does that will be his business. After a moment she observes, "There is something in the center of the circle, like concentric circles on calm water, a sense of washing black clouds clean, a tide gently washing away, wearing away." The session ends here. Leigh has identified the green mass as 'greed,' but as an opposite of the Exhausted one she could also be the unredeemed self who 'receives simply by asking.'

In the above sessions, since the Exhausted self is not separated from Leigh, she can express the willingness necessary for Christ to intervene. Likewise, the *experience* I am seeking to foster is the idea of turning to Christ for help rather than feeling she has to go it alone. Note, that in both interventions in the first two sessions, Christ is asked to inject himself. Essentially, I am looking to Christ to alter the Exhausted self's core belief by injecting the possibilities for recovery when he is an integral part of her life. I note all of this because, ordinarily, I do not ask that Christ be injected into the core belief, but rather that he injects the experience of the opposite pole, though in one very real sense he is the opposite pole of many of her beliefs. Finally, I would note that in the coming months she becomes increasingly prayerful for his succor.

In the next session Leigh reports that she is continuing to read a book by Florence Shinn, and that her business during the month has become unbelievably successful.[143] But she also has a cold, which she experiences as congestion in her chest. I suggest we focus on that. She lets Christ create a well of sensation and dome to bring the "cold" to the surface of consciousness. (Here, we are treating for sensation rather than belief.) She sees nothing. I ask, "what is keeping this cold from becoming a conscious self?" She replies, "I am conflicted about my success. I am not comfortable with it. I don't deserve it." (Her evaluation is a classic example of someone who suffers from the Bread of shame.) I encourage her to allow the cold-congestion into the dome. I assure her that it will not be released until she is convinced that it is not dangerous. "Yes. That feels better, lighter." I suggest she extract the core belief held by whoever is in the dome. "I keep thinking about the investments, not sure I have made the right investments. I feel a lot of doubt." I suggest that what is in the dome is her reason for doubt. First she says it is unknown to her, but then she adds, "My greed is in the dome. Anything not earned by hard work is suspect. It is not a pretty picture. It is an olive green mass like snot." I have her ask Christ what he sees, adding, "You will know what he sees by your disbelief of what he says." "He shows me a shaft of light looking down on this mess, a hand up and out, escape from a dungeon, hope and escape." The session ends here.

Leigh returns saying she has finished reading Shinn and asks about books dealing with gifts of the spirit. She complains about her house. She seems unable to finish any project around the house. "The house projects seem insurmountable, I don't know where to start; I can't deal with one more thing on my plate." I introduce the idea of opposites, the idea that there might be a self that is antithetical to the Exhausted part and rebels at home.

In the next session I return to the theme of opposites. Leigh conjectures that "The house reflects the victim part of me, the part that can't manage all of life, a passive reactor." I suggest she go inside and use concentric circles to separate from this part of her, and once separated to use a second circle to identify the opposite of this victim part. Essentially, I have her imagine she is home confronted with all her unfinished work projects. This allows her to 'step into the tension' created by the two selves. I then suggest that she look back and forth between the circles and tell me what she sees. "I *hear* characteristics. There is one figure sitting on the ground, pounding the ground. It is real hard. She is exhausted, despairing, not having fun. Her opposite is proactive, energized, alive, enjoying life, ebullient, taking things in strides." Clearly, 'the victim' is the part of her that feels constantly exhausted by the work-to-you-drop mentality. I suggest that she have Christ place a third circle between the two, which he will use to identify the bifurcating force that has split these two apart. Christ does this but Leigh says she does not see anything. I suggest that she walk into the third circle to get a sense of it. "I sense a lack of deserving an easier life. I have to be a workaholic. It is a parental teaching. Christ says it is not what he wants from me. He takes pleasure in my creativity." At this juncture I suggest that, if she is willing, Christ can remove the negative force from this third circle and then both images could join her there. Specifically, she is to "Let Christ place a portion of his *Light* in the center of the circle and absorb all of the parental authority. "It worked. His *Light* got bigger. Both poles started flowing together, like two bales of straw, swirling together into one. I have been having a lot of negative thoughts about being alone in the season (Christmas), but they are not true; many people have reached out to me. The opposites are mixing like paint, same substance like ying and yang, a peaceful feeling. It is nice to get out of pain."

The common thread weaving through the above sessions, which makes this seemingly disjointed series coherent, is Leigh's *belief* that she must work to exhaustion to be successful. This manifests in a variety of ways: initially in the symptom of feeling exhausted, followed by fears of 'exhausting' success leading to a nervous breakdown, the distrust of any success not connected to exhausting work, and a common cold found to be generated by the conflict between work and Christ's abundance. As a rule of thumb, while I generally prepare myself to pick up wherever we left off in the previous session, I look to the client for where to enter the process. Thus, for example, when Leigh came in complaining of exhaustion that is where we started. When she later came in complaining about a cold, that is where we started. When she came in complaining about never getting home projects done, that is where we started. Regardless of where I think the client needs to focus, we go inside in response to the presenting complaint if there is one, or if there is no pressing symptom, then I will encourage the client to pick up where we left of the previous session or further explore a recurring theme such as exhaustion. The goal is always the resolution of symptoms and/or the reconciliation of selves. Extracting core beliefs is always fruitful, but as the above sessions demonstrate, other interventions are equally fruitful and often necessary. Leigh's therapy sessions are continued in the last chapter of this book. Those verbatims follow her for a period of months as she comes off all the medications she has been taking for years to 'control' her bi-polar disorder, and our work toward resolving her mania and depression.

Relational Beliefs

It is possible to extract the core belief *controlling a relationship*, be it between selves or the client and another person. While this intervention always begins with a specific relationship, the extraction process will often reveal a belief that generalizes to other significant relationships. This intervention is helpful when the client complains about a significant relationship for whatever reason, or even a seemingly insignificant relationship if the client has reacted strongly to it. Most often, the intervention is used to identify the core belief governing a relationship between self and other. To begin, the client is asked to draw two circles. One will contain an image of the person stimulating the client's strong reaction; the second will contain the ego-aspect that *reacts most strongly* to the significant other (most often an ego-aspect that is fearful or angry or carrying resentment). Then Christ is asked to draw a *third circle* around the two circles, which he uses to extract the ego-aspect's core belief regarding the relationship, the belief that controls or regulates the relationship. The most common result of this intervention is discernment of a duality wherein 'self and other' represent opposite poles. Often it is a duality bespeaking a need evidenced by the self. This is illustrated in the following case example.

Tory. Initially, the focus of this session is work between two selves, one self in a dome and a second self that is 'repulsed' by (ashamed of) whoever is in the dome. ('Repulsing' is a Dominant self with the power to self-shame.) I have noted to Tory that, at some point, she must forgo this power to self-shame and open to Christ's discernment in order for the two selves to be reconciled. In this session, I suggest that Repulsing also be placed in a dome so Tory can focus on the disowned self in the other dome and gain a better appreciation of who she is and what she represents. (My suggestion will greatly complicate the process. It mutes Repulsing but a Regressive dominant – a younger version of

Repulsing, immediately takes her place. That particular dynamic is described in Chapter VII. It allows Tory to move forward but complicates the picture.) Tory obligingly places a dome over Repulsing, but then reports: "I can see the one in the dome but there is no energy. I don't feel any connection to her *or the Light*. There is no energy anywhere." At this point, the reason for 'no energy' is unclear to both of us. Very likely, it is the experience of another self that has emerged to replace Repulsing. The new self seems unwilling to proceed, and may also be the reason for the drain on Tory's energy. I suggest to Tory that she allow Christ to help her separate from this new self. Christ does this and Tory tells me: "I think the energy is all caught up in anger. I feel really angry with nowhere to put it. She (the angry self) is feeling like she gets the short end of the stick and deeply resents it." Tory then proceeds to talk about her father and husband asking her for help all the time while being thoughtless of her needs. This is a recurring theme in both relationships, which has ebbed and flowed for as long as we have worked together. But while her father is clearly selfish and self-absorbed, her husband has become more attentive as a result of therapy. I ask Tory what it is they have that she needs? "It is not energy. It is something to do with control." I suggest that she place her father and husband in a circle next to the separated part that is simmering with resentment. Then I have her ask Christ to draw a third circle around both circles and use it to extract her core belief of what the men control and withhold from her (the relational belief intervention). "Without them, I would not be OK. If I cut off the relationship I will not be OK. I could not exist. They prop me up. I am unable to stand on my own two feet." I ask if Christ believes that? "No. The idea is probably repulsive to him." This sounds like Repulsing speaking, projecting into Christ her own attitude. But I say nothing about that for the moment. Instead, I wonder out loud what duality is being expressed by this dichotomy? I note that the angry self seems to feel dependent. "It is more negative than dependent. She seems helpless." Now we spend some time identifying the opposite pole represented by the men. She considers several possibilities but settles on the idea of completeness, which she prefers over other descriptors I suggest. Finally, I ask what Christ could inject into this core belief that would allow the angry part to range freely between helplessness and completeness? Tory has no idea. I suggest Christ. I tell her that, when she feels dependent on men outside of herself, if she had Christ she could feel complete." Someone balks at this thought, I suspect Repulsing. "I am not liking this. I do not want to believe any of this." I point out that the angry self is telling her otherwise. Her anger is saying that she feels helpless when not propped up by these men, and fearful of expressing her resentment for fear of losing their support. But I also note that this is Anger's choice since she is the one experiencing the lack of support. (In effect, this is not the belief of the Repulsing part who probably feels self sufficient, though I don't say this.) Then I add that Anger is the one that has to be willing for Christ to inject himself into the belief that controls all the principles, then lower the raised circle down so they can feel the effect. Anger agrees and it is all done almost instantly. By way of a response Tory shares, "There was very clearly this reminder that God created me perfect and whole. There is a real sense of that creation. That the creation is complete and perfect." The session ends here. But in the coming weeks Tory begins to challenge all the men in her life, for appropriate reasons, and in appropriate ways. (Tory's therapy is continued in later chapters.)

Relational tension always bespeaks a sense of lack that the client believes can only be satisfied by another self or another person. Sometimes the lack is perceived in the 'other' who needs the self to satisfy it. More often, the lack – as in Tory's case – is perceived as residing in the self. If what is lacking is perceived to be in another, then the situation bespeaks a self-other split, which is discussed in the next section. In that case, further exploration generally uncovers a disowned ego-aspect projected into the other. Whether self or other, the difficulty is the same: *lack and satisfaction* are split. In my clinical experience, injecting Christ into that dichotomy affords the greatest degree of self-correction. Basically, it is the same as letting Christ baptize an ego-aspect. The particular advantage of this approach is that it simultaneously liberates self and other. Thereafter, the relationship is likely to become much more relaxed, at least from the client's perspective. Finally, I would note that a crucial variable in this process is the identification of duality. Often, this naming requires some reflection on the part of the client necessitating more than one session. Likewise, the perception of lack in the other bespeaks a self-other projection that must be teased out. The following case illustrates the projective aspect of this intervention.

Lydia. Lydia's younger brother is a marginally functioning physician in another state. His marriage is in shambles; he is self-medicating, addicted, and suicidally depressed. Lydia has cause for concern but other than being a long-distance sounding board there is little she can do despite her overbearing sense of responsibility for his wellbeing. When they were growing up, the father (deceased) physically abused his son; the mother, though alive, was psychotically withdrawn most of their lives. Lydia also feels responsible for the mother, though more reasonably so as a result of therapy. Lydia is asked to go inside to specifically identify the belief controlling her relationship with her brother. Lydia asks her *Light* to draw two circles, one for her brother, and one for the self most concerned about him. Even before Christ can extract the belief, Lydia has named it: "I see me at age five and every year thereafter. If my brother is left to his own devices he will do something to cause himself harm, get beat up by my father. I have to protect him from harm. His wife is a reincarnation of my father. He is unable to protect himself. As a child I watched after him and engaged him in play so as not to draw our father's attention. I did not get mad. I was very forbearing. A lot of egg shells here. I was afraid of father or mother's reactions." I press her to have Christ extract the core belief, even though she has named it. I want her to create a circle into which Christ can inject a new belief at some future point. I ask if her brother shares her belief? "Yes. I stand between him and his estranged wife and my father." I ask what belief would she need to make her brother fearless and her relaxed? What does her brother need? "Self worth. I perceive him as believing he lacks self worth. *I have felt the same thing for myself, but less so.* Maybe there is some part of me in him, but I rail against that part in him and myself." This seems quite insightful on Lydia's part. At this point I suggest that she have Christ put a dome over her brother and extract her brother from the dome leaving only the part of her that has been projected into him. (What she extracts is not her brother, but a sense of herself that gives her brother a backbone.) "I see a skeleton dancing. This is the backbone I try to give to him. He has no backbone, no inner structure." Now she describes an image of her brother: "Christ is holding him up *outside* of the dome. (Note that Christ has removed the brother who lacks backbone from the dome, but not the sense of herself who she projected into the brother.) Christ is holding him up, functioning as his backbone." I ask if she would be willing for Christ to provide him a backbone? "The skeleton is not willing for Christ to function as a backbone. It does not want to become useless. The skeleton is a gift from God. She values what she is, she has worth." I reframe what she has said: "A part of you has the gift; another part lacks the gift." I ask if she would be willing for Christ to extend the gift to the part that lacks it. If her answer is yes, then the skeleton part must express her willingness by giving Christ a portion of her *Light*. "She is willing. She is glad to give up the responsibility. The one who is afraid of hurting people (in the dome) actually holds the power. She needs a good dose of self-love. Christ is giving it but not in an overwhelming way. It is like a warm feeling. I have kept my brother from killing himself. I am glad there is someone else to take the responsibility." From my perspective this is far from resolved but we are well over the session so I must end it here. The part that has the gift still has no need of Christ so there is still no common ground for reconciliation. The other part will acquire a backbone but remains unseen. All this must be explored in later sessions. However, in the intervening weeks the brother's situation does improve considerably and Lydia becomes more focused on herself and her mother. She also comes down with 'mononucleosis,' which precludes her coming in for some weeks to address the unresolved issues; but also further frees her from caring for her mother and brother.

Identifying and altering core beliefs rarely occurs in isolation. It generally leads to the discovery of projections that must also be addressed, just as projections can lead to the need for altering core beliefs. As the above cases illustrate, having Christ raise a circle above the ego-aspect or relationship can easily access belief. Once a belief is identified Christ can be asked to inject a new belief that expands on the old, which allows the ego-aspect a fuller range of motion between a pair of opposites. Often, the greatest amount of time in session is devoted to actually identifying the opposites in question.

Identifying and Resolving Self-Other Opposites

A second kind of intervention regarding belief addresses the issue of self-other opposites. This is the condition wherein the individual experiences one pole of a set of opposites as existing permanently *outside the self*. The exclusion is most often generated by a parent who identifies one pole as an appropriate felt experience for an ego-aspect, and the opposite pole as belonging to others, or retained exclusively as the parent's prerogative. For example, a parent can judge a female child as unworthy of being heard and valued (not an uncommon experience for women in misogynistic patriarchies). Simultaneously, the parent judges male siblings, or others outside the family, as worth hearing and being valued, thereby anchoring the duality's other pole beyond the girl's reach. In effect, being heard and valued is attributed solely to males, never to a female. In such cases, 'being heard and valued' is more than disowned. It remains essentially undeveloped within the self, *and only possible in others*. Alternatively, parents can retain the quality within their own person. In that case, only the parent is to be heard and valued. This splitting can be observed to occur for a large number of opposites, e.g. respected vs. denigrated, dominant vs. submissive, achiever vs. loser, rich vs. poor, etc. Self-other opposites can be likened to projections since the denied aspect is always attributed to another. Wherever split-other opposites occur, they are likely to create a third ego-aspect that is rebellious, defiant, stubborn, *or* inordinately complaint, seeking to please or appease. An example of this is given further on.

The real problem for clients with split-other opposite projections is the inability to achieve any sense of balance. The valued other pole is always seen as outside the self, either retained by the parent or located in another person. With disowned ego-aspects the disowned pole can be experienced somatically or even experienced within the self under the influence of mind-altering drugs or alcohol. But in the case of split-other opposites, the positively connoted pole remains beyond the reach of the ego-aspect embodying the opposite pole. This state of affairs can be a life-long problem. But once it is identified it can be readily corrected by allowing Christ to inject a balancing belief into the belief core of the ego-aspect forced to function at the opposite pole. The following two case studies illustrate this intervention.

Michael. Michael is a divorced male in his late 30's, personable, thoughtful of others, striving to do well in several entrepreneurial businesses. He is the youngest of four children. He has a brother who is the oldest of four, and two older sisters. His father died when he was a juvenile. He has always felt within the family that neither his brother nor mother give him a serious 'hearing' (the typical plight of many youngest children). The night before our session he was restless and anxious, in anticipation of a business meeting that would follow our session. "Last night I felt a real loss of confidence, a feeding frenzy of anxiety." Michael is comfortable going inside. I suggest he have Christ draw a capturing circle, which he will walk through holding his own *Light*. When he gets to the center he will be asked to divide his *Light* in two and leave a portion for whoever is feeling so anxious. He will separate from this part when he leaves the circle and be able to identify it when he joins Christ and turns around facing the circle he has just left. The separation process seems to work well. "I see me in my mid 20's. Nobody believed in me or listened to me. No respect." What history, I asked, created this self? "The history within the family, especially, my mother and brother." Did your brother take your father's place? "Yes." What do you need from your mother and brother? "Their *acceptance*. They hold the power of acceptance. I hold a lot of fear regarding other people. Fear of being rejected by them, not being heard or believed." I suggest that Michael ask Christ to place a second circle around the unaccepted self so Christ can extract its core belief by raising it above everyone's head. Next, I have him ask Christ to inject into that core belief a counterbalancing belief in acceptance. "The circle has become energized. Initially, it was mattered, a dark color, slothful." After the self in the circle expresses willingness, I suggest that Michael allow Christ to lower the circle re-impregnating the fearful, unaccepted, self. "I am getting more of a mirror image of me standing next to Christ. The process seems to have shot me forward to where I am today. What hits me is that in the time we have worked together, I have grown in a lot of areas, but the business part of me has lagged. Today, that seems to have changed."

Michael was the first client for whom I sought to alter a split-other opposite. As we explored the unaccepted ego-aspect's history I suddenly realized that he was permanently stuck in that position without hope of balance because the mother looked only to another sibling – specifically the oldest brother, for advice. Despite the fact that Michael had been very solicitous of his mother's welfare and concerns, he continued to feel unheard and unvalued by both the brother and mother. (Over time the mother came to rely more and more on Michael.)

Since this first use of the intervention, I have added one additional component. The addition addresses the parent and others whose authority defines a positive pole as beyond the reach of the client. In effect, the parent retains the authority to define the 'other.' For that reason, before altering the core belief, Christ is asked to contain the parent(s) and anyone who symbolizes embodiment of the positive pole. Then Christ is asked to remove that authority from all of them so that it implicitly rests with him. Finally, he is asked to inject the new balancing belief into the ego-aspect's core belief. The second case illustrates all of these steps.

Monica. Monica is married to a man who is aggressively successful in his work. She is a woman of independent means who involves herself in a number of volunteer causes. She has a rebel streak, which she has always valued. She sees it as giving her energy and having been instrumental in getting her to move away from her family of origin who gave her status but were also constricting. The inner work has helped her to objectify her Rebel. In this session we focus first on her sense of self that the mother identified as 'defeated' based on her slumped posture. This 'sense of defeat' has stayed with Monica all of her life, although the Rebel appears to have mitigated the posture. I ask Monica what is the opposite of defeat? She is quick to answer, "Victory." But to her way of thinking victory is elusive. "People outside yourself define it. My mother saw it in other girls that were my friends, but not in me." Monica names one friend in particular. In response to further questioning, she confirms that her husband also personifies victory in his career. Interestingly, at this point Monica shares a dream that seems to confirm all that we are discussing, as if the dream anticipated her dilemma. As we examine the dream she becomes acutely aware that her Rebel is in large measure a rebellion against her sense of defeat. It can never actually achieve victory but it can repeatedly defy her felt sense of defeat. It is at this point that I suggest we set up an intervention. I review the steps for her in some detail. First, she will ask Christ to contain her mother and her power to define victory and defeat. Christ will include in that same circle images of others, which have symbolized victory in the eyes of the mother and/or Monica. This will include the girlfriend who was seen as most popular with boys, and her husband. Christ will then be asked to enter that circle and absorb her mother's authority and the authority embedded in girlfriend and husband. Next, Christ is asked to contain all manifestations of her sense of defeat as defined by the mother. Then he is asked to use a second circle to extract the core belief of this sense of defeat from whatever self personifies it. Finally, Christ is asked to inject a balancing sense of victory into the core belief and reintegrate the ego-aspect with this new balance. I now have Monica actually go inside and I walk her through the intervention process. When the core belief is extracted it appears to Monica as yellow, symbolic of fear, and the complement of purple, which she envisions Christ injecting into the extracted circle as symbolic of victory. She envisions the integration process as a swirling circle of Tao. This integration brings to mind an imagined memory of roller-skating vs. an actual memory of hiding behind bushes to avoid going into a roller rink when she learns that her parents have dropped her off at the wrong time. She also remembers a time when, as a flower girl in a wedding, she was a center of positive attention that left her feeling 'victorious.' She senses that it will take time to absorb the sense of victory as opposed to defeat, but senses it will happen. I ask her if she can name a good emotion for bridging these opposites. She immediately identifies, "Patience." I ask her if she can imagine the desired outcome of being guided by both poles of this duality. "I sense it is a freedom to be. I will be free to cease trying to always rebel. I don't have to fight anymore."

The session ends here.

THE CIRCLE OF RECONCILIATION

This intervention was introduced in the previous chapter in the section on bifurcating force, but I have waited to "name" the circle in the context of my discussion on opposites. It takes its name from the intent of the circle, and that is exactly how I describe it to clients. The repetitive association of an affective emotion with a particular pole produces polarization. That polarization limits an ego-aspect's movement within the range defined by the opposite poles. Shame is the primary emotion binding an ego-aspect or event to a particular pole. This restriction, in turn, necessitates the creation of other selves sufficient to span the range of duality. In theory, the circle can be used to reconcile any grouping of polarized selves. (The qualification is 'theoretical' because I cannot even imagine applying it to all opposites, and there may well be classes of opposites that are unaffected by this intervention.) In addition to reconciling selves, the circle can also be used to reconcile functions such as thinking and feeling, as I have already illustrated.

Basically, the circle of reconciliation is a circle of *light* created by Christ for the reintegration of polarized selves and other ego-aspects created as a consequence of their polarization. It tests the proposition that *all polarized selves can be merged because one ego-aspect is sufficient to span a duality; that the process of Ego fragmentation is reversible*. In practice, most circles of reconciliation are used to merge two ego-aspects at a time. In more complex situations three or more polarized selves can be merged. For example, the resolution of Moral authority issues generally requires the reconciliation of at least three ego-aspects. Merging does not always occur when this intervention is first used. 'Failure' is presumed to indicate that other selves within the duality – as yet unidentified, object to the merging; or that the parental bifurcating authority has yet to be terminated by Christ. In other words, instances of 'failure to merge' are not seen as an invalidation of the process. Rather, it serves to point out the necessary next step in the process, which is identification of objectors, and their healing.

The circle of reconciliation represents a major goal of psychotherapy. The final goal of any series of interventions is the merging of polarized ego-aspects identified and healed by use of the *Light* and a higher power. Stated another way, polarizations created by parental authority and/or trauma are said to be resolved when the polarized ego-aspects are free to merge, and do so successfully via a circle of reconciliation. While clients often report improvement prior to reconciliation, it is still seen as a necessary final step in the process.

In my early exploration of the circle of reconciliation I did not expect the client's selves to actually merge. It surprised me the first time they did. In retrospect, all the theoretical underpinnings of this chapter point to merger. The Ego begins as a unity. Fragmentation – the creation of ego-aspects – is a consequence of parental authority and/or trauma. Once the wounds have been healed, and the authority removed, the Ego is best served by the reconciliation of its parts; and the centripetal forces of homeostasis would seem to dictate it. But reconciliation is unlikely to occur in a significant way where only the Ego – even an Aware-ego as defined by the Stones – is the sole source of options. The reason for this is that many ego-aspects must be healed in significant ways before they are willing to merge with their polarized opposites, and most of those interventions require a higher power. This is especially true of prideful selves. If they are unwilling to forgo their power to self-shame, there is no chance of reconciling them with any other selves, even selves healed of shame. Prideful selves will only forgo their power if there is a higher power with more to offer them.

In reconciliation the first step is to have Christ contain the bifurcating parental authority between circles containing the polarized selves. Christ is then asked to enter the circle containing the parent(s), or surrogates, and terminate the authority constellated in the parents and/or surrogates. I generally suggest that Christ terminate the authority by placing a portion of his *Light* into the heart of the parent. Sometimes, the intervention 'absorbs' both the authority and the parental images channeling it, but most often the parents are merely observed to become more relaxed and/or diminished in size. The second step involves Christ drawing the circle of reconciliation to be used for merging the polarized selves. This is only done when the selves have been healed of whatever emotions have polarized them, e.g. pride, anger, desire, fear, guilt, shame, and their variants. The nature of the merging 'ritual' can vary. The therapist's conviction that Christ can reintegrate fragmented selves into one functional unit seems crucial. In my early explorations I was doubtful, so I set up interventions that allowed reconnection, but not merger. Fortunately, a few clients had greater faith in the process, and they showed me that merger was possible. In fairness to my doubt, merger is often not possible initially. More frequently than not, there are ego-aspects who were to cope with the polarized duality, who strongly object until their concerns are also addressed.

In no sense is merging a reinstatement of what was. The merging creates a new ego-aspect with the memory – but not the emotional restraints – of the polarized selves created to cope with the polarized duality. The new self still experiences all emotions but is no longer susceptible to polarization by emotions such as shame. Shame can still be experienced affectively but will no longer bind the pertinent ego-aspects to that emotional state, provided the disowned self has been baptized as part of it's healing.

I have used a variety of 'rituals' for merging polarized selves following Christ's depotentiation of parental authority. In one, Christ is asked to draw a circle, which includes him and the two or more selves. Each self is asked to give him a portion of the *Light,* which he mixes with a portion of his own *Light* and places in the center of the circle. Each self is then asked to merge with the others by stepping into the *Light*. A variant of this is to have Christ draw a circle between two or more selves. Each ego-aspect expresses their willingness for reconciliation by giving Christ a portion of the *Light,* which Christ mixes with his own *Light* and places in the circle between them. At that point, the Aware-ego is asked to enter this circle of reconciliation. The polarized selves are then asked to join him. Over the years I have employed variations of these two basic approaches as circumstances and intuition dictated. What all share in common is one or more circles created by Christ, or another higher power, for the explicit purpose of reconciling opposing selves. On occasion, I have even encouraged clients to do this between sessions after laying out the conditions that seem requisite. In every case, the first requirement is removing the parental bifurcating authority.

Christ's response to the process of

reconciling opposites is somewhat unique. In most of the interactions described in this work, Christ's interactions are not particularly notable in terms of his own emotions. But very often, in this particular intervention the client notes that Christ is emotionally active, he implores, and he appreciates, he offers pictures of what resolution will be like, and he is grateful for the willingness to agree to the reconciliation, especially from primary selves. I have not encountered any disowned opposites that are unwilling to be reconciled. Any reticence generally comes from the primary selves. Christ appears to acknowledge the need for their willingness by appreciation. Essentially, he acknowledges that the primary self must be willing for the process to proceed, that it is not automatic, and that it may constitute some sense of sacrifice *before* resolution is experienced. This is especially true in the case of Moral authority where the Dominant self must forgo the power to self-shame. I have already given several examples of reconciliation in this chapter; other examples will be given throughout the remainder of the book.

CHAPTER V ENDNOTES

1   Scarfalloto, Rodolfo (1997), *The Alchemy of Opposites,* New Falcon Publications: Tempe, AZ.

2   From Socrates to Sartre, philosophers have felt the need to define theories of emotion, to account for its ubiquitous presence in human consciousness and its capacity to dictate the behavior of human beings.

3   See Damasio, A.R. (2000), *The Feeling of What Happens: Body and Emotion in the Making of Consciousness*, Harvest Books.

4   See Pert, C.B. (1999), *Molecules of Emotion: The Science Behind Mind-Body Medicine,* Simon & Schuster: New York.

5   See Hillman, J. (1960, 1992), *Emotion: A Comprehensive Phenomenology of Theories and Their Meanings for Therapy*, Northwestern University Press: Evanston, Ill.

6   Greenberg, L.S. & Paivio, S. C. (1997), *Working with Emotions in Psychotherapy,* Guilford Press: New York.

7   Goleman, D. (1995), *Emotional Intelligence: Why It Can Matter More Than IQ*, Bantam Books: New York.

8   Even the Penguin Dictionary of Psychology finds the task formidable: "Historically this term has proven utterly refractory to definitional efforts; probably

no other term in psychology shares its combination of nondefinability and frequency of use. Most textbook authors wisely employ it as the title of a chapter and let the material presented substitute for a concise definition. The term itself derives from the Latin *emovere,* which translates as *to move, to excite, to stir up or to agitate.* Contemporary usage is of two general kinds: 1. An umbrella term for any of a number of subjectively experienced, affect-laden states, the ontological status of each being established by a label the meaning of which is arrived at by simple consensus. This is the primary use of the term in both the technical and the common language. It is what we mean when we say that *love, fear, hate, terror, etc.* are emotions. 2. A label for a field of scientific investigation that explores the various environmental, physiological and cognitive factors that underlie these subjective experiences. See Reber, S. R. & Reber, E. (2001), *The Penguin Dictionary of Psychology,* Third Edition, Penguin Books: New York, p.236.

9   See Greenberg, L.S. & Paivio, S.C. (1997), opt. cit. Their work references a number of studies in support of their conclusions.

10   Paul Ekman has spent much of his career documenting the universality of affective emotions in adults. Each of the affective emotions has a distinguishable set of facial characteristics. See Ekman, P. (2003), *Emotions Revealed: Recognizing Faces and Feelings to improve Communication and Emotional Life,* Henry Holt and Co.: New York.

11   See Ekman P. (2003), op. cit.

12   In theory, the Body does express *all emotion*, provided that 'expression' exceeds what is commonly understood as affective emotion. I assume that all physical diseases and health reflect emotional components. Someday. it even might be possible to create working matrices that can identify emotions and corresponding physical states. But such correspondences would greatly exceed the possibilities permitted by a limited set of affective emotions.

13   I draw largely on the work of Barbara Brennan in my descriptions of Chakra theory, but any book search will provide a long list of titles dealing with the many facets of Chakra energies. See Brennan, B. (1987), *Hands of Light: A Guide to Healing through the Human Energy Field*, Bantam Books: NY.

14   The Root chakra emanates from the perineum, which is located between the penis/vagina and anus. It is distinctly different from the other two in two ways. First it is seen as emanating downward rather than outward. Second, it has no will center per se. Its will manifests as instinct in the brain-body. In contrast, the Solar Plexus and Abdominal chakras have will centers on the back of the spine, which

can modify their function. See Brennan, B. (1987), op. cit.

15   McCraty, R., Atkinson, M., & Bradley, R.T. (2004), Electrophysiological Evidence of Intuition: Part 1 The Surprising Role of the Heart, *Journal of Alternative and Complementary Medicine,* 10(1): 133-143; and McCraty, R., Atkinson, M., & Bradley, R.T., (2004), Electrophysiological Evidence of Intuition: Part 2 The Surprising Role of the Heart, *Journal of Alternative and Complementary Medicine,* 10(2): 325-336.

16   See Childre, D., Martin, H., & Beech, D. (1999), *The HeartMath Solution,* Harper: San Francisco.

17   Brennan, B. (1988), *Hands of Light: A Guide to Healing Through the Human Energy Field*, Bantam Books: New York.

18   Bruyere, R. (1987), *Wheels of Light*, Healing Light Center: Glendale, CA.

19   See Brennan for measures of chakra activity. Brennan, B. (1988), op. cit.

20   Polarity therapy is relatively unknown, but a number of practitioners have been developing it since its introduction in the mid-fifties by Randolph Stone. It also has its advocates from Asian disciplines. Westerners tend to define it in terms of electrical currents while Easterners rely on more traditional references to Ying and Yang meridians. See Burger for a complete, contemporary, exposition of Stone's work. Burger, B. (1998), *Esoteric Anatomy: The Body as Consciousness,* North Atlantic Books: Berkeley, CA.

21   Over the past several decades a number physical rehabilitation therapies that treat the body as an energy system have also demonstrated effective interventions. Upledger was among the earliest with his discovery of the cranio-sacral rhythm. See Upledger, J. & Vredevoogd, J. (1983), *Craniosacral Therapy*, Eastland Press. See also, Hamwee, J. (1999), *Zero Balancing: Touching the Energy of Bone,* North Atlantic Books: Berkley, CA.; Roth, G. (2005), *The Matrix Repatterning Program for Pain Relief,* New Harbinger Publications: Oakland, CA.; and Giammatteo, S. (2002, *Body Wisdom: Light Touch for Optimal Health,* North Atlantic Books: Berkeley, CA.

22   For several hundred years Homeopathy has offered discernible cures for a multitude of physical and emotional problems, even as the method defies physical science. It treats like with like. It takes a substance known to produce a set of symptoms and dilutes it to something like 1:300,000, which leaves no discernible trace except its effect on the water used to dilute it. In this subatomic state it is then

used to heal the very symptom(s) it would produce if swallowed in a 1:1 ratio. Clearly, homeopathic remedies are being read and responded to by something far more subtle than Body organs, including the brain.

23 See Goodheart, G.J., Jr. (2002), *Applied Kinesiology: A Training Manual and Reference Book of Basic Principles and Practices*, Ronin Publishing: California; and Diamond, J. (1989), *Your Body Doesn't Lie*, Warner Books: NY.

24 The interested reader can purchase a hand held instrument that can reliably and precisely identify all known surface acupuncture points comprising the meridian system. Acupuncturists have known these same points for several thousand years. A trained acupuncturist can 'feel' them. What a point locator provides is objective, measurable, evidence for the existence of these points. The point locator can be purchased from any catalogue selling acupuncture supplies.

25 The Rolf Study is described in Bruyere, pp. 219-233. See Bruyere, R., (1987), Op. cit.

26 The etheric body is also referred to as the human energy field (HEF). A number of researchers have addressed its existence. See Becker, R.O. (1998), *The Body Electric: Electromagnetism and the Foundation of Life,* Harper (1st Quill Edition): New York; Gerber, J. (2001), *Vibrational Medicine: The #1 Handbook of Subtle-Energy Therapies,* Bear & Co. (3rd Edition): New York; and Oschman, J.L. (2000), *Energy Medicine: The Scientific Basis of Bioenergy Therapies,* Churchill Livingston: New York.

27 'New' is a relative term. Knowledge of chakras and meridians has been known for several thousand years. The 'new paradigm' refers to the *scientific community's* willingness to investigate the phenomenon defined by these theories.

28 Jung. C.G. (1971), *Psychological Types*, Collected Works, Vol. 6, Princeton University Press.

29 A notable exception is the work of M.L. Schulz, a physician well grounded in the scientific method. Schulz, M.L., (1999), *Awakening Intuition: Using Your Mind-Body Network for Insight and Healing*, Three Rivers Press: California.

30 In describing the etheric body I frequently equate it with Meridians but even that concept does not do it justice. A meridian point, i.e. acupuncture point, represents the confluence of numerous strands of energy. Such strands could easily number in the millions if they could be seen. The etheric body is comparable to the 'luminous egg' frequently referenced by Carlos Castaneda in his series of

books describing Juan Mateus's alternate realities. See, for example: Castaneda, C. (2008), *The Teachings of Don Juan: A Yaqui Way of Knowledge*, University of California Press; Castaneda, C. (1991), *A Separate Reality*, Washington Square Press; and Castaneda, C. (1991), *Journey to Ixtlan*, Washington Square Press.

31   Kirlian photography – though primitive, provides one way of observing this phenomenon. The oft-reported experience of phantom pain is also offered as evidence of the etheric body's blueprinting effect. See Iovine, J. (2000), *Kirlian Photography*, Images Publishing.

32   The interested reader is also referred to Becker's work on regeneration in animals. See Becker, R. & Selden, G. (1998), *The Body Electric: Electromagnetism and the Foundation of Life*, Harper Paperbacks.

33   Donna Eden uses Kinesiology to demonstrate dramatic changes in the body's physical polarities. Kinesiology is also used by David Hawkins to rank order emotions, as discussed in Chapter II. See Eden, D. (1998), *Energy Medicine*, Tarcher/Putnam: NY.

34   It is helpful to remember that the Root chakra is an auric body as well as a specific site of energy. As a site of energy it is located between the sex organs and anus, the area called the perineum. As a 'body', it has its own seven chakras. Every auric body, or chakra, has its own seven chakras.

35   Foundation for Inner Peace (1996), *A Course In Miracles,* Penguin Books, p. 3

36   According to Freke and Gandy, "The word 'syzygy' means 'yoked together'. A syzygy is one thing in two states, a pair of concepts which arise simultaneously. The primal syzygy is the archetype of all subsequent dualities of complementary yet irreconcilable opposites (p.133)." See Freke, T. & Gandy, P. (2001), *Jesus and the Lost Goddess: The Secret Teachings of the Original Christians,* Harmony Books: New York.

37   Note that energy, will, and emotion are not the same. Energy sustains an image, will actuates an image, and emotion is the Mind's medium for communicating intent-belief to other images, the Heart, and etheric body.

38   There is a very old book still in print, and currently available on the Internet free of charge, which describes seven basic principles of hermetic philosophy. Most of these principles address different qualities of opposites. See Three Initiates (1912), *The Kybalion: A Study of The Hermetic Philosophy of Ancient Egypt and*

Greece, The Yogi Publication Society, Masonic Temple: Chicago, Ill.

39   Three Initiates (1912), op. cit. p. 149.

40   See Raff, J. (2000), *Jung and the Alchemical Imagination,* Nicolas-Hays, Inc.: York Beach, Maine. Also, though very difficult to comprehend: Jung, C.G. (1970), *Mysterium Coniunctionis,* The Collected Works, vol. 14, R.F.C. Hull, trans. Bollingen Series XX. Princeton University Press: Princeton, NJ.

41   Kabbalah is particularly cogent to this discussion in their insistence that every manifestation is comprised of force and form, or intellect and desire, which represents all opposites as defined by the masculine-feminine polarity. See especially: Chambers, S.,(2000), *Kabalistic Healing,* Keats Publishing: Los Angeles.

42   See the reissue of a mid-century classic on Zen Buddhism by an English Psychiatrist: Benoit, H. (1998), *The Supreme Doctrine,* Sussex Academic Press: Portland, OR.

43   Hauck, D.W. (1999),*The Emerald Tablet: Alchemy for Personal Transformation,* Penguin Compass: NY.

44   Every 'miraculous' healing in the Gospels is a function of Spirit over Soul over Mind over matter.

45   See Cofer and Appley's chapter on 'Homeostatic Concepts and Motivation' in Cofer, C.N. & Appley, M. H. (1966), *Motivation: Theory and Research,* John Wiley & Sons: New York.

46   Not all 'lack' is the same. Back in the 1960's Abraham Maslow made much of the distinction between deficiencies needs and being needs. A comparable distinction is being made in this work between the needs of the Soul (the Soul's desire) and the Ego's desires, and the Body's desires. Needs infer a sense of lack at each level and are replicated at each level, but are different in kind as each level is different in kind. See Maslow, A. (1962), *Toward a Psychology of Being,* Van Nostrand: NY.

47   At the risk of getting too abstract, desire can also seek homeostasis at a higher level, but as it is used here it will generally refer to a *return* to mental homeostasis unless otherwise noted. See, for example: Odier, D. (2001), *Desire: The Tantric Path to Awakening,* Inner Traditions: Rochester, NY.

48   That is not true Hermetically speaking. Extreme fear can put us back to

back with the *object* of fear, but it is true enough as a descriptor of most fearful activity.

49   Scarfalloto, Rodolfo (1997), Op. cit. p. 25. Scarfalloto's sense of singularity is taken from astronomy: "The term "singularity" is borrowed from astronomy. It is the mathematical expression for a point in space where there is no space. In astronomy, a "singularity" has no "here", and no "there", no "now" and no "then". It is a singular point where time and space have merged into something beyond time and space as we know them (p.27)"

50   The complementary quality of all dualities also reinforces the need to always treat both poles with equal regard. All dualities reflect an admixture necessary for the existence of life, namely energy and definition. Taoists capture this essential admixture in their symbol of ying and yang (a circle with two tear drop shapes, one black, one white, each moving to become the other in a circular fashion). Each pole of a set of opposites is an admixture of energy and structure wherein one pole represents a *preponderance* of one or the other. I call this the principle of complementarity, which states that each pole needs the other to complete the whole. No pole can stand alone as an absolute. God can exist apart from manifest dualities. But life cannot exist apart from an admixture of energy and structure, be it spirit/matter, ying/yang, good/evil, heaven/earth, etc. Thus, for example, masculine (as yang) is commonly represented as a preponderance of energy relative to structure, while feminine represents a preponderance of structure relative to masculine energy. In this conception of duality, *fluctuations* around homeostasis are clearly the optimum function: movement away from homeostasis in both directions is necessary to insure that both energy and structure are replenished. Persistent reliance on energy sacrifices the flexibility of complex form while unremitting form strangulates energy. From this perspective, neither pole is more valued since both are absolutely necessary to the whole. The relationship is always complementary. The interaction is necessary to sustain the generative nature of the whole. Hot devoid of cold negates temperature; male without female provides no means for procreation. If a male plug lacks a female receptacle there is no flow of electricity. There is no evil apart from good, for the very reason that each needs the other to define it. Remove evil from the world and you remove the need for Christ. Remove the negative and the positive has no means of flow. The Tree of Life illustrating Kabbalistic relationships also captures this interdependence with its three pillars. The Pillar of Severity (feminine) and Pillar of Mercy (masculine) must be reconciled by the central Pillar of Equanimity, which is governed by will.

51   It is possible to talk about a *fourth* will implicit in the homeostatic paths created by the set of all opposites defining the limits of Mind: basically the Mind's will. But the Mind's will is only relevant in the context of ego-aspects that accede or deviate from it. Discussing it as separate and distinct will only further complicate

an already complicated set of theses.

52	Of note, the environment – the context in which a bodily organism is obliged to exist, can also frustrate or disrupt instinctual rhythms. Such disruptions can be societal as when a culture seeks to actively disrupt eating rhythms or sexual rhythms, or biological as when there is simply not enough food available within the environment (draught, scarcity, starvation). In this work we are only concerned with optional disruptions caused by culture (community, family, and mates) or those self-imposed by an ego-aspect, most often in response to culture's surrogates.

53	A belief validates itself by setting a limit on what is possible; this is particularly true of defeatist beliefs.

54	See Bertalanffy, Ludwig Von (1976), *General Systems Theory: Foundations, Development, and Applications,* George Braziller: NY; and Wiener, N. (1965), *Cybernetics, Second Edition: or the Control and Communication in the Animal and the Machine,* MIT Press.

55	Pearce, J.C. (1971/2002), *The Crack in the Cosmic Egg: New Constructs of Mind and Reality,* Park Street Press: Rochester, Vermont.

56	Brazier, D., (1995), *Zen Therapy: Transcending the Sorrows of the Human Mind,* John Whiley & Sons, Inc.: New York.

57	Brazier, D. (1995), op. cit. pp.87-88.

58	Kelly, G., (1963), *A Theory of Personality: the Psychology of Personal Constructs,* Norton & Company: New York.

59	In some clinical interventions, I have the client ask Christ to stimulate the Heart center of one of their selves with loving energy that flows through his hand. The idea for this intervention came to me while studying several papers and books put out by the Institute for HeartMath. The primary thrust of their work is the development of a biofeedback system. This program generates significant changes in Heart rate variability through a combined focus on the Heart coupled with the generation of positive emotions such as love, gratitude, and caring. The subject is literally asked to breathe into their Heart as a way of focusing on this center while imaginatively evoking a positive emotion. (With one client who had access to the biofeedback program, I had her imagine breathing in through her Heart while Christ continually placed small portions of his *Light* into her Heart chakra with each in-breath. The client completely mastered the biofeedback program in one session using this particular intervention.) Such emotions are shown to have a profound effect on Heart activity. What makes the work of the HeartMath group particularly interesting is a series of rigorous experiments that argue for treating the Heart as the center of emotion (as distinct from the brain), which is what the Old Testament and Kabbalah – among others, have argued for centuries. On average, the Heart beats sixty times a minute sending out electrical impulses that are 6000 times stronger than anything generated by the brain. It is argued that differential frequencies in the Heart rhythm can convey emotion throughout the body on an average of once a second.

Basically, the HeartMath group argues for the treatment of the Heart as the primary communicator of emotion. I expect this will be argued for some years to come as they are putting forth a new conception of the *physical* origins of emotion. What distinguishes them from other theorists is their rigorous and innovative peer reviewed experiments. For my part, what I found most intriguing was the thought that Christ might provide all the necessary ingredients for replicating their biofeedback program. By way of introducing this idea to a client, I explain that 70 percent of their body weight is water which can function as an ideal conductor of bio-energetic impulses generated by the Heart every second. Focusing on breathing through the Heart, and allowing Christ to stimulate a self's Heart with loving energy could give a stressed ego-aspect a breather, provided it is willing. Generally, this is done by simply having Christ place his hand on the ego-aspect's Heart center. I note that the client must allow this intervention to continue for at least a few seconds, that the effect is cumulative as the Heart "beats" out a new rhythm being channeled by Christ's love. The effects are often dramatic in reducing the client's sense of stress, in or outside of a session.

In sum, whenever an ego-aspect is stressing the physical body with symptoms, asking Christ to stimulate the Heart lovingly, is a good first step toward alleviating the stress. Anyone can use this intervention at anytime, once it is learned, and it is easy to learn. The client is asked to focus on their Heart, to imagine literally breathing in through the Heart center. Christ is asked to place his hand over the Heart center, or to begin 'feeding' it with his own *Light*, filling the Heart with his love. This generally alleviates the most intense curve of the stress within a few short seconds. I suspect it is short-circuiting the ego-aspect's control of the Heart, which accounts for the quick change. Once the stress is eased the therapist can focus on altering the belief system sustaining the stressful emotions. I would also note that the HeartMath people recommend their biofeedback system as a regular meditation for correcting a great many ills.

60   Jung. C.G. (1971), Op. cit.

61   It is likely that visual repression of a sensate image is necessary for complete repression as in the case of repressive somatization. Depersonalization is one

step short in that the client retains a visual connection to the sensate image.

62   Modi, S. (1997), *Remarkable Healings: A Psychiatrist Discovers Unsuspected Roots of Mental and Physical Illness*, Hampton Roads: Charlottesville, VA.

63   Bandler, R. & Grinder, J. (1979), *Frogs Into Princes: Neuro-Linguistic Programming,* Real People Press: San Francisco.

64   The sensate body has its Body counterpart in the ears, feet, and hands. Each of these appendages has points corresponding to the entire body, which can be manipulated by acupuncture and reflexology. Two German doctors, Kolster and Waskowiak, provide a detailed atlas for all three locations. See Kolster, B.C. & Waskowiak, A. (2003), *The Reflexology Atlas,* Healing Arts Press.

65   On rare instances, an ego-aspect may assert control over consciousness and report observing a self-image (sic) Aware-ego holding the Light. When this occurs, the first order of business is the containment of the self dominating consciousness. This usurpation is illustrated in several cases throughout the book. The kind of self most likely to usurp control of consciousness generally functions in an observer role. It does not act except in its power to control consciousness for the sole purpose of observing. In such cases, observation becomes a protective mechanism against being overwhelmed by negative feelings. An observer relies on depersonalization as its primary defense. An 'observer' is easily contained, but difficult to treat, as it must be reintegrated with its 'participant' counterpart, which is invariably in the thrall of overwhelming emotion likely to provoke numerous compulsive behaviors.
An ego-aspect that is 'purely mental' will have no discernible connection with sensation. Its demeanor is comparable to an out-of-body experience that is generally the result of severe trauma. Such a purely mental self – when discovered, will be found to observe *the self holding the Light*, generally from slightly above the scene being observed. The reconciliation of this self with its dissociated body sensation is often dramatic in the amelioration of long standing symptoms. The other more common exception, though still comparatively rare is the presence of a Dominant self that actively retains control of consciousness following the emergence of the Aware-ego holding the Light. In such cases, it reports observing the Aware-ego as an image of the self holding the Light. Both exceptions are illustrated in the book. These exceptions are most likely to occur in MPD cases, but not exclusively. I have observed the phenomenon in a client with strong characteristics of Asperger's syndrome.

66   There are notable exceptions to this rule as described in the preceding

endnote.

67   Napier, A. & Whitaker, C. (1980), *The Family Crucible*, Bantam Books.

68   Psychic healers who treat clients for chakra dysfunction describe chakras as chronically under-functioning or over-functioning or even traumatically wounded. See Brennan B. (1987) Op. cit; and Judith, A. (2004), *Eastern Body Western Mind: Psychology and the Chakra System as a Path to the Self,* Celestial Arts.

69   I first encountered the idea of 'felt sense' in the works of Eugene Gendlin. Peter Levine builds on his work in his book on shock trauma. See Gendlin, E. (1982), *Focusing,* Bantam Books; and Levine, P. with Frederick, A. (1997), *Waking the Tiger: Healing Trauma, The Innate Capacity to Transform Overwhelming Experiences,* North Atlantic Books.

70   Damasio is a research neurologist who has written a number of popular books on the subject of consciousness. He takes as his thesis the exact opposite of what I have asserted in this work: namely, that mind is the product of neural sets created by the combined function of body and brain. In effect, mind is caused by the activity of brain-body, not vice versa. See Damasio, A. (2000), *The Feeling of What Happens: Body and Emotion in the Making of Consciousness*, Harvest Books.

71   Pert, C., (1997), *Molecules of Emotion: Why you Feel the Way You Feel*, Scribner: NY.

72   Lipton, B.H. (2008), *The Biology of Belief: Unleashing the Power of Consciousness, Matter, & Miracles*, Hay House, Inc.

73   Levine, P.E. (1997), *Waking the Tiger: Healing Trauma,* North Atlantic Books.

74   Here, I am using the concept of shame in its most primitive somatic sense – the power to freeze ongoing activity; the response of complete powerlessness to overwhelming stimulation, terror, or attack.

75   See Levine, P, (1997), op. cit.

76   Depersonalization is by no means the only reason for PTSD symptoms. Dissociation will play an equal or greater role where present. But it is possible for depersonalization to occur in the absence of significant dissociation.

77 There are a number of therapies that address energy blocks in the Body. Myotherapy, Craniosacral Therapy, Rubenfeld Synergy, Acupuncture, Polarity therapy and Zero Balancing are just a few of the therapies currently practiced.

78 Of note, 'repression' can also be used to describe the dissociative effects wrought by a very punitive Voice-of-conscience or abuse of Temporal authority, though I will generally use the term as the primary defense exercised by a Dominant self. But the two uses are comparable in their exercise of shameful judgment. The difference is that dissociation results from the shaming judgment of an image constellated by the Empowering archetype, while repression proper results from self-shaming by a Dominant self.

79 Hamwee, J. & Smith, F., (2000), *Zero Balancing: Touching the Energy of Bone,* North Atlantic Books: NY; and Smith, F.F. (1986), *Inner Bridges: A Guide to Energy Movement and Body Structure,* Humanics Ltd. Partners: NY.

80 Burger, B. (1998), *Esoteric Anatomy: The Body as Consciousness*, North Atlantic Books: NY.

81 This was a very apt insight on his part. In the chapter on Moral Authority I describe the Addict, who is generally present in some form wherever a self has been shamed into exile. The Addict is best described as pure sensation cut off from intuition. This description aptly describes the Worker Bee.

82 These sessions took place before I finally decided that the Aware-ego is always merged with an ego-aspect in the early stages of therapy. Whenever one self is separated and addressed, another self - usually younger version, emerge to come center stage as needed. The Aware-ego is rarely strong enough to speak for any length of time until *after* the client has allowed Christ to enter the Heart, which can only occur when the Dominant self forgoes the power to self-shame in exchange for Christ's discernment. See Chapter VII for a description of those dynamics.

83 Peck, S. (1988), *The Road Less Traveled: A New Psychology of Love, Traditional Values and Spiritual Growth*, Touchstone Books: New York.

84 Peck, S. (1998), *The People of the Lie,* Touchstone Books: New York.

85 Moore, T. (1994), *Care of the Soul: A Guide for Cultivating Depth and Sacredness in Everyday Life*, Perennial: New York.

86 Moore, T. (1995), *Dark Eros: Imagination of Sadism*, Spring Publications:

New York.

87   Gibran, K. (1923), *The Prophet*, Knopf: New York.

88   Three Initiates (1912,1940), *The Kybalion: The Hermetic Philosophy of Ancient Egypt and Greece*, The Yogi Publication Society, Masonic Temple: Chicago, IL. p. 159

89   Three Initiates (1912), op. cit. p.160

90   This book is currently out of print, but other more current titles by them cover the same basics. See Hendricks, G. & Hendricks, K. (1993), *At the Speed of Life: A New Approach to Personal Change Through Body-Centered Therapy*, Bantam: New York.

91   Hanna, T. (2004), *Somatics: Reawakening The Mind's Control of Movement, Flexibility, and Heath*, Da Capo Press.

92   Post, A. & Cavaliere, S. (2003), *Unwinding the Belly: Healing with Gentle Touch,* North Atlantic Books: New York.

93   Caponigro, A. (2005), *The Miracle of Breath: Mastering Fear, Healing Illness, Experiencing the Divine*, New World Library: Novato, CA.

94   The opportunity for unlimited sexual activity is equally demanding for men and women. For men, it would soon exhaust them physically, if not emotionally. Rats able to directly stimulate the pleasure center of the brain will do so in lieu of just about all other activities including eating and sleeping. Women are equally at risk with continuous pregnancy, not to mention the toil and uncertainty of raising children while dependent on men. Interestingly, Chinese emperors were taught how to ejaculate inwardly in order to preserve their longevity against the ready availability of consorts and concubines. The same Taoist practices also offered women the ability to stop the menstrual cycle. See Chia, M., (1984), *Taoist Secrets of Love: Cultivating Male Sexual Energy,* Aurora Press.

95   See Chia and Abrams for a discussion of the Taoist alternative to ejaculation in men and the menstrual cycle in women. Chia, M. & Abrams, D. (1997), *The Multi-Orgasmic Man,* Harper.

96   Maines has written a very good book on the history of hysteria in women. Its cause – the denial of woman's capacity for orgasm, has been known for centuries, and patriarchy appears to have gone to great lengths to simultaneously foster and deny it. Women have long been expected to be objects of desire, but rarely

desiring objects. See Maines, R.P. (2001), *The Technology of Orgasm: "Hysteria," the Vibrator, and Women's Sexual Satisfaction*, The John Hopkins University Press.

97   See Maines (2001), op. cit.

98   See Hanna's work on the incessant stimulation of the fight-flight reflexes and their untold effects on aging. Hanna, T. (2004), op. cit.

99   John Upledger describes the craniosacral rhythm in great detail by. It is experienced by the therapist as a rhythmic expansion and contraction of all muscles of the body and treated as responsible for the continuous flow of cerebral spinal flow, hence its name. Upledger has been treating major disruptions of this flow for the past thirty years, and teaching his methods to other therapists. The book, *Craniosacral Therapy,* is very technical, but he has written a number of others for the lay public and as addendums to his work. See Upledger, J. & Vredevoogd, J. (1983), *Craniosacral Therapy*, Eastland Pr: New York.

100   A major difference is blood flow. In anger/fight/approach the blood flow is directed to the arms and upper torso. In fear/flight/withdraw the blood flow is directed to the legs.

101   See Levine, P, (1997), op. cit.

102   See Hanna, T. (2004), op. cit.

103   The reference is to Hans Selye who developed the concept of stress in medicine, and showed conclusively its effects on the endocrine system. Hanna's work focuses on the effects of stress on the neuromuscular system paralleled by the endocrine system. See, for example, Selye, H., (1978), *The Stress of Life*, McGraw-Hill: New York.

104   Hanna, T. (2004), op. cit., p. 47.

105   Hanna, T. (2004), op. cit. p. 50-51.

106   Hanna, T. (2004), op. cit. p. 53.

107   Hanna, T. (2004), op. cit. p. 54.
108   Hanna, T. (2004), op. cit. p. 65.

109   See Sarno, J.E. (1991), *Healing Back Pain: The Mind-Body Connection*, Warner Books: New York; and Sarno, J.E. (1999),*The Mindbody Prescription:*

Healing the Body, Healing the Pain, Warner Books: New York. Both Sarno and Hanna focus on fear and anger as responsible for neuromuscular problems. Hanna addresses the problem at that level, while Sarno argues that the patient must also address anger issues, particularly the inability to recognize and/or voice anger.

110   Hanna, T. (2004), op. cit. p. 69.

111   While recognizing that desire is the cultural choice, it is not a better choice. Learning to guide the angry force of an opponent so it becomes self-defeating is a far preferable solution. This is true whether the opponent is real or imagined. The method is described in every book on Aikido. See, for example, Westbrook, A. & Ratti, O., (1970), *Aikido and the Dynamic Sphere: An Illustrated Introduction,* Charles E. Tuttle Co.: Rutland, Vt.

112   Anger is more likely to show itself in the face and eyes, but again the client can be totally unaware of what the therapist is seeing. When queried about his anger one of my clients described himself as an intense person, not an angry person. He could own that he fantasized a lot of angry situations and responses, but thought his felt anger was hidden if not acted upon. This 'obliviousness' actually describes a number of clients I seen over the years.

113   If an ego-aspect continues to be fearful after accepting a garment of protection, it is because the object of fear is within them. In that case, as a second step, Christ can be asked to extract it from whatever part of the body is identified by the client, and place it in a separate circle.

114   Tory's treatment is examined again at length in Chapter VIII. In the extensive verbatims provided in that Chapter, I revisit the Gingerbread girl, who is identified there as Victoria. This is Tory's given name, and the one her mother always used. Everyone else who knows her, calls her Tory.

115   In a later chapter I describe an alternative method for releasing accumulated unexpressed emotion that I call the gift of salt, which appears to have a comparable effect.

116   In the first chapter I discussed Wink's idea that our culture lives out the myth of redemptive violence, the belief that violence can be used to defeat violence. See Wink, Walter, (1992), *Engaging the Powers: Discernment and Resistance in a World of Domination, Vol. 3*, Augsburg Fortress Publishers: NY

117   Crum, T.F.,(1998), *The Magic of Conflict: Turning a Life of Work into a Work of Art*, 2nd Rev. Ed. Touchstone: Los Angeles.

118   See Winks (1992), op. cit.

119   Lowen, A. (1970), *Pleasure,* Lancer Books, Inc.: New York.

120   Lowen, A. (1970), op. cit. p. 72.

121   "As excitement mounts on the pleasure side of the spectrum, the movements of the body become more intense and more rapid, maintaining, however, their coordination and rhythm. In 'pleasure' the person feels soft, vibrant, and buoyant; his eyes are bright and his skin warm. It can be said that the body *purrs* with pleasure. Joy denotes increased pleasurable excitement such that the body seems to dance. Its movements are lively and graceful. In ecstasy, the highest form of pleasurable excitement, the currents in the body are so strong that the person is 'lit up' like a star. He feels transported (from earth to the cosmos). Ecstasy is experienced in the full sexual orgasm, in which the movements also take on convulsive character but are unified and rhythmic." Lowen, A. (1970), Op. cit., p. 72.

122   The following is a brief summary of pain receptor physiology extracted from notes found on the Internet. The impulses perceived as pain are generated by the simplest type of sensory receptor- a naked nerve ending. Pain receptors are activated by strong stimuli that threaten tissue damage. They may also be stimulated by chemicals released when tissues are damaged (i.e., histamine). There are two basic types of nerve fibers. Slow, unmyelinated C fibers carry pain from deep within the tissues. The pain is felt as a dull ache, which is hard to localize. Fast, myelinated A delta fibers carry sharp, well-localized pain from the surface. Like all somatic sensory nerves, pain fibers enter the spinal column through the dorsal root. They synapse and cross over immediately (most sensory nerves cross over in the medulla). The nerves ascend in a spinal tract to the thalamus. Slow pain nerves may end in the thalamus. Fast pain fibers continue to the postcentral gyrus (sensory cortex). Some pain is "Gated" in the spinal cord and does not reach the brain. The gate theory holds that pain of C fibers may be blocked in the spinal cord by other nerves from the same area. Skin stimulation by massage can reduce pain. Nerves coming down from the brain can also block pain. Endorphins (natural opiate-like chemicals) may be involved in pain inhibition.

123   Levine, P.E. (1997), op.cit.

124   See Lowen, A. (1970) op. cit.

125   Olds and Milner (1954) first identified brain sites where direct electrical stimulation is reinforcing. Laboratory animals will lever press at high rates (> 6,000

times per hour) to obtain brief stimulation pulses to certain brain regions. The reinforcement from direct electrical activation of this reward substrate is more potent than other rewards, such as food or water. The potency of this electrical stimulation is most dramatically illustrated in a classic experiment where the subjects suffered self-imposed starvation when forced to make a choice between obtaining food and water or electrical brain stimulation (Routtenberg & Lindy, 1965). A second distinguishing feature of reward from electrical brain stimulation is the lack of satiation; animals generally respond continuously, taking only brief breaks from lever pressing to obtain the electrical stimulation. These two features (i.e., super-potent reward and lack of satiation) are important characteristics of direct activation of brain reward mechanisms. See Olds, J. & Milner, P. (1954), "Positive reinforcement produced by electrical stimulation of septal area and other regions of rat brain." *Journal of Comparative and Physiological Psychology* 47: 419-427; and Routtenberg, A. & Lindy, J. (1965), "Effects of the availability of rewarding septal and hypothalamic stimulation on bar pressing for food under conditions of deprivation." *Journal of Comparative and Physiological Psychology* 60: 158-161.

126   See Heath, R.G. (1964), "Pleasure response of human subjects to direct stimulation of the brain: Physiologic and psychodynamic considerations." In R.G. Heath (ed.), *The Role of Pleasure in Human Behavior* (pp. 219-243), New York: Hoeber.

127   See Lowen, A. (1970), op. cit.

128   Cofer, C.N. & Appley, M.H, (1964), *Motivation: Theory and Research,* John Wiley & Sons: New York, p. 620.

129   As I have noted elsewhere, the concept of Multiple Personality Disorder was documented in the late 1800's, but then eclipsed by the work of Freud who ended up treating memories of severe abuse as fantasies of the Id. Initially, Freud treated the 'abuse' as a memory, but after the Vienna, male dominated, medical establishment threatened to ostracize him he changed 'memory' to 'fantasy.' Patriarchy secured for another 100 years! Interestingly, we have seen a similar back peddling by a few researchers to label the recall of abuse memories a false memory syndrome.

130   While such emotions are most likely associated with a disowned ego-aspect, on rare occasions they may be autonomous emotions. Such emotions – which some therapists and psychics call spirits, can manifest as a nebulous forms that attached themselves to an ego-aspect. Seeing 'blackness' in a circle would constitute such a formless form, if the blackness is distinctly different from what is outside the circle. Whenever a shapeless form is identified, the first step is to have

Christ extract any ego-aspect, which might be surrounded or covered over by the formless emotion. Then Christ is asked to transform the 'emotion' into pure white light and return it to the source of light. Such a procedure often provides the client with a sense of relief although also frequently a sense of disbelief as to what they have encountered and dealt with. Since, for my part, I am unsure myself, I tend to emphasize their sense of relief and minimize any theological considerations.

131   Again, as in the previous footnote, the symptom may not be caused by a disowned ego-aspect. I have had a number of occasions when the client identified an image of another person. This is always unexpected however often it has happened. Where it occurs, I encourage the client to enter into a dialogue with this image and ascertain its reasons for being present. Regardless of what is revealed, the bottom-line remains the same: its separation from the client. In this matter Christ can always be called upon to take the image under his care and separate it from the client's Soul. Several authors describe a large number of anecdotal cases involving this kind of Soul attachment. See Fiore, E. (1995), *The Unquiet Dead: A Psychologist Treats Spirit Possession*, Ballantine Books: NY; McAll, K. (1999), *Healing the Family Tree*, 2Rev. Ed., Sheldon Press: London; and Modi, S. (1998), *Remarkable Healings: A Psychiatrist Discovers Unsuspected Roots of Mental and Physical Illness*, Hampton Roads Publishing Company: NY.

132   It is important to keep in mind that the Mind is intermediate between Soul and Body. While most of the interventions described here relate to the Mind-Body connection, the Soul can exert a powerful direct effect on the Body when conjoined with other Souls or spirits. The two previous footnotes are essentially addressing the Soul-Mind-Body connection.

133   Cancer is a prime example. Cancer is treated primarily with surgery where possible, followed by chemotherapy and/or radiation. This removes or reduces the cancer, though rarely without equally life threatening side effects. Moreover, these do not 'heal' the problem and unless there are significant life changes in the person being treated, the rate of resurgence remains very high. What is most in need of treatment is the Mind and Soul; and for these physical medicine has little to offer. I consider physical medicine complementary. It can be necessary, even life saving, in the initial stages of treatment, but remission is only assured if the client can call on a higher power and join wisely in their own healing.

134   I never do this in lieu of referring the client to a physician, but in most of the situations brought to my attention the client has already exhausted or received whatever medical science has to offer. That said, I also acknowledge that I rarely have the opportunity to work with severely sick people who are in the throes of their illness or terminally ill. Likewise, I am not averse to referring clients to a

psychiatrist for medication, though I will then work to treat whatever is necessitating the need so they do not become interminably dependent on drugs. I spent the first ten years of my professional career in a state psychiatric facility attempting to treat the most chronic patients in the hospital. Without question there is often a need for whatever psychiatry can offer by way of medication. But in that decade I saw too many people warehoused with medication straitjackets. It still goes on today. But again, I appreciate a law of diminishing returns, economically speaking. There will always be some adults whose life histories and genetic makeup make it near impossible to treat them by any means other than medication and incarceration. I also doubt that the methods described in this work would be permissible in a state institution since they often call for "spiritual solutions;" I did not begin this work until I was several years in private practice. In any case, I would never assert that this work is a solution to all the problems of physical and mental illness manifest in this world, or that it will ever offer hope to any but a small portion of the world's population. I work with a skewed population consisting of those people who have sufficient financial resources to engage me via insurance, or on a sliding fee scale, and get to my office on a regular basis, which is a small room on the second floor of an old house in a good neighborhood. Those conditions exclude a lot of people, even in my locale, not to mention the world's population. There is a law of diminishing returns for any discipline including my own; a point beyond which client and therapist are obliged to accept the mysteries that remain the hallmark of all life. But even then we are not without prayer.

135   See for example, Johnson, R., (1985), *We: Understanding the Psychology of Romantic Love,* Harper: San Francisco.

136   For many years I have hypothesized to clients that their parents will strongly identify them with one parent and grandparent based on birth other. The firstborn is always identified with the father and his side of the family regardless of the child's sex. The second born will be identified with the mother's side of the family. Since there are four grandparents, and each grandparent seeks to continue their family of origin, each grandchild will be claimed for one of those four families. Whatever side of the family the father is most strongly identified with will determine the extended family of origin for the firstborn child. In this case, the client – the firstborn of four children, was most strongly identified with her father. As a firstborn, her daughter was also identified with her father, the mother's ex-husband who was also seen as acting irresponsibly.

137   Bowen, M. (1985 reprinted), *Family Therapy in Clinical Practice,* Jason Aronson: NY.

138   Friedman, E.H. (1985), *Generation To Generation: Family Process in*

Church and Synagogue, Guilford Press: NY.

139   The HeartMath research group has developed a computerized biofeedback program that is easily self-administered. The program and research are described in their various publications. See Childre, D., Martin, H., & Beech, D. (1999), *The HeartMath Solution,* Harper: San Francisco.

140   Raff, J. & Vocatura, L.B. (2002), *Healing the Wounded God: Finding Your Personal Guide on Your Way to Individuation and Beyond*, Nicolas-Hays, Inc.: York Beach, MA.

141   J. C. Pearce has provided a number of dramatic examples in his groundbreaking book, *The Crack in the Cosmic Egg*. (Pearce, J.C. (1971), Op. cit.) As he amply demonstrates, belief can kill, but changing a belief can heal. The power of belief is well documented by the placebo effect. Double-blind studies of drugs must exceed 33 percent in efficacy to demonstrate potency greater than the placebo effect, i.e. *the standard measure of your belief* in the potency of any drug offered by authority to heal what ails you. In other words, 33 percent of subjects are expected to get better while taking a placebo! When a new drug comes on the market, doctors often prescribed it widely while it still works well (actual potency + plus placebo effect, minus the documented side effects). Like a placebo, changing a client's core beliefs can be expected to alter the emotional field generated by that belief. See Harrington, A. (Ed), (1999), *The Placebo Effect: An Interdisciplinary Exploration*, Harvard University Press: MA; see also Brody, H. & Brody D., (2000), *The Placebo Response: How You Can Release the Body's Inner Pharmacy for Better Health*, HarperCollins Publishers: New York.

142   This is the only time I have had a client describe this kind of visceral effect. I suspect it has to do with the 'upward' separation of an ego-aspect from the Aware-ego as well as the core belief. I did not intend that the ego-aspect would be separated in that way, but that seems to have been the effect. Normally, ego-aspects are separated while remaining on the same plane. However, that surmise is speculative; I am not sure what has caused the effect.

143   Leigh is reading this book at my suggestion. It was published in the early years of the 20th century. It is based on the premise that we 'receive what we ask for' and we must become mindfully deliberate for what we ask. See Shinn, F.S. (2008), *The Game of Life and How to Play It*, Dover Publications**.**

CHAPTER VI

CHRIST AND THE ISSUE OF TEMPORAL AUTHORITY

OVERVIEW

When we are children our parents are gods. If they are abusive then we quickly grasp that they are gods with the power to inflict pain, including the pain of toxic shame, abandonment and injury. Throughout infancy and childhood the power of parents is absolute. They can love us or not, beat us or not, feed us or not, send us to bed or permit us to stay up. Parents do not have to justify their behavior, do not have to be reasonable, do not have to account for their actions. And this is the power I have in mind when I speak of the Temporal authority of parents. One client related a memory of when he was nine years old that succinctly illustrated his father's awesome authority within the family. Both parents abused alcohol; they would both die at relatively early ages from its effects. On this particular afternoon the parents had been arguing with words and raised voices for several hours. The client and his brother were present in the background, very aware but also trying to stay out of the line of fire. Then, quite abruptly it seemed, their father went upstairs with their mother anxiously following him. They followed as well since their bedroom was upstairs. Once upstairs, they found themselves all gathered in the spare bedroom witnessing their father loading a shotgun. He said he was going to kill them all and then himself. He could see no other solution to the interminable arguments. The client remembers everyone pleading with him not to do this, and the relief he experienced when his father finally relented, unloaded the gun, and put it back in the closet. Reflecting on this experience as an adult, what stood out in his mind was the thought that, while it was all happening, no one really questioned the father's "right" to kill them if that is what he finally decided to do. All the family could do was plead for their lives. To the best of his recollection, it never occurred to him to go to a neighbor's for help. This story aptly illustrates the awesome power given parents — particularly fathers, by Temporal authority.

The Empowering Archetype

It is asserted here that an Empowering Archetype constellates both Temporal and Moral authority in the same parental images. This archetype assigns a 'god-like power' to the images it constellates, and the initial constellations are invariably parental in nature. By 'god-like power' I mean an image within the Mind that has the authority to judge, reward, and punish in parent-child relationships, e.g., parent, policeman, emperor, commander, pope, etc. The existence of this archetype can be demonstrated by the observation that *parental images are seen by most clients as the most powerful images in the Mind*, even more powerful than an image of Christ that the client believes is the 'son of God.' It can also be demonstrated by changes that occur in parental images when Christ is asked to terminate the parent's Temporal authority. In the course of development, parental images are normally the first and only images constellated by this archetype, though as a child grows, this authority can generalize to other adults or surrogates who are said to exercise it *in loco parentis*. As adults, the power is generalized by our voluntary submission to other adults who reenact the parent-child relationship in their interactions with us.

Temporal authority is the defining power of parent-child relationships. A parent is all-powerful in the eyes of their children whether or not s/he abuses this authority. Parents who do abuse it are likely to appear even more powerful. Fear of further abuse will keep children ever vigilant and fixated on the parent's moods and expectations. What use to amaze me about adult survivors of childhood abuse was that so many of them continued to interact with their abusive parents as adults. Now I understand that constellated parental images shape the ego-aspects controlling behavior, and those aspects reinforce the continued channeling of Temporal authority even when the client is no longer physically dependent upon the actual parent. More often than not, those ego-aspects are child-like or adolescent in demeanor. They are rarely adult. This truncated development of an ego-aspect *can emotionally cope* with the parental abuses, but it imposes untold difficulties on clients attempting to interact with family and adult peers. Ego-aspects in the throes of this arrested development can sit in a session and describe continuing abuse and exploitation at the hands of parents, and bemoan their fate, but be unable to seriously contemplate stopping it, i.e. confront and separate from the abusive parent (or parental surrogate such as a wife-beating husband). They seem unable to break the spell of their parent's power over them. As one client put it, "my father continues to treat me as a child even though I am now a single mother raising three children; and I continue to give in to him." Even clients who are physically separated or cut-off from their parents can remain victimized by this authority, which they project onto others in their life or continue to experience subjectively as a parentified Voice-of-conscience. In effect, the parent's abuse of Temporal and Moral authority appears to continue in one manifestation or another until the individual is able to staunch the flow of energy authorizing parental images, and heal the ego-aspects created by it. *The authority is perpetuated, as much by the ego-aspects created to cope with it, as it is by the parental images that channel it, so both must be addressed.*

Temporal authority can be *ritually* recapitulated in other adult images such as bishops, kings, queens, tribal leaders, and the like. In ritual subjugation, the individual voluntarily generalizes parental authority to a titled person, e.g. a monarch who confers knighthood, a bishop who ordains for ministry, an officer who commissions other officers. Such voluntary rituals recapitulate the parent-child relationship. Cultures will also foster the 'collective recapitulation' of Temporal authority in certain *groups* such as doctors, police officers, and judges, etc. In a Doctor's office, for example, the culturally sanctioned recapitulation of Temporal authority is what 'empowers' the doctor to physically or psychologically examine people of all ages (which few people would allow another person to do outside of a Doctor's office). Christ's termination of Temporal authority in a parent's image only removes the constellated authority from the parental image; it does not automatically remove it from other images. But termination of Temporal authority in a parent does give clients the wherewithal to challenge and question the authority of others; and *Christ will terminate any enthrallment to the Empowering archetype upon request*. I doubt that 'recapitulation' is equal in power to 'constellation.' Any learning that includes a strong emotional component is easily generalized, but that does not mean recapitulation is equal in power to the constellation, or necessarily reflects a separate and distinct constellation. What does appear to be generalized is the parent-child paradigm *reinforced* by the ego-aspects already created to cope with it.

The above observations are further complicated by the real possibility that some images – including self-images – can be constellated with archetypal energies other than the Empowering archetype. For example, Jung placed great emphasis on the Persona and its Contra-sexual aspect. These archetypal energies also have the power to enthrall self-images as well as the images of others. I will examine some of those enthrallments at some length in this and later chapters. Freeing an ego-aspect from other archetypal enthrallment – any manifestation of the Persona in particular – is often a necessary step toward a closer relationship with Christ.

An ego-aspect can defy constellated Temporal authority, even rebel against it, but does not have the power to staunch its flow. In my clinical experience, a parent or other adult image can only be divested of Temporal authority by a spiritual being such as Jesus Christ incarnated in the Mind. Paradoxically, an incarnated image of Christ will appear less powerful than the parental image initially, but that notwithstanding, once the client becomes willing, Christ can effectively terminate the Temporal authority constellated in the parent. Such terminations are generally a prerequisite to reconciling polarized opposites.

While I have not explored all facets of the Empowering archetype, *I am convinced it is not the source of Vox Dei, i.e. the Voice of God*. But very definitely, the archetype does create the prototypic, unredeemed, conscience defined as the Voice-of-conscience, Rejected-self, and Ideal-self; and these create a 'white noise' through which it is difficult to hear the Voice for God. The Empowering archetype is responsible for ego development in early childhood and the definition of good and evil when the child can finally grasp abstract opposites (the tree of good and evil). In response to the child's moral development, the parental image acquires the power to judge pride as good and the shamefully unforgivable as evil. A little later, the Ego will create a Dominant self that seeks to usurp that power by emulating it. All of those 'voices' will normally block a direct access to Heart conscience.

Christ never assumes Temporal authority when he curtails its flow in parental images and others. But regarding the archetype's manifestations as Moral authority, he will supplant that power with his power of discernment, if asked to do so by an ego-aspect, and provided the ego-aspect is willing to forgo its own power to self-shame. In the next chapter I describe the process of supplanting Moral authority with Christ's power of discernment. The process requires each ego-aspect to open the Mind to Christ for the explicit purpose of relinquishing the power to self-shame in exchange for his discernment.

Christ is asked to *terminate* the Temporal authority of parents for several reasons. First, it cannot be transferred to an ego-aspect without risk of enthrallment and hubris, and there is no value in assigning it to another human being since the authority only serves to perpetuate unequal, parent-child relationships. Second, Christ has no desire to assume Temporal authority for himself. He has never asked to 'lord' it over those he serves. In fact, the only deities likely to desire it would be Satan and his minions, who were reduced to seeking worldly power after being deprived of their heavenly powers; or human beings seeking autocratic leadership. Third, the moral aspect of this god-like authority is ideally a function of Vox Dei expressed as discernment and forgiveness, which is quite distinct from the Temporal and Moral authority exercised by a mere mortal. The latter is invariably judgmental and punishing and only pridefully rewarding. An individual is asked to be voluntarily receptive to Christ's discernment, not subject to his authority. Fourth, there is no need for an adult to be subject to any authority not freely chosen by that adult. When Christ terminates Temporal authority, he strips the parent of the power to continue exercising that authority unilaterally. Unfortunately, by the time a child becomes an adult, parental authority has been largely solidified in the unique responses of ego-aspects created throughout childhood and adolescence, so these too must be addressed.

The dilemma of every adult is that once the Empowering archetype has constellated the parental image with Temporal and Moral authority, the parent is then 'empowered' to shape and define the Ego in successive developmental epochs. The parent becomes, in a matter of speaking, the Ego's first and most empowered creator. Any ego-aspect defined by Temporal authority will experience the parent as the source of its definition, and cannot evolve far beyond that definition without the direct intervention of a higher power. The Ego can create other self-images – particularly during the juvenile period and later in adolescence – but they are most often emulators of the parent, or rebellious/defiant reactors to the parent.

Within a year or two following the emergence of the Voice-of-conscience, the Ego generally seeks to create a Dominant self that strives to usurp the parent as the Voice-of-conscience. A Dominant self can 'drown out' the parentified conscience by assuming the power to self-shame; but the parentified Voice-of-conscience will continue to be felt, if only somatically. It cannot be silenced by the Ego. Parents remain the initial and sustaining progenitors of the Voice-of-conscience until Heart conscience is redeemed by a spiritual power. The Ego cannot staunch the Empowering archetype's power by its creation of a Dominant self. That power can only be staunched by a spiritually embodied being. Free choice is limited here: we can either allow the parental voice to persist, or seek out a spiritual being to speak as Vox Dei. But whatever our choice, *conscience will have a voice.* Ideally, it will speak as Heart conscience, but failing that it will be obliged to speak through Ego conscience. Until the Ego is released from its enthrallment to the Empowering archetype, conscience is reduced to expressions of that enthrallment. Once activated, the Empowering archetype continues to sustain and constellate mortal images until staunched and supplanted by a spiritual voice for God. This means that, if authority is stripped from the parent but not supplanted by a spiritual higher power, the archetype will constellate other images, even Ideal personas (discussed in Chapter VII).

While it is clearly demonstrable that Christ can terminate the flow of archetypal energy constellating a parental image, it is not clear whether his own image is ever constellated by the archetype. There were definite historical periods when his image was portrayed as exercising Temporal authority: when, for example, he was perceived in the role of king or lord of lords. These epithets clearly reflect the attribution of Temporal authority to the image of Christ. But the gospels are equally clear that Christ, himself, rejected those powers while on earth.[1] At one stage in my thinking, I thought it would be necessary for Christ to assume Moral authority following its termination in the parent, but it never worked out that way in practice. Christ appears to eschew Moral authority as well as Temporal authority. He willingly offers the power of his discernment regarding moral issues, but as the unerring channel of the Holy Spirit his judgment is always toward love and forgiveness. Today, I refrain from suggesting that Christ assume either Temporal or Moral authority once it is stripped from the parent. Christ only appears receptive to a relationship that embodies love. When an ego-aspect willing opens to Christ – which I do strongly encourage – it is only for the purpose of receiving the power of Christ's discernment and ongoing grace as a loving response. This is not to say that the Empowering archetype cannot constellate either the Christ image or other images; only that I do not suggest it in the case of the Christ image, and find no reason to suggest it in the case of other images. Other mortals may actively seek to embody the archetype's constellating power. For example, bishops will emulate it when they confirm young confirmands or ordain priests. But I have not examined those kinds of rituals in this work; and, thus far, I have been unable to determine whether the Empowering archetype is actually called into play in ritual subjugations or is merely a generalization of the parent's Temporal and Moral authority with cultural approbation.

So far as I can determine, Christ's power and grace do not derive from the Empowering archetype. While the archetype may constellate *his image*, as Logos he is not subject to it. If he were merely a constellation of the archetype, he would not have the power to staunch its flow. The source of his power must be spiritual in nature, as distinct from soulful, insofar as discernment and forgiveness are both quintessential gifts of the Spirit. (Jung might describe the Christ image as psychoid, a creation of the spiritual realm adjoining the collective unconscious.[2]) This is why we speak of Christ as being born of the Spirit, baptized by the Spirit for his earthly ministry, and resurrected by the Spirit as a perfect conduit of the Spirit's discernment, grace, and forgiveness for all who ask.

Ego-aspects Created by Temporal Authority

In this chapter I explore the various ways in which Temporal authority manifests in active imagination. Initially, my interest was drawn to the images of parents exercising this authority. But I gradually came to see that Temporal authority manifests in two ways: first, as parental images empowered with archetypal energy; and, second, as ego-aspects created to cope with the demands and abuses of that power. Temporal authority is the initial creator of ego-aspects. The earliest Ego fragmentation is a direct consequence of shame and pain inflicted by parents wielding that authority.

All children develop *Coping-aspects* as an initial and ongoing response to fragmentation. 'Coping' aptly describes the Ego's primary accommodation to Temporal authority, what R.C.Schwartz might call the prototypic function of a manager or protector. Basically, a Coping-aspect seeks to satisfy the demands placed on it by parents and other adults who function in loco parentis. *A Coping-aspect is defined as an ego-aspect that relationally complements the image of a parent exercising Temporal authority.* A coping-aspect that is strongly related to a parent can be identified in a straightforward manner. First, Christ is asked to contain an image of the parent wielding Temporal authority, most often the father. Then, Christ is asked to draw a second circle next to the first, and place in that circle *the self-image most strongly related to that parent.* Almost without exception, this self-image will be found to play a pivotal role in the client's character and intimate relationships. This self is generally problematic for the client, often exhibiting character traits that prompted the client to seek therapy.

Pre-moral aspects and Mirror-aspects are a subgroup of Coping-aspects created by parental abuse of Temporal authority. They too are defined by the parent but cut off or estranged from the parent's image. Abusive neglect of an infant or very young child will create ego-aspects with a profound sense of lack. I call these very young selves Pre-moral aspects. When abuse of Temporal authority creates a Pre-moral aspect, the Ego will reflexively create Mirror-aspects intended to cope with the parent's neglect or abuse. Mirror-aspects tend to have an "eye for an eye" mentality by which they seek to protect the Pre-moral aspect from further wounding, though their opposition may be covert, e.g. anger expressed as pouting. Where Christ is allowed to intervene, the profound sense of deprivation experienced by a Pre-moral aspect can be satisfied by a numinous, maternal, archetypal image found by Christ. Finding this archetypal mother generally requires the cooperation of protective Mirror-aspects. The intervention is described later in the chapter. If clients have received adequate nurturing during infancy and early childhood they are not likely to develop a Pre-moral aspect or concomitant Mirror-aspect protectors.

A third kind ego-aspect distinguishable from the prototypic Coping-aspect is the Temporal persona. This persona is created when *an ego-aspect is given direct access to the energy of the Empowering archetype*. For most people, the active exercise of Temporal authority over individuals, other than their children, remains a latent potential. Normally, parents do not *assume* Temporal authority; they expect their children to mind as they minded. (It is the child's Empowering archetype that imbues the parental images with that power.) But there is a condition in which a son or daughter can assume the Temporal authority originally constellated in a parental image. The process is similar to Old Testament descriptions of 'birth right,' which entitled the firstborn son *to rule the family of origin or tribe* when given the father's blessing. In Western culture, the 'blessing' can be passed to the first-born of either sex. Being crowned the Queen is an apt example. In a number of countries that still organize around tribal connections, the assumption of Temporal authority by the firstborn is expected. But this covetousness of the parent's constellated power, while tempting, becomes a major impediment to further individuation if assumed. Temporal authority is unavoidable in parental images. Its constellation is necessary to insure the raising and safeguard of children. But the same authority cannot be assumed by children with impunity. When a growing child assumes *it within the family of origin*, even with the required blessing of the extended family, s/he invariably becomes enthralled by it. Of the few cases I have worked with that exhibited the constellation of a Temporal persona, all of them were in its thrall. Replacing a parent within a family of origin is invariably ego inflating, and generally detrimental to the individual's psychological development. Several examples are given further on.

Temporal personas need to be distinguished from Mirror-aspects. The latter emerge in response to early abuse, neglect, or rejection by parents. Mirror-aspects tend *to act like the parent in some way*; but in so doing generally seek *to stand against the parent*, not supplant the parent with the blessing of the extended family. Mirror-aspects attempt to defensively 'mirror' the parent, by exhibiting a 'stronger' quantity of whatever attribute the parent exhibits that is problematic for the child, i.e. anger, coldness, arrogance, etc. In contrast, a Temporal persona assumes the authority of an *absent* or *deceased* parent, effectively supplanting that parent in the extended family's dynamics. In effect, s/he seeks to assume a parent's place in the family of origin rather than leaving the family of origin and starting a new family. This anchors the self within the family. In contrast, most individuals normally develop ego-aspects that merely seek to cope with the parent wielding Temporal authority, rather than opposing or supplanting the parent.

The Temporal persona is a particular manifestation of the Ego that Jung referred to as the Persona. The Persona is the ego-aspect socialized by both parents to conform to their expectations within the family and other social settings. It can be identified by having Christ contain *both parents* and, in an adjoining circle, *the self-image defined by both parents in the family setting*. This is the 'mask' we wear when we are with our family or in social settings. It can be very powerful since it governs much of our behavior in family settings and other social milieus. As a rule, the core Persona is only unearthed following the redemption of a Dominant self. (The process for unearthing and working with 'the personality' is described in Chapter VII.)

The Voice-of-conscience and Rejected-self

The Rejected-self is most strongly identified with Moral authority, but is most likely created by the exercise of Temporal authority, i.e. before the age of reason. The Rejected-self is very nearly a universal occurrence. I suspect the Rejected-self is created by the adult with the most authority in a household, traditionally the father, but increasingly the mother. It is created by shaming the Ego with sufficient severity to force its dissociation thus obliging the Ego to create a new ego-aspect capable of avoiding the shameful pole of a set of opposites. The point I want to stress is that the Rejected-self, as well as the parentified Voice-of-conscience, *are both created* prior to parent's 'assumption' of Moral authority. A parent assumes the mantel of Moral authority when the child can fully grasp absolute opposites, which generally occurs around age seven (sic) the age of reason. At that point parental authority can define ideal selves as well as rejected selves. Because the Rejected-self is so closely allied to Moral authority, and so pivotal to the redemption of conscience, I have chosen to address it in the next chapter, even though it is most likely created in the early years preceding moral development.

Temporal Authority Sustains Cultural Institutions

No small part of the difficulty in working with Temporal and Moral authority is its nearly universal recapitulation in the culture at large. *While the Empowering archetype continues to be channeled predominantly through fathers, it sustains patriarchy by generalizing its power in gradients to all other males and patristic institutions*. (The person of God the Father as the sole parent of the 'Son' is a reflection of this imbalance.) In the normal course of events, patristic cultural values and institutions will both reinforce Temporal authority and actively resist the male's divestiture.[3] So far as I can determine, there are no recognized cultural rituals for removing either Temporal or Moral authority from 'the head of household' when a child comes of age.[4] If anything, the cultural rituals in place appear to support perpetuation of the parent's authoritative voice. Once a parent is empowered with Temporal authority, as must be the case if the infant is to survive, the archetypal energy will sustain the constellated images. It is reinforced by Coping-aspects and its generalization in loco parentis to such a degree that it is difficult to even discern the authority, i.e. separate the forest from the trees, much less remove it. In fact, I have only been able to do so where the client is willing to evoke an image of Christ or comparable higher power. *In the absence of a consciously evoked spiritual being capable of staunching the parent's Temporal authority, there is no merely human image or voice in the psyche with more authority than the parent or surrogate.* Without recourse to a spiritual being, the parental image – and its patriarchal surrogates, remain the most authoritative voices within the individual's Mind. This may surprise the reader, but it is easily observed using the *Light* and an image of Christ.

The Transference Phenomenon

All of my observations and interventions support the conclusion that Temporal authority underpins the transference phenomenon first described by Freud nearly a century ago. This phenomenon has been exhaustively documented in the psychoanalytic and psychodynamic literature, family systems, and work systems literature.[5] Insofar as someone is perceived to act like a parent, the client's *internalized image* of that 'someone' will be imbued with the parent's Temporal authority, and the client's Coping-aspects will react accordingly. In traditional psychotherapeutic approaches, the analysis and use of the transference phenomenon was the primary tool for correcting abuses of authority exercised by parents. It was assumed the client would quickly imbue the therapist with the characteristics and authority of a parent. It was further assumed that the client improved because the therapist responded as a 'good parent,' as distinct from the dysfunctional parent experienced in childhood. In effect, the therapist hopefully used that empowerment for the good of the client. Much the same appears to occur when supplicants seek out priests, masters, or gurus in the Christian, Buddhist and Hindu religions. But no analytic approach appears to offer a ritual for divesting the parent or surrogate of that authority either during the therapeutic process or at the completion of it.[6] Rather than setting out to deliberately remove that authority from parental images, and thereby freeing self-images to recreate, most therapists and religious have consciously or unconsciously used the transference to influence the client without altering the Temporal authority per se. However, where the therapist has access to *Light* methodology, and the Christ image, a much different approach can be offered. Through a series of interventions, Christ can divest the parent of that authority, and provide the client greater opportunities for self-definition. He can also provide significant healing for any ego-aspects created to cope with abuses of that authority.

Further Considerations in Working with Temporal Authority

The same parental image can be imbued with Temporal and Moral authority. Each authority needs to be addressed *primarily in terms of the ego-aspects it creates*. Since my practice is symptom based, I look to address whatever the client and I identity as the most pressing symptom in each session, which can include physical as well as psychological symptoms. Interventions are designed to identify the ego-aspects sustaining the symptom(s). Early on, this approach is likely to uncover Coping aspects identified with Temporal authority. This is likely the result of the client's unconscious transference of parental attributes to the therapist. However, the characterological issues shaped by Temporal authority are only likely to be addressed after working with a Dominant self, which is predominantly the creation of Moral authority. Relational authority (Chapter VIII) can be addressed before Temporal authority, but when this is done the clinician should be on the lookout for Temporal and Moral authority issues intruding into the process.

Phenomenally, the Coping-aspects created by Temporal authority often function as the precursors of ego-aspects shaped by Moral authority. Their similarities can be confusing if the therapist fails to discern the distinctions between different authorities. Temporal authority is the earliest authority consciously experienced by a child, being the one most strongly felt from birth through age seven. It is largely responsible for the creation of the earliest Ego formations described by Object Relationists. Those ego-aspects can be dissociated or overlaid by new creations designed to cope with the demands of Moral and Relational authority. But the overlays notwithstanding, Temporal authority remains foundational throughout the client's life unless consciously altered.

Once the client has learned basic uses of the *Light*, it is possible to go inside and contain a parent exercising Temporal authority. The request can be quite specific. The client is asked to use the *Light* to contain the parent in the exercise of 'parental authority.' What the *Light* contains is generally a characteristic stance or attitude of the parent whose 'look' or 'facial expression' or 'tone of voice' captures the behavior used to control or set limits on the child at different ages. The initial containment can be of one or both parents, but generally, only one parent will finally embody Temporal authority. That is most often the father, but not always, and perhaps even less so as more and more children are raised in single parent families. When a parent is contained by the *Light*, the authority often becomes quite palpable, particularly if the parent was dogmatic, overbearing, or abusive. As a rule, the father is the most visible embodiment of this authority. In past generations, the mother would only be seen as wielding Temporal authority by threatening the child with the father's authority. But note, the mother always exercises this authority directly during infancy and early childhood, and by her inadvertent, collusive, perpetuation of the father's authority in later development.

I have found it helpful to conceptualize Temporal authority in developmental terms. In infancy and early childhood it is primarily exercised by the mother's goddess-like power and experienced by the child in terms of nurture. The power of this role is immense but not generally appreciated because most abuses are hidden by the child's Coping or Mirroring ego-aspects, and the cultural expectation that the mother relinquish Temporal authority in favor of the father early in the child's life. Later in the chapter, I illustrate the effects of nurturing disruptions, and interventions for ameliorating them. The effects of disrupted nurture are profound, and generally account for some of the most severe problems encountered in clinical practice. While these abuses of nurture are easily attributable to the mother on first reading, their frequency and persistence into adulthood also appear to be a patriarchal issue. Some fathers (as well as mothers) severely abuse their infant children, but many culture-wide patriarchies are also abusive in their suppression of the numinous feminine. It is possible to correct early disruptions of nurture by fathers as well as mothers, but their correction has been traditionally opposed by patriarchies, which actively suppress numinous images of the feminine. Correcting disruptions of nurture requires the evocation of an archetypal mother whose numinous qualities are comparable to those found in goddesses; and patriarchy has a long history of diminishing the power of goddesses. Even so, I have found no better solution than the one offered by such incarnations. From a child's perspective, the mother's authority is all encompassing, which is nothing less than the role of Demeter, Quan Yin, The Virgin Mary, or a comparable goddess.

The adult client's problems are rarely with Temporal authority per se. The client's struggle is rather with the ego-aspects who react to or emulate that authority. These ego-aspects tend to act subconsciously and compulsively. In general, treatment seeks to make the client aware of these ego-aspects, alter their dependence on the parental image wielding Temporal authority, and remove restrictions on their nature dictated by that dependence. Thus, interventions are generally a two-tiered process. First, the client is helped to divest the parental image of residual Temporal authority; and second, the therapist helps the client heal the dualities most adversely affected by that authority. In this chapter, I am specifically concerned with 1) conscious Coping-aspects that remain relationally attached to parental images exercising Temporal authority, 2) Temporal personas created by the direct assumption of a parent's authority, 3) the Pre-moral aspects created by nurturing disruptions, and 4) the Mirror-aspects that inadvertently perpetuate abuses of early nurture.

Since culture – be it secular or religious – does not offer any rituals for the termination of Temporal authority once the child reaches adulthood, the individual generally feels compelled, often unconsciously, to maintain ego-aspects shaped by that authority. Normally, Coping-aspects will seek to 'pacify' the parental surrogates that receive the 'transference' of Temporal authority in relational and institutional settings. Only Mirror-aspects or rebels are likely to defy it. All of these ego-aspects are generally debilitated by this inadvertent capitulation to or defiance of the parent-child relationship. Institutional patriarchies only lose power when the energy of the Empowering archetype is separated from the father (or mother) and ego-aspects are given the opportunity to redefine.

Temporal authority is *always* exercised by parents. Resolving its residual effects – those effects that persist beyond an individual's minority – is always advisable before attempting to work on issues of conscience. *This is true even where the authority was not abused because our culture implicitly supports its generalization to patriarchal institutions at the cost of personal individuation.* In any case, it is nearly impossible to evade issues of Temporal authority. Because of the normal transference of parental attributes to a therapist, the ego-aspects most strongly shaped by Temporal authority will generally be the first encountered on going inside.

What Happens When Temporal Authority is Terminated?

This is a hard question to answer. I can tell you that Christ does not assume it, though it is often attributed to him or God the Father by religious, patristic, organizations that seek to exercise temporal power in his name. The images of parents are altered, but Christ's image is not. Therapeutically, its termination in parents appears to be a springboard for the long process of individuation. Following termination, the Aware-ego appears to be strengthened in its role as a facilitator of Christ's activity within the client's Mind. Issues suppressed by parental authority appear to come to the fore for treatment, particularly issues of abuse. As far as I can determine, the archetype does not automatically constellate other images to stand in the place of the parent. There are a number of instances wherein the individual may voluntarily allow the archetype to constellate a new image as when an adult is knighted by royalty, or ordained to holy orders by a bishop, or someone submits to the authority of a guru, or accepts a commission in the armed services; but it is not clear if the generalization is just that or a mew constellation. Historically, women were expected to become subject to their husbands when they married, but much less so – today – in America. I have not explored these voluntary subjugations, but recognize that most vows are taken seriously by the participants.

The authority is truly terminated only when the ego-aspects created by it acquire 'inner direction' of a different sort. In this work I encourage the client to turn increasingly to Christ or a comparable higher power for discernment and healing. In the beginning, most people will only trust an Egoic sense of self, failing to appreciate that ego-aspects have been largely shaped to cope with the very authority Christ is asked to terminate. At the outset, only the Aware-ego willingly addresses the effects of that authority and willingly allows Christ to terminate it. In the final analysis, it may simply be a process of attrition wherein ego-aspects turn more and more frequently to a higher power for guidance as their own solutions fail to provide the desired result. Most inner work will involve working with the ego-aspects created by Temporal, Moral, and Relational authority; and most of those ego-aspects will seek to lead themselves until it becomes painfully obvious that a higher power will better serve them. The sages refer to this as a period of purification. It can take years.

The Basic Intervention

The basic intervention can involve one or two steps. In the two-step process Christ is asked to contain the image of the parent exercising Temporal authority and then to separate or extract the energy of that authority using a second circle. This provides the client with an image of the authority's power. The second step is to have Christ place a portion of his *Light* into the heart of the parent exercising the authority. The extraction process is unnecessary for the actual termination of Temporal authority but does provide a visual analogue of the energy and what happens to it. In the one-step intervention, Christ is simply asked to place his *Light* into the heart of the parent, which staunches the flow of that energy in and through the parent's image. When this is done, the parent's image immediately changes. If the parent is still living, the image often changes from a younger image to their current age. If the parent is deceased, the image simply appears to relax.

I am quite satisfied with the action initiated by Christ – the placing of his *Light* into the parent's heart, but remain dissatisfied with the words I use to describe what he does. I have called it 'stopping the flow of energy,' 'staunching the flow,' 'separating the image from the flow,' 'reflecting the energy back to its source,' and 'terminating the flow,' to mention but a few phrasings I have used. All of them seem to work. I suspect the essential ingredient is the client's understanding that the parental image is not the source of this authority; that it is a collectively experienced archetypal energy which constellates the parental image early in life. Temporal authority is instrumental in keeping ego-aspects fragmented and willful, but its connection to the parent is arbitrary and can be dissolved by any higher power using their *Light*. I also consider it crucial to caution against any attempt to claim the energy for the Ego. It is always dangerously inflationary to assume it. However, once the authority has been terminated, the client can expect significant healing of any ego-aspects strongly attached to the parent or exiled by the parent's authority. In this way, the Ego is re-empowered; and thereafter, the Aware-ego is also empowered.

The God of Our Childhood

One last thought before moving to the clinical portion of this chapter. Temporal authority, as exercised by parents and culture, has a second effect on ego-aspects, which can also be addressed when Christ is asked to strip the parent of that authority. Parents and culture define the *'God(s) of our childhood,'* including our earliest understandings of the Christ image. The archetype empowers parents to name and define the gods we are expected to obey as children. Often, at least as I observe it in my clinical population, the gods of our childhood are often exceedingly judgmental, demanding, punishing, and distant; this can even be true of the Christ image if parents and culture have defined him as such.

During the course of therapy, if I discern that the client's conception of 'God' is harsh, punitive, distant, or adversarial, I will suggest that the client allow Christ to remove from the parent their power to define the 'god of their childhood.' Often, it may be necessary to include other early influences such as ministers, priests, nuns and Sunday school teachers. All of these 'adults' are placed in a circle that Christ enters with his *Light*. He is then asked to stand in front of each adult and place a portion of his *Light* into their heart which the client experiences as sufficient to cancel the image's power to define God.

Appendix II further explores the issue of God as a higher power. For most individuals, their 'God choice' appears to be an unconscious assimilation of familial and cultural mores. The Appendix strongly encourages the reader to reflect on what has been chosen for them and offers a ritual whereby they can consciously choose again.

THE POWER OF TEMPORAL AUTHORITY COMPARED TO CHRIST

My first encounter with Temporal authority, though I had yet to name it, occurred while using the Christ image to explore a client's relationship with her parents. When the client used her *Light* to contain an image of her father – an Episcopal priest, we were both surprised to discover that his imaged appeared to exercise more authority than her image of Christ! His image was more strongly felt by her; and in her Mind, his authority was unquestioned. She could not imagine a more powerful image than her father. Theologically speaking, one might expect the opposite. But in practice, I have since found that parental authority is initially experienced by most clients as greater than Christ's authority whether or not they are clergy. For most people, *parental images present as the most powerful images in the client's Mind.* When the parental figure with the most authority is contained – generally the father, that parent will appear much stronger and more powerful compared to the client's image of Christ. This observation is easily replicated by simply asking clients to have their Christ image stand next to the circle containing a remembered image of the parent exercising Temporal authority. In many instances where this suggestion is acted upon, the Christ image will appear smaller or otherwise less powerful than the parent wielding the authority. Most clients are chagrined to discover this since they would like to believe that an incarnation of God has more authority than a parent, abusive or otherwise. But, in fact, most clients discover, in their initial forays inside, that there are no images more powerful than that of their parents. It should be stressed that the authority vested in these parental images is more than just Temporal authority. When first encountered these images generally reflect an aggregate of Temporal, Moral, and Relational authority, although it is Temporal authority that appears to give them so much stature.

Whenever I have set up the above demonstration, I hope it will encourage the client to consider allowing Christ to use his *Light* to remove the parent's Temporal authority. I describe this authority quite simply as the parent's power to order the client without having to give a reason, e.g. you go to bed because your father tells you it is time to go to bed. Of note, it is easier to convince the client of the value of terminating the authority after s/he is asked to identify the Coping-aspect most strongly attached to the parent wielding the authority, since that image is generally found to be immature or undeveloped. This arrested development is the direct result of the parent wielding Temporal authority and can only be corrected by letting Christ remove the authority.

Before I fully appreciated the concept of energy inherent in images, my interventions relied simply on Christ terminating the authority from the parental image. This proved helpful to the client, but the idea of it was frequently threatening. Many clients intuit at some level that the authority must go somewhere once it is stripped from the parent, and they were fearful of the unknown quality of any new vessel. This was especially true for men whose mothers were seen as dominant. In their mind such a transfer would simply give another female the power to order/abuse them. Also, many clients tend to marry a spouse much like the parent wielding Temporal authority, e.g. the wife-beating husband. Removing authority from the parent might reasonably increase the power of the spouse. All of these concerns will have to be addressed concomitantly or prior to asking Christ to terminate Temporal authority in a parent.

Given time and reflection, most clients will acknowledge that Christ is personally immune to the temptations of Temporal power; that he is not tempted to use that power for good or ill. Repeatedly during his ministry, as described in the New Testament, he is offered and refuses temporal power (beginning with Satan's temptations in the desert). Thus, most clients will agree, in principle, that this aspect of parental authority might be safely terminated by their Christ image without his being tempted, in any way, to assume it. In therapy, I stress the word *terminate*. His intent is only to terminate this authority. Truly, Christ appears to have no interest in Temporal authority beyond unburdening the relationship between the parent and the adult child; and as far as I can determine, he is the only archetypal image in Western culture who has categorically refused to assume it (aside from Buddha whose teachings have made strong inroads in the West).

In the initial stages of inner work, the therapist needs to continually emphasize the distinction between Temporal and Moral authority. Though I am only addressing Temporal authority in this chapter, the two types of authority must be distinguished, because they are initially blended in the client's mind. This blending is another reason why clients are initially reluctant to allow Christ to terminate the parent's Temporal authority. They fear Christ would then use his authority to morally condemn rejected aspects of the Ego. I have worked with adults who were lifelong, devout, Christians who, nonetheless, were convinced that Christ would label parts of them as 'bad' and unforgivable, if he had the parent's power to judge them. Since I held a similar belief for too many years, I can appreciate how easy it is to conclude that Christ acing like a parent would be equally condemning. I always discuss these distinctions with the client to allay any fears in this respect. Christ may quicken conscience as a deterrent, but he never condemns after the fact.

Initially, I am only interested in dealing with Temporal authority, the authority that makes the parental image loom larger than the Christ image. Only later, will I endeavor to address the issues of unredeemed conscience. What I stress is that Temporal authority is about the arbitrary imposition of physical and gender limits, the power of 'no;' the power of force and law as distinct from morality.

The Client's Fear of Independence

Some clients are convinced that their well-being requires a continuing dependence upon the parent's Temporal authority. Such beliefs are generally reinforced by the parent and prognostic of childhood abuse. It is most pronounced where the parent is described as forcefully thwarting adolescent strivings for increased autonomy. As the following case illustrates, the issue may only become apparent when the client seeks to remove the parent's authority.

Anita. For several weeks, Anita had been struggling to clarify her feeling of having been raped as a child. She is convinced she was raped and wants to believe it was by a man next door who was known to have molested his stepdaughter. But in this particular session, she admits to ruminating on a terrible thought all the previous week: her father is the source of her *pain*. I suggest it might be helpful if she goes inside and asks her *Light* to contain *the source of her pain* in a circle, whoever it might be and whatever the reason for it. At this suggestion, and without actually going inside, she spontaneously recalls the memory of a thanksgiving dinner at the family home, during her college years, when she and her father were arguing. At some point in the argument, he sat close to her and said, "Don't you ever disobey me." As she recalls it: "He was really angry ... past the point of being angry ... over the line ... I'm not sure what he would have done if I had challenged him at that point." Given this deep-seated fear of him, I suggest she contain her father's Temporal power to hurt her. She agrees to go inside specifically for that purpose. Initially, she has difficulty re-orienting inside (indicative of feeling threatened), so I suggest she *sense* the presence of her *Light* and ask it to provide her with a circle of protection which she can enter upon going inside. This allows her to orient inward. Almost immediately, she reports seeing an image of 'Christ' outside her circle, *only it is older* than her normal image of Christ, and distinctly different in that the image is wearing a *cape* and *carrying a cane*. I ask her to have this Christ explain the meaning of his appearance but she is unresponsive to my question, which is unlike her, and she seems increasingly engrossed with the image. She reports hearing the suggestion from this figure that she is "to lean on and trust the cane" and then she goes on to say: "It can support...I can use it for the support I need." The image appears to be modeling this for her. But then the 'Christ' figure breaks the cane and she hears the words "broken trust." She then sees an image of the 'Christ' in a wheelchair, which reminds her of her paternal grandfather. I ask if he is the one we should be concerned about? She does not answer but seems more and more enthralled by whatever is going on inside. It is at this point that I feel a need to intervene. I attempt to refocus her by asking directly: "Are you willing to contain your father's power to hurt you if you disobey?" She answers "yes," but continues to be entranced by the cane, and saying: "It's new ... and more powerful than the *Light*." At this point I asked her to touch the cane and the 'Christ' with her *Light*. But instead, she again insists: "The cane is a part of the light – a new source of strength." I ask her if it is intended to replace her father? She replies: "It is a gift." Again, I insist that she touch the 'Christ' with her *Light*. Finally, she touches the image and immediately reports the appearance of her familiar Christ figure, and exclaims that whatever she has been dealing with is untrustworthy but very powerful – even to the point of falsifying her Christ image and having the cane mimic her *Light*, but when her Christ appears he seems more powerful. Again, I ask her if she is willing to contain her father's authority? This time she reports success and describes it as like a windstorm. I suggest she have Christ bind it with his own *Light* since I am not really sure what we were dealing with at that point. She replies that, "Christ has it ... but it's hard for me to let go of it ...it is easily bound ... but also unbound ... he has sealed it in a jar... it has the cane in it ... I've been using my father's authority *as a crutch not to stand on my own feet* ... it is very powerful ... almost as powerful as the *Light* (her willingness) ... this fake power is almost as strong as the real thing ... but it's cold, not as warm ... and really empty ... inside the cape is a facade ... I thought Christ was in it ... but it is empty and hollow ... that cape wanted me to fill it up." I ask if she was willing to keep it contained so she can examine herself apart from it? She answers "yes" but also notes that she feels naked and exposed. I suggest she ask Christ to stand as a buffer between her and the power. She agrees. A week later she allows Christ to remove her father's Temporal authority, but not without many distractions, and immediately afterward, she begins recovering a memory of having been violently struck by her father, as a toddler, during an argument between the parents. That session ends with her having Christ go to the stricken child to hold it, and protect it from any further harm.

In addition to illustrating the marked dependence created by abuses of Temporal authority, the above case also highlights several other points worth noting. Something in Anita strongly resists the divestiture of the parent's authority, very likely a Coping-aspect who remained merged with the Aware-ego. This session occurred long before I had gained an appreciation of the Coping-aspect's dependence upon the parental image for definition. What accentuated this parent's authority appeared to be the father's continuing threats of violence even when his daughter became a young adult. In such cases, the authority can truly seem unbreachable or god-like; and a Coping-aspect will be hard pressed to defy such power. In Anita's case, immediately on going inside for the explicit purpose of containing her father's power, that 'power' sought to convince Anita – yet again – that she needed to sustain the status quo rather than change it. It did so by *trying to appear like her Christ figure!* This adulteration of a Christ figure is a rare phenomenon, but I have encountered it on several occasions. It is one of the reasons why early on I began asking that the Christ figure (or any other figure intended to be helpful) be initially screened by the client's *Light*. If the figure is not threatening to the client, it will remain as it is even after being touched by the client's *Light*. If it is a threatening, bogus, or counterfeit image, this simple procedure dispels the figure. Of note, Anita herself was immediately aware that the figure that first appeared to her was different even as it seemed to enthrall her. Such occasions also call for a degree of discernment on the part of the therapist. I could sense 'wrongness' in what was happening, in part, because Anita kept getting caught up in the enthrallment to such a degree she was hard pressed to even acknowledge my questions much less respond to them. Wherever there is doubt, the therapist needs to insist that the client touch the figure with the *Light*; and only trust the image's veracity if it passes that simple test.[7]

The above example represents an extreme of what is likely to be encountered on going inside. Most parental images exercising authority are much less dramatic, but I have not encountered any who seemed willing or eager for Christ to remove their authority, though most appear remorseful, unburdened, or relieved afterward. It is also worth noting that a Coping-aspect never acquires direct access to Temporal authority when it is removed from the parent. When the Coping-aspect is redefined by a consensus involving itself, the Aware-ego and Christ, it will receive a recalibrated energy most suitable to its new definition.

The Effect of Grandparents' Temporal authority on Parents

The Temporal authority of grandparents can also have a discernable effect on the client. Interventions demonstrating the effects of Temporal authority on the *parent-grandparent relationship* are helpful in modeling its suppressive effects, especially on daughters. Asking Christ to terminate a grandmother's Temporal authority to define her grandchild's femininity can have a freeing effect on the client. Observing what happens when Temporal authority is removed from the grandparents also provides the client with a paradigm for what s/he can expect when Temporal authority is removed from the parents.

When applying this intervention from the perspective of a female client, I first ask her to contain her mother in a circle of *Light* as s/he appears to the client in a contemporary image (if the mother is still living) or as she is remembered (if deceased). Then, I ask her to place the maternal grandparents in a second circle beyond the mother's circle. Christ is then asked to enter the second circle containing the grandparents, and terminate any Temporal authority that has *suppressed* the mother's femininity, sexuality, or womanhood. The choice of words can be altered to fit the situation. For example, I worked with a woman who was very repressed sexually, so that quality was emphasized. If the maternal grandparents' Temporal authority has been operable in this regard then I would expect to observe changes in the image of the mother. As a rule, the mother will be described as appearing lighter or standing straighter. Essentially, the client reports shifts in perception that indicate a lifting of some form of oppression or compulsion. After working with the maternal grandparents, I might then focus on the client's paternal grandmother. Interestingly, removing authority from a paternal grandmother will often affect the father's image. His image is likely to change in a way that reflects his diminished authority to define the feminine. When a mother-in-law no longer exerts authority through her son, the husband's authority to define his wife's womanhood is also diminished. Often, this intervention will produce positive changes in his wife's self-image. Likewise, I have had a number of clients report positive changes in their relationships with significant others, including parents, in the weeks following this type of intervention.

I might also ask the client to examine the Inner dyads of the grandparents (discussed Chapter VIII), especially if I suspect that the client has been strongly identified with a particular grandparent within the extended family. In general, parents appear to raise grandchildren; that is to say, children will be very quickly identified with one of the four grandparents by the immediate and extended family. This should not be surprising. Each grandparent represents a 'family name' which seeks to continue itself through progeny. In most cultures, the first-born is generally identified with father's side, second born with mother's side, third born to the father's side, etc. If the father is identified with his paternal side then his first born will be identified with the paternal grandfather, and his third born will be identified with the paternal grandmother's side of the family. This can be tested as a hypothesis. Ask the client to have his or her parents identify the client with one of the four grandparents. The answer needs to be a forced choice: that is, the parent or parents are obliged to choose just one grandparent. This choice will frequently coincide with the client's self observation as well as the identity assigned by other members of the family.

THE TEMPORAL PERSONA

In working with clients around the issue of Temporal authority, one source of client resistance is the covert desire to *retain* the parent's Temporal authority as their own. Under special circumstances it is possible for offspring to assume the authority that the Empowering archetype constellates in a parental image. A Temporal persona only emerges when 1) the parent exercising Temporal authority in the family system dies or otherwise abandons the family; and 2) the sibling has 'the blessing' of other members of the family, including the other parent, to assume the authority exercised by the deceased/abandoning parent, or less frequently, a grandparent. It is not clear to me whether the assumption of a Temporal persona by a client results from the constellation of the Empowering archetype or is merely an 'authorization' by other adults within the family. But where I have encountered this phenomenon clinically, the client was clearly in the thrall of the power they appeared to covet.

Temporal authority within the family of origin is comparable to Cultural personas, which I discuss in the next chapter. An ego-aspect experiences itself as a Cultural persona when it accepts any *culturally defined* role of leadership, e.g. Emperor, King, Chief, Headman, Sheik, etc. Where the role has wide cultural import, it is generally highly defined and dependent upon the sustained 'blessing' of a significant group of adults. In contrast, the assumption of a Temporal persona only requires the blessing of those most immediately affected by the role of leadership within a family of origin.

I have had too little experience with the Temporal persona to assess its prevalence, though I am able to document its effects. It is probably less prevalent in the United States than in other cultures. In tribal cultures, such as Near Eastern Cultures (Iran, Iraq, Turkey, etc.), or cultures in which the firstborn son is given undue regard and authority (China, India, South America, etc.), the Temporal persona is probably quite prevalent. In such countries the Temporal persona seems to be culturally expected and reinforced. But that is a surmise based on reading about those cultures rather than first hand experience. Remember, the only requirements for the creation of a Temporal persona are a growing child's assumption of Temporal authority within the family of origin with the explicit blessing of the surviving parent and siblings. In America, most children are expected to *leave* the family and cleave to their spouse. But there are numerous circumstances even in our culture where families may elect to maintain the status quo by appointing one of the children to replace a strong patriarch or matriarch (following the death or abandonment by that parent or grandparent) rather than allowing the family to reorganize. And it is likely that there will be an increase in the prevalence of the this persona as we seek to acculturate increasing numbers of people from countries other than Europe.

Olivia. The nature of this persona was first highlighted for me by the astute self-disclosures of a client named Olivia. She is avowedly lesbian in her sexual orientation, and generally assumes the 'butch' role in her relationships. She is cognizant of her 'masculine demeanor,' which identifies her with butches as distinct from fems. She feels it comes from being strongly identified with her father by other members of her family. Their identification intensified following his alcoholic death in her early teens. But even before his death, her mother treated her as a father surrogate. Whenever the father was gone the mother insisted she sleep with her; and often stimulated her sexually. As an adult, Olivia experiences her 'father identification' as giving her a sense of specialness, a kind of "heady ego trip." She feels it most strongly as an officer in her military unit or with other butches. She describes it as making her feel self-centered, almost insatiable, and fearful of abusing the power it seems to impart to her. The day she described these feelings to me she was wearing her father's academy ring, which seemed to her a kind of signet ring representing a visible transfer of her father's authority. In listening to her, it feels as if her father's authority controls her as much as she controls it, that it might be more than she can handle in that it frequently threatens to overtake and rule her. Indeed, it seems to enslave her to care-taking her abusive, exploiting, mother and siblings, as well as her lover who was a practicing alcoholic for much of their relationship. The way she describes herself reminds me of hubristic dramas in Greek mythology: the experience of excessive pride or self-confidence verging on arrogance that overwhelms individuals when touched with 'god-like powers.' When Olivia finally goes inside to contain her father *and his authority*, she visualizes it as "cyclonic ... like a tornado ... a constant whirlwind inside of me ... my weight is a reflection of my inability to control it (she is struggling to control her weight), and its whirlwind quality makes it difficult for me to organize my thoughts." When she is finally able to ask her inner Christ to strip her father's image of this authority, she reports feeling a discernible difference in terms of calmness and her ability to focus her thoughts.

Olivia's case illustrates how I addressed Temporal persona issues early on. Today I would approach it more gradually, first separating the authority from the father, then separating it from the Temporal persona. Christ can then be asked to help redefine ego-aspects *suppressed* by this persona and reconcile them to the ego-aspect now separated from the persona energy. Examples of this more complex intervention are given in later sections on the transformation of Coping-aspects.

Olivia's case also illustrates an almost irresistible dilemma/urge faced by growing children. Parental authority is a god-like power not unlike the anima/animus energies described by Jung. As Jungians describe those archetypes, no human being is an adequate vessel of that power. It is hubristic to assume it, and invariably problematical for another to accept your projection of it. To project these energies onto another enthralls you to the recipient.[8] In cases of enthrallment by Anima/Animus archetypes, the client is said to be Anima or Animus possessed.[9] Clients are equally enthralled when the family encourages them to hubristically assume a parent's Temporal authority. The solution offered here is a third alternative: to ask Christ to terminate the authority in the ego-aspect and parental image, and then have him offer reconciliation to the previously enthralled ego-aspect and ego-aspects suppressed by it. But this is never an easy matter since it means individuating vis-à-vis the family of origin. Even where the client is willing, the family itself may actively resist, since any such separation will force them to reorganize. After my work with Olivia, she did separate from her family and lover by moving across country to pursue a music career.

Work with this hubristic condition is a delicate matter. Since the client tends to experience this authority as a form of strength, they will not consider relinquishing it until they have experienced its limitations. Normally, such clients are *strong*, but paradoxically, always at the expense of suppressing sources of real strength which they identify as *weak*. Suffice to say, this hubristic condition is most likely to be found where one or both parents abdicates their role during development, or where the client remembers having to defend one parent against the abuses of another, or having to take care of siblings and/or self because one or both parents were regularly absent, drunk, severely depressed or chronically ill. Such clients tend to be overly responsible toward others. Often, they come into therapy exhausted by their efforts to care for dependent family members. (Not surprisingly, these dependents are often seen as weak, and where that issue is explored, they are often found to be projective vessels for a disowned self.) As a rule, the issue of strength, or over-responsible functioning, needs to be examined at length before interventions are enacted. The intervention is only effective if such clients can appreciate the limitations of this 'false strength' and be willing to forgo it. In my experience, this is never an easy matter to resolve.

Temporal Personas Derived from a Grandparent

While Temporal authority is most often experienced by the child as flowing through the father, this is not always so. Sometimes his image remains unconstellated, as when maternal authority remains a dominant force throughout the client's development. Whenever the father's image is not the apparent vessel of this authority in an adult client, it is generally because the mother or a grandparent exerts it. Later in the chapter, I explore conditions in which the mother's Temporal authority is dominant throughout the life of the child. Here, I want to examine generational usurpation – conditions where grandparents retain or divert the flow of Temporal authority thereby circumventing its constellation in the father's image. This circumvention can also result in the creation of a Temporal persona. It is most likely to occur in families where two adult generations live under the same roof or practically next door.[10] The dominant grandparent may be male or female. Whenever the father's image does not appear to constellate Temporal authority, the therapist needs to ask: where is it embedded? The following case illustrates a situation in which the Temporal authority of the *maternal grandfather* (deceased) was delegated directly to a grandson with the family's blessing. Wherever hubristic manifestations of this sort are identified, the client must allow Christ to terminate the authority in the Temporal persona embodying it, as well as the grandparents' authority. This case represents a variation of the one described above. Such delegations of authority only seem to occur where the extended family seeks to perpetuate a particular constellation of roles rather than letting the family system reorganize following the death of a significant member such as a patriarch or matriarch.

Reese. In Reese's case, Temporal authority was exercised by the maternal grandmother following the death of her husband. Very quickly, the grandfather's Temporal authority passed directly to her grandson, Reese, who was expected to eventually replace the maternal grandfather as 'head of household.' This was only discovered when Reese agreed to go inside for the purpose of containing his father's Temporal authority. What he reports, on going inside, is an image of his father (also deceased) that is very vague – suggesting that he has very little authority in the eyes of his son. On reflection, this is not altogether surprising, since the father lived in a small house on his mother-in-law's property as a tolerated, practicing alcoholic. In contrast, Reese grew up in the maternal grandmother's house under her aegis and as something of an emotional substitute for the deceased grandfather. Over the years, the women in the family, including Reese's mother and sisters, delegated all Temporal authority to Reese.[11] He had, however, to pay a price. The authority he assumed made him rigid, opinionated, and perfectionistic, even as it also provided him an elevated status as the family hero. In the process he also appears to have displaced a firstborn brother. That brother, like the father, is also a practicing alcoholic who left the family circle early on and was rarely heard from. Reese appears to have a good deal of difficulty with other male authority as if his authority was tenuous outside the family circle or vulnerable to challenge by any 'first born.' I note Reese's case because it illustrates why the particular characteristics of a father figure should always be closely examined. In terms of treatment, Reese had first to forgo his claim to that authority. In doing so he had to relinquish his felt status within the family – a difficult decision; but in exchange he would go on to claim a better, non-defensive relationship with other males and a legitimate authority that encouraged growth, rather than perfectionism and the fear of shame.

Circumstances similar to Reese's case will have a comparable effect on a daughter. I suspect that a daughter's circumvention of a father's Temporal authority is very rare. A daughter can only circumvent her father's Temporal authority if her mother is dominant, or she is removed from the father's home and identified with a more dominant grandparent by her caretakers. I only have one case example of this occurring. The daughter was removed from the father's home and raised by a spinster, maternal great aunt. This great aunt, as well as other members of that extended household, appears to have *delegated the maternal great grandfather's authority* to the granddaughter. (He had been a wealthy landowner in a South American country.) She was raised in a highly patristic culture. She became very high achieving and quite successful, but never married, though she had several long-term affairs with successful men. Such a daughter must live in a constant state of tension. To marry, she must find a man willing to implicitly submit to her authority within the home; but what is more likely, she will not marry. She must forgo any strong identity with other women insofar as they are subordinate to males, unless she plays a clearly dominant role in the relationship. Likewise, while she evades being suppressed by her father's Temporal authority, she nonetheless must still contend with the legacies of her grandfather's authority and a sense of uniqueness that makes it difficult for her to fit into the culture; and she will feel obliged to support any of the extended family who look to her for support. I suspect this family situation would be very rare in America. It is more likely to be found in South American and Asian communities.

In sum, the assumption of a Temporal persona is likely to occur whenever a child is identified by family with a particular parent or grandparent, and asked to assume a 'head of household' role within the extended family system, rather than allowing the family system to naturally reorganize and evolve. In Olivia's case discussed earlier, she was delegated the role of her deceased father; in Reese's case just described, he was delegated the role of his deceased maternal grandfather. In both examples, the children are encouraged – from a very young age, to assume a Temporal persona. It is difficult, if not impossible, for the child to resist such an offer if all adults in the immediate family tacitly support it. But having acceded, whether consciously or otherwise, the child will become enthralled by it. In treatment, Christ must be allowed to terminate this authority enthralling the ego-aspect most identified with the deceased parent/grandparent, as well as terminating the Temporal authority constellated in parental figure.

The Ego is an archetypal energy that always constellates as an ego-aspect. 'Coping-aspect' is an umbrella term describing several kinds of ego-aspects that, in one way or another, are the Ego's *reaction* to Temporal authority. For example, Mirror-aspects are Coping-aspects specifically created by the Ego to shield and hide a Pre-moral aspect from further wounding by maternal Temporal authority. In sharp contrast, a persona is created by *the co-constellation of two archetypal energies*. Thus, a Temporal persona is specifically created when an ego-aspect is infused with energy from the Empowering archetype. It is not merely another ego-aspect or coping-aspect

THE MOST COMMON EGO-ASPECTS CREATED BY TEMPORAL AUTHORITY

Temporal personas are comparatively rare. Most of us are followers, not leaders. The most common ego-aspects are Coping-aspects. These are generally the selves first encountered on going inside, as they are strongly governed by the transference phenomena, which is most strongly evoked at the outset of therapy.

In both men and women, a Coping

-aspect, either seeks to comply with Temporal authority at some level, withdraw from it, mirror it, seduce it, or defy it. The quality of emotional response is generally a reaction to the parent's exercise of Temporal authority. Where parental affect is clearly abusive as in the case of repetitive rage, then the Ego will seek to withdraw if possible, comply as needed, seduce the parent and/or covertly mirror the parent, e.g. the bully. If the parent's exercise of authority has been relatively benign, then the individual is most likely to develop a Coping-aspect that seeks to comply with it. I am sure there are more than these five responses available to a child, but they appear to be the most prevalent. Until the onset of adolescence, most coping responses will be outwardly compliant. It is only in early adolescence that Coping-aspects will crystallize as rebellious in an effort to respond to the adult world on a more equal footing. What form that takes will depend on how the parent wielding Temporal authority responds at that point in the child's development. If a Temporal persona is actualized within a family of origin it is most likely to emerge in adolescence.[12]

Coping-aspects Co-exist With the Aware-Ego

Whenever the client focuses inward, the Aware-ego can evoke the *Light* of willingness and the aid of a higher power such as Christ. But most people are simply not use this degree of mindfulness. So who is the client when s/he goes inside, unaided and alone? Or even when s/he avoids the process with endless distractions? What self enacts the individual's ordinary sense of 'I'? I do not mean, who s/he is in fantasy, but rather who s/he is as s/he acts in the world, or rehearses alternatives, or contemplates tomorrow's activities, or relives a myriad of typical emotions such as fear, shame, pride, desire and the like. Coping-aspects guide us minute by minute, all the day long. They are defined as the set of all ego-aspects, except the Rejected-self that precipitated their initial creation. They must cope with all of our worlds – Body, Mind, Soul and Spirit.

Coping-aspects co-exist with the Aware-ego. They embody the conscious personality. Until the individual begins to exercise 'mindfulness,' these ego-aspects will dominate consciousness, and control much of our behavior. So long as these Coping-aspects co-exist without differentiation, their fears and threats will co-exist with the Aware-ego, often overwhelming it and thereby limiting the Aware-ego's ability to exercise willingness. That is to say, whenever an *undifferentiated* Coping-aspect is threatened, it will compete with the *Light*'s ability to act on suggestions. Discerning the existence of these undifferentiated Coping-aspects is the first step toward depotentiating them. While undifferentiated, their co-existence will not be readily apparent to the client who often confuses the feelings generated by these aspects with Aware-ego consciousness. As I have noted elsewhere, most clients will initially treat consciousness as a unitary phenomenon and, thereby, fail to differentiate between the Aware-ego and other ego-aspects.

A Coping-aspect remains enmeshed with the Aware-ego until consciously differentiated from it. They control significant segments of a client's emotional life, physical being, and motivation. They are invariably willful, meaning they tend to be stereotypic, situationally reactive, and compulsive. They can be so enmeshed, so much a part of how the client presents to the therapist, that even a therapist can overlook them, as I too often did in my early work, and continue to do so on a regular basis.

Coping-aspects must contend with all forms of parental authority. They come in all sizes and shapes and tend to be hierarchical. Those that develop later are generally superordinate, meaning they have the power to suppress the activity of another ego-aspect. 'Superordinate' is a term I borrowed many years ago from a theory of personality developed by George Kelly.[13] His cognitive theory was built on personal constructs of reality identified as superordinate or subordinate. Superordinate constructs controlled lower ordered, or less developed, constructs of belief. A similar process appears to be at work in terms of Coping-aspects. A Dominant self is generally the more developed than Responsible primary in a client's consciousness even as both emerge to contend with the constellation of the moral complex.[14] Mirror-aspects, by contrast, are considerably less developed and generally subordinate to a Dominant self, though they can definitely clutter the mind with emotional turmoil. This hierarchical process can be briefly illustrated with the following case.

Benedict. This illustration describes Benedict's first time inside. In recent years, I have frequently provided new clients with a Manual describing the use of the *Light*, which covers most of the material in Chapter III.[15] I have found this helpful in facilitating the process. Anyone who reads that chapter has begun imagining the *Light*. It would be hard to read the chapter without doing so. For Benedict, I used a much quicker induction then the one outlined in that chapter. I simply had him imagine his young daughter bringing him his *Light*. A parent's own children, particularly young children, are implicitly trusted by their parents. In any case, Benedict easily found his *Light* by this method. Next, I had him use the *Light* to contain and screen a Christ image. Our purpose for going inside on this particular occasion was to see if he could identify the source of his anger, which he often feels but hardly ever expresses. Basically, I ask him extend his Light to Christ who uses it to draw a double circle around his Aware-ego. I then have him ask Christ to separate a personification of his anger. He immediately reports sensing a 'sad face' indicative of disappointment. Then he reports that it is not possible to separate the circles. When he attempts to separate them everything goes black – a clear indication of threat. But it is not the angry aspect that seems threatened. On reflection, Benedict reports that as soon as the angry aspect began to separate, Benedict could feel himself 'shutting down.' The 'blacking out' only occurred when the two circles were about to separate completely. I surmise that the threat is a fear of liberating anger – though that was not the intent of the separation. Another self does not trust the angry aspect to remain contained apart from its own ability to shut down the expression of anger. Benedict now tells me that this is a typical response for him. He values this ability to 'shut down' and can identify a number of situations in which it normally comes into play, e.g. arguments with his wife, tense work situations, etc. What is significant, from my perspective, is not so much his valuing of it, but the occurrence of the reflexive response at the mere thought of consciously expressing anger even within the Mind. This shutting down points to control being exerted by yet another ego-aspect. In all likelihood, the angry part is a Mirror-aspect, and will be needed to find the Pre-moral aspect it is protecting. But before we can get to that, the Coping-aspect with the power to 'shut down' must also be contained, separated, and mollified. Otherwise, it will consistently abort any attempt to personify and dialogue with the angry Mirror-aspect.

Any therapist using the interventions described in this work is likely to encounter the active blocking of those interventions on a regular basis. In the particular instance above, separation threatens an ego-aspect created to shut down expressions of anger. That Coping-aspect is superordinate to the Mirror-aspect which seeks to express its anger. But even if angry expression was not threatening, and separation of the Mirror-aspect went smoothly, it is still likely that further on we will encounter other 'resistances.' If, for example, a Temporal persona has been created, it will assuredly come into play before Christ is allowed to terminate the Temporal authority of a parent. As a rule of thumb, older Coping-aspects control younger ones, e.g. adolescents control juveniles, juveniles control children, etc. Of note, there are very few adults in this hierarchy. If existent, they are generally young adults; and this is reflected in the observation that most people report feeling younger than their age much of the time.

The point to bear in mind, whenever clients go inside, is that the Aware-ego co-exists with a number of Coping-aspects of varying power. Individuation is a process of identifying each of them and their disowned opposites, healing them where that is called for, depotentiating inflation as necessary, maturing them as needed, and finding in Christ the best source of inner and outer guidance. These Coping-aspects persist in strength because the parental authority that created them remains active. So the work must focus on ego-aspects and parents alike.

Temporal authority and Subjective Age

I first became aware of the significance of subjective age while working with MPD clients, though I have since discovered it is a common phenomenon throughout the clinical population. Subjective age is the distinct feeling of being younger than our chronological age in a way that often incapacitates us in our interactions with significant others. We are most likely to feel this younger age in family situations, interpersonal relationships, or when interacting with authority figures. The phenomenon is most pronounced with MPD clients whose alter personalities can look, act and feel the age they report, such that a therapist can have the distinct feeling of working with an actual child. Often, in therapy, clients will spontaneously report feeling a certain age, and having felt that age for a long time, though not all of the time. For these reasons, *whenever a client describes a new ego-aspect I ask its age*. Clients can generally pinpoint it to within a year since the ego-aspect has a visual analogue. Common age ranges for all kinds of ego-aspects are 'infant' (ages 1-2), 'child' (ages 3-6), 'juvenile' (ages 7-13), 'early adolescence' (ages 13-16), and 'late adolescence' (ages 16 –20). Often, the aspect's age will correspond with the age of their creation or developmental fixation. In the case of MPD fragments, the age will usually correspond with the age when they came into being to cope with a specific trauma.

For most clients, the experience of subjective age is generally felt in recurring situations such as contact with parents or other long-standing relationships. But it can become more or less embedded in his or her demeanor if the client continually interacts with others who enact parent-child scripts. For clients who have geographically separated from families where parental dysfunction is ongoing (e.g. alcoholic, autocratic behavior), the feeling of age dissonance will be most pronounced in the presence of the parent or when talking to them on the telephone. In those instances, it is as if a trance state is triggered by simply walking through the front door of the parent's home or calling the phone number. I call it 'entering a trance state' because clients frequently report feeling overtaken with lethargy, feeling heavy, or drained of feeling, or numb when in the presence of parents; and these feelings begin to clear as soon as they are away from the home place or off the telephone.

These reactions can also be triggered by adults in authority who act like the parent. Most people are unaware that these feelings are sustained by a child or early adolescent self. They can distinctly 'feel' the self but be unaware of its subjective age and demeanor. This only becomes readily apparent when they go inside and separate from it.

Coping-aspects that remain children or minors clearly place the client at a disadvantage in an adult world. When you are feeling like a child among adults you can be blustery, defiant and rebellious, even childishly seductive or cute, but hardly effective in asserting your own authority. I have encountered this subjective age phenomenon in a variety of clients. Wherever it is encountered, my rule of thumb is to assist the client in raising the ego-aspect to the client's current chronological age. This 'growing up' process can be prolonged, however, because the experience of subjective age is closely tied to issues of Temporal authority and these must be resolved before the client permits Christ to raise an image to full maturity. At the very least, the parent's constellated authority must be terminated. Where that is permitted, it still takes an indeterminate number of sessions for a child image to grow through different developmental epochs, e.g. puberty, adolescence, early adulthood, etc. It is hard to appreciate how powerfully these child images effect a client's outlook and behavior until therapist and client can observe the changes that take place following each growth spurt. Almost without exception, the presence of a prepubescent or young adolescent aspect is indicative of a Coping-aspect strongly in thrall of parental authority. Prepubescent Coping-aspects are also likely exhibit gender and/or sexual maturation issues. Of note, the process of maturation does become quicker with repetitive use of the intervention.

Few clients are aware of how much their behavior is controlled by developmentally fixated ego-aspects. This is primarily the result of having never separated from the ego-aspect. Without the visual analogue provided by the *Light's containment,* it is difficult to achieve the perspective needed to appreciate the developmental immaturity of these selves. Subjective age illustrates yet another way in which Temporal authority can limit an individual's ability to function in the world. Truncated development is the direct result of a parent's inability to foster autonomy. This may be willful on the part of the parents or simply the inadvertent consequence of their own truncated development. It is to be expected that sons and daughters will begin to assert themselves in early adolescence, implicitly asking their parents for increased self-governance concomitant with their maturation. Where parents block this, the adolescent must either defiantly break away or become developmentally fixated. Where development is essentially blocked by the parent's authority, the stunted ego-aspect – in the guise of an adult, will too easily accede to the authority of others or ineffectively assert themselves in self-destructive ways.

In general, one or more ego-aspects will be strongly attached to the father and/or mother since our culture has yet to offer a rite of passage whereby parents divest themselves of Temporal authority when the young adult comes of age. Historically, the only way a daughter could stop cleaving to her parents was by the father's act of 'giving' her to her husband. In effect, her husband was expected to become the generalized manifestation of Temporal authority. Later in the chapter, I will discuss how this still manifests in the current culture. Where it is identified in therapy, Christ can be asked to place both father and husband in the same circle and simultaneously terminate the authority in both. Men are also vulnerable to this kind of enthrallment if the father's authority flows through the mother. In such cases both parents are placed in the circle and the authority is simultaneously removed from both.

However a Coping-aspect first presents itself, one goal will be its maturation to the client's chronological age. The only exception is a Pre-moral aspect. Generally, this aspect is left in the perpetual care of the archetypal mother, as described later in the chapter. But otherwise, the goal will be full maturation and autonomy. Four major developmental epochs are generally used as stepping stones to maturation: early childhood, the juvenile period, adolescence and early adulthood. Often, it is necessary to resolve the issues that fixated development in a specific epoch. In addition, the client will need to imbue the self image with the specific qualities necessary for full autonomy. That is done by asking Christ to provide the necessary attributes as the Coping-aspect becomes willing. Last, it is always advisable to ask Christ if he wants to imbue the ego-aspect with any specific qualities. Often, he will select qualities which the client clearly would value but is too timid to request.

One more point to consider. Many Coping-aspects appear to be fixated at prepubescence, particularly females. It is almost as if the parental authority blocks the maturational transition to womanhood. This issue must be addressed. Christ must be asked to bring the child into full maturation, specifically menses. In some cases it may even be necessary to explicitly discuss such issues as masturbation, orgasm, and the like. A juvenile Coping-aspect can only move into adolescence when she can claim her sexuality. With males this is also an issue as many males are stuck in the masturbatory fantasies of early adolescence.

The Transformation of Coping-aspects Most Strongly Related to the Father

In much of this work, progress is often made by asking the right question. In this instance, the right question is asking Christ to help the client identify the self *most strongly related to the father*. Procedurally, Christ is first asked to contain an image of the father using his *Light*. Then he is asked to draw a second circle next to it containing an image of the client most strongly related to the father. (Sometimes, I use the word 'attached' rather than 'related') The process could not be simpler, but amazingly, the results are often pivotal. Almost without exception, Christ will identify an ego-aspect that exhibits some of the client's most problematical characteristics. The next step is a bit more difficult for some clients to grasp, though none have failed to do so if they are willing for Christ to proceed. The second step asks Christ to terminate the Temporal authority flowing through the father's image, thereby releasing the relationship from archetypal enthrallment. Always remember that images are comprised of energy and definition. They are not made of flesh and blood even though the image appears as a physical being. In the case of Temporal authority, the termination only affects the flow of archetypal energy, not the energy which sustains the father's image apart from that energy. It is understood that while the archetypal energy continues to flow to the father, it empowers the father to define any image strongly related to him. Termination also achieves the goal of demonstrating that the father is a conduit of the energy rather than its source. It is the archetypal energy which empowers the father to define the ego-aspect. The father's image is said to be inflated by archetypal energy while constellated by the Empowering archetype. Neither the father's image nor the ego-aspect most strongly related to it will disappear when the energy is terminated. But significantly, though the father's image may or may not change in demeanor, it quickly becomes less figural. In every case I have investigated, the focus quickly shifts to the ego-aspect most strongly related to the father.

The therapist also needs to help the client appreciate beforehand that the archetypal energy of Temporal authority does not sustain the ego-aspect most strongly related to the father. An ego-aspect is sustained by its own source of energy. This should be noted to the client as some clients have expressed the fear that if the energy is terminated in the father it will also be terminated in the ego-aspect most strongly related to the father. The energies governing each are distinctly different, even though the father's behavior initially defines or shapes the ego-aspect. The energy governing the father is the more powerful of the two – until Christ intervenes, but it does not sustain the ego-aspect it creates. When the authority invested in the father by the Empowering archetype is removed, the ego-aspect is free to seek redefinition and reconciliation with its contra-sexual opposite. Actually, Christ can alter the ego-aspect's definition prior to removing the authority from the father, as when he baptizes an ego-aspect. But normally, in addressing issues of Temporal authority, it is better to terminate the father's authority before seeking to redefine the ego-aspect. On occasion, the ego-aspect will spontaneously evolve when the father's authority is terminated. All of the above holds equally true for ego-aspects most strongly related to the mother.

Once Temporal authority is terminated in the parent(s) the client is given two further therapeutic goals. First, s/he is asked to extend a portion of the *Light* to the ego-aspect identified as most strongly related to the father; and, finally, s/he is given the long-term objective of raising this ego-aspect to the client's chronological age and imbuing it with characteristics that would most benefit its future functioning. This second objective is not the sole prerogative of the client. Any alterations must be jointly agreed upon by the Aware-ego, the ego-aspect most strongly related to the father, and Christ. Often, I have the ego-aspect explicitly agree by giving Christ a portion of its *Light* prior to Christ intervening. This intervention always requires the ongoing willingness of the client, ego-aspect, and Christ.

Reconciliation with disowned opposites is not a primary objective at this point in the process, primarily because it is unlikely that any will have been identified. With the termination of the father's authority, and the evolution of the ego-aspect most strongly related to the father, the disowned aspects will emerge in subsequent sessions. The termination of Temporal authority invariably brings to light issues of polarization as inner dynamics are altered by the client's new sense of autonomy.

In Chapter VIII, I introduce a new intervention that involves conviction with the power of the Holy Spirit. That intervention is probably the most effective method for 'evolving' an ego-aspect most strongly defined by a parent.

Removing Temporal Authority Preemptively

Bertha. On occasion, I find it helpful to have Christ terminate Temporal authority without much focus on the ego-aspects most affected by it. As a rule, I only do this if the client is in a crisis clearly precipitated by a parent's Temporal authority. The following is a good example. Over the years I have worked with clients who have grown up in the 'hollers' of East Tennessee and never really left them. How they have found their way to my office is a wonder in itself. But something about them, the very grit that got them to me in the first place, has prompted me to work with them, often pro bono. One such client – Bertha, prompted me to move quickly rather than take the time necessary to raise up her Coping-aspect. Bertha is a 45 year old, white, divorced, female. For many years she worked as a welder on the night shift. For most of the time I have known her, she has lived in a trailer in a holler (a steep valley where you can holler across to kinfolk), above her son and his wife, and below the husband of her deceased sister. She has struggled with a number of issues, including chronic alcoholism, agoraphobia (it was a miracle she could even get to my office), and a severe history of physical, sexual and emotional abuse suffered by her and her nine siblings that left her extremely dissociative. In the recent past we addressed sexual abuse by her oldest brother who regularly took her – quite literally, to the melon patch for sex from age six till he moved away from home when she was eleven.

After several months' absence, Bertha returns to therapy close to mental collapse. She describes herself as incessantly tormented by her deceased father's voice telling her to kill herself. He fatally shot himself in the family's presence when she was twelve years old, after physically and emotionally brutalizing the family for years. In the presence of his wife and several siblings, including the client, he put a gun to his head and blew out his brains, which splattered the wall. The father's abusive behavior – if not his suicide, was a recapitulation of what he himself apparently experienced at the hands of his own parents. Bertha knew the grandparents. They were unmitigatingly rejecting of her entire family. In addition, all of the aunts and uncles were very much like her father in terms of drinking and abusing their children. After the father died, Bertha's mother became the matriarch. When Bertha began to lay bare the family secrets, specifically her molestation by the oldest brother, she was increasingly ostracized by her mother. As the firstborn, the brother replaced the father in the family's dynamics, if only because he was readily available during his many years on disability and chronic alcoholism. Bertha's revelations threatened to leave the extended family without a 'patriarch.' I sensed it was the mother's ostracism that was most threatening to Bertha, since Bertha's whole life has been pretty much defined by her place in the extended family.

My initial motivation for setting up the termination intervention was a desire to offset the mother's shunning by depotentiating her authority, though I actually begin by working with the father's parents since his voice was the one actively traumatizing her. Also, I anticipated that the first intervention involving the deceased father might serve as a model for Christ's removal of the mother's authority. First, I have Bertha ask Christ to contain the father. Then a second circle is drawn to contain his parents. Christ enters the circle and removes the grandparent's power to control Bertha through the father. Almost immediately, the father's face softens into a smile. The grandparents go from looking evil to looking sad and lonely, wishing they could make amends for what was lost by their actions. (These are all Bertha's descriptions.) Next, a third circle is drawn to contain the ego-aspect who is feeling shunned by the mother and traumatized by the father's voice. *Then her mother is placed in the circle with her father*. Bertha understands that Christ can remove the parents' power to control her activities within the family by shunning and guilting her. The mother seems to initially resist Christ's effort to terminate her authority. But in my experience, Christ's power in this matter has always proven absolute, and the mother – an ostensibly devout Missionary Baptist, cannot resist him for long. Also, Bertha has come to appreciate that beyond a certain developmental age, parents have no further right to Temporal authority, and therefore no rightful claim to it, even by her culture's standards. (Having been married and the mother of grown children she is no longer expected to 'cleave' to her parents.) After this session, her father's voice stops telling her to kill herself, and she is able to tolerate her mother and sisters' shunning. Although the shunning greatly abated in the months that followed, she was not free of it till the brother died about a year later. Thereafter, Bertha moved in with her mother and cared for her till she died.

When I first began exploring Temporal authority, I was quick to suggest to clients that they allow Christ to terminate the authority constellated in parents and grandparents. More often than not, the clients 'resisted' my suggestions for the many reasons I have described in this chapter. All of these resistances have taught me to set divestiture as an end goal rather than a first step. But sometimes, I still find it helpful to proceed with an immediate removal, provided the client is willing. The above is a case in point. In actual practice, I have also found it helpful to speak in terms of parental "control" and the demand for unquestioning "obedience" as well as "Temporal authority," and I will use the words interchangeably during the intervention. Even with explanations of what I think Temporal authority means, many clients have a better sense of the meaning when I refer to it as their parent's power to *control* their activities, thinking, and/or feelings, and to continue treating them as children, even though they are adults. Some adults still experience parental authority as a demand for unquestioning *obedience*. Also, I emphasize that the culture offers no rituals for ending this parental control; if anything, many institutions are dependent upon its recapitulation to support the many parent-child scripts we compulsively engage in daily. Lacking cultural rituals, most parents are not even sensitive to the need to release grown children from this authority, even if they were inclined to do so. Finally, in setting up this intervention, where I begin is dependent upon the client's history. Where social history suggests that a particular set of grandparents have played an active, aversive role, then I will first address their authority over the parent before addressing the parents' effect on the client. [16]

Even where removal of Temporal authority is the first interventional objective, I will still ask most clients to identify any ego-aspects strongly controlled by or related to that parental authority. (Bertha was a notable exception.) Prior to removing parental authority, the client is asked to closely examine the images in both circles so as to later ascertain changes in their demeanor. For example, one client saw her Coping-aspect as a teenager sitting in a straight chair but completely hunched over. Following the removal of the parents' authority the image was seen as sitting straight up in the chair. As regards parents, changes in the images will vary greatly. Quite often, individual parents will appear relieved or unburdened by the process. But almost as often, especially in the case of overbearing parents, they can appear quite resistant to the idea of giving up their authority, and afterwards, they may appear shocked, dismayed or ashamed. Generally, the Christ image is unaffected. In early experiments, where Christ was asked *to draw out the archetypal energy* using his *Light*, he often appeared to grow very large immediately after the removal of the authority while the parents became correspondingly smaller. The size differential appears to be more a reflection of how inflated the parents were beforehand than inflation on the part of Christ. This shift in Christ's image is most likely to occur when Christ is asked to *withdraw the energy* from the parental image, rather than terminating its flow by placing a portion of his *Light* into the heart of the parental image. In the early interventions, when Christ withdrew the energy, I had the client continue to watch the Christ image until he then released the authority *back to the Empowering archetype.* Immediately afterward, the Christ image would again appear normal vis-à-vis the parental images. However, where before the parental images appeared more powerful than the Christ figure, they now appeared less so. Today, I only request that Christ *terminate the energy flow by placing a portion of his Light into the heart of the parent.* Where that occurs, Christ's image does not inflate, but the parental image can be expected to diminish in demeanor.

I still use the intervention wherein the energy of the Empowering archetype is separated from the parents rather than just terminated. It gives the client a visual demonstration of my assertion that parents are conduits of the energy not its source. I explain to clients that separation in itself changes nothing. Christ must still insert his Light into the parents' hearts to terminate their connection to it. This simply allows them to see that it is an archetypal energy within them that has constellated the parental images, thereby inflating the parents' power. Once separated, I always stress the unsuitability of any ego-aspect assuming it. After terminating the archetypal connection, Christ is asked to "return the separated energy to a safe place of his choosing where it can no longer be abused by parents or others." He does this by entering the circle and using his Light to transfer the energy to 'that place.'

Maternal Temporal Authority

Most cultures designate one parent to exercise Temporal authority, generally the 'head of household.' Wherever a culture favors one gender over the other, Temporal authority effectively exaggerates the authority of the favored gender and suppresses the other. In our culture, patriarchy still appears to define this authority. Infancy and early childhood are the only periods in a child's life when a woman's Temporal authority is not suppressed by patriarchy. Following early childhood, given that we live in a patriarchy, whatever Temporal authority is still claimed by a mother, is seen to flow from her husband, father, father-in-law or grandfather. There are exceptions but that seems the rule.[17] If Temporal authority is clearly exercised by her husband, then the mother will relinquish it as the children grow older, and thereafter, only exercise it as a threat: "If you don't mind me, I'll tell your father." [18] In this section, I want to address what happens when *the mother continues to exercise Temporal authority,* in effect, refuses to acquiesce to any male in the household as the children grow older. Even then, the Temporal authority exercised by the mother will indirectly flow from a male: be it her husband, her father, grandfather, father-in-law or other male surrogate. Still, her effect on children is significantly different than would be expected had the father directly exercised that authority.

In this section, I want to consider four possible outcomes based on the presence or absence of the father and the sex of the child. These are tentative formulations. The situation is comparatively rare so I am extrapolating from very few cases. The first two conditions describe a mother exercising Temporal authority when the father is absent. His absence may be due to prolonged absence (e.g. war or work), death, abandonment, or divorce. The other two conditions involve a dominant mother where the father is present. Both conditions - father absent, father present, appear to have differential effects on sons and daughters and so the conditions are further defined by the child's gender. The following descriptions should be taken as suggestive only. I have seen too few cases to definitively describe this range of conditions, but it is clear from the cases I have work with that there can be significant differential effects.

To fully appreciate the effects of temporal dominance exercised by a mother, it is necessary to bear in mind the influence that the Gendering archetype has on the whole process. The Relational authority generated by the Gendering archetype is discussed at length in Chapter VIII. Let me just note here that the Gendering archetype uses parental interactions to constellate the Inner dyads defining a child's sense of self. These Inner dyads also provide templates for both interpersonal and intrapersonal masculine-feminine relationships. If the wife plays a subordinate role in her relationship with her husband, then this will be reflected in a number of ways. First, he will visibly wield Temporal authority. More importantly, the masculine aspect of a child's Inner dyad is likely to reflect this dominance. The same will be true if the roles are reversed: then the feminine aspect would be relationally dominant. In effect, Relational authority appears to reinforce Temporal authority; but may also 'trump' the cultural standard in future generations.

When the Inner dyads of both parents are not synchronistic, there will likelyced be considerable discord that generally results in divorce, abandonment or mayhem. With similar effect, single mothers who choose to remain single will likely reflect Inner dyads whose masculine aspect is in some way subordinate, and/or exhibit Temporal personas that exercise Temporal authority within an extended family. In effect, the dominance of a mother, or father, cannot be explained by Temporal authority alone. Relational authority always needs to be treated as a contributing factor.

Dominant Mother, Absent Father: Effect on the Daughter

The process of removing Temporal authority from a dominant mother is similar to Christ removing the father's authority. But the first time I observed it, a surprising turn of events took place. In retrospect, what I think I observed was Christ's acknowledgment that the feminine had been suppressed in both mother and daughter. He sought to show, in effect, that mother and daughter had their own authority quite apart from the Temporal authority wielded by the mother. Very likely, the Temporal authority wielded by the mother was also experienced by the mother in her own upbringing. Of note, the two cases reported here are the result of the two-step process wherein Christ is asked to first extract the energy rather than simply terminate it by placing a portion of his *Light* into the heart of the parent.

Loretta. Loretta has been raised by a functional, alcoholic mother. Loretta's father died when she was an infant. The mother never remarried. She clearly exercised Temporal authority in the household from Loretta's infancy onward. When Loretta uses her *Light* to contain an image of her mother exercising Temporal authority, she perceives her mother's authority as a "dark spirit" permeating the image of her mother. Christ appears to absorb or draw out this "dark spirit" using her *Light*, which Loretta has passed to him for that purpose. But then, a "woman in white" spontaneously emerges beside Christ. He appears to transfer "something" to her and then she disappears. As I came to understand this exchange, it was as if something controlled by the mother's Temporal authority belonged to a distinctly feminine element within both women that Christ acknowledges and respects. He seems to absorb the mother's exercise of Temporal authority and then acknowledges a personal authority suppressed by it – what I will call Loretta's individual authority. This two-fold process of removal and emergence has spontaneously occurred on several other occasions when Christ withdraws the energy from dominant mothers of daughters. Consequently, I have come to accept it as a possibility whenever Christ extracts the energy under those conditions. In effect, the successful removal of Temporal authority from a dominant mother appears to require both the removal of that authority and a concomitant, symbolic, acknowledgement of *a new configuration of the feminine in the mother and daughter.* All this is further illustrated by the experience of the client in the next verbatim.

Dourine. When Dourine's *Light* contains her mother's Temporal authority, what she visualizes is a pond contained by the circle. She extends her *Light* to Christ who uses it to 'draw off' the pond water symbolic of the mother's Temporal authority. What she then sees is a sparkly, golden stream running through the center of the circle. When she asks her *Light* the meaning of it she sees a tree in which she is the trunk and her mother a limb! She understands this to mean that the mother's individual authority is something they hold in common, that the stream symbolizes a shared power hidden by the mother's exercise of Temporal authority. These are my interpretations. What transpired could have numerous other meanings. That notwithstanding, whenever Temporal authority is terminated by Christ, the client generally experiences a discernible increase in their own sense of authority – what I am calling their individual authority.

When Christ withdraws or terminates the father's authority, the father's image diminishes in size and potency – as seen by both male and female clients, and Christ's image remains unaltered. But where the withdrawal is on behalf of a male client, there is no symbolic exchange indicating that the son is to claim his individual authority. In patriarchy, the son's claim to individual authority appears to be culturally sanctioned and reinforced; I cannot otherwise account for the difference. Also, there is the role of Relational authority to be considered. Even when a father's Temporal authority is removed, the Inner dyads will continue to sustain a masculine dominance. Historically, males appear to receive individual authority when they come of age. Clearly, culture and fathers-in-law, invest son's-in-law with authority over their daughters and grandchildren in traditional marriage ceremonies. Armies provide similar rituals in their transfer of authority to new commanding officers or 'change of the guard.' Clinically, male clients do begin to exercise a greater sense of *individual authority* following the divestiture of Temporal authority by Christ.

The idea of individual authority – 'being your own person' – is difficult to tease out in the context of Temporal authority, which is why I have kept it lower case. Temporal authority fragments the Ego, thereby delimiting the exercise of free will since fragmented ego-aspects are often at odds with each other. The constellation of parental images by the Empowering archetype will always result in a distortion, i.e. inflation of the parental image and unnatural suppression or inflation of Ego function. From my perspective, a major goal of therapy is the client's liberation from these arbitrary constellations, and the consequent freedom to choose a spiritual being that better serves him or her in all dimensions of being. What Christ seems to be demonstrating in the above case examples is that all authority flows from within; and it is within the individual's power to regulate that flow by calling on a higher power. It is also possible to realign the Inner dyads generated by Relational authority, if the client is willing to call on a higher power.

Mother Dominant, Father Absent: Effect on the Son

I have had too few cases in this category for anything but a tentative generalization. Dominant mothers, whether the father is present or absent, tend to raise 'good sons' whose masculine energy is diminished in a variety of ways. If the father is present, then the father's role is seen to be denigrated by the mother's dominance in the household. If absent, he is generally absent from a failure to provide, e.g. divorce, abandonment. Either way, the son's sense of the masculine is diminished. The sons I have worked with tend to be strongly identified with a narcissistic Coping-aspect that needs the mother's continuing affirmation – even in adulthood – to sustain it. Attempts to remove the mother's Temporal authority are strongly resisted. The son has had to spend much of his life being "not like his father;" which generally results in Not-me duplex (described later in the chapter). Any ego-aspect *identified with the father* will be seen as a 'first cousin' to the Rejected-self if not an actual embodiment of the Rejected-self. The mother's Temporal authority not only buttresses the son's Not-me duplex, but also serves to suppress knowledge of it. Premature removal of the mother's Temporal authority, before the client is prepared to address issues of a negative masculine identity, is likely to precipitate a severe somatic or emotional crisis. In such cases, it is best if the therapist begins by dealing with Relational authority issues first and, especially, with the healing of the father's Inner dyad. When the son has a firmer, more confident, sense of effective masculine energy, he will have less need of his mother's continuing exercise of Temporal authority.

There are notable exceptions to the above scenario. The mother can hold up the father or a grandfather as a role model. The absent father can be idealized by the mother. Also, in American culture today there are many divorced parents who share child custody such that the father, or mother, lives apart but is still present on a weekly basis. The above scenario only applies to situations where the father is clearly absent, implicitly denigrated, and the mother speaks with her 'own Temporal authority' rather than looking to a male as a role model of Temporal authority for the son.

Mother Dominant, Father Present: Effect on Son

There are families in which the mother is truly the head-of-household by force of will and demeanor. Where this is so, it will have an equally profound effect on all children. I am not speaking of a mother who is head-of-household out of necessity, i.e. the father absent, or deceased, or the parents divorced. In those instances, the father's image can still embody Temporal and Moral authority, or another male can be assigned that role, e.g. a grandfather, boyfriend, even an eldest son. What I want to highlight here are those instances when the mother is clearly dominant in the household even as the father is present. In the eyes of her children, she is clearly dominant by her force of will, spirit, and accomplishments. In such marriages, the husband is more like a house husband or introverted, quiet, and unassuming, even though he may be the bread winner. In any case, he will acknowledge her dominance in the marriage. One way she may be dominant is in her rages toward the children which the husband does not challenge even when they are clearly shaming. But this is only an example. Often the dominance, while frequently enacted in terms of disciplining the children, is more apparent in strength of character, high energy, determination and the like. She is likely to be the first born child of a father who is also first born. These are powerful women who 'do not take kindly to fools' or tolerate opposition even within the extended family. The maternal image will be clearly superordinate in the hearts of the children. And she, rather than the father, will exercise Temporal and Moral authority. Sometimes, this authority can be seen even more clearly from a third generation perspective. I recently saw a male client in which the Temporal authority was clearly exercised by the paternal grandmother. In that case, the client's father was clearly subordinate to the grandmother and demanded that the client's mother also be subordinate to her will when the family lived with her or near her.

In my clinical experience, *firstborn sons* raised by dominant mothers will seek to stand 'toe to toe' with their mothers. They are very mindful of their mother's power, but tend to focus on adolescent events wherein they stood their ground with her rather than submitting, as they did in childhood. There is, however, a distinct feeling of never being more than equal, and ever a fear of being overwhelmed if they are not continuously vigilant. In general, they will seek a higher ground – temporally or morally, whereby they can hold her at bay. This is in sharp contrast to a son whose father exercises Temporal authority. While the dominant father also demands submission, for most sons it is relinquished by the father when the son becomes an adult. Then, a son can generally expect to take his place in a paternalistic world and exercise both Temporal and Moral authority in his own children's eyes. In contrast, the son of a dominant mother cannot identify with that mother without a perpetual feeling of submission and loss of masculine identity. But nor can he identify with his father without also submitting to the mother, since the father has implicitly acknowledged his wife's authority within the family.

I have worked with two males who exhibited the above constellation, prior to my studies of Relational authority. Both terminated therapy while attempting to address their mothers' Temporal authority, ostensibly for other reasons, but I suspect to avoid letting Christ remove the mother's authority. Prior to therapy, one of them had had exceedingly contentious relationships with all of his wives and girlfriends. His mother was dominant, physically harsh, and shaming. The other client had essentially avoided intimate relationships with women. His mother was dominant, positive regarding his aspirations as a minister, but emotionally distant. In retrospect, I suspect that removing the mother's Temporal authority – without first addressing Relational authority issues – would have precipitated a crisis that they seem to intuit better than I at the time. Very likely, the clients' Inner dyads were replete with dominant feminine aspects that both clients held partially in check by allowing the mother to retain her Temporal authority, which allowed them to retain Mirror-aspects capable of standing toe-to-toe. I have since learned that once the Inner dyads are healed, clients are more willing to remove any residual Temporal authority from a dominant mother.

Mother Dominant, Father Present: Effect on Daughter

I have teased out several variables that

may account for a mother's dominance in the family, other than the absence of a father. In my studies of Relational authority it is clear that individuals can play out either role of a dyadic template (sic) the stereotypic interaction between a mother and father. Normally, the individual plays out the role identified by his or her sex. However, in a number of the cases I have examined, both genders of the Inner dyad were identified with the same sex. Moreover, where this occurs it seems to be true for the Inner dyads of *both* parents. This lack of sex differentiation may be what allows some clients to move from one role to another, i.e. for a mother to act as the "male head-of-household." Another factor that more likely plays a role is birth order. Ordinarily, the first born is most strongly identified with the father's side of the family, and the second born with the mother's side of the family. A first born daughter whose father is also a first born, will be very strongly identified with both her father and her paternal grandfather. These are the women most likely to exhibit the characteristics of a dominant mother even in households where the husband is present.

Bridgette. The following case is an example of a dominant mother exercising Temporal authority, but it is even more an example of the complexity unearthed in such cases. The discernment of Temporal and Moral authority can be a complex undertaking involving the uncovering of numerous projections among an extended family including grandparents, in-laws, and other authority figures intimately associated with a family. In this case, Bridgette's mother was pivotal in most of Bridgette's authority issues. The mother's Temporal and Moral authority appeared to flow originally from her own father (a rigid, authoritarian, Catholic). But the mother became estranged from the father when she joined a cultic church. From then on, the mother's Moral authority appeared to flow from the founder of that church. When the mother joined this cultic church, she appears to have unconsciously continued the now estranged relationship with her father by projecting his authority into the image of the cult's founder. The entire family became slavishly committed to this church. The client, the oldest of three daughters, abided by all its strictures and married a man whose family was also devoutly involved in the church.

Bridgette's mother died when she was a young woman. (The father quickly remarried yet another dominant woman within the cultic church.) The mother had suffered a long debilitating illness that demanded the family's constant attention and sacrifice, made worse by the mother's refusal to seek medical treatment in favor of God's deliverance. For many years afterward, Bridgette lived with an image of her mother as irritable, stern, and difficult, *all of which she attributed to the mother's long illness*. But, when her Christ image used his *Light* to terminate the *grandfather's Temporal authority* embedded in the mother's image, the image of the mother immediately became softer and lighter. This strongly suggested that much of the mother's demeanor may have come from a Mirror-aspect originally created to go 'toe-to-toe with the maternal grandfather, but now dominant in the mother's exercise of Temporal authority.

After her mother died, Bridgette drew closer to her in-laws even though she experienced them as very judgmental. When their images were explored, her sister-in-law's image was found to projectively personify Bridgette's Ideal-self, while the mother-in-law's image had projectively absorbed much of her mother's Temporal and Moral authority. By entering into dialogue with these images, Bridgette was also able to discern her Rejected-self – an image that was clearly antithetical to the puritanical image ascribed to her sister-in-law. After redeeming the Rejected-self, Christ could approach the mother's image and terminate her Moral authority. Only then was the most powerful source of the mother's authority revealed: it derived primarily from the father-like founder of the church who everyone in the extended family had idolized, and it was not until Christ was able to terminate *his* authority that Bridgette could finally reconcile the disparate parts of herself and be free of this oligarchy.

This was a complex case. It can be difficult to fully appreciate without a working knowledge of the interventions described in the following chapters. Even so, it serves to further illustrate how issues of Temporal and Moral authority embedded in a maternal figure are often multi-generational, and quite capable of biasing the images of extended family as well as institutional figures.

Maternal exercise of Temporal authority beyond age four is relatively infrequent in a patriarchal culture, so it is difficult to speak of it definitively. But it very definitely exists. The few cases I have worked with suggest that it has a negative effect on both sons and daughters since it suppresses the individual authority of both. It may be even more detrimental than the nominal exercise of Temporal authority by fathers, if only because it is at odds with the cultural norm and will create dynamics in children also at odds with the cultural norm. (I would assume similar detrimental effects from a father's dominant exercise of Temporal authority in a matriarchy.) Where mothers are the primary conduits of Temporal authority it appears to be as a consequence of strong identification with their own fathers, and marriage to a passive husband who is likely to be a youngest, an 'overgrown boy,' a 'mother's boy,' a 'good boy,' or otherwise pueristic in character. Such men are also likely to abandon a wife and child emotionally and physically, and leave her to function as de facto head-of-household. I do not mean to infer by any of these observations that the maternal exercise of Temporal authority is a bad thing, simply that it poses particular difficulties for children raised in that environment, but no more so than the numerous abuses of Temporal authority by fathers. What I consider far more detrimental to adult development is the continuation and generalization of Temporal authority beyond a child's coming of age, which is a nearly universal phenomenon, and equally detrimental whether upholding a matriarchy or patriarchy.

DISRUPTIONS IN NURTURE AND THE CREATION OF PRE-MORAL AND MIRROR ASPECTS

Thus far, I have examined the power of Temporal authority compared to Christ; its power to shape a Temporal persona; and it's role in the creation of Coping-aspects. Those effects are predominantly the consequence of a father's exercise of Temporal authority in a patriarchal culture, though significant variations can be observed if the mother's authority is dominant throughout childhood. In this section, I want to focus on the Temporal authority *universally* exercised by mothers. Any Temporal authority exercised by mothers is also controlled by patriarchal values, but that being said, there is one area where her Temporal authority is largely unchallenged: *the care of infants and toddlers*. Mothers nurture their young. Without this nurture the young would die. They exercise this power of life and death on a daily basis for a prolonged period of time. Even now, when many women have joined their husbands in the workplace, it is still the mother who shoulders the major responsibility for a child's welfare in the first years of life. The mother is considered *always responsible* for the child's care unless she can delegate someone to relieve her. Caregiving is a full-time job. Infants cannot be left alone very long without being at risk. They require 24 hour supervision, seven days a week. In this section, I want to examine what happens if nurture is disrupted willfully or otherwise. Clinically, the most profound effects are obscured because they are generally hidden by the Ego. But when found they are unmistakable. The image of a young child wounded by disruptions of nurture is classic in its personification of trauma. The child appears totally decimated by the experience. The Ego's response to this trauma appears to be markedly similar across a wide spectrum of clients. In the face of such trauma, the Ego will dissociate the part perceived responsible for the disruption. I call this part 'Pre-moral' because it is always created in the first three years, prior to the onset of morality. Without exception this aspect is always perceived as very young.

The dissociative creation of a Pre-moral aspect enhances the child's ability to survive abuses of Temporal authority during infancy and early childhood. But the continuing existence of such an aspect – as must be the case once it is created, represents a permanent scaring until it is healed. It is experienced as a deep sense of lack that is continually sensed, and defended against by the client. Such images can be healed when discerned, but once again, the Ego appears incapable of the task without the aid of a higher power – unless it is willing to incorporate dream images into active imagination. [19] So far as I can determine, the healing of a Pre-moral aspect requires *a mother image that is archetypal in nature*. That is to say, the mother image needed to rectify these early disruptions of nurture, will frequently be numinous or goddess-like in appearance. The child in need of this mother is rarely older than age three, and often younger. At this age, the child's perception of 'mother' is much different from our adult perceptions of 'mother.' For infants and toddlers, the mother is a goddess, the very giver or withholder of life force. There is no image more powerful in the life of an infant, whatever the actual gender of the primary care-giver. Remember that gender is largely irrelevant here since the child makes few such distinctions before the age of three. The primary care-givers are 'mother' regardless of sex.

Very likely, what I am calling the Pre-moral aspect is also the focus of a number of psychoanalytic theories offered by the Object Relations school. That being so, the numerous approaches described by them might serve the same purpose as the interventions outlined in this chapter. Almost without exception, their approach tends to be dialogic, rather than psycho-imaginative, and requiring years of effort since they tend to eschew the evocation of higher powers such as Christ or goddess-like dream images. But clearly their work intends the same outcomes I am describing here and it offers both collaboration and an alternative methodology for addressing these early disruptions of nurture.

When found in active imagination, Pre-moral aspects appear deeply wounded. The pain of nurture disruption is so severe that the developing Ego finds it necessary to separate the painful experience by dissociation, and create another ego-aspect that can shield the Pre-moral aspect from further wounding. These shielding aspects, which I describe as Mirror-aspects, are generally the first to be discovered. Their existence always infers the hidden presence of a Pre-moral aspect. Mirror aspects tend to evolve throughout the developmental process. Often, the latest manifestation will consciously co-exist with the client's Aware-ego as a dominant player in the client's daily life. Mirror-aspects must be worked with empathically throughout any process intended to heal the Pre-moral aspect, or they will sabotage that process. While these shielding aspects are tenacious in hiding (sic) protecting the wounded aspect, they cannot heal it. Only a 'mother' can heal this woundedness. To accomplish this, she must be experienced as something more than merely human. She must, in effect, be goddess-like in her powers, i.e. numinous, archetypal. In yesteryears, we called her goddess but monotheistic patriarchy forbids that. Thankfully, Christ has no qualms about seeking out such a mother on behalf of the child. What he finds for the child, he does not name as goddess, but it is quite clear to the client and therapist that she is something more than the client has known in his or her worldly life experience, and so something more than mere Ego can ever hope to offer.

The Pre-moral aspect generates a complex of feelings that the client may feel on a regular basis without being able to identify its source. Despair, aloneness, and isolation are examples. It co-exists with other ego-aspects, including the Aware-ego, but while it remains undifferentiated the client cannot distinguish its feelings from others. Until the therapist develops some facility for differentiating these particular aspects of the Ego, s/he is also likely to confuse them with other aspects such as those related to conscience. Healing a Pre-moral aspect is truly worth the effort in terms of the positive changes experienced by clients. It is one of the more powerful interventions I have discerned in working with the *Light* and images of Christ. It goes a long way toward affirming Christ's power to heal.

The Pre-moral Aspect

The Pre-moral aspect personifies a child severely wounded by abuses of Temporal authority. As D.L. Nathanson notes, behaviors typical of shameful affect can be observed in infants.[20] A parent rarely has cause to evoke such affect, unless s/he is essentially 'out of control.' Toilet training is one area where many children have experienced severe shaming at a very early age. Most Pre-moral aspects are probably created by a combination of parental abuse or neglect, as well as shaming anger. Infants and young children have little defense against severe shaming, or the terrible angers that often accompany it. This early traumatization may account for the terrible fear of shame experienced by many people throughout their life span.

The Pre-moral aspect most often personifies as a two year old. It will exhibit the effects of unmitigated shame, neglect, or abandonment as experienced in infancy or early childhood. These early experiences of shame traumatically interrupt the connectedness between parent and child. This creates an ego-aspect that reflects the total decimation caused by that trauma. *It may look like a lifeless rag doll, or a very small child in a fetal position, or a small child staring blankly in an empty room, or hiding in a closet, or in darkness.* Those are characteristic postures though I doubt they exhaust the number of possible manifestations. In some instances there may actually be a sense of soul loss in the image; and it may be necessary to ask Christ to retrieve the soul part. The shame pivotal to these experiences is not moral, except as regards the parent's inexcusable use of it. Rather, it is a force that traumatically interrupts the bond between mother and child.

If Temporal authority is abused in infancy and early childhood – and in clinical populations that is too often the case, it will decisively effect the client by forcing the Ego to dissociate, thereby creating a Pre-moral aspect. Concomitantly, the Ego will then seek to create a protective Mirror-aspect. (In Dissociative Disorders it may be forced to create several pairs.) The Mirror-aspect will seek to hide or cover up the Pre-moral aspect in an effort to 'protect' it. Initially, the Pre-moral aspect is only 'felt' by the client as something caused by their current situation rather than a specter of past neglect. This is because the Pre-moral aspect is covered or hidden and therefore unidentifiable as the source of severe angst. The negative emotions are generally the byproduct of repressive somatization. The Mirror-aspect fulfills its role by emulating (sic) mirroring the parent's wounding behavior. It uses that mirroring to shield the Pre-moral aspect from further attack, though significantly, the Pre-moral aspect may be hard pressed to experience the reactivity as protective. Essentially, the Mirror-aspect fosters an 'eye for an eye' response in the child that it directs toward the parent in a covert way. These Mirror-aspects can model paternal figures as well as maternal figures. Even though disruptions in nurture are caused by a traumatic severing of the mother-infant connection, adults other than the mother can be the cause. A father who physically, sexually, or emotionally abuses an infant or toddler, with the mother seemingly powerless to prevent it, will have the same effect as a mother who enacts such abuse herself. Remember, for an infant or toddler gender is not a distinguishing characteristic.

The Pre-moral aspect may function as a progenitor of the Rejected-self, but the Rejected-self is seen in this work as a universal occurrence.

Relatively few parents would traumatize a child in a way that forces the dissociation of a Pre-moral aspect. The Pre-moral aspect is a consequence of trauma, not merely shaming events in a context of abiding care and love. *It is created by inflicted pain that significantly and irreparably disrupts the nurturing bond*. A Mirror-aspect is created in response to this trauma in an effort to defend the child against further wounding by the care-giver. In this respect, a Mirror-aspect is very much like an Ego-in-conflict, which also strives to minimize the effects of shame enthralling a Rejected-self. Mirror-aspects may serve as prototypes for the Ego-in-conflict in later development. (This will be clearer in Chapter VII where I take up the discussion of the Ego-in-conflict.) Since the Pre-moral aspect can be mistaken for the Rejected-self, the therapist must become sensitive to the differences. Unlike the Rejected-self, the Pre-moral aspect is not considered universal whereas the Rejected-self always occurs as a function of conscience being quickened to activity (ages four to six). The Pre-moral aspect is only dissociatively created if there are severe abuses of Temporal authority in early development (birth to three years).

Early manifestations of the Mirror-aspect may go through several permutations such as those discussed in following sections, but the Pre-moral aspect appears to remain, essentially, unaltered. The Mirror-aspect will actively persist in some form to protect the Pre-moral aspect from further wounding. In clinical settings, the Mirror-aspect can manifest as any age though it often appears as a pre-teen (ages 11 to 13). But this is deceptive. In its formative stage it is always a young child. This is demonstrated by the intervention I most often use to access the Pre-moral aspect: regression to the source. This is done by containing the identified Mirror-aspect and asking it to remember its earliest memories. Often, this takes the client back to the juvenile period, then back to age six or seven, then back to age two or three. Each regression will revive an ever younger personification of the Mirror-aspect. (Note, these are not ages that I suggest, but the ages most frequently reported by clients.) Generally, the earliest memory held by a Mirror-aspect will point to the felt presence of the Pre-moral aspect that necessitated it's creation.

Abuses of Temporal authority can be inadvertent as would be the case where catastrophic or natural upheavals separated parents from small children. But regardless of the reason, wherever found, the Pre-moral aspect will need a higher power to connect it with a healing, archetypal feminine image. In almost all cases, *the client will need Christ's assistance in connecting the Pre-moral aspect to an archetypal mother image* such as Mary, the Deep Mother, Great Mother, Medicine Woman, or some Goddess-like manifestation such as Sophia, Tara, Quan Yin or Demeter. In clinical practice, this mother archetype can take a variety of forms, most of them numinous in quality. Often, a dream image will serve. On one occasion it finally manifested as an idealized image of the client, but that is rare.

In anticipation of later discussions, I would note in passing that baptism of the Rejected-self is considered indispensable for the release of that ego-aspect. It can also be offered to a Pre-moral aspect, but is generally experienced as irrelevant to its basic need for nurture; and that may be a distinguishing difference between the two.[21]

Finally, I would note that the Pre-moral aspect is a significant player in transference relationships. It can generate great demands on the therapist and this will continue unabated until the aspect is contained, differentiated, and actively nurtured by internal archetypes. I suspect that Pre-moral aspects are the root cause of many Borderline disorders.

Mirror-Aspects Defined

Mirror images were briefly described in Chapter IV in their function as protectors. They function as protectors by emulating the behavior of a parent experienced as abusive. In my clinical work, I have identified four kinds of Mirror-aspects: expressive mirrors, suppressed mirrors, hidden mirrors, and the Not-me duplex. *Expressive and suppressed* Mirror-aspects are the most easily identified. Often, they manifest as *a characterological behavior of the client's that copies the parental behavior experienced as abusive*, e.g. angry, fear inducing, shaming, etc. Quite often, it is some form of 'righteous' anger' acted out with an 'eye for an eye' sense of entitlement. Whether it is *expressed* or *suppressed* depends on the conditions in which it was learned. If, for example, a male child mirrored his angry mother in a household where the father also expressed anger toward the mother, it is likely to be an expressed aspect of behavior in adulthood, at least in relationships with women. If, however, it was solely a mirror of the father's anger, or a mother's anger that the father did not challenge, it is more likely to be suppressed if its expression provoked immediate retribution. Most often, suppressed Mirror-aspects are controlled by fear and manifest as persistent resentment. A common example would be 'smoldering' resentments that are nursed but rarely expressed except for pouting and the like. A suppressed Mirror-aspect can become expressive in adolescence. In effect, the adolescent becomes defiant, rebellious. This can become a more or less permanent state of affairs or a phase quickly squelched by the parent.

Both expressed and suppressed Mirror-aspects will have angry qualities easily provoked by current feelings of 'unjust treatment' or memories of parental abuse that are easily re-invoked by current situations. Where the therapist picks up on these qualities, s/he can ask the client to contain the Mirror-aspect reacting to that abuse. Then the client can repeatedly ask the *Light* to recover the earliest remembered instances of the mirrored behavior. This line of questioning will eventually put the client in touch with an early memory of being wounded by the Temporal authority of a parent. It is generally a well-remembered memory. This technique is called 'regression to the source.' It calls for a series of regressions that take the client to successively earlier ages. When the therapist senses that the client has identified the earliest memory, s/he then asks: "Who is the Mirror-aspect protecting in this situation?" Finding the Pre-moral aspect is critical. The Mirror-aspect cannot be treated while it continues to successfully hide the Pre-moral aspect since that is its raison d'être. Only as the Pre-moral aspect is healed can the Mirror-aspect become less reactive.

During the discovery process, it has proven helpful to emphasize to the client that the only objective in unveiling the Pre-moral aspect is to heal it, and to further emphasize that the Mirror-aspect can only hide it. This hiding is very much like allowing skin to grow over a deep wound before it has healed from the inside out. In all such cases the wound festers. The Mirror-aspect inadvertently maintains the wounded state of the Pre-moral aspect by hiding it. It has no power to heal. All a Mirror-aspect can do is suppress the hurt with its own negative emotions. When the Pre-moral aspect is identified, focus can shift entirely to its healing by Christ via the maternal powers that Christ will seek out. But the clinician needs to keep in mind that other aspects of the client's Ego can also collude in hiding the Pre-moral aspect in a mistaken belief that it is hopelessly wounded and even, in some instances, a justifiable target of attack. For example, a strong aspect can be very threatened by the existence of a Pre-moral aspect and it's dependency needs. The therapist needs to challenge this misperception wherever it is noted. Healing the Pre-moral aspect may take a number of sessions, and while those sessions do not require an undivided focus, a portion of each session needs be given over to the process. The Pre-moral aspect appears to heal in direct proportion to the conscious opportunities Christ and the archetypal mother are offered to work with it. This is not a one trial learning process. The client must be encouraged to 'visit' this ongoing interaction as often as possible once the Pre-moral aspect is reunited with an archetypal mother.

Any characteristic behavior of a parent can be mirrored by the client, and is likely to be, if it can function in a protector role. The earliest manifestations will be simple mirrors, i.e. anger for anger, blame for blame, etc. Later, the child may develop mirrors of the other parent, if that mirroring has the power to thwart the wounding parent, e.g. thinking like the other parent thinks. General fearfulness or psychosomatic problems such as migraine headaches are frequently emulated if they put off the wounding parent. Hypochondriacal and disphoric behaviors are other examples. Wherever mirroring is suspected, the therapist needs to regress the ego-aspect to the earliest memories of that mirroring. This is easily done by having the client ask their *Light* for the earliest memory when the client exhibited this behavior. A double circle can then be placed around this younger version of the Mirror-aspect, and Christ can separate out the Pre-moral aspect being protected by this behavior and place it in a protective dome.

The Pre-moral aspect will always manifest as a very small child. It appears to make no distinction between God and parents. It has relatively little appreciation of Christ as a manifestation of God. Rather, the Christ image is only experienced in terms of his parenting. For example, one client in reviewing what we had done in the previous session, which included asking Christ to join with her Pre-moral aspect, insisted that God - not Christ, had entered the circle protecting her Pre-moral aspect. When asked to examine this image of God, she reported it was God the father. Further scrutiny revealed that it was her understanding of God in the image of her father. In this particular case, the Pre-moral aspect, a two year old, had been created by her mother's repeated rejection of her in early childhood, in contrast to her father who appeared to 'adopt' her as his favorite among the siblings.

The Pre-moral aspect has a seemingly *insatiable* need for the parent, most often the 'mothering' parent, and clearly suffers from this lack. While Christ can comfort such a child, he cannot satisfy it. This is why I always ask Christ to augment his efforts by providing the Pre-moral aspect with an archetypal parent – most often a mother archetype, which is basically how the child experiences a parent in infancy and early childhood. Often, this quality of neediness, especially in cases of severe abuse, greatly disturbs the client. S/he may describe it as insatiable, shameful, disgusting. Their abhorrence is one reason why the client tends to support the Mirror-aspect's effort to hide the Pre-moral aspect, and why s/he may even fear the parent was justified in rejecting this child aspect. The client's fears in this matter can be greatly attenuated by having him or her assess Christ's reaction to the Pre-moral aspect, which is invariably unconditionally positive.

In working with cases of severe abuse, such as found in dissociative disorders generally, and MPD specifically, many child aspects holding memories, as well as major alter personalities, need to be treated as Mirror-aspect protectors. This is particularly true in MPD where a particular alter is angry or defiant. Two illustrations may help here. The first client – Zelda, who used severe psychosomatic symptoms to cope with her memories, personified the self with those symptoms as someone who actively resisted by pushing back or going rigid (not moving, clinching her teeth, staring blankly, holding her body tight). Several chronic illnesses served as physical analogues of these behaviors. What I finally came to appreciate in working with her was that this rigidity, or locked-in response, served primarily to protect a Pre-moral aspect. When this aspect was extracted from the earliest memory she emerged as a very needy little girl with grasping hands symbolic of her desperate need for connection, like a drowning person grasping for a life preserver. When Christ entered the circle containing her, he took her hands and said, "stop." This was not said unkindly, but more in the manner of someone saying it is ok now, you can relax, you are safe. In this particular case, the discovery of this Pre-moral aspect led to the further discovery of numerous alter personalities that until then had remained hidden or acted out as severe, chronic, physical symptoms.

The second example comes from work with another MPD client named Menta. Not all alter personalities are Mirror-aspects by any means, but if a particular alter exhibits characteristic behaviors that are angry, oppositional, or even seductive, then it may prove helpful to ask what they are protecting. In this case, the alter was one of the Menta's most confrontational personalities valued by other selves for her willingness to stand up to abusers. In this particular session, I suggested she might examine whether this behavior was serving to protect a wounded part of her. (I might note here that this was done well into the therapy. This is not something you do without a lot of preparation.) She understood that her anger was a protective mechanism against hurt and therefore there might be a part of her that was hurting – though she assumed it was another alter. She allowed the *Light* to put a double circle around her sense of self and extract whoever it was. What emerged was a six year old child. When asked what the child looked like, she said it was a younger, angry image of herself, and she then began to remember an event when she reported some of her abusers to their superior, but to no avail. According to her, thereafter, she did not have to come out to suffer any further molestations. But she had to witness the others suffering them, and this made her repeatedly angry and confrontational, particularly in adult life. Note that the younger personification is also angry. This suggested that it was not the Pre-moral aspect but rather the youngest version of herself as a protector. (Interestingly, Menta would later share that, until this session, she did not believe she existed before age six.) Having identified this six year old manifestation, I asked the adult alter if she would allow the *Light* to draw yet another double circle, this time around the younger, six year old self, and extract whoever was being protected by her anger. When this was done there emerged a three year old, tearful and frightened, very characteristic of a Pre-moral aspect. Significantly, this child was seen as being in a room all by herself. Menta had an Inner Self Helper (ISH), different from Christ, but exceedingly Christ-like, which she always evoked when the Christ image was called for. I asked what would happen if the ISH and child left that room. She said they would enter a house where the parents were always angry, fighting and attacking her. Eventually, she did allow the Pre-moral aspect to leave the room, but not before much nurturing by her Inner Self Helper. This case illustrates two points. First, alter personalities – as distinct from fragments – are three dimensional; that is, they have a developmental history, they do not just appear two-dimensionally formed. Second, in this particular instance attention had to be paid to the details. It should not be automatically assumed that what is extracted from the protector is a Pre-moral aspect just because it is younger. Often, the first extraction will simply be the earliest personification of the Mirror-aspect. Pre-moral aspects are never angry; they are wounded, deeply so.

As noted, a Mirror-aspect can evolve over time in terms of expression. It can, for example, go from *unexpressed to expressed anger*. The anger is felt, but unvoiced, until a critical developmental event galvanizes anger. This was illustrated by yet another client called Mally. As she got in touch with expressed anger toward her aunt, she was reminded of a time at age 14 when – for the first time, she openly and angrily defied her father's authority (he was drunk at the time). She rightly felt that his exercise of authority was arbitrary and unjust. Rather than comply with his demands she ran away to a relative's house. Interestingly, her father did not apologize, but through the mother he conveyed there would be no repercussions if she came home, that nothing more would be said on the matter. In this way he did validate her sense of injustice. Mally could not remember an earlier expression of this anger, but could immediately remember her earliest *unexpressed anger* when I asked her in just those terms. That memory was when she was age three and her mother seemed to consistently favor her older sister by giving her lollipops of a preferred color. This memory shaped her later behavior. Aside from hating lollipops of a particular color – the one she always had to accept, she also became obsessive about insuring that her children shared equally. When a double circle was placed around this 'smoldering' three year old, and Christ asked to extract whatever she was protecting, Mally immediately saw Christ picking up a very tearful two year old in the second circle.

Hidden Mirror-Aspects

Projection and dissociation are two ways of hiding Mirror-aspects. This becomes necessary if the mirrored behavior threatens to evoke severe repercussions. When projected, the Ego literally imbeds (dissociates, then projects) the Mirror-aspect into the image of another family member generally perceived as more powerful than the parent emulated by the Mirror-aspect. A grandparent is a typical example, but in later life, a spouse can also serve this purpose. In more extreme cases, the Mirror-aspect is 'hidden' by Repressive dissociation. 'Alter personalities' are examples of dissociated Mirror-aspects. A common example of a dissociated Mirror-aspect is whatever seems to overtake an individual during altered states of consciousness such as alcoholic blackouts. Generally, a Mirror-aspect is hidden because it cannot be consciously owned by the client. It could be that the identity becomes shameful to the client as in the case of the Not-me duplex discussed in the next section. Or, if the Mirror-aspect acted on its emotions, it would place the child at risk. Most mirror aspects are angry protectors; acting on that anger would likely incur an even angrier response from the parent. Dissociated Mirror-aspects are likely to manifest somatically, e.g. teen-agers with acne; or characterologically, e.g. individuals with persistent sadistic behaviors toward animals.

In projection, the family member is often a grandparent, but it can also be a parent, spouse, son or daughter. [22] This projection is most likely to occur if the client is in some way identified with the family member (each grandchild will be identified – or dis-identified, with a particular grandparent). To illustrate, a client described her maternal grandfather as an abusing, denigrating, womanizer who died when she was twelve years old. Her mother married a man (the client's father) in many ways like the maternal grandfather. This client was identified within the family as being like her maternal grandfather. In addressing Temporal authority issues with this particular client, I suggested she ask Christ to remove from the maternal grandfather any Temporal authority *oppressing her mother*. The client found herself strangely reluctant to allow Christ to do this, and after further discovery, she finally admitted her strong identification with this grandfather's authority even though it was perceived as cruel. Using a double circle of *Light*, she extracted a Mirror-aspect hidden in the grandfather. This image of herself was seen as a protector capable of standing up to her abusive father, and other men, and protecting the weak, feminine self likened to her mother. This particular case illustrates another point regarding interventions. Any particular intervention is as likely to reveal hidden resistances as it is to remove oppressive forms of authority.

As noted, Mirror-aspects are also commonly hidden by dissociation. This is most likely to be the case where the client exhibits dissociative behavior in several contexts, and almost always in the case of MPD. An alcoholic blackout will precipitate a classic examples of a dissociated Mirror-aspect assuming control of a client's behavior. While in a blackout, the individual can literally become the 'spitting image' of the parent who abused them. The Mirror-aspect is considered dissociated because in normal consciousness the client actively disowns any identification with the abuser. Instead, s/he self-perceives as the victim of this parent. Moreover, particularly as regards blackouts, the drinker will have no memory of how s/he acted during the blackout or will consciously disown the behavior. The dissociation hides this Mirror-aspect from the conscious self who is normally empowered to keep it repressed. All that is consciously felt is a compulsion to repeat an activity, such as drinking, that will release the dissociated ego-aspect. Hiding a Mirror-aspect by dissociation is different from hiding by projection. With projection, there is an implicit or subliminal identification with the family member who embodies the Mirror-aspect although this connection may not be apparent until an intervention is attempted. In cases of projection, the client will usually balk at having the Temporal authority summarily removed from the family member. But where the Mirror-aspect is dissociatively repressed, the conscious self has no problem asking Christ to remove the Temporal authority. But note, removing Temporal authority will not curtail the activity of a dissociatively repressed Mirror-aspect. It will continue to plague the client until it is consciously recovered and can ask Christ's assistance in identifying the Pre-moral aspect. It is the Pre-moral aspect that sustains the Mirror-aspect, not the Temporal authority it seeks to emulate.

Regardless of how the Mirror-aspect is hidden, the goal of treatment is still the removal of Temporal authority from the family member(s) wielding Temporal authority, and the Pre-moral aspect's healing. In the above case, where the Mirror aspect was hidden in the maternal grandfather, the client had to first allow Christ to terminate her father's Temporal authority. This was the authority that necessitated the creation and projection of the Mirror-aspect hidden in the grandfather. Without terminating that authority first, the client would have felt too undefended to proceed. Not surprisingly, the client was equally fearful of having the father's authority terminated because she sensed it was likely to release a flood of negative memories involving her parents. Where this kind of fear is encountered, the therapist needs to move slowly, but remain focused on the issue to the exclusion of much else. In this case, the father and his authority was contained in a dome; and the Mirror-aspect was given a garment of protection. This allowed the client to unearth the Pre-moral aspect and then allowed Christ to find the Pre-moral aspect a suitable mother. Thereafter, the client became willing for Christ to terminate the Temporal authority embedded in both the father and maternal grandfather.

The therapist needs to bear in mind that Temporal authority normally reinforces the Mirror-aspect and suppresses affect associated with the Pre-moral aspect. Consequently, any attenuation of Temporal authority will leave the client more vulnerable to affective emotions associated with the Pre-moral aspect. Whether clients sense this or not, the therapist should be prepared for it. Mirror images are never created without cause. Once the Temporal authority of a parent or family member has been removed, affect associated with the Pre-moral aspect will be very strongly felt by the client. Remember, a Pre-moral aspect can be felt without being seen. While it remains hidden (sic) 'protected' by the Mirror-aspect, the client cannot differentiate it from the Mirror-aspect. Instead, the client looks to the environment to account for how s/he is feeling. Viscerally, a Pre-moral aspect that sustains a hidden Mirror-aspect will be experienced by the client and therapist as excessively needy and demanding of nurture. The therapist will feel its demanding character in therapy sessions. The most common affects associated with a Pre-moral aspect – in and out of sessions, is crying without cause, general fearfulness, or feelings of despair. For all these reasons, it is generally wiser to forego removing Temporal authority from a parent if the existence of a Mirror-aspect is suspected. Removing that authority beforehand puts considerable pressure on client and therapist to find the Pre-moral aspect and heal it. One way or another, the process must be completed. But sessions will be a little less pressured if the therapist can wait till the last to remove Temporal authority from the parent.

In general, wherever Mirror-aspects are an issue, interventions generally require six steps to achieve closure:

1) Whether expressed or suppressed, the client must be able to personify the characteristic behavior at issue by separating out the Mirror aspect embodying that behavior. If hidden, whether projectively or dissociatively, the client must own the Mirror-aspect by extraction or containment.

2) The Mirror-image must be offered a shield of *Light* to protect it from further attack. In theory, containment of the abuser provides this, but sometimes it is helpful to further augment Mirror aspect in this way, especially if the Mirror-aspect has been suppressed or hidden.

3) Using 'Regression to the source,' the Pre-moral aspect must be identified and offered the protection of Christ and the *Light*.

4) The Pre-moral aspect must be healed. Healing will include, but not be limited to, a nurturing love that completely satisfies any sense of lack experienced by the Pre-moral aspect. This generally requires a specific mother archetype as well as Christ.

5) Christ needs to terminate the Temporal authority of the parent and/or other family member(s) that necessitated the creation of the Mirror aspects and Pre-moral aspect.

6) Christ needs to help the Mirror-aspect redefine itself at some point during the process, as described below.

As noted earlier, the primary objective of these interventions is the discovery and nurture of the Pre-moral aspect being protected/suppressed by the Mirror-image. Redefining the Mirror-aspect is often helpful but secondary. Like other Ego defenses, Mirror-aspects do not have the power to heal the Pre-moral aspect, remove the authority suppressing it, or facilitate its growth and maturation. As long as the Pre-moral self is 'obliged' to accept protection, it must remain a wounded child. Likewise, the Mirror-aspect, of whatever variant, injects an 'eye for an eye' mentality into much of the individual's thoughts and/or behavior that greatly impedes seeking more viable alternatives.

The Not-me Duplex

The Not-Me duplex is the most convoluted of the Mirror-aspect variations. It begins with a parent, generally the mother, creating a Pre-moral aspect through neglect, rejection, or other forms of emotional abuse. To protect itself from further wounding, the Ego generates a Mirror-aspect of this parent. But in this particular scenario, the Mirror-aspect's behavior is shamed by other members of the family, including the *other* parent who likely functions as the Voice-of-Conscience. In short, the Mirror-aspect is shamed *for acting like* the mother. In response to family's negative feedback, the Mirror-aspect is projected into offending parent's image, and an *antithetical* (not me) Coping-aspect is created to complete the dis-identification with the shamed Mirror-aspect.

The initial Mirror-aspect is an attempt to overcome the parent's wounding in much the same way as other expressed or suppressed Mirror-aspects. The difference here is that the parent being emulated is treated by others in the family as 'shameful' or otherwise to be shunned. (Of note, 'shameful' behavior can characterize a multitude of sins not the least of which are most forms of severe mental illness.) In effect, other family members validate rather than deny the abusive parent's behavior, but in so doing, point to the Mirror-aspect created to cope with it as *equally undesirable*. Consequently, the child is now obliged to evade similar ostracism by projectively hiding the Mirror-aspect in the image of the shameful parent, and then assuming a Coping-aspect that acts out the antithesis of the disowned Mirror aspect. As used here, the Not-me duplex consists of two images. It is, first, a Mirror-aspect projected into the abusive parent that it models, and second, a Coping-aspect that seeks to act in ways antithetical to the abusive parent. The Coping-aspect may model another surrogate, e.g. a grandparent, if the child is treated as also favoring that grandparent, but most often, the Coping-aspect is simply identified with *one or two opposite qualities* that the client compulsively enacts. The Not-me duplex is relatively easy to identify once the therapist is sensitized to its existence. The therapist has only to ask the client in a straight forward manner if there is any one in the family, specifically a parent that the client has actively striven to be *not like* as an adult.

The client's worst fear is that others – particularly other family members – will see them as being like the offending parent. (Very quickly, transference will add the therapist to that group.) The Not-me Coping-aspect becomes the client's primary protector against the Mirror-aspect hidden in the abusive parent. The client will slavishly enact this Coping-aspect in a concerted effort to not be identified with the offending parent. Acting 'selflessly' is a good example. In that instance, the offending parent would be seen *by others* as shamefully demanding and needy. Acting 'warmly' – where the offending parent is perceived as cold and heartless – is another example of a Not-me Coping-aspect. Initially, client and therapist may be unaware of the Not-me duplex because the Coping-aspect effectively hides the offensive image of the parent behind words of love and devotion. But eventually, the perceptive therapist will note that the parent in question hardly deserves that love and devotion. This usually comes out as the client describes how others in the family describe the parent in pejorative terms.

The Not-me Coping-aspect should not be confused with an aspect of the Ideal-self. The Not-me Coping-aspect is more interested in dissociating itself from the shameful parent than striving to achieve an ideal standard. Its intent is to erase from its repertoire anything that would make it like the offending parent *including negative judgments* of the offending parent. But the client is always clear that s/he does not want to be seen as like the shameful parent even while remaining, seemingly, devoted and attached. Almost without exception, if there are other siblings in the family, they will perceive the shameful parent accurately; and the client will be able to explain the reasons for their assessment even while denying similar thoughts. This negative perception of the parent by others in the family may be the best indicator of a Not-me duplex. Another clue is the therapist's own response to descriptions of the parent. If the therapist is responding negatively to descriptions of a parent, but the client continues to claim a dutiful attachment, a Not-me mirror image is likely embedded in the parent.

I have identified the Not-me duplex primarily in mothers and daughters, but it will also be found in sons and mothers. A determining factor may be the child's birth order identification with the parent by others in the family. The Not-me duplex requires some form of identification with the mother that then requires a dis-identification. A male child can be identified with a mother image before gender differentiation. But culture and most families will discourage a boy's overt identification with the opposite sexed parent; the same for girls. Boys who 'fail' to hide this Mirror-aspect may end up enacting 'sissy' roles. Even a daughter, discouraged from acting like her mother, is nonetheless expected to act like a girl and model some female in the family. For girls, it is truly a double bind. The girl seems to resolve the impasse by compulsively conforming to the Coping-aspect intended to effectively disown connection with the mother, but nonetheless be like the mother in surreptitious ways. If possible, she can identify with another surrogate such as a grandparent.

The major liability of a Not-me strategy is its likelihood of binding the client to lifelong servitude and torment. I have already mentioned one way this can happen, namely, by generating a Not-me Coping-aspect that obliges the client to act selflessly toward the offending parent. Female clients with negative mothers are prone to this type of servitude. The classic example are those clients who are vocally critical of the mother while continuing to 'honor' their filial obligations. To reject the shameful parent is paramount to acting like the parent, thereby revealing the Mirror-aspect kept hidden in that parent. Wherever a client continues to interact with a parent – whose behavior is clearly denigrating or abusive, the therapist needs to suspect a Not-me duplex. Projection demands that interaction with the offending parent or surrogate is sustained in order to continue hiding the equally offending mirror image of the self. If the parent changes in a dramatically positive way, or dies, the client is likely to hide the Mirror-aspect in a spouse, child, or significant other. Where no projective container is available, the individual is likely to be taken over by the Mirror-aspect and begin acting like the offensive mother.

Negative identities shared with a parent are among the most difficult to work with as they thrust the client into the role of perpetrator. This is especially true where the parent is physically and/or sexually abusive. The finding of a Not-me duplex must always be handled with great tack or the client is likely to terminate therapy prematurely. Even though clients with histories of severe abuse are likely to develop Not-me duplexes, suggesting the existence of a Mirror self-image that emulates the abuser is definitely like adding insult to injury. (This is true for all hidden Mirror-aspects.) If opportunity affords, it is best to start working with images of other people suspected of carrying shadow projections and have Christ work with those projections as a way of preparing the client. Frequently, clients with a Not-me duplex will be very critical of other people in their lives. Initially, the therapist can work with those shadow images. The positive transformation of shadow carriers offers hope of a comparable outcome when the client can finally identify his or her abusive-aspect in need of similar redemption. One client, for example, had a strong negative image of her adopted son's biological mother. This image was contained, and Christ was asked to redeem it. This was not immediate, but over several sessions the image became positive as Christ was allowed to work with it. At this level, no effort is made to identify what has been projected into the person that makes them so negative. Rather, the emphasis is on the power of Christ to redeem that person in the client's eyes and help the client to understand that no one is beyond redemption. In effect, the client is helped to understand, by example, that a comparable outcome can be expected as and when they identify a Mirror-aspect that is like their abuser. I would also note that, in cases of severe abuse, recovery of abusive memories is generally the first order of business. Asking Christ to intervene at the end of each memory, and heal the child image wounded by the event, will also set the stage for self-redemption. This healing effectively diminishes the abuser's power to do irreparable harm. And that is also true of any Mirror-aspect embedded in the abuser. If the abuser's 'trespasses' can be undone, then the same holds true for any actions of the hidden Mirror-aspect who is like the abuser. In any case, this recovery of memories cannot be short-circuited, so the first goal of treatment is the recovery and healing of those memories before attempting to extract any Mirror-aspects hidden in the perpetrator.

A Coping-aspect is the conscious part of a Not-me duplex. It is generally identifiable as an industrious youth. In periods when the client is feeling stress, this Coping-aspect is likely the one generating the stressful behavior. Since it co-exists in conscious awareness with the Aware-ego, it can be separated from it by placing a double circle around the Aware-ego and extracting the feeling that seems to be dominating the client's awareness. To illustrate, one client continually complained of feeling exhausted. When a double circle was used to separate that feeling from the Aware-ego, the *Light* personified a twelve year old driven to stay active and *not be like* her mother who was seen as sleeping all the time. These coping-aspects can also be used to recover the Pre-moral aspect, which is often felt simultaneously. Once the Pre-moral aspect has been reunited with an archetypal mother it is possible to extract the projected Mirror image and also take it to the archetypal parent for healing. Always bear in mind that however offensive a Mirror-aspect may appear, it is just as wounded as the Pre-moral aspect. The following case illustrates these dynamics, and adds some of its own.

Bonny. Bonny's mother died two years before this series of sessions. Bonny had seen me some years before about a failing relationship, and again immediately after the death of her mother. We parted well but I felt little was done to help her. She hardly mourned her mother's death though she was her primary caregiver in the last years of her mother's life. She considered her mother's life a source of embarrassment. Her greatest fear was that she might end up being like her mother who was seen as self-centered, lazy, and exceedingly needy. The year following her mother's death, her youngest son died in a auto accident. She came to therapy because she could not shake her own 'neediness' following his death. Her inactivity made her fearful of becoming like her mother. Bonny is a self-sufficient, take charge, person well respected in her vocational field. Despite this self-assured demeanor, she is very fearful of mental illness in others, especially her ex-husband who she sees as threatening her life if not placated. Early in our sessions, she identifies a twelve year old Coping-aspect who seems exhausted by her efforts to keep going. I suggest she let Christ separate this self from the Aware-ego to discover the source of her great tiredness. This twelve year old is oppositional, a fighter, determined not to be still. She is most fearful of being seen as like her mother who never seemed to leave the couch – a classic Not-me complex. Concurrently, Bonny also identifies a small child who desperately wants to be taken care of. This child is identified as a Pre-moral aspect. Christ agrees to undertake the task of finding a mother who can fulfill the child's lack.

In successive sessions, Bonny seeks to retain control of the mother quest by identifying images that might serve as an archetypal mother. Each of the images she selects seems worthy, but are not Christ's choice, and none of them satisfy the child carried by Christ. They are all choices extrapolated from the client's lived experiences. Of note, all of them do have archetypal vestiges. This effort to retain control of the quest is not uncommon. But as I note to Bonny, if an archetypal mother could be found among people already known to her, the child's need would have already been satisfied. Finally, she agrees to let Christ take the lead via an "experiment." I suggest she allow Christ to draw a circle and let each image thus far selected walk through the circle leaving behind their essence. Ordinarily, I would not have made such a suggestion. What prompts me to do so in this case is the archetypal qualities that Bonny has identified in the images previously selected. The images she has evoked accede to her request: "I can feel that each has left a part of themselves and formed something like a mound." I then have her ask Christ to step into the circle. Spontaneously, Christ walks back out of the circle carrying 'the mound' and takes it someplace to do something with it. She does not know where or what. After a short interlude, he returns with an adult image of Bonny who is nonetheless also seen as different because she embodies all the qualities of the persons she wants for the mother of the child. The image surprises me as much as it does her. But, she reports, "the child loves it and feels love." The self image is clearly affirming for Bonny and appears to satisfy the child's need for nurture.

By the next session Bonny is markedly better. The twelve year old Coping-aspect is still and thoughtful, rather than pushing herself to exhaustion, and almost ready to reach out to the mother image herself, but not quite yet. Even so, this is the first time in my clinical experience that Christ has presented a child with an ego-aspect of a client, and I remain a bit dubious. Clearly, Bonny has need of this affirmation. All of her sons had been scarred by alcohol or mental illness. Alcohol probably contributed to her youngest son's death. In fact, when she reflects on this new image of mother and child she uses early memories with her son to describe an interaction that is idyllic. Then she also notes, almost in passing, "I would like this mother to also mother the mother who was my mother." I am reluctant to encourage this, and ask instead: is there was a part of her that is like the mother? If so, where would she hide it? Initially, this brings a blank response, but as the idea is discussed she begins to consider the logic of hiding a part of herself in the image of her mother since *she and her mother were physically similar in appearance.* She agrees to let Christ extract any self-image from her mother.

Both of us are surprised by the initial result. I expect Christ to extract a negative image – a Mirror-aspect. Instead, he extracts a glowing light that she identifies as her spirit. All I can ask is why it has been hidden in her mother all these years? The answer is that her mother has needed so much help, that she was a weak, frail, spirit who needed Bonny's spirit to survive, that without it she would have collapsed and dissolved. Bonny then goes on to say: "I always felt responsible for her and resented it immensely. She could never take care of things on her own even though she was dominant in the sense of always screaming at us." I ask if there is an image that embodies the spirit. She says it reminds her of the time after her divorce when she felt free for the first time in her life, not in bondage to anyone. I then have her ask her *Light* if there is another image hidden in her mother? The *Light* says "yes" and Bonny becomes willing to extract that image as well. "This one" she says, "is not nice…a crazy, homeless, street person, tattered clothes, an adult who looks like and not like me, babbling." I ask how it got there? Bonny says it is the part of her she has always been afraid of becoming. "The whole time I was married to my husband he said he was the only thing between me and my going crazy." (In fact, it is her ex-husband who is finally identified as schizophrenic.) I suggest that she let Christ take this 'crazy lady' to the archetypal mother. Bonny agrees and then reports: "She is going to take care of her, clean her up, make her to understand she is ok. The little child is also going to help. The mother says, she is just dressed up like this, but is not really crazy, that she is ok." Before this session ends, I have Bonny ask Christ to assume responsibility for the care of her biological mother, and to release Bonny from all further obligation in that respect.

The above case illustrates a number of

the points I have covered regarding the Not-me duplex but also highlights several that are anomalous and do not easily fit the paradigm. First, the mother image found by Christ is a clearly a self image of Bonny. That is the only time I have found that to be so. But even Bonny is clear that, while the image looks like her, *it is much more than she imagines herself to be*. Next, the first image *extracted from the deceased biological mother* is a very positive image, where I was anticipating a projected, shameful Mirror-aspect. The negative aspect followed, but the first was truly unexpected. It reminds me of an embodiment of individual authority suppressed by the mother's Temporal authority. (As ineffectual as her mother was, she 'wore the pants' in the household.) That is the closest I can come to naming it. In most other respects Bonny's case highlights the various aspects of the Not-me duplex. Over the years, I have come to expect most cases to show 'anomalies.' Theory is to be valued for its identification of the major cast of characters, interventional endpoints, and potential obstacles to reaching the goal. But there is no way that the small case load I have worked with can anticipate all the variables at play in the lives of the population at large. The therapist must anticipate variance and trust the method rather than insisting that every case replicate the previous one. By method, I mean always calling on the *Light* and Christ to make the interventions.

To summarize, a Not-me duplex is to be suspected if a client reports either 1) an intense dislike of a same sexed parent but continues to interact with them on a regular basis, or 2) reports that other family members are critical of the parent while the client remains non-critical, or neutral, or 'selflessly' positive. This duplex will be comprised of a denied Mirror-aspect projectively hidden in the dysfunctional parent, and a Coping-aspect that acts the opposite of the family member's shameful behavior. The Coping aspect allows the client to disown any connection to the negatively perceived family member while continuing in relationship with that member. Were it not for the shameful behavior exhibited by the family member, the client might openly identify with this parent via an expressive Mirror-aspect. However, given the family member's shameful history, any open identification would immediately bring shame upon the client from other family members. But even open identification could be deceiving. Since identification is generally to the same sexed parent, it would seem to be a natural consequence of gender development. In fact, however, the mirroring represents an early effort to avoid further wounding of the Pre-moral aspect.

As a rule, strong dis-identification with a shameful parent will generally require excessive control on the part of the Not-me self to ward off being taken over by the projected Mirror-aspect. These controlling behaviors act as a substitute for the shameful gender identity with a parent. This was brought home to me by a client whose alcoholic mother acted shamefully in public throughout the client's childhood and adolescence. In order to protect herself from repeating such behavior, the client assumed a Coping-aspect in early childhood that was the opposite of her mother's behavior. When the shameful parent later changed her behavior (i.e. successfully maintained a recovery program, including attempts to make amends), the client married someone who acted like her shameful parent, and projected her disowned Mirror-aspect onto this spouse. This client was also identified with her maternal grandmother and her behavior was considered even worse than the mother's. It is very likely that this double identification with mother and grandmother contributed to her need to continue disowning the Mirror-aspect even when the mother recovered. She insisted she would never be like her mother/grandmother or her addictive spouse. Her Coping-aspect was ever fearful of being 'out of control' – like her mother or grandmother. Her ideal was to be selfless and helpful, always thinking of others, happy all the time, strong, brave, no desires, no need for anybody, no dependencies. Her husband's family was chronically addicted to a variety of substances, which provided her ample hiding places for her disowned Mirror-aspect. Of note, over the client's lifetime, there were periods when the Mirror-aspect broke through and the client acted out. Such acting out was only suppressed when the client could find another relationship that provided a suitable container for her disowned Mirror-aspect.

Nurturing the Pre-moral Aspect

To truly nurture a Pre-moral aspect, the therapist must encourage the client to let Christ seek out an archetypal mother image. These images often have a numinous quality. They are exceedingly powerful and potent images of the mother archetype. I have always found Christ a willing participant in this process. When asked, he will unhesitatingly help the client find the nurturing mother most needed by the Pre-moral aspect. Until then, he will function adequately as a surrogate. The need voiced by a Pre-moral aspect would be difficult, if not impossible, for most human beings to satisfy. It tends to be absolute: a mother who would *always be strong enough to hold the child forever.* These absolutes are impossible to satisfy in the real world of adults. The client's self-reports will often reflect this impossibility as they report vainly searching their memory for a real life image that could satisfy the child. The child will only be satisfied with an archetypal image. This is why the images found by Christ are so often numinous. One of the most common images is Mary, his own mother. One client, on being led to Mary by Christ, understood her to lovingly say, "He brings all the lost children to me." But whether it is Mary, or a generic image of the Great Mother, or a more idiosyncratic image of 'mother,' the response is always the same. From the child's perspective, it is a perfect fit. The child and mother completely connect and satisfy. It is a felt experience of connection noticeable in the child's demeanor, and felt by the client's Aware-ego. Even the Mirror-aspect, which frequently accompanies the child on Christ's search, will acknowledge that the new relationship completely satisfies the child. Henceforth, the child will lack for nothing in terms of nurture.

The greatest difficulty with this phase of the work rests with the client's own resistance. Generally, 'regressing to the source' will quickly identify the Pre-moral aspect. However, in successive sessions the client will actually seem to disown or distance itself from this Pre-moral aspect. To seek such a mother often challenges family loyalties and sense of self. For years, many clients will have striven to define their parents as adequate by denying the existence of this aspect. Its existence calls into question all their make-do definitions of love and parenting, including the parenting of their own children. Other clients will express feeling guilty over the idea of turning to an image other than their mother for mothering. And almost all of them will plead a lack of experience: How can they expect to find a nurturing mother having failed to experience it in their own life?

I have found one formulation of this intervention very helpful in guiding the client to a nurturing mother. I call it the child's *innate sense of rightness.* When the Pre-moral aspect is identified, it will express a sense of lack vis-à-vis the wounding parent. This sense of lack will be slightly different for each client, and the therapist needs to take some time helping the client define the specific sense of lack. In the process, the client will complain they have no idea what a nurturing mother would be like, their mother having failed them repeatedly in this respect. What I point out to them is that the child has some sense of its need or s/he could not express its lack. Eugene Gendlin developed this logic years ago in his book on focusing. [23] He pointed out that quite often a client cannot name what s/he is feeling but can, nonetheless, tell you what it is not. To illustrate, I can name a whole list of feelings. To each one, the client can reply that it is like or not like whatever s/he is feeling, even as she does not yet know the feeling's name. Moreover, when s/he – or I, can finally name the feeling, s/he will affirm it as a felt sense of release or rightness. It is as if the blocked verbalization creates a tension that the naming releases. In much the same way, the Pre-moral aspect has a built in sense of rightness about what is needed for adequate nurturing. When given the opportunity, Christ can take the Pre-moral aspect to the place where this 'sense of rightness' is most strong. This union, one might say re-union, can be quite profound.

Dory. The following case, illustrates the sense of rightness. In this particular session, Dory re-identified a young child curled up in a dark closet. She has previously identified this image and then lost track of it in successive sessions. However, during all this time, since the image was first identified, Christ has remained in the closet with the child. I suggest to Dory that she now ask Christ to take the child 'deep inside' to a mother both she and the child could trust. She reports that many images flash in front of her following this suggestion but none seem to fit. I introduced her to the 'sense of rightness' concept, and reiterated that Christ, not her, must lead them to the image. After a few moments, she reports feeling a presence. It feels loving and compassionate, but has no face and cannot be identified with anyone in her memory. The child is hesitant to approach at first. When asked why, Dory reports that the child believes this is the mother who deserted her creating her sense of distrust. But quickly the child overcomes her hesitancy as she experiences this mother's *great relief* at being reunited with her daughter. Whatever the original cause of separation, it is quickly dismissed as an impediment, as mother and child lovingly reunite. Clients will often report this sense of déjà vu. The mother is unlike any in their experience; but nonetheless, the experience feels like a re-union.

As noted, it is vitally important that the client be given ample opportunity to explore the child's sense of lack. This can take several sessions, though this necessary delay can be excruciatingly difficult for the client. The child's sense of lack – even vaguely identified, will be felt in the client's daily life, and often – though inadvertently, acted out. The client can become very needy or psychosomatic – what Object Relationists refer to as regressed. So once identified, the therapist needs to keep the client focused on this image till it is lovingly connected with a mother archetype. And until then, the child needs someone to cling to. In most cases, that will be the Christ image. But even Christ can only comfort, not satisfy. Truly, only an archetypal mother will serve here. The process cannot be shortchanged in that regard. Likewise, the client must come to terms with the failure of their own parent to satisfy the child's essential demands for nurture, and to name the specific sense of lack experienced by the child. For each client it will be somewhat different. For one, it may be the child's sense that the mother is not strong enough to protect. For another, it may be the child's sense of feeling like a burden or inconvenience. Christ can and will find a perfect fit for this sense of lack – whatever it is, but only after the lack has been named and felt. And again, as I have noted, the process will often be hampered by the client's desire to remain loyal to their birth mother's 'parenting,' and their long held fear that the child, not the mother, was lacking in something that precipitated the disruption in nurture.

In sum, only the Pre-moral aspect can determine if Christ's choice of a nurturing mother is sufficient to satisfy its lack. The Pre-moral aspect's response is the sole criteria for determining whether the search has been successful. It is the Pre-moral aspect's felt sense of need that must be satisfied, and the source of its generally manifests as an archetypal image of the nurturing, healing, feminine.

Redefining the Mirror-aspect

As a matter of course, I now ask any identified Mirror-aspect to accompany Christ and the child in their search for the archetypal mother. Quite often, following the re-union, the Mirror-aspect will also want to join with this mother. It goes without saying that I always encourage this as the best way to depotentiate its controlling behavior. But there are other ways to depotentiate its negativity. A Mirror-aspect has a set of core beliefs. These can be identified by having Christ place a second circle around it and lifting that circle above the aspect's head, thereby extracting its core beliefs, which can be read by simply having the Aware-ego look up into the raised circle. Once these are identified Christ can be asked to augment or balance the beliefs by injecting complementary experiences into the raised circle and then lowering it back down over the Mirror-aspect. This process does not take away anything. The Mirror-aspect can still believe as it has, but can now also believe the opposite. It now has a choice. This intervention can be offered to the Mirror-aspect at anytime, before or after the Pre-moral aspect is treated or before or after Temporal authority has been terminated.

SOCIETAL IMPLICATIONS REGARDING TEMPORAL AUTHORITY

The thoughtful reader may discern more implications regarding this matter of Temporal authority than I have addressed here. What has held my interest these past years is the power for healing that an inner Christ can offer individuals ready to address the various mental health issues promulgated by this authority. But it does seem noteworthy, when I reflect on it, that our culture has no rituals for divesting parents of Temporal authority when a child comes of age. I only know of one ritual where a father is explicitly asked to relinquish his authority to Christ. In the Roman Catholic church, in some religious orders, a woman becomes a bride of Christ when she takes her final vows. In years past, this often involved a ritual wherein the father gave her, dressed as a bride, to be married to Christ. [24] But even then, in another part of the same ritual, she is expected to take a vow of obedience to her superiors. So far as I can determine, we have no rituals by which parents are asked to return their Temporal authority to its archetypal source when their children become adults, or a ritual that allows an adult to remove that authority when s/he comes of age. Rather, such rituals as do exist are explicit acknowledgments of a *transfer* of Temporal authority for the maintenance of State or Ecclesiastical authority. The most common ritual for the transfer of authority is the Christian ritual of a father giving his 'authority' to a son-in-law at the altar when he 'gives up' his daughter to be wed. (Historically, until married, that daughter was expected to remain under her father's Temporal authority.) Other adult rites of passage explicitly transfer Temporal authority to the State as when a young man is inducted into an Armed Service, or a couple seeks a marriage license. Even when minor children go off to college it is understood that the college administration serves *in loco parentis*. In effect, the culture only delimits the parent's authority for the purpose of extending it to a State or Ecclesiastical authority.

From a clinical perspective, a significant finding of this work is the seeming emergence of individual authority, specifically in women, when Temporal authority is terminated by Christ. This emergence of individual authority may be the primary reason why patriarchy has no rituals that invite parents to relinquish their authority when the individual comes of age. So long as no rituals enact closure on this authority, it is retained by parents or transferred to anyone with the power to engage us in a parent-child relationship (e.g. a subordinate or submissive relationship authorized by parents, the church, or law of the land). Such transfers will tend to exaggerate the authority wielded by men and suppress that of women.

In theory, Temporal authority serves parents raising children who must learn to survive in a complex, often dangerous, world where no restrictions could sometimes be fatal. Running out into a street without looking can be a harsh and unnecessary teacher. But to indefinitely block self-volition in adults would appear to serve others at the expense of the individual.

I honestly cannot envision a world free of Temporal authority. Even in an androgynous society, there would still have to be specific rites of passage – at appropriate developmental epochs – that facilitated individual authority supplanting Temporal authority. But for a child, as with any immature mammal, adult actions expressing 'no' have got to be enforceable. There are occasions when disobedience can put all at risk, child and parent alike. The physical safety of children requires the archetypal investment of parental images with Temporal authority. At issue is whether this authority is needed indefinitely by parents and culture. Beyond a certain age, it seems to serve the proverbial 'principalities and powers,' at the expense of the individual. Unquestionably, in a patriarchy, it serves men at the expense of women. It is very likely that many adolescents, and even children, learn to *defy* abuses of Temporal and Moral authority. But over the long run, an individual is no better served by defiant/rebellious solutions since they are only reactive rather than proactive. In rebelling, the individual is still engaging the parent by 'pushing against' as distinct from being freed up to choose a new path. Likewise, the seemingly inevitable transfer of Temporal authority to the wider culture offers little more by way of alternatives. As Walter Wink argues, our culture still acts out the myth of redemptive violence, e.g. an eye for an eye. [25] The emotions defining that myth are pride and attack with 'righteous' anger, characteristics most likely to be expressed by Mirror-aspects. To my mind, any intervention that supports the emergence of individual authority is far preferable. Individual authority seems to dramatically increase the client's choices. At the very least, it strengthens their ability to choose such options as Christ's third way, [26] or the principles of aikido, [27] whereby aggression is used to defeat itself.

CHAPTER VI ENDNOTES

1 Three gospels describe Satan's temptation of Christ with Temporal authority following his baptism: Then Jesus was led by the Spirit into the desert to be tempted by the devil. After fasting forty days and forty nights, he was hungry. The tempter came to him and said, "If you are the Son of God, tell these stones to become bread." Jesus answered, "It is written: 'Man does not live on bread alone, but on every word that comes from the mouth of God." Then the devil took him to the holy city and had him stand on the highest point of the temple. "If you are the Son of God," he said, "throw yourself down. For it is written: " 'He will command his angels concerning you, and they will lift you up in their hands, so that you will not strike your foot against a stone." Jesus answered him, "It is also written: 'Do not put the Lord your God to the test." Again, the devil took him to a very high mountain and showed him all the kingdoms of the world and their splendor. "All this I will give you," he said, "if you will bow down and worship me." Jesus said to him, "Away from me, Satan! For it is written: 'Worship the Lord your God, and serve him only." Then the devil left him, and angels came and attended him. (Matt 4: 1-11)

2 See Raff, J. (2000), *Jung and the Alchemical Imagination*, Nicolas-Hays.

3 Abortion battles, i.e. control of the woman's body, suppression of homosexuality that connotes the emasculation of the male, and the right of every man to carry a gun, can all be seen as a valiant effort to sustain patriarchal dominance.

4 It is possible that the sacrament of Confirmation was originally intended to release the child from the Temporal authority of the parent, but in practice, only serves to place the supplicant under the authority of church leaders which have been predominantly patriarchal for many centuries.

5 See Bowen, M.& Kerr, M. (1988), *Family Evaluation: An Approach Based on Bowen Theory*, Norton: New York; and also, Friedman, E., (1985), Generation to Generation: Family Process in Church and Synagogue, Guilford Press: New York.

6 A notable exception might be Zen Buddhism. The first koan described in Zen Flesh, Zen Bones, seems to infer that enlightenment flows from moving

through the negative prohibitions established by Masters. See Reps, P. & Senzaki, N. (1998), *Zen Flesh and Zen Bones: A Collection of Zen and Pre-zen Writings*, Tuttle Publishing.

7   Anita's case illustrates why it is necessary to challenge any changes in the Christ image reported by the client. But as ever there are exceptions to that rule. Another case illustrates a rare instance when the image of Christ is altered unexpectedly and I end up facilitating its emergence rather than containing and testing it. I note it, first, because it is an exception to my general recommendation that changed images of Christ be contained. The reason why I did not follow my own guidelines in this instance was that the changes were generated by my suggestions though I did not expect this particular outcome. Normally, for this client – a Lutheran priest, the image of Christ appeared peaceful and calm. Most clients see him as gentle, loving, and forgiving, but in this particular instance, that typical image of Christ literally thrust the client toward another image of Christ whose appearance riveted his attention. The client has just accepted a new parish. He is ambivalent about going back into parish work but needs the transitional employment. When he goes inside to appraise an image of himself doing parish work, the ego-aspect he evokes is distasteful; he appears to himself as fastidious, suited man sitting with old ladies drinking tea in the afternoon. This image appears to grow out of his fear of disappointing others, of not being able to meet their expectations. After going inside and joining up with his normally expected image of Christ, I suggest he let this image of Christ give the suited ego-aspect a push in the back. This phrase, 'push in the back' has gained significance for the client who has been reading the works of Carlos Castaneda. In those books, Castaneda's teacher, Don Juan Mateus, would thrust him into different realities by giving him a push in the back. I hope my suggestion might at least create an openness to change, but to the surprise of both of us, his typical Christ image literally thrusts him into a new perception of Christ! It is, he says, a rude awakening. The push seems to thrust him into the presence of a Christ who looks like a beast. The image is lion-like, riveting, but asleep, snoring. The client senses that the image has been put to sleep by his own cautious, aloof, behavior. Moreover, he is very reluctant to wake him up. What further intrigues him – as we explore this new image of Christ, is the response of one of his favorite feminine images. He hears from her that she has repeatedly engaged the client in an effort to reach this archetypal Christ in him - another rude awakening. In successive sessions, this Christ image exhibits a power that inspires and heals the client, as well as showing him an ecclesiastical power structure that had been emasculating rather than empowering of Christ. I might note that while I did not screen this image, the client did test it in a variety of ways on his own, including using the Light. He was especially concerned that the image exhibit the stigmata which it did. Let me reiterate that my non-intervention in this case is an exception to the rule. Normally, I would have quickly had the client

contain any image whose appearance drastically alters, and I would encourage other therapists to adhere to that rule until they have grown comfortable working with Christ images.

8   See Johnson's excellent discourse on romantic love, which describes anima/animus possession as it occurs in the process of 'falling in love.' Johnson, R. (1985), *We: The Psychology of Romantic Love*, Harper: San Francisco.

9   Anima and animus possession are more common than most people like to think. It is most likely to occur in mid-life and generally manifests in men who take 'trophy wives' much younger than them selves. But it can also be seen in women who subject themselves slavishly to certain kinds of men, or seek out younger men as lovers.

10   The Amish have evolved an interesting solution to this problem of authority where two generations continue to live "under the same roof." Quite often, at least one child remains on the farm to care for the parents. When this caretaker marries and has children, the couple move into the home place and the grandparents move into a smaller detached house, signifying a transfer of authority. Also, Amish children are encouraged to go out into the world and explore it before settling down, and in any case, are not baptized until they are adults and prepared to enter a community of peers and elders with all rights and responsibilities attendant.

11   As the forgoing observations suggest, a parent's familial identity can attenuate their Temporal authority. This is most likely to occur when a grandparent is dominant in the family system. In my clinical experience, parents raise grandchildren. Of the first four children born to parents, each child appears to be identified with one of four grandparents, an identity which is often reinforced not only by the parents but as well by others in the extended family from the first week of birth onward. This identity will define whether they are most identified with the paternal or maternal side of the family, and appears to be assigned on the basis of birth order without regard to gender. Since we live in a patriarchy and model our own genealogies after European mores, the firstborn is always identified with the paternal side of the family, the second born with the maternal, etc. If the father is identified with his paternal side, then his first born will be identified with the paternal grandfather, if the father is identified with his maternal side then his first born will be identified with the paternal grandmother. The mother assigns an identity to the second born child dependent upon her own primary identity. The third born child will receive the father's secondary identity, and the forth born child will receive the mother's secondary identity. These identities are assigned without regard to the child's gender. In ascertaining a child's familial identity based on birth order it is necessary to count abortions, stillbirths and miscarriages if these events have

been shared by the parents; also the parents' birth order must also be assessed. Familial identity can play a significant role in shaping the parent-child interaction. For example, if a child is identified with a grandparent who abused the child's mother, the interaction is bound to be less than nurturing if those wounds have not been healed. What I want to emphasize is that having Christ absorb the Temporal authority of a grandparent does not erase the client's identity though it will help to ameliorate the effects of a negative identity. Issues of authority and identity require different interventions though they are definitely interactive.

12   I have observed some notable exceptions where it appears to emerge earlier, particularly among adult children of alcoholic parents, who relate stories of being responsible for the well being of both their siblings and the parents when the parents were drinking.

13   Kelly, G.A. (1963), *Theory of Personality: The Psychology of Personal Constructs*, WW Norton & Company: New York.

14   The moral complex was Carl Jung's term for Freud's superego. See Stevens discussion of The Shadow archetype, which addresses what Jung called the moral complex and the moral archetype – the archetype of good and evil. Stevens, A. (1982), *Archetypes: A Natural History of the Self*, Quill: NY.

15   Since most of my clients have access to the internet I have found it helpful to send them a PDF version of the manual. Even if I use the *Light* in the first session, which is rare, I would still encourage them to peruse the manual if they can download it.

16   A good deal of my post-graduate training was in family therapy. If possible, I use the first couple of sessions to gather information about the relevant extended family – the 'cast of characters' in a client's life. It is a good way of getting to know someone that often leaves them feeling at ease because the focus is elsewhere, though everything they tell you is related to them. If the client sees me for any extended period of time I will do a genogram that provides a capsulated form of what s/he has told me. For most people family is significant, whether for support or obligation, estrangement or enmeshment.

17   There are family systems that draw on matriarchal authority more or less exclusively, even in a patriarchal culture, but I have rarely encountered them clinically. I did work with a fourth generation daughter where the fathers abandoned the children or were pushed out, for three, possibly four, generations. This effectively made the family system matriarchal. Sons do not fare well in that kind of system, and daughters are likely to bear children, but not stay married. The client was raising her own daughter and son in the house belonging to her maternal grandmother

and mother. I suspect the major difficulty for such mini-matriarchies is the lack of emotional and institutional support for them in the larger patriarchal culture and their inability to effectively acculturate the males raised in the home.

18   Sometimes this threat can be so subtle as to be denied. A male client perceived his father as extremely labile and potentially violent. Growing up, the father was often gone during the week. His mother, a firm woman in her own right, would be disappointed if her son disobeyed but would not openly threaten him with his father's wrath. Instead, she sought to "protect" him from it. She would not tell the father whatever he had done to disobey her as long as the father did not catch him. For all practical purposes the son was very obedient. He clearly knew what his father would disapprove of and did not step over that line·

19   Another notable exception to that assertion might be the efforts of a psychoanalyst of the Object Relations School who becomes, de facto, a 'higher power' during the prolonged regression of the patient and, essentially, seeks to re-parent the regressed ego.

20   Nathanson, D.L., (1992), *Shame And Pride: Affect, Sex, and the Birth of the Self*, Norton& Co.: New York, ff.134

21   One client did identify a form of baptism, which is quite striking in its implications. Initially, the archetypal mother, identified by Christ, was only experienced by the child as a pair of loving hands. In the next session, this image was transformed into a woman kneeling by a lake with her hands in the water. The client understood this as the mother offering the child a form of baptism, which was enacted by the mother washing the child's face with water. This image set me to wondering about the significance of water in the baptism ritual. Does water symbolize the Mother as Spirit symbolizes the Father?

22   Mirror-aspects are not the only form of projected aspects. One client, for example, lost her mother after years of enduring her mother's unmanageable and debilitating headaches. Her strong identification with her mother created a painful aspect which was reactivated when her own daughter began to have severe medical problems. The client, in effect, had looked to her daughter to replace her mother (by projecting the mother's image into her daughter), and when the daughter began somaticizing like her grandmother this revived the painful aspect. This dynamic was only attenuated when the client could remove the mother projection from her daughter and allow Christ to begin addressing issues of both her mother and the painful aspect. The painful aspect was found by entering the 'darkness' which the client symbolically entered when suffering migraine headaches. In effect, projections can be complicated, both in their discernment and treatment, and are by no

means limited to Mirror-aspects.

23   Gendlin, E.T. (1982), *Focusing*, Bantam Books.

24   This ritual can be collusively compromised. In working with one nun it was discovered that the ring she used in her marriage ceremony was not one provided by her community, but rather the ring belonging to her deceased mother given to her by her father. This was rectified by a renewal of her vows using a ring provided by her community, which went a good way toward helping her to separate from her father's Temporal authority and move toward Christ as her intended groom.

25   Walter Wink's third book on addressing the Principalities and Powers of the world examines our strong belief in the myth of redemptive violence which asserts that one can defeat violence with violence which is what happens every time one of our heroes shoots the bad guy. What I most appreciate about Wink's book is his demonstration that Christ repeatedly addressed the issue of aggression with non-violent, but effective solutions a la Gandhi and Martin Luther King, See Winks, W. (1992), *Engaging the Powers: Discernment and Resistance in a World of Domination*, Augsburg Fortress Publishers.

26   Winks, W. (1992), op. cit. Basically, the third way refers to Christ's use of non-violent intervention to effect changes in a culture. The whole Christian movement, at least in the first three hundred years, is a profound example of this power.

27   Aikido is a defensive martial art that only comes into play when the individual is attacked. In principle, the defender uses the other's aggression to defeat them. Once learned, the individual is not likely to use aggression to solve problems. See Crum, T. (1987), *The Magic Of Conflict*, Simon & Schuster: New York.; or Dodson, T.& Miller, V. (1993), *Aikido In Everyday Life*, North Atlantic Books: San Francisco.

CHAPTER VII

MORAL AUTHORITY AND THE REDEMPTION OF CONSCIENCE

Christ incarnates in the flesh when he becomes the abiding power of our Mind, Heart, and Soul.
-Anonymous

No client has ever come to me asking help to change his or her conscience, much less to facilitate the emergence of a Christ conscience process. Aside from the fact that most people think it is impossible to alter their conscience, my clients come to me with 'psychological' problems, which contemporary culture tends to separate from moral and spiritual issues. If conscience is a glaring issue, then the client is likely to present with strong feelings of guilt or shame, but even then they may not appreciate the connection with conscience. This may also be true in a religious context, as even that population is likely to treat conscience as invariant. So, as with most psychotherapists, 'beginning the process' will be what the client points to as figural for them. As appropriate, I will introduce the use of the *Light*. For many clients, just the process of going inside can be a significant event. Generally, I only broach the issue of conscience when we have used the *Light* to explore other symptoms and, in the process, uncovered images and emotions (particularly shame) related to the Voice-of-conscience, Ideal-self, Rejected-self or Ego-in-conflict.

With some clients I may never address the issue of conscience, if only because their current world view is firmly irreligious and unable to encompass a relationship with Christ or comparable higher power. Hal and Sidra Stone, whose Voice Dialogue methodology is described in Chapter IV, have argued that it is possible to attenuate the effects of what they call the Inner Critic without recourse to a higher power, and this approach is probably advisable for individuals whose values do not allow for a higher power.[1] I can also recommend the work of Jeffrey Raff, a Jungian therapist who has written extensively and well on active imagination in an Alchemical context. His book on *The Practice of Ally Work* parallels much of my own work here. It does not reference Christ, per se, but the 'Ally' shares many attributes of a Christ image.[2] Fortunately, the 'fates' have sent me clients amenable to evoking Christ during inner work, which has provided me the clinical database for my study of conscience. I am equally grateful to those clients who have asked me to accept divergent spiritual paths. They have taught me to accept guidance from other higher powers for effecting change, including the ability of those higher powers to effect changes in conscience by channeling the Holy Spirit.

It all comes down to this: there is no single way to begin the process of redeeming conscience. *One must begin with what the client presents*, and that will somehow be different from whoever came before. I have never found two people the same. I sometimes think that even the 'similarities' only flow from my desire to impose order on the infinite variety of human nature. In response to whatever the client presents, I do insist that s/he employ the *Light* when going inside. But even that seems dispensable to the process of transforming conscience since its transformation has occurred repeatedly over the past two millennia without requiring the presence of a *Light* as I define it (though I suspect it has always required some manifestation of *willingness*). Nonetheless, all of the work described here is predicated on use of the *Light*. It is the pan I have used to sift for the gold. Most certainly there are other ways of redeeming conscience and they may be found or rediscovered as readers extract what they find useful here and adopt it to their own approach. If this work only affirms the real possibility of a Christ conscience, then it has served its purpose. And I cannot stress enough that Christ conscience is ultimately a function of the Holy Spirit who can access any means for its singular aim of bringing our wills closer to the love and care of God.

A Summary of the Basic Tenets

In the first chapter I developed the basic tenets regarding conscience. What most people experience as conscience is actually a Dominant self that preempts the parental Voice-of-conscience from about age seven onward. The Voice-of-conscience is constellated by the Empowering archetype. At about age three, this archetype imbues *parental images* with Temporal authority. Later in development – when the Ego first experiences an *interiorized sense-of-self* constellated by the Gendering archetype – it will concomitantly experience the interiorized voice of one parent. This interiorization marks the emergence of Moral authority. I call that disembodied voice the aural Voice-of-conscience.[3] The disembodied voice reinforces the parents' cognitive, emotional and gender values embedded in the child's interiorized sense-of-self, which I define further on as the Familial personality.[4] Until a child interiorizes this gestalt, the parents are only experienced as evaluating the child's *behavior*. With interiorization, the parental voice can now evaluate the child's unexpressed thoughts and feelings. The Familial personality is very responsive to the parental interiorization as this voice has the power to threaten dissociation. To evade the ongoing threat of further dissociation, the Ego quickly learns to create a Dominant self, which incorporates the Familial personality and power to self-shame. In this regard, the Dominant self can be likened to Prometheus who stole Zeus' fire; and like Prometheus, the Dominant self must suffer the god's wrath thereafter.

Conscience is said to be *unredeemed* so long as the aural Voice-of-conscience and Dominant self reign as judge and reinforcer. Conscience becomes *redeemable* when the image and voice of the parent are 'dethroned' and the Dominant self relinquishes its power to self-shame in exchange for Christ's discernment. Thereafter, Christ can enter the client's Heart, begin purifying it, and begin speaking as Vox Dei – the Voice for God. In my experience a redeemed conscience is very rare; but I deduce that from the examination of a very small clinical population, which may not be representative of the population at large.⁵

A *redeemed* conscience requires that all vestiges of the Empowering archetype's influence on the Ego be neutralized. This process is accomplished by each ego-aspect receiving a new voice of discernment and the Holy Spirit's felt forgiveness throughout the Heart. Stated another way, the parent must be dethroned as the aural Voice-of-conscience, and all ego-aspects shaped by parental authority must come to accept Christ's discernment instead of the parent's voice and image or their own power to self-shame. Given that the Ego constellates numerous ego-aspects to cope with a aural Voice-of-conscience, the process is probably a life-long goal, as every ego-aspect must eventually become *willing* to accept Christ's gift of discernment, and the Holy Spirit's power to forgive and correct self-defeating beliefs. The Ego creates Dominant selves in later childhood, adolescence, and even adulthood that seek to function as their own conscience, and it takes time to convince these ego-aspects that it is in their best interest to forgo the power to self-shame in favor of Christ's discernment. Likewise, if individual development has necessitated the creation of an Ego-in-conflict with the power to act shamelessly, then it too must become willing to forgo that power in favor of Christ's discernment. Each of these major players – facilitated by the Aware-ego's active participation – must be engaged by Christ and willingly accept his grace, forgiveness, discernment, and love.

In what passes as normal development for most children, shameful punishments inflicted by parents wielding Temporal authority invariably force the child's Ego to dissociatively reject one or more selves. This dissociative rejection by the Ego is tantamount to stripping an ego-aspect of free will since it leaves the ego-aspect in shameful enthrallment. In that dissociated state, the Rejected-self experiences itself as powerless, worthless, unforgivable, unredeemable, and void of self-esteem. Whenever the Ego dissociates an ego-aspect, it reflexively creates an opposite self. This is not an Ideal-self; merely an avoidant self such as a Responsible primary self or Mirror-aspect that can hopefully cope better than its shamed predecessor. But from about age six or seven onward, the Ego learns to better cope with parental shaming by preempting it. Preemption is accomplished by self-shaming and the incorporation of parental cognitive, emotional, and gender characteristics (i.e. the Familial personality). Once the Ego learns to self-shame, the dissociative phase of childhood development usually gives way to repression.⁶ The archetypal creation of a Familial personality and aural Voice-of-conscience provide the transitional bridge from dissociation to repression. The Ego preempts both by the creation of a self-shaming Dominant self. The self-shaming empowers the Dominant self to repress its emotions, thoughts, and experiences within the Heart or gut (abdominal chakra). Operationally, it is self-shaming that generates and sustains repression, as self-shaming effectively strips an ego-aspect's *cognitive/emotive associations* of their free will. The power of self-shaming also reduces the threat of dissociation by *preempting* the shaming power of the aural Voice-of-conscience, which might otherwise force the Ego to further dissociate.

Dominant Selves Assume The Function of Conscience

IIn clinical work, the initial focus is generally on dissociated selves. These are the earliest casualties of Temporal authority, whose traumatization has necessitated the creation of Coping aspects most likely to surface during the client's initial *transference* of parental authority into the therapist's image. As those Coping aspects are addressed, the therapist and client will begin to encounter the Dominant self. Dominant selves are created by the Ego to *repress* events, thoughts, and feelings with shameful emotion in an effort to *preempt* the aural Voice-of-conscience. By exercising *the power of self-shaming,* this ego-aspect becomes, de facto, its own unredeemed conscience. Later, it may reinforce that position with the creation of persona overlays. In this work, all selves capable of repression (i.e. self-shaming) are identified as Dominant selves. I have found Dominant selves in all of my clients so I feel safe in generalizing the existence of this self to the population at large. I confess that I did not appreciate their existence or power when I first developed my theory of conscience, which was initially based on a dissociative paradigm. I only became aware of Dominant selves when one of them actively resisted my suggestion that Christ reach into a client's Heart and satisfy an insatiable desire.

Dominant selves play a pervasive role in the client's daily activity by judging the behavior of self and others as shameful, and by assuming control of socially acceptable behaviors, which they use *in excess* to cope with the accumulation of shame in their chakras, particularly, the heart and abdominal chakras. They repress shameful events *within the Heart* to evade censure by the aural Voice-of-conscience. While this core of experience remains shamefully hidden in the recesses of the Heart, the Dominant self can be made to feel *ashamed* of it, but not be overwhelmed to the point of dissociation. The Dominant self avoids the fate of a Rejected self by exercising this self-shaming repression, which only *diminishes the free will of repressed contents.* However, the Body becomes vulnerable, in turn, to the excessive use of socially acceptable behaviors such as eating, which the Dominant self may use more or less constantly to placate the emotional and sensate pain of its repressed core.

While the power to shame allows the Dominant self to function as its own unredeemed conscience, its repression inevitably generates a 'wrathful' consequence (i.e. Zeus's punishment for stealing fire). The Dominant self has to use socially acceptable behaviors in excess to ease the angst of its shameful core, as it has no way of dispelling the core's accumulated shame. The excessive use of any behavior will generate 'wrath' by exceeding the body's lawful limits. Today, in America, Dominant selves appear to turn more and more frequently to food. For the past several centuries they used the nicotine inhaled with tobacco, which is still a behavior of choice in many other countries. Shopping – especially as reflected in credit card indebtedness, is another form of socially acceptable behavior often done in excess. (The latter causes wrath to the body via the mental stress of indebtedness, which the individual seeks to assuage by further excesses.) Watching television, playing video games, and Internet surfing are other forms of socially acceptable behavior often used in excess as hypnotics. The same can be said of the hyperactivity observed in people who are hard pressed to sit still or just be quiet. All such activities – if used excessively – point to an ego-aspect that seeks to placate the physical or mental angst of accumulated unexpressed shame within the Heart. When this strategy fails or is insufficient, the Ego can create an Ego-in-conflict, which can shamelessly use socially unacceptable, mind-altering, behaviors in excess.

Until the client willingly forgoes the power of self-shaming – in exchange for Christ's discernment – it will not be readily apparent that the Dominant self exercises that power in a concerted effort to *preempt* the aural Voice-of-conscience. Only when the Dominant self gives up that power does the aural Voice-of-conscience reassert itself as a discernible, punitive, voice; *but Christ can and will quickly and permanently silence this resurgence when asked.* I have developed a series of interventions that facilitate the transformation of Dominant selves. The process requires a good deal of forbearance by the therapist, and a growing trust in Christ by the client. Dominant ego-aspects are never easily redeemed. The interventions are described and illustrated in this chapter and the next.

In the same way that Ego uses sensation to communicate with the Body, the Soul uses the seven heart chakras and physical heart to communicate with the Mind. The Soul's directives are communicated, via the Heart by archetypal embodiments within the Mind. Images of others, particularly parents, are the most frequent embodiments of archetypal energy. Self-images, such as the Dominant self, become archetypal embodiments by incorporating the parental prerogatives as their own. Christ has the power to terminate archetypal flow in any embodiment, if the Aware-ego or ego-aspect affected by the flow willingly asks him to do so. But note that the source of power is not the image. Rather, it is the archetypal energy sustaining the image or hubristically assumed by the image, and that energy flows through the Heart. More to the point, Christ can enter that Heart and terminate any aural Voice-of-conscience found there. Imaginatively, he does so by 'pushing' into an ego-aspect's heart chakra, provided the ego-aspect is willing. The ego-aspect and Aware-ego can then follow him through. This is demonstrated in all of the following verbatims. The clinical difficulty is in gaining the ego-aspect's permission to enter. The Dominant self is initially highly resistant to the prospect because it has hidden all of its shame within the heart and abdominal chakras; and continues to do so while it exercises the power to self-shame.

The power to self-shame sustains the Ego's idolatrous stance insofar as it empowers the self to function as its own conscience. The Dominant self will frequently see itself as the equal of Christ, or see Christ as merely a teacher to be emulated, or simply does not see Christ in its field of vision. This hubris only becomes apparent where Christ can be imaginatively present for comparison. Without a Christ image for comparison, the Ego remains myopic regarding its hubris. A Christ conscience process requires the relinquishment of this prideful condition in exchange for Christ's discernment and the Holy Spirit's forgiveness. The transformation of Dominant selves is the most difficult part of the redemption process, often requiring a period of months.[7]

In sum, the redemption of a Dominant self requires that *Christ be allowed* 1) to terminate the Dominant self's power to self-shame in exchanged for Christ's discernment, 2) enter the Heart and heal its shameful core, and 3) terminate the parental voice that would shame the Dominant self when the redeemed self no longer *preempts* that voice. The enactment of this series of interventions vis-à-vis a Dominant self is always experienced as transformative, even as it may have to be repeated for several other selves. The crucial intervention is the client's willingness to allow Christ entry to his or her Heart. The first time is by far the hardest. Each time thereafter becomes easier. More to the point, repeated entry into the Heart greatly facilitates successive interventions. Within the Heart, ego-aspects are less likely to inflate their function or deny the Soul. And only the Heart provides an adequate domain for a partnered relationship between the sense of self most closely attuned to the totality of Self and his or her contra-sexual aspect.

THE FAMILIAL PERSONALITY

This section covers *new ground*. It is derived from clinical work based on the above tenets. When the Dominant self is redeemed, a new sense-of-self emerges *within hours*. I neither predicted nor anticipated this particular sense-of-self when I outlined my theory of conscience in the first chapter. At first, I thought it was a regressive Dominant self, since younger selves often emerge when a more developed self is redeemed. But what actually emerged is far more significant. Today, I refer to it by various names: the Familial personality, the 'personality core,' the amalgam of parental values and interactions, or the conscious sense-of-self that the client insists is "me." This new sense-of-self appears to be a *component precursor* of the Dominant self; and very likely, the personality core defining most self-images. I would argue that it is constellated by the Gendering archetype, which I discuss at length in the next chapter. But in any case, so far as I can determine, the Familial personality only becomes figural after Christ terminates the Dominant self's power to self-shame (in exchange for Christ's discernment) and the client then allows Christ to enter the Aware-ego's Heart and dissolve any accumulated shame found there. Shortly thereafter, the Familial personality appears to emerge as the new locus of consciousness (i.e. "I am me") along with an aural Voice-of-conscience that shames it.

Operationally, the Familial personality appears to be the second part of a complex comprised of 1) an *aural* Voice-of-conscience constellated by the Empowering archetype and 2) *an amalgam of personality characteristics* derived from the parents and constellated by the Gendering archetype. I call that amalgam the Familial personality. So far as I can determine, it is the archetypal substrate of Carl Jung's Persona. Jung made much of the Persona in adults. He was convinced it is responsible for major distortions of its *complementary contrasexual aspect* (Anima/Animus) and a primary obstacle to individuation.

I think of the Familial personality, primarily, as the child's *first interior, subjective experience of self*. This sense of self is not created by the Ego, but by the Gendering archetype. The Ego uses it as a template for producing a variety of selves, all imbued with free will and similar personality characteristics, and all of whom the client identifies as 'me.' This archetypal core enables the Ego to function in the Mind as well as in-the-world since it serves as a primary frame of reference for distinguishing itself from 'others' (not-me). Immediately after the Dominant self is redeemed, the client experiences the Familial personality as the *primary observer* of conscious processes within the Mind. This sense-of-self is distinctly different from a Dominant self, Temporal persona, or Ideal persona, which always manifest as Ego *personifications* of the Familial personality. Initially, the Familial personality only manifests as the *unadulterated substance* of an archetypal constellation; that is, in its manifestation as focalized consciousness prior to its incorporation by the Ego. In this initial manifestation, it appears to be the unadulterated archetypal core of personality derived from parental interactions constellated by the Gendering archetype. It may be present from the onset of therapy, but it only appears to become figural after the Dominant self is redeemed. So far as I can determine it is not a depersonalized ego-aspect, though it does seem to lack access to a sensate body, which the Ego apparently provides when it incorporates the archetypal core into an ego-aspect.

Two clinical findings point to the

Familial complex as the *precursor* of Ego conscience. First, the new sense-of-self (i.e. Familial personality) is invariably co-present with a shaming voice that is also *disembodied*, but nonetheless identifiable as belonging to a parent. This is the first time the aural Voice-of-conscience is actually *heard* in a therapeutic context. Second, the new sense-of-self is difficult to personify (imagine) until it is correctly identified as *the archetypal substrate of personality*. Very likely it was always present in its unincorporated state as an archetypal constellation, but camouflaged or 'overwritten' by the conscious presence of the Dominant self. (That last statement is speculative.) All I can assert here is that the Familial personality becomes the new locus of consciousness within the Mind following the redemption of the Dominant self. More to the point, when first encountered, the client cannot personify a self-image of this amalgam of personality characteristics, even with Christ's help, and despite the fact that s/he insists it is "me." In active imagination, s/he can only discern mental and/or emotional characteristics that Christ can 'capture' in a circle and help the client to identify (e.g. controlling, angry, anxious, etc.) But the Ego *can personify* this sense-of-self if the client asks Christ to capture an image that *most strongly embodies his or her personality*. It was that discovery that led me to identify the constellation as the Familial personality.

A third observation is worth noting in conjunction with the Familial complex as it helped me to discover the connection between the Familial personality and what is commonly referred to as an individual's personality. Initially, I continued to think of this new sense-of-self as an ego-aspect (specifically, a regressive Dominant self) and asked my clients to make repeated efforts to personify it with circles of *Light*. While all those efforts were unproductive, *persistent* attempts did stimulate the personification of an *impersonal image* that seems best described as a 'stereotypic gender role.' The stereotypic role is not seen by the client as a self-image, but can be used by the client to identify an ego-aspect that either copes with the stereotypic image or conforms to it. During this process of discovery I also observed that most of the self-attributes identified by the client were also attributes of the parents as I had come to know them in the course of therapy. It was this confluence of observations that finally led me to hypothesize that the client was experiencing a personality core unmitigated by Ego personifications.

In sum, once the Dominant self has been redeemed and Christ has terminated the aural Voice-of-conscience, the therapist must shift focus to work on the client's personality in its manifestation of as the Familial personality. This personality core is strongly reactive to the aural Voice-of-conscience until that is silenced by Christ. Then it appears to become the primary subjective observer who uses thought or feeling to vicariously live through the new ego-aspects that incorporate it. The original constellation generally lacks anything approaching a full range of functions (i.e. sensation, intuition, feeling, and thinking). Yet all are needed to be fully attune it to the totality of Self. Also, the Familial personality appears to have no connection to a sensate body. Even so, the Familial personality is a mandate, not a choice. The Ego may seek to augment the personality core once it has incorporated it into an ego-aspect (e.g. Ideal persona), or supplant it (e.g. the Not-me duplex), or even rebel against its by creating Mirror aspects, but it does not get to choose what amalgam the Gendering archetype will constellate. Any change of the actual constellation (i.e. Familial personality) requires the willingness to call on Christ or a comparable higher power.

Once Christ has silenced the aural

Voice-of-conscience, the Ego quickly learns to personify prototypic 'stand-ins' of the Familial personality that allow the constellation to vicariously experience events in the Mind and Heart. Insofar as the Familial personality shares its identity with an ego-aspect it can live vicariously through that aspect. But the stand-in cannot provide the Familial personality with the first-person experience that would allow the Familial personality to evolve. I suspect that Christ can provide a Familial personality with that experience, but a full exploration of that hypothesis is beyond the scope of this book, though I hope to offer some initial steps. More important to the present discussion, the personality amalgam objectified by the Ego is rarely, if ever, attuned to the totality of Self. It is – as might be expected – willful and devoid of any knowledge of its relationship to that totality. The last phase of therapy to be examined in this work will focus on reshaping the Familial personality with *Christ identified* contra-sexual pairs that are attuned to the totality of Self. When Christ is allowed to place Ideal pairs into the Heart and/or heart chakra, they gradually reshape Ego personifications with a new sense of personality offering potential access to all of the psychological functions. Ego-aspects incorporating this redeemed personifications of the Familial personality are expected to move more comfortably in the worlds of Body and Mind, and respectfully interact with the worlds of Soul and Spirit. In effect, the Familial personality's prima materia can be reshaped at the level of personification in a manner that facilitates a relationship with the totality of Self.

The primary difficulty with the 'Familial personality solution' constellated by the Gendering archetype in childhood is the Ego's inability to appreciate that the 'personality' imposed by the constellation rarely syncs with the child's *unique identity* as a human being. The Familial personality only expresses a sense-of-self *derived* from the parental interactions and shared genetics. In effect, the Familial personality is 'other' directed rather than 'inner' directed because it generally mimes *parental sync and/or conflict* rather than an *individuated* sense-of-self *attuned to the totality of its Self (Spirit, Soul, Mind, Body)*. Jung argued – and I would agree – that the Persona (i.e. Familial personality) – shaped as it is by parental values, actions, and cultural mores, normally makes it difficult for a growing child to comfortably relate to the forces *within* the Mind comprising the totality of Self. It is intended to 'help' the child conform to the 'outer world' of family and neighbors and an 'inner world' shaped by Temporal and Moral authority; it is rarely shaped to foster the child's unique potential. Leastwise, that is what I have found to be true for the clinical population I have served. The interventions described in this chapter seek to bring about a greater attunement between the individual's sense-of-self and the totality of Self.

I need to stress that the Familial personality is not constellated by the Empowering archetype. The Familial personality is constellated by the Gendering archetype; and discordant factors can play a significant role in its creation. A Familial personality can be heavily weighted to favor a parent who is denigrated by the aural Voice-of-conscience parent, or otherwise in conflict with him or her, or the amalgam can strongly model someone else at odds with the parental Voice-of-conscience (e.g. an estranged or dysfunctional grandparent). The latter is most likely to occur as a result of projections imposed by Temporal authority, which I discussed in Chapter VI. These unintended consequences can constellate a Familial personality that is intrinsically dysfunctional vis-à-vis the world or the parental Voice-of-conscience.

The Familial personality provides the

Ego its primary self-awareness, i.e. "I am me." It is debatable whether this sense-of-self is constelled in response to the aural Voice-of-conscience or precedes it. (Both conditions may apply with differing outcomes.) But in any case, the interiorization of both appears to mark the developmental transition from Temporal authority to Moral authority. The Ego responds to that complex by creating a new egoistic structure capable of *subjecting both components to its free will* (i.e. the Dominant self). This allows the Ego to effectively *preempt* the aural Voice-of-conscience with its own shaming voice thereby giving it greater latitude in coping with the parents' Temporal authority as manifest in parental images. It allows the Ego to use shame to repress errors within the Heart's interior, rather than living with the persistent threat of dissociation by Temporal authority. To further buttress this dubious gain, once the Dominant self is firmly ensconced in consciousness, the Ego can begin building an Ideal persona that will conform to the Familial personality or better cope with its strictures. But, when the Dominant self and its personas are redeemed and the aural Voice-of-conscience is terminated by Christ, the Familial personality once again becomes figural as 'I am me;' likely, for the first time in adulthood. This shift in dynamics appears to be both regressive and potentially transformative. The 'transformative aspect is largely dependent upon the client's increasing willingness to call on Christ or a comparable higher power. Unfortunately, calling on a 'higher power' is not automatic. Often, the ego-aspects incorporating the Familial personality are no longer bound by an aural Voice-of-conscience and seem strongly motivated to remain free of any restraining powers. By this point in the journey, however, most clients have acquired a wealth of Christ-related experiences and – hopefully – a therapist who can continue to guide them through the process.

As a primary focus of consciousness, 'I am me' is a very controlling first-person experience. The Ego can and will provide 'stand-ins' using it as a template. These are necessary for the exercise of free will 'in-the-world.' Stand-ins manifest a particular phenomenology, which become apparent to the client and therapist over time. Phenomenally, the sense-of-self seems to move back and forth between observer (i.e. archetypal constellation) and observed (i.e. ego-aspect). But keep in mind that the original Familial personality is also self-limiting. Free will and the sensate body remain limited by a personality structure derived from parental interactions. However, what I have also discovered is that the Aware-ego's personified Familial personality can be re-formed by Ideal pairs that provide it greater attunement to the totality of Self. In turn, any ego-aspects that have incorporated the unredeemed Familial personality can then be entrained to the redeemed personification by comparable Christological interventions. Christ can also begin providing the personified Familial personality with optimal access to all four functions and an enduring relationship with himself. This phase of therapy is described later in the chapter and illustrated in three verbatims (Marian and Tory's verbatims in this chapter and Leigh's in the next chapter).

In sum, I had to shift my focus in order to effectively work with the Familial personality. I had to appreciate that Ego conscience incorporates the individual's personality as well as the power to self-shame. I had to 'remember' that conscience is not the be-all of a person. A Dominant self makes the client's Voice-of-conscience a powerful part of Ego consciousness, but it is not the creator of its personality. The Dominant self *must also incorporate a Familial personality constelled by the Gendering archetype*. That archetype uses gender qualities derived from both parents to constellate a Familial personality, whose power to focus consciousness as "me" all but insures its role as a template for all future ego-aspect creations. Because this constellated sense-of-self is also responsive to the aural Voice-of-conscience, the Ego will seek to incorporate both the personality-core and power to self-shame as the best strategy for self-control. Once the Dominant self is redeemed and the aural Voice-of-conscience is silenced, it is possible to begin working directly with this archetypal substrate of personality. But all I can offer in this work is a glimmer of what I now suspect is possible.

The Familial personality, Temporal Persona, and Ideal Persona

As the Dominant self develops, it can be further infused with authority 'authorized' by a family group (in the case of Temporal personas), or by familial/cultural mores and ritual (in the case of Ideal personas). 'Mother,' which is a culturally sanctioned role in every culture, assigns considerable authority and responsibility to every woman who claims the role. The same is true of many other roles such as 'judge' or 'bishop.' Ideal and Temporal personas are, effectively, Ego integrations of the collective authority of adult groups. The collective unconscious provides the templates for the Dominant self, and family and culture provide its collective embellishments.

Carl Jung's descriptions of the Persona are comparable to my definition of the Dominant self. The Ideal and Temporal persona are *overlays* assumed by a Dominant self, and by far the most powerful selves encountered in therapy. (Spirit possession is conceivably more powerful than personas, but I have not worked with any cases of possession.) In much the same way that a Temporal persona is ego inflating, an adult also will experience an Ideal persona as ego inflating, though the client would rarely describe either of them as such.

When a Dominant self *slavishly* adheres to an Ideal overlay, it does so to further protect against shame by assuming a prideful role that is culturally empowering. This improves its odds against failures that would make it feel *ashamed*. Carl Jung assumed that *all adults exhibited a face* that they presented to the world, which he called the Persona. For most people, that would be a Dominant self, whose power to self-shame, gives it *self-perceived authority* to judge self and others. However, culture gives some roles inordinate authority, which further empowers any Dominant self that ritually acquires it. I refer to that authority as *culturally sanctioned*. In tribal societies, for example, tribal leadership or shamanistic powers confer a culturally sanctioned Ideal persona that allows the individual to exercise considerable Temporal and Moral authority within the tribe. In Western culture, presidents, judges, high ranking military officers, surgeons, persons known to be very rich, college professors, ecclesiastical authorities and the like, can acquire a culturally sanctioned persona that sets them above 'the masses' – at least in their own minds, and often in the minds of those around them. Culturally sanctioned Ideal personas give the individual power to wield Temporal and Moral authority over groups of individuals. I have found this especially true for doctors – particularly surgeons, who daily engage in life and death dramas. Culturally sanctioned Ideal personas can make an individual particularly susceptible to a hubris that is difficult to forgo. Like all Dominant selves, an Ideal persona has to accept Christ's power of discernment in exchange for his or her power to self-shame. But in addition, individuation also requires that the client forgo the culturally sanctioned authority and primary allegiance to the clan or group that confers the authority. For example, in the case of Roman Catholic clergy, their authority ultimately derives from the Pope. Christ must be allowed to intervene in a way that frees the ego-aspect from that authority. A client can respect authority without being enthralled to it.

But why is all of this necessary? So long as the individual remains in the thrall of a Dominant self, s/he is unable to access the Familial personality underpinning it. That persona is a major impediment to the client's ability to relate to the interior life of Self. The necessary transformation requires, first, that the *Heart of the Aware-ego* be provided an Ideal pair of images most closely attuned to the totality of Self. Next, any ego-aspect embodying a Familial personality will have to be purified and inculcated with an Ideal pair distinctly different from a parental dyad. Those two Ideal pairs will gradually reorient the personality in a way that will allow the client to fully engage the inner world of Mind, Soul, and Spirit, by reshaping the Familial personality from within. Finally, the Familial personality must be given full access to all four functions. Those changes will provide any ego-aspect embodying the Familial personality with the greatest breath of movement I have been able to envision up to this point.

Once it is appreciated that the identification of an initially un-imaginable sense-of-self signifies the emergence of an un-personified Familial personality, Christ can be asked to capture the client's *strongest sense of personality* and the contra-sexual aspect most strongly attached to it. The Ego will readily generate this in its effort to regain control of consciousness. Following the examination of this pair, Christ can be asked to *liberate* a previously *unseen opposite* that is most closely attuned to the totality of Self. In effect, Christ is asked to personify a self *opposite* the Familial personality assumed to most attuned to parents and culture. Christ can then identify the contra-sexual aspect most compatible with this 'liberated' self. That contra-sexual aspect is often archetypal in nature, not unlike Dante's Beatrice or a Mary Magdalene image related to the client's Christ image. The next step is to grant this Ideal pair permanent residence within the Aware-ego's Heart. The strong attraction between the 'liberated self' and his or her contra-sexual aspect, coupled with their conscious access to the Heart, insures the client will thereafter have mediated access to the inner world (i.e. Heart's interior). Next, Christ is asked to work directly with the ego-aspect and consort initially identified to embody the client's 'personality,' including the purification of that personification's heart chakra, and bring the pair into sync with the Ideal pair already resident in the Heart. Finally, Christ is asked to work directly with the Familial personality in the first person for the purpose of providing it unmitigated access to all four functions. These steps are illustrated in three verbatims found in this chapter and the next; but a fuller explanation must await a further work.

Other Tenets Regarding Moral Authority

The Ego-in-conflict

Later in development, the Ego may also create an Ego-in-conflict, which has the power to act shamelessly. This self can willfully (defiantly) engage in the shameful behavior that previously resulted in the creation of a Rejected-self. It does so by *stimulating desire* for mind-altering substances that are socially *unacceptable* when used in excess, and acting out shameful behavior under the drug's influence, or allowing the behavior to be acted out by another ego-aspect. The effects of mind-altering substances are generally sufficient to drown out awareness of the shaming emotions generated while under the influence of those substances. Egos-in-conflict are most likely to develop in familial environments that are repressive and model addictive behaviors. An Ego-in-conflict is most likely to assert itself whenever the coping strategies of a Dominant self become insufficient. Like the Dominant self, an Ego-in-conflict accumulates shame by its excesses. The difference is one of degree: whereas the Dominant self uses socially acceptable behavior in excess, the Ego-in-conflict uses mind altering substances that are *socially unacceptable* if used at all (e.g. cocaine) or in excess (e.g. alcohol). The shame it generates is cumulative insofar as the Ego has no way of discharging it while it remains unforgiveable; and no reason to be repentant while the 'pleasure' it creates masks the sense of shame it generates. Even so, the shame it generates will eventually manifest as physical and/or emotional wrath. Emotional shame generated by an Ego-in-conflict is most likely to accumulate in the abdominal chakra, particularly, the sexual organs. I discuss all of this in more detail further into the chapter.

Parents who use shame excessively, or add corporal punishments to the shaming, will generally necessitate the creation of an Ego-in-conflict. The most common manifestation of the Ego-in-conflict is addictive behavior, specifically, any behavior treated as socially unacceptable because it is likely to impair judgment or result in dangerous acting out, e.g. getting drunk, snorting cocaine, abusing prescription drugs, etc. The Ego-in-conflict uses *mind altering physical sensations* to mitigate the effects of emotional pain caused by a shaming Dominant self, particularly, shameful judgments previously reinforced with physical punishment or other forms of anger. In contrast, the Dominant self only uses socially *acceptable* behavior in excess to mitigate its self-shaming. The addictive solutions used by the Ego-in-conflict impair judgment to one degree or another. They are most often pleasurable, but can be painful, as in the case of self-mutilation and forms of masochism. The Ego-in-conflict acts in a knee-jerk fashion to stimulate and satisfy *physical desire*. When studied in detail the Ego-in-conflict is often found to be young and almost mindless in its reactivity. Nonetheless, physical desire is experienced as more powerful – less negative, than *fearing* the reoccurrence of the shameful punishments. It acts shamelessly to generate a *desired* 'pleasure' more powerful than shame or the individual's fear of it, since the Ego-in-conflict rarely experiences anything but its own desire in the throes of its dubious pleasure. In effect, while the individual is under the influence of an Ego-in-conflict, *active physical desire* can suppress the *fear* of shamefully punished acts and effectively blunt the power of self-shaming. Under the influence of alcohol, or any mind-altering drug, the individual is freed to engage in previously punished activities. But only so long as physical desire is *active*. Once the desire is sated or effectively exhausts the Body, the individual becomes subject to guilt and the re-experience of chronic fear.

Most significant to this discussion, the Ego-in-conflict can temporarily release a Rejected-self to range toward homeostasis thereby temporarily reducing the tension created by extreme polarization. Consequently, once an Ego-in-conflict has been identified, it can be used to identify the Rejected-self that spurred its creation. To that end, Christ can give it the necessary intuitive insight. Healing is another matter. The Ego-in-conflict is a rebel who seeks to overcome the strictures laid on the Self by a Dominant self. An Ego-in-conflict is only likely to relinquish its power to act shamelessly when Christ has redeemed other selves, and the client finally comes to appreciate the adverse physical effects that cumulative emotional shaming has on the body and relationships. However, insofar as an individual is actively engaging a power greater than the Dominant self and seeking self-actualization, an Ego-in-conflict is likely to remain quiescent.

perpetually at risk of shameful falls. If they can, those selves will use pride to detach from fears of shame, and anger to suppress fearful encounters (be it overt anger, or covert anger as in abiding resentments). Most other selves will simply rely on the *fear* of a shameful encounter to guide their social interactions, since even fear is far less onerous than the experience of *actual* shame. Fear will be more or less present in most selves that play an active role in the client's day-to-day behavior, including Dominant selves. Guilt can also be found in varying degrees among these primary ego-aspects. Guilt occurs when we have engaged in a shameful behavior *without getting caught*. Guilt always occurs after the fact, *after* we have eaten the whole cake, or *after* a night of too much partying, or *after* we have indulged in shameful sex, etc. Guilt is preferable to actually feeling shame since guilt can be mitigated by remorse and regret, or our 'swearing' never to do it again in response to its wrathful consequences (till the next time). Guilt allows us to make amends, if necessary. In Hawkins scale of emotions, guilt is only slightly less negative than shame; but it does not label us unforgivably shameful, only errant; and it does not banish us to a state of perpetual shame or force us to feel unmitigatingly ashamed. The Ego is generally limited to this pride-shame axis until it becomes willing to receive the forgiving grace of the Holy Spirit, which Christ offers unerringly to all who ask.

The Effects of the Law vs. Grace

St. Paul asserted that the individual is obliged to function 'under the law' until s/he willingly opens to Christ's grace and discernment.[8] In effect, *unredeemed* ego-aspects are obliged to adhere to the law defining sin and live

Physical and Emotional Disease

Physical and emotional diseases are the most common manifestation of the prolonged tension created by the chronic polarization of opposites. While I know this will be a contested thesis, all my findings point to the conclusion that all physical and emotional illnesses are the inadvertent consequence of selves that are unremittingly polarized and shamed. I would further assert – as a working hypothesis – that the specific 'sickness' will be a *conscious* symbolic representation of the unresolved conflict between one or more primary and disowned selves. Dis-ease is what St. Paul refers to as Wrath. Most people perceive illness as something that happens to them. We generally accept varying degrees of responsibility for its treatment, but not its cause (unless we accept a correlation as causal, e.g. smoking behavior can lead to cancer). Most people believe that disease is something that 'attacks' us, not something we bring upon ourselves as a direct consequence of our beliefs and lifestyles. But whenever a disease manifests, it is possible to discern severe conflicts sustaining it. That thesis is not the focus of this work, but case examples are provided throughout all the chapters because more often than not I willingly work with any physical, emotional, or mental symptom identified by a client; and most clients report recurring illnesses, or are called upon to deal with acute illnesses in themselves or family members in the course of therapy.[9]

Sexual Repression

No Rejected-self or shameful core is inherently shameful. It is made shameful by the parentified conscience or a Dominant self arbitrarily attaching shame to one or the other pole of a set of opposites, which an ego-aspect is likely to range toward in the course of development. Parents polarize dualities by shaming or priding the ego-aspect as it ranges toward one or the other pole. In the redemption process, the objective is to neutralize this polarization so a Rejected-self or shameful core can reintegrate with its polarized opposite and swing freely to and fro around a homeostatic center, guided by Christ's discernment and the perpetual forgiveness of the Holy Spirit. For this reason, the therapist is generally encouraged to identify the sets of opposites that have been polarized. Where this is done sexuality often becomes figural. For many people seen in therapy, at least one Rejected-self or component of the shameful core will manifest sexually. The shameful association will inhibit sexual feeling in significant ways. In severe cases it will force the creation of an Ego-in-conflict that expresses shamelessly in an effort to compensate for the repression.

The Ego-in-conflict needs specific mention here. If a child or adolescent is *shamefully caught* in the midst of a sexual act, the Ego will create a new ego-aspect intent on avoiding further shaming. Such a self can powerfully repress sexual desire if it exercises the power to self-shame. But the very act of repression will eventually necessitate the creation of an Ego-in-conflict able to satisfy the repressed sexual desire. In effect, much of the activity attributed to an Ego-in-conflict will have sexual satisfaction as its end goal. All cultures appear to regulate sexuality so it is not surprising that the sexual behavior of children is so often, and so strongly, shamed. But an instinctual rhythm cannot be shamed with impunity. Sexual behavior cannot be shamefully suppressed without generating hysterical effects, or compulsive expressions of the repressed.

Sexual energy ebbs and flows within the body *but never ceases*. It is the energy inherent in all masculine/feminine connections. Often that energy is channeled through the sexual organs, which the Mind and Body experience as arousal. The individual, if conscious of the arousal, will seek to discharge the tension by some form of sexual activity, or in rare cases, sublimate it in ways described by Taoists and Tantric yogis. But the individual strongly shamed for sexual expression may remain unaware of the tension being created by dissociated or repressed sexual arousal. This is when sexual arousal is most likely to result in hysterical and psychosomatic symptoms. I consider it significant that the two most common cancers in women are breast and cervical cancers; and prostate is the most common cancer in men. It is quite likely that all three are the result of a chronic accumulation of unexpressed shame associated with sexuality. Likewise, until the mid 1960's, Hysterical Personality Disorder, with its vague sexual references, was the most common diagnosis used to describe women with *mental* problems. But that diagnosis all but disappeared from the DSM literature following the 'sexual revolution' of the 1960's when women "re-discovered" their clitoris and g-spot and became free enough to touch them. Sexual energy can be channeled; it can never be blocked with impunity. Unfortunately, despite our increased knowledge of sexuality, families and communities continue to shamefully repress it rather than teach healthy regulation.

Suffice to say, redeeming conscience does open this Pandora's box. But however the Rejected-self or shameful core manifests, Christ will unerringly seek to free it from the bondage of shame. His *judgment* of any behavior associated with the Rejected-self or repressed core is to *forgive it as often as needed* while encouraging loving, harmonious, interpersonal and intrapersonal relationships. Wherever he is permitted, Christ will dispel the effects of shameful punishment with love, forgiveness, and discernment. And that includes our sexual proclivities.

Temporal vs. Moral authority

Given that Temporal and Moral authority both arise from the same Empowering archetype, how are we to distinguish their effects? Clinically, there appear to be three distinguishing characteristics: age of onset, types of ego-aspects created to cope with the particular manifestation, and the kind of interventions used to work with them.

Age of Onset. Temporal authority is the first emerge. It will have its greatest effect on ego-aspects created during the first five years of life. The only notable exception is the creation of a Temporal persona, which generally emerges in adolescence. Temporal authority constellates both parents as wielders of authority. Between the fifth and seventh year, the *interiorization* of one parental voice marks the transmutation of Temporal authority into Moral authority. One parent will then function as the aural Voice-of-conscience with the other parent becoming the delegated surrogate of that spouse's authority.[10]

Traditionally, age seven has been used to mark the onset of 'reasoning' in children, which is considered necessary for making distinctions between right from wrong. I also use this age as an arbitrary demarcation point for the emergence of Moral authority, though it probably begins to develop well before that. Studies by Piaget and his students confirm that by age seven children have mastered the basic constructs of thinking, which theologians have historically correlated with the onset of conscience.[11] With the onset of reasoning, children begin to grasp *abstract dualities* though they may not be able to state them as such at this age. This is the necessary prerequisite that a child needs to distinguish between good and bad, right and wrong; in effect, to begin eating from 'the tree of good and evil.' Children can make these distinctions in a concrete way prior to age seven, but after seven they can generalize abstract dualities and apply them to an interior sense of self and other. Finally, during this period children are considered old enough to 'move into the world' and accept direction from other adults and older children.

As the child moves into the world, other adults will assume the exercise of culturally sanctioned Temporal authority (e.g. policemen and teachers), while still others may be 'empowered' by parents to speak with Moral authority (e.g. Sunday school teachers and priests). These changes notwithstanding, Temporal and Moral authority will remain constellated in the parent. Ministers, teachers, and policemen gain authority because the parent attributes it to them, like a king knighting peers of the realm. Even the Dominant self, created by Ego to function as its own conscience, will most often emulate the parent wielding Moral authority.

Types of Ego-aspects. In general, ego-aspects are distinguished by the age of their creation and the type of authority primarily responsible for their creation, i.e. Temporal vs. Moral. The Rejected-self and Coping aspects are the most common manifestations of Temporal authority. As well, Pre-moral aspects and Mirror aspects are always created by abuses of Temporal authority. The Pre-moral aspect is created early in life and always manifests as a very young child or infant. The presence of Mirror-aspects generally indicates the existence of a Pre-moral aspect. A family system can foster the creation of a Temporal persona at any time in a child's development. It is so named because it authorizes a progeny to exercise the Temporal authority of a parent within the family. Its emergence is most likely in families that function as mini-tribes. It is like an Ideal persona described later in this chapter, which can exercise degrees of Temporal *and* Moral authority over groups of people *outside the family*. Stated another way, a Temporal persona only exercises his or her authority within a family group, whereas an Ideal persona can exercise authority will beyond the boundary of a family.

Some Coping aspects will mature over time into Responsible primary selves. These selves are created to *avoid dissociation* precipitated by a parent exercising Temporal authority. Dominant selves *use self-shame* to repress shameful experiences, thereby preempting the aural Voice-of-conscience and providing further defense against dissociation. The creation of a Dominant self is invariably a response to the interiorization an aural Voice-of-conscience which is the primary expression of Moral authority. Dominant selves are further characterized by *an excessive use* of socially acceptable behavior to assuage the angst of accumulated shame. Another distinction between the two is the way the therapist is encouraged to work with them. A Responsible primary self is generally separated from the Aware-ego as soon as it is identified. When working with a Dominant self, it is left merged with the Aware-ego for as long as possible so Christ can address its power to self-shame from a first person perspective.

When a Dominant self is redeemed, this resolution invariable precipitates the emergence of the complex comprised of the Familial personality and the disembodied voice of the aural Voice-of-conscience. That complex is seen as the archetypal precursor of the Dominant self. What sets the complex apart from other images of self is its distinct lack of Ego personification. The interventions I have normally used for separating selves only seem to extract 'symbolic contents' or feelings, but no image of the self. Sometimes the effort to separate will generate an adult, archetypal, idealized gender image. But the client will be unable to identify an Ego creation until asked to separate from the ego-aspect *that most strongly embodies his or her personality*. The emergence of this complex generally marks the beginning of a significant shift away from issues of Temporal and Moral authority, (except as they may manifest in Ideal personas) and a movement toward the client's individuation.

Different Treatment Interventions. The major thrust of treatment in working with Temporal authority is the termination of its flow through the parent and the reconciliation of ego-aspects polarized by that authority. Work with a Temporal *persona* further requires that the ego-aspect *voluntarily* forgo its Temporal authority. In the special case of a Pre-moral aspect created by Temporal authority, the goal is the Pre-moral aspect's nurture by an archetypal mother. For Moral authority the treatment approach is much different. Here the end goal is for Christ to 1) extend the power of his discernment to all ego-aspects open to it in exchange for their power to self-shame, 2) enter the Heart, 3) heal the shamed core, and 4) terminate any aural voice of the Voice-of-conscience. The process of redeeming conscience begins with the baptism of any Rejected-self, which releases that self from any shame preventing its full exercise of free will. Following baptism, the Rejected-self can ask Christ to terminate the Voice-of-conscience expressed through any parental image by having Christ place a portion of his *Light* into the parent's heart. Then the Rejected-self must *voluntarily* open itself to Christ's power of discernment. Finally, the therapist must engage the Dominant selves that actively resist Christ's entry to the client's Heart. A Christ conscience only becomes a discernible possibility when Christ is allowed to repeatedly and freely enter the Heart. The process of entering the Heart is described later in the chapter.

In working with Moral authority, there are *four basic interventions* that are simple in execution, but difficult for the client's selves to allow. The *first* is baptism of the Rejected-self, which is offered by Christ at the request of the Aware-ego. Remember, the Rejected-self is unable to ask on its own behalf. Shameful bondage all but strips it of free will and leaves it convinced that it is unforgivable. Baptism can also be extended to other ego-aspects who are made to feel *ashamed* of their actions, but in those instances, the self must express unequivocal willingness for Christ to do so. An ego-aspect who is made to feel ashamed can still exercise free will after the fact. Feeling ashamed has to do with prideful falls that threaten comparison with a Rejected-self and temporarily weakens the ego-aspect's willful resolve, but does not strip it away. In contrast, the Rejected-self is seen to be in the thrall of shame and unable to decisively exercise its free will.

The *second* type of intervention addresses the enthrallment of ego-aspects by *undue influences*. Frequently, the free will of ego-aspects can be constrained by undue influences, which can be archetypal or even spiritual in nature. This is discussed at length further on. Where it becomes apparent to the therapist that something of the sort is constraining an ego-aspect, the therapist can suggest that Christ be allowed to 'cauterize' or terminate the influence by placing a portion of his *Light* into the heart of the ego-aspect. This request is made by the client's Aware-ego. It is a second instance in which an affected ego-aspect does not have to be asked beforehand. Basically, the ego-aspect is treated as being in the thrall of the undue influence and unable to ask on its own behalf. (Note that the ego-aspect must first be separated from the Aware-ego before Christ can be asked to intervene.) Baptism would also release an ego-aspect from this type of enthrallment, but often the enthrallment prevents the ego-aspect from asking for it. In actuality, baptizing and releasing an ego-aspect from undue influences may be one and the same from Christ's perspective.

The termination of undue influence is often necessary before the ego-aspect can willingly open itself to Christ's discernment. That is the *third* intervention: the ego-aspect's opening to Christ's discernment. Christ does this by placing his fingers on the ego-aspect's brow, penetrating to the center of its brain, and implanting the *Light* of his discernment. This can be a powerful life changing intervention as it forges a lasting bond between the ego-aspect and Christ image, which the ego-aspect most often experiences as love and forgiveness as well as discernment. The major hurtle to this opening is the ego-aspect's willingness. The ego-aspect must clearly and unequivocally open to Christ before he can forge the connection. This is described in later sections.

For a Dominant self and any Ideal personas the process of 'opening to discernment' is more complicated and more profound. A Dominant self may suffer from undue influences, but once those are excised, it must willingly *give over its power to self-shame* in exchange for Christ's discernment. Both can be done in the same intervention, but termination of the self-shaming must precede the insertion of Christ's discerning power. Self-shaming is an act of free will. It will preempt Christ's power of discernment while it continues to control judgment. Also, in working with a Dominant self, the focus is on the Heart as well as on the brain. Conscience only has the potential of becoming a Voice for God when Christ is allowed full, unimpeded, access to the individual's Heart; and consequently, the aural Voice-of-conscience. A Dominant self will not accede to Christ's entering the Heart until it has allowed Christ to terminate its power to self-shame in exchange for Christ's power of discernment. I strongly suspect that it is the Aware-ego that opens the Heart to Christ. But that can only happen when a Dominant self accedes to it. The process of entering the Heart, absolving the shame found their, and terminating the aural Voice-of-conscience is the *fourth* intervention required for the actualization of the Christ conscience process.

It should be noted that the Empowering archetype retains its power to constellate other images following its termination in the parents. Christ does not prevent this archetype from constellating other images with Temporal or Moral authority. However, in adults, such constellations will have little effect on the individual if the constellation cannot shape/create new ego-aspects to be subject to it. As the originally created ego-aspects turn to Christ, the power of that archetype decreases proportionally. What also needs to be stressed here is that Christ does not assume the authority of that archetype. At no time is the client asked to become subject to Christ. Christ can become a client's freely chosen higher power (see Appendix II), but that is not a prerequisite for him to accomplish the foregoing steps. At one point in my thinking I thought that subjection to Christ would be necessary, but clinically and logically my conclusion proved incorrect. Christ is empowered by the Holy Spirit, not by an Empowering archetype. If his power was derived from the Empowering archetype, he could not terminate its flow in the parent. Stated another way, Christ cannot speak as a Voice for God if he, himself, is subject to the Empowering archetype. That is why my wording of the interventions has become very specific. The ego-aspect is asked to *willingly open itself to Christ's discernment and the forgiving power of the Holy Spirit*, first in its brain and finally, its Heart; the ego-aspect is never asked to become subject to Christ as an embodiment of the Empowering archetype. Children are subject to parents, and persons can be subject to the principalities and powers of this world, but all they can ever do is be receptive to Christ and the Holy Spirit. Christ came to offer a path back to the face of God; not to be a lord and master. Without question, ecclesiastical authorities and institutions have sought to exercise Temporal and Moral authority in Christ's name, but the gospels seem clear enough in their assertion that Christ eschews Temporal and Moral authority. Over time, the client's growing attachment to Christ can become profound. Clients often make references to Christ as their beloved or teacher, but all of such relationships are voluntary and freely ascribed to him.

Surprisingly, the client's willingness to allow Christ to function as his or her conscience is not tantamount to accepting him as his or her higher power. Very often, the client continues to treat 'God the Father' as his or her higher power. Where clients have verbalized this, I have suggested that they consider making a conscious choice, since most often 'God the Father' is an unreflected, osmotic, assimilation of cultural conditioning. I address this issue in Appendix II.

In sum, the Empowering archetype constellates parental images that then exercise Temporal and Moral authority. This empowers the parental image to precipitate the creation of ego-aspects by the Ego. In turn, these ego-aspects sustain the parent's authority. Christ can terminate that authority in the parent and heal the ego-aspects wounded by shame or hubristically inflated by pride. This begins the actualization of a Christ conscience process wherein ego-aspects are guided by the power of Christ's discernment and the convicting power of the Holy Spirit. The Empowering archetype can continue to constellate images with its authority, but will generally have little effect on the Ego following Christ's interventions. The redeemed conscience – what I call Vox Dei or the Voice for God – can only function as such if it speaks for the Holy Spirit. Only the Holy Spirit can be a Voice for God. For the past two thousand years we have accepted the person of Jesus Christ as the perfect conduit of Spirit's power for any and all who ask. I interpret this to mean that the redemption of conscience requires interventions that allow Christ to terminate the power of the Empowering archetype, baptize the shamefully unforgiveable, and abide within the Mind and Heart of the individual as an unerring channel of the Holy Spirit. The interventions I offer to my clients are intended to open the Mind to Christ's power of discernment, and open the Heart to the Holy Spirit's abiding presence as an ongoing source of grace and forgiveness. The redemption of conscience is a process, rather than an event. It is comparable to the years demanded by any discipline offering spiritual development. My approach is more 'earthy' in its focus on the problems of living, but the goals are much the same.

Chapter Outline for Addressing Moral authority

In the next section, I digress slightly to describe a new intervention that I have come to rely on in working with clients. As I reference it throughout the chapter, it needs to be described next. I call it 'the gift of salt.' It can be used without reference to Moral authority, but quite often it becomes another entrée to addressing those issues. It offers any ego-aspect a very effective way of releasing negative emotion, including *accumulated unexpressed shame and anger* generated by a Dominant self or Ego-in-conflict.

The remainder of the chapter is devoted to the clinical treatment of Moral authority: it's termination in parents and the transformation of selves created by that authority. Christ can be asked to terminate the Moral authority embodied in parents *after he has liberated the Rejected-self from shame, and later when it manifests as the aural Voice-of-conscience*. The initial request to terminate the archetype's constellated authority in a parent is expected to come from a redeemed Rejected-self. The Rejected-self is then offered the opportunity to open itself to

Christ's power of discernment. Following that, the therapist can then focus on those ego-aspects that have sought to preempt the aural Voice-of-conscience. Ultimately, the therapist must address any Dominant self blocking entrance to the Heart as well as any Ego-in-conflict that continues to shamelessly accumulate unexpressed shame in the emotional auric bodies. Dominant selves are the most problematical for clients because they play a significant role in the client's day-to-day life as well as blocking entry to the Heart. The actualization of a Christ conscience process requires that (1) Christ be allowed to enter the Heart of the Dominant self and release its shameful core; and (2) the repetition of those steps for each primary self that comes to the fore following the initial purification.

Often, conscience is first addressed by working with an Ego-in-conflict. This ego-aspect is easily accessible and often a primary reason for the client seeking therapy. The Ego-in-conflict provides an excellent entrée for addressing issues of Moral authority because once it is separated out, it can quickly identify the most pressing embodiments of the irreconcilable conflict that necessitated its creation. Thus, working with an Ego-in-conflict can quickly unearth a Rejected-self in need of baptism. Once identified, the Rejected-self becomes the focus of therapy. The initial goal vis-à-vis the Rejected-self is baptism at the request of the Aware-ego, who always exercises the *Light's* willingness when the client goes inside. That done, the Rejected-self can ask Christ to terminate the Moral authority embodied in the parents and ask Christ to instill the power of discernment within its brain, i.e. brow chakra. Christ becomes a viable conduit of Vox Dei when one ego-aspect willingly accepts his power of discernment; but a Christ conscience process is not actualized until Christ is also allowed to enter and purify the Heart. There is an experiential difference between work done 'outside the Heart' and work done 'within the Heart.'

The Rejected-self is always the first ego-aspect invited to accept Christ. When this is done Christ can begin offering the power of his discernment to other primary selves. Without any exception I can think of, the Rejected-self has always been willing to accept Christ as its voice of discernment, once it has been liberated from the bondage of shame. In sum, the initial termination of Moral authority in parents and the actualization of Christ's power of discernment both require the explicit willingness of a baptized, liberated, Rejected-self. This is how, "the stone rejected by the builders becomes the cornerstone."

All of the above is rarely accomplished smoothly. Primary and Dominant selves are prideful and/or fearful. They want nothing to do with the Rejected-self and are basically distrustful of Christ terminating authority in the parents. Their ambivalence must be anticipated, respected, and addressed, or they will surely sabotage the therapy as well as further aggravating the client's symptoms. But note, their permission is not required to baptize the Rejected-self, or ask Christ to actually terminate parental authority. Those steps are the prerogative of the Aware-ego and liberated Rejected-self. But their *fears* must be addressed before, during, and after, or they will surely sabotage the therapeutic process.

The ultimate goal of this process is an ongoing, internalized, daily relationship with Christ wherein the Ego feels comfortably yoked with this image. I consider Conscience operationally redeemed when Christ assumes the role of 'daily partner' in the client's interior life. It is an ongoing process that can take years. It is probably comparable to the Alchemist's completion of the first stage of work toward creation of the philosopher's stone.[12]

THE GIFT OF SALT

The inspiration for this intervention came while reading a book by W. Weston called *Emotional Release Therapy*.[13] Weston describes a method for healing negative emotions based, in part, on the work of pranic healers.[14] Prana is a name given to life energy in the Near East. It is comparable to chi in Chinese medicine. Pranic healing can be likened to other forms of energy healing such as Reiki and Therapeutic Touch. What sets it apart is the healer's use of light visualization and salt water. The healer visualizes different colors of light flowing from his or her hand into the patient, white being the color most commonly used. Equally notable, the healer will periodically rinse his or her hand in a bucket of salt water, which is thought to dissolve any toxic emotions *inadvertently drawn from the patient* in the course of the work. Weston alters this process in significant ways. He *actively seeks the release* of those negative emotions into his hand. He has the client envision any negative emotion, e.g. anger, fear, unforgiveness, etc. as a colored light flowing out of the body and released as light into his hand. He experiences this release as a burst of heat. He then dissolves the emotion, now held in his hand as heat, into salt water. Normally, this is salt water in a pail or dish. Often, Weston will hold his hand over a client's heart, which is most commonly identified as the part of the body where the emotion is most strongly felt. However, this process is also used for addressing the psychosomatic component of acute and chronic illnesses in which case the hand is held over the part of the body that is wounded or diseased. After the toxic emotion has been released and dissolved in salt water, Weston may then focus on replacing it with more positive emotions such as love and acceptance, which he does imaginatively by visualizing colored light flowing into the affected area. This is comparable to most energy therapies that seek to supplement the client's energy with the therapist's channeled energy. According to Weston, and Pranic healers generally, these interventions can be very effective in facilitating the healing of wounds and diseases of all types as well as post-operative healing.

While reading Weston's work, I was most intrigued with the use of salt water for the dissolution of negative emotions released into the healer's hand. It reminded me of Alchemical writings by Carl Jung and others. Alchemically speaking, salt, sulfur and mercury are considered the three primary forces of nature. To quote a contemporary Jungian:

> Salt is not strictly understood as common sodium chloride. It has a much greater significance. The alchemical salt is the ground upon which all creation rests. In human experience, it represents the principle that allows us to apprehend all natural phenomena. *It is life's flow experienced through the feeling function*. Refined salt allows us to penetrate our own depths, and there discover wisdom [italics mine].[15]

While much can be said about salt in alchemy, my primary purpose in referencing it here is to point the reader toward its symbolic, psychic, significance. 'Alchemical work' is comprised mostly of meditations in active imagination, which are used to dissolve and shorn impurities as the first stage toward recreating the Self. Alchemists refer to this process of purification as *solve et coagula*" (separate and recombine). [16] The properties of salt - such as dissolution, solvent, and crystallization, become metaphors for interventions at the level of Mind. All these thoughts inspired me to develop an intervention that used the 'psychic salt' of oceans and Christ. Basically, *the client is asked to take Christ to their most easily imagined ocean shore*. Just about everyone has visited the ocean and has anticipated returning when they could.

I introduce this intervention by speaking of Weston's work, focusing especially on his use of salt water to decompose the negative emotions, and imagining emotions as light. I note that the emotion can be any color and the colors can change as the process evolves. I ask the client to imagine being at an ocean shore, and then imagine Christ walking into the ocean with them. The client can stand or sit in the ocean or even float on a raft. On occasion, I have even suggested placing a massage table in the ocean. The goal of this intervention is to release into Christ's hands any negative emotion which may be wounding the client or preventing healing. The emotion can be related to a particular self – as in the clinical example below, or it can be seen as 'stressing' a particular part of the body causing it to malfunction. The client is directed to release the emotion as a colored light into Christ's hand. The emotion does not have to be named for the intervention to be effective, but it does have to be released as a colored light and the client needs to be able to report the color(s). Christ, in turn, releases the light into the ocean, which the client is also asked to observe and report upon. Alternatively the light can travel through Christ's body to his other hand, which is submerged in the ocean. One client even imagined it flowing through Christ's feet while he used both hands to receive negative emotions. Another client experienced it as simply dissolving into the ocean as Christ massaged an affected area. However it is done, the client is asked to report how the emotion is dissolved into the ocean. Most often, clients observe it leaving Christ's hand and flowing into the ocean to the point of complete dissolution. On occasion, Christ is observed to form it into a ball and throw it far out into the ocean. Sometimes, if the client considers the emotion particularly toxic, Christ may be observed to thrust it *deep* into the ocean. In any case, once released the client invariably reports a discernable sense of relief. The client may repeat this process as often as necessary; and in the case of chronic problems repetition is encouraged. It is one of the few interventions that most clients feel comfortable using at home on their own. Finally, once the negative emotion has been cleared from the body, Christ can be asked to replace it with healing by his *Light*.

Guilt-Shame

The gift of salt intervention was originally intended to deal with emotions other than shame. What sets shame apart is the pervasive sense in every culture that it is irremovable, in addition to being the most toxic of emotions; like being branded for life with a perpetually festering scar or scarlet letter. This is why most individuals go to great lengths to hide it as letting it be seen is tantamount to being condemned by it. And truth be told, individuals can do nothing on their own that is powerful enough to remove a sense of shame once it is experienced. The Ego can concoct numerous variants of defensive denial and minimization, but none of these can dissolve the toxic imprint. The gift of salt can dissolve accumulated shame but only insofar as the individual is willing to call on Christ or comparable higher power to act as a conduit for its release.

Shame is an emotion, a coalesced energy. If the body cannot discharge it then it remains in the body – both the physical body as well as the auric bodies, particularly the heart and emotional auric bodies. Most people think of shame as an infrequent event, like a memory of shameful things done to or by others in the past. Memories of shame are nearly universal. Because the experiences were both exceedingly painful and resistant to self-amelioration, the experiences remain perpetually painful 'to the touch,' and the individual will strive to protect them from being touched or repeated. Unfortunately, while such wounds significantly shape all future ego embodiments, they are not the most toxic vis-à-vis our physical and emotional bodies. The most dangerous repetitions are the Ego's own creation: its power to shame itself when it functions as its own conscience, and its power to act shamelessly in defiance of past shaming by others. The first is primarily a function of the Dominant self, and the latter primarily a function of the Ego-in-conflict.

By age ten, the Ego has learned to exercise the controlling power of shame. What it fails to learn is that this exercise continually inflicts toxic shame on its mental, sensate, and emotional bodies. It also fails to appreciate – which is true for the culture at large, that it has no power to undo the wrath this heaps on Body, Mind, Heart, and Soul. If such self-inflictions were an infrequent event then likely the Body could gradually dissipate the adverse energy. But for many people, self-shaming and acting shamelessly is a daily experience that is cumulative and progressively corrosive.

The intent of all *compulsive* desires is the active suppression of felt shame associated with a behavior. This is reflected in the fact that, for most people, eating the whole bag of Chips or knocking off a half-gallon of chocolate ice cream is guilt inducing. After the fact, s/he feels guilty. But s/he did not feel guilty while s/he was satisfying the desire, only after the act when the desire is satisfied. What the guilt tells us is that we have once again indulged in a shameful act without the shame stopping it. So the desire is satisfied in defiance of shame, but what can we say of the evoked shame whose consciousness was overridden by the desire? It is blocked from conscious awareness, but the telltale signs of guilt mark it as a manifest consequence of the behavior. (We don't feel guilt in the absence of shame.) More to the point, guilt cannot discharge the toxicity of the shame, even with penance and absolution. The issue here is not one of morality, but of energy. Guilt cannot dissipate the energy of shame. So, how are we to release our mental, sensate and emotional bodies from this self-inflicted and seemingly indelible toxicity? And what happens when the most toxic emotion in human experience is *repeatedly* injected into an individual's emotional field over a period of months and years with no viable means of discharge? Can the reader imagine the effect that cumulative toxicity has on the emotional and physical bodies? I would argue that – aside from making us 'feel bad,' most of the severe ailments plaguing humankind, whether the rages of war or physical cancers, are caused by the cumulative effect of toxic shame. And the real tragedy is that we do it to ourselves without any thought of an exit strategy, short of submitting ourselves to the surgeon's knife, or years of chronic pain, or a life of mental disorder and emotional poverty.

Thankfully, Christ channeling the Holy Spirit can reverse this inexorable drive toward self-destruction, which can be likened to Freud's death instinct. Christ can remove the shame from the emotional field and heal the scars of its imprint. The gift of salt and comparable interventions (described later) can ameliorate the cumulative effects of undischarged shame. But that effort will continue to be undone while the ego-aspects responsible for the shaming continue to re-wound the emotional and physical bodies. Even so, if any part of the Ego, particularly the Aware-ego, can acknowledge that other selves are polluting the body with toxic shame, then that self can ask Christ to begin the process of removing it by having it released into salt water. Hopefully, the client can then move toward identifying those selves responsible for the pollution and convincing them to forgo their dubious 'power.'

Clair. I will only give one clinical example of the gift of salt in this section, as I describe its use in different contexts throughout the chapter. This example is quite long and complex, covering two sessions over a two-week period, both two hours in length. I offer it because it demonstrates how its use can quickly lead to the discovery of other major issues. I see Clair every several weeks for two hours, as she has to travel a good distance to see me. She has a history of severe cultic and familial abuse in childhood, which she survived by developing multiple personalities. She is in a healing profession and *driven* to do well. Often, the 'inner work' portion of our session can last an hour or more. Interestingly, Christ has always joined with Clair at an ocean beach, though this session was the first time I have ever used the gift of salt intervention with her. Clair's chief complaint on this occasion is great tiredness and fatigue. Something is sapping her energy to the point where she feels like dying. What will emerge when she goes inside is a self who is being drained by her *caring for others*. I would also note, that Clair's Christ image is very active and more autonomous than found with most clients. Clair has made many journeys inward. Christ's increased autonomy seems to be a function of these repeated encounters over time. Her Christ is a living, breathing, figure of compassion and strength within her Mind whenever she becomes willing to call on him.

Using concentric circles, Christ helps Clair to quickly separate from the self that seems "tired onto dying," which she associates with Kierkegaard's "sickness onto death." When separated, Clair describes the self as very dark, "She seems to absorb the light." I ask if she can identify what is producing the darkness in her? "The darkness is her weariness. She has stopped living." I ask what emotion has stopped her from living? Clair answers with one word: "Caring." I asked if she absorbs the cares of others? (I am aware that this can happen in the healing professions. In fact, it is the reason why Pranic healers use salt water!) Clair replies that this self is "greatly affected by the feelings of others." My next question is pivotal: "Would she be willing to relinquish – not her caring, but the cares of others?" Her answer comes quickly: "She is willing, she never knew it was an option. It gives her hope. She is almost giddy like a kid at the prospect of giving up their cares." At this point I introduce Clair to the idea of releasing those cares into Christ's hand and he, in turn, releasing them into the ocean. Clair responds by describing an ocean scene. "She is on a huge rubber raft which keeps her afloat, but lets the ocean water lap over her giving her energy. The cares are oozing out of her pores, like an oil slick in water – greens, golds, pinks, and brownish stuff. Her muscles are relaxing. Christ just stands at her head, massaging it, helping her mind to relax." While all of this is happening Clair also becomes aware of another self, "A little girl, very panicky, trying to break through; she wants me to save her, keep her safe, she is really scared." (Remember, Clair is MPD. Even so, this kind of intervention is likely to activate other selves who also want release.) I suggest that she let Christ reach out for her. What is most disturbing to Clair is that this little girl's body has sexual feelings. I suggest that the little girl can feel them safely in Christ's arms and release them into his hand as needed. This appears to happen but I do not pursue it. My focus remains on the part of her that has been overwhelmed by the cares of others. In response to my refocusing her on this caring self, Clair reports that, "As she lets go of the cares, other things emerge, like the little girl with sexual feelings and a big block – not a box, not a door, but something encased in a big block." I suggest that she contain this big block and let the 'blockness' be dissolved so that only what is contained within it remains. "It is a flood of memories, all abusive. There is both awareness and *denial of that reality*. I started remembering them when I started reading the *Body Wisdom* book." [17] I suggest that Clair release the denial into Christ's hand and accept the reality of her memories. (I would not make this suggestion if Clair had not already dealt extensively with her memories. The issue here is not the memories per se, nor even the emotions directly associated with them – which have all been dealt with by and large, but rather the *denial* exercised by the Caring self.) I surmise that acceptance of the memories might prompt her to greater caring for *herself*. "I am almost there, but there is fear of letting go of the denial and allowing the awareness." I suggest that she ask Christ for *acceptance* of the memories. In reply, Clair reports that she can no longer see Christ, "I can't find him." I suggest that she open her eyes, sense the presence of her *Light*, and have it draw a circle of protection, which she will enter when she goes back inside. When she goes back inside she can again see Christ. I suggest that she give Christ the 'denial' and see what is left. "It washes away. I can see behind the barrier. It makes me feel kind of dizzy. There is a little girl in a blue denim dress lying on the floor." I suggest that she let Christ go over to the little girl and literally breath new life into her – like resuscitation. "He does that, he holds her. Now she is leaning up. She asks him what happened? Where is she? She has no memory of what happened before. He has wiped the slate clean. She is starting with a new mind, clean and pure. It was only the denial that made her impure." I reframe this slightly for Clair: "Denial walled her off from change. She must learn to modulate between denial and acceptance. Now Clair shifts her focus to another thought: "My heart hurts when I think about my parents and paternal grandparents (her primary abusers). Earlier in the week I remembered some good times with my paternal grandparents." I do not pursue this; again, I suggest that Clair refocus on the Caring self. "The Caring self looks like a deflated balloon, kind of empty." I suggest that she allow Christ to extend *his caring for her, and in the future she can extend to others what she receives from him, she can become a conduit of his caring.* "She is taking on some shape and movement. She is not giddy, but alive, peaceful, maybe balanced. She is now sitting on the edge of the raft with her legs in the water, being aware of all around her, but peaceful. She is aware of other parts of her that seem to be soaking up the peace she is experiencing. They seem anxious, fearful and crying. She is aware that they are not a part of her." I suggest to Clair that the caring part be given a circle of protection so as to not be overwhelmed by their needs. The session ends quickly afterward.

Taking on the cares of others is a way of feeling the emotions of disowned selves without admitting the existence of those selves. Denial allows a self to block the mental awareness of disowned selves and their memories, but not the emotions they generate. In Clair's case the strongest emotions appear to be sexual in nature, which is why that self is the first to be experienced. Hopefully, in this session the continuous effort needed by the Caring-self to deny her traumatic past has been attenuated by the idea that she can give caring vis-à-vis Christ rather than merely absorbing the trauma. But removing her *denial of reality* has also allowed for the emergence of other selves into her co-conscious existence. These selves will also have to be addressed in future sessions. Clair has been seen in therapy for a number of years. Responsible primaries such as her Caring-self, *whose primary purpose is the conscious denial of her abuse*, have been largely responsible for her survival. It is actually a good sign that this self has 'presented' for therapy at this time. It is a tacit acknowledgement that most of the abuse issues have been addressed and that she can now be healed which, in her case, would include the *acceptance* of memories she had to deny in order to pass as a 'normal person.' I would never ever attempt to remove defensive denial in the early stages of therapy, even if I thought it possible. The onslaught of memories would overwhelm the alters who have sustained the client as an adult while those memories remain unconscious and unaddressed. Where severe abuse is known or suspected, the recovery and healing of those memories must come first. It is better not to address issues of Temporal and Moral authority until the therapist and client have developed a paradigm for unearthing and healing the memories. Clair trusts her image of Christ implicitly because he has walked her through some of the most horrific cultic memories imaginable and unerringly healed the alters and fragments who suffered them.

In the next session, Clair reports feeling better, not overly tired. But very quickly, *I become tired*. It is a feeling I have come to associate with any client who is actively suppressing a disowned self. It makes me want to close my eyes. I find it difficult to focus. Our conversation becomes discursive. In passing, she mentions her high blood pressure, which I suggest we address, if only to get her inside and discover what is going on. I suggest that she go inside and use concentric circles to separate from whoever is *constricting the blood flow*. "It does not look like a person. Christ has placed its *Light* on a table, the one I left for it when I separated from it. The image is square with rounded sides, beige yellow, brighter in the center. I assume it is somebody rolled up in a ball. There are feelings associated with it of pain, fear, anger, and a need for comfort; a sense of feeling caught, hopelessness, trapped, constrained." I have Clair ask Christ if he can illuminate the nature of the constriction producing the trapped feeling? "The square goes from beige-yellow to charcoal gray. The life is being sucked out of me." The part that is speaking is whoever emerged when the painful aspect is separated but I have yet to appreciate that. Instead, I ask Clair: who is sucking the life out of *you*? "I don't have anything left in me. The inside is all empty, a shell." At this point I realize that I am talking to an alter personality that is feeling *psychically* drained. Our exchanges at this point are too confusing to capture in print. I ask numerous questions in an effort to tease out what is going on. Basically, I am finally able to discern that the 'drained' alter is someone looking at Christ and herself *from above*. This 'drained' alter experiences the self she sees as a mere shell because she is out of her body. She has depersonalized as a result of some trauma. I encourage her to float down, enter the body image she can see, and stand in front of Christ; then I ask her relationship to the yellow square: did it become charcoal gray when she left it? "Yes." I have the sense that this alter has been triggered by our work in the previous session. In some way this is all related to *caring for others* and opening herself to Christ. I suggest that she let Christ become the author of her caring, to let him put his hand over her forehead and open herself to him, to become the conduit of *his* caring rather than the source of caring. As part of this process, she is also encouraged to release any fear of opening to him. Unbeknownst to me, the idea of "opening to Christ" has triggered an abuse memory (probably in the last session), including the depersonalization that occurred during that memory, or this is what I surmise when Clair can finally report: "When you talked about opening to Christ, I saw somebody holding my legs open, and felt the pain. But Christ tells me I do not have to open my legs, and that he would not hurt me open or closed. So I have given him the fear and he has placed it in the ocean. I can feel energy flowing through me now, through my fingers." (From this point onward, there is a switch in perspective from the alter to the Aware-ego's perspective.) Clair proceeds to describe what is happening from her new perspective: "She gave him her *Light*. He breathed on her. It was like a red flame, but not like a fire. He breathed it into her mouth. She is standing. There is a bluish white, dark gray, band up behind her that is keeping her grounded." I ask if there is more he can offer her if she is willing? "He says she can use his energy to care for others, that he will recharge her if she calls on him. If she is unable to call him, he will tap her on the shoulder and ask if she wants it. She has to stay here. She cannot go away and die. *She was ready to die*. I don't know if she is convinced, but she is open to seeing what happens."

In the following weeks Clair begins to set serious limits on her clients and work schedule. Two months later she gives up her caseload to take over as the clinic supervisor of other care managers. She knew she was burned out and, had she not gotten the new position, she was preparing to quit. It would be several more months before she finally becomes willing to reconcile a major alter who defines herself by how productive she is and a disowned self who is suicidally depressed.

The forgoing sessions illustrates the repetitive use of the 'gift of salt' intervention, and some of its effects as well as unintended consequences. It is always good to anticipate the unintended when working with MPD clients. But with most clients this intervention will generally bring other issues to the foreground. Once the therapist and client learn to use it, the intervention becomes an integral part of the work, especially any work addressing anger, fear and shame issues, which are core to so many of our problems. Fear is by far the most common emotion addressed with this intervention. It can be used in tandem with the garment of protection described elsewhere and brain-stem massage described later in this chapter. Christ can provide a parallel intervention wherein he creates a dome and places a portion of his *Light* near the top of the dome. This *Light* is expected to absorb any negative emotion felt by the client while in the dome.

The above sessions were atypical in lasting so long. Generally, a client is only inside for 20-30 minutes, often less, though I also see most clients more frequently than I was scheduling Clair. Longer periods of inner work often generate this complexity, but frankly, it is taxing for the therapist as well as the client to be inside for so long.

The gift of salt intervention is most frequently used in the context of working with stress-*fears* that generate physical problems; or with accumulated unexpressed emotions such as *anger*; or with emotional defenses such as *denial*. The selves must be helped to release those emotions, and then helped to alter the beliefs that perpetually evoke the negative emotion. The selves must come to rely on Christ rather than their self-sufficiency, which has placed inordinate stress on the body. This is particularly true of prideful selves that are discussed further on. In the above case, the Caring-self appears to have been responding to the feelings of other dissociated selves, whose existence she has *denied* and then projectively experienced in her caseload of clients. Now that she can see these selves with a less-anxious presence, it will be possible to help each of them release their negative emotions into the ocean, thereby treating the source rather than projecting it.

The gift of salt – as I have come to call it, can be used to address any negative emotion including shame. In initial work with a Dominant self, that self may seek to 'rid' itself of its shameful core by having Christ draw the shame out of it's Heart without owning it. And it is possible for Christ to do this insofar as shame is a cumulative, unexpressed, emotion. But ultimately, the Dominant self must forgo its power of self-shame or it will simply re-pollute the Heart.

The Capturing Circle or Christ Drawn Circle

The capturing circle is essentially a circle created by Christ at the client's request. It will be used increasingly in the verbatims without my saying much about it. As I reviewed this chapter, it just seemed to insert itself into the process more and more. Christ's role in the client's inner life becomes ever more figural once he has redeemed a Dominant self, entered the Heart one time, and silenced the aural Voice-of-conscience. Just about everything the client does thereafter is done by asking Christ to do it. This happens in no small measure because the therapist also suggests that Christ intervene in this or that way, but also because the client is now sufficiently trusting of the Christ within. In any case, the 'capturing circle' is drawn by Christ at the client's request. Basically, this circle will capture anything *Christ intends for it to capture.* As the therapist, I can be quite specific as to what I would like to have the circle capture, and I trust that is true of the client as well; but ultimately it is Christ that defines what will be captured since he defines the intent of the circle when he draws it. Generally, the circle is drawn between himself and the Aware-ego. The Aware-ego enters and walks toward Christ. When the Aware-ego exits next to Christ and turns around, whatever the circle is intended to capture is personified in the circle for the client to observe. Even when nothing is seen, it is assumed that something is there as it is Christ who has drawn the circle. Normally, something is personified, but in cases where it is not, the therapist can assume that some defense on the part of the client is blocking awareness. Sometimes, the resistance is overcome by asking Christ to 'compress' the circle till whatever is present emerges. Or, the self that is merged with the Aware-ego can be queried as to why there is nothing in the circle; or Christ can be asked if he 'sees' something that, for whatever reason, the client is unwilling to see. If he answers in the affirmative, then he can be asked to provide a symbol or association that might allow the client to safely begin to approach what is in the circle.

Of note, a Christ-defined circle has many other uses, which I have only begun to explore. Christ can saturate a circle with any emotion, which allows an ego-aspect to experience it, often for the first time. He can also transform a circle into a circle of effect as a means of teaching a self the effects of its behavior. This has proven to be particularly helpful in working with depersonalized ego-aspects whose lack of sensate feedback often drives the body to the point of exhaustion; or in working with parental images that have traditionally overwhelmed an ego-aspect. Many such interventions will be used in the verbatims in this chapter and the next with very little preamble, which is why I am highlighting the use of the Christ-drawn circle here.

Initially, I only used the capturing circle with clients who have redeemed at least one Dominant self and allowed Christ to enter the Aware-ego's Heart one time. However, I find myself using it with increasing frequency with clients who are new to the process if they are willing to evoke a Christ image. I still supplant its use with double circles, concentric circles, and upright *Light* portals; and those remain the preferred choices for working with new clients. But frankly, the more a client and therapist are willing to turn the work over to Christ, the easier and more fruitful the process becomes. I give numerous examples of the capturing circle in verbatims provided throughout the chaper.

THE ADDICTED EGO-IN-CONFLICT

The Ego's initial defense in response to parental shaming is dissociation of the ego-aspect shamed by the parents. Later, prideful Dominant selves will cope with shame by exercising the power to self-shame, thereby pre-empting the aural Voice-of-conscience. Any emotion more powerful than pride, such as forgiveness, must be *received* from a 'higher power.' Since the Ego cannot forgive itself, it often uses pride to deny the need for forgiveness. Anger and fear are less powerful than pride, but even more frequently called upon in coping with a shaming environment. Between those two is desire – stronger than fear, weaker than anger, which is the modus operandi of the Ego-in-conflict. Note that the Ego-in-conflict and Dominant self both use desire for much the same reasons; but the Ego-in-conflict rebelliously engages in unacceptable types of mind-altering substances or quantities.

In its effort to quell the pain of polarized selves, the Ego can create an Ego-in-conflict that *rebelliously* uses physical desire for mind-altering substances, which are able override any interior shaming authority or feelings of shame while the brain remains in the altered state. The Ego-in-conflict generally models the behavior of a parent or grandparent. It seeks to repetitively achieve *physical homeostasis by using brain-altering substances that temporarily mask the tension created by polarized opposites*. The strategy temporarily reduces the emotional tension created by polarized selves, particularly dyads polarized by pride and shame. It can do so in two ways. First, the mind-altering effects of a substance such as alcohol counteract the *physical tension* generated by polarization. Second, the mind-altering *quality* of the substance often allows the Ego-in-conflict to temporarily move toward the shamed polarity by blunting fear of it. In contrast, socially acceptable behaviors used in excess are less effective in reducing the angst for more than a short period of time or allow the self to move toward the shamed polarity.

Often, the Ego-in-conflict will be seen to act collusively with another ego-aspect that is threatened with loss of control, e.g. a Responsible primary self, Mirror aspect, or Dominant self. The Ego-in-conflict is responsible for all our socially unacceptable addictive and compulsive behaviors. (Of note, the Ego-in-conflict is a *function* as well as a personification: it may have several addictions rank ordered in terms of availability and efficacy.) Of note, the Ego-in-conflict serves the same purpose as using socially acceptable behaviors in excess. It generally comes into play when those behaviors are experienced as insufficient. The Ego-in-conflict's use of socially *unacceptable* behaviors (i.e. illegal or taboo) is what distinguishes it from a Dominant self. The difference is one of degree: the Ego-in-conflict rebelliously uses unacceptable substances while a Dominant self seeks to overtly comply with social dictates by using socially acceptable behaviors *in excess.*

Physical desire allows an Ego-in-conflict to deniably generate shame. The mind-altered state is more powerful than the shame it generates. In effect, the Ego-in-conflict uses physical desire for mind altering substances to overwhelm the shame component of an experience, which is most likely generated by the aural Voice-of-conscience, and in so doing can 'act shamelessly;' but it nonetheless precipitates the generation of shameful emotion. It can ride 'rough shod' over the aural Voice-of-conscience and any self that seeks to shame it, but the Body cannot escape the wrath of toxic emotions it precipitates. While in the thrall of physical desire and concomitant 'pleasure,' the Ego-in-conflict will not feel the emotional shame it generates, except as another self may feel guilt after the fact. Nonetheless, as the Ego-in-conflict repeatedly turns to physical desire, it repeatedly precipitates the injection of emotional shame into the heart, emotional, and etheric bodies as well as damaging organs of the physical body by the excessive use of the substance. The emotion accumulates since the shame is effectively undischargeable without recourse to a higher power, and any long-term accumulation eventually becomes toxic to both the auric bodies and physical brain/body. The toxicity can manifest in a variety of ways. For example, any long-term abuse of drugs – illegal or legal – will have 'side effects' detrimental to our wellbeing.

Sexual pleasure is one of the strongest motivators of behavior in every culture. Every child would freely engage in self-stimulation if not shamed for it. Unfortunately, most cultures seek to restrict the activity by shaming it rather than teaching its regulation.[18] In fact, the shaming of self-stimulation may be one of the child's earliest experiences of shame. While such shaming may block socially acceptable expression, sexual arousal and satisfaction are too powerful to be blocked from all expression. If 'socially acceptable' outlets are unavailable, most individuals will simply act *shamelessly* to achieve sexual pleasure. Tragically, the repeated arousal of shameful outlets also injects repetitive bursts of emotional shame into the body, most often the first and second chakras, which will cumulatively affect the sex organs.[19]

The Ego-in-conflict is a significant player in the life of any client who seeks help for alcohol and drug related issues. Fortunately, it is also surprisingly easy to contain within a circle of *Light*; and once contained, it can be asked to identify the conflicting selves it seeks to physically reconcile. For that reason it provides an excellent entrée for accessing the major players creating the conflict it seeks to repeatedly obviate. But the Ego-in-conflict is also an integral player in the conflict – the other tip of a triangle – so beyond its role as an identifier of conflicting selves, it too must be redeemed. At some point, all three must open to Christ's forgiveness, discernment, and purification.[20] This is most likely to occur after a client has worked with a Dominant self. But it can also occur if the Ego-in-conflict becomes 'ashamed' of its role in polluting the body and asks Christ to release the body from the shame it has inadvertently injected into it. Basically, the Ego-in-conflict must forgo the drugs of choice that are precipitating the repeated injection of shame into the emotional field. Interventions involving the Ego-in-conflict will generally require the identification of all ego-aspects defining the triangle generating the shame and working with them in concert. I address this triangle in greater detail later in the chapter.

A defining characteristic of the Ego-in-conflict is its slavish attachment to physical *sensation* and the simultaneous, inadvertent, blocking of its *intuitive function*. Intuition is the polar opposite of sensation. For an ego-aspect to have a full range of choice it needs to have equal access to both poles. Christ can provide this, which opens the Ego-in-conflict to a new range of awareness. In working with the Ego-in-conflict this is generally the first intervention I offer the client since it often provides the Ego-in-conflict with much needed insight into the reasons for using addictive substances. Only later do I encourage the Ego-in-conflict to forgo its shameless use of the stimulant(s) in favor of Christ's power of discernment. As I have noted elsewhere, the Ego-in-conflict is likely to become quiescent if the underlying polarities can be addressed.

Christ's opening of the Ego-in-conflict to its intuitive function is much like the baptism of a Rejected-self in that neither ego-aspect is expected or required to give its permission. As is the case for the Rejected-self, it is the Aware-ego that asks Christ to intervene on behalf of the Ego-in-conflict. The Ego-in-conflict can choose not to avail itself of its intuitive function once it is opened to it, but refusing to avail itself would be comparable to the Rejected-self refusing to be free of shame. *Using* its newly acquired intuitive function is another matter. That will take practice and the willingness to access it.[21] But it is now available to offset a previously slavish bondage to sensation. As and when an Ego-in-conflict expresses contrition for polluting the body, and becomes willing to forgo that power, it can receive both baptism and Christ's power of discernment. Unlike the intervention that opens the Ego-in-conflict to its intuitive function, the Ego-in-conflict must be explicitly willing to receive the Holy Spirit offered by Christ.

In clinical cases involving alcohol and/or drug abuse, I am quick to help clients get involved with AA or NA. I tell the client that participation in AA is not a precondition of therapy, but they will have to put up with me making it a focus of therapy until they are actively involved. I am totally in agreement with AA that, "There is nothing so bad that alcohol does not make it worse." All 12-step programs are *spiritual* in nature. The program insists that finding a higher power is absolutely essential to sobriety. Therapists need to work in concert with these programs. It is a lot easier to address an Ego-in-conflict when the client can admit that the addiction has made his or her life unmanageable.[22]

Belinda. This case example offers a straightforward examination and use of the Ego-in-conflict to access polarized selves bound by shame and pride. When I first saw Belinda, she was recently discharged from a three month, inpatient, drug treatment program for addiction to pain medication. Her drug addiction followed on the heels of cancer treatment and continued for several years. The addiction ruled her life during that time. She finally admitted herself to inpatient treatment; she is currently in AA and fully committed to working her program. She is an RN by training. She was evangelically religious in the past, but not currently. She is committed to the spiritual aspects of AA and quite willing to call on Christ in our sessions. When I begin this session, Belinda has already been seeing me for six months and gone inside numerous times, often in regard to physical symptoms. When she presents with a dry cough, I suggest she might want to separate from the part of her who seems to be coughing so much. In this same session, prior to going inside, we have also begun talking about "Druggy," the Ego-in-conflict that used pain medication. That discussion arose as a result of Belinda expressing fear of using medications of any kind to control her cough. Once Belinda separates from "Cougher" (using concentric circles), I suggest she let Christ open Cougher's intuition so she can apprise the reasons for her coughing. (In this instance, I decided to treat Cougher as a first cousin of Druggy.) "The coughing creates a boundary. It holds people at a distance…like not having to talk to my youngest daughter on the phone…probably, my shrink, too. (She canceled the previous session.) It would also legitimize using drugs if I let myself. There was a lot of fear when I used drugs, fear of being found out. I can't be found out." The Cougher's desire for, and fear of drugs suggests that this may be a good time to begin working with Druggy. Belinda is quite willing and quickly separates from her. Christ steps into the circle and opens Druggy's intuitive function by touching her on the brow. I suggest she let Christ develop a relationship with Druggy. "Druggy seems to sedate the Cougher and whatever it is she fears. Druggy is drawn to Christ; she leans into him. She leans back and rests in his presence." I ask if it is Druggy's drug use that allows her to be so comfortable with Christ? "No, this is happening in spite of the drug use. She does sedate the body's fears." I ask if Druggy can use the *Light* to contain the object of fear? "It is a fear of being alone – profoundly alone." I ask if Christ is aware of this part that is so alone? "Yes." I am feeling pressed to end the session here, so I suggest that she ask Christ to commit to staying with "Profoundly alone" (whoever or wherever she is) till we can work with her. I suggest that Profoundly alone and Christ reside in a dome of *Light* so that her being brought into relational consciousness does not overly disturb any other selves.

When Belinda returns the following week, she is feeling better (not coughing), but when I ask her about 'Profoundly alone' she sheepishly admits that she has completely forgotten about her until I asked. Interestingly, she has reflected a good deal on Druggy. "I am not afraid of my addiction any more. At some level she protected me. Might not have been the best way, but she did the best she could. The year I underwent cancer treatment was a black, lonely, time; terrifying. I was profoundly alone. I feel like I can breath today, lots of light, some sadness, but not a black hole kind of sadness." I suggest that she go inside and let Christ baptize Profoundly alone so we can discover what has kept her so isolated all of these years. "I know what it is: it is survival. She is so thin, frail and sick." I suggest that she will revive quickly if Belinda allows her to remain in consciousness. My mention of regaining strength touches a cord in Belinda. She begins to reflect on the strong-weak dichotomy that shaped her in childhood. "She had to act one way – strong, even while she was feeling really weak. She feels physically weakened by having to be strong and alone. Because of my father's inappropriate advances, she felt she had to make decisions for both her and her mother even as a child. She was incapable of making those decisions but she had to." I ask if Profoundly alone has any relationship with Belinda's sexuality? (Belinda's father sexualized her in childhood, though as far as we can determine, he did not actually have sex with her. The mother could not protect her. Belinda has shied away from talking about sexuality whenever I have broached it.) "Profoundly alone does not know what to do with that [her sexual feelings]. That is when all the trouble started. A lot of shame to overcome about that." In effect, this Rejected-self embodies a strong sense of Belinda's sexuality. I suggest a ritual in which Christ is asked to purge Profoundly alone's sexual energy of all the negative emotions related to her father's behavior.[23] I add that, if she is willing for him to do this, then Profoundly alone would not have to be anorexic anymore. In making the suggestion I am thinking of Patrick Carnes' *Sexual Anorexia*, but Belinda takes me literally.[24] She immediately replies that she never told me about *that*, meaning that she was diagnostically anorexic when she was younger. In truth, she had not told me, and her current body weight gave no hint of it. The session ends at this point. In the following session, Profoundly alone is worked with directly and baptized.

As this case illustrates, working with the addicted Ego-in-conflict can 'quickly' allow the client and therapist to access a Rejected-self, in this case one with a shameful core of sexual feelings. I put 'quickly' in quotes because the actual disclosures can happen quickly once the Ego-in-conflict is addressed, but that is rarely done without considerable preparation. I worked with Belinda for a good six months before addressing her Ego-in-conflict. I closely monitored her AA program. We touched on and explored a great many issues involving her current life, extended family, and childhood. She had gone inside numerous times and was comfortable with the process. All of that takes time. As the Alchemists are wont to say: purification must precede transformation. If the addiction has been severe and clearly disabling, as was clearly the case for Belinda, the therapist must be sure the client has embarked on a program of recovery before working with an addicted Ego-in-conflict. Don't proceed until the client has learned to trust going inside by experiencing it, and is committed to the work. Every Ego-in-conflict works collusively with other primary selves who will sabotage therapy if the Ego-in-conflict's usefulness is threatened before their issues are addressed. Where the Ego-in-conflict must be addressed early on, the therapist needs to focus first on the collusive relationship between the Ego-in-conflict and primary self, which will generally be a Responsible primary self or Dominant self. Whichever it is, that self must be protected before approaching the Rejected-self.

The Rebel Variant

An Ego-in-conflict is the most problematic user of addictive behavior. However, there are ego-aspect variants that appear to use it for the same purpose. These variants are 'close cousins' to the Ego-in-conflict, and often work in tandem. Obviously, the most common variant is the socially acceptable behavior used in excess by a Dominant self. A less common variant is the Rebel.

Once the therapist is sensitized to the Rebel variant it is easy to identify. It is the stereotypic rebellious adolescent, though the image may be younger than adolescent. It is a self that defies parental authority in some way, sometimes openly and brashly, sometimes more subtly. Smoking is good example of the subtler; alcohol and drug abuse are examples of the more open and brash. The Rebel is most clearly defined by its stance against authority, less obvious in its use of addictions. For example, s/he may get drunk but not habitually. What makes the Rebel stand out is the client's compliance to cultural standards in most other regards. For example, one client, a nurse, was very responsible on the job, but smoked and drank off the job. The Rebel generally takes pride in defiance, hanging tough, standing up for self, etc.; but the behavior is generally circumscribed and not likely to jeopardize work or social position, and the overall effect is more self-destructive than anything else. Rebels tend to be argumentative and oppositional in therapy. Convincing a client to separate from a Rebel self can be difficult because the Rebel is generally vigilant in therapy and likely to take charge where its status is threatened. It is best if the therapist treats them as a kind of protector – which they are, and asks them to separate so the client and therapist can better appreciate whom they are protecting. As I have noted elsewhere, separation serves to objectify or personify a sense of self; it in no way diminishes it. If that self is dominant, then it will immediately reassert that dominance on leaving the office. Reminding a client of those facts will generally mollify a distrustful self. Finally, I would note that Rebels are most likely to be created when a Responsible primary self is too submissive toward a parental authority that is seen as flawed (e.g. an alcoholic parent).

Healing the Ego-in-conflict

The primary distinctions between an Ego-in-conflict and a Dominant self are as follows: The Ego-in-conflict engages in socially unacceptable behavior such as alcohol abuse and snorting cocaine. In that regard, it acts shamelessly, though that is not how it thinks of itself. Rather, it self-perceives as seeking a mind-altering sensation that has shown itself to be 'pleasurable and liberating.' Generally, it steps in when the socially acceptable behaviors used in excess by a Dominant self are insufficient for handling a current, potentially shaming stressor. I tend to treat the Ego-in-conflict as a Mirror aspect creation. It generally models the addictive behaviors of a parent or grandparent, which makes it most like a Mirror aspect.

Whenever an Ego-in-conflict is identified, it's healing must be addressed at some point in the process, since it is often a major source of accumulated toxic shame. The first step in the healing process is opening its intuition, which Christ is always asked to do as soon as possible. At some point, however, it will also need baptism, as it can feel shame and remorse for its actions once it is able to reflect on them. But unlike the Rejected-self this baptism must be voluntary. The need for baptism will only arise after the Rejected-self or repressed core have been baptized and freed of shame. At that point, the Ego-in-conflict is likely to express remorse or feel ashamed for its part in maintaining that status quo. Initially, it will have little awareness of the emotional shame it has obliged the Body to absorb. As the Ego-in-conflict becomes more reflective, it can be encouraged to ask Christ to release the Body's accumulated shame. Hopefully, before or during that release it will voluntarily forgo its power to act shamelessly in favor of Christ's discernment on how to address future conflict. In effect, it must fully open itself to Christ.

The Rejected-self

The Rejected-self can manifest in a variety of dissociated forms including various objectifications of the Dominant self's shameful core. What all of them share in common is bondage to shame and Christ's ability to liberate them baptismally. The most common form of a Rejected-self is the self-image, which can range in age from toddler to adult, though it is most often childlike in demeanor. It is most likely to be found in dark places, deep underground, in fetal positions, starving or similarly ego-dystonic. But significantly, it can also manifest as a dream image, especially a recurring dream image; or even as a self-image representing a past life. Most images of past lives are by no means shameful, but often those retrieved in therapy do come to the fore with shameful karmic burdens. Sometimes, both rejected and hubristic selves appear to be spiritually infested, which exaggerates their sense of shame or pride. All of these subtypes are illustrated throughout the chapter.

The Rejected-self is pivotal to the redemption of conscience because it alone willingly provides Christ access to the Voice-of-conscience channeled by parents. There can be more than one Rejected-self, but only the first one is needed to begin the process of terminating the parents' Moral authority and supplanting it with Christ's forgiveness and discernment. Once a Rejected-self is freed from the bondage of shame by baptism it can willingly allow Christ to terminate the parent's Moral authority and open itself to Christ's discernment. The Aware-ego can then approach any polar opposite and encourage it to reconcile with the Rejected-self by also opening to Christ's discernment *and forgiveness. In all likelihood this process will have to be repeated for several polarized sets of selves*, in addition to working with the ever-present Dominant selves. Those additional selves will spontaneously emerge over successive sessions.

Comparatively speaking, the baptism of a Rejected-self, the termination of parental authority by Christ, and a Rejected-self's opening to Christ's discernment and ongoing forgiveness, are the easy parts of the process. But nothing more can happen until those steps have been completed. The value in working first with an Ego-in-conflict, if present, is that it often provides direct access to a particularly problematical Rejected-self or shameful core as well as facilitating the early healing of this critical triumvirate. Also, any Dominant self collusively connected with an Ego-in-conflict is *less likely* to interfere with the process if it is begun from the perspective of an Ego-in-conflict and no immediate effort is made to change the Ego-in-conflict other than providing it access to its intuition. While focus is on other members of the triumvirate, a Dominant self can continue to look disdainfully upon the whole therapeutic endeavor. The Dominant self will not become deliberately figural until Christ is asked to enter the Heart and 'satisfy the insatiable.'

Shame and baptism appear to be covariant. With every baptism by Christ shame becomes less powerful. Today, in my clinical practice, I encourage my clients to ask Christ to baptize whenever a self appears in need. Most clients rarely name what they are feeling as shame. They use numerous synonyms which the therapist comes to recognize as shaming, e.g. disgust, disdain, low self-esteem, feelings of abandonment, hurt feelings, inadequacy, worthlessness, stupid, weak, unforgivable, despicable, etc. Whenever a self is described using a 'shame' word I encourage the client to permit Christ to baptize it, to fill it with the Holy Spirit and free it from that sense of shame. It is quickly done. Clients are encouraged to treat baptism as a recurrent event. Whenever in doubt ask Christ to baptize. The best indicator of its effectiveness will be the client's report of a felt change in the demeanor of the baptized self, which is always immediate. With every baptism shame becomes less powerful and Christ's role in the client's inner life becomes more central. Every baptism also weakens the power of the opposite self to dominate consciousness since it deprives it of the power to suppress the Rejected-self by treating it disdainfully (e.g. arrogantly, pridefully). Primary selves have other strategies for stymieing a Rejected-self – such as anger and detachment, but prideful disdain and disgust are the most pervasive.

There are at least five ways to bring a Rejected-self into consciousness. The first one is unbidden. The client goes inside guided by the therapist to look for the underpinnings of a problem behavior or situation, and what they unearth is a Rejected-self. Not surprisingly, this is most likely to happen as the therapy hour is drawing to a close. When this occurs it is best to immediately place that self under an opaqued dome so it will not overwhelm a primary self, whose fear of the Rejected-self can threaten the therapeutic process or motivate the cancellation of the next session. In addition, ask Christ to enter the dome and sit with it till the next session. Often, with those two interventions, the client will develop a kind of amnesia regarding this self until s/he returns and goes back inside, though as in the case of Belinda described above, there may be reflections that touch on it. When the client returns, be sure to focus on discovering any self that is threatened by the presence of the Rejected-self and address its issues first off.

A second way of identifying a Rejected-self is to explore dream images reported by the client that suggest the existence of a shamed self. I have always worked from the Gestalt Therapy premise that every aspect of a dream is a part of the self. If a dream reveals a part of the self that seems to function as a Rejected-self then the client can be instructed to re-enter the dream, contain that image, and begin working with it with it within the dream's perspective. It goes without saying that the client is always expected to enter the dream scenario with the *Light* and image of Christ.

At some point, however, the client must be encouraged to go inside for the specific purpose of unearthing and redeeming a Rejected-self. An addicted Ego-in-conflict is a common reason for many clients entering therapy. The only way to decisively attenuate its effects on the client's behavior is to contain the particular Ego-in-conflict and have it identify the Rejected-self or shameful core that necessitates its addictive activity. A fourth approach is past life regression. I use this rarely but it has proven effective in ameliorating persistent symptoms. It is described further on. The fifth approach is to directly seek out an early manifestation of the Rejected-self. Having the client *recall memories of early years in grade school* can do this. I describe that intervention later in the chapter.

THE IDEAL-SELF

The Ideal-self is an umbrella term for Ego manifestations that seek to preempt the shaming power of a Voice-of-conscience as distinct from merely fearing Temporal authority, which is the primary strategy of a Responsible primary-self. All Dominant selves and – most particularly – Ideal personas, personify the concept of an Ideal self. Originally, I reserved the term 'Ideal persona' for ego-aspects who perceived themselves as Christ-like. More recently, I have broadened the definition to include ego-aspects who acquire culturally sanctioned personas – such as tribal leader, priest/minister, bishop, judge, or doctor, which can further insulate them from shame.

The power to self-shame is only effective in hiding shameful actions not discerned by others. A Dominant self will use *prideful* strategies when others are the perceived threat. When shamefully exposed by or to another person, a Dominant self can feel *ashamed*. Most often it will react in a knee jerk manner. It will seek to stand disdainfully apart (pride) from the shaming or angrily attack whatever is shaming it if the other is a peer or perceived to be inferior; it is more likely to emotionally/physically withdraw if the person is perceived as superior. Later it can minimize the shaming by shaming itself and thereby hide all of the associated emotions within the Heart. Significantly, a Dominant self (and for that matter any self) can only hide shame in the dark recesses of its Heart; it cannot heal it. And over time it will continue to experience intimations of what is hidden without necessarily appreciating the original source or reasons. Pride and the power to self-shame are not solutions to the problem of shame, merely the most powerful defense available to an ego-aspect acting alone. When a client shares that s/he 'feels ashamed' or has 'felt ashamed' the therapist needs to focus on the issue *carefully and respectfully*, as the client is now speaking of a prideful self who *plays a dominant role* in the client's psyche. The first case below illustrates what can happen when a therapist moves forward too quickly, even for good reasons.

Illustrations of the Ideal-self

Below are two case examples of an Ideal-self. The second case illustrates its manifestation in a dream. Jung introduced active imagination into psychotherapy by encouraging his clients to use it as a means of working with dreams. The first case – Bracky, is a vivid example of an Ideal-self, but the same characteristics, somewhat muted, will be found in the Dominant selves of most clients. In this and the next chapter I will offer numerous examples of the Ideal-self.

Bracky. I had seen this 27-year-old client only six times when we began exploring the following glaring example of an Ideal-self. While this exploration is very telling it was also premature; Bracky stopped coming to therapy after being so revelatory.[25] The first several sessions were more of a counseling nature than therapy. I did have him go inside, learn to use the *Light* and evoke a Christ image. He scheduled the first session because of anger toward a girlfriend. However, he had all but broken off that relationship before coming to see me. Bracky is intelligent, attractive, very personable, charming almost to the point of charisma, and seemingly not ashamed to reflect on how he appears to himself and others. (He may come by it honestly; his mother is an actress and his father is in marketing.) He manages the branch office of a franchise company. Part of his anger stemmed from working too many hours, which was the primary focus of our early sessions.

Bracky no sooner ended his relationship with the first girlfriend then he met another and they fell quickly in love with each other. This new girlfriend lives in another state. Having spent two 'glorious' weeks with him she returned home. Two nights later he meets up with another girl and they seduce each other on the first date. I see him several days after that weekend. "She was wild. I felt naughty. Today I feel awful. It would not have happened if I had not been drinking." I sense a pattern here, a dangerous one insofar as he takes no precautions under these kind of circumstances. I suggest we go inside and meet 'Old Bracky' – what his peers call him when he is 'on the make.' Once he is separated from Old Bracky I ask him to observe the relationship between Old Bracky and Christ. "Old Bracky can't see Christ. Christ is observant of him. Old Bracky is caught up in the fun and convenience. It is not convenient to do Christ-like things. He can do Christ-like things when it is convenient; then he is open minded, considerate of others, wants to help others. *Then he is Regular Bracky.* Regular Bracky and Old Bracky overlap." I ask his attitude toward Christ when he feels like doing Christ-like things? "He accepts Christ, friendly toward him, a good guy to hang out with. He would like to be more Christ-like, more respectful of himself and others, think about the consequences of his actions, be less selfish. He understands other influences. The bible is not to be taken verbatim, but it is an excellent tool to live your life." I ask him who is Old Bracky's authority? "Old Bracky is his own authority. The counterpart is God Almighty who is with Regular Bracky." I ask how the two are different? "Regular Bracky has only a little charisma; Old Bracky is charisma to the wall. He does not need Christ dying on the cross for him (in response to another question I have asked). He is a power on to himself. He does OK on his own. He is not dependent on Christ for his strength and abilities – except when things go south. Then he meshes back with Regular Bracky who is willing to call on God for help." I note that the absence of feminine attention seems to activate Old Bracky. "Old Bracky did not come out till college. I finally got all the girls I wanted. I did not drink in High School. Old Bracky is strongest when there are men and women around, when he has an audience." I ask who is the opposite of Old Bracky? "The opposite is the guy who wants to be like my parents, my father." The session ends here. Bracky fails to keep his next appointment and does not call to reschedule.

Robert. This second example illustrates a dreamful encounter with an Ideal-self and Rejected-self. The dream is significant because it highlights a recurring theme in Robert's life – a continuing struggle between seeking a spiritual path and satisfying his aspirations for social and professional recognition. In real life he is an intelligent, attractive, well-married, skilled surgeon, who has devoted considerable time and effort to Jungian individuation. The dream he shares with me captures various aspects of the conflict between his shadow and Ideal persona, i.e. the Surgeon.

"I am in the inner sanctum of a research library. The head librarian shows me a blue folder. I knew it was important. It held the keys to everything, but I did not realize that at the time of the dream. He says I can have it. Next, I am part of a class learning how to use the library. Our goal is to find that blue folder. I believe I have an edge because I have at least seen it, though I did not appreciate its value at the time. I know it exists. Anthony is there. [In real life, Anthony is a fellow surgeon who has been forced to leave the group practice because of drug use.] I let Anthony follow me around. There is another guy in the room. He is young, very well built, unflappable, and always strong [the Ideal-self]. He has an inner strength that cannot be moved. I think he is gay, in the sense of being very self-absorbed. He says he is not moving. At first I think I am his equal. We joggle for position, but he is clearly stronger than me so I desist and apologize for trying to move him out of the way. Instead, I will work around him. I find 'the book of books.' It references all the other books. With it I can recreate the contents of the blue folder."

If this were a Jungian analysis, I would have Robert enter the dream as the dream body reporting the dream, and have that self enter into a dialogue with any of the images in the dream. Instead, I ask Robert to reenter the dream as his Aware-ego accompanied by Christ, who provides a frame of reference not afforded by an orthodox Jungian analysis. I have him begin by engaging the young man who has to be *worked around*. I tell Robert that this young man is probably the diametric opposite of Anthony, who undoubtedly carries Robert's shadow or Rejected-self. Robert is conversant with all of these concepts having worked with them before. Likewise, I note in passing a similarity between this strong self and an ego-aspect previously identified as the 'Surgeon,' who Robert has identified as an Ideal persona in previous sessions. The connection is easy to make because the young man stands in sharp contrast to Anthony, a 'fallen' surgeon.

I suggest to Robert that he give both Anthony and the young man a portion of his *Light*. Anthony takes his portion, but when the young man takes his it becomes a much larger *Light*. I ask Robert what he thinks this different proportion indicates? "That he is more aware, that he knows more. He symbolizes eternal youth. The knowledge is what makes him strong. He also has laughter, though he is not just fun. There is also a deep sense of calm." At this point I ask Robert to bring Anthony into the picture. How do the two relate when seen together? "The young self knows his way; Anthony has lost his way." What keeps them separate? "Me, the dream ego. In the dream I brought Anthony to this young guy, he followed me. Anthony is a reminder that I can always be lost." I ask if he can tell me the young man's relationship with Christ? "They know each other well. The young man was created to help me understand my true nature." Does he, I ask, consider himself Christ-like? "Yes. Christ is something I can personally comprehend now." I ask how the young man perceives Anthony? "He does not exist. He is *merely a symbol* of being lost." I ask if he can correct Anthony's sense of being lost? "No. He is around to remind me. I need Anthony to be lost in order for me to find myself." I ask what would it be like if Anthony could find himself? How might he do that? "He could go and feel the youth's strength. He would be transformed and disappear and reappear." I ask if the young man is ego? "No. He is part ego, capable of awareness, and part eternal (i.e. archetypal)." Now I have Robert focus more on his shadow, Anthony. I ask Robert if he can separate the part of himself projected into the image of Anthony? "I can see him. He has very limited awareness, basic awareness, unguided, unconnected. Definitely ego, lost ego." At this juncture I suggest to Robert that he allow Christ to baptize the lost-self extracted from Anthony. And when that is done he could then choose to identify with the young man or with Christ. "This baptized self feels the freedom to serve, be, live, listen, to be human. He has chosen to be open to Christ. He has the knowledge that he was created for a purpose, for experiences, and as a recipient of gifts from something greater than himself." He no longer has to be lost on behalf of the young man? "No."[26]

The above clinical notes are abbreviated. Even so, they seem to clearly convey the ego-inflation of 'the young man' and his need to keep 'Anthony' lost in order to elevate himself. The idea of being Christ-like is always a clear indication of ego-inflation. A Christ-like image has no need of Christ's salvation. But his inflation notwithstanding, he cannot transform Anthony except to make him 'disappear' and 'reappear.'

Christ-like self-images exercise tremendous power in shaping and defining clients. But those selves can only assume that stance by shaming their core, and perpetually risking a shameful descent. Robert struggles with his surgeon persona, which is a waking manifestation of the young man in the dream. Only by redeeming the shadow side of that Ideal-self can the therapist and client hope to loosen the Ideal persona's hubristic hold on the client and guide him away from catastrophe.

The above cases give an indication of the strength and entrenchment of the Ideal-self. Other examples will be given throughout the remainder of this chapter and the next. Most of the work in redeeming conscience requires focus on these Ideal selves, in their manifestation as Dominant selves and personas. The redemption of conscience is only possible when Ideal selves become willing to forego hubristic pride and the power to self-shame.

MEMORIES OF THE SEVENTH YEAR

Several developmental theorists, such as Lawrence Kohlberg,[27] Urie Bronfenbrenner,[28] and Jean Piaget,[29] have looked at the moral development of children and adults. Kohlberg, for example, speaks of the child's earliest development being the reward and punishment stage and then an exchange stage, e.g. I will scratch your back if you scratch mine. By the time children enter elementary school they are seen to function at the conventional morality stage (good and bad). Interestingly, this is seen by Kohlberg to be the functioning level of most adults as well, though he can identify three further stages. In this section, I want to explore this consolidation of conventional morality by age seven, give or take a year. The Roman Catholic Church calls this the 'age of reason' whereupon, having acquired an internalized knowledge of right and wrong, children are able to confess their sins and seek penance and absolution, and then allowed to receive their first communion. At this age they are seen to feel the pangs of conscience for doing, or merely thinking, the wrong. It is during this time – between the ages of six and eight, that one or more Dominant selves also begin to develop. Until then, the Rejected-self exists as a distinct entity unclouded, as it were, by the overlay of Dominant selves. In fact, it is relatively easy to identify this early manifestation of the Rejected-self by focusing on this childhood period of development. The most direct approach is sensitive questioning of clients about how they saw themselves in the early grades of elementary school.

The prototypic Rejected-self comes into being well before age seven but is often 'crystallized' in the social context of parental surrogates and other children. Whatever its origin, most clients can recover memories of feeling the pangs of conscience in a well-remembered episode or sense of self. Generally, when I make inquiries about these memories, I preface my questions, by remarking that this is the period of life when the individual develops a conscience, and then ask them if they can recall early experiences of their conscience. I am rarely more specific. This seems sufficient to direct the client's free ranging recall of those early years. (Significantly, early experiences of feeling ashamed are rarely forgotten.) For my part, I listen carefully for images and events suggesting the presence of a Rejected-self. When discerned, I have the client focus on that sense of self or event. If the client is already inside I suggest that s/he have Christ contain the relevant self-image. If the client and I are simply talking, I generally suggest s/he go inside. It goes without saying that this type of work is only done when the client is comfortable going inside and working with the Christ image, and has accepted the idea that Christ can perform interior baptisms. The following case examples serve to illustrate the process as well as the kind of images that emerge. These case notes do not describe the whole process, only the part where Christ is working with Rejected-self.

Miranda. I have worked with Miranda and various members of her family over the years. Her husband died about six years ago. Despite everything she has shared with me, she still has difficulty trusting me enough to do more than glance inside while her eyes remain open. If I had to give her a diagnosis, it would be atypical Dissociative Disorder with strong paranoid features. So far as I can determine, Miranda's paranoia is a concerted effort to avoid further abusive and often irrational punishments suffered in childhood. The paranoid self does this by fixing the blame outside of the self. The problem with this strategy is several fold. One, it leaves the self powerless to effect change except for fixing blame; two, it isolates the self by keeping it ever vigilant against external threats; and finally, as in the case of conflict with her daughter described below, it generally evokes a mirror response. *Fixing the blame* is often done with angry tirades or critical comments toward someone who has acted wrongly in a situation, in the opinion of the paranoid self. Fixing the blame seeks to insure that the paranoid self is not accused of whatever the other person has done. In Miranda's case, the other person is her daughter who messes up the house that Miranda keeps conscientiously clean. Very likely, the daughter is also a carrier of the part of Miranda that did 'mess up.'

In past years Miranda's paranoid self was often dominant in therapy and her daily life. It can still come out, but is far less dominant as a result of extensive work. In this session Miranda begins by complaining about her young, pregnant, unmarried, daughter, a slow learner who is living in Miranda's house, and will probably be financially and emotionally dependent on her mother for some years to come. In short, the daughter is a perfect vessel for the Miranda's, projected, disowned parts. Miranda describes her daughter as blunt and abrasive toward her despite all she does for her. I trust her description is accurate since the daughter is very likely coping with her mother's attacks by mirroring her. Miranda and I both know that other family members would describe Miranda as equally blunt and abrasive on occasion. And even as she continues to berate her daughter, Miranda can also admit she acted the same way toward her husband when he was alive. "Anything I said was not heard – null and void. Then I got spiteful – like my daughter. If I died she would see. I feel worthless, I am hurt too." I ask if she had these feelings growing up. I know her mother and sisters did not treat her well. "It has always been that way with family members, my mother and sisters. Nothing I said was important. Nothing I said carried any weight, it was like speaking into the air." I suggest she go inside, see her self at age seven, eight, or nine, feeling worthless, unheard. Miranda reports an image of herself feeling that way. I immediately have her ask Christ to baptize the image and see herself able to speak up. Next, I suggest that she let Christ terminate the parental authority that kept her 'unheard.' That is done, but then Miranda reports she is still pissed off, which I interpret to mean that a new sense of self is threatened. Even so, I keep her focused on the Seven-year-old and ask her to let that self open to Christ's power of discernment if she is willing. That done, Miranda then observes that, "My daughter acts victimized all of the time," meaning like the self Christ has just redeemed. I suggest that she have Christ place her deceased husband in a circle. Initially, my thought is to have Christ terminate her husband's authority over her daughter, but instead I am moved to suggest that she ask Christ to baptize him, his soul. So I say, " Let Christ release John from his shame." (Her deceased husband provided well for the family. But he was a workaholic who also ate and drank too much, was rageful, and died young of a heart attack. The family – especially his stepdaughters, were not greatly saddened by his loss since they were often the brunt of his anger.) When she sees Christ baptize her deceased husband, her first comment is "I can finally do something for him." Now a new part of her emerges expressing shame for her own addictive behavior. I suspect this is the part that has kept her angry even after the redemption of her Seven-year-old self. The addictive self used tranquilizers when Miranda's children were young; she finally had to go into a mental institution for detox. This new self is an Ego-in-conflict. She feels ashamed of her behavior, though it never stopped her from doing it. I suggest that this Ego-in-conflict can also receive baptism from Christ. When I sense this is done I ask how she is feeling? "It is love. Unconditional." The following week Miranda comes in feeling optimistic about her circumstances. Things are going very well for her and her daughter and the newborn grandchild. In fact, she has almost nothing to complain about despite everything that is going on in her extended family and work schedule, which is good because I am planning to leave on a two-week vacation.

I have rarely done so many interventions in such a short time as I did with Miranda. Unearthing the Seven-year-old seems to have been pivotal – along with many years of 'preparatory' work. The request to envision a Seven-year-old was injected in the midst of teasing out a projection. I had already worked with Miranda and her numerous projections, so she 'knew' where I was going almost from the beginning. Likewise, I had spent many therapy hours getting her involved with 12-step groups (AA and Alanon) in response to her recurrent use of drugs and alcohol during periods of stress. My biggest hurdle was her very limited willingness to go inside. Mostly, I had to 'guess' what was going on because she would report on so little, what with her focus divided between keeping me in her line of sight and whatever was happening inside. (After the session just described she was far more willing to go inside with her eyes closed!) There were two unexpected interventions in this session that I would like to emphasize. The first was my request to have Christ baptize her deceased husband. This was actually the first time I used this intervention, i.e. asking Christ to baptize the image of another, but I have since found it to be very useful in working with any 'image of the deceased' whose behavior in life has shamed a client. This kind of baptism is really a profound kind of forgiveness and a partial redemption of the client's masculine or feminine aspect. It implicitly recognizes that the 'shamer' was also shamed, and equally in need of God's grace. Today, wherever possible, I encourage clients to release their shaming parents from the shame that made them so wounding, though only after the Rejected-self has been baptized and the parents authority has been terminated.

The second observation I want to highlight is the spontaneous emergence of an Ego-in-conflict on the heels of Christ's redemption of a Rejected-self and baptism of her deceased husband. Shame leaves the Rejected-self all but paralyzed except when periodically released by the actions of an Ego-in-conflict. An Ego-in-conflict can act shamelessly as long as it is seeking to restore physical homeostasis through addictive desire. Feeling ashamed after the fact is rare, though the acting out can leave the self feeling guilty and remorseful. That was the case for Miranda. Having seen her Seven-year-old redeemed, and having forgiven her deceased husband, she became aware of her own role as a mother. What she recalls is her own abuse of drugs while raising her children. If the Ego-in-conflict feels unworthy of the baptism, then the therapist can have the client's Aware-ego ask on its behalf. But whoever asks, Christ's response will be quick and with visible effect.

Leigh. At the time of this intervention, I was seeing Leigh every other week. She is a single parent who works in the financial sector. In the previous sessions we have worked with two selves that were literally driving her to a mental and/or physical breakdown. She comes in reflecting on the last session and the intervening period. At the end of the last session she had a powerful insight, wrote it down, but did not want to share it with me. She hints at it in the beginning of this session. "Last time I got it. Christ does a better job. While I bitched about opening to him, I was able to finally do it. It bothered me that I had all of that physical stuff kicked up over the past months and had to take off so much time (a surgery that forced her to rest somewhat). Even so, I took off two more days since I last saw you. When I went back to work I could focus. I felt a shift; I feel more centered and no longer feel I am shortchanging my daughter." Since she is doing so well I decide to have her focus on memories of around age seven that might reflect the development of her conscience. "We lived in a very exclusive neighborhood. Another girl and I stole tomatoes and detergent and put them on someone's driveway. I was the instigator. She got in a lot of trouble. *I remember playing in the dirt and having suicidal thoughts*. I was a little thief; I stole candy daily from the corner store. I was a fat kid. I can remember trying to buy friendships. I was eating to fill an emotional hole." At this point I stop her free association and have her contain the sense of self that had the 'suicidal thoughts.' Then I ask her to determine, if she can, what was prompting those thoughts in this seven-year-old self. "Loneliness and not feeling valued. I see a picture of myself eating cold spaghetti out of the ice box. Not cherished or cared for." I suggest that she allow Christ to enter the circle and baptize this image. (We have done this before in other contexts so the idea is not new to her, but even so she balks at first.) "The Seven-year-old is not comfortable. She is afraid of the tall male stranger. (Leigh's father physically terrorized Leigh, her siblings, and mother, emotionally and sexually.) Now Leigh tells me that, "The image I have of her is *covered in brown*." I suggest that the part of her holding her *Light* enter the circle where the little girl is and bring her out of it. When she does this the brown blob is separated from the little girl. I tell her the brown blob is 'negative emotion' that attached to the little girl and suggest that she allow Christ to dissolve it into pure white light using his *Light*. He does this immediately and without any fanfare. Next I suggest that she can baptize the little girl using a portion of Christ's *Light* and the words, "I baptize you in the name of the creator, redeemer and sustainer." "It feels really good. She is happy." Can you and Christ approach her now without her being fearful? "Yes."

What this case illustrates is how quickly a free-associative approach can unearth a significant image of the Rejected-self. It also highlights that someone other than Christ can baptize in his name, using his Light; and have the same effect one might expect if Christ baptized her. Obviously, his role in this sequence was not minimal. He did remove the brown blob and share his *Light*.

Martin. Martin is a married male, with grown children, who has been seeing me every other week for two years. We have dealt with a great many issues that originally brought him into therapy. Since nothing is pressing in this session I suggest we examine his conscience in terms of memories of his early life. Martin had a strict religious upbringing in that his parents and grandparents were pillars of a mainline church and attended weekly services religiously. Over the years, he and his wife have continued that tradition. I simply suggest that when he goes inside and finds his *Light*, he can just begin by sharing whatever comes to mind regarding his conscience and early school years. I might note here that Martin has already shared his most shameful secrets as an adult. I would not pose such a question to a new client, or one that has not come to trust me. On going inside, Martin immediately starts free-associating: "I remember shoplifting in second grade. I hid what I stole in my drawer. My mother found it and made me take it back. I felt very *ashamed* giving it back. I started shoplifting again as a teenager. In 5th grade my father pushed me to join the Little League. I was fat then and got a lot of ribbing. I remember kissing a girl in 2nd grade behind a rock. I must have known it was wrong somehow, but felt excited at the same time. I was never spanked. I was made to feel ashamed of my big head, glasses, and flat feet." At this point I ask him to go back to the first shoplifting incident. "I was eight years old. I stole a penlight. I felt a need to hide the wrongness. I got scared after taking it. I knew I had done something wrong. Later, as a teenager, I got a thrill out of doing something wrong like shoplifting." I ask who defines 'wrong?' "My grandparents, parents, Sunday school nursery. Remember, I was in church every Sunday since a toddler, sitting right next to my parents and grandparents when I got too old for the Nursery. But I was also disgusted by my mother's drinking (alcoholically)." I ask if he hid things like his mother tried to hide her drinking? "I hid porno magazines, and I hid my using them to masturbate since I was a small child, and the thefts. I'm still hiding." I suggest that we identify the part of him that is still hiding, the part that wants to have sex with men (an issue that brought him to therapy). He quickly goes back inside and separates from the Hider. "It is an image of me hiding my erection while playing with myself in bed." I suggest he allow Christ to enter the bedroom and baptize this part of him. At the same time I ask whom he was hiding the erection from? "My younger brothers and my parents." I suggest that once Christ baptizes this part he then ask that part to let Christ terminate the parent's power to judge his erection as shameful. Next, I suggest that he also ask Christ to terminate the grandparents' authority, especially, the paternal grandmother. Finally, I suggest that the six year old open to the power of Christ's discernment. Martin finishes with the comment that he has seen all of this happen.

The significance of this intervention is that Martin has for many years been a self-employed professional who has under-functioned, secretly used marijuana on a daily basis, and had secret affairs with other men. The Hider is clearly a Rejected-self whose sexuality significantly shaped his life. I do not see Martin again for three weeks. He comes in to report that he has slipped on marijuana. He has taken all the right steps to rectify the situation vis-à-vis 'AA protocol,' but clearly something has been stirred up. He has acted 'very responsibly' in other respects and was quick to make amends where needed. I have him go inside, and identify the 'pot smoker,' which he describes as an 18 year old. In turn, this Ego-in-conflict quickly identifies the 'Responsible Family Man' vs. the 'Creative Artist.' This conflict is resolved over several sessions. Martin has become very productive since then.

Memories of the seventh year and working with an Ego-in-conflict are two of the best ways I have found for identifying the Rejected-self. Usually, the Rejected-self first identified by these interventions is the tip of the iceberg. That is, as the Rejected-self is unearthed and successfully reconciled, the Dominant self will emerge. That is a fairly predictable consequence of uncovering a Rejected-self. The Dominant self will quickly come to the foreground and challenge the whole process, or provoke an Ego-in-conflict to create a crisis, as in the case of Martin. The therapist needs to become sensitive to this probability and be prepared to address it. In a later section I give several examples of this shift and how to address it.

BAPTISM, CHRIST'S DISCERNMENT, AND THE ACCEPTANCE OF HIS RECONCILING POWERS

Once a Rejected-self is identified and baptized, it can ask Christ to terminate the parental authority that placed it in perpetual bondage. The client must be made aware of this possibility by the therapist and prompted to act through the Aware-ego. The process of redeeming conscience now requires that Christ begin assuming the function of conscience. That is formally begun when the Rejected-self willingly opens to Christ's power of discernment. As I explain it to clients, discernment is a gift of the Holy Spirit, which allows them to distinguish 'good spirits' from 'bad spirits.' It is an internal guidance providing them a way forward through the world: move toward this, avoid that. Discernment is intended to supplant the shaming directives of the aural Voice-of-conscience as well as the power of self-shame exercised by a Dominant self. Shame can only stop ongoing activity; it has no directional power beyond painfully stopping whatever we are doing.

The Rejected-self knows from the outset that its salvation is clearly with Christ and will not hesitate to let him function as his or her Voice for God, i.e. redeemed conscience. But in sharp contrast, the primary opposite of a Rejected-self invariably balks at the idea of giving up *fearful or prideful* self-sufficiency in favor of Christ's discerning power. Even so, it is a fear previously sustained by the ongoing angst of a Rejected-self. As Christ significantly alters those dynamics, the fearful avoidance exercised by the primary opposite really becomes unnecessary. With gentle persuasion these primary selves can be made aware of the self-imposed constrictions on their movement and become open to reconciliation.

In sum, to begin work with a Dominant self, Christ must first baptize a Rejected-self, terminate the parent's Moral authority, provide the Rejected-self with the power of his discernment, and reconcile the Rejected-self with his or her primary opposite, which is generally an avoidant self rather than a Dominant self. While these steps in themselves are insufficient for the redemption of conscience, they become the model of what Dominant selves can experience once they become willing. The presumption here is that an Ideal-self has no reason to even contemplate forgoing its power to self-shame until a dissociated self has experienced the first four steps.

I have found it helpful to ritualize the act of opening to Christ's power of discernment. Basically, every self is asked to express its willingness by standing in front of Christ, allowing Christ to penetrate his or her brow chakra and leave the *Light* of his discernment in the center of the brain. Explicit willingness is most easily expressed by asking the self to divide the *Light* and hold the arms open. Christ uses his fingers to penetrate the brow, opening a direct channel or conduit between him and the self. The ritual is the same for a Dominant self with the notable addition that a Dominant self must first relinquish its power to self-shame, which can be done during the same act of penetration. (Any self exercising a power that would directly conflict with Christ's discernment, such as denial, is also asked to relinquish during such a ritual.) Once a pair of selves has opened to Christ's power of discernment, Christ can then offer the two selves a reconnection ritual, if they have not simply merged into one self as a result of the their shared connection with him. What needs to be stressed about these two rituals is the free will exercised by the selves. The rituals are only enacted when a self expresses explicit willingness for Christ to instill the power of his discernment, which is also the power of the Holy Spirit.

In preparing clients to receive Christ's discernment, I also emphasize that discernment in no way preempts a client's free will. An ego-aspect can ignore such promptings even after accepting the gift. It may take an ego-aspect some time to appreciate the unerring value of the gift. But that is what life's lessons are for. In any case, Christ's promptings are nearly impossible to hear while the ego-aspect exercises the power of self-shame or other defenses such as denial, so relinquishing those powers is a necessary prerequisite.

Once a pair of opposite selves has accepted Christ's gift of discernment, all ego-aspects will – thereafter – fall into one of two categories: willfully self-sufficient or willingly open to Christ's discernment and grace. In effect, the successful execution of this ritual by any dyad defines a clear point of demarcation. Those selves that choose Christ's discernment and forgiveness are said to come under Christ's grace; those that choose to remain self-sufficient remain subject to the law.

When I first developed the above interventions, I imagined that accepting Christ's grace and discernment was tantamount to a client accepting Christ as his or her higher power. But in fact, most clients continue to envision 'God the Father' as their higher power even after accepting Christ as their 'Voice for God.' Their sense of 'God the Father' is inculcated at such a young and unreflective age that it will persist indefinitely unless consciously challenged. And quite often, that sense of God also keeps the individual bound to the law. That is why I make a distinction between 'opening to Christ' and the individual's 'acceptance of Christ as their higher power.' In the rituals described above, the client is only asked to open to Christ's discernment and willingness to channel the Holy Spirit on the client's behalf. I address the issue of 'God the Father' at length in Appendix II: Who Is Your Higher Power?

The Law Vs. Grace

The concept of law vs. grace is a vital part of Christian theology as defined by St. Paul in his Letter to the Galatians.[30] While an ego-aspect remains self-sufficient, its emotional expression is generally limited to the pride-shame axis, which automatically subjects it to the unforgiving judgment of the law. To a lesser extent, the unconscious acceptance of 'God the Father' as his or her higher power also continues to subject the client to the law. Only "in Christ" can the law's judgment be redeemed by grace. What this means, emotionally, is that only 'in Christ' does the Ego gain access to the full range of Soul emotions, e.g. willingness, acceptance, discernment, forgiveness, love, etc., as exercised by the Light and Christ channeling the Holy Spirit. This distinction is hard to appreciate because most people, most of time, function under the law, as distinct from grace. Culturally speaking, the law surrounds us and shapes our thinking. We continue to live in cultures that perpetuate the myth of redemptive violence: the righteousness of an "eye for an eye," the belief that 'righteous' anger can defeat 'evil' anger. Despite the dawning of a new era two thousand years ago, our societies have continued to live with beliefs that inculcate emotional shame, fear, greed, anger, and pride. We give lip service to love; we live in fear. Only when an ego-aspect willingly accepts Christ's grace can it work free of this impasse.

Paul made much of the distinction between the law and grace, as did the Gnostics who quoted him at length.[31] From Paul's perspective the law was to be valued only insofar as it led us to grace. To quote Barclay, an orthodox theologian:

> The law has its own place in the scheme of things. First, it tells us what sin is. If there is no law, we cannot break it and there can be no such thing as sin. Second, and most important, the law really drives us to the grace of God. The trouble about the law is that, because we are all sinful, we can never keep it perfectly. Its effect, therefore, is to show us our weakness and to drive us to a despair in which we see that there is nothing left but to throw ourselves on the mercy and the love of God. The law convinces us of our own insufficiency and in the end compels us to admit that the only thing that can save us is the grace of God. In other words, the law is an essential stage on the way to that grace.[32]...It was the function of the law to bring men and women to Christ by showing them that by themselves they were quite unable to keep it. But, once people had come to Christ, they no longer needed the law, for now they were dependent not on the law but on grace.[33]

St. Paul considered the law to be weak and poverty-stricken. "It is weak because it is helpless. It can define sin. It can convict a person of sin; but it can find neither forgiveness for past sin nor strength to conquer future sin...It is poverty-stricken in comparison with the splendor of grace."[34] The law, as St. Paul used the term, is clearly manifest in the functioning of an unredeemed conscience. The Voice-of-conscience – personified by parents and the ego-aspects emulating them – can shame, but is unable to forgive. Many people, reading Galatians for the first time, tend to think of 'the law' as Jewish Mosaic law, and certainly there are parallels. But the law seems best defined as the Ego functioning apart from grace, emotionally yoked to the pride-shame axis.

An Early Case Example

It is hopefully clear by now that the redemption of conscience is never accomplished in one or two sessions. It is an arduous process, for client and therapist alike, that can extend over weeks and months. Any therapist who endeavors to facilitate this process is advised to keep detailed notes so s/he can pick up wherever the client leaves off. A client can often be absent for weeks at a time for any number of good reasons. The greatest resistance will be found in Dominant selves that are fearful of giving up their power to self-shame. Be patient. Trust the process. My role as therapist is to facilitate the client's discovery of Christ and provide a therapeutic space for them to work together. The flow of treatment can range widely. Today, I may address a disturbing dream image; next week focus on Moral authority; and the week after focus on a physical complaint. The common thread is the client's growing relationship with Christ and the particular symptoms Christ is asked to address each time we meet.

Monica. Monica was one of my earliest clients to work through the initial steps for redeeming conscience. She does so *before I came to discern the near universal existence of Dominant selves*. In this series of sessions, Christ seems to work through Monica, teaching us both how to proceed. The Comparisor – described below, may be a Dominant self, but I cannot conclude that with any certainty. At the time, I lacked awareness of Dominant selves, so conceptually I imagined the Comparisor as part of a dissociative dynamic. Monica, for her part, attributes a strong archetypal quality to the Comparisor throughout the sessions. But whatever the Comparisor's true identity, Monica's Christ will bring the process to fruition. The following case notes cover a period of some four months punctuated by eight sessions. (Another several months would be needed to enter and redeem the Heart.) In the session before the first of these eight, Monica identifies a *feeling of dread* that regardless of what she does, *a voice inside will find her wanting*. This voice has been with her for as long as she can remember. We begin this session by examining that sense of dread in some detail. Monica quickly labels this voice the Comparisor. She asserts that, "The Comparisor always compares me to others. I can hardly ever be better than they are. Nothing could happen to me that would remove this self-doubt. I can't control this voice." Monica's conviction of powerlessness notwithstanding, I suggest she go inside and let Christ use concentric circles to help her separate from this part of her. Once this is done she begins to describe her: "She is bigger than me, more authority, I feel diminished in her presence. She is meaner than me. She definitely does not like being separated. Christ has his robe around me. He is also bigger than me. I am almost a child. Maybe, I do not feel safe without her. She is like a shield." I ask Monica if the Comparisor is aware that her actions diminish you (the younger self that has emerged to speak for Monica)? "She is a bully. I have no power to stop her." I ask how the Comparisor exercises her power? "She sends mental images to provoke envy, 'you would be happier if…' She has the power to define happiness and ruin what I am happy about. She is never content with who I am." At this point I suggest that Monica separate from the part of her that is perpetually diminished by the Comparisor. She does so and then describes it. "The diminished part is like a ghost, grayish-blue, a shadowy figure, almost transparent. So powerless. Zero success. She steps next to Christ. He gives her a *Light*." I suggest that she let Christ forge a connection between this self and Christ. "He is touching her forehead. She is still ghost like." We are over time; I am obliged to end the session here.

I need to preface this next session by noting that Monica often visualizes Christ and other selves in the chancel of her church. Just about all of her visualizations during this period appear to take place in the chancel. I begin the next session by asking Monica to again focus on the Comparisor. Without formally going inside she begins to describe her. "She looks like a woman principal, older, not pretty, always undermining by comparing. I also see the ghost figure; it is like my soul. The Rebel is smoking behind the pulpit." (Earlier in therapy a lot of work was done with a Rebel part, an Ego-in-conflict variant. In this session she spontaneously emerges along with the ghost-like image and Comparisor.) At this point, I suggest that Monica go inside and find her Light. "I am standing next to Christ. He is looking at the Comparisor. Next to me is the grayish-blue ghost figure that I am thinking is like my soul. I understand now that the Comparisor has truncated my soul's development. Christ goes to the Sacristy light, uses it to light a candle and places it into the Comparisor's Heart. *She crumples forward*. The grayish-blue ghost figure is getting less gray."

I am frankly baffled by what Monica has just reported. Christ appears to have brought the Comparisor to some awareness that crumples her forward. (Later, I come to understand this action by Christ as a purification of the Comparisor's heart chakra, or the traditional 'quickening' of conscience. Apparently, Christ has accomplished this by drawing heavily on Monica's understanding of Eucharistic symbology.) In retrospect, I am surprised that I do not address this rather dramatic and unsolicited intervention by Christ. Instead, I have Monica focus on the Ghost self. I have her ask Christ to give this grayish figure a portion of Monica's *Light*. "She reaches out for it." I suggest that Monica let Christ baptize her. "It reminds me of Ash Wednesday. The Ghost figure responds to the baptism by turning lighter and much more animated." We end the session here.

Monica cancels the next session because she is ill. She continues to visualize while bedridden, and reports this when she returns. Monica now imagines the Ghost figure is her 'soul.' She now sees it as quite animated, and dancing in the chancel. She describes Christ at this point as bigger than life size. Monica reports that during her illness she wanted attention. While meditating, she saw an angel, felt immense love, and had the realization that everything you really need is inside. Monica comes to this session convinced that the Comparisor is her enemy; that she 'killed' her mother (who died of alcoholism). (Indeed, the Comparisor – whether archetypal or a Dominant self, has striven to preempt and emulate the mother's aural Voice-of-conscience; but at the time of these sessions I have yet to appreciate the existence of Dominant selves, and so continue to treat the Comparisor as a dissociated aspect.) Now Monica switches her train of thought and tells me of the illness that required her to cancel the previous week's session: "My illness is in my stomach, but it is not a stomach virus. The Doctor cannot explain it, but prescribes antibiotics." I take an intuitive leap at this point and suggest that some other self does not want the Comparisor back in charge and their conflict is creating the stomach pain. Only later do I surmise that Christ has weakened the Comparisor's ability to shame other images when he placed the candle in her heart; and he likewise weakened her ability to repress the Ghost figure when he baptized that image. But the Comparisor has persisted in her efforts to shame and that is what has aggravated the abdominal chakra. In any case, another self is now challenging Comparisor's control as a result of these altered dynamics. This becomes clear when, in response to a question put to him, Christ identifies the 'source' of the stomach pain as the ghost-like image that is now actively resisting the Comparisor's effort to repress her. I suggest to Monica that she let Christ help her separate from whoever is supportively resisting the Comparisor. Monica identifies that part as "Me," so I suggest that she separate from Me so we can learn of her concerns. Once separated, Monica reports that, "Me is fearful of the Comparisor, and for good reason. She has been tormenting Me for 55 years and Me is not interested in rehabilitating her." (Monica is well aware of my penchant for having Christ forgive and heal any self identified in therapy!) I ask, who is Me? "She is the original version of my soul, the ghost figure." What, I ask, is *your* relationship with the Comparisor? (Note here that I have begun speaking directly to Me.) "I have been tormented by her for never measuring up." I ask Me if she would be willing to place herself under Christ's authority? Monica answers for her, "She does not like the word authority. She does not like judgment." [35] So instead, I suggest to Monica that she let Christ baptize Me. Monica envisions Christ taking her to the church's baptismal font and baptizing by sprinkling water. "He has baptized her. She becomes more flexible and happier. Playful. She is shaking the water off of her hair. Her hair is straight whereas mine has always been curly." Next, I suggest that, if Me is willing, she can ask Christ to terminate the authority in her parents that compared her to others and always found her wanting. She asks Christ to do this and then Monica reports that afterward her parents appear much smaller than Me. I end the session here.

Today, I might identify 'Me' as a reconstituted manifestation of Monica's Familial personality, since she is difficult to personify except as a ghost-like figure. In the above session I initially treat her as an unredeemed Rejected-self. But an unbaptized Rejected-self would never be strong enough to speak in the first person or reject the imposition of authority. Significantly, she is nonetheless 'open' to baptism, which transforms her. In addition, she gives Christ permission to terminate the parents' Moral authority.

In the next session, I begin by discussing the need for both the Comparisor and Rebel to accept Christ in order to be reconciled with Me. At this point in my thinking, I have yet to make the distinction between accepting Christ as a higher power vs. accepting his discernment; but even so, as I might have expected, the Rebel is defiant at the idea of accepting any authority. The Comparisor, for her part, is now dressed in a Battle Ax shirt. I suggest they begin by letting Christ take them both to the ocean where they can at least release their fear of acceptance. "They are each standing in the water. The fear is flowing out of their hearts and floating toward Christ. It is like dry ice smoking. He is placing his robe over the fear, which makes it balloon up. He turns around and puts the bubble underneath the water. Now the Comparisor and Rebel are frolicking together. Before they were suspicious of each other. All of sudden the bubble Christ was holding under the water went up in the air. Christ pulls it back down, unties some kind of knot and it dissolves into the water." I ask if there is any fear in Me? "Yes. Now she jumps into Christ arms. She is only a child. Christ kisses her chest, squeezes her, and the fear comes up out of her like a burp. All there is now are the two women in the cove swimming together in their clothes while Christ and the child watch." I ask if the clothes represent more fear? "No, it is just their costumes. They are not bothering them." I ask if they are aware they can let go of their costumes? But no one answers and I do not pursue it. The session ends here. (The costumes are significant in the case of the Comparisor. Basically, they represent her continuing power to self-shame, though I do not appreciate this as yet. But at least the fear of each other has been released.)

I do not see Monica again for two weeks. When she returns other issues are pressing her and must be addressed. And then I do not see her for another two weeks. This time she reports that when she looks inside she sees the Comparisor throwing rocks at her (sic) shaming her. I discuss the process of redeeming conscience with Monica. I explain that while she has terminated parental authority, all the selves that withhold their acceptance of Christ as their higher power remain 'under the law,' since the law originally shaped them. The Comparisor's actions are most likely the Comparisor's futile attempt to regain control of Me. I suggest that it is time for Me to accept Christ. Monica goes inside and Me opens to Christ. "Now Me is approaching the Comparisor, who is no longer throwing any rocks. The Comparisor realizes she is in the presence of a higher power and she is being differential toward Christ. "But," Monica says, "I am suspicious. The Comparisor is a night person; that is when she has been the most active." I suggest that she simply ask Christ to shield Me at night. The session ends here.

The following week Monica claims that nothing much as happened inside. Everyone is about the same. But she does have a dream she very much wants to share with me. "A man has fallen in love with me. He is Jewish. I am full of love and peace. My husband does not object to this. He is smooth faced with blond hair. He has fallen in love with me and I with him." I am thinking this dream is a 'god send.' It appears to reflect the altered relationship between Christ and Me. But I make no effort to interpret the dream. Instead, I encourage Monica to go inside. Almost immediately, Me is seen by Monica to approach the Comparisor and remove her Battle Ax shirt. "Now everyone is animated but Christ. His body is misty and vague, while the others are clear. It is helpful to see the Rebel and Comparisor so clearly." I ask Monica what is the relationship between Me and Christ? "Me is loved by Christ; the Rebel seems willing to reconcile with him. I think the Rebel is secretly an agent of Christ. There is still tension between the Comparisor and Christ. The Comparisor is an agent of culture and the gods of success; but her power was weakened when the parents' Moral authority was terminated." Then, almost as an aside, Monica remarks that, "I have never had a dream like the dream I shared with you today." I suggest that she give the Rebel a portion of her *Light*, if she does not already have one. Then, if she is willing, she can open to Christ by holding the *Light* to her brow. "She is willing. Christ has put his hand on her forehead." Can you sense any difference? "She wants to walk over with Christ to stand beside Me, but the Comparisor is resisting." The session ends here.

As the next session begins, I am aware of the Rebel's desire to shift her allegiance, but rather than broach it I simply suggest that Monica go inside and separate from whoever is merged with the Aware-ego. I am not sure it was just the Comparisor who resisted the Rebel's switching alliances. She separates using concentric circles. "This self looks like a patch of light in a dark space. I use to be called Patch. She is a person who looks like me, *my age*." I suggest to Monica that quite often this part may function as her. I am not quite sure why I say this. I reason it from the image's age and seemingly diminutive stature, which reminds me of an adult version of the Me. (This new self is very likely Monica's personality, but I have yet to appreciate that dynamic.) I ask her what is Patch's relationship to Christ? "She looks up at him, she is less wary of him than Me. She is bolder with the Comparisor, who is sitting on the floor with her back to the Lectern. The Comparisor knows that changes are being made that will lessen her power. Her power is cultural, the world, material things. Patch has power too." I take this opportunity to better understand the nature of Patch by asking what it was she was shamed for having? "The power to stand apart from culture. But her fear of others kept her from exercising it." What, I ask, is her secret? "Hard to tell." I suggest that Christ open up Patch's throat chakra and empower her to speak. If she is willing for him to do it she can hold her *Light* to her throat. "She has the *Light* to her throat. Everyone is quiet. Now Christ picks her up and holds her compassionately. She is the part that could most feel love and tenderness; she is the one who is vulnerable to the feelings of others toward her. She can know hurt as well as love. She has hidden from the hurt. She is lacking strength." This session ends with a question: what does she need to be strong?

(I need to make an aside here. Much of what is transpiring above will take me several years to appreciate. Patch is very much akin to the self most closely attuned to the totality of Self. Christ is revealing through Monica the entire process of redeeming conscience and *the Familial personality*. But as one of my mentors said: "The client will tell you everything in the first 30 minutes of the first session. But it will take you six months to figure out what s/he told you. In my case it would take several years, and by then I had been practicing nearly 40 years!)

The following week, Monica returns with another dream: "I walk through a series of rooms. Someone follows and I am terrified. It is a black man with a stubby beard. I beg him not to rape me, but rather go to bed with me and make love in his arms. I start talking to him." I merely reflect back what she has said: While you fear him he rapes you, when you no longer fear him he loves you. "Yes. It reminds me of my old image of Christ as Santa Claus with a sting." (This dream makes sense to me today; it did not at the time. I surmise the 'black man' is the masculine counterpart of Patch. Both need redemption so they can take up residence in the Heart. This dynamic is discussed in the next section.) I sense it is time for Monica to encourage the Comparisor to join with Christ, by asking her to release her fear of Christ into his hands and the ocean. (Without knowing it, I am also asking that she release her power to self-shame.) "I see her doing this. Her fear is a red light. He puts it in the ocean. It makes the water purple for awhile. Now she is standing next to him." I suggest that she ask him how he can enter her heart? "She asks and he turns to her and places his hands on her shoulders; and looks at her with compassion." I add my own thoughts at this juncture to the effect that she must open her intuition to him and when she does he will become her constant companion. (Intuition is identified with the third eye or brow chakra. It is what Christ penetrates when he places the power of his discernment into the brain.) "She wants this to happen. She is feeling much better. She can sit by Me. It feels fine. The Comparisor believed that the real self – Me, was not good enough, that she had to be someone else or she would be abandoned. Everyone would abandon them, if the Comparisor and Me were the same. That was her fear." I suggest a new intervention. First, I have them ask the Rebel to join them. Next, I suggest that each give Christ a portion of their *Light*, which he will mix with his own and place into a new circle he creates for this purpose. Monica has recently had a dream about four bottles of wine and this intervention seems to resonate with it. Her last comment before returning to me is that, "It really and truly feels good right now." This is the last session in the series.

I have described the above series for several reasons. First, the verbatims are a good description of how the work proceeds while the therapist treats all of the images as *dissociative aspects*, which was true for me while I worked with Monica during this period. In truth, all images are multivariate symbols. Their 'symbology' evolves with the therapist's ability to work with an increasing number of variables. Today, I name the images differently because I have learned new ways of discerning distinctions between the images. But I strongly suspect that even 'today's understanding' is a poorly drawn map of what the future offers. This must be a work in progress because it is Christ and the human Mind who are its authors; and Christ's role is nothing less than fulfilling God's vision for us. In the final analysis, all I can offer is a theory sparsely documented with case studies wherein each additional study provides 'evidence in support of the theory,' as well as data for its revision and refinement, and finally, it limitations.

Monica's series captures my transitional thinking as I begin to have intimations of how to work directly with the Heart and brow chakras. Even so, by following Christ's lead, I was able to offer Monica what Christ was attempting to teach us both in this series. Perhaps the most impressive aspect of this case is Christ's *active involvement and guidance* in both her dreams and active imagination. For example, without my asking, Monica spontaneously allows Christ to purge the Comparisor's Heart. This eventually leads me to formulate interventions for entering and purging the Hearts of other clients. This series also helped me to understand an ego-aspect's need to open to Christ, as distinct from being subject to him. Christ is able to guide us both during this transition despite my own conceptual shortcomings. Finally, as a result of this series, I came to understood that a Dominant self represses its shameful core within the Heart; that the Christ conscience process requires that Christ be able to enter and purify it, and make it the abode of both the Holy Spirit and unifying parts of the Self.

ENTERING THE HEART

The remainder of this chapter focuses on interventions for the transformation of conscience, which Christ finally accomplishes by entering and purifying the Heart. Throughout this work I have made references to the chakras, particularly the heart chakra. In active imagination Christ can enter this chakra space with ease *provided the client is willing*. But initially most clients resist his entry. Most people appear to live in fear of their Heart's interior because that is where their shameful secrets are hidden. They spend their lives actively barring all access to this space. The reader can wish it were otherwise, but in a clinical population, clients invariably fear the shame hidden in their Heart, though that fear generally goes unnoticed until the therapist asks the client to let Christ enter.

Just so the reader understands what I am talking about here, in active imagination Christ can literally enter the Heart by standing in front of any sense of self and pushing into its heart chakra. When this is allowed, Christ, the Aware-ego, and some part of the self that is penetrated all enter a space that is often cave-like in appearance. (Note that I say 'sense of self.' It is very likely that the Heart is only entered by Christ and the Aware-ego; that the self cannot actually enter until it is purified, but it can *witness* what occurs within via its sensed connection with the Aware-ego.) Once inside, Christ is asked to heal the shameful core and place a portion of his *Light* in the center of the space before he and the Aware-ego exit the Heart space. That *Light* is seen as an abiding presence of the Holy Spirit perpetually residing in the Heart thereafter. Some clients report later that they reenter this space on their own as it gives them an abiding sense of peace to be there. But once this peace is experienced it is not restricted to the Heart's interior. Often, it can then be experienced in a variety of interior and worldly contexts.

In the final analysis, working with images *exterior* to the Heart has a comparatively limited effect. Images exterior to the Heart mirror what has to be addressed and transformed, but all of that mirroring takes place outside the Heart. For several reasons, Christ only incarnates as our conscience when he is allowed to enter the Heart. First, as all esoteric and biblical references make clear, the Heart is the center of the self: it connects above with below. Second, while the Heart retains a shameful core, the client's conscious sense of self is obliged to live perpetually outside of it, ever fearful of being overtaken by shame if s/he enters. While that sense of shame persists, the person remains in a self-conscious state of un-forgiveness despite all outward appearances. Finally, the aural Voice-of-conscience appears to 'speak' from the Heart. The Dominant self preempts that interior aural Voice-of-conscience by assuming the power to judge something as shameful and thereby repressing it in the Heart's interior. The power to self-shame only preempts the aural Voice-of-conscience as expressed by the parent's Moral authority. When the Dominant self allows Christ to terminate its power to self-shame, and enter the Heart and purify it, then a parentified Voice-of-conscience is heard, often for the first time since childhood. But Christ will quickly terminate this voice as well, as soon as he is asked. In affirmation of the process, as this final stage of the work progresses, there is often a series of epiphanies and world changing perspectives that have lasting effects on the client's everyday life and relationship with Christ.

Re-entering the Heart

Only Christ's *Light* remains when he and the Aware-ego leave after first entering the Heart. And so far as I can determine, thereafter, only selves that are 'purified' can enter and abide there. The Aware-ego is always admitted. Likewise, any sense of the Body appears to be admitted, as it does not exercise negative judgments of itself. The Pre-moral aspect and its numinous mother can enter, as well the Rejected-self once it is liberated from shame and accepts Christ's discernment. And most significant, any self and consort identified by Christ as 'attuned to the totality of Self' can enter the Heart. But the Dominant self, Ideal personas, and any other ego-aspects manifesting the personality, must first go through a process of purification before they can enter.

It took me nearly a year to organize a process that can facilitate helping selves to obtain the necessary purification and enter the Heart. Much of that work requires an understanding of Relational authority, which is the subject of the next chapter. Basically, every image has a contra-sexual aspect, which Christ can 'capture' and bring into relational consciousness with that image. The contra-sexual aspect generally has a quasi-archetypal quality as it is derived from an archetypal amalgamate that 'underpins' the image, be it a self-image or image of another. Thereafter, as the client is willing, Christ can transform the relationship of self and consort until the relationship is shame free and optimally relational. Attaining a shame-free relationship is the primary prerequisite for any image or pair seeking to enter the Heart.

A distinction needs to be made here between self-inflicted shame, i.e. the power to self-shame, and a shameful relationship, which is always treated as 'an error in judgment' from the Holy Spirit's perspective. For example, parents can be shaming of each other as well as their children; and their relationship will reflect this. So too, will any self-image that embodies their relationship. Insofar as a Familial personality is derived from such a relationship, the self is inherently shamed by it and more or less powerless to change the relationship without recourse to a higher power such as Christ, who can transform any image or relationship with the power of the Holy Spirit. That process is addressed at length in the next chapter.

Asking clients to address images that manifest their sense of personality is the best way I have found to help a redeemed sense-of-self 'take up residence' in its heart chakra. After the imaginal relationship informing the personality has been purified, it can be entrained with Heart consciousness as a second Ideal pair. As noted in an earlier section, the process seems best begun by asking Christ to capture the self *whose dynamics reflect the client's sense of personality in daily life*. Basically, this is the client's adult adaptation of the Familial personality. The self is most easily identified by asking Christ to separate it from the Aware-ego using a capturing circle. Note, this self is different from the sense-of-self or Observer that emerges when Dominant self is redeemed. That personality-core appears to be an archetypal constellation of the Gendering archetype. That sense-of-self can eventually be worked with in the first person (discussed later in the chapter); but for the purpose of integrating Ideal pairs, it is necessary to work with images. Once the client's 'personality' is observed, described, and named by the client, Christ is then asked to cast a circle into the nether reaches of the client's Mind (i.e. active imagination) and retrieve the self's contrasexual aspect. These two are examined in relationship, but not worked with immediately. Instead, Christ is next asked to extract from the 'personality' the sense of self *most closely attuned to the totality of Self*. The client is made to understand that the 'personality' is that part of ourselves that has accommodated to family and community; and is likely to reflect constraints that block an awareness of the client's individuality or totality of Self. In contrast, the 'attuned self' or 'individuated self' is seen to move comfortably through all the Heart chakras as it is simultaneously attuned to the interior and exterior world (wherein the Heart portal is treated as the line of demarcation between interior and exterior). After the individuated self has been extracted from the adult personality, Christ is asked to cast another circle into the nether reaches of the Mind and capture the consort of this individuated self. After being observed together, the client is then asked if s/he is willing for Christ to bring both into the Heart and offer them untethered access to all its realms. These are the first selves invited to 'take up residence' within the Heart. I generally refer to them as the Ideal pair. Their entry is generally experienced as a positive change in the client's demeanor and reflections. In the ensuing weeks their felt presence becomes even stronger as the client accommodates to their assimilation.

Once the Ideal pair is permitted entry and residence in the Aware-ego's heart, I encourage the client to begin serious work on transforming the relationship between the adult personality and its consort. This will require two major steps. The first is *repeated conviction* of the pair until they embody an ideal relationship from the client's perspective. The second is purification of the adult personality's heart chakra. That is where the purified pair will reside. Once purified, that self and its consort will become the exterior counterpoint of the Ideal pair insofar as the personality will continue to reside exterior to the Aware-ego's Heart.

The relationship between the self embodying the Familial personality core and its consort is invariably conflicted in one way or another; so Christ must bring about the transformation of that relationship by repeatedly convicting the self and its contra-sexual aspect. That process generally requires two ancillary steps. The self is generally resistant to change. S/he needs to be encouraged to exercise *willingness* as Christ can only convict to the extent she is willing. To facilitate this willingness, I often ask the client to let Christ stand between the two aspects so he can *instantly* convict the moment she experiences an 'instant of willingness.' The second step requires that the personality allow Christ to enter the *adult personality's* heart chakra and witness what he finds there. While the Aware-ego's purified heart is currently out of bounds to the adult personality, any ego-aspect manifesting personality can enter his or her own heart chakra. This entry invariably illuminates *the major source of chronic resistance* and need for healing. Interestingly, some selves may initially question whether they even have a heart, but all ego-aspects appear to have a heart chakra; and as regards the adult personality, this is where his or her worse fear is hidden.

Once the adult personality's heart chakra and masculine/feminine relationship have been purified, the pair are invited to enter the Aware-ego's Heart with Christ. There, the purified pair can be integrated with the Ideal pair by inviting Christ to join their combined Lights. Generally, the pair defining the re-formed personality will then exit with Christ. Thereafter, they are free to enter or leave, but will generally abide in the personality's heart chakra, intimately connected with the Ideal pair via their shared Light. I assume here that the heart chakra of any ego-aspect is connected with the Heart of the Aware-ego via one of the Heart's seven heart chakras.

The adult personality's heart chakra is treated much the same as the Aware-ego's Heart. Christ identifies the source of conflict and generally collects it into a circle. Then, I generally suggest that he place a portion of his *Light* into the center of that circle, which is intended to purify it and thereafter provide *an abiding conduit of the Holy Spirit*. Essentially, this provides an ongoing source of conviction. When this is done, clients are simply asked to observe any immediate effect and their growing awareness, which is likely to evolve over a period of hours and days. Eventually, Christ and the client will use what is learned to define the further steps needed for further purification.

Prior to, or following the purification of a Familial personality and consort, I now encourage the client to also work with the parental relationship. The same intervention is applied: Christ is asked to convict the relationship between the parents until the client is comfortable allowing that relationship to also abide untethered within the purified Heart. As a rule, this pair will remain in the Heart once they have entered. Cumulative convictions must result in a parental pair that are clearly free of all antagonism and shame and are healthily engaged and intimate. This is a significant intervention as the parental relationship – aside from frequently being treated as initially irreconcilable – generally functions as the prototype for Ego self-images, as I demonstrate in the next chapter. To the extent that the relationship is conflicted, the images will also be conflicted. Redeeming the parental relationship and allowing it untethered access to all of the client's auric bodies will osmotically facilitate the transformation of those images.

The steps described above go beyond the redemption of conscience, as the final steps can only be taken after Christ has entered and purified the Aware-ego's Heart. In theory, all of the steps done exterior to the Heart can be done before Christ has entered the Heart and purified it; but the work is only truly effective when the images and their consorts are able to take up residence in the Heart chambers, which invariably requires Christ's prior purification of that space.

I cannot stress enough that the steps laid out above are only effective *after* the Dominant self has forgone the power to self-shame in exchange for Christ's discernment, and Christ has entered the Heart and purified it. 'Exterior' interventions can be done before that, but no one can safely enter the Heart before Christ has purified it and the selves in need of purification have accepted the need for it..

Other Chakras

The heart chakra is pivotal to everything done in this chapter. To a lesser extent that is also true of the brow chakra from which Christ extracts the power to self-shame, and supplants it with the power of his discernment. Before the Heart can be entered, the Dominant self must forgo the power to self-shame and allow Christ to supplant it with the power of his discernment. Otherwise, the Dominant self will continue polluting the Heart. Initially, the power to self-shame can be extracted provisionally while the client 'tests out' the power of discernment, but finally it must be given up *forever*. In effect, the client must imagine that s/he will never again have access to the power to self-shame. Instead, s/he must look to Christ to terminate the shaming voices of others wherever encountered, which the power to self-shame sought to usurp, as well as relying on Christ's power to discern the best way forward.

I might note here that it is possible for a client to experience shame after s/he has given up the power to self-shame. The client retains the ability to experience affective emotions, including shame, where it is aroused by others or situations outside its volition. Also, the core personality can embody the actions of a parent whose relationship to the spouse and children is inordinately shaming. Some ego-aspect will continue to experience this until directly addressed. Healing one, does not heal all of them at once, even when all of the preceding step s have been taken.

In this chapter and the next I also work with the root (sensation) and abdominal (emotional) chakra. While not directly related to sexuality, the root chakra is foundational to it and clients greatly benefit from letting Christ 'clear' it of shame. Finally, as I have already noted elsewhere, it has proven well worth the effort to allow Christ to clear the abdominal emotional chakra of any and all shame, particularly shame inadvertently injected by the activity of an Ego-in-conflict. It will take a whole other book to fully explore Christ's healing power vis-à-vis the chakras. In this work I do little more than point to the potential, though even that 'little' is crucial to the redemption of conscience.

I have recently developed two interventions for working with the 2nd chakra (emotional). Basically, I have come to treat that chakra as most often blocked by 'mini-beliefs' that are behaviorally conditioned stimulus-response associations. In this instance, the emotion in question is seen as strongly associated with another negative emotion or event. Examples would be arousal and shame or arousal and anger or arousal paired with an incestuous image. Other examples would be fear paired with innumerable stimuli such as high places, people and the like; or desires associated with particular foods, people, settings, etc. It is possible for Christ to open the 2nd chakra and clear it of these stimulus-response associations. Examples are given in Marion's verbatim later in this chapter and Leigh's verbatim in the next chapter. The other approach is a more piece meal approach but helpful if the client is too frightened of the prospect of letting Christ work directly with the 2nd chakra, or in working with a set of emotions such as humiliations associated with events in the client's life. That intervention has two components. First, the Aware-ego and whoever is merged with it is provided a garment of protection against fear. Second, Christ provides a dome that will repeatedly *trap* objects of fear. He also places a portion of his *Light* in the dome, which is intended to drain the object's energy once it is identified. This intervention allows the client to look at the object of fear, name it, and allow Christ to strip it of the negative emotion sustaining it. the object is 'trapped' with a circle drawn by Christ intended to capture it when the Aware-ego walks through the circle.

TERMINATING UNDUE INFLUENCES

Before approaching the Heart proper, I need to describe the series of interventions that finally leads to entering it. These interventions evolved from my efforts to work with prideful selves and the discovery of Dominant selves. The interventions include 1) the termination of undue influences, 2) working in the first person, and 3) instilling Christ's gift of discernment.

The first intervention grew out of my work with the Monica described earlier. Recall that she said her Comparisor prostrated herself on the floor after Christ spontaneously lit a candle from the sacristy light and placed it into her heart. The following intervention is very like the spontaneous solution Christ offered Monica.

The basic intervention is simple. Christ is asked to place a portion of his *Light* into the heart of *any image* – self or other – whose free will is thought to be compromised by 'undue influences.' The influences can be emotional, archetypal, or spiritual in nature. Emotional shame functions as an undue influence insofar as it has the power to strip thought and images of free will. Archetypal undue influences are most likely to be found in Ideal personas – Dominant selves overlaid with a culturally sanctioned role such as Nun, Priest, Doctor, or Career Army Officer, etc. In those cases, asking Christ to place his Light into the heart chakra of the image appears to sever the archetypal connection, which is generally a contrasexual Anima or Animus manifestation. If the undue influence is spiritual then – I presume – the autonomous emotion or spiritual infestation is banished. In every case where there is undue influence, the change is immediate or there is no change at all. I treat this intervention as homeopathic: if needed, the effect is immediately felt; if not, then there are no side effects. So I am always comfortable recommending it. However, as the following case illustrates, the effects can be quite profound.

Christ does not need the prior permission of a Dominant self before placing his *Light* in the Heart and that definitely sets this intervention apart from most others. But the ego-aspect rarely objects to the intervention. Where it does respond *fearfully*, Christ will first act to *extract* the undue influence before terminating it so as not to violate the ego's boundaries. As with the Rejected-self, Christ acts at the behest of the Aware-ego; so the therapist needs to direct the suggestion to the Aware-ego not the separated prideful self. This intervention is only used after the self in need of the intervention has been separated from the Aware-ego. It is not used while an ego-aspect remains merged with the Aware-ego. Later, the prideful ego will be asked to open its heart to Christ. That ritual does require the ego-aspect's explicit willingness. Undue influences are seen to compromise or inhibit a prideful self's free will, thereby blocking it's ability to work free of the influences by it's own volition. Essentially, Christ seeks to restore the ego-aspect's untrammeled access to its free will.

As a rule, I tell the client all of the above. I emphasize that Christ is asked to terminate any undue influence so as to insure that the self has full access to its free will. Christ's intervention will in no way compromise the ego-aspect's free will. If there are no undue influences present, then the client will observe no change in the image of the separated ego-aspect. I am generally vague about the 'nature' of the undue influence other than comparing such influences to the effect that the Empowering archetype has on parental images or the effects that shame has on a Rejected-self. (I have not had occasion to use this intervention before a client has experienced Interior baptism or the termination of authority in a parent.) In truth, I really don't know beforehand what effect the intervention will have, if any. Often as not, there is no discernable effect. But the intervention is quickly done, and if there is an effect it is immediately known, so I would recommend it whenever in doubt.

In this section I offer one example – Marion's case, which describes what happens when archetypal influences are terminated in a self. Following that, I describe – with further case examples, the potential effects of terminating undue influences in the images of others. More examples will be given in the remainder of this chapter and the last chapter.

Marion. Marion is an older woman who has remained active in her religious community since she was eighteen. She has never had an orgasm despite numerous attempts to achieve one through masturbation. Each time she has come close to orgasm some part of her has angrily suppressed it. Recently, her Gynecologist scheduled her for a biopsy to diagnose suspicious white spots in her vaginal area. In the first of five sessions covered by this series, Marion comes in saying she is calmer as a result of our previous interventions but remains non-orgasmic. "Actually, I have not masturbated this week. A little part of me is still fearful it will not happen." When I ask her to elaborate on this fear she describes it as a feeling of being stuck, "mired down, weighted down, paralyzed, immobile." I suggest that this is more than just stuck; it is more like shameful bondage. I suggest she ask Christ to identify the part of her that is shamefully stuck in her sexuality. She says, "I know that part. I can feel it. It feels urgent, desperate, angry, incompetent, strong." I ask if Christ can baptize it and release it from the stuckness? "No. *It is the part I have control over*. The real stuckness is my self-control." (A Dominant self has just made itself known to me for the first time. It claims the power to suppress her sexuality, placing it in a constant state of urgency, desperation, and hunger.) I ask to what extent her sexuality's deep sense of deprivation is a direct result of this control? "It feels like one hundred percent, but I am not sure." Do you believe your sexuality is not affected by this controlled suppression? "They are scary thoughts." In truth, the dialogue has disturbed Marion, but I have to end the session here.

Over the next three weeks our focus is repeatedly on Control and her suppression of sexuality. The machinations of this self are amazing. "I did think about masturbating. One reason for not experimenting is that I am afraid of insatiable desire. With my eating it is hard to stop myself. If I had an orgasm I would seek to have them all the time. (The implication being this is a bad thing.) I think what I have to do first is control my eating. Then I will know I can set limits." I point out that she has been setting emphatic limits on her sexuality all of her life. Other arguments are that she is too old to change; or that the white spots on her vagina are likely the result of her attempts to masturbate and if she continues now she "will do more damage." This litany of reasons goes on for this entire session and the next.

The fourth week begins as a continuation of the previous two. She complains of feeling stuck. I note that the intent of Control is to be 'stuck.' I ask if she feels at all sexual? "No." Then, I note, she continues to be in control. "I don't feel anger anymore, I don't feel anything. I don't have any feelings." I suggest this is a direct result of her ongoing and intensified suppression of sexual desire. Now she wonders, "Have I suppressed for too long?" I reply that she can only know if she stops suppressing. At this point, I shift the focus and ask her reason for suppressing deep hunger (the name I have given to her sexuality). "What comes to mind right away was that a year ago, when I was masturbating, and thinking that I was close to having an orgasm, I got scared. It felt like I was letting go of something. It was the only time in my life that I felt that close. I've never been as aroused as then. In my head I am not afraid." I ask if she controls her head or her groin? (In retrospect, this was an interesting choice of words as I was soon to learn). She agrees that the answer is obvious. Next I ask what is her fear? "I feel an overwhelming fear of giving up, giving in, letting go."

At this point I make one of those intuitive leaps that has been the source of most of the interventions in this book. I suggest that Control might well be in the thrall of some archetypal energy that is preventing her from choosing release. I suggest that she could let Christ terminate that enthrallment by placing a portion of his *Light* into her Heart; that the action would be homeopathic. If it is not what is called for, it will have no effect. Amazingly, it has a near instantaneous effect. "When Christ touched his *Light* to her Heart, *I saw a warrior disappear*, he just left. He had a shield and sword, a huge helmet, and guards on his arms and legs. He was a real warrior." From her descriptions I sense the image was male and when I ask she confirms that it was decidedly male. She then reports feeling having been mesmerized by the image of Control under undue influence. "She was mesmerizing me. I feel like I am seeing her for the first time. I sense a connection between us. She is the source of my identity with my family name, my family's mystique. Control is making that gesture of 'back off' that my father used so often. We have taken something away from her that was important to her. She has lost her way. She is alone. Something deep down is gone. There is a sense of deep loss for her. I wonder if I could feel an orgasm as deeply as she feels the loss." The session ends here.

I suspect the warrior described above was an Animus enthrallment. He is clearly a contrasexual male; and the warrior image is one of the four major Animus variants: king, warrior, magician and lover. I suspect this is a case of Animus possession because the warrior has sustained a sense of self strongly identified with a patriarchal family mystique that embodies pride, discipline and fidelity to religious values. In any case, its loss has deeply affected Marion. In the following session Marion seems disoriented. She has little memory of the previous session. When I suggest she go inside and ask what has happened she says she cannot. "If I ask and do not get answers it is like another failure. I feel totally stupid that I can't answer a question. I don't have your faith that I will get an answer." I ask what could possibly justify not asking? But none of my questions lead to insight. The self remains dominant but feels completely alone and unable to ask for any assistance, which is characteristic of Dominant selves.

In the next session there is more of the same, but also some reflection. "Control is like a box to keep things in order. But when I talk about it, it does not make sense. There is very little that we do control. Her control is limited to my immediate environment and me. She controls the questions and what ifs. She needs certainty." I ask her if she can identify the opposite of control? "It is freedom and breathing, a box vs. the flow of a river. I suggest that she could ask Christ for the gift of discernment so she could choose between freedom and control as the situation warranted. Her reply is telling. On the one hand she feels she has lost touch with herself as well as Christ. "There is no real motivating factor in my life any more. I wish I loved somebody. I once imagined an intimate relationship with Christ. I don't feel like I know him enough to ask him for something. I feel stuck. Nothing touches me." I reflect that such a position must be painful. "It is. But I don't have to risk anything anymore." Who values that, I ask, suspecting it is someone else who is also present and mediating her thoughts. "Touch is risky, but it is worse not to be touched. Whenever I see something poignant, I feel like it almost touches me." I suggest that maybe Control seeks to curtail feeling as well as thinking. "Well, I don't like to feel deeply." The session ends here.

In hindsight, Marion's reflections confirm the loss of an Animus connection. Such constellations tend to block more worldly connections as well as a viable connection with Christ. Having lost that archetypal connections, Marion can now bemoan the lack of male relationship and feeling.

Later in the chapter, I will pick up where we leave off here. As the reader can observe, the removal of undue influences does not result in an automatic acceptance of Christ, but it does diminish archetypal influence, which encourages the Dominant self to become more reflective as she seeks a new center; and over successive sessions Marion will move toward a heartfelt conclusion. Part of what Marion is feeling is a loss of the masculine energy that the Warrior provided. I was not so aware of that as I am now. In retrospect, I might have speeded the process by suggesting that Christ sustain her with his masculine energy until her own sense of the masculine could evolve. (That line of thinking will make more sense to the reader after reading the next chapter.)

Working With Undue Influence In Others

Sometimes, removing undue influence from the images of others can have a 'highly coincidental' effect. In this variation, the client is asked to contain an image – say a husband or wife, and ask Christ to remove any undue influence that may be having a negative impact on the life of that spouse (or child). Changes in the image following this intervention should not be surprising given how profoundly the same kind of intervention alters self-images and images of parents. What is surprising is actual change in the behavior of the spouse or child who often remains totally unaware of the intervention. The following two examples illustrate the phenomenon.

Eduardo. This first case concerns a couple I furloughed after several years of therapy. They were doing well when I stopped seeing them, but four months later the husband – Eduardo, returns to complain that his wife appears to be very depressed, has withdrawn from all major activities, and blames her disposition on his lack of emotional support. She had made similar complaints in the past, but has not previously withdrawn like this. I work with him for two sessions. The wife knows he is coming to see me, and although we have had a good rapport in the past, she insists that his coming is a 'waste of time.' Finally, in the third session, I suggest that he go inside, contain his wife in a circle, and ask Christ to place a portion of his *Light* into the wife's Heart terminating any undue influences. "Christ has done that. She looks more relaxed, less depressed. She had an intense stare, like her mother (recently deceased) use to have. That is gone." I suggest that he now ask Christ to terminate any soulful connections between his wife and her mother. In reply, Eduardo reports seeing a ball of light separate from his wife's image. I identify the ball of light with the soul of her mother and suggest he commend the spirit of her mother to Christ's eternal care. "The white light has diminished to nothing. I see a crystal clear ball. Christ says there is nothing left." The spouse's mother was an exceedingly shame-based woman who controlled every aspect of her own life in effort to avoid any hint of shame. The very next morning Eduardo's wife calls me for an appointment!

Our first session is basically a catch up. In her second session she shares with me that she had stopped just about all of her social and domestic activity to spite her husband for his seeming lack of attention toward her. But the day before she called me she came to the realization that it was not helping her at all. This behavior of spitefully stopping all interactions was characteristic of her mother. Calling me the morning after the intervention is a coincidence, but she also quickly resumes her social and domestic activity after our first session. (Eduardo's wife is Tory – whose case is described at length later in the chapter.)

Matthew. In this case, Christ is repeatedly asked to place his *Light* into the heart of a variety of family images whose behaviors seem strongly controlled by shame and fear of shame. Matthew's wife, who is a psychiatric social worker, referred Matthew to me. His wife is very fearful of being shamed by the opinion of others. In this she is much like Matthew's mother. Frequently, the wife goes into prolonged verbal 'rants,' again like Matthew's mother, which he submissively tolerates in both of them. In this session I begin by focusing on a 12-year-old image of Matthew standing with his mother. This 12-year-old is identified as the mother's golden child, who she nonetheless threatens to shame if he steps out of line, which is probably why the image remains prepubescent. Matthew – the youngest of three children, appears to function as the family hero, so failure to act as his mother dictates is also tantamount to shaming the family. Likewise, any missteps are also seen as embarrassing his wife. My first intervention is to suggest that Christ be asked to terminate the power of both mother and 12-year-old son to shame each other. Thereafter, neither would be able to shame the other. Christ will do this by placing a portion of his *Light* into the Heart of each image. Matthew reports what happens:

"When Christ places his Light into the Heart of the 12-year-old nothing happens, but when he places the *Light* into my mother the 12-year-old suddenly grows up to his mid 20's. That is when I got married." Next, I suggest that he imagine his wife and ask her to join his young adult self in the circle. I suggest that Christ enter the circle and place a portion of his *Light* into the Heart of each image. "Both images take in the *Light*; both look happier afterward; my wife looks more content." At this point I decide to go for broke and suggest we also terminate undue influences that might be affecting their two small children, both boys. I begin with John, the oldest. I assume here that Matthew's family will be having the most undue influence on the firstborn. I have Matthew ask Christ to terminate in his firstborn all undue influences flowing through Matthew from his parents. Then I have him do the same for his youngest son. Next, I ask him to invite his wife's image to do the same. To accomplish this I ask him to give her a portion of his *Light*. Interestingly, she takes both of their *Lights* and mixes them together and gives them to Christ who, in turn mixes it with a portion of his own *Light* before placing the combined *Lights* into the Heart of the youngest child, and then the oldest.

When Matthew returns two weeks later he shares a series of changes that have occurred between sessions. First, he has begun setting limits on his mother's demanding behavior. Second, he has begun challenging his wife's 'rants' for the first time in their relationship. He does not do this in anger. He just firmly challenges her generalizations with loving facts. For her part she has become less 'rantful.' At this point, I suggest that Matthew go inside and ask Christ to baptize his wife's shameful core so it is liberated and can gradually emerge in her. "I stand next to Jesus. He explains to my wife's image what he is doing. Then he places his hand over her Heart and then into it. I could sense a dark part of her Heart light up. There is a dark spot in his palm when he withdraws his hand. After withdrawing his hand he rubbed the spot with his finger and the spot disappeared. There is a small change in her image, she seems happier, but when he pulls his hand out I felt a *big relief in me*, a real sigh of release. I stood up straighter. The strongest reactions seem to be mine." In truth Matthew does visibly change over the next several sessions. He has grown comfortably firm with his mother and wife who in turn acquiesce to his new stance, to the benefit of both families. It is quite possible that his wife's image has functioned as a primary carrier of Anima energy, which Christ's intervention has purified. This conclusion is suggested by her interactions with Christ in combining their *Lights*; and by the effects that 'purifying' her heart has on Matthew.

FIRST PERSON INTERVENTIONS

'First person' is a grammatical term. It describes a speaker referring to self in the first person as *I* or *me*. It can refer to two different kinds of such experiences. Initially, it refers to any self in active control of the client who remains *fused with the Aware-ego* when the client goes inside; that is, before the self is separated from the Aware-ego and personified. It can also refer to the reconstituted Familial personality that is liberated following the redemption of the Dominant self. However, the emergent observer is not an actor or ego-aspect per se, though when it does emerge it becomes the client's strongest sense of 'I am me."

In first person interventions involving the Dominant self, the speaking self is left fused with the Aware-ego as long as possible; or, if separated, the client is asked to rejoin with the image for the purpose of these interventions. If this self has to be separated, then it is likely that the self that replaces its will have to undergo a similar series of interventions in later sessions.

The Rejected-self is always objectified when Christ baptizes it, and this process of objectification (personification) is initially used in working with most selves. When objectified, a self becomes a 'him,' 'her,' or 's/he' from the Aware-ego's perspective. One day it occurred to me that any intervention, including baptism and the removal of undue influences, could also occur *before the Aware-ego is asked to initiate separation*. Under this condition, any intervention would occur while the self co-conscious with the Aware-ego remained fused with the Aware-ego. The therapist – aware that s/he is talking to a co-conscious self, continues the dialogue without asking the Aware-ego to separate from the self. The major difference is that once inside, the Aware-ego is co-conscious with that self, and can be asked to exercise its own willingness using the *Light*. This co-consciousness defines a condition in which the Aware-ego and self are said to share chakra connections – particularly the heart chakra connection.

When going inside, the Aware-ego – the holder of the *Light*, generally emerges in the midst of the self currently directing the client. (There are notable exceptions, which I describe elsewhere.) This is true whether the therapist names the self while in dialogue with the client or senses it's co-conscious presence while the client is inside. Either way, the self remains merged with the Aware-ego until separated. In effect, the Aware-ego and co-conscious self continue to share the same Heart, the same psychic space, and the same Body. It is only when the Aware-ego collaborates with Christ to contain and separate from a co-conscious self that the co-conscious self becomes visually objectified. It is generally prudent to use separation procedures when the client is learning to go inside, and most especially when first addressing disowned selves. But eventually, and particularly in the case of prideful selves, leaving the Aware-ego and prideful-self unseparated can greatly facilitate the redemption of conscience, though it may also require that the therapist offer the prideful self a circle of escape as an option (see below).

As I began to explore this 'first person' condition, several effects became quickly apparent. First, it could be used to baptize as well as terminate undue influences in primary selves. Second, the effects seemed more vivid or more real to the client when the intervention is experienced in the first person. This is due, at least in part, to the fact that we are working with selves that generally dominate the client's conscious life. Most important, the client is encouraged to use the first person when receiving Christ's discernment and when Christ enters the Heart. The first person stance is the most viable for entering the client's brow and heart chakras with greatest effect.

I have very little to say about first person interventions involving the observer, i.e. Familial personality. The verbatims will provide a sense of my early explorations with several clients, but I can say little that would be definitive as I have only begun to tap the potential of this kind of intervention for working with clients who identify with a Familial personality core in the process of transformation.

Since I will be illustrating the first

person intervention in this and next chapter, I will only give two illustrations in this section. Both verbatims also illustrate a concept that highlights a particular sense of shame that I had not been consciously aware of until reading about it in Kabbalah. Its role will be more apparent to the reader if I briefly describe it before it is encounter in the verbatims. It is called the bread of shame.

The Bread of Shame

The Bread of shame is not unique to the first person experience but it is much more apparent in the first person, and addressing it offers another intervention for changing prideful ego-aspects. I first read about this concept in a book by Rav Berg.[36] Apparently it is well known in Kabbalistic circles but I had not come across it before in my earlier readings. It refers to the idea of feeling shame *for receiving something that is not earned*; what we commonly call charity. A colleague put it differently but just as succinctly: Shame is pride's response to the idea of forgiveness; it is shameful if not earned in some way. The Kabbalists insist that the receiver must come to understand that receiving is also a form of giving, since the giver cannot satisfy his or her own desire without a receiver. The desire of the giver can only be satisfied when the receiver is satisfied. Some prideful ego-aspects have great difficulty receiving from Christ what cannot be earned but only received; they often fear being shamed by its acceptance. This is especially true of those selves that believe reward is always proportional to effort, which makes them suspect any 'easy' solution that purports to bring great change. From the Kabbalist's perspective, the only way for the 'vessel' to be freed from eating the bread of shame is by learning to receive *for the purpose of sharing*.

Rav Berg describes humankind's current restrictions by shame in the following way:

> Unless there is a balance between donor and receiver, the original intention of the donor will not be realized.... A receiver who is not prepared to share [equal to what they receive], or one who is prevented from doing so [by shame], will inevitably reject the true intention of the donor. It was the Creator's wish and sole purpose to bestow abundance, but the Creator's creations could partake of this abundance only to the degree that their sense of shame would allow them. Therefore, the Creator complied and caused the desire to receive to withhold the Light so that it could redress the existing lack of balance [caused by the sense of shame].[37]

This has its parallel in the Genesis creation story. After Adam and Eve ate the apple they were ashamed and hid from the face of God. Eating from the tree of good and evil signified the creation of Mind, the world of opposites and knowledge of shame. Thereafter, Adam and Eve no longer felt worthy to partake of God's abundance. Hence God was obliged to clothe them and send them out of the Garden and receive only what they could earn by the sweat of their brow. 'Our fall' is our inability to receive the full abundance of the Creator's desire for us.

The Bread of shame is a state of mind, which seems to characterize some selves that emulate the Ideal-self. They believe that all reward must stem from the sweat of their brow. Nothing really worthwhile can be easy. There is no place for grace in this schema. To receive without proportional effort is shameful. 'God only helps those who help themselves.' The bread of shame theme plays out in different ways. The following cases only illustrate it. They do not define it. I have no statistics on the matter, but

I suspect this schema is present in many people, and a major impediment to Dominant selves accepting Christ as their higher power since, a priori, his grace threatens to shame their beliefs.

Remember in the following case studies that the intent is to illustrate first person interventions. Coincidentally, this approach appears to highlight 'bread of shame' issues.

Clair. Clair comes in and immediately begins complaining about a 'horrendous' week at work. She was recently promoted. Her new role as a clinical supervisor has placed her in an adversarial position with several clients and staff. As she relates the events of the past week, I feel she has handled herself quite well and tell her so. She appreciates the compliment, which others have also given her, but is most aware of how threatened she felt during the process and it is that which most concerns her. Such confrontations generate extreme anxiety and heart palpitations. She knows this stems from her need to do the job *perfectly*. I suggest she go inside and have Christ place all of her problematical staff and clients into the same circle. I then have her ask Christ to dissolve their image into a common denominator: what it is in her that they all share in common. (Note, I have yet to separate her from the part that strives to be perfect.) "I see several images at once: a road block on an otherwise smooth road, a big brick building that seems to represent authority and disheveled stuff. It is more a feeling than images. (The fact that Clair is only observing 'feelings' and symbolic images is further evidence that her Dominant self remains fused with the Aware-ego.) The feeling is 'I can't handle it,' 'I am going to fail,' 'I am bad, stupid, incompetent, and will do it wrong,' and then everyone will know I am all of those things." I ask how she feels about the compliments when she does it well, as she did this past week? "I like the compliments when I do it well." At this point,

I decide to focus on the Dominant self's relationship with Christ since she is undoubtedly an Ideal-self. I ask her, what is *your* relationship to Christ? "I know him, I believe in him, but I don't accept help from him." I ask her if pride plays a role in all this? "It is all over the place. If I do it well there are compliments, but if I fuck it up I can't show my face." I sum this up by observing: Pride does not need Christ and fuckup is unworthy to ask. I note to Clair that her perfectionism appears to be unaware of a recurring *consequence* of striving for perfection and prideful compliments: it repeatedly sets the stage for bouts of shaming or acute fear of shaming. At this juncture I suggest separation; that she now separate from Perfect and then allow Christ to enter the circle and place a portion of his *Light* into her heart to dissolve anything blocking her awareness of the pattern of prideful striving, which repeatedly provokes fear of shame or actual shame. She does this and then reports about Christ's entry into the circle containing Perfect: "As Christ entered her circle I saw three layers of light surrounding Perfect. The top layer is red to black, the second layer is yellow-beige to brown, and the bottom layer is black. These are all around her. She is in the center. The colors obscure her." It is not clear to me that the colors go completely around Perfect so I ask Clair to check this. "It does not go all away around. The back of it is all black." I suggest that she ask Christ to use his *Light* to dissolve these colors. "He does not dissolve them. Instead, he uses his *Light* like scissors to cut thru them. She stands there naked. She is about eleven years old. (Clair suffers from severe MPD, so it is not surprising that a Dominant self would be so young in age.) When Christ steps through the 'colors' he has cut she is too startled to be embarrassed. It was OK for her to be naked (ashamed) while she was concealed in the triangle of colors." (The colors appear to represent her prideful defenses.)

I suggest she ask Christ to baptize this eleven-year-old and release her from her sense of shame. "She does not know what to do with the reality of being accepted as she is. She has felt acceptance before, but that was always conditional on doing a good job. *She does not know what to do with acceptance that is not earned.*" I ask if Christ understands her dilemma? "She has collapsed into his arms." (This is the Bread of Shame issue I mentioned above. I do not tell her this but it helps me to appreciate the particular dilemma of this Ideal-self. She has only ever been prided for what she has done. The unconditional and complete acceptance offered by Christ far exceeds anything she has ever experienced by her own efforts. She cannot imagine how to sustain it without earning it.) "There are others inside who also need to feel this. *We don't want to lose this feeling.*" I suggest she can 'earn' this unconditional acceptance by sharing it with the others. If she is willing to open herself to Christ and become a conduit of the feelings flowing from him, then she can 'earn' the feeling by allowing it flow through her to the others. But she must forgo any pride that the feeling is from her rather than Christ; she cannot see herself as the source. Clair describes how it transpires: "Perfect asks Christ to make her a vessel that can channel this feeling to others. She holds her *Light* to her forehead and he opens her to him with his fingers." I now suggest that she invite any selves that also want to feel this into her circle. "Perfect sees them become much lighter when they enter her circle. It is pleasant for her to see it but she does not feel responsible for it." While this inner interaction continues, Clair – as Aware-ego, comments that it has become lighter where Perfect is in the circle but it is darker on the other side of the circle. I assume from this observation that another self has emerged who perceives the threat. I begin to talk directly to this emergent self, again, without asking the Aware-ego to first separate. I ask about the dark side of the circle. "It is behind her [Perfect], she does not turn around to look at it. There is stuff packed in the darkness." I ask if she would be willing for Christ to work with it? And if so, what would he need from her? "I am willing. He says that I need to go into it with him. But there is a fear of having to be honest about what is in there." I ask her what emotion might compromise her honesty? "Shame." So I tell her, "Hold your *Light* over your heart and he will baptize you and remove the shame underlying that fear." I am offering her baptism in the first person. She has not been separated from the Aware-ego. She still has a strong connection to the body and remains fused with the Aware-ego. "When Christ touched my heart, the darkness immediately faded. I see a big space with lots of boxes. There is nothing in the middle. It is a large warehouse with an uneven ceiling. It is black and the boxes are brown. The floor is gray. It is a storeroom. I need to decide what I will keep and what I will dispose of." I suggest that she ask Christ to get a box and open it so she can decide. "The idea is scary but I am willing. The box he opens has pictures, and toys, and memories. Some are good and some bad. I want to get rid of the bad memories." I suggest that she not do this. Rather, I advise her to consult with Christ how to handle this. "He asks me to give him the bad memories. He will stand between them and me. He will use them in a positive way for me. I do not have to carry them. I don't even have to necessarily see them now. He knows when a particular memory will be helpful. He can impart the insight I need from the memory when I need it. If a good memory tempts me then Christ can reveal another memory to balance that and shed a truth." I ask her if all of the boxes are full of memories? "I don't know." Clearly, there is more work to do, but for now I need to bring her back and get some closure on the session. I ask her how she feels when she comes back. "That room was very real."

Tory. Tory is very angry with, Eduardo, her husband. When I ask her to go inside and contain an image of him she describes his image as intolerable. But she is also aware that her feelings are 'bigger' than him, that something more than just him is bothering her. I suggest that it is her Gendering archetype's failure to constellate a fulfilling image of the masculine, based on what I know of her grandfathers, father, brother, and first husband. But, I stress, even if Christ could constellate a more satisfying image of the masculine she would not be receptive to it in her current state of mind. I suggest that she go inside and have Christ terminate any undue influences in her that would block the necessary receptivity. I explain to Tory that the Aware-ego will emerge into the midst of her when she goes inside and it will ask Christ to terminate through their *shared Heart* any undue influences in her that interfere with a greater receptivity to the masculine within her. This instruction is different than any I have previously given Tory. In the past I have always had her separate from the self before Christ intervened. Her response is telling. "I heard you but I did not do it. *Now I will do it on my own.*" Essentially, she has separated herself from the Aware-ego or is attempting to block the Aware-ego from emerging in her midst (this is rare but not unique). After a minute or so she goes on, "I am not getting anything. It is hard to even see the *Light*. In the past, when I went inside I immediately got the *Light*, but now it is hard for me to even sense it. I have a real feeling that there is nothing in me. When you were speaking earlier, I felt that I would need to go within me. In the past I always imagined it as something happening outside myself. *There is nothing within me* (Tory is close to tears at this disclosure)." Tory has rejoined me to share all of this. I suggest that she go back inside and *see Christ and the part of her that always holds the Light standing next to Christ*. This she can do. Then I tell her that I will be instructing her Aware-ego to place a circle around her and to enter that circle and give her a portion of its *Light*. Tory is able to do this with no difficulty, since this is like her longstanding role as an observer of what goes on outside of her. (Note, however, that she is still in the first person; the Aware-ego is the separated self.) Next, I explain that, if she is willing – which she will express by holding the *Light* to her heart, Christ will enter her circle and place a portion of his *Light* through her *Light* and into her heart where it will terminate any undue influences interfering with her receptivity to any masculine images formed by Christ. "He walks toward me. I feel a calming kind of feeling when his *Light* joins with mine at my heart." In effect, their *Lights* have joined, but Christ's *Light* has yet to penetrate her heart; so I suggest that she move her *Light* away from her heart thereby expressing willingness for Christ to penetrate it. "I feel *Light* that went deeper. I feel it inside. I feel the way I expected to feel when we first went inside." Finally, I suggest that she ask Christ to baptize her and dispel "any shame hidden within you." She allows this to happen but reports that nothing happens, so I suggest that I am going to ask the Aware-ego to ask this on her behalf, adding that she can resist the suggestion if she chooses. But she does not want to do anything more: "Let us leave it with the deeper feeling." I acquiesce leaving her unbaptized, and ask her to shift her focus to the image of her husband and tell me how she feels? (I am hopeful of some change but that does not occur except that, in focusing on him, she is more insightful.) "I feel disappointment, resentment, lots of questions, a sense of failure." I ask if she can identify the source of all these feelings in her self? "Incompleteness. A picture of me that has no needs; or that he could not meet them if I did. The more they go unmet, the more defined that picture becomes that I do not need them met. I tried to change the picture of not needing but I cannot." I ask if she can identify any image of her feeling very needy? "I hate that image. Whenever it was expressed it never changed things." The session ends shortly after this. I now understand that what we have to address is this hidden, despicable, *neediness*. But first we will have to address the pride that sustains her not needing.

Tory asks for a second session in the same week, which she has never done before. She returns three days later. She is now very angry at her father, who she fears is about the renege on a promise to set limits on her alcoholic brother. She has very little recall of the previous session, which is quite unlike her, though the anger toward her husband has abated somewhat. I begin by focusing on her anger, pointing out that anger can only push away; it cannot solve the problem of her *neediness*. She has all but forgotten about her 'neediness,' except to say that she hates it. Tory makes two telling comments during this discussion. First, she recalls visiting her PGM as a child with her mother. The PGM took them to her basement and pridefully showed them all of the vegetables she had canned for the winter. From her child's perspective there was a great deal on the shelves. She was particularly taken with the pickles in glass jars – her favorite, and remembers asking her PGM if she could have a jar. The PGM said, "If I gave all this away I would not have anything to eat this winter." The child did not get her jar of pickles and was shamed for asking. By way of contrast, Tory also remembers her MGM, who was divorced from the alcoholic MGF, and relatively poor, but would nonetheless take her granddaughter to the general store when she visited and let her pick out something which the grandmother would then buy on credit. That grandmother was her favorite, but the self that relates all of this then confesses: "I look like my PGM." This was the first time I had heard any of this. Interestingly, Tory also believes that her father is equally selfish and unwilling to share. (From the Kabbalist's perspective this inability on the part of the PGM 'to receive for the purpose of sharing' also shames anyone who would ask to receive. I suggest to Tory that she allow Christ to terminate any undue influences flowing from her PGM thru her father that produces in her any sense of scarcity. Tory goes inside but tells me she cannot see Christ. I suggest that she ask her *Light* to draw a circle and place an image of Christ within it. She cannot do this either. Next, I suggest that she place a small circle around "you" and a larger circle around the part of her that cannot see, that is blind to Christ. Next, I have her move toward the inner edge of the larger circle and completely separate from it. She can do this and immediately reports that she can see Christ but cannot see anything in the circle she has just left. So I suggest that she let Christ enter the circle and terminate any undue influences that are in there, even though she cannot see them. "I do not see who is inside the circle, but I feel her. She is really strong. There are powerful contractions, pulsating, and a lot of darkness. When Christ put his *Light* into her Heart there is just white light, then nothing, she disappears. There is white light everywhere. When it leaves there was no darkness, just nothing." I suspect some kind of spiritual infestation here – perhaps a soul part of the PGM, but do not focus on it. Rather, I suggest that she approach Christ and ask him to place a portion of his *Light* into her heart. Tory allows this and then reports, "In my mind there is a word that is echoing from all sides. The word is 'trust'." Finally, I suggest that she ask Christ to perform the same ritual on an image of her father. She does this but reports there is no discernible change in him.

I have reported all of the interventions used in this session. Some appeared to work, some not. The goal is to remove any obstacles preventing Tory from allowing Christ to shape a new sense of the masculine and an equally receptive feminine self-image, while striving to work with the co-conscious self in the first person. The most significant impediment uncovered in this session appears to be something that literally blinded the co-conscious self from even seeing Christ. Once Christ was allowed to dispel that defense, the self then allowed Christ to approach her and place a portion of his *Light* within her heart. This results in her experiencing a strong sense of trust. The object to be trusted is unknown at this point, though I surmise that it has to do with the needy self. The bread of shame aspect is less apparent in these sessions. Tory's self is identified with her PGM. But the PGM appears unable to share, even toward the fruit of her own womb. I suspect, but cannot prove, that what Christ has terminated as an undue influence, is a soulful connection with the PGM. A lot of this work only makes sense if the therapist allows a psychoidal connection with the world of Spirit that includes disincarnate souls as well as spirits.

Circle of Escape

Tory's case is also significant in illustrating the 'shock' a primary self can feel when obliged to reflect on itself. Until this series of sessions, Tory's Dominant self was use to being an observer. In these sessions she is threatened with the prospect of looking into herself. The process gives her a glimpse, which is very disquieting: she learns that her prideful sense of 'not needing' is hiding a despicable neediness. Between the first and second session she again represses what she has seen. This compulsion to reinstate the status quo is quite common when repressed contents initially break through. After working with clients for several months in the first person, I developed another intervention called the circle of escape, which is intended to lesson the 'shock' of imminent exposure. Now, when I anticipate that a self being worked with in the first person is likely to become resistant to my suggestions, I suggest that the Aware-ego draw a circle of escape nearby. Any part resistant to what I am suggesting can escape to that circle. This allows the self being worked with in the first person to separate from the Aware-ego, if threatened by my questions or suggestions. This is illustrated later in this chapter and the next.

CHRIST'S POWER OF DISCERNMENT

Receiving the gift of discernment from Christ generally precedes Christ's entry into the Aware-ego's Heart. A client can only receive the gift of Christ's discernment, if s/he is willing to simultaneously relinquish the power to self-shame. From an ego-aspect's perspective, receiving it is tantamount to accepting Christ and the Holy Spirit as the Voice-of-conscience. However, it is not the same as actualizing a Christ conscience. That can only be realized when Christ is then allowed to enter the Aware-ego's heart, and the Holy Spirit can dwell within as an abiding source of conviction. But no Dominant self will allow that entry until s/he has *relinquished* the power to self-shame and concomitantly received Christ's discernment.

Discernment is described as one of the gifts of the Holy Spirit.[38] Originally, it was seen as the ability to distinguish 'good spirits' from 'bad spirits,' which is how I often describe it to clients. But in this work I define it primarily as the ability to 'see a path forward' wherever both acceptance and rejection are possible; or more generally, *as seeing the way forward through any set of opposites that are potentially positive or negative in terms of outcome.* Discernment can be experienced in Mind and Heart. As used here, the gift of discernment will generally refer to mindful discernment. The Heart is said to be governed by discernment when Christ is allowed to place the Light the Holy Spirit within the Heart after entering it, healing the shameful core, and terminating the aural Voice-of-conscience. Those last steps are always dependent upon an ego-aspect first allowing Christ to insert the power of his discernment into the brain, i.e. mindful discernment.

The protocol for this intervention is the same for both coping and repressive aspects. Most coping selves are governed by fear, anger, desire or rebellion, to mention just four possibilities. When a Rejected-self has been healed, coping ego-aspects that were protecting, mediating, or avoiding the Rejected-self are often at a loss. Left to their own devices, these ego-aspects have no way of moving forward; all they can do is continue to avoid, push against, mediate, or suppress. This persistence of willful behavior is an obstacle to reconciling any pair of opposites. When confronted with this situation, Christ is asked to offer the gift of discernment, which is expected to provide the coping aspect the necessary guidance for finding a way forward. This gift is always offered to Dominant selves as well. In fact, it is absolutely necessary for the redemption of both kinds of selves.

In all cases, there must be a quid pro quo wherein the self willingly forgoes its primary ego defense in exchange for the gift of discernment. In the case of Dominant selves this requires that they forgo their power to self-shame. For other selves such as Responsible primary-selves or Mirror aspects, this requires that they forgo their primary defenses of fear, anger, and the like, as habitual responses.[39] I generally reframe those defenses as 'powers' as in principalities and powers. The most common would be the power of doubt, the power of denial, the power of distrust and the power of anger. What all of these defenses share in common is their blocking of forward movement. For example, distrust does not allow for trust, doubt does not allow for certainty, denial does not allow for acceptance, and anger merely blocks the underpinning fear.

The intervention is basically the same for both coping and repressive ego-aspects: they must allow Christ to extract the power from their brow chakra (brain) and supplant it with the power of his discernment.[40] Ideally, Christ is allowed to irrevocably remove the ego defense. However, for a number of selves I have found it helpful to let them *temporarily* retain the option. That is, the ego defense is extracted from the brain and placed in a circle, where it remains separated but still re-assumable. If the ego-aspect finds s/he does not prefer Christ's power of discernment over the previously used ego defense, then Christ will re-instate it. To paraphrase an AA slogan, "he will refund the misery." None of the clients who accepted these terms has ever asked for a refund. But I do stress to them that they cannot have it both ways. While Christ's power of discernment is far more powerful and effective than their ego defense, it is still – nonetheless, dependent upon their ongoing willingness. Generally, I ask the ego-aspect to allow Christ to make a simultaneous exchange. In that case, Christ first removes and absorbs the ego defense and immediately instates the gift of discernment in its place. The basic idea here is that the two options cannot simultaneously exist in the same place. The 'physicality' of the brain tends to reinforce this need to choose. Clients generally experience this gift as greater receptivity to Christ's direction. Christ's discernment is never forced, but the client becomes more willing to hear and follow his lead.

It is often helpful to extract the ego defense and place it in a circle in front of the self, and then have the self describe it. It has never been pretty, and is quite often gross. This objectification of the defense further encourages the self to allow Christ to exchange it for the power of his discernment.

Monica. This case example illustrates the process of offering and incorporating Christ's power of discernment. It is a continuation Monica's case described earlier. I have not seen Monica for almost a month, due largely to both of us taking different weeks off. She is doing quite well. We begin the session by discussing her blood pressure as she anticipates seeing her doctor in the coming week. She has taken blood pressure medicine for several years. It was a primary reason for coming to see me. She is taking much less now but is not yet willing to go off it. More important, at the moment, is her realization that her blood pressure is most likely to peak in the doctor's office. At first she thought it was in response to the authority of the doctor but now realizes it is the nurse who takes the reading and the two have always seemed comfortable with each other. When Monica takes her own pressure at home it reads normal. I suggest that we go inside and look for whoever is constricting the blood flow "in the doctor's office." "What I see is floating in the circle, like an angel, a female spirit. I sense it is supposed to be helpful." I ask whom it is attached to? "The Drab One, the Meek One." (Monica has decided to rename her redeemed Rejected-self, the Meek One.) I am wary of this 'angel' so I have Monica ask Christ to touch it with his Light. I will assume it is safe if it does not disappear. "It is safe." Next, I suggest that she touch her Light to the angel in order to get a better sense of the reason for its presence. "I feel it is benevolent; I was not expecting that." I ask who is reacting negatively to this angel. "It is the Rebel. She does not trust it. She is not buying into the program of trusting." I ask what is the Rebel's relationship to Christ? "She seems compliant toward him, but still distrustful of the world." I suggest that, if she is willing, she can open herself to the power of Christ's discernment and gain the ability to both *trust and distrust*. "She does this." Next, I ask what is her relationship with the angel? What if the angel did not exist? The Rebel replies with an insight that is quite unexpected, "I would not be here. The angel made us aware of the problem and the need to rebel." Then she adds, "The blood pressure uncovers the Meek One." I ask if any part of her remains fearful of the doctor discovering Meek? "The doctor's blood pressure cup is a tool for discovering Meek if he cares to." (In effect, constricted blood flow points to the hidden existence of Meek.) I suggest that the three of them – Comparisor, Meek one, and Rebel, stand in the ocean with Christ and release any residual fear of the doctor and his authority. They appear to do so willingly because very shortly Monica reports that it 'feels good.' We end the session here. When I asked Monica about her blood pressure several weeks later she shares that they took it twice in the doctor's office and both times it was normal. The doctor acknowledged the change but made no comment, apparently assuming it was solely the result of the blood pressure medicine, despite the fact that she has been taking it for years and always before it measured high in the office.

Further illustrations of the gift of Christ's discernment are provided throughout the remainder of the chapter.

WHEN A SELF FUNCTIONS AS CONSCIENCE: SATISFYING THE INSATIABLE DOMINANT-SELF

I discovered the Dominant self while looking for a new way to address obesity.[41] A number of my clients are medically obese. None of them have come to me with that as their presenting problem and they would probably not have addressed it had I not made it an issue. Despite my own willingness to address it, I was singularly unsuccessful in helping them lose weight. Let me confess at the outset that the following intervention has also failed to immediately solve that problem. But as my clients have moved through the series of interventions described in this chapter and the next, they have begun to lose weight. All that notwithstanding, my desire to find a 'weight reducing' intervention is what inspired me to begin asking clients *to satisfy the insatiable*; and it was this particular intervention that revealed the final necessary steps in the treatment of conscience. It taught me to see *how clients use socially acceptable behaviors in excess to cope with a repressed shameful core*. The accumulation of a shameful core appears to be a direct consequence of a Dominant self functioning as *its own conscience* in order to preempt an aural Voice-of-conscience, which is clearly heard *within* the Heart until it is silenced by Christ. A Dominant self will exhibit the full array of dynamics found in a the Rejected-self, Ideal-self, Ego-in-conflict, and Voice-of-conscience. It uses repression, rather than dissociation, to achieve this painful amalgam. Dominant selves develop after the seventh year. I don't know how pervasive it is in the population at large, but given the extent of obesity, smoking, and use of prescribed psychotropics in our culture, I would say it is quite ubiquitous.

I have identified at least one Dominant self in every client where Moral authority is addressed. While I discovered its existence in the context of working with obesity, I quickly learned that the interventions offered below are applicable to *any socially acceptable behavior used in excess*; and any of those behaviors, when used in excess, points to the existence of a Dominant self.

Eating – even eating too much at a meal, has no taint comparable to drinking alcohol in excess or snorting cocaine. Eating per se is not shameful; only obesity is treated as shameful. Eating to replenish the body's nutrients is treated as a desirable daily ritual by all cultures. Given our daily demand for food, any self charged with finding and consuming food is usually dominant within the Mind. Even when we are not actually eating we often think about our next meal, e.g. what we will eat, where we will go to get it, etc. We only know that someone is eating too much when they appear overweight; or we learn they are throwing up after meals (bulimia). But an overweight person eating a reasonable meal in a public place is not seen as acting shamefully, even though we suspect – based on their weight, that they are eating too much throughout the day. Eating can be 'disgusting,' as when someone eats a whole pie in one sitting, but that is almost always done in private, away from the public eye. In sum, obesity has all the earmarks of an addiction, but most people treat eating per se as a necessity. Thus, it can be done repeatedly and unashamedly in the light of day. This distinction between socially acceptable and unacceptable behavior is important. Excessive cocaine use is clearly an unacceptable behavior. For that reason it is generally a function of the Ego-in-conflict and only found in cases where parental conscience is particularly punitive. In sharp contrast, eating per se is rarely if ever considered shameful though it can result in body conditions that are perceived by others as shameful.

It is reasonable to assume that most people are overweight because they eat too much. It seems equally reasonable to deduce that most overweight people feel perpetually unfulfilled; that *some part of them* may even be feeling deprived, all but insatiable. In effect, food is being used to placate a hidden self by temporarily reducing the angst of its existence, but is ineffective as a source of lasting satisfaction. The food can placate but not satisfy, pacify but not heal. Feeling starved, deprived, or unfulfilled is an emotional state, not a bodily sensation, so attempting to satisfy it with food sensations will only temporarily sate the feeling. In fact, any effort to satisfy an emotionally repressed self with 'acts of sensation' will actually starve it because its need arises from its emotional deprivation and bondage rather than physical deprivation. *If this premise is valid* – that a part of the person is feeling emotionally starved or insatiable, might it be possible for Christ to satisfy it? Can Christ *satisfy an insatiable self* residing within the Heart? I decided this was a testable hypothesis that I could offer clients: *Let Christ satisfy the insatiable.* He would succeed or he would not. If he succeeded, then they could stop eating excessively. If not, then we would keep looking for another solution.

I made one assumption regarding my hypothesis: the self that ate excessively had to hide its insatiability within its person, that is, within an auric body. I decided the most logical place was the heart chakra since the Heart is the place most commonly identified as having dark recesses. Recall that the biblical Heart was treated as the center of the person and the source of conscience. Thus, my hypothesis assumes that the sense of 'hunger' *resides within the Heart of a Dominant self,* which Christ could satisfy by entering the Heart using the first person intervention previously described. Basically, I encourage the Dominant self – the self responsible for finding and eating food, to remain fused with the Aware-ego and simply stand before Christ. If the Dominant self is willing for Christ to satisfy the 'insatiable' within the heart, then it would express this by dividing the Light in two and opening its arms, explicitly granting entry to Christ. The simplicity of this intervention notwithstanding, clients invariably balked at doing it either before going inside or shortly thereafter. I have rarely encountered such active resistance to one of my suggestions! I knew I had touched a cord, but what was it?

There is one further assumption implicit in this intervention, namely, that the Dominant self responsible for eating excessively is co-present during the intervention. In my experience that assumption has a probability approaching certainty, especially for clients who are overweight. Without exception, I have found my overweight clients hypersensitive to the issue, as are most overweight people. Since any intervention is always preceded by some discussion of the issue as a preamble to setting up the intervention, it is generally safe to assume that the 'guardian of the repressed' is very present and hyper vigilant.

(There is an equally viable hypothesis embedded in my thinking that I was unable to explore at this point because it was clinically silent. The Dominant self could also be blocking entry to the Heart because, at some level, it knows the aural Voice-of-conscience is audible within the Heart. Once the Dominant self relinquishes its power to shame and allows Christ to enter and purify the Heart, that self quickly begins to hear an aural Voice-of-conscience generally identified as belonging to a parent. It is quite conceivable that the implicit threat of this aural Voice-of-conscience reasserting itself is the primary source of resistance. But that can only be appreciated after-the-fact, after the Dominant self gives up the power to self-shame and allows Christ to enter and purify the Heart. Very likely, the excessive use of desire is intended to squelch both the angst of accumulated shame and the shaming aural Voice-of-conscience.)

As I began to explore clients' resistances, what first emerged was their sense of despair at ever satisfying the insatiable desire. At first, I thought this despair was the actual source of their resistance. That emotion is only slightly less negative than guilt and shame. But as it turned out despair was a consequence rather than a cause. Clients' despaired because they could not ask Christ to intervene. As we continued to analyze their resistances and its consequences, what finally dawned on me was the realization that *clients were functioning as their own conscience*. They were using shame to repress the source of their angst; and they were unwilling to relinquish that power. All of this led me to further reflections on the concept of repression.

Freud made much of repression.[42] He saw it as the ego's primary defense against unacceptable impulses. I have always accepted repression as a viable, demonstrable, concept. But the modus operandi has always escaped me; and I suspect that is true for most adherents of the theory.[43] How does the Ego actually 'repress' something when the process itself is treated as unconscious? And what allows the repression to be lifted? I consider it significant that Freud had very little to say about shame. He focused on anxiety and guilt: which I have defined as the after-effects of satisfying a shameful desire. I finally concluded that shaming is the root cause of repression. In effect, self-shaming strips any component (mental, emotional, etheric) of an ego-aspect of its free will, which results in its 'will-less' banishment to the dark recesses of the Heart. Shaming leaves that part of the ego-aspect in a temporary or permanent state of impotence. And shame might well reinforce that repression indefinitely were it not for the contents of what is shamed: emotionally charged memories and traumas, psychic functions such as feeling, a polarized side of an archetypal duality, and/or instinctual rhythms (e.g. sexuality), all of which are vital sources of function and sustenance. As I have noted elsewhere, all of those functions and energies can be repressed, but never with impunity. If an *emotionally* charged part of the organism is obliged to remain buried within the Heart, its energy will manifest negatively as somatizations and/or compulsive behaviors.

When an ego-aspect represses – as distinct from being dissociated, the repressed remains within the domain of that self. It becomes a shameful core of that self rather than becoming an 'other' via dissociation or projection. When the client and Christ can enter the Heart, whatever is hidden there becomes objectified. It is also possible to extract it from the Heart, which also objectifies it. The shameful core is repressed because it is perceived as dangerous as a result of past shaming by the aural Voice-of-conscience or by others acting in loco parentis. Repression strips the object of shame of its free will, which effectively banishes it to the dark places of the Heart. Outwardly, this silences the repressed part, but consequently exacerbates the situation by generating a continuing sense of unfulfillment and angst within the Heart, where the shamed object is also quite susceptible to the aural Voice-of-conscience. To placate this tension or ongoing sense of lack the Dominant self then seeks socially acceptable, brain altering, remedies. In our culture food is easily accessible, highly sensate, and socially acceptable. But an *emotionally starved self* can only be *briefly* placated with food sensations. Hence, ever more food needs to be eaten. Oft times, food can be supplemented by other activities and/or drugs, but in our culture food remains the most easily accessible pacifier of distraught emotions. (Culturally, we previously 'swallowed/inhaled' nicotine, until it dawned on most of us that cigarettes had adverse consequences; just as we are now appreciating that food, as the new pacifier of choice, has equally adverse consequences.) The problem with using food and/or nicotine to placate the emotionally starved core is that it only pacifies; it never satisfies. *The disowned core remains chronically unfulfilled as a consequence of its will-less state and repeated bombardment by the aural Voice-of-conscience.*

When a prideful self is wounded by shameful exposure it is said to 'feel ashamed.' This reaction is near instantaneous and self-inflicted. An ego-aspect assumes the power to self-shame for one primary reason: it empowers it to preempt the aural Voice-of-conscience, which it often emulates. If it can supplant that voice then it can avoid dissociation, which is tantamount to a loss of free will. Self-shaming allows a Dominant self to maintain its integrity in the face of shame rather than being overwhelmed by the aural Voice-of-conscience. The Dominant self does not 'hear' the aural Voice-of-conscience as long as it can regulate itself through self-shaming. The problem with this solution is the untenable dilemma it creates. The Dominant self must thereafter avoid its own Heart. It cannot approach the toxic remnants of its self-shaming. And it cannot give up the power to self-shame without once again becoming vulnerable to exile by the aural Voice-of-conscience. All of this can be demonstrated after the fact. When Dominant selves give up their power to self-shame an aural Voice-of-conscience appears to return with a vengeance.

But at that point Christ can quickly contain any such voices and terminate their power to shame the self.

Revisiting the Seventh Year: Distinguishing Dissociation from Repression

Earlier in the chapter I described how it is relatively easy to access a Rejected-self by asking the client for any memories of their seventh year associated with the development of conscience. Frequently, this questioning will activate a Dominant self. The therapist needs to be mindful of this and decide whether to continue treating any Rejected-self identified by this questioning, or acknowledge the emergence of the Dominant self and proceed to work with it. To be frank, when I first developed the idea of identifying a Rejected-self via memories of the seventh year, I was not aware of the 'existence' of Dominant selves and how they might interfere with the process. So before I proceed to describe a definitive process for working with the Dominant self, I think it worthwhile to give two examples of 'misidentification.'

Clair. This is from the case files of the MPD client referenced earlier. I ask Clair what image of her self comes to mind when she started in 1st grade that might be associated with the development of conscience? "I can remember isolated events, *but I can't picture myself*. I remember the first time I did something wrong in school. It was kindergarten. When we got up from our chair the teacher said we were to push our chair back under the table, and tell her if anyone did not do that. I told her when one of the boys did not do it. She called me a tattle-tail, placed us both at the end of the line, and made me hold his hand. He was a dirty nasty little boy. By pairing us I felt dirty too. Everyone laughed.

I was mortified. (I could have begun by having Clair contain this sense of self, but she continues with an even more interesting revelation.) I had a *recurring dream* all through elementary school. In it I have on a blouse and shoes but no pants or skirt." I suggest that she allow Christ to contain 'Skirtless' in a circle. "I see her, the blouse she had on. It is the 3rd grade. She is missing a skirt. She has a slip on. I can feel those feelings of being ashamed, embarrassed, stupid, for not being aware of going to school without my skirt. (Note the transition here. In the first memory, the teacher and other students shame her. In the dream she is shaming herself, making herself responsible for the shame she feels.) I am standing in the classroom trying not to be noticed." At this point, her Christ spontaneously intervenes by emptying the schoolroom so it is just them. (For some years, her Christ image has functioned very autonomously and with exceeding sensitivity.) Interestingly, the dream self does not know who Christ is. I suggest to Clair that she enter the scene as her Aware-ego and act as an intermediary if necessary. "I don't know how to explain who he is, how will it have meaning? But now Christ is explaining to her *what* he can do for her. She is weeping...telling him it does not matter what he does...the damage is already done...they already know. He tells her that he can't change what people know, but he can accept and love her to the point that even people knowing will not make her a bad person. They can ridicule. She does not have to be embarrassed by it. She can hold up her head and laugh with them. He can heal her to the point where she can look at it as funny, rather than embarrassing. She cannot see how that can happen but does not see anything to lose. She walks up to him. He puts his hand on her head and kisses the top of her head. He holds her tight to him, like infusing himself into her. When he releases her she is fully dressed in appropriate clothes better than any she ever hoped to own as child. She is cute, witty, and perky. He takes her to a mirror to show her the transformation. We see her in a slip, she sees herself differently, and she walks out into the hallway. The others see her as she sees herself." (What Christ as done here is convict her of the Holy Spirit. I address this phenomenon at length in the next chapter. It is truly the most powerful intervention I have encountered and Christ was using it with my clients long before I could describe it and its import. In this case, the modus operandi was "infusing himself" into her.)

It is important to stress that the Dominant self described in this case is a dream image. But the dream was real enough all those years she had it. (Of note, many MPD alters make their initial appearance in therapy as dream elements.) Clair is also cognizant of the difference as she now plaintively observes, "I've never been able to see myself that way (redeemed); how do I translate that to now? I only know how to fake it." I suggest to the Dominant self who is now speaking – though at this point my theoretical position (dissociative dynamic) cannot distinguish her – that she give Christ a portion of her Light and let him separate from her the part she has to fake. (Essentially I am treating this Dominant self as a dissociated primary self that is seeking to hide a Rejected-self.) I add that she will have to ask Christ to baptize this Rejected-self. Clair replies, "That will be harder to do. I do see her. She is like a little ball, *afraid to move for fear* of getting into trouble. The rules keep changing in every environment – work, friends, kids, husband, if you change or move someplace else you have to figure it out all over again." This is actually a part of her paralyzed by fear of shame, but I mistakenly treat it as a Rejected-self. In my ignorance, I reiterate the idea that she can see the effects that repeated shame has on her by letting Christ baptize whatever part she is seeing. I add that she saw her one step removed in the dream and how Christ changed her in the dream. In reply she describes what happens. "He picks her up. Sits down in a chair holding her and rocking her. He tells her that he loves her and that she is worthy of being loved. She is looking at his face to tell if he is telling the truth. She knows that he is telling her *what he believes* and that others feel that way too because of the way she *faked* everything. Christ blesses her. They go to the ocean. It is the only place I know to go. He tells her they will walk out far enough for the waves to wash over them, and when she feels free they will walk back. Now they walk out. As the waves washed over them, the waves falling on the sand are full of creepy, crawly things. The wave action keeps happening over and over again. The sand turns black. It seems like a long time. Finally, the waves and waters pull back and they are standing on new sand. She is glistening. Her skin is like a baby's – new, soft and clear. The sand is white and pristine. She has an incredible smile on her face." I ask Clair if she is still afraid of her, and if not, is she willing to take her back inside? "I want to be like her." I suggest that she too can open to Christ by holding her *Light* to her brow. He will penetrate it with his fingers, touch her brow and open a direct connection between him and her. She attempts to let Christ do this, but the effect is unexpected by both of us. "Everything becomes squared off and brown. The *Light* left my hand. Something is blocking, something is unwilling." I ask if she is saying that someone is unwilling to be open to Christ? "Yes. I can say that though I am ashamed to say it." I have her recover her *Light* and ask it what is the issue? "My disbelief in Christ and God. Not wanting to buy into something that is not real. The disbelief has always been with me since I was a little girl sitting in church." (This is clearly the voice of a Dominant self, but I keep thinking it is the voice of the one who fakes. They are likely one and the same.) I suggest that she could ask Christ for discernment as to when and where to speak her truth in order to not always be worried about shame. "No. I will be made a fool of in the eyes of others. But I don't think I have ever realized how crippling that is, and how much it impacts on my relationships with other people. I would have done things much differently with my children if I had known." (Clair is getting in touch with her power to shame, but I am failing to fully appreciate that fact.) I note that she has seen the effects on her dream self and a Rejected-self. "Yes. The Dream self answers me that she will not do anything to embarrass me. Maybe it is my freedom I am afraid of…" At this point I have to end the session.

In this session we began by extracting a dream image, which Christ baptizes and transforms. Unbeknownst to me, because I had yet to conceptualize a repressing Dominant self, the dream intervention has brought a Dominant self to the foreground, which I mistakenly assume is a Responsible primary hiding a Rejected-self. Someone – the Aware-ego, Christ, perhaps even the Dominant self – objectifies a Rejected-aspect of the Dominant self in order for Christ to work with it in the ocean. But when I suggest that the Faking self (sic) Dominant self open herself to Christ, she balks and the *Light* reflects her refusal to allow the process to continue.

I have put the cart before the horse in a significant way. It was inadvertent. I had yet to conceptually identify the existence of Dominant selves. Significantly, Clair's Dominant self claims ownership of the faking from the outset. The Faker is neither a Responsible primary nor a Rejected-self, although in this instance it was possible for Christ to extract and personify her shamed core. This Dominant self has always been aware of her shameful core, and felt the need to 'fake it' in order to cover up the deeply felt inferiority. As such, it would be nearly impossible for her to open herself to Christ before she is willing to forgo her power to self-shame, which she believes is the source of her 'freedom.' Confabulations of the sort described above are probably inevitable without a working knowledge of Dominant selves. At each juncture it was her autonomous Christ that appears to salvage my own fumbling efforts to intervene.

Marion. I ask Marion – a life-long Roman Catholic, to name any strong associations with conscience following her first communion (which generally occurs between the age 6 and 8). "I remember somewhere during that time... my father telling me lovingly... that I was his little tub of butter. I knew it was not good. My brother sometimes referred to me as roly-poly." I ask if her body, thereafter, threatened to shame her? "I started to become a tomboy. It was easier to fit with the guys than the girls. The feminine was hidden. It was fat." I suggest that she let Christ baptize this part of her, release this sense of the feminine from shame. She has used the baptism ritual numerous times before in different contexts and generally resists whenever I first ask. This is no exception. Her resistance emerges in the form of a new self that begins to minimize the child's perceptions. "I was young in those years. I should not have been *ashamed*. (Feeling 'ashamed' is a definite clue that a Dominant self has taken charge of the interactions.) As a kid I loved my father so much, he was so handsome. I was so proud of him. Anything he said to me really affected me." Since Marion has terminated her father's authority in other contexts, I suggest she do so now, even though she holds back from letting Christ baptize her 'little tub of butter' image. But she leaves the session reluctant to move in any direction.

In the next session, Marion reports that she let Christ baptize the fat girl image. "He embraced her, she walked away. It is OK between her and Christ. I blew her out of proportion." For my part I am skeptical, as there seems to be no real change in the little girl. She just walks away. I suggest to Marion that she go inside and ask the little girl to come back, and ask her if she is willing for Christ to terminate the father's authority that shamed her in the first place? "There is no need. *We have a tacit agreement that she was just a kid and took the shaming to heart*." (This is clearly the voice of a Dominant self.) I persist in asking Marion to call back the little girl. When I persist Marion claims that, "I see her giving a part of her *Light* to her father and stepping over to Christ." To me, it feels like more attempts to evade. So again I persist that she honor the ritual and let Christ terminate the Moral authority of this father image. Inside, Marion now reports that the little girl has retrieved the *Light* she gave to her father and returned it to Christ. At this point there is a shift and Marion becomes very thoughtful. "I guess I did not realize how much his comment has influenced me in my life. There is a sick feeling in my stomach and a sense of stunted growth." I suggest that, since the Fat little girl can act on her own, perhaps she can give voice to what has been stunted? "Dad was like a god. What he said hurt. My sisters were so beautiful. I gave up trying to be feminine." Did he squelch that in you? "I was less than perfect for him. Isn't your father the first man you love as a girl? I worked other ways of getting his approval – sports, grades, friends, a religious life." Marion is a life long religious and her sexual repression has been a life long issue for her. I ask if her femininity is related to sexuality? "I am not sure I know the difference between the two." I suggest that she allow this nine year old to open her sexuality and femininity to Christ for healing and then let him raise her to sexual maturity. But it is only a suggestion for later, as she has not even allowed the little girl to terminate her father's authority.

Marion returns to the next session convinced that this time she has terminated her father's authority during the week. "Christ gave me his *Light*. I gave it to my father; told him I loved him, but I needed a new understanding of my sexuality apart from him…and then I went over to Christ. My father faded into the background. I wanted big changes to take place, but nothing has happened yet. I am more at peace. It feels calmer. I have not tried to masturbate this week. (Her frequent attempts notwithstanding she has remained non-orgasmic.) I need to just enjoy the calmness. There is a little part of me that is fearful that it will not happen when I do it again." At this point I suggest she go inside, go to the ocean with Christ and release this fear. "It is a fear of being stuck, mired, weighed down, paralyzed, immobile." I reframe this to her as the effects of shame. I suggest that she ask Christ to help her identify the part of her that is shamefully stuck in her sexuality. "I know that part. The part of me he can't release is *the part of me I have control over*. The real stuckness is my self-control." (Again, I am hearing a Dominant self assert herself but don't identify her as such.) I ask if she can see the part that she is controlling? "I feel her. It feels urgent, desperate, angry, incompetent, strong." (Note, she is talking about feelings within her. This is not a reference to a dissociated self.) I ask her, "To what extent are her feelings a direct result of your control? Do you believe the feelings are unaffected by your control?" I then answer my own questions by commenting that what she feels is a direct result of her control, which is merely another word for perpetual suppression. We stop here.

These sessions clearly reveal the onion-peeling flavor of the process: first we identify a Rejected-self identified as a 'tub of butter.' Her memory immediately provokes minimization by a Dominant self. This Dominant self sabotages my every effort to see the Rejected-self baptized and the father's Moral authority terminated. The one intervention that does prove helpful is the Dominant self's willingness for Christ to remove her fear in the ocean. It is this that finally allows her to begin examining the effects of her father's shaming on her sexuality. But it will be months before this Dominant self is willing for Christ to enter her brain and forgo her power to self-shame in exchange for his discernment.

If the therapist focuses on conscience by asking about memories of the seventh year – which I still consider a viable way to proceed, s/he must be prepared to engage a Dominant self. The dissociative phase is considered the earliest stage of conscience development and addressing it first lays the paradigmatic groundwork for tackling the repressive phase enacted by Dominant selves. But those selves will often emerge in the midst of the early work since they are always dominant, and will take charge if the work threatens them. If the therapist senses such an emergence, s/he needs to shift the work to the Dominant self as the 'Rejected-self' is likely an objectification of its shameful core. Note that, in Marion's case, this was by no means the first time we had worked with a Rejected-self. She had previously engaged these selves in their dissociated state, and allowed Christ to baptize them and terminate her father's Moral authority. Had I been more aware of what my questions of the seventh year would evoke, I could have addressed her sexual repression more directly. I will revisit this case later in the chapter.

REDEEMING THE DOMINANT SELF AND HEART OF CONSCIENCE

As already noted, 'satisfying the insatiable' is actually a series of interventions that will follow from the suggestion that the client allow Christ to satisfy an insatiable desire. The interventions are generally preceded by a discussion of the particular socially acceptable behavior used in excess. At some point, all of my clients have expressed resistance when offered these interventions. I anticipate this and continue by encouraging them to examine *their reasons* for resistance, e.g. their admissions of shame surrounding this insatiable part of them, or their intimations of how dangerous it would be if that part of them were freed from shame. The reasons are legion and seem to require several sessions for each client to examine them closely before they are willing to proceed. As they continue to procrastinate – and the opportunity arises – I point out that it is *they who are starving* this part of them. This is not something they can blame on others, not even their parents. They are functioning as their own conscience; they are the ones doing the shaming. Basically, I ask them to accept that they are exercising this power to shame as a primary defense against their fear of being overwhelmed by a shaming aural Voice-of-conscience or the dissociated aspects stripped of free will by shame; *and that there is little that Christ can do until they are prepared to forgo that power.*[44] I will also tell them, since it is a fairly predictable occurrence, that they are likely to encounter an aural Voice-of-conscience when they give up their power to self-shame, but Christ will immediately terminate its voice. Christ cannot prevent people-in-the-world from shaming us, but he can reduce their attempts to an affective response, and he can terminate the authority of any internalized image previously empowered to shame us.

Essentially, a Dominant self will strive to emulate the parent who functions as the aural Voice-of-conscience in order to preempt that voice. In so doing, the Dominant self seeks to usurp the power of conscience as Freud defined it. But like Prometheus stealing fire from the Gods, the power to shame becomes the torture of both Prometheus and the mortals who accept it. Humans assume the power of conscience to their detriment. The client must become willing to forgo this power or continue suffering the effects of hubris – in this case overeating, but there are many others. To work through this emotional impasse, the client must finally be encouraged to forgo the power to self-shame in exchange for Christ's discernment. I cannot express it more succinctly than St. Matthew: "Come to me, all you that are weary and are carrying heavy burdens, and I will give you rest. Take my yoke upon you, and learn from me; for I am gentle and humble in heart, and you will find rest for your souls. For my yoke is easy, and my burden is light" (Matthew 11: 28-30).

Only when the Dominant self is willing to relinquish the power of self-shame can the client take the next step of allowing Christ to enter the Aware-ego's Heart. Relinquishing the power of self-shame is the first necessary step in the final redemption of conscience. Initially this can be *provisional*. That is, the client allows Christ to extract the power to self-shame from the brain and place it in a circle in front of the self. But at some point the extraction must be finalized by allowing Christ to absorb it with his Light forever. Following absorption of the power, the client asks Christ to insert the power of his discernment in the place previously containing the power of self-shame. Then the client asks Christ to enter the Heart and purify the shamefully repressed.

The Dominant self needs to be fused or remerged with the Aware-ego when Christ enters the Heart. Initially, only the Aware-ego is able to offer its Heart for Christ's entry. At this point in the process, without purification, the Dominant self cannot even enter its own heart chakra much less the Heart, which is a far vaster realm than that lesser chamber. But while it remains fused with the Aware-ego, the Dominant self can sense what occurs within the Heart, though it is obliged to remain outside. (That conclusion is based on events that predictively occur in the hours following the initial entry into the Heart i.e. the consequent emergence of the reconstituted Familial personality.) Even so, the therapist needs to insist that the Dominant self and Aware-ego remain fused so Christ's entry is a first person experience that allows the Dominant self to sense what occurs. *If the Dominant self has separated from the Aware-ego, then s/he must be re-merged with it.* Once the Dominant self has forgone the power of self-shaming, and assumed the power of Christ's discernment, Christ can enter the Heart through their fused union, and the Dominant self can follow the sense of what occurs therein. The Dominant self's willingness is critical here, and that will only manifest after the Dominant self has given up the power to self-shame. In sum, the initial entry into the Heart is via the Aware-ego. In theory, this could occur without the Dominant self being fused with the Aware-ego, but it is difficult to achieve the first person experience without that fusion, since the Dominant self embodies the strongest sense of '*I and me.*'

Without fusion with the Aware-ego, the Dominant self cannot even sense what occurs after it forgoes the power to self-shame, and opens itself to Christ's discernment. Once the Dominant self forgoes the power to self shame, and Christ terminates the aural Voice-of-conscience, the Dominant self will revert to 'I am me' in its amalgamate state as the reconstituted Familial personality. At that point focus must shift to working with the personality, unless the client has Ideal personas that come into play. In the latter case, the process must be repeated. When all of the Dominant selves are reduced to reconstituted Familial personalities then one of them can be personified and used to create Ideal pairs.

The one invariant in this process is Christ's need to *penetrate* the brow chakra. In order for Christ to extract the power to self-shame and insert the power of his discernment, Christ must 'literally' penetrate the brain with his fingers. He does not merely rest his hand on the head, though this can be an intermediate step. *He must be allowed to enter the brow chakra in a tactile way*, which is best experienced in the first person. Several female clients have objected to my use of the word 'penetrate' because of its sexual connotation, but are mollified when I suggest that Christ be allowed to 'enter' the brow chakra with his fingers; so I am likely to use both verbs in describing the process.

The following case examples are highly condensed versions of the dialogues between the client and myself over a series of sessions that incorporate all the forgoing interventions. It goes without saying that I would not venture to offer these interventions until the client has done considerable work inside. It will have little value until s/he has allowed Christ to baptize one or more Rejected selves and depotentiated the parents' authority – be it Temporal or Moral. What sets this series of interventions apart from earlier interventions is the goal of receiving discernment in the first person while working with a Dominant self. Because this is the definitive process for finally redeeming conscience I am offering the reader several extensive case examples to illustrate the variety of issues encountered. Even so, any therapist guiding their own clients must be prepared for them to differ from these illustrations in significant ways. Their first client will be different in the way that each of these cases is different from the one before it. It will ever be so.

The following cases are among the first of my clients to enact the interventions. In significant ways, it was their responses that identified the necessary steps. As they progressed I learned. Repeatedly, their inner Christ lovingly corrected and redirected my mistakes. I have deliberately chosen to use their files because, however well prepared the therapist, the process must allow Christ to guide it, and these files highlight that imperative. His lead has always proven more valuable then my preconceived notions.

Marion. Marion is the first of my clients to work through the process. As is generally the case with 'firsts' it gets messy at times, and often surprises myself as well as her. A brief history. I have seen this client for some years. She entered the religious life at age 18 as a virgin and, despite temptations, has kept her vows of poverty, celibacy, and obedience for the past forty five years. The only vow that has ever really concerned her was celibacy, which she has continually railed against but not broken, except in her Heart. She firmly believes that her inability to achieve any kind of orgasm leaves her incomplete and unfulfilled as a woman. Late in life she began to masturbate, but every time a frustrated anger interrupts the act. She feels estranged from the church, though not her order. She has studied and integrated Buddhist meditation practices into her daily prayer life. She maintains a more consistent prayer life than anyone else I know. She has a love-hate relationship with Christ, but has never failed to evoke him when going inside. She has done more explorations using the *Light* than ninety-five percent of my clients. For my part, I have explored every nook and cranny of her Mind in an effort to see her satisfied, including past lives, undue influences, and every other intervention described in this book excepting the ones used in this and the next chapter. Marion, by her own admission is about 60 lbs. overweight. Some years earlier she had shed all of it but has gradually gained it back. The sessions described below reflect my own growing understanding of how to work with Dominant selves exercising the power to self-shame. In the first session described below, we continue a month long focus on a prideful self called Control and its strong resistance to becoming open to Christ's healing of Marion's sexuality. Marion sees this part of her as responsible for the control (sic) suppression of her sexuality. I have not seen her for three weeks as either she and/or I were on vacation or otherwise unavailable. When she returns, she is intent on continuing to work with Control.

In this session Marion begins by showing me a diagram she has made. It shows a box on the surface with rocks on top of it and tubes going underground to another box. I suggest she go inside, let Christ create a well of pure sensation, and bring the underground box to the surface. "There is a lot of power attached to that box and it is very connected to Christ. I can feel it far beneath the earth. It is awesome. It is above the ground now and surrounded by light. It contains understanding. The two boxes are connected. The stones on top of the other box weighed it down. Christ opens the box. In it are balls of light, almost fire; there is one for every stone that was on top of the box representing

Control." I have Marion ask how the stones and balls of fire are connected? "They represent my choices. I have only seen those choices from the perspective of Control, which insists on seeing them as stones." Who, I ask, sees the fire/light? "A deeper part of me. I don't know her." At this point, I suggest that she provide a opaqued dome of protection for Control and let 'Deep' come to the surface. There ensues a long silence. Finally, I prompt her to tell me what is happening inside. "I feel ashamed of the image that came to me. It feels childish, very childish. It is me as a 17 year old. I have never let go of my mother's death. The 17 year old feels angry that she died, and sad and resentful and self-pitying." I comment that Control suppressed the part of her that was feeling grief. Then I ask why she thought it was necessary to put those feelings underground? "I have a loving family. I did not know what else to do with her. I did not feel I had the right to be sad." Who said you did not have the right? "Everyone around me. Their silence. I wanted to be strong for the rest of them. I was silenced by the need to be like everyone else. The sadness was so new to me and I felt a need to keep a stiff upper lip like my father." (Marion's mother died when she was 17. She is the youngest of four siblings. The two oldest – sisters, were married. She remained at home with her father who looked to the church for comfort; he had two younger brothers who were priests.) I ask if the 17 year old thought she was weak? "She thought so, actually, she thought she was *needy*." At this point I suggest that she ask Christ to baptize the 17 year old to remove any shame that is silencing her. It is not clear whether this happens. What does happen is a reassertion by Control. "I don't want to get stuck there. I am ashamed of her." Who, I ask, are you? "I am a 63 year old woman who counsels families who are grieving. I judge her." My response is quite firm and equally judgmental: No, I reply, "You shame her to keep her silent. This is the most feeling part of you. You must let her live through her feelings. You collude with your family to silence her. She feels. You think." In turn, Control challenges me to tell her what to do with her. I suggest the only safe solution is reconciliation. In turn, Marion tells me she can picture the 17 year old with other selves that have been reconciled to each other and open to Christ. "But I feel so far away from them. I don't know how to live with sadness without fighting with it. It will overpower me if I accept it." I ask what the other selves will do if the sadness overpowers the 17 year old? "They will be there for her. But I cannot be there with them." The session ends here.

In the next session Marion begins by saying she has had a difficult week. A voice in her head has continually berated her: "Woman, get over it; don't be touchy-feely; don't be emotional." She goes on to say, "I am embarrassed by feelings. I have to be in control. I am not embarrassed by anger; but I am easily shamed by tender feelings. I did not choose this. It started after my mother died. If I let go of my heart I am afraid it will bleed to death. I want to feel without being ashamed of feeling, but allowing Christ to remove the shame is not easy. I need to stay in control. I need to earn this, be punished, or suffer a little. To let Christ take away the shame feels shameful. What do I do with all the years when I have felt embarrassed by my feelings? How do I become different?" (Her litany is an illustration of the 'bread of shame' in bold relief.) We go on like this for several more minutes until Control finally becomes willing. In setting up the ritual I make it clear that Control has to remain in charge and that she must express her willingness at each juncture. First, she allows Christ to place a portion of his *Light* into her Heart and absolve all shame hidden there. Then she is instructed to hold her *Light* to her brow so he can open a direct connection with her. After a long silence I ask her if she is having trouble? "No. I caught a glimpse of Christ for a second when he had his hand on my head. I felt like we connected. It was a strange feeling. That moment of connection felt right. It was not charity. He gave me something because he loves me. That took the shame out of it. I need to remember that." I ask her to have him strengthen his image. "He is not going anywhere. What I need to do is stay on top of that voice that wants to shame me." This is the shaming voice she commented on at the outset of the session. Her comment tells me that she needs to let Christ terminate the voice before she can open to him. I ask if she is willing for him to terminate the voice in her? Her answer is telling: "Does he do that? I thought I had to do it. I feel like I was born with it. It is my father, my uncles, my community, and the Church. It permeates my whole life. It is in my head. It is the order in my life." Christ has touched Control, but she is still striving to do it herself. I tell Marion that she must complete the ritual. To become completely open to Christ's voice she must allow him to penetrate her brain *deeply* with his fingers, not just place his hand on her forehead. Again, she holds the *Light* to her forehead, and afterward, describes what happened." I feel like there is a center to my brain, a whiteness that he can penetrate. He gets to the center and holds it. It feels like a new voice there. It is OK. I think it is OK." I ask how it feels? "It feels empty, but not bad empty. Quiet. New maybe. Am I going to be different?" I suspect so, but all I can add is "We will just have to see."

I do not meet with Marion again for three weeks. In that interval I have begun to conceptualize the intervention for 'satisfying the insatiable.' When I ask what she recalls of the last session three weeks earlier she is initially hazy about it. She has come to realize that she does not have to get mad at her sadness over her mother's death. "Attacking it is unproductive. If I let myself feel it then it passes. But before when I felt it, I would get embarrassed by it and push it away. While I was visiting my brother I was able to express the sadness to him." At this point I decide to introduce the idea of 'satisfying the insatiable,' which I have begun to explore with several other clients. Marion's initial reaction is to deny the existence of any part of her that is insatiable. "I don't feel like there is a part of me that is starving. I just eat the wrong things at the wrong time. I don't eat more than I need to." Marion continues with her rationalizations for a while and then confesses: "It would be a big step to ask Christ. If it is out of my hands and it does not work then I will feel twice as bad. It feels like a real commitment. From the beginning I think I knew the insatiable part has to do with my loneliness. I want to be needed by somebody, important to somebody. The idea embarrasses me, but it is real. What I really hate about this is that you make it seem so simple." The session ends here.

In this next session Marion becomes willing for Christ to reach into her Heart, touch, and satisfy, her sense of insatiability. Afterward, she shares what happened: "What I saw happening…Christ went deeper…very visual for me… he reached for a part of my heart…he is holding it very carefully, tenderly…he is putting his *Light* around it…there are no words…now he is backing out…it feels different…I don't know what really happened…that is what I saw…it is different. There is this whole area of my Heart… whatever you want to call it…now it is empty… except for the sexual part… the empty part feels warm and open…he changed the quality of the sexual part…it does not feel as heavy…more out in the open. One of my biggest hesitations in doing this was fear of losing control…but I did not feel that this time. I feel more accepting of my loneliness. It is a part of who I am… what happened was a very tender thing…can't be tender if you don't really love something. Mother Teresa had a tenderness toward people that can only come from what Christ just did for me. It feels like a whole new level."

I was completely caught off-guard by what Christ did for Marion in this intervention. I expected him to connect with a self, not the core of her sexual desire. He holds it 'tenderly' –which is a strong emotional word for Marion, and places his *Light* around it. The area surrounding this center of energy becomes warm and open. There is no self identified with it, just a sexual sphere of energy surrounded by his *Light*. I am cognizant of that absence of self when Marion returns the following week. She begins by reflecting, first, that she has recalled, on several occasions, the experience of Christ entering her Heart; and second, she has continually heard a recurring thought through the week: "I am because I am loved." She then goes on to say, "During the week I felt like I was getting soft. The rational side kicked in, but has yet to take over. I am staying with the thought that I am really loved. There is no place for shame or embarrassment in that. I have gone back – in my memory, to last week when Christ extended his hand and went deep and held my sexual desires in his hands. It is calming for me to go back to that." I hear that she is merely remembering and ask her, "You are remembering, but have you let him actually go back inside since last week?" She owns she has not, she has only remembered it. So I suggest she go inside now and let him return to that place within her Heart. "What I see most clearly is the picture of his hands, the gentleness, how he holds that space within me." Do you feel connected to that space? "Yes. There is a connection…this is a part of me…deep… the journey through my Heart brought him to this place…he is honoring it…he knows it…it is a feeling thing rather than a thinking thing… I don't know the words for it…it is calm and non-judgmental…sacred…things I don't usually associate with sexuality." At this point, I decide to move the process forward by asking her if there is a part of her that could join Christ in this space? "Yeah – the part of me that feels incomplete and needy." Is she there? "Yeah. There is no need for her to feel incomplete while she is there. If she could stay there it would be OK." I ask what would prevent her from staying there? "It is not a familiar place for her to be. There, you are surrounded by acceptance. It seems unreal." I ask, from whose perspective? "Mine, me, that part of me that is looking at her. It has a fairy-tale aspect. It is too new. It is real here in the room with you [the therapist], but it will seem unreal away from here." I tell Marion that I understand it is difficult for her to continue entering her Heart, but if she could enter more often perhaps the needy part could *begin to hold Christ's hands*. The session is quickly coming to an end. I again encourage her to enter her Heart during the week rather than just remembering it.

The preceding session seems pivotal for Marion. Christ has been allowed to enter the Aware-ego's Heart a second time, and this time Needy joins her within the core of her sexual desire. I have not the faintest idea how this will play out and do not blame Control in the least for her fear of 'injecting this new behavior into her life' between sessions. But I suspect she will, at the very least, be willing to move it forward when she returns.

Marion comes in and immediately begins sharing her experience of having a massage (her first ever), and the fact that she has hired a personal trainer to help her develop an exercise regimen and eat better. (This is a major commitment for Marion and only possible because her brother has provided the money.) Marion goes on to share that she has gone inside several times during the week and seen Christ, Needy, and – at this point her mind goes blank. "I have been working with them all week and now I cannot think of the name for the other one." A third self has joined the other two during the week. I suggest that she go inside and perhaps this will prompt her recall. "I am inside. Christ is holding my sexuality...totally embracing it. It is very poignant...he holds it lovingly, without reservation. Needy is watching but whoever is next to her is not clear to me, but it has been clear all week until I came in here." I can only comment that something is clouding her perception. "I remember other qualities. The other is not likeable. She embarrasses me. She has a weakness. I did not feel she could be held by Christ." I suggest that she give this part of her a portion of her *Light*. This action brings her to the realization of who she is looking at: "It is my incompleteness as a woman." (This is a code word for her desire for sexual fulfillment.) What follows is Control's angst at experiencing all this. It is difficult to describe. On the one hand she is face-to-face with the fact that Christ is holding her sexuality and prepared to baptize the two selves Marion has identified, but in order for this to happen she must – finally, relinquish her power to shame them. "It is hard to imagine not thinking of myself as incomplete (shamefully fulfilled). I have blown up that idea by being angry and frustrated at the thought of it. If Christ baptizes those parts of me it would be like a great exhale." Marion becomes willing, but because all of this is still new to me I insist that Christ enter her Heart – rather than her brow chakra, to terminate her power to self-shame. Interestingly, or so it seems to me, when she imagines standing before him, he first takes her hands in one of his hands and then places his other hand on her forehead! In retrospect, I suspect Christ is expressing his desire to terminate her power to self-shame, in fact he may even have done so, but I presume he has not and insist that she let him enter her Heart for this purpose. But Marion says it is Ok, "His hands gave off warmth that went all through me. Now he takes my hand and we walk over to the two images. He places his hands on Needy's head and heart. He lets her know that her neediness is her need for him, and he is there for her and will never go away. He is removing all of her shame at feeling so needy. It feels like so much going on and nothing going on, my mind is racing so, but Christ and Needy are not; they are calm. The clutter of my mind does not touch them. The session ends here.

Once again I have put the cart before the horse. I insist that Christ must penetrate Marion's heart chakra for the purpose of terminating her power to self-shame instead of penetrating the brow chakra. But rather than follow my suggestion, Christ places his hands on her forehead and Marion insists that this is sufficient; and certainly it is enough to allow Christ to proceed with the baptism of Needy. The reader needs to bear in mind that this is the *first* time I have ever done this with a client. In my ignorance Christ is directing us both! In the next session, Marion returns clearly in a different space. "I worked with the incomplete self during the week (the self that desires sexual fulfillment). Her image is very clear to me. She is definitely a female image of me. Needy understands that Christ is fulfilling her, encouraging her to look to him, use him, call on him often. With Incomplete, Christ just put his hand on her heart to let me know that my completeness was in him, *but there is something I need to learn from this part of me*. My mind went to a lot of places. I realized that the whole world is incomplete, and that I was never going to be whole in this world. The connection he made with me was very tender." At this point, I suggest a new intervention: I ask Marion to join/merge with Incomplete and let Christ into their shared Heart. I suggest this in part because Marion seems to continually merge with that self as she is speaking. I am not sure who is going to be merged with Incomplete: certainly the Aware-ego but I also suspect that Control is co-present. In any case, when Christ is asked to enter their shared Heart Marion experiences a sense of cloudiness within. I suggest that she ask him to dispel the cloudiness, and if she is willing, bring her sexuality in with him. "I agree to this, but now I am confused. It is clear and it is not. Joining with Incomplete does not help me. I have to make a connection between completeness and my incompleteness." (I suspect the struggle is between feeling and thinking.) "Christ's gesture is so filling. I can relinquish the sense of incompleteness regarding Needy, but I feel there is a bigger reason for feeling Incomplete." I suggest that she treat her incompleteness as a desire to know God, her body, and life. Marion grows very reflective: "Those two images have always been there [Incomplete and Needy]...now it is like night and day...going from shaming them to finding they are a part of me which Christ also blesses. These were the two worst parts of me, the source of all my previous reasons for control. All my problems have belonged to those images. It all feels new and fragile, almost too much to take in." We are short on time. I decide to leap ahead and suggest that she ask if Christ can connect the four of them (Christ, Control, Needy, and Incomplete) to the core of her sexuality? But, apparently, that has already happened. " If I visualize it, the four images are connected to it already. He holds it. A magnetism or string connects each of us to it. At the end of the string is our *Light*. The connection is very real and very strong. A lot of my neediness and incompleteness was in not being OK with my sexual part. I do have needs sexually that I will never fulfill...husband, children. I don't have to be ashamed or fearful of that anymore. Maybe celibacy is incompleteness." The session ends here.

This series of sessions is continued in a later section when I take up the issue of the reconstituted Familial personality –the self that appears to emerge following the initial entry into the Heart. Marion is greatly changed by the forgoing and in the coming weeks its effects seem to permeate many aspects of her life in a positive way. But in one regard there is a noticeable absence of change. She is still not able to orgasm. All the involved images are connected to sexuality, but sexual satisfaction continues to elude her.

Pearl. Pearl's case describes my second exploration of Christ's ability to satisfy insatiable desire. It overlaps with the Marion's case described above, so frankly, I have little idea what to expect when I begin the exploration. Pearl has been working with me for several years. She is essentially asexual. She can function well in a variety of work settings, but tends to isolate during her free time. Diagnostically, she seems best described as an Avoidant personality. In the first session of this series, I revisit her weight issue. (She has struggled with her weight since childhood. She is a tall woman who carries her weight well but she is overweight. In previous sessions I have treated her eating as an Ego-in-conflict issue. That led to the discovery and reconciliation of numerous conflicting selves, but failed to bring about any changes in her eating. It is only during this series of sessions that I come to realize that eating per se is not a shameful behavior, but rather a socially acceptable behavior used in excess.

(Of note, while eating per se is not a shameful behavior, I have since come to appreciate, that most over-eaters experience much guilt around their eating, or a shameful lack of control after the fact. The eating does inject shame into their emotional field. They are rarely aware of it while eating since the desire for food will normally drown out the shame aspect of the experience; and afterward they generally lack the awareness needed to discharge it. I will speak more of this later in the chapter.)

Every client I have worked with for any period of time seems to tolerate my penchant for posing questions 'out of the blue.' So Pearl is not taken aback when I opt to be direct, and simply ask if she thought there is a part of her that is *insatiable*? A part that could not be satisfied by food though that is all she is offered? Pearl responds: "That is not quite true. She also has access to reading and sleeping. Food, reading, and sleeping." I reply that at some level this part must be starving because Pearl is doing all of these things in excess, which suggests they are insufficient to satisfy it. I then suggest she could *let Christ satisfy that part of her which never gets enough*. Pearl is immediately and acutely aware of her reluctance. "I find myself very resistant. I fear any change would deprive me of sleep. That escape is my safety. I am not willing to let go of that part of me in order for Christ to satisfy her and draw her out. I am not willing to see her satisfied. I don't want to see what her need is. It will be made public to me and to you. The angel on my shoulder says Christ can meet her needs, but the devil on my other shoulder says not this one." I reframe what she is saying by suggesting that the resistant part of her is *personally responsible for this unmet need by actively denying its satisfaction*. Our conversation stimulates a memory in Pearl. "I have met her before. It was during a period of grief following the breakup of my affair. (This was her only real relationship; it lasted several years. As he was married the relationship was always hidden.) A voice in me said, "You can't control your sense of loss but you can *control* what you eat." In effect, she believes she is using food to placate a sense of loss. But I suspect it is more than a sense of loss for just that relationship.

When I see Pearl again two weeks later, we quickly resume our discussion. All of the session is taken up by her offering reasons for not allowing Christ to satisfy this part of her and my challenging those reasons. What emerges from this discussion is her observation that for as long as she can remember she has been alone, and that her shameful core is starved for connection. I suggest that her reasoning is a veritable Catch 22. While the insatiable self remains shamed she cannot hope to forge healthy connections because the very act of connecting is experienced as shameful. But it is she who shames herself; so it is in her power to liberate the shameful core if she is willing to forgo her power to judge this part shamefully. While I could appreciate this intellectually it took me, and Pearl, three more weeks before I fully appreciated that she was functioning as her own conscience. In this session she grows increasingly despondent over her inability to let go of her judgmentalness, which she recognizes as irrational and self-defeating; she asks for a second session later in the week, which is the first such request in our years of working together.

When Pearl returns she says she feels exhausted beyond all reason, but not so depressed. The prospect of releasing her power to shame herself is still frightening but she does not feel as willfully opposed to it. But for my part, I have yet to understand that the power to shame is a brow chakra issue rather than a Heart issue. So I suggest that she allow Christ to enter her Heart by moving her Light away from it. "A glass walled chamber seems to surround me. It feels like I open a door to it and he enters. The wall seems eminently reflective. It seems like a fragile protection if this is what I have built around my heart. It seems constantly endangered." What I sense is that Pearl is looking at am image of herself rather than looking out of her eyes at Christ. She confirms that she sees her heart as separate from herself. I reiterate that there can be no separation or dissociation. Then she says, "If I am to do this I need to surrender my *Light* to Christ not just move it aside." Again, I challenge her to follow the suggestion, otherwise she will be surrendering her willingness rather than exercising it." (What I still fail to appreciate is her intuitive understanding that something does need to be *surrendered* before the intervention can be effective; namely, her power to self-shame. It is all so clear in retrospect.) Pearl is quiet for some minutes. Finally, I ask her what is happening. "It is as if by moving my *Light* aside I removed all defense, revealed my belly. Christ wasted no time. He plunged into my very core…the hardest part was the submission…he filled a space waiting to be filled." What is interesting here is that Christ has entered her belly, not her Heart. I encourage her to let him show her what he is filling, what he is doing. "There is a certain sensuality to it, a masculine and feminine aspect…a part of me does not want to articulate it. It seems akin to planting a seed, a kernel left behind when he withdraws his hand, that has a huge potential."

Since Pearl is unwilling to look too carefully, or at least describe what she sees, I simply accept whatever has happened and focus her on what I believe is the next step. I ask her if she is now willing to let Christ satisfy the insatiable part of herself? In reply she says that she had a thought earlier in the session – unvoiced till now, that "This part of her is seeking definition, self definition, as distinct from being endlessly malleable. She desires to define herself. Christ is consistent, more so than any of the other stop gaps I [Pearl] have offered her. That gives me hope for her. He is consistent and persistent." So I ask her, if she is ready for Christ to enter and touch her and liberate her from her shameful embodiment? Pearl reflects that, having acknowledged her desire for definition, she should welcome Christ's hand. Again, I challenge her to move her *Light* away and experience the act. "All the barriers are down. He does not just touch her, he holds her, she is still trying to control her definition of herself and he is not resisting that." (Note the separation implicit in this statement. She has separated from this part of herself, and it is not clear to me what she has separated, as it feels more like a Dominant self than a shameful core.) That is all Pearl can tell me in this session.

When Pearl returns the following week, she shares that "I don't like my life." I'm surprised by this turn of events. As I begin to query her she becomes aware – seemingly for the first time, of a voice berating her for all of her failures. (This is her power to self-shame.) "I just realized the existence of this voice. I have been responding to it by being depressed, aware of my imperfections. Last night I spent time entreating God to help me. I cannot remember the last time I did that." For the moment, I choose not to address this voice. Instead, I ask Pearl to tell me what she recalls of the last session and what she is aware of in the present tense. "I am aware of Christ holding Insatiable. (The nature of that self remains unclear to me.) She has stopped shape shifting and is now in a malleable state for his shaping her and directing her. If that power to shape shift continues to be hers then she will continue to be shaped by external forces, society, culture." (This sounds like the very essence of the Familial personality, but it will be another year before I could recognize it as such.) Again, my own gut reaction is to insist that this self – Insatiable, retain the power of willingness, or she will be essentially trading one form of selflessness for another if she forgoes her willingness. I encourage Pearl to give Insatiable a portion of her *Light* so that she can express willingness to Christ in this matter of his providing her a consistent definition. Pearl does this and then reports: "I give her a portion of the *Light*. When she takes it she literally splits open

– literally breaks open and something gushes out. If she were human I would say it was blood. It might be poison. I don't know. Her external shape seems completely drained. Only a shell is left." I suggest that she let Christ catch whatever has flowed from her and, if necessary, deposit it in the ocean. I also suggest that she ask her *Light* to name whatever it is. Pearl replies that she cannot see what has happened to the *Light* she originally gave to Insatiable, so I encourage her to give her another portion of her *Light*. Pearl reports feeling that while before this part of her was waiting to be shaped now she is waiting to be filled. I, in turn, again insist that this must be willingly done, and for that she will need access to the *Light*. Pearl gives her yet another portion of the *Light*. Then she reports seeing two images occurring almost at once. "First, she kneels before Christ and offers her *Light* as an indication of her willingness. Then Christ moves forward and takes her hands into his – that is the first picture, and then raises her to her feet and takes his hands away. It is so hard...the instinct to defend is so engrained...I sense it in her...she needs to open herself...move her hands away... it is so difficult to allow that vulnerability...but she does...she drops her hands to her side. His hands are cupping his *Light* and then entering her chest...it is the same as last time but different...he is touching her Heart and dispensing the *Light* to all of her wounds...I had not recognized her woundedness till now. I can see flickers of the *Light* in the places where it has spread, like fireflies...she seems a little surprised, stiff, as with unused muscles...atrophied is not quite the right word, not quite immobile, but stiff from the lack of being active." At this point, I have Pearl refocus on her critical voice and ask if she can still hear it? She replies that she has not been hearing it, but is aware of it when I ask. "I know where it is...*in my head behind my right eye.*" (Later Pearl will tell me this is also where she experiences most of her headaches, including episodic migraines). I have her ask Christ to draw it out of her head and place it in a circle. What she reports surprises us both. In fact, she prefaces what she reports by saying she has never done this before. Essentially, she 'hallucinates' Christ drawing it out of her head and placing it on the coffee table between us in my office. "I have never done what I just did. Our work has always been internal. He has physically removed it and put it on the table, put it outside of me on the table. There is a circle confining it there. Whatever it is seems dark, oily, and poisonous. It has no shape." I suggest that she simply ask Christ to turn it into pure white light and return it to its source. (I have yet to appreciate that Christ has extracted her power to self-shame and treat whatever has manifested as an autonomous emotion.) "It crystallizes like dry powdery snow that you can blow away and he puts it in the ocean. When it hits the surface of the ocean it glitters for a moment and then disappears. This is weird. Where he pulled it out from my head is where I have always had my headaches." At this point, I wonder aloud if Pearl is willing to reintegrate with the insatiable part of herself? "I feel like the healing process is incomplete. I guess I am saying I am not ready yet. I want to watch a while longer." I tell her that is quite all right, but also remind her that she does not have to wait till she is back in session with me. (Pearl is quite right. She has allowed Christ to remove her power to self-shame, but has yet to have him supplant it with the power of his discernment, or entered her Heart to clear any shame found there.)

In retrospect, I am in awe of everything that has just transpired. Everything happening in this session is truly Christ working in Pearl. I am behind the curve from the word go. Only weeks later will I finally come to appreciate the dynamics. Truly, it is Christ guiding us both that is bringing Pearl to these major shifts in her world, and 'firmly' preventing me from forcing pre-mature closer. It is worth reiterating here that, if a client calls on the Christ image over a period of months and years, the Christ image will become increasingly autonomous; and the therapist would do well to increasingly accede to it, even when he seems to frustrate therapist's agenda.

Pearl returns the next week with interesting news. She has been promoted to a job her employer *told her to apply for*. When the job was initially posted, Pearl felt too inadequate to apply because she was being made to feel so inferior by her shaming voice. By the time she is encouraged to apply, Christ has silenced the voice. In fact, when I query her about it she really cannot remember feeling it or hearing it at any point during the previous week. Next, I ask her about Insatiable. "She is standing beside Christ holding his hand." I ask Pearl to please describe the changes she observes in Insatiable. "She has been purged of some kind of poison, but I don't know what it was. She is – like me, much more trusting and relaxed. Our need for self-defense has been largely eliminated. Whatever has happened to her has happened to me too, only it is more visible in her. Several times during the week I have asked Christ for a refresher by letting him place his hand into my Heart." I ask her if she is ready for reintegration? "It is time. Actually, I feel the process has already begun. Her qualities will serve me well. I am just not sure that I have anything comparable to add to the mix." I explain to Pearl that she represents the other pole in this and that both are needed to effectively range around a homeostatic center. I suggest that each of them – Christ included, place their *Lights* into a circle as an expression of willingness for the reintegration; and then each of them will step into the circle. I add that she needs to let Christ take the lead in how to proceed beyond that. "She and Christ are hand in hand. They come over to 'collect' me. I take his other hand." There is a few minutes of silence then I see Pearl smile and comment, "OK, that's weird." She goes on to explain: "When we placed our *Lights* in the circle they seemed to scoot toward each other and join as one. When we step into the circle, Christ links my hands with hers and then steps back. He may have his hands on our shoulders; I am not sure. Our two images are side by side. We begin to overlap and merge." I am a little concerned at this point that Pearl has dissociated so I ask her if she is in the experience or observing it? "I am out and in. she is much clearer to me, but there is also a bigger picture of the two of us in lesser focus. I guess I am also observing. Our figures are sliding into each other. We are overlaid." To reaffirm her first person experience I suggest that she join completely with this merged self, stand in front of Christ, and ask him to enter *their joined hearts* and seal the connection. "It is that touch that sustains us. It is stronger than any voices that could undermine it." I suggest that she take the time to write a prayer and pick a time each morning when she says it as an invitation for Christ to once again enter her Heart as 'daily bread.' The phrasing reminds me to ask her about her eating. "I have come to realize that I must change my eating habits. For one thing, instead of going out everyday to eat a big meal, I have started to pack a lunch and eat it at work with other employees. I use to look for immediate gratification, hope for it. Now I am planning to eat, preparing it, and eating it when it is time."

From my perspective, Pearl's promotion is the universe's 'answer' to this intervention, one of those coincidences in which God chooses to remain anonymous. Her employer has all but insisted she apply when she did not voluntarily respond to the posting. Beyond that, Pearl's own sense of inner change speaks a great deal for the intervention. As for the overeating, that will have to wait for the weeks and months to evaluate. But Pearl's response is typical. All of the clients who have successfully moved through these steps begin reporting spontaneous changes on the heels of it. For example, in Marion's case described previously she began an exercise program with a trainer.

When Pearl returns she reports that inside is good. She feels calmer and more peaceful, but she notes that she remains solitary in most of her pursuits and only occasionally goes out with a friend. (Her friends have tended to be very needy people who she is less interested in pursuing.) She shares that she has written a prayer, which she has placed on her bathroom mirror. "It is a great comfort experiencing that touch on a daily basis." Her statement about 'remaining solitary' prompts me to ask if there is a place of sexuality in her Heart? (I suspect this question was prompted by Marion's case described above.) She replies chidingly, "I knew you would get back to that! The question evokes discomfort in me. I feel like I have failed sexually. But yes, I think there is a place for it in my Heart." I ask if she would be willing for Christ to enter her Heart and take her to that place? "He can and does. I see him holding it. It is tiny, acorn size, a sphere, lead-like in quality, opaqued...completely...inaccessible. It is all of the same material. It is not a shell. It seems inert, a metal." I ask her if Christ can blow on it? Warm it? Awaken it? Pearl balks. A new self has emerged as we talk. Pearl tells me: "I am unwilling to allow Christ to act upon it. I don't have time for that." Even, I ask, if it were to draw you closer to Christ? "That was mean! I would do it for that." So I challenge her to let Christ awaken her sexuality. Pearl is now reflective. "This may be a case of being careful of what you pray for. I have been praying to him to make me aware and open my Heart. Intellectually, I am struggling with this. The idea of Christ and sexuality going hand in hand seems contradictory. My logical thought has made everything inside disappear." Pearl has become cognizant of a new self, which she proceeds to describe. "She is control, tradition, distance, disengagement. She is outside the Heart. Her self-stated mission and intent is to block and protect. She perceives sexuality as dangerous. My faith is vertical and her logic is horizontal. She flings herself between my Heart and me. But she has no control over my faith." I suggest that our goal become the reconciliation of this new self with her Heart, and the establishment a midpoint between faith and logic with a freedom to move back and forth freely. The session ends here.

Pearl returns the next week to report that she has purchased the book on Tantric sexuality that I have suggested, which is a first. In the past she has always demurred when I have recommended books that were implicitly or explicitly sexual, even when I have offered them off my own shelf. She comments that, "The fact that I have been reading it without rejecting it is testimonial to a shift in my Rational self. She is in retrograde, no longer dominant. The exploring Heart is dominant." For my part, I have finally deduced that Christ can offer the power of his discernment in exchange for the power of self-shaming, and now offer this to the Rational self. "That is not something she has experienced in the past. Her responses tend to be knee jerks. It would be a new experience, allowing her to think for herself rather than relying on the contradictions of tradition and culture. I am currently allowing myself more of the humanity that I have made allowances for in other people." I suggest she go inside and let the Rational self take the step I have suggested. Pearl quickly goes inside and immediately begins reporting: "The process has already begun. She is different than she was last week. She is more parallel with the exploring Heart. She is easier for Christ to access and penetrate than I would have imagined. The *Light* illuminates her from within. If we could let down the barriers a little more, it could radiate more." I ask what does she mean by 'barrier'? "There is a fear of being visibly different." I suggest that she release the fear into the ocean and then move into the Heart closer to Christ. "She is prepared to move in next door and visit frequently, to begin the process, like an overlay." I suggest that there may be a sexual self in the Heart, and that might be the reason for her reticence. "This is the first time I have had a glimmer of that, of accepting it as a possibility, of imagining pleasure. I have asked Christ to blow on that sphere. What is different is that I can imagine it flowering. Before I denied it totally." I ask if he needs an assistant, a female image? "It would confuse me. He says, 'no'." But I persist in this train of thought. I ask who will be the recipient of this energy? The Mind needs an image to reach the body. Pearl senses conflict but is willing to reconsider what I am saying. "Here is where the battle begins. I can serve as a vessel, but the Rational self does not like the body as it is, she does not see it as able to fill the potential that the Heart imagines." Even so, I encourage Pearl to present herself as a vessel, to give Christ a portion of her *Light* and let Christ mix it with the sphere of her sexuality. "I have done it. Visually, the *Light* surrounds the sphere...there is not a real blending...but I sense the edges will blur as the sphere softens. I am unable to predict or imagine the result at this time." Our session ends here.

With hindsight, I will come to appreciate that Christ's actions in the previous sessions has precipitated the emergence of a reconstituted Familial personality. That self will remain strong for the foreseeable future, but its ability to totally control Pearl is greatly diminished. Pearl calls the difference 'faith,' and I really have no better answer for the time being. When she is offered the option of relinquishing her power to self-shame in exchange for Christ's discernment, Pearl quickly accedes. The Rational self, though not overtly shaming, will now proffer doubts about the presumably overweight body being an adequate vessel for Pearl's sexuality. Here Christ appears to tell her that what is in the Heart can trump the Rational self's control of the body. I really don't know. What is clear are the dramatic changes taking place in Pearl's inner and outer life. Even with the Rational self intact, Pearl will go through a period of dramatic changes that culminate in her joining a church, receiving yet another promotion in a much better paying and more satisfying job, and meeting a new companion. But it will be months before her Rational self is finally willing to stop shaming her body. As for me, I am coming to trust the process, but frankly I also find it a little unnerving. Christ is guiding us both in ways I am still struggling to understand. It is not until the third case, discussed below, that I finally appreciate the need to terminate the 'power of self-shaming' before asking the client to let Christ enter the Heart. Both work as it turns out, but terminating the power first, and anticipating the need to terminate the aural Voice-of-conscience soon after entering the Heart, seems to shorten the processing time.

Leigh. This next case represents a significant departure from the first two in that weight has never been a significant issue for Leigh. She has maintained a healthy body weight throughout her adult life, primarily by skipping meals while working compulsively. I suggest to Leigh that her *excessive working* may be her attempt to cope with an insatiable desire. She shares with me that her "Mind went to loneliness. I am starving for a family life." I suggest to her that very likely this self resides in her heart, and that Christ can satisfy this insatiable part and then draw it out of her heart into a circle. (As with the above cases, I have failed to first address self-shame and the resistance that will result is all but inevitable.) After a few minutes inside Leigh reports: "At first I was really resistant. I did not want to look at it. I was very afraid it would be painful, a lot of shame. I turned to Christ and sat in his lap so I would not be afraid of his reaching inside. Then I remembered my father always grilling us when he got home. I am afraid of seeing myself as like him, not knowing how to do the relationship thing." I wonder out loud if maybe the starved part of her is crucial to being in relationship? "Of course you are right... my unwillingness to be vulnerable...it got used against me growing up." So, I ask, is its satisfaction at odds with her distrust? At this point I make several further suggestions all at once: 1) provide yourself with a garment of protection from the fear of being vulnerable; 2) delegate responsibility for the vulnerable part to Christ; and 3) insist that all of the vulnerable part's satisfaction flow through Christ, even when it comes from others. I imagine this last suggestion easing the Dominant self's fear. The idea is for Leigh to experience vulnerability as safely satisfying in order to know if the experience is worthwhile. Leigh accedes to all this to the extent that she is willing for Christ to place his hand on her Heart. "I am sitting with his hand on my Heart. I am in it. This is so painful and he just holds me. It hurts so much, beyond anything that is logical. It is purely emotional. But my defenses seem lower." (Leigh appears to be experiencing a phenomenon I call 'love breaking through the armor.') Leigh continues: "Now he has placed his hand on my back at the level of the heart, and he says, 'Lets do it from the back'." At this point Leigh distracts us both by commenting on her allergies. I accept her need for distraction – if that is what it is, and suggest that she let Christ take her to the ocean, which she has done before. There, she is to release the emotional sinus pains into his hands as light. She sees black oil being released from her eyes. She describes it as a headache, tension, and exhaustion. After a few moments I refocus her on the vulnerable part by commenting that in order for this intervention to be effective Christ has to be allowed to reach into her heart not just place his hand over her heart. This is too much for Leigh. She responds by telling me, "I have to work on that one." This is not an atypical response. Clients often express the need to reflect on this intervention, which seems to speak well for it insofar as the client can sense its potential for change. But in retrospect, I am also aware that the suggestion is pre-mature. She has yet to forgo her power to self-shame in exchange for Christ's discernment. And intuitively, she seems to have glimpsed her fear of such a step.

When Leigh returns she has indeed been reflective. She does not tell me this at first but she has returned intent on letting Christ enter her heart. What she does share at the outset is that she has been feeling tired the last two weeks – a recurring complaint. She also shares her belief that her power to self-shame has served as a kind of life preserver. Even so, she is willing to go inside so Christ can enter her heart. But once inside she immediately dissociates and sees an image of herself with Christ – "I observe myself with Christ." The problem here is my failure to first have Leigh extract her power to self-shame and accept Christ's power of discernment and she seems to cope with my premature suggestion of letting him enter her Heart by separating. I stress that nothing will come between her and her *Light* until she is willing. She tells me that the thought of letting go of the *Light* terrifies her. I ask what it is she is afraid will happen if Christ enters her Heart? "Christ seems so giant and I feel so small; I cannot see myself. I cannot get beyond being terrified." This is the voice of a new self who has emerged to take the place of the one who has been separated. I ask what is terrifying her? "I have to grow up and deal with all the freaky people out there. I feel like a 12 year old." I remind her that Christ can replace her power to self-shame with his gift of discernment. (But note, I am still directing the client to make the exchange within the heart rather than the brow.) At this point she makes a connection between discernment and intuition. In the past she has always felt well served by her intuition. This connection encourages her to move her *Light* aside and let Christ enter her Heart. "I can sense an opening...like a mail shoot...a lot of light...no visuals...now I have a fleeting image of the windows of Notre Dame lit up. I feel like a seed has been planted. I came in today maybe ready to do this. The past week has been boring, hot, monotonous...not what I want life to be about." We are well over our time so at this point I have to bring her back.

The above session was another illustration of my putting the cart before the horse. Early on in developing this intervention, I thought it would be possible for Christ to achieve everything if he and Leigh could enter the Heart. Some access to the Heart was gained, but note that Leigh is terrified at the prospect of entering her Heart in the first person. We will eventually discover a number of good reasons for that resistance in addition to her initial resistance at the thought of relinquishing her power to self-shame. It is also seems significant that when Christ terminates her power to self-shame in exchange for his discernment (which is not unlike intuition) it is as if he does it through a 'mail shoot;' as if he were sending his power to another chakra (sic) the brow chakra. This was one of the clues I would need to begin focusing on the brow chakra. Today, I would only suggest to clients that they enter their Heart without any preparation in order to demonstrate their anticipated resistance, which I would then use as an entrée to addressing their power to self-shame. Leigh's case is described at greater length in the next chapter where I will follow it through to its conclusion.

I can anticipate the reader's confusion on several levels at this point, which will somewhat reflect my own confusion as the clients and I struggle to enter, what I eventually call, the Aware-ego's Heart. Each of these will eventually experience this space via their connection to the Aware-ego, but none of them will actually gain access to it until a personification of the reconstituted Familial personality has allowed Christ to purify its heart chakra. These are now my treatment goals for any new client, though few others have yet to achieve them. What I am attempting to capture here is the process of 'accepting their resistance as the means of discovering an optimum path into the Heart.' Each of these cases was instrumental in helping me to discern a replicable path, which others can follow. In my mind, they and Christ are the true authors of these discoveries.

Tory. Tory is the next client to work through the initial stages of the process. She has just worked through a major reconciliation involving deeply disowned parts of her self identified as Victoria and Victor. Shortly thereafter, a new self emerges which I identify as Rational Understanding. She says of this self that, "It does not accept the new sense of me, though that does not alter how I feel about it. Rational Understanding definitely comes from mother, especially in terms of her rejection of anything spiritual. My mother always said that 'God never promised that life would be easy or good.' Rational Understanding has a real sense of scarcity. She is very fearful. There is only one right answer and she constantly fears she may not know it." I suggest to Tory that she separate from Rational Understanding, which she does.

"She is much like me. I thought she would look stern and rigid." I suggest to Tory that she teach Rational Understanding to use the *Light* as a garment of protection from fear. "When we did this before the garment appeared cloak-like. But this time it appears like a slip. No one else will know it is there." I ask Tory if Rational Understanding would be willing to meet Tory's sense of Jesus Christ? "I paused for a moment because she does have an understanding of Christ, but my sense of him really is different." I ask if she is willing to hold Christ's hands for just a little bit so she could get a sense of him? "It was hard for her to do until he actually took her hand and then it felt really good. When Christ took her hands I could physically feel myself relax. She may have been rigid." I suggest that she let Christ baptize her by placing a portion of his *Light* into her Heart and dissolving all sense of unworthiness about interacting with him. Tory tells me: "It is not going to happen now, but it will happen." The session ends here. Again, I am putting the cart before the horse in failing to first address self-shaming.

In the next session, I begin by further exploring the nature of Rational Understanding – who I have decided to treat as a Dominant self. I begin by asking how she copes with the irrational? "She can't combat it. She just lays low until it goes away and she can reign again. She is the default setting, not my typical mode of operating. She only has an intellectual understanding of the irrational, not a heartfelt experience." I change the tack of my questions by asking what she does with emotions? I suggest that she ask Christ where Rational Understanding keeps the emotions? "I wanted to say away from me, but Christ is pointing at me. They are inside of me." I ask how she keeps them locked inside? "I hear the word memory." You have the ability to lock memory away? "Yes. I discount it, refuse to think of it." What emotions do you use to discount something? "I don't trust the memory. I doubt it. I just explain it away." At this point, I ask Tory to reorient to me in the session. Her first comment is, "To listen to myself – God that is strange. What could be so terrible about memory?" I suggest that she is guarding against the emotional impact of memory. "Yes. That was true for so many years. Growing up I had nothing I could do with it if I felt it. No one to make it better, share it with, understand it." I suggest to Tory that she go back inside and ask Christ to create a dome that will absorb any feeling memory that might emerge as a result of our focus on it, so she can feel it without being overwhelmed by it, and feel free to talk to Christ or me about it. After she does this I end the session. This last suggestion is cautionary. I am not sure if there will be a surge of memory or not. The dome will probably foster recall as well as containing it.

Tory cancels the next session claiming that her sinuses are so severe she must go to her Doctor. [45] I schedule to see her the following day. When she returns she tells me that only the right side of her face is affected by the sinus congestion. I suggest that she go inside and have Christ place a tube that will allow it to drain. She feels a sense of pressure release. Then she goes on to report that after the last session she 'felt' a lot of images that *hurt*. "There was a memory of my mother offering to take me shopping downtown and then leaving without me as I was getting ready to go with her. Lots of Christmas images of mother 'cancelling' Christmas." I pick up on the *hurt*, which is so often a code word for feeling ashamed, and ask her who is shaming her over these events? "I think it is Rational Understanding." I suggest that she ask Christ to place Rational Understanding in an opaqued dome for a moment and then approach the other opaqued dome that has been 'absorbing' the feelings. Basically, I am encouraging her to identify what part of her is the recipient of the shame.

"I don't know who it is. The dome remains opaqued. Part of me says what is in the dome is negative and another part says positive." I have her ask Christ if he will heal anything she sees in the dome? When she affirms that he will, I encourage her to let him look inside the dome, determine if what is there that needs healing and then tell her if he can. Again, he affirms his willingness and ability. "What I see in there is a coil and something that is being squeezed. The coil is negative and what is running through it is positive. The coil started out as protection. It directed what was running through it. It determined the direction and quantity." I ask if the coil has a name? "Fear." I ask if she can identify the object of fear? "Whatever it is really is pure and valuable. It is fluid, not liquid, a real joy to it." I have her ask Christ to name it. "I can't ask him. What is going through my head are readings from the Course in Miracles, Marian Williamson, all of her essays on love. I want to say it is love. It has been a real struggle for me to receive love, and make people understand that love is my nature." I ask how it is that Rational Understanding finds it necessary to shame love? "It was an unequal balance. My parents never understood what I wanted or needed, or what I give to other people to this day. Today, I strive to act on love, but when I look back and remember I see the squeezing and strangling." I suggest that she allow Christ to dissolve the coil, but Rational Understanding will not feel the effects until she has given up the power of self-shame. Then I ask how the dome appears when the fear is dissolved? "I don't see the dome. I see that the flow has flattened out. There is a place for it now. Rational Understanding's dome is still intact." I note that when Rational Understanding is willing to give up her power to self-shame she can use the power of Christ's discernment to know how best to express this love. I am also aware from something else Tory has said, that her father's beliefs also sustain the fear of love, so I suggest that she ask Christ to terminate his power to define love for Rational Understanding. "When I asked Christ to do that, my father was close in, but then when Christ placed his *Light* into his heart, he zoomed out." The session ends here.

Most of the next session is taken up with a prolonged discussion of Tory's relationship and observations concerning her daughter and granddaughter. This theme will continue for the remainder of the sessions so I need to introduce Tory's daughter, Abby, and Mandy, her granddaughter of 24 months. The extended family believes that Mandy is developmentally delayed. Tory, who has had a distinguished career as a teacher of the gifted is reserving judgment. Another theme that may be playing out here relates to eating. Both Tory and Abby are overweight, Abby most decidedly so. In contrast, Mandy – her daughter, is a very finicky eater, whose developmental delays involve oral articulation. There is also a recapitulation theme being played out with this triad. Tory's maternal grandmother took care of Tory after her own mother had a second child, a son, who Tory's mother (two years deceased) always favored. Abby has recently delivered her second child, a son. She has all but excluded her mother from involvement with this pregnancy, except to call on her increasingly to care for Mandy. In this session I begin to weave these themes together. I strongly suspect that Mandy's developmental delays reflect her role in the family as a carrier of disowned selves for both Tory and Abby. To the extent possible, I will work with Tory to have her own any projections embedded in her image of Mandy. Tory begins this session by sharing her observations concerning Abby and Mandy. "Abby fears that Mandy is uncontrollable. She is developmentally behind. Her articulation is not good. Her tongue is always out. She seems to have oral sensory deficits. Abby does not know what to do with her. I feel like I have to make up for Abby with Mandy. Mandy does not get enough from Abby." I listen to what Tory is saying and begin to weave it into our work with Rational Understanding. First, I note that Mandy seems to be embodying a kind of emotional starvation, in her inability to eat, voice her needs, and in her oral sensory deficits. Since Tory understands the concept of projection from past work, I suggest that Rational Understanding needs to give up her power of self-shame and ask Christ to draw out whatever is 'starving' Mandy. (In making that interpretation – or intuitive leap, I am applying a basic working premise. Whatever a client introduces at the beginning of a session is in some way applicable to what s/he is working on inside. The current 'worldly' concerns of our lives are the projective vessels of our inner life. From that perspective, Tory's concerns about her granddaughter make her a ripe vessel for unconscious projections of any disowned opposite motivating Rational Understanding.) Tory does not go inside in this session.

In this next session two other themes are introduced. The first one concerns her grown brother, 'Mack,' the one favored by her mother. Over the past two years his alcoholism has cost him his job, and his wife is seriously threatening divorce. Mack is strongly identified (by me) with his MGF, a small-town drunk, whose public behavior humiliated Tory's mother throughout her life. Mack hid his alcoholism from the family while his mother was alive but has given up all pretence since her death. Tory tells her father, whom she always thought of as an ally while the mother was alive (though it required a lot of denial to sustain that fiction), that she is afraid that Mack will not live long, given how much he is drinking. "Daddy says he will be better off dead." (Within months of the mother's death, 'Daddy' took up with another woman who he has focused on these past two years to the exclusion of any real involvement with his son or daughter.) Tory is seeing her father in a new light of late and can now say that his comments reflect a real anger in him that has probably been there for a long time. Interestingly, her father denies that his father-in-law was the town drunk, but also says he hates drunks, has no use for him. The father has a brother who is alcoholic, and I suspect there are others in his extended family. Tory is "angry at him for being able to feel that way. He can just cut somebody off." I remind her that Tory cut off 'Victoria' for most of her adult life (the inner relationship we resolved before this series) and that Rational Understanding may well be cutting off a major source of love in her self. Tory replies that, "There is a real rage in him (her father). I cut off parts of my self, but he is cutting off his son. With the slightest provocation his anger can erupt. He was the one parent I felt I had a chance with, who was reasonable. I wanted to be more like him. I thought he would be there as a protector, even though he did not give me an indication that he might do that. In fact, he put me in situations that I did not need to be in." Tory goes on to share new memories of how her father used the pretext of taking her to town to meet with other women and then ask her not to share the episodes with her mother. "But he would not stand up for me with mother because he said he had to live with her when I was grown and gone. Mother said he did not care for us. Even so, I still saw him as the only chance I had." I wonder aloud if Rational Understanding has patterned herself after her dad? (As it turns out, the angry part of her is not Rational Understanding, but a part that will emerge when Rational Understanding is reconciled.) Once again, Tory avoids going inside, but clearly she is giving a lot of reflection to the family dynamics that have shaped Rational Understanding.

Tory returns again preoccupied with her brother, Mack. "I have cried a lot thinking about him, but I do not know why." I make a suggestion, which will prove to be significant in later sessions. I assume that Mack's masculine and feminine aspects are significantly shaped by the estranged relationship between Tory's mother and her alcoholic maternal grandfather. I suggest that Christ be allowed to extract these from her brother's image and work with them. (This might help her as well as her brother.) Tory demurs and says she would prefer to do that on her own later in the week between sessions. Instead she is ready to focus on Rational Understanding who, she believes, has been the cause of all of her tears. I suggest that she go inside and separate from Rational Understanding. "She looks like me. There is a real hardness about her." I suggest that this may be the consequence of her power to self-shame, and I have Tory ask Christ to draw out this power from Rational Understanding's brow chakra. I note that this only objectifies it, that she will still retain the power to exercise it. "What I feel from that circle is that *I'm a mistake*, I never did what I was supposed to do, and I still don't. It makes me feel like I could make up for the mistakes but I've never been able to do it. I see my daughter Abby acting toward my granddaughter Mandy as if everything about her is a mistake, that Mandy is a mistake. I am just amazed that there is such a connection between Mandy and mistake." Even so, when I suggest it, Rational Understanding is unwilling to give up her power to self-shame in exchange for Christ's power of discernment as a first step to Christ's entering her Heart and healing Mistake. So I modify my suggestion to make it provisional (this is the first time I have done so with a client). I suggest that, if she is willing, Christ will extract the power of self-shame and *provisionally* replace it with the power of his discernment. If Rational Understanding finds the exchange intolerable, then Christ will reverse the process. Rational Understanding agrees to proceed under this condition. "There was a lot of tension at first, but then a sense of relief and lightness. All I can see in the circle where Christ has placed the power [of self-shame] is something black and hard that seemed to grow when it got out. It is dark, like a heap [of cow manure]. The power of discernment generated the relief, or maybe a release." I ask Tory what she would like Christ to do with 'the heap,' hoping she will let Christ have it. "We need to leave it in the circle. Her willingness came because it is provisional." I ask if she is willing to let him enter her Heart and heal Mistake? "OK. So Christ and I are to go into her Heart?" I affirm her query and there is a long silence. Then she asks what is she to do? I suggest that she let Christ find Mistake and heal her. Tory becomes tearful. "Mistake is really, really little. She is trying to be unnoticed. Christ takes her hands and stands her in front of him. She is crying." I remind Tory that she must ask Christ to baptize Mistake and fill her with the Holy Spirit. "Yes. He does that. She is still small but she is no longer crying; she seems normal." In response, I pose a series of questions: What is her nature? What will feed her? Who is she when free of shame? "She is his child and she is loved. That is Christ talking. And she can grow in that feeling." I suggest that Rational Understanding can discern that growth only so long as she does not shame it. She – Rational Understanding, can still impede the experience of love in herself. "She is not thinking or feeling anything. I have to digest and think about all of this." I add that she allow Christ to leave a portion of his *Light* in her Heart before exiting. The session ends here. Three days later Tory e-mails a dream to me:

> Last night I dreamed that I was teaching at my old school. The school was close to my home. So during lunch, I decided that I wanted to go look at my

old house. I could not find it! I was looking for landmarks and not looking at the street names. I was lost. When I started looking for the street names, I finally found my street, but they had built a large, beautiful government building where my house was. I was frantic. I kept saying, "Why didn't I know about this? Why didn't someone tell me? Why didn't my Daddy tell me they were going to do this?" Soon this man came up to me and identified himself as the builder. He told me that I was upset over nothing. He told me that much of my home was included in the building – only in a more beautiful way. "Come on – I'll show you." When we went into the building, I immediately saw many of the things I recognized from home. It was really fun going through the building looking for things I treasured from my past! Even I can interpret this one!

When Tory returns a week later she fills in events surrounding the dream. "For three days after the last session my eyes felt like they had cried for a year. (Bear in mind that Rational Understanding has been dissociated and not remerged with the Aware-ego.) On Monday I felt so different and then I remembered the dream. My eyes were fine. I have had a really good week. I don't know how to understand the crying part. I saw Mandy [granddaughter] yesterday. She is precious! Abby [daughter] starts a new job next week and I have agreed to provide day care for Mandy and her little brother. I am excited to keep them. The teacher in me already has a month of lesson plans." I ask her if Rational Understanding is willing for Christ to absorb her power of self-shame? "I suspect her willingness will strengthen, but she is willing enough for now." I have her ask Christ to completely dispel it. "OK. He has turned it into pure white light. Rational Understanding feels a reserved good. She is not use to feeling. She thinks she is interested in knowing the changes it will bring." I suggest that Rational Understanding could ask Christ to baptize her and she can then merge with Mistake. "I think she would be more comfortable observing Mistake." (I suspect this is a new self speaking.) I suggest to Tory that she allow Christ to bring Mistake out of her Heart and into a circle. Tory agrees to this. "There is some fear on Mistake's part in accepting the Light which Rational Understanding offers her, but she did accept it. Part of the fear was in being out. Everything is so different. No sense of what to trust, almost as if there was never anything to trust before." I note that she did dare to trust the *Light*; and then ask what is Mistake's need at the moment? "Her need is to not be disappointed with the world. She has become very vulnerable." I ask what is the opposite of disappointed? "Embrace." I suggest that Christ can instill his power of discernment within her, which will allow her to assess what will embrace and what will disappoint. "That feels right. She wanted everything to embrace her, but understands that distinguishing will be better." This initial series of sessions ends here. It continues later in the chapter.

Transitioning From Conscience to Working With the Familial Personality

In the next section of this chapter, the verbatims provided by Tory and Marion are continued to their conclusion. Leigh's verbatim is continued to its conclusion in the next chapter. Both of the verbatims given below are extensive. Each spans more than a year of work with each client. Moreover, I quickly move beyond Moral authority proper into Relational authority issues, which are covered in the next chapter. The reconstituted Familial personality is most properly identified with Relational authority as it is a constellation of the Gendering archetype. But that sense-of-self is nearly impossible to identify and work with until the Dominant self is redeemed. Moreover, the Gendering archetype constellates more than images of the self and can be addressed in a general way before the Dominant self is redeemed; but not so the Familial personality. Essentially, the Gendering archetype is responsible for the creation of all images within the Mind, including self-images. It constellates the Familial personality by constellating an amalgamate of personality characteristic derived from parental interactions experienced by the client during childhood.

In sum, Tory and Marion's verbatims will be introducing the reader to masculine-feminine concepts underpinning the Gendering archetype as well as the Familial personality (which may be its most significant constellation as a governor of personality). In addition, the last chapter also provides the rationale for *convicting with the power of the Holy Spirit*, which has proven to be the most powerful intervention offered in this work. That too is repeatedly illustrated in the verbatims but not elaborated upon.

I have chosen to follow both clients through the entire process in this chapter even though it means getting ahead of the reader, because even though the Familial personality is a byproduct of the Gendering archetype, it is also the bridge that allows the client to begin major reconstructions of the personality, which the therapist is obliged to address soon after the redemption of the Dominant self. My suggestion to the reader is that s/he read the last portions of each case without having to fully understanding them, and then reread those verbatims after finishing chapter VIII.

I also include these particular verbatims because they illustrate my own struggle to understand the consequences of redeeming conscience. All too frequently, they will illustrate my missteps as I learn along with my clients. In significant ways, the redemption of conscience leaves the client stripped of many ego defenses learned in childhood, but leaves the client still grounded in whatever personality-core dysfunction stimulated the need for therapy. The redemption of conscience makes Christ and the Holy Spirit strongly figural in the client's inner dynamics; and now they must be called upon to help the client address core personality dysfunction. With Christ's help, the client can embark on the necessary personality change. And I cannot understate the need for Christ's help. The sought after changes are largely governed by archetypal constellations, which can only be altered by a higher power. Left to its own devices, the Ego cannot change its basic building blocks.

A Phenomenal Perspective of the Familial personality

I want to remind the reader and elaborate upon the unexpected emergence of the sense-of-self that comes to the fore when Christ terminates the aural Voice-of-conscience. What then becomes figural is the reconstituted Familial personality. Marion will initially prove the exception to that rule, as we will first have to address an Ideal persona; but all three clients will otherwise exhibit the same progression.

The client's personality amalgamate becomes figural within several hours or days of Christ first entering the Aware-ego's Heart and terminating the aural Voice-of-conscience. At first, I thought of this sense-of-self was merely a 'regressive' ego-aspect because it feels and acts like a younger, less developed version of the Dominant self, which the therapist and client have worked so hard to redeem. But when the client goes inside as Aware-ego, it is nearly impossible to personify this new sense-of-self, except by the client's repeated assertion that it is "me." Christ can contain a sense of mental attributes and feelings, but no image. It is as if the new sense-of-self remains inseparably merged with the Aware-ego or lacks any degree of sensate embodiment. When I finally decided to treat this sense-of-self as the personality-core, it then became possible to personify it. However, once personified the actual sense-of-self then assumed the role of participant-observer.

Following the redemption of conscience, the reconstituted Familial personality appears to become the client's preferred locus of consciousness. From that perspective, the client can observe and vicariously participate in the actions of Christ, the Aware-ego, and any ego-aspects embodying the personality-core. This is made evident by the client when s/he repeatedly refers to his or her sense-of-self as "me." The "me" is separate and distinct from the Aware-ego, but nonetheless actively identified with what is happening inside. Before the redemption of conscience, the client normally localized his or her sense-of-self within the Aware-ego and whatever ego-aspect was fused with the Aware-ego at the time s/he went inside. When separated from the Aware-ego, the separated consciousness was identifiable as an ego-aspect while the locus of consciousness normally remained with the Aware-ego. In contrast, there are now two potential loci of consciousness: the Aware-ego and a participant-observer. And often it is the Aware-ego that is personified, though this is not readily apparent until the therapist becomes cognizant of the participant-observer, who cannot be personified. In effect, the therapist must begin to take seriously the client's assertion that there is a second locus of consciousness that cannot be personified in its unmitigated state, and has the capacity to vicariously experience what is going on inside. Of note, the observer is not an 'actor,' s/he is only a participant-observer; which is one reason why its existence is not immediately apparent. What makes the observer a participant is its empathic connection with, and reactivity to any inner activity involving another self that has embodied its personality-core. That reactivity also sets it apart from the Aware-ego, which is simply aware and willing rather than empathic and reactive. In sum, the participant-observer is the archetypal substrate that gives each ego-aspect a sense of identity, which the client also accepts as "me." So far as I can determine, this archetypal substrate is an amalgamate of personality characteristics derived form parental interactions constellated by the Gendering archetype (described in the next chapter).

I eventually concluded is that the reconstituted Familial personality is most likely the core-personality of the self-shaming Dominant self and any other ego-aspect created after its constellation. Initially, it is hard to assess its age since it remains highly resistant to separation; but when finally personified it is generally identified as between the ages of seven and twelve. It is determinedly intransigent to change in its participant-observer state. Gradually, the Familial personality can be transformed, but not before it has sorely tested any therapist who thinks the client's previous changes were sufficient. Fortunately, the reconstituted Familial personality becomes the locus of consciousness in the context of all that immediately preceded its conscious re-emergence, including the client's progressive experiences of Christ's discernment and forgiveness and entry into the Heart. Even as the client struggles with this atavism, s/he remains mindful of transformative experiences that have redeemed the Dominant self, and her ongoing experience of Christ provides both daily reminders and new insights. These new experiences, coupled with further interventions, keep the client mindful that 'something better' is possible, even as she struggles with the atavistic nature of the reconstituted Familial personality; or, in the case of Marion, the emergent presence of an Ideal persona overlay.

The Core Personality

The emergence of an interior sense of 'I and me' appears to coincide with the constellation of an aural Voice-of-conscience by the Empowering archetype. It is unclear to me whether the constellated Voice-of-conscience precedes or follows the Gendering archetype's constellation of a core personality. But in any case, the Ego's incorporation of the Familial personality appears to represent its first successful effort to incorporate the sense-of-self identified as "me" or "I am me." In turn, the Dominant self, represents the further integration of this personality-core with a concomitant power to self-shame. I suspect the process of integrating those two is never an easy one, and quite painful for every child who must learn to shame his or her self.

My understanding of the reconstituted Familial personality did not emerge full-blown following the redemption of the Dominant self. I quickly grasped the regressive character of this new self, and the need for Christ to terminate the Voice-of-conscience (which the client could now hear clearly and aurally), but not the fact that this new sense-of-self was an unmitigated, archetypal constellation. What finally led me to this conclusion was nearly a year's work with the numerous permutations of Relational authority described in the next chapter. I developed most of the interventions described in that chapter, particularly the convicting power of the Holy Spirit, in an effort 'change' the reconstituted Familial personality, largely without any success until I could actually 'name' this sense-of-self as an unmitigated archetypal constellation.

It is important to appreciate that what emerges following the redemption of the Dominant self is an adult variant of the Familial personality, which incorporates the strife and union inherent in the parental relationship at the time it was constellated. The Gendering archetype uses the parental relationship to constellate an amalgamate of masculine/feminine personality characteristics, which the Ego then seeks to incorporate into an ego-aspect. Once this is appreciated, Christ can be asked *to capture the sense of self that best reflects the client's current personality*. (The development and use of a 'capturing circle' is described below.) Whatever is captured becomes, in effect, the prima materia that Christ initially uses to reshape personality through the generation of Ideal pairs. The reshaping process is intended to liberate the client from restrictions imposed on the reconstituted Familial personality by its slavish adherence to familial and cultural demands, which are most often at odds with the process of individuation. Later or concomitantly, Christ can be asked to awaken function deficits observed in the Familial personality.

Operationally, the personality 'captured by Christ' will objectively define the gender of the personified Familial personality. That gendered personality has a contra-sexual aspect, which Christ can also *capture* by casting a circle into the nether reaches of the client's active imagination and bringing it into consciousness beside or near the personified Familial personality. If the client is female, the contra-sexual aspect is expected to reflect the masculine animating energy sustaining the two images; and if the client is male, the contra-sexual aspect is expected to reflect the feminine defining quality of the two images. The two images captured by Christ (i.e. the personification of the Familial personality and its contrasexual aspect) are treated as the yin and yang of whatever self currently controls the client's behavior. They represent the masculine and feminine aspects of the personified Familial personality. The intervention process involves Christ working with these two personifications in several ways.

Once Christ has identified the personified Familial personality and its consort, the client is asked to describe the relationship. The long-term goal of these interventions is the dramatic alteration of that relationship, but initially, no effort is made to change it beyond identifying the tensions and dysfunction. Instead, Christ is now asked to *extract* from the personified Familial personality, the sense of self *most closely attuned to the totality of Self*. This is *assumed* to be, in significant ways, the opposite of the Familial personality, which is generally seen as most closely conforming to family and culture. Christ does this by first drawing a circle in front the personified Familial personality and then extracting the 'attuned self' from the heart chakra of the personified Familial personality and placing it in the circle. This attuned self will become the prima materia for an Ideal pair that Christ will be asked to place in the Aware-ego's Heart. Once the attuned self is identified, Christ is then asked to identify its contra-sexual consort, which he does by casting another circle into the nether reaches of the Mind that he then uses to draw the consort into consciousness next to the attuned self. In the few clients who have completed these steps the contra-sexual aspect appears to be archetypal in nature. The client is asked to closely examine this pair. Generally, I will end the inner work at this point so the client can reflect on them. Invariably, this Ideal pair is a sharp contrast to the 'unredeemed,' personified Familial personality and its consort. I explain to the client that, if s/he is willing, Christ will bring this Ideal pair into the Heart of the Aware-ego where they will reside with a portion of Christ's *Light*, which will function as a perpetual conduit of the Holy Spirit. Because the images are invariably positive, the client may be quite willing for all of this to happen in the session and that is fine, as it is quickly done. But often, I encourage the client to spend a week reflecting on the Ideal pair that Christ has identified as most suitably attuned to the totality of Self.

The enthronement of an Ideal pair and Christ's *Light* in the Heart of the Aware-ego becomes the paradigm for further work with the personified Familial personality and its consort. The transformation of that pair will require their repeated conviction by Christ. Some of the many possible permutations of that process are described in the next chapter. Clients who have gotten this far in the process will have experienced that kind of transformational work in other contexts, particularly the transformation of parental images. The most potent intervention I have discovered for effecting these transformations is the *simultaneous* conviction of the masculine and feminine aspects with the power of the Holy Spirit. Christ will convict them as often as asked by the client, until the client is totally satisfied with the transformed relationship. That Ideal pair is now ready to be placed into the heart chakra of the personified Familial personality. But first, the heart chakra must be purified. A purification of the heart chakra must always precede the placement of an Ideal pair in the heart chakra. Last but not least, the participant-observer is asked to merge with the Aware-ego and the redeemed, personified Familial personality and Christ connects the three by placing a portion of his *Light* into their shared Heart.

Whatever is in the heart chakra of a personified Familial personality is normally a real threat to it; an also blocks the heart chakra's connection to the Aware-ego's Heart. For those reasons it must be purified. The major difficulty is generally the strong resistance of the Familial personality to anyone entering the heart chakra and discovering what is hidden there. I have discovered two strategies that have proven helpful. The first is the client's understanding that Christ's sole purpose in entering the heart chakra is to place a portion of his *Light* into the heart's center where it will function as an abiding conduit of the Holy Spirit's forgiving grace. In practice, once inside Christ may be required to intervene in a variety of ways to neutralize and transform the negative energies found there. And this he will do unfailingly. The second strategy addresses the personified Familial personality's knee-jerk resistance, which can be considerable. Here the Aware-ego must be actively engaged to exercise its willingness for Christ to heal. The client (sic) Aware-ego must acknowledge that the Familial personality's intransigence is self-destructive and Christ can be asked to heal the *intransigence*, which is often a personality characteristic. In effect, Christ is asked to approach the personified Familial personality and heal him or her in whatever way Christ deems appropriate, to the point where s/he can willingly allow Christ to enter the heart chakra and purify whatever is found there. It may be helpful to bear in mind that the personification is a representation of an archetypal amalgamate embodied with free will by the Ego. The embodied personality-core is a given, not a choice. It is generated by the Gendering archetype and derived from the qualities of parental interaction, be they horrendous or optimal. The personified Familial personality is a simulacra. It may be a powerful governor of the client's behavior, but removing its intransigence will not alter the personality-core; it only provides Christ the opportunity to enter its heart chakra. The unmitigated, archetypal constellation, i.e. participant-observer, and all of its embodied identities can only be transformed from within the Heart and heart chakras.

Once the heart chakra is purified, Christ can be asked to approach the personified Familial personality and its consort, and begin the process of repeatedly convicting the pair. The end goal is another Ideal pair albeit a more 'earthy' version appropriate to the personality. When the client is satisfied with the transformations, Christ will bring them into the purified heart chakra. The particular characteristics of this dyad are difficult to describe as they appear to be unique to each individual, but I believe the following verbatims will capture the feeling and results of this process. The Ideal pair serves two functions. First, this pair provides the optimum definition of what is possible for an ego-embodied Familial personality acting in the world. Second, the Ideal pair will function as a 'tuning fork' that quickly entrains with the resonance of the Ideal pair in the Aware-ego's Heart. But note, healing a personified Familial personality is not the same as healing the Observer. That requires a first person experience.

The Aware-ego's Heart

The first difficulty in my work with the Familial personality was my failure to appreciate that I now had to work with a 'formless' archetypal constellation: a presence with the power to organize consciousness, as distinct from the images that normally embody it. The second hurdle was my prolonged failure to distinguish between the Aware-ego's Heart and the heart chakras of ego-aspects. I assumed all of them shared the same Heart. At some level they do, but the only sense of self that can initially enter the Heart with Christ is the Aware-ego, which is why I now refer to it as the Aware-ego's Heart. The other ego-aspects have great difficulty even contemplating entry of their own heart chakra, much less the Heart, which has access to the physical heart and the seven heart chakras of each auric body. Even after the Aware-ego's Heart has been purified and the aural Voice-of-conscience has been terminated, ego-aspects will only be able to experience the Heart through a mental connection (sans emotion and/or sensation) with the Aware-ego (I call this the vicarious connection). The Dominant self provides the willingness necessary for Christ's initial entry into the Aware-ego's Heart. But its personification cannot follow Christ and the Aware-ego into the Heart proper even where it remains merged with the Aware-ego. Though this may not be readily apparent, every ego-aspect invariably 'hangs back' and relies on a sense of what happens via its mental connection with the Aware-ego. A Dominant self's primary reticence is likely a fear of the aural Voice-of-conscience, whose archetypal energy flows through the Heart. But I also sense a real boundary limitation that is difficult for the Ego to breech. Even when a client 'goes inside' s/he remains exterior to the Heart and any of the chakra portals. So far as I can determine, only willingness allows a self to follow Christ into those interior realms. Ego-aspects can sense the journey of the Aware-ego to the extent they are merged with it by willingness (in the same way they can sense the brain-body). But ego-aspects (aside from the Aware-ego) seem constitutionally incapable of actually entering the Heart or heart chakra without the sensed connection to the Aware-ego. Even so, their role in the process is crucial. Ego defines the world of free will, which is our normal state of consciousness. Consequently, ego willingness is required for any intervention that will effectively transform it, e.g. relinquishment of the power to self-shame in exchange for Christ's discernment, the purification of the Heart and their own heart chakras, allowing Christ to begin transforming the Familial personality by injecting Ideal pairs into the Heart and heart chakras.

So far as I can determine, the Aware-ego's Heart and all chakra portals are best treated as archetypal in nature; they are energy chambers connecting Soul to Mind, just as the Meridian energy field appears to connect Mind to Body. To date, the only images that seem comfortable within Hear and heart chakras (aside from the Aware-ego and Christ) are Ideal gender pairs most closely attuned to the totality of Self. It is possible for Christ to extract, reveal, and transform such Ideal pairs once the client is able to personify the reconstituted Familial personality and its contrasexual aspect. Once an Ideal pair is identified they can be 'enthroned' within the Heart. Then it becomes possible for personifications of the Familial personality to be transformed by conviction of the Holy Spirit until they can entrain with the Ideal pair in the Aware-ego's Heart.

The Capturing Circle Offered by Christ

Before proceeding to the verbatims, which will also illustrate the early transformations of the Familial personality, I want to illustrate and elaborate upon the Capturing circle intervention. This intervention was developed late in the process as I struggled to understand and work with the Familial personality. I cannot explain why it took me so long to discover it. Nonetheless, I can provide sufficient examples of its efficacy in this chapter and the next. The intervention is deceptively simple. What continues to surprise me is its power, which appears to be a function of turning the process entirely over to Christ (which is probably why it took me so long to discover it).

I thought about naming it *The Christ Circle*, but 'capture' best describes the effect. Basically, the Aware-ego and Christ stand a comfortable distance apart facing each other. Christ draws a circle between them *using his Light*, which the Aware-ego then walks through and exits near where Christ is standing. Or Christ can draw the circle while standing beside the Aware-ego and then walk through it with the Aware-ego. (As the verbatims will illustrate, even more options than these two are possible.) What could be simpler? The kicker is the circle's purpose. Each time Christ draws this kind of circle the intent is *to capture whatever Christ intends it to capture*. This can be a particular emotion ranging from pride to shame, or an emotional pain, or whatever is responsible for generating the emotion in question. After the particular manifestation is examined – if it is an emotion, then Christ is asked to absorb it with his Light. If it is a self, then Christ is asked to provide other appropriate interventions. The capturing circle is very like the double circles and concentric circles used throughout this book. What makes it distinctive is that Christ draws it with his *Light* and defines what it will capture, though he always does so in response to a specific request of the Aware-ego, who is generally following up on a suggestion made by the therapist. An illustration will provide a helpful preamble to further discussion.

Rona. The following verbatim describes the first time I used this intervention. Rona is a single mother going through a contentious divorce. She is in a graduate program for Social Work and works part time. We have been working together off and on for the past year. She is very good at going inside. She is OK about calling on Christ but feels most comfortable when she can also evoke a feminine image called Medicine Woman. The two images seem to work well together in complementary ways. Rona tends to be overly responsible, which she rebels against by eating, drinking, and smoking too much. She also has a history of acting out sexually. In the first session of this series, Rona begins by addressing an issue that has left her feeling very ashamed. Christ quickly addresses it in a thoughtful and forgiving matter. But she is still feeling remorseful, and berates herself: "I do everything in excess; all or nothing." I suggest we shift the focus to the 'excesses' (eating, smoking, drinking, and sex) as they have to be accumulating a lot of unexpressed shame. I explain to her that it may be possible for Christ to remove all of the accumulated shame. This will not prevent the accumulation of more shame by whoever is self-shaming, but it will ease the 'weight' of the accumulated shame. Rona is agreeable. She allows Christ to draw a circle that will capture all of the accumulated shame in her energy fields when she walks through it. I am specific: all of the accumulated shame related to excessive eating, drinking, smoking, and sexual acting out. (In retrospect, and based on what she will report the following week, we are asking Christ to capture and remove a great deal of shame all at once. Based on her feedback, I would now limit the number of 'excesses' per session.) I ask Rona to closely examine the circle she has just passed through and describe what she sees and feels. "After walking through, I was anxious until Christ provided me with a brain-stem massage. I am seeing a black and white rock sitting on something bigger. It fills the whole circle and feels like the tip of an iceberg. I can see ripples of water at the edges." I have her ask Christ if he can dissolve it, release her from it, and give her a fresh start? "At first, I did not know if I wanted him to release me. I asked him to and then when he began, I stopped him; but then I finally let him do it. Now it is just a clear circle of water." I suggest that she walk back through the circle and see how it feels. Instead, she swims across. "It felt cleansing and refreshing." The session ends here.

I see Rona the following week. The first thing she shares is that for several days immediately following our last session she experienced a number of unusual symptoms: frequent bouts of shaking, excessive sleeping, and nausea at the thought of eating. She even goes to a doctor on the third day, but he can find nothing wrong with her. Finally, by the fourth day, the symptoms clear. She reports that she has decided to join a running club at the YMCA and that she is being much more reasonable about her eating. Also, on three or four occasions during the past week she reenacted the intervention by swimming through the circle. Each time, the water is a beautiful blue-green when she dives in, but turns a dark murky green by the time she gets out. In each case Christ restores the water to its blue-green color. I tell her my surmise that her symptoms were a manifestation of her body detoxifying from all of the negative emotion that Christ has absorbed; and that it might have been easier if I had anticipated that possibility and told her to drink a lot of water. (Masseuses always encourage clients to drink a lot of water for several days after a their first massage.) The repeated change in the water suggests to me that one or more selves continue to self-shame, thereby re-polluting her energy field; but nothing like the accumulation she had to address the previous week. I suggest that she ask Christ to contain whomever is doing so by walking through another Capturing circle that he creates for that purpose. "There is nothing in the circle after I leave it." I have her ask her *Light* if she is the one shaming herself? "Yes. I did get a glimpse of me as the Do-gooder. She has a strict set of standards. When I fail to meet them she gets sad. When I disappoint her she does not seem to get angry, but she does get smaller." I ask if someone else shames her when the Do-gooder gets sad? "Yes. I was initially reluctant to go into the new circle that Christ just created to contain this part of me. I have been having a temper tantrum in my head. This new self throws temper tantrums when I do not do what the Do-gooder wants. Temper tantrum is very loud. I hear her cussing quite clearly." I ask Rona to have Christ join the two circles together. "Do-gooder is standing beside Temper tantrum and cowering. She is afraid of her angry outbursts." I ask if it is a 'shaming anger'? "Yes, but I am not sure what part of me she is attacking." I suggest that there may be a part of her in deep shame; and that Christ can place it in a dome so it does not overwhelm the other two, and then baptize it. "There is a devilish figure in there that is definitely male. Christ caught him in the dome and baptized him. What is left is a skinny, more feminine, image. The sex is ambiguous. The image appears to be a 4-6 year old child, but I know it is older as well." I ask if this is the image that has been the target of Temper tantrum's anger? "Temper Tantrum has shut her mouth. She has witnessed all of this. It was as if Christ was performing an exorcism. He expelled the 'evil.' The Do-gooder and the 'devil' now seem to share attributes. Both are blond and girlish, and about nine years old." I suggest that she let Christ forge a safe heart-to-heart connection using the Do-gooder's *Light*. The session ends here.

As Rona's verbatim clearly illustrates, use of the Capturing circle can quickly bring the client into contact with selves struggling with Moral authority. But that was not my initial intent in using it. Rather, I generally introduce it as a very effective way to dispel accumulated negative emotions such as shame, fear, and anger. At the risk of being boringly repetitive, it is these emotions – not the content that attaches to them, that cause the client so much grief. Clients can be terrorized by their very 'success' at controlling self-generated fear and suppressed anger, and made to feel perpetually inadequate by their accumulated unexpressed shame. If a client merely seeks to 'control' those emotions, then the very act of controlling will produce an endless accumulation of the emotion. In effect, if the individual seeks to control fear, then the fear will continue to accumulate in the body until it manifests as psychosomatic dis-eases that continue to require ever more extremes of control, e.g. psychotropic drugs.

The Capturing circle is completely dependent upon the higher power that draws it. I am often very general and tentative in what I suggest is contained by the circle as I expect Christ to execute and capture what he deems appropriate. The circle's positive effect on clients can be measured by the frequency with which they will use it between sessions. Practically, every client who has been taught this intervention has repeated it between sessions. Even Rona, who suffered some strange symptoms from her perspective, continued to use it. And very likely, her continued use contributed to her equally quick recovery, as she swam through very healing energy. When Christ dissolves any accumulated emotion in a Capturing circle, he does so unhesitatingly, and as often as he is asked. Some clients will initially balk at entering the circle literally from fear, and particularly if fear is the emotion being addressed. Often, the Aware-ego must use a garment or circle of protection to sufficiently shield from the sheer terror of the whatever is generating the emotion (which in one instance was actually an autonomous emotion).

All clients are encouraged to drink water after using this intervention the first time, if a massive accumulation is removed, and also encouraged to attend to any physical urges or symptoms that may appear immediately after the session. For example, Marion – whose verbatims are given in the next section, initially uses the intervention to dispel shame accumulated by her striving to 'control' her weight. In the following week her eating was much better but she developed a strong urge to smoke, which then became the focus of her control. Likewise, removing *fear* may precipitate a surge of somatic anger suppressed by the *fear* of retaliation. If the client complains of this before or during the next session, it is easily addressed by asking Christ to draw a Capturing circle that will contain the anger and anyone generating it. Then he can be asked to dispel accumulated anger and work with the angry self. Finally, I would note that once the client has learned to use the Capturing circle they tend to prefer it as the modus operandi for separating from selves. Note, for example, that Rona spontaneously used it when she was asked to separate from two selves. I will add to this discussion when I provide further examples in the verbatims offered below and in the next chapter.

One last observation: this intervention appears to change the client's relationship with Christ in a noticeable way. It may be that it is merely 'the cumulative straw that broke the Ego's back,' but I suspect it is something more.

The instant removal of accumulated emotion such as shame is easily equated to 'absolution' or Christ's forgiveness. Sometimes, there is even 'penance,' as when the client must 'suffer' the body's detoxification. It also becomes quickly apparent that it is the individual who is attacking the brain-body by the continuing the generation of negative emotion, e.g. that the ego-aspect's continuing need for *control* is what accumulates the emotion. This particular intervention greatly facilitates the ego-aspect's awareness of its own culpability. In order for the individual to effectively stop polluting the Mind and Body, s/he needs to give up its particular control in exchange for Christ's discernment.

An Addictive Bond Hypothesis

My work with Tory and Marion's weight issues (illustrated in the last portion of each verbatim) also helped me to formulate what I hope will be a viable hypothesis for the treatment of significant compulsive behaviors such as addiction. This is the gist of how I explained it to them:

An ego-aspect requires three essential *components* for the free-will direction of the Body. These component correspond to the mental, emotional, and sensate consciousness generated by the mental, emotional, and root chakras. The unencumbered *interaction* of these components is absolutely necessary for an ego-aspect's adequate performance vis-à-vis the Mind and Body. A significant addiction or compulsive behavior indicates that two components of the triad – the mental and sensate – have been *forcibly disconnected* by familial/cultural shaming or emotional/sexual trauma. The most common 'victims' of component disconnection are ego-aspects that exercise a particular perceptual function (feeling, thinking, intuition, and sensation) or ego-aspects whose gender dyads are sexually expressive. The latter is most often split by familial shaming.

Component disconnection is generally the result of repressing the sensate component. The sensate component reads and directs the Body (brain-body) as free willed by the mental component. The sensate component provides the ego-aspect direct access to the Body's instinctual will, making it the most potent of the three components. When the sensate component is repressively disconnected from the mental component it is left *undirected*, except as a Pavlovian response. In effect, *shaming* paralyzes the emotional component thereby severing the sensate component's connection to the mental component, which the sensate component needs for self-direction. Stated another way, shame banishes the sensate component to root chakra consciousness (i.e. the sensate consciousness sustained by instinctual will). Equally consequential, although the ego-aspect's *mental* component remains conscious, it is effectively reduced to an *insatiable* desire for its exiled sensate component, which it needs to adequately function in the Mind and world-at-large. The mental component's desire becomes *insatiable* because it no longer has a way of satisfying its function while the sensate component remains in exile.

The Ego will always create a *new* ego-aspect to replace the disconnected ego-aspect. This new ego-aspect will seek to satisfy the angst of the mental component's insatiable desire using any substance that promises to ease the emotional *pain* of disconnection as experienced by the exiled sensate component. Unfortunately, the new ego-aspect is handicapped by a general failure to discriminate between the experience of its own sensation and sensations produced by the repressed sensate component. All it can do is strive to hold the angst of (mental) insatiable desire in check by seeking to repeatedly placate one or both components.

Taste provides nearly instant stimulus/response communication in the Mind and Body. Oral ingestion can instantly connect all three participants of the triangle comprised of the split-ego components and their unknowing manager. If the taste is *gratifying or rapidly mind altering*, it can provide all three a repeatable, if temporary, release from the angst generated by the mental component's unrelenting desire. In sum, these three – by acting out their respective motivations – invariably create and sustain an addictive bond, generally defined as the excessive use of one or more substances. Other sensate experiences such as adrenalin surges can also serve as reinforcers, but taste is by far the most powerful.

While exiled, the sensate component is restricted to sensate expression and affective volition. Most often, those are experienced as sensation, but not always. (Tory's verbatim in the previous section illustrates the exile of sensation, which necessitated an over-reliance on thinking and intuition.) The sensate component has the will to respond to all matter of stimuli including pain and pleasure. This is why the exile can be intermittently placated with sensory experiences generated by taste and mind-altering drugs. But the mental component only desires reconnection and that is the one thing a managerial ego-aspect's offered 'drug' cannot provide, except as a temporary promise. The best an ego manager can hope to achieve are sensory experiences able to evoke a satisfying response from the sensate component, which 'seems' to reduce the angst of both of them, if only temporarily.

A managerial ego-aspect can offer two kinds of sensate altering substitutes: the easily accessible and the less easily accessible. Food and, previously, nicotine are two of the most common substitutes in the 'easily accessible' category. Alcohol, marijuana, and medications (particularly psychotropics and pain relievers) fall into the 'less easily accessible' category. (Both sets of examples barely sample the complete lists.) The 'less easily acceptable' often require an Ego-in-conflict, who is most likely to come out when the manager's normal strategies are insufficient. The problem with either the manager's (or Ego-in-conflict's) proffered substitutes is that all of them are temporary, and their repeated use over increasingly shorter intervals is generally Wrathful, i.e. exceeds the body's lawful limits. The manager's solution is simply incapable of satisfying the mental component's desire for reunion, however frequently or infrequently the 'drug' is used. More to the point, repeated usage of the substance will strengthen a pseudo (Pavlovian) connection between the mental component's *desire* and the sensate component's *response*, which reinforces the manager's desire to continue procuring the substance. Inadvertently, this positive feedback loop also strengthens the sensate component's willful *resistance* to any attempts by the Manager to hold the frequency in check.

While a split-ego's two components remain irreconcilable, the addictive substance remains the most intense expression of their desire for reconciliation. The substance will be totally unsatisfactory as a viable means of reconnection, but a continual reminder to us of the intensity of that need; and the need will remain incessant while the sensate component remains in exile cut-off from its mental component.

If the client is willing, Christ can identify both of the split-ego's components. He can identify the mental component *by capturing the self who expresses the insatiable desire*. He can identify the sensate component by *capturing the self that most actively resists Dominant self's attempts to control the addiction*. (Most people who struggle with an addiction have spent a good deal of time reflecting on how to get free of it. In many cases they have experienced or intuited both components, but not been able to name them or their dynamics. Once the dynamics are described, my clients have been quite willing for Christ to enact these first two steps.) Generally, Christ will need to use a well of pure sensation or dome of pure sensation to bring a sensate component back into to relational consciousness. Initially, I suggest that the dome remain opaqued and the client only be aware of the 'risen presence.' I generally refer to a sensate component as the secret sharer, alter ego, shadow self, or evil twin. One of these appellations generally resonates with the client. Work with the mental component can be equally difficult. It has lost its connection to sensation and therefore has no feedback loop regarding its effect on the Mind and Body. So it can be incessantly demanding with impunity, and therefore unresponsive to change without drastic measures. Reestablishing a feedback loop is the first priority. This is done by asking Christ to place the mental component in a *circle of effect*, whereby it is obliged to *experience* the effects of excessive, unmitigated desire on the Body, which is invariably negative. Next, the Dominant self must forgo its use of shame if it has not already done so. Finally, the two components must be reconciled in such a way that each gains untrammeled access to other and can take up residence in a purified heart chakra if that is appropriate. Unfortunately, all of this is harder to do than it is to describe. Bringing the sensate component into relational consciousness requires that Christ raise it from the depths of sensate exile. The Dominant self is often fearful of being overwhelmed by all the negative emotions attached to the exile. It is never easy to convince a Dominant self or personified Familial personality that Christ can safely do the work. The forthcoming verbatims capture some of the effort involved. It is all doable, but never easy. In all honesty, given the complexity and effort involved, I cannot imagine this solution becoming a treatment panacea for addiction, particularly overeating; but the complexity has certainly helped me to appreciate why most treatment efforts have failed to address that problem.

Over the years, I have successfully worked with a number of addictive behaviors by incorporating the AA model into my treatment, but overeating has consistently resisted my best efforts even as it helped me to identify the Dominant self. As a culture, all the statistical evidence points to overeating as epidemic. For that reason I have persisted in my efforts because compulsive eating has clearly replaced cigarette smoking as the national drug of choice. Like all addictions, the bond between an overeater and his or her food can be intense, and the gradient of intensity is easily measured by the individual's age and girth.

Anyone who uses the methods described in this work will be working with overweight clients from time to time, not to mention the other addictions. I offer this hypothesis to those therapists willing to use the methodology, but I have no illusion it will become a panacea for the masses. As regards overeating, I expect some entrepreneurial spirit will invent a pill in the foreseeable future…and the culture will go on to find yet another substitute to temporarily mask the angst of component disconnection. But I doubt any 'drug of choice' will satisfy the underlying component disconnection beyond masking it at the price of eventually incurring the Wrath.

Back to the problem at hand: I am arguing here that an individual's particular addiction is the most intense relationship they have with themselves; and most people have such a relationship. Among any group of people gathered in a public space, a very large percentage of them will have an addiction of one type or another. Many addictions will be less obvious than eating and relatively benign (e.g. zoning out in front of a TV for hours at a time, spending comparable periods playing solitaire, video games, knitting, and the like). But many other addictions can be very problematical (e.g. overeating, taking prescribed psychotropics for years on end, daily smoking of marijuana or drinking alcoholically, seeking adrenalin highs, sleeping excessively, etc.). Whatever the 'drug of choice,' many individuals are hard pressed to give it up even when the 'drug' becomes detrimental to their health and wellbeing. The addictive bond can be so intense that the person caught up in this triangle would rather die than go without; and many, many people will die from the direct or indirect effects of their addiction, while also suffering numerous related dis-eases that are the precursors of such an ending. In sum, more people die from their addictions than recover from them.

Just about all of us blame the substance. It overpowers us. The *desire* that stimulates our impulse to procure and consume our 'drug of choice' always seems stronger than our unaided will. Even AA will be the first to tell you that only a higher power can save us. The *seeming* bond between the substance and desiring-self seems too intense, too strong, too binding, too 'addicting,' to be broken by our unaided will. That may be true as far as the thought goes, but I am now convinced that the real bond is a triangle between *two split apart components of an ego-aspect that share an intense desire for reunion*, and the ego-aspects created to cope with their split. Normally, a Dominant self enacts the third part of the triangle, but when its socially acceptable behaviors become insufficient, an Ego-in-conflict is likely to come out and seek more potent solutions.

Thinking and feeling, intuition and sensation, Mind-Body connections, arousal and satisfaction, and masculine/feminine interactions are examples of essential functions embeddable in an ego-aspect. They are the potential capacities of every ego-aspect. When an ego-aspect strongly embodies a particular perceptual function, any dissociative split of its components will produce an inordinate desire for reunion. Marion's verbatim will illustrate the effects of shaming the sensate component of a feeling ego-aspect; while Tory's verbatim will illustrate the profound effects of repressing the sensate component of an ego-aspect that strongly exercised the sensation function.

The integrity of every ego-aspect is dependent upon the emotional cohesion of mental and sensate components. The two structural components (mental and sensate) can be dismembered by repressive shame. Thereafter, the person becomes vulnerable to any substance that can forge a Pavlovian bond between a mental component's incessant desire for reunion and its shamefully repressed sensate component. The mental component is sometimes labeled too 'weak-willed' to resist its own desire. But in fact it is pure desire and only that, as it has no means of satisfying that desire while its sensate component remains in exile. In contrast, the sensate component, though exiled to the pure sensation of root chakra consciousness, still retains a potent will to act, though now lacking direction. Once a Pavlovian bond establishes a pseudo connection, the sensate component can decisively and repeatedly overwhelm *any ego-aspect that seeks to hold the mental component in check* by adding its sensate angst to the mental component's desire.

The 'controlling' or 'managing' ego-aspect tasked with addressing the component split has no way of reinstating ego integrity. All it can hope to achieve is a sensate experience that will temporarily assuage the sensate component and/or temporarily drown out the mental component's insatiable desire. A 'sufficient' sensate experience ('drug of choice') will meet the respective needs of at least two participants in the triangle. The 'perfect' drug will meet the needs of all three. But all too often, 'perfect' is also a death knell, e.g. opium, crack cocaine and the like.

Of note, a Dominant self does not create the mental-sensate splits it is required to manage. Those are fostered by circumstances beyond its control be they familial, cultural, or environmental trauma. Neither the aural Voice-of-conscience nor Familial personality are creations of the Dominant self. They are givens which the Ego assumes and models in order to garner the ability to organize consciousness and preempt the aural Voice-of-conscience. But a personality core can be dysfunctional by virtue of the parents that provide the template and the aural Voice-of-conscience can be unbearably shaming. The Ego must cope with what it is given to work with unless it can turn to a higher power.

The addictive bond is a pseudo connection. It can drown out the mental component, and/or placate the sensate component, but only so long as the drug of choice is repeatedly used. The two will only be satisfied when the split is healed. So long as the split remains unhealed it will demand the repeated use of the 'drug(s) of choice.' But the repeated use of a pseudo connection also strengthens the stimulus/response (Pavlovian) connection between the two split parts, and that ultimately works against the Dominant self's second task of holding desire and drug usage in check. All drugs have a cumulative negative effect if used indefinitely or too frequently. Unfortunately, once formed, the triad (comprised of mental and sensate components, and a managerial ego-aspect tasked with keeping them in check) becomes a very stable triangle with strong negative feedback loops. A managerial ego-aspect offers a modicum of control, even as it perpetuates the shame that keeps the two components separate. Its effort notwithstanding, the mental aspect will continually tempt the managerial ego-aspect with its insatiable desire; and the 'secret sharer' (e.g. evil twin, alter ego, shadow self) will repeatedly *tip the scale* in favor of physically seeking sensate satisfaction by adding its own sensate will to the equation. This is why resistance is so frequently futile. The secret sharer repeatedly tips the scale by lending its own will to the equation by demanding sensate satisfaction of the mental component's desire. In so doing it repeatedly overwhelms the managerial ego-aspect's resistance (already weakened by the felt angst and promise of momentary relief).

The mental component is generally disconnected from its sensate component by shock trauma of one sort or another. I suspect that shaming anger by adults or self is a primary cause. Because of that disconnection, the mental aspect can willfully and incessantly evoke desire without any fear of shameful repercussion (a sensate experience) but it will also be denied any chance of satisfying that desire. In effect, the mental component becomes pure impulse, pure desire, and totally immune to any affective shame or adverse effects on the body, but also cut off from the sensate component that could offer it true satisfaction. That is why its desire is insatiable. In a similar vein, the sensate component also seeks to reconstitute the connection between itself and the mental component, but is limited to Pavlovian responses while it remains in its repressed state. Temporary satiation provided by the current 'drug of choice' can only placate the sensate component's need for reunion while the drug's effect remains satisfying. In sum, both components can be silenced or sated, but rarely for long. And the longer they can be silenced, the more likely the drug is adversely affecting the brain/body.

The ongoing desire of a mental aspect combined with the sensate will of its 'secret sharer' will invariably trigger an addictive bond that reflects their need for reunion. And so long as this dynamic is not altered, the two will invariably overwhelm the one that seeks to control them even at the brain/body's expense. A managerial ego-aspect can alter that equation only if s/he is willing to seek *reconciliation* of the mental component and its sensate counterpart. Unfortunately, managerial selves are generally unaware of the nature of the split; and shame provides a false sense of control, even as it inadvertently sustains the bifurcation. More to the point, Dominant self does not have the wherewithal to heal the breach with its own resources; if it did so, it would not have to succumb to the addictive use of sensory experiences. That is why AA is quick to tell us that only a higher power can restore us to sanity.

In sum, there is a 'secret sharer' in every addiction, which is disconnected and sensate; and a depersonalized, mental component that incessantly desires reconnection with its sensate component. The lack of a satisfying reunion perpetuates the mental component's insatiable stimulation of the brain/body with desire. While split, the mental component's *desire* for its sensate component and the experience of *sensate* satisfaction, however brief, is the only conscious awareness of the need for reunion. (This need for reunion can be expressed in dreams and symbols and other transliterations; but only sensation offers the most unequivocal expression.) To free consciousness from their pseudo Pavlovian bond, the secret sharer must be brought into relational consciousness and reconciled with its depersonalized, mental component. Christ can identify both of them, and can liberate them from the addictive bond once the manager is willing to give up its power to shame. The secret sharer is relatively easy to identify once the client accepts the probability of its existence; Christ can also identify the mental component by using his *Light* to capture whoever stimulates desire for the substance in question. Finally, Christ can liberate the two from their addictive cycle once the client (i.e. managerial ego-aspect) is willing to give up whatever defenses are in its armamentarium, e.g. shame, denial, rebellion, prideful beliefs, etc. The most effective way of working with a mental component is for Christ to place it in a circle of effect that obliges it to feel the bodily repercussions of its excess. But note, the managerial ego-aspect must concomitantly give up its powers in order for Christ to effectively reconcile the 'secret sharer' and mental component.

The addictive bond hypothesis may be paradigmatic of most cases where a client's symptoms are sensation-based, including most physical symptoms, especially chronic pain. Its applicability to pain is illustrated in Leigh's verbatim in the next chapter.

I began testing this hypothesis in the last reported sessions of Tory, Marion and Leigh's verbatims. Those sessions offer evidence in support of it, but do not demonstrate its efficacy, which will require at least another year (in terms of measurable weight loss and other symptom amelioration). I know this makes the last sessions feel like the proverbial cliffhanger at the end of a TV serial. But there is simply not enough room to explore it in this book. The interested reader can go to the book's website (The Unredeemed Conscience.org) for the next installment.

The Familial personality and Depersonalized Mental Component

The Familial personality and depersonalized mental component (described above) are distinctly different entities. Both are experienced interiorly as depersonalized; that is, lacking a sensate component. But the reconstituted Familial personality is an un-embodied *archetypal constellation* with the inherent ability to organize consciousness. It provides a template identity for every ego-aspect that incorporates it. By virtue of this incorporation, the Ego makes the reconstituted Familial personality the Observer who can vicariously experience the activity of every ego-aspect that shares its identity. I would further hypothesize that, as the reconstituted Familial personality is altered, those alterations will change the ego-aspects that embody it. In contrast, the mental component of a disconnected ego-aspect experiences the incessant loss of sensate connection. Insofar as a particular ego-aspect embodies a critical activity such as perceptual function (sensation, intuition, thinking and feeling) or sexual expression, or a significant masculine-feminine connection, then disconnection will be a felt loss by the Mind and/or Body; and the Ego will be obliged to cope with that loss. Such coping appears to invariably manifest as addictive or other compulsive behavior.

Of note, following verbatims work a great deal with split-apart components and very little with the Observer. It might have been otherwise had I earlier discovered the full import of the Observer. But it was not to be, and my publisher has set definite limits on the size of this book. I do intend is to continue the exploration of this phenomenon as my clients are willing, and will post addendum to the book's website (The Unredeemed Conscience.org) for anyone who is interested. For better or worse, there is really no end to the process, merely arbitrary continuances.

Two Case Illustrations

I want to stress that both verbatims pick up where we left off earlier in the chapter and *well before I had acquired a working knowledge of the Observer or the addiction hypothesis*. I attempt to identify those variables as they make themselves felt in the each session, but all that is done with hindsight, and therefore speculative. These verbatims are intended to reveal the dynamics as they unfold and become known to me, rather than explicitly demonstrating a process where the therapist has an explicit knowledge of the dynamics.

Tory

When Tory returns, Rational understanding appears to be most conscious of a previously denied resentment toward her younger brother, Mack, who was favored by the mother, and is currently going rapidly downhill as a result of severe alcohol abuse. Despite this preoccupation, I feel prompted to ask Tory whether she ever did her planned work of extracting and reconciling the images of her mother and grandfather from her brother? This was 'homework' she agreed to do in the previous session. In reply, she tells me that something made her really angry at the thought of doing that so she has avoided going there. I suggest she go inside and separate from the source of this resentment. Significantly, whoever is co-present with the Aware-ego does not separate, though that is the intent of the intervention. Rather, this new self reports what she describes as 'scenarios.' She is emphatic about this: "I don't see a person. Scenarios run through my mind. Mother was always this wounded person who could not take care of herself. She was so needy and I felt so responsible for her. Now that she is dead Mack is taking up where she left off. I can't win." I inject an interpretation at this point to the effect that so long as she feels she can only cope there will be no way for her to change the situation. I ask this new self, which I initially call Resentment, to tell me her attitude toward Christ? "He has never been an option." Why, I ask, does she doubt Christ's efficacy? Would she be willing to give up her power of doubt? (Here I am treating doubt as a power much like the power of self-shame. Doubt, denial, and distrust, would all fall within the set of ego defenses likely to be used by a reconstituted Familial personality in tandem with self-shame.) Tory observes that she really does value doubting Christ's ability, and believes that her doubt has to do with being safe: "No one takes care of me, but me." I ask her if she can tell me the opposite of doubt? She says "Belief." I suggest, rather, that it is 'certainty.' The session ends here. (What is not readily apparent from the foregoing excerpts is that 'me' is expressing resentment in the first person but cannot be personified. This sense-of-self appears to have taken charge of Tory and is currently identified with an ego-aspect that harbors considerable resentment toward her brother.)

Tory returns to tell me that it has been a terrible week, with one exception. Early in the weekend, as she was driving to give a workshop on mentoring, she passed several houses on a main street, which she thought of as old, but 'having bones.' As she passed one of them, she became convinced that someone came out of the house that looked identical to her image of Christ. She was convinced she saw him and that he waved at her to catch her attention. Tory values this 'seeing' as a good omen, but from then on significant relationships are repeatedly mired in negative emotions. First she got a call from her brother intimating that he would likely commit suicide in the near future to avoid being kicked out of the house by his wife's filing for divorce. Tory believes him and at first she felt heartbroken that she had failed him, and then got angry with him. Next she got a series of calls from her daughter, ranting about her job and complaining she had nothing to be thankful for and even imagined running her car into a pole to get out of work. Next, she found herself at odds with two women in a support group she leads. "I cut them off because they were so full of God and really did not know what they were talking about." Finally, her husband had a wreck the night before our session. "He was driving furiously, which is so unlike him, and ran up on the meridian. He said he felt totally out of control. He felt the anger consumed him." I suspect he was reacting to Tory's anger in response to a cell phone call from her daughter that she answered in the car. Her response to my observation is that, "I have done everything I could do for all of these people, and it is not enough, not even enough for them to be pleasant." I comment that it has been a matter of pride for her that she does it all herself. It puts Tory in mind of her divorce many years before: "It was what I most disliked about the divorce. I felt totally alone – that I had to do it all myself, it was a horrible feeling for me. Last night I felt in the same place again." The session ends here. My only comment is that I suspect Christ was reminding her to keep him with her when she hallucinated him in the front yard of 'a house with bones.' [46]

Tory comes into the next session a week later to report a lot of anger at her brother, father, daughter, and husband, particularly her husband who has gotten the brunt of it for wrecking the car and several other 'unpardonable sins.' She knows that he did not deserve all of it and apologized afterward. I suggest to her that her anger is *shaming judgment* and she needs to come to terms with it. In response she tells me that, "I am just so overwhelmed. I am not OK in any way. I've been sick all week. I have had a high fever but no reason for it as far as the doctor is concerned. I am chilled too. And the pills for my heartburn are ineffective." To my way of thinking it all sounds like somaticized anger, and when I suggest that Tory agrees. I then suggest that she go inside and ask Christ to create a dome of *Light* for a safe place to absorb her anger. The dome can simultaneously absorb the anger and allow whatever is being held in check by it to emerge within the dome. She allows Christ to do this and then she remembers a self that we worked with awhile back. She calls it Frenzy. Frankly, I remember the name but not the particulars. She says that Frenzy is everywhere surrounding her. I walk her through the separation procedure, but again, only feeling is separated. "What I see is how I feel – chaos. Wild head to toe." I suggest that she let Christ place the feeling in a dome and reduce the amplitude enough to identify the feeling. "I can't identify the feeling. Now there is darkness, but the darkness is calm." I ask if 'frenzy' is something she does? "If I do, it is something I have done forever." For my part, I am mystified and the session is over time. I suggest to Tory that the dome containing the 'dampened down' frenzy needs to remain intact as long as the other dome holding the anger also remains intact and we will just have to wait and see what happens in the next session.

I have scheduled two sessions for the next week, which is two weeks before Christmas. She comes in to the first one telling me that she has spent the weekend being like her mother, awfully like my mother. "It dawned on me that I was acting like her and I decided to stop that. There was never a Christmas she did not get mad about something, and from then on nothing happened for Christmas as she would barely talk to anyone." Then Tory focuses on her husband and all of the things he has been doing that suggest a progression of his forgetfulness (possible Alzheimer's). I hear her out and tell her, I cannot rule out what she is inferring and I will address it with him when I next see him. Also, I know he is scheduled to see a specialist within the month that has been following him for the past two years. I agree with Tory that her husband may be getting 'worse,' but I also tell her that it is possible that her anger is not helping. Given his family history, her anger would put him in a high state of anxiety, which is likely to exacerbate his forgetfulness. She understands that she may, in fact, be contributing to his memory issues and finds that "depressing and oppressing." She says the thought of it threatens to close her down just as her mother did. To offset that feeling, I immediately suggest that she go inside, stand in front of Christ, and ask him to convict her Heart with the power of the Holy Spirit. (This is the first time I have used the intervention in just this way, though she has used variations of it on numerous previous occasions. It is described at length in the next chapter.) "I can stand there in front of him and say that, but nothing happens. I only see a picture of Christ." I suggest that she touch the picture with her *Light*. "When I did that I saw to the left of the *pictured* Christ an image of Christ from the house with bones." I suggest that she turn to her left and screen that image of Christ, which is animate. She does so and he appears safe so I suggest that she ask him to convict her Heart with the power of the Holy Spirit. "He has done that and there seems to be a greater sense of light between the two of us." As we are over time, I suggest that she ask him to repeat this conviction as often as she thinks about it between now and the next session. Hopefully, in the next session we can begin to focus on the two domes, though I am feeling an equally urgent need to focus on the dynamic between her mother and maternal grandfather (the small town drunk).

Tory returns very pleased with her granddaughter's progress. A therapist, who visits the home weekly, evaluated the granddaughter. Tory has been keeping her for the past month, four days a week, while her daughter works. "She was not 'frenzied' with me this week. (That is an interesting statement given that her own 'frenzy' was contained the previous week.) On Wednesday, when the therapist came to work with her, she was much more focused. The therapist feels her progress is equal to where she might be if the therapist worked with her everyday instead of just one day a week." I query her about her own homework. "I have repeatedly asked Christ to convict my Heart. I feel better, not great, but better. I am still edgy – anything can turn into a huge emergency." She also mentions that her father called with a 'deal' quid-pro-quo favor, which she politely but pointedly rejects. Her father is no longer a favorite, or the male who will rescue her from whatever. I mention that it might help her, as well as her brother, if she can eventually resolve the conflict between her mother and maternal grandfather (the town drunk). But I do not stress this. Instead, I have her ask Christ whether we need to go there first or begin dealing with the two domes containing 1) the frenzy feeling and 2) whatever is being suppressed by her anger. She goes inside and identifies Frenzy as closest, so that is where we start. "This is hard. I can feel what is in the dome. She [Frenzy] is just panicked that the next thing is going to be something she can't handle. Everything gets settled and managed and then something else comes along. It has reached a point where it is taking everything in her to manage it all. She feels at her breaking point and the next thing will break her." I ask why she feels so personally responsible? "There is no one else to do it." Who creates all the crises? "My husband, my father, my daughter, and sometimes me." How old are you? "I am an adult. We are one and the same." You identify with her? "Oh yeah. I think there was a sense of competency in the past, but not anymore. Maybe I lost it when I quit working. My only role now is managing everyone's lives, and I am doing a horrible job of it." I remind her that all of this started with her need to manage her mother's silences. That during those years there was no help from her father or MGM. "My MGM rescued me from my mother when I was a child (just as Tory is doing now with her own granddaughter)." I shift the focus slightly by asking her attitude toward Christ. (I am attempting to get a better sense of whoever is in charge.) Tory willingly describes her relationship with Christ. "Growing up I believed that Christ helped those who helped themselves. Since then I have tried to cultivate a relationship with Christ, but it is mostly a head process. The Heart is rarely involved. I struggle with that. I save Christ for the big things; there is a limited amount I can use him. I keep him in reserve." I ask what would happen if she used him daily? "I never have. *That would be weak*...not right...like seeing him as the genie in the bottle." I ask Tory what would happen if she could not manage, if she could not come up with the answer? "It would be a catastrophe." I tell her that she could always have an answer if she were willing to rely on Christ's discernment. Her response is to tell me she has learned some coping skills along the way though none of them are working. I ask her what is the worse thing that could happen if all her coping strategies fail? "The withdrawal I saw in my mother. I can see myself totally disconnecting from everyone and everything." I ask her to tell me more about this 'disconnection.' I ask if it is a protection from all of the circuits going out at the same time or fear of an explosion? "I use anger to disconnect, to end things." I paraphrase this by suggesting she is repeating her mother's relationship with the maternal grandfather, that anger made it easier for her 'to leave him' because he did not provide what she needed. "No. His not providing was the reason for my anger; when I cut him off it gave me the opportunity to do something that mattered, to control the outcomes more, to make a difference, to work with integrity." (I have the distinct feeling here that this is her mother telling me how she felt toward the MGF.) I ask her if this meant she was perceived by him as being less than she could be? "Yes. But I never really thought about totally disconnecting. That was the fear I had of my mother, that one day she would be gone, that she would have separated completely from reality. At first I thought about it in terms of myself, 'What would happen to me?' Later, I thought about it in terms of taking care of her, and lastly it just felt like a huge sadness for no good reason." I ask Tory if she would be willing to give up her power to disconnect? "Yes. I have never wanted to relate like that." I suggest that she ask Christ to extract it so she can see it in a circle. She does this but then tells me that she does not want to see it. "I know there is something there. I just want to be through with it. *There is such repulsion in that*. It is totally negative and non-productive." I encourage her, again, to look at it, to ask Christ to give her the strength by placing more of his *Light* into her Heart. "I was always the one who worked to bring my mother back from her silence until the day she died. It bothered me that she could go for days without speaking to anyone. If I did not call her no one else seemed to care. It changed my day and me. I could not stop thinking about it. I would not do something like that in retaliation, but I might become so injured that it could happen to me. Then I could not function well." Are you saying that we are asking Christ to save you from yourself? "Yeah." At this point I am aware that there is something terribly shameful in the circle, i.e. repulsive. I feel she must be able to name it before Christ can take it away. At first, I am thinking that she just needs a shield to protect her while she looks at whatever is in the circle, and then suddenly, I realize that this problem is of her own making. She is *judging whatever is in the circle as repulsive*; what she has to give up is her power to self-shame. She understands what I am saying, but says she needs to think about it. The session ends here.

Tory misses her next session and goes through the Christmas holiday without seeing me. Everyone gathers at her house – including her daughter and spouse, and grandchildren, her brother (drunk or just sullen) and his family, her father and his companion. They are all in character and she is truly and understandably miserable. To add to her situation her acid reflux is in high gear despite three new medications and she can barely tolerate food. (Interestingly, her compulsion to eat left her during the reconciliation work with Rational Understanding and she has lost 13 pounds, but now she has gone from eating moderately to hardly eating at all. I am concerned about her and arrange to see her before New Years. She shares all of this when she returns plus a few discoveries regarding her husband that appear to *mitigate* her conviction that his memory is increasingly impaired. Consequently, he is now the one person about whom she is not despairing. She tells me that, at one point, she was discussing her new meds with her sister-in-law. Her brother overheard her and generalized 'she had become her mother's daughter' (who was fanatical about taking her medications on time). "It was the most shaming thing he could have said and it made me furious, though I did not voice it." Then she goes on to comment: "For the past several weeks whenever I am tense I feel my whole body *arch* with my head back. It feels like the perfect picture of me reacting to *revulsion*." Tory is more than ready to go inside and address all of this.

I have her begin by asking Christ to extract her power to self-shame and place it in a circle in front of her. "It looks like a red hot ember – a huge chunk of red hot." I tell her that she needs to give this up forever and replace it with the power of Christ's discernment. If she allows him to penetrate her brain and place his *Light* within and she *observes that the ember disappears*, that will indicate that the exchange has been made. Silence. When I ask her what is happening, she tells me that, "I had a conversation with Christ. I told him that I can't do this any longer; and I know it is not what he would have for me. Then I asked him to replace it with his *Light* and my eyes rolled back into my head, and I could see the light he placed there. I relaxed. The ember is gone. That is kind of scary." I ask her why? "It leaves me vulnerable to being hurt, to attack." I have her confirm with him that he will strip the power from any shaming voices outside or within her Heart, since she believes such voices and thoughts come from both places. I suggest that she follow him into her Heart where he will collect together any voices and terminate their power. "I am not unwilling, but I cannot see it happen." At first, her response baffles me, but then I ask if she is seeing an image of herself in front of Christ or standing in front of Christ holding her *Light*? "I am seeing an image of me in front of him." I explain to her that this must be done in the *first person* and that it is a felt experience of entering into a new space. "OK, now I can feel it. OK…when I was doing that it felt like a darkness in front of my eyes, and then a kaleidoscope of pulsating waves, and now I am standing behind Christ in my Heart. I am looking around but there is nothing to see." I suggest to Tory that she take Christ's hand and let him draw her into the space. "This is crazy. Now I see an outside scene like springtime. There are all of these colors hanging on a clothesline. Beautiful colors drying on a clothesline."

I suggest that she run her hands through them. "Yeah. Sheets and towels and shirt tops in different colors." I ask about the size of the tops. "They are for a small child, no adult shirts; at first I thought they were for a boy, but they are for a girl; they are hung up so nicely." I ask if they belong to a part of you locked away in your Heart? "There is such a sense of perfection here. Not in a negative way. I mean in the sense of cleanliness and freshness; there is such a good smell about them. No one ever thought of me that way." But, I reply, something knows her to be that way in her Heart. I ask if there are voices in her Heart that would squelch this experience? "Christ shows me just one. She is four or five years old with cork screw pigtails. She is shaking her finger at me in a scolding, shaming, way." I suggest that she let Christ place a portion of his *Light* into her Heart and strip her of that power as if waking someone who has been in a trance. "What I saw was her disappear; that is what happened when he placed his *Light* into her Heart." I ask if the clothes were hers? "No. They are my clothes not hers." We are well over our time and I need to bring her back, but before doing so, I ask if there is anything in her Heart that would prevent her from returning there with Christ? When she answers in the negative, I tell her it is better to re-experience all of this rather than just remember it. The session ends here.

Tory returns the following week with a number of observations suggesting that the previous session has had a significant and beneficial impact but also brought a new lack of self-confidence to the surface. She begins by noting that, on several occasions since the last session, she has remembered events that greatly shamed her in the past but when she remembers them now it is in a completely different light. She remembers, for example, that early in her current marriage she made plans to attend a weekend retreat. In turn, her new husband and daughter made plans for an outing on their own. When her mother learned of this she was adamant that Tory not let her daughter stay in the same house with her husband overnight alone; the mother insisted that the daughter stay with her. The mother told Tory that 'she did not know anything. She could not possibly leave her daughter unattended with a man she hardly knew (despite their already being married for two years). That if she left her daughter with him, then the mother would never keep her again.' (The mother was regularly keeping her granddaughter while Tory worked as a schoolteacher.) "I gave into her. Last week, when I remembered that, it was with the certainty that I should never have given in to her; that the whole thing was her humongous problem." I ask her about her reflux. "It is better. I started taking an anti-biotic three days ago for a cold, which does not allow me to take an antiacid. I have gone to bed each night without it and had no problem." She then has a question of her own: "I feel totally inept. I have no confidence that I can do anything correctly. I don't trust myself, my own judgment. The other day I gave my granddaughter some medicine. When I repeated it the next day my husband suddenly accused me of giving her 5X too much the previous day. I knew I could not have done such a thing but immediately doubted my own judgment. Then I discovered he was reading a dropper, which measured 5 milligrams as well as one teaspoon. But in the past I would never have been so unsure of myself. As an adult I have loved driving my car, but as a teen-ager I hated driving. I had no confidence in my driving then, and I have no confidence in my driving now. Is this the result of our work together?" I tell her I suspect it is, that an earlier – regressive version, of her Dominant self emerged, likely one who shamed her own judgment, to the point of doubting it, in favor of her parent's judgments, particularly her mother's. It was probably why she was remembering giving-in to her mother earlier in her marriage and why she was feeling paralyzed with doubt now. I suggest we think of this self as 'shaming doubt.' I ask her where she thinks this doubt is felt most strongly? She can tell immediately that it always starts in her abdomen and shoots up to her brain. Interestingly, she then goes on to tell me that since the last session she has had little appetite for food but it is no longer *revolting*. Now, even when I have a desire for something – such as going out for a hamburger the other night, I only ate half and brought the rest home to eat the following day. And I have gone through my kitchen and thrown out a lot of 'comfort' food that my husband has brought home for me in the past." She is glad for the lack of craving in her life but remains preoccupied with how much her doubt drains her energy. I have her go inside and stand in front of Christ. I am deliberately vague because I would like Christ to take the initiative and tell her so. I assume he will extract the shaming doubt from wherever it is and place it in a circle and I mention that possibility but do not presume it. This is what she reports: "He went in through my navel and pulled it out. In the circle there is now a huge intricately woven mesh with just the smallest openings in it. It is really like a trap. It is not solid but meticulously woven. If it were thrown over you there would be no way to get out of it. If that is in my stomach no wonder I have had trouble with my stomach." Since her experience with revulsion is so recent, I simply have Tory ask Christ what he could offer as quid pro quo for her giving up this doubting enmeshment forever? "He would give me two things: assurance and clarity. That really resonates with me. I feel like I am on egg shells all of the time. When I was growing up, one misstep with my mother and you paid for it for weeks." I suggest she tell Christ that she is willing to give up the power to shamefully doubt her self in exchange for the power of his assurance and clarity. I add that she also ask him to terminate her parents' power to shamefully doubt her. "I don't see a change in them but I feel a change in me. I just felt a complete relaxation of the *arching* in me. It lessoned since the last session but had not gone away. Now it is completely gone." Since we have some time remaining, I have her ask Christ if there is anything more he would encourage her to do today? Silence. Then she tells me, "We have been in a dialogue. He has reminded me that I left the distrustful state before and liked it, and I could leave it again and like it as much." (Her comments are in reference to the reconciliation of other selves that resulted in a profound sense of trust for Christ and the self we were working with at the time. Unfortunately, the selves that took her place have gradually eroded that trust.) I ask her if she can sense where she is holding this distrust? When she becomes unsure – distrustful, I ask if it would be advisable to enter the Heart for this work? In reply, she tells me, "No. This is a head thing." So I suggest that she ask Christ to penetrate the brow and extract this power to value distrust over trust. "There is something in the circle we drew but I can't see it." I suggest that she is in an active state of distrust and this is probably contributing to the distrust of her inner sight (which is generally quite clear and distinct). I suggest that she draw a circle of escape and ask Christ to convict her distrust with the power of the Holy Spirit. Her distrusting part can accept the conviction or escape to the circle. "I have asked Christ if he would replace my distrust with the security of trust, but nothing has changed." I note that she is setting conditions. It would be better to just accept the conviction and see what happens. "I have asked Christ to convict me and he did. There is nothing in the other circle (of escape) but I felt a lot of light enter my skull." I ask her to focus on the circle containing whatever Christ originally extracted from her brain. "I see a misshapen glob that is under a covering." I have her ask her Light to identify the nature of the 'covering' that has been hiding the misshapen glob. "Rationalization…total misinformation… double misinformation." I ask if Christ wants to offer anything other than his discernment in exchange. "No. That is quite enough. It is gone." I ask how she feels? "I feel fine. But to really know, I have to go and do; and see how it plays out this week." The session ends here.

When Tory returns the next week she has good news and bad news. Interestingly, her reflux problem is a non-issue. What with her 'new medicine' she has had absolutely no problem, though the new medicine was supposed to be less effective then the one she had to discontinue. The 'good news' from her perspective has to do with the grandchildren she keeps four days a week. She decided after our last session that she needed to be different with them. She was simply not pleased with the quality of her interaction. So each morning she prayed that, "They see and feel Christ's love through me all day long. I want to be used in that way. I have never had such a wonderful week. My granddaughter repeatedly hugged me and said she loved me. My grandson was all smiles and giggles. It still felt disingenuous – genii in the bottle stuff, but even though I fought with myself all week over it, I still had the best week with the children." The bad news has to do with her husband. They went for his annual checkup with the Neurologist. Beforehand, she told him that she was going to tell the doctor her observations. What most bothered her was her husband's response to the effect that he felt he had nothing to live for, no real purpose in his life. Significantly, the doctor found no discernable deterioration; the results of the evaluation were good even when he checked him more thoroughly in response to her observations. I suggest that she take a completely different tack to the problem: that she no longer take responsibility for her husband's attitude, but she take complete – 100 percent – responsibility for her image of him. In effect, I encourage her to treat his image as a manifestation of her masculine, contra-sexual, aspect and begin a process of asking Christ to completely redeem it. We have discussed this idea before, only now she is completely open to it and actually accepts that her husband is 'extremely sensitive to her thoughts' and so both might really benefit for this intervention. We do nothing in this session, but she anticipates letting Christ simultaneously convict both her and her husband's image; and both of us anticipate following up on whatever she does in the next session.

(At this point, the case notes will be getting ahead of the reader. What they cover is work I will be presenting in the next chapter. I am including them here for the sake of case continuity. The reader may want to revisit these verbatims after reading the next chapter.)

I see Tory a week later. She is still doing amazingly well with her grandchildren and they by her – based on positive reports of her granddaughter's dental exam and the evaluation of her language therapist. Tory is pleased with herself *as well as her husband's role as a co-caretaker*. During the week, Tory has done some inner work regarding her masculine. She asked Christ to extract from her brow her *perception* of her masculine, or to paraphrase what I finally understand her to say, the lens by which she sees her masculine. Note, this is not the same as asking Christ to separate her masculine from her, and that distinction becomes clearer as we work. She reports that what Christ put in her circle was both a feeling and a visual. "There was a huge feeling of lack or deficit. The visual was a little claylike stick figure, rubbery and wimpy. It made me feel bad. I asked Christ to start changing that perception into something better for me, but I did not get very far. I did have the strange sense that 'better' would be a 'positive swagger' and that surprised me. In my life, there have been males I could control and all others have really frightened me. I never could control my first husband. There was always an element of fright in our relationship, a sense of not measuring up to his standard. The idea of a positive swagger both surprised and scared me." At this point, I suggest that Tory needs to give up this 'lens of perception' in favor of Christ's discernment and she readily does so. She does not see anything in the circle in front of her after Christ has made the exchange, but hears repeatedly that, "All things have become new – a new creation in Christ." Now, I suggest, she can ask Christ to separate out her contra-sexual aspect, her masculine counterpart. "Christ separated the circle from me. What I see is the opposite of wimpy-rubbery. This male image is huge, rough and burley, and it has a *negative* swagger. There is a sense of injury or harm to me. I am aware now that my dad personifies both of those images – the wimpy and the negative swagger. How is it I am now seeing the opposite?" I suggest to Tory that the initial image was a consequence of her effort to control the masculine by emaciating it, whereas this image of the male with the negative swagger is her fear of the male. I tell her that what she needs is a masculine that will *empower* her. "Wow. That is a new thought." I suggest that she ask Christ to convict both her and her Negative swagger simultaneously. "OK, the hulky guy is gone. I don't feel the feeling I felt toward him anymore, but I don't see any image either. What I am thinking is 'I came in here seeing rubbery which was surprising, and then I discovered Negative swagger, which was even more surprising and I just want to think about it all." I feel there is one more thing she needs to do if she is willing. I am cognizant that she has evolved beyond her previous sense of the masculine but has yet to visualized a masculine that can empower her. I suggest that she ask Christ to sustain her with his masculine energy while her new sense of the masculine evolves and materializes. "I feel really good about that. I really like that. There is a sense that if that connection is in place for awhile I will have the opportunity to see and feel what I really need." I ask Tory how Christ forged the connection with her feminine? (Remember, she is doing all of this in the first person. Christ is not working with a separate, dissociated, feminine aspect.) "He was right there in front of me. It was an instant connection with his eyes. They were so deep. It is so strange. I never saw Christ's face when we started all of this in therapy. Recently, since the 'house with bones' image, I have seen his face as from afar. Today, I could see through his eyes. Mine were locked on his." When Tory returns to me and we are discussing her experience, I reflect that perhaps she only saw him from 'afar' as that is all she could safely handle until today. The session ends here.

I am unexpectedly called away and am not able to see Tory again for nearly a month. I am able to exchange several e-mails and she seems to be doing well, but when we see each other again she shares her concern for her brother whose drunkenness has seemed to escalate. She also relates another experience, which is difficult for me to label except as she sees it. Tory has been steadily losing weight for the past several months by eating moderately. For some years she has been allergic to shellfish and must carry an antidote with her when she eats out if she inadvertently does eat it. During the previous week she got the feeling that she could eat a crab cake without suffering any adverse effects. She told her husband she wanted very much to eat at a seafood restaurant that served delicious crab cakes. She ate one and had no ill effects. She believes that her 'allergy' was a way of teaching her that she could immediately refrain from eating something if it was harming the body. Having learned this lesson she no longer has need of the allergy. I am tempted to focus on her Eater at this point, but decide that the most pressing issue is the life-long estrangement between her mother and maternal grandfather father who died as the town drunk, since this is defining both her masculine and her brother, who is most strongly identified with that side of the family. Tory agrees wholeheartedly and is quite ready to address them. She goes inside and I suggest that she place both mother and MGF in the same circle. "It is hard to see them together. My MGF is wearing the hat he always wore. He looks dirty; he always did. There is a certain smell about him. Mother looks younger than I ever remember seeing her. She has really tightly curled hair and she is looking away from him." I anticipate that some part of Tory may be resistant to her letting Christ convict the two images, so I suggest that she draw a circle of escape to address that possibility. Then I tell her that the goal of treatment is for Christ to convict both of the images until they can lovingly embrace. "I have never seen that in my life. I've never seen her even touch him. She was always so proud to never want anything from him. My uncle and his family did play up to him. I was afraid of him." I suggest that she ask Christ to convict her with the willingness to allow Christ to transform them. It is not clear that this happens, but in reply she tells me, "A part of me is really curious, like 'my gosh what could happen…. Now, I am aware of how cold they were, how awful they were together." I suggest to her that all she is giving up is the continuation of that 'coldness' into eternity. Again I encourage her to let Christ convict her with the words: remove any obstacle to my willingness for you to completely transform this relationship. In reply, she tells me that, "No one objects." Now I ask her to ask Christ to begin convicting the relationship. "Another thought comes to my mind when he does this. The idea of a father and child relationship. When I think of it in those terms, the distance is not so cold between them and my mother has turned around."

Tory returns a week later. She has been suffering some pain in her right arm. She reports that her right arm has gotten worse – the muscles are tighter and painful, and the Chiropractor has no explanation for it. I tell her of a Chakra therapist who believes that different parts of the body correlate with specific chakras of specific auric bodies; and that there is such a point on both arms. [47] This point correlates with the heart chakra of the emotional body. Since the muscles are painfully tight, I suggest that there may be a self that is constricting the emotional heart chakra of the Emotional auric body by its activity. Tory willing goes inside for the purpose of letting Christ reach into her Heart to the level of the Emotional auric body and extract any self constricting it. "There is a teenage self, age 13-14, who is extremely conflicted about her allegiance to her mother and father. The option is never there to be aligned with both of them so she bobs back and forth." What is making her active now? "A real sense that nothing good or pleasant can be discussed with daddy about mother. He seems to have closed a book on their relationship and that gives him permission to negate her." What is the major obstacle to the teenager releasing her hold on the heart chakra? "The fear of change. She feels she can handle this by bobbing back and forth. Right up until she died mother was always seeming to ask, 'are you with me or against me'? Bobbing back and forth was a way of maintaining a connection between the two of them." At this juncture I make two suggestions that 'Bobber' can ask of Christ: 1) If she gives up her power to 'bob' will he reconcile her parents as well as her mother and grandfather, so there is no reason to ever 'bob' again; and 2) will he sustain her energy and definition during the transition? Tory reports that he answers "Yes, he can and he wants to do this for her, but she cannot see Christ's eyes and there is no discernible change in the 'Bobber.' I suggest that she direct the Bobber to look into Christ's eyes and again make the request of him. "Looking into his eyes made all the difference in the world. It made the request easy. It's done."

Basically, in this session, Tory has struggled with a relationship between her mother and father that essentially recapitulates the relationship between her mother and grandfather, and the self that has coped with the life long estrangement of her parents by bobbing back and forth. What makes this such a difficult coping mechanism is that when she is unable to 'bob,' for whatever reason, she is likely to become depressed, as when for example, her mother would go silent for days or she became justifiably angry at her father's callous disregard of her feelings. Hopefully, in this next session we can refocus on healing the breach between mother and maternal grandfather.

When Tory returns her arm is both better and worse. "I have more strength in it and range of motion, but it is very tight and painful. Then she adds: "Every year about this time I have something wrong with me. Last year it was my hip, the year before the other arm was fractured, and the year before that I had food poisoning. I have not done any inner work. The kids have been sick all week." I am convinced this has to do with resistance to working on significant relationships defining her masculine and feminine. She is quite agreeable to going inside. I suggest that she first draw a circle of escape, and then ask Christ to convict her and be ready for a whole lot of insight to follow. The circle of escape will be for any self that is most resistant to change at this time. "I immediately saw a part of me enter the circle of escape. "It is not the Bobber. This self just feels beaten down as well as feeling a complete lack of connection. My birthday is this month and that made this month doubly hard growing up. I always got clothes from mother and I never knew if I would be able to wear them. If they were too small mother took it as a personal affront. This was also the month I had my miscarriage, and the month my mother died. This part of me never felt any connection with anyone who understood how I felt about any of those things. I hate this month." I ask the age of the self in the circle of escape. "She is about eight-years-old." I attempt to paraphrase the child's need: That she really needs someone who can understand her painful of lost connection, someone who can know this pain and help her experience reconnection. Frankly, at this point I have an idea but need to be sure that Tory is at least willing to consider such a person. I ask if there is any unwillingness on her part to satisfying the little girl's need? At first she says "No," that she is really tired of her arm hurting. But then she tells me that she cannot see Christ. I suggest that she come back to me and with her eyes open ask her *Light* to draw two circles, one for herself and the other for whatever resists seeing Christ, and then upon entering the first circle she is to ask Christ to convict her again. "I felt the conviction as a lightening. Now I can even see his eyes. There is nothing in the other circle. What needed to be convicted was my disbelief that it could be so simple."[48] That all I had to do was ask Christ. I think all of this is coming from the eight-year-old. She is such a *feeling* being, she needs a feeling, a heartfelt feeling that she can connect with another and be understood. She wants to feel that Christ wants her, that he cares enough for her to feel differently." I could not imagine a more perfect entrée to the intervention I have in mind, though I am still feeling very tentative about suggesting it as I have never done so before. But the time could not be more right so I begin by asking Tory to give the Eight-year-old a portion of her *Light*. Then I tell her that if she is willing the *Light* will take her to the foot of the cross. Tory does this. Her facial changes tell me it is having an effect on the Eight-year-old. I now suggest that the Eight-year-old step close to the cross and touch the feet of Christ as he hangs there. Tory is close to tears as, frankly, am I. Finally, I suggest that she step back from the cross and stand next to Mary. Through her tears, Tory begins sharing with me: "There is a special connection between Mary and the Eight-year-old. She is feeling for the first time that there is someone who understands how she feels. The understanding is complete; it goes all the way back. Mary is telling her 'you worried about clothes. Imagine how I felt when I had to tell someone I was pregnant with the Son of God. I know how you felt, your fear…At first, I thought the cross was the answer, but Mary is much, much, more the answer…This month will never be the same…There is still a little pain in my arm, but all of the tightness is gone." The session ends here. Two days later Tory sends me an e-mail telling how much better her shoulder is and how even her Doctor was surprised, and that our session was an experience she would not quickly forget. She then went on to relate a story of how, after our session, another person shared with a large group that it was Tory who had first given her the experience of someone who felt her pain and sadness and wanted to help her out of it instead of making her feel worse. Tory has always understood, now she can feel understood.

I see Tory two weeks later. She returns to complain that she is not sleeping, that her right arm is keeping her up at night, though better during the day. Also, she is 'angry at everyone' without good reason. What keeps her up at night is a 'tearing' sensation in her arm. I suggest she go inside and ask Christ to extract whatever is 'tearing' at her arm, and put it in a circle. "It's there, it is not a image. It is a pile, red and angry. It glows like a huge clinker that is rough as well." I suggest that she ask Christ to bring into consciousness whoever it belongs to? "It belongs to me. It is jagged and sharp and would really hurt if you touched it. I would like to not deal with it." I ask if she would be willing for Christ to show her who it connects her to? If so, I suggest that she ask Christ to bring it into consciousness within a dome. In response to several questions from me, she shares that, "No, the anger is mine. My anger keeps it away. It is fearful of my anger. Mother was silent when she was angry. I hated that. I have actively missed my mother this past week. I wanted her to see my granddaughter and share her with my mother." I tell Tory that there is no reason why she cannot bring her mother and granddaughter together in her imagination except that she has not. I suggest that the anger is keeping them apart. I suggest that she ask Christ to show her how *she can safely touch the anger in the circle*. Tory replies that, "It will really hurt, you can't touch it." The session ends here. What I surmise is that Tory is experiencing symptoms of repeated shock trauma related to her mother repeatedly disconnecting from Tory. And, in fact, what will follow are a series of recollections attached to strong fearful emotions much in need of discharge.

In the next session we continue to focus on Tory's hurting arm and the anger it holds. Tory is reflective about her anger. "I think it was born out of extreme frustration, silent frustration. Silence blocked connection and repair, and it had to be endured. In private, I could become angry in order to break into mother's silence, but it never changed anything. My anger would escalate and mother would say 'I can't live like this,' and threaten to send me to boarding school." I suggest that she let Christ reach deep into her anger, dissolve the feelings that perpetuate it, and draw out the event that started it. She can ask him to leave some residual of the feeling but not the full charge, but she will need to see him reach into the Heart of it. A long silence ensues. Finally, Tory begins to speak. "I was ten or eleven. Mother and daddy had a horrible argument that went on for days. Mack was two or three. Mother picked him up, took her pocketbook and left the house. She was gone for hours. I started getting scared she would not come back. When she came back I asked where she went. She said she went to a local restaurant for barbeque. That was the first time I wanted to scream and scream and I did not. It did not matter that I was scared. To this day Mack will remind me that she took him to the restaurant. After that things changed. If I played her game it did not make a difference, so I might as well let her know how I felt. My feelings seemed to have no effect on her. That is why they have to be so extreme." I suggest to Tory that she ask Christ to see behind her mother's silences, to let Christ dissolve the wall of silence. I add that we do not need her mother's permission for this. "I see her swallowed up with discomfort, never confident, on edge, fearful. I was the cause of the discomfort in her when I was an infant. She did not want to be who she was in Brecken (the small town where they lived). The mother I lived with was completely defined by her shameful judgment of her parents." I ask Tory if she is succumbing to her mother's shameful baggage? Tory attempts to deny this but ends with a confirmation: "I did succumb, but not now. I despise having accidents. It is a personal affront to fall and mess up my arm. My mother use to say 'My mother fell, I fall, you fall.' I hate being identified with her and my grandmother in terms of weakness. Right before I fell there was a sense of euphoria – pride before the fall." I ask her if she attaches pride to feeling good? "I can remember thinking this is a good day, then I slipped on the floor while carrying Mandy. My mother would say that pride keeps you out of heaven. I just realized what a concrete connection that is. When the pride comes it feels like somebody jerking on a leash." What I suggest at this point is somewhat paradoxical: I ask her to give up the power of shaming pride and anger in exchange for the power of Christ's discernment and feeling good? "Yes, and my shoulder is already feeling better." The session ends here.

Tory's arm continues to hurt at night. In this session I set up another intervention to get at the source. I suggest that she have Christ draw a Heart portal that the two can step through. There, he will provide a safe place for a true answer to the question of what is sustaining the pain in her arm. "It feels cold, void, a nothingness. I feel Christ is there." I ask if she has to address the cold void? "No. I have to address the feeling that says 'Nothing I do is effective.' I need to release the belief that I can change things with enough effort." I have her stand in front of Christ and say the following, which I slowly repeat to her: "I am willing to give up my conviction that I'm the only one who can do it in exchange for your discernment in these matters." I stress that she must feel Christ entering her brow and making the exchange. "OK. I can feel Christ inside of me, his fingers penetrating me. There is a sense of relief, of lightness, and closeness. What I like more than anything is that sense of closeness." The session ends here.

Tory returns three days later. She reports that she slept through the last two nights. "I can even go back to sleep if I get up. I quit the antidepressants cold turkey a month ago. That may have been contributing to my difficulty sleeping. I kicked my husband out of the bed because of his snoring and that allows me to sleep in a position that is easier on my shoulder so I am not sure we have gotten to the heart of the problem. I do have a sense that it is OK to feel good since our session last week." I suggest that she allow Christ to create a well of sensation and bring to the surface whatever is continuing to keep her shoulder sore. I further stipulate that he will place a dome over the circle and a portion of his *Light* into it to draw off any excessive negative charge. Finally, I encourage her to get assurances from him that this is doable. "OK. I could feel myself being real tense from the waist up when he was drilling. I am no longer tense. I don't have any interest in what is going on in the dome. My arm was aching but it is not hurting now." I encourage her to walk toward the dome with Christ. "The *Light* inside the dome was diffuse before. Now it is defined like a shaft only slightly smaller than the well hole. The shaft is very bright and glowing. Purification comes to mind and the idea that if purified nothing is a problem." I suggest that she step back and let the process go forward. "OK, that will work. The shaft of *Light* is almost like a sword." The session ends here.

I confess to the reader that I am surprised how long this process of healing her arm has taken. But the next session explains it all. She has been coping all these years with shock trauma. When Tory returns she tells me that "The night after I was here I awoke in a panic and a fear of losing my granddaughter and that she will not have me or anybody. The next night I was also afraid." I suggest that she go inside and separate from this fearful part. Very quickly, Tory goes inside and begins reporting on a memory. "There is this incident I remember at age six or seven. I was sitting outside the house, which was on a local road beside a highway. A bus on the highway stopped in front of our house to let off a passenger. He walked in front of the bus to cross the road. A car came up from behind the bus, passed around the bus, and hit the man. I saw him flying up in the air. I started screaming.

My mother came out. It was horrible, you can't imagine what it looked like. The driver of the car did not even stop. She said, 'It is over, he will be alright.' But I said to her what if that happened to me? She replied that, 'that I always imagined terrible things.' And I did imagine there would be no one there for me. Period. I could not count on mother to be there for me. She would be gone. I can trace all kinds of things back to that. I believed I made her life unhappy because she did not want me. I felt she would leave if she could. *The seven year old was traumatized. My mother brushed it away as if it was nothing.*" I ask Tory: Who did she brush away? "It felt like it was me. I think it is in the well, the part that truly felt that it was horrible." I paraphrase what she is saying: she brushed away a little girl who needed somebody to reassure her. I ask her two questions: will Control let this little girl out and will Christ enter the well and bring her up into consciousness? "She had to be banished. She felt it as if it could happen to her." Again, I encourage her to let Christ give her a second chance, to bring her back and give her the security she needs. "I see Christ holding her the way I love to hold Mandy. She is really little, younger than I expected, age three or four." I wonder aloud if there was an earlier trauma? "The trauma was ongoing from day one. My mother told me I almost caused my parents to divorce because I cried. It is deep in the little girl. I can remember at age two being woken up in the middle of the night to go get a puppy. My parents were excited. I remember just being scared." I sense this child needs maternal healing and encourage Tory to let Christ allow his mother, Mary, access to the child. "I can see Mary. She is not able to keep her hands off of her. She is touching her, hugging her, pushing her hair back. She is standing in front of Christ constantly touching the child." I ask if she is willing for Christ to pass the child to Mary? "I am not comfortable with that. I like the touching, but it feels good to just be held by Christ. It is a real secure feeling." I tell her there is no need right now. If Mary can satisfy the child's need for nurture, the child will let her know. "I tried to tell my dad, but he never understood." I reiterate my own thought that the child needs to know that the maternal can satisfy. The session ends here.

When Tory returns she is very reflective. "After the session I had a real sense of sadness, not just for what I missed, but for the way I raised my own daughter, which was much like my mother raised me. But I also felt real joy when I went back inside and watched the scene evolve. Christ kept holding me and Mary engulfed us both, playing with my hair, combing my hair. I never actually went to her, but there was a lot of joyful interaction." I ask if she thinks there is some reticence on her part? "Yes. But I have felt better than I have in a long time. I have slept well. I have tremendous energy. Thinking of mother I realize she could be either/or. She could be attentive and nurturing but it never lasted. I knew what it was to be nurtured, but then it would get shut off. I never knew which mother was going to show up. Later she would repeatedly tell me that she loved me because of all the things I did for her. My daughter says similar things to me now. The part of me who distrusts what they say seems crucial here." A new self has emerged who is distrustful. I suggest to Tory that she go inside and ask Christ to use a concentric circle to separate from this part that distrusts. Tory does so and quickly begins to describe her. "She is a young adult in her 20's. She looks like me but not like me at all. She looks like the opposite of me, a part that I do not like. I do not like the control and power she has. She is so negative and draining." I ask Tory if she can assess her reasons for being so negative? "She sees reality as it is: most times you will be disappointed, hurt, can't count on others; and no one really cares. They may say they do, but not the way it really is. I don't like to feel that way." I suggest to Tory that Distrust holds the memory of being deeply hurt and disappointed; and then I ask if she knows where she keeps those memories? "She keeps them in the feelings they evoke…the hurt she can recall instantly. The memories are in her feelings…a broken heart, pulled down, unable to move." I suggest to Tory that Christ could free her feelings of those memories; that he could absorb the negative emotions attached to them. "I like the idea of absorb." I ask if 'Distrust' can tolerate the child that Christ is carrying? "She is familiar with the child." When I ask if she can also tolerate Christ entering her circle, Tory replies that, "He can enter the circle. But she is reluctant about contact. She is afraid to even look at him." I suggest that Tory give Distrust a portion of her Light and teach her to create a garment of protection. "OK. Now she can look." We are very short on time so I suggest that Distrust, Christ and Tory work with the situation between sessions. Tory's last comment is telling: "That is fine with Christ. But the child is missing Mary. It is really obvious. She keeps searching for Mary." I do not make any suggestions because we are well over time, but plan to address that first thing in the next session.

I see Tory a week later. After a quick review of what has been happening in her life, I suggest that she go inside and ask Christ to give the child to Mary so he can work with Distrust. Tory shares her thoughts on the matter: "When we had them together, there was a strong sense of relationship, but I have no physical appearance of Mary." I suggest that she trust the process enough to watch it unfold. "Christ has handed the child to her out of view. I can feel her holding the child. I sense it; it is fine." I ask if she is satisfying the child? "I am not focusing on the child, but they are fine. I am not experiencing that. I am in the circle with Christ and Distrust." I decide not to press the point and direct her to let Christ work with Distrust. "Christ has gathered her cloak of protection closer around her. Now he has put his *Light* before her at her feet. I am not sure what that means. She is taking steps too where he puts his *Light*. He is going with her and I am watching. He is illuminating a path for her." I suggest to Tory that she bring her own *Light* up to her brow and ask it to clear her sight so she can see the path. "I knew Christ was in front of her. The *Light* is leading her to him a step at a time. I was not aware he was as far away from her as he seems now." I suggest that she allow the process to continue and return to me. The session ends here. I will not see her again for three weeks and I am quite curious how this will all evolve.

Our next session is delayed a week as Tory fights a flu bug with her grandchildren. She is on the mend when I see her. The issue that seems to have compromised her immune system was a call from her brother – the deteriorating alcoholic, asking if he can come live with her ostensibly because where she lives has more resources for recovery. She is able to say no, but feels very guilty afterward. She also tells me that over the past three weeks she has continued to work with Distrust, who finally 'reaches' Christ. "He reached out and she took his hand." I tell Tory that Distrust is unique in that she is the only self Tory has identified whose primary function appears to be feeling, even as she seems to negate her feelings with distrust. I suggest that she allow Christ to work with this self during the session. First, that Distrust – if willing, allow Christ to give her an experience of trust equal to her experience of distrust; and second, that she allow Christ to provide her the gift of discernment as a way of moving between these two poles vis-à-vis her feelings. Tory and Distrust are agreeable. Distrust expresses her willingness by entering a circle drawn by Christ. She can use the circle to express her willingness by stepping in and out and back in, which she does several times during the session. The moment Distrust stepped into the circle she reached out and took both of Christ's hands; in effect she wholeheartedly expresses her trust in him. Next, I suggest that she allow him to penetrate her brow and instill the power of his discernment. Initially, he lays his hand on her forehead. Tory reports that it is a good feeling, but I note that it is not the same as penetration. I ask if she has ever used distrust of her feelings to shame herself or others. Distrust affirms that she has. I point out that she will have to forgo this power to shame this set of opposites. She reaffirms her willingness by stepping out of the circle and then stepping back in. Tory reports that Christ's fingers penetrate to the center of her brain, then Tory tells me: "I thought the result would be a feeling of being free from distrust, but it is really a feeling of being free to do either one as the situation dictates." Finally, I sense it may be time to address the cutoff relationship between Tory's decease mother and maternal grandfather. I tell her we really need to accept that there is a self that has been strongly resistant in this matter, even as the divisiveness has clearly had an adverse effect on the dynamics of at least three generations. Tory agrees but goes on to defend her reluctance: "All my feelings of him were negative. A secrecy and mystery swirled around him. I was afraid of him. I loved my maternal grandmother so much and he was so mean to her. The idea of changing my attitude feels like a betrayal of her." Even so, I press her pointing out the potential effect it is having on her brother and daughter, neither of whom seem to have the wherewithal to do this themselves. She reluctantly agrees. I suggest that she go inside and ask Christ to contain her grandfather's soul, then I modify the suggestion by asking her to let Christ convict his 'soul, mind, and body.' Tory has a mixed reaction to my suggestions: "When you said I could just bring his soul into the circle, I felt his presence, but when you added 'body and mind' I could not get beyond that." I explain that the redemption of his soul would be reflected in a 'new body' so a body is necessary for that purpose. I suggest that she ask Christ to help her separate from whoever is 'unwilling' to see him embodied? Tory reports this quickly done and goes on to describe her: "Unwilling is a little girl, age 8-9. She has no positive connection with her grandfather." But, I reply, she has a strong *negative* connection. The session ends here. Tory agrees to flesh her out between sessions.

When Tory returns the following week, as soon as possible, I have her focus on Unwilling. "I don't see her. There is no connection, no response; no life or action. I don't see her in my mind. There is a real heaviness. It is too hard to bring her back into focus. This parallels the way I have been feeling all week: burdened and heavy. I felt it even more so when I went inside." I ask if this feeling has to do with Unwilling? "I don't know." (I have come to suspect that that particular phrase is a strong marker of unwillingness.) I suggest to Tory that she return to me, use her *Light* to create a circle of protection with her eyes open, and then ask Christ to begin the separation process once she is back inside. "OK. I can see her the way I saw her last week." I ask if Christ can give her an experience of willingness equal to her experiences of unwillingness. "I asked Christ, but this is not working. There is no feeling on my part. Everything seems dead, wooden. The lack of feeling is coming from me." I ask if she would be willing to give up her power to block feeling? "Isn't it appropriate?" I tell her that she believes that cutting off feeling is appropriate, that she has been doing it for 50 plus years. "I know the answer to this: shut off the feelings or just cry about it, and crying accomplishes nothing." I reply that crying would at least discharge the tension and she would not have to deaden by cutting off feeling. The session ends here. I schedule another for two days later. I am concerned that this self is depressed and painting herself into a corner. I anticipate that the next session will be a 'hard' one and I frankly pray for guidance and help before meeting again with Tory.

The next session is quite amazing. I might call it a prayer answered. Finally, after months of resistance Tory comes in *willing to do whatever I want her to do*. I immediately ask if that includes her going inside and allowing Christ to begin convicting her mother and maternal grandfather? When she says 'yes,' I immediately have her go in without further ado, not even asking the reasons for this shift. She will stay inside for most of the hour. Tory asks Christ to convict the two images and then reports: "After he did it, there was a more visible change in my mother, but as she started to soften my grandfather did become less stern. Mother reached out and took his arm as if to help him walk." I suggest that she ask Christ to convict their images again, noting that they need to become life enhancing and free in every way from the need for addiction. "I see my mother being positive and nurturing, but not my grandfather. He is not repulsed but not responsive." At this point I suggest that Tory have Christ move her grandfather into a circle *with the maternal grandmother* and convict the two of them. "Christ does it. My grandmother has a sense of gratitude toward him. I can't imagine why. He is hard; there is armor all around him." I note to Tory that he married her when she was pregnant with an out of wedlock child by another man. They conceived her mother after they were married. This might account for her sense of gratitude. I then suggest that she allow Christ to continue convicting the grandfather until all of the armor is dissolved. I stress that she is looking to release the generations from his 'sins,' especially any effect his history is having on her brother and daughter. "You could not change his mind about anything. That is certainly a characteristic of my brother. I don't want to work on this anymore." I query her as to why? And ask if she would let Christ convict her for insight? "There was never a relationship between us. He was a source of fear and total embarrassment." I suggest that she ask Christ to release her from that emotional connection of fear and shame, as it will otherwise maintain the status quo. My wording is quite specific: Ask Christ to release you from the negative emotions binding you to your MGF. Let him convict you both simultaneously. "I can see a lot *Light* in the circle. I have no insight into him. The armor is gone and he does not seem stern or hard. I do not feel ashamed or overtly negative. Nor am I positive; not loving, just neutral." I ask her about 'all the Light in the circle'? "It was created by the energies of the change. There was a lot of release. Now it has dissipated. I could feel the negative emotions before that; they were almost overwhelming." I suggest that she tell him to go back to his wife; that both of them need to be redeemed. I note to Tory that he could only have come into her life through her maternal grandmother, who chose to marry him for whatever reasons. "I see them both in the same circle. Before they were facing each other. Now they are standing side by side in front of Christ. I can see the same *Light* at the bottom of the circle after Christ convicted them. Now they are closer together. I never saw them like that. I never even saw them in the same location while they were alive. They seem normal, together, in rapport." I suggest that she now ask Christ to convict them for a comfortable intimacy. "No. Christ could do that, but it is not going to happen. That is too much." I point out to her that these images channel her image insofar as they culminate in her. "OK. I understand that. Convict for comfortable intimacy. I can see Christ doing that." How is it different? "The feeling is different. The body language is different, a sense of relaxation. I just see them differently, together instead of separately." At this point I suggest one more intervention: that she bring her mother into her grandparents' circle. "At first I sensed some anxiety from mother. But she goes inside and the three seem fine together. She links them with one hand around her own mother's waist and the other through her father's arm." I suggest that she ask Christ to complete the connection by blessing the three. "There is a huge sense of release, release and connection." The session ends here. This is probably one of the purest expressions of willingness I have encountered in a single session, all the more so because there were two separate bursts of resistance that might ordinarily have brought the process to a halting stop. At no time did we actually address the unwillingness that dominated the previous session. Very likely, the request that she experience willingness equal to unwillingness, and Tory's realization that her unwillingness was an effort to stuff feeling, were sufficient to bring her so strongly to the opposite pole. Nor can I rule out my fervent prayer the morning before our session.

When Tory returns the following week nothing is said about the previous week. Instead, Tory is majorly preoccupied with her daughter, Abby, and her granddaughter, Mandy. "I am having a lot of trouble with Abby; she has been sick with a stomach virus all week. I am not supposed to have any life but the kids. Keeping Mandy has become a real burden. She seems to fly off whenever she experiences the slightest frustration." I make several observations and suggestions. First, that Tory consider teaching Mandy to use the *Light* and begin teaching her about emotions such as naming her anger or sadness. I note that Mandy seems to be modeling her mother who is constantly upset and frustrated. I strongly suspect the core issue is Mandy's lack of attachment with Abby. I also note that, as the first born, Abby will be strongly identified with her father, Robert. Her father may well have suffered an attachment disorder. He was adopted at nine months. The biological parents seemed unwilling to raise him and pressed the adopted parents to take him. The adopted parents seemed to do so reluctantly and raised him with benign neglect. I tell Tory that very likely Mandy is carrying disowned projections from all three: her father, mother, and Tory; and that she needs to see Mandy in the hands of an archetypal mother. I am aware that Tory has yet to finally resolve the issue of her own nurture. Recall that Christ has handed her Pre-moral aspect to his mother 'off stage.' Tory has yet to see the mother and child together.

The next session is interesting in several respects. The primary focus remains on Mandy, but there are intimations of other changes. For one, the alcoholic brother has been visiting and staying with the father. He was in town for four days and as far as Tory could tell he never drank. Abby, Tory's daughter, has been pressing her mother to tell her what I have been suggesting vis-à-vis Mandy. (I saw Abby and her husband for several sessions, several years back, but never felt I got to first base. She has tended to minimize anything I have reportedly said in the past.) Tory tells her of my hypothesis that Mandy may be suffering from a lack of attachment. Abby in turn freely admits to her mother that she feels she has never bonded with Mandy. Tory knows this and resents the fact. I ask Tory if she would be willing to let Christ help her bond with Mandy? Tory considers this but has trouble getting beyond her anger at Abby for not bonding with Mandy. I suggest that she ask Christ to convict her anger; that her anger represents an error in judgment as it merely results in anger, which is unhelpful to Mandy. Conviction would allow the Holy Spirit to 'correct' this error in judgment. "I see Abby saying 'Mommy, you take care of it. She does not know how, but neither do I. I am feeling powerless." I suggest that she ask Christ to make a difference with Abby on behalf of all four of them (Tory, Tory's mother, Mandy, and Robert, her husband). Then I suggest that she show Christ an image of Mandy having a temper tantrum and let him show Tory how to 'attach' to her in the midst of that. "When I show him, Christ sits beside her on the floor. This surprises her. She quietens to look at him. He keeps talking but I do not know what he is saying. He is not reaching out. She is calming down and getting closer to him. She finally comes and sits in his lap but he has still not touched her. He becomes perfectly approachable and she is drawn to him. He is still talking to her and she is laughing; and I love it when she laughs and she does not laugh much anymore. I want that. The closest we come to it is when she sits on my lap and plays computer games." I suggest to Tory that she ask Christ to help her experience what makes him so approachable. "It's delight. He delights in her. I use to have that." I ask if she can identify the obstructing beliefs? "What has gotten in the way is my anger at Abby and my fearfulness about Mandy." I suggest she conclude they are not helpful emotions. I ask if she is willing to give up the anger and fear to Christ for a renewal of the delight? "Yes." The session ends here.

The following week Tory reports that Mandy has changed back to her 'wonderful self.' "Each day before she arrives at the house, I pray to be delighted in her. This week she could not cuddle enough with me." I suggest that we focus on Abby's masculine and feminine aspects. I suspect they are comparable to the unredeemed masculine and feminine found in Tory's brother. Tory has difficulty doing this. She is filled with anger toward Abby for her treatment of Mandy. "I feel like my anger is righteous. I fell in love with Mandy the moment she was born and feel very protective of her." I reply that she needs to alter her image of Abby so her daughter can make the choice to attach to her daughter. She reports that after Christ convicts her image of Abby, she seems a little more proactive, "with more energy than I generally attribute to Abby." But Tory remains essentially unwilling to work with Abby's masculine and feminine aspects. I suspect she is also being protective of herself, as what emerges will have flowed from Tory to Abby.

This next session is woven from numerous threads, which may be what makes it pivotal. I have not seen Tory for two weeks. In the interim her brother has visited yet again. His divorce is imminent; he has no job, no place to go, and has started drinking again. But he has also grown very attached to Mandy who he feels is one of the few persons who seems to love him unconditionally. Despite the fact that he has resumed drinking he is apparently giving serious thought to going to a halfway house for three plus months when he is forced out the house. During the previous week he also agreed to go with Tory and her husband, Eduardo, to a Celebration Recovery meeting. He was quite taken with the experience and hopes he can find one in his city when he returns there. All of this notwithstanding, Tory is most aware of her anger toward her daughter, who has added fresh oil to the fire by telling her mother that she and her husband are contemplating filing for bankruptcy. The mother knows that this is purely the result of unnecessary and excessive spending. I point out that Abby's excessive eating and excessive spending are clearly additive; that she is acting just like her great maternal grandfather (the town drunk). At first I think – out loud, that Tory is carrying her mother's identity and her daughter is carrying the MGF's disowned identity. In other words, Tory has unconsciously projected the masculine aspect of her mother's identity into her daughter. That will prove not to be the case, but the rational is sufficient for Tory to go inside and try yet again to separate out her daughter's masculine and feminine aspects. This time I phrase the request more specifically: that she ask Christ to extract the masculine and feminine aspects that are *the source of her daughter's addictions*. Basically, what she discovers is that the aspects are a personification of the GMGF and GMGM. "What I see about them is that both are so closed. There is a wall around each one of them, clear but soundproof." I suggest that she allow Christ to dissolve the walls around each one and convict their images until they are reconciled. I remind her that she has done this once before. "I watch the walls disappear. At first the images are shocked, anxious and fearful. Then Christ brought them together and reconciled them. It almost feels like they are experiencing mutual pleasure, but that is probably too strong." I suggest that she 'go for broke' and ask Christ to convict them for 'mutual pleasure in each other.' "I can see a difference. They are turning toward each other lovingly. Interesting…I don't think Abby finds pleasure in anything." I suggest that she allow her mother – whose image was previously extracted, to step into the circle containing her parents and assimilate the essence, but not the images, of her parents. Tory observes this and reports that her mother's image seems radiant. Then she seems to dramatically shift her focus by commenting on something her brother told her the night before. Her brother was upset when his father told him that he would not be going by Tory's house because 'those kids' were there. What I extrapolate from this comment is Tory's intuition that her mother's image is sustained by her father's energy and the father is unwilling to support this sense of 'mutual pleasure.' I suggest that she ask Christ to insure that her mother's dramatic redefinition is sustained by Christ's masculine energy until her father 'comes around.' (If masculine and feminine aspects are not simultaneously convicted, then it will be necessary for Christ to sustain any redefinition of the feminine until the masculine willingly accommodates to the change. All of this is described at length in the next chapter.) Finally, I have Tory encourage her daughter's image to enter the circle with the redeemed GMGF and GMGM. The daughter does so but is unable to assimilate the changes. The session ends here. I am not sure what is blocking that assimilation, but I note that Abby is an only child and strongly identified with her father's side of the family; and Tory's father is clearly an unredeemed masculine energy. It all suggests that the pendulum must now swing to 'the fathers.' The session ends here.

I see Tory a week later. She continues to complain about her daughter's sense of entitlement. After venting for a while she becomes willing to go inside and ask her mother to assimilate the new image of the maternal grandparents and then address the relationship between her and her husband. The mother seems quite willing. "When I ask she walks to them. They are close together. She embraces them and gathers them to her. At first I could not see a lot of detail but afterward there was a real softening of her outline and by the way she stands and holds her head. There is a fleshing out and greater lightness. When you first talked about bringing my father and mother together I thought she would be angry, but not now. Christ has forged a visible energy connection between her and my father. He asks my father to remember the way mother was when they lived away from their hometown. There is a visible change in him but not enough to make it the way it needs to be. Mother has a happiness about her and seems carefree. What I sense about daddy is that he has a real desire to be with mother and that is real different." The session ends here. I do encourage her to revisit this scene throughout the week and continue to ask Christ to convict her parents' relationship.

Tory reports several dreams when she returns, all of them positive toward males and particularly her father. She goes inside and asks Christ to convict the parental relationship till it conveys a total, soul-satisfying embrace. "I could see it before you said it. It is not how I have ever seen them together. It is very positive and pleasant. There is a sense of rightness about it, but it is not enough. It lacks a certain energy. I want to sense the feelings inside of them, from the inside out. I never saw them in that kind of embrace. I want to sense what caused it to happen." The session ends here.

In the next session, Tory reports that her daughter is looking to place the grandchildren in daycare. Tory and her husband are quite willing for this to happen. While they love the children, the constant weekly care is physically wearing. I summarize where we are with her parents, emphasizing that we are seeking their complete reconciliation because their images play such a vital role in shaping the flow of *her* masculine and feminine energies. (The reader will better appreciate my perspective after reading the next chapter.) The objective is for Christ to convict the relationship until it honors them and her as well, to release them from their 'fates' so they can realize their destiny. She asks Christ to convict them and then begins to describe the changes. "I can see them so differently. There is an excitement about them. I never saw them in an embrace. There is energy and expectancy, a smile on mother's face. It is a situation where I would like to be a part of it. I suggest that Tory enter her parents' circle in order to join them.

She finds herself surprisingly reticent. She is afraid it will have a dampening effect on their interaction. "There is not room for another person. Dad felt that mom made us kids a priority that excluded him." I stress to her that she must forgo this fear, as they must be reconciled 'through her.' (Remember, our ostensible goal is to pass these generational changes through Tory to her daughter, Abby.) The session ends here.

When Tory returns she tells me that her brother has finally left his home and entered a halfway house for alcoholics. She is quite bitter toward her father who is currently blaming his 'heart stress' on her brother. I suggest that his 'heart arrhythmia' is most likely the effects of a guilty conscience over his self-absorption with his girlfriend at the price of neglecting nearly everyone in the family, except when he needs something from Tory. After hearing her understandable vents against him I point out that his real life behavior does not have to reflect her interior image of him. Those images are as Christ would have him in her; Christ's gift to her. She goes inside with the intent to finally enter the circle containing her parents. "This is hard. I am in the circle, but not touching them, not close." I suggest that she allow Christ to convict her so she can receive them. "The circle is really big. Christ comes to me and begins to walk us both toward them. They begin to notice us. They turn and start to walk toward us, glad to see me. (This last is spoken with quiet but discernible emotion.) I'm really, really, close. I can see them as I saw them before. There is room for me too. I can feel it more than I can see it." I suggest that she will 'complete them' as they are by assimilating them into her. "Christ agrees with you, but I have no sense of it from them." I ask if she is ready to give them an interior life? "Yes." I suggest that she ask Christ to bring them into her. "Now I can feel what I felt but without them being their externally. There is a sense of expectancy, a wondering 'how good can this get...' I suggest that she kiss Christ by way of saying thank you. "I just want to kiss the hands that led me to them. It is a good feeling. And there is the thought that this is not finished. I want to see how this will make a difference in me." The session ends here.

Over the next several sessions, Tory reports a number of improvements on several fronts. She can tell me that her granddaughter has overcome most of her motor deficiencies and will soon be going to daycare. But the relationship with her daughter, Abby, continues to be contentious. The daughter's weight issues and sense of destructive entitlement seem to have no bounds; and all the interventions on her behalf, to date, appear to have had little effect. I broach the idea that Tory may need to work on her relationship with Abby's father. The couple have been divorced for many years. The father's involvement with his daughter has been minimal to non-existent. I realize this will be a very difficult reconciliation for Tory and do not press it. Instead, I focus on her comment that, "I see a lot of blah-ness in front of me." Despite her complaints about the time required for daycare, it has filled her days in a meaningful way. Now she is beginning to anticipate a 'retirement' with little meaningful work. I suggest that she go inside and let Christ use a Capturing circle to contain all of the emotions that impede her finding a renewed purpose. "When I look back in the circle, I see a huge dock area with piles covered by waterproof tarps. The piles seem to represent a sense of disappointment, regret, failure, resentment, and feeling victimized. When I ask Christ to absorb those emotions with his *Light*, the tarps fall flat to the ground." I now suggest to Tory that she ask Christ to draw another Capturing circle, this time, for the purpose of capturing all of Abby's anger, fear, and shame. After he has drawn the circle, I have her ask him to walk Abby through it. "Abby resisted at first, but then she acquiesced and let him walk her through. Now I see all of this swirling fog." I ask Tory if Abby sees the same thing? "At first, she resisted seeing it; but now I sense that she is seeing something really heavy and gunky." I ask if she would be willing for Christ to remove it? At first, Tory gives me an emphatic "No." It is not clear whether this is from her or her image of Abby. In any case, I persist by suggesting that *Christ give Abby* a portion of Tory's *Light* so she can express willingness for Christ to remove the gunk. Abby appears willing, so Christ absorbs it completely. Now, Tory reports that, "Abby wants to be done with this." I suggest that she release Abby so she can go about her business and reflect on what has happened. The session ends here.

The forgoing is difficult to interpret. The first part about 'removing self-defeating emotions that impede renewal' can only be measured by what happens in the coming weeks. As regards Abby, this is the first time I have used the Capturing circle to work with someone other than a self-image, though I cannot rule out that Abby's image is also carrying disowned selves belonging to Tory. For example, it is not clear who says 'no;' but when Abby is given the 'freedom' to exercise willingness, she allows Christ to remove the gunk. Likewise, it is not clear who is so anxious to end the session even though Tory insists that it is Abby.

***

During the following year, Tory's brother will successfully complete his three-month treatment program and pick up a one-year chip from AA. Her daughter, Abby, will have gastric by-pass surgery several months after the last session reported above. Tory will have "reconciled" with the image of her ex-husband. During Abby's surgery he will unexpectedly join with Tory to sit with her in the hospital as

Abby recovers. Abby will lose over a 180 lbs. Tory will become a cornerstone in her church's volunteer programs. There will continue to be significant frictions between Tory, her father, and daughter, but she and her husband will become much closer. The following verbatims pick up where Tory has begun to focus on her own weight, particularly, as it may be related to her lack of sexual desire. This series of verbatims begins with the identification of a new self we call the 'Head.' Tory believes this self acts like her mother. It suppresses sexual desire. Even more than that it cuts off everything below the neck. "My body shames me." The body has accumulated a lot of unexpressed shame, which is reflected in Tory's weight. I begin the first session by suggesting that she let Christ draw a circle that will capture the accumulated shame. "I have a lot of feelings as I walk through the circle. How can you expect me not to comfort myself in other ways. There is a real sense of dissociation, disappointment, and hurt." Does shaming your body generate a desire to eat? "Of course it does. There is a distinct sense of lack of comfort or satisfaction, a lack of pleasure. The shaming is insatiable."

In the next session I ask Tory if Christ can capture the Head in a circle? "I see a head, like a mannequin with a wig; no body." I ask if Christ can separate out the sexual energy being suppressed by The Head? This question elicits a fear response from somebody as Tory now reports that she cannot see anything. I suggest that she ask her *Light* to provide her with a garment of protection to shield her from the Head's reactivity. Now Tory or the Head – I am not sure which – insists that the sexual energy was not suppressed. It was given away. She willed it away…out of existence. It is no longer an issue." I ask her rationale for doing that. "It protects her from being hurt, from being denied. It eased the tension between what was and what was fantasized." How old were you when she did it? "Late 40's or early 50's. It is like if you have a blender: push harder and finally it goes away. It is gone, over, done, finished." I ask what would happen if she no longer had food to placate? "Things would be blah. There is a feeling of desire, wanting something and getting it. Comfort." And if that was taken away? "Blah would become dissatisfaction, unsatisfied desires. My life is simple. If it stopped being simple there would be nothing, and that is sad." At this point I draw a parallel between the Head and Tory's mother: Your mother used her will to avoid shame. She was willful. She could cut off anything she wanted to. And that is what the Head can do. And if the will is in the service of avoiding shame it has very few limits. The session ends here.

In the next several sessions Tory becomes obsessed with her granddaughter. For a host of reasons having little to do with Mandy, the parents constantly berate the daughter. Basically, they are recapitulating the way Tory's mother treated Tory. Tory's own maternal grandmother was her primary shield and Tory has assumed a comparable role in Mandy's life. In this session I suggest that Tory go inside and ask Christ to capture anything that the parents have projected into Mandy. "I can see it. It is the size of a leprechaun, evil, just evil. It is very active, a feeling of 'I gotcha'." I ask if Christ can place a portion of his Light into the leprechaun? "He can, but Christ says it has to be open. It is all bent over." In retrospect, I will come to appreciate that Tory is seeing a disowned part of herself, which is probably the reason why Christ is unwilling to act. But, apparently, Christ is willing to place his Light into the leprechaun's back at the level of the heart. I ask why it is bending over? "That is its method of attack. It attacks Mandy's calmness, her focus, it nips at her heels, destroys her peace. *It reminds me of Frenzy.*" (This is a self in Tory that we have previously worked with.) I ask if there is an anecdote? "This picture is very upsetting to me. She is not receiving the love she needs. It is even worse than abusive. It is actively negative."

In the next two sessions I attempt to identify the Head's disowned self, which Tory sees as a 1920's Flapper. It is hard to do any inner work, as Tory is increasingly preoccupied with her daughter's attitude toward her granddaughter, Mandy. She is afraid to be overly critical of her daughter but anguishes over the pain Abby and the father are causing Mandy. In this next session, she begins by berating herself. "I have done nothing positive." I am convinced she is being overwhelmed by the Head, and ask her to go inside and let Christ draw a capturing circle that will again separate them. "I have not walked through the circle. There are 10,000 things going through my head." I suggest that she ask Christ for a 'head shield' to shield her from the Head's thoughts. "OK, now I see her. She is a wild person, crazy, constant movement." What is agitating her? "It reminds me of Mandy's demon, but she looks like me." I take a different tack. I ask if the Head and Tory share the same heart? If so then Christ entering Tory's heart would draw in the Head and lesson its strength. But her answer is "No. There is nothing redeeming about her heart. The energy in that circle is fighting against everything. There is no energy left in me; it is all in the circle. She feels caged." I ask if Christ can release her? "Yes, but he hesitates. She needs structure or she will spin out of control. She has to be changed before she can be released." I suggest that she enter her heart chakra and leave the part of her, whose head is shielded, with a portion of Christ's *Light*. She does so, and when she exits the heart, I ask her how she feels? "It feels better than anything else." I then ask if there is a part of her that would be willing to take up permanent residence in the Heart? "Yes. There is a part that is loving and nurturing and cares." I ask if Christ can shield her from the 10,000 thoughts as well? "Yes. She is comfortable in the heart space. I am really surprised there was still something positive in me; that what I share with other people can be there for me as well. It is the first time I have felt that in a long time." I suggest that if she is willing, Christ can place the 'Wild one' aka the Head in a dome and offer the first of a series of convictions by the Holy Spirit. "She is in the dome. Christ enters, but I have no idea what he did." I suggest that during the week, whenever she thinks about it, she is to go inside, reassure herself of what is in her Heart and allow Christ to convict the 'Wild one' in the dome. I ask if she would like to bring her image of Mandy into her Heart? "That is a good idea. It is the part of me that Mandy sees anyway. I had not stopped to think. I am better to other people than I am to me." The session ends here. Frankly, the above interventions are intended only to give Tory some relief. But, significantly, they lay the groundwork for pivotal interventions I will suggest in the coming weeks.

In the next session I seek to work again with the Flapper who is undoubtedly identified with shameless sexuality. "I see her in the Head. She is risqué if not shameful." Christ extracts her from the Head. Then I ask if the Flapper is willing for Christ and Tory to enter her Heart? "Right before he started to enter, there was a sense of all of this light. Now there is a sense that he has entered but all I can see is light." I suggest that she ask the Flapper if she would be willing for Christ's *Light* to grow in her heart? "Yes. The light outside has filled that space. Now all I am aware of is light. I do not see her or Christ." The session ends here.

These next two sessions seem pivotal. They are scheduled two days apart. Between times, Tory will meet her daughter at a child psychologist's office with her granddaughter. In the first session Tory tells me that she has been having a hard time physically. She has gone to an Internist, who gave her a complete physical and found a lot of painful areas that he cannot account for. He has taken her off some medicine that may be the cause and will see her again in two weeks. I suggest that the pain is not new. Rather, as she focuses on the Head, the power of that self to deny the body has lessoned; that her 'high threshold' for all physical sensations has lowered. I ask Tory to go inside and approach the dome. Hopefully, she can help us distinguish between the Head and the Wild one who feels caged. Tory assures me that the caged part is a part of the Head, but uncontrollable outside of the cage. "There is a sense of danger, a global feeling of non-specific danger. There is a memory that if I was not where I was supposed to be, no one would bother looking for me, or notice that I was gone. No one would blame my mother if there was an accident and I was not where I was supposed to be. I could not be spontaneous." I suggest that Tory ask Christ to provide the Head with a garment of protection that would shield her from her fear of the cage. "OK. It is a scarf." I then suggest that, if the Head is willing to reveal her body, then Christ would provide it with a garment as well. "She panics. She is deathly afraid of the body. But she does not see it as her fear. She is afraid of some force outside of herself." Essentially, the session ends here. But Tory and I are agreed that the Head needs to regain her body and schedule the next session to do so.

Tory reports her visit to child psychologist's office. My sense is that the psychologist has quickly picked up that the parents are the primary problem and pretty much told the mother as much. But Tory is concerned with the parents' perception of her granddaughter as 'broken.' "Mandy's 'brokenness' is how my mother saw me as a baby. That was the bottom line. I had colic. She said my crying almost caused my father to lose his job, lose him, get a divorce." I comment that Abby appears to be raising Tory. "Since our last session I have thoughts of *despising and hating my body*. I hate everything physical about me." I reflect back that her descriptions tell me that the Head is shaming the body. I ask if Christ can give the Head an experience of the body free of shame? Could he removed the accumulated shame and temporarily stop her from shaming her body so she could see the 'world' free of shame and shaming. Tory allows Christ to approach the Head and place his hands on her head. Silence. I ask what is happening. She says she does not know. I see her lower lip quivering. "I am thinking that everything I have done has failed." I ask her what has failed? Can she complete the sentence? "Even when I was small I had the insight that I did not want my life the way it was. It was cold, rigid, empty, unloving, not giving, no fun, no joy. The body wanted those feelings: to be hugged and held. She severed her connection to the body. The worse time of the day was bedtime. I was supposed to kiss them good night, but there was never a response from them." I reframe what she is saying: the body could not rationalize the parent's treatment of her. It knows the truth. "My mother's only pleasure in me was to dress me up, the prettiest dress, spotless. When she had to start buying dresses I was constantly afraid they would not fit and she would blame me, my body." I ask if Christ can give the body the feelings it so dearly craves? If so, let the Head experience this temporarily. This evokes another memory, which she has shared before but without the detail she shares now. "When I was five years old my brother was born. He was a twin. His brother died at birth. My mother did not want an autopsy or embalmment. Someone had provided a baby outfit. My grandmother took me to the funeral home and let me touch him. I touched his hand and feet. They were stiff and un-giving. That is how the Head perceives the body: as dead, plastic, un-giving. Christ has given her a sense of life in the body." I remember that previously Tory has allowed a loving, caring part of her to take up permanent residence in her Heart along with an image of Mandy. I decide to build on that. First, I suggest that Christ could show the Head that, if she entered the Heart, Tory could satisfy the body. But in order to enter the Heart, the Head would have to give up her power to shame the body while she was in there. She can perpetually reside with the caring mother looking after Mandy, but she cannot enter while she continues to shame because there is no shaming in the Heart. "She is willing." I have her let Christ pick her up and enter Tory's Heart. "OK. There is nothing negative, but there is an awkwardness because she still does not have a body." I tell her that if the Head is willing, Christ can place the Head in the mother's lap and he will begin the process of revealing the body. "OK. It happened. The awkwardness is gone. But I don't know beyond that. I can't see what is going on in the Heart." At this point, I sense someone's fear. I suggest that she ask Christ to restore her vision by standing behind her and placing his hands (sensation) over her eyes. "OK. I can see but everything seems to be on pause." I suggest that she let the mother kiss the Head. "She pulled the head to her breast and kissed her. It is the first time I saw the body act like a body. Now she is just resting in her lap." The session ends here.

A great deal is left undone here. For the next several weeks Tory finds numerous excuses to avoid going inside. She spends most of each session focused on her granddaughter, Mandy. Clearly a new self has emerged on the heels of redeeming the Head. I have yet to define the reconstituted Familial personality or the need to purify its heart chakra, though we have been working with that sense of self in a variety of guises. In this session Tory is once again focused on her granddaughter. Tory is feeling 'paralyzed' by her fear for her. I ask her to let Christ capture the source of her paralysis. "I hear this voice identifying all kinds of fears regarding my granddaughter." At my suggestion, she asks her *Light* for a garment of protection to shield her from the *fear* of this voice and then she is able to see the image of a woman in a housedress. In response to my questions, she tells me: "She does not look like anybody I know. She has power. She does not have a soul. She just knows what buttons to push. Her appearance reminds me of the 1940's when all women seemed to wear housedresses."

In the next session Tory tells me that the 'Housedress woman' reminds her of growing up in her small town. Fear was much more motivating than encouragement. When asked about the woman's masculine counterpart, she senses that it is emasculated, but has no clear image of it. Christ is able to place the sense of it in a dome.

Interestingly, in the next session, she describes her husband as acting like a slave; willing to do whatever she asks. This leads to a discussion of males generally and the masculine counterpart of the Housedress woman in particular. She feels as if she has been at odds with men all of her life.

In the next session she continues to feel fear and now a sense of hopelessness regarding her granddaughter. I suggest a radical intervention: Christ will draw a capturing circle, which he will also define. She tells me: "I don't want to do this." To which I say, of course not, but so what? All she has to do is walk through. Basically, I am offering an intervention that even her fear, paralysis, and hopelessness, is hard pressed to resist because it asks so little of her. She agrees to let him do it and to leave a portion of the *Light* for whoever is captured. "It really touched me when I visualized him drawing the circle. It immediately reminded me of the woman caught in adultery. She would have felt fear of course, and humiliation at being used for someone else's purposes. But Christ has the opposite feeling toward her.

In this next session we are able to return to whatever was captured in the circle by Christ. I do this by introducing a new intervention, which I call the circle of growing awareness. Christ draws it and the Aware-ego steps in for as long as the client is willing. When done she steps out. While inside the circle, she will gain a growing awareness about the issue at hand. I ask: who is your Mary Magdalene, your adulterous woman? "I don't know. Last week I had him cover the circle with a dome. The circle he drew, he drew with his finger. I did not walk through the circle last week. What kept going through my mind was the lack of value everyone assigned to the adulterous woman. They were willing to kill her to make their point." I ask if someone was willing to 'stone' Tory in order to make a point? "It was how I felt growing up. The 'law' – the right thing – was important; it did not matter that it killed a lot of me; my competence, self-esteem, creativity, ability to explore. And it continued as an adult." I ask Tory who it is that Christ wants to release from that law? I know who I would like him to release. She constantly felt judged, even when she was out in the world in a capable way. It is really scary that I have lived my whole life like that." The session ends here.

The following week Tory shares that she cannot sleep. "I am anxious all night. I get so uptight; my skin feels like it is crawling everywhere. Feels like something is crawling all over me. I wake up and everything on my plate keeps going through my head." I suggest she go inside and ask Christ to capture whoever is waking her up at night and making her skin crawl? "He created a dome. In the past, the domes were tall. This one is really short and spread out. It reminds me of an anthill. It covers what I have created: fear, uncertainty, lack of control, anxiety. Trouble. I have always been a schemer, a plotter. I see lots of options to things, which gave me a sense of being in control, and take care of myself. Now everything that matters to me (i.e. granddaughter) is out of my control."

When Tory returns the following week she shares her reflections on the plotter, who she prefers to call the Manager. "The essence of the Manager has been my entire life. I never let anything happen naturally. I always managed my friendships and family. Periodically, I had to set a new course in my life that involved everything. The 'managing' has lessoned in the past several years, but it does not go away when there are important things." I suggest that Tory go inside and let Christ capture (personify) the Manager. "She is not anything human, more like a robotic transformer. There are gears and lights and buttons where the head would be. The things being fed in are her desires, but what comes out are plans." I ask her to let Christ identify the Manager's masculine counterpart. "I am not sure I can share it…. He dragged it out of the darkness. It is a fool, but not a jester. It is a foolish puppet type of thing, a scarecrow, goofy, foolish, limp." I wonder aloud, what part of her does her Manager hold captive? Tory can tell me that she has several 'visuals' in response to my question. "I see a child, age 7-8, joyful, active, perky, just playing. I see a young adult in her 20's who is trying to do the opposite of everything she had ever known, and a feeling of freedom to create. I don't know how I know this." I ask Tory to let Christ coalesce these images into a single image, and then ask her how that image might relate to the masculine scarecrow? "At first she seems neutral, not dismissive like the Manager. In a crazy way she can connect with the freedom, the lack of restraint, instead of seeing it as negative.

It is possible she can work with it." (Note here that I have yet to envision the possibility of letting Christ provide this liberated sense-of-self with her own contra-sexual masculine.) I ask Tory if she can identify the power that locks in the creative adult and dismisses the masculine as a fool? "Part is the woman in the housedress; and part is a nebulous overwhelming sense of fear that the woman controlled. It was not a fear of her, but the fear she continually introduces into situations. She turns everything fearful." I ask if the Creative one experiences fear. "Yes, it is a normal, reasonable fear; and the fool is never afraid because he has no sense of consequences." I wonder aloud if severing the connection between the Woman in the housedress and the Manager might allow her to be more human? Tory is willing for Christ to temporarily sever the connections. "OK. Everything about her was human except her head. When Christ shut off the power, he 'unplugged' it. It became a head and I could see the workings of the mind, but it is not like a computer. The energy to think is still there." I ask if this has an effect on the masculine? "He is not floppy like a puppet. Now he looks more like the scarecrow in the Wizard of Oz. The session ends here. (Basically, I an still working on the hypothesis that the Creative one – as she will come to be called, and the Manager can both be reconciled with to the same masculine image. I have yet to envision the liberated self with her own masculine and the two of them entering Tory's heart. At this juncture, I have yet to fully appreciate that we are working with the Familial personality .

I do not see Tory for two weeks. She is amnesic regarding our last session. This is not surprising as the Manager appears to re-assume a tight control after such a session as there have been no interventions apart from discovery. But Tory is quick to recall events once inside. "I remember her, the Creative one. She is older, in her thirties." I ask if she can identify a masculine counterpart. I word this to indicate something different from the scarecrow. "I really don't have a visual, but there are thoughts or words. I am really fascinated by her sense of self; and there is this sense of the masculine giving *her value and appreciation.*

In the next session Tory does not go inside. She is too preoccupied with matters related to her granddaughter, who I sense is a strong carrier of her un-liberated self. But significantly, she is making fewer and fewer attempts to 'manage' her daughter and being more open about the emotional pain the daughter seems to be inflicting on both Tory and the granddaughter.

I see Tory again two weeks later. (In the interim, I have finally begun to appreciate the definable parameters of this process, and can use it as an argument for challenging the Manager.) The situation with her daughter – Abby, and granddaughter – Mandy, has become even more stressful. The Manager is clearly in charge and expresses her belief that there is "No need for a masculine counterpart for the Creative one because there is no reason for her existence." I challenge this by telling Tory that several other clients have been significantly affected by identifying that masculine counterpart, and then letting Christ take them both into the Aware-ego's Heart. Tory tells me, "I can do that, but I don't see how she could live in the real world." I reframe that by identifying the 'real world' with the Manager and the Scarecrow and telling Tory that those two will stay outside, i.e. remain outside the Heart. Only the part holding the Light (the Aware-ego) needs to enter with Christ, the Creative one, and the masculine that extends value and appreciation. She finally agrees to let it happen. "The masculine is a non-descript person, nothing exceptional. He does exude a feeling of appreciation and respect for her. There is a real sense of partnership." I ask how they like this inner space. Tory tells me that, "I am tolerating it. I am glad for them but it is not me; it does not spill over to me." I tell her that if she gives each of them a portion of her *Light* they can flow throughout the Heart. Tory does this and then shares that, "It felt like a whole row of dominos falling even though they are still there. But their essence started going everywhere." I ask if she would like Christ to forge a connection between her and them? "OK. He has joined all of our Lights together, but I do not have any sense of difference. I am still just tolerating it." I ask her if she can name the opposite of intolerance? "Acceptance." I suggest that she ask Christ for the gift of acceptance; that she ask Christ to fill the chamber with an overwhelming sense of acceptance. "OK. I did. I know it is there." She returns to me. I ask if she prefers a Heart filled with acceptance rather than intolerance. She can tell me that acceptance is far better.

When Tory returns the following week she tells me about major changes in her granddaughter, Mandy. Where before Mandy was very mindful and loving toward her she is becoming increasingly oppositional. Her mother, Abby, has also decided to enter her in kindergarten. Tory laments that she does not trust Mandy to make good decisions. Tory also shares that her own first grade experience was horrible. "I never stayed in school the whole day. In my six year old mind I was concerned that my mother would not care if I got lost or the bus took me somewhere else." She also shares that she did attempt to work with the Creative one but found her 'unavailable.' I discuss the idea that Mandy may be carrying a part of Tory. I suggest that she (the Aware-ego) bring Mandy into her Heart. Christ does this quite willingly. Once there, Tory can tell me that, "We both suffer this lack of attachment, we both need to be healed of it, especially the part of me in Mandy." I ask if she is willing for Christ to provide a mother who could satisfy this need? When she says, "Yes," I add that only Mandy can judge if the mother is sufficient. "When I asked Christ I did not see anything, but I feel there is another presence." I ask if Mandy can see it? "I feel like I have lost Mandy." I ask if the presence feels feminine? "It feels sheltering. It feels like a positive presence." I ask if she can trust what she feels in her Heart? "Yes." Again, I ask if Mandy is feeling the presence? "I cannot connect with Mandy, I can only visualize a picture of her." I ask if Christ can use double circles to extract the self belonging to Tory that is hidden in Mandy? "I see a really young child – a toddler." I ask Tory if she is willing for Christ to pick up this toddler and place her in the arms of the Sheltering presence? "OK. He has picked her up and placed her in the arms of *the presence behind me*." When I suggest that she turn around and observe, she is clearly hesitant and finally tells me, "I just want to stop right here." (It hard to appreciate what is going on here in terms of what Tory can see and not see. For example, during the previous week the Creative one becomes "unavailable" to her. Now she loses her strong connection to Mandy once Christ takes her into the Aware-ego's Heart where she can connect with the sheltering presence. She is obliged to rely on a felt sense of what is happening, and this will continue to be the case until she can allow Christ to enter her own heart chakra and purify it.)

The next session, seems to be both pivotal and difficult to describe. Tory is terribly stressed by the week's events. Mandy has pulled away from her and *repeatedly* insists that she only "wants her mother." (This is quite amazing since she is imaginatively with the sheltering presence in the Heart of Tory's Aware-ego.) Her mother, Abby, seems oblivious to her daughter's need, and the lack of attachment is driving Tory to distraction. "There was a time when I could be that mother for her, but not now; I cannot take

Abby's place any longer. Abby says, 'I cannot sacrifice my career because Mandy cannot adapt to change.' When Abby was in kindergarten, I took her to a daycare where the director was also her Sunday school teacher. But even so, I had to peel her hands off me when I left. The next year, I only worked part time so I could be with Abby after school, and did not go back to full time until she was in middle school. All this week I could not stop crying." Tory continues to share events in her childhood and Abby's, which closely parallel each other and Mandy's as well. It is as if Mandy is expressing the cumulative effect of three generations of maternal attachment trauma. I ask Tory what she remembers of the last session. She remembers taking Mandy into her Heart and the Sheltering presence, but not extracting the Toddler (self-image) and asking Christ to place it with the Sheltering presence. I surmise that her 'intolerance' is keeping Tory (aka Manager) outside of the Heart. I suggest that she allow Christ to enter the Manager's heart chakra and bring her with him. This is clearly a different sense of the heart. The Creative one and consort are not present, though interestingly she can sense the Sheltering presence. In fact, she tells me that she has always felt that sheltering *presence* behind her. Now, she can imagine turning around and getting a sense of someone holding out a towel or blanket and wanting to enfold her with it. "As I move toward her I get the distinct sense of a woman who seems to embody love and protection. She is waiting for me to come into the towel." I ask if she can? Her closed eyes seem on the verge of tear and tremoring. "It is so strange. I need to do this, but I am just standing still. I even know how it would feel." I ask if Christ is present? When she affirms that he is, I suggest that she allow him to collect into one hand the source of her hesitancy. "OK. What I understand is that if I allow that towel to be gathered around me, some of me will no longer exist, maybe none of me. Such a stupid thing to say." I ask if she understands that her hesitance is keeping the Toddler and Mandy from also entering the towel? Then I ask: are you willing to make any sacrifice on their behalf? "OK. I can imagine it wrapping around me and sealing myself from feeling it. It would change everything if I felt it. The thought is I would just disappear." I suggest that she ask her Light to provide a garment of protection that will shield her from fear. I also suggest that the towel is actually a form of protection since it will act as a buffer between her and the woman filled with love and protection. "Christ says I can take the two children if I do not let them substitute for me not feeling anything. We will see. I take them with me. I have their hands. We walk into the towel. I reach down and pick them both up. The woman wraps the towel around us. There is a feeling of peace, nothing else, no conflict about the towel. The Toddler and Mandy are really enjoying this. They are animated, but I am just at peace, no animation." I ask if the girls can go into the woman's lap. "Not yet. Christ wants them to stay with me. He wants me to continue feeling how they are reacting with their bodies, skin on skin. Each time I reenter the towel during the week, I am to really notice how they feel and how the towel feels, since each is a different experience." OK, I suggest, give thanks and return here to me. The session ends here.

The following week Tory reports that Mandy is making an exceptionally good transition to public school much to the surprise of everyone. She also tells me that she has been visualizing the three of them wrapped in the towel morning and night. Her attention near the end of the session focuses on her father and brother, both of them irritants. But she does not go inside this session.

In this session Tory begins with a reflection on Joseph as the father of Jesus. She wonders aloud about God's effort in choosing Joseph as the father. When given a choice between working with her daughter's image and working with the Manager's sense of the feminine and masculine, she chooses the latter. She allows Christ to stand between her image of the Manager and the Scarecrow. I emphasize that this conviction only requires an instant of willingness from her, which Christ will express by momentarily placing his hands on the brow of each aspect. "OK...I am not sure...several things went on...I could see as he touched them....it is clear to me that there is something very opposite about them. The Scarecrow had no rigidity; the Manager was nothing but rigid. I never thought about it like that. Also, a part of me could breath when he touched them." Tory allows Christ to convict them two more times. Nothing observable happens after the second conviction, but there is a discernible shift after the third conviction. "They were both in their own circle, but as far away from each other as possible. The third time they had move closer to each other and to Christ. I saw that Christ did not have to stretch so far to convict them." I ask if she is willing to let Christ convict a fourth time? "No. My resistance has not lessoned any." I suggest she let Christ provide a circle of growing awareness so she can ascertain the reason for her resistance. "Because I don't have the answer to 'what if,' I don't know how I will change." I ask if Christ will still be there, if she changes? "Yes. He is always showing himself to me in mundane ways." I agree with her that the whole premise of her being could change when the dyad is healed and reintegrated into her heart chakra, but the changes would be assimilated and accommodated over time; it would not be instantaneous. The session ends here.

This is the Thanksgiving holiday. I do not see Tory again for two weeks. She returns to report some positive changes particularly as regards her daughter and son-in-law who appear to be much more involved with their children. Also, "Abby brought two dishes for thanksgiving this year. It is first time I ever remember her doing this." Tory remains peeved at her father and put out with her brother who is "in love." In the interim, I have come to appreciate the need to 'purify the heart chakra' before asking Christ to further convict the gender aspects. Tory is agreeable to letting Christ enter her heart charka. He will enter for the purpose of containing whatever he finds there. As I watch, her face becomes very sad and on the verge of tears. Finally, she tells me: "This is very upsetting. What I am seeing is a glob of putrid slime. I am really at the point to where everything is sickening. Mandy is my only pleasure. I am sick of my life, my relationships, the tasks I have to do. The best I can say is that things are neutral, not negative. The majority are negative." I tell her that it will make a real difference if she can allow Christ to place a portion of his *Light* in the center of her heart chakra that will be a perpetual conduit of the Holy Spirit. "OK. We are back inside. He places a portion of his *Light* in the center of the putridness. When we first did this I thought there was a finite amount, but the *Light* is showing me that it reaches into every part of the heart." I suggest that she ask Christ to release her heart from the bondage of this putridness. "OK. When I asked Christ gathered it all up from everywhere and now it is literally contained and under his control, and his *Light* is in the center. The *Light's* shadow covers it, but does not do anything with it." I ask her to come back. She goes on to tell me: "Something is going on in my head. It is the idea that 'I knew this would be upsetting, but my gosh why do you go to such extremes?' There is a real battle going on inside. The Manager is struggling. But like it or not the slime is in her heart. *She is not all there is to me.*" The session ends here.

Tory returns the following week. She has the beginnings of a cold. Over the past week she has reflected a lot about the Manager: "I can trace the Manager back to elementary school. In every example I can think of the outcome amounted to *settling* for something." I ask if she is been back in the heart or become willing for Christ to purify it? The answer to both questions is "No." I weave in what she has telling me by commenting that the Manager continues to settle for less. "I am not wild about going in there." (It is interesting to observe here that someone other than the Manager is doing the talking and will continue to report on the Manager.) I do note that Christ does need the Manager's willingness to enter the heart. "It bothers me how negative and extreme the heart seemed to me. The Manager kept trying to minimize it. I differentiate me from the Manager in this instance. That is where I came up with the idea of her settling for things. Then the back and forth stopped. She has settled for a putrid heart." I counter this by saying that her settling is shaping her personality, shaping her sense of the masculine, and generating Mandy's legacy. At this point, I address Tory as someone different from the Manager. I say to her: "If you ask, can Christ purify her heart? "Yes." Would she continue to generate the putridness? "Yes. He can purify at my request and the putridness could no longer grow or be sustained there." Does he recommend that course of action and do we need her willingness? "Yes he can and he will." So by way of encouraging her to proceed, I tell her this will be a kind of baptism. "I took your suggestion of baptism literally and expected him to completely immerse her (Tory has attended Baptist churches much of her life), but that is not what he did. He took her face and head in his hands and started putting oil on her face, forehead and hair. It is obviously a pleasurable experience for her. I can still see it going on. I am remembering her rigidity; with each stroke she becomes softer and more pliable. The oil does not grease her hair; it becomes lustrous. I can't see anymore, there are no more visuals." I suggest that she may be settling for more. "The words don't feel right but the feeling does. The feeling is more of releasing control, the need for control is being released. This is much holier and intimate than what I would expect from a baptism. The session ends here. I recall that in other churches such as the Episcopal and Roman Catholic, that an anointing with oil follows baptism. Tory is unfamiliar with the idea but researches it after the session and sends me an e-mail: I found the description of baptism you were talking about: You are sealed by the Holy Spirit in Baptism and marked as Christ's own for ever. Amen.

I do not see Tory again for two weeks. In the interim she is hospitalized for abdominal bleeding. The doctor finally gives her a clean bill of health. While hospitalized, I spoke with her on the phone, and guided her through an intervention to clear the heart chakra. I strongly suspect that the medical crisis has been brought on by her inner conflict. In any case, she is able to come to a session just before Christmas. She tells me that Christ has continued to stroke the Manager with oil and Christ told her that each time he has been removing a series of alliterations from her heart: "unfulfilled dreams, unreturned love, unwarranted shame, unanswered needs, unnecessary hurts, unneeded fears, unacceptable judgments, undeserved feelings of lack." Tory is convinced it was these that made her heart chakra so putrid. I encourage her to go into the heart chakra with Christ and the Manager. "OK. We can do that. It seems like it is a void but not in a bad or negative way. Neutral." I suggest that the Manager can approach Christ and ask for a portion of his *Light* that will provide a perpetual conduit for the Holy Spirit. "OK. She does this and places the *Light* in the center of her heart chakra. Now the energy is much more positive." At this point they exit the heart chakra and Tory returns to me. "It bristles me to come back and realize she is still in control; but she was willing to give up control and he was willing to assume it." I encourage her to be patient and allow Christ to further convict the image of the Manager and the Scarecrow. "OK. I remember that the last time the Manager got a little bit less stiff. This time the Scarecrow was not even in the picture. I had to ask Christ to bring him into the area so they could be convicted together. The conviction has brought them together." The session ends here.

I see Tory the week after Christmas, which she says has been her best Christmas ever in terms of family. I have her focus on the Manager and Scarecrow. "They seem normal together." I ask if they seem ideal? "No." I emphasize that she can seek an ideal pair that will entrain with the Creative self and masculine-who-values-and-appreciates that reside in the Aware-ego's Heart; that she can claim an Ideal pair that will manifest a personality linked with the Ideal pair most attuned to the totality of her Self. She goes inside and asks Christ to convict the two: "I can see them where they were before. This conviction gives them more life. They seem more engaged in the process rather than being passive recipients. They are seeking the conviction. Now they want to experience what they have just received. There is a lot of animation toward each other that surprises me. This change has stimulated a connection between the two. I have bought a new book called *Jesus Calling*. All of the selections I have read talk about willingness." The session ends here.

The following week Tory is still not ready. When she looks inside her Manager and Scarecrow look 'fine,' but she is still not ready to bring them into her heart chakra. I sympathize with her hesitancy by noting that their integration into the heart chakra can be expected to change her in significant ways.

Tory returns a week later enthusiastic about her daughter and granddaughter, especially the latter. Mandy likes to draw hearts signifying love. She will write short sentences like Mandy [heart sign] mommy. But this past week she drew a heart with her grandmother, mother and Mandy *within it*; and asked her mother to make a copy of it at her workplace and keep it there to remind her. Tory is ready to go inside and let Christ integrate her Ideal pair in her heart chakra. I have her imagine standing in front of Christ in the first person. Christ has each aspect standing beside him. Then Tory begins to share what happens. "He gathered them by the waist and walked the three of them in. Strange. I feel cut off; I have lost all visual sense of them. I have a physical sense of drawing a breath but not exhaling. It is not negative at all. The feeling is energy, and light, and presence, but not visible; I can only *sense* my *Light*." I quickly pick up that she is *sensing* what is happening rather than visualizing it. Tory is very visual. I do not recall her ever being this sensate in the past. In fact, I would say it is her least used function. I comment that sensation is her weakest suit and ask her about her drawn breath, wondering if some part of her is holding her breath. She agrees that sensation is her weakest suit, then goes on to tell me: "The drawn breath was surprise at my experience of the energy and pleasantness. I am accommodating to it, but still a pleasant feeling there." I ask if she is comfortable leaving the Ideal pair inside? "Oh yeah. I also sense that a portion of Christ's *Light* is already there." I suggest she exit her heart and describe any differences. "Now I can see us (Manager and Christ)." At the beginning of this session, Tory reported that her blood count is still low as a result of her recent loss of blood. I suggest that she ask Christ to capture the self responsible for the low blood count. In turn, Tory says she finds herself resistant to doing this, "I want to blame it on having lost so much blood; I do not want it to have anything to do with my mind, though I now know it does."

The following week, Tory returns with high praise for her granddaughter, Mandy, and *her husband*. She also tells me late in this session, that she went to a grocery after leaving the last session and was overwhelmed by all of the smells she encountered. She is willing to go inside but immediately encounters significant blocks. She cannot see or sense her *Light*. "There is craziness in my head. Static. I can't keep my eyes still. She can sense Christ but he is far away." Nothing I suggest is helpful and I am running out of suggestions. I have her ask Christ to tell us how to move forward. "I have to give up; and I am not willing to give up what he is going to tell me." For reasons I cannot explain, I have the distinct sense that all of this is related to her daughter, Abby, and say as much; that what is happening is related to her enmeshment with Abby. "I knew you were going to say I am responsible for Abby." In turn, I put forth the idea that they share something that is causing her inability to separate. This thought, in turn, reminds me of shielding techniques that Reiki and Pranic healers use to shield themselves from absorbing the negativity of others while working with them. Abby is very negative; her modus operandi is to blame everyone else for her problems. I tell her all this and suggest the technique: she is simply to imagine being encapsulated in a blue filtered light. Tory imagines it. "It feels much better. It also brought Christ to where I can see him." The session ends here.

This next session is intense and weaves so much together it may be difficult to follow without rereading. First, Tory initially wants to cancel this next session. Her gastroenterologist has told her that test results suggest there may be a problem with her aorta artery, the examiners could not find 'its origin' in a CRT scan or sonogram and it may be necessary to do an angiogram and place a stint. Her daughter is concurrently suffering acute stomach pains but refusing to take the necessary tests because she cannot tolerate drinking the prep for the test. I am able to convince Tory to come in and see me. I have a tentative plan, which I share with Tory when she arrives. She will go inside and ask Christ to place Abby in a domed circle with a blue filter over it. Next she will ask Christ to place a circle around both the dome and Tory and extract whatever the two of them share in common. Tory goes inside. She is able to make the requests without any visual impairment. "Christ has extracted a life-size boulder, as big as a person; it is crystal, beautiful and glowing. It has sharp points all over it; they are very sharp. There is really no way of accessing what is inside the boulder. You can never touch the boulder, though it draws me to do so, because the points are so sharp." I encourage her to ask Christ what it represents and can he change it? "It represents our relationship (Tory and Abby); the boulder is the good part, the love and enjoyment. But the points make it impossible not to be hurt by any attempt to reach out and touch it. Even so, the boulder keeps drawing me back." I note to Tory that apparently she has only been able to sense this with her newfound access to sensation. "That's true. I keep wanting to *touch* it; before I would just see it and judge it." I also suggest that this 'boulder' may be paradigmatic of her relationship with her own mother. "It use to be, but not so much any more." I suggest she ask Christ if it would be possible for him to dissolve the boulder and stand in its place? "Christ says the boulder cannot be perfect. Even if you sand down the points, the rounded edges would still be there." I ask if there is any way to move toward perfection? "The picture has to be changed. He says he needs a *peace* from me. (Tory is emphatic that he is saying peace, not piece.) He can give me peace; help me be at peace, in exchange for the boulder. Honestly, that seems neutral, blah." I ask her if that is what she imagines in *the absence of experiencing it*? "Honestly, I have no idea what it would feel like." (I hope the reader is appreciating that throughout this exchange sensation is being given equal weight with intuition in her reasoning process.) I comment that the boulder feels like a perpetual state of approach-avoidance, which has to restrict her heart. "The doctor told me that any aortic constriction did not cause my colitis but without it, they might not have discovered the aorta problem." I press her to let Christ act. "Christ is telling me this cannot happen in an instant. It will be a process. It must be done in small steps with my agreement at each step. If I am willing to take the steps toward being at peace it will replace the boulder." I ask if she is willing to take the first step? "Yes. Christ has drawn a circle and tells me that if I step in it will *relax me from head to toe*. I am game to do it, but not now. I want to do it at home when I have time." We are well over and definitely pressed for time. The session ends here.

I am not really surprised when Tory returns and confesses she has completely forgotten what she intended to do vis-à-vis entering the circle that will relax her from head to toe. She willingly goes inside to do so, but then immediately reports that, "I can't quiet my mind." I suggest that she ask Christ for a garment of protection. I also note that what we are addressing here is the sensation, which is the opposite of intuition (her strong suit); and the idea that Christ wants to use sensation to bring her closer to God. (Jung felt that the least developed function was the 'God function' as it was the least under control by the conscious mind.) "OK. I stepped into the circle. The noise in my head is quieted. I'm aware of breathing. I don't feel relaxed all over." I suggest that she let Christ join her and use his hands to make her more aware of tension and relaxation. "I don't do well with touch. The thought of his touching me makes me uncomfortable. I feel very self conscious with you present." I ask her to return. I recommend a book by Sharon Giammatteo called *Body Wisdom* that describes a very gentle kind of self-touch that can facilitate self-healing.

I do not see Tory again for two weeks. She is being required to provide full time childcare while her daughter recuperates from surgery. She does share in an e-mail her growing awareness that since she was a child she could suppress pain sensations both surgical and dental. In the interim she also attempts to reenter the circle. When I next see her she shares the thought that, "I absolutely hate my life." I ask if she has a sense of the self she hates? "Yes, I do. There is nothing to her except being someone else's slave. "My life consists of coming here (therapist's office), my Bible classes, and going to church on Sunday. Everything else is what I have to do for someone else. I hate it." I suggest that if she can allow Christ to capture this 'slave-to-others,' she could then ask him to convict the slave and hateful self until both are freed of the enslavement. "I don't believe the *facts* can be changed. She is enslaved to what I have to do everyday." I point out to her that *she* (whoever is in charge at the moment) is treating sensation's 'facts' as inalterable, though the Creative one (her intuition) would never be bound by such facts. I suggest that whoever is totally enmeshed with the sensation function (likely Slave-to-others) does not have the same access to thinking and feeling that the Creative one regularly draws upon. Also, it is likely that Slave-to-others does not know the pleasure that Tory experienced in her heart chakra. I ask if she would be willing to take Slave-to-others into her heart chakra? "Probably not. I hate her." At this point, I make a leap by suggesting that till now Tory has only connected with sensation when using it to suppress pain, *and through food*. I tell Tory that her belief in the inalterability of certain 'facts' may also account for her inability to overcome her compulsive eating. I surmise that Slave-to-others may be her shadow, her evil twin, and I challenge her to tell me I am wrong. "No, you are not wrong." Tory then adds that, "During the previous week I wanted to begin addressing her eating issues with you." I hear this but do not respond to it. Instead, I ask how the Creative one and her valuing male, and the Manager and Scarecrow, would respond to Slave-to-others, if they had access to her. "The Creative one and the appreciative male have no desire to have access to her. The Manager and Scarecrow are closely connected to her, especially the Manager." This makes sense since the latter two are in the heart chakra, which is giving them a strong link to pure sensation. "The Manager is between me and her. But the Manager is not working; she is no longer attempting to manage." The session ends here.

I make a note to myself that in the next session Tory and I need to identify whoever has emerged to take the place of the Manager, who is no longer managing. This new self hates Slave-to-others, who appears to represent the disconnected sensate part of triangle defining her self, Slave-to-others and the compulsive eater (mental aspect). The above session is one of my earliest attempts to address a new way of thinking about addictions (The Addictive Bond hypothesis). Essentially, for the past three weeks Tory has been focusing on *sensation*, as a result of the Manager's experience of it in the heart chakra. It has made her highly sensitive to her eating, among other issues. Very likely, the Manager's ongoing experience with pure sensation has precipitated the emergence of the disconnected aspects responsible for Tory's overeating. The new 'manager' expresses awareness of the sensate component by calling her the self she hates: a Slave-to-others. 'Hatefulness' is a common response to failed efforts at attempts to control addiction: 'I hate myself for binging like that.' It is essentially an impotent rage. It is likely that Tory's newly emerged sense-of-self is also 'famished' by the efforts she mistakenly directs to her family, who seem concertedly unreciprocating. She is 'starved' for appreciative valuing in the same way the compulsive eater is starved for conscious reconnection with her sensate component.

The following week, Tory calls to cancel her morning appointment. Her sinuses are "the worst ever" and she cannot talk without coughing. She knows this is psychosomatic, but goes into a coughing convulsion when she tries to tell me that coughing makes it nearly impossible to talk. We reschedule for later in the week. Two days later she calls again to cancel. She tells me she was able to place the cougher in a dome and that has relieved most of her coughing, but she is still feeling she needs to put off coming in till the following week. We reschedule and then I suggest that she allow Christ and the Manager to enter the dome and minister to the cougher. She is agreeable to doing that and promises to report via e-mail if something happens as a result. I make this suggestion because she told me in our last session that the Manager is now connected to Enslaved-to-others and acting as a buffer between her and Tory; and I suspect that the cougher and Enslaved-to-others are both the same. Interpretively, the 'new manager' is attempting to block intuitive awareness (brow chakra/sinuses) and but Enslaved-to-others (coughing) will no longer be silenced. Even if Tory is unable to allow the entry into the dome on her own, I will definitely push for this when Tory returns. But Tory has surprised me before with her ability to work between sessions.

Early in the next week, Tory sends me an e-mail: "I was not sure that I remembered the role that the Manager was supposed to play in my going inside. So-o-o, I went inside and asked the Manager if she would enter the dome with me. I also asked Christ if this was okay. When we went into the dome it was very dark and I didn't see anything, but I could hear something moving in there. I asked Christ to shine his Light into the dome and what I saw has me really puzzled. I saw a very sturdy black woman with burns on her arms and face. Some of the burns were recent and others were raised scars. I felt very sad for her and even started crying. I will go back inside, but this has kind of freaked me out." I reply: Tory, I am guessing she personifies Enslaved-to-others. The goal is to allow Christ to heal/liberate her and be reconciled in the heart chakra shared by the Manager and Scarecrow.

I see Tory two days later. She is doing much better physically. She decided the antibiotics she was taking were actually making her worse. She stopped them and immediately began to improve. She reports that her eating is much decreased. She is much more aware of Enslaved-to-others. "There is a rawness about her appearance. Her skin had never been cared for; it was just *scrubbed* clean." I tell Tory about my Addictive Bond hypothesis. I suggest that she ask Christ to capture the conscious counterpart to Enslaved-to-others, who is most likely, the binge eater. "Mother controlled my food and controlled me through her control of it. When I got out of the home I began to control what I ate. I could have chosen wild behaviors such as sex, drinking, and stuff. Instead, I assumed control of my eating. I can see anger, disgust and resentments toward the black woman." I assume these are being directed at Enslaved-to-others by whomever Christ needs to personify. I press Tory to let Christ capture the conscious counterpart of Enslaved-to-others. "OK. The person looks like one of those balloons in a parade that is held down by ropes." I ask if she knows she is like a blimp? "Yes." I ask if she is connected to Tory's body in any way? "No." She lives entirely in the mind? "Yes." (This is quite clearly the mental component.) Does she eat a lot? "Yes." Does she know the effect she has on your body? "No." What is her rationale for eating a lot? "That is all she does. She eats in search for satisfaction. She has always thought she would put something in her mouth and be satisfied; but she has never been satisfied." I suggest to Tory that she 'return to me so we can 'digest' everything she has learned. "I would have expected the black woman to be huge, but she is not. She is obviously sturdy, capable and strong, but not fat. That surprised me." I observe that she seems *grounded*; and that if reconciled with Blimp, she could ground her as well. I also note that Tory must become a growing awareness between the two. "I feel more connected with the black woman than I do the Blimp. There is no sense of connection with the Blimp. The black woman seems to be self-regulated in eating and living. The Blimp is pure rebellion. She is my mother's worse fear of pure impulse; nothing else matters but the impulse. If it comes into my mind I can get it and eat it." I reflect that one of the Manager's primary jobs was probably managing the Blimp complete lack of impulse control. "Yes, and what a job that was, but not anymore. The heart chakra is so pleasurable to her, I am surprised she left it to come into the dome where the black woman is, but she is now the part of me that feels the strongest connection to the black woman." I suggest a first step toward reconciling Blimp and the black woman: let Christ place Blimp in a circle of effect wherein she is obliged to experience her effects on the body every time she eats. "The original circle was large enough for the ropes that hold her, but she was actually bigger than the circle. The new circle has drawn her down to earth so that the circle now contains her and the ropes. I am also aware that nothing connected me with my body in the past. I was oblivious to temperature, pain, and food." The session ends here. Later in the day Tory sends me an e-mail. When she got home she opened a book she had just received in the mail. "The first chapter is titled 'Surprisingly satisfied: A Resolution to be content!' Interesting also, that driving home after our session, it came to me that Blimp was seeking a sense of being satisfied, not food. Food was just the place she looked for satisfaction. Satisfaction can come from many things."

I see Tory twice during the next week. In the first session, I suggest that she let Christ bring the Black woman into her heart chakra. This confuses Tory who insists that she has not done this before, even when I remind her of the Ideal pairs. She is mindful of the pairs but not of entering the heart chakra. So I suggest, instead that she ask Christ to create a shared space where the to Ideal pairs can gather and Christ bring the Black woman to that space. He does so with surprising a surprising result. "OK. It looks like a room, the walls are white and there is a lot of light. I image the four of them there. Interesting. I have an image of all five of them. The two couples are proportional, but the Black woman is much bigger, almost twice as large as the couples. They are not put out by her size, but I am. She is towering over them and taking up too much space. They are adapting to her presence by coming together so she has ample room." I ask her to locate Christ. "He is in the doorway, actually just outside. I am looking in with Christ. I only see her back. Even when we found her she had a backbone." I ask if Christ can move to around the front? "I just noticed that the four images act like people, but the Black woman is like a block of wood, a statue. She has been brought to the room." I ask what she needs to join with the two couples? "I don't know. I am fixated on the fact that she is so different from them. Her feet are not on the floor in this space. She is standing like a statue on a platform" I ask if this space is connected to sensation? "No." The session ends here. In this session, Tory appears to have no memory of the fact that her Manager and Scarecrow now abide in a heart chakra that is pure sensation. When the Black woman is removed from sensate consciousness, but not allowed entry into the 'heart of sensation,' she becomes like a statue. In the next session, I can hopefully convince her to let the Black woman enter the heart chakra of pure sensation.

I see Tory two days later. I ask her if the Manager is willing to bring the Black woman into the heart chakra where she now abides with the Scarecrow? Tory asks me why? I tell her because it is the heart of pure sensation. Tory replies, "That does not resonate with me, but OK." I suggest that she consult with everyone. "OK. The Manager and Scarecrow are willing. There is no hesitancy on Christ's part." I suggest to her that she stand in front of Christ, and he will move everybody into the Manager's heart chakra. Silence. "OK. Once the Black woman came into the heart she became the same size as the Manager and Scarecrow. She lost her statuesque appearance. Now she looks like a human being." I suggest that she leave her there with the Manager and Scarecrow and she and Christ exit and then she can rejoin me. I tell her that the Blimp and Black woman need to be reconciled, and ask if she can identify anyone who might object? "I will tell you something that I forgot. Some of the perspective I gained about satisfaction. I lost some of that. Maybe it was because the Black woman was ineffective, stone like. I felt bogged down the last two days. It has only been recently (the last two years) that things could touch me to where I could be happy or cry. Nothing previously evoked those feelings since childhood. I could not cry because I had to be in charge." I suggest that she allow Christ to capture whoever was responsible for the split between Blimp and the Black woman. "I hate to tell you what is there. The original split was caused by mother's shaming of everything to do with me. Her 'normal' was extreme. I can sense being lost as a young child, not having a clue of what I was supposed to say, experience,, or share. Just the way it was. My maternal grandmother was not that way, nor my out-of-wedlock aunt. I remember visiting my aunt as she was dying of Alzheimer's. All of sudden she sat up in bed and said: I love you; and then flopped back down in bed. It was the most sincere and unconditional love I experienced apart from my grandmother. When my mother disowned me after my first marriage, my Aunt became her surrogate and gave us a wedding party where all the rest of the family gathered. Saturday will be seven years since my mother died." The session ends here. I suspect in the next session we will discover a self much like her mother that has sustained the addictive separation between Blimp and the Black woman.

I see Tory two weeks later. She is doing well. She has glowing reports about Mandy in school and while staying with Tory after school. Even her daughter is bonding better with Mandy. She praises her granddaughter's teacher and this leads her to reflect on how two of her teachers in grade school and high school were positive 'mother nurturing' figures, in sharp contrast to her own mother's total lack of encouragement. At this point I am moved to ask her about the Blimp. "The Blimp in the circle has caused a lot of negative feelings. In my Mind, I did not look like that, but now I know that is how I look in reality. It makes me think that any significant body change is impossible. My mother equated food with outbreaks of pimples." I suggest to Tory that she go inside and capture any sense of self that has followed 'in her mother's footsteps.' "Would rebellion be a negative continuation? The Blimp is definitely the most rebellious part of me. The ropes are the rational side of me." I suggest to Tory that the Manager acted out her 'rational side' but she is now in the heart chakra with the Black woman experiencing pure sensation. I have her ask Christ if flooding the Blimp's circle with pure sensation would be helpful? "He says that flooding would not be helpful. It would be overwhelming. It would be better to introduce sensation a little bit at a time." I quickly rephrase the question: would she be willing to let him gradually introduce sensation. "It does make me anxious, but I trust him to modulate it. Now, the Blimp's circle has a small dome over it. It will contain the sensation and shield me as well." I ask how Tory will know what is happening. "It will be experienced in a positive way, though it is hard to imagine when all of our experiences of sensation have been negative." I remind her of the Manager's experience in the heart chakra. The session ends here. I am hopeful, but only time will tell.

Tory returns the following week. Over the weekend she and her husband spent two nights in a nearby resort area. "I was sick to my stomach the morning we were supposed to leave. I decided to not give into it and I was fine. Our Inn was delightful. I enjoyed the outdoors, which is unusual for me. It was gorgeous." I ask her about the Blimp? "She is rid of the ropes. Now she is sitting on the surface of the circle, not held down. She seems a lot more under control." I ask Tory to go inside and ask Christ if the Blimp could be 'trusted' with more sensation? "I am aware that the sensation is coming slowly into the circle, but I kind of like that. I did not finish anything (food) that I ordered. Nothing appealed to me. It is hard to be around my husband when I eat. He has a high metabolism and can eat everything and anything. I confess I could not pass up the lemon moraine pie." Tory's comments make me wonder if Christ could increase her metabolism via sensation. "No. He says he will increase my *satisfaction* but not my metabolism; that I really need to focus on the satisfaction of what I eat. That could mean a lot to me. I east so fast." So we agree that Christ will alter sensation to increase satisfaction. The session ends here.

(I employed the above intervention in three of the four major verbatims in this chapter and the next (Tory, Marion, and Leigh's in the next chapter). *The addition of pure sensation* to a mental component's circle of effect – after the circle has had its desired effect of constraining the mental component – has produced consistently positive results. In each case it immediately begins providing the mental component with a significant 'ground' (sic) sensate connection. In another case I used it with a chronically fearful component with comparable positive results.)

I see Tory two weeks later. She cancelled the previous week because of bronchitis. I start to work with that symptom, but she quickly tells me that she worked with dissatisfaction over the previous week. "I have had a real dissatisfaction with food. Nothing appeals to me. Everything seems unsatisfying. *I hate my life because it brings me no satisfaction.*" I suggest that hate is a an ineffectual rage. "We can agree on that; I feel powerless to change." I suggest that she ask Christ to provide us with a belief or emotion that will empower her to change her life. "The anger never gets out; it churns inside of me, *shoots my digestion to pieces*. I feel so stupid that I can't do anything about this and it is getting worse." I suggest that shame is not a good emotion for directing change. I ask her to let Christ draw a circle that will capture the self who hates. "I walk through but there is nothing there. When I ask Christ he tells me that is because I believe it is too huge to separate." I suggest another approach: she will stand in circle and Christ will place a portion of his *Light* in a circle whose frequency will dissolve the hate and empower her to change. "I am in the circle. When I ask he literally uses his *Light* as a wand and begins tracing my body starting at my toes, going up into my armpit, then down to my hand, up over my head and down the other side. I can feel its touch all the way. I feel encased in his *Light*." I ask her to tell me about the feeling of encasement? "It is not rigid; more like oil or cream on my skin." What is the intent? "It is meant to penetrate, not just soak in. It feels neutral." I note that he is acting on my suggestions and ask if he would like to add anything? "He also wants to deal with my mind. He wants to place memories in it that will dispute the way I am feeling, memories of joy and pleasure by giving me the ability to recall them. He wants to place a portion of his *Light* into my heart. I thought he would put it in my brain. But the memories will come from my heart. The recall will be of the feelings, not the events. When I agree, he simply reaches in and leaves a portion of his *Light*." I stress to her that she must allow Christ to renew this at least once a day, more often if it is satisfying, but at least once a day. I remind her that Christ gives us *daily* bread. I suggest that she come back, but still be in the circle. This is the first time I have made that kind of suggestion. Basically, I am encouraging her to be in both places simultaneously.

Tory returns a little horse, but does not complain about it; in fact, she minimizes it. She tells me, "I know my life is not terrible, though it is not what I want. This past week, I have repeatedly asked Christ to anoint my life." I suggest that she go inside and ask Christ to draw a circle that will dissolve all of the hate in her mind, heart, and body. She has only to step into it. "OK. I have stepped inside the circle. There is no change." But last week you told me you hated your life? "I don't, I changed all of that. It is not a word I use now." I tell her that she has used it all of her life. "I dislike some things, but as I sit here, if the dislike reached the level of hate, I would do something about it." I suggest to Tory that she allow Christ to add an emotion to the circle that would replace any residual hate. "OK. I am not reading it." I suggest that she ask Christ to add more till she can experience it. "What is clearest is moderation. Hate paralyzes; moderation turns down the intensity of it. Moderation facilitates movement, makes me able to move. When I am so bound up with hate, I can't get out of the situation. With moderation I might dislike something but it does not trap me. I can turn to something else and put the disliked situation on hold. I did not realize that was happening: that hate actively blocks change. Maybe, my previous statement was false that, that if I hated something I would do something about it. I think this is going to be much better, far more productive. Now there is an opportunity to change things." I ask her if she would like to stay in the circle and come back or leave it and come back to me? "Leave it. I got the value of the circle; it was a very teachable time. I do have a little bit of doubt – maybe more than a little – that I can change my life. I want to be happy, to feel joy, I want to have fun and experience fun. I want to fulfill purposes in my life. Mandy provides all of these things for me, but I want to move into situations beyond Mandy. I would like my house to provide me pleasure, but I feel trapped in it." Tory goes on to explain that she would like to move to another part of town, but that would put her further from Mandy and her daughter, who bought a house close to where they currently live when she moved back to the city. I suggest to Tory that she return to the 'circle of moderation' and ask Christ to stand in the center of it. Then, I suggest that she enter it and present him with her sense of tension between staying in her house – which she has wanted to move out of for years – and her desire to remain close to Mandy. "The moment I stepped in I realized that not moving is a choice. I made that choice but I don't care for it now." I suggest that she ask Christ to give her 'another choice' for the resolution of this tension; that she needs to see brand new options. As we are beginning to run over I have to ask her to return to me. Again, I give her the choice of staying in or leaving the circle when she comes back. "I will stay in the circle and come back." The session ends here. Reflecting back to the previous session, I have a strong sense that she has remained all week in the circle intended to dissolve hate; and it has had a decided effect. I suspect her decision to remain in her current circle with Christ at the center will have an equally strong effect.

(I have also begun using 'Christ defined circles of infused emotion' with Marion and Leigh with equally fascinating results. The general intent is to suffuse a circle with an opposite or deficit emotion [such as the need for a safe source of masculine energy], which allows the self within the circle to experience everything differently. Often, I am willing to leave the contents unnamed. With Tory, unbeknown to both of us, he filled it with a strong sense of moderation. The effects are generally immediate so the results are easily judged and, provided the client elects to remain in the circle when 's/he comes back to me,' the effect seems to continue through the week.)

The next session a week later takes a surprising turn. Tory begins by telling me how wonderful Mandy has been during the week that Tory has kept her and her mother has been away on business, but also how 'bad' her younger brother has become, "really worse than Mandy ever was." I suggest that she go inside and let Christ draw a circle and place her grandson in it. "He is his normal self, agitated and rash; he wants to be in control and have his way in everything, like refusing to go to sleep." Ask Christ to place a portion of his *Light* into the circle and set it to a frequency that will satisfy the lack in him. Let Christ tell you his reasoning and the *Light's* intended correction. "Christ says he just has to come closer to him. Christ gets his attention by walking slowly toward him. He is suspicious of his approach, but he has finally sat down in the middle of the circle. He is waiting for Christ to sit beside him. He is looking at the *Light* that Christ has brought. You know, my total attention has been on Mandy. I need to start doing for my grandson what I have did for Mandy." I ask Tory if she can identify the emotions that Christ is emanating? He may be sensing that Christ is someone who will meet him on his own terms, valued and accepted for who he is. It is strained between him and his father; and there is an unhealthy fusion with his mother. He needs a healthy supportive relationship. Christ is just interested in him." I suggest to Tory that she let Christ remain in the circle and she return to me. She tells me that I have been right about the relationship between her daughter and grandson: "It is so much like my mother and brother." At this point, Tory shifts her focus to her husband, and what follows is what will surprise me. "There is no intimate relationship between us; no kissing or hugging. At church when he is a Greeter, he is quite comfortable kissing or hugging other women, which is inappropriate, but he avoids being affectionate with me. When we were first married he could not stop touching me." I ask her if she is willing for her husband, who is exceedingly governed by sensation, to come together with her image of the Black woman? (This may seem abrupt, but sexuality and touch from any male is something that Tory has assiduously avoided every time I have broached it. Her growing experience of sensation has finally heightened this sense of lack in her. Allowing Christ to bring the Black woman into relationship with her husband's image will hopefully bring her to the point where she can desire it for herself.) "I want to be angry at him for withholding." I challenge her with her own desire: is she willing to see her desire consummated in her own mind? If not, she will not be able to experience it in life. "I have an acquaintance who recently remarried. They went on a river cruise. The more I thought about it, the more depressed I got. I missed the joy and intimacy we had." I suggest that her anger has generated her depression, as it has split her from the masculine energy that use to flow through her husband's image. I suggest that she let Christ draw a circle and stand in the center, and place a portion of his *Light* in the circle that will saturate it with Christ's unconditional masculine/sexual energy. Then she can step in and see how it feels. "I did not do it. I don't know why I am resisting." Are you willing to find out? "The thought of finding out is making me anxious." I suggest that she can assume a garment of protection and step into a circle of growing awareness. But we are over our time. I tell her that so long as she does not experience the energy she will not attract it. "I agree with that." The session ends here, but I trust it will be continued.

When Tory comes in she shares more sensation experiences with me. She has spent time in a Salt room (a room whose walls and ceiling are saturated with salt) and found the experience very 'cleansing.' Likewise, her granddaughter, Mandy, continued to be a real joy through the rest of her stay with Tory; but her daughter's continuing failure to appreciate Mandy is a source of despair. And, once again, Tory also despairs that she has become just like her mother who could go for days without speaking to her father. I am still desirous of having her experience her own masculine energy, but decide we must first focus on the thinker's capacity to 'experience' it. That thought, prompts me to suggest a new intervention: Christ will create a circle and place a portion of his *Light* into it, set at a frequency that will saturate the circle with sensation. I tell Tory that the intent of this intervention is 'the awakening' of her thinker's sensation function. I add that Christ will follow her in if she agrees. Tory agrees to let Christ do this and then reports: "What I felt as soon as we stepped into the circle was the awareness of a huge lack, a huge sense of what I have missed and I am missing." I ask if she means by this a sense of sensory deprivation? If so, then she needs to allow Christ to fill the void with sensation. "I have always coped by cutting off sensation." I ask if she is willing for Christ to add sensation to her sense of being, which I liken to the experience of 'love breaking through the armor.' Then I add: are you willing to *embrace* Christ (as I imagine such an action would definitely require sensation)? "That is strange. I have never had that thought. I can't do that...I have had times when he embraced me. In fact, I have lots of pictures of him doing that. But it would be presumptuous of me to embrace him." I sense this is a real struggle for Tory, particularly the idea of presumptuousness. So I ask if she would be willing to kiss his feet? "That I could do." Several minutes of silence follow, but it is clear from the strong emotions on her face that something is happening (what I call a love breaking through the armor experience). When she can speak again, she shares with me: "When I kneeled to kiss his feet my head was down. He reached down, touched my head and pushed my hair back. I don't have enough hair to push back, but I make that gesture all the time with Mandy. I really enjoy looking into her face and beauty and who she is. He evoked all of those feelings when he made that gesture." I ask if she wants to stay or leave the circle when she returns to me? "I need to leave the circle for now. It was so strange. I need to think about this." I comment that, you embraced him in the way you could and he responded. But thinking will not allow her to continue experiencing it; thinking can only evoke memory. She replies that, "I have thought negatively about my life before, but lately the thoughts are increasingly visceral and distasteful." I reply that today there was a moment in time when the void was filled by her experience (sensation) of Christ and she cannot have those experiences without sensation. "Mandy is the purest sensation experience I have ever had in my life." I ask if she can embrace her daughter in the same way. "No...OK, I will go back into the circle this coming week." The session ends here.

Tory returns the following week to tell me she has gone back to the Salt Spa. This time she got a massage: "The moment she touched me I could feel a difference and I thought: this is sensation. During the week I have gone back into the circle. I received an illumination of me. I am really a very negative person. It is not something I want to be or something I thought I was. But it is obvious I have gotten to be that way. I have talked to Christ about it. Especially, I have changed how I talk to Eduardo. I nag him; I am not pleasant with him. I am angry with him, there is no gratitude or respect for him." I suggest that she invite Eduardo into the circle with her so Christ can embrace him, but she is not ready yet. So I ask how the Blimp is doing. "She is on the ground; nothing is holding her. She is soft and squishy." I ask Tory if she can discern what she needs? "She wants a place in my life. The changes have diminished her." I ask if she is the source of negativity? "No. It's mine; but she is negative. All of the emotions surrounding her are negative: anxiety, judgment, and fearfulness." I suggest to Tory that she allow Christ to enter the Blimp's circle, purify it of all negative emotions and embrace her? Tory is agreeable.

"When he embraced her she just disappeared. He absorbed her." I suggest that the Blimp was a creation of her negative thoughts. Tory is not disturbed by her disappearance. Rather she refocuses on the memory of her own 'embrace' by Christ. "That memory…what really added to that experience was feeling my face. My cheek was against his breast and it felt so good." The session ends here. I will be gone for the next two weeks so we agree to meet again the following day. She returns with the desire to focus on Eduardo. "I have a totally negative image of him and yet I use to love to call him at work just to hear his voice." I suggest that she let Christ fill the circle with sensation and *her unconditional masculine energy*. This, I explain, is her masculine energy uncontaminated by males in her life. "OK. Eduardo and I are standing in front of Christ. It was hard for me to walk through the circle, but easy for Eduardo. I suggest that she let Christ embrace her till she is willing to embrace Eduardo. "OK. I can embrace Eduardo but I do not get a wonderful feeling from that. I feel sad." I suggest that she step back and allow Eduardo embrace Christ. "Eduardo is far more willing than I was. I feel that there has to be more change in me." I suggest that she allow both Eduardo and Christ to hug her at the same time. "His embrace of me felt much better than mine to him." Did you like it? "Yes. Both felt good." Is it something you would be willing to repeat? "Yes." I suggest that she leave both in the circle, where she can return to as often and she chooses. The session ends here.

I do not see Tory again for nearly three weeks. Overall, she is doing well. She is very pleased with Mandy's success in Kindergarten and has high praises for her teacher. "The only time I went inside was to ask Christ to be with Mandy during her dance recital. She has had good rehearsals. I did not go in to embrace Christ and Eduardo, but I consciously attempted to see Eduardo as I saw him in the circle and it was good relating to him. I did have another massage that was just as good as the first one." I remind her that our goal is for her to comfortably embrace Christ. "I did that once!" I suggest that it would be ideal if she could do it daily and encourage her to go inside for that purpose. "OK. The first time I embraced him he felt much taller. This time he was not so tall and the embrace felt more like a casual hug. The overwhelming love I felt before was not there." I asked if she had her guard up? "I did not think so, but probably, yes." I suggest that she ask Christ to suffuse the circle with equal measures of sensation, thinking and feeling. I tell her that sensation will give her the feeling of his body and her reaction to it. "There was o sensation before." I tell her that sensation that will allow her to feel his hands as he returns the embrace. "I could feel that before. This time was like the last. It may be the first time I felt him he was so much bigger than me. I feel reticence and reserve on my part." I suggest that she allow Christ to draw another circle that will capture all of the resistance. "I have a clear sense of where it came from now. As an adult, I have refrained from hugging others. I have not practiced this, but everyone else has." I ask her what remains in the circle? "I just see stupidity (shame). Stupid that you can't enjoy something that is naturally pleasurable." I suggest that she allow Christ to draw a circle that will help her separate from the family taboo against embrace. "OK. But there is another issue: my body. When Christ was bigger I felt small and that made my body small." I suggest that she also ask Christ to create a circle that will remove the sense of body that reinforces the taboo. "It is hard to remove." I suggest that she just step out, or just back out; that she can then evaluate from the perspective of being free of it. "OK. I have stepped out of the circle, and now when I embrace Christ it feels much better." I tell Tory that unless she allows

Christ to dissolve what she left in the circle she will reconnect with it when she leaves the office. "I do not mind his doing that, but do not care to look back. He does not think I need to look back. OK. He dissolved it, and now it looks like any other circle. I remind her that this is daily bread and suggest that a part of her remain in Christ's embrace while she returns to me.

Tory returns two week later negatively focused on her daughter, Abby. Tory and Eduardo have been 'vacationing' with Abby and her family, and it was not a good experience. "Seeing Abby with her family is not a pretty thing. She has started smoking again and drinking soda. She is not eating, but she has gained weight. She is so disconnected from everything. All she wants to do is love on her son." I suggest that Abby seems to lack empathy. "She is the most selfish person I know." Now, Tory shifts the focus to herself. "I felt a slight spinning the last time I went to the Salt room. It started back when I returned from the vacation. It felt like somebody was playing pinballs in the right side of my head. My doctor is sending me for an MRI and a consult with a Neurologist. I shift the focus back to Mandy by commenting that Tory has a hard time letting Christ work with her. "I wish I could kick her out of my life. I see her as so evil, so apart from Christ. It is really hard for me to ask him to work with her." The session ends here.

I see Tory early the following week. She tells me that her head is better, and also that, "I am trying to accept what Abby feels about me." I ask if she find's Abby's image of her painful? "Yes. She holds me in disdain and contempt. She wishes me well so she will not have to deal with me unwell. She has filled my life with hurt and fear of what she can do with the children. I would kind of like it if she left." It is clear to me that Abby is holding a disowned part of Tory. I suggest that the real problem is that her pride prevents her from letting Christ change Abby. I add that the only way Christ can reach Abby is through Tory, but (to paraphrase what Tory has been saying to me) 'You say it can't be done, I've failed, and I have the hurt and fears to prove it.' Then I add, 'Ask Christ where he stands on this?' Abby replies, "He tells me, 'First, why would I want you to be hurt and fearful, to live like that, knowing what you know about me, you know I would not want that; second, why are you willing to trust me with so much else and yet you don't trust me here.' I really do want this to change. I don't want to live crossways with Abby. But there is always something between us, some barrier." So, I reply, 'ask Christ to remove the barrier and put himself in its place.' Ask Christ to draw a circle with the two of you in it. "OK. But she is only there because I have brought my part of her into it. She is not 100% in the circle. Only my part of her is in the circle, and I am 100% in the circle." Ask him if that is sufficient? "He says it is." Do you have any reservations? "I guess." Do you have a sense of a barrier? "No. Christ is between us." Then your part is to remain mindful of where you are." Then Tory tells me, "I'll just come back here but that makes it easier to go back." I am not sure. The session ends here.

Tory returns the following week. She has learned that her daughter is applying for a promotion that will take her and her family to the Northeast, a two-day drive from where she now lives. Tory is really beside herself at the thought of how this will affect Mandy and effectively deprive her of an ongoing relationship with her granddaughter. But she also becomes increasingly nihilistic as I press her to allow Christ to work directly with Abby. I seem to intensify those feelings by confronting her with her projection: Let Christ redeem the part of your mother disowned by you both and projected into your image of Abby; let him stand between both of you and repeatedly convict you both. "I can't do it; I can't hold it in my head long enough to do it." I tell her if she will just step inside the circle with Christ and Abby that will be sufficient willingness for Christ to act. "I consider her evil." I ask her if she has the power to change evil? "I give up." Then turn it over, I reply, express the willingness for Christ to step in. "OK. I am leaving." I tell her, 'that is her mother speaking. Abby's image is forcing you to look at yourself.' "I am more than happy to say I am evil. Absolutely nothing works out. I wish she never had children." The session ends here.

I do not see Tory for another two weeks. My notes for this session indicate more despondency and nihilism, but no work inside. When Tory returns the next week there is more of the same. "I'm done, I am through; if my mother could just go silent and withdraw, I can do it better. Mandy tells me that she has the best mommy in the world. Mandy seems to adore Abby. All I wanted was a loving family, but there is no love for one another. I can give up better than my mother could give up." I tell Tory that if she does not address this nihilism it will become her granddaughter's legacy, her unfinished business. "Just one of many." Yes, I reply, but the governing one. "I don't feel the need to explore whatever I have projected onto Abby. Nothing will change it." You think that Mandy is not going to be affected by three generations of nihilism? At this point I suggest a new intervention that I hope she will accede to: Let Christ create a dome that will lift her negativity, absorb her fatalism, nihilism and aloneness. "How can that happen when nothing changes?" I reply that all it requires of her is an instant of willingness expressed by stepping into the dome. "OK. I will do that, but what will happen?" I tell her to just 'be aware;' that she has accumulated a negative core that Christ will dissolve. "What it feels like is that my emotional attachment to what is going on in my life has been changed from negative to neutral. But the facts have not changed. I am just not reacting with tears and hurt." I tell her that the love she has sought is beyond the ego's capacity. "Yes. On the floor of a closet in my house is a wooden picnic basket. I searched for it when Abby came back here to live. It has never been used. Mother had one when we were kids. Twice a year we would use it when the extended family gathered together. Everything was right on those occasions." I remind her that everything good she has gotten in therapy was provided to her by asking Christ to provide it and then go on to list a number of significant changes she has experienced over the years. I now suggest that she make a contract with Christ. She will stay in the dome if he will provide her with a usable picnic basket. If he agrees he will shake hands or maybe hug her. "OK. I said it. He reached around and put his arm around my shoulder." I tell her that a part of her must stay there when she comes back. The session ends here.

When Tory returns the following week I ask her to immediately go back into the dome where I will then explain what I think is happening. I tell her that the sense of self she has been experiencing is her personality-core. It is something she 'received' from her parents; and her mother's characterological flaws dominate it. It is manifesting in Tory as a Mirror aspect. If her mother cuts her off then this self will cut off her mother and anyone acting like her mother. But, I stress, this is not something you choose; you receive it when you are a child. It was all her mother ever had to protect herself because she was unable to call on Christ to intervene. But she, Tory, can call on Christ. "I agree with everything you say." Then look to Christ. If your ego control can only offer nihilism, what are your options? Invite him in. What does he bring into the circle? "I know what I want." Ask him to bring what you need. Now I see tears in her silence and ask her about them. "They are about me being the mirror of my mother." Do you want to continue being that? To not know what Christ can bring into the circle forces you to continue mirroring her. "I told my brother what was going on in my life. He said I sounded like mother. I said I was her daughter." But, I insist, she does not have to be like her. "Abby is the epitome of everything my mother did not want to be: white trash." (This seems to hit the mark. While Tory mirrors her mother, she unconsciously projects the mother's shadow into Abby.) At this point, I remind Tory that her brother and Mandy are both functional today because a higher power intervened. I ask her if she thought her mother ever asked a higher power to intervene? "No. I will be more than happy to allow it if it can happen. I will be more than happy to be wrong." Then, I tell her, look at Christ and tell him: I am willing for you to intervene. But at this point she is distracted by another observation. Tory teaches a bible class to a group of women living in a halfway house. She now tells me that three of the women are having similar experiences with their daughters and grandchildren. I reply by asking, of the four of you, who has the most experience with Christ intervening? Suddenly, it comes to me to have her ask Christ to place a portion of his Light into her heart chakra and feel its affects. "OK." Now all I can observe is a facial tremor and a long silence. And then she says: "I will purposely go inside and tell Christ I am willing to do this ongoing. The only other choice is I am going to die like my mother. Carolyn Myss talks about negative energy causing illness. She says that the chances of negative energy causing illness are great, but if you are aware of it and continue, then chance becomes a certainty." (Tory has been reading *The Anatomy of Spirit* by Carolyn Myss and has now taken it to heart.) All I can do is put my faith in Christ's intervention. The session ends here.

I am scheduled to see Tory two weeks later. My plan is to keep her focused on her reference to Abby as "white trash," as this is clearly the projection that is deeply wounding mother and daughter. But Tory's unconscious has other plans. Tory calls me about a half hour before our session and leaves a voice message to the effect that she has likely broken her ankle in the process of leaving to come to the session. I speak to her that evening. The break is severe. It has been set but will require surgery as soon as the swelling has gone down and approximately three months recovery time. I am both sympathetic and pro-active. We both agree that such accidents have happened numerous times before and mark a fatalistic connection between her and her mother. She shares that over the past two weeks she has begun sharing her fears and feelings regarding Abby with others; she is no longer keeping them secret (thereby breaking a maternal taboo). I tell her it is absolutely imperative that she begin addressing the 'white trash' projection.

Over the next two months we do weekly telephone therapy. Space does not allow me to enter the verbatims here. I can tell you that the results of her effort are life changing for Tory and her daughter; and I plan to post them in the Addendum section of my website (The Unredeemed Conscience.org.).

The Ideal Persona

I described the Ideal persona earlier in the chapter, but its characteristics bare repeating as it becomes pivotal in Marion's case, whose verbatim begins in the next section. It is essentially an archetypal overlay ascribed to a Dominant self and actuated by the client's culture. Any conferred title – especially in a religious context, is generally a highly ritualized event that grants the recipient a life-long authority or blessing in exchange for sworn allegiance, vows, and/or oaths. Marion's Ideal persona will play a pivotal role in her verbatim as it empowers her life long vocation as a nun. Marion became a novice in her late teens. This vocational choice was strongly supported by her widowed father and his two younger brothers, both life-long priests (recall that her mother died when she was seventeen). The role of nun is highly respected among Catholic school children and laity, if not necessarily in the patriarchal hierarchy of the Church itself. It is a less visible role today now that most nuns serve out of habit, but Marion wore a habit for many years. (She was brought up – if you will, in the old school.) This persona carries a great deal of authority as it taps into the role of hierophant or priestess. Her vows of poverty, celibacy and obedience to church authority also set her apart from the community at large. Her role is distinctly different from, say, the role of a doctor of medicine or career officer in the armed forces, but each is comparable in terms of the authority bestowed by a large group of people in the culture. As Marion's verbatim will illustrate, such a persona may often be a powerful obstacle to accepting Christ's discerning voice and the forgiving power of the Holy Spirit until it is directly addressed. But I would also note another aspect of her vows that few laity know about. A nun's final vows are made during an actual marriage ceremony in which she is betrothed to Christ. Essentially, she becomes a bride of Jesus Christ. But the vows of chastity, poverty, and obedience are made to the church. It is those vows that appear to empower the Ideal persona, which gains its authority by submitting to the church's hierarchy. Even so, the marriage vows are intended only for Christ; and ideally, she is expected to cleave to him and no other.

Marion

Marion, Tory, and Leigh are the soul of this book. They are the first to work through all the steps, each one of them sometimes leading and sometimes following the other two. Their sense of Christ has guided and inspired me. Along with several clients in 'supporting' roles, they are the primary teachers of this work. I have always accepted their 'resistances' as the prod to discover what I am failing to see, and their forward movement as a validation of the correct path.

I have used excerpts from Marion's case throughout this chapter. When this series begins, she has already worked through the acceptance of Christ's discernment by one Dominant self, who then allowed Christ to enter and purify the Aware-ego's Heart. All that has had a noticeable, positive effect on her daily prayer life and coping skills in the real world. Christ has become her daily companion and she has become acutely aware when her willful selves resist his ministrations. But it will be another year of often painful resistances, before I learn to *name* and work with her Ideal persona and its Familial personality. Both of those selves are 'thinking types,' whose gradual transformation can be measured by the increasing clarity of their thought and, more significantly, their increasing reliance on feeling. There are two themes that run through most of Marion's sessions. The first is her lack of sexual orgasm (which in her mind leaves her incomplete as a woman), and the second is her weight. These are the issues we return to time and again. They are the ostensible barometers of forward movement or lack thereof; but really, they only seem like the setting conditions of a deeper struggle to connect with Christ, and he with her. (Though it is never spoken of as such, all three of these clients seem to manifest repeated interactions with Christ that I can only describe as powerful moments of increasing intimacy and reward.)

I debated shortening Marion's verbatim as it is much longer than the others; and there are periods of seemingly dry and painful resistance (though much shorter than they use to be). The machinations of her Ego's shaming self-reliance have seemed endless at times. But my own ignorance is equally at fault; and the reader who would be a therapist needs to gain some insight into my failures as well. Thankfully, as ever, Christ redeems us both through his guidance and inspiration. In sum, it is possible to think of Marion's 'dry periods' as a reflection of therapeutic shortsightedness. Neither of us would achieve a degree of closure until we willingly turned it over to Christ and accepted his pivotal role in every transformation.

For several months preceding this series, Marion has worked with selves sexually repressed by her mother and father. This has brought about some changes in her parental images. (I describe these kinds of interventions in the next chapter. They have proven helpful with other clients who were sexually repressed, but not with Marion.) What that series of interventions did provide is a deduction that seems all but unassailable, namely, that it is Marion who is blocking Marion. Even though Marion's ego-aspects are a reflection of parents and culture, it is the exercise of free will by those selves that shame almost every expression of her sexuality. And the decisive reasons will only emerge when we are finally able to explore her Ideal persona and the reconstituted Familial personality called Control. I should stress, however, that at the outset of this series I have no real appreciation or understanding of Marion's Ideal persona or its Familial personality. Both of us must discover them as we work through her resistances. In a very real sense, her case amounts to original research for both of us. Hopefully, the reader will benefit from our perseverance.

In the first session of this series, Marion begins by reporting on inner work she did throughout the week regarding her father's power to repress her sexuality. Basically, in this kind of intervention Christ is asked to convict the image of a parent with the power of the Holy Spirit until it changes from one who represses to one who embraces and affirms the child's sexuality. In Marion's own words, "I asked Christ to take away my father's tightness and taboos about sexuality, his own and others. I kept asking Christ to convict my father. I saw Christ give my father portions of his *Light*, and my father kept getting lighter. Then I shifted to my father and mother. They were having fun being sexual and intimate, enjoying each other. It felt good. I can't change what was, but I like the way it is now in my mind." I suggest to Marion that she go inside and move the process forward. I have her ask Christ to convict the image of her father so he can completely affirm and embrace the sexuality of her child self. "The new image of dad is so different. I can picture him being affectionate toward me. He touches me. I feel closer to this image." I ask if she can climb into his lap? "Yeah. If we were in the neighborhood he would hold my hand – a father being *proud* of his daughter." I pick up on the word *proud* and it prompts me to ask about a father *loving his daughter*. "In the absence of love, pride is the best you could ask for. There is an easiness around him that was not there before. He is reciprocating. It is not just me reaching out to him. It can be different now, and maybe different in the next life." At this point, all of her comments are like a series of red flags to me. Who is this self that seems both glad at the changes but resigned about the limits on change she seems to be imposing on the relationship? I ask Marion if she is still hiding her sexuality from her father? "I'm just not dealing with it right now. I'm busy. It is not important." But where, I ask, do you keep it? "I do keep it somewhere in a box. Every once in awhile I open the box up when I am feeling useless, lonely, unproductive or lazy, and it makes me feel a lot of shame." Her statement confuses me. I ask her if she means that she has to be feeling really ashamed in order to feel sexual? "No. I only allow myself to feel sexual when I feel a sense of lack and then I can't feel sexual either. Sex does not drive me, but at that point the only thing I have is sexuality and it does not work either." I ask Marion to identify the self that thinks this way. "It is the self controlling me. Sex is one of the things you should have control of." I tell her that she seems to engage in masturbation for the purpose of frustrating it. That her 'control' is repressive, not directive. Then I ask what she is thinking about? "I am thinking about the new image of my parents. They have moved ahead and I have not. I am ashamed of never having an orgasm." I reiterate my assertion that her shaming interrupts her pleasure; that shame will always interrupt ongoing pleasurable activity. As a means of control, shame can only stop behavior. The session ends here.

In the next session Marion broaches a recurrent theme, namely, that her inability to have an orgasm leaves her incomplete as a woman. I ask if she is ashamed of this. When she says, "Yes," I ask what she believes is the effect of feeling ashamed? "The shaming is always there. It helps me to doubt myself. It reaffirms every time something goes wrong that I am not good enough." I suggest that she allow Christ to extract this power to shame her incompleteness and place it in a circle in front of her. "It is a scale that measures good and bad, right and wrong. It measures me." I ask her to describe the standard by which it measures her? "Completeness, the perfect, the ideal me, as I would want to be." I ask if she has ever been that? "No." I ask what happens when she fails to be complete? "It feels like more incompleteness is added to the scale, and the 'complete' side becomes less and less achievable." I suggest that she can ask Christ to give her the power of his discernment provisionally. (Remember that Marion has gone through this process once before some months previous; but not for this self.) I tell her that if she cannot see the scale in front of her then she must assume that it is back inside and re-supplanted his discernment. I tell her, further, that he will insert it in the place where the scale was inside her head; and, finally, that this discernment will provide an internal guidance system that would allow her to look into her heart, and he could enter her heart at some point in the future and heal whatever she has shamed. Marion is silent for some minutes. Finally, I ask her what is happening inside? "He placed his hand on my third eye and he said this would allow me to look into my heart and see what I am ashamed of. I saw it. I'm most ashamed that when John wanted to have sex that I did not and that when I masturbate I can't have an orgasm. I most regret that I did not have sex with him. I could hate myself that I have not let another person love me or love myself. I could have lived with breaking my vows." (John is another religious with whom Marion has been emotionally involved for some years. There was some petting. He is considerably older than her, charismatic, and very senior in his order.) I ask Marion if she can still see the scale? "Yeah. It is behind Christ. It has not changed; it is still very weighted." I ask her if she can follow Christ into her heart with the scale out there? Are you prepared for him to baptize your experiences with John and release them from shame? "I feel like they are so abnormal. I want them baptized." Even so, as I further describe the process to her, whoever is in charge now resists the suggestion and tells me, "I have to figure this out." I reply with the thought that, 'If that is what scales are for there will be no change.' I rephrase my suggestion by asking what Christ needs to move the process forward? "He needs me to be willing, but what I most feel right now are shame and anger at why I did not have sex with John." I suggest that she ask her discernment. "I was scared that I would not be enough for him. I was fearful of getting pregnant. I was afraid of hurting him, his vows." We are over our time. I decide it will be better to withdraw all of my suggestions. I ask her to have Christ bring her back out of her heart, if they have entered there, and give her back her scales. Lastly, I then ask her if the scales are her higher power. "A lot of times they are." The session ends here.

When Marion returns I am surprised by the amount of work she has done between the sessions. The reader needs to bear in mind that Marion devotes an hour or more to daily prayer, which involves her going inside. Her relationship with Christ has actually become quite constant and close since she allowed him to enter her Heart some months previous. In any case, this past week she has allowed Christ to enter her heart while Control remains merged with the Aware-ego. (It is not clear to me, in retrospect, which heart they enter or whether Control enters or remains outside.). She describes the heart's interior as cavernous. "In one section is a huge shadow, something dark. I imagine a cloak over it that is shame. Under it are negative emotions, my anger, frustration, impatience, and body image that I have made into negative things. I feel almost paralyzed by it all. I want to change it but I do not know what I want from Christ." I ask her if Christ thinks it is a good thing to have shame in her Heart? "No. But he is waiting for something from me. A part of me has screwed so much up; she thinks it is wrong to be without shame. I don't deserve to not have shame. How can I think to feel good about who I am and what I have done?" I tell her that, 'Yes you are a sinner, but even a sinner can feel good.

Then I ask if all her sin is that darkness? "Yeah. That is what it is. I did not think of it that way before. Some is almost intrinsic to what I am. What would it be like to say I am a good person and that God is *proud* of me?" I silently cringe at the word 'proud' but do not comment on it just yet. Instead, I encourage Marion to turn to Christ and ask him to forgive her sins. "Christ says it is forgiven. I have to forgive myself." (I take this to mean she has to give up the power to self-shame.) I ask if Christ can fill her with the grace of the Holy Spirit that will allow her to forgive herself? "A parade of stuff is coming out from under the cloak of shame. As it comes out I have to say out loud that I forgive myself for whatever it is that is there – the anger and judgmentalness and repression." At this point I suggest to her that she stand in front of Christ and relinquish her power to shame herself; the power was never intended to use on ourselves. "Does this mean I must give up the power to be angry at myself?" Yes, I reply, if you use the anger to shame yourself. "I feel like I am right on the line. What would other people think if I did this, if I stopped apologizing for who I am, stopped shaming myself for not living up to my or their expectations? Something about it is really appealing, but what will they think?" I reiterate to her that she will need guidance and can ask Christ to supplant her self-shaming with the power of his discernment. "I am ready to do this. I hand over all the crap in the corner. I give it to Christ. I need a relationship with him for real. I feel lightened. We are still in my heart in the cave. I thought it would be filled, but it is empty and waiting to be *filled*, it is empty of shame. It is the opposite of what I expected. Shame took up a lot of room. Now there is the fullness of grace but empty, a good empty, an illumination of sorts. It goes against the expectation of fullness but it feels full." I ask her about her power to judge. "Mine or other peoples'?

Right now I feel very less apt to judge myself. I am afraid of other people judging my not judging." I ask if she is sensing other people judging her, thinking she may be hearing an aural Voice-of-conscience. I suggest that she ask Christ to terminate the power of any voices that seek to control her in this way. "Christ's response is that when I feel that way I am to come back inside and be with him. I am not use to doing that. I am use to relying on my own devices. I feel OK with Christ in the cave. I need to feel intimate with him in my heart. I need that closeness and his strength. Strange for me to say that I could be a good person, that I am a good person, that I have what I need. I need to stop weighing; I need to know that my heart is OK. Old habits die hard. I can hear a voice in my head being critical." I immediately suggest that she ask Christ to terminate it. If you have his discernment do you really need that voice? "No. I don't need it, but it is new. My hesitation is the newness. I am almost afraid to let it go." I ask her to compare the voice to her judgment. "It is where my judgment comes from. Is it not innate to have this voice shaming you?" (So far as I can determine, this is an aural Voice-of-conscience.) I affirm to her that it is not innate. "To replace it would feel too good. Months ago when we talked about being convicted with the power of the Holy Spirit I would ask for it each day and have continued to do that. Sometimes I feel it as living in another sphere. If I consciously lived without the ability to shame I would be living at another level. I don't deserve it." I tell Marion that, indeed, it is undeserved grace, but she does have to allow Christ to terminate any shaming voice whenever she hears it, beginning now with the voice in her head. "Yeah. I feel like it will be testing me pretty quickly." I encourage her to proceed, her reservations notwithstanding. "OK. He put his hands on my head. I told him I don't want to be led by that voice anymore. He just put his Light in there. I have to make that a conscious effort. Everything I have said today is different for me. This is not a calm time for me, and yet I really want to be calm, and I feel calm right now in my Heart. Is this rational?" I reply 'absolutely not' and then suggest that she ask Christ to terminate 'that voice' as well. "I feel like I'm in a place I've never been before and I want to hold on to it, just be able to return to it." The session ends here. Frankly, it is not clear to me if she has allowed Christ to terminate the voice. In the following weeks we will repeatedly return to her struggle to stop self-shaming so I must presume that someone blocked him.

The next session is interesting on several levels. Basically, it illustrates Marion's need to reinstate ego defenses against the aural Voice-of-conscience because she was unwilling to let Christ terminate the critical voice. First, in this session she immediately launches into a 'confession' that she *controlled* all of last week's session but cannot remember what transpired, other than having been in her heart and seen the shame bundle. She has not gone back into her heart since the last session. She appears to have exercised 'control' by forgetting. I suggest that she go into her heart and see if it will facilitate her remembering what happened during the previous session. She goes inside and reports that "I see the bundle covered in cloth with shame on it. It is over to the side, not in front of me. What is in front of me is space, nothing there." (Basically, she seems to be both acknowledging and denying the 'empty space.') I ask her what it is like to walk around in the empty space? "The bundle reminds me of a white elephant in a room that everyone pretends is not there." (It may be difficult for the reader to grasp what is going on here. Entering the Heart alters dynamics. Basically, once inside the Heart, the Aware-ego can observe and speak free from Control, and will retain that power so long as Marion remains in her Heart. But Control remains co-conscious and can also speak from outside the Heart when I address her directly.) I ask Control if *her forgetfulness* is a way of dealing with the bundle? "I have forgotten because I had to control it." At this point, I equate her power to forget with the power to self-shame and tell her that she has to relinquish the power to self-shame in exchange for Christ's power of discernment. "Yeah. I would like somebody else to be responsible for me." I encourage her to let Christ extract the power to forget and place it in a circle in front of her. "I see fog, gray and smoky. I can't see or remember clearly. I feel like I have to go back and deal with the shame bundle." I suggest that she let Christ liberate whatever is behind the cloth of shame and baptize it. But Marion is focused on her own thoughts and does not pick up on my suggestion. Instead she reports that, "Christ says I am here because all that stuff has made me who I am. It is the shadow side of everything that I am. Till now it has always been covered. I really took it for granted. This week I did a review of scripture to see how often it speaks of God's love for us as a person. I found a lot of references." I suggest that she let Christ take the 'fog.' "He goes over to the circle where there is a big cloud of fog. He just takes it into his *Light*." I ask if this changes anything? "I think something happened to the bundle of shame. I do feel more of a connection between Christ and myself." As this session ends I suggest only that she see what she can remember during the week. This 'two steps forward, one step back' is very characteristic of Marion.

Marion comes to the next session with the remnants of an obvious cold. She tells me she came down with it right after seeing me the previous week. She believes she got it to keep her home and thereby facilitate her *remembering*. "I remember Christ and I putting people in a circle who I would be fearful of if I gave up the power of self-shame. That power allies me with them. If I am ashamed of myself then no one expects a lot of me. I also remembered feeling a sense of incompleteness. I remembered the bundle of shame in my heart. I put the blame for that shame outside of myself by programming other peoples' responses. I expect them to shame me. I realized the shame is in me. If I can give up shaming myself it does not matter what is outside. I picked up the bundle and owned it and told Christ that I needed his forgiveness and my own. Christ put his hands on my hands and the bundle turned into sand that sifted through my fingers. I felt more complete. I have acknowledged it was me that is shaming me and not anyone else. I was my own worse enemy." Marion has not only remembered, she has also moved the process forward in significant ways! I suggest that she allow Christ to directly penetrate her brow chakra, terminate her power to shame evermore and replace it with the power of his discernment. "OK. I'll do that. It is like hearing another voice. I am conscious of another way, a different way of looking at things. I just keep thinking that there are two ways of living. Instead of holding my head down and saying I failed again, there is another way. Instead of seeing change as getting me off course, I can see it as a new way. I get so rigid about everything. What I see now is that every time the road goes different it is not something to be ashamed of, but something to be explored. What is hard is the lack of certainty. I have in my mind what is good and I can be so rigid about that – work, relationships, and sexuality. I get rigid about it all and that is where the shame comes from. Rigidity does not fit life." (The source of this rigidity is her Ideal persona, but it will be a good while before I can name it and address it.) I suggest that she and Christ penetrate her heart and discern if there are any shaming voices within it. "We are in the cave. There are voices but I give them the power and I do not have to give it. There is a shield in front of me now." I suggest that she allow Christ to cauterize the source of those voices in the heart. "You know, I feel that they will always be there." I suggest to her that she is attempting to control the voices and that she needs to let Christ terminate them. At this juncture she has an insight: "Oh, you are talking about the voices in my head! (She thought I had been talking about the voices of people-in-the-world.) The voices in my head are everyone sitting at the picnic table *before they were baptized*, constantly correcting and scolding and telling me how to be better. I thought they were gone. (What Marion is referring too are four archetypal embodiments that were all worked with previously and baptized. They all sit around a picnic table where Marion, Christ, and others have joined them from time to time. Each has been worked with – *outside the heart*, baptized, and healed. But apparently at least one of their 'voices' have continued within the Heart.)" I suggest to Marion that she ask Christ to baptize the interior of her heart. I have never suggested this before and have not the faintest idea what will happen. After a few minutes' silence I ask what is happening? "Christ goes to each of them and touches the forehead and they join with the baptized part of them. That feels right. They are fine." (This reference to feeling is significant and no mean feat for a client who has relied almost exclusively on thinking.) "It is no longer me and them, it is more 'us.' They can help me." I refocus Marion and ask her to listen carefully and discern if there are any other voices that would shame her. "No. Not on the inside." On the outside? "No. We are strong enough. I want this to last." I ask her if she is having misgivings? "This is such a good place to be. I want it to be real (on the outside). I don't want to get knocked down." I surmise that she is anticipating masturbating and still not having an orgasm, so I encourage her to ask Christ if that will happen? "I am worried about how I will feel if I don't." And how will you feel if you do? "Pretty good. All of us at the picnic table think so." What, I ask, would she use to stop herself? "I used shame and anger in the past." The session ends here, and once again I am quite curious as to what will transpire during the week.

Allow me to step 'outside the frame' for a moment. What I still fail to appreciate is that Marion's Ideal persona will continue to exercise *her control* outside of the Heart, as that archetypal energy is conferred and sustained by culture, by the expectations of others. More to the point, for some time to come, I will confuse this Ideal persona with one of the archetypal aspects (Sr. Regina) sitting around the picnic table. Having failed, as yet, to name the archetypal energy conferred and sustained by culture, I will continue to treat two different manifestations of Sr. Regina as one and the same.

Marion is hard to read when she returns. She seems more relaxed, even though I know she is very concerned about her financial prospects for the future. She is currently unemployed, running out of funds, and has no real prospects. She tells me straight out that she has not masturbated because she is afraid to. I do not belabor the point. Instead, I suggest she let Christ take her within her Heart *to a place where she can hear her Soul's desire for her*. "It is the same cavernous space I have been to before, though all of the shame is gone from it." I suggest that Christ take her further in, closer to the place where she can hear her Soul's desire. "I get an immediate picture of a maize of obstacles – strings, brambles and fallen logs. There are too many things in the way. Questions about what is the good or better thing to do concerning financial security, fear of not getting a meaningful job, everything other people will tell me to do." I comment that none of this seems to be of the Soul's making, and ask if she is willing for Christ to dispel these obstacles so she can hear her Soul's desire? "I wish he could." I am quick to say that only willingness will do. "I can see beyond that stuff to where Christ would lead me, where everything is OK – working a meaningful job that sustains me, staying in this part of the country and also remaining a part of my religious community, volunteering in the evenings, *but it is not real*." (Even so, months later all of this will come to pass.) I ask her if any of her obstacles will achieve this desire? What emotions do the obstacles symbolize? "Fear." I ask again if she can identify what her Soul desires through her? "To know I am making the right decision and being the person I am supposed to be; Christ and I working together define that from the depths of who I am." I suggest that she let Christ take her to the place where she can hear that depth. "It is not a place I am familiar with." That is why I suggest that you let Christ guide you. Let him take you by the hand and take you there. (Silence.) "It feels like it has been hidden away. He leads me to this other space that feels both spacious and close. I almost feel a little embarrassed to be there because I don't know it and I should know it." I suggest she probably wants to get over that. "Yeah. Christ says my embarrassment is not what I am here for. He does not say it in a mocking way; rather, lets just deal with where we are." I suggest that she just 'be there' for a while and feel it. At this point, Marion begins to obsess about repeatedly losing her sense of 'professional identity' as she has been obliged by circumstances to make career changes. I suggest that she is functioning out of a pride-shame perspective and needs to be receptive to her Soul's perspective. "I am still in that place with Christ but I don't see anything." I ask her to *listen*. "I hear a song that has a line in it to the effect, 'I will hold you in the palm of my hand,' the idea of God accepting me. I can believe that." I tell her to forget about believing; she needs for Christ to take her deep enough for her *to know that kind of acceptance*. "I feel like I am going down and down and *I keep wanting to say, but*." I ask her if she is willing to give up the power of *but*. She tells me that, 'it is the real world' inferring that what precedes it is a fiction. I rephrase this by commenting that all of her life she has asked her Soul, and its desires for her, to play second fiddle to the 'world.' I ask her if she can tell me what emotion 'but' generates? "Fear and hesitation, denial and paralysis." I encourage her to ask Christ to terminate the *but* in her head in exchange for his power of discernment. "I can't clear my head enough to believe it, even as I can remember getting those three checks in three days." (In the recent past, when she was faced with the prospect of no income, she received three large checks in the mail from three unexpected sources over three successive days.) I tell her she is experiencing the first-hand paralysis of *but*, but in a moment of willingness she can change that. I remind her of how often in the past this 'but' has paralyzed her in therapy for weeks at a time. "Every time I give up something here I first get to this place where I fight and resist. I know I am different for giving up the shame. I feel different. But each new 'giving up' feels like the biggest one." The session ends here.

This next session takes place several days before Christmas. (A note to readers attempting to fit a timeline to these verbatims. Retrospectively, this will be *last* Christmas. The process will come to fruition during the *next* Christmas holiday. The remainder of sessions in this verbatim will span a whole year and one half.) Marion's concerns about money have been greatly eased by *two more* large gifts of money – completely unexpected. Coupled with that she has learned that she can start her Social Security in January and get nearly twice what she expected to receive. All this financial news has come on the heals of inner work she did during the week. As she describes it, "I finally let Christ penetrate my brain. I went inside and we both entered my Heart. I asked Christ for his discernment. He penetrated my forehead. I knew it happened, but nothing happened. Then, the next morning, I remembered the mantra I had been saying daily for several months, but have recently stopped saying: 'I am willing and grateful to be convicted with the power of the Holy Spirit.' That is the gift of Christ's discernment, to say and live that everyday. I stopped praying that because I had stopped feeling 'real' about my inner life. I have confused staying calm with doing nothing. I was learning to stay calm without getting panicky and it seemed unreal to me." I ask Marion about 'but;' I suspect she has still not let go of it. She tells me that 'but' still feels like the real world. I suggest that it is an arbitrary definition of the real world. In turn, she contrasts the real world with faith. At this point we enter into a discussion of real vs. faith, which takes up the better part of the session. Gradually, she actually provides more and more arguments against 'but.' "Instead of being grateful for what I have – which is ample, I live in the fear and anxiety generated by 'but.' I did not think I would even get through October and here it is almost January. Something or somebody expects me to be panicky. If I am calm about it, I am not doing what I am supposed to do. I was thinking that the Soul's desire and God's will for me are opposites, but they are not." I rephrase this by noting that her Soul's desire flows through her, it is not from the 'real' world. As we are nearing the end of the session I ask if she wants to do anything today? "Yeah. Give up the 'but'." I tell her she needs to go inside for that, which she immediately does. "I am inside my heart with Christ. I see two figures with him. There is *me that has let Christ penetrate my brain and convict me with the power of the Holy Spirit* and this other that is the 'but.' Christ goes to the 'but' figure and I hear him say to her, 'Fear not, I bring you tidings of great joy.' That is what Christ just said to her. I don't have to live in fear and panic. He just gently moves her over and she is enveloped by the *me* who believes in living in the Spirit." I suggest to Marion that she needs to ask all this in the first person standing in front of Christ. "I am that figure." If that is so, I say, then let him penetrate her brain. "His penetration is solidifying the two images." I ask her if she is giving up "but" forever? "Yeah, Yeah." (Silence.) "Its good. I think it is going to be different. Feels funny inside. It *should* feel loose, but it feels tight. I just had a terrible thought that I am afraid of what I just did. There I go with the 'but' again. I know it was right. It really feels more like putting a puzzle together. It feels balanced. What I did was right and I don't want to move anything. I need to treat *me* gently. I don't have to have it fixed for a year or even a week. I just need to remember that today is sufficient." The session ends here.

I see Marion two weeks later. She is both up and down. "I felt good after the last session. I keep reminding myself that I don't have to live in fear. I have the present moment; I am alive. I have been going into my Heart. Before, the emptiness felt spacious. Now it feels empty, as if nothing is in balance, nothing works. I am aware of putting on weight – eating too much. I don't know what I am. I have not even tried to masturbate." After listening to this litany, I decide to offer her three options: 1) go further into her Heart and seek out her Soul's desire for her, 2) let Christ work with her root chakra (i.e. sexuality), or 3) bring the Eater into her Heart and work with her there. She gets to choose which one she works on. "I don't want to deal with the Eater; I would like to know what my Soul's desire is for me." In other words, she is also not ready to deal with her sexuality. I have her go inside and ask Christ to take her to the place in her Heart where she can hear her Soul's desire. Silence. I ask her what's happening? "I went into the big empty space and felt an opening, a tunnel. There are phases to the tunnel. In the first phase I heard 'I want things the way they were'." I ask her who is saying that, you or her Soul? "Me. I had a steady job and liked what I was doing." I ask if this is her Soul's desire for her, or Christ's desire for her? "It was something I was good at." I ask if they are telling her that? I suggest that Christ 'refresh' the power of his discernment within her. After he does this she can tell me, "It is what I was supposed to be doing for the time I was doing it. But I don't have any control over now." I suggest that may be a good thing as powers outside of her control have been financing her for the past four months. She hears this but minimizes it by saying she is being taken care of 'by people who love her.' I tell her it reminds me of the AA joke where a recovering alcoholic prays for God to deliver him from a flood. First one boat and then a second comes by and he shoos them off saying God will rescue him. When he is on a roof a helicopter offers to save him and he shoos that off. Finally, he drowns, goes to heaven and complains to God that he did not save him. God replies that he sent him two boats and a helicopter. She understands my rationale but continues her complaint, which is becoming clearer to both of us. "A part of me needs to be reconnected to being needed. I am not 'officially' anything (meaning she lacks a meaningful job sanctioned by an institution). When I worked, I belonged, I could do something. I don't know if I will ever have a purpose again." I encourage her to commence walking in the tunnel. "As we walk the air gets heavier and foggier." I suggest that she take Christ's hand. "When I took his hand, the first thing I heard was 'be at peace.' It sounds like such a glib band aide for reality." I suggest to her that she can be a source of peace if she allows peace to flow through her. Then I ask if 'peace' is her Soul's desire. "Christ and the *Light* say no. It is part of it, but not what I am to seek. I am drifting. I need a reason to be." I suggest to her that, if her Soul needs a sense of purpose, then she can let Christ convict her soul with the power of the Holy Spirit. "Strange, that was not hard to do. What I immediately saw was that my Soul, Christ and the Holy Spirit are very connected. The problem is my connection." If that is the case, I ask, who is resisting the connection? "I don't think I am resisting. I have had to hear from my Soul this morning that I need a reason to be, how basic that need is for me. I disguise it in words like I need a job, that I am not doing anything, that everyone is taking care of me, but the truth is I need a reason for being, something that makes my life meaningful." I ask her if she is willing to receive her purpose from Christ and the Holy Spirit? "I have no purpose. Mary had a purpose when the Holy Spirit came to her and said she would conceive." I paraphrase what she is saying using her analogy: Your problem seems comparable to Mary exercising her own judgment and saying such a thing is impossible rather than accepting the impregnation of meaning by the Holy Spirit. The only way you can know Christ and your Soul's purpose for you is by being willing to receive it, but your judgment says it is not possible.

When Marion returns a week later she tells me she has spent a lot of time *thinking* about her Soul's desire for her. I reply that 'we cannot think our Soul's desire; we can only receive it or resist it. Moreover, her 'thinking' appears to be judging her shamefully insofar as she has been very self-critical in the past week toward her vocational ideals, which she has also been berating. I suggest that she go inside and let Christ extract her shameful thinking – objectify it so we can have a better sense of how it functions. Marion immediately reports seeing a ruler in the circle that Christ has drawn. "It measures what I think and who I am. Outside the ruler is 'not good.' It measures me in terms of the universe. It is even critical of the fact that I have received yet another $1200 gift this past week." I suggest that she also subjects Christ's discernment to this ruler. "I don't know what else to measure truth by." I insist that she does know: Christ's discernment or the ruler. She cannot have it both ways. "It feels like I would be forgiving everything I do. I know it would be a lot less stressful with Christ as my ruler, but another voice is saying, 'Oh yeah. You would get away with murder if you went along with Christ.' I have never had this much free time or money or been the person I am right now." I ask her how 'Shameful thinking' evaluates that? "She is coming down pretty hard on me." I ask her what she would think about Christ not coming down hard? "She believes he would be too easy on me. She believes that a part of me needs to feel shame. I only know to feel guilty about the way I am living." I note to Marion that 'Shameful thinking' is real but not the totality of her. I suggest that she draw a circle of escape and ask Christ to convict her (Aware-ego) and 'Shameful thinking' with the power of his discernment. Shameful thinking can escape to the circle, but either way Christ will permanently exchange his discernment for the ruler. I remind her that it is her brain as well as Shameful thinking's brain. Finally, I note that she cannot imagine living free of shame while she is obliged to think under its direction. Marion replies by telling me that 'she has asked Christ to remove the ruler *to the best of her ability.*' I immediately challenge this wording and she rephrases it. "I am ready for Christ to be the measure of who I am." I remind her that this is an experience. He penetrates her brain. If he is effective then the ruler will disappear and his image will stand in its stead within the circle. "OK. The ruler is gone and I hear him say, 'Be still and know I am your God'." The session ends here.

Marion's next session – a week later, moves beyond the scope of this chapter and well into the next one as it takes up the exploration of Marion's contra-sexual aspect. As such it provides an entrée to the next chapter. Basically, any client - when functioning as an Aware-ego, can ask Christ to extract their contra-sexual aspect using his *Light*. Following an exploration of that aspect, Christ is asked to simultaneously convict the contra-sexual aspect and Aware-ego till the relationship is seen as definitely fulfilling. A client needs to assume 100 percent responsibility for whatever s/he sees. This is particularly true of a female client who remains merged with the feminine aspect as the feminine always defines the relationship between the masculine and feminine aspects. Marion has been changed by the previous session and this is reflected in her beginning comments. When I ask what she wants to work on in this session, she both acknowledges and evades the need to work on her weight; so I suggest that she work on her contra-sexual aspect instead. She is familiar with the concept having worked with the masculine and feminine aspects of other images including both parents.

Marion tells me she has been reading the Gospel of Mark. She notes several chapters in which Jesus critiques the limits of literal thinking, particularly as regards the Sabbath. She is particularly mindful of Christ's warning 'Beware of the yeast of the Pharisees': the idea that faith in Christ multiplies the loaves whereas the literal thinking of the Pharisces creates a sense of scarcity. "Things fell into place this week. I know that I will be OK. I have to trust Christ when I get anxious." I ask her what issue she would like to address. "I am aware of eating as an issue I need to address." I counter with the suggestion that we first work with her contra-sexual aspect. She is quite willing, if only because she feels the eating issue is all but insurmountable. Once inside, she allows Christ to immediately extract her masculine aspect. "I see a block of wood, long and rectangular. I thought it was strong, but it feels tough rather than strong. It is not likeable." Her first descriptions make me wonder if it is anything other than a block of wood so I ask if it has any human characteristics? "It is human. It has my face on it, hands and feet. Its physicalness is not well defined." I ask how she would describe her relationship to it? "I relate to it when I need to be strong. I am starting to feel sorry for it. It is not as bad as when I first envisioned it, not 'just a chunk of wood.' It does give me aspects of myself. I don't dislike it. I really don't want to run it down." I ask her if she could imagine a really intimate close relationship with this masculine aspect? "Yeah. I know that I need it. I think I can. My fear is that in the past I have relied on it more than my feminine. I have overly used it. Now I see the need for a balance." I ask her to consider allowing it to be more strongly defined by the feminine, but note that the feminine would have to evolve with any change in the masculine insofar as the feminine redefines the masculine – like yin and yang. "The more I think about it, my first visual of it as a 'chunk of wood' was definitely a mistake. We need each other. In the past I have seen it as a protection, a shield. I do not have to do that anymore. I can balance better." At this point I suggest that she allow Christ to simultaneously convict both her and her masculine aspect and observe the changes in the relationship by the sense of change in her masculine aspect. (To fully appreciate what transpires the reader needs to recall that Marion had an emotional affair of the heart with a charismatic male religious who seems to have felt the same way about her. There was some petting and a lot of guilt. They still maintain sporadic contact). After my suggestion there is silence and a discernible softening and smile on Marion's face; but note in what follows that she has also separated from the feminine counterpart to the masculine. "She is surprised to see that after the conviction by Christ her masculine aspect has assumed many of the characteristics of John. When Christ reached out and touched us both what came to mind was John, a masculine figure with his qualities, much more human than the block of wood was. I would like to have his characteristics. It would be a wonderful masculine to be intimate with. A gift." I suggest to her that she step inside the circle containing her masculine-John and see how it feels. "It feels like coming home; very comfortable, a long way from that block of wood. I never got in a circle with a masculine like that within me. I am remembering something a friend said about a TV personality always saying that 'people need a soft place to land.' That is what being inside the circle feels like. I never thought of my masculine like that before." At this point I gently shift her focus to her appetite and suggest that she ask what the three of them can suggest to do? Can Christ and John provide for her sense of lack? "Is that what it is? What I heard in the circle was to be gentle with myself, but I feel *repulsed* by my lack of will power." I ask her if being tough with her self turns John into a stick of wood? "Yeah. But I can't stop it." I ask how John responds to 'I can't'? "It disappoints him." Well, I comment, that may be preferable to turning him into a stick of wood. I have her ask again what will work between the two of them? "If I am gentle with myself." I suggest that she assume 100 percent responsibility for his well-being because she has that authority by virtue of her choice to ask Christ's intervention.

When I see Marion the following week, she seems to be doing well overall. I ask her about her eating. She tells me that, "Actually, I've been real good about eating this week – no sugary stuff, I have been eating fruit twice a day. But even as I strive to do better something happens and I need to eat." I do not belabor the point with her but suggest instead that she go inside and work more with her masculine aspect. "I go directly into my Heart now when I go inside, even at home. I feel strange looking at the masculine figure. It feels different. Last week I felt comfortable with it. This week I feel standoffish, afraid of it. I don't want to touch it. I want Christ at my side." I suggest that she let Christ provide brain-stem massage to lesson the fear so she can further identify it. (That intervention is described in the next chapter.) "I am afraid I don't have enough to live in balance with the qualities that the masculine has and I don't want him to be overbearing." Why would he need to be overbearing? "Because *they* always are. It is the nature of the masculine and I let it be." Is Christ overbearing? "No. I am thinking of men like my brother who is always taking charge of my life and how I always capitulate. I am the baby in the family, the little girl." I ask if she is willing for the little girl to become a full-grown woman in the eyes of Christ and her masculine? "I am and yet I have always made it by being that little girl. I am afraid to give it up, but I don't want him overpowering me." I state the obvious: she cannot have it both ways. She has to give up this 'little girl power' forever and see her masculine through the eyes of a woman. "But I still need her sometimes." Yes, I reply, but right now she is all you have. I ask what brings her out? "I get mad when I use her and then treat myself like a child." I suggest that she let Christ penetrate her brain with his *Light*, terminate the image of the child, and supplant it with a new sight. "I want the new image to be my mother; but it is not because I don't understand how she lived with my dad." I comment that she did not live, referring to the fact that she died of breast cancer when Marion was seventeen years old. Now Marion reports another image: "I see the Samaritan woman who tells Christ that even he can give her the crumbs from the table. She has the strength to speak up and also humility and faith. Christ says to me, 'You got it right.' It was more intimate than the story tells. What a moment for her to be so accepted and he got a kick out of her courage. I want to know when to be humble and when to push ahead." I sense that she is on the verge of letting him supplant the images and equally tempted to put it off, so I say to her, 'you have one minute left before I have to end the session.' "It has happened and I have to work on it." The session ends here.

I am unexpectedly called away and do not see Marion again for another three weeks. Again, she is doing well on a number of fronts. In the interim, I have been formulating my hypothesis that excessive use of socially acceptable behaviors inadvertently injects more shame into the emotional field. Like many clients with whom I will come to share this hypothesis, it resonates with her and she becomes quite willing to go inside and work with her Eater. "The Eater is a female doughboy. She is aware of wanting to eat and then after eating I say I really didn't need that." I ask if there is a way of making her aware of the consequences of her behavior? Can she be made aware of the shame it is continually injecting into the body's emotional field? "Christ is telling me that I have to connect with her. We are two totally different people when the eating happens. I am in my mind and she is in my gut. I just got the feeling that I don't like her. But Christ says I have to nurture her. I feel like she is my enemy and I get mad at her and judge her. I am more dominant than her. She allows me to use her like a scapegoat." Again I reiterate her observation that she lives in the brain and Doughboy lives in the gut, but both share the same body; and again, I encourage Marion to let Christ extract the self-shaming into a circle. "It is mud. It is all those feelings I have of incompetence, not good enough, not living up to my own expectations, ashamed of being happy for no good reason." We are near the end of the session. Marion is still unwilling to let Christ supplant the shame, but she is determined to reflect on it. And she does. Several days later I receive the following e-mail:

> I want to tell you what has happened since I saw you on Tuesday. I've been reflecting/praying with the 'little dough girl' since then. I see how I've blamed and shamed her a lot for 'her' eating. I realize that it's easier than to shame 'me.' Then I was thinking she is really young! And who can blame a little child for what she does...I mean they don't understand the consequences of their actions yet, not fully anyway. So she served me well in that respect. Then I started thinking about the times I eat and the reasons why I do; you know the whole – I'm lonely, I'm a failure, I'm not a good nun, etc, etc. But when I do eat I go to her; I don't take the moment it would take to ask why I'm feeling like I am and what else could I do about it other than eat? I just eat! So, this morning I asked Christ to take us both, dough girl and I, to the water and to baptize us both so we could start anew. I had hold of her hand and as Christ started to pour water over us I looked at her and she was no longer 'dough girl' she was me...a reflection of me! So, I think I'm ready to approach eating as an adult. Perhaps taking the moment to ask why and what I can do otherwise.

The following week Marion returns to tell me that she has lost six pounds over the month. She also shares that overeating has finally begun to take a toll on her body. The results of her annual physical the month before showed her cholesterol exceeding normal limits for the first time, her blood pressure significantly increased since the previous physical, and her Thyroid deviating from the normal range. She then goes on to report that over the weekend she was filled with fear about her financial future. "I let the fear flow over me. I was covered in it." (Later in the session she will tell me that *once again* she can expect a new source of income – this time from social security that far exceeded her expectations. But between now and then we will begin to address this fear.) After listening to Marion describe her fear I reflect back to her that it sounds like a self that 'only trusts her fear to give an accurate reading of the world.' I suggest that she go inside and let Christ extract this self with concentric circles. "I am almost embarrassed by what I see...a teenager, age 17, experiencing a sense of abandonment after my mother died." I ask if this teenager has an experience of love in anyway equal to her experience of fear? "She felt very loved all those years her mother was alive. She feels abandoned by love since her mother left her. Now she will only trust her fear of being left alone. It is not something she wears on her sleeve or is desperate about, but it is there at her core." I suggest that she ask Christ to extract from her body the cumulative effect of this fear of abandonment. "It permeates her whole body. Christ is combing it out. It is her life. It is the anger, fear, and sense of rejection at always having to prove herself. I don't think she was aware of those consequences." I ask if any of those emotions have contributed to her eating excessively? "When I feel her presence I do not want to feel her presence, and then I need to do something. I feel sorry for myself and those are the times I eat. I need to put something else in its place." Are you saying her fear of abandonment stimulates the addictive cycle? "Yeah. It controls everything – smoking, drinking purposely, because I did not want to be touched by her fear. I still don't want to be." I suggest that she allow Christ to convict this fearful sense of self, but another self immediately resists, herself fearful that the conviction will 'sugar coat' the sense of loss. Anything that would ease the sense of loss is seen as 'sugar coating.' (This 'other self' is Marion's religious persona. We will not encounter it directly for several more weeks. It is very powerful and has been the primary source of much of her shame.) Basically, the session ends here. There is no resolution, but Marion does continue to struggle with it and sends me this e-mail several days later:

> I think I realize something. The feeling I have is not abandonment since my Mom's death - everyone dies and it wasn't anyone's 'fault. It's more a feeling of just being left alone. And all that I do or don't do is proving I can or can't make it on my own [alone]. The 17y.o. is alone; I've left her alone except when she demands attention and then I let her get angry, depressed, feel inferior, etc. which I think only exacerbates her feelings of aloneness. She was alone, or at least she felt the aloneness back then and she is stuck in it. It's like we are two different persons instead of one; basically, I don't feel alone but when I get anxious and scared she immediately comes to the front and I let her take over. How can Christ take away? Dissolve? Change? Confront? That feeling of loneliness. Just thinking out loud.

What Marion does not say, is that the self that is shamefully evaluating the teen's neediness gains strength from emulating her father who appears to make it 'alone,' unneedful of another. When that stance becomes periodically unbearable, the teenager makes herself felt and the Eater self steps in with food, anger, cigarettes, whatever, to temporarily assuage the teenager's angst, giving her a respite until the Dominant self can 'regain her strength' and once again go it on her own. The real issue for Marion is the Dominant self who insists she can 'go it alone' as her father seemed to do. (He never remarried; and if he dated it was a well-kept secret. He seems to have followed in the footsteps of his brothers – both religious, who outwardly honored their lifelong vow of celibacy.) Until this Dominant self is willing to give up her 'power' to 'go it alone' the teenager will have no choice but continue being a periodic scapegoat, i.e. an older version of 'dough girl.'

When Marion returns the following week she seems to be ready for work so I begin by challenging her minimization of the Teen's emotions and introducing, yet again, the idea that Marion's 'going it alone' is the real obstacle to change; the Teen is expressing in a negative way her deep need for connection. Marion understands what I am saying intellectually: "I put her down and ignore her and put her out of sight after eating." In response to my asking where the Teen is most strongly felt, Marion replies that, "She is in my gut – my core, right at the belly button, very deep." (This is the physical point identified by Paulson as correlating with the emotional chakra of the emotional auric body, which I discuss in the Chapter VIII.[49]) I tell Marion that the Teen needs desperately to experience connection and Marion keeps her perpetually isolated. "But I am embarrassed by her existence. I don't allow her to connect. I get mad at her, embarrassed, scared by her. She is not a part of me I like." I ask Marion if she can tell me where the emotions go each time she attacks the Teen. "I get tighter and withdraw more into myself." I suspect she is talking about the Teen as well as herself. I suggest that she allow Christ to extract the effect her attacks have on her emotional field. "The first thing I see in the circle is a sense of distance. My anger creates a greater distance between us. I also sense knots in a big ball, and fear in that circle, and more loneliness." I ask her to tell me more about the knots. "They are mental and physical. Five years ago I would not have been able to see this. Today, I am not comfortable with how I treat her. There is a sense of tightness in my body. I can't relax my neck or back, especially at night. I am sure it is affecting my blood pressure." I reiterate here that Christ cannot override her shaming. "But I am *afraid* that if I give it up I will still not be able to connect." In reply, I tell her there is no way for her to connect until she is reconciled with the Teen who personifies her power to connect. If she wants connection, she must forgo her power to attack and shame the Teen *forever* in exchange for Christ's discernment. As Marion begins to rationalize how she could do that, I tell her that her 'rational approach' will not work here. "What you are asking is such a leap of faith." Again, I suggest that she must stand in front of Christ and accept the exchange just as she has observed her other selves doing it. "No way to do it but do it." I have her repeat the words verbatim: I am willing to give up my anger, shaming, and fear of not rationalizing, in exchange for the power of your discernment. Silence. When I finally ask she begins by telling me that Christ put his hand on her forehead. At first, I thought this meant she remained unwilling to let him penetrate her brow but her continuing description suggests that a complete exchange has, in fact, taken place: "I feel weak instead of strong. I felt a penetration throughout my body. Maybe what I am feeling is not weakness but vulnerability. It was like Christ has removed something that cloaked me. I feel more *exposed* to Christ, almost a sort of dependence that I didn't feel before, but it is OK. It feels like I am standing in front of him naked but not afraid; it is not a fearful thing. The cover up I used is not there anymore and this is really me. I want it to be me with Christ." I ask her to focus on the circle that contained the 'effects of her shaming' and tell me what she sees. "Actually, I see the Teen in the circle. There is not that much difference between the two of us right now. I can easily approach her with Christ. I need to understand her, what she needs from Christ and me. In some crazy way she was ahead of me. She has been vulnerable all along, her real self, but I didn't pay attention to that. We are on a par now. I need to love her. I have done to her what she felt from everyone else in the family after my mother died. Christ and she know each other." The session ends here.

Marion is in good spirits when she returns the following week. Her Social Security and Medicare benefits are about to begin easing her financial concerns and she has the prospect of a part-time job. She reports spending time inside exploring the relationship between the Teen and her 'Go-it-alone' self. "Christ has blessed the relationship between the two of us. I am getting more familiar with her; I don't avoid her. I wanted the relationship to become dramatically different, but it has not." I ask her how willing she is for the Teen to become active in her? Does she have equal access to the hands and body that the two of them share? Using this as a frame of reference, Marion admits that she is still treating the Teen as inferior. So I rephrase my question: If the Teen were to 'touch the body' to feel herself (sexually) would Marion slap her hand? "OK. You made your point." So I ask her if she is willing to give up unilateral control of the body forever in exchange for both of them relying on Christ's discernment as to how to proceed? Marion says "Yes" and then tells me that she has gotten to the point of masturbating without feeling guilty, but still no orgasm. I reply that orgasm requires a sense of connection, which is embodied in the Teen; going it 'alone' is insufficient. At this point Marion introduces what seems to be a tangent: "A part of me feels sorry for myself." (A new self is expressing, but I miss that and proceed as if the 'feeling sorry' is coming from one of the two already identified.) I ask if Marion would be willing to give up the power of 'feeling sorry' for herself in exchange for the unencumbered free will to be connected? Both Marion and the Teen are ready for something. So I suggest that she go insider and let Christ initiate the process. "Christ takes my left hand and her right hand and puts them together. Then he tells us that we have to go ahead together. In the past I have put her behind me." I ask what each of them has to give up for this to happen? "I have to give up my sense of superiority and control and individualism. She has to forgive the aloneness and anger she felt *as a result of feeling abandoned by her mother*. She wears it to explain her shame and her belief that abandonment is forever." I ask if the Teen would be willing for Christ to convict her belief that abandonment is forever? If true, the Holy Spirit would affirm her belief. "When Christ convicts her the first thing I register is the heaviness of being abandoned. Her holding that belief has weighed heavily on her. The Spirit is getting across to her that everyone does the best they can, including the members of my family. Instead of staying stuck in that pain she can come out of the fog; she can let it go. Maybe she was abandoned or felt that way at the time, but she got stuck there, and everything has fed into it since then, the anger, shame, and guilt. Anytime she did something wrong it made her feel even more abandoned and proved why she should be abandoned." I ask if she is willing to give up the power to continue building that wall? "She is giving it over to the Spirit. She has moved away from the stuck place. Both of us have been so stuck. I blamed much of my life on my mother's death. I carry her death as a burden and a scapegoat. I have used my mother's death as a crutch for so much, for my isolation and lack of feeling. I even blamed my misdeeds on it. " I suggest that she allow Christ to convict her again and again until she can transform the sense of abandonment into something positive. Marion leaves feeling deeply reflective. The session ends here.

I do not see Marion again for three weeks as both of us are out of town at different times. When she returns I suggest that she go inside and work at reconciling Go-it-alone, who I identify as masculine, and the Teen, who I identify as feminine. She quickly goes inside but then becomes distracted and, finally, confessional. She is still non-orgasmic. Something continues to block her. We explore possibilities during this and the next session. She allows Christ to extract whatever is blocking her. She sees a pretty cloud that gets dark and stormy as she approaches orgasm. I suggest that she ask Christ to teach her how to touch this cloud at its worse.

Prior to the next session I have an insight while reviewing my notes. I recall an event that Marion shared with me years earlier. As a young teen she had actually begun experimenting with masturbation. One evening her mother walked in on her while she was – very likely, close to orgasm. She immediately felt great shame. Her mother said nothing. She sat beside her on her bed and took her hand and said good night. The mother could not affirm the act – being a devout Catholic in the 1950s', but neither did she condemn it. Yet Marion's reactions have all of the earmarks of shock trauma. Some part of her holds the tension of that near orgasm being cut off by self-shame. When Marion returns I share my thoughts on the matter and suggest that she ask Christ to create a well of sensation and a circle of escape. Christ will use the well to extract the pent-up negative charge from that night. "The first thing I see is a box." I ask Marion whose perception is that? "It is Go-it-alone. She will have to see what we have done. I need to let her be there." But she does not have to interfere? "Right. The shame and guilt is like a bubbling up, like the bubbling of the witch's cauldron. Not good stuff." 'Just let Christ's *Light* absorb it,' I reply. "I feel so exposed and guilty." I tell Marion these are the feelings she felt when her mother walked into the room. "Anytime there is sexual touching I have felt it as pleasurable and guilty; it has always been that way. Now I feel the connection with that event and those feelings. I feel mesmerized by it." I suggest that she take Christ's hand. She responds with a deep sigh and exhale. "He does not hate me for it. He puts his other hand on the dome and draws it all in through his hand. It just isn't anymore. It's not." I ask Marion if this negative energy has kept any self underground? "I do feel an angry self within the guilt and shame. The three emotions are rolled together. I'm angry that I always felt shame and guilt with the arousal." I suggest to her that the anger has to go as well and that she needs to let Christ draw it up the well. "Seeing it in the dome I realize that I have been my own worse enemy. When I was younger and thinner in Boston, one of my supervisors referred to me as a 'bitch in heat.' I loved it. I even knew that he knew I could take what he said. But it was scary." I begin to focus Marion on clearing her sexual energy and emotional chakra of any further impurities. "Christ says there is no need to work on the sexual energy, but what I see regarding my stomach is a neediness that needs to be fed." I ask if Christ can remove the accumulated 'neediness'? "I feel like I need to do it." I ask if that is like saying 'I need to go-it-alone'? "To say that the neediness is there embarrasses me." Even so, I suggest that she let him redirect the well of sensation so it can begin to bring all that neediness to the dome where his *Light* can absorb it. "We are doing it and reflecting together. When I talk about guilt, shame, and anger, I can feel them. They energize my life. I don't know anything else that energizes the way they do." I comment that the three stimulate adrenalin surges. If you mix sex with chi (breathing) you get arousal and orgasm; if you mix sex with shame, anger, and guilt you get adrenalin surges. "I am asking Christ to take the anger and neediness the way he did the guilt and replace it with something – a better diet and physical exercise. It's OK. He did the same thing with his hand and cleared it. I feel empty. I feel like I am looking at myself for the first time in a long time. I don't know what I feel, just me. We have taken a lot of clothes off. I want to like me, but right now I just feel empty. I have never been as unstructured as I have this past year. I ask if she wants it all back? "No." The session ends here.

Marion is doing well. She complains – without any sense of embarrassment, that she is enjoying masturbation but still not able to achieve orgasm. I sense that a basic block is her inability to imagine sexual connection with another person; that she is still trying to Go-it-alone, in large measure from a dearth of experience. I suggest that she go inside and see if she can identify who prevents her from imagining being with another person. "It is the person who feels I should be able to do this without pictures, a feminine side that feels it is natural to women. But all I have are times when John touched me and there is still a lot of guilt around that and hardly any arousal, even then. After last week, I do feel differently about the whole masturbation thing. Now it seems more natural than unnatural. I repressed the feminine because I wanted the masculine power." I suggest that arousing pictures are in the eye of the beholder. I ask her how she sees arousing pictures? "Most people see it as shameful, cheap, not relational, lustful." But then I ask her, 'How does Christ see it'? "They have the power to keep him out of the circle." I am not clear who 'they' is. I ask if 'they' would be willing to subject their judgment to Holy Spirit'? "They are not willing. But I don't want pure lust and animalism to be what will arouse me. That is pornographic." I suggest that she consider evoking Christ at each step in the process. "I am not sure I have that intimate a relationship with Christ." So, I ask, whatever he did would be pornographic? "I have a relationship with him, *but my moral monitors are not relational.* They stand at the gates judging what comes in and out. They are very factual, black and white, full of 'shoulds.' But it is an interesting thought: that whatever Christ did would be pornographic." The session ends here, but I have underlined her reference to 'moral monitors' and hope to pick up on it in the next session. (Unfortunately, the 'moral monitors' are significant in a way that will not become clear for some months. In the next session, Marion and I address Sr. Regina for the first time, but fail to appreciate that this self will endure until she is able to forgo her allegiance to the Temporal and Moral authority of the Church and 'God the Father.')

To fully appreciate this next session the reader will need some additional background. Several years earlier in therapy, Marion identified and worked with four personifications, which are almost archetypal in nature. As each was addressed they joined the others at a picnic table. The first one was Sister Regina, who is the interior sense of her religious persona complete with the habit of her order, and strongly modeled after her father. Another is the Professional woman who is modeled after her mother who went to work when Marion was a juvenile. The other two are sexual. One is called the Lutheran woman who is bisexual, and the other is called the Placard lady, who is heterosexual. All of them were discovered and initially worked with prior to the development of the interventions used in this and the next chapter. Returning to them now will begin to tie up some loose strings and potential. Sr. Regina emerges in this session as the 'moral monitor.' She is a Dominant self and then some, though I still fail to appreciate her role as an Ideal persona. Given her role as a 'model Christian,' she is full of contradictions. When Marion returns she is immediately preoccupied with her financial situation. This morning she heard Christ say, 'be still,' which she understands to mean 'be aware, be receptive, listen.' So I asked if she listened? "No. I am too anxious about my finances." I ask Marion who is stimulating all this fear? "It is Sr. Regina and all of her expectations. She is also the moral monitor. She has standards and requirements." I ask if her thinking is intended to make Marion anxious? "No. It is just her job. She feels I am not measuring up to her standard, which makes her feel ashamed of me. I shame her by being out of work for so long." (In effect, Sr. Regina is also the source of her angst about her loss of 'professional identity.') I ask Marion how Sr. Regina sees shaming as helpful? "She believes it will push me to do something. She uses it to disown me and distance herself from me." I ask if she considers that Christian? "She can rationalize it." I reply that she puts herself out to the world as a model Christian and here she is using shame. "She knows that shame works well with me." I suggest to Marion that she ask Christ to simultaneously convict their shared identity in shame with the power of the Holy Spirit. "I am OK with that but I feel a big 'but' coming from her." (So she is also the primary source of 'buts.') I suggest that she be encouraged to voice her 'but' in Christ's presence. "Christ is looking at her gently. I don't know how to describe it…she is telling Christ he does not get it; that she needs to wake me up to reality. Compassion and the Spirit are not waking me up. It has to stop. He almost feels sorry for her, like the rich young man who walked away from him." I have Marion ask Sr. Regina what her fear is regarding the Holy Spirit? "She is the rational part of me. She believes that *her thinking already is subject to the Holy Spirit.*" What, I challenge, if it is not in this matter of you? What if Christ were to convict your shared identity in thinking? "She is afraid that the Holy Spirit would let me off the hook." I press Sr. Regina by asserting that, if Marion's thinking is in error, the Holy Spirit will correct that as well. "OK. Christ reaches out his hands to touch us both on the forehead. I just need him to keep his hand there; she does too. It is like drinking in strength and compassion. I just want to hold onto his hand, but it feels strange to her. It is a first for her, *slower* for her." I reiterate that she is allowing the Holy Spirit to inject its discernment into the process of thinking. "She is becoming more comfortable, less afraid of it, not fighting it like she was." The session ends here.

When Marion returns she is quick to report that during the week she asked Christ to convict her and Sr. Regina twice a day, everyday. "The teacher is teaching her a kind of gentleness. She is very opinionated, but she is stepping back into quiet. I have stopped wearing a watch. I only wear my Buddhist prayer beads. The time is now. Marion also 'confesses' that she has been going to Mass for several months 'in order to provide transportation for an older acquaintance.' Marion has only attended church sporadically for the last several years. I suggest she go inside, approach the four selves at the picnic table and ask them to help her achieve an orgasm. "My hero is the Placard lady. I admire her now, her acceptance of her body and sexuality. I think it could happen." I ask what prevents Marion from surrendering the Body to her? "It is not a matter of surrendering. I have to become comfortable with my body first. I need to chill out about the orgasm. She is a lot thinner than I am." I suggest that she allow Christ to create a dome containing a template of the Placard lady's sensate body. Then, I suggest that she enter the dome. When she does so she will temporarily separate from her sensate body and merge with the Placard lady's sensate body. When she leaves the dome she will rejoin with her sensate body but retain her experience of the Placard lady's sensate body. "I can imagine what it would feel like. It feels good. It does not feel like me; it feels like I am in somebody else's body; experiencing hers does not make mine any easier." I suggest that she ask Christ how she can use this new knowledge to reshape her sensate body? "I feel a confidence in her body vs. having to prove myself in mine. Her body just is. I don't like feeling inferior to her body." I ask if Christ can use her Body as a template for healing Marion's? "I can learn from her. There is a real connection between her and Christ. She is confident in her relationship with Christ. The session ends here. (Later, in this series Christ will extract the self most closely attuned to the totality of Self that she will call Belonging. In this session, Marion seems to experience that sense-of-self for the first time.)

In this next session, which takes place three weeks later, I broach the idea of Sr. Regina becoming a bride of Christ. For those not familiar with the ritual, most nuns become wedded to Christ as part of their vows and thereafter wear a wedding ring signifying this marriage. Marion reports on her return that she has 'looked in' on Sr. Regina on several occasions and reports that, "She is tired of being the bad cop; it takes away from who she was meant to be." I ask if Sr. Regina would be willing for Christ to convict her role as a bride of Christ? I note that she did agree to become a bride of Christ some years ago (when she took her final vows), but I have no sense that she 'consummated' that relationship. Marion admits that, "No, she has not. She has been wife *and husband*." Is she ready to acknowledge Christ as husband? I suggest that Mary stand with her and aid in whatever way seems appropriate. "I can picture us three (Aware-ego, Mary, and Sr. Regina). I am really just a by-stander. Mary knows that Sr. Regina wants to change her relationship with Christ. It has got to be real. She only knows one way of being. Whenever Christ steps back she is quick to take over." I suggest that the 'by-stander' might be having this problem as well. "I don't know how to make it different." To which I answer: 'You can't on your own.' "Maybe, I need Mary and Christ... Sr. Regina has been much more the masculine. I need Mary to be the feminine in Sr. Regina. The relationship between her and Christ has been missing the feminine. The Spirit and Mary are two strong feminine sources... Hum, what both of us need. Sr. Regina is kneeling in front of Mary and Christ is behind her. Mary has her hands on both sides of my face and tells me the Spirit is mine...it is all very simple...things are in their proper place balancing the masculine and feminine better. The feminine was lost." I ask Marion if it would be appropriate for Sr. Regina and Christ to renew their vows? Marion is agreeable to this but it does not happen in this session. Marion wants to shift focus as we are running out of time in order to discuss the Placard Lady, who she sees as the epitome of feminine sexuality and sensuality. She has felt that the more she focuses on her, "the more I experience her sensate body the harder it is to value her own body." I suggest that she ask Christ to help in the blending of the two. The session ends here. For some reason I am not picking up on Marion's focus on her own body. She is experiencing considerable shame about it.

When Marion returns the following week she begins by sharing her reflections. "I don't feel as hostile toward the church. I am using Jesus more in my prayers. He is opening himself to be something different to Sr. Regina; and she is seeing a different side of his personality. The relationship is calmer. She does not have to prove herself always right or have the last word." She goes on to talk about a job possibility and the feeling that 'she will not be good enough for the job.' I suggest that she go inside and identify the voice that is doubting her ability. "Thinking I'm not going to be good enough feels like a life-long portrait of myself. This self bases her predictions on past failures. She keeps me from being at peace; and she keeps me from giving my all to everything and anything." I suggest that she ask Christ to give this self an experience of trust equal to her distrust. I note that Marion cannot give her this, as she believes her. "This reminds me of a line from John Michael Talbot (a Christian musician): like a child at rest on its mother's knee. Let me reflect on it." The session ends here.

During the week, Marion has been considering applying for work within the church, but returns with the thought that it would not be a good fit. "I don't think I can work in the Catholic Church again." I ask if Christ has something else for her? She goes inside to find out. "We are sitting by the ocean. He is telling me that it would probably be difficult to work in the church unless I changed. He is telling me that I have become global and the church is parochial. He is happy with what I have done so far. He says that the church is very exclusive rather than inclusive; that he has exposed me to something bigger. It is where he wants me to be. The church is bigger than the Catholic Church. He has shown me a bigger world. (What follows will make more sense if the reader knows that Marion has been reading a memoir about Montana and ranching.) He has been holding a rope in his hands while we have been talking.

Now, he tells me that 'whatever I do next...' While he is speaking he throws out the rope and then begins to draw it in. He tells me that he has been letting me go on my own a lot, but now it is time to consciously include him in what I do. It will be easier if I do it by letting him be involved in the decision-making. He is telling me that he is beyond the paper they had me sign (a lot of strictures she would agree to keep if hired to work in the church); that it is just their way of keeping him in a box. I am looking at the ocean horizon, an endless ocean with endless possibilities. I recall a line from a daily meditation I read recently: 'can you trust enough to know that Christ is birthing you each day? It stuck with me." I suggest that she let Christ penetrate her brow and let him supplant her power to fail for the power of his discernment. I note that he has obviously been supporting her throughout the past year. "It is not as complicated as I have made it. We are still sitting. I tell him I give up; that I do not have control any more and I need to put my trust in him. He takes one of my hands with one of his and places his other hand on my brow. He just says, 'be still and trust in me.' As he said that it felt as if I released a breath from my whole being and I can believe he is really there for me. I have not let him be the way we are now. I need to believe, see, and live this experience in-the-world, not just in my mind." the session ends here.

In the next session I am able to move Marion quickly to a focus on trust vs. distrust. All week she has been aware of an 'attack voice.' I ask if this facilitates moderate eating? "Definitely immoderate. When people ask me how I am doing, I tell them I'm ashamed of myself for not working. I beat them to it. It is definitely a voice in me." (It is very definitely Sr. Regina or a variant, but I do not recognize it as such.) I ask if Christ could terminate the voices of the others from whom she anticipates shaming?

Marion is willing to go inside for this reason but once inside she tells me that the 'Attack voice' cannot be put in their circle. She then proceeds to tell me the underlying cause of discomfort regarding her body. "There is a bundle of shame in me, mostly in my stomach." I suggest that once she is willing to give up the power to attack her self that Christ can permanently clear it. I agree with her that it is toxic. "I can feel the toxicity. I can visualize this glob of shame in me and it has a lot of energy. It is always ready to speak and feel." I encourage her to at least ask Christ to draw out the accumulation in her stomach. "When I ask Christ, he places his hand on my stomach. The shaming energy is drawn to his hand like a magnet. I feel heat coming from Christ's hand. The heat is turning the glob from a gray to transparent. Now the energy feels as if it is going into his hand." I suggest that Christ can dissolve it in the salt water. "It is not there anymore. What is different now is my realization that I have a choice to shame myself or not. Before I did not seem to have that choice; I just automatically did it. Often, when we go inside I do not understand what the change will be. Now I understand that it is to give me a choice. Christ gives me a choice. Before I listened to shame and agreed. Now I can have another response. This week I went back and forth between attacking myself and accepting myself. Before, I did not have a choice." I tell Marion that 'external voices' may still try to shame her but if she gives up her power to self-shame their power will be automatically diminished. "OK. I am face to face with Christ. I need his touch. When he penetrates me, what I hear is 'to remember what we are doing, live with it, and remember it.' Again, it is that choice thing. There is still choice even with his discernment. Right now I feel strong enough to not feel ashamed of who I am and what I am doing. But it also feels like it goes against the grain (of Sr. Regina's persona); that it would be so much easier to claim shame instead of love. We are brought up to shame, trained to it, taught it. I have to make this choice conscious in my life." I suggest that she ask Christ to 'terminate the other shaming voices.' "It was not hard for him to do. They were all coming from me. He put his hand toward the circle where all of them were contained and now the circle is empty. The voices came from me; they were all my fears of what I 'thought' would happen. I hope I meet somebody I know today so I can tell them that I don't have a job and smile. I think I will call one of the sisters who e-mailed asking about my recent job." The session ends here.

Marion returns the following week seemingly relaxed. She has job prospects but nothing definite. I ask about her eating? "I continue to eat comfort food. I stimulate the eater by the way I feel." I switch the subject by asking about her sexual activity. "I still cannot fantasize." I suggest that she enter into a dialogue with Christ by suggesting that she ask him if he would forgive her if she used pornography? Or, can he tell her of a better way to arouse and satisfy her self? "I'm the biggest obstacle to the porn stuff (implying that Christ is not). *I have this ideal.* I don't want to be cheap. It is *shameful* to look at porn (Sr. Regina's moral monitors)." I ask what is accumulating the shame in her? And what would it look like apart from her shaming? (Here I envision that she is imagining *something* that shamefully puts her down whenever she imagines her self as sexual.) "Christ says that sex without pornography would be intimate sex." I suggest that she ask Christ to draw a large circle for all of her sexual energy that is bound up in pornography. My assumption here is that her years of identifying sexuality with pornographic images has bound a good deal of energy to those images, even as she has rarely if ever looked at pornographic images. Now I ask her to describe what she sees. "It looks hard, cheap, lustful, animalistic; there are images of men and women who are not emotionally connected." I ask if she can sense any sexual energy in the circle? "There is an animalistic drive between the people and an exhibitionistic part." I suggest that she ask Christ to place a second circle over the first and separate out all of the sexual energy bound up with the 'pornography.' "Now what I see and feel is a calm flow, like a calm river, but not quite. It has a fire to it, but it is directed, not random." Now I suggest that she ask Christ to separate out the emotions attached to the images in the first circle. "They are loud emotions, anger, lust and greed, sadness, hurt, a lack of respect of people for themselves, and shame." I have Marion ask Christ to enter that circle and absorb all of those negative emotions with his *Light*. "It changes the whole picture. Where it was loud, there is softness about it now. The people are not pornographic anymore." I now ask if she will give the 'people' a portion of her *Light* so they can safely connect with the sexual energy in the separated circle. (Basically, I am following the protocol described in Appendix I.) "I am having a problem connecting with them." I remind her that they are figments of *her imagination*, and therefore aspects of her masculine energy and feminine definition. "Maybe, but they are parts of me that I am ashamed of." So, I ask, is there still a 'you' judging them, even as you can see that Christ has changed them? "Yeah." Essentially, the session ends here. I reiterate my conviction that her self-shaming is distorting her perception of the male and female images in the circle that are apparently sexually attracted to each other in a way that is not pornographic. She needs to give up that self-shame in exchange for Christ's discernment regarding what she is seeing. I tell her that I will send her a copy of Appendix I, which may help her to move the process forward during the week. A day after I send it, she sends me an e-mail reply.

The following day I send a reply. Both are give below:

> From Marion: I haven't been able to do this intervention; I don't think I can. I thought I understood what you've been writing and I read it over a few times. Then when Christ and I drew the circle for the sexual energy something weird happened: what appeared in the circle were two separate 'entities', instead of one there were two sides to the circle; what I mean is there was a line dividing the circle in half that made two half circles. I didn't understand it and it has been on my mind. I think I get it. My sexual energy has two sides to it; there's the side that sees sex, arousal, pleasure as bad, dirty, almost repulsive. Then there's the side of it that wants so much to enjoy sex, arousal, pleasure, almost to the point of being promiscuous. (Not that there's much of a chance of that at my age.) It's like each keep the other in check. You mentioned that sexual energy makes no moral judgments so how come mine does. It, the different sides to it, looks different; one side is like a steep mountain range... endless, sharp and high; the other is clear, calm, and almost stagnant. They are both positive in their own right so perhaps there is no judgment after all. I found myself, when I separated the feelings from the memories connected with sexual encounters or whatever we call them, that they themselves were almost identical. Resentment stood out to me in both circles, resentment that each one exists. I find myself feeling angry and emotional when I'm working with the circles right now. Discovering this 'other part' of my sexual energy really bothers and yes, even shames me. So, here I am.

My reply:

> Step back a moment. Remember Pogo: we have met the enemy and it is us'ens. Christ has already separated your sexual energy from the circle – if you are still working with that same circle. He has also separated and absorbed the negative emotions you have accumulated around whatever was in the circle. What you are experiencing now are the effects of your self-shaming. That lens is distorting everything you are seeing. You need to turn that over to Christ once and for all in exchange for his discernment. We have been here before. You know what to do

Marion returns complaining about conflicting voices in her head: "I think I'm so good, and I'm so bad." Whoever it is that struggles with that conflict, Christ has apparently put in a dome and silenced it for the moment. She goes on to recall what Christ did in the last session and later in the week. "Christ suctioned up the negative feelings. That circle ended up empty. I asked him to do something with the 'porn' circle. The two people in it became 'everyday people'." I ask if they are clothed or naked? "The are naked everyday people, but not connected." I suggest that she go inside and ask Christ to convict the two 'everyday people' until they are uninhibited, mutually aroused, and satisfied with each other. Marion remains reticent. So I then ask her to query Christ: In his wisdom, is there any redeeming value in shaming her sexuality? "It is such a habit with me. When I do something sexual I revert to my childhood. What are my parents thinking, what are the nuns thinking? There is the fear that if I don't shame myself then they will." I point out to her that Christ will terminate their authority to shame her if she forgoes her own power to self-shame in exchange for his discernment. "I hear your words, but all of these other people have authority. As a religious I (Sr. Regina) am responsible to others. It is such a different way of living and being, letting Christ be the authority. He does not judge." I inject a reframing here by noting that Christ does judge but much like a GPS that simply directs us to correct our course when we have missed a turn. As Marion reflects on this she has an insight: "I just got this feeling that I was created by God who does not create shameful things. When I took a vow of celibacy, I made sex shameful for me. I closed off a whole portion of myself. Anytime it was awakened, I squelched it with shame; and eventually a part of your body stops growing; it turns black and falls off. I just felt Christ saying that I have stopped paying attention to a vital part of me that not only is OK, but healthy. It is me that makes it shameful, not him. It makes me mindful of a love scene in a movie that brought tears to my eyes. I'll never have somebody touch me with that tenderness and love. I've chosen to not let that happen." All I can say by way of reply is that she is in an ideal position to let Christ touch her in that way; but I stress, not until she can willingly give up her power to self-shame. Nor can Christ convict the 'every day' people until she gives up that power. "If I give it up I do have Christ's discernment. I have been educated to have other authority figures. Never Christ. They spoke for Christ. As long as I have them there seemed no need to hear Christ. Now, at 65 years old, you tell me I don't need the middleman anymore. Everyone else's voice is so loud that the voice behind them is lost. I don't think sex is bad, but I have bought into their beliefs all of my life." The session ends here.

When Marion returns two weeks later she voluntarily reports that she has been comfortably aroused a number of times. I suggest that she go inside and ask Christ to convict whoever objects to freeing her mind so she can fully experience sexual arousal. She can draw a circle of escape for that part, in case it is unwilling to receive the conviction. "Christ and I are at the ocean walking together. He draws the circle of escape. (This seems to be spontaneous on his part; that is, without her asking him directly.) Christ uses a combing through to free my mind. What goes into the circle is a phrase, 'impatient peppermint patty.' Now I see a female figure, not well defined, but familiar." I ask Marion if she values her? "My immediate thought is 'yes'; but maybe I don't. There are times when she may be helpful, like when I need to clean the house. She pushes me to get it done and then it is finished. She motivates me to not put things off, but I can see that she might interfere with the flow of sexual energy. She is a compulsive motivator. Basically, she makes me impatient by wanting things done right now. There is such a gap between her and Christ's discernment. She goes around holding her breath and Christ exhales. When it comes to sex, I know she is around. She wants something to happen quickly, and she has the ability to shame me if nothing happens when she thinks it should. These last two weeks are different. I am getting to know my body, but her shaming does discourage me. I cannot separate her from who I am. I'm still into the idea that I should climax in two minutes. She feels like a microcosm of my whole life, the idea that I want it yesterday." At this point I suggest that she ask Christ to exchange her power to shame with impatience for the power of his discernment. I emphasize that she must let him penetrate her brain to make this exchange. "Wow. He went over to her and I – we, and I remembered when he entered my Heart and held my sexuality in his hand, and OK'd it. He is showing it to her. It is completely OK; there is no blame or shame. She looks at it and it is good. He is imbuing her with that sense of it and re-imbuing me. It is an energy that comes over us both. I need for it to stay in my heart. We both share a total acceptance of it." The session ends here.

When Marion returns the following week, she reports that, "I feel so different masturbating now, like discovering another part of me. Orgasm is no longer the goal, just being comfortable with my body. Christ and I worked with Peppermint Patty in my heart this week. Christ does not have me on a timer, she did." Our conversation shifts to her eating. I ask if she involves Christ in the issue of her overeating? "I am ashamed of my overeating. I don't involve Christ in that part of me. I isolate that part of me." I point out that she has probably accumulated a lot of shame over the issue and suggest that she at least allow Christ to take her to the ocean and draw it out. "I can see myself with the accumulated weight, like a body in a casket, gray and heavy with it. I feel heavy walking into the water with it. The 'grayness is so clear to me. It is the first time I have seen it that way. Christ does not see a need for it. He puts his hands on the thing around me. As he draws his hands down that shape it dissolves. Now there is just a little fat 'me' standing there." I ask if she has accumulated any sexual shame? "I know that I have, but I have been released of that. I justify the weight with the feeling of 'who cares,' the idea that no one cares for me intimately, there is no one I am important to in an intimate way. I need someone who can care for my sensate body. The fat little girl needs touch. Christ is asking me *to step into her completely*. But I cannot totally accept her, the lack in her." I point out to Marion that the 'lack in her' may be what she is withholding from her; that she trusts her judgment over Christ's. I suggest that she ask Christ to convict her judgment in this matter with the power of the Holy Spirit. The session ends here, without Marion asking for Christ's conviction or following his suggestion; but before the day is out I receive the following e-mail:

As soon as I left today I 'continued' our session in my head. I couldn't believe what I had said about "leaving Christ out of this, the Fat girl part of me!!! How could I even say, I 'should' be able to handle this part of me and I don't need Christ to help me. Gads! Did you want to hit me over the head at least, when I spoke those words? I am willing and I will ask Christ to give me his discernment so I can forgive this part of me. I do need to open up the little Fat girl to Christ and me. Just needed to tell you how I felt about what I said.

Over the next two weeks, Marion continues to work with her acceptance of the Fat girl. Concurrently, she has been hired for part-time work that is a wonderful fit for her counseling skills, and will also allow her to volunteer the rest of her time in another ministry. She remains somewhat hostile toward the Fat girl, though she is now coming to realize that this aspect has been the scapegoat for her excessive eating. (If all this seems repetitious, it is; a new sense of self is struggling with this issue.) I suggest that she let Christ raise the Fat girl to adulthood so she can challenge Marion's shaming rather than submitting to it. She allows this. When the Fat girl steps out the circle Christ has created for that purpose, she has a garment of protection and an aura around her. In the ensuing dialogue between Marion and the Fat girl, what Marion comes to appreciate is that the Fat girl takes the shaming to heart (feeling it), while Marion rationalizes it away (thinking). I suggest that she allow Christ to create a circle that can capture all of the Fat Girl's accumulated shame. "When the Fat girl leaves the circle I see lots of goop. When I ask, Christ puts his hand over the circle and all of the goop just disappears. It is not there anymore and he is not ashamed of me for allowing it to accumulate." The session ends here.

When Marion returns, she observes that her eating is better, but she has really struggled the past week with a strong urge to smoke again! She is also feeling irritated at Christ. She feels that, "I am letting Christ take over. It feels like I am coping out." (This is Sr. Regina, but again I fail to recognize her.) I suggest that she go inside and allow Christ to draw a circle that will capture all the shame she generated in past years as a result of her controlling her smoking. "I see a big lobster box in the middle of the circle. Christ invites me to walk through it. The netting is like a combing *Light*. After I exist the circle what I see in the box is a smoky, gray, drabness. As I look at it a lot of things come to mind. There was a lot of pride involved with my smoking, a kind of defiant pride, the idea that I am in control of what I am doing. There is a lot of gunk at the bottom of the box. The smoke represents my prideful defiance; the gunk is my shame. For the last week I have had a choice about my eating. I have been mindful of what eat." I suggest that she first let Christ remove all the negative emotion in the box and then give up the power to judge her smoking in exchange for his discernment. "Christ goes into the circle and picks up the box; it becomes small in his hands. He throws it into the ocean and when he pulls it out it is empty. It becomes large again when he sets it back down in the circle. Now he sits on the edge of it and invites me to join him. He asks me what I want to do with the box? I realize that I have constructed it as a collector of shame. I could walk through it everyday and leave shame in it." I have her ask Christ what would release her from the bondage of this box. "He seems quite clear that the choice is between him and the box. Holding onto the box allows me, and others (i.e. Church authority), to shame me. Christ can touch it, sit on it, but he can't stay there for long. Right now it is clean and free. Why do I want to hold onto this power to shame? With masturbation I feel free of it, no shame or anger. My life would be so different without this lobster box. I am willing to give it up, but I want to reflect more on it too. I want to realize that I have constructed it; that it is my prison box."

(What continues to escape me in the preceding series is that Sr. Regina is an Ideal persona. I have yet to grasp or fully appreciate the archetypal power inherent in any self that is culturally sanctioned and reinforced. In this next session, only when I offhandedly ask Marion to name her higher power do I begin to appreciate the authority underpinning this Dominant self. I expected her to name Christ – as Marion is positively engaging him daily, but she unhesitatingly names 'God.' With careful questioning we both come to the realization that she really means 'God the Father.' I ask other clients the same question and they give me pretty much the same answer. And for all of them, 'God the Father' is essentially an osmotic assimilation reinforced by family, religion, and culture. For the reasons addressed in Appendix II, which are essentially my reflections on the concept of 'God the Father,' I begin to challenge this choice. Most of my clients are open to the idea of making a *conscious* choice, and to that end I write an appropriate prayer to be read by someone on their behalf, other than myself. The major exception is Sr. Regina. For a number of reasons, she has difficulty giving up her allegiance to the Church fathers. It will take Marion six months before Sr. Regina is willing for the prayer to be said on her behalf. In the interim, Marion goes inside most of the weeks I see her. During this period Christ is thoughtfully and graciously present. A part of Marion is acutely aware that 'God the Father' is a poor choice as a higher power, but it is Sr. Regina who must consciously choose. At one point, Marion (Sr. Regina) observes: "When I speak of 'God the Father,' I go to a place of authority and judgment. But what if Christ and the Father are one? The Father that Christ reveals is different from my conception of 'God the Father.' By declaring the Father a person he is made separate from Christ rather than being revealed by Christ.")

The verbatims resume several months after the above session. As I struggle to help Marion find a path forward, I increasingly encourage her to focus on different conceptions of her masculine and feminine. This session begins with a query as to what her father and two uncles (both Catholic religious) share in common? Marion quickly identifies her paternal grandmother. "She was fierce. You did not want to know her. She did not like my mother. She ruled her family. She was a strong looking person, stoic, tough." I suggest that Marion ask Christ to separate out the PGM's masculine aspect. Initially, it looks fearful, foreboding and sad. Marion asks Christ to purify it and offer it back to her. It becomes clear and showers over her. She becomes a totally different woman, laughing and smiling. Marion is astounded. "I saw an immediate change in her. She was released from something. My whole body right now feels like my skin is stretched. To see the similarities between her and I is scary." Marion is struck by how much Sr. Regina is like her PGM. "She controlled her sons. She was dominant in the family. She had religion but not relationship. She was a semi-god. Sr. Regina is doing the right thing. She is following the rules, the laws." I encourage Marion to read St. Paul's letters to the Ephesians and Galatians; to meditate on the difference between law and grace; and how her PGM has been changed by grace. When Marion returns she describes Sr. Regina as defiantly compliant regarding the Church's rules. I ask her, whose rules? "The Church's rules, the Pope's rules, Christ's representative on earth." I suggest that she ask Christ to place a portion of his Light into the Pope's heart and terminate his authority over Sr. Regina. Marion immediately sees the Pope in a circle. He is German (like her PGM). "He is angry. He is holding to tradition. The same dark cloud is above his head. But Christ does nothing." I ask what she sees? "Christ's *Light* is quivering. I know that Christ loves him. The Pope is staunch. He believes what he is saying and doing." I ask if Christ needs the Pope's permission to terminate his authority. "No, but he does not do it." I ask if Christ can terminate the Pope's authority over Sr. Regina? "Yes." I ask if Sr. Regina is willing? "Yes. Christ turns to her, places his *Light* into her Heart. Now, he places his hands on her shoulders. The two of them see the Pope and his army of clergy. It feels different. She does not need that anymore. If Christ is for us who can be against us. The Spirit of God is on our side. Why has she given so much energy to her religion?" I tell Marion that this is not a one-time fix. Sr. Regina must begin to put that energy into her relationship with Christ. When Marion returns for her next session she shares that, "I feel less guilty about not doing church things. Not so judgmental. It feels like I am growing up in my feelings about faith. I do not need all that my religion teaches."

In the next session I have Marion focus on Sr. Regina's masculine and feminine aspects. Christ extracts them. "The masculine is heavy and lumbering, a robot made of steel. The robot seems rule-bound. The feminine is a woman with children gathered around her. She is very loving and nurturing, comfortable and touchy-feely with the kids. The aspects are the antithesis of each other; as distant as they can be. The masculine feels like a burden. It is heavy and plodding with no beating heart." I suggest that she let Christ re-integrate them into Sr. Regina just as they are. "They feel like a conflict. It is probably why she goes to rules and regulations, and what people think. She hides behind those rather than address the conflict. Whenever we talk about Sr. Regina I see her in a habit, but our order stopped wearing the habit years ago. It allows her to avoid dealing with the conflict. Habited nuns don't have conflict, no human parts." I comment that the habit can hide the conflict but not resolve it.

During the week between sessions Marion uses her meditation periods to repeatedly ask Christ to convict Sr. Regina's feminine aspect with the power of the Holy Spirit. "First, she became a spinning cloud. Then I got lots of images of women in the Bible and other places. The idea of clothing became immaterial. There are so many different women and cultures. The feminine is all of these. The robot melted down to an energy source. First it was Christ. Then the Christ image disappeared and it became a heart of pulsing energy. What the women have in common is this Yahwistic energy." Sr. Regina's masculine and feminine aspects have become very archetypal. I tell her that reintegrating these energies directly would greatly inflate Sr. Regina's ego-aspect. Even so, Marion is insistent that something needs to change. "I and Sr. Regina need a change. Her paradigm is the old images of authority and conflict. These new images do not exclude." I ask her to query Christ: can he safely integrate these profound images of the masculine and feminine? "I have the feeling that Christ is bringing me back to the core, what all of us share in common, the creation element. What all of us have the potential to be. All of those women in the Bible are tapped into that. What is basic to them is basic to Sr. Regina as a woman. I got an image of the Great Mother that seems to encompass all of them. She would be all encompassing of them." I am still hesitant to have these new images re-integrated into Sr. Regina, and reiterate my concerns regarding ego inflation. I do suggest that Marion again consider having the prayer said (Appendix II) on Sr. Regina's behalf. My thinking is that is she can shift to Christ as her higher power than he could channel those energies. The session ends here.

My notes for the next session are uncommonly sparse. We talked about dominance. I put forth the idea that Sr. Regina must go from being a dominant force to serving a power greater than her self. Marion comments that Sr. Regina feels her dominance is her institutional entitlement for being compliant with the rules. Once again, I suggest to Marion that she go to a weekly healing service that she has attended in the past and ask the priest – who is familiar with the prayer, to say the prayer for Sr. Regina.[50] I note that Sr. Regina will not allow Marion to go to the alter rail until she is willing. I am very surprised when Marion calls me later in the day to tell me she went to the service and asked for the prayer. When she returns the following week she is different. Her first comments are about Sr. Regina. "The Spirit is holding a place for me, holding the masculine energy and the numerous women on the feminine side. These are two powerful images. Christ knows I need something there. The Spirit will hold them till I find the images or he provides something fitting for what I need."

I feel that Sr. Regina has played a significant role in repressing Marion's sexuality and ask her if there have been any changes in that regard. I begin by asking if she has thought about sexuality during her reflections? Would Christ sustain an image of the feminine that is sexual? "The majority of Old Testament women were sexual. They are flesh and blood people. Sr. Regina is asexual, always in habit…though we did look like women in our habits. I have thought about how those women were used by their husbands sexually, but still retained their own strengths and weaknesses." At this point Marion shifts her train of thought to a book she has been reading about a mother and daughter. It has reminded her of the loss of her mother as a teenager. "There were times in the convent when I wanted to cry about my mother and what I missed." I suggest that if she has that urge to cry, she needs to let Christ hold her and allow the feelings to flow. I then suggest that she might ask Christ to capture whatever or whoever stops her from crying. "I feel ashamed of crying. The first image that comes to mind is something I learned as a child – to be strong and not need to cry. Sr. Regina felt it was necessary to do away with emotions; or the nuns would send her home from the novitiate for not being strong enough." I ask if Christ could draw another circle that could capture her weakest part? "Sr. Regina's strength comes from a need to be loved." I ask if she feels this love? "She feels liked." I wonder out loud what would happen if Marion allowed Christ to give the weak part a total experience of being loved, as much as she could tolerate? Would the strong part object to that? "No, but I can't. I know he loves her." Again, I ask if Sr. Regina is willing for Weak to experience as much of Christ's love as she can tolerate? "I felt her going to Christ, wanting to go to Christ, have him embrace me, I felt it in my whole body. *But I felt it like a porcupine and it reminds me of when I masturbate*. In both instances there is a mental and physical pain about getting that close. I felt it all over my skin. I don't know where that connection came from." I suggest that she return to the healing service and ask Christ to love the weakest part of her. "The porcupine is the weakest part of me." The session ends here.

When Marion returns the following week she has little memory of what transpired. I reflect that Sr. Regina must be amnesic; that she could not assimilate what was learned and had to forget it. Slowly, Marion begins to recall: "Approaching Christ was painful; I related it to masturbation; how painful it gets as I approach an orgasm." I decide to take a different tack. I remind Marion that she has allowed Christ to enter her Heart in the past, and now ask if Sr. Regina would be willing for him to enter her Heart? I suspect Marion hears my suggestion but chooses to stay focused on her train of thought regarding the part of her self that is so conflictual. "There are lots of parts that are good, but not this part." I ask where she hides this part? "Very close to her, in her core deep down. It is so little and so powerful. All of her reserves and authority and independence, her fear of intimacy and strong expectations, all of them compress this part of her into something little. It is in her gut, not her heart." I suggest that, if that is the case, would Sr. Regina be willing for Christ to enter her 'gut chakra'? "From the outside, that part seemed impenetrable, but in the cave it is sparkling and shiny, alive, emanating light. It is not what I thought it would be." I reflect back her realization that 'outside' she is looking at it one step removed; that she needs to get to know it from the inside. And then I wonder aloud, 'How does she feel about masturbation 'inside the chakra'? Marion allows Christ and Aware-ego to enter the gut chakra. "I don't know how to relate to *that*. It looks like a cut diamond, hard and beautiful. I cannot connect with it. It is a dead weight. I don't feel connected to it." It is unclear whose perception Marion is offering. Even so I ask what happens if Christ touches it? "It reacted." She is unclear how it reacted, but she clearly does not like it. "I resent his spending time with this part of me. I could almost get angry at this setup, but I hate saying that. Why is he wasting time here?" I ask who is speaking and shaming? "It is *me*, not Sr. Regina. Sr. Regina let it happen; I am watching." Unfortunately, we are well over time so I have to end the session here not even knowing who has emerged.

In the next session Marion begins discussing Sr. Regina almost immediately. "All along I have associated my sexuality and femininity with another self, the Placard lady (another archetypal figure identified earlier in therapy). But Sr. Regina has more say than anyone else. She is the captain, the ruler. She rules my femininity and sexuality. To her the 'the diamond' are negative traits, that are nonetheless valuable to her because they allow her to maintain her position." I ask what happens when another self gets close to these 'negative traits'? "She plays her superior part, takes control and makes things black and white. 'Its wrong and we do not need to discuss it.' (That is something her father would say.)" So, I ask, she relies on your father's authority? "The way he was, not too loveable or compassionate. The more I work with her the harder she gets, the stiffer she gets. I am not Sr. Regina, but she can cause havoc." I ask if she has accepted Christ as her higher power as it does not sound like it. "In her mind she thinks she is doing the right thing. She has accepted a fundamentalist type of Christ. Not Jesus. Not the Christ that is standing in front of her. She is trying to be in charge of me again. The Christ next to me is not fighting for control of me. I am struggling with her." I ask Marion if she and Sr. Regina share the same heart? "Yes." Then she can follow you if you enter your Heart? "She does not have a choice. We share the same heart." I encourage Marion and Christ to enter her heart. After a few moments I ask what is happening? "I feel the space we are in. It is hard for Sr. Regina to be in this space. She is in the far reaches of the heart. She is not big anymore. I feel sorry for her. She feels very confined, less powerful, and a little scared. I ask if Christ can show Marion the 'diamond' as it is seen within the heart? "It is totally changed. Now it is a block protecting Sr. Regina from us." I ask Marion if she can identify the emotions comprising the block? "Fear is a big one, and anger." I have Marion ask Christ to remove the accumulated fear and anger, then ask what is left? "Sr. Regina is left." What is she protecting with the block? "The only thing I get back is she knows she is not good enough to be loved. They are irrational thoughts. I felt, when my mother died, that she left me and everyone else too. *I disappeared.*" (The desire to 'disappear' is a penultimate expression of extreme shame such as mortification.) What, I ask, was the great shame that made her disappear? "Everybody else had grown up except for me. I did not matter enough." I ask if sex is a part of what she is talking about. At this point I am convinced that Marion is talking less about her mother's death per se and more about how she felt when her mother left the room after saying good night. "Sex is a deep feeling of loving and being loved. I lost someone I loved a whole lot and I still had to grow up. She did not love me enough to stay around till I grew up." I remain convinced that Marion needs to make a connection between the night her mother came in and found her masturbating and the feelings she is expressing toward her mother now. I ask Marion what is the most significant sexual moment between her and her mother? "Her death. She did not love me enough to stay, and I did not love her enough to let her go." I insist that Marion identify the moment. "I know what you are thinking: the time she found me masturbating." How close do you think you were to orgasm? "I just felt good. After she left I was embarrassed and ashamed. I knew it was wrong." Was it unforgivably wrong? "*It was wrong enough that I would not do it again or get caught.*" How did it affect you and your mother? "Not my mother; it affected me. It became a secret about me, a part of me I had to keep secret, the fact that I enjoyed it. When I was sad it became a place I could go for comfort." Who disappeared that night? "The sexual part of me." The session ends here because we are well over time. But I tell Marion that I can see her the following day and she willingly agrees.

Marion returns with a dream: "I am in a habit back at the mother house. I am supposed to interview people who come to the door. A number of them have unexpectedly come with requests and are growing impatient. I have four hats. I write their requests on one of them, but then I misplaced the hat with the names. Two people request to meet with a postulate, Linda Z. I called Joan, the postulate supervisor, because ordinarily people are not allowed to meet with postulates. (Joan is the name of two significant older women in Marion's life.) We talk about the weather and then Joan gives Linda Z. permission to meet with the two people. I told Joan I would find her, but then I became afraid to go back to the group of people because I had lost their names and requests." I ask Marion to share what happened after the previous day's session? "I started beating up on myself. A voice says all this is stupid. I did not go back inside." I began to weave her dream into what she is telling me by commenting that she was afraid to go back to the 'two people' who have asked to see Linda Z. and been given permission by two older women she highly regards. She replies: "I can feel Sr. Regina back in control." In turn, I ask if she is now aware of Sr. Regina's reason for control? I suggest that Sr. Regina cannot be objective and that Marion allow Christ to place her in a circle. Then I ask Marion, what truth is Sr. Regina attempting to hide, repress? "She does not want to look at what we talked about yesterday. Yesterday, I thought about what happened that night with my mother. I closed off a part of myself (made it disappear). Thereafter, I was never comfortable with best friends when we talked about sex. I never really joined the conversation. I could not talk about that part of me. I never talked to my mother or family about sex. Everyone else had grown up. They were married and had sex." I reframe what she has been saying: she silenced herself. Her father, PGM, and Catholicism also silenced her. I ask if she is ready to enter her heart and find the part of her that was made to disappear. I add that Sr. Regina could come or stay behind. "I don't know what that would mean for me at my age." I ask if there is any reason – apart from age, why this part of her should remain perpetually shamed? Marion remains reluctant. I suggest she has two choices: beat herself up for the foreseeable future, or find that part and let Christ baptize it. Even so, she decides to put off entering her heart till the following week. But at least we have agreed that there is a sexual part of her and it resides in her heart. Marion is finally coming to appreciate that it is not so much her mother, but herself and other images of authority that have conspired to suppress her sexuality.

This next session surprises me by its elegant resolution. I anticipate a simple intervention, but Marion and Sr. Regina have their own agenda. Marion begins by reflecting on what she has learned over the past week. "I thought a lot about my mother. Her reaction did have an affect on me. 'I was caught, not good, it was wrong.' I don't like talking about sex or intimate relationships. I really don't have any. When I was with John I was ashamed that he would feel what my mother felt – something shameful about me." I ask who is shaming her? "Me. I am not sure my mother was shaming me then. It was the silence between us that I filled in with shame. I have carried that shame through my life. Sr. Regina is the keeper of that shame. She kept me where I am sexually. She became an institution onto herself, even after we took off our habits 32 years ago. She is hiding from who she is too by continuing to wear the habit. She disappeared into the habit. She is stuck. I turn my sexuality and relationships over to her because she is the loudest. I want Christ to pull her out of the habit, but I do not want her to disappear. She can be Sr. Marion.

She has been a part of me for fifty years. I don't want her to disappear." At this point I suggest a simple intervention that could quickly bring "Disappeared" to the surface. Marion and Christ would enter her heart and she would ask Christ to find Disappeared, baptize her, and bring her to Marion and Sr. Regina. Marion goes inside and Sr. Regina follows them into the heart but remains at a distance. Marion feels a strong need to speak on behalf of Sr. Regina. "Sr. Regina is the key. She wants to be a part of us." I suggest that, if that is so, she can give Christ a portion of her own *Light* as an expression of her willingness. She does so and this brings her closer to Marion and Christ. But now, Marion has another request: Sr. Regina wants to be baptized. I remind Marion that Sr. Regina exercises her own free will so she must make the request. Marion can ask that Christ place a portion of his *Light* into Sr. Regina's heart to terminate any undue influences, but aside from that Sr. Regina must be willing. "I feel sorry for her. She will have to start over. She was so strong and righteous, now she will be on par with the rest of us, but she is willing if a little shaky. Christ is in front of her now. She kneels in front of him. This is the first time. She has always been level with Christ. Now she is humbled before him, connecting with him, needing to ask him for something. His hands are on her shoulders. I am really struck right now with how she really wants Christ, needs him. It is a whole different flavor of her...and Christ really likes her. It is not just love. That is the baptism: a heart connection between the two. It is the first time she has ever knelt before Christ." Marion is silent. I suggest that Christ can help Sr. Regina up, but Marion demurs, saying that Sr. Regina is "soaking it in." Finally, Christ helps her to rise and she goes to stand beside Marion. "When she looks at me, what comes to me is that we can do this differently, live differently." I ask about Christ now working with the part that disappeared. Marion reports that there is an 11 year old in a circle nearby. "It is me before that night. There was a time when I was not guilty or ashamed of who I was. The Placard Lady has also appeared. She is the child grown up. The Placard Lady has always been OK with her sexuality, but I do not bring her into consciousness in a good way. Even though we baptized her months ago, Sr. Regina continued to push her to the back. She was too earthy. Now Sr. Regina is OK with her, she is welcoming her. She wants to get to know her. She regrets now knowing her." I ask who has been carrying the shame all of these years if not the 11 year old? "The child that night became Sr. Regina. She was authoritarian and always right and in charge. She made up for the shame of her body and its desires. She stayed strong and isolated from everybody. I – she – need to get out of that habit. It represents too much of an authoritarian character. She does need to retain the title of 'Sister' and be sexual as well, and capable of deep relationships and open to people." While I agree with this train of thought, I press Marion to discern how the child is to make the transition from where she was before 'that night' to where the Placard Lady is today? How does she make it through that night without having to disappear? How does she cross the chasm? Did she shame herself? "Yeah. She got caught doing something unacceptable and laid it on herself. She was *not scolded*. When I stop and go back to then, I suddenly realize that it could have been an affirming moment...if I had not shamed myself...an awesome moment of my mother affirming my sexuality...like my mother saying 'yes,' this is an important part of who you are. *I remember that she kissed my hand*. That does not say shame, but that is what I saw it as. It was me who put the brakes on, not my mother." I ask if the 11 year old would be willing to give up her power to self-shame in exchange for Christ's discernment? "Yeah. She wants to experience it as I have described it. Christ goes over to her and simply says 'welcome.' He takes her hand and brings her over to the Placard Lady. They embrace happily, as if they have been waiting for each other. I never saw it that way before… now Sr. Regina wants to change her name." I suggest that she consult with Christ. "She wants the child to name her. The child wants her to be called Sr. Mara. When I was a child my friends called me that in a loving, playful, way. It is more open, and definitely less superior. Sr. Regina is OK with this. The session ends here.

***

This portion of the verbatim commences about six weeks after the above session. It is late summer. Marion's sessions have been sporadic as both of us have been gone a lot. Overall, she is doing well, though there has been little movement regarding weight or sexually. This phase of treatment focuses on the redemption of the Familial personality . That self will 'morph' over the following sessions. Initially, Marion will identifying it as 'living safe.' Quickly, it will be identified as 'intolerant,' which describes its denial/shaming mode of being, and finally it will come to be known as Control. In the session preceding this final series, Marion has reflected that she lives a 'safe' life, far from the 'pain' of the masses. In this session she begins with the assertion that, "I've been conditioned to be safe, not take risks. I grew up feeling safe." I begin to suspect that 'Safe' describes her Familial personality, *which emerged shortly after the redemption of Sr. Regina and has been playing it safe in her therapy sessions.* I suggest that she ask Christ to capture Safe. "It is me in my home, age 14. It's me, safe with friends. I see light instead of dark. Christ is in the safe, not in the unsafe." Her description suggests she can imagine 'unsafe' someplace away from her. I have her ask Christ to capture 'the unsafe out there' and place it in a dome. "I sense somebody who is a shadow in the night that could attack me. *He* is violent. He will beat me up. I am alone with him; that is what is scary about it. The figure reminds me that I am alone. He is the source of my fear, and he is within me, and I feel less and less safe." Essentially, the session ends here. Marion has spontaneously identified her reconstituted Familial personality and its archetypal masculine counterpart. Aptly, she calls it Shadow. (Over time, Shadow will morph into the 'bullying masculine.')

When Marion returns the following week, she is both impressed and scared by the idea that, "The shadow character is really me. It makes me mindful of how I seem to 'hang' with people with 'big personalities'." I suggest an intervention based on work I have been doing with another client. I ask her to contain Safe in a circle and Shadow in another circle beside Safe. Then I suggest that she let Christ liberate a truer sense of self by extracting it from Safe and placing it in a third circle. Today, I would rephrase the suggestion by asking Christ *to liberate the self most closely attuned to the totality of your Self.* But my phrasing to her seems to work just as well. Rather quickly, she tells me: "Funny. When he came over to me – my Safe self – he unzipped me and out came this person. She is comfortable in her own skin. Safe had a tough skin. In this person – I could really like her – I don't see any of the aggression, anger, fear, or inferiority that I sense in Safe. If I could give her words, it would be a strong sense that 'I belong here.' That is really important. She does not have the angles, lines, or stoniness of Safe. Her sense of belongingness is so real it is bigger than Shadow's presence. She has an awareness of practical fear, like being cautious late at night on a dark street. With her, Shadow becomes a companion." (Note here, While Marion remains identified with this sense of belonging, her sense of the masculine alters. This happens before I have even suggested that she ask Christ to bring the new self's masculine counterpart into relational consciousness.) Marion continues to 'flesh out' this new self, which hereafter we both refer to as Belonging. "There is a sense that *belonging* can overcome most negativity. Safe does not have that and that is why things are so fearful for her. Belonging wipes out fear." I suggest that Marion refocus on Safe to see if we can better understand her power to enthrall Belonging. I suggest that she ask Christ to put a double circle around Safe and extract the enthralling power. In response, Marion reports that she hears words being pulled from Safe. The first is 'distance': "I keep seeing a strong connection with Shadow that generates a fearful distance between her and others. Another word is 'pride': "Distance and pride give her power. Being safe keeps you from failure. Also, Safe is empowered by anger. Belonging is less affected by externals." The session ends here. I will not see Marion again for three weeks, which is probably a good thing as I have yet to develop a paradigm that might guide us. (Anger appears to be different from Safe, but I will not register that 'fact' for several months.)

When Marion returns, she has little conscious memory of what we did three weeks earlier. I expected this. Safe has regained her dominance and suppressed conscious awareness of what she probably perceives as a threatening perspective. I gently guide Marion to remember. She finally remembers about Belonging and can tell me that, "Belonging has always been an ideal for me." Safe has effectively 'distanced' herself by treating Belonging as an 'out of reach' idealization. Marion's identity with her reconstituted Familial personality is so strong that without the next step of bringing Belonging and her contra-sexual aspect into the Aware-ego's Heart it will be nearly impossible to work free of the Familial personality's perspective. Those steps are realized in the next session.

A week later, Marion returns with a dream fragment: "It is a scene from *The Lion King*. Mufasa, the father, takes his son, Simba, to the highest hill of his kingdom, and tells his son, "Everything, that the light touches will be yours." Marion then tells me that she got very involved with studying The Lion King after having the dream, and even remembered that Christ was the Lion of Judea, which carried her off on yet another track. But now she catches herself and can tell me that her mini-query was engaging, but also a distraction; something that Safe could really get into. I suggest that she go inside and first ask Christ to capture Safe and Shadow in the same circle. Now I have her, once again, extract Belonging from Safe. She sees her as a 15 year old. Now we enter new ground. I suggest to Marion that she ask Christ to 'cast a circle' into her archetypal consciousness, and bring Belonging's masculine counterpart into relational consciousness. "What I see in the new circle is a mixture, of hero, lion, Christ, and warrior. It is a strong, but gentle, presence." The Christ quality bothers me. But Marion assures me, first, that Christ is standing beside her; and, second, that the Christ quality is part of an admixture that includes the other qualities defining Belonging's contra-sexual masculine. Marion goes on to tell me that, "During the week my Safe persona kept looking for a masculine counterpart for Belonging *in the world*, but I kept feeling that it had to be Christ. Christ is strong – like the Lion of Judea, but he would not overwhelm. The "Christ" in the circle with Belonging is the 'Christ of the Gospels.' These two belong together. It reminds me of going home to visit my brother. We hug; I'm home. That is the feeling of what happened when Belonging is joined by 'Christ of the Gospels' only 1000x magnified. Safe is watching this whole thing. She is feeling more isolated than ever, even though Shadow is now with her. Her thoughts are jumbled. She both wants and resents what she is seeing. It undoes everything that Safe and Shadow have put together; it is a totally different way of being." I suggest that Marion enter the circle with Belonging and 'the Gospel Christ.' "I can see Safe in the other circle. She looks like someone with a wet suit that has now collapsed onto ground. There is nothing inside. But Shadow has grown." I ask how Belonging and Gospel Christ have responded to Shadow? "They are calm. I am getting strength from them. Shadow will always exist, but Belonging always was and her masculine is sufficient. In the past, whenever Christ intervened, I wanted the negativity to disappear. But Shadow will always be there. You cannot have the light without the dark. But the weight is on the side of the circle I am in." At this point I ask a crucial question: I have her ask Christ if it is appropriate for her, Marion, to assimilate Belonging and Gospel Christ. "Christ says I need to bring them into my Heart." In effect, Christ and Marion suggest the next step. I have her stand in front of Christ and give him a portion of her *Light* as an expression of here willingness. She does, and all four of them enter her Heart. "Yeah. He did. I don't know what to say." I suggest that she say nothing; just reflect on it. The session ends here.

Marion did her work in the midst of my effort to formulate the paradigm I finally discovered with the help of Tory, Leigh, and Marion. Her verbatims are providing me considerable guidance. The first thing that impressed me was the fact that when Belonging emerges she is much less threatened by Shadow, as if her perspective automatically diminishes his negativity. Even so, I came to appreciate – during Marion's three-week absence – that the 'attuned self' needed her own contra-sexual aspect, which Christ can readily provide. I was also struck by the fact that, when Safe appears to 'evaporate,'(collapse on the ground) Shadow remains. I suspect this is because Shadow is pure archetype, whereas the Safe persona is built on a fabric of cultural expectations that really cannot hold a candle to any self attuned to the totality of Self. But note, Safe only crumbles while Marion is within the circle containing Belonging and while she is feeling her fully and unhampered by Safe's defenses. Safe will return as soon as Marion exits her heart. And Last, I want to highlight Marion/Christ's suggestion that Belonging and her Gospel Christ be brought into Marion's Heart. This is the first time I explicitly used this step, which I have since incorporated as the next step of this series of interventions.

Marion returns the following week. With little prompting from me she begins sharing the changes she has observed over the past week. "At some point it ended up just being me and Gospel Christ. The image of Belonging seems to have merged with me. That doesn't mean I have changed a lot. I do seem to have more insight about situations I am in. I find myself stepping back and thinking 'I belong where I am to do what I need to do.' I feel calmer. It feels better."

When Marion returns the week after I am prompted to ask her if she has a physical sense of her body? "It is heavy, useful, sometimes painful, not too ugly." I suggest that she ask Christ to bring this sense of the body into the Heart with him and Belonging and reconcile the two. "Christ is disappointed in my self-image. He created me to be Belonging. He is disappointed in what I see myself as being." I ask if she would be willing for Christ to intervene on behalf of her body image? "I am not true to myself if I let him do that." I am not sure who is speaking here, but observe that Belonging will have difficulty 'being in the world' if Marion is at odds with her body. "I want Christ to meld them." I suggest that she reflect on this, as my sense is she is trying to make the body disappear. Marion then tells me that, "The sense of body is safer in the Heart; otherwise, I will beat up on it." So, I ask Marion, she is *intolerant*? "Yeah. Christ is protecting it in the Heart." I suggest that she ask Christ to fill the Heart chamber with 'acceptance.' "I already feel safe and accepted there." I suggest that, maybe, what needs to change is her *judgment* of the body; that, maybe, it is her judgment that is distorting her physical sense of self. The session ends here.

The following week Marion begins by sharing a quote from one of Richard Rohr's books: If we don't transform our pain, we will definitely transmit it. The quote has stimulated a lot of reflection about what she could have done had she "been open to accepting" all of these past years. She also owns that she still finds it difficult to talk about her own body. "Intolerance of my body generates a lot of emotions: guilt, shame, pride in its strength; it makes me feel righteous. If I were not intolerant, I could be accepting of it." It is at this point that I suggest a totally new intervention. I suggest that she allow Christ to enter her 'intolerant heart' and she follow him in. I surmise that this is somehow different from the Heart holding Belonging and her physical body. (This is where I finally make the distinction between the Aware-ego's Heart and an ego-aspect's heart chakra.) At this point Marion strongly identifies herself with ego and asks if the ego even has a heart? She believes that the heart is a sacred space. I remind her that the Heart can be polluted, as hers was when Christ first entered it months earlier. "OK. Christ has entered my heart and I have joined him. I get a visual. A place with many strings; connected strings that make it difficult to move around. Some of them form pockets. If I fall in one of the pockets I feel a negative emotion such as shame. The pockets are traps that cause you to fall in them. It is hard to get a clear vision when you fall. When you look up, all these strings are in your way. I am not comfortable standing there with Christ looking at it. I see how stupid it is. I imagine he could just wind up the string." But, I note, you would just generate more. "Yes, the intolerance could bring it back, but hopefully it would be more difficult to layer each time. It would be freeing to not have to deal with my body so intolerantly." We are both clear that this is her heart, not Belonging's, so I suggest that she would need something more than just the absence of intolerance to enter Belonging's Heart. By way of moving this forward I suggest that, first, she allow Christ to collect together all of the strings. "He is doing it slowly, slowing me down, reminding me that changing all this will take some time. Now he has a pretty big ball in his hand; and now the rest of the space is just clear space." I ask her what she would have him fill it with? "I know what needs to be there. The intolerance is wrong. Acceptance and understanding are what need to be there." I reformulate all of her thinking into a single request she can address to Christ: ask Christ to fill the space with acceptance and understanding of your intolerance. "He has done it. I feel it as an invisible force. I know in my head that Christ has done what you suggested." (This is another step of the protocol I will develop based on our work here: the purification of the heart chakra.) I suggest that she exit her heart and now seek to enter the Heart where Belonging and the Body are abiding. "As you suggested that, it just came to me that I've always thought of my body as stronger than me, but that seems the opposite of what we believe or know to be true. Just the same, I have always thought my strength was in the physical body. Maybe, my soul has taken a second seat to that. My body has been a scapegoat. I feed my body to make myself strong, a bulldozer. I also can blame my body, get angry at it. When it comes to all I am, I only deal with this outside layer. I can blame my body instead of tending to what is inside; it is a major source of distraction. Now I am aware of seeing it in layers: the outer body and inner mind and soul; spirit and heart are the deepest layers." The session ends here.

I have made a significant discovery during this intervention. Any self whose heart chakra is not cleared will have difficulty entering the Heart that Christ has previously entered and purified. In Marion's case this is the Heart that Christ purified some months ago, and that Belonging enters with her Gospel Christ because they have a complete sense of 'belonging' there. Marion's sense of body also appears to enter effortlessly, I surmise, because it simply 'is' when freed from Intolerance's judgments. The discovery is actually two discoveries. First, the self that emerges following the entry of an individuated self, such as Belonging, is likely to be uncomfortable for one reason or another if s/he follows the others in. Second, it has its own heart. This can be entered and whatever emotions or beliefs are blocking its entry to the purified Heart can be discovered relatively quickly; and since it is Christ who brings the self into the 'unredeemed' heart he is also available to assist in its redemption. Likewise, any discernible movement toward redemption can be gauged by the self's success in relating to the purified Heart.

Bear in mind, as this next session begins a week later, that Marion and I are literally *discovering* the protocol in these sessions. Marion says that she remembers Christ clearing the space of her heart chakra, but Intolerance still does not like it. I suggest that she cannot enter the purified heart chakra while she is still filled with the negative emotions that attack the body. "Yeah. It feels separate right now, more divided. I can't be whole as long as I have this negative body out here. It is Intolerance's sense of body, but very real." At my suggestion, Marion goes inside to re-enter her heart chakra. "I sense the heart chakra is energized, but something or someone is holding back, some part of me. Christ is offering the heart chakra to me to embrace it, include it and bring it all together. The big heart is where Belonging is. I am not embracing this smaller, but necessary part. My body is in the background behind us." I ask what it is she needs to embrace? "Everything from my neck down. This morning, I am seeing my body as my weakness. I don't know if I can continue to talk about this; I am feeling a lot of shame and anger. It feels too close." I encourage her to ask Christ to release her from the emotions preventing her exercise of free will; to convict her and those emotions with the power of the Holy Spirit. I tell her to just be willing for him to touch her. "Yes, I let him touch me; now I don't know what I feel." Ask him to touch you again? "Ok. I think I feel calmer. I feel almost like a child, the way we were meant to feel. Innocent, in the sense we are OK. Before I started being so negative. But when Christ touched me it was OK. I was OK. I can will myself to be in this space right here, right now. It is a good space, but it is an unreal space. In the real world my body pays for what I think and do not think about it, do and do not do. My body is a visible sign of who I am. It shows what is going on with me." I encourage her to let Christ convict her again. "My body becomes my whipping board. It is always there to be punished." I encourage her to think otherwise by insisting that Christ can alter that perspective. The session ends here.

A week later I ask what she remembers of the previous session? "I remember very well. Belonging has become a grounding point for me. Christ was blessing my body. But every time I step out of her circle a group of 'demons' shake me into reality and ruin everything." (I surmise that the Aware-ego is doing the reporting here and accurately capturing the struggle within Marion.) I suggest to Marion that she go inside and let Christ capture this 'group of demons.' "A clear voice is saying to me that it is a matter of control. I did not want to deal with 'control;' I want back to being with Belonging. I have been eating a lot. I take control by being out of control." I ask her about Intolerance? "It's me, how I see myself." I suggest that she ask Christ to identify her masculine counterpart. "What came right away; it is an almost identical twin, only male. He has more bullying traits and a lack of sensitivity. He is a bull in a china shop." I ask about their relationship? "Intolerance is not very vocal about it. I don't like the masculine." I suggest to Marion that in order for these two to enter the purified heart chakra the pair would have to be stripped of their history: all the developmental layers that have led them to this point. "I am looking at the two images as they are. Belonging is much more of who I am." At this point I weave in the quote she gave me from Rohr to the effect that she can transform them or they will continue to transmit who they are now. Even so, she questions whether conviction will have the desired effect. "It is such a big step." I reply that she can ask Christ to do it in the smallest steps she can tolerate. "So many things they need to change. They don't even like other. They are so out of whack with what we have done, so dysfunctional, separate. I know they are a part of me, but they are so disconnected. But I also know that when I do not treat my body well they are in charge. I become the bully." I suggest that she simply allow Christ to stand between them till she can find an instant of willingness for him to convict. "Christ is saying, 'just let me do it.' I am sitting here trying to anticipate." Silence. I ask what happened? "The air was taken out of both of them; a deep exhale. It is the first time they really looked at each other. They don't really know each other. Christ is still touching both of them. That is why the process is still happening. Intolerance started to feel shame. But Christ has intervened stopping her from going there. It was coming from her head. A greater heat came from Christ's hand, like the overwhelming love of the father toward the prodigal son. I can only feel what is going on with Intolerance. She is feeling exhausted." I remind her that Intolerance's source of energy has been the masculine just altered by Christ. "It is a different kind of exhaustion. It comes from putting up a front as to who she is. The shame kept her standing straight and strong, unaffected and untouched. Christ took away the barriers. It is the first time she has felt love to be who she is, rather than that ramrod of shame and strength. Christ has allowed her to let that go. She reminds me of the woman who came in and washed Christ's feet, that she was able to be that open and he was able to be that open. That is what I feel has happened." I suggest she focus on the masculine but she tells me there is no rush. "He is still there. I just did not know she could respond to Christ that way. I know he is there and she needs to do something. What has happened to her feels so alien. I can't believe it is the same person." Then Marion asks me: "What can Christ do with him?" I tell her it will be primarily determined by what Intolerance can receive from the masculine. "Now I understand what you have been saying about definition, the feminine providing that. I was just thinking about the twins (Intolerance and the bullying masculine); I have provided the definition of how much I was able to receive from him. I was intolerable. I was ramrod and afraid to receive." The session ends here.

The following week Marion comes in and begins by sharing her reflections. "I keep trying to figure out the masculine. Last night I imagined Christ moving the masculine into a circle with him. I got a visual of the Wizard of Oz. A bullying mask fell away and he was just a regular person. I knew that would not be sufficient. Christ pointed to the prodigal son. The masculine has forgotten how much he is loved. Christ is not holding me/him accountable or judging me. I was open that he does love me." I suggest to Marion that she go inside and let Christ convict Intolerance and her masculine while both are in the same circle; that she let Christ convict them till it is painful for her to keep them apart. "It is not painful. There is no reason for them to be apart because of who they are now. But in the real world this is 'too smooth'." I inject here that passion is a natural way of coming together. "Too easy, their whole history just dissolved." I inject that maybe it would be easier to feel pain in separation so she could find a reason to bring them together? "The pain is in their newness. These new images are floaty, not concrete, not a map. They do feel right; the old images feel black and white. The old feels like me. When I just concentrate on them I do feel passion in both of them. Exciting. The old are steady, my back up. I like reflecting on the new. The two sets are different as night and day. The new images are 'comfort food'." I have Marion return to me. She continues her reflection, though now strongly shaped by her Intolerant self: "If I had not come into the session today, I would have gotten where we are by being practical. I don't know where I am. I feel like I have been duped; that I have given myself over to some thing. It felt real at the time, but I don't like where I am now. The old images are in a *square* beside the circle with the new images. I am regressing. The square is making fun of the circle." I ask if any part of her is holding the *Light*? "The new images are holding the *Light*. I am closer to the square." I ask if she has the will to move back and forth? "I am not powerless. When I move toward the circles, I think of last night when the mask came off of the bully, and the prodigal son being welcomed home, and loved enough to want to stay there." The session ends here.

This next session begins with Marion describing a 'bread of shame' scenario: "I feel guilty for letting the Spirit (conviction) work in my life, but everything I am reading talks about God's love." I press Marion to enter her heart chakra and discover what is there. "It is a funny picture: images clamoring for attention, jumping up and down. They are so opposite me; chaotic, attention seeking. They remind me of St. Paul's clanging symbols. If I was loved they would not be there." I ask who is responsible for them? "The practical side; she is intolerant of being loved as God would love me. Conviction would dismiss the clamoring." So, I suggest, let Christ convict and see what the heart chakra is like without it. *Allow Christ to place his Light in the circle with the 'clamoring' and let it be a channel of the Holy Spirit.* (This is the first time I have made this suggestion to a client: that Christ's *Light* be used as a perpetual fountain of the Holy Spirit.) I tell her it is an experiment and she can observe the result. The circle will contain everything so she will not be overwhelmed by what she observes. Silence. Finally, I ask her what is happening. "All of the images are clamoring around the *Light* trying to put it out. They can't. Now they are moving to the edge of the circle. They seem fixated; no longer clamoring." I tell her it is only an experiment. She can ask Christ to remove his *Light*. "I don't want him too, yet. It feels peaceful in there now." I suggest that if he does not remove it, the awe-stuckness might dissipate and they will attack again. "What happens to me? This is in Intolerance's heart. The deepest part of me is with Belonging. Before, they were loud and boisterous; now there is only mumbling, cowering, and embarrassment. They are like the Pharisees in the story of the adulterous woman after Jesus has convicted their conscience. They have lost their individual voices. They are feeling shame because the Light came and found them. Wow. I just got a real feeling of shame. I was 'caught' too. That is a strong feeling." I immediately encourage her to let Christ convict them and her. "I cannot right now. The feeling is too strong. It feels like when Adam and Eve were caught. *I just went back to being caught by my mother*. It is the first time I felt the shame. I never really felt that shame till just now." The session ends here.

Marion returns in much the same state as when she left the week before. I ask her if she can tell me Intolerance's age? "She is a younger person, age 8-9. I see her as an adult, but that is her foundation." I ask her what she has been most aware of this past week? "Intolerance and the Bully feuding would be less scandalous; I don't know how to love that much. Love like that is too much." (She is referring to Christ's last conviction of Intolerance and her masculine.) We enter into a kind of dialectic where I attempt to give her choices; she can agree intellectually but remains essentially intransigent to change. I suggest that she go inside so Christ can show her choices. "All I can see is last week when Christ entered the circle and placed his *Light* in the center of the chaos and everything went to the edges. I don't remember anything from last week but the shame. The shame is powerful, demoralizing and humbling. It makes me want *to supersede it, rise above it*." I ask if she has the power to dissolve it? "I do not think so." What effect did it have when you connected with it? "It made me draw in and concentrate on my head." What created Intolerance? "The power to rise above it. It reminds me of a guinea pig running around a circle. I don't get out." I ask if shame is the foundation of Intolerance? "Yeah (spoken in a whisper)." I ask her if she can imagine Belonging entering her heart chakra in its current state. "No. OK. Christ's *Light* is in the middle of the circle. The crazy things are all around it. I am outside with Christ. I am getting there." But I tell her that we are way over time; and she will have to do it in her own time. The session ends here.

When I reread my notes of the previous session, I find myself reflecting on the concept of intransigence when Marion returns the following week. She has been working during that time. She tells me: "I was outside the circle, but also outside the heart. Christ tapped me on the shoulder and told me to open my hand. It held a cinderblock comprised of the fear of failure. As soon as Christ took it from me, it turned to sand and flowed through his fingers. A dome of light embraced the circle and Christ asked if he could do it his way? Christ says he could love me enough to take care of the circle. He says I always have the choice to feel the shame or look to him. I feel the shame does not belong in my heart, but I don't think I'll ever be free of it. It is easy for me to get angry with the Church because of how often they shame women, and me; how often they lay the shame on us. I am embarrassed that the whole shame thing is in there. I want to put it outside of myself." So, I comment, you project it onto the Church. I suggest instead that she let Christ purify her heart. "OK. We are standing next to the dome. It is warm. I'm just a little scared. Christ moves closer to me. I told him it was OK and that I want his help to get rid of the shame. As soon as I asked the dome became empty. The *Light* and the warmth are still there. Christ is just smiling. I feel like what he has done is show me that I can live without shame. I have this powerful energy from the dome being offered me. I am grateful. It is almost too much, but I am not rejecting it." I ask if she is willing to share this new energy? And then ask her to step out of the heart. I then suggest that she let Christ convict Intolerance and her bully masculine until they are worthy of the heart he has made for each of them. I add, almost as an aside, that this new heart is sexual as well. "I see the bully masculine outside of the dome. Christ asks if I am willing to bring him in as a part of us. I hesitate and then say yes. Christ goes over to him and embraces him." Silence. After a few moments I ask what is happening? "I am just standing there. I've been so rejecting or angry with this person for so long. Christ does not make sense. He is just loving this image. It was dark and now it has the same glow as the dome. I want to stand back and look at what has happened. Who am I now in reference to all that has happened? I have taken on a whole new sense of clothes. I don't have to be ashamed of who I am or what I am. I can say that? It is so out of character for me to say that." I tell her: thinkers assimilate and then accommodate. "Yeah. It is new. If I understood the full impact it would be too much. I have lived with shame all of my life. It is why I fight and run. All because I was ashamed of what I am. Now I have been accepted. I have to go over this piece by piece." The session ends here.

Marion returns the following week, which is just before Christmas. She shares feeling really good. "I feel positive and good. I am trying to get use to a new skin...how awesome it is...to think I don't have to shame myself and I am loved. It is not something I can grasp all at once." I ask if she is tempted to let the shame back in? "It was a 'natural' part of me for 60 plus years, but God loves me. She [God] is not ashamed of me or my actions." I gently shift her to a focus on the Intolerance and her masculine. I tell her that she needs to see herself in relationship with the masculine so she can connect with Belonging and the Gospel Christ. I suggest that Belonging and the Gospel Christ are like a tuning fork; that she needs a 'tuning fork' in her heart chakra that can entrain with them. "I can feel what has happened. Intolerance is a container. When the masculine changed she also changed. But now I also see Intolerance as masculine. It is all masculine." Well, I suggest, maybe the masculine would welcome a feminine counterpart? "The masculine is loving. What I feel is not what I want. It is merely practical and substantive." I suggest by way of asking: What would the Holy Spirit offer as a fit? Adding, s/he might surprise you. "I can tell you exactly what happened. Christ says, let go of your father and take hold of your mother." So I suggest to Marion that she let him convict the images and see what happens. "Thy will be done. There is an immediate bonding of my mother and her new life in me; it is my mother enlightened and offering me the best of her, as a feminine image here in this life. She provides love with the right balance. It is compassionate and relatable; not gushy or over overpowering. The dynamic is synchronous; it works. They make each other better; neither blots out the other." So finally, I can ask if she is willing for Christ to bring this pair into her heart chakra where it will take up permanent residence? "Once they entered heart it was roomy, spacious, open in a good way, bright, warm, welcoming...a lot of things my heart has never been. Belonging and Gospel Christ are connected, but a deeper part of it. Love and the enlightened image of my mother are like angels' wings surrounding me." I tell her that I don't think we can continue to refer to her as Intolerance and ask if she would like to choose a new name? "I would like to aspire to... *compassion*, an openness to self and others. It is so different from how I held my heart in the past: constricted, filtering, and cave like vs. this spaciousness." The session officially ends here, but later that day I receive an e-mail from Marion telling me, that on reflection, she thinks she would like to aspire most to *wisdom*, which is probably a better fit for a well-adjusted thinker.

We pleasantly catch up when Marion

returns after spending the holiday with her extended family. At one point she tells me: "I see Christ more in the (real) world where I belong. I found myself not reacting to stuff or having to get in the last word. I did not have to change my family. Time is slowing down in the sense of what is important. Being there was important, not so much what was said." The session ends here.

***

This verbatim is already long and I wanted very much to end it with the above session. But as illustrated by Tory's verbatim preceding Marion's, there are real consequences to letting these Ideal pairs take up residence in the Aware-ego's Heart and the heart chakra of a personified Familial personality. Two weeks later, Marion returns fearful. The chronic pain in her knees has become unbearable and she is finally willing to get shots that may ease it. Also during the week she has experienced breakthrough bleeding, which she is fearful may point to cancer (or other punishment for using a vibrator). Basically, Marion has always been healthy, but her weight has begun to tell on her as well as her denial that her 'strong' body could hurt or be ill. "I have a hard time dealing with my body (owning it)." I comment that her denial may be a luxury she can no longer afford. I suggest that she let Christ capture her sensate body. She goes inside but then corrects me: "You mean my feeling body, right? I have walked through a hoop that Christ is holding. It is holding a vibrating body filled with fear and shame, denial and dread, and a lack of control. It is a pretty sick body." I suggest that she ask Christ to place the body in a circle by laying the hoop on the ground. I then suggest that she ask Christ, 'What can I do so you can do whatever will make a difference'? "I have a strong image of a door slamming. I tend to deny stuff. I shut the door in my head because I do not want to know; but in denial all I do is spin my wheels." Marion then makes a reference to doctor appointments she has made that she believes counteracts her history of denial. But I tell her that a doctor cannot treat her emotional body. "When I opened that door I was starring at the negative emotions. I don't know what to do about them. I do need his help." The session ends here.

The verbatims provided by Tory and Marion both illustrate an immediate consequence of addressing the Familial personality. In both cases, each client gains access to her 'god function.' This is their least developed function which was previously suppressed/repressed; that is, previously the antagonist of the dominant function. Tory repressed her sensation function; Marion repressed her feeling function. Now Christ is helping them to use both for the *conjoint* evaluation of pressing issues that have so far resisted solution. Frankly, this was a totally unexpected consequence of the process, which is why I feel the need to illustrate it with the verbatims.

By the following week, Marion has gotten shots for her knees and feels great relief. During her weekly meditation she was able to further observe the 'door-closing phenomenon.' "I was able to look around the door. I got a small picture of someone crouching behind it. I felt the presence of Wisdom who calmed me. I started to think that the crouched one is a part of me and that I do not like it. I try to keep her quiet behind the door. I know she is a part of me, and maybe not all wrong. If she could talk to anybody, she would say she is scared. I already have this terrible scenario in my head about what is happening to my body and I could use a couple of people who care." I suggest the crouched one is not polluting the emotional body in the room with her, but she must take the brunt of the pollution. I suggest further that Marion give her a portion of her *Light* and a garment of protection, and allow her the voice of Christ's discernment. "Christ enters the room. He walks over to her, takes her hand, and helps her up. *He gives her a portion of his Light and steps back; he is no longer in the room.* His *Light* is in the room but he is not there. They can see each other but he is not in the room. I don't remember any self ever receiving a portion of *his Light*. Christ is asking her to let him work through her. She is willing. She is standing and confident. She is looking out at all those feelings. She knows she is OK and protected, but it is daunting to look at all of that crap. What is she to do?" I suggest that she begin placing the *Light* into her eyes, ears, brow, throat, and heart chakras. "She went slowly to the top of her head (which I had failed to suggest) and heat went through my body. She is almost illuminated, fitted with Christ's *Light*, stronger. I feel like I have to face each of the emotions, and say out loud that they scare me. They keep the little person in the corner. *I can name them but not feel them*; I only feel the guilt for never questioning my body's need, never taking care of it." I suggest that she address the shame first. "The shame is there because I grew up a tomboy and remained so until I fell in love (with John) and started masturbating. I am scared about this whole thing." The session ends here.

When Marion returns the following week she tells me about her meditations. She now imagines that the two Ideal pairs join her in a circle when she meditates. Christ initially remained outside with the emotional body. "I told Christ that I needed to get beyond it (undefined). He went over to the body and collected gobs in his hand, closed his hand and when he opened it there was just light. Everything went away except shame and fear. He brought those into the circle with the two Ideal pairs and asked if they wanted it. They said *it does not belong in their circle*. He picked it up and transformed it as well. I find a lot of strength in those four. Then I stepped into the circle and Christ put his hand on my head and they joined around me. While I can feel shame or trust in my qualities, it makes no sense to feel shame in their circle. It does not fit them or who I want to be. I go back there a lot." I praise her for her insights and ask about the self behind the door. I surmise that she must do the work of keeping the emotional body clean on a daily basis. "I completely forgot about her this week. She is my alter ego, the person who says 'I need others.' She really wants help and support now. I am just not comfortable with that part of me." I ask her to go inside and ask what her knees are telling her (now that the shots have removed the pain)? "Christ and I are sitting across from each other. He is telling me that I can run away again now that my knees are fixed. In truth, I forgot all about her this past week." I cannot resist commenting, that she really is good at slamming the door on her. "I am going through a purifying process. I do need help. The shots have taken care of the knees, but the whole thing about my body is coming to a head." So, I ask, what is the way forward? Who has the key? "I would like to say me, big and strong, but I have a feeling it is the person behind the door." I suggest that the two of them need to be reconciled; that Big and Strong pollutes the body and will continue to do so since she is the one who generates the shame and fear. "This is old stuff. Christ shows me the self behind the door and – I am embarrassed to say it – when she needed people, they were not there for her. (What follows is a reference to her mother's death.) Everybody was strong, and I was scared of being seen as weak and needing comfort. I shut the door on her then. Her neediness was not acceptable. I was praised for being strong. Whenever I feel the need for help I go back to when it was not acceptable to feel that need. I do not know how to do it in moderation." I ask her, what emotion does she use to shut the door?

"Shame and feelings of inadequacy. Christ says I cannot have what is in the circle (with the Ideal pairs) while I remain dependent on shame and fear." The session ends here.

Marion is suffering from a bout of bronchitis but is able to get to the session and assures me she is no longer contagious. I ask who is feeling the bronchitis the most? "Me, Big and Strong. I did work this week. I asked Behind-the-door to join me in the circle with the two ideal pairs. She feels more deeply than I do. I don't know why I have kept her behind the door." I have her ask Behind-the-door if she can tell Big and Strong why she has the bronchitis? "She says it is cleaning out, getting rid of the junk, which are memories. I keep getting the image of clearing away memories and grudges. At the time of my mother's death, if I had felt deeply then my whole life since then would be different. The last time I felt deeply was when my dog was sick (a couple months back). It surprised me. I did fall apart." I observe that people can put off grief indefinitely, but only at the price of forgoing the ability to feel fully. "The two pairs feel safe and good." I ask if she is with them or only observing them? "When I go to that place I stand and observe. I only sat down when I was with Behind-the-door. I do not want to use that place as a crutch. I know that Christ has given me a portion of his *Light* in the past. If I had his *Light*, I could sit in the circle with them. That was not hard. He came over and gave me a portion of his *Light* and invited me to sit down. My first feeling is that I am surrounded by the feeling of being perfectly protected and loved. I need to feel it outside the circle. Christ is in each of those five images (including Behind-the-door). It is what makes them so huge that they cover me completely. I need to bring this into the world." The session ends here.

This next session, a week later, exhibits all the vestiges of the 'old Marion' in control, but not wanting to be. When she returns, she "confesses" that she was in control of the whole previous session, that she never entered the circle, but remained outside. She observed Christ bringing Behind-the-door into the circle. "Once inside the circle, Behind-the-door sat with each of the four selves comprising the two Ideal pairs. Nothing was said. There was just an energy that past through them. In the end she was still in the circle and I was not. I wanted to make her dissolve into me. Instead, she became one of them. I do not know their place in my life. I know they are important. They are parts of me. I want to model each one. I am surprised she has a place there." So I pose the question to her: how does she express them from outside the circle? Marion has also shared that numerous family and close friends called in response to learning about her bronchitis and she cut each of them short. I tell her at the very least she needs to call each one and apologize for rejecting their overtures. "So, I need to…risk connecting. What if I take the risk and do not connect?" I suggest that she only takes the risk when she actually does connect, when she actually steps into the circle. "I don't feel right sitting in the circle with them. They are such strong images to me. If I really went in there I would be safe anywhere." I suggest to her that maybe she needs to receive the feeling in small doses; that she is really not prepared to indefinitely experience what is in the circle. "How do I do that?" I suggest that she step in and then step out; and whatever is learned she can bring back with her. She briefly steps in and then tells me, "I feel very strongly their openness to me, and abundance, and characteristics of pure love, and no hesitation on their part." I reiterate that she cannot stay there. That, maybe, after ten years of practice she can be in there for longer periods of time. However, every journey begins with the first step. When she first enters the circle all she can tell me at first is that it is overwhelming, but definitely not bad. She goes on to describe the experience: "It is like a miniature football stadium. I am in the bleachers. I have to get up and walk over to them. I do ask Christ for his *Light*. Actually, he is going to come with me. We sit between Belonging and the Gospel Christ. I feel like I want to withdraw into myself. I am embarrassed to be there." I interrupt to challenge whether she really wants to be controlled by that emotion? "No. I feel Belonging strongly. It is OK. As I look at each one, I feel so much *acceptance*." Her face and long silence seem to convey strong cathartic feelings. Finally, she tells me, "I am there for this time. All I need from them is right now. I have gotten permission to be there. No, I am accepted there. They accept me. I need to be more accepting of family and friends. I go into situations with a shield so I have felt unaccepted even before I join with people." Before Marion returns I suggest that she do a part of her daily meditation in the circle. The session ends here.

Marion returns a week later pretty upbeat. "I went into the circle quite a bit this week. It is such a safe place to be. I need to use it as an oasis. I cannot stay there indefinitely; I need to bring it out here. If I can share love and belonging with people I meet out here, then I can be replenished when I go back into the circle." Nothing seems to be pressing Marion so I ask about her weight by way of telling her about the new hypothesis I am developing about addictions. After sharing some of that with her, I ask if she can identify the part of her who periodically thwarts her best intentions to eat moderately. "It is a lonely self. She is like me, but not as sharp as I am, not as confident." Since Marion has gone inside to get a better sense of her, I ask if the self has her own *Light*? "No, but I can give her a portion of mine." I ask if the two of them could enter the circle with the others? "I want to keep her outside the circle. Everything in the circle is good. She is embarrassing to me. My shadow. She is self-pitying. Wow...I just felt this intimate connection between us. She is intimately related to me; my evil twin." I ask Marion if she has held onto the power to shame her? "I know I am shaming myself. I do it because she exists. I can do well with my eating for so long; then I feel something deeper and spin out of control. She allows me to do what I shouldn't do. I know it is wrong to overeat. She is what I know I really weigh, but I have a fantasy that I do not look like her. I deny that we are the same person." I ask Marion to let Christ convict her. "I am afraid of losing her. Where will I find my strength if not there." I suggest that she can ask Christ to simultaneously convict both of them. But Marion is unwilling in this session to do anything more. The part in control is convinced that she needs to keep her 'secret sharer' just as she is so she can remain strong in her denial.

The following week, Marion begins her session by telling me she has started keeping a food journal. I commend her, but suspect this is also an effort to maintain control of the Lonely self. I note that both parts collude in the overeating. One part seeks to 'control' overeating but invariably Lonely 'tips the scales' and once again Marion overeats. One part that is "very rational and disciplined" (Marion's words) fights the desire to overeat, which invariably 'starves' Lonely. Marion replies that, "I don't like the description of her as lonely, she seems to personify nothingness or emptiness. I need to use the circle to better understand her, but there is something missing in that space." I reinforce this by saying that there is a lot of wisdom in that circle. "Why don't I want her in there?" I suggest that any reason she finds in answer to that question, while outside the circle, will only reinforce her reluctance to let her in. I suggest to Marion that she go inside and ask her *Light* for a garment of protection so she can see Lonely free of fear. "OK. I have the garment and I am looking at her. She is always going to be a part of me, and that is my fear. I need to accept that. But how can I feel alone when Christ is with us?" I ask Marion: if Christ does not satisfy her what does she need to feel connected? I encourage her to ask Lonely that question. "She says I have kept her away from Christ. I don't think that is true. She says she is trying to teach me something. She says, if I give her access to the circle, then I think everything will be perfect, but she says nothing is perfect. I think I would be at peace." I challenge Marion: so anything less than perfect is un-peaceful? "Yeah." So she has to battle your perfectionism? By way of answering, Marion complains: "What if I bring her into the circle and then feel her again at some point in the future?" I reply, Well...you could practice humility. Then I ask if it is 'perfect' in the circle? "It is good in the circle." Both of us can agree that good is not perfect, but definitely good and peaceful. Finally, Marion lets Lonely enter the circle, though at first she hangs back just wanting to observe. Reluctantly, she joins everyone. Significantly, her first comment is that, "The six of us are standing around the circle." At first, I understand this to mean she has yet to enter. But no, she is inside with the other five (the two Ideal pairs and Behind-the-door). She corrects me by telling me that Lonely is in the *center* of the circle. "When she goes in she is welcomed by everyone. We are all inside and she is in the middle, the center, she is filling the center. Wow. I use food to fill the center when she is not there. Wow." Marion is having a hard time digesting all of this. "I need to use her rather than reject her. No, I need to accept her. There is a strong connection between her and Belonging, even though they seem to be diametric opposites." I suggest to Marion that there are two experiences of Lonely. The experience Marion is most use to is the one in which she has actively kept Lonely away from Christ and out of the center. The other is the one she is experiencing now. "Yes. Outside, she is isolated and negative. Inside, she is receiving a lot of energy from the others, which is embracing her." I cannot resist injecting here, that perhaps, she *completes* the circle. All of what is going on inside Marion reminds her of a dream she had the previous week which she has been attempting to figure out since she woke from it. "I was masturbating. It was so vivid in my mind. Everything was leading to a climax, but then I woke up because I was in intense pain (in the dream). I was so close to orgasm. I ask Marion to go back inside and ask everyone in the circle to interpret the dream, in particular, to help her identify who was the source of her pain? "Now I remember. There were other people in the dream. I am angry about something... they are not paying attention to me. I masturbate to punish myself. I am mad that I want people to pay attention to me. Control is the actor in the dream. She does not accept that it is OK to want the attention of others. It is a balance she does not have. My thinking self feels something and does not know what to do with it." I suggest by way of ending the session that completeness seems a small price to pay for accepting the moderation of Lonely.

The following week Marion comes in feeling quite satisfied with her self. She has sat inside with Lonely and explained to her how she came to be, how after her mother died she became embarrassed to talk about her death. "I put Lonely aside and developed a tough, stand alone, angry self." I tell her it sounds like her "dialogue" was a monologue. She agrees. I suggest that she go inside and ask Christ for the empathy to understand from Lonely's perspective. "The first thing I felt is she had a sense of not fitting in with who I was, of not belonging. I became ashamed of wanting my mother." I suggest to Marion that she ask Lonely how it feels to be the recipient of those shameful feelings? Maybe, she experiences the events as something totally different? "She loved my mother. I use shame to block her sadness at losing my mother. I don't feel the connection with my mother." I remind her that shame severs connection. I suggest that she ask Christ to convict the shame between her and Lonely. "I am thinking. I am not asking; I am trying to figure it out." I reply that this is an 'action step' that Christ can only take when she is willing; that there is a shameful bond between the two of them that he needs to dissolve. Silence. "He gave both of us a portion of his *Light*. The *Light* he gave us is very specific. The only way we will be able to see and be with each other is by exchanging our *Lights*. We each have a different part of the other. We have now exchanged them. She is to have access to my head and I will have access to her heart. I will put her *Light* into my heart and she will put my *Light* into her head. Yeah, it is a new feeling. She feels...she feels...she feels and I think. We have to blend that. I can see what she feels and that she does feel. But I don't understand it. This is not as big a deal as I am making it. I love my mother. We both love my mother. I can feel it. I don't have to think about it." The session ends here.

The following week, Marion begins by sharing her growing awareness of her feelings over the past week. "I am aware of my feelings; particularly, how I respond to them with anger and frustration. This week I prayed for people who made me angry. I was aware of eating when I got sad and lonely. I was aware of how I screwed up love and relationships in the past. I generally dealt with it by moving away and isolating. Inside, I am aware that the five are a resource that I can use; but outside I expect magic to take over." I suggest that she go inside and ask Christ to capture whoever is the least aware of her need to have access to her inner circle. "It is the part of me that gets angry even before I stepped inside. Anger is my first response to loneliness and sadness. She is my knee jerk response to those feelings as well as intimacy and sexual arousal." I ask if Marion can identify Anger's problem with them? "She has never taken the time to feel them." I ask if she has ever felt her own anger? "I get a visual of her suppressing it and expressing it at the same time." I suggest to Marion that she allow Christ to turn Anger's circle into a circle of effect. "That turned the circle into a chaotic circle. I can see people getting hurt, Anger getting hurt, yelling, screaming, crying. It is what Anger sees and what she is in the midst of. It is the awareness she keeps away from herself. The anger hurts her too, puts her down in the eyes of others and herself. It is hurtful. The circle feels like I am looking at my anger for the first time. How can all of those things be a part of the anger? It is like seeing a rock break open and seeing what it is made of. It is strange to see how screwed up my anger is. I see it as anger, but it is chaos, out of control. It is made of my fear of chaos. Chaos is lack of control. I justify my anger with the belief that I have to stand my ground or I will look stupid or submit to something I don't believe in." I note here that Anger can act out the feeling with impunity because she never experiences the effects of her anger; she is unable to make the connection between cause and effect. Her anger is insatiable and there is nothing to stop her. She has access to consciousness and no need for Christ or the five inside. "I was able to step back this week and pray for the people who made me angry." I speculate that Anger's use of anger may be cutting her off from something, and ask Marion if she would be willing for Christ to help her discover it? "Yes." I suggest she also ask Anger if she is also willing? "Yes. The feeling cuts us off from who we are. Christ draws a circle standing up. I walk through it like a comb. What is left behind is the deepest part of my soul. (Note, Christ created a similar portal a year or so earlier that allowed Marion to step through and approach her soul with a question.) I just know it is that part of me. I feel like I am that close to it." I ask how Anger reacts to it when the circle is brought close to her? "Anger exhales. A sigh of relief. She has no belligerent feelings toward it. It is almost freeing, like bricks coming down around a wall. I just had a flashback. My mother died in July. I was a senior when school began in the fall. I remember hearing some kids talking behind me. One girl said, 'She will always be weird. Her mother died.' I am looking at myself, the part I never became. Anger feels so connected to this part of me in a good way." I ask Marion when was the connection lost? "When my mother died. I knew my mother loved me. I had to be different after that. My mother nurtured me, my soul. She understood me." I ask Marion if she is willing to leave Anger in the circle of effect and the portal containing her soul next to her so the two can work it out? "Yes. I wanted to be like my mother, but I became so unlike her. I really lost her." The session ends here. Marion's Anger is very much like the mental component hypothesized to be responsible for the insatiable desire found in addictions. But in Marion's case it suppresses desire which makes the desire insatiable. It has definitely been an integral part of Marion's behavior for as long as I have known her; and always appears to take over when she seeks sexual satisfaction. In years past it was exceptionally strong and controlling of her behavior. Historically, it only appears to be placated by excesses such as overeating. What is unexpected here is its seeming relationship with Marion's sense of soul.

I see Marion two weeks later. She wants to share her reflections on her mother and I encourage her to express them. "When my mother died I lost a part of me, my feminine side, the nurturing part of her. It has taken me a long time to look at her death. I shut off that part of me and the masculine became dominant in my life, strong and stoic. I don't think I operated that way before my mother's death. I never put together that losing my mother meant losing a part of me. I don't want to lose that anymore and I do have time to change it, to be more like the woman my mother was. I need to stop blaming her death and start honoring her life." What about Anger? I can let go of it now. It was a defense. When my mother died I did not think I had a choice except to become strong and angry." I suggest to Marion that she ask Christ to add pure sensation to Anger's circle of effect. "There is more energy in the circle, a vibration, and a sense of aliveness. I can feel my body getting uptight, withdrawing in the face of the anger, clenching my teeth. That is the effect on my body when there is anger. The anger is conflicted: a push-pull thing, a sense of coming close and pushing away." I ask if there is any sense of gender? "There is a sense of masculine, of trying to be strong, in charge, powerful, but conflicted. I don't like the feelings that go with it. I thought it was strong, but feeling it now there is a sense of weakness. How can it be strong and weak? I never thought of it as conflictual. Even with eating, I take food in and my anger goes out. I always thought of anger as outward, but the sensate part is inward." I suggest to Marion that she allow Christ to capture the feminine counterpart of anger? "The first thing I saw was a very free floating river, confident, the soul image." I ask if Christ can convict them so they can be truly interactive? "Now I have a visual of Christ building a bridge and asking both images to cross over. Now I have a sense of Christ beginning to overlap the circles. The bridge was my sense of it. He is telling me that he is not taking 'choice' away (each crossing over the bridge to the other side). Merging the circles is how it must be done. He is making it possible if I am willing. It is such an odd configuration. There seems to be more physical sensation in the masculine anger than in the feminine. I feel the feminine is at peace and calm; but the masculine can feel more sensation. The bridge is thinking. Not what is needed here. He has taken the bridge away. Now he is waiting for my understanding of what is happening. I am hesitant; they seem so different." I end the session here with the suggestion that Marion reflect on the two circles during her daily meditations. I suspect this process of discovery has highlighted a core conflict. When sensation is added to Anger's circle of effect, it brings its conflicted nature into sharp relief. As feeling, Anger expresses "outward," but as sensation it appears to attack the deepest part of Marion, her very soul, the feminine sense of self. Briefly, Marion seeks to resolve the conflict with thinking, e.g. the bridge, but quickly concludes that this conflict cannot be resolved with her preferred function. Christ will hold the tension of this conflict until she gains the necessary insight. I have not the faintest idea how it will be resolved but suspect intuition will play a significant role.

Marion returns the following week. She tells me about the work Christ has done with the two circles during the week. "I asked Christ to help with Anger. He put a filter or sieve under Anger's circle. Then he opened a part of the feminine's circle from the top; and like the floodgates in scripture, all the yucky stuff in Anger's circle went down through the filter. Now there is water flowing in Anger's circle with three large boulders. They represent good anger that we feel when people are treated unjustly. But I was also aware of being angry at a woman who I saw in the ER this past weekend who was on drugs and had been raped by the person who sold her the drugs. (Marion counsels rape victims). It is easy to counsel victims but hard to work with someone who seemed to bring it on herself. I stepped away from her for a bit and became mindful. My body and soul seemed to come together in the circles and I was able to get free of my anger toward her and be helpful." I ask about the rocks? Are rocks the most suitable form of interaction with the flowing water? "I see them as two different kinds of strength, the flowing water is moving, reflecting, thought…the other strength is the strength of my father. But honestly, that is no longer satisfying. It is more like digging in my heels." I suggest that over a long time the water would dissolve the rocks, but wonder if Christ could speed up the process? "Christ is waiting for me to let go of the boulders. I value the water, its flow and aliveness, but a part of me wants to hold on to the boulders." I suggest that she ask Christ to *name* the boulders. "They are control, courage of my convictions, and stubbornness." I ask if she can name the opposite of control? "Acceptance and Truth." I have her ask Christ if he can add those attributes to control's boulder? "Before he added them, the boulder was jutting out of the water, sharp and uneven. Now it is flattened and just below the surface, like a stepping stone that allows me to step into the water." I ask about 'courage of convictions?' "Christ adds tolerance and the same thing happens to that rock; it also becomes a stepping stone." And stubbornness? "Again, he adds acceptance; now all three are stepping stones. But they do not cross the water. Rather they are aligned with its flow." I ask her to step out onto them. "It feels very freeing. (Silence) It feels. Period. It is how I felt on Saturday night in the ER when I could be aware. I know I am meant to be who I am. Funny. I am out in the middle of the stream. I imagine that everything around me must be beautiful, but this is the spot where I go into the deepest part of me surrounded by love and beauty. I am me, fully alive, with people around me fully alive, unafraid, and unencumbered. Christ is there too. He makes it what it is. It is like my mother brushing my hair as a child, only magnified a hundred times." I cannot resist asking: can Christ tell her about sexuality in that space? "There, sexuality is in the stream; it is different from when I am back here. It is bigger than sex or an orgasm." I ask if Christ could place 'that stone' in the water? "Christ has shown me that the water is sexuality. It is not a stone. It is the water flowing and alive." I comment that his word is gospel. "Yes. Write that one down. And that is good news…I could not resist that." I ask her to put her hands in the water. "It always feels good." The session ends here.

It is the following week and Marion has just returned from her 50th high school reunion, but we barely talk about it. Instead, she quickly relates that she has gone inside a number of times during the past week. She reminds me that, "We ended up talking about sexuality. I would still like to have an orgasm, but guilt interferes." I ask her what emotion neutralizes guilt and shame? "Acceptance." I ask if Christ can capture the self that feels the most guilt/shame about masturbation? "I don't feel guilty about it." I take a different tack by suggesting that she ask Christ to collect into one circle all of the pictures contaminated by guilt and shame. "As I see them now, it is a mixture of feelings, great while I am doing it and guilt after." Who is the self with the memories? "I know who she is. I see her. It is me as a nun in my habit. I feel distant from who she is. I wonder if I keep a little bit of her alive as an excuse. She is my excuse when I do not have an orgasm. *I think it is impossible to have one.*" I immediately sense that a new self has taken charge. I have Marion ask Christ if this is a healthy belief? The new self replies: "I think it is real. I can't hear him." I ask Marion if this self is willing to test her belief in the circle with the water and rocks? "Yes, though she is tentative. She is standing on the rocks. I do not feel connected to her." What is happening here? As soon as the 'realist' steps into the circle a new voice seems to take charge and describe the 'realist' in the third person. The new voice also reports that she 'needs to connect with her.' So far as I can determine, the 'new voice' is a personification of the feminine identified with the water. She will described herself as 'belonging' to it, but Marion will call her Peace. Without knowing who she is I nonetheless suggest that Marion ask Christ to connect the two. "She is now sitting down on the rock Indian-style; and I am sitting next to her." I suggest that she also invite the Nun to join them. "Oh Lordy, she may as well come in. The Realist is starting to get frustrated with everybody. She needs is saying, 'Look, this isn't going to happen physically (an orgasm).' This is her belief." I point out that the stream is experiential knowledge of sexuality. It might help if she entered the water. Her belief will not be altered by entering the water unless her experience of the water is different from her belief. At this point it also occurs to me to ask Marion to identify the woman beside the Realist. "I will call her Peace. She considers the water ideal. It is not a problem or a barrier for her. She can dive deep and swim in it. The water *belongs* to her. She is so whole and complete. The stones are compassion, tolerance and acceptance." I ask if she can bring the Realist into the water? "The Realist says, 'OK, I'll put my feet in the water. I will forget what I feel.' The difference between the two is startling. Peace is very much at ease. The Realist is …very uncomfortable. She says she wants to get beyond her desire for an orgasm. To her the water is cold because she is not at peace. For her to feel peace she must be untrue to herself; she would have to become unrealistic." The session ends here, but I anticipate that Marion will be struggling with it all week long.

As I predicted, Marion has struggled with her 'triangle' throughout the week. "I woke from a dream this morning. In it, everyone was yelling at me to grow up, get over it. I got angry. I wanted to figure it out for myself. I believe that I am unable to have an orgasm." I ask her to identify the consequence of her belief. "Peace feels a part of the water; the Realist thinks there is a time and a place for the water. She is not dressed for the water. She does not want to get messed up by the water. Now she is getting angry." I suggest that Marion invite her to leave the circle containing the water and rocks. "She is always going to get that way and hold everything back with her anger." I suggest to Marion that she let Christ put the Realist in a circle of effect and she focus on the Nun. "She feels different about the water." Is she willing to join Peace in the water? "Where she is on the rock, the water is sparkly and beautiful and she is attracted to it. It is almost a soul connection. I did not expect that of her. I thought she would be more critical." I ask if she would care to join Christ in the water? Could she take his hand and go in with him, robes and all? "No. I know what it is. Peace believes it is more than sex or orgasm. All three of them are part of me. The Nun can look and like from a distance, but she is encumbered by her habit. If she gets in the water her coif will collapse. (This is a starched white band that her order wore around their heads with a black covering over it that was likely to 'collapse' if they got caught in the rain.) It made you look stupid for a week until you could replace it. She has lots of clothes; she would sink in the water. Her Rosary would rust." I fain sadness when I comment that it sounds like Peace will have to swim alone. Then I ask if Christ would swim with her? "I am sure he would." The session ends here.

The next session a week later has a third act quality to it. "I have reflected a lot on the water during the last week, especially at night. I had a dream or something, embarrassing to tell you. The Realist has remained in her circle of effect. I have repeatedly asked the Nun to go into the water. She finally went in frustratingly, after taking off her clothes. Christ was on a sandbar. She swam to him. She was being seductive; that is what it looked like to me. Christ just stood there. That got her more frustrated and angry. She started beating on him. He still did not do anything. She finally collapsed in front of him. It ended there. She is worn out with grief, half in and half out of the water." I comment that her emotions are negative. He accepts them, but how can he respond to her negativity, aside from accepting it. The Nun's negativity would deny the experience of the water. Peace claims it. The water is life. She approached Christ in anger and it wore her out. The Nun needs to apologize and choose again. "She has a fear of rejection." I suggest to Marion that she let Christ place her in a circle and infuse it with acceptance, give her a choice. "But I keep thinking 'you did not love me when I was angry'." I challenge her to explain how he is to love her when she is attacking him, aside from absorbing her blows? He can see through her anger but she cannot. "He could have stopped her, like a parent holding a child who is having a temper tantrum." No, I reply, he could not stop her without going against her free will. Howe does he respond to her when she accepts him? "It has always been a contest about how far she can go, how good or bad she can be, and then asking him to prove he loves her." I ask Marion to tell me what Christ wants from the Nun? "Her anger." I ask Marion if the Nun is willing for her anger to crucify him? (This is the week after Easter.) What else can her anger do but crucify him? "OK. That is a different picture. I have been seeing it in a self-centered way. She needs Christ to love her." Has she ever said to him, 'I need your love'? "No. I always wanted him to read my mind." Can she own her love for him, or will she only give him her anger? "I should be ashamed. Another nun would go to him clothes and all." What has been the problem all of these years? "Anger. But I blame Christ for making me the way I am." So being you is being angry and blaming God? If you choose anger, it will always have the same effect of pushing away and crucifying. Ask Christ, what will cancel all desire to be angry? "He did not say anything. He just opened his arms. She accepts his arms, but it is not who I am. (Notice the immediate shift as soon as the Nun enters Christ's arms. The Realist has immediately taken her place, almost in mid sentence.) I see it as childish. It scares the hell out of me." Now you know the source of all your judgments: fear. "He wants me to go to him more often instead of feeling I have to prove something." What emotion interferes with your relationship? "Pride. I have to be perfect. I have to present a perfect person to him, I cannot need him, he will not want that. I am a co-worker with Christ, on the same plane. He is in charge and I am in charge, both of us working for the same thing. I do not depend on him; that would be a bad thing to do. But for the Nun dependence is a strong thing. Dependence on Christ is like dependence on people. That is why I do not like it. I do not relate to him." I challenge her by saying that as his co-worker she does relate to him. "But it is not what I want." Then what stands between you and the relationship you desire? What emotion? "Pride." So what has to change? What sustains your perfectionism? "My pride and anger. I need to understand this. I need to think about it." I can only remind her that 'thinking about it' will only reinforce the status quo. The session ends here. Two days later I receive the following e-mail:

Question: Is it really as simple as asking Christ to take the anger and pride that has been within me for so long away? The three of us, Nun, Realist and Peace, are on the sandbar with him and are willing, even anxious, to ask forgiveness but there seems to be something else, to just ask forgiveness seems too simple. What else do I need to do?

I am frankly impressed with how quickly the three have joined Christ on the sandbar, but I keep my reply very short: Find the willingness to ask.

This is what Marion tells me when she returns the following week: "Christ called the Realist and Peace to the sandbar. The Realist did not swim there, but she has been changed. The Nun was naked. Christ told her to go back and get her habit. The habit is unaffected by the water even though she swam back to the sandbar with it on. Me, *the observer*, told Christ I was sorry for my anger. I remember asking his forgiveness before. It was a great breakthrough when I asked his forgiveness the first time. I asked him what I could replace my anger with. He told me to use the three people in front of me. The realist was not as stubborn or angry as she had been. I need to use her as my groundedness. I have to learn from Peace that nothing lasts forever. Nunny Bunny...Christ sent her back for her habit for a reason. Last week she could not go through the water as a nun. He sent her back to understand that being a nun does not exclude sexuality as a part of life. These three have replaced the people around the picnic table; they combine all of them. I make progress, but I don't keep on top of it. I know that a few months ago I did something similar with my anger and had moments of enlightenment. But I don't keep it in front of me." I tell Marion my reservations: that I am not clear about the Realist's pride issues. Does she still feel 'I am in charge, Christ is in charge?' How comfortable is she swimming in the water? "It is weird. She was OK on the sandbar. She felt above it all." Does she know how she got there? "He called her." Does she know how she will get back? "She is not as flexible.

I thought she provided grounding, a sense of rootedness. She has a connection with Christ." What is it? "It is strength and conviction, more masculine than feminine. Like a light house." Is she also the light? "Yeah, she gives direction." I comment that she does not need Christ, that she is the light and the lighthouse. Then I ask, of the three, who are you most like? "OK. She is isolated. Now she is in the water. She is walking around in it. But I feel like I have set up an artificial situation; that she will do whatever I tell her to do. We have made her into a monster but she is not. She is not perfect, she is just trying to hold a line or something." Whose line? "I don't know. She is like a bulwark in a storm, only a little bit separate from the others." Separate from who? "From them, from Christ. She believes she gets her strength from Christ." It makes her his equal? "Yeah." She can be like Christ? "We all aim at being Christ-like." I comment that the Nun and Peace have *embraced* Christ. Could the Realist embrace him? "I feel sorry for her; all of sudden she looks very lonely and tired of being perfect; of staying away and not touching people. She really would like being embraced by the other three. She is the part of me that is always hesitant." So, I ask, can *you* embrace Christ? "I know it is about willingness, but it seems to be so much more than that." I point out that willingness in this case includes feeling the effects of the embrace. But we are once again over time. She will have to settle this on her own. When all is said and done, she will need to embrace him in the first person.

When Marion returns a week later she begins, almost immediately, to report what has occurred inside during the week. "The Realist fell into the water. She gave up. Peace and Nun are surrounding her. She is saying to us, 'here I am, now what do I do?" I am aware of Marion functioning as an observer; that is, standing back and observing what is happening and vicariously *experiencing* everything through the Realist. I tell her as much and suggest that she enter the water, swim to the sandbar and embrace Christ. "It feels good, it feels like being home." I suggest that she take his hand and draw him into the water with the others. "He is pouring water over me gently; it is refreshing, nurturing, just feels good. But I do keep getting distracted by them. I feel sorry for the Realist; comfortable with Peace and Nun. I comment that the Realist feels like the 'odd man out.' Marion, surprises me by saying that, "I am very aware of her being feminine now." I suggest that, maybe, she is just not use to feeling feminine. "She is just not use to feeling. I have a sense from her of surrender. She is saying, 'her I am in the water; change me'." It suddenly strikes me that she may not have access to sensation. (This turns out to be the case; and based upon what will transpire, I will apply the same hypothesis to Tory in her verbatims.) I ask if she has access to sensation? "I am not sure. When she fell into the water it was all about what was going on in her head, not her body." I suggest that she return to the sandbar with Christ and allow him to draw a circle that will awaken her sensation function. "I do not think she is afraid of it; rather, it is simply unknown to her. What's happening to her reminds me of a sponge being filled with water, but not fast." I tell her that she has another 30 minutes in this session and the whole rest of her life. "I am watching. I am feeling what is happening to her." I suggest that she might step into the circle herself. "Yeah, I am going to stand in the circle with her and hold her hands. We can do it together. I am very aware of Christ's *Light* generating the sensation. I can feel the heat of the *Light* in my feet on the sand. It is not burning. It is a warm heat. It is beginning to flow up my body and her body as well. This may say a million things about us, but she is not ready for it to flow into her vaginal area; it needs to bypass around there because she needs to feel the sensation in other parts of her body first. The heat is flowing through our arms and around our hearts. It is important that the heat and Light are in our hearts. Our bodies are glowing. Now the heat and *Light* are flowing down to our gut. It is OK for me, but she is getting a little shaky. For her the sensations are new. I am familiar with gut feelings such as nausea. The problem is with its going down further." I suggest to Marion that she give them both a garment of protection from the fear of sensation entering her vaginal area. "I just heard the words, 'stay away, don't go there'." Who is voicing the words? "Everybody, the church, my vows; but not my mother. Her voice and visual are saying it is OK." I challenge these voices by phrasing them as 'this masculine authority' that ostensibly serves on behalf of the Christ within her. "No. my Christ put his *Light* in the circle, got us this far." I have her ask her Christ if the voices are speaking for him? "No, he just smiles as if to say it is ridiculous to think that they do." I ask her, 'Who are your vows intended for,' the church or him? I suggest that she allow him to enter their circle and give them peace in this matter. "I feel aligned with Christ in this." I suggest that the Realist approach Christ within the circle of sensation and embrace Christ. "It is what she has wanted to do for so long. She is in Christ's embrace and a part of us now." I tell her to stay there and come back to me. She is grinning about something but does not tell me what it is. She does tell me that, "It is a big move." The session ends here.

Marion is reflective when she returns the following week. "Sexual intercourse is emotional for me. I do not feel an emotional tie with Christ. I feel Christ's love for me; but I have trouble reciprocating. I don't know how to return that kind of love." I suggest she might want to surrender to it. I then go on to suggest that she has fallen back on her self-sufficient self and it has not had the desired effect. "I do it when I don't feel I have measured up." I ask if she finds 'not measuring up' helpful? "No." I suggest that she ask Christ to help her with her negative thinking. "Going inside I see myself with my back to Christ. I have never seen that before. I am feeling sorry for myself and want to be left alone, but another part of me wants him to come over." I ask who is generating these thoughts? Can she own responsibility for them? (What she will say next has to do with an event that occurred many years ago. She attended the funeral for the mother of another nun. Her father went with her. During the service she felt a strong need for her father to hold her, but she could not ask and he was insensitive to her need.) "When I saw me with my back to Christ, I immediately went back to the funeral of Martha's mother and the need for my father to hold me." I suggest that she is still turning to the wrong source of masculine energy (sic) her father. "I use these thoughts to feel OK when I did not feel OK." I tell her that her solution has isolated her all of these years, and that I imagine her father's soul must be in anguish right now. "I do not blame him; I wish it could be different." Ask Christ if he can remove your power to shame your feeling of need? She is making her moments of need despicable. "I bury them." I tell her that her father was emotionally crippled. "As am I" Yes, I reply, insofar as she follows in his footsteps by mirroring him. When, I ask, did your father ever hug you? "In that circle Christ is my father." I tell her that is a projection, which is turning her to stone. Essentially, the session ends here. Marion remains unable to turn around.

I do not see Marion again for three weeks. She returns to share her reflections: "It took a couple of days to get beyond my last visual. I hate to repeat stuff. But I do get a little further each time. I felt a lot since our last session, instead of just thinking. I have used the picture of my dad and me at the funeral to shape my response to people: I would be a good listener but not open to how I feel about them. But seeing me with my back to Christ is a sad, lonely, image. I remembered the feeling that when Christ embraced me he really embraced me, and that scared me. I ran away from that. Most of my religious life has been spent proving something to myself, in control of myself, self-serving and self-centered. It is supposed to be about transforming life through Christ. I was on the fringe of where Christ was happening. I do not bring him into what I do and who I am. I pray and then I do what I need to do to listen, but not feel. I concentrate on being good and self-sufficient, but not being with Christ. I am afraid to turn around and ask him. I am afraid he will ask too much of me." I tell her that I sense there is a painful cyst in her that has been kept inflamed for years. I encourage her to let Christ provide her a garment of protection against fear and let him dissolve the cyst. But then I reframe my own thinking. I suggest instead that she is wearing her father's defense against feeling; that she needs to let Christ capture it. "He draws a circle around me and when I step out of it, I see this black energy. I feel cold and exposed without it. I feel like a child without it. I don't want to feel like a child who is seven years old." I press Marion to stay focused on the child and her need. "Christ is holding a lamb's wool blanket in his hands. He just wants to wrap her in it and hold her. She allows him to wrap her up. She is exhaling and she turns around and embraces him back, almost like a death grip. She feels safe. The image of me watching them…I do not know what to feel. I feel so ashamed and also that I could also turn around." I suggest that she ask Christ to convict her with the power of the Holy Spirit. "Christ just came up behind me, lays a blanket on my shoulders and turns me around. I know the black energy is gone. I am just enveloped by him and telling him I am so sorry that I carried that inside of me instead of him." The session ends here.

Marion tells me she has had a good week when she returns. "I kept going back to our last session. It was good and comfortable. A part of me would say that it was too touchy-feely, but then I would say it is what I need right now. I know who the other "I" is, she is not connected to feeling." I ask if she would be willing to work with her feeling chakra? Marion is agreeable. I suggest that he have Christ take her to the ocean place with her massage table. Of note, an Observer sees the thinking self on the massage table and the feeling self standing beside it and reports what Christ does with the self on the table. (But I also sense that at different points it is the feeling self that speaks or dominates consciousness.) "Christ is using his hand to warm her body and calm her down. He is getting ready to do surgery without anesthesia. He places his hand on her abdomen and it opens. He is taking out yarn that seems to go on forever, but now it is all gone. I did not expect this. Most of it is just past memories. It looks like dead stuff, kind of repulsive. It does not surprise me that it is dead. She has just held on to it, the part of me that holds onto things. I understand why she has been afraid to feel what with all of that inside of her. It had to dull her senses and feelings, every part of her. How could she enjoy anything? I am looking down the table at her. Christ is finished. It is an empty space; Christ has cleaned out her stomach." I suggest that she get off the table and embrace Christ. "She is not quite as emotional as I was last week. There is still a feistiness in her, but she does hug him, which is more than she has done before. There is no embarrassing shame." I suggest that she get back on the table and now let Christ work with her root chakra, but she is not yet willing to go there. The session ends here.

The following week Marion begins by telling me she has looked up information on the root chakra. "It is the grounding charka, Mother earth. When it is cluttered there is anger and fear and the lower extremities are adversely affected. You don't trust your emotional life when it is cluttered. You are quick to feel fear and can't let go of things like grief. It is the chakra of passion. An unclean root chakra inclines you to shame." Personally, I could not have put it better. But for my part I have finally realized that the reconstituted Familial personality is exercising a degree of conscious dominance and needs to be addressed. I ask if the sense-of-self that observes everything on the inside is connected to Marion's body? "I see her as a head thing, as the intellect. *I see her as me.* Everything takes place outside of her. But it does not feel right. She does not think she needs to be affected by anything, but she does. She has the power to stop the process by refusing to engage in it." I ask Marion how she judges the sexual and whether she has the power to stop it? "I do not want to go there, again." I tell Marion it sounds like her father. "It is cleared up by not engaging it (sexuality)." But, I note, she has discovered there is more to the root chakra than sex. I ask if she has a root chakra in need of clearing? Does she have a horse in this race? Is she connected to the body? I then suggest that she lives vicariously through Feisty (the thinking self who embraced Christ the previous week after emotional self was cleared). To which Marion replies: "I do feel a little superior to Feisty." I tell Marion that I do not see how she can be a 'complete' woman by standing back and just observing. "Yeah, it does feel separate. I did not see till you brought it up. I get the information and impose it on Feisty. But I also keep her from things by being disconnected from the Body." I tell Marion that the Observer lives in the solar plexus unconnected from the 1st and 2nd chakras; that she has done good work as the intellect, but she cannot be sexual or help Cathy lose weight while she remains disconnected. "How do I bring her in, how does she bring herself in, where does she start?" I rephrase her question: how does an observer become a participant? This question prompts a lot of reflection from the Observer. She admits to living vicariously through personifications. The 'thought' of actually entering the heart chakra or root chakra generates an experience of slowness and heaviness. This is probably true as intuition is most suitable for hearing the Soul speaking through the heart chakra; and sensation most appropriate for reading and responding to the root chakra. In effect, she is obliged to own that thinking is not very comfortable anyplace but in head. The session ends here.

When Marion returns the following week she tells me that, "I'm feeling like an empty shell; I do not know where to go with this." I explain that she does not have the functions needed to directly access the heart or body. "I felt like a was making progress; now I feel like I am directing a play and I want to be freer and more open than that." I reinforce that thought by noting that she was only getting it variously through 'stand-ins.' In effect, she shares her identity with ego-aspects; but that only allows her to experience what happens vicariously. (For my part I am choosing to treat her as the unmediated constellation of her Familial personality, altered by the two sets of Ideal pairs placed in the Heart and heart chakra, but otherwise deficit in terms of function.) I suggest that she allow Christ to create two domes. One will provide her an intuitive body and the other a sensate body. Marion, and I presume the Observer, is agreeable, and chooses to first enter the dome with the intuitive body. "I feel like I am in a mist shower, an Irish rain; it is damp and uncomfortable. Christ is a distance from me. I want to call to him, but I don't. I need his help. I can't move.

Why do I have to stand here alone? I can feel the mist getting wetter and wetter. I know I need to call him, to just say 'come.' I don't doubt he will come. It is all about letting go of all the stuff in my mind. I know that if call Christ that I'll be able to let go of all the stuff. It is just letting go of a plan, of having everything in place, my way, my decisions; and being open to changes, surprises and amazement. I know what it means to call Christ to invite Christ in and not trying to be in control of everything. It would be so much simpler in a lot of ways." I hope the reader has been picking up on her expressions of 'knowing' rather than 'thinking.' In any case, I tell her that it only requires an instant of willingness for Christ to come. Then, intuitively, I suggest a solution. I tell Marion to fall flat on her face and let him pick her up. "I did. I did not have to call him. He just came. I do not know how to feel right now. I feel safe. Inside, something important happened." Ask him? "I surrendered. I willingly gave it up. I fell. I had a weighted backpack on me. He took it off and I fell forward. He knew what I want; I did not have to ask." I ask, in turn, if she can nonetheless voice it to him? "I want to give up living in the past, just listening to myself. I want to be free." OK, I reply, but these are just wants. "They are what I gave up. I need to listen to the inner voice I hear and dismiss my rationalizations. I need to want to feel his love and love from others and not have my guard up. I have to see the forest and not just the trees. I need to be what I was created to be." When Marion exits the dome she feels that something is missing. I tell her my surmise that it is the sensation she needs to act in the world, and I assure her we will address it in the next session.

I am gone for three weeks. Marion sends me an e-mail the first week I am gone that wonders if alcohol would loosen her up. She does not say for what, but I surmise it has to do with helping her achieve an orgasm. Even before I reply, she sends another e-mail asking me to not respond to her thoughts. But I do, telling her it might help, but only if she can use it without anger.

Several days later she sends the following e-mail:

> Well, I've had time to think about your suggestion with regard to using alcohol. I hear what your saying and for whatever reason it doesn't sound right for me. I've been praying about it for a couple of days now and something in me, intuition (?), is saying that I've worked for so long now with Christ that I can do this "feeling" thing with him instead. Then this morning I had this perhaps insight that I really DO feel! What I don't do is allow myself to do the feeling. I've been pleasured and felt good about my body, I've been saddened and felt emotional pain, I've felt both and all. What I haven't done is allowed the feelings to remain so that I find the source of the feelings and what is going on in my body when I do feel. I immediately feel embarrassed, shamed, angry, confused, frightened. Then I stop feeling! I can feel but I don't allow myself to do so. And I believe this has probably come up in sessions but I get it, I hope, this time. I haven't stopped praying about this as I haven't 'finished' this part of me but realizing I do feel, 'feels" like a step forward. And so I continue...do you have a thought for me? Marion

I reply:

> Lets agree that shaming emotions stop the feeling of whatever you are feeling. My thought is to ask Christ to provide a dome with a portion of his

Light set in the top. This dome and *Light* will absorb any experiences of anger and shame that would block you from exploring your sexuality with him.

I mention the above because when I see her three weeks later she begins by reporting the work she did with my suggestion. "I went into the dome. Christ's *Light* was above me, washing over me. I watched this film of anger and shame being sucked up by the *Light*. Next, I felt the presence of my mother beside me telling me this is what she wanted for me all along: no shame and no anger. All of this happened to *me*. I ask if she went into the circle more than once? "I repeatedly brought it to mind, but now that you talk about it, I am afraid of the vulnerability in there. I would be vulnerable to…feeling and sensation in there, very much like entering the Heart." But, I add, without stand-ins. I suggest that she needs to become a participant-observer. The dome will provide her access to feeling and sensation without fear of shame and anger. I encourage her to go inside and enter the dome. "There are two of us there now: me and the person who had the wonderful experiences." I suggest that she ask Christ to gently merge the two of them. "I feel like I am in her, that I need to relax in her. I just need to breathe. I am getting more comfortable… the space between us is getting thinner. Christ is doing a kind of Reiki. He is passing his hands around our outer body. I feel energy. I am present as an energy. I am thinker and feeler. I am this energy with the body…thinking energy, the ability to feel the sensate part of me. I have not been this before. I always separated my head from my body. I do see as one. I am a mind inside that body, together. Christ is not done; he is still working. It is all new to me. When I am in the dome now my head is all over me; my mind is all over me. My whole body is thinking and feeling, not just my head." At this point I ask her to step out and assess whether the body comes with her? "No." The session ends here.

When Marion returns the following week she can share that she has returned to the dome numerous times and can distinguish the difference between observing and being present in the body without shame or anger. For my part, I have come to a conclusion regarding her desire for completeness, i.e. orgasm. I tell her that at this point it will be impossible for her to have an orgasm with anyone other than Christ. And that such an orgasm, however it is experienced, must happen in the dome when she is embodied and he is present. I tell her that she must make a new vow to him: Tell Christ that you are alone without him. "In my best moments I do feel that way." Tell Christ that you do not have to pay attention to anyone else's rules; that the body is God's gift for me to decide how I want to treat it. "I never thought of myself as owning my own body. Throughout the centuries people have given it over to others, which accounts for the shame I have felt when I masturbated, etc. I feel free with my body and I am taking better care of it. I will always want to have an orgasm; our bodies are made for that; it is a little late for me." At this thought I remind her that Abraham's Sarah said the same thing….then I add: 'Christ has unlimited access to the universe's resources. Your control is so miniscule it is less than a grain of sand by comparison. Turn it over. This orgasm – however it manifests – will have to be his doing. "Why is it so important to me?" I tell her my conviction that her soul has made it so, and only Christ can satisfy that desire. It is at this point that events begin to seem very synchronous. "I had a dream last night. I was not going to tell you about it, but now I must. I was in a school taking classes. There was a man behind the teacher's desk and another man beside me. The teacher was going to teach me how not to be a person (read personality). The classmates were exuberant about being in the class. I was not sure I wanted to tell it to you." I suggest that she ask her *Light* to identify the males in the dream. "In the dream they are both people I care about. The guy behind the desk is older and the one beside me is younger. Not people I could identify. One teaches and the other participates with me. He was talking to the one next to me. It was all very public, a little too much for me. The guy next to me took me in his arms and kissed me, really kissed me. Something dropped out of my vagina. I do not know what." I suggest she ask her *Light*. " The teacher said it was esoteric. It is a gold disc; I do not understand it." I suggest that she touch her *Light* to it. "It is valuable. I am supposed to pick it up and hold it. I keep seeing the teacher encouraging me to pick it up. I do not understand it." I tell Marion she cannot understand if she does not experience it. "OK. I pick it up." I ask her to name what it means. "A new relationship, a pure relationship." I ask if it has kept her a virgin? "Wow. Yeah, but now it is out. I cannot keep it within me anymore." Who will you give it to? "Christ. It is a golden relationship, almost unfathomable." At this point, I have her come back and comment that it is hers to give, but she can only give it to one person. The session ends here.

Marion's dream seems to synchronize with my assertions in ways that defy chance. Even more so because for years I have imagined that she could only have an orgasm when she could emotionally connect with a male, though I remained ambivalent about that being Christ despite all of my own esoteric reading. But *the morning of the above session* I realized that there are many kinds of 'orgasm' including ecstasy; and (given all of the work we had done and her recent rejection of other options) her image of Christ seemed the only viable image in her mind who stood any change of 'completing' her. The final vows of her novitiate were given to the church, but given in the context of being 'married' to Christ. After all of these years, the church could no longer claim to be 'his representative on earth.' Her body was now her own and she could choose to whom she gave it; in effect, she could now choose to 'consummate' her marriage vow to Christ. Or so I had come to understand it when I told her my conclusion.

I do not see Marion again for two weeks. She has not gone back to the dome in the interval and I have a sense that Sr. Regina has taken over. I tell her my sense of it: when she does not move the process forward Sr. Regina will take over. If Marion refuses to be the bride, Sr. Regina will be the nun. I suggest that she go to the picnic table – where her major selves have always gathered – and query Sr. Regina regarding the consummation of her relationship with Christ. "Sr. Regina says I did that a long time ago when I said my vows." I ask if she said them to Christ or the church? "The church." Who were they intended for? "Christ. I intended the vows for Christ. I see Sr. Regina right now as an adult nun in the church; and I see me as a flaky 16-year-old teenager who is rash and impulsive. Neither of us seems ready to enter the circle where Christ is standing." I remind her that for many years she was "married to her father" (her community allowed her to use her mother's wedding ring when she took her final vows). Currently, she is married to the community (church), which occurred when she renewed her vows with a ring provided by her community (and much prompting by me). But, I stress, neither is a consummation of her relationship with Christ. "You are right. Outside that dome is what Sr. Regina sees. The flaky teen is her creation." But, I wager, the Teen is willing to go into the circle with the coin? "Yes, but I hold the coin. I have gotten so far away from the dome. I remember coming out with no anger and no shame. But I lost the feeling because I was afraid to deal with the shame of being seen as a flaky teen." What are you going to do now? "I need to go into the dome. The Teen is coming with me. I feel like the Teen is a part of me. She is really inside of me. I want to accept her without shame. This is the part of me that Sr. Regina does not like in me, and her feelings overtake mine when I am outside the dome. The Teen can make people laugh, I can be funny delightful, lovable. She accepts the caring of others. Sr. Regina says 'you are a grown woman.' But in the dome Christ loves her, she is whom he wants, though not totally. I can be an adult as well, I can be both, but without having to stand apart like Sr. Regina and her church authority. I am there as the whole person who I want to give to Christ. This time Christ is in the front of us. I gave him the gold coin, but now he is handing it back to me." I suggest that she ask him to transform it into two rings. But Marion tells me: "That is not what it is. He blessed it and gave it back to me. There is something I need to understand about it. I need to know it better. He does not want to change it. I do not yet understand the power in the coin. For the last two weeks I have been distracted. Now, he has given it to me again. This time a part of me will remain in the dome when I come back." The session ends here.

I see Marion the following week. "I went into the dome many times this week. I kept giving him the coin and he kept giving it back. I had to forgive Christ for all the times I got angry at him, like my mother's death. It was meant to be and it has brought me to where I am today. I don't trust Christ. I keep taking control and second guessing him." I ask how she can be intimate with somebody she does not trust? Can Christ convey his trust of you? "I know it." I suggest that both exit the circle and Christ place a *Light* of unmitigated trust into the circle so she can experience it when they reenter. I tell her she must allow Christ to hold her hand so she remains in the first person. "When we enter it is like walking into a fog; I am totally drenched by it. I feel me receiving his trust. It is almost overwhelming. I can feel and see all of the times he has been there for me." (silence) I need to step out of the circle because it is almost too much. Even out of the circle I keep feeling his trust of me. He has always gotten me through." I tell her that Christ can give her the capacity to know what to trust and distrust. Do you trust his capacity to trust you? "Yeah." Can you say: I trust you implicitly to know what to do with this (the gold coin)? "It feels like a big move." I suggest that she ask Christ to infuse the coin with the capacity to trust. "I feel like I am retaking my vows for life…to be able to return that trust. OK. The drama queen did it. I gave him the coin so he can give me just a piece of the trust he has in me. He held it in his hand. It lit up, came alive. And he gave it back to me. He just said: just trust me and then gave me back the coin. It feels liberating. I feel a weight has been taken off me. I don't feel I have to be in control anymore. It feels right." At this point, I question if her, or a personification has enacted all this? "For the past two weeks I have been the Observer. I bring me into the circle." Having answered my question, she then goes on with her train of thought: "I make everything complex because I have to figure it out. If I read the gospels today, I would have a new, different, understanding. He really means those words: 'I am in you, and you are in me, and I and the Father are one.' What is different too is I think I feel it, and yet I know it; and I am not embarrassed by feeling it or knowing it. If I am really going to be in an intimate relationship with him, then I can tell him what I am feeling, even feelings I would not share with others."

This verbatim is continued on the website (the unredeemed conscience.org).

The Import of Dominant Selves And the Reconstituted Familial Personality

I wrote my theoretical chapter on conscience some years ago. Helpful as that theory has been, for many years I remained frustrated in my efforts to help clients actualize a Christ conscience. Gradually, I was forced to the conclusion that it would never be a one-step event; that there were significant layers to be unearthed and addressed. I had to accept that numerous selves would remain quite resistant even after Christ terminated Moral authority at the behest of a Rejected-self. It was only when I focused on the prideful selves, and developed interventions to facilitate their opening to Christ, that I learned to identify Dominant selves and the Familial personality. What stumped me for so long was a myopic focus on dissociation. This is the most primitive of all defenses, and very likely the first defense used by the Ego to cope with shame and trauma. It is found most glaringly in cases of severe physical and sexual trauma, which were my primary teachers in those early years.

Severe shame and trauma in early development will generate extensive dissociation. But the characteristic response of all shame in early childhood is to precipitate dissociation, not just the extremes found in MPD. Moreover, in active imagination, dissociative personification (the imaginal creation of ego-aspects) is easily replicated by the willing Ego as the safest way to explore the Mind by compartmentalizing emotion and belief. What I failed to appreciate was the Ego's evolutionary development; particularly, it's later ability to garner a host of defenses within one ego-aspect in an effort to preempt the shaming of an aural Voice-of-conscience. This defense empowers a Dominant self to repress shameful events within the Heart – and other chakras, rather than being overwhelmed by them. Self-shame is the modus operandi by which a Dominant self represses shameful phenomenon. With that power the Dominant self becomes, de facto, its own shaming conscience. All of these discoveries highlighted the need to address the Empowering archetype's constellational voice as well as its personifications (i.e. parental images and other authority figures). To curtail the activity of the Empowering archetype *in an adult* Christ needs to become the governor of that archetype, which he can only accomplish by purifying the Heart, as the aural Voice-of-conscience is only clearly heard after the Heart is purified. Several interventions are offered to that end. First, a Dominant self is asked to forgo its power to self-shame in exchanged for Christ's discernment. That allows Christ to enter the Aware-ego's Heart and remove the shame found there. Working within the Heart appears to be the functional equivalent of working with the Soul's 'etheric body' or constellational powers. These steps may be repeated a number of times for different Dominant selves (such as Ideal personas). Following termination of the aural Voice-of-conscience, all further work requires that Christ be allowed to work with the heart chakra of each self that is then addressed. Dominant selves are heartfelt gatekeepers. As long as they unwittingly hide their shameful experiences within the Heart/ heart chakras, the Dominant self obstructs the optimal guidance provided by the Holy Spirit and Soul. It is possible for Christ to effect changes in the Heart proper, without entering it, by placing a portion of his Light into the heart chakra of a self, but the Christ conscience process requires that he gain unimpeded entry to the Aware-ego's Heart, which allows him to purify it and terminate the aural Voice-of-conscience. In the final analysis, the test of optimal movement toward a Christ conscience process is whether the Heart is easy or difficult to enter. At any given time the self that impedes entry is the self most in need of work.

The Ideal Persona

In Chapter VI, I identified the infrequent occurrence of a Temporal persona in an extended family. In sharp contrast to this idiosyncratic familial sanctioning, the Ideal persona is *culturally and widely reinforced*. At least I suspect it is much more pervasive than I have documented here as I have only had the opportunity to knowingly work with two of them. While I have worked with ministers, priests, doctors, judges, and army officers in the past, I was frankly unaware of the role of an Ideal persona in their lives. I am sure it was present, but I had yet to discover the prominence of Dominant selves on which the Ideal persona is overlaid. Another culturally sanctioned role I have yet to address are the roles of 'mother' and 'father.'

My theoretical considerations did not anticipate the existence of an Ideal persona other than its 'equivalence' to the concept of Ideal self. I gradually came to appreciate its dominance of the personality after learning to identify the nearly universal presence of Dominant selves. This is a Dominant self that has acquired *culturally sanctioned* Moral and Temporal authority; thus, it generally arises later, when the Ego can aspire to achieve such accreditation. Marion's Sr. Regina is the only example offered in this book. I have only worked with one other client who I was finally able to identify as strongly controlled by an Ideal persona: a doctor whose surgeon persona was clearly infused with archetypal energies.

It is difficult to generalize from two cases, though I have worked extensively with both. But there is ample ancillary evidence to support the hypothesis that Ideal personas are pervasive and very hubristic. Any earned title, e.g. doctor, priest, nun, judge, Army officer, legal counselor, archbishop, senator, general, president, tribal leader, etc. that is generally conferred for life and includes culturally sanctioned prerogatives, is likely to infuse archetypal energies into any Dominant self that exercises those prerogatives. Such individuals are seen by the culture-at-large as qualified to exercise an inordinate amount of Temporal and/or Moral authority. Sr. Regina saw her authority as flowing from every clerical authority in the chain of command from the Pope downward. Most doctors are daily imbued with Moral and Temporal authority by both their patients and fellow practitioners. It is what *authorizes* them to make life and death decisions. The selves embodying those powers are exceedingly vulnerable to hubristic infusions of archetypal energy. Those energies appear to be most easily teased out by extracting the Ideal persona's masculine and feminine aspects. That process is described at length in the next chapter. The more difficult task is convincing the Ideal persona that those archetypal energies must become subject to a higher power. Otherwise, the Dominant self constellated by those energies remains vulnerable to inflation and unwilling to accept the redemptive grace of the Holy Spirit. While an Ideal persona's constellation by archetypal energies goes unmediated, the persona remains in the thrall of those energies; and it can become a dangerous enthrallment for the persona and any who are subjected to it. The only way I have found to dispel those archetypal energies is to ask the Dominant self to consciously accept

Christ as his or her higher power and accept the power of his grace and discernment. A prayer of conscious declaration is offered in Appendix II.

The Familial Personality

The reconstituted Familial personality was neither predicted nor anticipated in the theoretical theses presented in the first chapter. It is a 'reconstituted' existence that only appears to become consciously figural when the Dominant self gives up the power to self-shame and Christ can terminate the aural Voice-of-conscience. It is quite probably the constellation that defines the personality core of most ego-aspects. As Marian's verbatim attests, it appears to morph into different ages. Its original manifestation appears to be quickly incorporated by a Dominant self along with the power to self-shame. In this work it is argued that the Gendering archetype constellates a personality amalgam derived from parental interactions; the Empowering archetype constellates the aural Voice-of-conscience; and the Dominant self personifies the incorporation of both by the Ego. The process of Ego incorporation can be decisively shaped by shameful trauma – as was the case for Marion – but will also emulate the defenses modeled by parents. Characteristically, the reconstituted Familial personality is young, visceral, generally rigid in its defenses to the point of intransigence, but rarely explicitly shaming. It can model visceral expressions of shame such as repulsion, disgust, and the like, but it only has to contend with self-shaming, as the aural Voice-of-conscience is silenced by the time it reemerges. It can be decidedly intransigent, but not dominant. That is, it can be strong, but not strong enough to overwhelm all the changes brought about by the redemption Dominant selves and the Aware-ego's Heart.

The little work I have been able to illustrate in this book vis-à-vis the Familial personality only hints at Christ's power to redeem this personality core. But it has provided my clients and myself with a sense of closure regarding long-standing clinical problems. Entering the Aware-ego's Heart, and purifying it, is the necessary first step. But the space is left empty when Christ exits. It needs a manifestation of archetypal masculine and feminine ideals, which can provide the unifying king and queen of Alchemy. These are the archetypal embodiments most closely attuned to 'the totality of Self.' They are intended to provide a Mind-Soul connection or bridge. In sharp contrast, the unredeemed Familial personality has sought to conform to family and culture at the expense of Self. But once a personification becomes cognizant of the Attuned self and consort, the personification can begin the process of claiming its own Ideal pair, which can provide it an entraining resonance with the Heart's Ideal pair.

In its reemerged state, the reconstituted Familial personality is seen to function as the 'opposite' of whatever sense-of-self is most closely attuned to totality of Self. Effectively, the reconstituted Familial personality contains the 'seed' of that attuned self within it. I deduce this from the clinical observation that Christ can extract an opposite sense-of-self when he is asked to extract the self most closely attuned to the totality of Self. Once identified, Christ can then bring its contra-sexual aspect into relational consciousness. The attuned self and its consort can then be placed in the Aware-ego's Heart with a portion of Christ's *Light*, which is expected to serve as a perpetual fountain of the Holy Spirit. This Ideal pair, in turn, will serve as the entraining 'tuning fork' for any Ideal pair intended to take up residence in a Familial personality's heart chakra.

An Ideal pair derived from the reconstituted Familial personality can provide a 'real world' tuning fork, which can entrain with the Ideal pair in the Aware-ego's Heart. The process of purification and transformation of the heart chakra comprise the final, major steps illustrated in this chapter and the next. Christ's work with the prima materia provided by the reconstituted Familial personality is what allows him to manifest and transform feminine or masculine selves and their consorts into Ideal pairs. Christ is asked to repeatedly convict the personality and its consort with the power of the Holy Spirit. This is expected to gradually transform them into an Ideal pair. Concomitantly, he is expected to facilitate the purification of the personified Familial personality's heart chakra so it can provide a suitable 'abode' for this Ideal pair and a portion of Christ's *Light*, which will serve as a perpetual fountain of the Holy Spirit.

Hopefully, the verbatims offered in this chapter and the next affirm that all of the above is possible, though none of it quickly done. I am reminded of a similar thought expressed in *A Course In Miracles*: we determine the time it takes but not the curriculum. Christ, or a comparable higher power channeling the Holy Spirit, is the mediator of all forward movement from beginning to end. The difficulty for most Ego manifestations is acquisition of the willingness to accept the guidance and interventions of the Christ power needed for each step. Few, if any, of the changes described in this book can be effected by the unaided will. The time consuming aspect of this process is the nurture of our willingness to accept the need for Christ at every turn. Hopefully, the reader has gleamed from the verbatims that this willingness is the necessary prerequisite for all major transformations.

A Summary of the Protocol

Generally, I begin this final series of interventions by asking the client to let Christ satisfy the seemingly insatiable within his or her Heart. Hypothetically, any socially acceptable behavior used in excess points to the presence of something insatiable. Christ is asked to satisfy the insatiable by entering the client's Heart, while the client – as Aware-ego – stands in front of Christ and makes the request (first person perspective). Invariably, a co-conscious self will resist, which sets up the condition for the rest of the interventions.

The clients resist because a Dominant self is sustaining heartfelt repressions by exercising the power to self-shame, and is unwilling to give up that power. It generally takes several sessions to tease out the specific reasons for the resistance, which always include the individual's valuing of the power to repress with self-shame. Of note, at the outset, the client rarely identifies what s/he does as shaming; rather, it is perceived as some form of judgment such as disgust, revulsion, or righteous indignation at weakness. But the root of all such judgments is shame, and the intent is a sustained effort to blunt the activity of whatever is being shamed. Once the particular manifestation of this self-shaming is understood as such, the Dominant self is asked to forgo this power in exchange for Christ's power of discernment. This exchange is necessary because the Dominant self will need an internal guidance system other than self-shame. The exchange can happen in one of two ways. Ideally, the Dominant self remains merged with the Aware-ego and allows Christ to penetrate the brow chakra. During this penetration Christ cauterizes the power to self-shame, and supplants it with the power of his discernment. Most clients will initially resist this direct swap even as they might accept the need for it in principle. The second more viable option is to have Christ penetrate the brow chakra and *extract* the power to self-shame, and place it in a circle in front of the Dominant self (whether that self remains fused or separated from the Aware-ego). The client is made to understand that this extraction only objectifies it. This extraction can be very helpful in convincing the client to proceed, as whatever Christ extracts is invariably noxious. The power of self-shame has no redeeming value when visualized. Once the power is extracted, the client is then invited to let Christ insert the power of his discernment into the brow chakra. The client understands that this allows him or her to experience the difference. As I have already stressed, if the client gives up the power to self-shame, which is essentially a power for controlling behavior by shaming it, then s/he will need a new power for guiding behavior. The power of Christ's discernment can guide the client through choice points, whereas the power to self-shame can only stop specific behaviors. The client is warned beforehand that termination of the power to self-shame generally results in the resurgence of a critical voice that becomes clearly audible once the power to self-shame is relinquished. But wherever this is felt, the client can immediately ask Christ to terminate it. One way of addressing critical voices is to have the Aware-ego stand in front of Christ and ask the Aware-ego to point to the part of the body from whence the critical voice seems to be emanating. Christ is then asked to insert his *Light* there. Another, more powerful, method is for Christ to enter the Heart and terminate any aural manifestation of the Empowering archetype. That is the definitive solution. Such terminations can occur at any time and regardless of how they manifest. If the critical voice is identified as one or more images of others, then Christ can be asked to gather them together in a circle and place a portion of his *Light* into the heart of each.

In terminating the power to self-shame, the goal is termination *forever*. In preparation for that finality, I have invited clients to begin by making the transfer provisional. The power is extracted from the brain center and placed in a circle. Christ is then asked to temporarily insert the power of his discernment so the client can experience the difference. But as I note to the client, the Dominant self will likely reassert its self-shaming once s/he leaves the office. A Dominant self only has permanent access to Christ's discernment when the client allows Christ to permanently terminate the power to self-shame and purify the Aware-ego's Heart. The termination of self-shame becomes permanent when Christ inserts his *Light* into the brow and the 'power' within the circle simultaneously disappears. If the exchange is not done in the first person, then it will have to be repeated in the first person, most probably in response to the emergence of an Ideal persona. But however the therapist proceeds, each step is a step closer to the goal of the client more fully accepting the guidance of Christ's discernment.

Once Christ's discernment is in place, the client is generally comfortable enough to ask Christ to enter the Heart and heal whatever is found there. Christ does this by literally pushing into the Aware-ego's Heart as if it was a portal. The Aware-ego is expected to follow him in with or without the Dominant self in attendance. Even if separated from the Aware-ego, a Dominant self remains mentally tied to the experience via the Aware-ego. A co-conscious sense-of-self will continue to be threatened by any shame within the Heart, and whether conscious of it or not, s/he will also be fearful of the aural Voice-of-conscience that expresses the Empowering archetype from within the Heart (at least until the voice is cauterized by Christ). For those reasons, any co-conscious self is strongly encouraged to assume a garment of protection and only expected to experience Heart entry mentally. Again, it is most desirable if this can be done in the first person, but in the first series of interventions, even working with a separated co-conscious self will have a telling effect on the client. Almost immediately, the client can describe an inner space, quite often a cave or cavern, or a space that has the definite characteristics of an interior space. Once inside Christ is asked to seek out the shameful core and baptize it in whatever form it manifests. Finally, he is asked to leave a portion of his Light within the Heart when he and the Aware-ego exit and return to the therapist. His *Light* is expected to function as a perpetual fountain of the Holy Spirit.

A phenomenal perspective may be helpful here. In this first series of interventions we are working with the Dominant self. The goal is to gain the Dominant self's willingness to allow Christ's entry into the Aware-ego's Heart. But quite honestly, once the Dominant self has relinquished its power to self-shame, it is hard to tell who is the actor. The Aware-ego, a Dominant self, even the reconstituted Familial personality, may be co-conscious with whoever is exercising willingness while the client is engaged in the process. That is why, in the above paragraph, I refer to whoever it is as the 'conscious self.' That sense-of-self can change from moment to moment. The issue is one of willingness vs. resistance. The Aware-ego and Dominant self can both express willingness at this point, and any number of other selves, including the Dominant self or Ideal persona can express resistance. If there is no resistance, then Christ can easily enter the Heart of the Aware-ego. But I suspect that a substantial part of the Dominant self hangs back; that it only enters mentally. The Dominant self, or its successor – the reconstituted Familial personality – must first allow its own heart chakra to be purified before it could comfortably enter the Aware-ego's Heart. Labels, such as 'Dominant self,' are helpful for distinguishing kinds of selves and their characteristics, but in the midst of the process, the 'conscious self' is in charge, whether this is the Aware-ego, Dominant self, or someone else; and who it is can change from moment to moment. For that reason, I hope for willingness and stay alert for resistance. If a circle of escape or garment of protection cannot quickly address resistance then it will usually be necessary to ask Christ to draw a capturing circle in order to identify the source of resistance and gain the cooperation of that part of the Ego.

In successive sessions after the initial entry into the Heart, a number of issues will have to be addressed. If the power to self-shame is only extracted provisionally, then the Dominant self must ask Christ to absorb it *forever*. The Dominant self then needs to be reconciled with the inner core, if it has manifested as a self. Finally, the client is asked to *reenter* the Heart in the first person. This suggestion will eventually stimulate the resistive presence of the reconstituted Familial personality (e.g. Tory's Manager) or Ideal persona (e.g. Marion's Sr. Regina) that has emerged following the redemption of the Heart. Suggesting reentry into the Heart is actually the best way of discovering who has emerged to supplant the redeemed Dominant self.

Working with an Ideal persona and/or reconstituted Familial personality will be as time consuming as working with the Dominant self. Often, its power to self-shame is 'augmented' by more primitive defenses such as shaming anger, denial, distrust, forgetting, depersonalization, or sense of entitlement. A personified Familial personality tends to work from the gut and the brain and both must be addressed. All of these 'lesser powers' must also be extracted and given over to Christ in exchange for the power of his discernment. But the fruits of this particular labor are significant. And frankly, in practice, they are unavoidable if client and therapist are seeking closure for long standing issues.

RE-ENTERING THE HEART

As the foregoing verbatims illustrate, most clients will actively resist entering their Heart when it is first suggested. But once done, the client knows s/he has experienced something valuable and repeatable. After s/he has done it once, the ongoing goal of therapy is the facilitation of re-entry for all of the purposes described above. Other ego-aspects will emerge to resist re-entry for a number of reasons. But that resistance is now counterbalanced by the client's *experience*. Now s/he knows it is possible and rewarding. Even a resistant self shares a heartfelt connection with the Heart of the Aware-ego via its own heart chakra. If the Aware-ego is willing for Christ to enter its Heart, the resistant ego-aspect is more or less obliged to experience whatever is happening. Normally, an ego-aspect can follow Christ and the Aware-ego into the Heart chamber via a mental or sensory connection with the Aware-ego, or the experience as derived from memory. Entering the Heart shifts perception. The Heart's interior frequently provides a better understanding of the distorted perspective held by a resistant self. While willfully functioning exterior to the Heart, a sense of self can seem to dominate consciousness, but s/he looses much of that dominance when seen from within.

Once a client's Aware-ego has penetrated the Heart with Christ, a totally new dimension is added to the work. Thereafter, even though the client 'goes inside' s/he will be outside of the Heart or willingly in it. From the perspective of active imagination, everything exterior to the Heart then seems to become an extroverted perspective, while entry into the Heart and its chakras becomes a truer sense of the Mind's 'interior.' Entering the Heart or heart chakra is possibly the ultimate expression of the Mind's permeability. I have only begun to explore the power afforded an individual who is willing to follow Christ through to this inner chamber.

Here I will briefly summarize the protocol for further work within the Heart and heart chakras, as I understand it today. When the Dominant self and any Ideal persona have given up the power to self-shame in exchange for Christ's discernment, and allowed Christ to purify the Heart's interior, the next goal is working with the Familial personality. The first step is asking Christ to capture it. Note that initially it may only manifest as particular qualities. The exploration needs to persist until those qualities are 'reconstituted,' which appears to be greatly facilitated by treating them as the personality-core and asking Christ personify it. Next, Christ is asked to identify its consort (i.e. contra-sexual aspect) by casting a circle out into the far reaches of the Mind and bringing that self into relational consciousness next to the personification. Ultimately, Christ will be asked to convict the pair until they become and an Ideal pair, but several steps must precede that work. First, Christ is asked to extract from the *personified* Familial personality *the self most closely attuned to the totality of Self*. Once extracted, Christ is asked to again caste a circle into the furthest reaches of the Mind and bring that self's consort into consciousness. These two are, by their nature, the Ideal pair that Christ is asked to bring into the Aware-ego's Heart, where they will take up permanent residence. Next, Christ is asked to focus on the personified Familial personality and its masculine or feminine consort, which Christ has previously identified. First, Christ is asked to gain entry to the Familial personality's heart chakra in order to purify it. This will generally entail the personified Familial personality forgoing its particular defenses including self-shaming. Once the heart chakra is purified, Christ can be asked to convict the personified Familial personality and its contra-sexual aspect until they too become an Ideal pair. (Note, work with dyadic pairs is described in detail in the next chapter.) Finally, Christ is asked to bring them into the purified heart chakra where they will take up residence along with a portion of Christ's *Light* channeling the Holy Spirit. Eventually, they are expected to entrain with the Ideal pair in the Aware-ego's Heart. I can describe all of this in one paragraph, but truth be told, it can take months to accomplish.

The final phase of work described in this books involves a first person focus on the Observer: the unmitigated, archetypal constellation, of the Familial personality. Work with its personifications, makes it possible to clearly discern the presence of the Observer, since the client will frequently move back and forth between being the personification and being the Observer of the personification. The client must be made aware of this movement and engaged in a discussion of its import. In particular, I emphasize that the Observer is the personality-core derived from an amalgamate of parental interactions and characteristics, which the client has been seeking to alter in the preceding set of interventions. Up till now that constellation has been a 'given'; a sense-of-self wholly defined by the Gendering archetype and inalterable, except by Ego reactivity. But it may be possible for Christ to offer the Ego a degree of choice by greatly extending the constellation's range of functionality and other variables. This requires that the Familial personality be worked with in the first person. The verbatims give a hint of that potential, but extensive work is beyond the scope of this book.

Penetrating A Soul's Heart

Clair. The following intervention is so unique it is difficult to know where to introduce it. I address it here because it was developed during the period in which I was developing other interventions related to entering the Heart. It focuses on *the soul of a deceased parent*. Clair's mother died two days before our session. She is expecting to travel to the funeral the following day. Throughout their relationship the mother has denied any knowledge of the fact that Clair's father and paternal grandparents sexually abused her throughout her childhood and adolescence, including Clair's involvement in a satanic cult by her grandparents. Her father died the previous year. The mother was suffering from Alzheimer's and assorted physical problems. Clair visited her the previous week with the expectation that it would be the last time she saw her alive. During our session she recalls her mother saying, in a seemingly lucid moment, "I am so lonely." Clair senses that this is a reference to her entire life, not just her current situation; and reflects that this is the first time she could ever remember her mother telling her how she felt. Clair is understandably distraught, partially as a result of being so conflicted in her feelings toward her mother. I decide to focus on her mother as a soul. I note that her mother did not live a good life; that her lifelong denial undoubtedly contributed to her senility; and inadvertently her senility has left her soul in a fogged state. I strongly encourage Clair to envision Christ striving to bring clarity to her mother's soul. Then it occurs to me to suggest that Clair *let Christ penetrate and heal the heart of her mother's soul*. This is the first time I had ever suggested such a thing to a client, and I have no idea what will happen. But based on years of work with Clair, I implicitly trust her Christ image to respond in way that will not endanger her or her mother. By way of buttressing my suggestion, I speak of the idea that each chakra body contains all seven chakras. Above the heart chakra are the three soul templates for the body chakras below the heart chakra. Essentially, Christ will be penetrating the heart chakra to the 5th, 6th, and 7th chakras. Frankly, I am not sure how much of this Clair grasps, or even if it is correct from a metaphysical perspective. But she is willing to envision her mother's image in a circle and let Christ enter the circle and enact the suggestion as he sees fit. My suggestion is very specific at this point: *Let Christ penetrate the heart of her Soul and satisfy her insatiable desire for connection.* What follows is an almost verbatim transcription of what Clair imagines and reports.

"She is tiny, fearful, alone, lost. She does not seem to know what to do or where to turn for guidance. Christ enters her circle. She has a mixed reaction. She does not sense that he is a dangerous person, but she does not know him. He takes her hand and asks her to sit down with him. He tells her what we are doing. She does not have a clue, except to have a sense that someone wants to help her and not leave her stranded. She seems to feel relief at being guided. This stimulates other scenarios in me. I identify with her desire not to have to be in charge and make decisions. I am suddenly aware of how much I am like my mother in that. Till now I always saw myself as being more like my father. I would like to be able to acquiesce as well."

"Christ continues to sit with her just to let her become comfortable with him. He talks to her and asks her about herself. I cannot hear what they are saying. I see a light in her eyes like a connection and the realization that he does not want anything from her. He just cares about her because she is. That is how he will reach her soul. He is letting her experience on the outside a sense of what he wants to give her. Once she embraces it and recognizes its existence he will move forward. He holds her hand, looks into her eyes, talks to her and she opens up to him. He wants to give it to her so she has it forever. He reaches into her Heart. There is this outpouring, a flowing of mud, gunk, oil-like sludge. It comes out of her Heart…all of the pain and crap, the stuff she has endured, denied, and pushed away in order to survive. It just flows away. At first she is *ashamed* and tries to clean it all up. He takes her hand, puts his finger on her mouth and whispers to let it go. No one will think badly of her. The outcome will be good. She relaxes and a whole lot more comes out. Now he makes contact with every cell of her Heart and shows her that it is all out. Now there is room to replace it with life. He enters her Heart. It is strong. It glows and she feels energized. I can see it on her face, a change in her being. As he is in her Heart it beats and sends him to every cell of her body, and her body is transformed. She is free, a glowing white bird, soft and graceful and free. She flies away. Now she is with God. Free. Now Christ is standing in the circle telling me that she is all right. She is joined back with God. Now everything in my mind is blank." Clair returns several weeks later with reports of 'little miracles' surrounding her mother's funeral. We soon move into other more pressing issues.

As I reflect back on the earliest stages of this work, I am repeatedly struck by how much more Christ can accomplish than I first imagined. Over the period of years my sense of his power has grown immeasurably. The above intervention with Clair is but one example. Can I say Christ has actually transformed a living soul? I will only know that when I consciously live once more between lives. But I have become a firm believer in interactive prayer. Christ is asked and Christ responds. That is very definitely so for Clair whose sense of her mother is completely altered by the experience. And as I will show in the next chapter, dramatically altering the image of a parent is often a necessary step for liberating the ego-aspects most strongly defined by the parent.

Accumulated Unexpressed Shame

The forgoing case examples demonstrate the discharge of accumulated unexpressed emotions especially shame. In this section I want to put forward the hypothesis that all physical and mental disease is a consequence of accumulated negative emotions, most especially shame. To the extent that accumulated shame and reactive emotions interfere with the function of chakras and meridians, such emotions will ultimately interfere with the proper functioning of the Body's muscular-skeletal functionality and organs including the brain. If the accumulation continues over months and years the emotions will adversely affect that part of the Body where it is most concentrated, resulting in the dis-ease of that physical function. Thus, for example, the hypothesis would assert that heart ailments are a consequence of an inordinate accumulation of shame ('stress') in the heart auric body and its meridian field. Likewise, accumulations of shame in the solar plexus or abdominal chakras will cause cancers of the sexual organs and aortic aneurysms to mention only some of the more common possibilities. The concentration of accumulated unexpressed shame and reactive emotions is hypothesized to account for every terminal, chronic disease, whether physical or mental. It is the penultimate cause of Wrath; and the result of our failure to resolve the shame that drove us from the Garden of Eden.

It is difficult to grasp the enormity of this hypothesis (to distinguish the trees from the forest) as all of the world's cultures continue to live in the silent thrall of shame. But it has been addressed for the past two thousand years in the person of Jesus Christ. A careful reading of the gospels will show that one third of all gospel passages describe Christ healing all manner of physical and mental disorders by touching the sufferer with his power. Medical science has made great strides in the past hundred years. My own body can attest to it, but it is nothing compared to the power of healing offered by Christ, because only a higher power has the wherewithal to remove the cancerous poison of accumulated shame, fear, anger, and the like. Medicine offers palliative care, repair, and remission. It buys the Mind time to change and heal or continue its inexorable course toward a painful death. As the Mind goes so goes the Body.

Allow me to relate the simplest of examples from Tory's case files. Although seemingly insignificant in the big scheme of things, it will touch a cord in every parent. I offer it as Tory recorded it in an e-mail. It deals with fear not shame, but emotionally speaking, and from Christ's perspective, the difference is only one of degree.

E-mail from Tory: The other day when I took Mandy [her granddaughter] to the doctor, something amazing happened. All day I had worried about taking her because she was going to have to have blood taken from her arm and this is bad enough for adults and terrible for 2 year olds. In fact, she had it done once before and it was a terrific ordeal for all.

All day, I tried to figure what I could do to help the situation. Finally I decided that I couldn't take the hurt away, but maybe I could work on the fear that she would have. You know I pray each morning that Christ will let her see, hear, and feel His love through me that day. I am also praying that He will be in her Heart, as well as mine. I thought that perhaps Christ could use His *Light* to remove the fear from Mandy. So as we went into the room, I started visualizing Christ with His Light going everywhere there could be fear in Mandy – her Heart, her mind, her eyes, her ears, her arms and body. I just watched as He soaked up the fear before it could take hold of her.

And it was an amazing experience. Mandy never likes to be laid down, but today the nurse laid her down on the table and she was fine. Mandy watched as she prepped her arm and gave no resistance to anything. Mandy and I named the colors on the wall. When the nurse started fishing for her vein, big tears rolled down Mandy's cheeks, but no crying. When the nurse decided she would have to use the other arm, she just turned Mandy around and laid her down in the other direction. Mandy cooperated with her totally. She and I started counting the spots on the dog in a mural beside the table as the nurse readied everything. Mandy cried when the nurse put the needle into her arm and started drawing the blood. But when the nurse told her there was nothing to be afraid of now, it was all over, she stopped.

The nurse was amazed. She kept telling Mandy she was so brave. She also said that she never had a 2 year old who behaved like this. I just thanked Christ for removing her fear and allowing this to be just another "oowie" in Mandy's life.

Accumulated unexpressed shame can be generated by a Dominant self's excessive use of socially acceptable behaviors and/or an Ego-in-conflict's use of socially unacceptable behaviors. Both act 'shamelessly' (i.e. oblivious of the shame they are generating) in an effort to squelch the pain of shameful states through the use of physical desire. But every act that uses desire immoderately will inject shame into one of more chakra fields. The shame will not be felt as such because the physical desire temporarily overrides both the shame injected and the shame that necessitated the excess in the first place. Only the tell-tail experience of guilt after the fact informs us that we have satisfied a 'shameful desire' to temporarily squelch a felt state of shame. And even guilt will diminish if usage becomes repetitive; but not so the consequences, the Wrath. In the early stages, the accumulation may express itself as weight gain, the smoker's cough, the hardened Heart, the impaired judgment, rages and impulsivity. If we allow that to persist, the accumulation will become the obesity-related-diseases and discomfort, the emphysema and lung cancer, the heart attack, the fatal car accident.

The major difficulty with using desire to temporarily abate the angst of a shameful state is the near invisibility (aside from the guilty aftereffect) with which it injects shame into the Body. Desire suppresses *all sense of shame while desire is active, both the shame it seeks to abate and the shame injected by our knowingly using the behavior in excess*. And once the latter is injected it will seem as irremediable as the shame it seeks to squelch. If the Ego had a way to discharge shame it would never have to resort to the excessive use of Mind or Body damaging behaviors in the first place. But left to its own devices it has no remedial powers. Only by calling on a power greater than itself can the Ego hope to be freed from the shame that forces us to turn from the face of God. Christ can and will free our Soul, Mind and Body from all shame, provided we are willing to call on him and grant him the power of the Holy Spirit, which is the source of all forgiveness.

The process of removing shame from the Body requires that Christ be allowed to work with all of the chakras. In this chapter I have focused on his work with the heart and brow chakra, and peripherally with the abdominal and root chakras. Each of these must be cleared of any strongly accumulated negative emotions, most especially shame. And to insure that they remain clear, the Dominant selves and Ego-in-conflict must be worked with extensively to insure they forgo the power to self-shame, and the shaming use of their 'drugs of choice,' in favor of Christ's discernment and Christ's willingness to release the Mind and Body from accumulated unexpressed shame.

Shame underlies our felt experience of sin and evil. When we ask Christ to remit our sins and save us from evil, we are asking to be freed from our shame. And Christ will do this with the power of the Holy Spirit wherever we can give up the pride of self-sufficiency and ask. And we can never ask too many times.

THE ROLE OF OTHER HIGHER POWERS [51] IN REDEEMING CONSCIENCE

As I have noted throughout this work, I am open to clients seeking out higher powers other than Christ. Most of my clients have eventually called on an archetypal maternal image such as the Virgin Mary, Mary Magdalene, or Earth mother to work in concert with their Christ image. My only reservation in solely using maternal figures concerns the ability of those higher powers to facilitate transformations dependent upon the Holy Spirit. But even a maternal image could easily channel the Holy Spirit in the name of Jesus Christ; and mythologically, the feminine has always claimed powers of healing.

I have only worked extensively with two clients who relied heavily on a higher power other than Christ. The first client was severely abused in childhood by priests and nuns as well as her father and uncles. She identified those priests 'as the representatives of Christ on earth' and that association made it nearly impossible to trust any male image of Christ during our therapy. In lieu of Christ, she found another higher power we called the Loving Voice, which I have described elsewhere. This Inner Self Helper always seemed ready to step aside as and when the client became willing to call on Christ, but that occasion did not arise during our therapy. In the year following therapy this client read *Teach Only Love* by Gerald Jampolsky,[52] which I had recommended several years earlier. This book and her subsequent correspondence with Jampolsky, coupled with her decision to trust a relationship with a man for the first time, all conspired to transform her from a lonely isolate into a woman willing to truly forgive all of her abusers and engage life with a 'renewed spirit.' I have rarely seen such a transformation in a client, which continues to this day. Early in the process of putting Jampolsky's suggestions into practice, she also allowed Christ into her life to act in partnership with her Loving Voice. I would note that none of our work involved the redemption of conscience as described throughout this chapter. I did see her one time at the beginning of the year she started her transformation. We agreed to exchange a series of e-mails regarding my protocol for redeeming sexual energy, which is described in Appendix I. She seems to have followed it religiously and communicated the results via e-mail, which are also included in Appendix I. Her usage of that protocol did precede the changes I have just described, though I doubt that intervention could fully account for them.

The second case of a client calling on a higher power other than Christ is much more complex and does illustrate many of the interventions described in this chapter. In her series of sessions, which specifically focus on the redemption of conscience, Christ is asked to 'assist' the client's chosen higher power. In effect, two higher powers 'partner' to help her; but by-and-large she relies on her chosen higher power. It will probably be easier to summarize those findings after presenting them

Lee

This case is noteworthy on several levels. First, throughout the course of therapy, Lee's higher power is an imagined spiritual being called Teacher who is channeled by a group meditation leader. Lee has participated in this meditation group for several years. Later in this series of sessions Lee also calls on Christ. Lee and I both refer to her higher power as Teacher. In my own mind, I imagine him as distinct from Christ, but I often use my understanding of how Christ functions with others to guide me in making suggestions. As my notes will indicate, Teacher is quite effective in helping Lee. But at a crucial point in the therapy – described below, I personally experience considerable dissonance (call it counter-transference) when her outcomes diverge from what I have come to expect when working with Christ channeling the Holy Spirit. At that point I felt obliged to discuss contrasting outcomes with Lee. Knowing she was raised in the Catholic Church, and it had sorely failed her as a child, I understood the source of her distrust in Christ. Until she joined the meditation group she was essentially agnostic. Were it not for the divergences described below, I would not have suggested that she entertain letting Christ partner with Teacher. But I do suggest it, and she agrees, and the resulting 'partnership' provides for a fascinating series of exchanges.

This case further illuminates the gift of discernment, which I have already discussed. It is also noteworthy in two other respects. The first series of interventions addresses a 'tenderhearted' self, a phrase I have often heard from clients. The second series describe interventions that address cluttering, which perpetually overwhelms Lee's efforts to 'get her house' in order.

Prior to these sessions, I have already seen Lee for several years. She is in her early fifties. She has worked most of her adult life as a nurse. Recently, she married a psychiatrist after being single for a good fifteen years. During the period covered by these sessions I was seeing Lee and her husband in marital therapy while continuing to see her individually. All the sessions describe our individual sessions but from time to time she will make reference to joint sessions that generally precede an individual session. At the outset of this series of sessions, she is complaining about the previous week's marital session with her new husband. "My adult self is bruised from bumping up against my husband's energy. He is unwilling to be there for her (note the third person distancing). I wanted to build a wall against him. Our last session seemed to trigger a lot of defenses in both of us. Saturday night I screamed at him. I am turning into his mother." As I listen, her comment about feeling bruised by 'his energy' draws my attention, as it seems an effect of shaming. I suggest she go inside and see if she can figure out which of his emotions is most bruising? I suggest she let Teacher place the 'bruised one' in a dome, which can simultaneously help to deflect the painful emotion and also read it. I then suggest that she imagine her husband expressing the bruising energy and ask if she can identify it. "The self in the dome is *tenderhearted*. She felt responsible for making things joyful, but she can't, it pains her." I ask Lee, what is the difference between tenderhearted and 'hearted'? "Tenderhearted is *painful caring*." What, I ask, is wounding her Heart? "My husband's critical energy. It is hurtful and makes Tenderhearted fearful of speaking up. It is draining her." What emotion hurts the most? "Not being able to express love. He burns her fingers when he works from his head. He withholds his heart and offers only judgment instead." What is her earliest memory of her finger's being burnt? (I suspect a projection here, knowing what I do of her family history.) "As we speak I hear another voice in the background that is harsh, critical, trying to protect Tenderhearted from being hurt." I immediately ask her to contain this voice and name it. "It is Harsh. My husband uses a lot of sarcasm [read shame]. I have it in myself. My dad and mom were both critical. I got a lot of criticism from peers in school. Harsh mirrors my parents she is how I acted to survive." I ask her what is the effect of this harshness on her heart, *whether she voices it or another speaks it*? What emotion has the power to burn the heart? "Fear of losing love, not being lovable, not being loved." I ask if Harsh knows what it is like to be unloved? "Yes." To be loved? "No. She would not let anyone love her. It would make her vulnerable to hurt." Is she, then, doomed to live in a loveless world? "In grade school I had a hard time feeling part of a group. What I did was put up a really big wall." At this point I suggest two interventions. First, Teacher will be asked to heal Tenderhearted. Next he will offer both selves the gift of discernment. For Tenderhearted this will help her to know when it is safe to open her heart or avoid a person who would wound her. He will offer the same to Harsh. I suggest that she let Teacher start with Tenderhearted and let Harsh observe. "I have asked Teacher to give her healing and extend the wisdom of discernment. There is a sense of calmness. Tenderhearted smiles and blows a kiss to Harsh (the smile on the clients face is quite evident)." Now I suggest that, if Harsh is willing, she also receive discernment so that 'belonging' can balance her sense of 'separation.' If willing, Harsh is to place her *Light* in front of her brow. I have assumed here that she needs to know when it is safe to belong vs. building a wall that separates her. "Harsh's sarcasm comes out. 'What am I supposed to do with this *Light*?' Teacher chuckles. This seems to disarm her. She got to the edge of 'maybe I will,' and then 'OK, I'll do this'." Lee goes on to describe the change in Harsh: "My original vision of her was of someone dressed in white starch shirt, stiff, and masculine. When Teacher touched her brow her clothing changed to hiking clothes, and finally, she has this joy on her face, and she can see the humor in herself." We end the session here. Lee is quite pleased with everything. Over the following weeks she revisits this experience, strengthening it; and feels its positive effects in her relationship with her husband

and others.

(The gift of discernment can be offered to any ego-aspect at any time provided they are willing to become open to the higher power that provides the discernment. The only requisite is the self's willingness. Generally, by the time it is suitable to make such a suggestion, the self has become sufficiently frustrated by its old ways. I also emphasize that the self does not give up their 'negative ability,' such as distrust of a situation, or painful caring, or choosing to isolate. Rather, the gift of discernment is meant to extend the range of possibility to its opposite pole; as the song says, 'To know when to hold them, to know when to fold them.' Life is always about choices and consequences. Discernment is the ability to know when to choose and when to refrain. Discernment is a gift because the necessary prescience can only come to an ego-aspect that has become open to a 'discerning power.' I often attempt to be specific as to what opposite is acquired with the gift of discernment, e.g. trust to balance distrust, approach to balance withdrawal, love to balance fear, humor to balance the serious, etc. But not infrequently, I will also be vague leaving it to the client's unconscious to provide the best reframe. Both ways seem to work equally well, provided the self is willing. This use of the gift is different from the exchange asked of a Dominant self, who must first focus on giving up the power to self-shame.)

Lee returns two weeks later with an unexpected crisis. Her dog, Shadow, has become seriously disabled by a cancerous tumor pinching the nerves in his hind legs. It is expected he will have to be put to sleep in the near future. Lee is beside herself with grief. This dog has been her companion through the many years she was single. Knowing her strong attachment, I treat this as someone losing a loved one. Lee believes her dog is staying alive "because he still has a job to do, but he is scared." I suggest that she go inside and visualize Shadow with her and Teacher. My thought is that at some point Shadow's role can be transferred to Teacher. Lee is agreeable to this. Lee goes *deep inside* as she is wont to do as a result of her meditation practice. I rarely question her until she returns to report whatever has transpired. "The moment Teacher came into our circle I saw Shadow excited to see him. I heard that he will be OK. He no longer seems scared. It is as if he is home. I wanted to know more but heard, 'No, I just need to trust him'." I ask if she thought Shadow has been serving Teacher all of these years? "I think so. It is hard for me to watch his pain, but I know it is not yet time to put him down. He seems to have some more work to do." I ask what stance she needs to take in the coming days, weeks, or months? "I need to share his love for me, to share what he teaches. I keep seeing him with Teacher." I suggest that while she is inside she might check on the status of Harsh and Tenderhearted. "I have taken inventory of them several times since the last session. It is amazing to me. I have not felt the same kind of tension toward my husband; I am not feeling a desire to run off and hide, or needing to run back to my house here. I am in a better place, more comfortable letting the little stuff go, less compulsive about projects. We are getting ready to talk to an architect about major renovations of his house. What really concerns me is the clutter." The session ends here.

As to the clutter, both husband and wife have admitted their inability to get rid of stuff; and this has become a real point of contention as they anticipate combining households. I have worked with Lee to some good effect but she still struggles to get her 'own house in order.' In previous sessions, we identified 'Clutter,' a rebellious adolescent type, but were sidetracked by more pressing premarital issues. My hope is to return to it in this next session. One of Shadow's "uncompleted tasks" is also made clear in this next session.

The session begins with Lee telling me she has found a Vet who seems able to minimize Shadow's pain with acupuncture. She then goes on to share that during the week she began to feel very angry. She knew it had something to do with what was going on inside. When she went inside she discovered her 'little girl,' who I had forgotten about since she was addressed several years ago. (Were it not for my notes I would have a hard time remembering what we did the previous week!) This little girl was the first self we worked with. At the time, Lee had no higher power she could call on. I suggested that she place the 'little girl' under the protection of a power animal. She had chosen Shadow to be the little girl's protector. Lee goes on to update events brought about by Shadow's looming death, "Now the little girl is angry that Shadow is leaving her. She has been with him in a circle of protection this whole time. Tenderhearted has reached out to the little girl who has responded by grabbing Tenderhearted's legs. Tenderhearted has said she will take care of her. The little girl had Shadow on a leash. She has given the leash to Teacher. Shadow now seems transformed by their play. My own sense of clinging to Shadow seems to have past. I am worrying less about him, relaxing, just being with him." Obviously, this relationship must still be played out in further sessions, but for now, I feel we can once again focus on Clutter.

Even before Lee goes inside, she can imagine Clutter as an adolescent sitting atop a big pile of paper. I suggest that Clutter is a protector, like Shadow; and that our goal is to heal rather than hide whomever Clutter is 'covering up.' (More likely, Clutter is a Dominant self since her characteristic trait is to be always making piles; but I have yet to appreciate the role and characteristics of the Dominant self during this phase of treatment.) In response to my comment about 'covering up,' Lee unexpectedly jumps to recalling her childhood difficulty with homework. When queried, her earliest memory is from kindergarten. She sees her father *screaming* at her, calling her stupid when she cannot grasp his instruction on addition. "My mind went blank. All I could do was keep calling myself 'stupid'." I surmise that Clutter is protecting/hiding Stupid. At this point I bring Lee back to me and outline a process for addressing Clutter and Stupid. I literally describe the entire series of interventions that will be needed to alter the Moral authority of her father. I tell her it is not likely we will get through them all in this session but we can begin. I go into this detail for two reasons. Since Lee goes deep when she goes inside, our interactions are minimal during that time. Also, she is already familiar with some of the steps. But I also warn her that once inside we may encounter the 'unexpected' and so may have to improvise. I explain that my first concern is protecting Clutter from being overwhelmed. So when she goes back inside she needs to initially focus on Clutter who she is to instruct in using the *Light* to create a garment of protection. The next task will be to release Stupid from the pile of paper and baptize her. At that point, Stupid can ask Teacher to terminate her father's Moral authority, and accept Teacher as her higher power. Next Clutter can be asked to accept Teacher as her higher power. She will be asked to accept Teacher in exchange for the discernment that will allow her to 'release' clutter as well as 'hold' it. I note that Clutter's goal is to 'organize,' but it is near impossible to organize if you are unable to get rid of stuff. (I confess that at this point I have some reservations regarding Teacher's ability to baptize, but keep them to myself and trust the process will either work as expected or we will have to improvise.)

When Lee goes back inside I instruct her

to first approach Clutter and explain that, after she has learned to provide herself with a garment of protection, Clutter needs to delegate her responsibility for protecting Stupid to Teacher. "Clutter has moved off of her pile. Teacher has given her a portion of my Light. Her clothing has changed. It is radiating. She is now sitting down next to the pile in a meditative stance. Her Light arcs to Teacher giving him permission to work with Stupid. Now she is even more meditative." I now instruct Lee to let Teacher create a dome over the pile of paper. He can then dissolve the paper and let Stupid emerge. When Stupid appears she is very deformed, not even recognizable as a self-image. "Stupid is exposed, deformed, hideous looking, very small, about two feet, but with the features of an adult. Her feet are very big, and though her arms appear small they have a long reach. She is drooling, and her teeth are bad. She has nasty hair." (This is without question one of the most vivid images of cumulative shaming I have ever come across.) At this point, I suggest that Teacher baptize her. Lee understands that this means to fill her with the Holy Spirit and release her from the bondage of shame; and that someone other than Christ can ask this. Ordinarily, I would expect a discernible change in any self that is baptized. But I hedge here because I am not sure what Teacher can do, although I trust something positive will transpire. I simply ask her to describe what happens. What change does she observe? "Teacher picked her up, wrapped her in a cocoon of *Light*. I cannot really see her in the crook of his arm. I sense she initially felt fear of being hurt again, but all she really feels is tenderness, and her fear has changed to calmness and peace. She is still in the cocoon. She feels very safe and she is not ready to come out yet." The session ends here.

It was at this point that I began having reservations regarding Teacher's ability to baptize Stupid. Normally, when Christ is asked to baptize a Rejected-self the change is an instantaneous, immediately felt, change in the character and demeanor of the self. That has not occurred here. Essentially, the self is covered in light and hidden in the crook of Teacher's arm; it is placed in a cocoon of protection, not unlike whatever has been offered to Clutter. In the next session I begin by tactfully asking about Teacher's understanding of the Holy Spirit. Lee replies that he sees the Holy Spirit as love. I cannot gainsay this but my own concern is that Stupid be released from shame, *forgiven*. So I ask if Teacher could allow Stupid to be infused with the Holy Spirit. Lee is quite taken with the response. "Wow. I asked and Teacher said it was no problem. He lay the baby down in front of him. *The Holy Spirit came down as a dove and melded with the cocoon*. The cocoon melted away and now I see a child that looks like a nymph with wings, wholesome and naked. She has started to fly and hover, almost as if she were a fairy." I ask Lee if she can identify this as a part of her self? "Yes. I can feel the lightness and sense of spontaneity, the playfulness. She is filled with heart for others and life." Having said all of this, Lee becomes distracted by her awareness of another part that has emerged 'in the shadows.' "There is a prideful part that is angry, very angry and constrained. She is sitting in the shadows. She obsesses about details of organization. *She gets bogged down and unable to finish*. She is very control oriented. She wants to manage everything and get it perfect." I suggest that Lee contain her and bring her out of the shadows. I am not sure if Lee does this, but she does continue to assess this new self, "Her authority comes from her mother and father. Her rants and rages are from her mother. Her dad made clutter and piles. Mom would get fed up with them and rant and rage." Finally, Lee reports that she can use concentric circles to separate from this new self that we end up calling OCD. "She is pissed and pouty. She does not want to change. The thought of change is anxiety provoking." At this point I am frankly caught off guard. The emergence of OCD is unexpected. I am still trying to get my head around Stupid's transformation into a nymph. We are close to the end of the session. All I can do is ask if Teacher would be willing to let an image of Christ baptize Stupid? Since Lee does not have time to go back inside the question is left essentially unanswered. For my part, I am anxious that I have overstepped a boundary and imposed my beliefs on a client.

The next session is hard to describe because I did most of the talking and it is hard to talk and write notes at the same time. Basically, I set out my qualms about how the process was proceeding. I began by reiterating my respect for Teacher's role in Lee's life these last several years and my continued willingness to work with him as her higher power. At the same time I was concerned about his use of Interior baptism. I noted that the creation of the nymph was what I would call a symbolic synergy in contrast to the transformation of a self-image, which normally occurred when Christ baptized a Rejected-self; that normally – when Christ baptized – the distorted image became a discernible self-image, in contrast to the mythic figure created by Teacher. I told her that while I had worked with other 'guides' that functioned as 'higher powers,' none of them had been involved in working with selves created by Moral authority and the transformation of conscience; that the baptism of the Rejected-self seemed crucial to the process of transforming conscience, since the liberated Rejected-self was the one who asked Christ to terminate the parental authority. I speculated that a Christ image would very likely be willing to baptize any Rejected-self and terminate the Moral authority of a parent without needing to fill the role of higher power. Whoever asked for the termination of the parents' authority had to be free to choose their new higher power, and I speculated that Christ would play any part he was asked without preconditions. That is, if allowed to act, Christ would then step back allowing the self to choose Teacher, or altogether another image. I did stress that it was not advisable to permit an ego-aspect to assume that authority. Interestingly, Lee appreciated that temptation from personal experience and understood the need for a mythic container. As it turned out, Lee had been quite willing to have Christ play a role in her therapy even before I outlined all my concerns. She said she had given much thought to my comment of the previous session and felt that calling on a Christ image no longer threatened or irritated her. For my part, I was concerned about Teacher's reaction. In reply, she told me that she did not believe that Teacher would have any problem working with Christ. We agreed to resume the work in the next session beginning with Teacher and Christ coming together.

A week later, Lee returns with an unexpected crisis involving one of her long-time friends, who has been living in her house for the past year and now accompanies her to the session. Most of the hour is spent resolving this conflict. After the friend leaves, I decide to let us run over sensing a connection between the crisis and the OCD-self we previously planned to address. Lee is quite agreeable. She tells me that Teacher and Christ are agreeable to working together. She also reports that when she meditated on this during the week she was aware of resistance. At first she thought it was Christ, Teacher or OCD, but when she went inside what she discovered was "a little Catholic nun who is very rule bound and is having a lot of trouble with the idea of Jesus and Teacher working together." I suggest that we begin by placing both OCD and the little Nun in separate circles and ask Christ and Teacher to cauterize undue influences, which I explain to Lee prior to her going inside. I am not specific as to who will do what, leaving it all to them to work it out. Apparently, Christ and Teacher will share the work. Teacher begins by placing his *Light* in OCD's Heart. She immediately disappears. Christ follows by placing his *Light* in the heart of the little Nun. This immediately changes her habit from black to white. I am concerned about OCD's disappearance, but Lee assures me when she looks back inside that OCD has reemerged. "Her energy seems less; it is more flowing; she is no longer angry. The energy is different. The intensity is gone. I hear a voice saying, 'I am OK, I am doing my thing'." At this point I decide to go for broke and suggest that Teacher and Christ change places, each to work with the other self. I am frankly curious to see if there will be any further effects. "Teacher put his *Light* into the Nun's Heart. She appears to react with a kind of charismatic ecstasy surrounded by an aura of light. Then she sits down in a meditative pose. Jesus approached OCD and hugs her, then places his Light into her Heart. She stops what she was doing, looks at Jesus and says, 'I feel loved'." Finally, I suggest - if Teacher is willing, that Christ be allowed to baptize the nymph. "The nymph was floating to the left of Teacher. Teacher took her hand and placed her in front of Christ. When Christ placed his *Light* into her Heart she was transformed into a Seven-year-old girl, wearing a white dress, holding both of their hands." I ask if she is a self-image? "Her hair is full of red ringlets. My mother use to make them like that for me, but not so many curls. She is quite angelic, but does look like me."

The following week Lee returns with her husband. They have both taken pictures of each of their houses to show me the 'clutter' in each one. This could have been a very tension filled session. Instead, I experience Lee as completely non-defensive, able to point out gains and things needed-to-be-done. I have rarely experienced such a transformation. Even her husband is able to be objective and non-defensive as she guides the three of us through the exploration. I have no opportunity to actually discuss the previous session but feel I am definitely experiencing its effects on her. This series of sessions ends here, to be continued in the next chapter.

Recently, I came across a quote related to the Jesus prayer.[53] What struck me about it was the Saint's conviction that the Mother of God was the catalyst for this prayer being constellated in his heart:

> I had great faith in my lady, the Mother of God, and besought her with tears to grant me the grace of mental prayer. Once I came to her temple as usual and fervently prayed to her for this. I went up to her icon and reverently kissed her image. Suddenly, I felt as if a warmth fell into my breast and heart, which did not burn, but bedewed and delighted me, and stirred my soul to compunction. From that moment my *heart* began to say the prayer within itself, and my *mind* began to delight in the remembrance of my Jesus and the Mother of God and have Him, the Lord Jesus, constantly within itself. Since then the prayer has never ceased in my *heart*.[54]

Teacher is not the Mother of God. But like her, he may well have served as a handmaiden for the Holy Spirit's entry into Lee's heart, just as her dog, Shadow, acted as a protector of her little girl until Teacher could assume that role. I think the same could be said of my other client whose higher power was also so pivotal in her spiritual journey. The redemption of conscience is an ongoing process of teaching the Ego to become guided by the Holy Spirit and lovingly subject to God and Soul. In my experience, the Holy Spirit will speak unerringly through Christ, but also through any image willing to give it a voice. It is quite possible that, if I had been less insistent on 'how it should be done,' Teacher would have managed to effect the same ends without Christ's interventions.

But my counter-transference has also taught me something quite valuable: all higher powers (even God the Father), who are willing to channel the Holy Spirit (rather than claiming to be its source), can work in concert. For now, that is all I can say on the matter of other higher powers.

Afterward

Theory strives to provide a new paradigm. But there is really no end to this process. Any attempt at closure is arbitrary. I have decided to continue the verbatims on the book's website (the unredeemed conscience.org). The continuing work by Tory, Marion, and Leigh exceeds every deadline I have set for myself, so the interested reader will just have to go to the website if s/he is interested in following their verbatims further. The website offers other addendum as well. A whole other book will be needed to flesh out the Familial personality, not to mention the Heart, which is at the center of most religions. I am grateful that the *Light* and Christ image have carried us this far, and hope it is sufficient to provide evidence in support of the hypotheses. While not the simple journey my 'desire for closure' envisioned, it is far richer. Even so, it is humbling to accept what feels like a life-long process.

My current work with clients is far more fluid than what is described in this book for the simple reason that I now have the benefit of all that I have learned. God only knows what you – the reader, will do with all this as your starting place. Finally, my Christ has convinced me that 'the response of others' is his responsibility. I know that releasing the book will free me to move more deeply into the process.

CHAPTER VII ENDNOTES

1 Stone, H. & Stone, S. (1993), *Embracing Your Inner Critic: Turning Self-Criticism into a Creative Asset*, Harper: San Francisco.

2 The referenced text is the third of a series of books based on Jung's perception of Alchemy as the practice of individuation. I will list them here in order of publication. They are all three exceptionally fine and readable treatises. Raff, J., (2000), *Jung and the Alchemical Imagination,* Nicolas-Hayes: Berwick, ME; Raff, J., & Vocatura, L.B., (2002), *Healing the Wounded God: Finding Your Personal*

Guide on Your Way to Individuation and Beyond, Nicolas-Hayes: Berwick, ME; and Raff, J., (2006), *The Practice of Ally Work,* Nicolas-Hayes: Berwick, ME.

3   The other parent may also exercise this authority but to a lesser extent, and generally as a role delegated by the primary parent.

4   So far as I can determine, this sense of self is not an ego-identity, but an amalgam of parental gender values and actions constellated by the Gendering archetype as an impersonal collective image.

5   Frankly, none of my clients have exhibited a Christ conscious process prior to working with me. I assume it must exist in the world, at the very least, in great religious teachers, saints, and the humble in spirit.

6   The notable exception are Dissociative disorders, which can continue to create alter personalities and fragments to cope with ongoing abuse, though they too can develop Dominant selves when the abuse is no longer a current issue. Those selves will generally serve to provide the individual with a sense of normalcy and denial that the abuse occurred.

7   The identification of the Rejected-self, its baptism and opening to Christ's discernment, and the dethronement of parents as the Voice-of-conscience, can be accomplished in a relatively short period of time. But the process of redeeming conscience can take years as the client struggles to identify and 'convert' ideal selves. This is analogously illustrated by the life of Christ, wherein he is driven into the desert for 'forty days' to struggle with the Temporal authority of Satan immediately following his baptism by John the Baptist. It is similarly illustrated in the life of St. Paul. Following his baptism in Damascus, he briefly witnesses to the change in him but then returns to Taurus for fifteen years before undertaking his mission to the Gentiles.

8   This is the primary thrust of Paul's Letter to the Ephesians. See Barclay, W. (2002), *The Letter to the Galatians and Ephesians*, Westminster John Knox Press.

9   It goes without saying that these assertions do not argue for psychotherapy being offered in lieu of diagnosis and treatment by a medical doctor. I generally encourage the medical route because the client can more readily discern the limitations of most diagnoses and treatments in terms of cure. As a rule, psychotherapy is most effective when the client has exhausted or is unwilling to proceed with medical treatment options; and least effective while the client believes there is a readily available and relatively painless cure.

10   In some instances, a grandparent may become the Voice-of-conscience. Adults other than a parent can be constellated with Moral authority, especially grandparents, if the child is being raised in their home and/or the parent clearly delegates that authority to them.

11   Piaget, J., (2000), *The Psychology of the Child*, Basic Books: New York.

12   The interested reader is referred to Raff, J., (2006), *The Practice of Ally Work,* Nicolas-Hayes: Berwick, ME.

13   Weston, W., (2006), *Emotional Release Therapy: Letting Go of Life's Painful Emotions,* Hampton Roads Publishing Co.: Charlottesville, VA.

14   Sui, Choa Kok, (1990), *Pranic Healing*, Red Wheel Weiser; or Sui, Choa Kok, (1999), *Miracles Through Pranic Healing*, Blue Dolphin Publishing, 2nd Edition.

15   Cavalli, T.F., (2002), *Alchemical Psychology: Old Recipes for Living in a New World,* Penguin Putnam, Inc.: New York, p.142.

16   To quote Michael Stavish: *"Solve et coagula,"* meaning "separate and recombine," is a term you will hear repeatedly in alchemical work, and it is the key to all occult work. Alchemists are constantly separating and recombining the various essentials and elements of plants, minerals, and, more importantly, themselves, to understand Nature's hidden laws and how they work (p.20-21)." See Stavish, M., (2006), *The Path of Alchemy: Energetic Healing and the World of Natural Magic,* Llewellyn Publications: Woodbury, MI.

17   The client is referring to *Body Wisdom* by Sharon Giammatteo (2002), North Atlantic Books: Berkeley, CA). The author was herself severely abused as a child and recommends a gentle, very effective, energy therapy for clearing such memories. I had recommended the book to the client in a previous session.

18   An Ego-in-conflict can use sex compulsively whether by acting out or obsessively masturbating while stimulating itself pornographically. But if it does use sex in this way, it is usurping the role of the disowned self held in bondage by shame, very likely a self shamed early in life.

19   I have noted this elsewhere, but it is worth repeating: the highest incidence of cancer in women are cancers of the breast and pelvis; and the highest incidence in men is prostate cancer.

20   These selves accumulate a great deal of undischargeable shame. It is vital

that Christ be allowed to purify the chakras that have been forced to accumulate the shame, most often the heart, mental, emotional, and root chakras.

21   I rely very strongly on intuition and it is hard to imagine an individual functioning without it, even as I know there are many individuals who have very little knowledge of intuition as a function. As such, I have found it helpful to encourage clients with little awareness of intuition to read on the subject. Clients addressing Ego-in-conflict issues have welcomed such recommendations. One book I can highly recommend is Schulz, M.L., (1999), *Awakening Intuition: Using Your Mind-Body Network for Insight and Healing,* Three Rivers Press: New York.

22   The 1st Step of AA: Admitted we were powerless over alcohol and our lives had become unmanageable.

23   The details of this intervention are described in Appendix I.

24   Carnes, P. & Moriarity, J., (1997), *Sexual Anorexia: Overcoming Sexual Self-Hatred,* Hazelton.

25   It is very rare to find a young client who has the stamina and financial resources to engage in depth therapy. A close friend of his parents referred Bracky to me. His immediate life problems were severe enough to warrant the initial investment. But to paraphrase an AA perspective, Bracky was far from hitting his bottom and so had little reason to change. By the time I ventured to explore his ideal sense of self, the reasons that brought him to see me were past events in his mind. Very likely, our exploration contributed to his decision not to return, but was not likely the only reason.

26   This case is continued in the last chapter where I examine the concept of Ideal persona in greater depth.

27   Kuhmerker, L., Gielen, U., Hayes, R.L., (1993), *The Kohlberg Legacy*, Religious Education LLC.

28   Bronfenbrenner, U., (2006 Reprint Ed.), *The Ecology of Human Development: Experiments by Nature and Design*, Harvard University Press: Boston.

29   Piaget, J., (1965), *The Moral Judgment of the Child,* Free Press.

30   See Barclay for an orthodox interpretation of this epistle. Barclay, W.,

(2002), *The Letters to the Galatians and Ephesians,* Westminster John Knox Press: Louisville, KY.

31   See Pagels, E., (1992), *The Gnostic Paul: Gnostic Exegesis of the Pauline Letters,* Trinity Press International: Harrisburg, PA.

32   Barclay, op. cit., p. 7.

33   Barclay, op. cit., p. 38.

34   Barclay, op. cit. p. 44.

35   In this early series of interventions I was struggling with how to word the transition. Initially, I thought it would be necessary for an ego-aspect to become *subject* to Christ's authority. Monica's Me understandably balks at this. Today, beginning with these sessions, I began to understand that Christ does not ask us to exchange one archetypal authority for another, but rather to open ourselves to the guiding discernment of the Holy Spirit.

36   See Berg, R., (2005), *The Kabbalah Method: The Bridge Between Science and the Soul, Physics and Fulfillment, Quantum and the Creator*, Kabbalah Publishing: NY.

37   Berg, R., op. cit., pp 47-48.

38   There are numerous books on the gifts of the Holy Spirit. The one I have found most helpful is by David Pytches, probably because I attended one of his weeklong conferences. See Pytches, D. (1987), *Spiritual Gifts in the Local Church*, Bethany House Books: London.

39   A self cannot give up their affective responses, but they can relinquish their habitual emotional reactions to situations in favor of discernment or detachment as an initial response.

40   This is one of the few instances when I use the word 'brain' instead of, or synonymous with, Mind. Even though the intervention takes place in the Mind, I have the client ask Christ to penetrate to the center of the brain where he first extracts the ego defense and then supplants it with his gift of discernment, which is most often visualized as a portion of his *Light*.

41   There are a great number of behaviors that are socially acceptable (or marginally so) that can be used in excess to temporarily reduce the dis-ease of a

repressed self. Recently, I interviewed a new client whose presenting complaint was bereavement following her mother's death. As I reviewed her history and that of her parents a number of socially acceptable behaviors emerged. What I found noteworthy is that she maintained a healthy weight despite being raised in a family where her father and his sibs were all 100 plus pounds overweight. She also noted, almost in passing, that her father use to gamble a lot, and seemed to be lucky. I would consider this a marginal, socially acceptable, behavior. (I had another client who could spend hours/days sitting in front of a slot machine.) What this client appeared to rely on for herself – as taught and encouraged by her mother, was a love of horror movies and books that offered frequent adrenalin surges, as well as shopping till they dropped, and a work environment that also insured weekly, if not daily, adrenalin surges – all socially acceptable behaviors. I have not yet had the opportunity to examine the role of these other behaviors in placating insatiable aspects, but I suspect they are equally powerful – especially those providing adrenalin surges. The above-mentioned client had also taken tranquilizers for a period of time – another socially acceptable behavior, for the control of painful and fearful emotions, which also correlate with insatiable dis-ease. I would also note that while the primary thrust of the interventions described here were developed for the treatment of overeating, that behavior will often be augmented by other socially acceptable behaviors used in excess. For example, another overweight client also relied heavily on excessive sleep and reading romances.

42   "**Repression**. The basic meaning derives from the root verb, *to repress*, which in various contexts means to put down, suppress, control, censor, exclude, etc. Hence: 1. In all depth psychologies from the classical Freudian model onward, a hypothesized mental process or operation that functions to protect the individual from ideas, impulses and memories, which would produce anxiety, apprehension or guilt were they to become conscious. Repression is considered to be operative at an unconscious level; that is, not only does the mechanism keep certain mental contents from reaching awareness, but also its very operations lie outside of conscious awareness. In classical psychoanalytic theory, it is regarded as an ego function and several processes are included under it: (a) *primal repression,* in which primitive, forbidden id impulses are blocked and prevented from ever reaching consciousness; (b) *primary repression,* in which anxiety-producing mental content is forcefully removed from consciousness and prevented from re-emerging; and (c) *secondary repression,* in which elements that might serve to remind the person of that which has been previously repressed are themselves repressed. An important corollary of this analysis is that that which is repressed is not deactivated but continues to have a lively existence at the unconscious level, making itself felt through projections in disguised symbolic form in dreams, parapraxes and psychoneuroses. Within these analytic psychologies, the term has a fairly clear referential domain and should be contrasted with other seemingly synonymous terms such as

suppression and inhibition (p. 625)." Quote taken from Reber, A.S. & Reber E., (2001), *The Penguin Dictionary of Psychology,* Penguin Books: NY.

43   While a college senior, I took a course in physiological psychology and learned about the physiological substrate of emotions being uncovered and explored in the 1950's. I still remember writing a long paper seeking to correlate those findings with a theory of repression. It was my first foray into theoretical explanation and it was a heady experience. The Professor gave me an A+ for my efforts, but I doubt he even read it. What it taught me was to appreciate the difference between purely explanatory determinants and finding manageable determinants that allowed someone to change the situation. Working at the level of physiology does not offer much latitude for changing what is observed.

44   Christ can be asked to dispel accumulated shame, even shame residing in the Heart. But the shame will continue to accumulate until the individual gives up his or her power to self-shame.

45   Many of my clients complain about sinus conditions. To be fair, I live in a part of the country that regularly has a very high pollen count, so they may come by it honestly. But their sinus conditions are also frequently cleared up in sessions where I address sinus conditions as a psychological defense.

46   I want to at least highlight this observation of hallucinating. Another client, Pearl, experienced something similar when she imagined Christ pulling something out of her head and onto my coffee table in the office. A few other clients – primarily MPD clients have reported similar phenomenon. It is rare and unclear to me why one event is experienced as distinctly out of the Body rather than in the context of active imagination. It is definitely more palatable but other than that I have yet to account for it. In neither of the clients does it become a recurring phenomenon.

47   See Paulson, G.L. (2008), *Kundalini and the Chakras,* Llewellyn Publications.

48   A beliefs validates itself by setting limits on what is possible; this is particularly true of defeatist beliefs. Fortunately, in this instance the belief was neither superordinate nor integral to the Eight-year-old's belief system, so it is easily dispelled by conviction. Where the belief is central, as in the case of a Dominant self's judgment, then the self must voluntarily give up the belief.

49   Paulson, G.L. (2008), op. cit.

50   I pray that God Ineffable/ With the power of the Holy Spirit/ Consecrate your image of [Jesus Christ]/ As the God of your personal salvation and / With the power of the Holy Spirit/ Guide, forgive, and inform you evermore. Amen.

51   Throughout this work I have referred to Christ as a high power. Most of this work was written before I discovered that most people unconsciously accept 'God the Father' as their higher power and continue to do so even after working extensively with a Christ image. For those clients, Christ was not – strictly speaking, their higher power. I never had the occasion to ask Menta or Lee – the two clients referenced in this section, to tell me the name of their 'higher power.' 'God the Father' could well have been their higher power as well. Any image that is archetypal in substance can function as a higher power. Most of the responses attributed to the Christ image in this work were enacted before the client consciously accepted him as their higher power; that is, as superordinate to any other archetypal image within the Mind. 'God the Father' is a person of God, an archetypal image. He is not to be confused the totality of God as embodied in the Tetragrammaton, i.e YHWH, Jehovah, Yahweh; but as a person of God he can function as a higher power.

52   Jampolsky, G. (1984), *Teach Only Love*, Bantam Books.

53   The origin of the Jesus Prayer is attributed to the Russian Orthodox Church. The story can be found in *The Way of a Pilgrim*, which has numerous translations in print. The author is anonymous. Basically, a Russian surf is taught to read byreading the bible. One exhortation by St. Paul to 'pray unceasingly' captures his attention. Following the death of his parents, who he has cared for, he sets out on a journey to discover how one is to pray unceasingly. He finally meets a very wise priest who tells him it is done by repeating the Jesus prayer over and over again – Lord Jesus, have mercy on my soul. Many miracles follow on the heels of his learning to do this. He says it unceasingly as a mantra until his heart speaks it effortlessly.

54   Brianchaninov, I., (2006), *On the Prayer of Jesus: The Classic Guide to the Practice of Unceasing prayer as Found in The Way of a Pilgrim*, New Seeds: Boston.

CHAPTER VIII

RELATIONAL AUTHORITY

*How can we know God
while still separate in gender?*

-Anonymous

OVERVIEW

This chapter describes my progressive understanding of Relational authority and the Gendering archetype, and the Inner dyads that manifest both of them. It describes and illustrates three distinct phases of discovery, all of them stimulated and confirmed by clinical interactions. The first phase grew out of my discovery that clients can extract a contra-sexual aspect or consort from a sexed-image. A sexed-image is any image that is biologically male, female, or hermaphroditic. A contra-sexual image would be its gender complement. I quickly learned it is actually possible to extract both gender aspects (masculine and feminine) from the sexed-image of a self or others. That discovery led to a prolonged exploration of the relationship between the two gender aspects and their effects on the sexed-image when Christ alters the aspects and then re-merges them with the sexed-image.

In the initial studies, Christ was only asked to work with the feminine aspect of a sexed-image's Inner dyad. He willingly 'evolved' the feminine aspect and sustained those changes with *his own masculine energy* until the sexed-image's masculine aspect could accommodate to the changes in the feminine aspect. Eventually, I discovered that Christ could *simultaneously* convict any dyadic pair with the power of the Holy Spirit; and that repeated conviction invariably resulted in profound transformations. The conviction process appears to work equally well with self-images and images of others and with all setting conditions. In effect, Christ can convict any sexed-image standing alone, or simultaneously convict a sexed-image and its contra-sexual aspect, or simultaneously convict two extracted gender aspects. All these setting conditions will result in equally profound alterations of the sexed-image. Those findings marked the second phase of discovery. The third phase of discovery followed on the heels of discovering and working with the Familial personality. Work with that sense-of-self demonstrated that providing Ideal pairs (i.e. Christ transformed dyads) unrestricted access to the Heart or heart chakras could also have a positive, demonstrable effect on the personality-core (i.e. Familial personality). I suspect there is much more to learn, but any further findings will have to await another book.

The early studies provided a conceptual paradigm for all that follows. Foremost, was the discovery that Inner dyads underpin all sexed-images constellated by the Gendering archetype. The Gendering archetype is the *image-maker* that constellates all sexed-images accessible through active imagination. The early studies demonstrated conclusively that every sexed-image constellated by the Gendering archetype is sustained by an Inner dyad, which can be transformed and, in turn, transform the sexed-image. The early studies also demonstrate that change is effected by altering the complementarity of the gender aspects. In effect, each dyad is comprised of a feminine aspect that *defines the image*, and a masculine aspect that *animates* the feminine form. Whether male or female, all sexed-images are sustained by a feminine *defining aspect* animated by a masculine *energizing aspect*. Together, the aspects *conjointly sustain* the sexed-image. Using the *Light*, a client can observe this by extracting them, letting Christ change them, and experiencing the effect of reintegration.

During childhood, the Gendering archetype constellates an amalgam of personality characteristics derived from the parents' demeanor and interactions, which manifests in the Mind as the child's Familial personality. This is what the Ego uses to create images of itself (i.e. self-images), which organize its consciousness and free will. (Always bear in mind that the Ego is also an archetype separate and distinct from the Gendering archetype. Invariably, it incorporates, i.e. embodies, the Familial personality constellated by the Gendering archetype, but it is not its creator.) *Relational authority is the power invested in parents by virtue of their roles in the creation of the Familial personality by the Gendering archetype.*

I have not been able to extract masculine and feminine aspects from the Familial personality unless it is *personified* by the Ego. At best, all the client can provide while experiencing the Familial personality qualities and attributes of that personality and a *disembodied* sense of self. Following the redemption of Dominant selves, the client is only able to consciously experience the disembodied Familial personality in the first person. I call this the *Observer's perspective*. When asked, the client will emphatically insist that the Observer is "me." The Familial personality is considered willful when first encountered. After Christ has Integrated Ideal pairs into the Heart of the Aware-ego and the heart chakra of at least one ego-aspect, it appears to become a willing observer of events. As a 'willing observer,' the Observer and Aware-ego appear to be phenomenonally indistinguishable while functioning in the first person.

The later studies focus on Christ channeling of the Holy Spirit to *convict* sexed-images and their Inner dyads. Repeated conviction reliably transforms the sexed-image and its Inner dyad into an Ideal pair; and those transformations are *enduring* and can alter the client's inner dynamics and relationships with others. The most recent studies document the effects that an Ideal pair can have on the Familial personality when the pair are allowed to assume permanent residence in the Heart or heart chakra. An Ideal pair is any masculine/feminine dyad that has been repeatedly convicted by Christ until it manifests an ideal state from the client's perspective. Normally, the dyads are extracted from ego-aspects, but Christ can also be asked to identify an Ideal pair that can take up permanent residence in the Aware-ego's Heart. Christ identifies that Ideal pair by first extracting a personification 'most closely attuned to the totality of Self;' and then identifying its contra-sexual consort. (Note that all of these steps are described in greater detail in Chapter VII.)

The primary difference between the early and later studies is the power of the Christological interventions used to transform sexed-images and/or Inner dyads. In my early work, Christ altered the aspects without reference to how he did so, i.e. his modus operandi. The later studies demonstrate Christ simultaneously transforming both aspects of the Inner dyad and/or the sexed-image by convicting them with the power of the Holy Spirit. Convicting with the power of the Holy Spirit is the process whereby the Holy Spirit corrects an ego-aspect's errors in judgment at the dyadic level. Most errors in judgment are the result of shaming judgments accepted by an ego-aspect. It is very likely that the Holy Spirit is operative in both the early and later studies, but its power is made explicit when Christ is asked to convict an image.

The verbatims describing my work with Tory, Marion (Chapter VII), and Leigh (this chapter) illustrate all of the foregoing interventions plus one more: the Holy Spirit's *consecrating* function as I currently understand it. Near the end of the process described in this book, Christ brings an Ideal pair into the Aware-ego's Heart or the heart chakra of an ego-aspect. These pairs are expected to permanently reside in those places and gradually entrain to each other. I also ask that Christ leave a portion of his Light in the center of each of those spaces that will function as *a perpetual fountain of the Holy Spirit's forgiveness*. The client's willingness for Christ to do this, allows Christ to *consecrate* the space as a perpetual fount of the Holy Spirit's will for us.

The positing of a Gendering archetype is the most heuristic explanation I have discerned to account for the universal generation of sexed-images in the Mind, be they self-images, images of others, or their gender aspects. Normally, a sexed-image manifests on the *psychological* level, which embodies the *gestalt* of an Inner dyad. The *Light* is the only methodology I have found that can provide access to the gender aspects underpinning the psychological sexed-images. Unlike a sexed-image at the psychological level, gender aspects are explicitly interdependent and complementary, and therefore require each other to be fully appreciated. It is there relational interdependence and complementarity that sets them apart from the sexed image.

To access the dyadic level underpinning the psychological level, an image – say a mother image, is placed in a circle. Then the *Light* is asked to create two more circles overlaying the first circle. Christ or the Aware-ego uses one of those circles to separate the mother's masculine aspect from her image; and the other circle to extract the feminine aspect from her image (the actual order of extraction is immaterial). *The critical point here is that, using the Light, a masculine and feminine aspect can be extracted from any sexed-image*. As a rule, Christ is asked to perform the extraction process, though it is also possible for an Aware-ego to do so using its own *Light*. The dyadic level can look like the psychological level in that gender aspects are likely to be sexed (male/female). However, the pair can be same-sexed as well as opposite sexed or one aspect can be so ephemeral as appear sexless. Those variations notwithstanding, the masculine and feminine aspects will be inherently relational as both are needed to sustain a sexed-image. In contrast, a sexed-image on the psychological level can meaningfully stand apart from either or both gender aspects, since the both are only partial personifications of its gestalt.

However they manifest, the gender aspects of an Inner dyad will be *complementary* and *interdependent*. The aspects are complementary in that each manifests a different function required to create and sustain a sexed-image; and interdependent insofar as changing either one requires a concomitant change in the other. This complementarity and interdependence makes all sexed-images functionally androgynous – however 'masculine' or 'feminine' the sexed-image may appear. While several theories postulate the existence of Contra-sexual aspects in all of us,[1] I have not found a methodology – *other than the Light and Christ image* – that demonstrates the inherently androgynous nature of all sexed-images. Nonetheless, anyone willing to use the *Light* and image of Christ will be able to extract masculine and feminine aspects from any sexed-image, transform their relationship, and thereby enduringly alter the sexed-image they sustain.

In this chapter, I explore the relational dynamics of Inner dyads, their effects on behavior and object choices, and the interventions I have found helpful in healing dysfunctional Inner dyads. Individuals, who become aware of the gendering process that creates and sustains their ego-aspects and the sexed-images of others, can ask Christ to transform any relevant Inner dyad. But lacking that awareness, the individual appears fated to repeat the relational dynamics initially shaped by the Gendering archetype.

The protocol for examining Inner dyads is quite straightforward. Circles of *Light* are used to extract masculine and feminine aspects from any sexed-image. Once extracted, each aspect of the Inner dyad can be differentiated by gender (masculine/ feminine), sex (male/ female), age (child/ youth/ adolescent/ adult), and their dynamic relationship to each other. The dyadic pairings revealed by this process can be quite varied, complex, and often painfully discordant. Treatment seeks to alter the relationship between the masculine and feminine aspects by changing an aspect's sex, age, definition, energy, and relationship, as deemed appropriate by the client and therapist. Often, the therapist must take the lead in suggesting the direction of changes (until the client learns to appreciate the profound malleability of images), but in all cases involving a *self-image*, the ego-aspect is the final arbitrator of those changes since the changes cannot be forced upon it. To be affected by changes at the dyadic level, the sexed-image must willingly step inside the circle containing the transformed Inner dyad and re-meld with it (or allow the dyad to enter its circle). Of note, only self-images require voluntary reintegration. The reintegration of other images (e.g. parental images), after a dyad that have been altered, does not require the other's willingness.

The gender aspects of an Inner dyad are most often sexed (male/female), *but they may be same sexed or opposite sexed*. In effect, a sexed-image can contain gender aspects that are *both* male sexed, or *both* female sexed, or opposite-sexed. Opposite-sexed gender aspects are the most common and desirable. If the gender aspects are opposite-sexed, the masculine aspect is male sexed and the feminine aspect is female sexed.[2] At the dyadic level, the sex of an aspect is alterable by Christological intervention. Thus, for example, it is possible for Christ to transform a masculine aspect that is female sexed into a masculine aspect that is male sexed. Such transformations are not possible at the psychological level, except by actual sex change operations or cross-dressing. Unless physically altered in some way, the sexed-image of a client is expected to embody their reproductive sex.

All clinical interventions are designed to effect changes in *the characteristics and relationship* of an Inner dyad. Once the masculine and feminine gender aspects have been extracted from a sexed-image their circles are *recombined* so the client can observe the two aspects interacting. The characteristics and interactional 'body language' of the two aspects is used to infer the nature of the relationship.[3] *The goal of treatment is an interaction that is non-incestuous, heterosexual, adult, and mutually satisfying.* I elaborate on those qualities in the next section. Recently, I have begun suggesting that the interaction also be 'unabashedly intimate,' but not necessarily sexual.

Parents acquire their Relational authority because they are the most visible role models in a child's worldview when the archetype begins constellating sexed-images of the self. The Anima and Animus have already constellated the mother and father sexed-images that will serve as the bedrock of the child's self-images. As regards the shaping of personality, the effects of the Gendering archetype are easily the equal in power of the Empowering archetype. But the two archetypes require totally different remediational strategies. A parental image can be *stripped* of its Moral and Temporal authority, which frees an ego-aspect to look elsewhere for guidance. But an individual's Inner dyads – derived from the sexed-images of parents – must be *transformed* to bring about the desired changes. An ego-aspect cannot be 'stripped' of its Inner dyad because that is what defines and sustains it. The Inner dyad must be reshaped to embody more desirable qualities. I have relied on the power of Christ channeling the Holy Spirit to transform the sexed-images of parents and selves. It is possible that alchemical processes, especially those described by Jungians, can achieve the same goal, but I will leave that exploration to others.

At the dyadic level, I have only been able to effect changes in dynamics by offering Christological interventions or the interventions of a comparable higher power. The conscious healing of Inner dyads is beyond the Ego's power acting alone, though the Aware-ego can separate out the aspects using the *Light*. The dyadic level is purely archetypal. The age, sex, definition, energy, and relational dynamics of Inner dyads must be altered at that level and the unaided Ego cannot penetrate to that depth on its own. A client can alter the physical sex of its sexed-image by having a sex change operation or cross-dressing, which might make his or her psychological appearance more congruent with what s/he is experiencing at the dyadic level; but the transformation of an Inner dyad always requires the intervention of a higher power.

Some therapists may consider Christological interventions a limitation. While Christ is seen to draw upon the personal and collective unconscious for new definitions, it is likely he also draws upon the dyadic *relationship* informing his own masculine and feminine aspects.[4] Thus, any new relationship between gender aspects must be treated, in some measure, as 'Christ inspired.' Clients who permit this find it rewarding beyond anything they could accomplish with their unaided will. Other 'higher powers' can also be asked to elicit these changes. I have only observed this in rare instances where a comparable higher power worked in concert with a Christ image. Lee's verbatim presented later in the chapter is an example. I will leave it to other therapists to explore the evocation of 'higher powers' other than Christ.[5]

What sets this chapter apart from the others is the transformational power of the Christological interventions. The images are dramatically and permanently changed beyond anything the client could have hoped to achieve with their unaided will. This is true whether Christ works with the Inner dyad, or directly with the sexed-image and its contrasexual aspect. What the transformation of Inner dyads demonstrates is that changing the gender aspects generates a lasting change in the sexed-image once the aspects are reintegrated with the image. But even where Christ only works with the sexed-image he can bring about comparable transformations by *convicting* the image with the power of the Holy Spirit or *reordering* it by injecting the Holy Spirit into the image at the subatomic level. (Both are illustrated in the later studies). Today, I am likely to work in all of the above contexts. The major difference is that in the early studies Christ is only asked to alter the feminine aspect and use his 'masculine energy' to sustain the redefinition until the masculine aspect can accommodate to the changes; and no explanation is given as to how he alters the feminine aspect. In the later studies, he is always asked to *convict* whatever level or combination of levels he is working with. It is likely that the Holy Spirit is operational in both sets of studies, but only explicitly so in the later studies. Also, it is likely that Christ's 'masculine energy,' evoked in the early studies is distinctly different from his power to convict but I do not attempt to parcel out the distinctions. In both the early and later studies, the 'photo' is changed, but transformation by conviction with the Holy Spirit is more definitive; and moving the Ideal pairs into a purified Heart and heart chakras seems comparable to generating a three dimensional holographic image.

Lastly, I would note that the sexed-image dictates much more than interpersonal relationships. Its Inner dyad also dictates major personality characteristics and character traits, as well as underlying causes of psychosomatic illnesses. These will also be significantly ameliorated or transformed by the Christological interventions described in this chapter. In psychotherapy, my objective is not simply to change an image, but rather to alter the psychology, physiognomy, and energy of the person being controlled by those images. The power of these interventions is their ability to dramatically change the person, as well as the symptoms that brought them to therapy. Altering the Inner dyad and sexed-image gestalt directly affects the person's character, personality, and physical wellbeing, as will as their interpersonal interactions and object choices.

THE INNER DYAD

This section provides a general discussion of findings regarding the Inner dyad. The next section will provide case illustrations of the early studies. This is a complex topic with many potential links to the esoteric and religious literature of the world. I report the findings of the early studies because they have helped me (and hopefully the reader) to better understand the assertions of other perspectives such as Hermeticism, Alchemy, Gnosticism, and Kabbalah; and major yogic and medical disciplines of the Near and Far East.

In this work gender is treated as distinctly different from sex. Gender denotes the complementary, interdependent interaction of the masculine and feminine aspects underpinning all sexed-images. It is asserted here, that both aspects are required for the creation of a sexed-image in the Mind. The complementary interdependence of that Inner dyad is a core premise of both Kabbalah and Far Eastern metaphysics. As with those disciplines, in this work the feminine component always provides the definition of the sexed-image, even when the sex of the image is male; and the masculine component always provides the energy for the sexed-image, even when the sex is female.[6] Electricity passing through a light bulb illustrates the relationship. Electricity and bulb are both needed to create light, which is the bulb's raison d'être. Electricity provides the masculine or energic component, and the bulb provides the feminine or definitional component. The bulb defines the purpose to which the electricity is put. Without the bulb, the electricity has no vessel of expression. Without electricity, the bulb cannot function as defined. In effect, each is complementary in function and dependent upon the other to generate light. Too little electricity and the bulb dims; too much and it is likely to explode. The masculine and feminine gender aspects of every Inner dyad enact a similar complementarity and interdependence. For every human image, the masculine provides the energic component and the feminine its definitional component.

The Inner dyads described by clients are almost like snowflakes in their variations, even when limited to the small set of variables I have studied. What makes it all manageable – from my perspective, is a definite set of treatment goals. These are admittedly arbitrary insofar as they assign very definite valuations to each variable. My goal of treatment in working with Inner dyads is *an adult, non-incestuous, heterosexual, relationship between two mutually consenting and life enhancing gender aspects*. This goal is based, first, on the observation of numerous, painfully 'deviant,' Inner dyads, and secondly, on Christ's ability to achieve it. Occasionally, for example, the aspects of a dyad will manifest as parent and child (incestuous). In such instances one of the sub-goals of treatment will be raising the child to adulthood and changing the identity of either or both aspects so there emerges a non-incestuous relationship. In a similar vein, gender aspects can be same-sexed as often as they are opposite-sexed. Such aspects will convey masculine and feminine characteristics, but both be of the same sex, e.g. macho and effeminate male, butch and fem female, tomboy, transgendered, etc. Same-sexed aspects generally point to a difficulty in relating to the opposite sex. Less frequently, a gender aspect – most often the masculine, can appear sexless as in ghostlike. But again, the goal remains an adult, sexed, image that matches the gender of the aspect. Relationship is by far the most crucial variable. The body language of the two aspects when seen together is the most telling in terms of treatment goals. For example, if the two images are standing far apart, or back to back, or clearly in a dominant/submissive stance, then the two images must be worked with until they can mutually interact with unconditional positive regard.[7]

All gender pairs can be defined by the *quality* of their connection. The preferred connection is one in which neither overwhelms the other, and the connection is mutually and positively reinforcing. Ideally, I would argue that the aspects be able to 'lovingly embrace' or exhibit an 'unabashed intimacy.' But regardless of the quality, *no Inner dyad can long function without an ongoing point of contact* however negative or positive. Prolonged withdrawal, or other active interference with a connection, invariably leads to *depression* of the individual if the dyadic pair underpins a dominant ego-aspect. For example, any ego-aspect created to cope with sexual abuse will embody a masculine-feminine interaction that either accedes to or resists the abuse. Either way, the sexed-image embodying the interaction will be conflicted. Resistance will be painful, while acceding is only achieved by morally conflicted sexualization or submission. In either case the probability of eventual psychosomatic illness is near certainty. The Ego is likely to create a number of sexed-images in an effort to cope with sexual abuse – particularly if it is ongoing, in an effort to sustain the least painful connection between the masculine and feminine aspects. Even though one becomes the preferred choice, the others will continue to exist in a repressed or dissociated state. In the remediation of dysfunctional Inner dyads, abusively created Inner dyads are probably the most problematical. This is especially true if the abuse is sexual since the sexed-image is obliged to re-experience the dysfunction at some level every time the individual is aroused. It is possible to put an end to the toxic effects of sexual abuse on ego-aspects; and imperative that therapists do so, if possible, in order to clear the emotional fields of accumulated unexpressed shame that is an inevitable consequence of such conflict. Interventions for ameliorating the effects of sexual abuse are described in Appendix I.

Sometimes, clients will report a lack of form regarding a particular gender aspect, but in all such cases, there is an *acknowledged sense of presence*, what I call a nebulous or sexless presence. When that presence is finally allowed to manifest it is generally opposite-sexed. The existence of a sexless presence generally reflects denial on the part of the client, who has difficulty allowing the gender aspect to have apposite sexed attributes for fear of experiencing those gender qualities in his or her own makeup or parental image. But if queried, the client can generally recall at least one event or trait that characterizes an otherwise sexless aspect. That event or trait generally serves as a first approximation of the opposite-sexed aspect. Wherever the client has difficulty imagining an opposite-sexed aspect, the therapist needs to treat it as a fear of the opposite sex. That fear needs to be addressed and ameliorated before proceeding. In many cases, the fear – particularly for men, is a fear of perceived weakness in their sense-of-self, or fear of an overwhelming power attributed to the opposite sex.

The Flow of Life Sustaining and Sexual Energy

The flow of life sustaining energy is neither masculine nor feminine, but appears to be governed by both. The meridians, for example, upon which acupuncture is based, are divided into feminine and masculine; and *all meridians* are needed to sustain the Body. Too much yin or yang, or too little, is always considered detrimental to the health of the individual. In most cases, the goal of acupuncture is an optimum flow of energy within and between meridians. It could be said that life energy is masculine insofar as the masculine gender aspect always personifies the energy of an Inner dyad; but it is difficult to prove since every sexed-image has a feminine component, and that component will govern *the quality of flow* as it manifests in the sexed-image. Even where a masculine aspect appears to overwhelm feminine governance, in actuality what is also being observed is the feminine aspect's resistance to that particular flow of life energy. But whether the observer chooses to identify the feminine as resistant or overwhelmed, the long-term consequence will be pathological. Both aspects of the Inner dyad – their chronological age, parity, and quality of contact, determine the flow of life energy (e.g. chi, ki, prana) permitted by a particular ego-aspect or image of another.

Sexual energy is treated as a distinct manifestation of life energy flowing through sexualized images and organs. Sexual energy appears to be the most consistent manifestation of Kundalini energy, which is also widely posited as the source of life-energy. As sexual energy, life energy will be most often limited in expression to the Emotional auric body.[8] Some Inner dyads draw heavily on sexual energy to maintain a point of contract that would otherwise be too painful and centrifugal. For example, a sado-masochistic relationship is inherently painful. If not for the sexual component there would be little to attract the masochist. Without the sexual attraction, the masochist would be inclined to terminate a relationship with a sadist; and without other manifestations of imagined contact between the sexes, the masochist would eventually become depressed. It is literally like being between a rock and a hard place. Without a sexual attraction, the contact would be too painful to bear, and without the contact depression would ensue. This is why students of sexuality note that every sadist needs a masochist, and every voyeur needs an exhibitionist.

All sexed-images are potential channels of sexual energy. The quality of flow appears to be determined by the sex, maturational development, and relationship of the aspects comprising the Inner dyad. All else being equal, masculine and feminine aspects that are *both* male-sexed will generate a greater flow of sexual energy than two aspects that are opposite-sexed or female-sexed. All else being equal, two *adult* male gender aspects will generate a greater flow of energy than two prepubescent males. While two adult male gender aspects theoretically channel the greatest amount of sexual energy, this flow is seen on several levels as dissipating rather than optimal. Essentially, the relationship lacks the fuller definition offered by a feminine female aspect. Two male gender aspects exemplify force relating to force, which fails to provide a sufficient container for relationship beyond the sexual encounter, much like water flowing onto a sand dune. I can imagine exceptions, specifically, instances where the feminine aspect – though male sexed – is clearly feminine in the gender relationship (i.e. effeminate male or 'shemale'). But I can only speculate here since I have not worked with enough gay males to generalize.

Remember that masculine and feminine aspects express functions – the one predominantly energic and the other predominantly definitional. Whether we are talking about a male person or a female person, their sexed-image will have a masculine and feminine aspect. It is the complementary function of the two aspects that defines the flow of energy. Stated another way, at the dyadic level, *sex, gender, age and relationship* all combine to express the complementarity of two aspects. Masculinity reflects the force and form of energy, and femininity reflects the definition that the energy is expected to sustain. For example, egg and sperm are alike as carriers of chromosomal strands, but still different in their contribution to the whole. The female provides a definitional contribution at all levels – from the determination of sex to embryonic development and birth. But note too, that too rigid a definition can restrict the flow of energy. Rigid definition leads to entropy. Whereas two male gender aspects tend to dissipate the flow of sexual energy by providing too little definition, the presence of two female gender aspects can constrict it by providing too much definition. But a very 'butch' (female) masculine aspect could approach a heterosexual pair in terms of energy flow, and comparably, a very 'nurturing male in a gay relationship could also approach that standard.

While a masculine male aspect engaging a feminine female aspect generally indicates an optimal flow of life energy, there are notable exceptions to that as well. One pertinent example is an *adult* feminine female aspect and a *prepubescent* masculine male aspect. An undeveloped youth (e.g. puer), cannot adequately sustain the definition of an adult feminine female aspect whether familial (a mother) or non-familial. Dyads comprised of such 'mother-puer' pairs are likely to generate a male *sexed-image* that is 'effeminate,' ineffectual, lacking strength or power; or a female *sexed-image* that is low energy and domestic. At the other extreme, an

Inner dyad defined by a father-like masculine male aspect and a prepubescent daughter-like feminine female aspect will create a female *sexed-image* that is both emotional and relatively undiscerning (e.g. daddy's little girl), or a male *sexed-image* that is overly forceful and controlling (e.g. the proverbial male).

Normally, the selves that present for psychotherapy are not particularly sexual in nature. They are personas: sexed-images created to act in public. Some personas can be highly sexualized as when an individual dresses provocatively for all-the-world to see. But I have seen very few clients that present in that way, and those that do have shown little interest in the explorations described in this work. But even clients who come to psychotherapy in non-sexual personas are nonetheless sexual. They just strive to obscure it from most people-in-the-world. What can be problematical is their hiding it from themselves. Individuals appear to function better when they have conscious, unconflicted, access to Inner dyads that facilitate the flow of sexual energy.[9]

The Inner dyad and Object Choice

The Gendering archetype appears to draw on parental sexed-images, constellated by Anima and Animus, to constellate the Ego's most enduring Inner dyad, i.e. the Familial personality. The earliest sexed-image of self will be the *Familial personality*, which the Ego eventually incorporates as part of the Dominant self. This Dominant self will initially govern many of the client's interactions in the extended family; and strongly determine the individual's partner choices in adulthood. My clinical observations lead me to conclude that the Familial personality is generally the *recapitulated* image of a grandparent reinforced by the modeled behavior of both parents. Stated another way: the Familial personality generally recapitulates the parent whose extended family makes the strongest claim on a child. Each child has four biological grandparents, each of whom seeks to continue their lineages through grandchildren.[10] This modeling of the grandparent is rarely a perfect identity as it is actually a recapitulation of a grandparent's Inner dyad *reactively filtered through the parent and reinforced by the other parent's role enactments*.[11] That is, the Familial personality constellated in the child is the recapitulated effect of the claiming parent's reaction to his or her own parent. The child's birth order most frequently determines which grandparent provides the recapitulated dyad for the child's Familial personality.[12] If the parent and grandparent are positively bonded, and everyone the same sex, then the child's Familial personality could be very much like the grandparent's personality. If, however, the parent and grandparent have a strained or cutoff relationship, the child's personality could manifest as a not-me complex or one in which the child is treated as a black sheep or rebel in the family. However, this is not an either-or situation. As noted in the endnotes, there are a number of possible permutations in this set of hypotheses that allow for numerous variations between those two extremes.

The Relational authority of parents will also manifest in the child's unconscious modeling of interactional roles modeled by the parents. Those role assimilations can reinforce or mitigate the Inner dyad of the Familial personality. When the client becomes an adult, his or her Familial personality will strive to enact one of the *interactional* roles modeled by the parents (or set of grandparents or parent-grandparent combination). That interactional role and concomitant Inner dyad will greatly influence the adult's choice of partners. The roles are repositories of stereotypic interactional patterns learned from both parents. In theory, the child learns both roles and can assume either one as an adult, but in practice, s/he will generally prefer to reenact the parent/grandparent who constellated the Familial personality. The Familial personality's preference for one role will oblige it to seek partners willing to assume the role of the other parent or grandparent. This can decisively limit the individual's choice of mates insofar as it limits choices to parameters defined by parental roles and the Familial personality's preference for one role over the other.

Few clients appreciate the Familial personality's investment in a particular parental role until it is consciously visualized. Yet it is easily done. The therapist has only to ask the client to visualize both parents in the same circle of *Light* in a way that reflects their marriage or life together. The observed interaction is generally stereotypic in nature and somewhat timeless as it is rarely affected by events unless consciously addressed. This interaction – the parental 'dance' – is a byproduct of the parents' own Inner dyads, which tend to dovetail each other in a synchronistic way, even if the synchronicity is traumatizing for them and others. The client's own interactions with significant others will likewise dovetail the parental interactions in a way that is, often, painfully obvious. Interactional roles generally encapsulate a series of scripted interactions for entering into and sustaining a relationship with significant others. I imagine it as an album of snapshots showing a husband and wife interacting together. Grown children tend to compulsively reenact these stereotypic interactions in their own relationships with others (even if the parental relationship was, and remains, woefully inadequate). These scripts will extend to the raising of children as well as dictating the relationship with a spouse/lover. Essentially, interactional roles provide the dialogic scripts for two interacting Familial personalities.

The need for a complementary 'fit' governs the individual's selection of mates. The Familial personality normally demands someone whose Familial personality offers a complementary role. In certain circumstances such a partner could even be expected to enact the qualities of an opposite-sexed parent. For example, the firstborn daughter of a firstborn father will be most strongly identified with the paternal grandfather and seek out a spouse most like her mother and/or paternal grandmother. Ideally, interactional roles reflect mutually affirming actions between parents. But that is rarely the case in a clinical population.

If there is severe dissonance or cutoff between a parent and grandparent, the parent is likely to project a not-me self into the image of the child identified with that grandparent. Such projections are likely to generate Bi-polar, Borderline, and/or Paranoid disorders in the child, if the grandparent's legacy is truly dysfunctional. (Alternatively, a miscarriage, stillbirth, or abortion will frequently correlate with a birth order position that would have identified the fetus with a disowned grandparent.[13] Where there is an ongoing, but strained, relationship between the parent and grandparent, the child's Familial personality can be repressed and projected back into that grandparent, and a grandparental identity offered by the other parent can assume dominance. In other words, instead of being identified with the birth order grandparent, the child actually represses the personality in favor of one offered by the other parent. However, if a child is obliged to repress the Familial personality of the parent/grandparent who makes a primary claim, there is a high likelihood that the adult client will find a spouse who will function as a suitable projective 'vessel' for the disowned identity. In one guise or another, 'the sins of the parent will be visited on the children for three onto four generations' unless successfully ameliorated by a higher power.

Regardless of which interactional role a client enacts, that role will dictate the need for a complementary, interdependent, counterpart. This is why repeated choices generally repeat past mistakes when it comes to partner choices. Of note, an individual choosing a second spouse can assume the less preferred role dictated by an interactional script, but the relationship will be just as painful and the role a less comfortable fit. Fortunately, interactional roles can be dramatically altered by Christological interventions. That is the basic thrust of both the early and later studies. The only way to free our selves from the 'sins of the fathers and/or the mothers' is to redeem the fathers and/or mothers and the Familial personality emulating them. Christ can be asked to transform the Inner dyad of each parent as well as the Inner dyad of any self that is identified as a personification of the Familial personality. Christ can be asked to convict with the power of the Holy Spirit until the client is totally and completely satisfied with the new image or Inner dyad extracted from any of those images. Then Christ can be asked to convict the relationship between the parents until the client is totally and completely satisfied with that relationship. The transformation of parental images and/or their Inner dyads does not automatically alter the Inner dyads of the client, which are self-willed in adulthood; but initial work with them demonstrates that it is possible to do the same for the Familial personality and any other self-image. More to the point, clients are more comfortable with the process if asked to first work with images of parents. Finally, I should stress that the Dominant self's compunction to function as its own conscience overlays the Familial personality or Personality, such that it is near impossible to work with and repair a dysfunctional Familial personality until the power to self-shame is addressed.

The Interventional Processes for Early and Later Studies

In the early studies, the interventional process evolved through two stages. In the earliest work, I focused on identifying and altering the contra-sexual aspect *of a sexed-image*. The extraction of a contra-sexual aspect is illustrated in the first two case examples. In the second stage of those early studies, I came to understand that it was possible to extract both gender aspects from the same sexed-image – the Inner dyad.[14] Once one or both gender aspects are extracted, the two images are examined in detail as regards their physical characteristics, sex, age and relationship. In the earliest studies, Christ was asked to begin the process of transformation by working with the feminine aspect. Since the feminine aspect determines the definition of the dyad, Christ was asked to change her till she achieved an ideal proportion, relationally speaking. Although it was Christ who shaped her, the self from whom the Inner dyad was extracted would have the final say in determining when the Inner dyad was reintegrated. What made all of that possible was Christ's willingness to transform the feminine aspect and then *sustain the changed aspect with his own masculine energy until the dyad's masculine aspect accommodated to the change in the feminine*. In the earliest studies, wherein the client did not work directly with the masculine aspect, I always emphasized to the client that Christ would sustain his transformation of the feminine with his own masculine energy until such time as the masculine aspect accommodated to the change. If Christ did not sustain the transformed feminine with his own masculine energy, the aspect would have been forced to revert back to her original form in order to maintain a continuing a point of contact with the energic masculine.[15] In the early studies where both aspects were extracted, following the transformation of a feminine aspect, I would shift the focus to the masculine aspect. That aspect was helped to understand that, unless it changed to accommodate the feminine aspect in her new form, it would eventually dissipate from lack of a container; and another sexed-image would supplant the current one. When the Aware-ego was satisfied with the new relationship between the two aspects, s/he would then ask Christ to reintegrate them into the sexed-image. That reintegration could be enacted by the Aware-ego, if the ego-aspect remained merged with it, or by a dissociated image if it was separated from the Aware-ego. Predictably, the sexed-image would change to reflect the new relationship. I always described the steps of this intervention to the client before we started as well as reiterating them throughout the process. Working with the first Inner dyad could take several sessions, but after the first dyad was reintegrated the process moved more quickly. I would also tell each client beforehand that the goal of treatment was a non-incestuous, heterosexual, adult, relationship between the two aspects that was mutually enhancing and satisfying; and I discourage them from accepting anything less.[16]

In the later studies, which take up the bulk of this chapter, Christ always convicts with the power of the Holy Spirit. That conviction is always *simultaneously* applied to both gender aspects, whether they remain embedded in the sexed-image, or one is extracted and the other remains embedded, or both are extracted. Interventionally, that is the only real difference between the early and later studies.

Functional androgyny has been repeatedly dismissed or denied by Western culture. The *apparent* sex of most images supports this denial. As well, when the client looks inside, s/he sees images of males or females. But using the *Light*, the client can observe a complementary, contra-sexual, aspect embedded in all sexed-images. So denial notwithstanding, individuals who fail to discover internalized masculine-feminine aspects that are interactionally healthy, run a high risk of psychological disorders, psychosomatic illness, or actual suicide. The inability to sustain viable, internalized, masculine-feminine connections is treated here as a potential death knell. Chronic psychic trauma is perceived as inevitable when these complementary masculine and feminine aspects are perpetually at loggerheads, or where one is dominant at the expense of the other. Not surprising, in examining complementarity in a clinical population, it is rare to find Inner dyads that are healthy and mutually empowering. Such distortions may be the primary reason why most individuals enter therapy though they are rarely able to verbalize it as such, except in terms of relational issues with others. Those 'relational issues' are always a reflection of Inner dyad discord. When I am able to work directly with the Inner dyads the client's relationships improve. Equally often, I find that working at dyadic level also has an ameliorative effect on psychological symptoms such as depression, bipolar disorders and substance abuse.

The masculine and feminine gender aspects of the most dominant ego-aspects are initially shaped by parental images. This is why parental images are so critical. Thus far I have not been able to determine whose aspects – mother or father – will be most pivotal for a particular client. Regardless of whom the client identifies as most problematical, when we commence work with the other parent, its role becomes – if anything, equally pivotal. For any particular individual it is reasonable to expect considerable overlap in the Inner dyads of both the parents and client. For example, a son's feminine aspect is likely to dovetail with his father's feminine aspect as well as the mother's. But in conflicted relationships the parents' Inner dyads can be dramatically different. Even if circumstances lead me to address one parent's Inner dyad first, I still push to work with the other parent's Inner dyad as well. They are interlocking. Hence, the greatest shifts occur when all three are addressed (i.e. the Inner dyads of mother, father, and Familial personality). Often, the client will "resist" making changes to any ego-aspect strongly defined by a parent until the parental dyad is also addressed. I suspect this is partially so because that parent's Inner dyad has unilaterally dictated the client's Inner dyads.

Anima/Animus And The Gendering Archetype

Here I want to differentiate between the Gendering archetype and Carl Jung's belief that each of us has an Animus or Anima archetype that constellates images with contra-sexual energy that strongly complements the conscious self. 'Contra-sexual' is a term used by Carl Jung to denote an archetypal energy that constellates images of the opposite sex, imbuing them with the power to capture and hold an ego-aspect's attention and interest. The archetype is active throughout our lifetime. The images it constellates can be negative as well as positive. The intent in either case is a binding attraction. Jung asserted that all males have an archetype that constellates female images with *Anima* (soul) power to attract; and that all females have an archetype that constellates male images with *Animus* (spirit) power to attract. The contra-sexual image can range from the merely human to images of gods and goddesses. Jung believed that an individual could only be affected by the archetype generating contra-sexual energy. But in recent years an increasing number of Jungians have argued that individuals must be prepared to address both Anima and Animus constellations in inner work.[17, 18]

In my work, I have assumed that the archetypal attractions generated by the Anima/Animus archetypes are *conjointly expressed* via the Gendering archetype. Jung did not treat them as normally relational or modulated by a Gendering archetype. Instead, he identified constellations in which a contra-sexual image *compensates* conscious relational opposites. Our differing perspective may be accounted for by the observation that Jung found these inordinately powerful constellations in his dreams and the dreams of his patients, in alchemical processes, in the myths of different cultures, and in Ego-enthrallments. In contrast, I have explored these energies by asking Christ to extract a masculine and feminine gender aspect while consciously aware of images in active imagination. My understanding does not contradict the thesis put forth by Jung, if the reader can accept that the Anima/Animus archetypes can manifest as modulated expressions of the Gendering archetype as well *as in extremis*, especially during dreaming. The Mind can experience them in a relatively balanced way when they manifest as the underpinning of an image; or in extremis when they manifest as an enthralling attraction. I think of Inner dyads as the human experience of Unity's *first division*. Unity encompasses all opposites – the positive and negative of creation, what Jung called the Syzygy. Anima and Animus provide the elemental forms and energies needed by the Gendering archetype to inform and sustain every image within the Mind. *But there are times when one or the other of these core energies exceeds a balancing threshold and effectively overwhelms its opposite. When this happens the energy becomes identifiable as flowing directly from the Anima or Animus archetype.* Ego enthrallments such as those found in Ideal and Temporal personas and during periods of being 'in love,' are primary examples of such an infusion. The desire to submit to a powerful male or female would be another example of animus/animus enthrallment. Numinous images actively sought after in the treatment of a Pre-moral aspect would also fall into this category. In effect, the image becomes supersaturated with Anima or Animus energy, which generally imbues it with an archetypal demeanor. Last I would mention the contra-sexual aspect of an Ideal pair found by Christ for residence in the Aware-ego's Heart. This aspect is also, frequently, an archetypal image.

Super-saturation generates an image that is a full octave above the normal activity of an ego-aspect. It creates an image more resonant with the Soul than the Mind, though otherwise human in its qualities. When experienced *in extremis*, the Anima or Animus archetype *transforms* an image in a way that grants it inordinate power to influence the individual. Jung believed that the Anima (feminine) was most pronounced in its effects on men; and the Animus (masculine) was most pronounced in its effects on women. However, insofar as both are needed to create and sustain an image, I would argue that both gender energies can be felt in extremis and transform images of both sexes in the same individual.

When Anima/animus infuses other images – as distinct from infusing ego-aspects – the images become 'larger than life.' Generally, an ego-aspect that relates to an anima/animus image will experience it as more powerful or ascendant than itself. For a discerning individual, it will seem less powerful than a mythic image such as Christ, but more powerful than mere Ego.[19] For the undiscerning, such an image is simply enthralling. If it is the image of a real person in the world then that enthrallment is likely to be experienced as 'anima/animus possession.' The classic example is 'falling in love' wherein the individual willingly deconstructs a life path in pursuit of his or her 'love.' But note, archetypal energies can also play a significant role in the 'veneration' of figures such as the Blessed Virgin or Mary Magdalene, and it seems immaterial whether the person 'venerating' them is a male or female. The same is true for men and women whose followers treat them as avatars or saints.

But the Archetypal Energy Belongs to the Client

Every image that *exercises power over an ego-aspect* has been constellated with archetypal energy that belongs to the client. *It is his or her archetypal energy* that imbues any particular image with power over the Ego. Any father within the Mind is not inherently 'God the Father' or even his first cousin. Rather, a father image is the constellated effect of one or more archetypes such as the Animus, Gendering, and Empowering archetypes, which imbue the image with god-like powers. The source of that constellating energy abides *within the child, not the image; and under special circumstances the archetypal connection can be removed from the image or transformed*. Since the archetypal constellation of images in early childhood precedes even the creation of a Familial personality intended to cope with those constellations, the most enduring self-images will be created by circumstances well beyond the child's control. If a father repeatedly abuses a child, then his constellated image will necessitate the creation of ego-aspects capable of coping with those interactions. These coping aspects will likely to be slavishly, rebelliously, or submissively bound to that father. *But the energies sustaining the image of that father do not belong to the father; they reside in the child*. Insofar as Christ is allowed to transform any image in the Mind, he can alter the quality of the masculine/feminine bond sustaining the image. In the parlance of acupuncture, he can adjust the flow of yin and yang energies. Once the client has grasped this understanding of archetypally infused images – that it is his or her archetypal energy being channeled by the image, s/he can begin asking her Christ incarnation to transform any negatively charged image or relationship. The Ego does not have the power to transform archetypal constellations with its unaided will, but it can exercise willingness to ask a higher power to do so on its behalf.

Gender-Sex and Age Congruence

A gender aspect is defined as 'contra-sexual' if its gender qualities are the opposite of an image's *biological* sex. But some gender aspects can be "sex deviant," meaning they can exhibit contra-sexual gender qualities but present as the same sex. Consider, for example, the Inner dyad of a female ego-aspect whose feminine aspect is wearing a sundress, and whose masculine aspect (her contra-sexual aspect) is also female but wearing a farmer's overalls. Another example would be the extracted feminine aspect of a male image that is essentially an effeminate male or shemale.

Primary masculine attributes – whether found in a masculine or feminine aspect, are generally expressions of strength, force, or power, or wear masculine apparel, or engage in traditionally male activities. (But note, it is a misnomer to think of the feminine as contrastingly weak or passive. The feminine is only passive in being *receptive* to the energy the masculine aspect generates to sustain her definition. Her 'receptivity' can be decidedly firm.) As a rule, I treat gender/sex disparities as problematical. If disparate, they need to become congruent. For example, if a male client describes his feminine aspect as feminine in gender but male in sex, then one goal of treatment will be the aspect's transformation into a female, feminine aspect. There can be numerous reasons for sex/gender disparities. A common reason is the perception of contra-sexual attributes as shamefully weakening. Such fears impede the optimal expression of dyadic interaction and bonding. Wherever possible, Christ is asked to remove that fear so the aspect can manifest as gender and sex congruent. In this work, the human image is always treated as androgynous, i.e. bi-gendered and bi-sexed at the dyadic level. Every sexed-image I have explored has been shown to have a contra-sexual gender aspect embedded within it. In order to be completely healed, the contra-sexual aspect needs to become sex congruent if it is not so when it first presents. All Inner dyads, when healed, are expected to reflect a heterosexual relationship irrespective of the client's sexual proclivities.[20]

In the later studies involving contra-sexual aspects, I may have the client extract his or her contra-sexual aspect while the Aware-ego remains merged with the same sexed aspect (the aspect that is the same sex as the client). Since most of my clients are female this means extracting the masculine or animus aspect. However this manifests, the goal will be for the masculine to evolve by the *simultaneous conviction* of the masculine aspect and the feminine aspect that remains merged with the Aware-ego. In this particular intervention, the client assesses Inner dyad changes by observing changes in the personified contra-sexual aspect and felt changes in response to those changes.

Age incongruence is another quality of gender aspects that must be addressed in treatment. Diagnostically, the most common manifestation of age incongruence is where one aspect of the Inner dyad is a child, prepubescent, or adolescent and the other is an adult. Quite often, in addition to being an age issue, these relationships are also incestuous. In these conditions the goal is to reshape the images so that both are adult and the relationship is non-incestuous. It goes without saying that only a higher power such as Christ could effect such changes.

In a clinical setting, *prepubescent* gender aspects are generally indicative of childhood abuse or sexual repression. (I suspect they are also prevalent in pedophiles, but I have not worked with that population) except from the perspective of the adult children they abused. If the abuser is a parent or close relative, and sexualization occurs over a period of time, then the interaction can forge a powerful masculine-feminine dyad in the child that must be corrected in therapy. I have only been able to do this successfully by evoking a Christ who can desexualize and reshape the incestuous relationship.[21] The most difficult part of this process is appreciating that what is being addressed is not the relationship between the relative and child, but rather the relationship between the child's masculine and feminine aspects, which condition client to repeat those encounters imaginatively or act them out in order to sustain those particular connections. In all cases of childhood sexual abuse, it is imperative that any Inner dyads created by the abuse be addressed and reconciled using the Christ image. I am hard pressed to suggest how this is to be done apart from a Christ image or comparable higher power (i.e. Sophia-Christ, guardian angel, Inner Self Helper, etc.). Often this needs to be done in concert with the sexual interventions described in Appendix I. It needs to be stressed and stressed again that we are dealing here with archetypal energies that are simply not amenable to Ego manipulation, expect by defenses that inevitably cripple the Mind and Body. The Ego's willingness is always required for the transformations, but that willingness is always an expression of the Ego acceding to a higher power.

Sexual Fantasy as a Counter Balance to Discordant Inner Dyads

Relational authority plays a significant role in the client's choice of sexual fantasies and preferences.[22] Sexual fantasies serve to overcome, or compensate for, stereotypic discord between parents that threaten to derail the unitive striving of the Gendering archetype. An harmonious, unitive striving of masculine-feminine connections is all-important to the individual's well being. Sexuality – especially as manifest in fantasy, appears to overcome disruptive interactional roles. When used thus, the primary purpose of sexual fantasy – be it pornographic or romantic,[23] is to maintain masculine-feminine connections that would otherwise deteriorate under the assault of negative emotions expressed by stereotypic marital discord or disengagement. Stated another way, where the unitive striving of an interactional role is threatened by disruptive emotions, then sexual fantasy can temporarily overcome the threatened dissolution by injecting sexual attraction. In effect, imaginative connections, particularly of a sexual nature, help to maintain connections at a psychological level that might otherwise threaten to become centrifugal.[24]

The Final Step

The final step is always the same: gender aspects must be reintegrated with the sexed-image to effectively alter the image. If the client is working with the image of another person, then the reintegration can be done with or without the image's willingness. However, if the client is working with a self-image, then the self-image must willingly accede to the reintegration. The self is not changed until it willingly melds with the transformed Inner dyad. This is most easily done by the Aware-ego or self-image stepping into the circle containing the Inner dyad, or by inviting them to enter its circle.

CASE ILLUSTRATIONS

Being thorough here would require a whole other book. Working with Inner dyads generates myriad variations. The entire process can be lengthy, often extending over several months, in part because numerous other issues are triggered, or emergent life events divert attention from it. But mostly it is the variations that make illustration so difficult. Whatever I offer by way of examples will not even scratch the surface. And frankly, I do not want to bog the reader down in detail here. The major thrust of this chapter is the later work – the conviction of sexed-images by the power of the Holy Spirit. I will leave it to others to write the book on Inner dyads. Hopefully, the following cases will illustrate the process. All of the interventions and issues discussed in the forgoing sections play an integral role in the later studies and are amply illustrated in those later sections. The examples given here are from studies preceding my awareness of Christ's ability to convict images with the power of the Holy Spirit.

Bethany. This case illustrates a severe distortion of the feminine extracted from a father image. During this period of time I was still working only with contra-sexual extractions. Bethany needed a felt sense of the feminine that could speak to her father and be heard by him. Bethany's father had been dead for several months. He died as he had lived, never really hearing his daughter. Bethany has little difficulty extracting the father's contra-sexual aspect and she is not surprised that it models how she always felt in her father's presence. "Her posture is one of 'tell me what to do.'… she does not want to show her face…her posture is twisted, going inward, down…I felt it deeply with him a lot…the image of not having a face, not having a posture (opinion), not having my own voice." Shortly after this description, I suggest she begin the process of letting Christ heal the contra-sexual aspect of her father's image. In response to Christ's ministrations, she describes the image as straightening up, becoming lighter and energetic, but the image still does not have a face. Bethany insists she is most in need of a voice. (I would note here that this client had great difficulty being heard. Often, I had to ask her to repeat herself. Speaking up was a real issue for her.) As Christ continues to heal this image, the image grows in size and, concomitantly, the father's image becomes smaller. This symbolizes for her that in order for her to have more voice the father will have to have less. At this point, I suggest she allow Christ to connect the two images heart to heart. She seeks to do so but immediately loses both images (fear or resistance, I am not sure which). Bethany then voices considerable conflict. Initially, she thought it would be better if Christ connected her father's ears to the feminine image's voice, but then considered that this might be a limitation on the image's voice. This conflict would not be resolved till the following session. Often clients will delay reintegration in order for the Mind to assimilate implications. Implicitly, the client recognizes that reintegration can dramatically alter, not only the parent's image, but his or her self-image as well. In the next session Bethany opts for a heart to heart connection that afforded both her and her father more latitude in speaking and hearing. It definitely improved her ability to be heard in future sessions.

Most of my female clients can extract contra-sexual images from their parental images. For men, it seems more difficult. Men sense, as do women, that these images have had a significant role in shaping the masculine identity. One man, whose father abandoned him at birth, and who lived with his mother most of his adult life, could not imagine his mother having a masculine aspect. (After saying that, he commented that she frequently had to shave the hair from her upper lip.) He felt that, if he had a feminine aspect, it would make him a "sissy." This fear gave his mother undue influence in his sexual development. When he was finally able to identify his mother's contra-sexual aspect, he discovered an effeminate male, much like an image of himself at fourteen, which she had tacitly supported. He remembers consciously forgoing that identity when his father shamed him for it, but encountered it later in his sexual fantasies.

Today, I rarely restrict the process to extracting just the contra-sexual aspect from a sexed-image. If an ego-aspect – usually a Dominant self, resists change by Christ at a psychological level, I will shift the focus to the dyadic level. In that case, I will initially have the Aware-ego extract the contra-sexual aspect first, but invariably, I will then encourage the extraction of the same sexed aspect. (Of note, this extraction process does not need the permission of a self that has been separated from the Aware-ego. But any changes to the dyad absolutely require the ego-aspect's willingness to reintegrate them; and there will be no real change in the sexed-image until there is reintegration.)

The above illustration is an example of the earliest work, which eventually led to the discovery of the Inner dyad and interactional roles; and those, in turn, set the stage for the most powerful interventions I can offer in this book – transformations by the power of the Holy Spirit. The next two verbatims illustrated the exploration of Inner dyads.

Patty. Patty is a grade school teacher and divorced mother of two children (both young adolescents). She lives near her parents and relies heavily on her father for emotional support and work chores. She is attractive and fit, with a wiry, muscular, frame. She came to see me for help working through her feelings about dating, and how to respond to her ex-husband who remains actively involved with the kids and occasionally expresses lukewarm interest in her. Both were virgins when they married. She gets on well with female co-workers, wants to date, but is anxious around men. In describing the functional differences to her between masculine and feminine, I used the analogy of a car engine and chassis to differentiate the differences between masculine and feminine. When she first describes her parents she applies the analogy concretely and begins imagining cars that describe her parents. She describes her father as a curvy, old model, Corvette, and her mother as a 'four cylinder' Cadillac. She is strongly identified with the masculine of both parents and, not surprisingly, she balks at treating the masculine as energic and the feminine as defining. I encouraged her to take another stab at describing them. Instead of a Corvette, she now sees her father as a Hummer. She is hard pressed to define her mother. She finally ends up describing her as a small piper cub airplane. I gently point out to Patty that my analogy should not be taken literally and ask if she would go through the process again, this time using human images.

First, her father's feminine side:

"bubbling, smiling, sympathetic...needs to be taken care of...wearing a dress, knee length, dark hair, in a 60's page boy, very thin, so thin she is weak, lacks strength, not smart about worldly stuff, innocent, not sexual." But now she adds: "My dad tells me I'm like him, strong, never met a woman like me." He does not shame you for being weak, I ask? She replies: "I'm not allowed to be weak." I ask her to describe her father's masculine side: "Really smart, takes care of the family, anticipates gratitude, muscular, really big - proud looking, very sexual - wearing an old roman shirt - big stick, stuff draped over one of his arms - the spoils of war. Even so she sees two sides of her father: she can see him being feminine, nurturing, sharing tender feelings, but only when they are alone. "In public, he is male and I am female."

She then goes on to described her mom's feminine side. "Women are the rock of Gibraltar, a hard look on her face, gladiator stance, does not need anybody, bossy - like directing traffic." When I ask about her mother's masculine side, she replies, that "It is difficult to do, don't see it. She is far more feminine than anything. Innocent, prudish, extremely ladylike, vulnerable, helpless, nonsexual." If the forgoing description seems confusing, it was so for me as well. Basically, she has reversed the order of description. Both have female bodies. The masculine is the bossy rock of Gibraltar, a director of traffic; and the feminine is "vulnerable, helpless, and non-sexual. Quite perceptively, she adds that it is nearly impossible to see them together.

A great deal can be read from this first attempt to describe her parents' masculine and feminine aspects. It reminds me of a Rorschach test. Patty tends to be very concrete which is not surprising in a grade school teacher. The masculine is clearly dominant. Patty is going to have trouble dating men. She is not allowed to be sexual as a woman; only masculine aspects are imbued with sexuality. She is not allowed to be feminine, without being seen as weak; and she over values her father's perception of her as strong. This was her last session with me. She claimed money had become an issue, when she canceled the next session, and I knew her funds were limited. But I also suspect she was frightened off by what we had tapped into in this session. Knowing money was an issue, I was torn between working safer and slower vs. examining dynamics that might be able to help her resolve her issues more quickly. In retrospect, I would not recommend this series of interventions unless the client can financially commit to six months treatment. The psychological commitment is always iffy, but given six months the therapist can work slower and safer.

Roger. Initially, I saw Roger and his wife in therapy. The couple have been married for 34 years and have two grown daughters – also married with children, who live nearby. The couple came to see me because Roger has rekindled a romantic attachment with a woman he knew before he married. She lives several states away so the 'affair' is mostly by Internet exchanges. Roger's wife is basically a passive, introverted, woman who has never worked since marrying and does little else than keep house. For the last several years she has been drinking heavily, is extremely moody, very sensitive to any criticism, and prone to temper outbursts followed by long silences. She was raised Methodist but is an indifferent churchgoer. Roger is a devout Catholic who attends church weekly. He experiences a great deal of emotional conflict over his love affair which, nonetheless, he seems unable to withdraw from emotionally, although he has studiously avoided any contact with her as he attempts to reconcile with his wife. At my suggestion the couple separate. Roger moves into his own apartment, though he remains in close daily contact with his wife.

Roger has no difficulty extracting the Inner dyad from his wife's image. Her feminine aspect is seen as a mother caring for children and clearly submissive to a stern, reserved masculine image, male in sex. It is noteworthy that the aspects are sex appropriate and the parental roles are clearly dominant/submissive, patriarchal, distant and strained. But note, the masculine image in no way fits Roger's demeanor in or out of therapy, and his demeanor will be found to be very congruent with his own parents' Inner dyads. The Inner dyads extracted from both of his parents are quite compatible, close and caring, though in both cases, same-sexed. Roger describes his father's feminine as a male who is compassionate and sensitive – when others are deeply hurt he cries, though not for himself. The masculine side of the father is also male, strong, hardworking, honest, fair, and sincere, with strong family ties. When the masculine and feminine are seen to interact, they seem to fit well together, the sensitive feminine is seen as impacting the honesty of the business man while the protective qualities of the masculine give comfort and strength to the feminine side. Examining his mother's Inner dyad, he sees the feminine side as a devoted, loving mother who enjoys friends and likes to do things, who likes associations beyond the immediate family, extroverted to some degree, a loving wife and mother who has a tenderness about her, but she also has a stronger feminine able to deal with difficulties. She is happy, very pleasant, and beautiful (and I might add, clearly idealized). Her masculine side is also female, strong, determined, bright, stands her ground, but does it with diplomacy, who can be aroused to the point of being – if not angry, very firm, independent, and able to meet life head on. When her masculine and feminine sides are seen to interact, the masculine side is seen to be in control but not contradictory. With little prompting on my part, Roger is able to see a role reversal true for both parents: whereas his mother's masculine aspect 'diplomatically' dominates her Inner dyad, the father's feminine aspect dominates his Inner dyad.

The above images were quite vivid as Roger describes them to me. Both parents were deceased and this felt like the first time he had clearly visited with their images. When he was done describing this father's Inner dyad his face showed a strong feeling. When I asked him about this he said that he felt his father's disappointment about his love affair. But then he adds, "He would not have had an affair, but he would not have tolerated my wife either." Similarly, when he is done with reviewing his mother's dyad, he comments that his mother would have told his wife to get lost, although she was never outspoken like that in real life, she was always more a lady. At this point, I ask him to contain his paramour with the Light and extract her feminine and masculine aspects. They are essentially an idealized amalgam of his parents with the exception that her masculine aspect is male in sex, which seems significant given that neither Inner dyad of the parents exhibits a heterosexual stance.

My question – given the configuration of his parents' dyads, is why did he not marry his paramour when he had the chance, and she was apparently quite willing? Why, instead, did he marry his wife of 34 years who is clearly unlike his parents and whose dyad is clearly unlike any of the other dyads we have examined? (I must confess here that I also tended to side with his parents in their response to his wife. The client and his wife seem totally incompatible by any criterion, other than their 34 years of shared history and two grown children.) Why has he stayed married to her all this time? One clue is in the idealization of the images. There is no negativity in any of the Inner dyads, except his wife's. It is as if he needed her to carry a repressed side of himself. But whose qualities? It was at this point that I began to ask about his grandparents, particularly his grandfathers. He said he knew nothing of his paternal grandfather who died just before he was born, but his maternal grandfather had actually lived with him for some years when he was a child following the death of the maternal grandmother. And what was he like, I asked?

Roger's description of his maternal grandfather goes a long way toward explaining his marital and familial dynamics. Note first, that Roger is the second oldest of two boys, therefore most strongly identified with his mother's side and most likely her father (See Endnote 12). Roger describes the maternal grandfather as a very stern man who never reached out. According to Roger, "He never asked us boys to sit in his lap, I don't know as he ever held me...totally different from my dad who was a touchy/feely type of guy...I imagine my mother and her sibs were expected to be seen and not heard." Not surprisingly, this description fits his wife's *masculine aspect* to a tee. Essentially, his Roger's wife provides a vessel for the projection of his *disowned familial identity* with his maternal grandfather, while he reenacts his mother's not-me Inner dyad.

My intent here has been to briefly illustrate the extraction process and some exploration of the dynamics encountered. The following sections offer case examples that follow clients for a year or more, and illustrate all of the interventions in the context of later work and previous chapters.

CONVICTED BY THE HOLY SPIRIT

There is a seven-year span between the early studies described in the previous section and the interventions described in these later sections. During that period, I focused primarily on working through issues related to Temporal and Moral authority. That focus led to the discovery of the Dominant self, which seeks to function as its own conscience. With the redemption of the Dominant self as a Voice-of-conscience, my long-term clients developed a much closer relationship with their Christ. But it was not all I hoped it would be. It seemed to lack the power of my own experience of resting in the Spirit. For me, that was a life-changing event that set me on my current path, as it inaugurated Christ as my higher power.[25] I hoped the redemption of conscience would provide a similar turning point for my clients; and it did move them toward that kind of a relationship with Christ, but that still seemed insufficient of itself. Moreover, my clients' persistent character issues pointed to continuing parental influences of an archetypal nature having little to do with Temporal or Moral authority. When I turned my focus back to the study of Relational authority, I encountered a confluence of events that pointed to what I had failed to see for so long: *the transformational power of the Holy Spirit*. Through most of this book, the Holy Spirit has been overtly restricted to its baptismal role, wherein it releases selves from the bondage of shame. (While Interior baptism seems a small step today, I remember thinking when I first began advocating it, that the concept of Interior baptism verged on heresy.) In retrospect, I can see where the Holy Spirit was present in many of the interventions enacted by Christ, including the transformation of Inner dyads. But once

I was able to explicitly ask Christ to convict with the power of the Holy Spirit, the transformations I had sought for so long began to occur.[26]

The 'confluence of events' leading to this last series of interventions is difficult to describe, though it remains clear to me that they all came together during a two week period in January, a time of year when I have come to expect a fermentation of ideas for the coming year. It began with my thinking about revising the early studies described in the first section. During this time I came across a book describing the experience of *deeksha*.[27] The interested reader can find a large number of references on this subject on the Internet. Basically, I would liken the idea of receiving deekshas to being touched by the Holy Spirit numerous times. But I have not personally experienced it so that is a deduction on my part. While I was reading the book describing the deeksha experience the word 'convict' kept running through my mind. I knew it was pointing me to a prayer I have kept on my writing desk for years. The prayer evokes the Holy Spirit and asks that it 'Convict us, convert us, and consecrate us, until we are wholly thine.'[28] It occurred to me that Christ convicting an inner image with the power of the Holy Spirit might have a profound effect on that image – be it a parental image, self-image or image of another.

The concept of being 'convicted by the Holy Spirit' is difficult for clients to grasp the first time I mention it because 'convicted' is most often associated with guilt. It is a strong word with definite negative connotations. Under the law, when one is convicted, they are found guilty as charged. But the noun form – 'conviction,' is much broader. It can mean guilty, but also 'convinced,' 'won over,' 'belief altering.' As I have come to use the word it always means a *direct experience* of the Holy Spirit offered by the Christ when he touches an image within our Mind. When Christ convicts by placing his hands on the forehead of any image or sense of self, the Holy Spirit irreversibly alters *our judgment* of the image, which judgment was previously condemnatory or delimiting to some degree. The Holy Spirit *graces* the image, and that gracing is always transformational in the sense of releasing the image from our erroneous judgment. Without exception, some degree of transformation can be expected whenever the client willingly asks Christ to convict an image with the power of the Holy Spirit, be it a self-image or image of another, be it a dissociated image or experienced in the first person. Moreover, Christ can be asked to repeat the process as often as necessary until the client is totally satisfied with the result.

Clinically, the effects of conviction by the Holy Spirit are a magnitude greater than any other intervention offered in this work, excepting its 'companion' intervention, which is described in the next section. Hopefully, my case reports will adequately document that assertion. When Christ baptizes, he releases an image from any shame that binds it. Conviction is expected to be *transformational*. Clients sense the difference almost immediately even without my defining it. It is the difference between merely *believing* what the gospels say about the Holy Spirit and *experiencing* it first hand.

I generally introduce this intervention by asking the client to identify the parent *who most strongly defined them*. Most clients are initially disbelieving that conviction can dramatically alter that parental image and a bit anxious that it might. Invariably, it often does so in profound ways, which leads the client to deduce that conviction could have a similar effect on any self-image strongly defined by that parent. I always begin this process by having Christ convict a parent because it is easier to assimilate these often, dramatic, changes one step removed.

This intervention can be introduced in a variety of ways, but I have found the most productive way is to pose a question: "Which of your parents *most strongly defined you*? Ultimately, the answer is immaterial since I expect to work with both parents using the same protocol. But I start with whatever parent the client identifies. However, this protocol is by no means limited to the conviction of parents; it can also be used to transform the images of children, lovers, and problematical relationships between the client and others. Once the client is comfortable with the process it can even be used to convict self-images in the first person.

Protocol for Convicting Sexed-images

As noted, this series of interventions generally begins by asking the client to identify the parent who most strongly defined them – mother or father. Ultimately, both parents will be worked with, but this format has proven the best place to start. If, for example, the father is identified, then Christ is first asked to create an opaqued dome with his *Light* and place within it the self-image most strongly defined by the father. Christ is asked to keep the dome opaqued, since initially the focus of the work will be on the father (or mother as case may be). If some thoughts come to mind concerning this self, the client is asked to share them, but initially, that self is not the focus.

Next, Christ is asked to draw a circle near the opaqued dome and place the parent's image within it. This image will be the initial focus of the work. The client is encouraged to describe the image in some detail. Then, Christ is asked to enter the circle and convict that image with the power of the Holy Spirit. Normally, Christ convicts by placing his hands on the head of the parental image, by which action he courses the Holy Spirit into the person of the image. But the therapist needs to allow wide latitude here as the Christ image can become quite autonomous during the process.

In some cases the transformation is quick and complete. In others, it may take a series of actions initiated by Christ and – as necessary – repeated convictions. Let me be emphatic here: *Christ cannot convict too many times*. He could convict one of the client's images of self or other every day for the rest of the client's life and it would not be too much. Once the client becomes comfortable with the process, s/he may voluntarily convict an image repeatedly between sessions. In cases where the defining influence of a parent was experienced as negative or the parent lived a bad life, the initial 'conviction' may serve to gently dissolve the parent's defenses before stimulating transformation.

Completed conviction is a subjective evaluation made by the client. Christ is asked to repeat the process until it feels total and complete. As a rule, I prompt the client to continue until the parental image seems completely healed of all defects of character. That assessment will be mitigated by what the ego-aspect merged with the Aware-ego can tolerate. That limitation notwithstanding, when the client feels the transformation is complete, then Christ and the Aware-ego approach the Dome containing the self defined by the parent and enter it. The objective is now to completely convict the self most strongly defined by the parent. That self is given a portion of the *Light* by the Aware-ego. The self in the dome must be willing for Christ to convict of the Holy Spirit. (Note, that is not the case for parental images or gender aspects of an Inner dyad. They can be convicted whenever the Aware-ego is willing for it to occur.) If, for any reason, the self-image seems resistant or reluctant, then Christ and the Aware-ego must engage the self in dialogue to discern the reasons. If s/he is fearful, the Aware-ego can ask the self-image to go with Christ to the ocean and surrender those fears or other negative emotions including any shame; or s/he can be instructed to use the *Light* to create a garment of protection. If the therapist senses that the self-image's free will has been compromised by undue influences, then s/he can ask Christ to place a portion of his *Light* into the heart of the self-image. This will terminate any undue influences – including shame, which may be compromising the self-image's free will. If there are none, then there will be no effect. If, finally, the therapist discerns an issue of pride, then the self-image must become willing for Christ to cancel its effect. That particular intervention is discussed further on. When any or all of these interventions have successfully dissolved the resistance, the self-image must then express its willingness to be convicted by Christ with the power of the Holy Spirit. I generally suggest that willingness be expressed by asking the self to take Christ's hand and place it on his or her forehead.

The act of conviction is always transformative to some degree and the process needs to be continued until the client – as Aware-ego, decides it is total and complete. Remember, Christ cannot be asked to do this too many times.

Next, the process is repeated by containing the other parent within a circle, and asking Christ to identify the self most strongly defined by that second parent. The same dome can be used to contain this new self, or a new one erected. Again, focus is initially on convicting and transforming the second parent. When the client feels that parent is also completely and totally convicted, Christ is then asked to focus on the second self within the dome. Again, the self must express willingness.

The transformation of a parent by conviction frees up any self defined by the parent so its own nature can evolve. But the transformation of self-images is never automatic. In each instance, the self in the dome must explicitly ask Christ to be convicted by the Holy Spirit. I would also note that it is possible for self-images to be convicted of the Holy Spirit without first asking Christ to convict the parent(s). If that is done, then it needs to be done in the first person; that is, the Aware-ego and whoever is co-present with the Aware-ego approaches Christ and opens to being convicted by him. But generally, the best time for conviction of the Aware-ego, and whoever is co-present with it, is after the parents and selves contained within the domes have been convicted.

Finally, Christ is asked to contain both parents in the same circle. He is then asked to enter the circle and convict the parental *relationship* by placing a hand on each of their heads as they kneel or stand side by side. This last conviction is always done with the expectation that the two will be reintegrated within the self of the Aware-ego. The integration step can be affected in several ways. Initially, I would have the client ask Christ to place a portion of the client's *Light* in the heart of each parent and then into the heart of the Aware-ego. More recently, I have begun to suggest that the Aware-ego enter the circle containing the parents and allow their images to meld with it.

Bear in mind that the above protocol is intended to facilitate the therapist's initial use of the conviction process. Many different combinations have evolved from the above protocol; and the therapist/reader is expected to develop variations as the clinical situation and experience dictate. For example, in one of the case studies described below, the client contains the parents of her spouse and then asks her higher power to convict them both until she is satisfied with their relationship. Basically, Christ can be asked to convict any image or relationship. The only qualification is that when the conviction involves a self-image, that image must give its willing consent when convicted. Christ is respectful of the images of others but does not require their willingness; in working with others he only needs the willingness of the Aware-ego.

What is conviction? It is Christ 'judging' with the power of the Holy Spirit; it is the judgment of the Holy Spirit channeled by Jesus Christ. It is any self-image or image of another receiving the direct experience of the Holy Spirit as channeled by the Christ within us. *The Holy Spirit never convicts with shame or guilt. Only the law convicts us with shame and guilt.* The Holy Spirit convicts us with the truth of ourselves; it convicts us by grace; and it is irreversibly transformational. The image – be it parent or self, or other is altered by the experience inside and out. And it is an experience. It is not merely what we believe the Holy Spirit can do. This is the experience of what it does, so do not be surprised if you hesitate or want to 'think about it' for a while. Just know that it is within you to receive it.

The above protocol for convicting sexed-images was developed *before* I discovered and began working with the Familial personality. Work with that archetypal constellation requires extensive work with gender aspects, consorts, and potential Ideal pairs, all of whom are repeatedly convicted *simultaneously* with the power of the Holy Spirit. Today, I am less likely to ask Christ to convict sexed-images without one manifest gender aspect. At the very least, I expect to work with the sexed-image's consort. These are contra-sexual gender aspects that a psychological ego-aspect allows to be separated from itself while retaining its same-gender aspect. A consort can also be a gender aspect brought into relational consciousness by Christ. The forgoing protocol demonstrates that the process of conviction can transform sexed-images as well as gender aspects; but working with dyadic modes seems more efficacious. Today, I am most likely to ask Christ to work with dyads and relationships. The conviction process and necessary conditions of willingness remain the same. At the time I developed the above protocol and the one below, I was still attempting to effect changes from outside the Heart and had not even seriously considered that each image would manifest its own heart chakra in need of individual work and an Ideal pair. As ever, it is an ongoing process of discovery.

REORDERING AT THE MOLECULAR LEVEL

This next intervention also involves Christ explicitly channeling the Holy Spirit. I initially offered it in response to emotional or physical distress (acute and chronic).[29] Most of my clients have taken to it quite readily and frequently repeat it at home. Over time, I have begun to offer it for a wider range of issues, including characterological issues defining particular selves. I really do encourage them to 'make it their own' and apply it to any area where there is a felt sense of dis-ease. Over time, I have begun to offer it for a wider range of issues, including characterological issues, such as overeating, that define particular selves such as Egos-in-conflict. The client can also offer it to images of others by envisioning 'the other' standing in front of Christ and receiving it.

The protocol is straightforward. I begin

by noting that – at the physical level – matter is perceived as quite dense. I emphasize this by lightly jabbing at my own arm. But – I stress – at the sub-atomic level this *same matter is highly organized energy*. When functioning correctly that energy is organized and orderly. Where there is pain, or congestion, or trauma, it is easy to envision the sub-atomic space as disordered, or constricted, or tangled, or otherwise damaged. To correct such disorder, Christ is asked to inject the Holy Spirit into the center of the painfully disordered space where it can re-order the ill-formed energy. In this intervention, *Spirit interacts with the organized energy that underpins our perception of physical matter*. Atoms are the bedrock of reductionistic science. Think of Spirit as able to permeate all atomized matter and reorder it instantly, provided the client is willing for that to happen within some span of time necessary for optimal healing.

For most people, it is hard to imagine how the Spirit can heal *physical matter*, heal flesh and blood. The Spirit does so by working at the sub-atomic or molecular level, which is the energic blueprint for all flesh and blood. When directed by Christ, the Spirit can easily permeate any disordered field of energy envisioned by the Mind and unerringly bring order to whatever it encounters. I simply encourage the client to imagine standing, sitting, or lying down beside Christ and letting him infuse the Spirit into whatever 'physical space' is the source of dis-ease. Christ touches the space, or places his hand over it and the Spirit enters for the sole purpose of healing the disorder envisioned by the client. It is that simple, and it can be asked for time and time again until the malady is healed. It is quite possible for such healing to occur instantaneously, but rarely so quickly without scaring the recipient. So there is generally a period between the Spirit's instant response, and the client's growing awareness that something is truly happening.

What is infused into the physical space is pure, unconditional love, and the intelligence to order and re-order whatever the Spirit encounters. It only needs our permission to enter. Initially, the client feels a sense of peace almost immediately after Christ is allowed to touch the area in need of healing. This may be followed by a sense of heat radiating from that part of the body. The latter is very likely if there is a need to discharge stored negative energies such as fear or anger.

If the reader is willing to enact this intervention all s/he has to do is imagine Christ standing next to the Aware-ego and separated self-image (front, back, beside, leaning over, kneeling) in whatever position allows him to comfortably access the painful site. It is best if you imagine all this sitting down or reclining. Now feel his hand(s) on the site – and as soon as he makes contact – accept his infusion of the Holy Spirit. I generally suggest that the most appropriate response to his touch is to relax into it.

Recently, I have begun offering a further refinement for selves that are likely to resist this offer of healing at the molecular level. After the self is identified using an intervention such as a capturing circle defined by Christ, the separated self is offered a portion of the Aware-ego's *Light*. It is instructed to use that portion of the *Light* to draw a circle of protection around itself. It is understood that Christ can only enter that circle when the self becomes willing for Christ to infuse its molecular energy with the Holy Spirit. As often as not, Christ is initially barred from entering, which initiates a dialogue with everyone present. On several occasions, the circle created by Christ has captured two images that the client comes to appreciate as working in collusion. The collusion is that one is generally perceived as strong and the other as seemingly weak, but the weak one seems to actually govern the resistance. In those cases, the resistance is resolved by the reconciliation of the two.

The inspiration for this intervention came from my reflection on miraculous healings wherein the recipient is completely healed in short order or gradually recovers from terminal, untreatable, chronic injury or illness as diagnosed by one or more physicians and tests. Doctors call this a 'spontaneous remission.' What that means, essentially, is that physical medicine can verify the 'cure,' but not explain it. What – I wondered – could possibly cause such an event since the modus operandi appears to defy the laws of physical matter? It suddenly occurred to me that those 'laws' might be very amenable to nearly instantaneous change at the molecular/ quantum level: the level of energy and definition. I hypothesized that it is possible for Christ to infuse any image with the loving, ordering, power of the Holy Spirit, and instantly transform any traumatized space constricting that image. That is the thesis. The intervention is intended to test it as a hypothesis.

THE PRIDEFUL HEART

For most clients, pride becomes a major impediment at some point in the process of convicting with the power of the Holy Spirit. There are a group of selves - primarily Dominant selves, which invariably resist the above interventions, until their pride is addressed. Not surprisingly, there are a number of verses in the Old and New Testament that also see pride as the greatest impediment to allowing the will of God to work through us. Here are but two examples: "But when his heart became arrogant and hardened with pride, he was deposed from his royal throne and stripped of his glory [Daniel 5:20]"; "The pride of your heart has deceived you, you who live in the clefts of the rocks and make your home on the heights, you who say to yourself, 'Who can bring me down to the ground?' [Obadiah 1:3]." Quite often, the self in question is not aware of pride as a major impediment. Instead, the ego-aspect simply feels the need to be 'in constant control' so as to avoid 'chaos.' This resistance is illustrated in all of verbatims provided in the chapters.

The struggle is always between a self that insists on functioning 'under the law' and the Holy Spirit's offer of a graceful alternative. In one form or another pride is a judgment: an emotion that trusts self-judgment – however constricting and condemning, over the judgment of God's grace. In my clinical experience, conviction by the Holy Spirit is *always* positively transforming. Consequently, the client's struggles are often painful to watch. Even the client can anguish, knowing that transformation is possible but continuing to fear the loss of prideful judgment. What the client fails to appreciate is that his or her self-image, or image of the other, is not a 'fact' but a judgment sustained by pride. The Holy Spirit's correction of this error inevitably shows the client a viable image free of *prideful* judgment.

Normally, when issues of pride are encountered, it can be traced to a first person voice that remains merged with the Aware-ego when the client goes inside. Generally, this prideful self makes itself known in the process of working with another self already contained in a dome or otherwise separated. Essentially, the prideful self resists letting Christ convict that self in the dome or infuse a disordered space with the Holy Spirit. This resistance is what initiates a dialogue between therapist and client that strives to understand the reasons for resistance. I have developed three interventions for addressing this impasse. Their varying use is illustrated in the verbatims.

The first intervention is actually the obverse of releasing a self from the *bondage of shame*. Christ is asked to release the self within the dome from the bondage of pride being exercised by a Dominant self. In effect, the separated ego-aspect is seen to be shamed by the prideful judgment of the Dominant self. Often, the severing of this pride-shame connection can be quite dramatic. Christ accomplishes it by entering the circle of protection and severing the connection by convicting or infusing the self with the Holy Spirit. This is very much like being baptized except that what is being convicted is the relationship between the Dominant self and the part being released from prideful bondage. (Shameful bondage is often the same as prideful bondage as the latter frequently expresses its judgment in shaming terms.) I am careful in using this intervention. The Dominant self's prideful resistance must still be addressed and can still sabotage therapy.

The second intervention involves the use of humility as the perfect anecdote to pride. At some point, the Dominant self can be offered the conviction of humility as an alternative choice to pride. Here, humility is not seen as supplanting pride, but added as an experiential alternative to pride, thereby providing the Dominant self with a choice between the two. In effect, the Dominant self is expected to *experience humility* in a measure equal to the experience of pride so that choice acquires an *experiential* – as opposed to merely hypothetical – foundation. It goes without saying, that the actual experience of humility can be quite mind altering. The *experience* of humility and the *fear* of humility are distinctly different states of Mind. From the perspective of a prideful self, humility is – at best, humbling, and - at it's feared worse, humiliating. Pride can see no real value in humility. To offset that fear, I encourage the prideful self to expand its choice: to allow itself to experience humility free of its prideful assumptions. It can still choose pride over humility in any future choice. But it is not really free to *choose* until it can experience humility equal in measure to its experience of pride. One way of enacting this choice is to have Christ create a circle infused with humility. The co-conscious self can empty the circle stay as long as it chooses, then step back out.

The third intervention is called the *circle of escape*. This intervention is used when the self co-conscious with the Aware-ego expresses long suppressed anger or another intense negative emotion in addition to pride. Christ is first asked to draw a circle of *Light*. Then he is asked to convict the Aware-ego and any self co-conscious with it. If the co-conscious self is unwilling to be convicted it can 'escape' into the circle of escape provided by Christ. The client and Christ then proceed to work with that image until it is willing to be convicted. Occasionally, when I am required to use this intervention, the ego-aspects contained in the circle of escape will be found to have spiritual issues requiring some form of deliverance.

I cannot stress enough that pride is the primary source of resistance in this process of being convicted by the Holy Spirit. Often the client is totally unaware of this fact. Rather, s/he feels it would be irresponsible to act otherwise, or 'letting go' would risk humiliation or other sense of shame. And all of this is 'true' from the perspective of a prideful self. To stop whatever s/he is doing would be 'humbling,' if not humiliating. Both possibilities describe pride's understanding of humility. Invariably, these selves always discover that quite the opposite is true once they become willing for Christ to give them a taste of humility. But persuading them to open to that choice is never an easy task. As the verbatims illustrate, issues of pride take the most time.

THE CLINCIAL STUDIES: 'LOOSE ENDS'

The next section comprises the bulk of this chapter. It provides yearlong verbatims of weekly sessions for two different clients, comparable to the yearlong verbatims offered in the previous chapter. Before presenting them, it will be helpful if I briefly address several loose ends by way of a 'heads-up.' Otherwise, it may seem that I am taking the reader into totally new areas without much preamble.

Parental Images and Self-images

In the case studies below, the parents are still living, divorced and remarried, or deceased. Whatever the parental status, the process transforms the image of the parent into one that invites reciprocal caring, often in sharp contrast to previous estrangement or cutoff. This dramatic shift appears to be irreversible and quickly supplants more negative images that the client has held for years. The process even facilitates the reconciliation of otherwise estranged parental relationships. The transformational effects are equally true for self-images. For any therapist who has worked with clients and their parental relationships, this shift is quite amazing. It is not delusional. If the parents are still living, the client perceives them as continuing to enact habitual patterns. The client is simply less reactive, more tolerant, and definitely more open to relationship, but generally non-reactive to negative scripts. In some cases, where idealization was a factor, the client may becomes 'less tolerant' if other person previously bore actual faults such as selfishness in daily life. Until I came across this series of interventions, the best I could offer a client was a parental image that was less powerful, but otherwise unchanged, coupled with changes in self-images that were less reactive. That is why I see these interventions as a magnitude greater in effect than everything that precedes them. They allow for the complete and total transformation of parental images that shape – not only parent-child interactions – but also the masculine and feminine aspects of many self-images. The client no longer needs the physical parent to change in order to experience a comparable change in his or her self-image. The very first time I saw the effects of conviction and re-ordering, I 'knew' these interventions would complete the work of this book and that has proven to be the case for all clients willing to engage in the process.

The Feminine Face of God

Alchemists – whom Jung considered the medieval equivalent of depth psychologists – have long insisted that individuation requires the redemption of Sophia and her marriage to God in Christ. According to Jeffrey Raff, she is indispensible to the creation of the Philosopher's stone, which is the goal of Alchemy.[30] As the therapist and client work with the masculine and feminine aspects of parental and self-images, a point is reached when clients begin to seek the feminine face of God in Christ; and Christ has always seemed willing to accede to this request. Sometimes, the extracted image is quite profound. On other occasions, however, the client is shown an image of self or parent that must first be addressed. I have yet to decipher why one kind of image and not the other is extracted from the Christ image. The intervention itself is quite simple. If Christ is willing for the Aware-ego to extract his feminine aspect, he gives that self a portion of *his Light*, which the Aware-ego then uses to draw a double circle and extract the feminine aspect of Christ. The opposite is also possible: a Christ image can be extracted from a Mother of God image. I have not had the opportunity to explore this discovery process very much, so there is very little I can say about it. What I have observed in some of my female clients is that, as they proceed through the process, they increasingly evoke Sophia-like images as a companion of their Christ image. This appears to be a felt need on their part; I do not normally suggest it, though I always accede to it. The feminine imagery is by no means restricted to images of Mary. They can be Earth mothers, Goddesses of Compassion, Mary Magdalene, and the like.

The Extraction of Masculine and FeminineAspects From First Person Selves

Generally, I only offer this intervention after the client has worked with parents and images of the self defined by the parents. By then, the client can fully appreciate that every image has a masculine and feminine aspect. In the 'first person' intervention one or both aspects are extracted from whatever self is co-present with the Aware-ego at the time of the intervention. It can be executed in one of two ways. The first option asks Christ to separate out both aspects of the merged self/Aware-ego. The second option asks Christ to only separate out the client's contra-sexual aspect.

In the first option, Christ is asked to begin by extracting the client's same-sexed aspect (the feminine in a woman, the masculine in a man). Then Christ is asked to extract the client's contra-sexual aspect. When both aspects have been separated Christ is asked to recombine both circles so as to observe the interaction. Of note, as each aspect is extracted the client is encouraged to describe it and then finally to describe their interactions once the two circles are rejoined. The goal, as ever, is a non-incestuous, adult, heterosexual, and totally satisfying relationship. If the images and their relationship reflect anything less than that, Christ is asked to enter the circle and simultaneously convict both images with the power of the Holy Spirit, and to continue doing so until the client is totally satisfied with the images and relationship. Then, and only then, is the Aware-ego/merged self asked to enter the circle and reintegrate with them.

The second option is much like the first except that *only the contra-sexual aspect* is extracted from the Aware-ego/merged self. The same-sexed aspect remains embedded in the Aware-ego/merged self. In this option the contra-sexual aspect becomes a *mirror* of the relationship by virtue of its demeanor and attractiveness to the client. If it is seen to fall short in any way, then Christ is asked to *simultaneously convict* the contra-sexual aspect and Aware-ego/merged self, until the client feels desirous of reintegrating with the contra-sexual aspect.

Early on, I asked all of my clients working in the 'first person' to extract both aspects – the first option. But I have found that the second option works equally well; so I am inclined to use either one today as seems appropriate. Of course whenever the contra-sexual aspect is worked with alone the same-sexed aspect can still be drawn out and examined – and sometimes the client will do this spontaneously – but I think that leaving the same-sexed aspect embedded with the Aware-ego/ merged self may have a more powerful intermediate effect on the client since it strengthens the idea that this is *my contra-sexual aspect like it or not*. And if it is not valued then it is adversely effecting 'me.'

It is quite possible that what is being extracted in the above interventions are the gender personifications of the Familial personality. I developed this series of interventions before I discovered the existence of that entity and I have yet to determine is this process and working with a personification of the 'personality' would produce the same result.

The two case studies presented in the next section illustrate a number of variations based on the two options as do the two verbatims offered in the previous chapter.

Grandparents and Great Grandparents

Often, the process of working with parental images, self-images, or even images of grandchildren, leads to a study of relationships going back to the great grandparent generation. Cutoffs and abandonment issues going back that far can necessitate forgiveness and reconciliation over several generations. The process of working with several generations is illustrated in the verbatims.

Massaging the Brain Stem

Several months into working with the cases described below I developed a new intervention based on observations made by proponents of the Oneness Blessing.[31] They contend that Deekshas have a dampening effect on the parietal parts of the brain, which are seen as responsible for chronic stimulation of the brain stem. The brain stem is commonly referred to as a reptilian brain or the fight-flight brain. Physiological observations of the Deeksha process observe a dampening of the parietal areas, which effectively reduces brain stem stimulation.

In the physical world, the brain is only accessible through surgical intervention. However, in active imagination is quite accessible and mutable to interventions by Christ and/ or images of the feminine such as Mary, Mary Magdalene, Sophia, Quan Yin, etc. For example, in active imagination Christ can be asked to insert his hand under the skull and beneath the cerebellum of the Aware-ego – and the self co-conscious with it – so he can gently cover and massage the brain stem with his hand. The clients invited to use this intervention have found it quite easy to imagine; and it has a *very calming effect*. It is especially effective, if the client is feeling terror at the thought of working with a particular self. Part of the calming effect may be due to the fact that it is hard to concentrate attention in two places simultaneously. Asking the client to begin by focusing on letting Christ massage the brain stem, then focusing on the source of terror, appears to abate the palatable sense of the terror. If, at any point, the terror reasserts itself, the client can refocus – as long as necessary – on Christ's calming massage of the brain stem. In this intervention, I imagine Christ actively severing or blocking negative emotional feed back loops between the parietal areas and the brain stem. This does not dampen terrorizing thoughts, only the connections that are forcing the body's unnecessary participation in the memory. It is the bodily reactions to fear that make the terror so difficult to address. Christ's severing of those etheric connections allows the client to sustain focus on the trauma without being undone by the physiological responses generally accompanying such trauma. The associated emotions can be fully felt and released without terrorizing the body. Of course, this is all speculative. I really don't know how Christ or his feminine counterpart accomplishes this intervention; only that they can do so with consistent effect. This intervention is illustrated in the following verbatims.

Infusing a Circle with Sensation or Emotion

I have already noted this intervention above when I described a circle created by Christ, which he infused with humility. A Christ defined circle can be tailored to many, many situations. One kind of circle, which I use repeatedly in the verbatims, is a circle infused with sensation. This is particularly helpful in working with mental components whose sensate component has been shamefully repressed, or with selves whose ability to feel sensation is denied or woefully underdeveloped, e.g. a highly developed thinking self. Use of such a circle can be voluntary or involuntary. In the case of a mental component cutoff from its sensate component it may have be involuntary as the only way to set limits on its insatiable desire. In other instances it can be voluntary as, for example, for a self whose sensation function is woefully underdeveloped. In theory, Christ can suffuse any circle with specific emotions or sensations including unconditional regard, love, or any emotion that a self has habitually avoided. Infused circles allow the client to experience any emotion or sensation missing from its repertoire. It seems to have myriad applications, which I have only begun to explore.

A variation of this intervention is a dome intended to *absorb* excessive negative emotion. Basically, Christ places a portion of his *Light* in the top of the dome or on the floor. He infuses the *Light* with a specific task such as absorbing one or more emotions. The ego-aspect or image of someone else is expected to remain in the dome until the negative emotion is completely absorbed by the *Light*.

Asking Christ to Find a 'Soul Mate' From Within the Heart

This particular series of interventions builds on the idea that working within the Heart is closer to the Soul than working outside it in the Mind. The Heart is a waypoint, deeper than the Mind and more clearly accessible to the Soul chakras. In working with clients that have suffered significant neglect, shaming, or abuse in childhood, and even those who have not seemed to suffer, young selves are discovered who are very fearful of the opposite sex. Essentially, these selves are estranged or threatened by contra-sexual aspects, and tend to live in a perpetual state of lack. Since all of the verbatims describe female clients, the young selves are invariable female. As a first step, Christ can heal these self-images and sustain them with his own masculine energy. As a second step, I have found it *very helpful* if I then suggest that Christ take the child into its heart chakra and bring it a 'soul mate' or 'play mate.' I do not suggest that what he offers has to be a contra-sexual image though it most often is contra-sexual. Basically, I am asking Christ to provide an anima/animus image that will reflect the healed status of the child. In practice, I do not limit this to child images. Particularly, as regards my male clients, I will invite them to let Christ select an anima image for any of their healed self-images. I have done this too few times to generalize, but the reports are consistently positive for the clients who have done it.

The Universal Projection Hypothesis

Finally, I need to put forth an hypothesis of universal projection. In working with masculine and feminine aspects I have gradually come to the conclusion that regardless of *what image is worked with*, all relational images are vessels of the client's masculine and feminine archetypal energy. *The clients are always working with their own masculine-feminine energies.* This is true whether the client is working with a mother-in-law, a grandfather, sibling, child or first person self; a stranger, god, goddess, or devil. All are expressions of the client's masculine and feminine energies. We inherit the unfinished work of our parents and grandparents and we marry our owned and disowned parts. If I ask a client to work with the masculine and feminine extracted from her brother and this turns out to be an image of their mother and drunken maternal grandfather…it is likely akin to her own sense of them. If a client is angry with her husband, then I am quite willing to focus on his masculine and feminine aspects, or even the aspects of either of his parents. Eventually, such a focus on others will bring the client to the first person scenario; and it is amazing how those others are also changed in the process, both in the world – if they are living – and most definitely in the mind of client. Please bear this hypothesis in mind as you read the following verbatims. It will help the reader to understand why I am quite willing to focus on whatever the client's seemingly 'free associative' process brings to the session.

Two Clinical Cases

Most of what I can say about working with Inner dyads and convicting or re-ordering images with the power of the Holy Spirit is derived from the clinical effects of the interventions. The best explanations I can give are the experiences of clients. In this section I offer two clinical cases each spanning a year or more. Two cases reported in the previous chapter – Marion and Tory, also spanned this time period and illustrate the same interventions. During this period I developed many of the interventions described in this chapter and the one preceding it. These clients were literally pioneers as they gamely worked through the process as I was developing it, often as a result of their work. The process is often dramatic and always transformational, but not quick; and frequently it is messy as I struggle to clarify what we are about. In the last section, I will attempt to summarize the findings and their implications. The clients described below are both in their fifties. During the period of *their work* with me they have become much more spiritual, but not particularly religious. In the initial stages of this process, if several weeks have passed they may have very little recall of what transpired. But more often than not, they are quickly reminded once inside. Occasionally, I will read them my notes from the previous session. One has suffered from a fairly severe bi-polar disorder; both have had significant relational difficulties. Both are female. Both have been married and divorced. Both appear to spend increasing amounts of time going inside between sessions (which is in sharp contrast to most clients who tend to avoid going inside between sessions). What they all come to share in common is a radical transformation of parental and self-images as a consequence of letting Christ convict or re-order those images with the power of the Holy Spirit; and a decidedly more centered and at-peace sense of self, despite the slings and arrows of everyday life. Individually, they also experience remissions in physical and psychological symptoms and much better relationships with peers and family. What is also likely to capture the reader's attention is the increasingly powerful interactions between Christ and client.

Lee

These case notes continue the therapy of the client who, in the previous chapter, evoked both Christ and a spirit guide called Teacher. This guide sees himself as both older than Christ and his mentor. The two images work differently but in concert. As the case notes will illustrate, both Christ and Teacher seem able to convict with the power of the Holy Spirit. In history, the Holy Spirit also precedes the incarnation of Christ, as seen throughout the Old Testament. I am ethically bound to report this case because the interventional results are comparable to all the other cases I have described in this work, even though Teacher is clearly from a different tradition and claims to be a mentor to Christ. But truth be told, I value the experience of Teacher and Lee, whatever the tradition. Lee was raised Roman Catholic. Her father was devout. Out of respect, Lee chooses to call on Christ when convicting her father, but for herself, and her mother, she chooses to call on Teacher with equally profound effects. Actually, as therapy progresses, her old animosity toward Christ and the Catholic Church dissipates and she becomes equally comfortable calling on both higher powers. Of note, the work with Lee covers an earlier period when I began actively working with Inner dyads but before I began working with the Familial personality.

I begin this series of sessions by telling Lee that I am developing a new set of interventions in which Christ is asked to convict images with the power of the Holy Spirit. I am not sure if this is something that Teacher can also do, but I am willing to entertain the idea that he can as well. Currently, Lee has been addressing issues of transference – seeing her new husband as like her father. I suggest that we might begin by asking Christ and/or Teacher to convict her father's image with the power of the Holy Spirit. (Lee's father studied to be a priest for several years, but left before completing his studies and later married Lee's mother. He remained a devout Catholic through his short life. He died of cancer when Lee was eleven years old.) Lee asks Christ to convict her father. She sees Teacher in the background. "Christ steps up to the edge of my father's circle. My father kneels on one knee and lowers his head. Christ puts a hand over him. It feels like a 'dove light' came down from above. The circle is filled with light. Father looks calm and peaceful. He has a soft smile. Now Dad pulls me into his circle, gives me a hug, and tousles my hair. Then he gives me a loving tap on my bottom and says it is OK with him and us." I ask why Christ did not enter her father's circle? "There was no need. There is no space, no separation, between them." I ask Lee to ask Christ if Teacher has the same power to convict with the Holy Spirit. "Christ says it is not for him to answer. Teacher could choose to do it, work the same 'magic,' but it would look different from your Christian mindset. Teacher has mentored Christ." I ask if Teacher is pleased with his mentoring? "His answer is neither yes nor no. He just gave me a big smile and chuckled." I ask if Christ is pleased with Teacher's mentoring? "He says 'yes' without qualification. It is good." I decide at this point to shift the focus to her new husband and ask who – Teacher or Christ, will enter his circle and convict his image? "Teacher." So I ask Lee to have Teacher convict her husband with the power of the Holy Spirit with her as the willing witness. "He stepped into the circle and placed his hand on the frontal lobe (Lee is a nurse; her husband a doctor). He was kneeling on one knee even before Teacher entered. His head is looking straight, but his eyes or downcast. My husband looks up when Teacher places his hand on his forehead. A light came from Teacher's hand surrounding my husband. I sensed a connection. When the vision cleared, my husband reappeared as a seven-year-old child fidgeting and bouncing, shifting his weight from one foot to another. He could not quite contain himself. As Teacher continued he calmed down and became more focused. There is a sense of peace about him." (At this point, Lee tells me that her husband started taking a psychotropic drug for anxiety and depression two or three weeks previous. He is more cheerful, sleeping better, and going to bed earlier.) Earlier, I told Lee what I knew about Deekshas.[32] Now I ask her if she can query Teacher about them. "You have to listen to the blackness in the darkness. A tangible feel to it, a brief sense that I was looking at myself in all of us. It is a third-eye energy. That is as much as I can get from him right now." The session ends here.

In the following session two weeks later, Lee is willing to begin exploring the part of her most strongly defined by her father. In this session Christ continues to provide the interventional conviction. Teacher remains present but in the background. First, Christ creates a dome to contain the part most strongly defined by the father. Lee divides her *Light* and gives a portion to Christ to extend to the self in the dome. "She is fearful. She is younger than me, but no perceptible age. She is fearful of being ridiculed or faulted." I suggest that Christ teach her to create a garment of protection and test its effect. Then, if she is willing, for Christ to convict her. She can express her willingness by holding the *Light* to her heart; and Christ will place his hand on her forehead. "Her appearance has changed; she seems more at peace. The thought that has come to her is 'there is no need to defend.' My interpretation of this is that she does not have to defend against the attacks of others because she is protected against them." The session ends here.

My goal for this coming session is to begin focusing on the mother and the part of Lee most strongly defined by her. However, when Lee returns she is preoccupied with her addiction to computer games, which can absorb her for hours. This sense of self is seen as an adventure seeker who is also engaged by rock climbing and kayaking, and other activities that give her an adrenalin rush. The downside is the sense of never finishing work tasks she starts. This time, Lee wants Teacher to provide the interventions. Teacher creates a dome. Then Teacher puts the Adventurer to sleep so that whatever part of Lee is being suppressed by her 'adventures' can emerged within the dome. Now Lee relates that, "As she was released into the dome, I felt the suppression dissipate, like an intense heat on my back. A part of me is grieving that whoever has emerged is dead, and also a fear that she can be resurrected again. It is a part of myself that has been shamed, and that I hide from myself." I suggest that she let Teacher baptize this part and release her from all shame so that Lee can observe her nature free of shame. "I asked to see this part of me before he released her and felt her pain and was deeply saddened by it. At the same time I have such distain and dislike for that part of me. It is hard to look at it." I ask if there is a prideful part judging her? "Very much so. But I also sense that what will heal her is my ability to not judge her and let her be loved." I suggest that she ask Teacher to convict her pride and then ask Teacher how to proceed. "When I ask, 'what do I do here?,' the thought came to me that she is dead because I have slain her with my pride. At first, I thought this was Teacher speaking but then realized it was my thought. I saw her come back to life when I realized that. She did not look haggard or weighted down; she has a sense of vitality when freed of the shame. All this happened before Teacher entered the dome, so I said to him, 'go inside and fix it.' When he entered the dome there was a sense of lightness, uplifting, joy; no harshness or sadness. She is a response to my mom's harshness growing up, my inability to feel like I had her approval. I have worked hard over the years to disconnect from my mom and her harshness. This is the part of me that desires connection." I suggest that she focus on her mother's image and ask Teacher to convict it as often as necessary until the part of her that desires connection, is satisfied that it can happen. "Wow…God is just…it feels like connection (sigh)…my mother looked small and distant as if she was dodging Teacher. I asked the Holy Spirit to convict her and that brought the realization that I was also dodging, so I let the Spirit convict me as well. I said, 'I surrender' and let us surrender – meaning my mom and me. Then the sense of separateness disappeared. That is where the 'wow' came in, the sense of love connecting us both." At this point, I tell Lee that the 'hard-hat psychologist' in me needs to test all of this by bringing her mother into the dome with the part desiring the connection. "Our sense of connection is so refreshing. It makes me realize that I have had difficulty following through on tasks because of my need to disconnect from her in order to avoid her harsh judgments. But there is no sense of judgment coming from her now." I suggest that she ask Teacher to instill humility in her to provide a viable option to her shaming judgment. "It is a balance to have the balance. Having humility toward myself is to have some slack. Having humility is like having love for yourself." The session ends here.

I see Lee a week later. She has just finished a weeklong intensive of meditation study with the man who channels Teacher. During the intensive she was reminded of a "dark angry self" that she had experienced the previous year while on this retreat, and her fear that it would overwhelm her. During the intensive, she reports being able to acknowledge it, and let it go, and experience it's opposite as love. I do not pursue this as there seems nothing to pursue at the moment. She also shares that she has deleted the computer games from her computer; and that she is more at peace with the clutter at home. "It is not tormenting me. I am paying attention to getting it cleaned in little increments and enjoying doing it. Also, I keep checking how I feel inside and it feels really good. I have warm feelings about mom; I actually miss her. I never thought like that before. She is claiming the part of me that desires connection. I see them walking together, holding hands, and hugging." I suggest that she go inside for the purpose of letting Teacher bring her parents together and convict their relationship with the power of the Holy Spirit. "OK. They both came into the circle. They are sort of facing each other. Now they both kneel down and bow their heads so Teacher can convict them. Then they stood up and dad hugged my mother. It felt really nice." I suggest that she divide her Light and place a portion into the heart of each parent so she can gradually assimilate these changes in the relationship. "I did not want to come out. It felt really serene inside. I felt surges of energy in my root chakra, not sexual. I am noticing a definite difference in connectedness, acceptance, and love." The session ends here.

I see Lee two weeks later. On the whole

she is feeling very good about herself and the world, but reports that she is still not good about completing projects and still has anxiety around deadlines. I suggest a new intervention for her. She will let Teacher draw a circle of escape and then convict her in the first person. The part of her who dreads deadlines can remain merged or escape to the circle. As Teacher approaches to convict her she is to imagine a task such as mowing the lawn or doing the laundry. I suggest that she ask Teacher to convict both selves: 'firm intent' and 'anxious at the prospect.' (Remember that Lee is one of those clients who go very deep when she goes inside, so I generally have to wait till she returns to learn what has transpired.) "I was aware of some shift to the circle of escape. I was totally willing to surrender to the conviction. I became aware of my difficulty saying 'no.' I over book and over schedule. I use to be distracted by this over scheduling, now it makes me anxious. This part of me needs the power to say 'no' to these distractions, the power to strike a balance between free time and structured time. But I have no sense of how to do it." I suggest that she ask Teacher to help her move through this conundrum. "He says it will be OK. I am creating this difficulty by not doing what I intend. Just go and do what I intend to do." I ask if she is being distracted from something deeper? "The Distracter is well established. She is most likely to emerge around paperwork anxiety." I suggest that she use concentric circles to separate from the Distracter and then describe her to me. "She is tomboyish, a white rumpled shirt, black slacks and wild eyes. Her hair is mussed and she is looking around everywhere. She can't stay focused. She has drumming fingers and a tapping foot." I sense a need to terminate undue influences, which she and Teacher agree to do. Afterward, she reports that the Distracter's hair seems smoothed out and her eyes more subdued. I next suggest that Teacher convict her of the Holy Spirit so she can experience centering equal to her distractibility, so as to maximize her free will. "She does not resist Teacher in this; now there is a sense of needing to rest. It seems easier for her to focus."

Lee returns a month later. She is doing well. I have been asking other clients to ask Christ if he will allow them to see his feminine aspect. I suggest to Lee that she ask the same of Teacher. At first she feels unworthy. "I don't have any right to request this. There is a sense of being seen, but not heard." I suggest that if that is so, then she can ask Teacher why it is so. Teacher merely smiles at her discomfiture assuring her that it is OK. He gives her a portion of his *Light*. I ask if she can tell a difference between her *Light* and his. "I feel lighter experiencing it. It seems more active." She uses his *Light* to draw two circles around Teacher and then separate them. She seems to go very deep and completely silent for an extended period of time. She returns to report that, "It is hard to put into words. Almost looks like a human body, like a fetus. There is an umbilical cord attached to a sac, which outlined the energy within. I heard the words, 'source of life.' It was very calm. It is our connection to our higher power, a distinct sense of 'no strife'." I have her ask Teacher if she can keep his portion of the *Light* and can she revisit this feminine aspect? He answers 'yes' to both requests. The session ends here.

I need to note here that I am seeing Lee and her new husband between our individual sessions. (The couple is unable to consolidate into a common household, in large measure because Lee is unwilling to move to his lake house in another state, which she feels would isolate her. For a variety of reasons I have to agree with her. I have been attempting to help them find a third alternative, which would involve refurbishing a house owned by her husband in another city much closer to the lake home he considers his primary residence where they could reside during the week and one that she could consider 'her' home.) Lee comes into this next session saying that her husband is 'draining' her. I appreciate that he can be overpowering but note that her reactions may be contributing as well to the sense of being drained, particularly as she imagines him in her own mind. I suggest that, imaginatively, he may have become a major image for the expression of her masculine energy, given there are so few other men in her life. I suggest that she treat his image as an embodiment of her contra-sexual aspect, and allow Teacher to convict both him and her simultaneously. She and Teacher are both agreeable. Initially, her husband's image is very resistant. "OK, you can convict me, but don't expect me to give in." Eventually, he goes down on one knee and does not question it. She, in turn, thanks him for his change of heart. I suggest that she ask Teacher to convict them both again, adding that I do not think resistance is ever an appropriate relationship for masculine and feminine aspects. "I felt more of an acceptance on the part of us both, a sense of healing." I suggest that she ask Teacher to convict one more time in order to discover what they need to live together. Finally, I ask her to return and share what she has learned. "I saw us standing side by side in partnership. I am as guilty as him in not joining into a partnership." When I see the two of them later in the week, she is much more engaged in expressing her needs and negotiating how they can both get what they want. For his part, he seems to hear her better.

Lee returns two weeks later and shares a dream, which suggests to me that we need to address the feminine; very likely, the feminine counterpart to her husband's masculine. I approach this by suggesting that she allow Teacher to separate out the masculine and feminine aspects defining her husband's image. Of note, Teacher has continued to convict her husband's image between sessions. Teacher quickly extracts both images. Not surprisingly, they are images of his parents who are living out a very painful relationship. "His mother's image looks crippled with a bent broken back, hurt in many places, weighted down, feeling very suppressed, using a lot of energy to keep control. She is furious, absolutely furious. She is running and she does not know why she is angry. She seems to be running to keep the pain at bay and the anger keeps her walled off from her pain." Now I have her focus on the masculine aspect: "He is indifferent; he does not understand. He wants control. Both of them have gentle sides but they never go there. He will not listen to her. He never listens. She wants to be heard." Now, I suggest that she ask Teacher to bring both images into the same circle. "He is facing away from the center and walking around the edge of the circle. She is following him but stays close to the center of the circle. She is trying to get his attention. Her back is hunched; she is slamming her cane as if to say 'listen to me'." At this juncture I suggest two options: she can ask Teacher to convict both images simultaneously or work only with the feminine at this time. I add that, of course, Teacher can elect a third alternative of his choosing. A long silence ensues. Finally I query her as to what has happened? "I saw her stand straighter and stop banging her cane. She has asked three questions of herself. How can I do it better? How can I do it different? How can I be loving? Each question seemed to open or extend her sense of self. Her anger seems to have dropped away. What I visualize now is her standing still in the circle." I ask if Teacher is in the circle? "Yes and no, he is on the edge but his energy is there as needed. The question I am hearing is how do I celebrate this gift of life, this opportunity to live life?" For the moment the question is going unanswered. I ask how the father appears to her? "He is on the periphery looking out, but he is no longer walking around the circle. He stopped when she stopped." The session ends here. As I reflect on this session I make a plan to continue working with these aspects until they can be reconciled and reintegrated into her husband's image.

Between this next session and the last, I have seen Lee with her husband. He is more willing to talk about his relationship with his mother. I would also note that he is also participating in his wife's meditation groups. In the interval between these two sessions, Lee has also continued to work with the images of her husband's parents. She has asked Teacher to convict them repeatedly. She tells me that the results were very powerful. "The masculine turned and faced her and then stepped toward her. The feminine stood next to him and leaned her head on his shoulder. That image has helped me when I have felt tension between my husband and myself. It is very comforting and safe and embracing." I suggest that she go inside and invite her husband to meld with this new sense of his masculine and feminine. "OK. He did not resist the idea; he is absorbing them." I ask if she can perceive any difference? "He has a big smile on his face and a twinkle in his eye. This is what I want from him." Lee now turns her focus to remembrances of another meditation workshop the couple has attended. This group was led by a leader who channels a spirit guide called Quan Yin, which is the Asian name for the Goddess of Compassion. "I did not want to hear what she had to say to me, that I don't have to be happy all of the time. The dragon in me – she was out this weekend, growling and hissing on all fours." I explain the brain-stem massage intervention to Lee and suggest that Christ or Quan Yin can provide this while Teacher is asked to extract from her the masculine and feminine aspects that sustain the Dragon in her. "Quan Yin is providing the massage. I have this sense of a melting of the tension. Teacher extracts the two. The feminine is a monster. The intensity of her rage is viscous and raw. The masculine is very small, like a tiny, tiny, person. It is an image of my father and he is saying 'please, please, don't eat me.' She wants to snap his head off. Her rage make me want to crumble in tears, but when I see it in the context of my father's pleading image I want to laugh." Lee goes on to tell me that she has always resented the color pink. I frankly do not remember how this got into the dialogue but it becomes relevant later. She then proceeds to tell me that during the weekend she also felt extreme grief of the death of her dog who died the year before. Lee has always been devoted to her pets. The session ends here.

In the next session two weeks later, Lee begins to spontaneously focus on her extended family, particularly her grandparents. "Mom grew up feeling trapped and beholden to her parents. She did not want that for us, but then got angry if we did not follow the rules. She seemed to feel an impotent rage that only came out when she was enforcing the rules. I feel like the Dragon has been holding an incredible sadness in check." I suggest that Lee needs to know her mother free of anger and grief regarding the maternal grandfather, who had a drinking problem and was a very strict disciplinarian. Lee replies by telling me there is a voice in her head saying "I don't want to go there" but it has to do with her *paternal grandmother* not her mother's father. "I feel really angry at dad's mother. I was always afraid of her, never comfortable with her. Mom shared that she meddled in the marriage. All of her twelve children either moved away or were ruled by her. She tried to raise me when dad was so sick and mom had to work, but she died. My paternal grandfather had Parkinson's and had to be put in a nursing home. Dad died six month later. My paternal grandmother ruled with an iron hand. At my 5th birthday party all the adults were giving me pats on my butt, but she walloped me." I ask her about the feminine aspect of the Dragon. "There is no longer an overwhelming urge to devour the masculine father, but she is still snarling and pacing as if to say, 'you can't intimidate me, nothing you can do to me that will keep me down.' She feels as if she has to devour the masculine to get its energy." I suggest to Lee that she go inside and ask Teacher to again extract the masculine and feminine from the Dragon, while Quan Yin provides calming brain-stem massage. "I could not really see anything at first. I felt this calming protective detachment from the Dragon. (Lee has personified the feminine aspect as the Dragon.) She seems to be protecting something that is wounded and in a cave." I suggest that she ask Teacher to heal whatever it is whether it is in a cave or in her. "I don't know how to explain this. There was a sense of moving, of traveling a great distance very fast. When I look at the Dragon now there is a sense of calmness. She is no longer pacing. She is wagging her tail, a good sign. She has won the battle." I ask about the father. "When I go to look at him he is not small anymore. He is the same height as the Dragon, who is physically changing into a normal woman." I suggest that she ask Teacher to convict their relationship with the power of the Holy Spirit. "Now they are smiling and dancing – in step. I almost feel that if I use too many words it will sever the connection; they will not fit right." I suggest that she can meld or assimilate them. I add that if they are prototypic male and female, then she is likely to only assimilate, not absorb. "When I stepped into the circle we all began dancing, the three of us. Then it turned into a spin with me alone in the middle. I will miss not seeing them dancing but they are always there for me to see. All I have to do is look." I suggest that she can affirm that by looking inside again. "I am. I see the three of us dancing." The session ends here.

I see Lee again two weeks later. She is reading a book on Deekshas called Awakening into Oneness.[33] She tells me that she has felt a real shift at work since our last session. "The panicky feeling is gone. I have the time needed to get the work done; and I have more patience with my husband." In light of what she is reading, I decide to give her a completely open ended suggestion: that Teacher will decide the intent of the conviction when she goes inside. It will be completely self-directed. "OK. I keep visualizing him holding my head…a sense of energy and lights moving…an experience of peace…I could ignore my ego direction…and ego-watcher…I can step back and detach and know it does not serve constructive purpose to be so bound to them…there is enough time for whatever." The session ends here.

I do not see Lee again for another month. On returning she begins by talking about a new set of opposites. "I am more consciously aware of the burrs under my feet. I feel disconnected from a rageful part of me as well as a silly girl. These alter egos have not gone away but my reaction to them is different. The Ranter rants because she feels powerless." I suggest that she go inside and sit with Teacher and the Ranter in a circle and ask to know the seed of her sense of powerlessness. "It is interesting what came up. She is pouting but calmer after I gave her a portion of my *Light*. Nobody will listen to her, others are not hearing me. Especially my husband who is passive-aggressive." (I need to note here that her husband is exceedingly opinionated, argumentative, and has a hard time hearing anyone's voice but his own. But he is changing, though slowly; and his mother was ragefully abusive in his childhood, which could account for his difficulty hearing any woman.) I suggest to Lee that she ask the Ranter's permission to separate out her masculine aspect and feminine counterpart.

"He is elderly, in his seventies, frail looking, leaning on a cane. His clothes are worn. She is younger than him, matronly looking, a little overweight. She is dressed in a late 1900's dress. Life has been hard. She reminds me of Olive Oil, complaining and whining." There is a sense that Lee is identifying this couple with her husband's extended family because she now goes on to tell me that her husband's maternal grandfather very likely suicided in an alcoholic stupor. (Alcohol was a problem for her husband in the past, but he has been abstinent for some years, though not what AA would call sober.) I decide to shift the focus and have Lee ask Teacher if he can recover the soul of her husband's maternal grandfather who suicided and redeem it? "Teacher says yes, if the soul will allow it." I rephrase the request by asking if Christ might intervene here instead? She is agreeable. I then suggest that *if there is redemption of the soul*, then Christ can be asked to present this to the Ranter and her masculine counterpart. "At first there was no specific image. Rather a dance of light moving in and out, a sense of energy, neither painful nor enjoyable…no strong emotion…a sense of loss as I reflect on it…then I felt myself trying to detach from the outcome so I could know his path. I asked to be a witness and know. Then I was the maternal grandfather dressed in white walking as if he was coming out of clouds of light. My feeling is one of joy, my tears were of gratitude and joy for being in the light." I suggest at this point that she ask Teacher to convict the Ranter and her masculine counterpart with the power of the Holy Spirit. "The look on her face is much different. They look more like a matched set. I heard the words: 'I am here to partner with him.' My feminine has had a strong sense of butting heads with males." The session ends here.

    I see Lee two weeks later. She feels on the verge of a real crisis with her new husband. He wants her to move to his lake house in another state. Her husband is OCD and has trouble giving up anything and so the house is full of clutter. Admittedly, Lee also has this problem – which she has been working to address, but even at her worse he makes her look like a piker. "My husband's brain is always dissecting and pulling apart. I have a hard time with his needling me about moving to the lake house. I don't have any sense of personal space there. I can't find shit there. The clutter makes me livid." As I listen to her a phrase comes to mind: the heart of the clutter. Lee's reaction to the phrase is that "It scares me shitless." I ask her to describe 'Scared Shitless.' "She is like me but very small. She is standing next to a huge pile of stuff." I suggest that she step back and let Teacher put a dome over it. Then I ask if she feels responsible for whatever is in the dome? "Yes. She is supposed to manage it, but she has no control over it." I ask if she would be willing to delegate her responsibility for changing it to Teacher? "She is struggling with Teacher. She does not feel *worthy* of asking for his help. There is some sense of shame for letting it get out of hand and not staying on top of it." I ask if she shames herself or is she shamed by others? "She shames herself. It stops her from addressing it and then she gets to keep her piles." I ask what she imagines would happen if she gave up her power to shame the piles? "She would have to face her fears." I offer her a proposition. If she is willing for Teacher to remove her power to self-shame then he will give her the power of his discernment. If she is not satisfied with the change, then he will return her sense of unworthiness. She and Teacher both agree to the conditions of the exchange. After the intervention has been effected, I have her and Teacher walk through her house and examine each of her piles. "Interesting. Instead of dread and feeling overwhelmed, I felt love and acceptance of my piles." I talk about the idea of inner piles vs.

outer piles suggesting that she start getting rid of the outer piles and begin transforming the inner piles. The session ends here.

I do not see Lee again for nearly a month as she is spending increasing amounts of time at her husband's lake house after they agreed to renovate his house in a nearby city, rather then immediately attempting to fix up the lake house. It is understood that this will be 'her house.' "My husband is a little better to work with, not so contrarian. I am primarily responsible for working with the contractors. I do get homesick for here (her house in Knoxville)." In a previous session with the couple, they are finally able to discuss their 'sex life.' As might be expected, it has grown contentious. I have suggested that they use The Zorba rule: There is one sin that God will not forgive, if a woman calls a man to her bed and he will not go.[34] In effect, Lee will be responsible for clearly calling him to bed and he must punctually respond or forfeit. This seems to be helping. I offer a way to move it forward by suggesting that Lee now go inside and ask Teacher to identify the child most sexually repressed by her mother and convict the mother until she can totally embrace her daughter's sexuality. Lee goes inside and Teacher convicts mother and child. A long silence ensues. Finally, I ask Lee if she can tell me what is happening. "A part of me is observing and thinking 'wow.' The toddler, probably two years old, is amazed and curious at everything around her. She wants to touch and explore. Initially, mom is watching her be curious. Then she picks her up and begins playing with her, gives her a belly kiss, letting the toddler touch and explore her face. Mom seems to be joyfully accepting this, even the pulling of her hair. The observer in me reflects that I have no memory of mom doing that with my younger sister, though she is able to do it somewhat with her granddaughter." I ask Lee to go back inside and ask Teacher to convict them both again so the child can become an older version of itself. "I see a four year old squatting on the floor and peeing and my mother laughing at her and letting her taste it. She is playing in it but not tasting it. Mother is making a game out of it while also cleaning it up. I am in awe of this." I have her ask Teacher to convict the two another time. For a while Lee is silent and tearful in a way that I sense is good. Finally, she is able to share with me: "The child is six years old. This time mother is in a rocking chair rocking the child and stroking her hair. The child is feeling very loved and secure. She reaches up and hugs her mother around the neck." I have her ask Teacher if there can be more? Lee goes back inside. "The child is now older – preteen, then teenager, then a young adult. There is a sense of her and her mother walking hand in hand on a journey, sharing and journeying together." At this point Lee becomes too emotional for words. Finally, she is able to say: "The journeying is never over and open to many possibilities." The session ends here.

I see Lee again three weeks later. She has no recall of the previous session until I have her go inside and 'look around.' Then she remembers the toddler playing with her pee. She tells me that she has had bladder spasms for years because she frequently 'forgets' to go to the bathroom, but now "I am more conscious or attuned to the need to go and it is no longer problem. And I have had some really good phone conversations with my mother. I have even come to miss her, and I am physically enjoying sex more with my husband. My dad was the one who disciplined and humiliated me over wet pants. Mom protected me over that. I remember having accidents and hiding it." Her reflections seem a perfect entrée to having Teacher convict her father, and the child he sexually repressed, so that her father can completely affirm her sexuality and body functions. "The conviction was instantaneous. This child felt much younger, perhaps ten months of age. She sat on the floor in a diaper, fearful of her dad, crying when he approached her, her diaper needing to be changed. He was tender with her, he cleaned her up without being upset or stressed about it. While he was changing her diaper, she began to pee. He picked her up and held her while she peed telling her that 'daddy loves you.' I started masturbating in the third grade. I lived to masturbate. They shamed me into stopping it in public places. I quit doing it in school and church, but not in the bedroom." I suggest that she ask Teacher to convict them again to help her find channels of regulation rather than repression of her sexuality. There is a long silence. Then she tells me, "The girl is older, perhaps nine years old. Dad is playing baseball with me. He picks me up and tosses me in the air and catches me. When he helps me with my homework, I am no longer whining. He looks over my shoulder with words of encouragement. 'You will make mistakes and it is OK. You are my princess.' There is a sense of going out in the world and exploring instead of being fearful of my own shadow." The session ends here. I suggest that next time we can experiment with Teacher healing her root chakra, but she is free for him to work on it between sessions.

I see Lee again two weeks later. First she shares a dream: "It was a dream of evil lurking…a demon-like figure and the fear that it will consume me. On awakening, I instantly asked for Teacher to bless it, and it instantly melted away. It was a part of myself. I also did your homework. When I first asked Teacher to work with the root chakra it was frozen. It was a black square. I noticed some physical energy in my back muscles and a tightness in my left hip. The third time I went inside for this work I noticed my vagina started to spasm, a post orgasmic feeling. Then I had the black square visualization. A white light emerged in the midst of the black square and there was something indistinct in the center of the white light." Based on what she has shared I sense that she is reticent to let Teacher touch her 'down there,' and ask her if that is so? "Yes I am. Laying down so he could do that seems disrespectful in his presence; but I visualized his energy opening it up." I ask if she is feeling a sense of disrespect or a sense of shame? And whether the feelings are tied to her early Catholic upbringing? If so, she might ask Christ to do the work. "I am hearing a voice telling me to 'not ask for too much.' I was taught not to ask, that I was not worthy. The ego will get overindulged by asking." I suggest that she ask Christ to extract from her brow chakra the idea of 'don't ask for too much' and replace it with the power of his discernment. She is agreeable so next I ask her what she sees in the circle in front of her? "At first I could not see anything. Then I asked. Now I see very interesting colors and a heavy, large, marble looking, stone. It is dome shaped like a stone smoothed by the ocean. It is pretty. It started to collapse in on itself becoming coin-like, a shield." I ask if this object has any limitation? "The only limitation is what I put on it." I suggest that she allow Christ to insert the power of his discernment into her brow so she can better read what is in the circle. "I asked. Then I felt physically uncomfortable. My skin began itching. I felt tension in other parts of my body. Then I started to relax with it. Christ tells me that what is in the circle is my discomfort of asking." I suggest that she may want to permanently give up this discomfort, but do not press her to do it just yet. Instead, I have her ask Christ to gently, safely, open the root chakra." She is silent for a good while. For much of the time she is uncharacteristically rotating her head. I finally ask what has been happening? "I did not see a lot. I felt a lot. My root chakra was moving counter clockwise and then I felt a release. Just a release and a softening." The session ends here.

I see Lee one month later. She feels she is in a good place. The house renovations are almost done and she is anticipating moving in after the New Year. "I am working on my root chakra and connecting with my family. I love my husband, but I'm mixed about initiating our sex. My libido is down with all the traveling and work. I know it is an important part of our relationship, one of the few ways we can connect. He is so walled off in a lot of ways. Teacher is touching my root chakra. It is so intense. I have been so disengaged from it for so long. And I am enjoying the feeling of actually missing my parents and wanting to see them." I suggest to Lee that she go inside and ask Teacher to open connections between her root chakra and abdominal (2nd) chakra. When she does this, what I hear are sounds, smiles, and humming notes, all of which are uncharacteristic of Lee's response while going inside. Finally, she shares what has been happening. "Wow. That was nice. I saw the root chakra as a round energy. When I asked for connection I saw a beam that went up. Then there was this incredible sense of calmness flowing through every part of my body, every fiber, peace and stillness, light and happy. This is why we meditate." The session ends here.

I see Lee a month later. She is open to exploring her contra-sexual aspect so I suggest we begin there. She is inside for a long time and silent. I finally bring her back so she can share what has transpired. "I could not visualize an image. What I got was an abstract feeling of rigidity that I felt in my upper back and shoulders; and the color red, a glowing orange-red. Then I realized I was standing there as the feminine and the masculine dissipated. I got a sense of bluish-green colors and pinkish. The feeling was different. My shoulders felt slumped, my head down, but not excessive. There was a sense of heaviness…compassion, caring, and heaviness. I wanted to cry. She seems so weak and vulnerable." I make two suggestions: first, that Teacher sustain her sense of the feminine with his own masculine energy; and second, that he begin convicting her and her sense of the extracted masculine with the transformational power of the Holy Spirit. "The center of my energy, the tension, is gone. I feel energy in my head in the front and base, more in the front. The masculine's colors have changed to orange-yellow and a little more pinkish; more like a starburst or burning sun that is round in the center with fire rays close together. He does not feel pumped up, rather he is much lighter." I ask if she feels connected to this sense of the masculine? "Yes. The colors are more muted and swirling with a white energy. There is a sense of strength and calmness, a restfulness. I want to use the word 'joy' too (smiles)." I suggest that she divide her *Light* in two and give a portion to Teacher. Then she is to ask Teacher to place one portion into her heart, another portion into Teachers own heart, and a third into her sense of the masculine so the masculine can flow safely through Teacher to her. "The masculine's color has mixed more and more with white light so it is now an incredible glowing yellow. I think I saw Teacher with his hand on my forehead. Then the light changed to pink moving from the center of a blue eye. That is when you asked me to come back. There was a distinct sense of Teacher connecting us. I associate all of this with the brow chakra, but I also felt this dancing rhythm in my hips connecting with the root chakra." I am hard pressed to interpret any of this except that it is definitely satisfying for Lee. I will just wait and see what unfolds.

I am unexpectedly called away and not able to see Lee again for almost a month. She is spending more and more time at her husband's lake house and the time is fast approaching when she will have to commit to moving into the remodeled house in a nearby city. But she continues to struggle with resentment. "I resent being at the lake house because my husband cuts me off so much. He finishes my thoughts and always seems to have better ideas as to how I should do something." She then goes on to relate a recent dream. "I am toting around a rambunctious seven year old boy. There is a female Asian woman who is mentoring me, and a masculine figure that is not at all helpful. The boy acts out and I get rigid. My mentor asks why am I so hard on the boy. I immediately have the sense that my dream image is my 'Victorian lady,' the rule maker." I suggest to Lee that someone may be actively blocking the evolution of the masculine aspect that she shares (projects) with her husband. "I can hear all of the voices of shame and humiliation growing up, the idea of never getting it right. There is a sense that this self is angry at the masculine because she feels it has always failed her. It is tied with my father dying when I was so young. She wants to beat the shit out of him for deserting her." Leaving her to do it herself? "Yeah. He was never there to support her. I have no sense of what a supportive masculine looks like. She did not get support when she accepted his suppression, and she is angry at the patriarchal overtones of everything that expects suppression but does not support in turn. Her mindset is that she does not need the masculine except to beat up on. My husband has been beaten up on by his mother all of his life; he was a perfect choice in that regard." I pose the possibility that Teacher could provide an uninterrupted flow of masculine support provided she gave up her power to beat up on images of the masculine. "When you made that suggestion the seven year old boy immediately grew up to a thirty year old adult and the Victorian lady became much softer and is now the same age as the young man." I suggest that she bring Teacher into their relationship and if she is willing to give up her power to angrily suppress the masculine, then he will forge a *Light* connection between himself and both of them as well as a direct connection between the both of them. "My reticence is about having compassion and love fill the space left by the anger. She does not have those experiences." I suggest that she ask Teacher to give her feminine self the experience of giving and receiving love from the masculine. "The two of them went from standing apart to standing side by side, each holding the other. She leaned into him and hugged him and then relaxed again. I feel how the masculine feels when I do not beat up on him – a sense of peace and strength and guided determination. The colors went to intense red after I saw them together." I suggest at this juncture, that the feminine 'give up her capacity for prolonged resentment in exchange for Teacher's discernment of how to approach and receive from her inner masculine.' "What I heard was that the release of all residual resentment would allow for joy between the masculine and feminine. It felt like that is what was happening. As I released the resentment there was a surge of white light that got brighter and brighter and a surge of sexual feeling. I could feel the white light pulsing as it washed downward and then I felt the sexual energy rise up to meet it." The session ends here. Something has definitely transpired, but as ever only time will tell.

I do not see Lee again for five weeks. She is doing well but still playing on the computer, though a lot less. I ask her if she can identify the internalized recipient of all her 'warring,' who she is shooting at inside? (Who is the recipient of her aggression?) "It is the ego self that makes excuses. She is afraid of doing it wrong. She is on the front lines; the Dragon Lady is not. She can kill safely on the computer." I suggest that she ask Teacher to show her who is always being shot? "Mmm. The bad little girl." What, I ask, is the effect of all this shooting on her? "She is wounded, standing there with all these arrows stuck in her and feeling hurt, dejected, looks like depression, hopelessness, loveless, no spirit or sparkle, wants to lay down and die, no engagement with anything around her. I recognize her. She comes up a lot for me in viewing today or tomorrow. Life is a wonderful gift but not for this part of me. She comes up a lot in the lake house. She has no way to express there." I suggest that she ask the Dragon Lady why she is doing this? I also suggest that Lee tell her that all of the arrows are striking a part of 'me.' "The part carrying the arrows has no sense of self; she is the part that wants to hide from everyone else. She is very self-centered. She carries the qualities that are obnoxious to others, the shadow side." I ask if the Dragon Lady is punishing her for perceived sins? "Funny, the Dragon Lady holds the anger and the other part holds all these qualities, but without anger. The Dragon Lady uses her anger to separate herself from all the negative qualities. The Dragon Lady has disdain for the wimp because she does not get angry. She, at least, can be angry." I ask Lee what she believes is needed here to reconcile the two? "To surrender to the power of healing." I concur, and propose the following request: We can get through this impasse if both of you willingly surrender to the power of Teacher's healing. "Dragon Lady got into Wimp's face and said, 'If you would just stop feeling sorry for yourself…' and Wimp transformed from corpse-like to a fun-loving, giggling, flower child. Wimp says, 'Is that what you want?' and Dragon Lady says, 'That's better'." I suggest that Dragon Lady still needs to surrender her anger in exchange for Teacher's discernment. "They are standing next to each other with their arms linked. Teacher says it feels like they are working together. I can no longer sense the strong separation. Teacher says it is not a bad thing to play the game." The session ends here.

Lee returns two weeks later. She notes in passing that her husband's mother also lost her own father when she was a small child and was raised by grandparents. I ask Lee if she and her husband have noted the parallel between the death of Lee's father and her mother-in-law's father? "Not much. I have a fear I could become like his mother. She carries my shadow." The previous session has given Lee food for thought in terms of projecting shadow. I suggest that she ask Teacher to simultaneously convict the shadow shared by Lee and her mother-in-law. "It was instantaneous. My mother-in-law embraced the shadow, which is so unlike her. I sat with it. Then I stepped in and embraced it as well. It looks like a three dimensional shadow, a muddy brown silhouette." I ask what she is embracing? "My mother-in-law says my hurt, fears, and weaknesses; those things in ourselves pointed out to us as not good enough. Qualities labeled by others as shameful." I ask if Teacher could baptize this shadow and release it from the shame imposed by others? (Long silence.) "When I asked, the shadow transformed into white roses. I sat with it. First they were flowers and white light and then those muted into swirling colors, which mutated into a younger, more engaged, woman. I physically felt energy moving into the root chakra, and a sense of connecting with family or others. The session ends here.

I see Lee a month later. She continues to complain about her husband 'cutting her off and finishing her sentences.' I will be seeing them as a couple the following day and sense that things must change here or Lee is likely to separate from him. I decide to focus on her husband's image as a conduit of her masculine energy, a fairly powerful conduit given that there are few positive male images in her life. I suggest that she ask Teacher to contain her husband's image and begin convicting both of them (he and Lee) until his image can provide a sustainable connection to her masculine, her animus. "The feeling has changed. His image did not change, but the feeling for me changed. It feels like I have been disengaged from the emotional triggers. It is very calming. It seems as if what he does or says will not disturb that. I don't feel like I have to go back to the emotional battlefield. I need to be strong and take care of myself. (Earlier in the session she remembers Teacher telling both of them in one of his recent meditation intensives: you do your thing and let him do his thing.) I ask her, if her husband's image were to fade for any reason (I am thinking separation but do not say that), will Teacher continue to sustain this connection with her masculine? "Yes. As long as I do my part and follow my heart." The session ends here.

I see Lee three weeks later. In the interim I have seen both her and her husband in conjoint therapy. Since that session, according to Lee, "He wanted me to talk and he listened. He let me tell him how I was feeling. He has been reflecting on the idea that he sounds like his father speaking to his mother and he does not like that. I am thinking it is time to sell my house or rent it and move into the house we have renovated. But I confess that I am afraid to go back to work. I know I *should* be looking for a job, but I am ashamed to admit that I don't want to go back into intensive nursing." I suggest that she go inside and separate from 'Should.' Lee becomes tearful. "I hear this litany of shoulds, but then I hear a very emphatic: I do not want to be a nurse; I never wanted to be a nurse. She is really, really, angry at the idea of having to be a nurse. She is terrified of failing on the job." I ask Lee if this self can identify who – inside, has the power to terrify her with a fear of failure? "She knows the source." I suggest that Lee give her a portion of the Light and teach her how to create a garment of protection so she can approach the source with Teacher. Also, I add, this self can go to the ocean and let Teacher help her release all the accumulated fear. As this is happening, Lee begins to share her understanding of the 'source' of her fear. "A lot of the fear has to do with feeling responsible for everything. My father died…" Lee seems to be releasing a lot of tearful grief at this point. I ask if she was trying to keep him alive or felt responsible in some way after he died? (Lee was eleven when her father died.) "She did not know what to do. She was supposed to help him get better." I wonder aloud if there was anyone she could ask? "She did not know how to ask." I suggest to Lee that this part of her needs someone who she can ask. Is there anyone inside who can step in and be there for her – Teacher, Christ, Quan Yin? In response, Lee seems to sigh and release. "She is sitting in a circle. I am sitting next to her. Teacher is standing there too. My dad is just holding her. I never got a chance to say goodbye and I can't remember if I said I loved him the last time I saw him. Life gets in the way; I don't remember the last time I saw him at home. I remember the morning he died. I was at church. I felt something was wrong. Mom told me when we got home. But he has always been there. There may be a different way to be a nurse." I ask Lee, 'If he has to go on, is there someone he can designate that this part of her can easily ask if there is a need?' "She is terrified of letting him go." I suggest that she let her father select the person. "She is not letting him speak. She keeps screaming, 'no daddy, no, no, no…" I gently tell Lee to be patient with her, give her all the time she needs to feel her way clear of this. (silence) "He tells her that he loved her very much. She tells him that she loved him. He put her hand into Teacher's hand and said it was time for him to go. She is OK. Time to grow up. And she is not alone." The session ends here.

Essentially, the series ends here. The following session, Lee reports that she is actively looking for work. She spontaneously reflects on the last session: "It feels like I got my chance to say goodbye till we meet again. I feel like dad is gone, at peace, our relationship is good. My nurse terrors were her fear of not doing it right. The fear is gone. I'm conscientious and careful. I feel enthusiastic about getting a job. I spend very little time on the computer of late. My husband and I are doing things differently; better. I have decided to go visit my family and old friends without taking him along, so I can just be with them as a daughter, sister, aunt, and friend."

Leigh

Leigh is a divorced woman in her early 50's. I have worked with her off and on for the past ten years. During all that time she has been diagnosed Bi-polar (with strong manic features) by all of her psychiatrists and heavily medicated by them. Earlier in her life she was successful in the finance field. She gave up that career to follow her husband to Knoxville. After the divorce, which he initiated, she found work in various financial positions until she finally decided to on her current job. She has done very well despite being heavily medicated to the point where she has to write down nearly everything to remember it. Often, when she comes to see me in the afternoons, she all but falls asleep when she goes inside. Whenever possible, I push to schedule morning sessions. Her own father was a very successful corporate lawyer when he was younger, but his own Bi-polar disorder, coupled with heavy drinking, left him emotionally and financially bankrupt at the end of his life. He died when Leigh was 42 years old. Her mother survived him by nearly three years. She was actively alcoholic while raising Leigh, and remained so till she died, though she drank less after the death of her husband. Leigh is the youngest of five children. The second youngest, a sister, died several years ago of cancer. She has difficulty relating to her middle sister; gets on better with her older brother. She relies very heavily on her assistant at work, but their relationship is very strained. It becomes an issue during the sessions described below. While I have 'tolerated' her psychiatrist's medication regimen for some years, I am convinced that it does nothing for her constant lack of sleep, and greatly impedes her ability to function cognitively. In this series of sessions begins with my encouraging her to withdraw from all of her medication. I refer her to a very competent physician who is also an acupuncturist and, because of a severe brain injury, had to take similar medication for a period of time. As we begin these sessions, Leigh is taking 250 mg. 3x daily of Depakote, an anti-depressant, Adderall for ADD, and Ambien at night to help her sleep. None of them really help her to sleep.

This series is longer than the other three. Leigh's case is by far the most severe. Her mother was a life-long alcoholic who conceived Leigh when she was forty. Her father was a life-long workaholic and alcoholic who was physically and sexually abusive to his wife and children. Basically, Leigh had to 'survive' these parents from infancy onward. They have scarred every stage of her childhood development. What she did not experience herself she had to witness her older siblings and mother enduring. As the therapy progresses it will seem like the same themes are being repeatedly visited. Just remember that Leigh's scarring began in infancy and continued throughout her development. The therapeutic process is essentially peeling away layer by layer and healing it. The process will draw on most of the interventions described in this book.

I need to make one other point. Leigh is manic-depressive. This 'disease' is treated as incurable by Western medicine and progressive: it is expected to get worse with age. The only accepted treatments are medication which essentially seek to 'strait jacket' the mania and attenuate the depression. This is why she is so heavily medicated. The general consensus is that 'seeking remission' is out of the question, but that is my goal; or, at the very least, to give her a renewed access to healthy energy and cognitive memory and a flexible regimen of medication.

Leigh is scheduled to be evaluated by the physician who will help in reducing her medications so I can evaluate her drug-free. I have worked with Leigh for a number of years and feel she can handle being off the drugs. And if it turns out that she cannot, then I will tell her and she can restart her regimen after a drug holiday. Leigh comes into this session reporting that she feels like she is walking through syrup. Leigh has no recall of the previous session. While not my usual practice with clients who forget, I read her my notes. I suggest that this time we take a different tack and have Christ contain the image of her father that has shaped a father's daughter – the compulsive workaholic. (We identified and contained this part of her the previous week. This image of herself will 'return' time and again throughout the verbatim. I suspect it is the primary source of her manic episodes.) I explain that this image of her father is also shaping the masculine within herself. I go on to explain that the purpose of containing the father is so Christ can enter the circle and convict his image with the power of the Holy Spirit. She will remain outside the circle as a witness. Leigh is disturbed by my use of the word 'convict.' She hears it as judgment and condemnation. She has always seen her father as evil. It would be fine by her if he's convicted of evil, but not fine if some part of her (the masculine) is also convicted. In her experience, the word conviction means guilty as charged (her ex-husband is also a lawyer). I stress that conviction does mean judgment, insofar as the Holy Spirit lovingly corrects Ego errors in judgment. However, if she leaves things as they stand, her self-image will continue to convict/condemn her father just as the father convicts the self-image he has defined: a no-win situation. Leigh goes inside. A long silence follows. I finally break in to ask what has happened? She replies, "Just what you thought would happen." Again, another silence, broken by my gently asking her to explain. "When I first went inside I immediately understood it is all about the disease (Bi-polar disorder). We both have it. I realized that no one wants to act the way he has acted or I have acted. But outside of his circle, I am angry. I am really anchored in seeing him as a son-of-a-bitch. But now Christ has asked me to imagine what it was like for him. He knew what he had done to us all; and when he was alive and growing up there was no comprehension of his disease or how it might be treated. Any form of mental illness was a stigma. But I don't want to hear it. I am so invested in maintaining this image of him as evil, and the belief that he has ruined my life. If he changes, then I must take an active role. I must totally shift my view of him 180 degrees. I have defined him purely by his behaviors instead of how it must have been for him. I am feeling like a spoiled brat right now." In the midst of these reflections, I ask Leigh if there have been any changes in her father as a result of Christ convicting him of the Holy Spirit? "My father was an atheist during his life, but in the circle he has fallen on his knees before Christ. His image is looking better and better and younger and younger. (At this juncture Leigh shares with me that she has been reading about Bi-polar disorder in adolescents. It is the first book she has ever read on Bi-polar disorder despite having been treated for it for the past 10 years. She picked up the book in the library after our last session. I suspect it has been contributing to her inner experience over the past twenty minutes.) I suggest that she go back inside and let Christ re-maturate the image of her father. "I see him in mid-life, still on his knees. Christ is holding his head and kissing his forehead, bathing him in *Light*." I ask what she is experiencing as she witnesses this? "I see him stroking my father's head in a gesture of healing and forgiveness. My congestion is cleared up, just like that!" I briefly ask Leigh to return to me and ask her about the congestion, which she had not shared with me beforehand. It had gotten so bad that she finally called the doctor for medication. The moment Christ touched her father in a healing way it instantly cleared up. It was still clear 30 minutes later when she left the office. But who knows, perhaps the medicine kicked in during the session. Leigh goes back inside and reports, "Christ is turning to me where I am standing outside the circle. He is asking about me. Healing is available for me as well. He steps out and comes to me. Draws a circle around us both. I am on my knees. Now he is stroking my head. I had a headache in my temple area; it has gone away (again, not something she mentioned previously)." I ask if he is making her mindful of anything? "He squats down in front of me – eye to eye and tells me to listen! 'You have to be a better parent to yourself. Your parents were not good models to follow. I can be your father. You have to actively do your part. It will not come naturally. You will need to keep turning your will and life over to my care.' (Leigh has been attending Al-Anon for years. This is the program's Third Step.) He says two things are going on. He will parent me and I must learn to parent myself; and a third thing: I must actively let go of my judgmental, unforgiving, attitude. That resentment is no good and does a lot of harm. A lot of my depression stems from my anger toward my dad." Leigh returns to me and we process what Christ has told her. I ask her to go inside one more time and focus on the 'father's daughter' in the dome. "I still see her in the rain, but now she is coming into a brightly lit area, and she is having fun splashing puddles with her boots. Its corny, but I can also see the dawn coming." We end the session here.

Over the next two weekly sessions I monitor Leigh as she begins stopping a number of medications under the direction of her new physician, who maintains active contact with her psychiatrist. (Both are women. The physician is senior and widely respected in town. I will be triangled in later. It gets hairy for awhile, but in serendipitous ways we will all manage to work together to get her off all medication.) This promises to be a difficult time. There will be withdrawal effects, which will take several weeks to manifest; but even more - from my perspective, there will be all the issues that have been suppressed by the medication. In the first week she stopped taking her sleeping pill, and could report sleeping through the night. She also began cutting down on her anti-depressant. By the third weekly session she has stopped the anti-depressant, as well as her medication for ADD and has begun cutting back on her primary medication, Depakote, for the Bi-polar disorder. She has been taking these medications for years. She reports having more energy and greater focus, though not manic. (She sees the mania as seasonal so its non-appearance is not surprising.) Her behavior at work is reportedly better. The weekend before her next session she goes skiing, which she has not done in years, and sprains her back. (This 'sprain' will become chronic and debilitating over the next year.) While in some pain she is able to go inside and do some work. So I decide to have her focus on letting Christ identify the part of her most strongly defined by her mother and then have Christ begin by convicting her deceased mother with the power of the Holy Spirit. She gets a brief glance of the self contained within the dome. Later she tells me that she immediately identified it as the 'victim' part of herself. Leigh's father physically and emotionally abused his wife throughout their marriage, as well as Leigh and her siblings. Leigh visualizes the mother sitting in her favorite chair. She crocheted compulsively, which seemed to ease the pain in her arthritic hands. The mother suffered from systemic arthritis in her later years. Leigh describes what happens when Christ enters the mother's circle: "Mother looks up as Christ enters her circle and stops crocheting. Christ stands in front of her and makes the sign of the cross on her forehead. She immediately begins to change." Leigh is first aware of her mother's hands becoming younger and free of arthritis; and then the rest of her – even her face, becomes clear and younger. "She is made new. Now mother takes his hand. She stands up. Christ draws her to him and begins hugging her. She is crying. It is a sense of release but also a sense of why could she not feel this way while alive. Christ directs her to the thought that it is enough that she can feel it now." Leigh goes on to share the mother's other regrets, and to each Christ redirects her to the present and how she can feel now. After awhile, I direct Leigh to her 'victim' self in the opaqued circle. Leigh says she is aware of changes in the domed self as her mother has changed. Initially, she seemed stooped over. Now she has started jumping up and down. When Leigh enters the dome with Christ and gives this self a portion of her Light, the self immediately expresses her willingness to 'receive the grace of the Holy Spirit through Christ.' She has been joyful but now she kneels reverently in front of him. Leigh sees her being bathed in a luminous light. When Leigh returns to me she does not want to speak a lot. "I just want to savor what has happened."

Leigh returns two weeks later. Her back is much improved after several visits to a chiropractor. She has now been off her antidepressant for three weeks, and is only taking half of her Depakote for the Bi-polar disorder. "I am sleeping through the night. I can focus. I feel like I have my brain back!" What most impresses me, however, are her next comments: I have been having positive sexual fantasies. But I have also begun to feel as if Satan is using my sexual pleasure to distract me from Christ. I never thought of Satan as being real till these past two weeks."[35] The positive sexual fantasies seem particularly significant as previously Leigh could only arouse herself with masochistic fantasies. I have her imagine Christ convicting this sexual part of her. She quickly replies that this part is now associated with Georgia O'Keefe paintings, which she thinks of as pure. So I ask her who is dwelling on the idea of Satan? "I sense a part of me which has low self-esteem, who recognizes her imperfections and weaknesses, and desires to be a *good* child of God. She fears Satan." As she speaks, I sense pride here in a self that desires to be a good child of God. But I do not address this directly. Instead, I speak to Leigh about the idea that experiencing the actuality of Spirit, pushes us to dwell on the idea that there can be bad spirits as well as good spirits; but that Christ can easily transform any bad spirits into pure white light as they are acknowledged. I then note that I also sense a secret pride in this desire to be a good child of God and suggest that she might want to separate from that part and convict her of her pride. Once inside, Leigh responds, "The Good child feels she has no choice, if she wants to be free of her fear of Satan. I am talking to her about willingness." I ask her if she has given Good child a portion of her *Light*? "No. I forgot to do that. She looks more like a tent, a head on a pyramid of cloth. The cloth is ripped, cold, and black. My *Light* makes everything very bright; there is a circular whirling." I ask if Christ has touched her? "No. Let me start again. This seems all wrong." I suggest that she let Christ place a portion of his *Light* into the heart of Good child to terminate undue influences, if there are any. "Now Good child is a self-image, submissive, calmed down. The image is more human and she is on her knees, focused and penitent." I ask if she is willing. "She does what she is told and holds the *Light* to her brow. Christ places his hand on her head in a comforting way. Now he has gotten down on his haunches and is hugging her. She has the feeling of overwhelming acceptance and love." The session ends here.

Leigh continues to improve. She seems more rested and alert than I have ever seen her. In this session I focus on having Christ convict the parental relationship. I tell her that when that is done she can begin the process of integrating their healed relationship into herself using her *Light* as the conduit. When Leigh goes inside and has Christ place the parents in a circle, her imagery surprises me. Normally, the images are parental images healed by Christ's previous convictions. In this instance, Leigh evokes a series of memories of her parents when she was six years old. She sees them both as working very hard. She visualizes her mother in wool and red bandana cutting a hedge in the summer. She sees her father coming home from work looking ten years older than his chronological age. "Their respective lives were all about hard, hard, work…lives of survival…any sense of intimacy was far away from how they looked at life." But then she focuses on her mother – an excellent seamstress, making a party dress for her when she was six years old. While this seems to be a diversion, it becomes quite central when she then focuses on letting Christ convict her parents' relationship. "I keep trying to imagine an earlier image of my mother. Of course it is not working. I realize I am trying to control the process." I reiterate that she really needs to be a witness to the process and only decide after the fact whether the changes are sufficient. (Long silence.) I ask what is happening? "I am having trouble concentrating. I can't see the circle, or I can't see Christ, or I can't see them both." I suggest she accept that there is someone co-present with her who is at odds with this. She is quickly able to separate from this self using concentric circles. What she senses is quite emotional for her. "I see a six year old. It is so sad. The only parenting I ever got was up to that age." What are you feeling? "Angry and bitter, not fair. I was the littlest angel (youngest of five). Mother loved to see me dressed up. I seem to be really invested in there not being a graceful alternative. She never said anything explicitly bad about my father – except when we could hear her pleading with him not to hit her. My relationship with her was probably unhealthy but you take it from where you can. I did not know the difference." At this point, I note to Leigh that the child's judgment regarding her parenting stunted her growth. If she was willing to accept the Holy Spirit's judgment, perhaps she could grow to full adulthood and have parents that facilitated that growth. I suggest to Leigh that she go back inside and see if the Six-year-old is willing to be convicted? "The moment I closed my eyes I saw her divide her Light (indicating willingness). Then Christ touched her and she was bathed in light. Now she is in a small dark circle. I have based my whole life on her judgments." The session ends here. I will not see Leigh for another two weeks but she understands that she can proceed with letting Christ convict her parents' relationship – assuming the Six-year-old does not object.

Leigh returns after two weeks. She has attempted to see her parents inside but cannot visualize them together. She has attempted to obtain Christ's help in her relationship with her assistant, which has been strained for months, but to no avail. She is off all medication except her Depakote, and taking one third less of that.

She is sleeping through the night, and no longer feels frazzled by work. She is much more able to focus. I have her reflect on the previous session. She reports that she still cannot see her parents together. She can evoke images of each one separately. She comments that she never saw them touch each other – ever. "One time, I did walk in on them making love, at age 14, but even that was doggie style. They initially slept in twin beds and later they slept in separate bedrooms." Leigh wants to focus on her relationship with her assistant. She comments that she, herself, has won a trip because of her performance, but is unwilling to give her assistant the bonus she agreed to pay her. "I know I am being small (petty) about this." I suggest that her unresolved issues regarding her parents' relationship may be bleeding into her workplace. As I draw a number of parallels Leigh reluctantly agrees. I suggest that she give the Six-year-old a choice by asking Christ to convict the parents' relationship. "I am having trouble seeing them together. Dad was always working; I never saw them together. My image of Dad is twenty years later. Mother seems to be looking through a window trying to connect with him." At this point, I realize there is one occasion when Leigh did see them together – when she was 14 and walked in on them making love. I suggest she let Christ enter that bedroom and let Christ convict them there. "That is disgusting. I don't want to go there – see them naked." (This client was fearfully touched by her father, but was finally able to rebuff him. She suspects he also molested her older sisters; and all of the siblings had to witness the sounds of the father beating the mother and then having sex with her. All of that will make the following changes even more significant.) I suggest she let Christ precede her into the bedroom, convict her parents, and attire them modestly. A long silence ensues. In response to my queries she begins to describe what has transpired. "When I entered the room, they were like two different people. There is an easygoing air about them. They were touching. Their body language was like two people who care for each other and have just made love. I don't see their faces clearly, but I can see the setting very clearly. I could sense Christ coming into the house and bedroom before I went in. I know it is his effect. I did not realize the tension between them had been 24/7 all the time they lived together. My parents were really uptight about their bodies." I ask her how they respond to her presence in the bedroom." They do not seem to mind. My father invites me to come into the bed and cuddle with him." How do you respond? "No way!" I suggest that she might allow Christ to convict her so she can be more in sync with this image of her parents as if they have always been this way. Are you willing for him to do that? "Oh, Yeah." There follows a long silence, then a sigh and sense of release. At my suggestion she comes back to me. Still, she does not speak. I have to ask if she got in bed with them? "Oh, yeah. But not under the covers." Did it feel good? "Oh, yeah." I ask her if she would invite the Six-year-old to join the parents. It is then she tells me that she has already been with them. That while she was inside she saw herself as a Six-year-old and a 14 year old cuddling with her parents, and then she adds, "Just now I saw the two of them together in the bed with my parents." The session ends here. Leigh assures me that between now and our next session she will revisit this scene.

Now it all begins in earnest. Over the weekend, Leigh calls in something of a panic. She is sleeping less. This is the time of year when she has historically become quite manic. She is suffering recurring pains in her abdomen related to a surgery eight months earlier. She knows she needs to go for a follow-up exam but keeps putting it off. Given her steady decrease in medications and my recent interventions, I am concerned that she is at a cusp point; that the previous session has precipitated this panic. (My surmise will prove correct but it will take a few sessions before she is able to resolve the issue upsetting her.) I suggest a session over the phone as both of us have the time then and there. It will go on for over an hour. I begin by suggesting that she ask Christ to help her separate from the 'pain in her abdomen' and/or the part of her that is waking up earlier in the morning. I suspect they are one and the same. Immediately on separating from the 'abdominal pain' she briefly sees a wildfire or flame. But no self-image emerges in the separated circle. She does hear, almost immediately, a voice saying 'not going there.' Whoever it is perceives the flame as being like hell fire. I suggest that she ask Christ to help her separate from the fearful 'Not going there'; then have him put that part of her to sleep and/or give her a garment of protection for her fear so Leigh can obtain a more 'objective' assessment of the fire. Instead, her Christ improvises by first taking her to a beautiful waterfall and then to a very still pond close to the waterfall, all of which has a very calming effect on her. He invites her to look into the pond. Initially, she is fearful. She sees a beautiful, multi-colored, fire with a light in the center that scares her. (Some months later, Leigh will finally 'touch' this fire, which symbolizes severe trauma in infancy.) I suggest that she use her *Light* to control what she is receiving by looking into the pond over her *Light*; in effect, letting the *Light* screen what she is receiving so she is not overwhelmed by it. When she returns her focus to the pond the first thing she 'receives' is confirmation that she needs to keep her follow-up appointment with her Radiologist. Next, she understands that the wild fire image is the combined energies of her parents acting in concert – a strength that she can draw upon, if she chooses. The prospect excites her, but also makes her fearful it could precipitate a bout of mania. (It does, but not for the reasons she believes.) At this point she shares with me that for the last couple of days there has been a third self – an older version of the Six-year-old and 14 year old identified in the previous session. This new self owns that she is prideful and fearful of 'hellfire' if she does not give up her pridefulness. I suggest – as an alternative, that she allow Christ to give her an experience of humility equal to her experience of prideful judgment. (At this point in the series I had yet to work out the need for these selves to forgo their self-shaming.) She seems open to that and as far as I can discern accepts the intervention from Christ. Finally, I suggest that she can ideally access the wild fire by asking Christ to become her constant companion and letting him be the guardian of that flame. That way she can have constant access to it without fear of being overwhelmed by it (made manic). She agrees to this and allows Christ to touch her forehead by way of sealing the agreement. A long silence ensues. Essentially, she reports feeling very good. Shortly afterward, we end the telephone session. This is a very abbreviated version as it is hard to write and hold a telephone. I sense that overall she has come to some resolution vis-à-vis her parents' relationship and Christ. But as ever, only time will tell. (What I will not learn till several weeks later is that about this time she will begin to masturbate to climax for the first time in years. It is likely the arousal is stirring up abuse memories.)

I see Leigh at the end of the week. At the beginning of the week she kept a scheduled follow-up MRI. She apparently has a reaction to the medication given in connection with the exam. She schedules two sessions with her acupuncturist physician who is also closely following her medication withdrawals, and she decides to take off the remainder of the week. This is unheard of for her. In the past, she would have pushed beyond the point of exhaustion or illness before taking some time off. Since lack of sleep is still the primary issue, I have her focus on who is keeping her awake. Immediately, she can tell me it is the Vigilant one, the willful one that does not want to submit to God. (This is a new self. It is especially fearful of men; and appears to have emerged with the sexual reconciliation of her parents.) This sense of herself is new to me, at least in its guise as the one who does not want to submit to God. At this point, I suggest a totally new intervention that I only just discovered that morning. I tell Leigh that the Vigilant one is very likely co-present with her. In a moment I am going to ask her to go inside and ask Christ to convict them both. Before doing that, however, I am going to ask her to draw a circle of escape. If the Vigilant one does not want to be convicted of the Holy Spirit, then she can escape into that circle. Leigh goes inside and reports the following: "I drew the circle and approached Christ. What immediately came to mind was one of Georgia O'Keefe's paintings of flowers and stamen. It represents the part of me that is willing to be convicted (her sexuality). The Vigilant one surrounding the real me is like a petal dying off, not in the picture anymore. I saw 'me' standing before Christ who is there purely to support me, rubbing my back, holding me. I also visualize the Six-year-old and 14 year old. He put his hand on my forehead and put me to bed with his hand on my forehead. Very restful." Leigh reports nothing in the other circle. I decide to have her reenact the scenario. "This time I see me like a kid skipping down into a garden, me as one person. I also felt the image of the dying flower wanting to bargain, make him promise that we will not flip out anymore (manic episode). The real me, not the bargaining one, asks him to convict us. I have to go through all of her mental chatter to get to that point. Out of the blue, I felt him drawing a cross on my forehead. It felt so soothing." I ask if the Bargainer was also convicted. "I gave her a choice to stay or leave. I told her *I was going to be convicted.* She vaporized again." I press Leigh to tell me more about the Vigilant one. "She is afraid to trust God. She trusts herself more. She is the part of my father in me; the part that has been molested by men." I note to her that her image of her father has been healed, which she affirms. I suggest that the Vigilant one may not have experienced this healed image of the father. I suggest that she use concentric circles to separate from the Vigilant one, the one who distrusts men. "I am not seeing a human image. Words come to mind. When I was in the center of her circle all of me wanted to run out to Christ. The circle is a dark green slime pool. There is feeling of a self older than me, suspicious, fearful, distrustful." I ask if there is any sense of her in the pool? "Oh yeah. This is the part of me that has been treating my assistant so shabbily. She is modeled after my mother. She is a victim; attached to property and prestige. I see an old woman with an upraised umbrella ready to beat off the men. She is reacting to my parents as they were before the change." I suggest that she ask Christ to place the reconciled parents within a circle and insert that circle into the circle with the Vigilant one. "I get a couple of cool pictures. I see my parents healed, like 20 year olds in love, not forty years old when my mother conceived me. The images went in like a drop of water into the pool. They are in a capsule of *Light*. The distrustful figure moved toward the bubble, intrigued and curious, knowing it is good. I sense she knows she has a choice. She can become the old lady with the umbrella or embrace my parents' healing." At this point I make one more observation and suggestion. I point out that this Vigilant self still has the power to either keep her awake or wake her up in the night. Either way, whenever that happens she is to immediately ask Christ to convict them both. I point out that the only way this self can allow herself to be convicted will be by making herself felt, so conviction will serve to change her, or oblige her to return to her circle.

Leigh's psychiatrist calls me several days later to express her concern. She writes a letter for Leigh prescribing two weeks medical leave, and places her on Abilify in addition to the Depakote. Her physician is also expressing concern. I am feeling torn. I avoid the psychiatrist by playing phone tag until I can see Leigh for two more sessions. In effect, I bow to the new medication and hope I can resolve the crisis necessitating it. I am grateful Leigh has so willingly acceded to the medical leave; it is an ideal solution that buys us all some time. After carefully reviewing my notes, I am also aware of an unaddressed issue: the green slime pool. I ask Leigh about this when she returns. She believes the pond is gone, that the Vigilant one is with her most of the time, and that she is looking at the parents healed and is in awe of it. I suggest that she let Christ just remove any vestige of the green slime, just to be on the safe side. (In retrospect, I suspect that the green 'slime' symbolizes her power to self-shame but have yet to formulate it during this period.) Leigh is hesitant. "It feels like the Vigilant one is invested in keeping things just the way they have always been. She is afraid she cannot be who she is if the pool is cleansed." Even so, Leigh is willing to go inside and ask Christ to cleanse the pool. In the process she will come face to face with a fear that has been gnawing at her for months. "I can sense his presence in the circle and feel it change to a white sandy beach with an ocean breeze. It is relaxing. Then I feel blinds casting shadows over everything and a strong resistance to change. In the past three months *I have felt like I am fighting for my soul*." I immediately suggest that she let Christ clean her mind completely of the slime. "Christ is just inside the circle with me. He called the Vigilant one and she came right over. He held us both. I ask him to clean the slime. It looked like a fried egg. I'm aware of trying to control the process." I suggest that she let Christ convict her 'control' by taking his hand and placing it on her brow. "I immediately saw myself in my bedroom trying to fight it alone. Now he is working on my headache. I am definitely understanding this at a deeper level. I am not strong enough to fight this evil. It is the spirit of my father that is not yet healed. So many nights growing up I would be freaked out by something awful from him, like his getting me up at 2 a.m. in the morning to wash the dishes. At night, when I saw him pulling into the driveway, I would turn off my light and pretend to be asleep. I have to give up my avoidance of him and let Christ heal it. I have been investing so much energy in avoiding the terror in the night. He is healing my father's insanity in me now. Christ is clearing it out. The remembered terror is what has been waking me up. I was his prey at night. Christ's Light is washing through my brain. The session ends here.

I see Leigh two days later. She has gone to an Alanon meeting and one of the participants has prayed a deliverance prayer over her. She believes now that the 'devil,' or someone very strong, has been controlling her. I agree there may be issues. I suggest that the Vigilant one has probably suffered from Post-traumatic stress disorder all of these years, and that could make her vulnerable to harassment. I suggest that the best way to address this in our session would be to let Christ convict any spiritual forces with the power of the Holy Spirit. I stress that we do not need the permission of any selves for this to happen. "Oh good, we don't need her permission. I caught myself trying to control the process again. I'm exhausted." I suggest that she again ask Christ to convict her control by taking his hand and placing it on her brow. When she reports feeling better I suggest that she have him step into the circle and 'clean house.' "Mostly the space is now clear and very bright. There is a corner off to the right. There are two portals and beyond that is darkness. The Vigilant one was in the shadow but I do not see her there now. The shadow area beyond the pillars is a choice. The Vigilant one's history kept her focused on the darkness. Now she is with Christ." I suggest that she ask Christ to baptize her and place his seal on her. "He placed his hand on her forehead. She is so tired from all the fighting. Now he has placed the sign of the cross on her forehead, and claimed her in that way. She asked to be claimed by him." The session ends her. Later in the day I speak with her psychiatrist. She accepts my interpretation of the crisis and tells me that she will begin withdrawing Leigh from her Depakote once she is stabilized on the new medication, which is expected to produce less memory impairment.

When Leigh returns she reports that her psychiatrist has further reduced her Depakote. She is sleeping better, but still unable to go back to sleep if she wakes early. She tells me that she has checked in on the Vigilant One who seems both afraid and excited at the prospect of getting off the medication. She equates it with getting sober, turning her will and life over to the care of God. "Christ is telling me how to take care of myself. I experience his words as 'go home and eat lunch. I did not want to quit working but I did and I worked better the rest of the day. I still believe there is an element of the devil using my weakness, playing on my fears of my father at his worse. That is my Achilles heal. It probably has to do with sex because I do not want to talk about it." Her comment suggests to me that maybe the unresolved darkness in one of Vigilant's circles has to do with a disowned sexual part. I suggest that she go inside, ask the Vigilant one to again accept conviction from Christ and then tell us about the dark portal in her circle. (Recall that in the previous session the dark slime pool in the Vigilant one's circle was pushed back but not completely transformed.) "I see the Vigilant one with Christ. She is on her knees. He is putting a cross on her forehead and then holding her. At one point she had a feeling of unworthiness. He is washing that away. As the Holy Spirit was washing through *me* we became one, washed clean. (Notice Leigh's merger with this self). I did not think it was sin, just darkness. I became transparent, a sense of exhaustion being wiped away, a willingness to stop being willful, a healing from being deadly tired. It is a lot easier when I can plug into the power rather than fighting it." At this point, I have Leigh return to me as I have just had a thought that I want to share with her and get her response. I ask if the Vigilant one, in addition to being fearful of male approaches, might also be fearful of any part of her that would invite 'attack' from a male by being attractive to males? "That nailed it", she replies. I suggest that she go back inside and ask Christ to illuminate whatever is in the shadow. "Christ is in the light area. There is a sense of buoyancy and celebration there. When he approaches the darkness with his *Light* it feels like we are in a dark cellar. There are slimy things there and crickets that jump out at me. Christ says these are my fears of being sexually molested, which I hold on to even if it means living alone for the rest of my life. It is true I have no interest in sex outside of marriage, I want commitment and security with it." At this point Leigh and I enter into a discussion about sexuality generally. I suggest that she really does need to bring it out from the shadows or it will continue to be a 'weakness' that could be preyed upon by spiritual forces, that the Vigilant one needs to embrace it rather than avoid it. I suggest that she allow this disowned part of her to emerge into an opaqued dome. When Leigh goes back inside she sees Christ contain the darkness in a separate circle. I suspect this is where the disowned sexuality is residing. For the moment that seems sufficient, since it is now clearly contained and separated out whatever it is. The session ends here.

Leigh returns three days later. She reports having slept eight hours the night before, but is still taking three meds in the evening, including a sleeping pill. She seems clearer in her thinking. I suggest that she go inside and ask Christ to place a dome over the circle containing the darkness and, I surmise, her sexuality. Then I have her ask Christ to enter the dome and transform the darkness into pure white light and/or convict it of the Holy Spirit. It is not clear to me what is needed here. She says that immediately after I made the suggestion she saw a dark figure popping out of a black well in the dome. Then she tells me her belief that the darkness has to do with her *shame* about sexuality – something she realized in the previous session but had not voiced to me. What she describes next confuses me, even after I have her return and draw it on paper. She reports seeing three arcs, like the iron on a Victorian greenhouse. The light is so brilliant it almost has a fearful quality, as if it was very cold or hot. The shadow in the dome went from black to white and then disappeared. Within the dome she sees only the arc of a circle, not a complete circle. In the past, I have come to associate an incomplete circle with the loss of a soul part in need of recovery. But for now, I choose not to pursue it as the dome is complete. Instead, I focus on her sexuality. I reiterate my thesis that sexuality can be moderated but never repressed with impunity. Leigh grasps my meaning. I note further that in order for Christ to liberate her sexuality, the Vigilant one must allow Christ to convict her negative judgment of sexuality as dangerous. She can do this by taking Christ's hand and placing it on her forehead. What follows is the long silence I have come to associate with conviction of a self by the Holy Spirit. When I finally ask her what has happened she says: "When you get me that deep, I don't want to come back. It felt really good." I suggest she go back inside and ask Christ to convict her once again. She does and comments, "It happened quicker that time." I assure her she can go inside and ask for this conviction as often as she wants. She then goes on to tell me that I might phrase it differently for my clients. "I have difficulty deciding which of his hands to take and how to place it. Instead, he took me in his arms first and kissed me on the forehead. It was extremely intimate, a really private thing." I told her that others have had similar experiences, but it probably would not have been a good idea for me to suggest that to the Vigilant one at the outset. The session ends here.

In the next session Leigh shares that she is sleeping better, but still wakes up in the night. She also shares for the first time that she has started masturbating during the day and has been doing so for the past week or so. I suggest that she do it again before going to sleep and see if that helps.

Two days later she comes in for our last session before I go on vacation. She reports that she has increased her "regimen" to twice a day, once before sleep, and that she has slept from 9:30 pm till 4:30 am. She woke up, called on Christ, rolled over and went back to sleep till the alarm went off at 7:30 am. She says that her psychiatrist wants to increase her new med – Abilify, by having her take it in the morning as well as evening. Then she will take her off the Depakote. Leigh decides it will only interfere with her cognition and not really help her to sleep any better than she is. Before leaving for vacation, I fax a letter to the psychiatrist summarizing the previous two weeks and diplomatically ask that she not insist on increasing Leigh's meds at this time.

When Leigh returns she tells me that her psychiatrist is planning to take her off of the Depakote. She complains that her back is hurting. I have her go inside and ask Christ about the pain. She immediately sees a picture of herself holding up a leg bone and using it to club her work assistant. I suggest that she have Christ contain the two of them in different circles and then convict both images simultaneously. "In my anger at her I have treated her unfairly. I have not given her the bonuses I promised. I am ashamed of that. The anger is related to being ashamed." I suggest that she approach Christ and ask him to convict her sense of shame with the power of the Holy Spirit. "He says that he is undoing it; that it need not be this way. I can see myself being washed clean of it." I ask if the relationship can be repaired? "I do not sense any closure here. I can make amends. My back does not hurt as much. The hipbone is back in place. I am aware of my assistant being overweight. She plays the victim too. I'm stepping back instead of being alpha." I ask if 'being alpha' is a handicap? "Me being in charge instead of her, oh yeah. But the alternative seems to be getting stomped on by her. I suggest she tell Christ that she is willing to give up her either/or, no-win belief for a third alternative. "I immediately have a sense of heart and head coming together, but also of that being fearful." I suggest that she let Christ keep his hand on her forehead for awhile till something emerges. "I sense it has to be him, but my head is arguing." I decide to shift her focus. I am beginning to suspect that her masculine sense of self is struggling with feminine alternatives. I suggest that she ask Christ for a portion of *his Light* as an expression of *his willingness* for her to extract his feminine aspect. I phrase it as her separating out the feminine side of Christ, the feminine side of God. He gives her a portion of his *Light* and she initiates the extraction. "I see the circle and a brilliant light inside. There is no image, but definitely a female presence. When he gave me his *Light* it also felt brilliant, buoyant, playful and glowing. Now it is bathing me and healing – the caring that a female presence gives, attentive to my needs, a tender hand on my back. My eyes – I did not realize how tired I am – they are a window to my soul. She is healing my inner eyes and my physical eyes and it is going into my soul." I suggest that she get her assistant and bring her into the presence of this feminine and, if Christ is agreeable, Leigh can share a portion of his *Light* with her. "Wild. Initially I did not see a positive image of her. Then I gave her the *Light* and she took it like a new toy. She put it all over her body. Now I envision her sharing it with her family. I see them at a dinner table. The *Light* surrounds them. They are happy together. I sense myself letting go of jealousy toward them. I am happy for them. She has made a choice to place her family first." I suggest that she take the assistant's hand and bring them both closer to the feminine presence. "My hand is tingling. She is embracing the circle of the feminine presence with a strong sense of physicality. She likes, needs, wants the feminine. She needs it, wants it, likes it." I suggest that she thrust her tingling hand into the circle. "Immediately, an image came to me of the fires of hell. My job is hellish. This is my dominant hand, my work hand. I don't know what I would do without my right hand." I suggest that her hand is expressing resistance to the feminine side of Christ, but perhaps through the week she can place her hand into his *Light* for healing. The session ends here.

Leigh reports that she left the last session free of hip pain; and that she is planning to give her assistant her bonus as soon as she is paid. I have her go inside and revisit what her hand experiences when placed in Christ's *Light*. She has a number of images in response, which frighten her. I finally have her provide herself with a circle of protection and an image of Christ, which she screens and trusts as safe. Next I suggest that she draw a circle of escape, and have her again place her hand into Christ's *Light*. She still feels pain, but no longer believes it is related to drug withdrawal or a side effect of the new drug she is taking. I ask if there is anything in the circle of escape? "I see some little black sheep part of me. It is active and small. It has low self-esteem. It is like a lamb. Christ takes it into his lap and strokes it, and it becomes white. It is really nice just to see him holding and stroking it." The session ends here. I decide not to press for more as she is going on vacation, and it seems best to leave off in a good spot.

    Before actually seeing her in this next session, I decide beforehand to examine her masculine side if the occasion presents itself. The idea of her 'dominant right hand' being so essential for work, suggests the masculine feminine relationship of her current Dominant self may be at issue. She comes in to tell me that she is still angry with her assistant, but has promised she will pay her bonus. No change in her meds; she expects her psychiatrist to take her off the Depakote next week. I suggest that she go inside and work with her masculine side by letting Christ extract it from her 'right hand.' She immediately has an image of sliding a glove off of that hand. When she goes inside Christ is able to quickly extract the masculine. "You were right in saying the masculine has not been serving me well. He is kicking and screaming, like a temper tantrum from a child; and *I am angry with him*. He is not protecting me. I have turned to Christ and asked him to hold me. There is more than anger on both sides'…frustration and despair. I feel like I have hit bottom; despair with a capital 'D.' I have been feeling like this for a while. If it were not for my daughter, I'd be doing stupid stuff." (Her sense of despair is quite pronounced; the medication is no longer masking these kinds of feelings.) I suggest to her that she let Christ convict both her and the image of the masculine. I note that Christ does not need the permission of her masculine side to do this so long as she is willing. (Silence) "I see the visual of Christ putting his hands on both our foreheads." (Silence) "While I want to be sure that my circle is safe, I do not see us as physically so far apart. I say to Christ 'this is really hopeless.' Christ replies to me that wherever he is there is hope." I tell her that each time she allows Christ to convict there will be further results. "The first time he convicted us, he put a half-nelson on the masculine's head making it quite clear who was in charge, which was comforting to my female side. Now my protecting circle does not have to be such a thick wall. Now it is more like transparent glass with two children trying to touch each other through it. Christ kisses us both on the forehead." I suggest that she just let Christ convict them again. "I see the wall dissolve. Now I don't see either of us, just blackness. I have been invested in hating the masculine side of me. I am being told that it will be transformed if I will continually ask Christ to convict us both." I suggest that she ask Christ to convict one more time. "I lost my concentration. I feel OK, but not centered, my thoughts are all over the place." I suggest that she is searching and scanning for clues to what kind of masculine will emerge. I suggest that she go inside one more time to receive Christ's assurance that he will sustain her with his masculine energy until the new form of the masculine emerges; that her requests for conviction will be like receiving her 'daily bread.' When she comes back to me I ask how she is feeling? "Better…glad that you are here." The session ends here.

    I do not see the Leigh again for almost a month. In the interval her psychiatrist has taken her off her Depakote, but continued the Abilify and has added Wellbutrin, at Leigh's request. She reports feeling a lot of fear and terror. I introduce her to the brain-stem massage. I suggest that she let Mother Mary work with Christ when she goes inside. "I see them both. I was really scared. I feel her hand as a caress. It is making me aware of how I feel – fearful, despairing, and angry at my disease." I suggest that she just allow herself to feel those feelings for a bit. "Inside, it is just boiling up. I can feel Mary drawing it out. There is so much there, like a miasma. It has got to be cleared out." I suggest that she give her undivided attention to Mary drawing it out. "She is making a gesture of holding and clearing out. I feel like both of my eyes are sore and tender, my brain is tired." I suggest that she let Mary give healing energy to her brain. "There is still a lot of anger there. I have an image of myself looking out of a window at rain and pounding on the glass." I suggest that she let Christ open the window. "I saw a white Lilly and sunshine; a part of me is fighting against that image. Now a bush is growing over the window and shading me from the sun. I realize that I can choose sun or darkness." I am aware that Leigh has extracted her sense of the masculine, but has yet to examine her sense of the feminine. I suggest that she let Mary continue to calm and clear her negative emotions and then ask Christ to extract her feminine sense of self. "I am not seeing anything clear, but from the moment you suggested this I had a distinct sense of a lack of development, almost fetal. There are some bright spots…a sense of something getting lighter…rising like dough…afraid of what would happen if it grew up…it was terrorized into not wanting to ever grow up…that rings true of a good portion of my personality…I skipped growing up and escaped into drugs, like my parents escaped into alcohol…it has made me overly cautious in everything…I see the danger of going so slowly, never really participating in life." I suggest that she allow Christ to remove feminine aspect's terror of growing up so she can enter a self-confident adulthood. "It is unbelievable that I am still so terrified of my father. I saw a plastic pet cage holding the terror. When it opened up all that came out were these harmless, plastic things. I sense Christ raising me up. Now I have a sickening image. I am terrified of heights. It is nauseating." I suggest that she refocus on Mary working behind her and look down. "I looked down and threw up. Then I backed away and sat down. I am concentrating on her helping me. I just keep retching… fear, hatred, anger, and resentment. Christ holds me and that feels better. Both of them are encouraging me to let go of it all. Mary is holding a bucket. Now I have this awful image of throwing up frogs and insects. They are creatures of terror. I feel like I am going crazy." At this point, I briefly distract her with a bantering comment. Then refocus her on letting Mary and Christ help her. "The retching has turned to clear water and now light. I can go back if I need to. I probably have more to get out. I feel both drained and exhilarated, and a little fearful. What started all of this was your reference to the reptilian brain (a comment I made at the beginning of the session in describing the brain-stem massage). The session ends here. Hopefully, in the next session, we will be able to start redressing the imbalances between her masculine and feminine aspects. It is no wonder the masculine has terrorized her. All this feminine aspect has wanted to do was evade and escape and remain essentially a terrorized child.

Leigh returns the following week. She reports that her psychiatrist wants to double her Wellbutrin. "My Assistant and the stock market are depressing. I am going on my vacation to Ireland in ten days." (It will be her first vacation in years.) I suggest that her 'depression' is a reflection of her current state of being which the Wellbutrin may mask, but cannot heal; and that she needs to go inside and let Christ convict her feminine side; and let Mary massage her brain stem. "I used the massage several times during the week. I have a toothache." I suggest that she let Mary work with the nerves of the tooth; that she let Mary reach in and 'read' the nerve. This is not so difficult given that Mary's hand is already able to penetrate her skull. "It is a different kind of retching." I suggest that she ask Mary to release it; that she think of it as an 'energy cyst.' "I feel as if I am being held down or jailed and a feeling of quicksand." I ask her what emotion is she attempting to evade? "Anger and resentment." I suggest that she allow herself to experience the anger with the assurance that it will not overwhelm the body. "Terrifying. Images of being underwater and drowning, images of water moving really fast and me being caught underground." I suggest that she let Christ swim with her sense of self that is feeling this. I then suggest that she let Christ teach her how to 'breathe' the water. "No. I feel alone like I was little. How terrified I was when I was little. Now I am letting Mary comfort me." I suggest to her that this 'little child' felt the feelings she has just experienced. I suggest that she ask Christ to rescue the little child, to dive down and get her. "That is exactly what he did. He got her out of there in a heartbeat. He has taken her to a beach and is comforting both of us. She is going back inside of me. I was really scared. I had no idea how afraid I was of deep water. There was no safe place growing up. Any time I went to mother and she was too drunk. I could be angry at her as a teen, but this is me as child. I am also angry (meaning her current sense of self)." I suggest to Leigh that the world would be a safer place if she will allow Christ to raise up her feminine sense of self and connect it with a safe masculine. "I see her getting larger and running to someone her size and age." I suggest that she have the feminine bring the male to Christ and ask him to convict them both into a safe relationship. "They both went from 20 to 30s' and got stronger when he convicted them. I then saw them growing to the wisdom of middle age. They feel capable and calm, sturdy and serene." I suggest that she 'update her body' by re-assimilating these images. "I feel shy for some reason, but OK. I see all three being playful together. (Note the dissociation.) Now the three are becoming one. I feel calm now, which I have not felt all day." I ask about the tooth. "I think it will require a root canal." I suggest that she ask Mary to 'drain it' completely by tomorrow morning when she wakes up. The session ends here.

I see Leigh again the following week just three days before she goes on vacation. She has decided that her toothache is the result of TMJ and is going to a dentist tomorrow. I suggest she go inside, let Mary massage her brain stem and then touch the tooth and see what comes to mind. "I see stairs and the feeling of running up and down them; lots of book pages turning, the idea that time is fleeting and getting away from me. A male client has offered to take me to dinner." At this point, I am moved to suggest a radical intervention: that she let Christ convict her mother during the period when she was pregnant with Leigh, as well as convict everything built on that foundation. "I need to do that more, it is giving me a totally different perspective. She was forty when she had me. She was drinking and really tired. I could see her putting the drink down and really tired. Christ is getting her to rest. I can see Christ combing energy through her belly and head, getting her to rest. It was hard for her to rest. Both parents were drivers. Amazing what she accomplished while being drunk all the time. My jaw really hurt while we were doing that, but it feels better now." I suggest that she go back inside and ask Christ to convict the conception so she can be born fully into the world without hindrance. "I am feeling pain and having trouble getting past it. I see a plane wreck." I suggest that she move into the pain and let Christ relax what is constricted. "When I went into the pain it got worse." I suggest that she let Mary massage her from the back and let Mary point out – touch, what she needs to know, let her use both of her hands. "It feels like TMJ on both sides of my face. I am aware of a Worrier." I suggest that she offer it a circle of escape. "It goes directly to the circle." I suggest that she let Christ enter that circle and terminate any undue influences. "I do not see an image of me. I see 'gremlins' and 'pirates.' He is terminating the 'pirate stuff.' When I was a teen my father had to declare bankruptcy twice. I have a fear of it happening to me." I suggest that Christ step back out of the circle where the teen seems to have emerged, and if she is willing, she can leave the circle and come to him. "I see her disappearing." I suggest that Leigh stand in front of Christ and let him convict the Worrier in her. "I can't, I can't, I can't." I suggest that she can at the very least ask Christ to give her the experience of 'can' equal to her experience of 'can't' so as to have a real choice. The session ends here all very unresolved as she is leaving for Ireland in two days. I will not see her again for three weeks.

Leigh returns three weeks later having 'survived' her vacation. I decide to focus as quickly as possible on 'I can't,' and suggest to Leigh that she go inside and have Christ create a circle of escape and then convict the Aware-ego sense of self with the power of the Holy Spirit. "She ran into the circle as soon as I closed my eyes. She is real young, small, and terrified. Age four, huddled up, arms around the knees, just like the fear of when my father came home." I suggest that she let Mary enter the circle and provide the four year old with brain-stem massage. "She jumps into Mary's lap. She is rocking *me.*" Leigh says this holding back strong emotion. I tell her that she does not have to express whatever she is feeling but to allow herself to feel it. "She is just really comforting me, working with the fear, reminding me that I am loved. She too [Mary] lost someone…the pain of it… it was terrifying and painful. Negative emotions are OK but not to dwell on them 24/7. The four year old says it is not fair. She hops off of Mary's lap and pounds the ground. She is having a tantrum. Mary is encouraging her to come back into her lap and calms her down. Mary tells her that she can thrive in an 'unfair' world without being a part of the unfairness, but not a victim of it either. Mary's hands on *my* head are so calming. I see Niagara Falls – how fast life goes by. Mary says that she and Christ are a way out of the terror. I see a sliding pole like a fire escape. I slide down to the bottom and Christ is there with open arms to catch me. Mary is holding me while another part of me slides down the pole into Christ's arms." I suggest that she let this child self repeat the experience till she is completely relaxed; that he is offering her the release from fear. I ask what is happening inside. "It has become a slide. I am going down all sorts of ways…on my back, head first, turning in circles, somersaults, like an airplane with my arms out. That part of me has grown up and now I even saw her going down in a bikini. Christ is telling me he is here for me. 'I convict you and that other part (bikini), all of you. You two can learn to play together.' He is showing me a musical instrument unlike any I've seen before. He is telling me that music is my life; that increasing the Wellbutrin is not the answer. That if I come to Christ he will really heal me, surprise me with how much I can be healed, exceed all the limits I place on my self. I will be loved and looked after." The session ends here.

Despite the previous session, or perhaps because of it, Leigh returns the following week feeling like a failure professionally. "In 18 years it has never been this bad" (Indeed, this is 2008 and the stock market is going to 'hell in a hand basket.') I suggest she go inside and ask Christ to convict her for insight. Initially, she is so fearful she cannot find Christ or her *Light*. So I have her sense a circle of protection and enter that. She immediately starts telling me how she is feeling. "The job has worn me out. I am really tired. It makes me feel old, tired, and exhausted. I am fighting it. It is not fundamentally rewarding. I may be through in this field. It is too exhausting; zero quality of life." I have her ask Christ what, from his perspective, is the major impediment to a quality of life? "Energy and passion. I don't feel strongly about anything. I am so absorbed with survival; I am terrified of economic insecurity." I ask her if she is willing to be released of her fear of economic insecurity in favor of a quality of life? "It is so much of who I am. I feel bound to it literally. I feel tied to a pole with rope; my hands are tied." I note that this belief guided her father all of his life. I suggest that she let Christ convict the tied-up sense of self with the power of the Holy Spirit. "I see myself going into a laundry shoot, falling into the unknown. It is uncomfortable. I see him at the bottom to catch me. This past week I have been thinking that this is not what I had in mind in terms of a life. I feel immobilized, but I also see I am where my choices have led me." I affirm her perception by noting that she is squarely where her parents shaped her to be. I suggest it is time to get over them; better, to love them free of their baggage. Let Christ liberate them and their fear of economic insecurity. "For a moment I saw them dancing. It felt good. Then I saw myself looking up stairs and Christ's light at the top. Whatever door I choose he will be with me. Where I am now is no longer meaningful to me." The session ends here.

Leigh returns a week later to report that she has upped her Wellbutrin by a third and that she feels better. "But I am still in survival mode; everyday is a grind." I suggest that she go inside and separate from whoever feels she needs the Wellbutrin. "I am observing myself lying down in a circle. It is the Driver. She is pounding on the ground angry and tired. She is dominating me now. She is impatient with the process. She just wants to be well. Christ is stroking her hair. She plays the victim. It is a habit. She does not know any other way and she cannot turn it over. She is too afraid." I suggest that she ask Mary to enter the circle and provide brain stem massage. " She had her head on Christ's lap for awhile. Now it is on Mary's lap." I suggest that she let Christ convict her role as 'victim' to provide insight. "I see him doing that. She turns on her back and looks up at clouds as a child would on a summer day. It comes to her that she needs to dream. She fights the idea but now she sees a cross covered with gauze. There is lots of light around it and Mary is there decorating it with flowers. It is a resurrection cross. I have an image of stairs again going up and down and a sense that I am really changing what I want to do during the day. The stairs are lined with shelves and boxes suggestive of that changing; there are grocery bags full of excess clutter in my home. I sense a bright light coming through a window, a dream or new direction is coming to me having to do with stairwell stuff. The Driver is sleeping. I think what she has lacked is the ability to connect with her dreams. I had a dream of lots of trees this past week that were real crowded together. Some started to uproot themselves and start walking. I have not looked forward for a long time. I need to start simplifying my life; that does not have to be bad." The session ends here.

Leigh returns a week later complaining about her sleep pattern. "I am in bed by 9 p.m. and then up at 2 or 3 a.m. sometimes I am awake till 4 a.m. It is hard to drag myself out of bed in the morning. I don't want to do my job. I just lost a million dollar account." I suggest she go inside and separate from the part that has trouble getting out of bed. "She feels younger than adolescent, age six or seven. She is sitting on her haunches in a fetal-like position. Not the way I wanted my life to turn out. *I am being so hard on her*. She is immature. She needs to shape up and grow up and do the work. She feels overwhelmed; can't do anything about any part of her life. She seems to wake up every morning depressed. She is terrified, immobilized by her fear of failing. I am watching myself fail. She feels suicidal." I suggest that Leigh let Christ enter the circle of this Six-year-old and identify her need. "She has a need for basic human companionship and eating right. She feels out of sync." I ask Leigh who it is that is shaming her? My parents and my office assistant, and the Driver. "I can see Christ terminating their power to shame. And I am asking him to convict me for willingness. I am afraid to give up that power. How will I relate to her." I suggest that he can offer her a quid pro quo. She gives up the power to shame and he will give her a path to love her – discernment in exchange for her power to shame. I tell her that Christ has an unerring sense of judgment in these matters. Leigh is silent. I ask her what is happening inside. "I am questioning him how it will take place." I suggest that if she is willing for anything to happen, then she is to walk up to him and let him place his hands on the side of her head for a few moments. (At this juncture, I have yet to discover the penetration and exchange process.) I add that when he takes his hands away, she is to come back to me. "While he was holding my head I saw a bright light coming out of his heart and into me and then back. I felt him holding me close to his body. We are standing on a stair landing. Just above I see a door brightly lit. There is a feeling of change in the air." I ask her if she wants to go through the door? "Yes. I suggest that she let him hold her head again and feel the heat of his hands. "There are lots of images. I kept praying for discernment. Where would I be living? I see myself walking into a neat bedroom, a bread and breakfast. I would be happier in new surroundings." The session ends here.

I see her again in two weeks. She is still taking the Wellbutrin and Abilify. She tells me that she is feeling terrified, meaning I suspect, the Six-year-old. "She is most afraid of abandonment by me." I ask how Leigh continues to abandon her. "I stop eating, I've lost ten pounds, or I sleep." I contend Leigh is using shame to banish and I tell her so, and ask her why? "She is so honest. My life is not a life. It is too frightening to contemplate." I tell Leigh that she must give up the power to shame; it is terrifying the Six-year-old. It is the most corrosive emotion she can use. It destroyed her father and crippled her mother and is doing the same to her. It has no socially redeeming value for the doer or the receiver. "I guess that explains my feeling of despair." Silence. "I am angry and frustrated." I tell her that those emotions will not deter Christ, only her unwillingness to stand before him and let him remove the power to shamefully banish. "It is a control issue." I have her ask Christ if he would accept her power to shame in exchange for his power of discernment. "He says 'yes,' people are always giving him odd gifts and he takes them." I have finally figured out the needed intervention and so tell her to focus on his fingers going into the center of her brain, drawing out the power to shame and replacing it with the light of his discernment. I add that it is like the brain stem massage only now he is entering her brow. "I sense some penetration, but now I am resisting. I see a file cabinet being pulled open like one I had as a child. A sense that all these bad things about me will come out; things

I am ashamed of, my deep dark secrets. Now I have the image of a water wheel. His Light is right behind the water coming down as if I was at the bottom of a cave." Ask Christ if he can baptize all of the shame hidden in your heart? "When I handed him those shamed things they became roses…a glimpse of heaven…a millisecond of real intimacy with him. He is baptizing me. I did not feel his fingers in my brain." I ask her if she is ready to feel them now? "I think so. I have oddball images of summer time with wicker porch furniture and a picnic. It is all around me and I can't get willing enough." Then she breathes deeply as if experiencing a release, but the session ends without a true sense of closure. I schedule to see her the following day. We both know she is on the cusp, so she is willing to come.

Leigh returns the next day to tell me "She is not optimistic about doing this today." I reiterate that Christ is able to terminate other shaming voices, to which she replies, "I can remember yesterday clearly hearing my father say, 'shame on you, shame on you.'" I immediately have her go inside and ask Christ to contain the shaming image of her father and terminate his power to ever shame her again. I tell her to see her father shaming her and then seeing Christ place a portion of his *Light* into her father's heart. "I saw bird's wings, a sense of a burden lightened, and then I saw him sitting down, more mellow, but he also looks beaten by life, crushed." I ask here if she is fearful she will also be crushed if she gives up the power of self-shame? "No. But I have felt shaky yesterday and today. "Now my father looks like a young man. He has jumped up and started doing ballet." I reiterate to her that self-hatred is not worth whatever power she seems to feel it offers her. "I saw my self in front of Christ, him holding me and conveying to me that it is all about trust, my core issue. We are both on planks of wood over a stream. We are coming from opposite sides. My plank cannot support me but he is supporting me. It has the flavor of walking on water. Now I am standing on the land and asking him for conviction. I was asking for an image of change rather than conviction and that is what was holding things up." Silence. "My whole forehead feels like it was bathed in light. I looked backward at my job. He says my worries are just a second in time; not what is important here. The job will work itself out one way or another. This is true." I reiterate that she needs to let his *Light* penetrate her mind. Silence. "For a split second it felt like great sex and then relief. Lots of images of water flowing down…a great amount…a giant hole…like Niagara Falls. I keep begging for conviction and get more comfortable with the images he wants to give me. Now I see a tree trunk cut off, a stump. I have to get comfortable. I see a serene pool of water, dusk, a farmhouse. The stump symbolizes the cutting away of how I had been living. I have been head strong for a long time; pining away for a long time. Now I do not see that tree at all just the stump." I ask about her child-self? "Before you mentioned that I saw an alpine lake, then me or the child in a rowboat quite relaxed. I see the child running along the dock, carefree, and then meld with the spirit in the rowboat. I see her – the adult, holding the child and becoming one with her. The message I am getting from Christ is that, 'It is not so hard; I do not have to be ashamed for shaming myself; it is all I knew.' Then he tells me, 'I have created this beautiful world; you need to take advantage of my world.' I feel like I have been on a real vacation. I just need to choose where I want to spend my mind, and I do not have to do it alone. And I need less drugs to do it, I need to own my own mind." The session ends here.

I see Leigh again in two weeks. She is doing well. She has reduced her anti-depressant to once a day and cut back on her sleeping pill. I suggest that we begin examining the part of her that clamps down on her sexual desire. (Antidepressants, whatever else they do, invariably suppress the sexual libido. As Leigh comes off this medication she needs to resolve any remaining sexual conflicts.) When Leigh goes inside she finds herself under the stairs of a general store afraid to come out. She can see the part of her that holds the *Light*. I suggest that this part will extend a portion of the *Light* to the part hiding under the stairs. "She rolls the Light to my feet." I ask her if she knows Jesus Christ? "Yes." I tell her that I am going to ask him to join her under the stairs so he can teach her how to create a garment of protection against the fear of exposure. "At first everything seemed murky. As he put the *Light* around me I felt comforted. I can see light when I look up. I can sense myself saying, 'I am so scared.' It feels like I am in a minefield of discarded furniture that is all broken up and jagged." I decide to treat this sense of Leigh as a shamed part of her sexuality and ask her if I could have her permission to ask Christ to baptize her? "Yes." So I ask him. "It is really abstract. I am not seeing my body; I am seeing arches of light and darkness. I am trying to distance myself." At this point it is not clear to me who is speaking, only that it is fearful of being shamed. So I ask her if she can tell me what is shaming? "When I was really little – age 3, I was ashamed to have sexual thoughts, ashamed for acting on those thoughts (playing with herself), being little and weak. Dad said 'shame on me'." I ask her if she would be willing for Christ to contain her father and terminate his power to shame her sexuality now and forever so that here after the only one who could shame her would be her, and I don't advise that. "I have been really angry at my father for doing that. He was being hateful. I boarded him up." I am not sure what she means by this but tell her that the three year old will be under Christ's protection hereafter.

The session ends here.

I feel the need to make an observation here regarding Leigh's selves. An overriding characteristic of Leigh's interior life is the large number of selves age six and younger. As each emerges, the feelings and defenses they enact dominate Leigh's emotional life. Each self must be respectfully worked with. The large number is indicative of the trauma wrought by both parents when Leigh was a child. I have only seen this quantity of young selves in MPD clients. Leigh is bi-polar, not MPD, but the limited coping skills of these children definitely exacerbate her mood swings. The only 'adult' in the group appears to be the Teenager or Driver, who is largely responsible for Leigh's manic episodes. This work does call for patience. As each self is addressed another will emerge to take its place. There is a distinct 'regressive' quality to it that cannot be avoided. It would be impossible to get to this depth with all the medication she was previously taking, but I am also asking a great deal of her as she struggles with these selves, a very demanding job, parental responsibilities, and life's general hassles.

I see Leigh the following week. She tells me that she has begun to dream again about her future, which includes holding babies, volunteering to work in a hospice, and helping people to the next spiritual level. Then she relates how she has become concerned about floaters in her eyes because her father had macular degeneration. I relate the story of a client who recently told of a 'miraculous' healing when he let Mary join her hands with his hands that were over his eyes. When he took his hands away all of the floaters in his eyes were gone. I suggest to Leigh that she ask Christ to free her from the fear of her father's legacy; to convict that fearful legacy with the power of the Holy Spirit. Silence. "I picture myself kneeling before Christ asking him to lift my fear. I immediately saw I have been trapped by all of these 'spider webs.' They were pulled off to the upper right and then to the right. Now I am asking him to put his fingers on my forehead and calm my brain, massage it. I see myself looking down on a palisade. This past week or two I have been thinking of fun things to do. The palisade is a symbol for fun." I ask about her sexuality or lack of it. "I see a line across my right eye. The lack of sex is just about the drugs. I am taking too much." The session ends here.

When Leigh returns the following week she tells me that she has further reduced her Wellbutrin but now is having trouble getting out of bed in the morning. I suggest we continue focusing on the father and the child whose sexuality he repressed. "I cannot deal with both at the same time so I have asked Christ to just work on me. But then I just see a very young carefree child, so I have asked Christ to work with my father. After Christ convicted him I see my father much younger – maybe eighteen years old. Christ is helping him to make different and better choices. I see him pushing my older sister in a swing, which is something he would have never done. Now he is helping my brother with his studies, another thing he would never have done, and affirming him. My brother's life as a bad student and asthmatic is totally different as a result. I see dad's life evolved so that he can now be affectionate with our mother in front of the kids. I feel compassion for him; I appreciate how lonely it was for him. Even if he evolved, my mom would still have been an alcoholic. At age twelve my father gave me a pink mini-slip. I felt it was inappropriate, too sexual coming from a father; something a mother would give to you privately. But I loved it. I just realized this. I never thought of it as an invitation from him." I ask her if she can tell her father she appreciated the slip? "My mother abandoned me to him; she turned a blind eye, got drunk and passed out. I am angry about it." I ask her if Christ can convey to the child that this was not a healthy environment in which to learn about sexuality. "Christ does. My mother's reaction is to sob and feel ashamed. Christ is trying to comfort her." I suggest to Leigh that she tell her mother that it is nearly impossible for Christ to comfort her while she continues to shame herself. She needs to give up her power to shame her sexuality, her husband's, and Leigh's. "When Christ draws out her power it looks like shit on a rock. It definitely casts a pall over everything. She is willing to give it up for Christ's discernment. The *Light* just came and replaced everything. As sick as she was with alcohol, she did have a good heart. I suspect the root of her sickness was all of that shaming." I suggest that she offer her father the same option. "I don't think it can happen; he was basically evil. My father worked side by side with very important people who hurt the country. His self-shaming drove him to work 36 hours straight at one stretch. He had self-hatred and hatred for whole groups of people. It was insane." I ask again if Christ can help him see the effects of his self-shame? "I see a big hole, straight down, emptiness." I ask her if he really wants to retain that power if this is the effect? Silence. "He would get into terrible dark depressions. In those episodes he saw what he was like. He is choosing Christ now, but as I see the light filling the hole it only goes from dark to gray. It is not the dazzling light I saw for mother." I suggest that he was very sick and this may take some time. "The hole is gone now but I don't know if he is willing to accept Christ's discernment. He had no spiritual life while he was alive." The session ends here.

When Leigh returns a week later, I decide to take a different tack and invite her to let Christ work directly with her root chakra. She tells me that it feels shameful 'down there.' I ask her to let Christ do whatever he needs to do to free it from shame. "It is shame. He is making it clear to me that I need to be comfortable for him to do this. The shame started with my father shaming me and it became a habit where now I do it to myself." I ask her if she can give up the power of this habit? "It would be hard to do." I suggest that she allow Christ to extract it from her head and observe its effect on her root chakra. "It keeps me bowled over in a fetal position." I tell her that I do not believe he can clear the root chakra while she keeps shaming it. "I am feeling healing energy in the circle where I am in the fetal position. I see a beach and a big sailboat up the beach. When he started I just wanted 'to get out of here,' but then he put his hand on my root chakra and I had this feeling of healing. His discernment is such a more comfortable choice, so much more loving to myself than that power to shame. Now I see a giant ship pulling onto the beach, a black hull. It seems dangerous. I scurry to get out of the way. It is an example of where I am not to go with my thoughts; that I must focus on the healing. Discernment is a choice. Now I see the black-hulled ship as a toy on a pond – that is the power of discernment, I can choose how I look at things. Christ wants me to get back to healing the spot. He has been drawing something out. It has been all tangled; the nerves have been stunted in growth when they should be free like hair. It was like they were burned off; now there is a sense of cleaning and straightening. Christ says that he has been waiting to do this for me." The session ends here.

When Leigh returns the following week she summarizes her 'progress': "I am off Wellbutrin. My libido is back and everything works...for the first time in months." I suggest that she let Christ work with her abdominal chakra (sexual). "Christ still wants to focus on the root chakra. I am anxious over talking about sex with you." I suggest that her fear is arbitrary and she can ask Christ to identify the part that is anxious and release it from fear. A long silence ensues. I tell her that I need to know she is working, not sleeping. "I am not sleeping." More silence. I ask her if – whatever it is, feels good? "Yeah. Not sexual. The shame is being lifted and cleansed. Funny, I see the edge of a square table suggesting that I am on the edge of something. Everything around the corner is hazy. The tip is bright. I am on the tip of a freedom, a butterfly comes to mind, the idea of flight and change, bluffs and a really blue sky, and Victorian houses perched on a bluff." I have her ask for discernment of what she is seeing. "It signifies liberation from the Victorian attitudes of my childhood. There is a feeling of release and expansiveness." Her free associations continue in much the same way for the remainder of the session.

I do not see Leigh for another three weeks. She reports sleeping well but still taking ¼ milligram of Ambien. She is off all antidepressants, but still taking 2 ½ milligrams of Abilify. She tells me that both her niece and sister have been diagnosed as bi-polar. She does not look forward to work, which is understandable given the whole country is going deeper into recession. I suggest that she go inside, lie on a massage table in her imagination and let Christ do whatever he has been wanting to do for a long time – obviously, a very open ended suggestion that picks up on his saying that he wanted to work with her root chakra for a long time. "He is working with my root chakra drawing out more energy, evil, bad feelings. He is pulling out self-destructive feelings. Now he has stopped." I ask why? "I thought we were out of time." I have her tell him she was mistaken. "Now I see some sort of box, an obstruction. It is where the heart is." I suggest that she let him enter her heart and for her to follow. "He is inside. There is something wooden, like an arch with light coming out." I ask if it is 'good light'? "It has a greenish cast."

I ask if it is sexual? (Sexual energy often has a greenish cast.) "Yeah. It is a core issue. I am still confused about what is good and bad." I ask if she would be willing for Christ to penetrate the box containing the greenish energy with his *Light*, purify the energy and begin the process of altering her false beliefs and attitudes? "Yeah. He has cleared it. The box has become a sleigh in the snow with a feeling a speed and going fast." The session ends here.

I see her the following week. "I am thinking more about sex. I have been sexual on the weekends. I did not want to be here today." I suggest that she consider dividing her Abilify in half. We talk about the coming holiday. I encourage her to make more plans. I do not see her again till after Christmas, just before New Years. She tells me she has cut her Abilify in half and stopped her hormone replacement therapy. (I do not say so, but the latter may be a mistake as she had a complete hysterectomy the year before.) She tells me she is feeling sad, that she needs to get people in her life who will not grow up and go away (a reference to her daughter becoming a teenager). I suggest that she go inside with Christ, enter her heart, and let him take her to a place where she can learn her soul's desire for her. "Christ is comforting me. I have not a clue what my soul wants for me. Years ago I attempted to find out by journaling a la Ira Progoff. I saw my soul as a little slip of a thing surrounded by sharks in the water." I ask her if she worries that she might be at odds with it? "No. Well, maybe. What am I doing with my life?" I suggest a partnership with Christ and her soul. "I don't feel passionate about anything. I can't put my soul into anything. It is not even there. Now Christ is reassuring me that I have a soul, that I have been going through a period of darkness, maybe even estrangement." I ask her if he can help her reconnect? "I need to do some stuff on my own, too. I need to make decisions regarding my church membership. Do I want to be there or not. I am so passive. I let things slide." I ask her what prevents her from being more active? "Too much energy." I ask her if she can identify the source of her energy drain, but we are out of time.

I see Leigh again two weeks later. She tells me that she has stopped taking her Abilify. She is off all medication except ¼ milligram of Ambien to sleep. But, she says, "I have no interest in doing anything at all and I don't want to work." My sense is that her 'energy drain' is due to her relationship with her masculine aspect. (It may also be the result of her stopping her hormone replacement regimen, but I fail to see this.) I suggest she go inside and let Christ extract her contra-sexual aspect. "I see a crumpled up figure lying on its stomach on the ground in a fetal position." I suggest that she lie down beside this male figure and let Christ convict the two of them simultaneously. She lets this happen and then reports that, "The male figure is relaxing. It has turned onto its back and stretches. I feel more relaxed and more uptight." I suggest that she ask Christ to convict again for greater insight as to what it all means. "He went back into his fetal position." I ask if he reminds her of anybody? " I am depressed by all of this. The image is of a younger man in his 30's with a beard. It feels like my ex-husband. I realize that I am causing him to be in the fetal position. I have all of these negative thoughts. I don't want to go on doing this for another ten years. I don't have the energy." I pose a hypothesis to her: if he is energy and she has hardened herself against him how can he energize her? I suggest that she say to him 'I am sorry, please forgive me, I do love you.' [36] Emphatically, she tells me, "No. I don't love that part of me. I am angry that he let me down. He does not give me energy." I ask her if she can appreciate the paradox she is creating for herself? "I do feel like someone who does not want to do their part and grow up. Why am I so resistant?" I suggest that she ask her Light if she is willing to hear the answer to that question? "I am pissed off at all males. That figure represents my father. I have nurtured that anger all of my life. It is so self-defeating." I remind her that this is *her masculine that she is attacking, her source of energy*. "I see myself comforting him. He is sitting up. It feels different." I suggest to her that she let Christ convict her till she becomes one hundred percent responsible for him. "If I let Christ do that then I can no longer be a victim." I tell her that if Christ gives her the authority commensurate with this responsibility, then she will probably have to repent of her past attitude, but his need for her is equal to her need for him so I am guessing he will be quick to forgive her. "I will work on it." I push her to ask; that it only takes an instant of willingness. "OK." The session ends here.

I see Leigh two weeks later. She is feeling 'wired, fried, and panicky. All the masculine wants to do is sleep. She also shares that after attending Alanon for 14 years she is finally going to tell her story. She underplays this but I know it is a major step for her. She also reflects on how she has nursed all her anger-resentment toward men. "I don't like the word repent. It is strong word. To look at my part in all this is depressing. I have not looked inside with Christ present." I suggest that she go inside and let Christ convict her and her contra-sexual aspects for 'embracing balance.' "I could see Christ putting his hand on both our foreheads. I could see energy flowing from the masculine to me and from Christ to me. There is a triangular flow from Christ to the masculine, and Christ to me, and the masculine to me. And I need to give him energy too. I need to concentrate on the energy being lighter and cleaner." I suggest that she allow Christ to effect the necessary change. "What I see is that the center of the triangle is white, yellow, and hot." I suggest that she ask Christ to name what is in the center. "It looks like a campfire, it feels like Christ's power. I want to draw close but there is an element of danger. I could burn myself. Christ is saying, 'Yeah, my power is pretty powerful. There are levels of my power that would be dangerous in your hands.'" I suggest that she ask Christ to insert the power of his discernment in both of them. "The masculine is sitting up by himself. I have been so aware the last two weeks of being manic." This is the other time of year when she has historically experienced manic episodes. The session ends here. I am unexpectedly called away and do not see her again for three weeks. However, I do talk to her on the telephone and actually have her come to my house for some CDs. She is going through a manic episode without medication. She manages to stay focused at work and even to tell her story in Al-Anon for the first time in fourteen years. She also manages to sleep through the nights. I ask her to go inside and re-embed the feminine sense of self within her person and then ask Christ to sustain her energy. "Her first thought is that, "I get to go shopping and I get to leave by 5 pm. Christ will provide the energy and light the fire as needed. I will continue putting the well being of my clients first…and maybe Christ will provide enough points for me to go on a cruise." Basically, she is through the worst of it. We schedule weekly sessions for the next three weeks. What most impresses me about the previous session is Christ's uncharacteristic warning about getting too close to the fire. She seems to have heeded it without benefit of drugs.

When Leigh returns a week later she seems much the same – what I might call a controlled manic state, but reportedly able to sleep and maintain focus. I suggest that we go inside and ask Christ to place the fire, which the three images previously circled, into a dome. I tell her my suspicion that this fire may be responsible for her manic episodes insofar as she finds its 'warmth' very tempting and I think it would be helpful if we can explore it in greater detail. On going inside she immediately associates it with 'pride wanting to play god.' I suggest she use concentric circles to separate from the part of her most strongly drawn to it. "I see a small child, age 3-4, terrified and afraid she will not be taken care of. I tried to mother her but it does not satisfy her." This is clearly a Pre-moral aspect as described in Chapter VI. I suggest that she allow Christ to enter the circle and taking the child by the hand lead her to a mother who can provide her with a 'safe warmth.' "He immediately takes her to a room with a hearth and cozily burning fire and a woman in a rocker. The child is in her lap. I see her being rocked and cuddled instead of being freaked out and freezing. The woman is stroking her back like my mother sometimes did to me as a child. It feels like a good start but the child wants to see her face, which is covered with a shawl. She wants to be able to touch the face and look into her eyes." I immediately begin to suspect that this is an image created by Leigh based on her best memory of her mother. I ask if she can see Christ? "I want him to be there but it is hard to see him." I suggest that she focus on Christ taking the child. "Yes. Now he has the child and is sitting in the rocker with her." I tell Leigh that she is attempting to control the outcome – a typical response by most clients, to the suggestion that Christ find an archetypal mother for the child. I suggest that she must let the child be the judge just as, in this instance, the child continues to feel a sense of lack. In reply, Leigh comments that she has thought a lot about the female aspect of Christ, his Shekinah, and she remembers quite clearly that when this sense of Christ cradled her in recent weeks she could quickly go to sleep. I tell her that if she will give over control of the process to Christ he will find this feminine presence for the child and in the interim he will carry and keep the child warm. We are well over time and I have to hurriedly usher her out. When I have my new client comfortably situated in my office I excuse myself for a bathroom break. I pass by Leigh who has remained in the waiting area savoring the last of her coffee and a cookie in a very relaxed state, and clearly in no rush to let go of whatever she is experiencing inwardly.

Leigh asks for another appointment three days later. I anticipate that she wants to move the process forward but mostly she needs to vent, and feels a little insecure as to what may be pushing her buttons. The stock market is going crazy (which she seems to be handling both assertively and professionally) and her assistant is both somatic and even more OCD than Leigh, and all but telling Leigh that she is looking elsewhere for work. I suggest to Leigh that she tell her assistant, 'that if she is looking elsewhere for work, Leigh will be glad to give her a good recommendation, but if she chooses to stay, her attitude toward Leigh must change starting now.' Leigh is aware that she must move the process forward and let Christ find an archetypal mother for the infant. She also tells me that she has been assiduously avoiding the dome where the white core of energy is contained. I reiterate that the infant will know the 'satisfying mother' when Christ is allowed to bring them together. That there is a point on the cheek that correlates with the heart chakra of the physical auric body, which is an infant's primary experience of the world.[37] That is why the infant became agitated when she could not touch it. The session ends here.

Leigh returns the following week. We discuss the infant. I tell her my sense of it: the infant got enough attachment from her mother to keep her alive but not enough for a firm foundation. Now she needs a mother who can nurture her 'taste' of attachment into a totally satisfying meal. Leigh goes inside and is quiet for a long time. I finally ask what is happening. "I've been trying to quiet myself, submit to Christ and find the willingness to be willing. I sensed the infant and a quick flash of a child being totally happy, sitting on a knee totally relaxed, which it will not do unless it is totally satisfied. Prior to that I had images of how exhausted and strung out we are. I need this through her. I can see an infant who could sit up with a happy gurgle." I ask if any part of her is averse to allowing such a feminine sense of nurture into her life. "No. I like an occasional frill." That phrasing catches my attention so I ask 'how much is too much'? And then go on to ask if she would be willing to give up this power of judging 'how much is too much' forever - in this matter of the infant and her need for nurture, in exchange for the power of Christ's discernment in judging such matters? Leigh grows very quiet in response to my questions. Finally, at my prompting, she tells me that, "This judging is pretty strong in me. I am all about being a strong female, and you are talking about a weak yielding side." I reply, that her power will always limit the infant from being totally satisfied. At this point, Leigh's 'inner clock' is convinced that the session is over and we need to stop. I assure her otherwise and send her back inside. "I am working on being willing. I got this flash of 'Thank God, now I can get to sleep through the night followed by a moment of elation. But I cannot tell you there has been physical contact between Christ and me. I saw myself kneeling in front him." I tell her that Christ has been giving her vicarious experiences of what she can expect, but she still needs to willingly accept his intervention in the first person. I give her an analogy. I ask her to imagine she is in a church where congregants can go up for an alter call. She observes a person beside her doing it and how profoundly it effects her, but she will only experience it herself when she accepts the call to go to the altar. The session ends here.

My verbatim for this next session is quite long. Even so, it is difficult to convey what finally happens. When Leigh returns she tells me more about the strong woman in her: "She was strong enough to walk away from a very successful career and follow her husband here to Knoxville; she was strong enough to give 'lip service' to nurture by adopting a child; and she has been strong enough to accept the burden of a Bi-polar diagnosis and its medication handicap…I almost went to the altar this past week. Christ came to me from two sides. I felt total healing around me – like a cloud. But as soon as I try to control the process it dissipates. Then my mind goes to the business of earning money." My comment on all she is telling me is that she does not seem to have the strength to let a helpless child be totally nurtured. Then I suggest that she go inside and let Christ personify her sense of strength. Without going inside she immediately describes it as a gremlin that is blatantly addictive. Then she begins to reflect on how, for years, when she went inside on her own she would go to a column of light, her inner core, for strength and centering. " I learned it from Ira Progoff.[38] I saw it as the Christ in me. But now the light is not a light. It is a fire and it is not in me at all. I cannot go there. I have also developed a splitting headache since coming here from the acupuncturist's office." I think I have been fighting the flow of energy she was attempting to stimulate in me. Our dialogue goes on in a similar vein for another twenty minutes. Finally, she is ready to go inside. I ask her to have Christ draw a circle of escape. Then I suggest that she ask Christ to convict her with the power of the Holy Spirit for the purpose of removing all obstacles preventing Christ from bringing the infant to the mother who can satisfy and heal her. Anyone objecting can escape to the circle beside her. I even have her repeat out loud what I have suggested.

A long silence ensues. Finally, I prompt her to share what has been happening inside. "I got to a place that I did not want to leave. I kept asking the Holy Spirit to wash through me. My headache is gone. I just felt healing from Christ on different levels of my being, my feminine side, different forgotten hurts melted away. It all happened so fast. I am understanding that all of those hurts do not matter. There is a sense of closure. I am asking for help." Clearly, something has happened, but I will have to wait till the next session to evaluate exactly what has occurred.

I see Leigh three weeks later. It is clear that she has yet to relinquish her judgments of 'how much is too much nurture.' She attempts to do so again. She reports feeling that this time Christ has penetrated her brain, but I am feeling more and more that there is a significant resistance that is unaccounted for. All we can determine in this session is that she is afraid of finding her way, and fearful of running after it blindly; a true double bind.

In the next session she is preoccupied with an MRI report that says she has a 'mass' in her brain, which her doctor tells her could have been there from birth. She is also preoccupied with pains in her toes, which she is attributing to meridian dysfunctions. I suggest she go inside and ask Christ to draw out any emotion associated with the 'brain mass.' "My fear of males and females comes together in it. I am really afraid of this brain thing." I encourage her to let Christ intervene. "His hand came into my brain over and under the mass. He is combing it, which is having a rippling effect. It feels enormously healing." She commits to letting Christ repeat this two or three times a day for as long as she is concerned. We do nothing about the child in need of maternal nurture.

I see Leigh again a few days later. She is calm enough to at least make another attempt at letting Christ find a nurturing mother for the child. She has accepted that she cannot do this and that it has to be done blindly. But nothing seems to happen. I see her again two days later. She is again distracted by fearful diagnoses from doctors. I listen sympathetically, but I'm increasingly convinced that she is doing all of this to herself to avoid some trauma related to the child connecting with an archetypal mother. She has allowed Christ to hand the child to a woman who is unknown to Leigh. She senses the child is in much pain; but again she is distracted by the pain in her toes. I suggest that she say to Control: you focus on the toes and I will focus on Mary and the child. Control is directed to hold points that may be related to whatever meridians are creating the pain. I have her move back and forth between checking in on what is happening with Mary and the child and whatever Control is doing for the pain in her toes. "You are right. I can move back and forth. The baby looks little, no more than nine months. She is not quite asleep. She is getting healing energy from Christ and comforted. Control seems to be setting criteria but the child is comforted. She is quiet even when traffic runs by her." The session ends here.

In the next session two weeks later Leigh reports that she has seen her gynecologist and has gone back on her hormonal meds on his recommendation; and she feels better. I suggest that she go inside and ask Christ to 'personify' her resistance to letting Mary nurture the child. "It is no big surprise. I am fearful of being vulnerable, a terror of exposure. I ask if Christ can *help her to safely touch the exposure and vulnerability*? (For some time I have strongly suspected some kind of shock trauma.) "It is raw, red, and painful. It does not want to be touched and I don't want to touch it. There is a sexual aspect; it may be vaginal. I can ask Christ to heal it. It is a burning redness. It feels like an internal view of an organ, an exposed heart; a part of me is repulsed by it; it is dangerous to get too close to it. It will hurt the organ and me." I have her ask Christ: if she gives up the repulsion can he heal it? "Of course, I know that my shaming is a big part of it. He says that I can do the judging or he can. If he does it, then the outcome will not be negative. It was not my fault." Again, there is a seeming struggle between retaining control vs. giving it over to Christ. "For a moment, instead of red, I saw a naked, healthy infant sitting up, healthy and happy." Again, Christ is showing her a positive outcome, but it is still not clear to me that she has relinquished control. The session ends here.

Leigh returns the following week seeming very relaxed. She reports having spent a good weekend with her brother who visited. She is exercising and continues to be sexual. Still using Benadryl to sleep at night and, occasionally, when she cannot sleep, she finds that soaking her feet in hot water helps. The 'sexual' is something she treats like an exercise, which she does even when she does not feel like it. It offers release. Apparently, Christ is her partner in this and she finds his presence healing. Over the past several days she has checked on the infant who seems to be in a good way. It is not with a mother, but the mother's presence is sensed as watchful and nearby. The infant is about nine months old. When she checks inside her sense is that the red rawness is not completely healed. I reiterate that she needs to relinquish her power to be repulsed by it in order for Christ to heal the red rawness completely. When she goes inside, she becomes aware that the repulsion permeates her body; one image in particular grabs her: her feet seem reptilian. She also remembers herself saying for years that 'she should have fought that off; and she can remember her father saying, 'In case I figured it out, it was my fault, not his.' I tell her that the 'who' is unimportant at this point. It could have been her father or mother, or any of her siblings, all of whom were at least ten years older than her. The important thing is that *her repulsion* is preventing Christ from healing the red rawness completely. Leigh goes inside and begins reporting: "I have a sense of Christ's hands pulling a rope of green slime out of a well. I am saying 'take it all.' Now Christ is pulling more with both of his hands. I am impatient for him to take it all but he is telling me to be patient. He says this is a big change and I have been heavily invested in not changing it. He is getting more and more with each pull. I feel I need to write this down so he can continue over the next week." She returns to me and immediately starts writing down what he is doing and what she is asking. I have her add that, if she hears any other voices being critical of her during the week, she can immediately ask Christ to terminate them. She writes down the idea that Control has been functioning as her own conscience in order to preempt such voices. The session ends here.

Leigh returns a week later and tells me she feels "anxious and depressed;" but frankly she seems much calmer and more alert than I have ever seen her. She tells me that when she imagines people who make her anxious, she is asking Christ to place a portion of his *Light* into their hearts. "It works. I can sleep better when I let Christ 'cool' the voices." I suggest that the infant is still in need of connection with a mother of her choosing. Leigh agrees to go inside. Immediately, she reports being frightened and unable to see the child. After Christ provides her with a garment of protection, she describes her feeling as one of "being cornered, trapped, vulnerable." I suggest to her that she let Christ help her to safely touch this early trauma so he can discharge it. "I see a closet. My siblings told me that when I was little they put me in a closet. I have this feeling of being in a closet and terrified." I ask if Christ can enter the closet, rescue her from that fear, bring her a portion of

Light and protection? "I see several closets from my childhood." Again, I reiterate my suggestion that she let Christ go to each child, give them a garment of protection from fear. I note that the 'who' is unimportant; that what is crucial here is her willingness to let Christ discharge the negative emotions attached to these memories. Leigh responds with a sigh of release and a long silence. Finally, she shares with me that "I saw a younger version of me with Christ, age 4-6. I felt Christ comforting me, reassuring me it was not my fault; that I don't need to carry the shame over what happened. I felt anger and the unfairness of it. I am not seeing the youngest one." I ask Leigh if she can share what she remembers: what is 'not fair'? "It was my brother and father molesting me. She is mad about it; for being shamed about it." At this point I take a different tack. I have the sense that this ego-aspect has been sexualized; that the father created a lot of sexual tension between the two of them. I suggest that she ask Christ to separate out the sexual energy that may be connecting them. Leigh responds with the insight: "That is how he bonded with me!" I reiterate my suggestion that she ask Christ to separate out the sexual energy connecting them and let him purify it so that, thereafter, it will no longer serve as a connection between them. Only she will have access to the energy as she chooses. After she does this I ask how she feels? "Revulsion and pity. She sees him as a sick old man." I ask if she can feel connected to the energy apart from him? "Yes. It feels healthy." I ask if she would like Christ to become the gatekeeper of masculine access to this energy insuring that no male can forcibly access it? "When I answered 'yes,' a division of light grew up between me and my father. His image was 'drowned' in light. Now he has disappeared behind a fenced area." The session ends here.

Leigh returns a week later reporting that she is feeling 'tense.' "Mostly, I have just been going to Christ. I saw the infant crying out reaching up to be comforted. No mother is responding to her. I am sleeping a lot more." I tell her my sense is that she is still holding on to her power to repulse herself and this control is blocking the child's ability to connect with the mother. Leigh agrees to this interpretation and is willing to give 'the turning over' a good faith shot. But once inside she again becomes resistant. I suggest that she literally take Christ's fingers and push them into her brow. "When I picture doing that some part of me becomes really afraid, nauseous, and frightened." I suggest that she ask Christ to show her how to safely touch that fear; then I add: can Christ bring peace to that part of you? "He wants too. I see him combing through the black fear in the closet, but now I feel this thing in my stomach." I suggest that she let him provide her a garment of protection so he can safely dispel the fear in her stomach. I remind her that fear has no power to heal the infant or her stomach, only to avoid what ails them. More silence. Finally, after several more comments of encouragement, I ask her 'what is the sticking point?' and then tell her she just needs to 'grit her teeth and do it,' and she does. "There is a big hole in the center of my brain. Now I see it bathed in light and love. I say to myself, 'test it.' I look over at the infant. A youthful mother is picking her up. She is young in features, but wise. She is putting the infant's head close to her chest. This gesture is calming the child. I cannot see her clearly; she has a covering over her head. The infant is really relaxing. She takes her head covering and puts it over the infant. It is very soothing. Now it seems as if the infant has grown from four months to one and a half years. I feel calm and tired from all the internal struggling. I continue to sense a young baby and loving presence. I can see the child crawling around. There is sense of safety. The 'sticking point' was my lack of trust. The child is definitely trusting the mother." The session ends here.

Leigh returns two weeks later still struggling with a sense of self-hatred. Going inside, she visualizes the child crawling toward the archetypal mother and into her lap. Leigh seems to experience this – at first, with sighs of comfort and silence, but then focuses on her own feeling of being wired and tired. "I go to Christ and feel him comforting me. My brain is irritated at me and others; that is where the self-hatred lives. The irritated brain feels like a kind of sponge." Leigh allows Christ to dissolve some of the accumulation in the ocean, but is unwilling to address the issue of judging herself hatefully. The session ends here.

Leigh returns two weeks later again complaining of insomnia. "Someone inside is having another temper tantrum. I'm so angry and tired. She cannot get off the floor." I suggest to Leigh that she let Christ calm her and give her some energy so she can stand up and speak coherently. "I've reached the end of myself. I'm so sad." Even so, I note, this part of her remains very powerful. I again make suggestions about sleep including taking a short nap after work that would allow her to stay up till 11 p.m. As we discuss the pros and cons, I suddenly realize that her father also suffered from driving himself to *exhaustion and probably insomnia as well*. He often came home very late from work and might then be up at 2 a.m. It seems quite possible that her father is providing the masculine energy for the self-hating self in Leigh, and I tell her as much. I suggest a series of interventions. First she put the overworking, insomniac, father in a dome and then ask Christ to enter the dome and put her father into a deep sleep. Then I suggest that she access the part of her that is so tired and have Christ bring her into the dome with her father and let Christ show her that he can put the father into a deep sleep the moment he is asked. Then I have Christ, Leigh's Aware-ego, and the temper tantrum girl step back outside. Christ then wakes the father up. The three are instructed to go back inside wherein the Temper tantrum girl asks Christ to put him back to sleep. The Temper tantrum girl observes Christ successfully enacting her request. I then go on to explain that she is to ask this of Christ each time she goes to sleep and specify the period of time he will be kept asleep, i.e. eight hours. I explain to Leigh that it is her masculine energy flowing through her father that is keeping everyone awake at night, but Christ can control the flow of that energy through her father. If this intervention is effective, then I will have Leigh work with the insomniac father in the next session as well.

I see Leigh a week later. She reports sleeping better. When she wakes up, she says the Jesus prayer and goes back to sleep. "I have checked in on the child when I wake up at night. She is a little restless, but there is a feminine presence with her. That image is still not clear to me beyond a sense of presence. This weekend it felt as if I had crossed over into the depressed side of my disorder. I hardly got out of bed." I ask if she did her homework. She does not remember. Though she wrote it down, she did not read what she wrote. When I remind her that she was going to put her father in a dome every night, she replies that, "Actually, I did do that. I did it Thursday and Friday. I did ask Christ to put my father to sleep in the dome and to convict me." I suggest that she go inside and check on the Driver (aka Teen) who seems to be so identified with her father. At first she is unable to find her *Light*. I suggest that she sense it with her eyes open and have it draw a circle of protection that she will enter on going back inside. This seems to work. Next, I have her invite Christ into the circle and *connect her to his masculine energy by having him place a portion of her Light into her heart and his.* I explain that her depression may be the result of not receiving masculine energy from her 'sleeping father.' She reports that the experience of Christ's energy "Feels good." When she then locates the Driver she describes the image as "Old and shriveled and lying on its back; an old way that does not work anymore; all used up. She just wants to lie down and go to sleep." It is not clear to me if she is speaking about the Driver or the part of her merged with the Aware-ego. I decide to treat them as equally co-present. I ask if her father is awake or asleep? "He is awake and haranguing like Fidel Castro. Some part of me is saying 'why don't you just die'." At this point I decide to take a different tack. I presume that these images are being defined by her father's feminine; and that is what I tell Leigh. I suggest that she let Christ redefine her father's feminine in a way that is more attune to how Christ would see it. She reports that her father's immediate response is to pull back saying, "Oh, that is a sensitive, private area." Even so, she allows Christ to convict her father's feminine aspect and then reports what she observes: "I feel a nurturing kind of energy, loving and creative, regenerative and human, not at all like him, youthful." I ask if she can see the effect on Driver? "Yeah. It is mirrored in her...restorative, hopeful, and enthusiastic. I am asking 'why was he the way I knew him.' I am still nurturing that anger." I ask if her anger is pointing to something that his old behavior withheld from her (the part of her merged with the Aware-ego)? "Yes. He did not give her positive direction." I ask if she is willing to be connected to his healed feminine definition? Quite astutely, Leigh asks about his masculine side. I tell her that Christ will sustain what he has redefined in her father. Leigh now shares an insight. "Until I am comfortable with the feminine in my dad, I will not have a clear image of the mother comforting the child. It is interesting that the one seems dependent upon the other. But I'm more comfortable with Christ's energy; I distrust my father's definition. But Christ is reminding me that it was my *Light* that he took to connect us. He is encouraging me to stay with what you are suggesting. Christ is saying that I am so tired and this is the only way to change that. 'You are at the end of your rope and this is the way back.' Christ keeps nudging me toward my dad. I am seeing a precipice. Dad is on the other side. Christ has made a bridge of light." I suggest that Christ can help her *to touch him safely*. I also encourage her to provide herself with a garment of protection against any fear of her father. "I don't see an image of him, but I sense that he is pleading with me to touch him as if his salvation is on the line. But what part of him would I want to touch? There is fear on my part. I try to touch his cheek, but if I actually do he will become a monster." I suggest that she let Christ touch him first on the cheek and if he becomes a monster then Christ can absorb that definition. "When Christ does that my father seems to mellow. His desperation was greedily wanting me; but now he seems instantly accepting of the next step. His eyes get intense when I get close. Christ puts his hand on his head to calm him down; and he puts his fingers on my brow. Christ goes into my brain and pulls out the fear. Then he puts his hand on my shoulder and I put my fingers on my dad's cheek. It seems safe while Christ has his hand on both of us to absorb any toxicity. My dad gives me a one armed hug so I don't get a trapped feeling. Christ conveys that his intensity is sufficient. My dad puts his hand on my cheek and looks into my eyes. Instead of the desperate greedy self he is now conveying a sense of steadiness. There is gratitude and self-assurance and a desire to comfort me that I never saw before. For myself, there is a sense of curiosity about what I am seeing in his eyes, and a gratitude." I ask Leigh to cross back over the bridge of *Light* with Christ before returning to me. I also encourage her to cross back several times in the coming week and allow this reconciliation to evolve. The session ends here. The interventions in this session are a blend of working with shock trauma and her father's feminine aspect in order to alter his masculine energy. Basically, Leigh is asked to approach a man she has spent her whole life fearfully avoiding. It is significant that both she and Christ focus primarily on her fear of her father. This session also highlights my thesis that the attenuation of a strong masculine/feminine connection is likely to lead to depression. Leigh experiences her father's masculine energy as a greedy, intense, desperation. Imagine that kind of energy having to sustain your feminine sense of self. It is no wonder that she sees her Driver as old, shriveled, and used up; but even so it is the only masculine energy she has had access to. Hopefully, all this will change for the better in the coming weeks.

***

Over the next six months Leigh will continue to discover, explore and ask Christ to redeem numerous selves. Her psychiatrist will retire and her new psychiatrist, also a woman, will change her meds to a very low dose of Risperidone. Her assistant decides to stop working with Leigh and is quickly replaced by a competent, pleasant woman. Leigh continues taking dancing lessons, and walking or bicycling most days. She takes another vacation with her daughter which is much more pleasant. But she is still having problems sleeping. She has a cycling accident, which stains her back. Gradually, the back pain becomes more persistent and the inflammation produces sciatica. The doctor gives her prednisone. The combination of stimulant, back pain, and lack of sleep precipitate a psychotic break requiring her hospitalization.

This is her first psychiatric hospitalization; and I suspect it is an unconscious push for short-term disability. Her psychiatrist temporarily ups her Risperidone and releases her within a week. She is placed on short-term disability. The psychiatrist treats the cause of the hospitalization as a drug reaction to the prednisone, but it is very clear to me at this point that the Driver (Teen), who remains in charge of Leigh's behavior, has pushed her to the point of exhaustion by keeping her sleepless at night and driven during the day. Over the next two months Leigh continues to struggle with unremitting back pain; and I struggle to understand and resolve the Driver's issues. In the process of helping her to find relief from the back pain, I begin focusing on helping her to find an Ideal pair for the Aware-ego's Heart. She identifies a pair of youths who she calls the wise youths, who were extracted from the Driver. The verbatims resume as I attempt to work more directly with the Driver's heart chakra.

Intuitively, I have sensed a disconnection between the Driver and the physical body, but cannot name it as such. Instead, I attempt to address it by encouraging Leigh to bring her 'medical body' (her current physical sense of self) into the Aware-ego's Heart where Christ can work with it. That is where this session begins. Leigh immediately feels a sense of congestion that will not allow her to bend her back or legs. "I have to stretch out the heart really long. I can't bend. The right side feels unyielding and congested. Christ wants to loosen it up. He wants to take me to the water and run his whole hand though that part of me. More than cleansing it, he wants to free it up. It is a tight pain. His hands relax it. He is telling me that he can really help when I trust him. I see myself in my heart bending now so I can move throughout my body. (When the Wise youths were inserted into the Aware-ego's Heart Leigh had experienced an immediate sense of fluidity throughout her body.) The youths are this free flowing energy that goes to all of the chakras. Christ encourages her to leave the 'body' in the heart. The session ends here.

In the next session, Leigh immediately goes back into the Heart. "I immediately lie down beside the water and Christ rubs his hand over the leg with the sciatic pain. There is a piece of wood stuck in my leg. It is my stubbornness; a small child that wants to be in control again who is fearful the pain will never go away. She wants to be in charge of the pain. She wants to control it. She says I have given all of the other control to Christ. The pain is all she has to hold onto." I ask if she can identify the opposite of control? "Giving up the pain would mean she is nothing. I want to be somebody. I don't want to be a no-body. I want to be in charge of something. She is six years old." I suggest that she be given responsibility and authority for *her body*. She likes that. She says that her body is *not feeling any body*. (This is significant, but I miss it. The six-year-old is saying she wants a body that does not feel the body, i.e. depersonalization.) The six-year-old wants to remain in the Heart, literally asleep in Christ's lap. While she remains in the Heart, this self will not feel the body's pain. This self appears to be the analogue of the Driver who actually does achieve a pain free existence by depersonalization. But I am far from appreciating in this session. Instead, I continue to quixotically to seek healthy pain-free solutions for Leigh.

Leigh returns the following week complaining that the pain has not stopped. She is pain free while she is in the Heart letting Christ work with her 'body,' but outside she continues to feel the pain. I am aware that she must begin working with a heart chakra, but still not clear whose heart chakra. I suggest that she allow Christ to enter the heart chakra of whoever stops Christ from healing the body when she is not in the Heart. She willingly goes inside and stands in front of Christ for that purpose and he pushes into her heart chakra. "I see him in a big cavern brightly lit. It is empty. There is fear and aloneness. The fear is that the pain will go on forever. It hurts in this heart space. It holds all of my fear and aloneness and it has no end." I suggest that she allow Christ to collect it all in circle and temporarily insulate her from it in such a way that she can also see it. "It becomes dark like a chunk of coal. I feel like I can breath easier; I am not so frightened. I want to touch it, but not. I have some connection with it. Christ does not want me to touch it. With his other hand he is drawing out the pain, the pain of that connection. The pain and fear feed on each other. The pain brings my fear to the surface. It is a long comfortable pattern. I am used it." How can he intervene? "He is doing that now by lessening the pain. But it is ultimately up to me. I must continue turning to him for a solution instead of always turning to fear and loneliness."

The following week she complains that the pain is getting worse. "Not a lot of success with going inside. When I did get in I would see turbulent waters that scared me." She has no recall of what we did last week. She has been attempting to reenter the Aware-ego's Heart and I have a sense that she cannot do so until she has purified the heart chakra she entered last week. I suggest she go inside and let Christ take her into her heart chakra. "I see us in a brightly lit cavern. He is running his fingers through my brain." There is a long silence here and a sense of concentration. I ask her what is happening. "I am feeling this sense of gloom. It is a longstanding bad habit. When I feel it, I don't want to take care of myself, I can't be bothered." I ask if she can remember how old she was when it started? "About age five. I was playing in the dirt and felt really sad; feels like there is one to make a difference. Christ is hugging her." I ask if he can take her to someone who can lift her spirits, turn this around? "He gets her out of the dirt and takes her to Mary. She sits her down and gives her some milk and cookies." For some reason I am prompted to ask if she has been squatting all of this time? "I can feel it in my hip as we speak. I know in the past weeks that Christ has wanted to repeatedly work with my thighs. The child is sitting in Mary's lap. She immediately bonded with her. She has a real deep need for that. I did not realize how deep and ongoing that need was. I have had a rash under my arms and down my chest for the past week. I feel it is clearing up now that she is with Mary. I really like the feeling of that child with Mary. I had no idea she needed that much attention. Christ says I still have a long way to go." The session ends here. I will not appreciate this till some weeks later, but what seems to be hidden in this heart chakra are sensate connections of the physical pains that Leigh is feeling in her body. Eventually, she – herself – will identify it as tissue memory. Whatever self is dominant outside of the sessions has little or no access to these sensate correlates to emotion or, for that matter, the emotions that would connect her to the sensate tissue memories. All of the significant emotions and sensations appear to have been repressed into the heart chakra.

When Leigh returns the following week she tells me that she will be getting a shot in the lower spine later in week that should greatly lesson the pain. She also shares that the rash has not abated, but has not spread. "My leg hurts like crazy." I suggest that she allow Christ to capture whatever self is looking to the shot on Friday as her only source of relief. "I get elements of her. She is the lazy one. She does not want to fight the pain, but hopes the shot will make it better. She has given into the pain. It is all there is in her world view." I ask if Christ can sever her connection with the body. "No she is too integrated with the pain and it is in charge." I am prompted to ask if the pain is *masculine*? "Yes. It is all around her." I suggest that she ask Christ to collect it into a circle and give it a masculine form. "All I see is a rocky, hard form. This masculine is in charge and all it does is inflict pain." Again, I ask, is it her masculine? "Yes." I suggest that Christ bring the circle containing the form close to her; and convict both with the power of the Holy Spirit. "My mind goes to the fear that I will have to live with this pain forever. It is what my old age will be consumed by." I challenge her by saying that it seems she is unwilling for them to be convicted. "I am afraid that messing with it in any way will make it worse." You trust your fear over Christ? "He touched the masculine but not the feminine. The masculine is taking a more human form and chatting with Christ." But, I note, he will still be the source of pain in her eyes till she is also willing to receive the conviction. "It relaxes me to see him as different. I don't feel as threatened. She seems to be relaxing a little bit. Christ has convicted both of them. She is now sitting comfortably in a chair with Christ and the masculine. Christ convicts them again and now they are dancing. Incredibly, my leg does not hurt." The session ends here. She leaves pain-free but it will be short lived.

I see Leigh two days later, the day before she is scheduled to get her shot. I strongly suspect that the 'masculine pain' is related to her father. I suggest that she allow Christ to convict her parents until they are sufficiently purified to abide in her heart chakra. Leigh replies that, "It is a tall order. I still resent them." I suggest that her attitude places grave limits on her. As her father's daughter, she is condemned to their existence unless she can allow Christ to alter their images. "The willingness is there for my mother to change, but not my father. Christ convicts her.

Electricity goes through her and she now seems relaxed and beautiful. I am praying for the willingness to let Christ convict my father as well, but aware of how invested I am in my unwillingness. OK. I see him convicting my father too. I see a gradual softening of his features. *It feels like he is convicting me too*; and saying that I have no right to judge him. It wears me out for him to keep doing that. Now I am seated with him and more relaxed. Christ is still standing. He says, 'I have been waiting to do this for a long time.' Then he told me that I am stubborn, historically speaking." I ask if she is willing to let Christ bring them into her heart chakra? "I don't feel that yet. Dad is quite ready. My mom is passive. She says, 'when I [Leigh] am ready'." The session ends here. Unbeknownst to me, we are working with a teenage self that is the Mirror aspect of her father. This is why she feels the father's conviction so strongly and why for reasons of 'other tissue memories' she remains unwilling to absorb them into her heart chakra.

I see Leigh two days before Thanksgiving. She is still feeling leg pain despite her shot on Friday. By Sunday she was 'manic,' which she correlates with reading three books that day. She is aware of making lists. I suggest that she let Christ capture whoever is in charge today? "First, I see her as a five-year-old, not in control, not knowing how to make the holiday happy. Now I see her as an adolescent, during a powerless and difficult time. She is trapped, trapped." I ask Leigh to let Christ identify the masculine counterpart of this adolescent. He is a bully. He is younger version of my father, an SOB. He picks on anyone smaller than him." I suggest that she let Christ 'alter' him. "When you said altered I was really willing. She is now moving around happy. The bullying characteristics have been lifted. Now he is a nice young man. The two of them want to join up in the same circle. Christ thinks it is safe for them to do that. I see them walking together like beauty and the beast; the male is now blond, slim, well manner and not driven." Note, these changes are not inculcated into the heart. They address the same theme as the previous session and once again point to the father as pivotal. Moreover, I am increasingly aware of their symbolic, almost fanciful, wish fulfilling quality.

I see Leigh a week later. It is after Thanksgiving, which she claims is the best she has had in the last 20 years. She spent it with her ex-husband, adopted daughter, and the daughter's birth father who always comes to visit this time of year. "I have always had trouble relating to men, but I have realized my 'ex' has become my best friend. We worked like an incredibly functional family this year." She has been relatively pain free since our last session, but that will be short-lived. Our conversation turns to her efforts to keep her teenage daughter on the straight and narrow. I wonder aloud if she is hiding some part of herself in the image of her adopted daughter, but then immediately shift to a focus on the part of her that seeks to constantly 'control' her daughter's behavior. I encourage Leigh to let Christ contain Control and enter her heart. "I am sobbing inside because I am so afraid. The interior of her heart is dirty, yukky and dark." I suggest that she allow Christ to place a portion of his *Light* in the center of the heart that will function as a perpetual channel of the Holy Spirit. "Christ and I swim into the heart chakra. He is comforting me. I am scared of not being in charge. I see the image of a drop of light in a pool of water." Basically, that is all that happens in this session. I tell her that the 'drop of light' will allow the Holy Spirit to begin interacting with Control's dynamics from within the heart chakra.

In the next session the following day Leigh shares that her back seems much better. She has an image of Control in a cage wanting to burst out, "Like a lion's claw reaching at me." I have her ask Christ if she is talking about the interior or Control's heart? And wonder aloud if the Holy Spirit is willing to dissolve the cage? I suggest that wherever the cage is, she can ask Christ to contain it in a circle of *Light*. "I am scared, I want to cry and run out of here. The fear is in my stomach, but it is in my heart chakra. The world is not a safe place. I suggest that she allow Christ to absorb the pent up emotion of whoever is in the cage. "Christ is comforting me. We are arguing. It is abandonment. This part embodies abandonment." In other words, you fear it and this part embodies it? "It is so powerful; it feels like it must be male. But it is tired and old, hoary, sinking to its knees, asking for relief. It wants the feeling of being cared for. Christ puts a kitten in its cage. It was wounded when it was little. He tells me I need not be afraid of it." Again, while the work seems positive, it still has a symbolic, fanciful, air about it. The session ends here.

The following week Leigh reports that her daughter precipitated a significant crisis over the weekend. "Christ got me through it; and he has started raising the six-year-old. This morning when I asked him to do that, I saw myself taller, fully grown, about 20 years old. I also sense I can deal with this coming week (meeting with psychiatrist concerning her disability and return to work, and taking a professional test). I suggest that she go inside and see what the masculine is about. "I see Christ and me sitting by a comfortable campfire," which Leigh identifies as her masculine. "Christ says it will burn me if I get too close to it, unless he acts as a buffer. It could not be my consort." Essentially, Christ continues to affirm her and caution her. The session ends here.

When Leigh returns two weeks later she reports on inner work. "Christ raised me to adulthood. I asked him to check on the six and four year olds' as they were anxious. I asked him to hold and calm them, which he did. When we checked in on Control/Abandoned it felt like a raging sand storm. I asked for Christ to put us under a dome for protection and for him to deal with the dust storm. Eventually, he rose above it and sent a great wave, which washed it clean. A peaceful landscape then appeared. I don't know if I feel raised up to adulthood or not, or that I am doing what I am supposed to do. Even when the ice was thin and I fell into the water I did get right back out." I suggest to Leigh that she enter her heart chakra with Christ and just tell me what she sees? I see Christ in me, the four and Six-year-olds. We are all huddled around the campfire getting warm. I am fearful. I feel that I am between fourteen and twenty years of age; that I am physically grown." I ask if she is afraid of her sense of the masculine? "I don't understand what has happened. I don't remember. The fire starts to get out of control. Christ puts it back." I ask her what made her anxious at fourteen? "My dad coming home always made me anxious. And I worried whether I would ever have friends." What about sex I ask? "Fourteen is when my father climbed into bed with me. At the campfire I am telling Christ I do not want to talk about this. My experiences were not a good way to start a life of intimacy with a man. I start shouting it at Christ. I am pounding his shoulder. I just want to mad." I suggest that her anger indicates to me that she is threatened with shame and suggest she ask Christ for a garment to shield her from the fear of shame. When she says she feels a little calmer I ask her what could shame her at this age? "My father would say 'shame on you.' He thought I was a little slut." I suggest that she needs to allow her sexuality to manifest in her heart and then allow Christ to remove all vestiges of her father's *slander* of it. "My sister called it mind rape. My father had more power than a stranger doing it. Now I am standing before Christ. He is drawing his *Light* through me, and cleaning it out. My image gets bigger and bigger." I suggest that she 'rejoin' with this image so she can experience this in the first person. "Yes. I've done that. Now, Christ is comforting and reassuring me. Yes, he says, it happened you told him [therapist], but it was not the real me. It is time to set it all down; too much for me to carry. It has shaped my relationship with myself for too many years. All he needs for this to be done with is my willingness." I suggest that she ask him to draw a circle that will express her willingness. When she becomes willing she is to step into it and stand before him in its center. "I see it happen. I leave a lot of dark, heavy, something or another, a lot of baggage. I leave it in the circle where I was standing and step over into Christ's circle of willingness. He holds me." I suggest that she ask him to dissolve it and safely remove it from the body. "He just dissolved it. That was an important step." The session ends here.

    I failed to mention this in the forgoing verbatim: in the previous session Leigh identifies the fourteen year old as an ice skater. In this session she first tells me that, "I have an attitude that is not going to get better." But she does not provide any context for the statement. In turn, I ask her if she can identify her masculine? Leigh replies, "I just see the fire. The skater is afraid of it." I have been thinking about Leigh's lack of a masculine image, which is what prompted me to ask in response to her negativity. Now, I tell Leigh that she needs a masculine that can *corporally* relate to the skater. She immediately tells me that whoever holds the negative attitude has "gone to Christ as a whimpering Six-year-old." When I suggest that she ask Christ to raise her up to adulthood, she replies, "I asked him, but now I see myself as a sad adult." This exchange reminds me of the Six-year-old who has remained in the heart chakra detached from any sense of the body. My suggestion that Leigh needs to find a *corporal* male has sent her into a tizzy of confusion and despair. I suggest that everyone enter the heart chakra. Christ takes them into a black cave. There is no fire there. The campfire has only been envisioned from outside the heart chakra. Christ provides everyone a light when I suggest it. I ask if the Skater banished the fire? "Of course, I would rather just be with Christ." I sense this is the Six-year-old talking and challenge her to tell the Skater that this fear of the fire is responsible for her sadness and anxiety. Leigh tells me, "Do you think I care? Let me tell you about that fear. She is sobbing; she is feeling it is hopeless. Some of you have made peace with the masculine, but they need a connection they do not control. Yes, the skater is manic. Her fire is out. Now Christ catches the Six-year-old and holds her." I suggest that she can ask Christ to convict her till there emerges a masculine she can connect with. "She asks, but now she is impatient and insisting that it happen right now. Christ is telling her that she has to be patient; that it will only happen in his time not hers. She wants it to happen now. He says that 'want' is not powerful enough; she needs to give him an instant of willingness. Apparently, the Six-year-old becomes willing as the *Skater*. This allows the skater to envision standing in front of Christ and receiving conviction, which lifts a lot of hatred and anger. The skater sees the six and four year olds' warm around the fire. She feels another hand take her hand and it is warm, but there is no visual presence, only the sensation that she is no longer alone. She then reports a feeling of feeling hands on her hips and being kissed lightly, and hands run through her hair. "While I do not see him I can put my hand on his face even though I can't see him. He wants me to be at ease." The session ends here.

    I need to make some sense of the above session, if only in retrospect. It will soon become apparent that the manic, driven, teenage part of Leigh (most recently manifest as the Ice Skater) is a disembodied self identified as the Six-year-old (aka Driver, Teen, Ice Skater, etc.). The depersonalization represents a continuing effort to repress both a strong, mirror-like, masculine identity with her father, and a 'tissue memory' of feeling his erect penis in the small of her back when he climbed into her bed that fateful night. Very likely, her strongest and most consistent manifestation is as the Teen, who was promiscuous and driven at that age. I will not become aware of all these connections till sometime later; but Christ is and will not allow Leigh or me to address them prematurely, even as he brings us closer and closer to her self revelation. This depersonalized self appears to be both intuitively symbolic and concomitantly fanciful. She also mirrors her father's own manic behavior. She uses prescription drugs rather than alcohol, but she is just as psychologically and physiologically addicted to them. Her lack of connection with the body allows her to drive it mercilessly to the point of exhaustion. Last, but not least, she must be brought to heel; she must be obliged to feel the effects her dissociative behavior is having on the body. But believe me when I tell you she is subtle, baffling, powerful, and very slippery. She has been 'slipping' through my fingers for years.

The next session is just after Christmas. We discuss her concerns about the crisis that her daughter is going through. She does not go inside. She tells me that, "Sometimes the skater falls down and sometimes she is with Christ or her sense of the masculine."

I see Leigh a week later. She tells me, "I go in all the time and ask Christ to convict the male and female skaters. My leg is getting worse. They seem fine." I ask if they seem 'ideal' to her? "Yes, except I can't see him as more than as a shadow." I suggest she allow Christ to create a 'circle of growing awareness' so she can willingly grapple with any resistance regarding the masculine. "I am afraid of intimacy." I tell her that their intimacy will only effect her as and when she reintegrates them into her heart chakra. "As soon as you said that I saw them putting their hands on each other's faces, but he is not much more substantial." I suggest that she allow Christ to bring the three of them into each other's line of sight. "He wants to keep a little distance from me. Both of them are wary of me. All of us are not sure we want to be within each other's space. I do allow Christ to convict us and then they say, 'do you want to see us skate, see what a good couple we are?' when I say, yes, they begin doing all this inter-dependent skating." I ask how it feels? "I wish I could be her." I ask if she would like them to be an Ideal pair in her heart chakra? Her apparent unwillingness breaks her focus and she immediately returns to me. She claims to have been distracted by thoughts of her daughter. Leigh goes back inside to ask Christ to convict them so she "can have an Ideal pair for her heart chakra. "I seem more comfortable with them. He is just kissing her. It was really important for me to get a sense of how tall he was. He is not overwhelming her that way. They are telling me that they would still have this good of a relationship in my heart. " I tell her that if she is willing, Christ will stand in front of her with one of the skaters on each side of him. He will then push through and all of you will follow him. "Yes (good sigh). He has already set his *Light* in the center of the heart. They want him to stay. He says that he is leaving the Holy Spirit with them via his *Light*. So they are OK with it. But we can visit." The session ends here. I do suggest that she arrange to see a Physical Therapist whose methods appear to be helpful in ameliorating sciatic pain.

Leigh returns the following week. She is still in pain. I decide to focus on her sensate body and suggest that she allow Christ to capture whatever he thinks we need to address. "My heart chakra is sad." Clearly, a reference to the Six-year-old. I ask her for a visual. "It looks like an ethereal ball, like a cloud. It is all of who I am and really lost. A lot of my life is not looking good. I don't want to live the rest of my life with this much pain." I ask if she is referring to a specific pain? "The pain in my right hip." Can Christ capture it? "It is a screaming monkey baby; that will not stop crying. No one gives a damn about it." Are you willing for someone to care about it? "Yes, I am asking Mary to go and pick it up. She says that is not easy. It is kicking and screaming. And it runs away form her. It is climbing the wall it is so out of control." I suggest that she give them both a dome of *Light*, which immediately relaxes the 'monkey' baby. "Mary has entered the dome now and is just holding the baby, settling it down. My pain is easing. I must have been neglected as a child... the youngest of five kids of an alcoholic mother." I suggest to Leigh that she ask Christ to identify who has disowned this child and place her in a dome? "It is myself when I was 14-17 years old. I was not taking care of myself." I suggest that she ask Christ to convict this Teen till the baby is healed. "She does not want to be judged. She hates it (the child). So instead, I suggest that Christ be allowed to place her in a dome that will oblige her to feel the effects of her attitude. "She does not like that. She is feeling totally alone and helpless, the misery of abandonment." I suggest to Leigh that she ask Christ to identify the Teen's masculine counterpart. "It is just like my father at his most judgmental. They like each other; they glom together. She is modeling her father." *Finally understanding that this self is a Mirror aspect*, I reinforce her observations by saying she is out-fathering her father. I suggest to Leigh that she ask Christ to extract the Teen's feminine. "It is an ethereal nothing. There is hardly any feminine left. It hurts me to look at them. At first, I felt it was too hard, too revolting, but then I heard that I am finally well enough to deal with this core issue. The Teen goes to her knees when Christ convicts her, but she is rebellious. She is speaking like her father telling Christ 'I made her what she is and I don't want to change. The baby should be abandoned. It is not even his; he cursed its seed. It is a devil kind of talk. She is openly challenging Christ, telling him 'I can go to hell, I don't care.' Now I see Christ convicting her and her father; and now both of them are on their knees. This is not going to happen in a second. I have to pray for his soul. I want this conviction and I don't. I am biting my nose to spite my face." I am frankly at a loss for words. Basically, the session ends here. In every sense of the word, this Teen is defined by her father's definition of the masculine. It is so overpowering, not to say incestuous, that there is no room for the feminine either figuratively or definitionally. She is a mental construct of pure energy unbounded by any feminine definition that would connect her to the physical body and the pain she is inflicting on it by her incessant activity. This seems to be as succinct a definition of mania as any I can muster. But how to address it?

The evening before our next scheduled session I get a call from Leigh. She is in intense pain. I suggest that she ask Christ to place a portion of his Light into the energy center that connects her with the Teen. She thinks he should place it in the brain, but *he places it in her root chakra*. Next, he places a portion into the Teens root chakra. Leigh begins to feel her self relax. The next morning she gets a Lidocaine patch and a week off from her doctor. She is still in too much pain to drive herself to our next session so I conduct it over the phone. I tell her that, eventually, the Teen will have to choose a new higher power in lieu of her father (See Appendix II). I have Christ place the Teen and father's circle touching each other with him standing between them. "Christ is gently holding the Teen's head and bathing her in light. His hand on the male's head is loving, but very firm, like holding a two-year-old having a temper tantrum firmly in place. There is a sense of gears falling in place." Leigh agrees to continue letting Christ convict the two whenever she looks inside. And she will also read the prayer in Appendix III in the presence of the three of them. The session ends here.

When Leigh returns the following week her back is as bad as it has ever been; and her leg pain is getting worse and worse. "The teen seem incredibly determined and I am tired of fighting with her. She is so fucking willful." I ask Leigh who she thinks would take the Teen's place if Christ put her to sleep for awhile? "Christ would take her place, but she never sleeps. I am so angry at her I use all of these swear words at home and then I crawl into his lap. He loves her and asks if she is OK." I suggest that she allow Christ to create a dome for the Teen that will dissipate some of 'her heat.' "I am afraid to have her cornered; the pain can be intense when she gets agitated. I am saying both things to him: I am thanking him for putting a dome over her and telling him I am scared. He puts a prayer shawl on me." I suggest that she ask Christ to sever the connection between the Teen and whoever. Christ is to decide which connections to sever. "He has a giant ax that he is using to cut again and again. He is severing her connections to spiritual contaminations, hatred, killer drive, mental calculating...." I refine the suggestion by encouraging her to let Christ sever any connections that prevent him from giving her a healthy sense of the masculine. "Now the shooting pain and numbness are gone. Now Christ lifts up the dome and goes in to convict her. The Teen is kneeling in front of him. She has her hands on her face, weeping with gratitude and saying 'home, home at last.' Christ asks her if she is ready for a new sense of the masculine? He puts his hands around her shoulders and on her face. She is bathed in this light from head to feet. She knows that it is good coming from Christ." At this point I suggest that she needs to let Christ convict her parents till they are redeemed, till here images are no longer a threat. "Christ has each one in a circle and his hands on each of them. Both of them scare me. I focus on Christ. I can't focus on both at once." I quickly remind her that she is not doing this; Christ is. "They embody so much for me...my mother at her worst...inside a reptile and sea monster...and all the terrors of my father." Again, I encourage her to let Christ do it his way. "The little person in me is so terrified of being blown away like a tumbleweed. It is so painful to realize the images have to be completely dried up, nothing left, not even the crumbs of connection. Now I see Christ embracing two indistinct figures. The little one says 'this is going to be good.' The female is young, in her early 20's, she has a cute figure (strong upwelling of emotion) and running pants. She is healthy looking. She seems full of vitality with a feeling of her whole life ahead of her." We are well over time. I encourage Leigh to allow Christ to continue the convictions at home; but I am wary. It feels like another fantasy fabricated by a mental self.

Leigh asks me to call her in the evening. She is in great pain – 8 on a scale of 1 to 10. She has pushed herself and the stress is threatening to send her to the ER. Her solution to the pain, actually the Teen's solution, is to focus on collecting the reports asked for by a neurosurgeon who will see her in two weeks. I begin by noting that she has put her faith in the surgeon and so no help can come till then. It comes to me to make a suggestion that has worked in other contexts. I suggest that she ask Christ to place the Teen in a new circle that will obliged her to feel the total effect that her behavior is having on the physical body. Almost instantly, the teen is crying out in pain behaving like a woman at the height of labor. I keep Leigh focused on the Teen's reaction. The teen's response does not surprise me as it simply indicates that the circle is having its desired effect. What does surprise me is Leigh's comment that she is not feeling any pain; that her own pain is gone. When I have her focus on herself for a minute or two she reports that, yes, it is like a .5 or 1 on a scale of 1 to 10. She is lying in bed as we speak, I have her get up and move around. She reports pains ranging from 2 to 3. The Teen in the circle continues to experience severe pain. I can make a clear distinction: The pain from 0 to 3 is her body's complaint in response to all the abuse the Teen has heaped upon it. The pain from 3 to 8 is a direct consequence of the Teen's behavior, and from hereon out it will be the Teen's problem to solve. Leigh's job will be to manage her experience of the body (the pain from 0 to 3); and allow Christ to work with the Teen to the extent the Teen is willing to accept his help. Leigh can measure the Teen's progress by her experience of the Teen's pain: all pain rated 3+ is to be attributed to the Teen. I will repeatedly remind her of this distinction when she tells me the pain is more than 3 on a scale of 10.

In one regard, the drama of Leigh's travail is not caught so much in the sessions as in telephone calls – like the one above, and her discovery and frequent use of texting (learned from her daughter). At first, I found the texting annoying, but gradually discovered it could be quite useful in addressing the Teen's machinations; and I was quite willing not to respond or only respond when I felt the time was right. (I also levied a texting charge above and beyond my customary charges). Basically, for the remainder of this series I made the Teen totally responsible for the back pain. I also insisted that she remain in the circle of effect and challenged Leigh any time I thought she had gotten out.

I see Leigh the following day. We work inside for the better part of her session. Leigh is still in pain. The Teen readily accedes to everything I suggest and the inner life seems to get better and better (e.g. the Teen gets a 'white knight' and the parents seek to become more worthy), but nothing has changed on the outside. I think our 'mental construct' is deluding herself and us, but doing the best she can under the circumstances. She needs to become a more active participant in healing the body.

I see Leigh a week later. She is being driven by a neighbor as she can no longer drive herself. She goes inside and describes the changes in her parents. They have become archetypal. It is all very idyllic. I go with it, as I suspect it is helpful rather than harmful, but it lacks substance.

Between this next session and the last I receive a text from Leigh. She has been working with the Physical therapist I have recommended and during one of their sessions she has what she is calling a 'tissue memory.' When I see her a week later, she can tell me that when her father crawled into her bed, she could distinctly 'feel' his erect penis in the small of her back. "That is how I learned what an erection is." We discuss this and, particularly, the idea that such a body memory could be significantly contributing to her back pain. I also crouch it as a chakra issue: that very likely the Teen has closed down her root chakra in a concerted effort to disconnect from that particular memory and all its ramifications. Leigh now reports that she can see the Teen lying in bed with the parents kneeling at each side of her praying for her recovery. "I also see Christ coming out of the dome where the Teen is and reassuring the Six-year-old and asking Mary to hold her. I have told Christ that you want him to begin healing the Teen's root chakra." I sense it would be premature to ask

Christ to work directly with the Teen's root chakra. Instead, I suggest that he create a dome of pure sensation that will allow him to access whatever she has felt oblige to dissociate. "I see a black twisted figure." I reassure her that Christ can separate and purify all of the emotions and sexual energy bound up in that figure, but first he must be allowed to bring it to the surface. "I keep seeing an amorphous light in the dome; my heart is beating very fast." I suggest that Christ give both of them garments of protection. "He has given the Six-year-old a baby blanket." Again, I encourage her to let him show her what he can do. Christ gently guides her toward a clear vision of what is in the dome: "I see a black shape like a volcanic rock with green ferns on it. I am not now in pain but beg Christ to heal it. I sense of tremendous rushing of light and air over it that has blown it away. Now I am looking down on a deep flower. He asks me again if I am willing to let go and turn my life over to him. I feel his *Light* surrounding the dome; Mary has joined us and even my parents are looking from where they are standing. I see the remains of the island turned into brilliant white clouds. But now I see another black volcanic thing, but without ferns. Everyone is supporting my willingness. Something like shit – disgusting – is coming up out of it. I keep asking Christ to heal it. He tells me that this is my root chakra and shows me a tunnel of light like a penis. I know it is the sexual part of all this; like the awful memories I have been experiencing for the last week or two. The light is going away leaving a light gray image of the island oozing shit…that may be the emotional part of it. Christ's *Light* is over the island again and it is growing larger and larger in my field of vision. It stops and I ask again for it to continue." I tell her at some point the Teen must actually experience the reconnection with the root chakra; she still needs to experience it open. "When you said that I felt another rush of sexual release. The island has been blown away. Now it is only mist and light and rain washing the rest away. Now everything is frozen and white. I pray for him to melt the ice. He is encouraging me to look into the pool and see myself healthy and restored. I'm afraid to look; that's probably the Teen. It's the part of me that needs to be brought to the surface." Frankly, I am not sure what the last means, but we are overtime. The session ends here.

I see Leigh the following week. She tells me that she has scheduled a minimally invasive surgery in three weeks. The surgeon will shave a small piece of bone from the vertebra pressing on the nerve. She also tells me that the Teen is feeling a lot of pain and is very restless, and it too frightened to identify the source. I suggest that she may be anticipating Christ working directly with her root chakra. Leigh is willing to go inside. I explain that the root chakra is between the vagina and anus, and that the feeling of it is distinctly different from those two; further, that Christ will be obliged to touch that area and even enter the chakra with his Light in order to clear the space. I ask her to identify whether the root chakra is closed or open? She tells me she sees 'white puffs of smoke' coming out. This is likely an association to the work we did the previous week when Christ worked symbolically with the root chakra/volcano. However, I intuit that the root chakra is open and turning counter-clockwise; that it is expelling energy rather than drawing it in, which is its normal function. I ask her if she is willing for Christ to reverse the flow? "Christ is asking her. She says yes." I tell her that Christ needs to place his hand there and also in the small of her back on the pain. "She is embarrassed for him to place his hand there." I gently challenge Leigh: does she really want to be guided by shame? How will it be helpful here? "She is calming down. *The root chakra is not connected to her. It is separate from her body*. I am telling her that letting the energy flow out may kill her. I am thankful that Christ is working anyway she will allow. We are both concerned about the disconnection." I assume that the Teen has lived exclusively in the mind as distinct from mind and body. So I suggest to Leigh that Christ might helpfully 'clear a path' between the mind and root chakra. "Yeah. She is open to that. I see a canal. First it was filled with light and then the darkness of shame and fear... the experience of my dad climbing into bed." I start to make several suggestions, but decide she must ask Christ to resolve this issue. "I see Christ placing his hand on her face. He is emanating love and encouraging her to relax. She says she is powerless to dispel the shame and hatred and asks him to dispel them. She begs him for forgiveness. I saw an image of the cross. Now I feel myself in an underground sewer with dark pipes surrounding me, lost. Christ says this is where I have been and asks if I want to get out? I take his hand. At first I only see a single candlelight and then there is light all around him that is getting brighter. He is showing her the way out. He is pulling me up by my jumper straps." I now ask if he can work directly with her root chakra? "He says I have been in the abstract." I reiterate my thought that he must also be allowed to work directly with it concretely; that she has to experience the sensations. "I see a big hole in her chakra. She is not ashamed anymore but she is afraid of too much energy. Christ reassures her. He puts his hand into her chakra. It is like he has entered her whole body, and his *Light* has cleared out a connection to her brain. He is cleansing her whole body and she has tears of gratitude." The session ends here. Over the weekend there are a number of text exchanges. In the first she reports that: "I am seeing peaceful light-filled images of Teen and her space. Very comforting." The next day she asks for suggestions about working with the Teen. In return I ask about the Teen's pain level. "If I am lying down it is between 1 and 4. When I am up it ranges from 4 to 6. If I continue to stand it is 8." I ask her what the Teen is doing when she is up? Leigh replies, "Screaming for me to lie down." My first response is 'Hmm...' But then I add: 'Give the Teen the opportunity to work with Christ in healing your shared body. Healing requires focus, concentration and willingness, which she can provide. Allow the two to collaborate on your behalf.'

I see Leigh later in the week. She remains in pain and seems convinced that nothing will change short of whatever miracle surgery can provide, though that is still two weeks off. I challenge her that looking to surgery for her salvation insures there is no release till then. This angers the Teen. "She is pounding the bed with her fists and saying, 'what did I do to deserve this?' She insists the continuing source of her pain is her father climbing into bed with her. Her father's penis is still causing the pain." I reply that her masculine energy does not get any release from this belief. I make what must seem an audacious proposal. I conclude that her father's erect penis describes the state of her own masculine energy. Therefore, I suggest that, if she is willing, Leigh can ask Christ to release the sexual tension reflected in her father's erect penis and thereby reduce its effect on her. "I saw him ejaculate and then she kicked him out of bed and got clean sheets. Now the pain is not so bad. I did not see Christ. She was willing and it just happened. Now I see Christ holding her face and telling her it was not her fault. He is directly addressing her pain telling her it will not go on forever." I ask if it has registered with her that her willingness was sufficient to reduce the tension of her masculine? "She gets it now." I ask if she can do it again as I suspect there may have been a lot of sexual tension stored up? "Yeah. Christ is there encouraging her to just let it keep happening and the pain will go down. She says, 'wow,' I did not realize I was holding all of this in. Her father is ejaculating time and time again; and she is sobbing with her head in Christ's lap. He is reassuring her it is not her fault and she is not to feel guilt or shame about it all. She gets up and runs across a field to Christ symbolic of running free." I further encourage her by saying that Christ can direct the release if she is willing to stop blocking it. I have her check the emotional chakra to ascertain if there are any blocks. She tells me that they are clear front and back. I ask her how her back feels? "She is calmly resting in Christ's arms. Her back has no pain. I feel pain in my legs, three on a scale of 1 to 10." I suggest that she allow Christ to work directly with her sensate body by placing her in a dome of pure sensation. When Leigh enters the dome she reports that the body's right leg is glowing green from hip to toe. "It is attacking me. I want to cut it off. I can't seem to love it." I ask her, who is the leg that you want to cut it off? I suggest, that she can use her *Light* to express her willingness to see this 'other' by drawing two circles in the dome, one for it and the other for her. They both share the same leg. (This is a variant of the addictive bond hypothesis discussed in the previous chapter. Pain is treated as equivalent to an addiction shared by the conscious self and a secret sharer.) "It is the male part of me like my father, hateful, who only knows how to cause pain and offers no comfort. It is willful." I reply that he is *her masculine* and she defines him. So right now the only way he can connect is through the painful right leg. If she allows Christ to convict her and him, then to the extent that he changes she should also observe a change in the sensate body. "I sense more positive characteristics now, a can-do attitude; he can take care of me, fix things. The leg is not glowing anymore. It is bare, new, and pink; not covered by pants. It is still getting a lot of attention from Christ who runs his hand down it. I need to keep working on this. The male is sitting in a rocking chair. He can patiently wait for the leg to heal. I see me standing up strong. Christ is encouraging me to stay with the process." The session ends here.

Unfortunately, but not surprising, Leigh returns the following week in severe pain and completely amnesic of everything that occurred the previous week. I suggest that she go inside and let Christ capture whoever is blocking her memory. "I let him draw the circle and I walked through it, but I do not see anything." I suggest that she ask her *Light* to provide a garment of protection. She then asks Christ to draw another circle, which she runs through. This time: "She looks like a bear, very threatening. We are all scared of her." Even so, I challenge Leigh to learn how this 'bear' can repress Leigh's memory of the previous session? I surmise that she may be using pain to suppress the memory and suggest that she ask Christ to provide a sensory block against her use of pain. Christ does something that reduces the pain somewhat. "Yes. She is using pain to repress the memory. She will use anything." I suggest that she ask Christ if he can tell Leigh the particular threat arising from last week's session? "I have no idea." I suggest that she ask Christ to transform the bear's circle to a circle of effect. "Yes. She is howling now; and that relieves the pain for me. The Teen is restless but no longer out-of-her mind with the pain. The bear is female. She has claws like a bear." I ask Leigh to ask Christ if the bear has been *cut off* from a vital part of herself? "I hear her say, 'you bet your sweet ass I have, but then she gets real silent. The cut off has stunted her." I ask if she knows the cut off has stunted her? "She has never thought about that. She is really malevolent. She wants to go back into her den." (Note: my unspoken surmise is that the Leigh is cut off from her sexuality; and the bear is an ego-aspect called Control, who appears to be a Mirror aspect of the father.) I tell Leigh that she needs to recover whatever the bear has cut off from her. Leigh becomes reflective: "Why is she desperate to keep me from remembering?" I suggest that it is her way of maintaining control. I wonder aloud if she also control's Leigh's father? (My thought here is that she might be a manifestation of his mother, but Leigh's answer points to the bear being a Mirror aspect.) "No, but she is his surrogate. They get along fine. He goes into her circle and they start dancing together. He likes what she is doing. He does not think that it is a problem. But she says there is a problem now that she is required to take the pain. He tells her we will deal with it." I have her ask Christ if he can insure that he also feels the pain? "I did not realize how much I still hate him. Christ asks me if I am sure I want him to make my father feel the pain? I say damn straight. But as I look at the Teen and six-year-old I begin to cry because I realize I have become just like him." I ask if Christ can show her, but not them, what they cut off? "It has to do with sex, but that is all I know." I ask if she has gone along with them all these years? Has she also cut off sex? "The pain is worse for me but not the Teen. It has to do with shame, their shaming me all of these years. He acted so wrongly and made it my fault. He repeatedly said 'shame on you' and I took it in." I suggest here that he cut himself off from his own sexuality and blamed the women in his life for it. Then I challenge her: what did we do last week that upset the cut off? You have a choice here, pain or knowledge. What do you have to give up in order to remember? "Control." How do you control? "Fear of pain. They use pain and shame. I use shame and pain." I tell her that Christ does not inflict her with pain; she inflicts herself. She is doing what they taught her. "I don't remember (what happened last week)." I reply: You insist on holding on to your pain and shame; and no amount of surgery or drugs will protect you from that. The session ends here. I have decided to tell her nothing about the previous session. Leigh leaves the session angry and in much the same amount of pain she was in when she began, except for the period of time when she was willing to place the bear in a circle of effect. The next day I get a text asking me to call her. When I do she tells me she left angry, but over the next 24 hours she recalled that the pain had something to do with sex. She masturbated and that seemed to release a lot of the pain. But she still could not recall the previous session. I am not sure how this will work itself out. I will be gone the following week and Leigh is scheduled for a neurosurgical intervention while I am gone. The surgery may ease the pain, but I have a strong sense that this will not be resolved until the sexual issue is resolved and Leigh can find a suitable masculine counterpart for the Teen.

I see Leigh two weeks later. She is recovering from the surgical intervention a week earlier intended to reduce the pressure on the sciatic nerves. The surgeon considers the operation successful. The first day after the surgery Leigh experiences tremendous relief but for the rest of the week the pain is as bad as ever. She finally starts taking muscle relaxers the day before she sees me, and that has helped some. She is now using a walker. It is not easy to get to my second floor office but she manages the stairs. I ask if she has recovered any memory of the previous two sessions? She says "No." I ask about the Teen? "She is asleep. Abba (God the Father) is curled up behind her." What? I have never heard of this image. It is totally new. I immediately surmise it is a 'morphed' image of the Teen's masculine that Christ identified and transformed during the now 'repressed' session. Leigh's explanation for him is that the Teen 'needed' him and he came from her prayers, which always include references to God the Father, who she identifies as Abba. "He has been with the Teen for much of the past week. She needs him and accepts instruction from him." Based on Leigh's history it is a perfect fit. All I can do is accept it and work with it. I suggest that she ask Christ to add pure sensation to the circle of effect containing the Teen and Abba. My hope is that this will provide the Teen with a sensate grounding she has lacked. Leigh does as asked and then reports that "Now the Teen is restless. She wakes up and remembers that the pain is still there but leaving. 'I am doing so much better.' Abba says the surgery was good." I suggest that she now ask if Abba can place his hand on the Teen's back and provide healing energy? "The Teen is awake. She turns to Abba and tells him she is so grateful that he is taking care of her every step of the way. He kisses her on the forehead. She snuggles in tighter to him." I ask if she likes the sensations? "She loves them." Leigh is quiet for a while. I ask what she is thinking. She tells me that she is obsessing about the drugs she is taking, especially the muscle relaxant, which makes her dizzy. She experiences little pain in her legs when she is sitting, but it goes to a 6 or when she stands up to walk. I ask if, perhaps, Abba and Christ could balance her energies better so there is less tension? (Frankly, I am remembering that before the surgery, her resumption of masturbation reduced the tension but make no mention of that.) "Christ says 'yes,' all of the chakras need to be balanced. One of them says that I need more sex. They remind me that it helped a lot before the surgery. I have stopped it since the surgery. Both are telling me it will not harm the body and I need to make it a priority now." I ask if the Teen is ambivalent? "No. She says, 'I understand;' she accepts instruction." I ask if there is a part that is prudish about this at all? "No, not at all. Now I pray to Christ and Abba all the time rather than going for the drugs. They are affirming me in every way, and telling me that now I need to take time for sex." I suggest that she ask the Teen to allow Abba to place his hand on her back so he can provide healing energy. "She turns toward him. He has placed his hand on her back…and the other hand on her root chakra." The session ends here. Leigh has a friend who has driven her to the session. They manage to get her and her walker down the stairs without any incident. I might also mention that Leigh has gone into her office to work during the past week and received 'unprecedented' new accounts during the few hours she has worked. On reflection, I am also struck by the fact that during the preceding months, while Leigh has experienced a great deal of pain as the Teen has been forced to feel the effects of her behavior and slow down, there have been no manic episodes.

I see Leigh the following week. She is still using a walker. Not surprising, she has no recall of the previous session, though she still calls on Abba and Christ daily. When I have her go inside and press her for what she does remember, she says, "I remember dad climbed into bed with me; I don't know if he ejaculated or not. I think I kicked him out before he did." I encourage Leigh to ask Christ/Abba if she remembers last week's session? "They are telling me that, of course, I remember. I am pissed and I am expressing it. I am angry at my father. The anger has been expressed by back pain. I have been fooling with this back pain for a year." I suggest to Leigh that she ask Christ to capture any self that may be interfering with her remembering. "I am afraid. When I try to enter the circle it gives way instead of letting me in. now it is convex." I suggest that she ask her *Light* for a garment of protection and assistance from Abba. "I am backing up. Now the circle looks like a circle." I suggest that what she is experiencing is her 'control.' "Now my legs and back are really hurting. I see an iron cylinder about the height of my body. It is an 'iron will.' Abba says I can walk around it. I am afraid that if I walked in it would close me off forever. Christ is rooting for me. The cylinder is about being in charge. It is male. The open part looks safe to walk into but then it clamps shut." I tell Leigh that, she was given explicit instructions last week by Abba and Christ, but she is still in pain because Control remains in charge. I ask her how the Teen feels about this? "She is still grateful that the parents remain on either side of her bed praying for her, and for Abba and Christ too. She is thrashing." I suggest that rebellion and control are flip sides of the same coin. I suggest that that Control and the Teen both need to be convicted by Christ. "I see us both on our knees accepting Christ's conviction." I tell her that the conviction will be sufficient when both of them can remember. I also tell them that if they cannot remember they are likely to suffer another week. "The Teen says, 'I don't like it when he talks like that, but he is right. Christ holds my face and says, 'It is Ok,. Everybody gets to this point. You are just slower than the rest.' A wonderful feeling of energy and light is coming into my face. I am so exhausted. I am remembering that Christ said, 'Come back to me and I will give you rest.' I remember Abba putting his hand over the incision when I laid down each night." The session ends here. I'm guessing I have angered Control, but with everyone inside contributing their input, I am not sure what will remain figural.

Leigh returns the following week. She is managing without a walker. When she looks inside she can see herself on her knees receiving conviction from Christ. "The Teen is looking at me. She is comfortable. The parents are on each side of her bed praying for her." But she has no real memory of the previous three sessions. I ask her, why the need for this control? "I get fearful. I am afraid of the pain." I ask if she can tell me the opposite of fear? "Love." I ask if she is willing for Christ to give her a major infusion of love? "Yes. I saw this rush of energy coming into me. I tell him I need more." I ask if the energy has the power to melt the fear and pain? Or does her belief in them reject the possibility? "I am reminded of lying on the beach in the warm sun. Christ is only giving me the doses I can manage. He is really ready to give me more." I ask if she knows the memory she is protecting herself from? "It was the time my dad climbed into bed, but also something earlier. I was five years old. He said I did not need under panties in bed. I told him did. And a sense of me as an infant, somebody penetrating me with a finger in the crib. Christ is saying that I am whole and not cut off from my sexuality." I ask if Christ can neutralize the negative emotions associated with the memories so she can remember them clearly? "Yes. He is taking a big net or screen through what he did to me and my sister, and the stories I heard. He captures the emotions and casts them out. I can see what happened without getting worked up. I am thanking him for that. That is so wondrous. All week the Teen has been on the bed. She tells me to get on my knees and accept conviction. She names the truth." I ask her who is interfering with recall of the sessions? "Christ says its me." I ask if she is willing to give up this power to block memory? "It is a mainstay. I am afraid I will freak out, that it will be too horrifying for me." I suggest that she ask Christ to collect all the imagined horror in a circle. "I see images of cockroaches, big trucks on the highway, my father running after me with a belt. All of that authority." I ask her how Christ would have her perceive all of this? What emotion would he have you use? "His love. His love is more powerful than mine." Is there a way for him to flood that circle of horrors with his love? Can he give you the power of choice? Convict you for the power of choice? "It is really good now that I see what I am asking for. Looking back without staring at the memories, choosing not to look back. I can choose to ask him to help me. Ask him to show me what I can remember. His hand is on my head, gentle but firm. I just threw off my clothes running free in the rain, dancing with Christ. I see him bike riding with me. Now he is telling me to remember. We are walking and I am pouting with my lower lip stuck out. I see the Teen and a handsome companion. Christ is putting his hand on my root chakra. I am aware that my father and I both cut off our sexuality." I ask if the object of Control's power is to cut off her sexuality? "Yes. That rings true." I ask if that has been a painful choice? "Christ say, yes! You were created to love sex." I ask if Control also cut the Teen off from her sexuality? "I took in what my father said, that I was a slut." I suggest that she let Christ capture the slut, the part that embodies her sexual expression? "The circle starts to bend, but I am finally able to walk through. I see someone with curly hair. Christ takes her face and says, 'It is OK. No one got hurt." I tell Leigh, that the Slut is her father's creation; can Christ make her his creation? "He convicts her. She is so grateful." And sexual? "Yes. Christ introduces her to the Teen and me. It is like old home week. He blesses us all." The session ends here. I have not the slightest idea what to expect of the coming week.

    Leigh returns the following week. She is doing better but complaining of great weakness from overexerting herself. She tells me that the Teen is ready to throw up from nausea. She blames Control for "putting me in this state." When she goes inside, she immediately complains that Control is beating herself up and complaining to Christ." Whoever is in charge – most likely Control – is not aware of the Slut or cannot offer any recall of anything that occurred the previous week. But she is very aware of Christ and Abba. "They are what I focused on all week. I saw incredible love from them." Frankly, I am suspicious. I have a real sense that Control is being manipulative. I suggest that when Leigh goes inside again, the part of her who 'holds the *Light*' needs to ask Christ to place Control into a circle of effect. "Christ did it, but now *he* is a wild beast, really angry, raging that I would have done that; and now *he* is sweating. He looks ashamed for a moment, but the other part of him is manipulative, wanting me to feel sorry for him. I did not know I had such an anger in me. I am asking Christ to convict me; I am more than just control. This is new: when I previously asked him to convict me I was on my knees and he held my head *firmly*. Now he is not holding my head firmly and it feels really good. Our eyes are meeting. He says I do not have to be afraid of authority. He is holding me and I am fine. There are tears of relief and gratitude. I am really afraid of Control. Christ says that he and Abba can be in charge." I ask her to name the opposite of control. "Control is all about fear, so love must be its opposite." I suggest that she let Christ infuse her with his love and see what effect that has on his fear? "Funny, I am a little afraid of that." Ask for a garment of protection? Ask the Teen if she would like some? Test it on her? "He is sending her rays or warm sunlight. She says it is great. Our stomach is calming down. Like being in a spa together. Christ is saying he will help me deal with Control, that he will love me back to health." At this point I tell Leigh that she must address Control. That when she leaves the session, Control's circle of effect will dissolve unless we do something more. "Christ is reminding me of your idea of control of *affects*." Frankly, I do not remember ever talking about it as such, but willingly go along with the idea. I suggest that she ask Christ to place a portion of his *Light* into Control's circle that will neutralize all of his negative affects. "It relaxes him almost immediately. It is like he wants to take a nap. I don't feel angry at him now. He was doing the best he could. It is good to see how angry I was at him. Christ loves Control as much as he loves me." I ask if Christ can sustain the neutralization indefinitely? "Yes, but he needs my cooperation. I need to ask Christ to be in charge every day. I am practicing and getting better at that. But he says I have a ways to go. I will have to remind myself that I have asked for this. I need to let go of my pride. He will give me a life that is less *clutching*." I reiterate the intent of Christ's *Light*: it is set at a frequency that cancels out the negative affects generated by Control. "I am aware that Control tries to control through worry." The session ends here. Later in the day I receive two texts from Leigh: she remains nauseous and has thrown up twice. I suggest that she ask Christ to place a portion of his *Light* into Control's heart that will terminate any undue influences. Her whole session suggests a real struggle going on within Control.

A week later, Leigh calls me the morning of our scheduled session. She has been diarrheic for the past 24 hours and is too weak to come in. As she is relating this, I intuit that the problem is a lack of masculine energy. Control is her primary source of masculine energy, and the circle of affect is diminishing its conditional flow, which is why she continues to be 'weak' and diarrheic. I suggest that Christ draw a circle around her and infuse it with sexual energy. We agree that she can call me for a telephone session during her scheduled hour. Surprisingly, she is in my office at our scheduled time; she has regained sufficient strength to get there (with the help of a driver she has been employing to get her around for the past several weeks). She tells me that late last week her Doctor stopped a pain medication with opiates because it appeared to be adversely affecting her parasympathetic system and replaced it with another. I ask her if she has been 'sexual' during the past week? She recalls relieving herself afterward for the first time in a good while. I suspect the drug withdrawal and tension release have precipitated the diarrhea. But I am also convinced more than ever that Control does not want her to be sexual and that he generally sets too many conditions in exchange for giving her access to his masculine energy. I have her ask Christ and Abba how often they have encouraged her to be sexual? "Never. But I remember that Christ loves the slut." So she still does not remember, but she does. I ask her if she has relied on Control for her sexual energy? "Yes." That, I tell her, is the problem. I ask if Abba and Christ can provide an alternative source of sexual energy that will allow her to unconditionally and freely choose to be sexual? Leigh imagines a cloud like a blanket. Then she remembers a picture of a Greek god in the shape of a cloud raping a woman. I suspect Control is still able to generate such images. I suggest, instead, that she ask Christ/Abba to create a circle suffused with sexual energy. When Leigh steps into it, she can bring any fantasy she chooses. She steps in an imagines a naked 9-14 year old running, and another image of her bicycling. I have her move that circle near to the circle containing Control and ask her to compare the two. "When I first moved the circle next to each other, Control fought it, but now he is resigned. I turn my back on him. I can be as sexual as I want in the other circle. Now Mary is in my circle. She confirms that sex is good; like appetite and good things to eat. I don't need Control to drive me." I reinforce these thoughts by noting that Control has set a lot of conditions on his supply of masculine energy: worry, obsessiveness, manic-depression, fear of sex. To this list, Leigh adds "He kept me too busy to think about it. He is horrified that he has been revealed for what he is." I suggest that she ask Christ to terminate any undue influences in Control. Apparently, he does so because Leigh notes that, "He looks thankful for that." Even so, I suggest that he be kept in his circle of affect for the foreseeable future. Finally, I have her focus on the Teen. "She is curled up sleeping like a baby." I ask if it would be appropriate to provide her access to this energy. "She is grateful. She wakes up. She likes it." The session ends here. Over the next two days I receive texts from Leigh, telling me that the effects have continued to provide her improved ability to exercise and work and appreciate her surroundings.

It is easy to fit what has been happening into my addiction bond hypothesis put forth in the previous chapter. Control has been Leigh's primary source of masculine energy. He has used a host of defenses – even more than those listed above – to suppress her sexuality in response to its historical expressions by the slut. The above intervention finally provides her Teen and dissociated Slut an *unconditional* access to masculine/sexual energy. Now, we have to consciously reconcile the Teen and Slut – the mental and sensate components, and devise a way to integrate them with a 'reformed' Control.

When Leigh returns the following week she is quick to tell me that she had sex five times the previous week (with herself). She is walking. It is painful when she stops, but the pain quickly subsides. I tell her my thesis that the three selves need to be reconciled; that Control needs to become unconditional in his giving of masculine energy. "He has been learning a lot this past week. I pray daily for Christ to place his *Light* in Control's heart, and shield him from undue influences. I have a sense that a lot of spiritual forces have been in control of Control." I ask if she can identify what it is about Control that makes him so vulnerable? "He likes to be in charge. He has to submit to Christ's authority. Control sees himself as his own higher power. Like my dad, he does not have one. Satan stepped into the void and took advantage." What about the Slut? "When I look in on her she is unconditionally loved." I ask if she has access to masculine energy. "When we were having sex I would see shameful arousal, but then it would dissipate. It is not what either of us wants." I suggest to Leigh that she focus on the Slut and Teen, and bring both of them to the circle that Christ is suffusing with masculine energy. "The Teen is out of bed now; she is curious about the circle. I did see her out a couple of times this past week in a bikini. She looked hot. The Slut is 25 years old. She sees what is in the circle as a pool of water. She looks at it with wonderment." I have Leigh ask Christ/Abba how to proceed? I am particularly concerned as whether the Teen should have direct access to this energy. "Christ says to include the Teen." I suggest that each connect to Christ – Heart to Heart – using his Light. Leigh adds that she would also like them to be connected to other. "Both are standing outside the circle." I suggest to Leigh that the circle will become permeable to each one as they are willing to accept Christ/Abba. "She (not clear to me who) indents the circle, but she cannot penetrate it." I suggest they accept conviction from Christ. "The Teen needs more discipline. She is on her knees, in her bikini, in front of Christ. She is very grateful for the energy to get out of bed. Christ is kissing her on the forehead. He tells her that she is 'his chosen one' and is bathing her in light. She is really feeling the healing. She is tired. She curls up right next to the circle on the outside. She did not realize how exhausting it was to do it on her own without help. Christ offers to let her in, but now she is rebelling. Christ says, 'OK. I will still bath you in healing light. Now, she can't go to sleep." I suggest to Leigh that she focus on the Slut. "The Teen says, 'don't leave me. Now the circle looks like a dotted line, very permeable." I suggest it will be permeable when she is willing to embrace Christ. "I see her in the circle embracing Christ and he is saying 'welcome home.' She is asking if she can leave. He says, 'Of course, but why would you?' So, she asks, 'can I go topless down here? She is imagining being on the beach at St. Barts. Christ says the circle can enlarge for this. Now the Teen is asking us to look to the Slut, who sees the circle as a fenced in area; she wants to go in to the topless beach." I ask if she understands the rule that she must embrace Christ to gain access to the circle? Actually, Christ has come out. She has felt out of the circle (sic) mainstream all of her life. She is happy with her life choices. Christ is bathing her in healing light and embracing her. She says it felt so good." I note that she still has to embrace him. "She recognizes the rule. She does not want him to go back inside. *I want him to hug me till I can hug him back*. I did not realize how wounded she was." I tell Leigh that the Slut needs to open herself up to all of the energy, not just the sexual. Her value is more than sex. She is loved for more than her sexuality. The session ends here, sort of. That afternoon I get a text: What was the rule that the Slut has to adhere to? Was it that she needs to submit to Christ's authority, that she must be willing to embrace Christ back, or that she must consciously choose Christ over Control as her higher power? My reply was longer than I expected. Very likely I wrote it to clarify my own thinking as well: 'When she enters his circle they need to embrace each other so she can receive the optimum flow of energy – masculine as well as sexual, and so she is no longer dependent on Control's energy. She could accept him as her higher power, but the flow of energy Christ is offering is not dependent on that. Likewise, the flow is not dependent on embracing him, but it is likely to be much more satisfying if she does. Eventually, the offer may be extended to Control, but for now I would leave him in his circle of effect so the Teen and Slut can be firmly assured that they are no longer dependent on his masculine energy.'**

Leigh has been working inside during the week: "My leg hurts when I have sex but it helps me to sleep. There is overflowing love coming from Christ and Abba for the Slut and Teen. At first, the Slut was outside the circle of masculine energy. She did not seem to respond to all the love Christ was giving her. She was emotionally dead. But then she began to respond a little. Yesterday, she entered the circle. Now, she likes being in the circle with the Teen and me. She likes Christ's hand on her root chakra. She is experiencing her value as a person rather than as a sex object. We still need to work with her to increase her comfort level in the circle. I had no idea how wounded she was. She is so fundamental to my being and so wounded. There is a lot of shame stuff in her that now seems about 80 percent cleared." I tell Leigh that I am convinced that the remaining pain in her leg is psychosomatic, and will abate when we have successfully worked with Control and Slut. "Control is anxious to get to the part where Christ blesses him. He wants Christ to convict him too." I tell her that all of them can gain their Christ perceived nature in that circle. "When you said that I got a visual of the Teen dancing and me riding on my bicycle." I have Leigh ask Christ what Control lacks. "He says 'good orderly direction' (An Alanon name for God). Christ loves him. If he can learn to love back it will be better than staying attached to Satanic forces and insisting on being in charge." I suggest that she let Christ place the appropriate *Light* in Control's circle. "Control backs away. He is still a beast. Now he is lying on his back totally relaxed. My leg is not throbbing anymore, which it has been doing for most of this session. Christ and Abba are rubbing Control's belly. Now, I am totally pain free." At this juncture, I suggest a new intervention based on what she is telling me. I ask her to let Christ place a 'screen of *Light* over the place on her back that will block Control's access to their shared sensation, and prevent him regaining access till he is proven safe. The session ends here, sort of. Later in the day I get a text: Control has been transformed into a cute, white, rambunctious puppy, which Christ has allowed into the circle of masculine energy. But the Slut is scared of him and hiding behind Christ. I immediately texted back that Christ needs to put him on a leash for the foreseeable future. Leigh texts again to tell me it happened as soon as she read my text; and now he is 'heeled' next to Christ, but snarly toward the Slut. (I might add here that Leigh has really gotten into texting. To offset her enthusiasm, we have agreed to a 'text-charge' for these mini-sessions, though I would have answered in any case.)

This series ends here. The sessions are continued on the website: The Unredeemed Conscience.org.

What strikes me, as I reflect on the verbatims thus far, is the strong focus on the regulation of masculine energy, whose unmitigated intensity appears to be largely responsible for Leigh's mania and depressions. Leigh has a number of selves that appear to mirror her father. In the verbatims I find myself repeatedly striving to rebalance their masculine and feminine aspects. The masculine containers have made her exceedingly strong willed, prideful, and resistant to change, even as they repeatedly drove her to the point of exhaustion. This past year, Leigh has been able to function on a minimum of psychotropics as a result of this work, maintain her job, and struggle with some truly complicating issues in her immediate family that I have left out of the verbatims. I expect we will be at it for several more years.

SUMMARY AND REFLECTIONS

The forgoing verbatims are extensive. All four verbatims – Marion and Tory in Chapter VII, Lee in both chapters, and Leigh in this chapter – span two plus years. Hopefully, they provide the practitioner a better idea of how the therapy process ebbs and flows on a weekly basis. As I noted at the beginning of this work, what is offered here clearly cannot be done in twelve sessions or less, though I know based on current work that it can be shortened. For example, I now use infused circles with most of my clients once they are familiar with the process, but I had not developed them till late in my sessions with the above four. It may be that future practitioners will find other creative ways to lessen the time, but it will remain a journey as well as a treatment. As *The Course in Miracles* asserts: We can choose when to do the work, and how much at any given time, but not the curriculum. It is possible to focus on Relational authority early in therapy, provided the client has done a modicum of work with the *Light* and Christ image. Wherever the client and therapist start, the most pressing issues will find a way to be 'heard' until addressed. But the more time the client has spent addressing psychosomatic and character issues, as well as Temporal and Moral authority issues, the easier the relational work will be. Even more than the client, the therapist needs to have some experience with all facets of this work. You can start anyplace in the process once you – the therapist, have been through it, but trust me when I say, a full appreciation can take years. At least initially, it is good to move through the process as it has been outlined in the chapters. It has taken me twenty plus years to discover the interventions in this book, and believe me when I say I am still learning. Using what I have learned, but not being bound by it, a clinician could demonstrate competence in far less time, but not by attempting end runs. As the above verbatims demonstrate, if you start by working with Relational authority, then relevant issues of Temporal and Moral authority will emerge in the midst of those interventions and you will need to shift focus accordingly. In the final analysis, there is a force in every human mind directing the process of *redeeming the person*, not just their conscience; what Jung called the Transcendent function that seeks to unify all opposites. That function will use whatever means we offer to achieve its goal. It will guide both client and therapist, provided the therapist is open enough. Keep good notes. You will definitely get 'sidetracked' by the pride and fear of ego-aspects.

The four verbatims describe clients who experienced most of the interventions outlined in all eight chapters. There was improvement in all of them as a result of that earlier work, but frankly, nothing we accomplished compares to the results described in this and the previous chapter. At least from my perspective, the interventions described in these last two chapters definitely move the process forward. There is much more to be explored, but I must leave that to other books and clinicians.

It is difficult to highlight everything discovered by the process of repeated conviction beyond what I noted. But that said, six sets of observations become quite discernible in the verbatims: 1) the progressive power and autonomy of Christ and the Holy Spirit, 2) shock trauma, 3) the conviction of negative bonds defining a relationship, 4) the various interventions involving auric bodies, 5) anima-animus actualizations; and finally, 6) the use of infused circles.

The Increased Autonomy of Christ and the Holy Spirit

There is a definite shift as one moves through the verbatims of the last two chapters. The relationship between Christ (Teacher) and the Aware-ego becomes a dialogue; he is no longer merely a representational figure standing silently by until called upon. He becomes increasingly co-present whenever the client goes inside, in the session as well as between sessions. The more he is in engaged, the more active he becomes as a partner in the process. There is a felt shift after a primary self accepts the gift of Christ's discernment and allows him to enter the Heart. Once Christ has entered the Heart and redeemed the shameful core, the client becomes more willing to enter the Mind between sessions, which is rarely the case beforehand. There is a comparable shift vis-à-vis the Holy Spirit. The client *comes to expect* that if s/he asks for conviction, there will be insight or transformation.

Christ and the Holy Spirit working together acquire the power to reconcile and transform any image within the human Mind. I challenge the reader to find another methodology that readily and consistently offers this redeeming power. I cannot claim this power as a therapist. It is an inherent aspect of the methodology; it is of Christ, or a comparable higher power, working in concert with the Holy Spirit. It is transformative in a way that points out the real limitation of any therapy that relies solely on Ego and therapist.

Conviction becomes a process whereby the Holy Spirit *corrects* errors of judgment sustaining self-condemning polarizations. The Holy Spirit is asked to convict numerous times because the process is progressive. With each conviction, the Holy Spirit guides the client toward an altered relationship with self or other that liberates both from self-condemning negative emotions. Once the effects of this progression are grasped, the client seems willing to extend the intervention to any situation within the imagination.

Shock Trauma

The concept of shock trauma is taken from Peter Levine's work, which I described in Chapter V.[39] This phenomenon can be likened to the concept of cathexis as described by traditional psychoanalysts. Basically, 'cathexis' refers to the unhealthy concentration of mental energy around the image of a particular person, idea, or event. For Levine, shock trauma results from the *abrupt blocking* of intense fight-flight energies when that response seems about to fail. An organism is seen to block the energy of that reflex in order to 'play dead' as a last ditch effort to evade a predator. This is analogous to the process of repressive dissociation. The fight-flight reflex galvanizes the body for intense activity so when it is blocked the accumulated undischarged energy must be released soon after the blockage. Most animals can be observed to 'shake it off' soon afterward, if the 'playing dead' strategy allows them to escape. Humans have difficulty shaking it off. From a psychodynamic perspective, the Ego's response to such trauma appears to be dissociation of the ego-aspect that directed the initial fight-flight response, leaving it in a perpetual state similar to shameful enthrallment. Many individuals come to 'fear' the self that is dissociated, which prevents their helping it shake off the excess energy. While most shock trauma is the direct result of dissociating intense anger, fear, or pain, shame seems to exacerbate the trauma by producing a concomitant sense of *defectiveness* that makes it difficult for the individual to overcome their fears regarding the trauma. Shame can also be directly responsible for a repressing response when it is used to block intense arousal that was near climax.

More than fifty percent of my clients have suffered shock trauma events. Of the four cases examined extensively in this and the previous chapter, all four of them discover and work through shock traumas. In the previous chapter both Marion and Tory needed to address shock trauma issues. Marion's life-long struggle with masturbation and lack of orgasm can be traced to her mother walking in on her while she was masturbating. Her humiliation was extreme, especially since the mother said nothing in attempt to minimize what she saw. In Tory's case, she witnessed a man being hit by a car that then sped away. She felt it as if she had been hit. Her mother completely denied the effect it had on her daughter by shaming her response. Of the two clients whose cases are presented in this chapter, one of them – Lee, reports trauma of a lesser degree that must be addressed, and the second, Leigh, must confront a major trauma in connection with her father's molestation of her as a very young child and her early teens. In each of these cases, the discharge of pent up emotion greatly reduces their compulsivity, guardedness, and need for control. Suffice to say, any therapist doing long-term therapy is likely to encounter shock trauma events in the lives of their clients.

Shock trauma most often emerges as the root cause of prolonged resistance; or in the context of working with strong undischarged emotion discovered while using a well of pure sensation. The primary goal in working with shock trauma is the discharge of strong pent up emotion, most likely, accumulated unexpressed anger, fear, shame, and/or pain; the actual event or 'memory' is secondary. Once the emotion has been safely discharged some selves may express anger, which can be treated as a healthy venting of residual emotion, but also bear in mind that continuing anger suggests that the experience may have to be revisited until the client feels it is completely cleared.

The energies accumulated in the course of dealing with shock can be spontaneously discharged. One client shared the experience of coming home after major surgery that required a short hospital stay. As soon as he got in the car to go home he began shaking. By the time he got home his hands and fingers were numb with shaking 'cold.' Climbing into bed under numerous covers he continued to shake for a good twenty minutes when it stopped as quickly as it began and his temperature returned to normal. While in the car, he had the sudden insight that he was discharging all the accumulated undischarged fear he had been 'manfully' controlling in the days leading up to, during, and following the surgery. Getting in the car and going home seemed to mark for him that the crisis was over. *He reported having to go through a similar, less intense, 'shaking off' the following week.* But this spontaneous 'shaking off' is more difficult if the event precipitating it is familial/social and threatens to repeat itself.

I do not have a particular protocol for working with shock trauma. Its emergence is generally the unintended result of other interventions. But I am always quick to suggest that Christ help the client *safely touch* whatever it is that has riveted their attention, e.g. the red rawness; in effect, Christ is encouraged to take the lead in *reducing the intensity of the emotion* and insuring that any self fused with the Aware-ego has a garment of protection against the fear of it, which is invariably the primary impediment to discharging the emotion. The client must become free enough of fear to *consciously* connect with the emotion in question. Christ's *Light* can absorb most of it but the client must 'touch' the residual in order to name it and bring the experience fully into consciousness where Christ can further resolve it.

Convicting the Negative Bonds Defining a Relationship

In Chapter II, I described the law of connection: the idea that everything in the Mind is connected to everything else. Whereas, in-the-world a wall *separates* us from whatever is behind the wall, within the Mind a wall connects us to whatever is on the other side. Affective emotion is a proverbial wall. Hate, for example, binds us to whatever is hated. It is a particularly onerous bond since it leaves us helplessly angry with the recipient of our hate, and repetitively pollutes the Body with anger. The same is true of every other polarizing emotion. However onerous, such emotions bind us to the recipient who, in turn, continues to provoke the same negative emotions. Even fear, which seeks to evade, perpetually binds us to the source of fear.

Once a client has learned to ask Christ to convict with the power of the Holy Spirit, s/he can ask Christ to convict any relationship defined by a negative bond until it becomes one of wholesome embrace or at least neutral. As the above cases illustrate, the intervention can be applied to any 'judgment' that negatively affects the client. However *justified* a negative judgment may seem, the negative emotion it generates ends up polluting the client. The Body will suffer the Wrath of the accumulated emotion. This is true whether the emotion is generated by self-shaming a disowned self, or by perpetually resenting the imagined sense of another. In the case of relationships between self and other, Christ is asked to stand between the Aware-ego and other and simultaneously convict both.

Conviction by the power of the Holy Spirit is essentially the correction of erroneous judgments made by an ego-aspect. The judgments are considered erroneous because they condemn the client to repeatedly experiencing the negative emotions resulting from the judgment. The Holy Spirit cancels those judgments in favor of less onerous images until, finally, the image achieves an approachable, desirable, cast. *Any polarizing emotion that pollutes the Mind and Body is considered an erroneous judgment amenable to conviction by the Holy Spirit*. What I want to stress here is how quickly the client becomes willing to extend the power of this intervention to all kinds of relationships, be they self-self, self-other, or other-other. Anyone using this intervention the first few times will hesitate; it will seem as if the therapist is asking for the impossible. But each time the client allows Christ to convict with the power of the Holy Spirit, and the image changes, s/he becomes less hesitant and disbelieving and increasingly willing to extend the intervention's range.

The Forty-nine Chakra Points

Throughout this book I have introduced a number of interventions 'transliterated' from the work of others. Once the therapist has grasped the centrality of Mind and power of the *Light* and Christ channeling the Holy Spirit, just about any didactic therapy can be added to the therapist's options. This is so, because all such therapies are dependent upon conscious or subliminal images evoked by their therapy. Working with the concepts offered by Levine's discourse on shock trauma is one example. The ideas offered by the concept of forty-nine chakra points is another.

Throughout much of this work I have referred to chakras mostly in the abstract. But the need to resolve Ego polarization and defenses has led me to explore chakras imaginatively as well as conceptually. For example, from the outset, I have treated *Heart* as the combined effect of seven auric bodies connected by their heart chakras whose expression culminates in the regulation of the physical heartbeat. Stated another way, the physical heart is the primary transmitter of emotion experienced by the Body, and the physical heartbeat is directed by the combined activity of the Heart's seven auric heart chakras. Over time, I discovered that Christ could work with the Heart auric body and clear it of undue influences; that he can actually enter the Heart and clear it of shame, guilt and anger; and that if the client was willing, Christ could even use the Heart as an avenue for moving the client within hearing of the Soul's desire. Likewise, I gradually found myself encouraging clients to allow Christ to work with the Root auric body, because the literature identifies it with Body acceptance and the capacity to hear the Body's needs. It is also the chakra energy most likely to be damaged by early childhood trauma. Concurrent with those discoveries came the realization that Christ could 'penetrate' the Brow auric body and replace the Ego's willful powers of defense with the power of his discernment. Finally, in this and the previous chapter, I demonstrated the accumulation of negative emotions in the Brow, Heart and Abdominal auric bodies as a consequence of immoderate and willful desire; and the need to clear those fields of negative emotions to stave off the Wrath of their accumulation.

The in-depth clinical use of Chakra theory is beyond the scope of this book or my current expertise. But the felt need to extricate the Body from the toxic effects of accumulated emotions such as shame and fear, have pressed me to delve ever deeper into the subject. That exploration has convinced me that any reader interested in using the interventions described in this book will also need to accept the existence of auric fields of energy and acquire some knowledge of Chakra theory. Grasping Chakra theory can be difficult given its subjective nature and the heavy reliance of its expositors on psychic powers; few of us are psychic. But that is equally true of our efforts to understand the path Jesus Christ directs us to follow. Initially, we must take his direction on *faith* in order to finally *experience* it as truly pointing in the right direction. And what my interventions have demonstrated is that it is possible for 'ordinary people' to work imaginatively with auric bodies and their energy centers in ways that facilitate the healing of psychological, psychosomatic, and spiritual issues.

In Chapter I, 'Consecrating the Heart for the indwelling of the Holy Spirit' was set as a final goal of treatment in the redemption of conscience. I have satisfied myself that this has happened for my clients; that Christ can be asked to place a portion of his *Light* in the Heart of the Aware-ego and the heart chakra of any ego-aspect, which will serve as a perpetual fount of the Holy Spirit. If one imagines the first four heart chakras as separate chambers of the Heart, then the goal is for Christ to move through the first three heart chakras to the heart chakra of the Heart auric body, the fourth chamber of a four-chambered heart. I know it is possible for Christ to enter the Heart. And my sense is that his initial entry is always at the level of the Heart auric body. Likewise, Christ can be asked to take the client further into the Heart to a point where s/he can hear the Soul's desire. How far is that? Those few clients who have ventured to do this describe the 'space' as much different from the place of initial entry. Where the initial entry is generally described as a cave-like, cavernous, space, moving closer to Soul's voice is described as a brighter, warmer, more enclosed space.

The concept of 'forty-nine chakras' derives from the work of Genevieve Paulson.[40] I have not seen it reported elsewhere. Most diagrams and commentary on chakras leave the reader with the impression that there are seven major chakras. In fact, what the diagrams infer but rarely show is that there are seven major *auric bodies* each of which is primarily sustained by the energy centers identified in most chakra charts. Each of these seven auric bodies has their own set of seven energy centers connecting them to the other six auric bodies. In total, the system is actually comprised of forty-nine primary energy centers connecting and sustaining seven auric bodies, which in turn form and sustain our physical brain and body.[41] What sets Paulson's work apart from others I have read is her identification of each of the forty-nine chakra centers with points on the physical body.[42] Thus, for example, the heart chakra of the Root auric body manifests as points on the cheeks of the face just below the upper jaw, which babies are often seen to touch on the mother. Each chakra of each auric body is similarly identifiable by points on the human body. Theoretically, 'painful' areas on or near these points will correlate with an auric energy center or entire auric body that is out of balance, i.e. too open or too constricted. (A cluster of painful points on the physical body that correlate with a particular auric body will generally point to a strong unbalancing conflict that threatens to precipitate or sustain a physical or mental dis-ease.) More to point, once a correlated chakra point is identified, Christ can be asked to extract and personify whatever is unbalancing that particular energy center. This use of the points is illustrated in Tory's case described in Chapter VII, and Leigh's case in this chapter. In sum, these diagnostic points have proven helpful in the identification of ego-aspects whose defenses are disrupting the proper function of an auric body.[43]

Another source of auric dysfunction is *unwillingness*. I have not actually addressed unwillingness in this book except as regards an ego-aspect's refusal to enact a suggestion. But I have come to appreciate that it too can be *actively* used by the Ego to obstruct communication between chakras. To be *unwilling* is distinctly different from willfulness, which is the Ego's exercise of will in the context of the pride-shame axis. Unwillingness is the *active withholding* of will as in being 'unwilling to understand' (crown) or 'unwilling to see' (brow) or 'unwilling to speak' (throat) or 'unwilling to feel' (heart). It is tantamount to shaming an auric body in that it curtails that body's ability to communicate by the Ego's refusal to receive. This active withholding of receptivity is the *negative* exercise of willingness. It is most likely to block the Soul chakras (crown, brow and throat), which give conviction, emotion, and 'voice' to the expression of willingness. In effect, unwillingness can be used to 'hold in check' or prevent expression by withholding the will needed to sustain receptivity. This withholding will generally manifest as a constriction of muscular activity at related points on the body.[44] In sum, unwillingness appears to block our conscious experience of the Soul in our Mind.

Implicit throughout this book is the further assertion that: free will that is willful is not free. It is bound up by negative emotions and self-limiting beliefs that prevent the full exercise of free will. Only will unencumbered by negative emotions and denial can provide the fullest access to free will.

Images Infused with Anima or Animus

Anima and Animus are different from the Gendering archetype. They are separate and distinct archetypes. Like the Gendering archetype, an image infused with anima (soul) or animus (spirit) is not something we choose; but with Christ's help we can choose to reduce its effect or facilitate its evolution. It is not the same as the contra-sexual aspect of an Inner dyad or even a contra-sexual aspect extracted from a self in the first person. Those may provide the 'bones' for an archetypal infusion of anima or animus, but the actual constellation most often emerges spontaneously during active imagination, real life experiences, or dreams. What I want to focus on here is Christ's ability to defuse the effect or facilitate the evolution of an image constellated by either archetype. When Christ is allowed to work with these constellations they tend to become very actualized human beings that offer the client a fitting vessel for anima or animus with whom the Aware-ego can partner without risk of enthrallment. Candidates for this type of evolution can to be strongly sexual at the outset, but they can also manifest as powerful healing figures. However they manifest initially, quickly 'pairing' them with Christ is what assures their evolution. If allowed to evolve, their primary influence will be felt within the Heart and Soul chakras (e.g. crown, brow, throat, and heart chakras).

Never underestimate the power of Anima or Animus to enthrall the Ego, or Christ's ability to mediate that power. Recently, one of my client's, who I had not seen in awhile, called in something of a panic. When I saw him the next day he shared with me that he was 'making a fool of himself' with a young woman, with whom he had been exchanging text messages the past six months. The previous week they finally connected for a date. He became quite smitten very quickly. The following night he joined her and another couple at her home where he felt in complete rapport with her. He left the house anticipating many such nights to come, but then heard nothing more from her. Finally, after numerous attempts to reach her by voice mail and text, she finally replied asking him to stop all communication, without any real explanation. (We surmised that she could not handle him in addition to a current boyfriend, ex-husband, and young son.) But even his sense of humiliation was insufficient to keep him from obsessing about her. He had a cursory understanding of the idea of Anima possession. I told him his experience of this woman was an Anima infusion if ever I saw one. Rather than trying to get her out of his mind, he needed to accept that her image was being used by his Anima to connect with him. He willingly went inside and asked Christ to forge a safe connection using a portion of his *Light* to connect him with her image, heart to heart. Then I suggested that he let Christ simultaneously convict the two of them with the power of the Holy Spirit. Immediately, she changed from a girl in shorts and a ponytail to a serious woman in a business suit. He agreed that any time he thought about her in the coming week he would immediately go inside and ask Christ to continue convicting the two of them. When I saw him the following week he could report having been very productive during the week and no longer obsessing about her or wanting to contact her, even as he felt comfortable with her image in his mind. This image could quite possibly endure as an Anima image for my client. Dante's Beatrice – one of the most notable Anima figures in Western literature, was drawn from a brief, chaste, encounter with a married woman some years before Dante wrote *The Inferno*. Only time will tell. But I am convinced he would still be obsessing about her if Christ or a comparable higher power were unavailable to mediate.

Ideally, every person needs an 'other woman' or 'other man' in their life that is not their spouse, lover, or Christ image; someone who can strongly embody their Anima/Animus and channel the powers of that archetype on behalf of the individual. The image's relationship with the Aware-ego will be greatly nurtured by allowing Christ to enter into a non-competitive relationship with both. In Western culture, there are relatively few figures tailored to receive infusions of Anima/Animus energies in ways helpful to the individual. For men, the Virgin Mary and Mary Magdalene readily come to mind; but most men initially pass them over in favor of Anima figures they can sexualize. The need to initially sexualize feminine images may account for our perennial attraction to myths in which Christ is married to Mary Magdalene. For women, Christ definitely has the potential of serving as a vessel for Animus, which may also account for their attraction to the same myths. But on the whole we lack a pantheon comparable to ancient Greece and Rome, or the contemporary pantheons of Hindu and Buddhist gods and goddesses. Consequently, whatever *prima materia* is offered up by the unconscious will to be tailored to what the individual can tolerate and accept at any given time. Christ can and will facilitate its evolution and transformation. Christ's willingness to reveal his own feminine aspect is one more example of his willingness to engage us at this level.

Infused Circles

The use of infused circles evolved from my reflections on a group of exercises described in *The Healing Code* by Alexander Loyd and Ben Johnson.[45] The book echoes much of my own work. Basically, they ask their clients to use a series of exercises intended to heal an immune system compromised by stress. It is their contention, based on well documented studies, that 95 percent of all disease is stress related; that stress compromises the immune system's ability to heal. Their exercises are intended to generate a 'healing frequency' within the brain and adjunctive hormonal glands. Basically, they are drawing on the directed use of chi or prana found in therapies such as Reiki and Healing Touch. It occurred to me that Christ could provide a comparable experience for my clients. If asked, Christ can 'set' his *Light* to any emotional frequency as well including optimum flows of masculine and sexual energy, and use that specific *Light* to saturate or suffuse a circle. An ego-aspect can, in turn, step into the circle and experience that healing frequency. The effects appear to be immediate and ongoing for as long as the client chooses to remain in the circle; and renewable if s/he chooses to leave it, and then periodically return to it. With the discovery of these infused circles, I began to reword my closure statement. Instead of simply asking the client to 'return to me,' I now give them a choice: They can stay in the circle and return to me, or simply leave the circle and return to me. The first choice appears to partially anchor them in the circle even as they reorient to a face-to-face encounter.

What has most impressed me about this intervention is Christ's power and willingness in executing it. Essentially, Christ sets the frequency of emotion to be experienced. Sometimes my suggestions are quite specific; more often they are very general. But in each case it is Christ saturating the circle with a frequency intended to ameliorate whatever negativity the client is experiencing. I use this intervention repeatedly in the last sessions of Leigh, Tory, and Marion's verbatims. Space does not allow me to explore it further, but I have already begun a series of observations and further applications will be posted on my website (unredeemedconscience. org.).

Final Thoughts

Pride, and the fear of falling from pride, are the major impediments to a harmonious inner life. I am not speaking of pride as most understand it, i.e. issues of self-esteem, arrogance, idolatry, and the like, but rather the pride implicit in all Ego self-judgments: the pride that trusts self-judgment over and against the discernment of a higher power, particularly the Holy Spirit as channeled by Christ. The Ego's use of physical desire, guilt, and shame to evade further experiences of shame invariably induces Wrath. The prideful judgments required for these defenses cannot evade the Wrath of an unredeemed conscience. Prideful self-judgment is the means by which the law described by St. Paul becomes manifest: the same law whose implicit sense of lack always condemns us. Only by grace are we liberated from that law.

The thrust of these final thoughts can be summed up by the following assertion: *Any ego-aspect, whose defenses abuse the Mind or Body, must accept transformation and give way to the Aware-ego's choices.* Throughout this work I have treated ego-aspects as constellations of the Ego archetype. I have been exceedingly respectful of these constellations because they control the daily lives of most people. But in the final analysis, they are mutable images, as is amply demonstrated by Christ's transformative convictions of them. If they are destroying the Mind/Body, they must be brought to heel.

If any manifestation of the Ego is altered, the Ego is not destroyed. In fact, it will itself readily abandon any ego-aspect enthralled to shame or compromised by component dissociation, which is probably the preeminent argument for its status as an archetype. The Ego can constellate new ego-aspects as necessary. The need to reconcile or transform an ego-aspect only arises if it is abusing the Body and refuses to relinquish its control. By abusing the Body, I mean any ego-aspect's behavior that precipitates or aggravates physical dysfunction, or harbors a belief that blocks healing. To the best of my knowledge, there are very few medical maladies, other than 'acts of God,' that have proven to be *100 percent fatal*. Even where the cure is considered miraculous it can nonetheless be counted a cure. If an ego-aspect can be shown to play a role in precipitating illness – spiritual, psychological or physical, then it is argued here that it must come to accept reconciliation or transformation. It defeats its intended purpose of protecting the Mind and Body if its defenses actually abuse the Mind or Body.

When the Aware-ego first emerges in the active imagination of the individual, it is generally a fragile force easily overwhelmed by the willful emotions of the ego-aspects merged with it. As the Aware-ego learns to call on the Light and Christ, it becomes stronger in its willingness to turn to them. Initially, it turns to them out of need. But if this interaction is allowed to continue over time, a point is reached where the Aware-ego automatically turns to Christ to contend with willful ego-aspects. I, for one, can feel this change in the verbatims offered in this and the previous chapter. Even in the midst of willful angst, the Aware-ego can be heard as quite willing to call on its *Light* and higher power.

Finally, the therapist's willingness to encourage acceptance of a higher power with the power to convict with the Holy Spirit allows the client to work with Inner dyads. Every working day, therapists hear histories of parents fighting, distancing, estranging, separating, cutting off, or abandoning. For many clients, the experience is unbearably painful, and for good reason: the parental dyads that lead to those discords have also shaped the client's Inner dyads and interactional roles. The tumult without becomes the tumult within. Yet it is difficult to appreciate the full effects of such chronic discord while *the denial of bi-gendered images remains a cultural standard*. It is hard to see the trees from the forest. I do not know of any nation or people who seek harmonious interaction of their inner masculine-feminine as a cultural standard.[46] So long as we continue to support a patriarchal standard with its emphasis on "one sex - one gender" the resulting discord will be perpetuated at the expense of realizing harmonious, androgynous, interaction. While we remain mired in our cultural resistance it is impossible to know how many untold health problems, deaths, and emotional traumas are attributable to this inner discord and distortion; and we will not know until some headway is made in acknowledging our androgynous status and fostering harmonious Inner dyads. In this chapter, I have described a number of interventions for identifying and rectifying these inner relationships so they can truly reflect a full partnership. As with other interventions described in this work, Christ channeling the Holy Spirit (or comparable higher power) must be an indispensible participant in the process. At all the critical junctures, his intervention is requisite to a full partnership between opposites. That such interventions are helpful is validated by the fact that they are often instrumental in correcting the client's most significant symptomatology and interpersonal discord.

CHAPTER VIII ENDNOTES

1 Carl Jung examines anima and animus in most of his writings, as do all of his expositors.

2 I need to stress here that this conclusion concerning the sex and gender of

opposite-sexed aspects is based on a very finite set of observations, namely, the clinical population I have worked with over the years. That population has not included individuals who are transsexual or transvestite. It is possible that when this population is studied there may be found a number of instances when the sex and gender of opposite-sexed genders are much different from what I have found in my clients.

3   The interactional scene between the two aspects is often 'frozen,' not unlike the sculpting techniques developed by Moreno in Psychodrama. See Dayton, T. & Moreno, Z., (2004), *The Living Stage: A Step-by-Step Guide to Psychodrama, Sociometry and Group Psychotherapy*, Health Communications, Inc.: NY.

4   Jeffrey Raff asserts that Sophia – Divine Wisdom, is the feminine aspect of Christ; and that when Christ manifests in active imagination it is also possible for Sophia to assume a unique form as his consort. It is hard to appreciate his 'wording' out of context but the following quote captures the idea somewhat: "Although Sophia and God are two halves becoming one in the ally [Christ], Sophia does not disappear as an individual being, but she is simultaneously part of the ally. As one with the ally, Sophia ceases to be a collective goddess and becomes unique and individualized. Therefore, rather than creating a new collective image of the feminine, psychoidal alchemy personalizes the experience of that image." Raff, J., (2003), *The Wedding of Sophia: The Divine Feminine in Psychoidal Alchemy*, Nicolas-Hays, Inc.: Berwick, ME.

5   Kabbalists appear to use angels to achieve understanding and experience of the higher realms. There appears to be a long tradition wherein each sefirah is associated with a specific angel and specific manifestation of God. In Kabbalah, each sefirah is identified with one of the ten names of God identified in the Torah. Christians tend to treat the "God of the Old Testament" as singular, but Kabbalists are very clear that in Hebrew there are ten different names of God and these ten comprise the ten sefirot of the Tree of Life.

6   There is a comparable analogy in the quantum paradigm of the New physics that has supplanted Newtonian physics, at least at the level of cellular Biology and the atom. In that paradigm, the masculine would be equated with the wave and the feminine with the discrete. See Lipton, B.H. (2008), *The Biology of Belief: Unleashing the Power of Consciousness, Matter & Miracles,* Hay House, Inc.; or Malkouski, E.F. (2007), *The Spiritual Technology of Ancient Egypt: Sacred Science and the Mystery of Consciousness,* Inner Traditions.

7   I have worked predominantly with clients who were in opposite-sexed relationships or expressed that preference, as distinct from gay or lesbian relationships. While I find nothing inherently wrong with same-sexed relationships,

gender aspects of the same sex are seen as making it difficult for the sexed-image to relate intimately with an opposite-sexed spouse or lover. If I were working with a same-sexed couple or an individual with a desire to only enter into same-sexed relationships, I would be less concerned with the sex of the aspects defining the Inner dyad, unless it was adversely affecting the personality, character, or physical wellbeing of the client. In any case, I not sure that heterosexual aspects would in any way alter an individual's proclivities regarding the same sex. It is a completely untested hypothesis; and I have found no reason to test it.

8   While sexual energy may be the most common manifestation of Kundalini energy, it is by no means the optimum expression of that energy, especially in its fixation at the abdominal (2nd) chakra. Kundalini energy, which can be exceeding dangerous when aroused, is only safe when it can flow unimpeded up the spine and through the crown chakra. It seems possible for Christ to eventually clear that path; but the process is well beyond the scope of this work. It is touched upon to the extent that shame is often the major impediment to its safe rising and many of the interventions used in this work actively strive to remove that shame from any and all chakras.

9   Sexual energy can be sublimated, even spiritualized. All my readings suggest that is possible but difficult. For many in celibate religious orders success appears to be a life long struggle. Tantric and Taoist practitioners have long asserted it is possible to spiritualize sexual energy, but in every case the practitioner is obliged to begin by first arousing it and then channeling it 'upward' rather than 'outward.'

10   I generally refer to this modeling as the theory of generational recapitulation.

11   The quality of recapitulation is difficult to describe, in part because so many variations are possible. Basically, it is a grandparent's Inner dyad filtered through the experience and reactivity of the parent. The Familial persona is modeled after the Inner dyad of the parent, whose own Familial persona models the grandparent with the greatest claim on both parent and grandchild. The parent's model could be an Inner dyad comprised of grandparents or even great-grandparents. (See the footnote below for a description of the claiming process.) What complicates the process is that family secrets often oblige the individual to consciously disown a Familial persona conferred on them by the parent and extended family, but that proviso notwithstanding, tracing the process backward allows us to study the effects of the 'sins of the father for three onto four generations.' In the final analysis all such findings are probably immaterial. They tell us what Christ and the Holy Spirit are empowered to transform, but in no way does this history place limits on that power. Where this understanding may be of value is in appreciating

what Christ accomplishes when he convicts the relational dynamics of Inner dyads found in parents, grandparents, and great grandparents.

12   Over the years, I have developed a number of hypotheses to account for the differing attitudes of parents toward their children and spouses. These hypotheses have helped me to understand why a particular child is favored or disfavored by a parent, or a particular child is seen as the black-sheep of the family, or "a chip off the old block", etc. These hypotheses were developed before I discovered Relational authority. The hypotheses are introduced here because they serve to support a particular hypothesis concerning Relational authority, namely, that most children are delegated a Familial persona characteristic of a grandparent.

The following hypotheses are identified as 'familial' to distinguish them from birth order hypotheses documented by Toman. (Toman, W., 4th Edition (1992), *Family Constellation: Its Effects on Personality and Social Behavior*, Springer Publishing Co.). Where the familial hypotheses have proven helpful vis-à-vis Relational authority is in highlighting the need to focus on grandparents as well as parents in both the diagnostic and intervention phases. The hypotheses can be summed up in the idea that parents raise grandchildren. Every child is the blood relation of four families represented by the four grandparents. Each of those four families seeks to continue their family of origin (their "line", "name", legacy, heritage) through their grandchildren; and our culture appears to reinforce a claiming process whereby each child can be claimed for a particular family. Under normal circumstances, this process favors a modified patriarchal norm. The first-born child, regardless of sex, will be most identified with the father's side of the family. The father's own birth order will determine whether his first-born is most identified with the paternal grandfather or grandmother. Very likely, one reason for the enduring popularity of British royalty is that it models this claiming process: the first born, regardless of sex, becomes king or queen. Interestingly, this modified form supplants an absolute patriarchal norm that gave priority to the first-born son regardless of birth order - as was the case in the Old Testament. The parents' second born child will be most identified with either the maternal grandfather or maternal grandmother. Which one depends upon the mother's birth order. (This assignment of the second born to the maternal side tacitly recognizes that no mother is likely to invest her life in raising children solely for the perpetuation of the husband's families.) This claiming sequence is repeated back and forth until all four grandparental families have been assigned one child to continue their line. The sequence commences again with the fifth child. A number of subsidiary hypotheses have been found to modify this sequence. For example, parents generally count abortions, miscarriages and stillbirths in determining who belongs to which family. (Not infrequently, such deaths also highlight cutoffs between the parent and a particular grandparent.) The parity issue is also reflected in second marriages. If, for example, a father has children by a first marriage, then divorces, and marries a woman with no children, then the first born of that second marriage will be hers to claim on behalf of one of her two families of origin. Out of wedlock children would also be counted in this process, though the counting may be a secret that only manifests itself in a seemingly out-of-sequence assignment.

The claiming process described above often takes place even before the child is born. Name selection is a good example. But whatever the infant's name, within the first few weeks of birth s/he will be seen as like certain members of the immediate and extended family. Often, the child will know their identity with a particular grandparent from an early age and may show a partiality toward them if they are living and in the good graces of the parents. But note that sometimes the identity can be negative in the sense that the child is identified with a particular family member who has brought shame upon the family, or whose relationship with the parent is strained, estranged or cutoff. If a child and parent both share a primary Familial persona with a particular grandparent, and that grandparent is part of a traumatizing Interactional template (discussed later in the chapter), then the child is likely to replicate that *relationship*, i.e. act it out in their own choice of marital partners. Under normal circumstances, the Interactional template most likely to control a child's choice of mates will be the one generated by his or her parents. The exception is identification with a parent-grandparent legacy wherein the parent felt obliged deny their Familial persona shaped by grandparent.

If a parent - say the father, was traumatized by the parent who shaped his Familial persona, then any of his children who are identified with that grandparent is likely to replicate the traumatizing relationship of the grandparent. As an adult, the child will enact the role of the grandparent with whom it is identified and choose a mate to act out the role of the other grandparent. The reason for this appears to be the parent's need to deny the Familial persona shaped by the grandparent. Any disowned persona has a very high probability of being projected into the child identified with the grandparent.

I would also note, that even though a child, say a son, is identified with a maternal grandfather, this in no way precludes identification with his own father. The old adage that we marry our mothers, or our fathers, is frequently born out in examinations of the Interactional template. A woman who marries a man like her father and then identifies a son as like her father, is also reinforcing the son's identity with his own father. But note, a girl can 'marry her mother' as well as her father. If she is identified with her grandmothers, then she is likely to marry a man like her father. But a first-born daughter identified with her paternal grandfather is likely to exhibit an Inner dyad with a strong masculine cast and likely to marry a man more like her mother.

The above hypotheses provide an added dimension to birth order probabilities and can often account for tensions between parent and child. Many clients spend their lives attempting to be 'not-like' a particular parent or grandparent who has shamed the family, only to discover disowned selves acting like that person or married to someone just like them. Interventions at the archetypal level permit the client to become like that parent or grandparent in healthy way. As ever, the overall thrust of my work is to "honor the parent," and the best way I have found to do that - via Relational authority, is to heal the parent's Inner dyad rather than reject it. What familial birth order hypotheses highlight is the occasional need to focus on the sexed-images of grandparents as well as parents. This is particularly germane when the client appears to idealize their parents or themselves while perceiving their spouse or a particular child in a very bad light. In such cases, they have projected the disowned identity of a grandparent upon the spouse or child. Healing the grandparent's image can redeem those projections.

13   See 'claiming process described in preceding footnote.

14   The paradigm for this intervention is derived from Kabbalah. They assume we integrate masculine and feminine qualities at all levels of being. The feminine, defined by the pillar of Severity, provides the "container" or "definition" for masculine force and power. It provides structure, form, and limits for masculine energy. As the setter of limits, the feminine manifests as the Wrath of God at the level of body, but not only that. The feminine also provides judgment, logic, feeling and thinking. At the highest level it provides Reason. This Pillar of Severity is best thought of as the pillar of form, which shapes, defines and limits the active energies of yang power and force. The masculine Pillar of Mercy is best thought of as affective, emotive, an active energizing force. In effect, feeling evaluates and passes judgment on affect and emotion. Put another way, the masculine pillar provides energy; the feminine pillar provides its definition or container. Without feminine definition, masculine energy dissipates; without renewing energy, feminine definition becomes rigid, dried up, arid. Clearly, each requires the other. In clinical practice, I share these distinctions with clients as they work with masculine-feminine dyads. The reader is referred back to Chapter one for a more detailed discussion.

15   Energy is not a formless state. Heat is not the same as electromagnetism or the power of gravity. New forms of definition generally require new kinds of channeled energy.

16   I have not had the opportunity to explore the Inner dyads of gay/lesbian clients. Such clients may have a preference for same-sexed Inner dyads. If that were so and they had no desire to alter that configuration I would certainly respect their choice. My hope is that other clinicians - who work with gays or lesbians - will be able to explore the Inner dyads of their clients and shed light on any differentiating dynamics.

17   The idea of androgyny remains a heated issue even among Jungians. To quote Stevens: "several writers agree with this stance [androgyny]...and suggest that the time has come to reject Jung's generalizations concerning the Logos qualities of male consciousness and the Eros qualities of female consciousness, and to endow everyone, regardless of sex, with an animus *as well as* an anima: anima and animus, should be equally accessible to all, whether they be men or women. Understandably, these developments have promoted interest in the notion of androgyny, which, since primordial times, has been represented by the symbol of the hermaphrodite (p.215)" Stevens goes on to argue against this proposition believing that biology as well as psychology dictates the differences between sexes. My own studies support the analysts that advocate for androgyny. See Stevens, A.,(1990), *On Jung*, Routledge: New York.

18   A series of papers on this issue – both pro and con – can be found in Stein, M., Editor (1991), *Gender and Soul in Psychotherapy*, Chiron Clinical Series.

19   The resurrected Christ, who incarnates as the Holy Spirit birthed by the Virgin Mary, is clearly mythic in aspect, but considerably more powerful than mere archetype as his progenitor is the Spirit of God. But the historical, pre-resurrected Christ would have an indeterminate Inner dyad, to be determined by the archetypal energies flowing through the perceiver.

20   I have not worked with gay or transvestite clients vis-à-vis Relational authority, so I have no idea what effect, if any, these interventions would have on their gender issues or same-sexed preferences. These interventions are not expected to alter sexual proclivities, only to extend the range of object choice to *include* adult, non-incestuous, heterosexual relationships that are mutually enhancing. I personally have no problem with gay and lesbian relationships. I am comfortable working with them in individual and couples therapy and expect them to retain their sexual proclivity throughout therapy.

21   These and kindred interventions are described in Appendix I. Prolonged sexual abuse is likely to create a potentially large number of ego-aspects with generally negative responses to sexual arousal, i.e. fear, anger, despair, terror, etc. Sexual interventions offer a way of decoupling the sexual energy from the events and emotions, and allowing the ego-aspects to 'start over.'

22   The Psychoanalyst, Robert Stroller provides some anecdotal evidence for this argument. See Stoller, R.J., (1985), *Observing the Erotic Imagination*, Yale University Press: New Haven. It is Stoller's contention that we all construct scripts that are meant to undo childhood traumas, conflicts, and frustrations by converting these past painful experiences to present fantasized triumphs.

23   With the advent of the Internet anonymity, pornography has become pervasive. Morally, I make no judgment of it except where it involves children, which I cannot countenance under any circumstance. Romantic novels and tabloids appear to serve the same – though socially more acceptable, purpose. Both provide the viewer/reader with fantasy material that uses *desire* to bring together otherwise painful or shamefully conflicted relationships.

24   The disruption of marital ties in a child's formative years is likely to result in an increasing need to compensate discordant Inner dyads with a greater degree of imaginative sexual bonding. Our continuing high rate of divorce among families with children and the rampant expansion of pornography on the Internet seems to support that thesis. I do not point this out as a reason for couples to stay in bad marriages. Either option places the child between a rock and hard place. I note it to highlight the need to correct the dissonance created by the Gendering archetype.

25   Appendix II addresses and formalizes the idea of consciously choosing a higher power. My own conversion was 'more impulsive.' Shortly before I went up to the alter to be prayerfully offered an 'indwelling' of the Spirit, I made the conscious decision that the Spirit, in turn, would commit me to Christ as my higher power. Since that day, Christ has been a daily image in my Mind.

26   There is one other variable that I do not address here, but I do address in Appendix II. Most people treat 'God the Father' as their higher power. Most often, when they use the word 'God,' they are not referring to Christ or an ineffable expression of the Godhead, but rather 'God the Father.' That sense of God is rarely experienced as a direct and loving channel of the Holy Spirit. The unreflected choice of 'God the Father' as a higher power is more likely to impede the flow of the Holy Spirit than offer it lovingly and unconditionally. Christ will offer it when he is asked as often as he is asked. But if he is not present in consciousness as a client's incarnation of God, he can only do so with conscious intentionality. Where the client becomes aware that s/he has unreflectively chosen 'God the Father' as his or her higher power, it is possible to choose again. A ritual for 'choosing again' is offered in Appendix II.

27   Windrider, K. & Sears, G., (2006), *Deeksha: The Fire from Heaven,* New World Library. Based on the description given on the back cover, I could not resist reading the book: "On a trip to India's Golden City, psychotherapist Kiara Windrider discovered that enlightenment – whether called Christ consciousness or that experienced by Buddha – is not based on a particular teaching, morality, or effort, but is in fact a neurobiological process. Under the guidance of Sri Bhagavan

and Sri Amma, he learned that over time, humans developed a membrane that separates their individuality from the collective consciousness. Deeksha – the transfer of enlightened energy from person to person – begins to puncture this membrane, allowing humans to experience oneness and divine grace. In Deeksha, Windrider describes his journey to enlightenment, and explains how readers can experience it as well – and how they can pass the gift on to other seekers. The book also includes seven case studies of others who have experienced Deeksha, an interview with Bhagavan, and two essays on the science of Deeksha." Given a careful reading of this book, I could not gainsay its claims. I was struck with the fact that the authors and case studies described people who had been intensely searching and meditating for a good number of years, and that the repetition of deekshas brought intense highs and deep lows. It is not a free ride. You still have to go through a period of 'purification' requiring intense inner work. Of further note, since reading this book others have been published which now call the process 'the oneness blessing.' See, for example, Ardagh, A., (2007), *Awakening into Oneness: The Power of Blessing in the Evolution of Consciousness,* Sounds True: Boulder, CO.

28   Come Holy Spirit, come/ Come as your fire and burn us/ Come as your rain and cleanse us/ Come as your light and reveal us/ Convict us, convert us, and consecrate us/ Until we are wholly thine. Amen.

29   I would like to credit Dr. Issam Nemeh's work for inspiring this intervention. See Zagrans, M. P. (2010), *Miracles Every Day: The Story of One Physician's Inspiring Faith and the Healing Power of Prayer*, Doubleday.

30   See Raff, J., (2003), The Wedding of Sophia: The Divine Feminine in Psychoidal Alchemy, Nicolas-Hays, Inc.: Berwick, ME

31   Ardagh, A., (2007), *Awakening into Oneness: The Power of Blessing in the Evolution of Consciousness,* Sounds True: Boulder, CO.

32   As I noted in my introduction to this chapter, it was reading about Deekshas that prompted me to have clients begin to ask Christ to convict images with the power of the Holy Spirit. See Windrider, K. & Sears, G., (2006), Op. cit.

33   Ardagh, A. (2007), op.cit.

34   This is a quote from the movie *Zorba the Greek* based on a novel of the same name by Nikos Kazantzakis.

35   I have had other clients express similar fears after their initial experience

of being convicted with the power of the Holy Spirit. It is as if the world of Spirit becomes much more real to them – good spirit as well as bad spirit; and not unlike Christ's experience of being tempted in the desert following his own baptism by John the Baptist.

36   The Hawaiians have what they call the ho'oponopono method, which means to set something right. The mantra for doing this is: I am sorry, please forgive me, I thank you, and I love you.

37   This point is identified as such by a Chakra therapist whose work I discuss in the last section of this book. See Paulson, G.L. (2002), *Kundalini and the Chakras,* Llewellyn Publications.

38   Ira Progoff was a Jungian psychotherapist, popular in the 1980's and 90's, who promoted self-discovery by having clients keep daily journals. See Progoff, I. (1992), *At a Journal Workshop: Writing to Access the Power of the Unconscious and Evoke Creative Ability*, Tarcher.

39   Levine, P.E. & Frederick, A. (1997), Waking the Tiger: Healing Trauma: The Innate Capacity to Transform Overwhelming Experiences, North Atlantic Books.

40   Paulson, G.L. (2002), op. cit.

41   Some authors actually identify ten chakras – three above the crown chakra, which makes the theory comparable to Kabbalah's ten sefirah found in the Tree of Life.

42   Barbara Brennan, who I have referenced in other chapters also provides excellent descriptions of the auric bodies and their concomitant chakras, but as far as I can determine makes no reference to physical counterpoints on the body. See, for example, Brennan, B. & Smith, J.A. (1988), *Hands of Light: A Guide to Healing Through the Human Energy Field*, Bantam.

43   My clients regularly report allergies and colds of varying duration. When these are closely examined they frequently point to a conflict between head and heart that manifests in the throat (5th chakra) by coughing, soreness, rawness, etc. It is relatively easy to ask Christ to draw out the source of the irritation, place it in a circle in front of the Aware-ego and identify its emotional quality. A recent example will illustrate the process. Joan has suffered from severe respiratory conditions since childhood. She has been treated for 'allergies' all of her adult life. I always know when she arrives for a session because of her distinctive cough heard from

the waiting area. I ask Joan to focus on her throat, particularly the phlegm she is constantly attempting to cough up that keeps irritating her airway. I have her imagine that if the phlegm were an emotion, what emotion would it feel like? "I feel resentment toward my son." I interpret this to mean that 'she doesn't want to feel that and keeps trying to clear it out, but some part remains resentful, and has been for a long time. I suggest that she use concentric circles to separate out the part that generates the resentment aka phlegm. "It is an image of me with a big frown on my face." I ask where it holds the power to keep generating all this resentment. "In my head, all of my sinuses." I ask if 'Frown' is masculine? When she affirms that it seems to be, I suggest that she ask Christ to extract the resentment from out of her brow and objectify it in a circle in front of Frown. "It is a black blob." I ask her how he thinks that black blob is affecting his brain? "Painful, like a wet blanket." I ask if he has ever known his vision free of this resentment? If he is willing, Christ will clean the *accumulated* resentment so he can visualize free of it for a little while. "He is willing for Christ to do that." What, I ask, does the black blob look like when it is not filled to overflowing? "It is a resentment that I could not control things. I work hard at controlling. I was sick so much as a child. I was kept home most of the year in third grade. I got so bored and resentful that I was sick." What was causing the sickness? Did resentment or anger contribute to it? "I wailed when my mother left me in the hospital for a little while to get a bite to eat." I ask if resentment is attempting to cope with her felt lack of nurture. (The mother went back to work when Joan was a year old leaving her in the care of a black maid; but she would come home to check on her daughter when she was sick.) I suggest that perhaps Resentment uses its anger to cloud his mind to cover up what he needs but does not know how to get. Then I suggest that if he released the denial of his need into the ocean, Christ could offer him its satisfaction. "What he needs to release looks like a stone lying on my heart", to which I add 'and blocking the upward flow of heart energy.' I suggest that she ask Christ to remove the stone, place it in the ocean, and watch it dissolve. "He has done that and now the frown is gone from my image." I suggest that she now ask Christ to return him to the beach and see how he responds. "He is looking renewed and sees hope all around him." I suggest that she ask Christ to give this masculine sense of herself the necessary feminine connection needed to maintain his sense of hope. I further suggest that she let Christ plant the seed of fruition in the heart so he can eventually realize that hope.

44   Loyd, A. with Johnson, B. (2011), *The Healing Code*, Grand Central Life and Style.

45   India may be a notable exception. While strongly Patriarchal, their religions and culture have embodied an inner masculine-feminine mythos for millennia; and they are described as a happy people, their abject poverty notwithstanding.

APPENDIX I
WORKING WITH SEXUAL ENERGY

Allow me to begin on the light side: A world-renowned sexologist was the keynote speaker at a conference. The person introducing him went on at great length about the speaker's credentials, laboriously so, to the extent that people were beginning to leave. Finally, the person introducing him allowed the speaker to talk. The speaker got up, went to the podium, and said, "Ladies and gentlemen, it gives me pleasure. Thank you and good evening". Then the speaker left the podium and the stage.

Most human beings are smart enough to realize that sex can result in procreation. But what prompts us (and every other species) to engage in its myriad manifestations is desire: the pleasure of arousal and satisfaction. And that desire is exceedingly powerful. Advertisers have been using it to sell just about everything under the sun from time immemorial. Sexual desire may result in impregnation, but that is not what drives us to arouse it time and again. Because the desire is so powerful and arousing stimuli so pervasive, a normal person is hard pressed to avoid it, even if the arousal has been associated with painfully shameful events. And that is the case for a number of my clients whose earliest experiences were highly conflictual, painful, and shaming. That kind of early experience can generate two extremes and everything in between. At one end of the continuum are individuals who shamelessly reenact those early experiences of arousal. At the other end are individuals who strive to suppress their sexual desire to avoid its painful associations. Most of my sexually abused clients fall into the latter category. For them, even solitary activities such as masturbation are painful.

Several years ago I was able to develop a set of interventions that have proven helpful to a number of clients who were severely sexually abused as children. By 'severely sexually abused', I mean children who were used sexually from infancy onward by a number of adults including parents, grandparents, and strangers; and forced to engage in various cultic practices that are beyond the pale of most peoples' imaginations. The wonder is that they even survived to tell it. By and large, my clients have not acted out their sexual travail. If anything, they are - for the most part, asexual. Arousal brings them too close to the memories that first stimulated arousal, so they tend to avoid it.

One of my earliest uses of this series of interventions was with a client, Menta, who had stopped seeing me a year earlier. She is MPD and used an Inner Self Helper called the Positive Voice as her higher power. We worked together for several years. She came to see me about a year after we stopped meeting on a regular basis. In that session, which occurred at the beginning of the month, I told her of recent work with other clients in helping them to heal from sexual abuse and told her that I would send her a protocol via e-mail, if she was interested. I knew she was strapped financially and could not afford to continue seeing me on a regular basis. A day later I received an e-mail from her requesting the protocol, which is given below. This is what I sent to her:

The following intervention addresses the sexual abuse of your many alters. Some of the alters enjoyed – took pleasure in, their early and later experiences, but the majority of alters associate sexual arousal with physical pain, fear, shame, and/or dread. For those, sexual arousal has repeatedly re-evoked those same negative emotions since they have no other experiences to counterbalance the negative.

This intervention is built on the premise that sexual energy can be treated as *separate and distinct* from the contents it infuses and from any emotions experienced concomitantly with it. When the sexual energy is aroused it becomes *arbitrarily* attached to stimuli associated with the arousing events. No particular content or emotion is an inherent quality of sexual energy, except the desire to arouse it from time to time. Sexual energy can be attached to a myriad of contents, which accounts for the wide range of things that arouse people. Further, while the associated stimuli are often considered pleasurable, they can also be painful and/or extremely conflictual. Sexual energy does not make a moral judgment about what contents will arouse it, or what it will be associated with when aroused. When aroused, sexual energy simply infuses concurrent events. Some events can evoke pain or fear as well as arousal; and those too will be re-experienced when arousal is re-experienced, *even if the circumstances of the second arousal have nothing to do with the first.* Thus, a second arousal can be entirely pleasurable and free of all fear and pain, but nonetheless *evoke fear and pain in other alters who were created to cope with a previous arousal that was painful in the extreme.*

Because some alters have positive associations to sexual arousal this intervention must be completely voluntary. It is only offered to alters who desire to be free of the sexual arousal previously paired with negative emotions such as pain, fear, shame and the like. Basically, the intervention severs the connection between negative emotions and the sexual energy that re-energizes those emotions via the memory. The memories remain intact and can be recovered, if necessary. But lacking a sexual and emotional connection, the alter is no longer forced to cope with the memory every time the body is sexually aroused. The alter will no longer have to dread sexual arousal for fear of re-evoking all the painful emotions that might be associated with it. Those connections will have been severed. Basically, the associations that are severed are concomitant *emotional connections and the involuntary arousal of sexual energy.* The mental contents are left intact, though they will be harder to recover if sexual energy has played a major role in re-evoking them.

Of note there are two 'sources' of sexual arousal, which are capable of re-evoking negative emotions and involuntary arousal. Sexual arousal can be experienced as residing in someone else (e.g. your father or a priest) or within yourself; that is, as something forced on you rather than something you voluntarily evoke as pleasurable. The intervention is effective in both cases: it severs the connection to sexual energy in 'the other' as well as the self, if the self experienced it as conflictual. Effectively, 'the other' becomes neutered. If experienced by the self, then the self voluntarily forgoes the arousal.

Here is how the intervention will proceed. The Positive Voice will create a circle with her *Light*. Those alters who want to sever sexual arousal with negatively charged memories will enter the circle with their *Light*. Each alter can only enter the circle if they have a portion of the *Light*. Entering the circle with the *Light* provides an explicit expression of willingness to separate from the sexual energy as well as any negative emotions associated with the energy. Some alters may come forward and ask you for a portion of your *Light* in order to participate. Don't hesitate to give it to them, even if you do not know their memories. They may also obtain a portion of the *Light* from other alters. None need your permission to enter the circle. They all have free will and will enter the circle of their own volition or not at all. The first time you do this intervention there may a lot of alters, or only a few, who want to be free of the painful experiences associated with sexual arousal. Note, that this intervention can be repeated as often as you deem necessary so it is not critical that all enter the circle at this time. Some may hold back and watch what happens. Others may choose to retain all of their associations intact as they experience them as pleasurable on the whole. This intervention is for alters – most of them children, who have experienced sexual arousal, primarily in others, as painful in some way.

When all the alters who elect to participate in this intervention are in the circle drawn by the Positive Voice, then you will ask her to draw two more circles on top of the first one. That done, you will ask her to use the second circle to separate all of the negative emotions associated with their abuse memories. When this is done you will ask her to separate the sexual energy attached to the memories, using the third circle. In effect, there are now three distinct circles. One circle holds the alters and their memories. Beside it, a second circle holds the negative emotions associated with their abuse memories. And on the other side of the alters' circle will be the circle holding the sexual energy previously attached to the memories. It needs to be stressed that sexual energy is never treated as negative. It can be strongly associated with negative emotions but of itself it is always seen as neutral or positive.

First let us deal with the negative emotions. The best way I have found to address these is to ask the Positive Voice to enter that circle and absorb those emotions with her *Light*. Essentially, she dispels their power by transforming them back into pure white light and returning them to the source of all light, or by absorbing them into her *Light,* which is seen as having an equally purifying effect. Basically, I would let the Positive Voice use whatever she deems best. For your part, you need to observe a noticeable change within the circle. Since these emotions generally manifest as dark colored energies, usually the circle 'clears' as a result of the Positive Voice's actions. At that point the circle itself can be dissolved.

Next, you ask the Positive Voice to focus on the circle containing sexual energy. It is difficult to say much about it beforehand. Sometimes, the energy appears contaminated. This must be a judgment call. Basically, it has to look 'healthy' to you. If it does, leave well enough alone. If it does not, then ask the Positive Voice to enter it and remove all contaminants until it attains a healthy color and dynamism. The sexual energy will remain separate from the alters in the center circle. Hereafter, they will access it in one of two ways. They can divide their *Light* and have the Positive voice place a portion of it directly into the circle containing sexual energy. This is probably the safest way of accessing the sexual energy since the *Light* will only permit a safe flow from the circle to the alter. The alter can also access the energy by self-stimulation of the clitoris and other erogenous zones, e.g. masturbation, or by mutual stimulation with another partner.

Accessing sexual energy with the *Light* provides the alter with access to its health benefits without the alter having to arouse it. A number of esoteric sects treat sexual energy as health giving and life sustaining. The two that come to mind are Taoism and Tantric Yoga. For that reason, it might be a good idea to encourage these alters to use the safe connection afforded by the *Light* even if they have no interest in self-stimulation of mutual stimulation with a partner.

Menta, if you use this intervention I would very much appreciate your written description of what goes on inside when you do, as well as a follow-up in a week or two of what you experience as a consequence of doing it. Please feel free to ask me any questions regarding it, before, during or after.

I receive several e-mails from Menta over the next month. During the month Menta repeatedly uses the intervention to very good effect. What follows is a portion of an early e-mail report.

I am doing this intervention again even though I have now done it several times. I see the Positive Voice and she draws a circle with her light. I ask if any alters want to come into the circle and there are a few. They each have a portion of their own *Light*. The Positive Voice draws two more circles. She takes from the alters their negative emotions attached to their sexual energy and puts it into the second circle. She then takes the sexual energy and puts into the third circle. The second circle is black and grey and she puts her *Light* into the circle. I wait for several seconds and slowly the color begins to change. Usually at this time everything turns clear but right now there are other colors underneath the black and gray. I am not sure what this means. The colors seem to be red and yellow. The Positive Voice still has her *Light* in this circle and it becomes pink. The other circle with sexual energy is yellow but dull. The Positive Voice puts her *Light* into the sexual circle and the color becomes orange and then changes to pink. The last few times I did this procedure the sexual energy circle was usually orange. I don't know what it means. I am just writing what I see right now.

Right now I feel safe and clean. Dr. Vreeland I want to tell you briefly what I have experienced after using this procedure a few times. I have masturbated a couple of times since then. Each time I have noticed that either myself or an alter will access the sexual energy using their *Light* while I am touching my clitoris and immediately I feel a tremendous surge of sexual energy and the orgasm has been even more dramatic for me. Both of these times I did not have the shameful feeling that I once had when I would masturbate and I have not cried.

In the remainder of this e-mail Menta shares her experiences with a male friend, which are decidedly positive. The fact that she is even dating is major for her. At the end of the month she asks for another appointment. The verbatim of that session is given below. I touched on Menta's case in a previous chapter. She was raised in an intercity slum and attended Catholic Parochial grade schools. Unfortunately, a group of nuns and priests at her school abused her, her sister, and a number of other students. One reason why she had so much difficulty evoking a Christ image stemmed from the priests' telling her that they were Christ's representatives on earth. She believed them. I mention this only because she references it in the session. In years following this series of interventions Menta would keep me updated by e-mail. Her transformation has been phenomenal. She has been able to forgive those men and women as well as her parents. In the process she was finally able to invite Christ to partner with her Positive voice. But I am getting well ahead of her story. Our last session took place in my office a month after she started using the interventions.

Menta. Menta has been making considerable progress on her own; she has scheduled one more session to 'touch base.' Most recently, she has been using the intervention to address a herpes outbreak. She discovered two alters who were experiencing her current sexual relationship (with a man older than herself) in the context of earlier abuse with an older man. She is able to help these two separate the sexual energy and dispel the negative emotions associated with the memories. Next I suggest that she might ascertain if their are any alters who seem resistant to separating sexual energy from abuse memories. The Positive voice helps her separate them. She discovers a number of child alters. The one who speaks on their behalf – a boy, says they felt all the sexual stuff she has been doing lately was like what they did with the priests and nuns. I suggest to the Menta that she let the Positive Voice separate the sexual energy from the children but not the emotions associated with the memories. When this is done the boy alter says he feels numb; that is the effect of separating the sexual energy. Before he had felt 'love' from the priests and nuns when they paid attention to him. Apparently they have not been able to distinguish between sexual interest and love interest on the part of the adults. I have her ask the Positive Voice if it would be possible for her to give them a taste of her sense of love. Of course. But some of the child alters now express fear of the Positive Voice. Some of the children told the priests and nuns about this Inner Self Helper, who was present even when the Menta was a child, and the religious said that such an inner voice was wrong, bad, of the devil. So some of the alters have a real fear of her that hurts their stomachs. I suggest that they use their *Lights* to provide garments of protection. This only helps a little. Next I suggest that the Positive Voice contain the priests and nuns in the circle that have the power to threaten these alters. Without my suggesting it, she adds her parents and an ex-male friend. I have the Positive Voice enter the circle and remove their power to threaten the children, but nothing much changes. When I ask why not, Menta replies that one other is missing – the therapist who sexually abused her, though again, his sexual interest had been confused with a love interest. (Her initial reason for coming to me was to help her report that therapist.) When his authority is also removed the children become willing for the Positive Voice to enter the circle. I first have her separate the negative emotions from the children. Not surprisingly, that circle is full of darkness. Next I suggest that the Positive voice enter the children's circle, and that each child who is willing touch their *Light* to her *Light* to safely experience the love she would offer them. At this point Menta becomes quietly emotional. She says the children are tearful, but they are good tears. When things settle a bit I suggest that the Positive Voice temporarily leave the circle to dispel the negative emotions in the other circle, which she does without fanfare. Then I suggest that she return to the children and that Menta return to me, as we are well over the time.

The Basic Thesis

The basic thesis for working with sexual energy is exactly as I described it to Menta in her protocol: *every memory and emotion associated with sexual energy is arbitrary*. The energy and any associated emotions can be separated from the memory. Once separated, Christ can be asked to absorb/dissolve the negative emotions. If necessary, Christ can also be asked to purify the circle containing sexual energy until it is perceived as 'healthy' – as perceived by the client. Thereafter, the affected selves can reconnect with the sexual energy by placing a portion of their *Light* into the circle containing it, or by arousing themselves thereby creating new memories. The primary argument supporting this thesis is the immense variety of associations that arouse people. The energy is universal; but what arouses is a function of the individual's life experiences. Different experience, different arousal. Clinically, the thesis is supported by a number of clients who have benefited from Christ's *Solve et coagula*.

While we can easily assume that sexual energy is instinctual, in human beings ego-aspects decisively mediate it. Unfortunately, many of those ego-aspects seek to repress it from fear of shame or pain. I would certainly not begrudge a culture its need to control procreative sexuality. But I do feel its citizens will be better served when it stops using shameful repression, in lieu of education. Sexual energy cannot be repressed with impunity. Like water flowing through rock, it will find a path. Repression invariably generates the accumulation of toxic shame by narrowing the individual's choices to shameful desires.

In my clinical experience, the Christ within us is clearly on the side of releasing sexual energy from shame and pain; and given the high incidence of sexual abuse in our culture, he has a lot of work ahead of him. But there are many more than those who have been overtly abused. If one considers the consequences of sexual repression – the toxic accumulation of shame, then all too many people are in need of release.

A Confession

This book has barely addressed sexuality. I do not mean its abuses or biology, but rather its soulful nature. Tantric Yoga and Taoism probably come closest to describing it's potential, but both – based on my own limited reading – fail to provide me a way of consummating my relationship with Christ. Some Jewish scholars consider The Song of Solomon the holiest of holy books. Gnostics, such as Tau Malachi, strive to understand Christ's nature by partnering him with Mary Magdalene. Christian mystics such as John of the Cross and St. Teresa of Avila encourage us to see Christ as the bridegroom. Thankfully, while I still draw breath all things are possible.

APPENDIX II

WHO IS YOUR HIGHER POWER? [1]

Any discussion of higher powers will be biased from the outset by the beliefs of the writer. For that reason, the least I can do is share them. They are expressed in the following prayer, which I strive to say each morning: "Almighty, ineffable source of all being and non-being. Gracious Father and Gracious Mother of all creation who by the power of the Holy Spirit conceived our Lord, Jesus Christ. Enter, Jesus, my Heart, and be the God of my personal salvation. Thy will be done on earth as it is in heaven. Give us this day our daily bread. Forgive us our trespasses as we forgive those who trespass against us. Save us in time of trial. Deliver us from all evil. For thine is the kingdom, and the power, and the glory, forever and ever. Amen."

One day, I was prompted to ask a client if she would name her higher power. I was surprised by the answer. For the past several years she had evoked an image of Christ every time she *went inside*, so I honestly expected her to name him. But without hesitation she named God. I asked if she could be more specific, how did she imagine or think of God? "It is God, the Almighty, omnipotent…God the Father… our Father in Heaven." Over time, I would ask most of my clients this same question, and with few exceptions, they gave me the same answer: God the Father. Not Christ, but God the Father. In their therapy, all of them regularly called on their image of Christ channeling the Holy Spirit to effect changes in their lives; but this reliance on Christ notwithstanding, their higher power remained God the Father, *the first named person* of the Holy Trinity.

Theologically, there is no '*first person*' of the Trinity. The Father does not precede the Son in power or precedence. Father, Son, and Holy Spirit are three co-eternal *persons* comprised of the same spiritual substance.[2] As co-equal manifestations of God, their relationship is circular not hierarchical. But as one client observed, practically all of the formalized prayers in church liturgies – especially the Nicene Creed, explicitly or implicitly address 'God the Father.' There are very few prayers addressed to Christ. We are Christians who pray to 'God the Father.' In no small measure this is so because, while he lived on earth, Christ instructed us to pray to Abba 'who art in heaven.' Variants of the Lord's Prayer are offered in two different gospels.[3] Both begin by addressing 'Our Father in heaven.'

Any religion that traces its origin to the Old Testament needs to accept that YHWH – or the equivalent name, and 'God the Father' – as a *person* of God, are two different experiences. YHWH is ineffable, inexpressible, and ultimately unimaginable; YHWH is without form and substance and all form and substance; YHWH is the Godhead, the uncaused cause, the first cause, the source of all being and non-being. In contrast, 'God the Father' is a godly father, who is sometimes given the attributes of a mother, but in his default mode is definitely a father. YHWH is both all-substance and non-substance. 'God the Father' is a particular manifestation of the substance. In contrast, Jesus Christ is asserted by the four gospels and Letters of Paul to be the living incarnation of YHWH.[4]

In Jewish cosmology, any incarnation of God *that is not the totality of YHWH* is an unpardonable sin.[5] Before Christ, YHWH was assigned many human attributes in the Old Testament, feminine as well as masculine, but no image. Even the Old Testament's primary *name* for God – YHWH, is not spoken out of respect for the awesomeness of the name. Some Jewish scholars would argue that we no longer know how to say the name as it was only verbalized once a year in the Temple, which was destroyed in 60 C.E. When YHWH's name is read in the Synagogue, this name of God is called *Adonai* – Lord; and in conversation, most devout Jews refrain from using either name when referring to God. Instead, they use HaShem, which means 'the name.' There are five primary names for God in the Old Testament, and numerous variants.[6] None of them refer to YHWH as father. Insofar as early Christians equated 'God the Father' with YHWH, they were understandably reluctant to image him. To equate YHWH with a father image would be an unpardonable violation of the First commandment. But since the Council of Nicaea YHWH has been divided into three idols of God, i.e. three distinct *persons* of God comprised of the same substance. And insofar as 'God the Father' is a *person of God*, it is possible to anthropomorphize him; and images of 'God the Father' have been created since the 15th century. The most famous is the mural of 'God the Father' touching the hand of Adam in the Sistine Chapel.

The Council of Nicaea adulterated the New Testament's assertions regarding 'God the Father.' ('Adulterated' is a strong word, but even that may fall short of the near blasphemous confabulation wrought by Constantine and the Nicaean Council.[7]) The theologian, Richard Bauckham, makes this abundantly clear in his treatise on Jesus and the God of Israel.[8] Bauckham's exegesis clearly demonstrates that well before 200 C.E., St. Paul and the Jewish exegetes who wrote the Gospels had developed a high Christology within the construct of Jewish monotheism – the belief in and worship of the One God.[9] In the New Testament YHWH is referred to as 'Father.' This was the name for YHWH chosen by Christ when he directs us to pray to Abba,[10] who is in heaven. It is comparable to the Jewish use of 'Adonai' in naming YHWH during their prayers.

While the Nicaean confabulation – equating YHWH with a person of God, makes it permissible to image 'God the Father,' Christ in the Gospels clearly cautions us against doing so when he tells us:

> "I am the way, and the truth, and the life. *No one comes to the Father except through me.* If you know me, you will know my Father also. From now on you do know him and have seen him." Philip said to him, "Lord, show us the Father, and we will be satisfied." Jesus said to him, "Have I been with you all this time, Philip, and you still do not know me? Whoever has seen me has seen the Father. How can you say, 'Show us the Father'? Do you not believe that I am in the Father and the Father is in me? The words that I say to you I do not speak on my own; but the Father who dwells in me does his works (John 14:6-10, *italics added*)."

Luke and Matthew express the same caution in their gospels when they assert that no one knows the Father except the Son and those to whom the son chooses to reveal the Father.[11]

What can we deduce from the foregoing?

As a Nicaean *person* of God, 'God the Father' cannot be equated with YHWH. Either the Father is YHWH or – as a mere person – he is a blasphemous expression of YHWH. The same is true for Christ: he is either the human incarnation of YHWH, or as a mere person of God he is a blasphemous expression of YHWH. In effect, Christ cannot be the earthly incarnation of YHWH, if he is merely a Son of 'God the Father.' If Christ's very words are heeded, we can only know the Father through Christ. As Christ himself cautions us, only he can be the living incarnation of YHWH, as YHWH has never incarnated on earth apart from Christ and the felt presence of the Holy Spirit. Consequently, there is a problem with choosing 'God the Father' as a higher power. A higher power needs to be accessible to the Mind in order to relate to our conscious sense of self; and the Mind cannot conceive without imagining. Unlike Christ, and except for Christ, 'God the Father' lacks a consensual image, which must be the case, as YHWH has never incarnated apart from Christ.

Christ's cautions notwithstanding, most Christians appear to assign various attributes of YHWH from the Old Testament to their understanding of 'God the Father.' Many of those attributes are contradictory; and none of them are definitive. Even more problematical, many people appear unable to differentiate between the Moral authority of their own fathers, which can be unmitigatingly harsh, and the Moral authority they attribute to 'God the Father.'[12] Moreover, as Jesus rightly observed, 'God the Father' abides in heaven, so it is difficult to imagine him as immanent (e.g. pervading us; here present) as opposed to transcendent (e.g. beyond or above the range of normal physical human experience).[13] The person of 'God the Father' has never become human, except in Christ. Unlike the contradictory images of the Father, images of Christ are consensually definable by the vignettes of his earthly life in the four gospels; and via his human form he is potentially immanent in all of us.[14]

The role of the Holy Spirit is also at issue here.[15] Those who have read my book know that the convicting power of the Holy Spirit is crucial to the most significant interventions it offers. Like 'God the Father,' the Holy Spirit has no anthropomorphic form. In active imagination, it must have a conduit, be it another person-in-the-world who prays on our behalf in the name of Jesus, or an interior image of Jesus Christ. Christ is Christ because he is conceived by the Holy Spirit of the Virgin Mary, he is anointed with the power of the Holy Spirit by God,[16] and by completely submitting his will to God, he can extend the Holy Spirit's discernment, forgiveness, and miracles to any who ask in his name. Stated another way, Christ is the ever-living incarnation of YHWH and channel of the Holy Spirit. Christ is God, not merely the Son of God.

I am careful when clients assign the Holy Spirit's convicting power to a higher power other than Christ, but I do not exclude the possibility. In the last two chapters of my book I examine one higher power other than Christ who seems to effect changes comparable to Christ when he convicts with the power of the Holy Spirit. I assume that the Holy Spirit can use any vessel in the world or in active imagination to bring us closer to the Godhead; that the source of the Holy Spirit is YHWH. S/he is the 'Spirit of God over the waters.'[17]

We are "indoctrinated" from early childhood to accept the *person* of 'God the Father' as our higher power because he is so often confabulated with YHWH. It is an osmotic assimilation reinforced by family, religion, and patriarchal values. The formalized prayers and Nicaean creed of the Christian faith assert a hierarchical relationship (i.e. the throne[18]) that subordinates Christ and the Holy Spirit to the Father; and most

Christians appear to unreflectively accede to it. But so far as I can determine, few Christians *consciously* choose 'God the Father' as their higher power. Given a choice between a distant, judgmental, person of God and an abiding presence within us who is loving and forgiving, I believe most people would choose the latter, especially when they understand that YHWH and the Holy Spirit incarnate through Christ. He is, after all, the reason for our faith and the instrument of our salvation.

One final observation: In 315 C.E. Constantine was intent on making Christianity *the official religion of the Roman Empire*; and that did not require the Jewish Christian insistence that Christ be the human incarnation of YHWH. By 315 C.E. most Christians in the Roman Empire were non-Jewish. Making Christ *a person* of God would make him much more palatable to the Greek/Roman understanding of God. Zeus, for example, had numerous progeny by human mothers. One of them, Dionysus, was worshipped in the Greek and Roman cultures long before Christ, and his life story has numerous, uncanny, parallels to the life of Christ.[19] Orthodox Jewry also pushed for separation. The Jewish Temple, and the culture organized around it, was completely destroyed in 60 C.E. This destruction forced the Jews to reorganize their religion around the Torah of the Old Testament rather than the Temple and its sacrifices. To that end, and even before Christian Jews wrote the New Testament gospels, the Post-Temple rabbis formalized the Torah and Hebrew Bible and declared it whole and complete.[20] That formalization discouraged any assimilation of the Christian apocrypha written afterward, though the Old Testament writings remained vital to an understanding of the New Testament and therefore could not be set aside. Post-Temple Judaism disowned Messianic Judaism, but Christianity could not disown its Biblical origins. The Nicene solution redefined Christianity obliging the Orthodox Christians (circa 315 C.E.) *to accept two different understandings* of Christ. The first one, derived from the Old Testament and explicit in all the Gospels, asserts that *Christ is God* and the living incarnation of YHWH. That is the essential statement of faith put forth in our orthodox Gospels and the Letters of Paul. The second understanding is that Christ is merely a person of God. The latter is promulgated by the liturgies of most churches that accept the particular Trinitarian formulation established by the Roman church. These are radically different conceptions of God. The Nicaean creed encourages the confabulation of YHWH with a Zeus-like 'God the Father.' In sharp contrast, the Yahwistic understanding holds that any *personage* of God is idolatrous. From the Yahwistic perspective, *Christ must be the human incarnation of YHWH* or he is only an idol promulgated by Greek and Roman paganism. Most people believe that the Nicene creed summarizes the faith expressed in the Gospels and Letters of Paul. In fact, it dramatically alters our understanding of God incarnate in Jesus Christ. In the Roman assertion, Christ is merely the Son of God, not God incarnate. And 'God the Father' is either a totally new person of God or an idolatrous image of YHWH.

Most of my clients can attest that 'God the Father' is an unreflected choice. But they would also attest that making a conscious choice for Christ or any other higher power – other than 'God the Father' – is exceedingly difficult after decades of indoctrination. Soon after discovering that most of my clients named 'God the Father' as their higher power, I began drafting an interventional prayer that would give them a conscious choice. Few were eager to act on it; and most of them actively resisted. One reason is that I make it difficult. I insist that they ask a person, other than me, to vocally pray it on their behalf and act as a witness of their conscious choice. But I also suspect another more gut wrenching reason. 'God the Father' is supported by the entire foundation of the Nicaean church. He is a backbone of a subordinating patriarchy. In 2010, that is less so in America, but still apparent; and most of my clients were born well before 2010. In other parts of the world patriarchy is still a largely unquestioned cultural precept with the force of law to back it up.

Those of my clients who have opted to freely and consciously choose a higher power have only done so after weeks or months of soul searching and reflection. Some are finally "driven" to it by a renewed need for a higher power or the growing awareness that sitting on the fence has become unceasingly painful. I have given each of them the following prayer to be prayed out loud by someone of their choosing – other than me. I tell them that any portion of the prayer can be altered to fit their needs, including who they designate as their higher power;[21] but I do encourage them to consider their higher power's potential as a conduit of the Holy Spirit,[22] for I am convinced that this is the source of forgiveness and discernment as well as the reason for Christ's incarnation on earth and in the Mind. I would also note that this prayer is addressed to God Ineffable – YHWH – not God the Father. The *person* of 'God the Father' can be the God of your personal salvation, if you so choose, but not the ultimate source of the Holy Spirit's convicting power as that must remain with YHWH.

> I PRAY THAT GOD INEFFABLE,
> WITH THE POWER OF THE HOLY SPIRIT,
> CONSECRATE YOUR IMAGE OF [JESUS CHRIST]
> AS THE GOD OF YOUR PERSONAL SALVATION;
> TO ABIDE LOVINGLY WITHIN YOUR HEART AND,
> WITH THE POWER OF THE HOLY SPIRIT,
> GUIDE, FORGIVE, AND INFORM YOU EVERMORE.

This prayer is only a beginning, but for the clients who have taken it, it has proven a significant first step.

APPENDIX II ENDNOTES

1   'Higher power' is the term used in AA and comparable support groups to identify the 'God of your understanding': the power greater than yourself who can free you from the bondage of your addictions and shame, and restore you to sanity. It is always a personal choice and never challenged by other members. But it is also rarely if ever discussed publicly or privately. The closest comparable concept that I am aware of is Ista Devata, which is a Hindu word meaning *the God of your personal salvation*.

2   Tertullian, who lived in the late 2nd Century, is purportedly the first to define the Holy Trinity as three persons and one substance. He is called the father of Latin Christianity as he wrote extensively in Latin as well as Greek. See Barnes, T. D. (1971), *Tertullian: A Historical And Literary Study*, Oxford Clarendon Press.

3   See Luke 11:2-4 and Matthew 6:9-13.

4   See Bauckham, R. (2008), *Jesus And The God Of Israel: God Crucified and Other Studies on the New Testament's Christology of Divine Identity*, William B. Eerdmans Publishing Company: Grand Rapids: MI.

5   The first commandment: I am the Lord your God, who brought you out of the land of Egypt, out of the house of slavery; you shall have no other gods before me. You shall not make for yourself an idol, whether in the form of anything that is in heaven above, or that is on the earth beneath, or that is in the water under the earth. You shall not bow down to them or worship them; for I the Lord your God am a jealous God, punishing children for the iniquity of parents, to the third and the fourth generation of those who reject me, but showing steadfast love to the thousandth generation of those who love me and keep my commandments. (Exodus 20:2-6).

6   I have yet to find a definitive reference text that authoritatively describes the names of God in Judaism. They do exist and a number of them can be purchased from Amazon, but I have not read through them all. However, in the interim, the interested reader can simply 'Google' the phrase *names of God* on the internet and find numerous descriptive sites describing the 'names of God' in Judaism and Christianity, as well as sites that address 'God the Father.' Google can also be used for definitions of 'HaShem' and 'Ista Devata,' which I use earlier in the endnotes and text.

7   The interested reader is referred to *Constantine's Bible* by David Dungan to gain a fuller appreciation of Constantine's inordinate role in shaping Christian faith in the West. Dungan, D.L., (2007), *Constantine's Bible: Politics and the Making of the New Testament*, Fortress Press: Minneapolis; see also Richard Rubenstein, who writes from the Jewish perspective as someone interested in conflict resolution: Rubenstein, R. (1999), *When Jesus Became God: The Struggle to Define Christianity during the Last Days of Rome*, A Harvest Book from Harcourt, Inc.

8   Bauckham, R. (2008), op. cit.

9   Even today, devout Jews begin their prayers with the Shema: the passage in Deuteronomy (6:4-6) which begins, "Hear, O Israel: YHWH our God, YHWH is one," and continues with the requirement of total devotion to this one God: "You

shall love YHWH your God with all your heart, and all your soul, and with all your might."

10   'Abba' is a term of endearment used by Jewish children to their fathers. It is still used today in Jewish households.

11   "All things have been handed over to Me by My Father; and no one knows the Son except the Father, and no one knows the Father except the Son and anyone to whom the Son chooses to reveal Him (Matthew 11:27; Luke 10:22)."

12   For many clients, the image of their father, or mother, *is the highest power in their Mind.* This is easily demonstrated by juxta-positioning the father with an image of Christ. Invariably, and often with some chagrin, the client will own that the parental voice is the more powerful of the two. The interested reader is referred back to Chapter VI of the book.

13   The theologian, Marcus Borg, devotes an entire book to the exploration of God as immanent and transcendent. See Borg, M.J. (1998), *The God We Never Knew: Beyond Dogmatic Religion To A More Authentic Contemporary Faith*, Harper One: San Francisco.

14   I say 'potentially' because he has to be invited to incarnate within the Mind, although he does not have to be invited as the individual's higher power for the incarnation to occur.

15   This is true in ways that I had not even begun to imagine when I started thinking about 'God the Father.' It appears that our attitude toward 'God the Father' can have a negative effect on the flow of the Holy Spirit. A surprising number of my female clients have negative feelings toward 'God the Father' that seem to stem from developmental issues with their fathers. They have learned to detach from those fathers and be less reactive to them, but still find it difficult to relate positively to 'God the Father' even as they continue to treat him as their higher power. Of course, it would be difficult to relate to him in the best of circumstances since he is supposed to be invisible and transcendent and essentially without form. But one of his primary roles in the New Testament is directing the Holy Spirit. I asked these clients if their negative attitude toward 'God the Father' might in any way inhibit the flow of the Holy Spirit? Might their negative images of 'God the Father' be blocking the flow of the Holy Spirit in their lives? I have suggested that Christ be allowed to contain any negative feelings or images of 'God the Father' that have any potential to block the flow of the Holy Spirit, and then dispel whatever he captured so the Holy Spirit could flow unblocked through Christ. In a number of instances this intervention had a noticeable positive effect on the client.

16   Matthew 3:16-17 – "As soon as Jesus was baptized, he went up out of the water. At that moment heaven was opened, and he saw the Spirit of God descending like a dove and lighting on him. And a voice from heaven said, "This is my Son, whom I love; with him I am well pleased." If my surmise is correct, this reference to God is not 'God the Father.' Any Jew writing this – or reading it, would immediately equate it with YHWH who also spoke to Moses through the burning bush; and first appeared before the beginning of time as the Spirit of God (Genesis 1:2).

17   Genesis 1:1-5 - In the beginning when God created the heavens and the earth, the earth was a formless void and darkness covered the face of the deep, while a wind (Spirit) from God swept over the face of the waters. Then God said, 'Let there be light'; and there was light. And God saw that the light was good; and God separated the light from the darkness. God called the light Day, and the darkness he called Night. And there was evening and there was morning, the first day.

18   According to the Nicene Creed, Christ is seated at the right hand of the Father. This is a place of honor not to be confused with actually sitting on the throne, which is the Father's seat. Four books of the New Testament assert that Christ rose to heaven and sits at the right hand of the father (Mark 16:19, Luke 22:69, Matthew 22:44 and 26:64, Acts 2:34 and 7:55). The New Testament was written before the development of a Nicaean God. As such, any reference to the 'Father' has to be treated as a synonym for YHWH. That being the case, Christ cannot share the throne until the end-time when all returns to heaven. Until then he sits at the right hand of YHWH. See Bauckham, R. (2008), op.cit, especially, *'The Throne of God and the Worship of Jesus, pp.153-181.*

19   See Freke, T. & Gandy, P. (1999), *The Jesus Mysteries: Was the "Original Jesus" a Pagan God?* Three Rivers Press, New York.

20   This formalization culminated in a malediction injected into the Jewish community's daily prayers known today as the Birkat ha-minim. The insertion of this one malediction into the heart of the daily prayer services amounted to a de facto spiritual excommunication of Messianic Jews. See Skolnik, F. (2006), *Encyclopedia Judaica*, 22 Volume Set, Macmillan Reference USA, 2nd Edition.

21   While I have not explored this extensively, I have come to appreciate that Christ can comfortably co-exist with a feminine counterpart that enriches and succors the client's sense of self, be it goddess, archetypal mother or consort.

22   To the extent that any of my clients have experienced the Holy Spirit through Christ, or another freely chosen higher power, while working inside, they

have done so *before using this prayer to consciously acknowledge their higher power*. The prayer is not a pre-condition for evoking Christ or asking him to grace them with the Holy Spirit. He willingly enters any Mind when invited, whatever his initial stature in the individual's pantheon. The changes that take place after a client has freely chosen Christ as their higher power are subtle. Basically, they seem to walk closer and more frequently with Jesus as a daily companion of their interior life, and more readily accede to his discernment in matters put before him.

www.ingramcontent.com/pod-product-compliance
Lightning Source LLC
Chambersburg PA
CBHW062122160426
43191CB00013B/2170